Trevor Bench-Capon   Giovanni Soda
A Min Tjoa (Eds.)

Database and Expert Systems Applications

KU-318-520

10th International Conference, DEXA'99
Florence, Italy, August 30 – September 3, 1999
Proceedings

Springer

Series Editors

Gerhard Goos, Karlsruhe University, Germany
Juris Hartmanis, Cornell University, NY, USA
Jan van Leeuwen, Utrecht University, The Netherlands

Volume Editors

Trevor Bench-Capon
Department of Computer Science, University of Liverpool
P.O. Box 147, Liverpool L49 3BX, UK
E-mail: tbc@compsci.liverpool.ac.uk

Giovanni Soda
Department of Systems and Computers, University of Florence
Via S. Marta, 3, I-50139 Florence, Italy
E-mail: giovanni@ingfi1.ing.unifi.it

A Min Tjoa
IFS, Technical University of Vienna
Resselgasse 3, A-1040 Vienna, Austria
E-mail: amin@ifs.tuwien.ac.at
        tjoa@garbo.ifs.tuwien.ac.at

Cataloging-in-Publication data applied for

Die Deutsche Bibliothek - CIP-Einheitsaufnahme

Database and expert systems applications : 10th international
conference ; proceedings / DEXA '99, Florence, Italy, August 30 -
September 3, 1999. Trevor Bench-Capon ... (ed.). - Berlin ;
Heidelberg ; New York ; Barcelona ; Hong Kong ; London ; Milan ;
Paris ; Singapore ; Tokyo : Springer, 1999
  (Lecture notes in computer science ; Vol. 1677)
  ISBN 3-540-66448-3

CR Subject Classification (1998): H.2, I.2.1, H.3, H.4, H.5

ISSN 0302-9743
ISBN 3-540-66448-3 Springer-Verlag Berlin Heidelberg New York

© Springer-Verlag Berlin Heidelberg 1999
Printed in Germany

Typesetting: Camera-ready by author
SPIN: 10704240   06/3142 – 5 4 3 2 1 0   Printed on acid-free paper

Preface

The Database and Expert Systems Applications (DEXA) conferences bring together researchers and practitioners from all over the world to exchange ideas, experiences and opinions in a friendly and stimulating environment. The papers are at once a record of what has been achieved and the first steps towards shaping the future of information systems.

DEXA covers a broad field, and all aspects of database, knowledge base and related technologies and their applications are represented. Once again there were a good number of submissions: 241 papers were submitted and of these the programme committee selected 103 to be presented.

DEXA'99 took place in Florence and was the tenth conference in the series, following events in Vienna, Berlin, Valencia, Prague, Athens, London, Zurich, Toulouse and Vienna. The decade has seen many developments in the areas covered by DEXA, developments in which DEXA has played its part.

I would like to express thanks to all the institutions which have actively supported and made possible this conference, namely:

- University of Florence, Italy
- IDG-CNR, Italy
- FAW – University of Linz, Austria
- Austrian Computer Society
- DEXA Association

In addition, we must thank all the people who have contributed their time and effort to make the conference possible. Special thanks go to Maria Schweikert (Technical University of Vienna), M. Neubauer and G. Wagner (FAW, University of Linz). We must also thank all the members of the programme committee, whose careful reviews are important to the quality of the conference.

June 1999

T.J.M. Bench-Capon, The University of Liverpool, UK
General Chair

Program Committee

General Chairperson:
T. Bench-Capon, University of Liverpool, UK

Publications Chairperson:
V. Marik, Czech Technical University, Czech Republic

Conference Program Chairpersons:
G. Soda, Unversity of Florence, Italy
A M. Tjoa, Technical University of Vienna, Austria

Workshop Chairpersons:
A. Cammelli, IDG-CNR, Italy
R.R. Wagner, FAW, University of Linz, Austria

Program Committee Members:
H. Afsarmanesh, University of Amsterdam, The Netherlands
B. Amann, CNAM & INRIA, France
F. Andres, NACSIS, Japan
K. Bauknecht, University of Zurich, Switzerland
B. Bhargava, Purdue University, USA
J. Bing, NRCCL Oslo, Norway
J. Bubenko, Royal Institute of Technology, Sweden
L. Camarinha-Matos, New University of Lisbon, Portugal
W.S. Cellary, University of Poznan, Poland
S. Christodoulakis, University of Crete, Greece
B. Croft, University of Massachusetts, USA
J. Debenham, University of Technology, Sydney, Australia
P. Drazan, RIKS Maastricht, The Netherlands
J. Eder, University of Klagenfurt, Austria
T. Eiter, University of Giessen, Germany
G. Engels, University of Paderborn, Germany
E. Fernandez, Florida Atlantic University, USA
A.L. Furtado, University of Rio de Janeiro, Brazil
G. Gardarin, INRIA, France
F. Golshani, Arizona State University, USA
A. Hameurlain, Université Paul Sabatier, France
I. Hawryszkiewycz, University of Technology, Sydney, Australia
M. Ibrahim, University of Greenwich, UK
S. Jajodia, George Mason University, USA
Y. Kambayashi, University of Kyoto, Japan
M. Kamel, Naval Postgraduate School, USA
N. Kamel, City University of Hongkong, Hong Kong
G. Kappel, University of Linz, Austria
D. Karagiannis, University of Vienna, Austria

Table of Contents

Fundamentals for Applications II

Advanced Databases II

Object-Orientation III

Query Aspects III

Fundamentals for Applications III

Advanced Databases III

Object-Orientation IV

Query Aspects IV

Fundamentals for Applications V

Advanced Databases V

Heterogeneous, Distributed and Federated Database Systems I

Transactions I

Applications I

Data-Warehousing and Data-Mining I

Heterogeneous, Distributed and Federated Database Systems II

Transactions II

Applications II

Data-Warehousing and Data-Mining II

Heterogeneous, Distributed and Federated Database Systems III

Transactions III

World Wide Web Applications II

Invited Talk

On Tractable Queries and Constraints

Georg Gottlob, Nicola Leone, and Francesco Scarcello

Institut für Informationssysteme,
Technische Universität Wien
Paniglgasse 16, A-1040 Vienna, Austria
{gottlob,leone,scarcell}@dbai.tuwien.ac.at

Abstract. Evaluating a conjunctive database query is known to be equivalent to solving a constraint satisfaction problem. These problems are NP-complete in general but become tractable, and actually highly parallelizable, if restricted to acyclic or nearly acyclic queries.

This paper surveys recent results by the authors on tractable classes of conjunctive queries and constraint satisfaction problems and presents a new decomposition algorithm for such problems.

1 Introduction

This article is about the database problem of evaluating a conjunctive query (CQ) and – at the same time – about the AI problem of solving a constraint satisfaction problem (CSP). In fact, it is known that these problems are equivalent [22, 25]. While CQ and CSP are NP-hard problems (whose Boolean versions are NP-complete) [7], there are important polynomial subclasses of practical interest.

Most prominent among the latter are the acyclic CQs and CSPs, i.e., the classes of conjunctive queries and constraint satisfaction problems whose associated hypergraphs are acyclic. Yannakakis [32] presented an algorithm for computing the result to an acyclic CQ in output-polynomial time, i.e., in time polynomial in the size of the result (which may be exponential). This algorithm was later used to compute the solutions of acyclic CSPs. In the case of Boolean acyclic queries, Yannakakis' Algorithm computes the result (yes or no) in polynomial time. Similarly, the *satisfiability* of an acyclic CSP, and even the computation of a single solution in the positive case, can be done in polynomial time by a minor variant of Yannakakis' algorithm [11].

The good results about acyclic CQs and CSPs extend to very relevant classes of *nearly acyclic* queries and CSPs, such as for example queries or CSPs whose associated primal graph has *bounded treewidth* [27], a *cutset* [9] of bounded size, or a bounded *degree of cyclicity* [22].

In the present paper we survey recent results by the authors on acyclic and nearly acyclic CQs and CSPs (Sections 4-7) and introduce a new algorithm for computing a decomposition of a hypergraph associated to a CQ or CSP (Section 8).

The recent results surveyed here are mainly from the following three sources, where formal proofs and a large number of further details can be found:

– Reference [17], where the precise complexity of Boolean acyclic conjunctive queries (ABCQs) is determined, and where highly parallel database algorithms for solving such queries are presented. In particular, we show that answering ABCQs is complete for the very low complexity class LOGCFL and we exhibit parallel database algorithms for solving ABCQs and for computing the result to restricted classes of nonboolean acyclic conjunctive queries. The results and algorithms in [17] are mainly formulated for Boolean conjunctive queries. That paper is complemented by another recent paper [18], where parallel algorithms for computing the result of general nonboolean acyclic conjunctive queries are discussed. In the present paper, we will not discuss parallel algorithms and refer the interested reader to [17] and [18].

– References [20, 19], where we study *query width*, a measure for the amount of cyclicity of a query introduced by Chekuri and Rajamaran [8] and where we define the new (more general) concept of *hypertree width*.

It follows from the results in [8] that Boolean conjunctive queries and CSPs of constant query width can be solved in polynomial time. However, Chekuri and Rajaraman left open whether for a given query Q and constant k it is possible to *recognize* in polynomial time that Q has query width k. In [20, 19] we give a negative solution to this question by proving this recognition problem NP-complete. However, we were able to find a yet more liberal measure of cyclicity, *hypertree width*, which shares all positive properties of query width, and for which the above described recognition problem is polynomially solvable. Hypertree width and the related concept of hypertree decomposition will be described in Section 6 of the present paper.

– Reference [21], where we establish criteria for comparing different CSP decomposition methods and where we compare various methods including the method of hypertree decomposition. The comparison criteria and the results of the comparison are reported in Section 7 of the present paper.

In [20, 19] we presented an algorithm running on an alternating Turing machine for computing a hypertree decomposition of bounded width of a given hypergraph. The purpose of this algorithm was to prove that the problem is solvable in polynomial time (and actually in LOGCFL). Based on this alternating algorithm we also presented a datalog program for computing a bounded width hypertree decomposition. In Section 8 of the present paper we introduce a more sophisticated algorithm which computes an *optimal* hypertree decomposition of a hypergraph H, provided that H has bounded hypertree width.

Due to the limited space, we will not include full details of all issues and will refer the interested reader to the relevant literature when appropriate.

2 Conjunctive Queries

One of the simplest but also one of the most important classes of database queries is the class of *conjunctive queries (CQs)*. In this paper we will adopt the standard convention [1, 29] of identifying a relational database instance with a logical theory consisting of ground facts. Thus, a tuple $\langle a_1, \ldots a_k \rangle$, belonging to relation r, will be identified with the ground atom $r(a_1, \ldots, a_k)$. The fact that a tuple $\langle a_1, \ldots, a_k \rangle$ belongs to relation r of a database instance **DB** is thus simply denoted by $r(a_1, \ldots, a_k) \in$ **DB**.

A (rule based) *conjunctive query* Q on a database schema $DS = \{R_1, \ldots, R_m\}$ consists of a rule of the form

$$Q : \quad ans(\mathbf{u}) \leftarrow r_1(\mathbf{u_1}) \wedge \cdots \wedge r_n(\mathbf{u_n}),$$

where $n \geq 0$, $r_1, \ldots r_n$ are relation names (not necessarily distinct) of DS; ans is a relation name not in DS; and $\mathbf{u}, \mathbf{u_1}, \ldots, \mathbf{u_n}$ are lists of terms (i.e., variables or constants) of appropriate length. The set of variables occurring in Q is denoted by $var(Q)$. The set of atoms contained in the body of Q is referred to as $atoms(Q)$.

The *answer* of Q on a database instance **DB** with associated universe U, consists of a relation ans whose arity is equal to the length of $\mathbf{u}$, defined as follows. ans contains all tuples $ans(\mathbf{u})\vartheta$ such that $\vartheta : var(Q) \longrightarrow U$ is a substitution replacing each variable in $var(Q)$ by a value of U and such that for $1 \leq i \leq n$, $r_i(\mathbf{u_i})\vartheta \in$ **DB**. (For an atom A, $A\vartheta$ denotes the atom obtained from A by uniformly substituting $\vartheta(X)$ for each variable X occurring in A.)

The conjunctive query Q is a *boolean conjunctive query (BCQ)* if its head atom $ans(\mathbf{u})$ does not contain variables and is thus a purely propositional atom. Q evaluates to *true* if there exists a substitution ϑ such that for $1 \leq i \leq n$, $r_i(\mathbf{u_i})\vartheta \in$ **DB**; otherwise the query evaluates to *false*.

We will, in the first place, deal with *Boolean* conjunctive queries (BCQs) represented by rules whose heads are variable-free, i.e., propositional (see Example 1 below).

Example 1. Consider a relational database with the following relation schemas:

```
enrolled(Pers#,Course#,Reg_Date)
teaches(Pers#,Course#,Assigned)
parent(Pers1, Pers2)
```

The BCQ Q_1 below checks whether some student is enrolled in a course taught by his/her parent.

$$ans \leftarrow \texttt{enrolled}(S, C, R) \wedge \texttt{teaches}(P, C, A) \wedge \texttt{parent}(P, S).$$

The following query Q_2 asks: Is there a professor who has a child enrolled in some course?

$$ans \leftarrow \texttt{teaches}(P, C, A) \wedge \texttt{enrolled}(S, C', R) \wedge \texttt{parent}(P, S).$$

In the general case, evaluating Boolean conjunctive queries is a very difficult task. In fact, Chandra and Merlin [7] proved that this problem is NP-complete.

If Q is a conjunctive query, we define the hypergraph $H(Q)$ associated to Q as follows. $H(Q) = (V, E)$ where $V = var(Q)$ and E contains a hyperedge e_i

for each atom $r_i(\mathbf{u_i})$ in the body of Q, such that e_i is the set of all variables occurring in $\mathbf{u_i}$.

Decision problems such as the *query-of-tuple* problem (i.e., checking whether a given tuple belongs to the result of a CQ), the *containment problem* for CQs, and the *clause subsumption* problem are all equivalent via simple logspace transformations (see [17]) to the the *evaluation problem* of Boolean CQs.

Another fundamental problem equivalent to CQ is the *Constraint Satisfaction Problem* [5, 22, 9, 25], described in the next section.

3 Constraints

An instance of a *constraint satisfaction problem (CSP)* (also *constraint network*) is a triple $I = (Var, U, \mathcal{C})$, where Var is a finite set of variables, U is a finite domain of values, and $\mathcal{C} = \{C_1, C_2, \ldots, C_q\}$ is a finite set of constraints. Each constraint C_i is a pair (S_i, r_i), where S_i is a list of variables of length m_i called the *constraint scope*, and r_i is an m_i-ary relation over U, called the *constraint relation*. (The tuples of r_i indicate the allowed combinations of simultaneous values for the variables S_i). A *solution* to a CSP instance is a substitution ϑ : $Var \longrightarrow U$, such that for each $1 \leq i \leq q$, $S_i\vartheta \in r_i$. The problem of deciding whether a CSP instance has any solution is called *constraint satisfiability (CS)*. (This definition is taken almost verbatim from [24].)

Many well-known problems in Computer Science and Mathematics can be formulated as CSPs. For example the famous problem of *graph three-colorability (3COL)*, i.e., deciding whether the vertices of a graph $G = \langle Vertices, Edges \rangle$ can be colored by three colors (say: red, green, blue) such that no edge links two vertices having the same color, is formulated as follows as a CSP. The set Var contains a variable X_v for each vertex $v \in Vertices$. For each edge $e = \langle v, w \rangle \in Edges$, the set $\mathcal{C}$ contains a constraint $C_e = (S_e, r_e)$, where $S_e = \langle X_v, X_w \rangle$ and r_e is the relation $r_{\neq}$ consisting of all pairs of different colors, i.e., $r_{\neq} = \{\langle red, green \rangle, \langle red, blue \rangle, \langle green, red \rangle, \langle green, blue \rangle, \langle blue, red \rangle, \langle blue, green \rangle\}$.

The *structure* of a CSP is best represented by its associated *hypergraph*. To any CSP instance $I = (Var, U, \mathcal{C})$, we associate a hypergraph $\mathcal{H}_I = (V, H)$, where $V = Var$, and $H = \{var(S) \mid C = (S, r) \in \mathcal{C}\}$, where $var(S)$ denotes the set of variables in the scope S of the constraint C. We will often use the term *variable* as a synonym for vertex, when referring to elements of V.

4 Acyclic Queries and Constraints

The most basic and most fundamental structural property considered in the context of conjunctive queries and CSPs is *acyclicity*. It was recognized in database theory and in AI that *acyclic* CQs or CSPs are polynomially solvable. A conjunctive query Q (resp., a CSP instance I) is *acyclic* if its associated hypergraph is acyclic.

Let $\mathcal{H} = (V, H)$ be a hypergraph. The *primal graph* of $\mathcal{H}$ is a graph $G = (V, E)$, having the same set of variables (vertices) as $\mathcal{H}$ and an edge connecting any pair of variables $X, Y \in V$ such that $\{X, Y\} \subseteq h$ for some $h \in H$. $\mathcal{H}$ is an acyclic hypergraph iff its primal graph G is chordal (i.e., any cycle of length greater than 3 has a chord) and the set of its maximal cliques coincide with $edges(\mathcal{H})$ [3].

A *join tree* $JT(\mathcal{H})$ for a hypergraph $\mathcal{H}$ is a tree whose nodes are the edges of $\mathcal{H}$ such that whenever the same vertex $X \in V$ occurs in two edges A_1 and A_2 of $\mathcal{H}$, then A_1 and A_2 are connected in $JT(\mathcal{H})$, and X occurs in each node on the unique path linking A_1 and A_2 in $JT(\mathcal{H})$. In other words, the set of nodes in which X occurs induces a (connected) subtree of $JT(\mathcal{H})$. We will refer to this condition as the *Connectedness Condition* of join trees.

Acyclic hypergraphs can be characterized in terms of join trees: A hypergraph $\mathcal{H}$ is *acyclic* iff it has a join tree [4, 3, 26].

Acyclic CQs and CSPs have highly desirable computational properties:

1. Acyclic instances can be efficiently solved. Yannakakis provided a (sequential) polynomial time algorithm solving BCQ on acyclic queries[1] [32].
2. The authors of the present paper have recently shown that BCQ, and hence CS, are highly parallelizable on acyclic queries, as they are complete for the low complexity class LOGCFL [17]. Efficient parallel algorithms – even for non-Boolean queries – have been proposed in [18]. They run on parallel database machines that exploit the *inter-operation parallelism* [31], i.e., machines that execute different relational operations in parallel.
3. Acyclicity is efficiently recognizable, and a join tree of an acyclic hypergraph is efficiently computable. A linear-time algorithm for computing a join tree is shown in [28]; an L^{SL} method has been provided in [17].
4. The result of a (non-Boolean) acyclic conjunctive query Q can be *computed* in time polynomial in the combined size of the input instance and of the output relation [32].
5. *Arc-consistency* for acyclic CSP instances can be enforced in polynomial time [9, 11]. From such arc-consistent instances, it is easy to obtain the solutions of the given CSP with a backtrack-free procedure.

Intuitively, the efficient behaviour of acyclic instances is due to the fact that they can be evaluated by processing any of their join trees bottom-up by performing upward semijoins, thus keeping small the size of the intermediate relations (which could become exponential if regular join were performed).

5   Decomposition Methods

The important speed-up obtainable on acyclic instances stimulated several research efforts towards the identification of wider classes of queries and constraints having the same desirable properties as acyclic CQs and CSPs. A number of different methods based only on the structure of the associated hypergraph have

---

[1] Note that, since both the database **DB** and the query Q are part of an input-instance of BCQ, what we are considering is the *combined complexity* of the query [30].

been proposed. We call these methods *decomposition methods*, because each one provides a decomposition which transforms any hypergraph to an acyclic hypergraph. For each decomposition method D, this transformation depends on a parameter called *D-width*. Let k be a fixed constant. The tractability class $C(D, k)$ is the (possibly infinite) set of hypergraphs having D-width $\leq k$. D ensures that every CQ or CSP instance whose associated hypergraph belongs to this class is polynomial-time solvable.

The main decomposition methods considered in database theory and in artificial intelligence are:

- **Treewidth** (short: TREEWIDTH) [27] (see also [25, 17]). These are hypergraphs whose primal graph has treewidth bounded by a constant. The treewidth of a graph is a well-known measure of its tree-likeness introduced by Robertson and Seymour in their work on graph minors [27]. This notion plays a central role in algorithmic graph theory as well as in many subdisciplines of Computer Science. We omit a formal definition. It is well-known that checking whether a graph has treewidth $\leq k$ for a fixed constant k, and in the positive case, computing a k-width tree decomposition is feasible in linear time [6].

- **Biconnected Components** (short: BICOMP) [13]. Any graph $G = (V, E)$ can be decomposed into a pair $\langle T, \chi \rangle$, where T is a tree, and the labeling function χ associates to each vertex of T a biconnected component of G (a component which remains connected after any one-vertex removal). The *biconnected width* of a hypergraph $\mathcal{H}$, denoted by BICOMP-width($\mathcal{H}$), is the maximum number of vertices over the biconnected components of the primal graph of $\mathcal{H}$.

- **Cycle Cutset** (short: CUTSET) [9]. A *cycle cutset* of a hypergraph $\mathcal{H}$ is a set $S \subseteq var(\mathcal{H})$ such that the subhypergraph of $\mathcal{H}$ induced by $var(\mathcal{H}) - S$ is acyclic. The CUTSET width of $\mathcal{H}$ is the minimum cardinality over all its possible cycle cutsets.

- **Tree Clustering** (short: TCLUSTER) [11]. The *tree clustering* method is based on a triangulation algorithm which transforms the primal graph $G = (V, E)$ of any hypergraph $\mathcal{H}$ into a chordal graph G'. The maximal cliques of G' are then used to build the hyperedges of an acyclic hypergraph $\mathcal{H}'$. The *tree-clustering width* (short: TCLUSTER *width*) of $\mathcal{H}_I$ is 1 if $\mathcal{H}$ is an acyclic hypergraph; otherwise it is equal to the maximum cardinality over the cliques of the chordal graph G'.

- **Queries of bounded degree of cyclicity** [23, 22]. This is an interesting class of hypergraph which also encompasses the class of acyclic hypergraphs. For space reasons, we omit a formal definition. Computing the degree of cyclicity of a query is feasible in polynomial time [23, 22].

Another generalizations of acyclic hypergraphs is the class of hypergraphs having *bounded query width* [8]. This notion yields a very wide class of tractable CQs (resp. CSPs). However, no efficient algorithm for computing a query decomposition of fixed width was known. In fact, it has been recently proved that checking whether a query has width $\leq k$, for some fixed constant k, is NP-complete [20].

Further interesting methods that do not explicitly generalize acyclic hypergraphs are based on a notion of *consistency* as used in [12,13]. [10] introduced the notion of *induced width* w^* which is – roughly – the smallest width k of any graph G' obtained by triangulation methods from the primal graph G of a hypergraph such that G' ensures $k + 1$-consistency. Graphs having induced width $\leq k$ can be also characterized as *partial k-trees* [14] or, equivalently, as graphs having treewidth $\leq k$ [2]. It follows that, for fixed k, checking whether $w^* \leq k$ is feasible in linear time [6]. The approach based on w^* is referred to as the w^*-Tractability method [9]. Note that this method is implicitly based on hypergraph acyclicity, given that the used triangulation methods enforce chordality of the resulting graph G' and thus acyclicity of the corresponding hypergraph. It was noted [11, 9] that, for any given hypergraph $\mathcal{H}$, TCLUSTER-width$(\mathcal{H}) = w^*(\mathcal{H}) + 1$.

6 Hypertree Width

A new class of tractable conjunctive queries, which generalizes the class of acyclic queries, has been recently identified [20]. Deciding whether a given query belongs to this class is polynomial-time feasible and even highly parallelizable. In this section, we review from [21] the generalization of this notion to the wider framework of hypergraphs, and how to employ this notion in order to define a new decomposition method we will refer to as HYPERTREE.

A *hypertree for a hypergraph* $\mathcal{H}$ is a triple $\langle T, \chi, \lambda \rangle$, where $T = (N, E)$ is a rooted tree, and χ and λ are labeling functions which associate to each vertex $p \in N$ two sets $\chi(p) \subseteq var(\mathcal{H})$ and $\lambda(p) \subseteq edges(\mathcal{H})$. If $T' = (N', E')$ is a subtree of T, we define $\chi(T') = \bigcup_{v \in N'} \chi(v)$. We denote the set of vertices N of T by $vertices(T)$, and the root of T by $root(T)$. Moreover, for any $p \in N$, T_p denotes the subtree of T rooted at p.

Definition 1. A *hypertree decomposition* of a hypergraph $\mathcal{H}$ is a hypertree $\langle T, \chi, \lambda \rangle$ for $\mathcal{H}$ which satisfies all the following conditions:

1. for each edge $h \in edges(\mathcal{H})$, there exists $p \in vertices(T)$ such that $var(h) \subseteq \chi(p)$;
2. for each variable $Y \in var(\mathcal{H})$, the set $\{p \in vertices(T) \mid Y \in \chi(p)\}$ induces a (connected) subtree of T;
3. for each $p \in vertices(T)$, $\chi(p) \subseteq var(\lambda(p))$;
4. for each $p \in vertices(T)$, $var(\lambda(p)) \cap \chi(T_p) \subseteq \chi(p)$.

A hypertree decomposition $\langle T, \chi, \lambda \rangle$ of $\mathcal{H}$ is a *complete decomposition* of $\mathcal{H}$ if, for each edge $h \in edges(\mathcal{H})$, there exists $p \in vertices(T)$ such that $var(h) \subseteq \chi(p)$ and $h \in \lambda(p)$.

The *width* of the hypertree decomposition $\langle T, \chi, \lambda \rangle$ is $max_{p \in vertices(T)} |\lambda(p)|$. The HYPERTREE width $hw(\mathcal{H})$ of $\mathcal{H}$ is the minimum width over all its hypertree decompositions. The hypertree decompositions of $\mathcal{H}$ having width equal to $hw(\mathcal{H})$ are the *optimal* hypertree decompositions of $\mathcal{H}$.

Intuitively, if $\mathcal{H}$ is a cyclic hypergraph, the χ labeling selects the set of variables to be fixed in order to split the cycles and achieve acyclicity; $\lambda(p)$ "covers" the variables of $\chi(p)$ by a set of edges.

Example 2. The hypertree width of the cyclic query Q_1 of Example 1 is 2; a (complete) 2-width hypertree decomposition of $\mathcal{H}(Q_1)$ is shown in Figure 1.

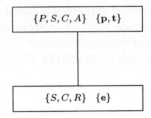

Fig. 1. A 2-width hypertree decomposition of hypergraph $\mathcal{H}(Q_1)$

Example 3. Consider the following constraint scopes:

$a(X_{ab}, X, X', X_{ac}, X_{af}); b(X_{ab}, Y, Y', X_{bc}, X_{bf}); c(X_{ac}, X_{bc}, Z); d(X, Z); e(Y, Z);$
$f(X_{af}, X_{bf}, Z'); g(X', Z'); h(Y', Z'); j(J, X, Y, X', Y')$

Let $\mathcal{H}_3$ be their corresponding hypergraph. $\mathcal{H}_3$ is clearly cyclic, and thus $hw(\mathcal{H}_3) > 1$ (as only acyclic hypergraphs have hypertree width 1). Figure 2 shows a (complete) hypertree decomposition of $\mathcal{H}_3$ having width 2, hence $hw(\mathcal{H}_3) = 2$.

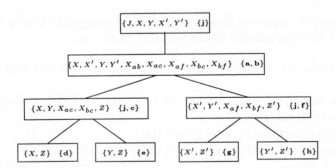

Fig. 2. A 2-width hypertree decomposition of hypergraph $\mathcal{H}_3$

It is easy to see that the acyclic hypergraphs are precisely the hypergraphs having hypertree width one.

We say that a hypergraph $\mathcal{H}$ has k-bounded hypertree-width if $hw(\mathcal{H}) \leq k$. From the results in [20], it follows that k-bounded hypertree-width is efficiently decidable, and that a hypertree decomposition of $\mathcal{H}$ of width k can be efficiently computed (if any).

In Section 8 we will introduce an efficient algorithm which decides whether a hypergraph $\mathcal{H}$ has k-bounded hypertree width and, in this case, computes an optimal hypertree decomposition of $\mathcal{H}$.

Any CSP instance I is efficiently solvable, given a k-bounded complete hypertree decomposition HD of $\mathcal{H}_I$. To this end, we define an acyclic CSP instance which is equivalent to I and whose size is polynomially bounded by the size of I.

For each vertex p of the decomposition HD, we define a new constraint scope whose associated constraint relation is the projection on $\chi(p)$ of the join of the relations in $\lambda(p)$. This way, we obtain a join-tree JT of an acyclic hypergraph $\mathcal{H}'$. $\mathcal{H}'$ corresponds to a new CSP instance I' over a set of constraint relations of size $O(n^k)$, where n is the input size (i.e., $n = |I|$) and k is the width of the hypertree decomposition HD. By construction, I' is an acyclic CSP, and we can easily show that it is equivalent to the input CSP instance I. Thus, all the efficient techniques available for acyclic CSP instances can be employed for the evaluation of I', and hence of I.

Theorem 1 ([21]). *Given a constraint satisfaction instance I and a k-width hypertree decomposition of $\mathcal{H}_I$, I is solvable in $O(n^k \log n^k) = O(n^k \log n)$ time, where n is the size of I.*

The same result holds for Boolean conjunctive queries [20].

7 Comparing the Different Methods

For comparing decomposition methods we introduce the relations $\preceq$, $\triangleright$, and $\prec\!\!\prec$ defined as follows:

$D_1 \preceq D_2$, in words, D_2 *generalizes* D_1, if $\exists \delta \geq 0$ such that, $\forall k > 0, C(D_1, k) \subseteq C(D_2, k + \delta)$. Thus $D_1 \preceq D_2$ if every class of CSP instances which is tractable according to D_1 is also tractable according to D_2.

$D_1 \triangleright D_2$ (D_1 *beats* D_2) if there exists an integer k such that $\forall m \; C(D_1, k) \not\subseteq C(D_2, m)$. To prove that $D_1 \triangleright D_2$, it is sufficient to exhibit a class of hypergraphs contained in some $C(D_1, k)$ but in no $C(D_2, j)$ for $j \geq 0$. Intuitively, $D_1 \triangleright D_2$ means that at least on some class of CSP instances, D_1 outperforms D_2.

$D_1 \prec\!\!\prec D_2$ if $D_1 \preceq D_2$ and $D_2 \triangleright D_1$. In this case we say that D_2 *strongly generalizes* D_1.

Mathematically, $\preceq$ is a *preorder*, i.e., it is reflexive, transitive but not anti-symmetric. We say that D_1 *is $\preceq$-equivalent to D_2*, denoted $D_1 \equiv D_2$, if both $D_1 \preceq D_2$ and $D_2 \preceq D_1$ hold.

The decomposition methods D_1 and D_2 are *strongly incomparable* if both $D_1 \triangleright D_2$ and $D_2 \triangleright D_1$. Note that if D_1 and D_2 are strongly incomparable, then they are also incomparable w.r.t. the relations $\preceq$ and $\prec\!\!\prec$.

Figure 3 shows a representation of the hierarchy of DMs determined by the $\lll$ relation. Each element of the hierarchy represents a DM, apart from that containing *Tree Clustering*, w^*, and *Treewidth* which are grouped together because they are $\preceq$-equivalent as easily follows from the observations in Section 5.

Theorem 2 ([21]). *For each pair D_1 and D_2 of decompositions methods represented in Figure 3, the following holds:*

- *There is a directed path from D_1 to D_2 iff $D_1 \lll D_2$, i.e., iff D_2 strongly generalizes D_1.*
- *D_1 and D_2 are not linked by any directed path iff they are strongly incomparable.*

Hence, Fig. 3 gives a complete picture of the relationships holding among the different methods.

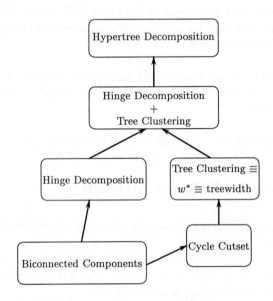

Fig. 3. Constraint Tractability Hierarchy

8 An Algorithm for Computing Optimal Hypertree Decompositions

In this section we describe a new algorithm, called opt-k-decomp, which, given a hypergraph $\mathcal{H}$, computes an optimal hypertree decomposition of $\mathcal{H}$ of width $\leq k$ (if any). The algorithm returns 'failure' if no such a decomposition exists (i.e, if $hw(\mathcal{H}) > k$).

We introduce a normal form for hypertree decompositions. Let $\mathcal{H}$ be a hypergraph, and let $V \subseteq var(\mathcal{H})$ be a set of variables and $X, Y \in var(\mathcal{H})$. X is $[V]$-adjacent to Y if there exists an edge $h \in edges(\mathcal{H})$ such that $\{X, Y\} \subseteq (h - V)$. A $[V]$-path π from X to Y is a sequence $X = X_0, \ldots, X_\ell = Y$ of variables such that: X_i is $[V]$-adjacent to X_{i+1}, for each $i \in [0...\ell\text{-}1]$. A set $W \subseteq var(\mathcal{H})$ of variables is $[V]$-connected if $\forall X, Y \in W$ there is a $[V]$-path from X to Y. A $[V]$-component is a maximal $[V]$-connected non-empty set of variables $W \subseteq (var(\mathcal{H}) - V)$. For any $[V]$-component C, let $edges(C) = \{h \in edges(\mathcal{H}) \mid h \cap C \neq \emptyset\}$.

Let $HD = \langle T, \chi, \lambda \rangle$ be a hypertree for a hypergraph $\mathcal{H}$. For any vertex v of T, we will often use v as a synonym of $\chi(v)$. In particular, $[v]$-component denotes $[\chi(v)]$-component; the term $[v]$-path is a synonym of $[\chi(v)]$-path; and so on.

Definition 2 ([20]). A hypertree decomposition $HD = \langle T, \chi, \lambda \rangle$ of a hypergraph $\mathcal{H}$ is in normal form (NF) if for each vertex $r \in vertices(T)$, and for each child s of r, all the following conditions hold:
1. there is (exactly) one $[r]$-component C_r such that $\chi(T_s) = C_r \cup (\chi(s) \cap \chi(r))$;
2. $\chi(s) \cap C_r \neq \emptyset$, where C_r is the $[r]$-component satisfying Condition 1;
3. $var(\lambda(s)) \cap \chi(r) \subseteq \chi(s)$.

Theorem 3 ([20]). *For each k-width hypertree decomposition of a hypergraph $\mathcal{H}$ there exists a k-width hypertree decomposition of $\mathcal{H}$ in normal form.*

The normal form theorem above immediately entails that for each optimal hypertree decomposition of a hypergraph $\mathcal{H}$ there exists an optimal hypertree decomposition of $\mathcal{H}$ in normal form.

For any hypergraph $\mathcal{H}$, we will call k-vertex any set of edges of $\mathcal{H}$ having cardinality $\leq k$.

Figure 4 shows the algorithm opt-k-decomp.

Let $\mathcal{H}$ be a hypergraph. The procedure *Compute-CG* computes a directed weighted graph CG whose nodes are partitioned in two sets N_e and N_a. Each node in N_e is a pair (R, C) where R is a k-vertex of $\mathcal{H}$, and C is an $[R]$-component. $(root, V)$ is a special node, because V is the set of all vertices of the hypergraph $\mathcal{H}$ and *root* does not correspond to a k-vertex of $\mathcal{H}$. It will be the root vertex of any hypertree decomposition computed by opt-k-decomp. This node has no outcoming arcs.

Intuitively, for every node $(R, C) \in N_e$, the algorithm solves a subproblem associated to the $[R]$-component C, and then employs these partial solutions to determine an optimal hypertree decomposition of the whole hypergraph.

Formally, for any node $(R, C) \in N_e$, we define the hypergraph $sub_\mathcal{H}(R, C)$ as follows. If $R = root$ then $sub_\mathcal{H}(R, C) = \mathcal{H}$. Else, let $k' = |R|$ and let $\{X_0, X_1, \ldots, X_{2k'}\}$ be a set of fresh vertices. Let R' be the set of k' edges $\{h \cup \{X_0\} \mid h \in R\}$, and let *Clique*$(k')$ be the set of edges $\{\{X_0, X_i, X_j\} \mid 1 \leq i < j \leq 2k'\}$. The set of edges of $sub_\mathcal{H}(R, C)$ is

$$edges(C) \cup R' \cup Clique(k') \cup \{h \cap var(R) \mid h \in edges(\mathcal{H})\}.$$

ALGORITHM opt-k-decomp
Input: A Hypergraph $\mathcal{H} = (V, H)$.
Output: An optimal hypertree decomposition
of $\mathcal{H}$, if $hw(\mathcal{H}) \leq k$; $failure$, otherwise.

Var
$\quad CG = (N_e \cup N_a, A, weight)$: weigthed directed graph;
$\quad HD = \langle T, \chi, \lambda \rangle$: hypertree of $\mathcal{H}$;

Procedure *Compute-CG*
$\quad N_e := \{(root, V)\} \cup \{(R, C) \; : \; R$ is a k-vertex
$\quad$ and C is an $[R]$-component $\}$;
$\quad N_a := \emptyset; \quad A := \emptyset$;
$\quad$ **For each** $(R, C) \in N_e$ **Do**
$\quad\quad$ Let $rc := (\bigcup_{h \in edges(C)} var(h)) \cap var(R)$;
$\quad\quad$ **For each** k-vertex S **Do**
$\quad\quad\quad$ **If** $var(S) \cap C \neq \emptyset$ **And** $rc \subseteq var(S)$ **Then**
$\quad\quad\quad\quad N_a := N_a \cup \{ (S, C) \}$;
$\quad\quad\quad\quad$ Add an arc from (S, C) to (R, C) in A;
$\quad\quad\quad\quad$ **For each** $(S, C') \in N_e$ s.t. $C' \subseteq C$ **Do**
$\quad\quad\quad\quad\quad$ Add an arc from (S, C') to (S, C) in A;
$\quad\quad\quad$ **EndIf**
$\quad\quad$ **endFor**
endProcedure;

Procedure *Weight-CG*
$\quad weight((R, C)) := \infty$, for any $(R, C) \in N_e$
$\quad\quad$ having no incoming arcs in CG;
$\quad weight((S, C)) := |S|$, for any $(S, C) \in N_a$
$\quad\quad$ having no incoming arcs in CG;
(* For any $p \in N_e \cup N_a$, let $in(p)$ denote the number of
arcs incoming to p from unweighted nodes *)
$\quad$ **While** there is some unweighted node in $N_e \cup N_a$ **Do**
$\quad\quad$ Let $p = (S, C)$ be an unweighted node s.t. $in(p) = 0$;
$\quad\quad$ **If** $p \in N_e$ **Then**
$\quad\quad\quad weight(p) = min(\{weight(q)| \ (q, p) \in A\})$;
$\quad\quad$ **Else** (* $p \in N_a$ *)
$\quad\quad\quad weight(p) = max(\{|S|\} \cup \{weight(q)| \ (q, p) \in A\})$;
$\quad$ **EndWhile**
endProcedure;

begin*(* MAIN *)*
$\quad$ *Compute-CG*;
$\quad$ *Weight-CG*;
$\quad$ **If** $weight((root, V)) = \infty$ **Then**
$\quad\quad$ **Output** *failure*;
$\quad$ **Else**
$\quad\quad$ Create a vertex $root'$ in T;
$\quad\quad \chi(root') := \emptyset; \lambda(root') := \emptyset$;
$\quad\quad$ *Compute-hypertree*$((root, V), root')$;
$\quad\quad$ **Output** HD
end.

Fig. 4. Computing an optimal hypertree-decomposition

Procedure *Compute-hypertree*(p : *CG*node; r : *HD*vertex)
    Choose a minimum-weighted predecessor (S, C) of p;
    Create a new vertex s as a child of r in T;
    $\lambda(s) := S$;
    $\chi(s) := var(S) \cap (C \cup \chi(r))$;
    For each predecessor q of (S, C) **Do**
        Compute-hypertree(q, s);
endProcedure;

Fig. 5. Procedure *Compute-hypertree*

Each node $(R, C) \in N_e$ has some incoming arcs from nodes in N_a. Let (S, C) be any of these nodes, where S is a k-vertex. S represents a candidate for "breaking" the $[R]$-*component* C of the hypergraph, or equivalently, for decomposing the hypergraph $sub_{\mathcal{H}}(R, C)$. The evaluation of this choice requires the solution of smaller subproblems, one for each $[S]$-*component* C' of $\mathcal{H}$ such that $C' \subseteq C$. For this reason, (S, C) has an incoming arc from any such a node $(S, C') \in N_e$.

To assign a weight to (R, C), *Weight-CG* will choose the best-weighted incoming node (S, C), and take $weight((R, C)) = weight((S, C))$. The nodes in N_a behave differently, because there is no choice to be done. Every $[S]$-*component* $C' \subseteq C$ must be decomposed, hence the weight of (S, C) will be determined by the worst-weighted incoming node (S, C''), i.e., $weight((S, C)) = weight((S, C''))$.

Lemma 1. *Let $\mathcal{H}$ be the input hypergraph to* opt-k-decomp. *After the computation of* Weight-CG, *for any node $(R, C) \in N_e$, weight((R, C)) is equal to the hypertree width of $sub_{\mathcal{H}}(R, C)$ if $hw(sub_{\mathcal{H}}(R, C)) \leq k$, and ∞ otherwise.*

Note that, in particular, the weight of the special node $(root, V)$ will be the hypertree width of $\mathcal{H}$ if $hw(\mathcal{H}) \leq k$ and ∞ otherwise.

After the execution of the procedure *Weight-CG*, the weighted graph *CG* contains enough information to compute every optimal hypertree decomposition of $\mathcal{H}$ in normal form, if $hw(\mathcal{H}) \leq k$. Figure 5 shows the procedure *Compute-hypertree*, which selects one optimal hypertree decomposition of $\mathcal{H}$ in normal form. It proceeds top-down, starting from the special node $(root, V)$ and recursively descending along the graph, choosing at each step the best-weighted nodes. Indeed, these nodes corresponds to the best solutions of the subproblems associated to the nodes of *CG*.

opt-k-decomp runs in $O(n^{2k}m^2)$ time, where n and m are the number of edges and the number of vertices of $\mathcal{H}$, respectively. This bound can be easily obtained by inspecting the procedures of opt-k-decomp. Note that there are $O(n^k)$ k-vertices of $\mathcal{H}$, and for each k-vertex R, $O(m)$ $[R]$-components. It follows that the graph *CG* has $O(n^k m)$ nodes in N_e and $O(n^{2k}m)$ nodes in N_a. Moreover, each node in N_e has $O(n^k)$ incoming arcs at most, and each node in N_a has $O(m)$ incoming arcs at most.

For space reasons, a formal proof of the correctness of opt-k-decomp will be given in the extended version of this paper. The proof is based on some results about the normal form of hypertree decompositions in [19], and on Lemma 1 above.

Theorem 4. opt-k-decomp *is correct.*

Acknowledgements

Research supported by *FWF (Austrian Science Funds)* under the project Z29-INF and by the *CNR (Italian National Research Council)*, under grant n.203.15.07.

References

1. S. Abiteboul, R. Hull, V. Vianu. *Foundations of Databases*, Addison-Wesley Publishing Company, 1995.
2. S. Arnborg, J. Lagergren, and D. Seese. Problems easy for tree-decomposable graphs. *J. of Algorithms*, 12:308–340, 1991.
3. C. Beeri, R. Fagin, D. Maier, and M. Yannakakis. On the Desiderability of Acyclic Database Schemes. *Journal of ACM*, 30(3):479–513, 1983.
4. P.A. Bernstein, and N. Goodman. The power of natural semijoins. *SIAM J. Computing*, 10(4):751–771, 1981.
5. W. Bibel. Constraint Satisfaction from a Deductive Viewpoint. *Artificial Intelligence*, 35,401–413, 1988.
6. H. L. Bodlaender. A linear-time algorithm for finding tree-decompositions of small treewidth. *SIAM Journal on Computing*, 25(6):1305-1317, 1996.
7. A.K. Chandra and P.M. Merlin. Optimal Implementation of Conjunctive Queries in relational Databases. In In *ACM Symp. on Theory of Computing (STOC'77)*, pp.77–90, 1977.
8. Ch. Chekuri and A. Rajaraman. Conjunctive Query Containment Revisited. In *Proc. International Conference on Database Theory 1997 (ICDT'97), Delphi, Greece, Jan. 1997*, Springer LNCS, Vol. 1186, pp.56–70, 1997.
9. R. Dechter. Constraint Networks. In *Encyclopedia of Artificial Intelligence*, second edition, Wiley and Sons, pp. 276-285, 1992.
10. R. Dechter and J. Pearl. Network based heuristics for CSPs. *AIJ*, 34(1):1–38, 1988.
11. R. Dechter and J. Pearl. Tree clustering for constraint networks. *Artificial Intelligence*, pp. 353–366, 1989.
12. E.C. Freuder. A sufficient condition for backtrack-free search. *JACM*, 29(1):24–32, 1982.
13. E.C. Freuder. A sufficient condition for backtrack bounded search. *Journal of the ACM*, 32(4):755–761, 1985.
14. E.C. Freuder. Complexity of K-Tree Structured Constraint Satisfaction Problems. *Proc. of AAAI'90*, 1990.
15. M.R. Garey and D.S. Johnson. *Computers and Intractability. A Guide to the Theory of NP-completeness*. Freeman and Comp., NY, USA, 1979.
16. N. Goodman, and O. Shmueli. Tree queries: a simple class of relational queries. *ACM Trans. on Database Systems*, 7(4):653–677, 1982.
17. G. Gottlob, N. Leone, and F. Scarcello. The Complexity of Acyclic Conjunctive Queries. *Proc. of the IEEE Symposium on Foundations of Computer Science (FOCS'98)*, pp.706–715, Palo Alto, CA, 1998.

18. G. Gottlob, N. Leone, and F. Scarcello. Advanced Parallel Algorithms for Acyclic Conjunctive Queries. Technical Report DBAI-TR-98/18, available on the web as: `http://www.dbai.tuwien.ac.at/staff/gottlob/parallel.ps`, or by email from the authors.

19. G. Gottlob, N. Leone, and F. Scarcello. Hypertree Decompositions and Tractable Queries. Technical Report DBAI-TR-98/21, available as Paper cs.DB/9812022 in *The Computer Research Repository*, http://xxx.lanl.gov/archive/cs

20. G. Gottlob, N. Leone, and F. Scarcello. Hypertree Decompositions and Tractable Queries. In *Proc. of Symp. on Principles of Database Systems (PODS'99)*, pp. 21–32, Philadelphia, May, 1999.

21. G. Gottlob, N. Leone, and F. Scarcello. A Comparison of Structural CSP Decomposition Methods. To appear in *Proc. of the International Joint Conference on Artificial Intelligence (IJCAI'99)*, Stockholm, August, 1999.

22. M. Gyssens, P.G. Jeavons, and D.A. Cohen. Decomposing constraint satisfaction problems using database techniques. *Artificial Intelligence*, 66:57–89, 1994.

23. M. Gyssens, and J. Paredaens. A Decomposition Methodology for Cyclic Databases. In *Advances in Database Theory*, volume 2, pp. 85-122. Plenum Press New York, NY, 1984.

24. P. Jeavons, D. Cohen, and M. Gyssens. Closure Properties of Constraints. *Journal of the ACM*, 44(4):527–548.

25. Ph. G. Kolaitis andf M. Y. Vardi. Conjunctive-Query Containment and Constraint Satisfaction. In *Proc. of Symp. on Principles of Database Systems (PODS'98)*, pp.205–213, Seattle, Washington, 1998.

26. D. Maier. *The Theory of Relational Databases*, Rochville, Md, Computer Science Press, 1986.

27. N. Robertson and P.D. Seymour. Graph Minors II. Algorithmic Aspects of Tree-Width. *J. Algorithms*, 7:309-322, 1986.

28. R.E. Tarjan, and M. Yannakakis. Simple linear-time algorithms to test chordality of graphs, test acyclicity of hypergraphs, and selectively reduce acyclic hypergraphs. *SIAM J. Computing*, 13(3):566-579, 1984.

29. J.D. Ullman. *Principles of Database and Knowledge Base Systems, Vol II*, Computer Science Press, Rockville, MD, 1989.

30. M. Vardi. Complexity of Relational Query Languages. In *Proc. of 14th ACM STOC*, pp. 137–146, 1982.

31. A.N. Wilschut, J. Flokstra, and P. M.G. Apers. Parallel evaluation of multi-join queries. In *Proc. of SIGMOD'95*, San Jose, CA USA, pp.115–126, 1995.

32. M. Yannakakis. Algorithms for Acyclic Database Schemes. In *Proc. of Int. Conf. on Very Large Data Bases (VLDB'81)*, pp. 82–94, C. Zaniolo and C. Delobel Eds., Cannes, France, 1981.

Instances Evolution Vs Classes Evolution

Dalila Tamzalit & Chabane Oussalah

LGI2P / Site EERIE – EMA   Parc Scientifique Georges Besse 30035 Nîmes Cedex 1,
France
{Dalila.Tamzalit, Chabane.Oussalah}@site-eerie.ema.fr

Abstract. we propose a model developed to have inherent capabilities for auto-adaptation between classes and instances. Our two main objectives are: to allow objects to evolve their structures dynamically, with all necessary impacts on the database schema; to allow, similarly, the creation and display of different plans for evolving the design, like ways of schema evolution, giving in this way a simulation tool for database design and maintenance.

Artificial Life and Genetic Algorithms inspired the idea of objects evolving and adapting to their environment. A model evolution is then considered in an auto-adaptive loop between classes and instances. Change is two-way: that coming down from class to object instantiates in *development processes;* that coming up from object to class in *emergence processes* which concern evolved instances which become not conform to any existing class.

1. Introduction

Experience gained in object oriented databases systems and applications development has brought to light specific gaps, in particular a weakness in matching the model to the reality. Indeed, certain application requires new data which have not been specified at the class level and which must be taken into account at instance level. Instance evolution is the focus of this paper. It appears to us crucial in the development and exploitation of real-life applications.

The aim that we set ourselves is an evolutionary model able to handle both unforeseen and inaccurately anticipated needs. This will allow an object to evolve autonomously using internal and external information and to permit the creation of new abstractions. With this in mind, we propose to extend instance evolution from simple value modifications to structural modifications (addition and deletion of attributes). We will study for this the evolutionary processes, which allow objects to adapt by themselves when change takes place.

1.1. Object Evolution Vs Artificial Evolution

Operations of addition, deletion or modification of data or functionalities in an OODB or application lead automatically to evolution. Thus, changes in a class hierarchy or class definition must be propagated to instances and subclasses involved. Many strategies have been developed to manage impacts. We have studied the most important ones in three categories[18]: *class evolution* ([3], [12], [1], [14], [10], [7], [19],

17

[2]…); *impacts of class evolution on instances* ([1], [9], [16], [4]…) and *instance evolution* ([10], [15]…).

The main conclusion of this comparative study is that the principal gap in existing evolutionary models is their incapacity to cope with unidentified or poorly defined needs and incomplete data. Moreover, instance evolution is always limited by class hierarchy - a rigid and unnatural aspect of their evolution.

1.2. Artificial Evolution

We have brought together under the title of Artificial Evolution all research work concerned with the definition and implementation of evolutionary and adaptive artificial systems. Artificial Life and Genetic Algorithms fall under this head [8] and constitute a basis for this study:

1. **Artificial Life:** its principal objective is simulation and synthesis of biological phenomena [5]. It attempt to generalize the principles underlying biological phenomena and to recreate them. It borrowed the concepts of GTYPE (genetic information of a system) and PTYPE (representative individuals of a system) respectively from the genotype and the phenotype of biology. GTYPE and PTYPE are interacting together unceasingly, enriching themselves through the processes of *development* (of GTYPE to create new individuals) and *emergence* (of new individuals properties to be inserted into GTYPE).

2. **Genetic Algorithms:** are particularly adapted to searching for better solutions to a given problem, iteratively, evolving "blindly" by reproducing and then perpetuating best genes through new individuals [6]. Genetic mechanisms are used: random *selection* of adapted individuals (implies a quantitative measurement of this adaptation); *crossing-over* of their genetic code in order to recover best genes; *mutation* to mutate a gene favorably.

1.3. Object Evolution and Artificial Evolution

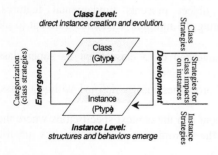

Fig. 1. Object evolution processes under Artificial Evolution viewpoint.

Taking into account the role of classes and instances in the makeup of a real or artificial system, we liken class to genotype and instance to phenotype. We propose to present the general evolution of an object model as a retroactive and iterative loop (Fig. 1.). For our part, we consider that object evolution presents an insufficiency in the evolutionary process - namely in the emergence of new properties from instance evolution.

2. A Genetic Evolution Object Model

We propose to adapt artificial evolution concepts to those of object evolution through the GENOME model[18]. In order to illustrate the concepts and evolutionary processes, we use the example of Fig. 2. :

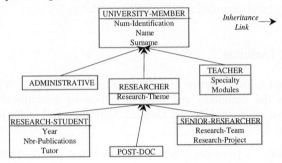

Fig. 2. Members of a university described at the class level.

2.1. Concepts

2.1.1. Basic concepts: population, Instance-PTYPE and Class-GTYPE

– *Population and Genetic patrimony:* a group of classes representing various abstractions of one and the same entity forms a *population* (like the population of members of a university). All the attributes constitute its *Genetic Patrimony*.
– *Instance-PTYPE:* instances are the phenotype and represent entities called upon to evolve.
– *Class-GTYPE:* classes define instances features, their genetic code.

2.1.2. Advanced concepts: Fundamental, Inherited and Specific Genotypes

In a class, not every gene plays the same role or has the same prevalence. We consider that any class is entirely specified through three types of genotypes:
– *Fundamental Genotype or FG:* any object presents fundamental features, represented by particular genes representing the minimal semantics inherent to all classes of a same population.
– *Inherited Genotype or IG:* properties inherited by a class from its super-class constitute the *Inherited Genotype*.
– *Specific Genotype or SG:* it consists of properties locally defined within a class, specific to it.
  IG and SG are issued from the environment and the context specificities where the "species" lives whereas FG corresponds to the transmission of characteristics specific to the whole species.

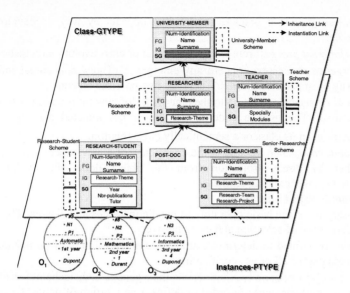

Fig. 3. Classes and instances model in GENOME.

2.1.3. Concept of scheme

The concept of scheme is borrowed from genetic algorithms. It is an entity having the same genetic structure as the represented population. Each feature is represented by 0, 1 or #: 0 for absence of the gene, 1 for its presence and # for its indifference. The scheme is a simple and powerful means to model groups of individuals. We consider two kinds of schemes:

- *Permanent scheme:* with each specified class is associated a permanent scheme. It also contains three parts: fundamental, inherited and specific genotypes parts.
- *Temporary scheme:* it is a selection unit of one or a group of entities (instances or classes). It is especially useful during an instance evolutionary process and is used like a filter allowing selection of adapted entities.

2.2. Evolutionary processes

An evolutionary process is triggered when a change, envisaged or not, appears in the model. The process must be able to detect this change, find the entity implicated in the evolution and reflect this change adequately. Let us recall here that we place ourselves within the framework of the instance evolutionary process:

2.2.1. Phases

We consider that an instance's evolutionary process is carried out in three phases: an *extraction* phase, an *exploration* phase, and finally an *exploitation* phase:

- *Extraction Phase:* it consists of the detection of an instance evolution and the extraction of the object's genetic code within a temporary scheme.
- *Exploration phase :* it explores all the model's classes to locate adapted, even partially, classes. In order to avoid fruitless searches, this exploration follows precise steps: first it selects the set of populations concerned, then it carries out the search in that set.

– *Exploitation phase:* it manage the various impacts by way of development or emergence:

- *Development process:* represents the impact of class evolution on instances.
- *Emergence processes:* concern any emergence of new conceptual information, by way of impacts on classes. There are two possible outcomes:
  - *Local emergence:* relating to the emergence of new information within existing class(es). The genetic code of the object has mutated and this can force mutation[1] in its class or a semantically close relation.
  - *Global emergence:* related to the emergence of a new conceptual (class) entity either by direct projection from the object doing the evolving or by crossing-over existing entities.

2.2.2. Genetic object operators

It is necessary to define basic operators to handle instances and classes. The two most important are those of selection and crossing-over:

– *Selection:* is defined to determine, after structural evolution of an instance, which class holds part or all of its specification.

– *Crossing-over:* works on two entities via their genetic code (scheme) to allow them to interchange their genes in order to define a new group of genes. Crossing-over works indifferently on classes and instances. It constitutes the core of the emergence process.

– *Adaptation value Av:* allows calculation of the semantic distance between the evolved object and semantically close classes, thanks to a function having as input parameters two schemes of the same length. The first represents the entity having evolved and the second represents a closely related class. Denoting the evolved object's scheme by Sch_{obj} and the close class's scheme by Sch_{param}, the adaptive function is defined, using the operator $\wedge$ (and_logic), as:

$$Av\ (Sch_{param}) = \sum\nolimits_{(i\,=\,1 \to\,n)} \{\ Sch_{obj}[i] \wedge Sch_{param}[i]\}\ /\ n$$

Where n is number of genes specified in the evolved object; i is the variable index from 1 to n, defining, at each stage, the position of two respective genes of the analyzed schemes. Two schemes are initially compared in their FG. The other genes are then compared.

In the following section, we present the architecture of GENOME as well as the operation of its evolution processes:

2.3. Operation of the model

Extraction, exploration and exploitation phases follow one another. Each phase is unrolled on an example.

2.3.1. Extraction Phase

It extracts the scheme of the evolved instances. New introduced attributes, which are reified, are created with a transitory status (their value is preceded in by a ~). Then all the attribute references are joined together to create the temporary scheme.

---

[1] We consider a mutation as every appearance of a new information inside a model, and that will provoke changes in the genetic patrimony.

– Example: the three instances of Research-Student (example in Fig. 3.):

Genetic Patrimony		Instances of Research-Student		
		O₁	O₂	O₃
FG	Identification-Num	#3	#8	#4
	Name	N1	N2	N3
	Surname	P1	P2	P3
	Research-theme	Automatic	Mathematics	Computing
	Year	1ˢᵗ Year	2ⁿᵈ Year	3ʳᵈ Year
	Nbr-Publications		1	4
	Tutor	Dupont	Durant	Dupond
	Research-Team			
	Research-Project			
	Specialty			
	Modules			

These instances will evolve to become (Attribute is a deleted attribute):

Genetic Patrimony		O₁	O₂	O₃
FG	Identification-Num	#3	#8	#4
	Name	N1	N2	N3
	Surname	P1	P2	P3
	Research-theme	Automatics	Mathematics	Objet
	Year	1ˢᵗ Year	2ⁿᵈ Year	3ʳᵈ Year
	Nbr-Publications		1	4
	Tutor	Dupont	Durant	Dupond
	Research-Team	Vision		Object
	Research-Project			
	Specialty			
	Modules	Segmentation		

New Attributes	Rank	Professor		
	Position		Engineer	
	Responsibility			Supervisor

The new attributes *Rank*, *Position* and *Responsibility* take transitory status and temporary schemes (TS) are:

$TSO_1=[11110001001\bar{~}100]$ - $TSO_2=[111000000000\bar{~}10]$ - $TSO_3=[1111000100000\bar{~}1]$.

2.3.2. Exploration phase

It is carried out within the selected population. Note that the new attributes (marked transitory) are not concerned in the selection since they are not in the possession of any class.

– **O₁'s Temporary Scheme:** An Av. is calculated for each class:

Entity	Scheme (IG and SG)								Av.
Objet O₁	1	0	0	0	1	0	0	1	
University-member	0	0	0	0	0	0	0	0	0/3
Researcher	1	0	0	0	0	0	0	0	1/3
Research-Student	1	1	#	1	0	0	0	0	1/3
Senior-Researcher	1	0	0	0	1	#	0	0	2/3
Teacher	0	0	0	0	0	0	1	1	1/3

With : ■ IG, and : ☐ SG

University-member (Av=0), Researcher and Research-Student are ignored, because they are in the same branch as Senior-Researcher which has the best Av. In contrast, Senior-Researcher and Teacher are partially adapted, and are thus selected.

– **O₂'s Temporary Scheme:** Calculation of each class's Av. gives:

Entity	Scheme (IG and SG)								Av.
Objet O₂	0	0	0	0	0	0	0	0	
University-member	0	0	0	0	0	0	0	0	0
Researcher	1	0	0	0	0	0	0	0	0
Research-Student	1	1	#	1	0	0	0	0	0
Senior-Researcher	1	0	0	0	1	#	0	0	0
Teacher	0	0	0	0	0	0	1	1	0

No class is adapted. They are all ignored. Only the University-member class remains because it has the same FG as the object.

– **O₁'s Temporary Scheme:** Calculation of each class's Av. gives:

Entity	Scheme (IG and SG)								Av.
Objet O₁	1	0	0	0	1	0	0	0	
University-member	0	0	0	0	0	0	0	0	0
Researcher	1	0	0	0	0	0	0	0	1/2
Research-Student	1	1	#	1	0	0	0	0	1/2
Senior-Researcher	1	0	0	0	1	#	0	0	1
Teacher	0	0	0	0	0	0	1	1	0

The Senior-Researcher class is completely adapted: it can contain the object in its new state, if it takes into account the new attribute.

2.3.3. Exploitation Phase

2.3.3.1. Local Emergence processes

O₃'s Temporary Scheme: an existing class, Senior-Researcher, holds the genes of the object O₃ after an evolution step, which introduces the new attribute of *Responsibility*. This will have: to be inserted into the Senior-Researcher class by local emergence; to enrich the genetic patrimony and to lose its transitory status.

2.3.3.2. Global Emergence processes

The emergent abstraction can be defined by crossing-over or directly:

1. Crossing-over:

The permanent schemes of the selected classes constitute the starting population for the crossing-over, and fixe its length. The new schemes will replace their parents.

Two schemes are randomly selected to be crossed. The choice of crossing-over point is significant. It is based on the *uniform crossing-over* of the genetic algorithm [17]. It amounts to granting a weight relating to each parent for the transmission of genes to one of the children. This weight is calculated according to the Av. of each scheme (see example). After this, a random number is generated, then compared with the weight. If it is lower, the scheme 1 gene is transmitted to child 1 and the scheme 2 gene is transmitted to child 2. This operation of random bonding is repeated until all the genes have been reviewed.

We add to that a significant constraint which enables us to ensure coherence for the crossing-over operation: a permanent scheme presents at most two significant blocks (without considering the FG): IG and SG, which must be respected and transmitted. We thus impose a constraint of *blocks of genes*.

– **O₁'s Temporary Scheme:** Senior-Researcher and Teacher schemes are selected:

– The first iteration:

O₁	1	0	0	0	1	0	0	1	
Random bonds	0.1	0.5	0.63	0.24	0.58	0.95	0.15	0.48	*Av.*
Senior-Researcher	1	0	0	0	1	#	0	0	0.65≈2/3
Teacher	0	0	0	0	0	0	1	1	0.35≈1/3
Child Scheme1	1	0	0	0	*1*	#	0	0	2/3
Child Scheme2	0	0	0	0	0	#	1	1	1/3

Since the Child Scheme 1 (or 2) has more chance to inherit genes of the parent 1 (or 2), each child scheme inherits the block constraints of its predominant parent.

– Second iteration:

O₁	1	0	0	0	1	0	0	1	
Random bonds	0.65	0.58	0.23	0.47	0.95	0.28	0.64	0.75	*Av.*
Child Scheme1	1	0	0	0	*1*	#	0	0	0.65
Child Scheme2	0	0	0	0	0	#	1	1	0.35
Child Scheme3	1	0	0	0	*1*	#	0	1	*1*
Child Scheme4	0	0	0	0	0	#	1	1	1/3

Child Scheme3 could be the parent scheme of O_1: it is the *emergent scheme*.

- O_2's **Temporary Scheme:** the scheme belongs to the population but cannot be deduced from any existing class. So it represents a new abstraction.

2. Global Emergence processes:
It can provoke the emergence of a simple class or of a collection of related classes. Necessary attributes (existing and new) are specified within the new abstraction. The methods, which call upon these attributes, are integrated and proposed to the user for validation. The user will validate and complete the specifications of the abstraction. O_1's Temporary Scheme is thus a *simple emergent object*.

Now, the question is where this new abstraction must be inserted? There are two possibilities:

- Within the hierarchy branch of Researcher, as a sub-class of Senior-Researcher, with a mutation on the *Module* gene defined by Teacher.
- Within the hierarchy branch of Teacher, as a sub-class, by integrating together, by means of a mutation, *Research-Theme*, *Research-Team* and *Research-Project*. The most judicious choice can be easily deduced from the Av.(section 2.4)
- O_2's **Temporary Scheme:** The object O_2 defines a new abstraction, that of Engineer, which is created and attached to the root University-member population.

2.4. Integration of the emergent entity and notion of semantic distance

The insertion of a new abstraction must reflect the influence of its parents but also the semantics carried by the emergent entity. It is logical that an abstraction, which takes the greater part of its genes from another abstraction, has to be in the same hierarchy as this last. In order to infer such information, we have recourse to the Avs already calculated during the exploration phase. The parent having the strongest Av. will influence the final scheme the most. All the more so if the emergent scheme contains the IG of the parent scheme. Likewise, in a global emergence, the emergent abstraction will be attached to its branch. But in the case of Avs are around 50% (±10%), multiple inheritance is the solution. When the IG of each of the parent schemes is found in the emergent scheme is also another criterion.

That's why the corresponding emergent abstraction of the object O_1, in the example, will be attached to Senior-Researcher, and this for two main reasons:

- the emergent scheme presents the same block of IG as Senior-Researcher.

- the emergent scheme is closer to Senior-Researcher than to other classes. This proximity is evaluated by comparison of the two schemes, using the adaptive function. The obtained value is the *semantic distance* between the two schemes:

Child Scheme3	1	0	0	0	*1*	#	0	1	*Semantic distance*
Senior-Researcher	1	0	0	0	1	#	0	0	3/4
Teacher	0	0	0	0	0	0	1	1	1/4

Once the emergent abstraction is inserted, the object O_1 is attached to it and an evolution link is created from its initial class to its new class: *the model has learned a new behavior and a possible direction of evolution.* Having concluded these evolution processes, the model becomes:

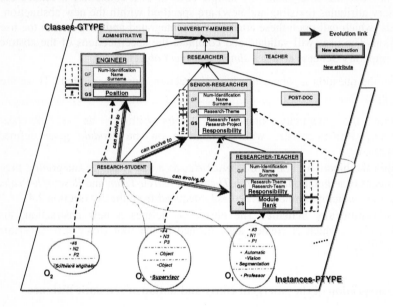

Fig. 4. The example model after evolution in GENOME.

3. Conclusion

The proposed and studied evolution processes are based on models organized around the inheritance link. We aim to extend GENOME to manage also complex objects. We have to study the emergence processes according to other structural links: composition and association links, implying like this, several populations.

Another future extension of the model is the evaluation of the quality of the emergence. In fact, many ways of evolution can be proposed and a choice must be done among them. We want to develop semantical metrics of emergence to make the best choice among several emergent abstractions.

It seems to us that this new way of considering object evolution is promising for analysis and design, and can provide new tools of design and simulation of complex systems.

Bibliography

[1] BANERJEE J., KIM W., KIM H., KORTH H.F. *"Semantics Implementation of Schema Evolution in Object-Oriented Databases"* ACM 87.

[2] BRATSBERG E. *"Evolution and Integration of Classes in Object-Oriented Databases"* PhD thesis, Norwegian Institute of Technology, jun. 93.

[3] CASAIS E. *"Managing Evolution in Object Oriented Environnements: An Algorithmic Approach"* Thèse - Université de Genève. 91.

[4] CLAMEN S.M. *"Schema Evolution and Integration"* in Proceedings of the Distibuted and Parallel Databases conference, vol 2, p 101-126.Kluwer Academic Publishers, Boston, 94

[5] HEUDIN J.C. *"La Vie Artificielle "*. Edition Hermes, 94.

[6] HOLLAND J. *"Adaptation in Natural and Artificial Systems"*, University of Michigan Press, Ann Arbor, Mich., 75.

[7] KIM W., CHOU H.T. *"Versions of schema for object oriented databases"* In Proceedings of the 14th VLDB Conference, Los Angeles, Californie, 88.

[8] LANGTON C., TAYLOR C., FARMER J.D., RASMUSSEN S. *"Artificial Life II"* proceedings vol in the Santa Fe Institute studies in the sciences of complexity, New Mexico, February 90.

[9] LERNER B.S., HABERMANN A.N. *"Beyond Schema Evolution to Database Reorganization"* Proc. ACM Conf. OOPSLA and Proc. ECOOP, Ottawa, Canada. Published as ACM SIGPLAN Notices 25(10), pp. 67-76. October 90.

[10] MEYER B. *"Object-Oriented Software Construction"* International Series in Computer Science. Prenctice Hall, 88.

[12] NAPOLI A. *"Représentation à objets et raisonnement par classification en I.A."* Thèse de doctorat, Nancy 92.

[13] OUSSALAH C. & ALII *"Ingénierie Objet : Concepts et techniques"* InterEditions, 97.

[14] PENNEY D.J., STEIN J. *"Class modification in the GemStone object-oriented DBMS"* SIGPLAN Notices (Proc OOPSLA'87) Vol. 22, No. 12, pp. 111-117. 87.

[15] RECHENMAN F., UVIETTA P.*"SHIRKA : an object-centered knowledge bases management system"* In A. Pavé and G. Vansteenkiste ED. AI in numerical and symbolic simulation, pp 9-23., ALEAS, Lyon, France 89.

[16] SKARRA A.H., ZDONIK S.B. *"Type Evolution in an Object-Oriented Databases"* in Research Directions in Object-Oriented Programming, MIT Press Series in Computer Systems, MIT Press, Cambridge, MA, 1987, pp. 393-415. 87.

[17] SYSWERDA G. *"Uniform Crossover in Genetic Algorithms"* dans les actes de Intl. Conf. On Genetic Algorithms, pages 2-9, 89.

[18] TAMZALIT D., OUSSALAH C., MAGNAN M. *"How to Introduce Emergence in Object Evolution"* OOIS'98, , pp: 293-310, 9-11 September 98, Paris.

[19] ZDONIK S.B. *"Object-Oriented Type Evolution"* in Advances in Database Programming Languages, François Bancilhon and Peter Buneman eds, pp.277-288, ACM Press, New York 90.

Dynamic Relationships in Object Oriented Databases: A Uniform Approach

Awais Rashid[1], Peter Sawyer[1]

[1]Computing Department, Lancaster University, Lancaster LA1 4YR, UK

{marash, sawyer} @comp.lancs.ac.uk

Abstract. In this paper we present a uniform approach to dynamic relationships in object oriented databases. We present our relationship categorisation based on dividing the object database into three *virtual* spaces each hosting *entities* of a particular type and show how relationships from the modelling domain map onto relationships in our categorisation. We present a relationship model and the semantics of relationships. The relationship model is complemented with a meta-model for implementing dynamic relationships in an object oriented database. The applicability of the dynamic relationships approach is explored by employing it to implement the database model for a system in order to achieve dynamic schema modification capabilities.

1 Introduction

Relationships are at the heart of the relational model [6] and semantic data models such as the entity relationship model [5]. They also play a key role in object oriented modelling techniques such as UML [2, 16], OMT [23] and SAMMOA [10]. Unlike their relational peers, relationships in object models exist among objects and not attributes. A relationship is: "an abstraction stating that objects from certain classes are associated in some way; the association is given a name so that it can be manipulated. It is a natural concept used in ordinary discourse" [21].

Object databases are considered to be suitable for supporting complex applications such as computer-aided design (CAD), etc. In order to address these complex applications involving correlations across data representations, object databases must incorporate functionality to create networks of semantically related objects. In addition, change propagation and referential integrity should be managed by the DBMS [17]. The highly interactive and evolutionary nature of these complex applications dictates the need for relationships to be dynamic. Facilities should be available to dynamically define new relationships in which instances of existing classes can participate. It should be possible to dynamically modify or remove any relationship definition and to dynamically add and remove participants from a specific instance of a relationship. Applications and objects created using existing classes for which a new relationship is defined or an existing relationship definition removed or modified should not become invalid.

In this paper we present our approach to dynamic relationships in object oriented databases. Object oriented modelling techniques identify several kinds of relationships such as *association*, *aggregation* and *inheritance*. Concrete instances of these relationships occur within an object oriented database. For example, the *defines*/*defined-in* relationship between a class and its members is an aggregation relationship. The *derives-from*/*inherits-to* relationship between a sub-class and its super-class is an inheritance relationship. Our relationships approach treats these concrete relationships uniformly regardless of whether they are association, aggregation or inheritance relationships.

2 Relationships: Objects and Meta-objects

Relationships in our approach are based on the observation that three types of entities exist within an object database. These are: **objects**, **meta-objects** and **meta-classes**.

Entities of each type reside within a specific *virtual space* within the database. Objects reside in the *object space* and are instances of classes. Classes together with defining scopes, class properties, class methods, etc. form the *meta-object space* [20]. Meta-objects are instances of meta-classes which constitute the *meta-class space*. Fig. 1 shows the object space, meta-object space and meta-class space in an object oriented database. For simplification we have only elaborated the *instance-of/has-instance* relationship which is represented by the solid arrows.

From fig. 1 we observe that relationships in an object oriented database can be categorised as: *inter-space* **relationships** and *intra-space* **relationships**.

Entities participating in inter-space relationships reside in different virtual spaces. Inter-space relationships can be further classified as: **relationships among meta-objects and objects** and **relationships among meta-classes and meta-objects**.

The *instance-of/has-instance* relationship in fig. 1 is an example of inter-space relationships. Note that the *instance-of/has-instance* relationship is a one-to-many relationship directly since each class can have many instances. It is, however, a many-to-many relationship indirectly because the substitutability semantics of object orientation mandate that an object is not only an instance of a particular class but also an instance of its super-classes. The same applies to meta-classes and meta-objects. We regard the *instance-of/has-instance* relationship as a one-to-many relationship.

Intra-space relationships are those where the participating entities belong to the same virtual space. These relationships can be further classified as: **relationships among objects**, **relationships among meta-objects** and **relationships among meta-classes**.

Fig. 1 also shows the virtual spaces that will be of interest to different *actors* [2, 16]. A novice application developer is interested in achieving object persistence and manipulating relationships among the persistent objects. S/he, therefore, will be interested in the object space and its intra-space relationships. An experienced application developer or a database administrator, on the other hand, is interested in manipulating all three spaces and the various inter and intra-space relationships. For example, an experienced application developer might be interested in evolving the schema of the database by adding or dropping meta-objects or by modifying existing intra-space relationships for the meta-object space. S/he may also be interested in introducing some new meta-classes and their instances hence introducing new inter-space relationships between the meta-class space and the meta-object space. We will discuss the introduction of new meta-classes in section 4. We will now discuss how the conceptual division of the database into virtual spaces helps shield a novice application developer from information not of interest to him/her.

Fig. 3 shows a simple UML object model [2, 16] to be implemented in an object oriented database. Our approach allows the novice application developer to define the class hierarchy in the database at the same level of abstraction as UML and to transparently manipulate the persistent objects and the relationships among them. Once the class hierarchy has been defined the system extracts the various explicit and implicit relationships in the hierarchy and generates the corresponding meta-objects and the various inter and intra-space relationships.

Fig. 2 shows the database from an experienced application developer's viewpoint. For simplification the object-space has been omitted. Note that an implicit aggregation relationship exists between a class and its members (methods and properties: attributes and relationships) which is extracted by the system in the form of *defines/defined-in*. Similarly, the inheritance relationship is extracted in the form of *derives-from/inherits-to*. The system also extracts the implicit recursive relationship *is-inverse-of* which exists between the two edges of a relationship. The implicit *has-type/is-type-of* relationship between a property and its data type is also extracted. Note that *defines/defined-in* is a many-to-one relationship, *derives-from/inherits-to* is a many-to-many relationship (our approach supports multiple inheritance) and *has-type/is-type-of* is a one-to-many relationship. We will discuss cardinalities, recursive nature of relationships and other semantics in the next section. Fig. 2 also shows the system generated *has-instance/instance-of* relationships between meta-classes and meta-objects. It is necessary for the system to extract the various types of relationships since they have different propagation semantics. The system can then provide propagation semantics specific to each type of relationship at the same time treating the various relationship types in a uniform fashion.

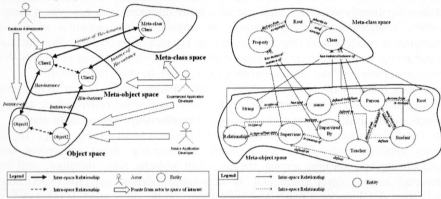

Fig. 1. *Virtual Spaces* in an object oriented database

Fig. 2. An experienced developer's view of the database (the meta-class space and the meta-object space)

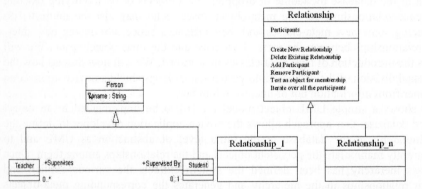

Fig. 3. UML object model for a simple application

Fig. 4. The Relationship Model

3 The Relationship Model

This section first describes the various features desirable of relationships in an OODB. This is followed by a description of our relationship model and the meta-model used to implement the relationship model in an OODB. Change propagation, referential integrity and the semantics of relationships are also discussed.

3.1 Desirable Relationship Features

Relationships in an ODBMS should satisfy the following set of requirements:

- Relationships should be dynamic i.e. it should be possible to dynamically define new relationships or remove existing relationship definitions. It should also be possible to dynamically modify a relationship definition and to dynamically add and remove participants from a specific instance of a relationship.
- Relationships can be n-ary.
- Relationships should have inverse traversal paths and these should be implicitly created by the DBMS except for uni-directional relationships. For a bi-directional relationship the application explicitly creates the relationship in one direction and the ODBMS implicitly sets the relationship in the opposite direction.
- Relationships can have a cardinality, either one-to-one, one-to-many, or many-to-many; many-to-many relationships cannot be uni-directional [17].
- Relationships can have ordering semantics [17].
- Relationships can be recursive. Participants of a recursive relationship are instances of the same class.
- Relationships can have different propagation semantics depending on whether they are aggregation, inheritance or association relationships.
- Change propagation and referentially integrity for bi-directional relationships should be maintained by the ODBMS.

In section 3.3 we will discuss how closely relationships in our approach satisfy the above set of requirements.

3.2 The Relationship Model

Relationships in our approach are both semantic constructs and first class objects. Fig. 4 depicts the class Relationship used in our system. The model also outlines the various operations that can be applied to a relationship. This is the model visible to all actors and is of particular interest to a novice application developer.

The class *Relationship* is an abstract class. Relationships are created as instances of classes *Relationship_1* and *Relationship_n*. These instances act as edges of the relationship; an instance of class *Relationship_1* represents an edge cardinality of one while an instance of class *Relationship_n* represents an edge cardinality of many.

Fig. 8 shows an example scenario: the many-to-one *supervises/supervised-by* relationship from fig. 3. The domain of *participants* is *student* for the *supervises* edge of the relationship and *teacher* for the *supervised-by* edge. The traversal paths for the relationship are managed transparently of the application programmer. It should also be noted that the *Relationship* instances are *existence dependent* on the objects related through them; the *Relationship* instance representing the edge of a relationship ceases to exist once the object that employs it to participate in the relationship dies.

3.3 The Meta-Model

We now present our meta-model that can be employed to implement the relationship model described in section 3.1. This is the model that is visible to an experienced application developer or a database administrator and not to the novice developer.

Relationships are treated in a uniform fashion regardless of whether they are inter-space or intra-space relationships. Intra-space relationships are treated in the same manner whether they exist within the object space, the meta-object space or the meta-class space. No distinction is made between inter-space relationships; i.e. relationships among meta-objects and objects are treated the same way as those that exist between meta-classes and meta-objects.

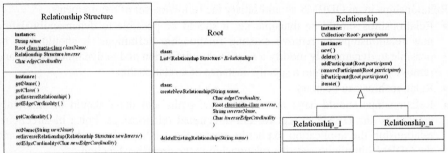

Fig. 5. The class *Relationship Structure*

Fig. 6. The class *Root* from which all classes and meta-classes inherit

Fig. 7. The Relationship Model implemented

In order to treat relationships in a uniform manner, all classes and meta-classes in the system inherit from the class *Root* which is shown in fig. 6. As shown in fig. 2 the class has replicas existing in both the meta-class space and the meta-object space. The meta-classes inherit from the meta-class *Root* which exists in the meta-class space while the classes (which are meta-objects) inherit from the meta-object *Root* which resides in the meta-object space and is an instance of the meta-class *Class*. Inheriting from the *Root* replica in the meta-class space allows dynamic introduction, removal and modification of relationships in which meta-objects participate while inheriting from the *Root* replica in the meta-object space allows dynamic introduction, removal and modification of relationships in which the various objects participate.

We now discuss how the class *Root* allows dynamic introduction, removal and modification of relationship definitions. Note that the **class:** tag in fig. 6 indicates class-level (static) properties and methods while the tag class/meta-class indicates that the value of the parameter has to be a class (which is a meta-object) or a meta-class. Inheriting from the class *Root* allows the particular class or meta-class to use the class-level (static) methods *createNewRelationship* and *deleteExistingRelationship*. These methods allow the dynamic addition or deletion of relationships in which instances of the class or meta-class participate. It should be noted that the inverse traversal path is implicitly created when *createNewRelationship* is invoked. Uni-directional relationships can be created by specifying a null value for the last three parameters of *createNewRelationship*. Recursive relationships can be set up by specifying the same class or meta-class on which the method is being invoked as an inverse. The inverse traversal path is implicitly deleted when *deleteExistingRelationship* is invoked on one of the classes or meta-classes whose instances participate in the relationship. Later in this section we discuss how propagation of this change to the affected instances is managed by the system.

Fig. 6 also shows the class-level (static) attribute *Relationships* which is inherited by all the sub-classes of the class *Root*. This class-level attribute is a *List* of instances of the class *Relationship Structure*. For each relationship, which the instances of a class or meta-class participate in, a *Relationship Structure* instance is created and appended to the *List* of *Relationships*. These instances are used to store and dynamically modify the structure of the relationship. The class *Relationship Structure* is shown in fig. 5. The **instance:** tag in fig. 5 indicates instance-level properties and methods. Note that the *Relationship Structure* class does not inherit from the class *Root*. The instance-level methods *setName*, *setInverseRelationship* and *setEdgeCardinality* can be invoked on instances of the class in order to dynamically modify the structures of relationships whose details they store.

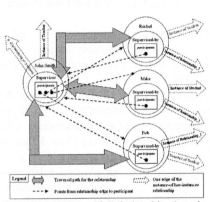

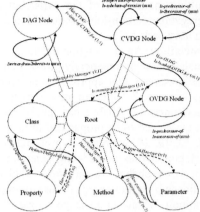

Fig. 8. Instances of Relationship_1 and Relationship_n representing edges of a many-to-one relationship

Fig. 9. Meta-classes in SADES and the relationships their instances participate in

Fig. 7 shows the relationship classes in the meta-model corresponding to the classes in the relationship model presented in fig. 4. Note that ordering semantics for relationships can be provided by using an ordered collection, such as a list or an array, for *participants*. Almost all object database management systems offer facilities to create ordered collections and provide methods such as addAsFirst, addAsLast, addAtSpecifiedPosition, etc. to operate on them. Note that only the instances of classes or meta-classes that inherit from the class *Root* can participate in a relationship. Also note that the relationship classes in fig. 7 do not inherit from the class *Root*.

We now describe the semantics of relationships in our approach and discuss how closely they meet the requirements set out in section 3.1. We also discuss how we address the various evolution problems arising from dynamically defining new relationships or modifying or deleting an existing relationship definition.

Our approach allows all actors to introduce, modify and delete relationship definitions dynamically and in a uniform fashion regardless of whether they are interested in the object space only or the meta-object space and meta-class space as well. Furthermore, it is possible to dynamically add and remove participants from existing instances of a relationship. Again, this is managed in a uniform fashion regardless of the nature of relationships whether inter-space or intra-space. Inverse traversal paths are created and managed transparently. The cardinality semantics described in section 3.1 are fully supported besides allowing ordering semantics for relationships. Our approach also allows the creation of recursive relationships. Change propagation and referential integrity is managed transparently of the user. Our approach, however, only supports binary relationships as n-ary relationships can be implemented as a layer on top of binary relationships.

We now discuss the propagation semantics for inheritance, association and aggregation relationships. It should be noted that the user does not need to concern himself/herself with these propagation semantics. The three types of relationships can be manipulated by the user in a uniform manner.

Aggregation: [26] provides a discussion of relationship semantics. For aggregation relationships it provides a number of propagation alternatives to choose from. We have chosen to propagate operations from aggregate to part, with deletion of the aggregate resulting in deletion of the parts, but not vice versa. It should be noted that the aggregation relationship is transitive in nature; i.e. an aggregate has parts which may in turn have parts [26].

Association: An association relationship requires that changes to one edge of the association are automatically propagated to the other edge. Cardinality semantics need to be preserved. Our approach transparently propagates changes from one edge of the association to the other, so preserving the cardinality.

Inheritance: Inheritance has special propagation semantics. Changes to the structure of a class need to be propagated to its sub-classes. We have chosen a class versioning [12, 13, 19, 24] approach to propagate changes along inheritance relationships. Class versioning avoids invalidating objects and applications created using class definitions prior to the change. It, therefore, addresses the issues that arise when adding a new relationship definition to a class or modifying or deleting an existing relationship definition. Whenever a change is made to the structure of a class a new class version is created for the class and all its sub-classes. Objects and applications created using the older class versions remain accessible through their respective version. They can then be attached to the new class version. [19] proposes a framework for such re-association. Our class versioning taxonomy is the subject of a forthcoming paper.

4 Application to Evolution

[9] characterises relationships among classes as static since these are fixed at compile-time. Relationships among instances are comparatively dynamic in nature and can be changed at run-time. Our approach differs from the viewpoint presented by [9]. Relationships among classes do not need to be fixed at compile-time. These can be dynamic in nature and can be changed at run-time. Therefore, the schema of an object-oriented database can be dynamically modified if the various meta-objects (classes, etc.) that form the schema are interconnected through dynamic relationships. Dynamic schema changes can be made by dynamically modifying the various relationships in which the meta-objects participate. These can be the *derives-from/inherits-to* relationships between classes or the *defines/defined-in* relationships between classes and their members. If relationships exist among meta-objects and objects they can be used to propagate schema changes to the affected objects.

We have employed our dynamic relationships approach to implement the database model and achieve dynamic schema modification capabilities for our Semi-Autonomous Database Evolution System, SADES [18]. SADES is being built as a layer on top of the commercially available object database system *Jasmine* from *Computer Associates International* and *Fujitsu Limited*. It provides support for: class hierarchy evolution, class versioning, object versioning and knowledge-base/rule-base evolution.

Dynamic relationships are needed to provide the above-mentioned evolution facilities. This serves a two-fold purpose. First, evolution can be achieved dynamically in a uniform fashion. Second, a coherent view of the conceptual structure of the database is provided making maintenance easier.

The SADES conceptual schema [19] is a fully connected directed acyclic graph (DAG) depicting the class hierarchy in the system. SADES schema DAG uses *Version derivation graphs* [11]. Each node in the DAG is a *class version derivation graph*. Each node in the class version derivation graph (CVDG) keeps: *reference(s) to predecessor(s), reference(s) to successor(s), reference to the versioned class object, descriptive information about the class version such as creation time, creator's identification, etc., reference(s) to super-class version(s), reference(s) to sub-class version(s)*, and *a set of reference(s) to **object version derivation graph(s)***.

Each node of a CVDG keeps a set of reference(s) to some object version derivation graph(s) (OVDG). An OVDG is similar to a CVDG and keeps information about various versions of an instance rather than a class. Each OVDG node [11] keeps: *reference(s) to predecessor(s), reference(s) to successor(s), reference to the versioned instance*, and *descriptive information about the instance version*.

Since an OVDG is generated for each instance associated with a class version, a set of OVDGs results when a class version has more than one instance associated with it. As a result a CVDG node keeps a set of references to all these OVDGs.

Fig. 9 identifies the various meta-classes in the system and the relationships in which their instances, the meta-objects, participate. The dashed block arrows indicate that all meta-classes inherit from the class *Root*. The line arrows, both solid and dashed, represent the various relationships meta-objects participate in. A solid arrow pointing from a meta-class back to itself indicates a recursive relationship. The dashed line arrows representing relationships among certain meta-classes and the class *Root* indicate that the relationship exists among instance(s) of the particular meta-class and instance(s) of a sub-class of the class *Root*. An instance of the class *OVDG Node*, for example, manages an object which is an instance of a sub-class of the class *Root* (since all classes inherit from the class *Root*). Similarly, a class *Property* or a method *Parameter* will normally have a sub-class of the class *Root* as its type.

The various relationships among instances of meta-classes shown in fig. 9 can be dynamically modified to achieve dynamic schema modifications. It is possible to introduce new relationships and even new meta-classes if desirable. For example, it might be desirable for an experienced application developer trying to extend the database model with active features [7] to introduce a meta-class *Rule* which can then be used to define classes (meta-objects) of rules which in turn will be used to create the various rule objects. Schema changes are propagated to the instances using the *has-OVDG/is-head-of-OVDG-for* relationship that exists between a class version and its associated OVDGs. Class versioning allows dynamic schema modifications without rendering existing instances invalid. Instances associated with one class version can be associated with another one using the framework we described in [19].

5 Related Work

Pioneering work to extend OO models with explicit relationships has been carried out by [1, 21]. [21] discusses incorporating relationships as semantic constructs in an object oriented programming language. [1] proposes inclusion of relationships and declarative constraints on relationships in an object oriented database programming language. [22] addresses propagation of operations by defining propagation attributes on relationships. [26] aims at incorporating relationship semantics into object-relational data models. Although the approach by [26] is applicable to pure object oriented data models the applicability has not been explored. All the work concentrates on semantics and propagation. The dynamic nature of relationships has not been considered. Neither is there an attempt to treat the various types of relationships in a uniform fashion or to extract the implicit relationships that exist within an object oriented model.

The object database standard, ODMG [3, 4], mandates both uni-directional and bi-directional binary relationships as semantic constructs in a database schema. The ODMG specification requires the DBMS to maintain the referential integrity of these semantically related objects. Relationships are treated in a uniform manner whether they exist among meta-objects or objects. Although relationships in ODMG are semantic constructs, they are not first class objects. Neither are they dynamic in nature. ODMG compliant bindings of commercially available object database management systems POET [15], Versant [25] and O2 [14] support binary relationships and maintain the referential integrity for bi-directional relationships. Referential integrity for uni-directional relationships is left to the application. Although these ODBMSs offer dynamic modifications to the database schema [20] dynamic creation, deletion and modification of relationships are not possible as relationships are not semantic constructs in the schema. Instead, they are mapped onto class attributes. Meta-objects in these systems are not semantically related either. As a result an actor such as an experienced application developer or a database administrator tends to lose sight of relationships in the system. Also, it makes maintenance a problem because it is easy to make errors.

In contrast to ODMG which mandates binary relationships among the various objects and meta-objects in the system, the Iris object oriented database management system [8] uses n-ary, inverse traversable relationships to model information about objects and meta-objects residing in the database. Referential integrity is maintained by the DBMS. In contrast to the ODMG compliant systems discussed earlier, both objects and meta-objects in Iris are semantically related. Types are treated as first class objects. Therefore, a conceptual equivalence exists between relationships among meta-objects and relationships among objects. Each type bears relationships to its sub-types, super-types and instances. However, relationships are not semantic constructs in Iris. Furthermore, relationships in Iris are not highly dynamic in nature. For example, new sub-type/super-type relationships among existing types cannot be created.

Relationships in our approach are both semantic constructs and first class objects. In contrast to the above-mentioned approaches it is possible to introduce, modify and delete relationship definitions dynamically. Relationships are treated in a uniform fashion regardless of their type. Participants can be added and removed dynamically from specific instances of a relationship with referential integrity and change propagation managed by the system. Propagation semantics for aggregation, inheritance and association relationships are provided by the system transparently of the various actors.

6 Summary and Conclusions

We have presented an approach to incorporate dynamic relationships in an object oriented database. The novelty of the work is in the dynamic nature of relationships and on treatment of the various relationships in the system in a uniform fashion. We have divided the database into virtual spaces in order to present an actor with relationships of interest to him/her. We have also presented a relationship categorisation on the basis of this virtual division and have automated the extraction of the various explicit and implicit relationships in the modelling domain in order to map them onto our relationship categorisation. Our approach allows new relationships to be defined dynamically and to remove or modify existing relationships definitions. We have used a class versioning approach to ensure that applications and objects created prior to the introduction, removal or modification of a relationship definition do not become invalid. Participants can be added and removed dynamically from instances of the various relationships.

We have also presented the semantics of relationships in our system and the various operations that can be applied to them. A meta-model has been presented which is used to implement dynamic relationships in an object oriented database. The meta-model can be layered on top of any existing object database management system hence incorporating dynamic relationships into the underlying system.

We have explored the practicability of our relationships approach by implementing the database model for the SADES system and exploiting the dynamic nature of relationships to achieve dynamic schema modification facilities.

Future directions include incorporating n-ary relationships into the system. These will be implemented as an additional layer on top of binary relationships. We plan to explore the applicability of the approach to object-relational data models and to employ learning mechanisms to extract implicit and explicit constraints on relationships in a high level object oriented design and incorporate these constraints into our system without affecting its ability to treat the various types of relationships in a uniform manner.

References

[1] Albano, A., Ghelli, G., Orsini, R., "A Relationship Mechanism for a Strongly Typed Object-Oriented Database Programming Language", Proc. of the 17th Int. Conf. on Very Large Databases, Sept. 1991, pp. 565-575

[2] Booch, G., Jacobson, I., Rumbaugh, J., "The Unified Modelling Language Documentation Set", Version 1.1,Rational Software Corp., c1997

[3] Cattell, R. G. G., et al., "The Object Database Standard: ODMG-93 Release 1.2", Morgan Kaufmann, c1995

[4] Cattell, R. G. G., et al., "The Object Database Standard: ODMG 2.0", Morgan Kaufmann, c1997

[5] Chen, P. P., "The Entity-Relationship Model - Toward a Unified View of Data", ACM Transactions on Database Systems, Vol.1, No.1, Mar. 1976, pp.9-36

[6] Codd, E., "A Relational Model for Large Shared Data Banks", Communications of the ACM, Vol.13, No.6, Jun. 1970, pp.377-387

[7] Dittrich, K. R. et al., "The Active Database Management System Manifesto: A Rulebase of ADBMS Features", Proc. of the 2nd Workshop on Rules in Databases, Sept. 1995, LNCS, T. Sellis (ed.), Vol. 985, pp. 3-20

[8] Fishman, D. H. et al., "Iris: An Object Oriented Database Management System", ACM Transactions on Office Information Systems, Vol.5, No.1, 1987, pp.48-69

[9] Gamma, E. et al., "Design Patterns - Elements of Reusable Object-Oriented Software", Addison Wesley, c1995

[10] Hesse, W., Mayr, H. C., "Highlights of the SAMMOA Framework for Object Oriented Application Modelling", Proc. of 9th Int. Conf. on Database & Expert Systems Applications, Aug. 98, LNCS 1460, pp. 353-373

[11] Loomis, M. E. S., "Object Versioning", Journal of Object Oriented Programming, Jan. 1992, pp. 40-43

[12] Monk, S., Sommerville, I., "Schema Evolution in OODBs Using Class Versioning", SIGMOD Record, Vol. 22, No. 3, Sept. 1993, pp. 16-22

[13] Monk, S., "A Model for Schema Evolution in Object-Oriented Database Systems", PhD Thesis, Computing Department, Lancaster University, 1993

[14] "The O2 System - Release 5.0 Documentation", Ardent Software, c1998

[15] "POET 5.0 Documentation Set", POET Software, c1997

[16] Quatrani, T., "Visual Modelling with Rational Rose and UML", Addison Wesley, c1998

[17] Rashid, A., "An Object Oriented View of the Department of Computer Science", MSc Dissertation, University of Essex, September 1997

[18] Rashid, A. & Sawyer, P., "SADES - A Semi-Autonomous Database Evolution System", Proc. of 8th Int. Workshop for PhD Students in Object Oriented Systems, Jul. 98, ECOOP '98 Workshop Reader, LNCS 1543

[19] Rashid, A. & Sawyer, P., "Facilitating Virtual Representation of CAD Data through a Learning Based Approach to Conceptual Database Evolution Employing Direct Instance Sharing", Proc. of 9th Int. Conf. on Database and Expert Systems Applications, Aug. 1998, LNCS 1460, pp. 384-393

[20] Rashid, A. & Sawyer, P., "Evaluation for Evolution: How Well Commercial Systems Do", Accepted at the 1st Int. Workshop on OODBs to be held in conjunction with ECOOP '99, June 14-18, Lisbon, Portugal

[21] Rumbaugh, J., "Relations as Semantic Constructs in an Object-Oriented Language", SIGPLAN Notices, Vol.22, No.12, 1987, pp.466-481

[22] Rumbaugh, J., "Controlling Propagation of Operations using Attributes on Relations", SIGPLAN Notices, Vol. 23, No. 11, 1988, pp. 285-296

[23] Rumbaugh, J., et al., "Object Oriented Modelling and Design", New Jersey, Prentice-Hall Inc., 1991

[24] Skarra, A. H. & Zdonik, S. B., "The Management of Changing Types in an Object-Oriented Database", Proc. of the 1st OOPSLA Conference, Sept. 1986, pp.483-495

[25] "Versant Manuals for Release 5.0", Versant Object Technology, c1997

[26] Zhang, N., Haerder, T., Thomas, J., "Enriching Object-Relational Databases with Relationship Semantics", Proc. of the 3rd Int. Workshop on Next Generation Information Technologies and Systems (NGITS), Israel, 1997

IFOOD: An Intelligent Object-Oriented Database Architecture

Murat Koyuncu[1], Adnan Yazici[1], and Roy George[2]

[1] Dept.of Computer Engineering,Middle East Technical University,Ankara,Turkey***
[2] Dept. of Computer Science, Clark Atlanta University, Atlanta, GA, USA

Abstract. Next generation information system applications require powerful and intelligent information management that necessitates an efficient interaction between database and knowledge base technologies. It is important that complex data and knowledge incorporate uncertainty that exists in the data objects, in integrity constraints, and/or in the application. In this study we propose IFOOD, an environment for modeling intelligent object-oriented databases for such applications. This permits flexible modeling of complex data and knowledge with powerful retrieval capability.

1 Introduction

In recent years, in order to satisfy the requirements of the newly emerging applications including CAD/CAM, office automation systems, engineering designs, etc., new database models, such as the Object-Oriented Data Model, and the Deductive Database Model have been developed. The object-oriented database model which provides powerful data modeling features has gained popularity in recent years [2],[5]. The deductive database model is another modeling approach to achieve intelligent behavior[6],[7], an important requirement of the next generation information systems. While these two models are being developed separately, the interaction and/or integration of database technologies and knowledge base technologies is also an important requirement towards the development of the next generation information systems. This is reflected in the continuing research towards the development of deductive object-oriented database models since late 1980s.

However, most existing database models, including the deductive object-oriented database models, are designed under the assumptions that the data stored is precise and queries are crisp. In fact, these assumptions are often not valid for the next generation information systems since they may involve complex information with uncertainty in data and knowledge. In general, information may be both complex and imprecise when representing subjective opinions and judgments concerning medical diagnosis, economic forecasting, or personal evaluation. Also, in natural languages, numerous quantifiers (e.g., many, few, some,

---

*** A part of this study had been done during Dr. Yazici's visit to Dept. of EECS, Tulane University, USA.

almost, etc.) are used when conveying vague information. There have been various studies in recent years giving much attention to the representation and manipulation of complex objects in the frameworks of database models [12],[15], in knowledge-based systems [6], [12]. Many of the existing approaches dealing with uncertainty are based on the theory of fuzzy sets [16].

There have been also previous efforts related to integration of object-oriented database and knowledge bases technologies [8],[9],[10],[13]. However, almost all of them assume crisp domains and ignore uncertainty. In these studies objects have to be defined with a high degree of crispness, which makes it difficult to model the real world information systems. Although the approach taken in this study has some similarities with some of the approaches of those studies, this study mainly differs from all of them in having capabilities to handle uncertainty in a tightly integrated environment. A good survey of current approaches to handle imprecise information in databases and knowledge bases is given in [12]. In that study, Parsons outlined the work carried out in the database community and work carried out in the artificial intelligence community. Among other approaches, the one developed by Baldwin et al. [1] is the most relevant one. A system called Frill++ that combines logic programming, uncertainty and object-oriented methods was developed. Frill, which is a logic language with capability of handling uncertainty, was enhanced similar to the object model proposed by McCabe [10]. Another related study by Ndouse [11], proposes a model embedding fuzzy logic into object-oriented methodology in order to deal with uncertainty and vagueness that pervade knowledge and object descriptions in the real world. An intelligent fuzzy object architecture based on the uncertain object-oriented model proposed by Dubois et al. [4] was described and enhanced with fuzzy relationships, generalization, specialization and aggregations. The object includes fuzzy *if-then* rules to define knowledge. He uses possibility theory for representation of vagueness and uncertainty.

In this study we aim to tightly coupling the Fuzzy Object-Oriented Database (FOODB) system [14],[15] with a KB. The FOODB is used to handle large scale of complex data and KB is used to handle knowledge of the application domain. The work described here differs from the others (one in [1] and in [11]) in the way that databases and knowledge bases are coupled with the handling of uncertainties. An environmental information system is chosen as the case study here since it involves uncertainty and requires subjective judgements to solve problems.

This paper is organized as follows: In Section 2, we provide a brief description of the architecture of our approach. Section 3 discusses the proposed fuzzy object- oriented data definition and query language with a special focus on uncertainty. The issues related to coupling are included in Section 4. Section 5 concludes the paper.

2 The Architecture of IFOOD

The architecture of the proposed environment for an intelligent fuzzy object oriented database (IFOOD) modeling is given in Figure 1. The architecture is based on the integration of the fuzzy object-oriented database (FOODB) system [14],[15] with a knowledge base (KB) system and the development of a common interface/language. At the lower level of the architecture, there is an explicit FOODB system for data management and a knowledge-base system serving as the knowledge server for knowledge management. The communication and interaction between the database and the knowledge base is performed by the bridge interface. The bridge provides the desired interoperability between two systems to achieve the management of data and knowledge.

At the higher level, a single user interface provides a unified environment for both data and knowledge management. The reason for providing such an environment for both data and knowledge management is that user has the capability to use data and knowledge manipulation and query facilities in a unified but powerful environment and does not have to be aware of the underlying architecture. A single language which supports OO and logic language features is developed as a unified environment for both data and knowledge management.

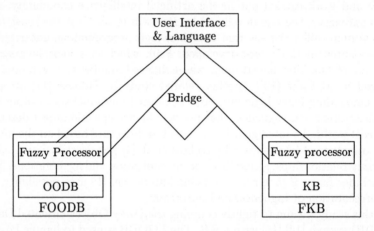

Fig. 1. The architecture of the proposed environment

We handle uncertainty issues through the fuzzy processors. Fuzzy processors are used to handle uncertainty at both OODB and KB. We have the solutions to the following issues to be able to handle uncertainty: 1) Handling uncertain type definitions; fuzzy, range, and null, 2) Definition of fuzzy domains, membership functions, and similarity relations, 3) Calculations of membership degrees, 4) Definition of fuzzy rules, and 5) Evaluation of user queries having uncertain values.

The definitions of domains, similarity relations, and membership functions are stored in the FOODB. The methods related to calculations such as membership functions are defined as methods of a utility class that is inherited by the entire user defined classes by default. In this way, the definitions related to uncertainty will be generalized for all the system and users do not have to define class-specific definitions for uncertainty.

In IFOOD, we see the KB as a natural extension of the FOODB. A class definition includes definition of inheritance, attributes, methods and rules. The KB processes rules while the FOODB processes the others. The KB should handle uncertainty since objects have uncertain attributes, rule descriptions include uncertainty or user can formulate queries with uncertainty. We provide required facilities to access to the definition on the FOODB from the KB and use them. The fuzzy processor constructed on the KB includes the facilities to access the uncertainty definition in the FOODB. For example, if the KB needs the similarity of two fuzzy terms from a domain, then it gets this value via the fuzzy processor of the FOODB. The KB has fuzzy inference capability to handle fuzzy rules.

3 IFOOD Language

The IFOOD language is an object-oriented database language extended with declarative rules. The language includes basic building blocks to define and manipulate the objects. The declarative rules are used for derived classes, derived attributes, and integrity constraints. The language is enhanced with additional capabilities to handle uncertainty. In this section we only focus on uncertainty related components of the language.

3.1 Uncertain Types

The IFOOD language of the environment includes atomic types such as integer, real, and complex types such as object type and set type, which are not discussed further. There are three types for representing uncertainty in the model. These are null type, range type, and fuzzy type.

The domain of a null type is an extension of a basic crisp domain by including the various null, the "unknown", "notexist" or "nil". More formally, if domain D_j consisting of crisp values $\{a_1, a_2, ..., a_n\}$, then D'_j is the domain of a null-valued type: $D'_j = D_j \cup \{unk, dne, ni\}$. These definitions are incorporated with the basic data types and the *nullinteger*, *nullreal* and *nullstring* types are introduced in the system. For example, *soilType* can have either a string value or one of the three null values as follows:

```
define soilType : nullstring;
soilType = ''loam''; or soilType = unknown;
```

Range type is used to represent incompleteness (a type of uncertainty). It is defined between two values from the same type. Values within the range must be countable and ordered. More formally, if D_j is the domain of an incomplete (range)- valued type whose values may be atomic or an interval. Interval representation is $[a_{j1} - a_{j2}]$, where a_{j1} is the minimum and a_{j2} is the maximum of the range. Both values are taken from the domain D_j. For example, *population* can be defined as an integer range value.

```
define population: range integer;   population=9500-10000;
```

Fuzzy type is another type of uncertainty that allows the representation of descriptive form of uncertain information. This type has either the atomic value or the fuzzy value as a set with various semantics (i.e., "AND", "OR", or "XOR" semantics). More formally, if D_j is the domain of a fuzzy-valued type, then the domain subtends a set of fuzzy linguistic terms. A fuzzy attribute value is a nonempty subset of D_j and represented as $[a_{j1}, a_{j2}, ..., a_{jm}]$. Fuzzy type is one of the three semantics of "AND", "OR", or "XOR" given to the object attributes. The details of the semantics of the fuzzy-valued type are given in [14]. For example, a fuzzy type, *fuzzyTemp*, can be defined and used as follow:

```
fuzzyOR integer fuzzyTemp {hot,mild,normal,moderate,low,frigid}
define temperature : fuzzyTemp;   temperature =[hot, mild]
```

An object attribute defined of this type will have either an integer value or a set of fuzzy values given in the type definition. It is necessary to define the user defined fuzzy type before the usage of it in the attribute definitions.

3.2 Classes

In this environment, classes are defined using the *class* predicate. A class definition includes class name, class abbreviation, inheritance list, attribute descriptions, rule descriptions and method descriptions. We illustrate this with an example, rather than giving the complete syntax of it. Let us consider the specification of the *pollutants* class in an environmental information system.

```
Class pollutants Abbr pol;
   define location : string;
   define dose : fdose[extremlyHigh,veryHigh,high,midHigh] 0.9;
   define exposureTime : ftime [veryLong, long, medium] 0.8;
   define contaminant  : fcont [barium, cadmium, mercury] 1;
   define wasteType    : nullstring;
   define structure    : string;
   defrule X.status=[dangerous](Y):- pollutants(X),
     X.dose([extremlyHigh,veryHigh]),X.exposureTime([veryLong]),
     X.contaminant([cadmium, mercury]);
endclass;
```

Abbr is the abbreviation of class name that is used to assign object identifiers. The *pollutants* class has different attributes defining various properties of the objects. We extended normal attribute definitions to handle uncertainty as following:

```
define <attribute name>:<type><attribute template><relevance>;
```

where *attribute name* is an identifier that identifies the attribute of objects, and *type* defines the type of the attribute. *Attribute template* and *relevance* are two new extensions to the object-oriented model to handle uncertainty. *Attribute template* indicates the ideal values of the fuzzy and range types for full membership. However, an object can take any value from the related domain. *Relevance* is a real value between 0 and 1 that denotes the weight of the uncertain attribute in determination of the boundary of an uncertain class. *Attribute template* and *relevance* are used to calculate the membership degree of objects to classes and membership degree of classes to superclasses. In the given object definition, the *dose* attribute is defined of *fdose*. *Fdose* is a user defined fuzzy type and it must be defined before the class definition. The set consisting of the fuzzy terms *extremlyHigh, veryHigh, high* and *midHigh* is the attribute template. The relevance value of attribute dose is 0.9.

New attributes can be derived defining deductive rules in the class definition. The *status* rule that derives the actual state of the pollutants from existing attributes is associated to the class definition in the given example. The attributes of uncertain types can be used in rule definitions. For example, *dose* is a fuzzy attribute that has fuzzy values. Y is the membership degree of the rule conclusion that is calculated from antecedent clauses.

Access and modification to objects are performed via one of the predefined methods. In this model, encapsulation is applied by restricting direct attribute modifications. Users and other objects have to modify the attribute values using predefined methods. The methods to update the attributes are created automatically. However, if a method requires some calculations instead of direct updating then user has to define the method explicitly.

3.3 Virtual (derived) Classes

An object-oriented model organizes the objects into a class hierarchy. Objects are stored into the database according to this defined class hierarchy. However, a database serves many users that have different demands. Such user demands may result in a complex class hierarchy that is hard to be handled by database system and to be understood by users. Defining virtual classes on the existing ones can satisfy this requirement. There are different alternatives to define virtual classes.

A virtual class may be a specialization of the database class with the same attributes and contains a subset of the objects of the database class. The objects may be selected by the constraint defined in the virtual class definition. For example, a virtual class that includes the *gaseous_pollutants* is defined as follows:

```
vclass gaseous_pollutants;
   inherits pollutants;
   condition X=gaseous_pollutants:-pollutants(X),
                 X.structure(gaseous);
endclass;
```

In this example, all the attributes of the *pollutants* class are inherited, but only the objects being in the *gaseous* structure are derived.

Furthermore, a virtual class may include only a subset of the attributes of a real class or may include attributes from different classes to form different views of the objects. The relationship between the virtual class and its superclass may be fuzzy as it is in the database schema and the objects of this virtual class may be instances of this class with a certain membership degree. For such cases, the uncertain attributes should be redefined with their template and relevance values to determine class/superclass and object/class membership degrees as shown below:

```
vclass dangerous_pollutants (0.6);
    inherits pollutants;
    define dose    : fdose [extremlyHigh, veryHigh] 1;
    define exposureTime: ftime [veryLong, long] 0.8;
    define contaminant  :fcont[barium, cadmium, mercury] 0.9;
endclass;
```

The *dangerous_pollutants* class is a subclass of the *pollutants* class. Its uncertain attributes are redefined in the attributes section with new attribute template and relevance values. The types of the attributes should be the same type of the inherited class attributes. Therefore, it is not necessary to specify attributes types and to redefine uncertain attributes if its attribute template and relevance values are not changed. The objects of the *pollutants* class which have a membership degree equal to or greater than 0.6 are derived as instances of the *dangerous_pollutants* class. The object threshold level may be given by the user to determine the level of the object selection as it is in the given example above. If it is not specified it is 1 (one) by default. Class/superclass and object/class membership degrees of virtual classes are calculated as explained in [14], [15].

3.4 Additional Definitions for Handling Uncertainty

The uncertainty may occur at three different levels in an object-oriented model. These are the attribute, object/class and class/superclass levels. How we handle uncertainty at each level can be found in [14], [15]. Fuzzy and crisp types are handled together utilizing the membership functions and similarity matrices. It is also possible to query the database both with fuzzy and crisp conditions. In order to handle both the crisp and fuzzy values uniformly, the membership functions are used to calculate the membership degree of crisp values to determine the corresponding fuzzy set which the crisp values belong to. Each fuzzy term is associated with a membership function in the system.

```
membershipof <ftype> <fterm> <function declaration>;
```

For example, the membership function definition of the fuzzy term *hot* that belongs to the *fuzzyTemp* type is given below:

```
membershipof fuzzyTemp hot triangle 20,40,60;
```

Similarity matrix represents the strength of the relation between every pair of the elements in a domain D. A similarity relation $\mu_S(x,y)$, for domain D, is a mapping of every pair of elements in the domain onto interval [0,1] and is defined as follows:

```
simmat <ftype name> <matrix entries>;
```

where *matrix entries* is a real list whose elements are between 0 and 1.

3.5   Object Queries

We introduce an SQL like query syntax in which declarative formulas are used, i.e., we adopt a *select ... from ... where ...* constructs for extracting information from the database. Rather than giving the complete syntax of the language, we will discuss the uncertain querying and illustrate it using an example:

```
select X.location from pollutants(X, 0.7)
where X.dose([veryHigh],0.6),X.exposureTime([veryLong],0.8);
```

where *pollutants(X, 0.7)* gets the pollutants which have a membership degree equal to or greater than 0.7, and *X.dose([veryHigh], 0.6)* selects the objects which have very high dose with a membership degree equal to or greater than 0.6. The statements in *from* and *where* parts are expressed in a declarative way.

The defined declarative rules can be called in the queries. For example, consider the *status* rule which is a derived attribute in the class definition above. In the following query, the pollutants having an object membership degree equal to or greater than or equal to 0.7 are selected and then the *status* rule is fired and the objects whose status are dangerous with a membership degree 0.8 or above are selected.

```
select X.location from pollutants(X,0.7)
where X.status([dangerous],0.8);
```

4   Coupling Properties

We provide an integrated language to manage data and knowledge at the user interface level. The operations related to object creation and manipulation are done directly in the FOODB through the data definition language. However, if the definitions include some kind of knowledge, then these knowledge definitions are processed through the KB system. The knowledge stored in the KB is seen as an extension of the object definition in the FOODB. The object and rules are bind together through the bridge that provides a virtual clustering of the objects. If one of the rules connected to one of the class is fired without bounding to a specific object, then only the objects of that class and its subclasses are evaluated according to object-oriented concepts. When a rule is fired on the KB, the objects to be evaluated are transferred from the OODB to the KB.

4.1 Interaction between the FOODB and the FKB

Data transfer is an expensive process and a great deal of time is spent for data transfer. To increase the performance of the system, the data transfer between two systems must be minimized. On the other hand, the OODB systems have efficient access structures to fetch data from secondary storage and they employ sophisticated optimization techniques to choose efficient algorithms to execute queries. We use this power of database and have the query be evaluated at the database side as much as possible.

Fuzzy queries require more objects to be transferred from disk to the memory. Since we aim to minimize the number of query and the amount of data in response, we develop methods to satisfy this requirement. Therefore, we use the membership degree to reduce the number of objects to be transferred in case of a user query. Consider again the *status* rule defined in class definition above. The rule clauses are connected by AND logical operator and its values are fuzzy. It is not possible to determine the status of a pollutant with precise predicates and measurements, since most of the attributes are fuzzy-valued. Assume the user formulates the following query:

```
select X.location from pollutants(X, 0.7)
where X.status([dangerous], 0.6);
```

This user query will fire the status rule in the knowledge base. The relevance values should be given for the *dose, exposureTime* and *contaminant* attributes respectively in the class definition. The rules are resolved using similarity matching instead of pattern matching in this model. The user specifies a threshold level for the rule conclusion and the system determines a threshold level for each attribute to retrieve the objects from the FOODB to the KB memory. The query also applies a threshold level for object membership level. Both the object threshold and attribute threshold levels specified in the queries can be used to increase performance of the system. However, this requires fuzzy indexing methods in the FOODB to benefit from this property effectively.

4.2 Class-Rule Bindings

KB system handles the knowledge part of the class definition and FOODB system handles the data. There should also be a way of handling a class definition in its integrity. That is, a rule that defines a derived attribute or a constraint in a class is a part of that class and this relationship should be defined in the system. To satisfy this requirement, the classes and the rules related to each other are connected through a binary relation which shows class and rule bindings and this relation is maintained by the bridge.

The KB handles the virtual (derived) classes to satisfy different query requirements. The virtual classes are connected to the base class schema, which is maintained by the FOODB, through one of the specialization, generalization, aggregation or association relationships. Therefore, the bridge that provides interoperability between two systems also keeps the relationship between a virtual class and the base class schema.

5 Conclusions

The main motivation of this study is to develop a powerful environment for complex applications with uncertainty. In this research we introduced an integrated architecture for an intelligent system that allows users to specify their application with uncertain properties, such as membership functions, similarity relations, and uncertain types. The classes defined in the environment may have uncertain attributes and rules. Virtual classes that are created to provide different views of the class schema and objects may have uncertain characteristics like database class schema and objects. Users can query the data/knowledge base that includes uncertainty by either crisp or fuzzy queries. At the lower level of the architecture, FOODB handles the large scale of complex data and KB handles knowledge definitions and uncertain deduction. These two systems are coupled through a bridge that provides interoperability. Improvement of the language and the architecture and development of an efficient fuzzy inference mechanism are current subjects of study.

References

1. Baldwin, J.F., Martin, T.P.: Fuzzy Objects and Multiple Inheritance in Frill++, in EUFIT'96, (1996), 680-684
2. Bancilhon, F., Delobel, C., Kanellakis, P.: Building an Object-Oriented Database System, Morgan Kaufmann Publishers inc., (1992)
3. Dubois, D., Prade, H., Rossazza, J.: Vagueness, Typicality, and Uncertainty in Class Hierarchies, Int. Journal of Intelligent Systems, (1991), 167-183
4. Elmasri, R., Navathe, S. B.: Fundamentals of Database Systems, The Benjamin/Cummings,(1994)
5. Kershberg, L.: Expert Database Systems, Proc. of the 2nd int. Conf., Benjamin/Cummunigs,(1989)
6. Krishna, S.:Int. to Database and Knowledge Base Systems, World Scien.,(1992)
7. Li, Q., Lochovsky, F.H.: ADOME: An Adavanced Object Modeling Environment, IEEE Transactions on Knowledge and Data Engineering, (1998), 255-276
8. Liu, M.: An Overview of the Rule-Based Object Language, Journal of Intelligent Information Systems, (1998), 5-29
9. McCabe, F. G.: Logic and Objects. Prentice Hall, (1992)
10. Ndousse, T.D.: Intelligent Systems Modeling with Reusable Fuzzy Objects, Int. Journal of Intelligent Systems, (1997), 137-152
11. Parsons, S.: Current Approaches to handling Imperfect Information in Data and Knowledge Bases, IEEE Trans. on Knowledge and Data Eng.,(1996),353-372
12. Urban, S. D., Karadimce, A.P., Dietrich, S.W., Abdellatif, T.B., Rene Chan, H.W.: CDOL: A Comprehensive Declarative Object Language, Data and Knowledge Engineering, (1997), 67-111
13. Yazici, A, George, R., Aksoy, D.: Design and Implementation Issues in the Fuzzy Object-Oriented Data Model, Information Sciences (Int. Journal), 1998, 241-260
14. Yazici, A., George, R.: Fuzzy Database Modeling, Physica-Verlag, Heidelberg, NewYork, (1999)
15. Zadeh, L.A.: Similarity relations and Fuzzy Orderings,Inf.Sciences, (1971),177-200

An OODBMS-IRS Integration Based on a Statistical Corpus Extraction Method for Document Management

Chung-Hong Lee[1] and Lee-Feng Chien[2]

[1] Department of Information Management, Chang Jung University,
396,Sec.1, Chang Jung Rd, Kway Jen, Tainan, 711, Taiwan
leechung@mail.cju.edu.tw
[2] Institute of Information Science, Academia Sinica
Taipei, Taiwan
lfchien@iis.sinica.edu.tw

Abstract. The maintenance cost is a critical issue for the success of integrating database and *information retrieval systems* (IRS). For a robust integration of search engines, the signature file filter can effectively eliminate the maintenance cost and offer a more natural fit between the database and text retrieval systems. Extending the usability of merged database and signature based text-retrieval systems by building on an *object-oriented database management system* (OODBMS) provides better and complementary advantages to both databases and *information retrieval systems* (IRSs). In this paper, we present a new approach for integrating OODBMSs and IRSs that maintains the flexibility and avoids overheads of mapping process, by means of encapsulating the documents and signature based IR methods into storable objects which are being stored in the database. In addition, we develop a novel signature file approach based on a statistical corpus extraction technique, which can effectively reduce false drop probability for text retrieval from the underneath document database.

1   Introduction

To combine the merits of databases and information retrieval systems (IRS) for document retrieval, a number of different integration approaches have been developed in recent years [4][12][6][7][16][3][15]. For achieving a more robust integration, several information retrieval techniques have been considered to meet the special requirements of implementing content-based retrieval functionality in the document database systems. The inverted file approach, for instance, allows the cost of processing a query much less than that of a sequential search through a large document collection. However, it suffers from a serious problem due to the high cost of establishing and maintaining the inverted file, particularly when updating the document database. The contents of inverted file and document pointers vary as documents are added and deleted from the database. Thus, the related indexed term parameters and retrieval algorithms should be calculated dynamically. This produces a rather high cost of system maintenance. Alternatively, the other IR approach considered is to employ a signature file in which documents are represented as a number of fixed length signatures stored in a data collection. The difficulties of maintaining the signature file and database maintenance are eased through the appending operations in the signature file. As such, the maintenance cost is relatively minimized and a more natural fit between the database management and requirements of text retrieval is obtained.

The signature based IR search combined with the original database queries allows to produce very powerful queries, going beyond regular expression search based on structural relationships or associated attributes. Unfortunately, the signature file methods have a distinctive drawback, the *false drop* issue. False drops are text blocks that the signature file identifies as containing the query terms but indeed they don't. In this paper, we describe an OODBMS-IRS integration based on a novel signature generation approach, namely *statistical corpus extraction* method, which does enhance the original database query functionality and reduce the false drop probability. The experimental results reveal a better performance provided by the system, especially in the reduction of false drops, space overhead and the retrieval time, etc.

1.1 Fundamental Concepts of Signature File Techniques

Signature file methods are algorithms to construct a signature filter from a document as a pre-processor of IRS or DBMS search engines for searching documents, with the purpose to screen out most of the unqualified documents stored in the database in order to increase the search efficiency. In the past, these techniques have studied extensively as an access method for textual databases [13][1][9]. In the signature generation method, each word in a text block is hashed into a word signature. A document signature (S(P)) is computed by superimposing all word signatures from the block. Similarly, the query terms in a query are hashed and superimposed into a query signature. Then the query signature is matched against each document signature in the signature file.

Conventional English signature file approaches generally rely on well-tuned hash functions in the transformation of word signatures [5]. However, in terms of optimization, it is not easy to utilize such functions to process the characteristics of various documents and occurrence possibility of word pairs to form sensible searching terms in determination of appropriated word signatures, the false drop probability therefore cannot be effectively reduced. In addition, the generated document signatures are only served as a filter for full-text searching, but rarely as feature vectors for best match searching at the same time. To remedy the weakness of conventional signature file approaches, we propose a new signature file approach which substitutes the use of hash functions by a statistical corpus-based signature extraction method. Through such an approach, it is possible to deal with the characteristics of various document databases in the generation of signatures. Meanwhile, each bit of the signatures has more semantic meaning, which is often vague through the conventional methods. The approach will be described later in detail.

1.2 Background

The system development is based on the scenario of an ongoing project in developing a multi-lingual information retrieval system which handles English and Chinese document collections. These documents are stored in an object-oriented database. The main aim is to integrate the developed IR technique with the OODBMS in such a way that it migrates the unstructured documents to the object database with regard to the integrated functionality of many existing approaches. Besides, it also requires a specially designed data model which considers the requirements of both database and our specific IR queries for document retrieval.

1.3 System Features

The features of the integrated system are highlighted as follows:
- a data model that encapsulates the individual document and its associated IR methods to allow the textual or multimedia type of documents to be stored in the object database.
- a novel approach for the generation of a signature scheme based on a statistical corpus extraction technique for document retrieval, which can effectively catch relevant documents from the underneath database system and eliminate the false drop probability.
- a *signature file* filtering approach designed for pre-processing the IR queries, and further transform the IR queries into OODBMS queries for document retrieval from the underlying database.

The rest of this paper is organized as follows. In Section 2 related work is reviewed and our distinctive approach for the integration is discussed. Section 3 describes the system architecture. The functions of each module within the system are discussed in detail. Section 4 addresses the proposed signature approach, the statistical corpus based signature method. Some experimental results are discussed in Section 5. Section 6 discusses the conclusions.

2 Related Work

There have been several research efforts at establishing retrieval systems that have aspects of both traditional text-retrieval systems and database systems. Some of them focused on the relational data model, such as [14][6][7], and there are also some commercial products available recently, such as Oracle SQL*TextRetrieval. However, for the management of multimedia documents, the retrieval and storage functions of the complex objects in the relational databases are relatively cumbersome and difficult. Besides, it is inefficient to satisfy the demands of semantic modeling for the complexity of document structures. Object-orient database management systems (OODBMSs), with their strengths in dealing with complex objects and close connection with the programming languages, are considered as a better solution for the development of the integration platform.

A text-search extension to the ORION object-oriented database was described by Lee [8]. It described an implementation of text search capability within the ORION framework that is compatible with the general ORION query processing functionality. The integration of the INQUERY text retrieval system and the IRIS object database proposed by Croft, et al. [4] was also an earlier implementation for this. Several research efforts have been focused on mapping the SGML document structures into OODBMS's data models [3][10][15]. The Refus system [12] handles autonomous text stored in conventional file. In Refus, attributes are extracted from the corresponding documents and then classified class in the OODBMS. Differing from some of the above efforts with the aims to model only structured SGML documents in relational or object-oriented databases, our system is particularly aimed at handling heterogeneous types of documents, such as textual and multimedia documents, and providing content-based retrieval functions to describe the stored document objects.

3 System Architecture

The system extends in layers the implementation of an existing search engine of the OODBMS (see Fig. 1). The system integrates the signature file based IR and OODB search engines. As a result it retains the simplicity of the original OODB queries while offering the functionality of the IR queries. In particular, the signature extraction of each document is performed automatically by our signature generation algorithm. Alone with the documents, the methods used to represent individual document signatures are encapsulated into storable objects which are being stored in the database. Besides, the resulting document signatures associated with the target paths that indicate their storage addresses in the OODBMS are stored in the signature file.

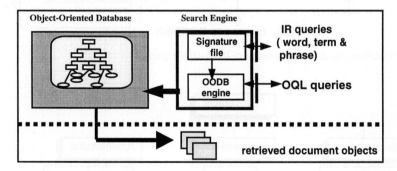

Fig. 1 System Architecture

Prior to insertion of documents to the database, each document is parsed into a set of signature representations that can be referenced in queries. The signature file acts as a pre-processor of the document database for filtering the query information. In order to quickly filter out non-qualifying documents and to avoid the difficulty of key word extraction, a novel approach by means of corpus based signature extraction is proposed. Such an approach will be described in detail later.

3.1 Signature File Scheme and Query Process

In this section, we describe the mechanism of the signature file processor in association with the query process of the OODBMS engine. As mentioned above, a document signature was computed and then recorded in a signature file. Once a query arrives, the query terms in a query are similarly transformed into a query signature. Then the query signature is matched against each document signature in the signature file. A signature failing to match the query signature insures that the associated document can be ignored. Thus, unnecessary database accesses are prevented. After the signature matching process, a list file that stores all matched signatures and their associated documents represented in path expression of the OODBMS is produced for the document objects in the database. The list file acts as a pointer file in which each item points to the associated objects for further retrieval task performed by the OODBMS queries. Fig. 2 shows the mechanism of signature file processor and the list file for object retrieval. Fig. 3 shows the designed document class hierarchy.

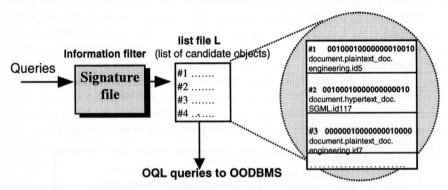

Fig. 2 Signature file as a pre-processor of the database queries

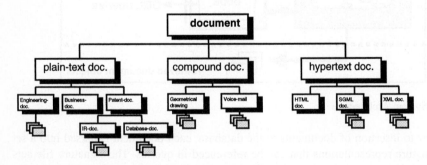

Fig. 3 The document objects in the class hierarchy

4 A Corpus Based Signature File Approach for Document Retrieval

4.1 Improper Signature Sharing Caused by Hash-function-based Approaches

The design of the proposed approach is primarily based on the analysis of improper signature sharing shown in Fig. 4, where three major types of improper signature sharing which may occur in conventional hash-function-based approaches are examined. Most of English signature extraction methods rely on hash functions in the generation of word signatures and determination of their signature sharing (one-bit assignment in the generated signature patterns). In fact, without sufficient information of the database content, there may exist some improper '1' bit sharing among the signatures of frequently used keywords or searching terms, which enlarges the number of false drops. For instance, as shown in Case (1) of Fig. 4, the words "information" and "retrieval" shouldn't have shared '1' bits in their assigned signature patterns, because they often appear together for forming the searching term "information retrieval" and thus more false drop situation will occur. In the same situation in Case (2), it should not allow the indexed terms, e.g., "retrieval" and "system", which have shared frequently associated indexed terms, e.g., "information", have shared signature patterns. Furthermore, it is also improper to let the indexed terms whose different frequently associated indexed terms have shared signatures, have shared signatures, too, such as "retrieval" and "processing".

Through the corpus-based approach, the characteristics of the document collections can be modeled in the generation of signatures and more proper document signatures can be produced. In particular, the design of the corpus-based signature extraction method is basically independent of the application domains and utilized languages. This approach consists of an algorithm for *dissimilar indexed term grouping*, *a character-level signature extraction method for Chinese database access* and a sophisticated design for both *exact match* and *best match searching*. In the following, we will introduce the key concept and algorithm of the first part. The rest of the corpus-based approach can be referred in our previous work [2].

4.2 Grouping of Dissimilar Indexed Terms

The goal of the algorithm is to group all of the indexed terms in the database domains into a pre-specified number of clusters, according to the statistical parameters extracted from the prepared corpus. Terms grouped in the same cluster can be suitably to have shared one-bits in their assigned signature '1' bits to reduce the signature size and numbers of false drops.

(1) Case (1): It is improper to let those indexed terms which frequently occur together have shared signatures, such as "資訊(information)" and "檢索(retrieval)" .

資訊(information)　　◁▷　　檢索(retrieval)

(2) Case (2): It is improper to let those indexed terms which have shared frequently-associated indexed terms have shared signatures , such as "檢索(retrieval)" and "系統(system)".

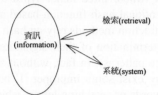

(3) Case (3): It is improper to let those indexed terms, whose different frequently-associated indexed terms have shared signatures, have shared signatures, too, such as "檢索(retrieval)" and "處理(processing)".

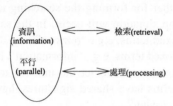

Fig. 4 Three cases of improper signature sharing which may occur in conventional hash-function-based signature file approaches, where the indexed terms within a circle already have shared signatures.

Firstly, using the algorithm the indexed terms grouped in the same cluster should be as "dissimilar" as possible and should rarely occur together in a single document. This would be very effective in reducing the occurrences of many possible false drops. Secondly, indexed terms that are frequently associated with other common indexed terms should be grouped in disjoint clusters, in order to reduce the occurrences of other possible false drops. For the above purposes, a similarity function is then presented and its definition is given below.

The similarity estimation function $TermSim(I_i, I_j)$ is defined below:

$$TermSim(I_i, I_j) = w_1 * f_{ij} + w_2 * \sum_{k \neq i, j} f_{ik} * f_{jk}$$

where I_i and I_j are a pair of indexed terms, w_1 and w_2 are predefined weight values, f_{ij} is the average frequency of both indexed terms I_i and I_j occurring in a document, and f_{ik} (f_{jk}) is the average frequency of I_i (I_j) and other indexed term I_k occurring in the same document (These frequency parameters can be obtained from the statistics of the document collections or some related documents.)

This function estimates the similarity of a pair of indexed terms with their co-occurrence and the frequencies of their shared associated terms. According to its definition, a pair of indexed terms which frequently occur together such as "資訊 (information)" and "檢索(retrieval)", will have a higher similarity value, and terms which contain many shared indexed terms such as "檢索(retrieval)" and "系統 (system)" have a higher value, too. These terms are not suitable for grouping together because they will produce many false drops. The cluster similarity estimation function ClusterSim(Si, Sj) is defined below:

$$ClusterSim(S_i, S_j) = W_1 * F_{ij} + W_2 * \sum_{k \neq i, j} F_{ik} * F_{jk}$$

where S_i and S_j are a pair of clusters with selected terms, W_1 and W_2 are pre-defined weight values, F_{ij} is the average frequency of both clusters S_i and S_k being in a document, and F_{ik} (F_{jk}) is the average frequency of both clusters S_i (S_j) and S_k being in a document (These frequency parameters can be obtained from the frequency parameters of characters, e.g., $F_{ij} = \Sigma\Sigma f_{\alpha\beta}$).

The grouping algorithm based on the extended cluster similarity function above is then proposed and briefly described below. The algorithm uses the greedy method. Initially, every indexed term belongs to a unique cluster, and all of these clusters constitute the cluster set. Each pair of clusters in the initial cluster set, e.g., S_1, S_2, has a cluster similarity value, ClusterSim(S_1, S_2), equal to the term similarity value of their composed terms, e.g, C_1, C_2. That is, ClusterSim(S_1, S_2) = TermSim(C_1, C_2) at the initial stage. Then, it starts with a three-step iteration. In the first step of each iteration, a pair of clusters, S_i and S_j, in the cluster set which has a minimum cluster similarity value is selected. In the second step, the two clusters are then combined as a new cluster, S_n, which is appended into the cluster set in the second step. During the second step, all of the cluster similarity values related to S_n are computed with the above definition. At the third and final step of the iteration, clusters S_i and S_j are removed from the cluster set. The entire iteration will be performed until the pre-specified number of clusters have been grouped. Since the combined clusters selected in each iteration are least similar to each other during that time, the similarity between each pair of the terms in the same cluster are then as low as possible. With the above grouping algorithm, the grouped indexed terms are allowed to share common one-bits in the document signature of the database. The signature size of a document database, thus, can be adjusted with the average length of each document and the number of possible false drops. Basically, the above grouping processing can be further improved based on some approximation methods, such as SVD [11].

5 Experimental Results

Currently we have successfully implemented a number of IR systems based on the proposed signature file approach. The implementation of the proposed approach has demonstrated that it has a better performance in many aspects, especially in the reduction of false drops and space overhead, acceleration of retrieval time, and a capability to perform best match searching of quasi-natural language query. In this test, the experiment environment includes a news database containing 32,000 news items (about 45 MB) and 300 randomly selected test queries with an average size of 3.0 characters, the test results indicate that the average number of false drops for each query is effectively reduced using the proposed signature extraction method, in compare with the one using conventional methods which simply rely on hash functions. On the other hand, our system also shows that the space required for a signature file based on the proposed approach is around 15% ~ 20% of the document database in a lot of tests.

6 Conclusions

The maintenance cost is a critical issue for the success of integrating database and *information retrieval systems* (IRS). For a robust integration of search engines, the signature file filter can effectively eliminate the maintenance cost and offer a more natural fit between the database and text retrieval systems. Extending the usability of merged database and signature based text-retrieval systems by building on an *object-oriented database management system* (OODBMS) provides better and complementary advantages to both databases and *information retrieval systems* (IRSs). In this paper, we present a new approach for integrating OODBMSs and IRSs that maintains the flexibility and avoids overheads of mapping process, by means of encapsulating the documents and signature based IR methods into storable objects which are being stored in the database. In particular, we develop a novel signature file approach based on a statistical corpus extraction technique, which can effectively reduce false drop probability for document retrieval from the underneath database system. The algorithms of the signature scheme and query techniques developed can also be applicable to the construction of multimedia-document based digital libraries.

The proposed corpus based signature generation method offers a significant reduction of false drops and space overhead, acceleration of retrieval time, and a capability to perform best match searching of quasi-natural language query. The implementation addresses some improvements in conventional IR methods, but still remains several issues with the integration architecture, mainly related to efficiency. This framework, however, is regarded as a starting point to allow for identifying the fundamental functionality and theories of both IR and database disciplines, in order to produce quality document retrieval and storage systems.

References

1. Chang, W.W. and Schek, H.J.: A Signature Access Method for the Starburst Database System, Proceedings of the 15th VLDB Conference, Amsterdam, The Netherlands (1989) 145-153

2. Chien, Lee-Feng: Fast and Quasi-Natural Language Search for Gigabytes of Chinese Texts, Proceedings of the 18th Annual International ACM SIGIR conference on Research and Development in Information Retrieval, (1995) 112-120

3. Christophides, V., Abiteboul, S., Cluet, S. and Scholl, M.: From Structured Documents to Novel Query Facilities, Proceedings of the ACM SIGMOD'94, (1994) 313-324

4. Croft, W.B. Smith, L.A. and Turtle, H.R.: A Loosely-Coupled Integration of a Text Retrieval System and an Object-Oriented Database System. Proc. ACM SIGIR Conference. (1992) 223-231

5. Faloutsos, C., Access Methods for Text, ACM Computing Surveys, (1985) 49-74

6. Fuhr, Norbert.: A Probabilistic Relational Model for the Integration of IR and Databases., Proceedings of the 16th Annual International ACM/SIGIR Conference on Research and Development in Information Retrieval, Pittsburgh, (1993) 309-317

7. Fuhr, Norbert.: Integration of Information Retrieval and Database Systems., Proceedings of the 17th Annual International ACM/SIGIR Conference on Research and Development in Information Retrieval, Dublin, (1994) 360

8. Lee, W.L. and Woelk, D.: Integration of Text Research with ORION, Database Engineering, Vol. 9. (1991) 58-64

9. Lee, D.L. et al.: Efficient Signature File Methods for Text Retrieval, IEEE Transactions on Knowledge and Data Engineering, Vol. 7, No 3, (1995) 423-435

10. Macleod, I.A. and Narine, D.: A Depository for Structured Text Objects. Proc. DEXA '95, (1995) 272-282

11. Schutze, H. Part-of-speech Induction from Scratch, In Proceedings of the ACL'93, (1993) 251-258

12. Shoens, K. et al.: The Rufus System: Information Organization for Semi-Structured Data, Proceedings of the 19th VLDB Conference, Dublin, Ireland, (1993) 97-107

13. Stanfill, C. and Kahle, B.: Parallel Free-Text Search on the Connection Machine System, Comm. ACM, Vol. 29, No 12, (1986). 1229-1239

14. Stonebraker, M., Stettner, H., Lynn, N., Kalash, J. and Guttman, A.: "Document Processing in a Relational Database System." ACM TOIS, 1(2): (1983) 143-158

15. Volz, M. et al.: Applying a Flexible OODBMS-IRS-Coupling to Structured Document Handling, Proceedings of the Twelfth International Conference on Data Engineering, New Orleans, Louisiana, USA (1996) 10-19

16. Yan, T.W. and Annevelink, J.: Integrating a Structured-Text Retrieval System with an Object-Oriented Database System, Proceedings of the 20th VLDB Conference, Santiago, Chile (1994)

Controlled Hypertextual Navigation in the SgmlQL Language

Emmanuel Bruno, Jacques Le Maitre, and Elisabeth Murisasco

GECT, Equipe Systèmes d'Information MultiMédia
Université de Toulon et du Var, BP 132, 83957 La Garde Cedex
{bruno, lemaitre, murisasco}@univ-tln.fr
Tél : (33) 04-94-14-26-21   Fax : (33) 04-94-14-26-33

Abstract. Due to the growth of networks, the notion of document has evolved to the notion of hyperdocument. It is usual to fragment documents in a set of files referencing each other, distributed over a network. Manual navigation remains the most usual way to browse this graph-like structure to query documents either from a known URL or from the output of an index server. Nevertheless, it is difficult to avoid digressions and even getting "lost in the cyberspace". Moreover, it is mandatory to read each accessed document to check its reliability. We present in this paper an extension of the SgmlQL language. The purpose of this extension is to define a specific operator to express and control hypertextual navigation. Path filters are defined and can be restricted according to the structure of the path, the followed links and the traversed documents.

1 Introduction

The treatment of electronic documents is becoming more and more important particularly because of the technological progress which facilitates the exchange and the manipulation of complete documents on networks. It is the reason why specific and efficient tools are developed for searching, using and processing distributed documents. This efficiency depends on (i) the representation of a document (ii) its accessibility on networks (iii) its manipulation.

Languages have been proposed to represent documents (SGML [5], XML [13]), they mainly define the logical structure of a document independently of any processing. After that, languages have been developed to manipulate these structured documents. SgmlQL [9] is one of them. It is a OQL-like functional language which manipulates the tree-like structure, it can be used with any kind of document from which a tree-like structure can be extracted, in particular SGML, HTML or XML documents (or even RTF...). SgmlQL enables to extract fragments of documents, to reuse them for building new documents, either by putting them together, or by modifying their structure. Moreover, SgmlQL makes it possible to query documents distributed over distant sites.

Otherwise, due to the growth of networks, the notion of document has evolved to the notion of hyperdocument. It is more and more usual to fragment documents in a set of files referencing each other and these files can be distributed over a network. The manipulation of the whole document requires the ability to browse this graph-like structure. Manual navigation remains the most usual way to browse it either from a known URL or from the output of an index server. Nevertheless, it is difficult to avoid digressions and even getting "lost in the cyberspace". Moreover, it is mandatory to read each accessed document to check its reliability. Finally, it is difficult to take advantage of hypertext particular organisations such as lists or trees.

Initially, SgmlQL offers operators for documents with a tree-like structure. In this paper, an operator for hyperdocuments with a graph-like structure is defined. Our proposition is to extend the language SgmlQL with a navigation operator. This operator uses path filters with associated constraints. These constraints can be set on the links to follow, on the content of documents or even on the structure of the followed path. Therefore, any component of each traversed document can be used to controlthe navigation, all these components can also be extracted and reused in new documents.

This paper is organized as follows : section 2 presents SgmlQL characteristics; section 3 is an intuitive approach of our proposition: it shows how a path filter in a SgmlQL query can be expressed and used to browse a hypertext and to extract parts of it; section 4 formally defines the navigation operator; section 5 proposes a mechanism to check constraints during the navigation, which is a first step to the optimization of navigation queries. Section 6 focuses on the problem of cycles. Related works are discussed and compared with our proposition in section 7. Section 8 concludes.

2　The SgmlQL language

```
<!DOCTYPE ANTHOLOGY [
    <!ELEMENT ANTHOLOGY (POEM+) >
    <!ELEMENT POEM (TITLE, STANZA+) >
        <!ATTLIST POEM AUTHOR #PCDATA #REQUIRED >
    <!ELEMENT TITLE (#PCDATA) >
    <!ELEMENT STANZA (LINE+) >
        <!ATTLIST STANZA NUM NUMBER #REQUIRED >
    <!ELEMENT LINE (#PCDATA) >
<ANTHOLOGY>
    <POEM AUTHOR="William Blake">
        <TITLE>The SICK ROSE<TITLE>
        <STANZA NUM=1>
            <LINE>O Rose thou art sick.        </LINE>
            ...
        </STANZA>
        <STANZA NUM=2>
            dots
        </STANZA>
    </POEM>
    <POEM>
                <! more poems go here >
    </POEM>
</ANTHOLOGY>
```

Fig. 1. An SGML document : DTD and instance

For example, the expression (E1):
```
navigate node("http://www.univ-tln.fr")
(→ as $1,_ as $d) | ((→ as $11,_).(→ as $1,_ as $d))
```

- filters all the paths of length 1 or 2 starting from (the node built from) the URL ''http://www.univ-tln.fr''.
- for each filtered path, variables are instantiated and an environment is generated.

The user can use an easy-to-read presentation : the expression → as var is the same as the expression var and the expression _ as var is the same that the expression var. For example, (E1) can be rewritten in this way :
```
navigate node("http://www.univ-tln.fr") ($1,$d)|(($11,_).($1,$d))
```

The **navigate** operator is embedded into SgmlQL and can be used in particular in the **from** clause of **select...from...where**. Thus, constraints can be set on the filtered components in the **where** clause. For instance,

Query 5 *Titles of documents reached from the Toulon Web server following one link the label of which matches "phone book"*
```
select first TITLE within $d
from    navigate node("http://www.univ-tln.fr") ($1, $d)
where   $1→label match "phone book";
```

Thus it is possible in a query to use the hypertext structure and to extract fragments according to some criteria.

4 The navigate operator

4.1 Hypertext model

A hypertext (it could be the Web) is a set of documents on a network. It can be viewed as a graph, the nodes are documents and the edges are links between the documents. Nodes can have different formats and heterogeneous structures (text/html, image/jpeg, ...). Links – embedded into documents – are monodirectional : so the graph is oriented. Moreover, the graph is dynamic, some nodes and links can be added at any moment. Navigation enables to access to documents by following links. We are particularly interested in SGML, HTML and XML nodes because it is this type of nodes which contains links leading to other documents. Document servers provide different information without accessing these documents. So, we define graph nodes as follows:

Definition 1. *A node is an instance of an* SGML *document. Some pairs (attribute, value) are added to the root tag of that instance:* URL: *string*, MIMETYPE: *string*, LENGTH: *string*, MODIF: *string*. MODIF *gives the date of creation or last update of the document.*

A *link* component is defined by the URL which references the source document, the URL which references the target document, and a label can be useful to take into account the semantics of this link with the two REL and REV attributes (see HTML). To represent such links, we define an SGML element.

Definition 2. *A link element is an* SGML *element defined as follows(the* BASE
URL *must reference a valid document, but the* HREF URL *can be wrong):*

```
<!ELEMENT LINK Empty>
        <!ATTLIST LINK
                BASE        URL         #REQUIRED
                HREF        URL         #REQUIRED
                LABEL       string
                REL         string
                REV         string              >
```

4.2   Path filters

We consider a path as a list of pairs *(link, node)*.

Definition 3. *A path filter is defined as a regular expression:*

- *A link filter is either* → *which filters any link, or* = *which filters the null
  link. The null link binds a document with itself.*
- *A node filter is either* _ *which filters any document, or an* URL *which filters
  the referenced document.*
- *If F_l is a link filter and F_d a node filter then (F_l, F_d) is a path filter. It filters
  any path (l, d) such that l is filtered by F_l and d is filtered by F_d.*
- *If F_1 and F_2 are path filters, then F_1. F_2 filters any path composed of two
  consecutive paths C_1 and C_2 such that C_1 is filtered by F_1 and C_2 is filtered
  by F_2.*
- *If F_1 and F_2 are path filters, then F_1 | F_2 filters any path which is filtered
  either by F_1 or by F_2.*
- *If F is a path filter then F^* filters either the empty path or a path composed
  of n (n>0) consecutive subpaths filtered by F. To impose a bound on the time
  t or the length l of the navigation, a F^* filter can be suffixed by [t, l]. These
  two parameters ensure that the number of filtered paths is finite.*
- *The expression (F) is equivalent to the expression F.*

For instance, the expression $(\rightarrow,\_).(\rightarrow,\_)^{*[0,3]}$ filters paths of length ≤ 4. The
timeout value (set to 0) is not specified.

Variables can be bound to any component of a path filter, using the keyword
as. These variables are used to define constraints on the followed links or on the
content of the documents accessed during the navigation :

- *link* **as** *var* : a link is bound to the *var* variable
- *node* **as** *var* : a node is bound to the *var* variable

Note that variables defined in the F subfilter of a F* filter are only visible in
F (the need for such variables will be explained in section 5 below).

4.3   The "navigate" operator

In order to produce the set of all paths matching a pattern starting from a given
node, we proposea specific operator called **navigate**.

Definition 4. *The* **node** *operator applied to an* URL *returns the node associated with the document indicated by this* URL.

Definition 5. *The expression* navigate n F *starts from the node n and instantiates the variables of F for each path filtered by F. Therefore, the* **navigate** *operator produces a list of environments.*

For example, the expression

```
navigate node("http://www.univ-tln.fr/") ($l,$d)
```

- filters all the paths of length 1 starting from (the node built from) the URL ``http://www.univ-tln.fr/''
- produces the list $[\{\$l = v_{11}, \$d = v_{12}\}, \ldots, \{\$l = v_{n1}, \$d = v_{n2}\}]$ if n paths are filtered and if for each filtered path i, v_{i1} is a link element and v_{i2} a node component.

The **navigate** operator is embedded into SgmlQL and can be used in any place where an environment is generated.

Let same_server($url1,$url2) be a boolean function checking if the URL $url2$ and $url1$ are on the same server.

Query 6 URL *and titles of sections[1] of documents which are referenced by a given document. These documents must be on the same server*
```
element RESULT content:
        let $start = node("http://www.univ-tln.fr/~gect")
        in
            select [ element URL content:$d→URL ,
                     element TITLES content: every H1 within $d ]
            from    navigate $start ($l, $d)
            where   same_server($start→URL,$l→HREF);
```

The **let** clause instantiates the variable $start, starting point of the navigation. The **where** clause checks if the followed link from $start is on the same server. The **select** clause builds a list of pairs of elements specifying the URL of the accessed document and its list of H1 elements. An answer could be :

```
<RESULT>
    <URL>http://www.univ-tln.fr/~gect/informations.html</URL>
    <TITLES><H1>News</H1><H1>Access to the university</H1></TITLES>
...
</RESULT>
```

4.4   Using index server

Up to there, we only saw some navigations starting from a given and unique URL[2]. In fact, it can be useful to navigate from a list of URL. Sometimes, a user

---

[1] We suppose that they are embedded into H1 tags.

[2] More precisely, the navigation starts from the node built from a given URL.

only knows some keywords about a given topic to start his search. The list of URL can be returned by an index server. Like [10], we define an operator to add the flexibility of an index server to an SgmlQL query (see section 6 for a complete example).

Definition 6. *The value of the expression $id* **about** *m is a list of environments [{$id= node_1},..., {$id=node_n}] where node_1, ..., node_n are returned by the default index server[3] in answer to the m query.*

5 Guards

In the above examples, all constraints are set in the clause **where**. Setting the constraints in this way delays their checking after the generation of each path. But most navigations can be interrupted as soon as possible if conditions are checked during the navigation. One solution is to add guards to link filters, node filters and path filters, as it is done with the Caml [6] functional language.

Definition 7. *Let C be a boolean expression and F be a filter, the expression F* **when** *C is a filter which restricts the list of environments filtered by F to environments where C is true.*

In the expression
navigate $node ($\rightarrow$ as $1 when 1\rightarrow$HREF match ".fr",_as $d)
only links leading to french Web server are followed. (only needed documents are loaded in main memory). Guards are mandatory to set contraints on F in a F* filter because variables bound in F cannot be seen outside F, in particular in the **where** clause.

Query 7 *Titles of documents organised as a list. The next document is pointed with a link, the label of which is "next"*
```
select $d
from    navigate node("http://www.first.element.list/")
                    ($1 when $1→LABEL match "next",_)*     (1)
                . (=,$d);                                  (2)
```

Lines (1) and (2) provide access to each document within the list (the variable $d will successively contain each document). Line (1) filters each path starting at the node ''http://www.first.element.list/'' of length 0 up to n (number of documents of that list). For each path, line (2) gives access to the last document (null link =).

6 Dealing with cycles

In hypertexts, lot of documents are referencing each other. Consequently it is necessary to be able to deal with cycles to avoid infinite navigation.

---

[3] Altavista for example.

The first solution could be to forbid traversing twice the same document. This is easy to implement but is semantically inadequate because the same document can be differently processed at different steps along the navigation. Note that this solution does not avoid cycles due to mirror documents.

The best solution would be to take into account the way each document is accessed : not only the link reaching the document but also the whole navigation before. This needs an in-depth study of the semantics of the links. This remains to be done.

Between these two solutions, we have chosen to keep track of the links reaching a document and to avoid returning to the same document by the same link.

7 Related works

Other works deal with the querying of distributed documents over networks. Their approach is generally to see the Web as a database and to develop specific languages. These languages are not usually based on document query languages and they focus more on the navigation between documents than on the querying documents. For example, they do not provide specific operators to query documents in-depth. W3QL [7], WebSQL [10], Weblog [8], RIO [12] are some of these languages.

In these languages, the Web is generally viewed as an oriented graph, the nodes are documents and the edges the links. For WebSQL, nodes and links which are reduced to some of their properties (an URL, a label, or a title) are not in-depth queried. In other languages (RIO, Weblog) the content is more finely queried (as opposed to a mere plain text search). The W3QL language does not directly constraint the content of a document but it offers external tools for that purpose (UN*X tools). These languages have an SQL-like syntax, except Weblog which has a Datalog like syntax. SQL is extended with specific clauses to express navigation patterns. These patterns are always defined in the **from** clause, either with a list of variables referencing traversed documents and links (W3QL), or with regular expressions (WebSQL, RIO). WebSQL's regular expressions precise start and final documents and only specify intermediary links. Thus, it is not possible to constrain traversed documents without splitting the expression of navigation. RIO's regular expressions constraint any component of a navigation pattern, but conditions are not checked during the navigation. Weblog expresses the navigation with rules.

Otherwise, each language offers specific functionalities like index servers call (WebSQL), automatic inputs for the forms encountered during the navigation, result refreshment mechanism (W3QL), connections with classical databases (RIO).

We propose an extension of the SgmlQL document query language, adding to it navigation capabilities, and not a mere language for the navigation over networks.

8 Conclusion

We have presented in this paper an operator [2] making it possible to manage fragmented data easily. This operator uses a path filter with associated constraints, to carry out a controlled navigation over a hypertext from either a start point (a valid URL) or the URL returned by an index server. Combined with standard SgmlQL operators, the user can express a query which (i) specifies a navigation where conditions are set on the followed path, and on the traversed links and documents, (ii) extracts hypertext fragments and (iii) reuse these fragments with classical SgmlQL operators to build new documents (or hyperdocuments). This paper also focuses on the problem of cycles and presents a detection mechanism. Finally, guards mechanism is proposed (i) to check space and time constraints as soon as possible during the navigation, and (ii) to make possible query rewriting for optimization. All the functionalities described in this paper are implemented and validated [11].

The perspectives of our work are to produce new hypertexts in order to offer dynamic views (which could be specific to user profiles), to propose connecting capabilities with server processing documents to add metadata [4, 1]. Finally we want to study the semantics of links, in particular to solve the cycles problem.

References

[1] L. Berti, J. L. Damoiseaux, and E. Murisasco. Combining the Power of Query Languages and Search Engines for On-line Document and Information Retrieval: the QIRi@D Environment. *International Workshop on Principles of Digital Document Processing, Lectures Notes in Computer Science 1481*, pages 116–127, 1998.

[2] E. Bruno. Un opérateur de suivi de lien pour SgmlQL. Technical report, SIMM.

[3] V. Christophides, S. Abiteboul, S. Cluet, and M. Scholl. From structured documents to novel query facilities. In *Proceedings of ACM-SIGMOD '94*, pages 313–324, Minneapolis (US), May 1994.

[4] *Dublin Core MetaData Initiative.* http://purl.org/dc/.

[5] C. Goldfarb. *The SGML Handbook.* Oxford Clarendon Press, 1990.

[6] INRIA. *CAML manual.* http://www.pauillac.inria.fr/caml/man-caml/.

[7] D. Konopnicki and O. Shmueli. W3QS: a query system for the world wide web. In *Proceedings of 21th Very Large DataBases conf.(VLDB'95)*, Zurich, Suisse, 1995.

[8] L. V. S. Laksmanan, F. Sadri, and I. N. Subramamnian. A declarative language for querying and restructuring the Web. In *Workshop on research issues in data engineering, (RIDE '96)*, New Orleans, USA, 1996.

[9] J. L. Maitre, E. Murisasco, and M. Rolbert. SgmlQL, a language for querying SGML documents. In *Proceedings of the 4th European conf. on Information Systems (ECIS '96)*, pages 75–89, Lisbonne, Portugal, 1996.

[10] A. O. Mendelzon and T. Milo. Querying the World Wide Web. *Journal of Digital Libraries (JODL)*, 1(1):54–67, 1997.

[11] *SgmlQL manual.* http://www.univ-tln.fr/~gect/simm/SgmlQL/.

[12] A. M. Vercoustre and F. Paradis. Reuse of liened documents through virtual document prescriptions. In *Proceeding of Electronic Publishing, (EP '98)*, Saint Malo, 1998.

[13] W3 consortium. http://www.w3.org/TR/REC-xml/.

SECONDO/QP: Implementation of a Generic Query Processor*

Ralf Hartmut Güting[1], Stefan Dieker[1], Claudia Freundorfer[1], Ludger Becker[2], and Holger Schenk[1]

[1] Praktische Informatik IV, FernUniversität Hagen, D-58084 Hagen, Germany
[2] Westfälische Wilhelms-Universität, FB 15 - Informatik, Einsteinstr. 62, D-48149 Münster, Germany

Abstract. In an extensible database system, evaluation of a *query plan* is done in cooperation between a collection of *operator implementation functions* and a component of the DBMS that we call the *query processor*. Basically, the query processor constructs an operator tree for the query plan and then calls an *evaluator* function which traverses the tree, calling the operator functions in each node. This seemingly simple strategy is complicated by the fact that operator functions must be able to call for the evaluation of parameter expressions (e.g. predicates), and must be able to process *streams* of objects in a pipelined manner.

Although query processing along these lines is implemented in most database systems, and certainly in all extensible database systems, the details of programming the parameter passing, organizing the interaction between stream operators, etc. are tricky, and seem to be buried in the code of the respective systems. We are not aware of any simple, crisp, clear published exposition of how one could implement such a query processor. This is what the paper offers.

Moreover, we feel the solution presented here is particularly simple, elegant, and general. For example, it is entirely independent from the data model being implemented, admits arbitrary parameter functions, and allows one to mix freely stream operators and other operators. The construction of the operator tree, shown in the paper, includes complete type checking and resolution of overloading. The query processor has been implemented within the SECONDO system; the source code is available.

1   Introduction

Extensible database systems have been studied since about the mid-eighties. The main motivation has been the support of new application areas, especially by making it possible to introduce application-specific data types (e.g. polygons or images), and the achievement of a cleaner system architecture which allows

* This work was partially supported by the CHOROCHRONOS project, funded by the EU under the Training and Mobility of Researchers Programme, Contract No. ERB FMRX-CT96-0056.

for easier changes such as the introduction of new access methods or query processing algorithms. Two main directions can be distinguished. The first one is to select a specific data model and to implement for it a system with well-defined interfaces for user-defined extensions. This approach was taken, for example, in the POSTGRES [22], Starburst [13], Gral [11], PREDATOR [20], and Paradise [16] projects as well as in commercial systems like Informix Universal Server [15]; in these cases, the model is an extended relational, or as it is called today, object-relational model [21].

The second approach strives for more generality and attempts to even leave the data model open. In that case, no system is offered; instead, a *toolkit*, a collection of powerful tools for building database systems is provided, for instance a general storage manager or an optimizer generator. Major proponents of this approach are EXODUS [5] and its successor SHORE [6], GENESIS [1], DASDBS [19] and Volcano [9]. Toolkits "have essentially proven to be dead-ends"; this is at least the view of Carey and DeWitt [4]. The main reason was that it was too difficult to construct a DBMS using the toolkit; also the tools offered were in some cases not flexible enough to entirely match what was needed in the application DBMS.

The goal of SECONDO is to offer a generic "database system frame" that can be filled with implementations of a wide range of data models, including, for example, relational, object-oriented, graph-oriented or sequence-oriented DB models. The strategy to achieve this goal is to separate the data-model independent components and mechanisms in a DBMS (the *system frame*) from the data-model dependent parts. Nevertheless, the frame and the "contents" have to work together closely. With respect to the different levels of query languages in a DBMS, we have to describe to the system frame:

- the *descriptive algebra*, defining a data model and query language,
- the *executable algebra*, specifying a collection of data structures and operations capable of representing the data model and implementing the query language,
- *rules* to enable a query optimizer to map descriptive algebra terms to executable algebra terms, also called *query plans* or *evaluation plans*.

A general formalism serving all of these purposes has been developed earlier, called *second-order signature (SOS)* [12]. It is reviewed in Section 2.

At the system level, definitions and implementations of type constructors and operators of the executable algebra are arranged into *algebra modules*, interacting with the system frame through a small number of well-defined support functions for manipulation of types and objects as well as operator invocation.

This paper reports on the core part of the SECONDO system frame, the *query processor*. The task of a query processor is the evaluation of a query plan, that is, an expression of the physical algebra. The basic strategy is to first construct an operator tree for the expression, and then to call an *evaluator* function which traverses the tree, calling *operator functions* in each node. This is complicated by the fact that operator functions must be able to call for the evaluation of parameter expressions (e.g. predicates) and must be able to process streams of objects, working interleaved.

The paper is organized as follows. In Section 2, we review the concept of second-order signature. Section 3 describes the interaction between the query processor and algebra modules from the algebra implementor's point of view. Section 4 describes the evaluation of queries, explaining the construction of the operator tree, type checking, resolution of overloading, and evaluation control. Section 5 discusses related work, and Section 6 concludes the paper.

2 Second-Order Signature

We can give here only a very brief introduction to second-order signature. For a more complete exposition, see [12]. A sophisticated OO and graph data model has been specified in SOS in [3]. The basic idea is to use two coupled signatures to describe first, a data model and second, an algebra over that data model. Recall that a signature in general consists of *sorts* and *operators* and defines a set of *terms*.

In SOS, the first signature has so-called *kinds* as sorts and *type constructors* as operators. The terms of this signature are called *types*. This set of types will be the type system, or equivalently, the data model, of a SECONDO DBMS. The second signature uses the *types generated by the first signature* as sorts, and introduces *operations* on these types which make up a query algebra.

As an example data model specification we choose a small relational model at the execution level (physical model and algebra) which will be used further in the paper. Although the purpose of SECONDO is not to reimplement relational systems, it makes no sense to explain an unknown formalism using examples from an unknown data model.

kinds IDENT, DATA, NUM, TUPLE, REL
type constructors

	→ DATA	*int*, *real*, *bool*, *string*
	→ NUM	*int*, *real*
(IDENT × DATA)+	→ TUPLE	*tuple*
TUPLE	→ REL	*rel*

Any term of this signature[1] is a *type* of the type system. Hence *int* is a type, and

$$rel(tuple(<(\text{name}, \textit{string}), (\text{country}, \textit{string}), (\text{pop}, \textit{int})>))$$

is a type as well, describing the type of a relation for *cities*. Since this is a physical model, for each type constructor there must be a representation data structure in the system.

---

[1] We write signatures by first giving argument and result sorts, then operators, with typing conventions as follows. Kinds are denoted in capitals, type constructors as italic underlined, type variables in italics, and query operators in bold face.

The second signature uses the types generated by the first signature as sorts, and defines a collection of *operators*, in this case for a query processing algebra. Since there are in general infinitely many sorts generated by the first signature, we use *quantification over kinds* to specify polymorphic operators. Hence kinds play a dual role: They control the applicability of type constructors, and they are used for the specification of operators.

operators

∀ num_1 **in** NUM. ∀ num_2 **in** NUM.

$num_1 \times num_2$ $\qquad\qquad\qquad \rightarrow$ *bool* $\qquad\qquad <, >, \leq, \geq, =, \neq$

This defines comparison operators for any combination of *int* and *real* types. Here num_1 and num_2 are type variables that can be bound to any type in the respective kind. A type is *in* the result kind of its outermost type constructor.

∀ *tuple* **in** TUPLE.

rel(*tuple*) × (*tuple* → *bool*)	→ *rel*(*tuple*)	**scanselect**
rel(*tuple*)	→ *stream*(*tuple*)	**feed**
stream(*tuple*) × (*tuple* → *bool*)	→ *stream*(*tuple*)	**filter**

These operators implement selection on a relation by scanning it[2], feed a relation into a stream, and filter a stream by a predicate, respectively. Note that the kind IDENT and the type constructor *stream* are not defined in the data model above. They can be viewed as predefined since their meaning is in fact hard-coded into the query processor, as we will show in Section 4.

Finally, we will use an example *attr* operator to access components of a tuple:

∀ *tuple*: *tuple*(*list*) **in** TUPLE, *attrname* **in** IDENT, *member*(*attrname*, $\qquad\qquad\qquad\qquad\qquad\qquad\qquad\qquad\qquad\qquad\qquad\qquad$ *attrtype, list*).

$tuple \times attrname \qquad\qquad\qquad \rightarrow attrtype \qquad$ **attr**

Here *member* is a *type predicate* that checks whether a pair (x, y) with $x = attrname$ occurs in the *list* making up the tuple type definition. If so, it binds *attrtype* to y. Hence **attr** is an operation that for a given tuple and attribute name returns a value of the data type associated with that attribute name. — Type predicates are implemented "outside" the formalism in a programming language. An example expression, or *query plan* using these operators, would be:

cities **scanselect**[**fun** (c: city) **attr**(c, pop) > 500000]

This assumes a *cities* relation of the type shown earlier, with tuple type *city*. Note that there is a general notation for function abstractions, of the form

fun $(x_1 : t_1, \ldots, x_n : t_n)$ *expr*

where the x_i are free variables in *expr* and the t_i their types.

---

[2] Notice that we do not advocate the creation of intermediate relations as selection results, but rather introduce operator **scanselect** in this paper to give a simple example of an operator using a parameter function, with an evaluation function implementation as brief as presented in Section 3.2.

A SECONDO system executes a fixed set of commands. Its most important *basic commands* are:

- **type** <identifier> = <type expression>
- **delete type** <identifier>
- **create** <identifier> : <type expression>
- **update** <identifer> := <value expression>
- **delete** <identifier>
- **query** <value expression>

Here the first two commands manipulate named types, the next three named objects in the database. *Type expression* refers to a type of the current type system and *value expression* to an expression of the associated algebra. Note that this is the way how the fixed set of SECONDO commands cooperates with the variable data model. Hence we can create the cities relation by commands:

type city_rel = *rel*(*tuple*(<(name, *string*), (country, *string*), (pop, *int*)>))
create cities: city_rel

The implemented query processor manipulates all commands, type expressions, and value expressions, in the form of *list expressions*, as in the language *Lisp*. In this notation, type constructors and operators are written as the first element of a list, followed by their arguments. Hence the type of the *cities* relation is represented as

```
(rel (tuple ((name string) (country string) (pop int))))
```

and the query shown above is represented as

```
(scanselect cities (fun (c city) (> (attr c pop) 500000)))
```

3 Interaction of Query Processor and Algebra Modules

3.1 Overview

Type constructors and operators are implemented within *algebra modules*. The algebra implementor must provide a fixed set of support functions which are registered with the system frame, thus becoming callable by the query processor. In the scope of this paper, we are only interested in the support functions presented in Table 1. An overview of the entire SECONDO system, including a complete list of support functions, can be found in [8].

The query processor, on the other hand, offers primitives which can be used within implementations of evaluation functions as listed in Table 2.

In the rest of this section we show how evaluation functions are implemented using the query processor primitives (Section 3.2) and explain the basic techniques for the implementation of type mapping functions (Section 3.3). We omit a detailed description of the implementation of *Select* functions, because they are an easier variant of the *TransformType* functions.

Table 1. Operator support functions (subset)

Evaluate	Computes the result value from input values. In case of overloading, several evaluation functions exist.
Select	Selects the correct evaluation function in case of overloading by means of the actual argument types.
TransformType	Computes the operator's result type from given argument types (*type mapping*).

Table 2. Query processor primitives

Handling of parameter functions	argument	Gives access to the argument vector of a parameter function.
	request	Calls a parameter function.
Handling of stream operators	open	Initializes a stream operator.
	request	Triggers delivery of the next stream element.
	received	Returns true if the preceding request was successful, otherwise false.
	close	Closes a stream operator.

3.2 Implementation of Evaluation Functions

The interface for *Evaluate* operator support functions written in Modula-2 is defined as follows.[3]

```
PROCEDURE alpha (arg    : ArgVector;
            VAR result : WORD;          (* out *)
                message: INTEGER;
            VAR local  : ADDRESS        (* in/out *)) : INTEGER;
```

Here *arg* is a vector of operands; each function knows how many operands it has. Each operand is represented in one word of storage.[4] The result value is returned in the same form in the parameter *result*. The *message* and *local* parameters are needed only for stream operators; they are explained below. The return value of the function is 0 if no error occurred; for stream operators it has an additional meaning explained below. This interface is sufficient to implement "simple" operators that just take some arguments and return a value, operators with parameter functions, and stream operators. We give an example implementation for each kind of operator.

---

[3] SECONDO supports algebra module implementations in C and C++, too. We prefer Modula-2 for code examples because it is best suited to show technical details while not requiring specific programming language expertise.

[4] To achieve uniformity and simplicity in the query processor, we assume that any type of any algebra can be represented in a single word of storage. For simple values such as an integer, boolean, etc., this is the case; for larger structures, it can be a pointer; for persistent values currently not in memory, it can be an index into a catalog table describing how the persistent value can be accessed.

Example (Simple Operator). Consider a simple addition operation on integers. The signature is:

```
int x int -> int     +
```

The evaluation function is trivial, but shows how the generic interface is used:

```
PROCEDURE add (arg     : ArgVector;
               VAR result : WORD;          (* out *)
                   message: INTEGER;
               VAR local  : ADDRESS        (* in/out *)) : INTEGER;
BEGIN
  result := INTEGER(arg[1]) + INTEGER(arg[2]); RETURN 0
END add;
```

Type casting is necessary to consider the arguments as integers when accessing the argument vector.

Example (Operator with Parameter Function). The parameter function will be given by an address within the argument vector *arg* in the proper position (e.g. *arg*[2], if the second argument is a function). Hence the argument vector contains values as well as what we call *suppliers*; a supplier is either a function argument or a stream operator. (In the implementation, the parameter function is represented by a subtree of the operator tree, and the supplier is a pointer to the root of that subtree).

A procedure implementing an operator with a parameter function will at some point have to call this function explicitly (perhaps several times); for each call it has to set the arguments and to receive the result using the *argument* and *request* primitives, respectively.

Let us illustrate this by a procedure implementing the *scanselect* operator of Section 2 with signature:

```
forall tuple in TUPLE.
    rel(tuple) x (tuple -> bool) -> rel(tuple)    scanselect
```

We assume the existence of the following operations for reading and writing the relation representation:

```
CreateRelation      Append       CreateScan       Next
DestroyRelation                  DestroyScan      EndOfScan
                                                  Get
```

Then the evaluation function could be coded as follows.[5]

```
PROCEDURE scanselect (arg     : ArgVector;
                      VAR result : WORD;          (* out *)
                          message: INTEGER;
                      VAR local  : ADDRESS        (* in/out *)): INTEGER;
    VAR r: relation_scan; s: relation; t: tuple; value: INTEGER;
      valid: BOOLEAN; vector: ArgVectorPointer;
```

---

[5] VAL is a type transfer function in Modula-2; it converts from INTEGER (compatible with WORD) to BOOLEAN.

```
BEGIN
  r := CreateScan(relation(arg[1])); s := CreateRelation();
  ALLOCATE(t, TSIZE(TupleRec)); vector := argument(arg[2]);
  WHILE NOT EndOfScan(r) DO
    t := Get(r); vector^[1] := t;
    request(arg[2], value); valid := VAL(BOOLEAN, value);
    IF valid THEN Append(s, t) END; Next(r)
  END;
  DEALLOCATE(t, TSIZE(TupleRec)); DestroyScan(r); result := s;
  RETURN 0
END scanselect;
```

The essential point is the treatment of the parameter function of type (*tuple* → *bool*) which is the second argument of *scanselect* and therefore represented by *arg*[2]. This function has a single argument of type *tuple*; hence the first argument of its argument vector is set to *t*.

Example (Stream Operator). A stream operator somehow manipulates a stream of objects; it may consume one or more input streams, produce an output stream, or both. For a given stream operator α, let us call the operator receiving its output stream its *successor* and the operators from which it receives its input streams its *predecessors*. The basic way how stream operators work is as follows. Operator α is sent an *open* message to initialize its stream state. After that, each *request* message makes α try to deliver a stream object. Operator α returns a *yield* message in case of success, or a *cancel* message if it does not have an object any more. A *close* message indicates that α's successor will not request stream elements provided by α any more.

When we try to simulate stream operators by algebra functions, one can first observe that a function should not relinquish control (terminate) when it sends a message to a predecessor. This can be treated pretty much like calling a parameter function. However, the function needs to terminate when it sends a *yield* or *cancel* message to the successor. This requires the function to be re-entrant, using some local memory to store the state of the function.

In the general evaluation function interface given above, parameter *message* is used to send to this operator one of the messages *open*, *close*, or *request*, coded as integers. Upon *request*, this procedure will send in its return parameter a message *yield* or *cancel* to the successor. The parameter *local* can be used to store local state variables that must be maintained between calls to *alpha*. If more than a one-word variable is needed, one can define and allocate a record (type) within *alpha* and let *local* point to it.

Let us now consider the implementation of the stream operator *filter* using the primitives for stream processing introduced above.

```
forall tuple in TUPLE.
  stream(tuple) x (tuple -> bool) -> stream(tuple)   filter
```

The *filter* operation has an input stream, an output stream, and a parameter function. It transmits from its input stream to the output stream only tuples fulfilling the condition expressed by the parameter function.

```
PROCEDURE filter (arg     : ArgVector;
                  VAR result : WORD;          (* out *)
                      message: INTEGER;
                  VAR local  : ADDRESS        (* in/out *)) : INTEGER;
VAR t: tuple; found: BOOLEAN; value: INTEGER;
    vector: ArgVectorPointer;
BEGIN
  CASE message OF
    OPEN:      open(arg[1]); RETURN 0                              |
    REQUEST:   request(arg[1], t); found := false;
               vector := argument(arg[2]);
               WHILE received(arg[1]) AND NOT found DO
                 vector^[1] := t; request(arg[2], value);
                 found := VAL(BOOLEAN, value);
                 IF NOT found THEN request(arg[1], t) END
               END;
               IF found THEN result := t; RETURN YIELD
               ELSE RETURN CANCEL
               END                                                 |
    CLOSE:     close(arg[1]); RETURN 0
  END
END filter;
```

3.3 Implementation of Type Mapping Functions

In SECONDO, we exploit the concept of nested lists, well known from functional programming languages, as a generic means to represent type expressions, queries, and constant values. Nested lists are very useful for the representation of query expressions or type expressions, since they are flexible and easy to manipulate. We have written a little tool called *NestedList* which represents lists as binary trees and offers the basic operations like *Cons*, *First*, *Rest*, etc., as in the language Lisp. This tool has Modula-2, C, C++, and Java interfaces. The tool considers the *atoms* occurring in the lists as typed, and there is a fixed set of atom types:

– *Int*	70, -5	– *String*	"Hagen"
– *Real*	3.14	– *Symbol*	filter, >
– *Bool*	FALSE		

Actually, there is a sixth atom type called *Text* to represent long texts which is not relevant here. The *NestedList* tool allows one to read a list from a character string or a file.

An operator's *TransformType* function is called during query annotation with a parameter of type *ListExpr* which is a list of the types of the arguments. The tasks of *TransformType* are

(i) to check that all argument types are correct, and

(ii) to return a result type, again as a list expression.

In addition to that, a *TransformType* function may

(iii) extract argument type information which might be useful for the operator's evaluation function.

Since query expressions may be entered by users directly, *TransformType* should be prepared to handle all kinds of wrong argument type lists, and return a symbol atom *typeerror* in such a case. — As an example, here is the *TransformType* function for the *filter* operator. The transformation of type lists to be performed is

```
((stream x) (map x bool)) -> (stream x)
```

This is implemented in procedure `filtertype` as follows.

```
PROCEDURE filtertype (args: ListExpr) : ListExpr;
VAR first, second : ListExpr;
BEGIN
  IF ListLength(args) = 2 THEN
    first := First(args); second := Second(args);
    IF (ListLength(first) = 2) AND (ListLength(second) = 3) THEN
      IF (TypeOfSymbol(First(first)) = stream) AND
         (TypeOfSymbol(First(second)) = map) AND
         (TypeOfSymbol(Third(second)) = bool) AND
         Equal(Second(first), Second(second))
      THEN RETURN first
      END
    END
  END; RETURN SymbolAtom("typeerror")
END filtertype;
```

Here *Equal* is a procedure which checks for deep equality of its argument lists.

In *filtertype* we did not need to make use of the possibility to pass argument type information to the *TransformType* function (task (iii) above). But consider, for instance, relational operators which allow the user to identify attribute values by name like the *attr* operator or a projection operator. For example, using *attr* the user would like to write an attribute name, as in (`attr c pop`). However, the *Evaluate* function does not have access to the tuple type any more, and needs a number, the position of the attribute called *pop* within the tuple, to access that component efficiently. For that purpose, the *TransformType* function of *attr* computes the information needed and returns it in addition to the pure result type *t* using the keyword APPEND: If a *TransformType* function returns a list (`APPEND inf t`) rather than just *t*, where *inf* is a sublist containing the additional information, *inf* will be appended to the original list of arguments during annotation of the query, explained below, and will be treated as if it had been written by the user. In Appendix B the implementation of this mechanism is shown.

4 Evaluation of Query Plans

4.1 Structure of the Operator Tree

The operator tree has three kinds of nodes called *Object*, *Operator*, and *Indirect-Object*. An *Object* node represents some kind of value (a database object or a constant), an *Operator* node an algebra operator. An *IndirectObject* node represents a value accessible through the argument vector of a parameter function, hence, a parameter to that function. The actual definition of the data structure is given in Appendix A.

Each kind of node has a field *evaluable* which is true iff this node is an object, an indirect object, or an operator which is neither (the root of a subtree representing) a function argument nor a stream argument. This means the value of this subtree can be computed directly. A node can then have one of the three forms mentioned above. It can represent an object (a simple value or a pointer); in that case a field *value* contains that object. It can be an "indirect object" accessible through an argument vector attached to a subtree representing a function argument; then a field *vector* points to that argument vector and a field *argIndex* is the position of the object within the argument vector.

Finally, the node can represent an operator with information as follows. Fields *algebraId* and *opFunId* identify the operator's evaluation function, *noSons* is the number of arguments for this operator, *sons* is an array of pointers to the sons, *isFun* is true iff the node is the root of a function argument, and *funArgs* is a pointer to the argument vector for a function node, only used, if *isFun* is true. Field *isStream* is true if this operator produces an output stream, *local* is used to keep the *local* parameter of a stream operator between calls, and *received* is true iff the last call of this stream operator returned YIELD.

The three kinds of nodes are represented graphically as shown in Figure 1. For an operator node, the top left field shows the operator rather than its *algebraId* and *opFunId*. The other fields in the top row are *noSons*, *isFun*, *funArgs*, and *isStream*; the last two fields are omitted in this representation. The bottom row, of course, shows the *sons* array.

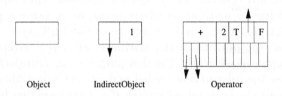

Object   IndirectObject   Operator

Fig. 1. Types of operator nodes

The structure of the operator tree is illustrated by the representation of the following query plan:

```
(filter (feed cities)
        (fun (c city)
             (>   (attr c pop .)
                  500000)))
```

Here *attr* is an operator with three arguments, namely, a tuple, an attribute name within that tuple, and a number giving the position of the attribute within the tuple. However, the user does not have to supply this number; it will be inferred and added in type checking (see Section 3.3). This is indicated by the dot, which is not written, only shown here to indicate the missing argument. The operator tree for this query is shown in Figure 2. Here oval nodes represent data objects represented externally from the operator tree. At the bottom an argument vector is shown.

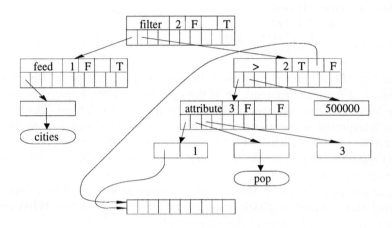

Fig. 2. Sample operator tree

4.2 Constructing the Operator Tree

The operator tree is constructed following two major steps:

1. The query is analyzed and *annotated*, i.e. an expanded list expression is returned with additional information about all symbols and substructures occurring in the query. Annotating the query requires interaction with the algebra modules in two ways. First, whenever an application of an operator α to a list of arguments is recognized, the *types* (type expressions) of the arguments are collected and the *TransformType* function for operator α is called with this list of types. *TransformType* checks that the argument types are correct and returns a result type (or the symbol "typeerror").

   Second, *overloading* of operators is resolved. An operator always has at least one, but may have several evaluation functions for different combinations of argument types; in the latter case we call it overloaded. Hence, whenever an application of operator α to a list of arguments is recognized, α's *Select* support function is called. It is given the list of types of the arguments and the *index* of the operator (the number of the operator within its algebra); it returns the index of the appropriate evaluation function.

2. The operator tree is constructed from the annotated query.

In the rest of this section, we discuss annotating the query, type mapping, and finally the actual building of the operator tree from the annotated query.

Annotating the Query Expression. A query or query plan is given as a nested list. Here is once more the example introduced above:

```
(filter (feed cities)
        (fun (c city)
             (>    (attr c pop)
              500000)))
```

It may have been entered by a user directly in this form, or be the result of processing of a parser frontend, or of the optimizer. Given a query in the form shown above, we can distinguish between the five types of atoms. The first four will be interpreted as constants of four basic types offered in a *StandardAlgebra* within SECONDO. The fifth, *Symbol*, is used to represent operators, object names, special symbols like *fun*, etc. In the query above, only 500000 is an *Int* atom; all others are *Symbol* atoms.

In annotating the query, the meaning of every atom and of every sublist is analyzed and returned explicitly together with that atom or list. What are the possible structures of a query? An *atom* can be:

(i) a *constant* of one of the four data types *int*, *real*, *bool*, or *string*
(ii) an *operator*
(iii) the name of an *object* in the database (which is not a function object)
(iv) the name of a *function* object in the database (see [12]).
(v) the name of a *variable* defined as a parameter in some enclosing *abstraction* (function definition) in the query
(vi) an *identifier* (used, for example, as an attribute name)

A *list* can be:

(vii) an *application of an operator* α to some arguments of the form
(alpha a1 ... an)
(viii) an *application of a database function* object f to some arguments:
(f a1 ... an)
(ix) an *application of an abstraction* to some arguments:
((fun (x1 t1) ... (xn tn) expr) a1 ... an)
(x) an *abstraction* (function definition) of the form
(fun (x1 t1) ... (xn tn) expr)

(xi) a *list of arguments* for some operator: (a1 ... an). Operators in SECONDO may have arguments that are themselves varying length lists of arguments (for example, a list of attribute names for a projection operator).

(xii) an empty list: this is interpreted as an empty *list of arguments*.

A procedure *annotate* does the annotation; for a given subexpression (atom or list) *s*, it returns in general a structure of the form

```
((s <descriptor> ...) <type>)
```

The descriptor is a keyword identifying the cases (i) through (xii) above, keywords are

```
constant, operator, object, function, variable, identifier,
applyop, applyfun, applyabs, abstraction, arglist
```

After the descriptor there can be further list elements giving specific information for this descriptor. For example, a constant is annotated as

```
<value>        ->        ((<value> constant <index>) <type>),
7              ->        ((7 constant 1) int)
```

Whenever a constant or a database object is annotated, its value, given as a WORD, is entered into a global ARRAY OF WORD *Values* at an index *valueno*, and *valueno* is incremented. The 1 after the descriptor *constant* is the index under which this constant was stored.

The second element of the annotation is always the type of the element annotated, except for operators, where no type is needed. Operators are annotated as

```
<op>           ->        ((<op> operator <algebraId> <operatorId>) none)
```

For an operator + as in Section 3.2 this would result in

```
+              ->        ((+ operator 1 1) none)
```

The application of an operator to some arguments is annotated as

```
(<op> <arg1> ... <argn>)
        ->     ((none applyop (ann(<op>) ann(<arg1>) ... ann(<argn>))))
               <resulttype>
               <opFunId>)
```

If a list *s* is annotated, then the original list *s* is not repeated in the annotation, instead we have a symbol *none* in the first position of the first sublist. The third element of the first sublist is the annotated version of the operator application. The *resulttype* was determined by calling the *TransformType* function of the operator. The *opFunId* is the index of the evaluation function for this type combination and has been determined by a call of the *Select* function for this operator.

Hence, for example, the complete annotation of a query expression (- 7 1.100) would be

```
(     (none applyop
          (    (    (- operator 1 2) none)
               (    (7 constant 1) int)
               (    (1.100 constant 2) real)))
     real
     6)
```

Here the result type is *real* and the evaluation function for *int* and *real* arguments has index 6. A shortened version of procedure *annotate* is shown in Appendix B. Most cases are omitted, but the overall structure is given, and annotation of an operator application, including the calls of the operator's type mapping function and selection function, is shown completely.

To annotate abstractions of the form (fun (x1 t1) ... (xn tn) expr), *annotate* calls a procedure *annotate_function*. This procedure first increments a global counter for function definitions *fno*. Then it processes each parameter definition $(x_i\ t_i)$ by entering name x_i, position i, function number *fno*, and type expression t_i into a table for variables. Finally, it calls *annotate* again to annotate *expr*. Within *expr*, occurrences of the names x_i will be recognized and annotated as *variables* with all the information mentioned above, so that variables can be translated into *IndirectObject* nodes of the operator tree later. *Annotate_function* also collects the types $t_1, \ldots, t_n$ and the result type t of *expr* (returned by *annotate*) and builds the type expression of the whole abstraction, which is (map t1 ... tn t).

Building the Operator Tree. The operator tree is constructed from the annotated query expression by a procedure *subtree*. This is a relatively simple matter, since all necessary information has been collected in the annotation. A part of procedure *subtree* is shown in Appendix C; that part gives the flavor and should be sufficient to process the little annotated query discussed above.

After annotating the query, it is known how many *abstractions* (function definitions) it contains. Before *subtree* is called, a corresponding number of argument vectors is allocated and assigned to the fields of a global array *ArgVectors*. Since the annotations of *abstractions* as well as those of *variables* contain function numbers, procedure *subtree* can set pointers to the argument vectors indexed by that number when nodes for *IndirectObjects* and root nodes of function expressions are processed.

4.3   The Evaluation Procedure

Evaluation is done in close cooperation between a recursive function *eval* of the query processor, applied to the root of the operator tree, and the operators' evaluation functions. Function *eval* has the basic structure as follows.

> **function** *eval* (*t* : *node*): WORD;
> **input:** a node *t* of the operator tree;
> **output:** the value of the subtree rooted in *t*;

method:
    if t is an object or indirect object node **then**
    lookup the value and return it
    else $\{t$ is an operator node$\}$
        for each subtree t_i of t **do**
        $\{$evaluate all subtrees that are not functions or streams$\}$
            if the root of t_i is marked as function (F) or stream (S)
        then $arg_i := t_i$
        else $arg_i := eval(t_i)$
        end
    end;
    Call the operator's evaluation function with argument vector arg
    and return its result
    end
end *eval*

The actual source code for *eval* can be found in Appendix D. The basic strategy is, of course, to evaluate the tree bottom-up, calling an operator's evaluation function with the values of the argument subtrees that have been determined recursively by *eval*. In case of parameter functions (F) or stream operators (S), however, evaluation control is passed to the evaluation function of the superior operator, which in turn uses the *request* primitive to call for specific subtree evaluation, as demonstrated in Section 3.2.

5 Related Work

We briefly compare with four projects that have studied generic query processors more deeply, namely GENESIS, EXODUS, Starburst, and Volcano. All these projects have lots of interesting concepts and results, but we can only consider the issue of this paper here. GENESIS [2] early on emphasized stream processing; they even adapted the data model level, a functional model similar to DAPLEX and FQL to use stream rewriting rules ("productions") as a querying primitive. A production is implemented by a *stream translator*, a box with input and output streams; such boxes are arranged into a translator network to describe a query plan. Translators communicate via mailboxes (shared variables). A translator is implemented by a function which branches on the various kinds of input *tokens*. An important feature not found in the other approaches is that streams have a nested structure; delimiters (braces) are part of the stream. In contrast to SECONDO, *all* operators have to be expressed as stream operators, even simple arithmetic or comparison operators. Parameter expressions are treated as streams as well. Mechanisms for setting up the translator network and for controlling execution are not shown.

    EXODUS [17, 18] offers a language E, an extension of C++ designed for implementing database systems. E provides an *iterator* construct which allows one to initialize a stream, then request elements in a loop, and terminates when the stream is exhausted. An iterator actually consists of the *iterator loop* construct and some *iterator functions* called in the loop. An iterator function sends results to the caller by means of a *yield* command. This is all very similar to our stream protocol which was certainly inspired by EXODUS. Operator functions written in E are slightly more elegant than those of SECONDO. However, the environment for executing such functions is much more complex since it relies on compiling the language E. Implementing operators that need access to type/schema information requires a rather complex interplay between the operator function written by the database implementor, and pieces of code generated by the E compiler which has access to schema information. E is also firmly tied to the C++ environment and the compiling strategy, which would make it difficult or impossible to design a query processing system as a collection of algebras which can be written independently and in various languages (currently Modula-2, C, and C++ are supported in SECONDO, we plan extensions for Java and possibly other languages).

Starburst [13, 14] uses query plans composed of algebraic operators called *LOLEPOPs* (low level plan operators). A LOLEPOP has several associated routines (e.g. a cost function, property mapping) and especially an interpretation routine (= evaluation function). These take one or more input streams and produce an output stream. However, the implementation of this concept, and the interface for writing interpretation routines is not shown in the papers. A specialty is that parameter expressions (predicates) are translated into programs for a stack machine.

Finally, Volcano [9] is the closest in spirit to SECONDO. Volcano also emphasizes data model independence (as already EXODUS did). Operators are implemented as iterators observing an *open - next - close* protocol equivalent to our stream protocol. A slight technical difference here is that an operator is realized by three different functions, e.g. *open-filter()*, *next-filter()*, and *close-filter()* instead of our branching on messages in a single procedure. Parameter expressions are made available to operator functions as so-called *support functions*. However, it is not clear how support functions for expressions are constructed, and the precise mechanism for calling them is not given. In Volcano, *all* operators are stream operators (operators like $+$, $>$ in expressions seem to be viewed as a different category). A difference to SECONDO is also that the environment recursively calls all *open* (and later *close*) functions, hence this is not controlled by the operator implementations as in SECONDO. Mixing stream and non-stream operators is not possible. Constructing operator trees from textual query plans is not shown. On the other hand, Volcano offers very interesting concepts such as *dynamic query plans* and transparent switching to a parallel execution, and is already a much more complete system than SECONDO, including an optimizer generator [10].

6 Conclusions

SECONDO is a generic development environment for non-standard multi-user database systems. At the bottom architecture level, SECONDO offers tools for efficient and comfortable handling of nested lists and catalogs, a simplified interface to the underlying SHORE storage manager, a tool for efficient management of tuples with embedded large objects [7], and an SOS-to-NestedList-Compiler. Algebra modules for standard and relational data types and operators as well as simple user interface clients have been implemented. In [8] a more detailed overview of the entire system is given.

In this paper, we have described the core part of SECONDO: the extensible query processor. Its main new aspects are the following:

- Other approaches lack a formal basis like SOS to describe a generic query plan algebra. This makes it impossible for them to give a clear algorithm for translating a query plan into an operator tree, as we do here.
- Functional abstraction is a well-defined concept in SOS. This leads to a very clean, simple and general treatment of parameter expressions of operators.
- *stream* is a built-in type constructor in SECONDO. Simply writing the keyword stream in the type mapping of an operator lets the query processor automatically set up calls of the evaluation function for this operator in stream mode. For this reason, SECONDO can handle uniformly streams of anything, not just tuples. Also, a query plan can mix freely stream and non-stream operators.
- SECONDO includes complete type checking, type mapping, and resolution of operator overloading.

For the time being, algebra support functions dealing with type expressions, like *TransformType*, have to be coded manually. In the future, an SOS specification compiler will create those functions automatically. Other future work will focus on the completion of an extensible rule-based query optimizer.

References

[1] D.S. Batory, J.R. Barnett, J.F. Garza, K.P. Smith, K. Tsukuda, B.C. Twichell, and T.E. Wise. GENESIS: An extensible database management system. *IEEE Trans. on Software Engineering 14*, pages 1711–1730, 1988.
[2] D.S. Batory, T.Y. Leung, and T.E.Wise. Implementation concepts for an extensible data model and data language. *ACM Trans. on Database Systems 13*, pages 231–262, 1988.
[3] L. Becker and R.H. Güting. The GraphDB algebra: Specification of advanced data models with Second-Order Signature. Informatik-Report 183, FernUniversität Hagen, Praktische Informatik IV, 1995.
[4] M.J. Carey and D.J. DeWitt. Of objects and databases: A decade of turmoil. In *Proc. of the 22nd Intl. Conf. on Very Large Data Bases*, pages 3–14, 1996.
[5] M.J. Carey, D.J. DeWitt, D. Frank, G. Graefe, M. Muralikrishna, J.E. Richardson, and E.J. Shekita. The architecture of the EXODUS extensible DBMS. In *Proc. of the IEEE/ACM International Workshop on Object-Oriented Database Systems*, pages 52–65, 1986.
[6] M.J. Carey, D.J. DeWitt, M.J. Franklin, N.E. Hall, M.L. McAuliffe, J.F. Naughton, D.T. Schuh, M.H. Solomon, C.K. Tan, O.G. Tsatalos, S.J. White, and M.J. Zwilling. Shoring up persistent applications. In *Proc. ACM SIGMOD Conf.*, pages 383–394, 1994.

[7] S. Dieker and R. H. Güting. Efficient handling of tuples with embedded large objects. Informatik-Report 236, FernUniversität Hagen, 1998.

[8] S. Dieker and R.H. Güting. Plug and play with query algebras: SECONDO. A generic DBMS development environment. Informatik-Report 249, FernUniversität Hagen, Praktische Informatik IV, 1999.

[9] G. Graefe. Volcano - an extensible and parallel query evaluation system. *IEEE Trans. on Knowledge and Data Engineering 6*, pages 120–135, 1994.

[10] G. Graefe and W.J. McKenna. The Volcano optimizer generator: Extensibility and efficient search. In *Proc. of the 9th Intl. Conf. on Data Engineering,*, pages 209–218, 1993.

[11] R.H. Güting. Gral: An extensible relational database system for geometric applications. In *Proc. of the 15th Intl. Conf. on Very Large Data Bases*, pages 33–44, 1989.

[12] R.H. Güting. Second-Order Signature: A tool for specifying data models, query processing, and optimization. In *Proc. ACM SIGMOD Conf.*, pages 277–286, 1993.

[13] L.M. Haas, W. Chang, G.M. Lohman, J. McPherson, P.F. Wilms, G. Lapis, B. Lindsay, H. Pirahesh, M. Carey, and E. Shekita. Starburst mid-flight: As the dust clears. *IEEE Trans. on Knowledge and Data Engineering 2*, pages 143–160, 1990.

[14] L.M. Haas, J.C. Freytag, G.M. Lohman, and H. Pirahesh. Extensible query processing in Starburst. In *Proc. ACM SIGMOD Conf.*, pages 377–388, 1989.

[15] Informix Software, Inc. *Extending INFORMIX-Universal Server: Data Types*, version 9.1 edition, 1998. Online version (http://www.informix.com).

[16] J.M. Patel, J. Yu, N. Kabra, K. Tufte, B. Nag, J. Burger, N.E. Hall, K. Ramasamy, R. Lueder, C. Ellman, J. Kupsch, S. Guo, D.J. DeWitt, and J.F. Naughton. Building a scaleable geo-spatial DBMS: Technology, implementation, and evaluation. In *Proc. ACM SIGMOD Conf.*, pages 336–347, 1997.

[17] J.E. Richardson and M.J. Carey. Programming constructs for database system implementation in EXODUS. In *Proc. ACM SIGMOD Conf.*, pages 208–219, 1987.

[18] J.E. Richardson, M.J. Carey, and D.T. Schuh. The design of the E programming language. *ACM Trans. on Programming Languages and Systems 15*, pages 494–534, 1993.

[19] H.J. Schek, H.B. Paul, M.H. Scholl, and G. Weikum. The DASDBS project: Objectives, experiences, and future prospects. *IEEE Trans. on Knowledge and Data Engineering 2:1*, pages 25–43, 1990.

[20] P. Seshadri, M. Livny, and R. Ramakrishnan. The case for enhanced abstract datatypes. In *Proc. of the 23rd Intl. Conf. on Very Large Data Bases*, pages 66–75, 1997.

[21] M. Stonebraker. *Object-Relational DBMSs: The Next Great Wave*. Morgan Kaufmann Publishers, 1996.

[22] M. Stonebraker, L.A. Rowe, and M. Hirohama. The implementation of POSTGRES. *IEEE Trans. on Knowledge and Data Engineering 2*, pages 125–142, 1990.

A   Definition of the Operator Tree

```
TYPE
  OpTree      = POINTER TO OpNode;
  OpNodeType  = (Object, IndirectObject, Operator);

  OpNode      = RECORD
    evaluable : BOOLEAN;
  CASE nodetype : OpNodeType OF
      Object:
        value: WORD;
    | IndirectObject:
        vector : ArgVectorPointer;
        argIndex : INTEGER;
    | Operator:
        algebraId: INTEGER;
        opFunId: INTEGER;
        noSons: INTEGER;
        sons: ARRAY [1..MAXARG] OF OpTree;
        isFun: BOOLEAN;
        funArgs: ArgVectorPointer;
        isStream: BOOLEAN;
        local: ADDRESS;
        received: BOOLEAN
  END (* CASE *)
END; (* OpNode *)
```

B   Structure of Procedure *annotate*

```
PROCEDURE annotate (expr    : ListExpr;
                    VAR varnames: NameIndex.NameIndex;   (* in/out *)
                    VAR vartable: varentryCTable;        (* in/out *)
                    VAR defined : BOOLEAN                 (* in/out *))
                                                          : ListExpr;
VAR ...
BEGIN
  IF IsEmpty(expr) THEN ...   (* empty arg. list, case (xii), omitted *)
  ELSIF IsAtom(expr) THEN ... (* treatment of atoms, cases (i) - (vi), omitted *)
  ELSE (* expr is a nonempty list *)
    IF NOT (TypeOfSymbol(First(expr)) = fun) THEN (* not an abstraction *)

      (* first annotate recursively each element of this list: *)
      first := First(expr); rest := Rest(expr);
      list := OneElemList(annotate(first, varnames, vartable, defined)); lastElem := list;
      WHILE NOT IsEmpty(rest) DO
        lastElem := Append(lastElem, annotate(First(rest), varnames, vartable, defined));
        rest := Rest(rest)
      END;
      last := lastElem;       (* remember the last element to be able to
                                 append further arguments, see below *)

      (* At this point, we may have for a given expr (+ 3 10) a list such as
         (((+ operator 1 6) none) ((3 ...) int) (( 10 ...) int))        *)

      first := First(list);               (* first = ((+ operator 1 6) none) *)
      IF ListLength(first) > 0 THEN
        first := First(first);            (* first = (+ operator 1 6) *)
        IF ListLength(first) >= 2 THEN
          CASE TypeOfSymbol(Second(first)) OF
            operator:                     (* operator application, case (vii) *)
              alId := IntValue(Third(first)); opId := IntValue(Fourth(first));

              (* extract the list of types into "typeList" *)
              rest := Rest(list);
```

```
            IF NOT IsEmpty(rest) THEN
              typeList := OneElemList(Second(First(rest)));
              rest := Rest(rest); lastElem := typeList
            END;
            WHILE NOT IsEmpty(rest) DO
               lastElem := Append(lastElem, Second(First(rest))); rest := Rest(rest)
            END;

            (* apply the operator's type mapping: *)
            resultType := TransformType[alId]^[opId](typeList);

            (* use the operator's selection function to get the index
            (opFunId) of the evaluation function for this operator: *)
            opFunId := SelectFunction[alId]^[opId](typeList, opId);

            (* check whether the type mapping has requested to append
            further arguments: *)
            IF (ListLength(resultType) = 3) AND
               (TypeOfSymbol(First(resultType)) = APPEND)
            THEN
              lastElem := last; rest := Second(resultType);
              WHILE NOT IsEmpty(rest) DO
                lastElem := Append(lastElem,
                annotate(First(rest), varnames, vartable, defined));
                rest := Rest(rest)
              END;
              resultType := Third(resultType)
            END;

            RETURN ThreeElemList(
              ThreeElemList(SymbolAtom("none"), SymbolAtom("applyop"), list),
              resultType, IntAtom(opFunId))

        | function: ...          (* case (viii), omitted *)

        | abstraction ...        (* case (ix), omitted *)

        ELSE ...                 (* argument list, case (xi), omitted *)
        END (* CASE *)
      ELSE RETURN SymbolAtom ("exprerror") END
    ELSE RETURN SymbolAtom ("exprerror") END

  ELSE (* is an abstraction, case (x) *)
    RETURN annotate_function(expr, varnames, vartable, defined, 0,
      TheEmptyList(), TheEmptyList())
  END
END (* nonempty list *)
END annotate;
```

C   Structure of Procedure *subtree*

```
PROCEDURE subtree(expr : ListExpr) : OpTree;

VAR ...
BEGIN
  CASE TypeOfSymbol(Second(First(expr))) OF
    constant, object:
      ALLOCATE(node, TSIZE(OpNode));
      WITH node^ DO evaluable := TRUE; nodetype := Object;
        valNo := IntValue(Third(First(expr))); value := Values[valNo]
      END; RETURN node;
  | operator:
      ALLOCATE(node, TSIZE(OpNode));
      WITH node^ DO evaluable := TRUE; nodetype := Operator;
        algebraId := IntValue(Third(First(expr)));
        opFunId := IntValue(Fourth(First(expr)));
```

```
          (* next three fields may be overwritten later *)
          noSons := 0; isFun := FALSE; funNo := 0; isStream := FALSE;
      END; RETURN node;
  | applyop:
      node := subtree(First(Third(First(expr))));
      WITH node^ DO evaluable := TRUE; opFunId := IntValue(Third(expr));
        noSons := 0; list := Rest(Third(First(expr)));
        WHILE NOT IsEmpty(list) DO INC(noSons);
          sons[noSons] := subtree(First(list)); list := Rest(list)
        END;
        IF NOT IsAtom(Second(expr)) AND
          (TypeOfSymbol(First(Second(expr))) = stream)
        THEN isStream := TRUE; evaluable := FALSE
        END
      END;
  | ...                        (* other cases, omitted *)
END subtree;
```

D Procedure *eval*

```
Procedure eval(tree   : OpTree;
               VAR result : WORD;          (* out *)
                   message: INTEGER);
VAR i: INTEGER; status: INTEGER; arg: ArgVector;
BEGIN
  IF tree = NIL THEN Error ("eval called with tree = NIL!"); HALT;
  ELSE
    WITH tree^ DO
      CASE nodetype OF
        Object:          result:= value; RETURN                          |
        IndirectObject: result := vector^[argIndex]; RETURN              |
        Operator:        (* First evaluate all subtrees that are not
                            functions or streams. Then call this
                            operator's evaluation procedure. *)
          FOR i := 1 TO noSons DO
            IF sons[i]^.evaluable THEN eval(sons[i], arg[i], message)
            ELSE arg[i] := sons[i]
            END
          END;
          status :=
                Execute[algebraId]^[opFunId](arg, result, message, local);
                (* Execute is an array of pointers to all operator evaluation
                   functions, maintained by the system frame. *)
          IF isStream THEN received := (status = YIELD)
          ELSIF status # 0 THEN  Error ("eval: operator failed"); HALT;
          END; RETURN
      END (* CASE *)
    END
  END
END eval;
```

Hybrid Simultaneous Scheduling and Mapping in SQL Multi-query Parallelization

Sophie Bonneau, Abdelkader Hameurlain

Institut de Recherche en Informatique de Toulouse (IRIT), Université Paul Sabatier
118, route de Narbonne, 31062 Toulouse cedex, France
Tel: (33) 05 61 55 82 48, E-mail: {bonneau, hameur}@irit.fr

ABSTRACT. In the context of the database query optimization on a parallel architecture, we focus here on the problem of dynamically mapping the tasks making up several SQL queries onto a shared-nothing parallel architecture. The main contribution of this paper lies in the proposal of an incremental parallelization strategy which carries out simultaneously both scheduling and mapping in co-operation with memory allocation in a dynamic multi-user context. The paper functionally describes in terms of components our dynamic PSA/MEG-based parallelization strategy in a multi-user context, as well as one of the two incremental memory allocation heuristics, called ModDeg, which are integrated into the MEG mapping method, and presents a sum-up of the performance evaluation of this heuristic.

1 Introduction

In the context of the database query optimization on a parallel architecture, we focus here on the problem of *dynamically mapping* the tasks making up several SQL queries onto a shared-nothing architecture.

The shared-nothing architecture, well-known to be scalable and offering high data availability [9, 27], mainly suffers from (i) high communication, (ii) programming complexity and (iii) workload imbalance.

Workload imbalance [6, 26] is due to the data skew phenomenon and/or the static determination of the relational operator parallelism degree achieved by a cost model. This one may, indeed, make mistakes [16, 22] leading to a severe performance degradation of the developed processor allocation strategies to the query operators. The workload balancing problem at the intra-operation level has already been intensively studied [15, 25]. As to processor allocation specific to the operators, also called "operator/task mapping" in literature, many allocation methods have been developed, distinguishing static approaches (i.e achieving operator mapping at compile-time) [7, 10, 14] from dynamic ones (i.e realizing mapping at run-time) [20, 23].

The parallelism degree determination methods and the processor allocation methods for query join operators have been intensively studied and carefully evaluated [7, 8, 10, 14, 20, 23]. Several statement can be made from a detailed state of the art which can be found in [3]: (i) the parallelism degree adjustment is performed [23] from the optimal number of processors which is generally calculated from a more or less complex analytical expression (i.e. single-user or multi-user mode) associated to the most adequate join method. At completion of this adjustment, keeping the same join algorithm may not be assured because a best algorithm is likely to exist for this new number of processors; (ii) several heuristics [10] are suggested to realize static simultaneous scheduling/ mapping of operator fragments by taking into account multiple pre-emptive and non preemptive resource sharing between concurrent operators, the different pipeline, independent and intra-operation parallelisms, and data placement, in single- and multiuser contexts. However, the heuristics proposed, based on quite drastic assumptions, remain only valid in a static context; (iii) the algorithm in [18] detects sub-optimality of a complex query execution plan while the query is being executed, and attempt to correct the troubles. However, the processor allocation to operators, the scheduling priority rule and the physical allocation method used, for instance, are not dealt with.

We can notice that [4, 5, 18, 20, 23] emphasize the importance of a dynamic re-adjustment of the strategies generated at compile-time, and underline how important it is to take additional resources to the CPU one, more particularly the memory resource, into account.

As we also wish to be more realistic towards the SQL query parallel processing problem [3], it is suggested to have the already designed static PSA/MEG (Parallel Scheduling Algorithm/Modifiable Estimated Greedy) scheduling and mapping heuristic [1, 13] evolve to a dynamic context. The main contribution of this paper lies in the proposal of an *incremental parallelization strategy* which is *"hybrid-like" and centralized,* in a multi-user and dynamic context: it carries out PSA/MEG *scheduling and mapping* as well as *memory allocation* thanks to two heuristics (ModDeg and RelaxIndic), onto a shared-nothing architecture. Only one of these heuritics (ModDeg) is presented in this paper for lack of space: the second one is detailed in [3].

This paper is organized as follows: first, after briefly introducing in section 2 the main features of the PSA/MEG static scheduling and mapping method already proposed in a single-user mode, section 3 details the functional description of our PSA/MEG-based dynamic parallelization strategy in a multi-user context. Then, the ModDeg modification heuristic of the intra-operation parallelism degree integrated into MEG mapping method is dealt with in section 4. Lastly, section 4.2 provides the key-results of the performance evaluation of the ModDeg heuristic, before concluding with a synthesis of the work achieved and an overview of related prospect.

2 Overview of the PSA/MEG Static Scheduling and Mapping Method

In [1], we have suggested the PSA/MEG static scheduling and mapping heuristic of the tasks making up a SQL query onto shared-nothing architecture processors. After proposing a model for the application and the target parallel architecture, we briefly remind of the application assumptions and the allocation constraints as well as the features of the static solution already designed.

2.1 Models of the application and of the target parallel architecture

To more accurately represent opportunities for parallel execution, the SQL decisional query model is a *directed bushy dependence graph* [24] whose nodes represent tasks (i.e.

Scani, Buildi and Probei[1]), and edges, information (data and control messages) communication and/or time-related dependence links. The communication link between two tasks I and J is either of the "precedence" or of the "pipeline" type. Only tasks Buildi and Probei are constrained by a precedence type communication. In addition, this graph is *valuated* by each task local response time, each task couple communication cost (estimated from the number of deduced tuples), and the number of processors required to execute each task (i.e. partitioned parallelism is taken into account), which is given by the cost evaluator [12]. The communication mode (i.e. distribution, broadcast, propagation) of each bound task couple is also known.

The target *shared-nothing architecture* is characterized by the number of its processors, and its interconnection network topology. Let's remind that this architecture is difficult to administrate because of the required data partitioning on each memory space, and that communications which depend on the interconnection network topology, can generate parallelism overhead.

2.2 Formalization of the static mapping problem

The mapping assumptions are as follows:

H1: shared-nothing architecture; H2: unreconfigurable architecture.

H3: processor homogeneity (no communication overlap).

H4: single-user context; H5: static mapping.

To ensure the best possible operating conditions, certain allocation constraints due to the target parallel architecture and the application type specificity have to be respected:

C0: data locality constraint: tasks Scani are operated at the very place where data they use are stored.

C1: data localization constraint: Alloc(Buildi) = Alloc(Probei)

C2: independent parallelism constraint: if $i \neq j$ and $\exists$ a time when Ti and Tj are simultaneously processed then Alloc(Ti) $\neq$ Alloc(Tj).

C3: pipeline parallelism constraint (relaxable):

Alloc(pred(Probei)) $\neq$ Alloc(Probei) et Alloc(pred(Buildi)) $\neq$ Alloc(Buildi)

with   Alloc: task physical allocation function onto processors, Ti: task i,

pred(Ti): task i predecessor task in terms of dependence graph data flows.

In other terms, C0 and C1 allocation constraints aim at limiting the communication volume between certain tasks, whereas taking C2 and C3 constraints into account shows the exploitation of both inter-operation parallelism types: independent and pipeline.

2.3 Features of the PSA/MEG static method

The PSA/MEG static scheduling and mapping method takes into account the features of both the application type to be mapped and the target parallel architecture. MEG physical allocation process is performed "simultaneously" with PSA list-scheduling algorithm [13] at compile-time, i.e. scheduling and mapping *co-operate* in order to minimize the query response time. This method respects (i) the initial data placement,

1.   i.e. tasks respectively reading tuples from disk, building and probing the hash table of a simple-hash join node.

(ii) the C0 to C3 allocation constraints that enable to minimize inter-processor and inter-task communication costs, additional I/Os, and to maximize fragment execution, and (iii) the *mapping clues*[1] provided by the *pipelined task pre-handling* which aims at limiting the pipeline start-up cost impact to ensure a better fragment response time [2]. Static PSA/MEG operates in an *incremental* way: it repetitively (i) assigns an execution starting time and (ii) physically "greedily" allocates *a processor set* to each fragment task of each *scheduling list*[2], until all query tasks have been handled. However, unlike a strictly greedy method, some mapping choices are allowed to be *revised*, so that the tasks are definitively mapped only once all those involved in a relational operator could have been physically allocated satisfactorily towards the allocation constraints onto the *"possibly allocatable"*[3] processors.

Fig. 1. sums up the various handlings that contribute to a valued dependence graph simultaneous mapping and scheduling. The performance evaluation of PSA/MEG compared with a given PSA/"greedy" strategy, has provided promising results [1].

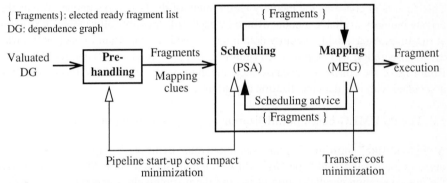

Fig. 1. PSA/MEG static simultaneous scheduling and mapping

3 Description of our dynamic parallelization strategy proposal

After precising the assumptions and constraints added to the mapping problem formalization described in section 2.2, the PSA/MEG scheduling and mapping adaptation to the dynamic context is formalized in section 3.1, and functionally detailed in section 3.2.

3.1 Formalization of the dynamic mapping problem

Now that a multi-user context is considered, the dynamic optimization goal aims at

---

1. A *mapping clue* is some processor logical allocation information concerning two pipelined tasks, specifying whether it should be better, in terms of couple global response time, to map these tasks onto the same processor set ("collapsed" tasks) or onto two different processor set.
2. A *scheduling list* is a list of fragments elected according to the increasing latest ending date (deadline) PSA priority rule.
3. A *"possibly allocatable"* processor for a task T is a system available processor that respects both the allocation constraints and the mapping clues related to T.

minimizing the response time of several queries submitted to the system while maximizing the system resource utilization. The H4 and H5 mapping assumptions are then replaced as follows:

H4: multi-user context; H5: dynamic scheduling and mapping.

As we are mainly interested in execution incidents (i.e. join product and redistribution skews [21]), the execution skew is only considered, which H6 means:

H6: there is no initial tuple placement skew.

Moreover, the following C4 constraint is added:

C4: *"task memory requirement" constraint:* let availmem(P), the available memory amount of the processor P from the "possibly allocatable" processor set EP of task T; reqmem(Ii), the memory amount required by instance[1] Ii from task T:

$$\forall Ii, (\exists P \in EP)/(reqmem(Ii) \leq availmem(P))$$

i.e. each processor allocated to each task instance owns enough available memory to execute its instance.

This constraint concerns the memory requirement of the task to be mapped versus the private memory available amount owned by each task "possibly allocatable" processor at run-time. An available memory deficit has, indeed, an important impact on the way the join operation will be processed (multi-bucket processed or not) and its cost. Only Buildi tasks are concerned because their mapping is also that of the Probei they are associated with (C1 data localization constraint).

3.2 The PSA/MEG-based parallelization strategy in a dynamic context

A "hybrid-like" solution. To make maximum reuse of the particularities of PSA/MEG, our solution is suggested to be *"hybrid-like"*: it consists of a *static phase* during which the intra-operation parallelization phase and the mapping clues generation are carried out, followed by a *dynamic phase* which enables to schedule and map the application as well as to take into account every unforeseeable execution incidents during the static phase thanks to a dynamic re-adjustment.

When to re-optimize in case of estimation or/and discretization errors. We could decide to interrupt pipeline execution of the fragments to re-optimize the "remainder" of the query (i.e. the tasks not executed yet) as soon as an estimation or/and discretization error has been detected. As the tasks of a fragment are supposed to start executing at the same time, this "break" would lead to serialize certain tasks of this fragment. Well, interrupting pipeline execution consists in non-respect of the mapping clues provided by the static phase. That's why, to establish a trade-off between the re-adjustment additional cost and the response time saving assured when mapping clues are respected at run-time, this re-optimization is chosen to be performed *only once the fragment is fully executed*. Moreover, we will be able to correct significant and prejudicial enough incidents which might not have been easily detected at the fragment task level. Further explanations can be found in [3].

---

1. We say that an *instance* is a parallel task which is executed by one of the processors allocated to the relational operator at stake.

Functional description. Fig. 2. gives the functional schema of our enriched "hybrid-like" adaptation of the PSA/MEG static scheduling and mapping method in a multi-user context.

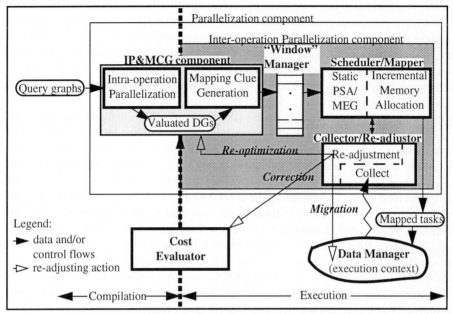

Fig. 2. Functional schema of the PSA/MEG -based dynamic parallelization solution

This dynamic strategy is *centralized*: it is performed by the Parallelization component which is executed by one of the target machine processors.

The Parallelization component input is a query graph corresponding to "the best sequential plan". The first time such a graph arrives (i.e. compile-time static phase), it is applied the intra-operation parallelization phase by the IP&MCG (Intra-operation Parallelization & Mapping Clue Generation) component, which produces a valuated dependence graph: this graph is then handled by the pipeline link pre-handling phase in order to generate mapping clues. The fragments, deposited by the IP&MCG, are managed by the "Window" Manager in a way to assure that no more than a maximal number of queries be simultaneously handled.

The Scheduler/Mapper removes from the "window" a maximum number of fragments which can be from queries that are not currently being re-optimized. The PSA/MEG heuristic adapted to the dynamic context co-operates with the incremental memory allocation to schedule and map satisfactorily the removed fragments: only the fragments (i) from queries which are still not currently being re-optimized, and (ii) whose mapping has succeeded, will be sent to the Data Manager. The execution of these fragments is triggered in accordance with the allocation choices made by the Scheduler/Mapper. Each fragment whose execution is over, is signalled to the Collector by the Data Manager: the latter sends to the Collector the system and application information which this component has taken of thanks to an adequate information collection policy. This information reflects the state of the system (system information) and the one of the application (application information) on completion of a fragment execution (e.g. the identifier of the fragment whose execution has just been completed, the available processors, their available memory amount, and the values of the metrics prone to error such as the number of tuples deduced by each instance of the ending task of a fragment). The Collector requests the Execution Context Manager ECM to store the application and system information received from the Data Manager, and informs the Re-adjuster. The ECM component identifies the fragment whose execution has been completed the most recently, the number of queries currently being handled, and the state of both the fragments and the query which they belong to, in order to know which query(ies) is(are) currently being re-optimized.

Once informed by the Collector, the Re-adjuster then judges whether it could be worse re-optimizing the query whose fragment F execution has just been completed. This estimation is, indeed, required because re-optimizing causes an overhead which is worse avoiding when the handling significance is not obvious. Intuitively, re-optimization should only be triggered if the sum of the time spent to re-optimize the query and the response time of the "remainder" of the query based on the information collected at run-time, is less than the response time of the "remainder" of the query based on the estimations provided at compile-time. If re-optimization seems to be required, it is applied by the Re-adjuster to the query which F belongs to, by ordering the IP&MCG component to launch the query optimization again in a *priority* way.

As soon as re-optimizing is over, the IP&MCG component informs the Re-adjuster. The IP&MCG component then naturally requests the "Window" Manager to deposit the re-optimized fragments into the "window" for the query handling to resume.

The Scheduler/Mapper can also request the Re-adjuster to re-optimize a query Q: such is the case when the memory allocation heuristic ModDeg (see section 4.1) had to be carried out to map at least one fragment of Q, and that this process has succeeded. In this case, the Re-adjuster does the same as if the re-optimization order was sent by the Collector, i.e. the relevance to launch this re-optimization is judged by the Re-adjuster. However, if re-optimizing Q appears to be needed, this re-optimization will be carried out while the fragment(s) that have required ModDeg application will be executed.

Let's go back over the query re-optimization process: this process consists in (i) removing (i.e. *purging*) from the "window" these query fragments, (ii) correcting in accordance with actual values previously collected, mistaken or obsolete values estimated or used by the cost evaluator associated with its tasks not processed yet, and (iii) performing optimization (i.e. intra-operation parallelization and mapping clue generation) to this task subgraph. It must be noted that re-optimizing *doesn't change the choice of the join algorithm,* and that this process is more likely to be required just before the query execution end than at the beginning.

As for workload imbalance, a mechanism migrating data (including data replication if the operation at stake is a join) is required for the Data Manager to solve imbalance at the very time when and where it happens while the fragment tasks are being executed, only if the saving brought by migrating is higher than the required inter-processor data transfer overhead in terms of time. For the time being, we need to further study the proposals provided by the community in order to determine whether we could adapt or extend an existing solution to solve the problem [19, 21].

The PSA/MEG scheduling and mapping method adaptation in a dynamic context.
In order to always be able to obtain a solution, the allocation constraints and the communication cost minimization handling in terms of inter-processor transfer times are assigned a handling priority. This point is detailed in [3].

Moreover, the following modification was made to PSA scheduling algorithm to adapt to the dynamic context: if no fragment could be elected at the current execution starting time, or if mapping the fragment tasks of the current scheduling list has succeeded, PSA waits for completion of a fragment execution before resuming. Anyway, whether the current scheduling list includes tasks to be mapped, whatever the mapping issue may be, PSA attempts to remove new fragments from the "window" before resuming scheduling.

As far as the MEG mapping heuristic is concerned, the static algorithm described in [1] are the same in the dynamic and multi-user context. Nevertheless, the mapping revision mechanism is given up. Moreover, the fragment tasks successfully scheduled and mapped, belonging to the queries which are still not currently being re-optimized, are sent to the Data Manager to be executed: in this meaning, scheduling and mapping are "real-time" executed, i.e. a fragment is triggered and executed on the available processors at the very time when it is mapped onto.

Finally, as we want to take the C4 "task memory requirement" allocation constraint into account, an *incremental memory allocation* has been devised and integrated into mapping Build tasks: it is proposed to be detailed in the following section. Section 4.2 will briefly present the performance evaluation of one of the heuristics used by the memory allocator.

4 Presentation of the incremental memory allocation heuristics

Memory allocation is carried out *at the very time when the Build tasks of the current scheduling list are mapped*: in that it is qualified as "incremental" because this memory allocation doesn't concern the whole query tasks at the current time. The Build tasks from the current scheduling list fragments are processed in decreasing order of their required memory amount. The available processors "possibly allocatable" to each of these tasks are, as for them, chosen in decreasing order of their available memory amount.

Memory allocation uses two heuristics in an exclusive way. The ModDeg modification heuristic of the intra-operation parallelism degree is exploited to map only non "collapsed" Build tasks whose C4 constraint cannot be respected. The "collapsed" Build tasks are carried out by the RelaxIndic relaxation heuristic of the mapping clues, only if the scheduling process allows to do so.

Both these heuristics assume that the data handled by the tasks which the heuristics are applied to, are uniformly distributed among the processors allocated to the tasks. In addition, they need to request the ECM to make themselves acquaintance with the system and application information associated with the fragment executed the most recently.

Lastly, it is specified that we qualify as a "possible" mapping of a task T a physical allocation of T respecting the allocation constraints (but the C4 "task memory requirement" constraint) and the mapping clues associated with T. A "valid" mapping is defined as a "possible" mapping that also respects the C4 allocation constraint of T.

The ModDeg heuristic is detailed in the following sub-section. The description of the RelaxIndic heuristic can be found in [3].

4.1 The ModDeg modification heuristic of the intra-operation parallelism degree

If the task memory requirement C4 constraint cannot be respected at the very time when a join operation (i.e. Build task) is mapped, it is necessary to attempt a modification of the number of processors to allocate to this task so that the memory required by each instance be available on each processor the task is mapped onto, in order to avoid extra expensive I/Os due to multi-bucket join processing.

In this perspective, we propose the ModDeg heuristic which is integrated into MEG mapping method whenever a fragment ending Buildi task *from the current scheduling list* cannot be mapped satisfactorily towards its memory requirement onto its "possibly allocatable" processors. The ModDeg mainspring is as follows:

for each Buildi task of the current scheduling list whose C4 constraint cannot be respected, sorted in decreasing order of its required memory amount, either handling (i) or (ii) is started;

(i) *if there are available processors left once the current scheduling phase is over (i.e. Dmax>0);* the task parallelism degree is attempted to be *increased*. If this modification led to no solution, the initial degree is then *decreased*.

(ii) *if there is no available processor left once the current scheduling phase is over (i.e. Dmax=0)*; the task parallelism degree is attempted to be only *decreased*.

Both the parallelism degree increase and decrease are done within a *parallelism degree adjustment interval*: this one is limited by the maximal and minimal numbers of processors around the initial economical intra-operation parallelism degree [8, 11] assuring that *the join algorithm chosen at compile-time is always the best,* i.e. doesn't need to be changed. ModDeg will be said to be successful if a "valid" mapping will have been found: it will probably be necessary to re-optimize the "remainder" of the query while executing the fragment. If no valid mapping has be found, ModDeg has failed: the parallelism degree remains the same, a "possible" mapping is determined, and the join will be multi-bucket processed.

In order to show its relevance and efficiency, the following section recapitulates the performance evaluation of the ModDeg heuristic.

4.2 Performance evaluation of the ModDeg heuristic

In [3], a detailed peformance evaluation presents the comparative results between the RT1(deco) response time of a simple-hash join multi-bucket performed by deco processors (i.e. deco is the economical intra-operation parallelism degree [11]), and the RT2(dnew) response time of a simple-hash join not multi-bucket processed on a different number dnew of processors determined by the ModDeg heuristic. This study was conducted for three different system configurations in terms of disk access and/or network transfer performance.

When observing the ModDeg average success (i.e. solution obtaining by ModDeg) percentage, it can be seen that the heuristic finds a solution in 24% to 30.4% cases on average. Fig. 3. and 4. illustrate ModDeg behaviour for J1= join(R1,S1) (with 2.5 millions tuples for each relation) for the system configuration SC3 (i.e. both efficient network transfers and disk accesses: network bandwidth = 250 MB/s, average disk access time = 9 ms): this join is, indeed, representative of ModDeg behaviour over the four joins tested [3]. These results allow to moderate this percentage smallness.

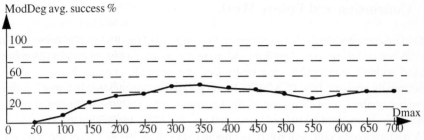

Fig. 3. ModDeg avg. success percentage for J1 in the case of SC3

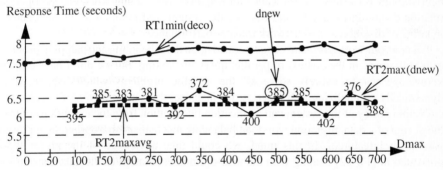

RT1min: the minimum value of the response times when J1 is multi-bucket processed by the economical number deco=307 of processors [11],
RT2max: the maximum value of the response times when J1 is executed by dnew processors found by ModDeg,
RT2maxavg: the average response time of the TR2max for all the possible values of Dmax.

Fig. 4. RT2max and TR1min for J1 in the case of SC3

Both these figures show that, the higher Dmax is, the more likely ModDeg is to find a solution dnew such that the RT2max join response time executed by dnew processors is *better than* else *closer to* the RT2maxavg average of the maximum response times observed for all the possible values of Dmax. For instance, ModDeg average success is 40% for Dmax greater than 350, and the RT2max response times are then generally closer to or better than the RT2maxavg average. However, ModDeg may also frequently find a solution for low values (and thus more likely to be found in real systems) of Dmax such as 150, 200 or 250: it can then be observed that the TR2max response times are closer to RT2maxavg than really better than it. As a consequence, the higher Dmax is, the more likely ModDeg is to provide a solution assuring a "stable" RT2max response time, even though "good" solutions in terms of TR2max response time can be found with a good success percentage for lower values of Dmax. As a conclusion, when a solution can be found, this heuristic offers a significant join response time saving whatever the operand relation cardinalities may be and whether the system configuration is "homogeneous" in terms of disk access and network transfer performance. However, this time saving might be more sensitive in case of "heterogeneous" system configurations.

5 Conclusion and Future Work

The main contribution of this paper lies in the proposal of an incremental strategy which carries out simultaneous scheduling and mapping, as well as memory allocation onto a shared-nothing architecture, in a multi-user and dynamic context. Mainly, we have functionally presented the PSA/MEG-based parallelization strategy in a multi-user and dynamic context, as well as one of the heuristics achieving the incremental memory allocation co-operating with and integrated into the MEG mapping method.

A performance evaluation has been conducted to study the join response time versus the join multi-bucket one after applying ModDeg. When a solution can be found, this heuristic always offers a significant join response time saving whatever the operand relation cardinalities may be and whether the system configuration is "homogeneous" in terms of disk access and network transfer performance.

Till now, our work has mainly concentrated upon the scheduling and mapping problem of a SQL query in the context of parallel query processing. So, we don't have enough knowledge yet to entirely solve all the satellite problems which happen when dynamically parallelizing SQL queries: for instance, the determination of an adequate collection policy of the system and application information from the execution context, the design of a data migration workload balancing mechanism appropriate to our target parallel architecture,... In this mind, we could take advantage of the recent work presented in [17, 22] dealing with the near-optimal estimation of the data distribution and result size of relational operations by means of specific histograms building, and its application to balance the operation workload: it could be adapted to not only produce improved and relevant estimations related to the query while this one is being executed (which would decrease the current cost of collecting application information), but also assure workload balancing of joins currently being executed.

References

1. Bonneau, S., and al., "A Greedy Modifiable Mapping Heuristic of a SQL Query onto a Shared-Nothing Parallel Architecture". Revue Calculateurs Parallèles, numéro spécial : "Bases de Données Parallèles et Distribuées", Sept. 1997, Vol. 9, N° 3, 285-304.
2. Bonneau, S., and al., "Database Program Mapping onto a Shared-Nothing Multiprocessor Architecture: Minimizing Communication Costs", EuroPar'97, Passau, Germany, August 1997, LNCS N° 1300, pp. 1154-1158.
3. Bonneau, S., and al., "Hybrid Simultaneous Scheduling and Mapping of SQL Multi-Query Parallelization", Tech. Report , N°. IRIT/99-15-R, Lab. IRIT, UPS, June 1999, 21 pages.
4. Brunie, L., and al., "Control Strategies for Complex Relational Query Processing in Shared-Nothing Systems", ACM SIGMOD Records, Vol. 25, N° 3, 1996, 34-39.
5. Brunie, L., and al., "Integration of Scheduling Heuristics into Parallel Relational Query Optimization". Revue Calculateurs Parallèles, numéro spécial : "Bases de Données Parallèles et Distribuées", Ed. Hermès, Vol. 9 , N°.3 , Sep. 1997, 327-346.

6. Bouganim, L., and al. "Dynamic Load Balancing in Hierarchical Parallel Database Systems", Proc. of the 23rd VLDB Conf., Bombay, August 1996, 436 - 447.

7. Chekuri, C., and al., "Scheduling Problem in Parallel Query Optimization", Symposium in Principles of Database Systems PODS'95, 1995.

8. Chen, M.S., and al., "Scheduling and Processor Allocation for Parallel Execution of Multi-join Queries", Proc. of the 8th Intl. Conf. Data Eng., Tempe, Arizona, 1992, 58-67.

9. Dewitt, D.J., and al., "Parallel Database Systems: The Future of High Performance Database Systems", Communication of the ACM, Vol. 35, N° 6, June 1992, 85-98.

10. Garofalakis, M.N. and al., "Parallel Query Scheduling and Optimization with Time- and Space- Shared Resources", Proc. of the 23rd VLDB Conf., Athens, 1997, 296-305

11. Hameurlain, A. and al., "An Analytical Method to Allocate Processors in High Performance Parallel Execution of Recursive Queries", Intl. Conf. DEXA'92, Valencia, 1992, 44-47

12. Hameurlain, A. and al. ,"A Cost Evaluator for Parallel Database Systems", Intl. Conf. DEXA'95, London, 4-8 Sept. 1995, LNCS, N° 978, 146-156

13. Hameurlain, A., and al., "Scheduling and Mapping for Parallel Execution of Extended SQL Queries", 4th Intl. Conf. on Information and Knowledge Management, ACM Press, Baltimore, Maryland, 28 Nov. - 2 Dec. 1995, 197-204.

14. Hasan, W., and al., "Optimization Algorithms for Exploiting the Parallelism-Communication Tradeoff in Pipelined Parallelism", Proc. of the 20th Intl. Conf. on VLDB, Santiago, Chile, Sept. 1994.

15. Hua, K.A., and al., "Handling Data Skew in Multiprocessor Database Computers Using Partition Tuning", Proc. of the 17th Intl. Conf. on VLDB, Barcelona, Spain, 1991, 525-535.

16. Ioannidis, Y.E., and al., "On the Propagation of Errors in the Size of Join Results", Proc. of the ACM SIGMOD Int'l. Conf. on Management of Data, Denver, 1991.

17. Jagadish, H.V., and al., "Optimal Histograms with Quality Guarantees", Proc. of the 24th VLDB Conference, New-York, USA, 1998, 275-286.

18. Kabra, N., and al., "Efficient Mid-Query Re-Optimization of Sub-Optimal Query Execution Plans", ACM SIGMOD Intl. Conf. on Managementof Data, Seatle, June 1998, 106-117.

19. Lu, H., and al., "Dynamic and Load-Balanced Task-Oriented Database Query Processing in Parallel Systems", Proc. 3rd Int'l Conf. Extending Data Base Technology, 1992, 357-372.

20. Mehta, M., and al. , "Managing Intra-Operator Parallelism in Parallel Database Systems", Proc. of the 21th Intl. Conf. on VLDB, Zurich, Sept. 1995, 382-394.

21. Mehta, M., and al., "Data Placement in Shared-Nothing Parallel Database Systems", The VLDB Journal, 1997, N° 6, 53-72.

22. Poosala, V., and al., "Estimation of Query-Result Distribution and its Application in Parallel-Join Load Balancing", Proc. of the 23rd VLDB Conference, Bombay, India, 1996, 448-459.

23. Rahm, E. , and al., "Dynamic Multi-Resource Load Balancing in Parallel Database Systems", Proc. of the 21st VLDB Conference, Zurich, 1995, 395-406.

24. Schneider, D., and al., "Tradeoffs in Processing Complex Join Queries via Hashing in Multiprocessor Database Machines", Proceedings of the 16th VLDB Conference, Brisbane, Australia 1990, 469-480.

25. Walton, C.B., and al. "A Taxonomy and Performance Model of Data Skew Effects in Parallel Join", Proc. of the 17th Intl. Conf. on VLDB, Barcelona, 1991.

26. Wilshut, A.N., and al., "Parallel Evaluation of Multi-Join Queries", ACM SIGMOD Intl. Conf. on Management of Data, San Jose, CA, 1995, 115-126.

27. Valduriez, P., "Parallel Database Systems: Open Problems and News Issues", Distributed and Parallel Databases, Kluwer Academic Publishers, Vol. 1, N°. 2, 1993, 137-165.

Cluster-Based Database Selection Techniques for Routing Bibliographic Queries

Jian Xu, Ee-Peng Lim, Wee-Keong Ng

Centre for Advanced Information Systems
School of Applied Science, Nanyang Technological University
Singapore 639798, SINGAPORE

1 Introduction

Given a user query and a set of data sources at different locations, **query routing** refers to the general problem of evaluating the query against most relevant data sources and integrating the results returned from the data sources. As Internet is now populated by a large number of web sites and databases, query routing is fast becoming one of the most important problems to be addressed on the Internet. Depending on the type of queries and the type of data sources, different forms of query routing can be defined.

In [10], the overall query routing problem has been divided into three inter-related sub-problems, namely *database selection*, *query evaluation* and *result merging*. The three sub-problems also represent the three sequential steps to be performed in query routing.

Database selection refers to the problem of analysing a user query and determining one or more appropriate data sources at which information satisfying the user query can be located. In order to address the database selection problem, *essential* knowledge about the content of individual data sources has to be acquired. Query evaluation refers to the problem of dispatching and evaluating the user query to the data sources chosen in the database selection step. Due to possible heterogeneous data representations at different data sources, the original user query may have to be translated into different local query statements to be submitted to the remote data sources. Result merging refers to the problem of integrating results returned by different data sources. Apart from standardizing the local result formats, one may have to re-compute the rank information of the integrated query result because of the different ranking formulas adopted by the data sources.

1.1 Objective and Scope

In this paper, we focus on the database selection problem in the context of a global digital library consisting of a large number of online bibliographic servers. Each server hosts a bibliographic database that contains bibliographic records each of which consists of text values for a number of pre-defined bibliographic attributes such as *title, author, call number, subject*, etc.. Each bibliographic database supports user queries on the bibliographic attributes. Since bibliographic records are relatively small in size, we only consider bibliographic databases that support boolean queries on the bibliographic attributes, and the query results are not ranked. While focusing on bibliographic databases, we believe that our proposed solution can be extended to handle other databases that contain searchable text attributes.

Formally, we define a general **database selection problem** as follows:

Definition 1. Let D be a set of databases, q be a query, and M be the number of databases which should be selected (or query q should be forwarded to). Compute $E \subseteq D$ such that ($|E| = M$ and ($\forall F \subseteq D$ such that $|F| = M$, $Goodness(q, E) \geq Goodness(q, F)$)).$\Box$

Goodness measures the degree of relevance for the combined result returned by the selected data sources. Gravano and Garcia-Molina, in [3, 4, 5], proposed a few possible *Goodness* functions that can be adopted by database selection. In routing bibliographic queries, we have adopted a *Goodness* function defined below:

Definition 2. Given a set of bibliographic databases $\{db_1, \cdots, db_N\}$ denoted by E and a query q,

$$Goodness(q, E) = \sum_{i \in E} s_i$$

where s_i denotes the result size returned by db_i for query q.$\Box$

Several database selection solution techniques have been developed for a collection of full text databases, e.g. NCSTRL[1] and TREC[2] collections. Very few techniques, on the other hand, have been proposed for bibliographic databases which contain multiple text-based attributes[5, 10].

The crux of the database selection problem is to construct a knowledge base that captures the content of local data sources well enough that the degree of relevance of each data source with respect to any given query can be determined accurately. Usually, the knowledge base maintains some statistical information that characterizes the content of each data source. In [5] and [10], term frequencies from each bibliographic server have been used to construct the knowledge base. Nevertheless, in a large database, database records can often be classified into different groups such that each group of records share some common or similar values for some attributes. Using clustering techniques, we would like to discover such grouping of database records. By capturing some essential statistics about each cluster of records, we hope to further improve the accuracy of database selection techniques.

---

[1] NCSTRL (Networked Computer Science Technical Reference Library) [7] consists of distributed online collections of technical reports that can be queried through web interface.

[2] TREC (Text REtrieval Conference) [1] consists of specially selected collections of text documents provided by NIST (National Institute of Standards and Technology).

In this paper, we investigate the use of clustering to improve the accuracy of database selection. Several cluster-based database selection techniques have been proposed to route bibliographic queries. Unlike other non clustered-based approaches, cluster-based database selection techniques involve clustering of database tuples before the content of each database is summarized. We have proposed different database selection techniques by coupling three clustering techniques known as *Single Pass Clustering* (SPC), *Reallocation Clustering* (RC), and *Constrained Clustering* (CC) with two database ranking formulas namely Estimated Result Size (ERS) and Estimated Goodness Score (EGS). Due to space constraint, the performance evaluation of these proposed techniques has been excluded from the paper.

2 Related Work

2.1 Database Selection for Text Collections

In the gGlOSS project[3, 5], the document frequencies of terms found in every text collection are computed and included in the knowledge base for database selection. Using the document frequencies, the relevance of each text collection can be estimated for a given user query.

Based on the document frequency knowledge, Yuwono and Lee proposed a unique database ranking formula based on Cue-Validity Variance (CVV)[11]. The proposed database ranking formula essentially incorporates the discriminatory power of keywords across collections. It was shown that the CVV-based database selection technique out-performed the database selection techniques in gGlOSS.

2.2 Database Selection for Collections with Multiple Attributes

In the GlOSS (*Glossary of Servers Server*) project[4, 5], a database selection technique for collections containing multiple text attributes has been proposed. Different from gGlOSS, the *boolean* retrieval model is adopted for querying collections in GlOSS. The queries for such collections consist of keyword predicates on the different attributes such as *author, title*, etc. Given a collection and an attribute-term pair, the number of records having the attribute values containing the term is known as the *frequency of the attribute-term pair*. This frequency information has been further used to estimate the rank of each database.

2.3 Database Selection for Collections Accessible Through Query Interface Only

In our recent research[10], we have designed new database selection techniques for distributed bibliographic databases using training queries and their query results. It was shown that using statistical information compiled from query results, it is possible to perform database selection with reasonable accuracy. These techniques are hence applicable to databases that can only be accessed through some query interfaces.

3   Overview of Cluster-based Database Selection

Clustering refers to the grouping of database records based on the degrees of similarity between the records. In order to route queries to a set of databases each with multiple text attributes, the content of each databases has to be summarized properly. Nevertheless, as the databases contain wide range of information, direct summarization of their content may result in inaccurate summary knowledge. In such cases, clustering may be applied to discover the hidden grouping of database records. By summarizing the content of different groups of database records, we believe that the accuracy of summary knowledge can be improved.

In this paper, we therefore propose a few cluster-based database selection techniques and apply them to the query routing problem over a set of bibliographic databases. Our proposed cluster-based database selection techniques involve two steps namely *knowledge construction* and *database ranking*. In knowledge construction, bibliographic records from each database involved are clustered and the content of each cluster is summarized. Database ranking is then performed for a given query based on the summary information of the clusters from each database. The query will be matched against the clusters from each database and a matching score will be computed for each cluster. When a query matches well with a cluster, it is likely that many records in that cluster will be relevant to the query. Furthermore, when a query matches well with significant number of clusters from a database, it is likely that the database will be more relevant to the query. In this case, the rank of each database will be determined by the matching scores between its clusters and the given query as well as the cluster sizes.

4   Clustering Techniques for Bibliographic Databases

4.1   Similarity Between a Bibliographic Record and a Cluster

Clustering can only be performed on the bibliographic databases when the similarity between a bibliographic record and a cluster can be determined and quantified. In this section, the similarity measures used in our proposed clustering techniques are defined.

Several attributes can be found in a bibliographic database, e.g. *title*, *subject*, etc. In this paper, we only deal with text attributes and assume that all databases contain the same set of attributes[3]. An attribute value can be described by an attribute descriptor (to be defined later) which is essentially a text vector. A database record can be represented by a set of attribute descriptors, one for each attribute. Similarly, a cluster can also be represented by a set of attribute descriptors. Hence, the similarity between a bibliographic record and a cluster can be defined based on the attribute descriptor information representing the record and the cluster.

---

[3] If different attribute sets are found in different bibliographic databases, an uniformed attribute set still can be adopted by integrating the different attribute sets.

Definition 3. Let $t_1, t_2, \cdots, t_W$ be all possible terms in our term dictionary, an **attribute descriptor** is defined by a vector $v = (w_1, w_2, \cdots, w_W)$, where w_j denotes the term weight of term t_j.□

Apart from being used to represent bibliographic records, attribute descriptors can also be used to represent clusters and queries. In the case of bibliographic records, term frequencies are used as term weights (denoted by w_j's in the above definition).

Definition 4. Let $A_1, A_2, \cdots, A_l$ be bibliographic attributes, a **bibliographic record** r is defined by a vector of attribute descriptors, one for each attribute,

$$r = (vr_1, vr_2, \cdots, vr_l).$$

□

Since each term will be counted at most once for each attribute with respect a record, vr_k's are binary vectors. A term weight of 1 will be assigned when term t_j appears in the record for the respective attribute. Otherwise, a term weight of 0 will be assigned.

Definition 5. A **cluster** consisting of a set of bibliographic records, $r_1, r_2, \cdots, r_{N_c}$, is defined by a binary tuple

$$c = (N_c, D_c),$$

where D_c is a list of attribute descriptors

$$D_c = (vc_1, vc_2, \cdots, vc_l),$$

and

$$vc_k = vr_{1,k} + vr_{2,k} + \cdots + vr_{N_c,k}$$

where $vr_{i,k} (0 \leq i \leq N_c)$ denotes the kth attribute descriptor of r_i.□

In the above definition, D_c captures the representative content of all bibliographic records belonging to a cluster.

Definition 6. The **similarity between a bibliographic record** $r(= (vr_1, \cdots, vr_l))$ **and a cluster** $c(= (N_c, (vc_1, \cdots, vc_l)))$, denoted by $SIM_{r,c}$, is defined as:

$$SIM_{r,c} = \frac{1}{l} \sum_{k=1}^{l} SIM_{vr_k, vc_k} \tag{1}$$

where the SIM_{vr_k, vc_k} denotes the **similarity between the bibliographic record and the cluster with respect to attribute** A_k, and is defined by the cosine distance[4] between the two vectors:

$$SIM_{vr_k, vc_k} = \frac{|vr_k \cdot vc_k|}{|vr_k| \cdot |vc_k|} \tag{2}$$

□

---

[4] The Cosine coefficient is originally proposed to calculate the similarity between two document vectors. We have borrowed the formula for measuring the similarity between a bibliographic record and a cluster.

As shown in Formula (1), the similarity between a cluster and a bibliographic record is defined by averaging the similarities between the record and the cluster for all bibliographic attributes.

Example 1. Consider a bibliographic database that contains two attributes namely $A_1 = $ title, $A_2 = $ subject, and a term dictionary of $W=3$. Let the terms be `information`, `retrieval`, and `clustering` assigned with term ids 1,2 and 3 respectively. The two bibliographic records below can be represented by $r_1 = ((1,0,1),(0,0,1))$ and $r_2 = ((1,1,0),(1,1,0))$, respectively.

record ids	title	subject
1	information clustering	clustering
2	information retrieval	information retrieval

Let $c_1 = (10,((2,2,3),(2,1,5)))$ be a cluster containing 10 bibliographic records. The two attribute descriptors $(2,2,3)$ and $(2,1,5)$ contain the term weights for the title and subject attributes, respectively.

Using Formula (1), the similarity between the bibliographic record r_1 and cluster c_1 can be computed as follows:

$$SIM_{r_1,c_1} = \frac{1}{2} \cdot \left(\frac{(1\times2+0\times2+1\times3)}{\sqrt{(1^2+0^2+1^2)\cdot(2^2+2^2+3^2)}} + \frac{(0\times2+0\times1+1\times5)}{\sqrt{(0^2+0^2+1^2)\cdot(2^2+1^2+5^2)}} \right)$$
$$= 0.885$$

The similarity between the bibliographic record r_2 and cluster c_1 is:

$$SIM_{r_2,c_1} = \frac{1}{2} \cdot \left(\frac{(1\times2+1\times2+0\times3)}{\sqrt{(1^2+1^2+0^2)\cdot(2^2+2^2+3^2)}} + \frac{(1\times2+1\times1+0\times5)}{\sqrt{(1^2+1^2+0^2)\cdot(2^2+1^2+5^2)}} \right)$$
$$= 0.537 \ \square$$

4.2 Proposed Database Clustering Techniques

Single Pass Clustering (SPC) and Reallocation Clustering (RC) are two straightforward clustering techniques used for text documents. To cluster bibliographic databases, the two techniques have been modified to cater for bibliographic records consisting of multiple text attributes. In addition, we have proposed a Constrained Clustering (CC) technique that generates for a bibliographic database a fixed number of clusters specified by the user. These three clustering techniques have been used with two different database ranking formulas given in Section 5.

Single Pass Clustering Technique (SPC) Single pass clustering technique is basically a greedy algorithm that always assigns a bibliographic record to the most similar cluster. Since each bibliographic record is read only once, SPC technique is efficient and easy to implement. Nevertheless, SPC technique requires a similarity threshold TH specified by the user. TH is used to determine if the similarity between a record and a cluster is high enough to assign the record to the cluster. When TH is small, each cluster can accommodate records that are less similar. Hence, a smaller number of clusters will be generated.

Although the single pass clustering technique is simple, it has been criticized for its tendency to produce large clusters early in the clustering process. It is because that the clusters generated by the SPC technique depends on the order in which bibliographic records are processed.

Reallocation Clustering (RC) Reallocation clustering[2] operates by selecting an initial set of clusters followed by some iterations of re-assigning bibliographic records to the most similar clusters. Through the iterations, the cohesiveness among records in a cluster is improved.

In reallocation clustering, it is difficult to decide how many iterations should be executed. For simplicity, we have chosen 9 iterations in our experiments. Like SPC, RC relies on a user specified threshold to indirectly control the number of clusters generated.

Constrained Clustering (CC) For both SPC and RC, there is no control parameter that directly controls the storage requirement for the generated cluster information. The number of resultant clusters is controlled indirectly by the threshold TH. To overcome this shortcoming, we proposed the **Constrained Clustering** (CC) technique. CC is able to generate a fixed number β of clusters for each database where β is specified by the user. Like in the case of RC, CC requires an initial set of clusters to be first generated followed by iteratively improving the similarity among records within the clusters.

5   Cluster-Based Database Ranking Formulas

In this section, two cluster-based database ranking formulas are given. They are defined based on the similarity between a given query and a database represented by a set of clusters.

Definition 7. A **query** is defined to be a list of attribute descriptors, i.e.

$$q = (vq_1, vq_2, \cdots, vq_l),$$

where vq_k is an attribute descriptor with respect to attribute A_k.□

Each attribute descriptor vq_k of a query captures the search terms specified for attribute A_k. (Since a search term will only appear at most once for each attribute in the query, vq_k's are binary vectors.) A term weight of 1 will be assigned when term t_j is given in the query for the respective attribute. Otherwise, a term weight of 0 will be assigned.

Example 2. Consider the bibliographic database in Example 1, a query consisting of the following predicate: *subject* = (`information` *and* `clustering`) can be represented by $q = (\mathbf{0}, (1, 0, 1))$. $\mathbf{0}$ denotes a zero text vector for the title attribute while $(1, 0, 1)$ denotes the text vector for the subject attribute.□

Once a set of clusters have been generated for each database, we can apply the following two database ranking formulas to compute the rank of the databases for a given query.

5.1 Cluster-based Database Ranking based on Estimated Result Sizes (ERS)

This database ranking scheme computes the database rank by estimating the query result size returned by a database. The estimated result size returned, originally proposed in GlOSS[4, 5], can be computed by summing the estimated query result sizes returned by clusters belonging to the database.

Definition 8. The **estimated result size (ERS)** of a given query q from database db_i is defined as:

$$\mathcal{E}_{db_i,q} = \widehat{Size}_{(db_i,q)} = \sum_{n=1}^{|C|} \widehat{Size}_{(c_n,q)} \tag{3}$$

where $C = \{c_1, c_2, \cdots, c_{\beta_i}\}$ is a set of clusters generated for database db_i, and $\widehat{Size}_{(c_n,q)}$, the estimated result size of a given query q returned from a cluster c_n, is defined as:

$$\widehat{Size}_{(c_n,q)} = |c_n| \cdot \prod_{\substack{k=1 \\ vq_k \neq 0}}^{|A|} \prod_{\substack{j=1 \\ w'_{j,k} \neq 0}}^{W} \frac{w_{j,k,n}}{|c_n|} \tag{4}$$

where $w'_{j,k}$ denotes the weight of the jth term in the attribute descriptor vq_k for query q, $w_{j,k,n}$ denotes the term frequency of the term t_j in the attribute descriptor vc_k of cluster c_n, and $|c_n|$ denotes the number of records in the cluster c_n. $\square$

In the above definition, we assume that all attributes in a cluster are independently distributed and all terms in an attribute domain are also independently distributed. The predicates $vq_k \neq 0$ and $w'_{j,k} \neq 0$ indicate that only terms appearing in the query q and their corresponding terms appearing in cluster c_n will be considered in the computation. Note that Formula 3 and 4 can be seen as an extension to the goodness function adopted by GlOSS[5]. When $\beta_i = 1$, i.e., there is only 1 cluster for db_i, our proposed ranking formula reduces to that of GlOSS.

5.2 Cluster-based Database Ranking based on Estimated Goodness Score (EGS)

Instead of estimating the query result size returned from each database, the EGS ranking formula, extending that adopted by Yuwono and Lee[11], computes the goodness score of a database with respect to a given query by using CVV to rank databases with multiple attributes.

Definition 9. The **estimated goodness score (EGS)** of database db_i for a given query q is defined as follows:

$$\mathcal{E}_{db_i,q} = \sum_{n=1}^{|C|} \mathcal{E}_{c_n,q} \tag{5}$$

where $C = \{c_1, c_2, \cdots, c_{\beta_i}\}$ is a set of clusters generated for database db_i.

The estimated goodness score $\mathcal{E}_{c_n,q}$ of cluster c_n with respect to query q is defined by:

$$\mathcal{E}_{c_n,q} = \prod_{\substack{k=1 \\ vq_k \neq 0}}^{|A|} \sum_{\substack{j=1 \\ w'_{j,k} \neq 0}}^{W} CVV_{j,k} \cdot w_{j,k,n} \tag{6}$$

where $CVV_{j,k}$ denotes the variance of $CV_{i,j,k}$'s, the *Cue Validity* of term t_j, for attribute A_k across all databases, $w'_{j,k}$ denotes the weight of term t_j in attribute A_k for query q, $w_{j,k,n}$ denotes the term frequency of term t_j with respect to attribute A_k in cluster c_n.$\square$

6 Experiments

To evaluate the performance of database selection techniques that are built upon various combination of the three database clustering techniques and the two cluster-based database ranking formulas, a number of experiments have been conducted based on a set of ten synthetic bibliographic databases and 2000 test queries.

From the experiments conducted, we have several findings as described below:

- Cluster-based database selection techniques using ERS significantly outperform those using EGS. The exact database clustering technique used does not even affect the performance of database selection techniques using EGS. This case occurs especially when a larger number of clusters were generated. When the number of clusters increases, database selection techniques using ERS outperforms those using EGS. In [11], the GlOSS database selection technique is shown to perform better than the database selection technique using CVV for a set of text documents. In our experiments, we notice that the same phenomenon also occurred in the case of databases containing multiple text attributes.
- All database selection techniques using SPC and RC with similarity threshold $TH = 0.2$ usually outperform those using different similarity threshold.
- Database selection techniques using RC perform slightly better than those using SPC. The clustering becomes more accurate after several iterations using RC than using SPC which only processes each record once.

7 Conclusions

In conclusion, we have proposed several cluster-based database selection techniques (SPC, RC and CC clustering combined with the ERS and EGS database ranking formulas). Unlike our previous database selection research that were proposed to route bibliographic queries using training queries, these database selection techniques are derived by combining three database clustering techniques with two database ranking formulas. Through experiments, we have shown that cluster-based database selection techniques outperform non cluster-based database selection techniques. However, clustering techniques require storage space more than their non cluster-based counterparts. In cases where accuracy of database selection outweighs the storage overheads, cluster-based database selection techniques could be applied.

References

1. Text REtrieval Conference(TREC). *http://trec.nist.gov.*
2. M. Goldszmidt and M. Sahami. A Probabilistic Approach to Full-Text Document Clustering. Technical Report ITAD-433-MS-98-044, SRI International, 1998.
3. L. Gravano and H. Garcia-Molina. Generalizing GlOSS to Vector-Space Databases and Broker Hierarchies. In *Proceedings of the 21st International Conference on Very Large Data Bases(VLDB'95)*, pages 78–89, Zurich, Switzerland, September 1995.
4. L. Gravano, H. Garcia-Molina, and A. Tomasic. The Effectiveness of GlOSS for the Text Database Discovery Problem. In *Proceedings of the ACM SIGMOD International Conference on Management of Data*, pages 126–137, Minneapolis, Minnesota, May 1994.
5. L. Gravano, H. Garcia-Molina, and A. Tomasic. *GlOSS*: Text-Source Discovery over the Internet. *ACM Transactions on Database Systems(To Appear)*, 24(2), June 1999.
6. K.A. Hua, Y-L. Lo, and H.C. Young. Considering Data Skew Factor in Multi-Way Join Query Optimization for Parallel Execution. *VLDB Journal*, 2(3):303–330, July 1993.
7. NCSTRL. *http://www.ncstrl.org.*
8. M. Sahami, S. Yusufali, and M.Q.W. Baldonado. SONIA: A Service for Organizing Networked Information Autonomously. In *Proceedings of the 3rd ACM International Conference on Digital Libraries (DL'98)*, Pittsburgh, Pennsylvania, USA, June 1998.
9. G. Salton. *Automatic Text Processing, The Transformation, Analysis, and Retrieval of Information by Computer.* Addison-Wesley Publishing Company, 1988.
10. J. Xu, Y.Y. Cao, E.P. Lim, and W.K. Ng. Database Selection Techniques for Routing Bibliographic Queries. In *Proceedings of the 3rd ACM International Conference on Digital Libraries (DL'98)*, Pittsburgh, Pennsylvania, USA, June 1998.
11. B. Yuwono and D.L. Lee. Server Ranking for Distributed Text Retrieval Systems on the Internet. In *Proceedings of the 5th International Conference on Database Systems for Advanced Applications (DASFAA '97)*, pages 41–49, Melbourne, Australia, April 1997.

Developing Patterns as a Mechanism for Assisting the Management of Knowledge in the Context of Conducting Organisational Change

Nikos Prekas[1], Pericles Loucopoulos[1], Colette Rolland[2], Georges Grosz[2], Farida Semmak[2], Danny Brash[3]

[1] Department of Computation, UMIST, P.O. Box 88, Sackville Street,
Manchester M60 1QD, UK
{prekas, pl}@co.umist.ac.uk
[2] Centre de Recherche en Informatique, UFR27, Université Paris 1 Panthéon-Sorbonne,
90, rue de Tolbiac, F-75634 PARIS CEDEX, France
{rolland, grosz, semmak}@univ-paris1.fr
[3] Department of Computer and Systems Sciences, Stockholm University/
Royal Institute of Technology, Electrum 230, S-164 40 KISTA, Sweden
danny@dsv.su.se

Abstract. In a constantly evolving business environment, knowledge management is becoming increasingly important. The shareability and repeatability of experience gained in change situations can prove an invaluable tool for the evolving enterprise. We advocate the use of the pattern paradigm as a means to capture and disseminate this type of knowledge. We place particular emphasis on representing both the ways in which an enterprise can conduct change (the process of change), and the states to which this change can lead the enterprise (the product of change). Our approach to pattern development is based (a) on the existence of a pattern template and (b) on a co-operative and discussant way of working, so as to ensure that a maximum of domain knowledge is captured. The approach is illustrated with examples from a case study of change management in the electricity sector.

1. Introduction

Today's turbulent business environment requires organisations to modify and extend their traditional practices. Businesses now have to undertake change and transform themselves into adaptive enterprises able to respond to increasing complexity and uncertainty. Conducting change in an organisation is not a straightforward task. Experience has shown that change is only possible, when those involved engage in an incremental and managed change process. This places an emphasis on changing behaviour and sets a demand for adopting the right practices in order to achieve preferred behaviour. The organisational context which supports the preferred behaviour should be enhanced [1]; this move needs positive reinforcement, as everybody involved needs to be convinced of the advantages to themselves [2]. In this demanding and ever evolving setting, the sharing and management of knowledge become essential, as change more often than not encompasses multiple aspects of a business environment. A global and thorough understanding of the situations at hand is therefore required before embarking on the process of change, but also during the process and after its completion.

In this paper we advocate the use of patterns as a mechanism for assisting the management of knowledge in situations of change, and the dissemination of experience gained from similar situations. The framework that we propose is based on a view of patterns as organisational design proposals that can be repeatedly used in different enterprise settings.

This research is part of the ongoing European research project ELEKTRA, which aims to tailor a methodology for managing change in Electricity Supply Industry (ESI) companies and to discover patterns of change management for reuse in the sector. Following a worldwide wave of deregulation in the sector, electricity companies nowadays need to reinvent themselves by building a profile based on market principles and by redefining their structure and operation. This changing environment has created a pressure on electricity companies to adapt many practices and structures and it has had an impact on almost all aspects of business. The framework presented here draws on the existence of a wider knowledge management methodology, namely the Enterprise Knowledge Development Methodology (EKD) [3], [4].

The paper is structured as follows: Section 2 presents an overview of the pattern concept. Section 3 completes this view by presenting how to encapsulate knowledge in the pattern template. In Section 4 we present the use of patterns in change management, and in Section 5 we explain the way-of-working for developing patterns. Section 6 concludes with a summary and our directions for future work.

2. Background to Patterns

Much of the contemporary work on patterns has been inspired by the work of Christopher Alexander who wrote a seminal book on the use of patterns within the domain of architecture. This book, 'The Timeless Way of Building' [5] sets the scene on the importance of patterns in such a way that, in many respects, it transcends the field of architecture. Alexander presents in this book the main arguments for the discovery of patterns and their use for achieving quality of designs. He defines a pattern as describing *"a problem which occurs over and over again in our environment and then describes the core of the solution to that problem, in such a way that you can use this solution a million times over, without ever doing it the same way twice"* [6]. Here, the emphasis is put on the fact that a pattern describes a recurrent problem and it is defined with its associated core solution.

More recently, an increasing interest in the use of patterns has been expressed within the software development community and in particular by those advocating and practising object-oriented approaches and re-use. This recent interest in patterns has its origins in [7] and has subsequently permeated into software programming [8], [9], software and system design [10], [11], [12], [13], data modelling [14], and more recently into systems analysis [15].

Despite this move towards the use of patterns in different problem domains, there has not been any significant application of patterns in the organisational and business domain. The idea of developing and reusing patterns to solve recurring business problems is relatively new and therefore there are no standard components for use in the enterprise world. As more emphasis is put on the management of change, and as the focus of attention in the IT community is shifting from software engineering to business engineering and the integration of business with IT, this situation is starting to change. The analysis patterns, for instance, that are presented in [15] are as much business-oriented as they are software-oriented.

In the context of enterprise development and change management, Coplien argues that *"patterns should help us not only to understand existing organisations but also to build new ones"* [16], [17]. Patterns in the enterprise setting can be used to describe anything that presents regular, repeatable characteristics: formal organisational and contractual relationships, informal relationships, responsibilities, work practices etc. In electricity companies, for instance, there is usually a business process dedicated to the collection of data on customer consumption of electricity. We can represent this knowledge as the Meter Reading business process pattern.

While in the traditional pattern literature a pattern is described as a tested solution to a problem, in EKD we use this term with a slight variation in meaning. Our study is focused on the enterprise setting, therefore the patterns that we propose are essentially organisational designs. These designs are solutions to specific problems within the context of an organisation, problems that are important and recurring in a variety of cases. Whereas it is possible to argue that some of these designs are tried and tested throughout a sector, some others will only be proposals for organisational solutions, whose degree of applicability will need to be tested. Therefore, in the scope of our approach we place the emphasis on the fact that patterns are *generic and abstract organisational design proposals*, solutions to recurring problems within the sector of interest, that can be easily adapted and reused.

3. Encapsulating Organisational Knowledge in Patterns

The main benefit of the pattern concept is reusability. A pattern is a component whose purpose is to be reused whenever a problem arises that matches the context of the pattern. The process of reuse can be divided into two activities [18], [19]. The first one deals with the process of defining reusable components (known as *Design for reuse*), whereas the second concerns the effective usage of the reusable components (known as *Design by reuse*). As this paper deals with the development of patterns, we concentrate on the activity of 'design for reuse'.

In developing patterns, we place equal emphasis on developing meaningful knowledge components and on providing enough information about these components so as to make them effectively reusable. Thus we aim to produce patterns that propose useful solutions to recurring problems and at the same time to describe these patterns in a way that facilitates the reuse process. We therefore make the distinction between the *body* of a pattern and its *descriptor* (Figure 1); these two elements constitute the pattern *template* [20], [21]. The former is the part of the knowledge that is effectively reused (*knowledge element*) whereas the latter aims to provide sufficient information on the pattern and to describe the context in which the pattern can be reused (*usage element*). A pattern is thus completely defined by its descriptor and its body.

In our framework the *body* of the patterns is in most cases an EKD model fragment, i.e. the patterns that we develop are cognisant of the semantics of the EKD methodology. In case that an EKD model is not available or feasible, the pattern can be described by natural language or a multimedia element (e.g. a drawing, a video etc.). As far as the *descriptor* is concerned, it consists of three elements:

- *the formal signature*: The formal signature is necessary during the reuse process in order to retrieve patterns which are appropriate for a given situation having a given usage intention in mind. A formal signature comprises the *domain* of activity in which the pattern applies, the *type* of the pattern and the *usage intention* of the pattern.
- *the informal signature*: The informal signature of a pattern contains detailed information about the problem at hand and the proposed solution; it is composed of mandatory and optional components. The mandatory components include the name of the pattern, the context of its application, the problem that it is trying to solve, the forces characterising the problem and the solution to the problem. The optional components are the consequences of applying the pattern, the rationale behind the solution, related patterns or documents, hyperlinks and known applications of the pattern, as well as additional annotations.
- *the guidelines*: Each pattern should reflect its applicability conditions within a real situation. This is achieved through pattern guidelines. The guidelines are usage tips to the potential user of the pattern about how the pattern can be tailored to fit into particular situations or needs. In a sense, using EKD terms, the guidelines aim to give an idea of how the pattern can be tailored to create an enterprise model.

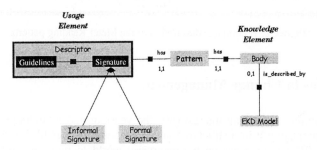

Figure 1: The pattern template

For describing the formal signature, we use formalised natural language, while the informal signature and guidelines are represented using free natural language. Figure 2 presents an example of a pattern, the Meter Reading pattern. This pattern is of Actor-Role type, a modelling mechanism devised to represent organisational and operational affinities in an enterprise setting (more on Actor-Role Modelling can be found in [4]). All the elements of the pattern template can be seen in this example (only the mandatory components of the informal signature are shown).

We have placed much emphasis in organising patterns using a meaningful and coherent mechanism. The mechanism that was preferred for pattern organisation is that of a *hierarchy* [20]. The hierarchy of patterns is built using the formal signature of patterns and specifically by associating the usage intentions, i.e. it is organised in an *intentional* manner. This mechanism facilitates the storage and retrieval of patterns through an *on-line pattern repository* (more on this issue can be found in [22], [23]), thus addressing to some extent the issue of 'design by reuse'. By organising and storing the patterns we develop a *knowledge base* for the domain of interest (what in other pattern frameworks has been termed the *pattern language*).

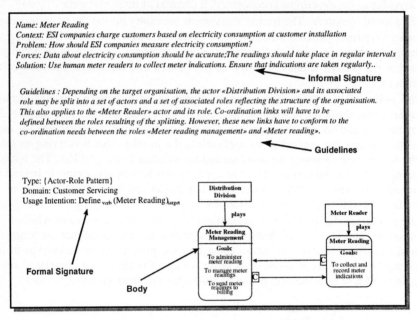

Figure 2: A complete description of the Meter Reading pattern

4. Patterns in Change Management

There has been an increasing interest over the years in understanding organisational change and managing it in a structured and systematic manner [24], [25], [26], [27], [28], [29], [30]. The pressure on the enterprise world to move towards leaner and more efficient business solutions has led to the development of increasingly sophisticated change management frameworks.

4.1 The process and the Product of Change

In our approach [31], [32], in order to deal with the task of consistently and systematically managing change, we impose upon the activity of conducting change the view of the *process-product cycle* (see Figure 3). The essence of this view is that an initial state of affairs gives rise to an intention for change; this change intention can lead to a new state of affairs through a set of alternative ways of achieving change. The way of conducting the change is the *process*, while the states that we start from and arrive to are the *products*. This cycle is intention-driven in that it is triggered by the needs for change that characterise the initial state of affairs.

What we want to achieve through the development of patterns is to ensure the repeatability of the process-product cycle. This involves identification of possible products (or states) that can be of interest to organisations in the domain of interest and of repeatable processes that can be followed to reach these states. In other words, we aim to disseminate the experience that we gain by applying the EKD methodology in a change management case. In ELEKTRA, our interest has focused on the ESI sector, and in particular on identifying *'generalised patterns of change management for re-using them in similar settings in other electricity supply companies'*.

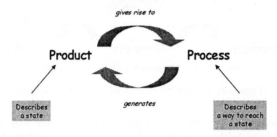

Figure 3: The product-process cycle in change management

4.2 Using Patterns to Represent the Elements of Change

EKD addresses both the description of the enterprise (in terms of organisational, operational, and informational components) and the description of the change process. This leads to the definition of two types of patterns:

- Patterns dedicated to modelling the change process in the domain of interest. We call these *change process patterns*. Change process patterns refer to the transition process, the choices and alternatives that one may have in reaching an objective. We use an extended goal model as a means to represent the body of change process patterns. The transition process, therefore, is viewed as a *teleological* process whereby the goal graph is a model of the design process.
- Patterns dedicated to modelling the domain of interest itself. We call these *product patterns*. Product patterns are further subdivided into types, according to the modelling aspect of EKD that they convey; thus, we can have goal patterns, actor-role patterns, business rule patterns etc.

A change process pattern constitutes a proposed solution to the problem of designing a new situation by describing the steps necessary for the implementation of the new situation, i.e. by offering a way of achieving the future state of affairs. A product pattern on the other hand describes the situation itself by detailing individual aspects of the business involved. Product patterns and change process patterns can then be viewed as complementary elements, in that they both contribute towards solving the greater design problem.

This dual nature of patterns is illustrated in Figure 4 and reflects the view of change management outlined above. Product patterns describe a state of affairs (i.e. a way in which the enterprise can conduct its business), whether it is the current or the future one. Change process patterns express the ways in which a transition from one state to another can be achieved.

Let us consider an example from the case of change in the ESI sector. An electricity company operating in a competitive environment with multiple electricity producers and suppliers will need to establish a business process for procuring electricity from the producers in order to sell it to the consumers.

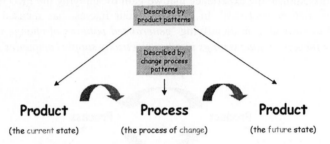

Figure 4: The role of patterns in change management

Figure 5 shows the change process pattern Introduce the buying and selling of electricity, which illustrates the options of how the company's Supply division (dealing with the retailing of electricity to consumers) can implement this process. The pattern has the form of a goal graph where the leaf goals represent four alternative ways (mutually exclusive in this case) of organising a business process of electricity procurement. The third leaf goal of the change process pattern proposes the introduction of a purchasing activity from multiple sources. The details of how such an activity can be configured are presented in Figure 6. Here, a product pattern is shown that explains the buying-and-selling activity when multiple sources of electricity are involved. Together these two patterns constitute a design proposal for answering the electricity procurement problem.

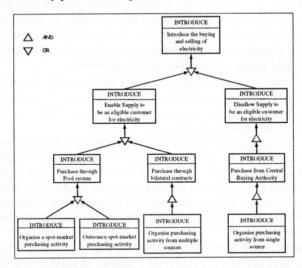

Figure 5: Change process pattern - the introduction of electricity trading

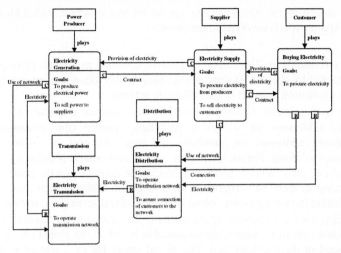

Figure 6: Product pattern - trading of electricity with multiple sources of procurement

5. Developing Organisational Patterns for Change Management

Developing patterns that encapsulate enterprise knowledge is a task of increased complexity. Domain knowledge, sometimes only implicit and vague, needs to be captured and represented. In the case of change management there are additional constraints. The conditions that characterise the change process need to be identified, so that the applicability of the patterns in similar cases can be determined. Thus, the context of the particular situation and the directions for change have to be captured.

5.1 The Way-of-working

In order to tackle the demands of pattern development, we devised a process that is iterative and involves domain experts and method experts (analysts) in close co-operation. The process consists of the following four steps: (a) *Elicitation of candidates*, (b) *Suitability evaluation*, (c) *Documenting*, and (d) *Verification*. We will now briefly examine each step (for a more detailed description, see [33]).

Elicitation of Candidates. Collecting candidate patterns aims at identifying potential change process patterns and product patterns. The objective is to describe the candidate pattern at a sufficient level of detail in order to proceed to its evaluation. The output of the elicitation process is a list of candidate patterns each having an initial description of major components: name, problem, solution and context. A first draft of the formal signature and body is also produced. Potential *sources* of knowledge for pattern elicitation range from enterprise-specific documentation (e.g. current-state models of a particular company) to domain-wide documentation. An important source of candidate patterns can be the not-yet-documented knowledge of various domain experts involved in the process.

Suitability Evaluation. The candidate patterns obtained as a result of step one need to be evaluated by domain experts so that their further development can be decided upon. The evaluation consists of the following actions:

- *Grading the pattern:* Grading is based on three criteria: *usefulness* (the candidate pattern addresses an important problem), *quality* (the proposed solution effectively addresses the problem) and *cost* (the cost of implementing the proposed solution). For each criterion, a set of sub-criteria is defined, which helps to evaluate the candidate pattern in detail. The domain experts grade the pattern according to these sub-criteria. A set of decision tables is then used in order to summarise the voting results into a single numerical score per criterion.
- *Deciding on the suitability of the pattern:* The decision on whether to accept a candidate pattern for further development is based on the global numerical scores produced in the previous step. The global rating for each pattern is the sum of these values for each criterion and ranges from 0 to 6. The pattern is accepted if the global rating of a candidate pattern is greater than or equal to 4. The pattern needs to be corrected if the global rating of a candidate pattern is between 2 and 4. Finally, the pattern is rejected if the global rating of a candidate pattern is less than or equal to 2. These values can be negotiated among the participants.
- *Correcting the pattern:* For each criterion we have defined a set of corrective actions that give guidelines about how to improve the pattern. When the corrective actions have been performed, the pattern is re-evaluated.

Documenting. At this stage the pattern template needs to be completed. More precisely, the domain experts, in co-operation with the analysts now provide the remaining elements of the informal signature (i.e. forces, rationale, consequences etc.) and a set of initial guidelines. The formal signature is also finalised at this stage, which allows the pattern to be included in a hierarchy on the basis of its usage intention. The pattern is now part of the knowledge base and any relationships with other patterns become apparent and explicit.

Verification. After a pattern has been fully described (i.e. all components of the pattern template have been described), the pattern is verified by domain experts. The wording of all elements in the pattern template is carefully studied and modified if necessary, as are interconnections between related patterns.

5.2 An Example From the Case Study

In the context of ELEKTRA, we concentrated on the study of change in the domains of Distribution and Human Resource Management of electricity companies. In developing a pattern knowledge base we used information from the various phases of the ELEKTRA project [34], [35], [36], [37], knowledge about practice in the ESI sector world-wide [38], and current understanding of domain experts involved in the project. The outcome is a knowledge base for change management in ESI, detailed in [33].

As an example of applying the methodology, we shall detail the development of the change process pattern Introduce structural unbundling, taken from the Distribution case study. This pattern addresses a significant problem of the Distribution division of an ESI company, with respect to deregulation and customer servicing. Specifically, an understanding is needed of how a horizontally and vertically integrated ESI company can undertake steps towards entering a deregulated and competitive electricity market. This is representative of the kind of thinking required for developing patterns in a similar environment.

Elicitation. The choice of candidate pattern was driven by what was considered as being essential toward the evolution of the ESI sector with respect to the deregulation rules being applied in the European Union. Existing EKD models, developed during earlier phases of the project, were used as the source of knowledge for this pattern. Initially, the elements of the informal signature were identified as:

Problem: An electricity distribution company in a monopoly environment must enter into a competitive market.

Context: The management of the wire and supply businesses of Distribution is currently fully integrated. All business-related activities are handled internally. The proposed services are restricted to electricity supply.

Forces: The deregulation rules for the European electricity market issued by the Commission of the European Union force an electricity distribution company functioning as a monopoly to enter a competitive market.

The initial version of the solution suggested considering four aspects of unbundling: (i) wire business and customer services are unbundled, (ii) new technical services other than electricity are introduced, (iii) outsourcing of customer and wire services are considered, and (iv) new customer services not related to electricity are introduced.

Evaluation. The pattern was evaluated by domain experts with knowledge of strategy issues. The pattern was deemed important for the ESI knowledge base because it addresses an essential problem in deregulation of electricity companies. During the evaluation corrective actions were proposed, particularly with respect to introduction of new services (both wire-based and customer-oriented ones).

As an interesting result of the evaluation process, the participants noticed the need to introduce a completely new pattern, complementary in nature, namely Introduce new means to increase market share. This pattern suggests a strategic view of how to face the results of structural unbundling and the introduction of competition.

Documenting/Verification. After further discussions it was decided that part of the pattern, dealing with the introduction of new services, contained sufficient information to be treated as separate patterns. The final version of the body of the pattern is presented in Figure 7. The remaining information is now contained in two additional change process patterns Introduce new services based on network assets and Introduce new customer services.

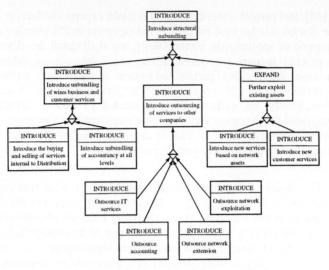

Figure 7: The final version of the pattern body

6. Conclusion

Managing change in organisations is becoming a crucial issue due to the rapid change of today's business. To this end, we propose patterns as a means to assist in the management of knowledge in change situations. The result of our work takes the form of a framework where a pattern contains an organisational design proposal that can be re-used in different enterprise settings. These proposals are based on the EKD methodology. We have applied the framework in the context of the European research project ELEKTRA for supporting change management in two particular domains of the Electricity Supply Industry sector.

A pattern couples a problem to a solution. The problem is described within the pattern descriptor whereas the solution, the organisational design proposal, constitutes the body of the pattern. We consider two types of patterns: change process patterns and product patterns. A change process pattern suggests how to conduct and manage the process of change in an organisation, whereas a product pattern describes a (part of the) solution implemented by the change. Patterns are organised within hierarchies that facilitate search and retrieval.

Using the proposed framework, a set of patterns has been developed for managing change in the Distribution and Human Resource Management domains of electricity companies. We have found one of the main contributions of patterns to the management of organisational change to be that they may supply decision-makers with semi-structured information in the face of choosing between alternatives. Since these alternatives are organised in an intentional hierarchical structure, browsing through them is more intuitive than, say, relational or object-oriented database searching. Problems and solutions are searched for according to a structure defined by the domain experts. This can make a difference in the case of participants that are not expert computer users, as is often the case with management personnel.

We are currently further elaborating on how patterns can be effectively reused ('design by reuse' activity). The final objective of our work concerns the implementation of the proposed framework within a consultancy toolset for change in the ESI sector [39]. We are also envisioning means for disseminating the knowledge embedded within the patterns through the WWW [20], [21].

Acknowledgements

The research presented in this paper has been funded by the European research project ELEKTRA (ESPRIT project no. 22927). The authors wish to thank all the partners involved in the project for their Cupertino and contribution to the results, and especially the participants from the two user companies, the Public Power Corporation of Greece and Vattenfall of Sweden. We also thank our colleague Vagelio Kavakli for her useful comments and recommendations.

References

1. Scarbrough, H.: The relevance and Contribution of Socio-technical Systems. http://bprc.warwick.ac.uk/focus4.html, Business Processes Resource Centre (1996)
2. Kautto-Koivula, K: The Pitfalls of Knowledge. Information Strategy, Economist (1998)
3. Bubenko, J., Brash, D., Stirna, J.: EKD User Guide. ELEKTRA Project Report (1997)
4. Loucopoulos, P., Kavakli, V., Prekas, N., Rolland, C., Grosz, G., Nurcan, S.: Using the EKD Approach: The Modelling Component. Research Report (ELEKTRA project), Report No. ELEKTRA/WP2/T2.1/UMIST/3 (1997)
5. Alexander, C.: The Timeless Way of Building. Oxford University Press, New York (1979)
6. Alexander, C., Ishikawa, S., Silverstein, M., Jacobson, M., Fiksdahl-King, I., Angel S.: A Pattern Language. Oxford University Press, New York (1977)
7. Coad, P.: Object-Oriented Patterns. Com. of the ACM, Vol. 35, No. 9 (1992) 152-159
8. Buschmann, F., Meunier, R., Rohnert, H., Sommerland, P., Stal, M.: Pattern-Oriented Software Architecture - A System of Patterns. John Wiley (1996)
9. Beck K.: Smalltalk Best Practice Patterns, Volume 1: Coding. Prentice Hall, Englewood Cliffs, NJ (1997)
10. Coplien, J., Schmidt, D. (eds.): Pattern Languages of Program Design. Addison Wesley, Reading, MA (1995)
11. Gamma, E., Helm, R., Johnson, R., Vlissides, J.: Design Patterns: Elements of Reusable Object-Oriented Software. Addison Wesley, Reading, MA (1995)
12. Vlissides, J.M., Coplien, J.O., Kerth, N.L. (eds.): Pattern Languages of Program Design 2. Addison-Wesley (1996)
13. Eriksson, H.-E., Penker, M.: UML Toolkit. Wiley, New York (1998)
14. Hay, D.C.: Data Model Patterns. Dorset House Publishing, New York (1996)
15. Fowler, M.: Analysis Patterns: Reusable Object Models. Addison-Wesley (1997)
16. Coplien, J.: A Development Process Generative Pattern Language. AT&T Bell Laboratories, WWW Publication, http://www.bell-labs.com/people/cope/Patterns/Process/index.html, (1995)
17. Coplien, J.: A Generative Development - Process Pattern Language. In: Coplien, Schmidt, (eds.): Pattern Languages of Program Design. Addison-Wesley (1995) 183-237
18. Bellinzona, R., Fugini, M.G., de Mey V.: Reuse of Specifications and Designs in a Development Information System. In Prakash, N., Rolland, C., Pernici B. (eds.): Information System Development Process (A-30), IFIP (1993)

19. De Antonellis, V., Pernici, B.: Reusing specifications through refinement levels. Data and Knowledge Engineering, Vol. 15, No. 2 (1995)
20. Grosz, G., Loucopoulos, P., Rolland, C., Nurcan, S.: A Framework for Generic Patterns Dedicated to the Management of Change in the Electricity Supply Industry. 9th International Conference and Workshop on Database and Expert Systems Applications, DEXA '98 (1998)
21. ELEKTRA-UP1, ELEKTRA-UMIST: The Patterns Model. ELEKTRA Project Report, Report No. ELEKTRA WP5/T5.1/UP1-UMIST/2 (1998)
22. Rolland, C., Grosz, G., Loucopoulos, P., Nurcan, S.: A Framework for Encapsulating Best Business Practices for Electricity Supply Industry into Generic Patterns. 2nd IMACS International Conference on Circuits, Systems and Computers - IMACS-CSC '98, Athens, Greece (1998) Vol. 1, 330-336
23. Rolland, C., Grosz, G., Nurcan, S., Yue, W., Gnaho, C.: An electronic handbook for accessing domain specific generic patterns. IFIP WG 8.1 Working Conference: Information Systems in the WWW Environment, Beijing, China (1998)
24. Medina-Mora, R., Winograd, T., Flores, R., Flores, F.: The Action-Workflow Approach to Workflow Management Technology. Conference on Computer Supported Cooperative Work (1992) 281-288
25. Davenport, T.: Process Innovation: Reengineering Work Through Information Technology. Harvard Business School Press, Boston, MA (1993)
26. Lee J.: Goal-Based Process Analysis: A Method for Systematic Process Redesign. Conference on Organizational Computing Systems, Milpitas, CA (1993) 196-201
27. Yu, E.: Modelling Strategic Relationships for Process Reengineering. PhD Thesis, University of Toronto (1994)
28. Ould, M.A.: Business Processes - Modelling and Analysis for Re-engineering and Improvement. John Wiley and Sons, Chichester, UK (1995)
29. Wieringa, R.J.: Requirements Engineering - Frameworks for Understanding. John Wiley and Sons, Chichester, UK (1996)
30. Hsiao, R.L., Ormerod, R.J.: A new perspective on the dynamics of information technology-enabled strategic change. Information Systems Journal, Vol. 8, No. 1 (1998) 21-52
31. Kavakli, V., Loucopoulos, P.: Goal-driven business process analysis - Application in electricity deregulation. 10th International Conference on Advanced Information Systems Engineering, CAiSE '98, May 1998, Pisa, Italy (1998) 305-324
32. Rolland, C., Nurcan, S., Grosz, G.: A Unified framework for modelling co-operative design processes and co-operative business processes. 31st Annual International Conference on System Sciences, Big Island, Hawaii, USA (1998)
33. Molière: ESI Knowledge Base Specification. ELEKTRA Project Deliverable (1999)
34. Athena: Initial Requirements Model for PPC ELEKTRA Project Deliverable (1997)
35. Carolus: System Design Specification for Vattenfall. ELEKTRA Project Deliverable (1998)
36. Demetra: System Design Specification for PPC. ELEKTRA Project Deliverable (1998)
37. Freja: Evaluated Design for Vattenfall. ELEKTRA Project Deliverable Document (1998)
38. Prekas, N., Loucopoulos, P., Dimitromanolaki, I.: Developing Models of Reform for Electricity Supply Industry Companies. 2nd IMACS International Conference on Circuits, Systems and Computers - IMACS-CSC '98, Athens, Greece (1998) Vol. 1, 337-342
39. Ikarus: Design of the ESI Toolset. ELEKTRA Project Deliverable (1998)

Knowledge Acquisition for Mobile Robot Environment Mapping

Miroslav Kulich, Petr Štěpán, and Libor Přeučil

The Gerstner Laboratory for Intelligent Decision Making and Control
Department of Cybernetics (K333)
Faculty of Electrical Engineering, Czech Technical University
166 27 Prague 6, Technická 2, Czech Republic
e-mail: {kulich,stepan,preucil}@labe.felk.cvut.cz

Abstract. This paper deals with methods of creating entities used for a geometric description of robot environment. These entities (primitives) are extracted from scene-depth measurements gathered by a mobile robot sensor system. The overall goal is to achieve efficient data fusion through extraction of specific geometric features - boundaries of obstacles - from sensor data. Although the geometric level of abstraction belongs to low level representations, it offers efficient reduction of data amount. This contribution overviews two different approaches. The first method has been designed for processing probabilistic sensor-based world models which integrate data from multiple sensors and multiple- sensor positions. The other approach handles cases of reliable ranging when navigating a nearby obstacle. The main features of both methods are discussed with respect to on-line updating of the global world model and simple sensor-based planning and control of the robot. The approaches presented are optimized towards performance robustness and are accompanied by experimental results with the GLbot[1].

1 Introduction

The main task for the autonomous mobile robot is to execute collision-free missions through the operating environment. For example, this incorporates a task of achieving a certain location or covering a particular region (in the robot path). The definition of the mission path is derived from the user-specified goal in a 2D environment, and navigation is executed respecting existing obstacle unknown to the robot. To perform this task, the robot must be able to detect and recognize new (unknown) and old (known) obstacles in order to correct inaccuracies/update its internal representation of the environment by understanding the sensor data.

The autonomous mobile robot typically has multiple representations of knowledge concerning the environment on two different levels of abstraction: global world map and the local sensor-based map. As the main task for the autonomous

---

[1] The Gerstner Lab Robot

mobile robot is navigation in a partially known environment, activity planning is similarly split into two major subtasks, global and sensor-based planning. The global planning module prepares a globally optimized plan of how to reach the given goal by using the global world map containing knowledge at a general level. On the other hand, the sensor-based planning module modifies the global plan according to actual needs during execution. Typical requirements for execution of the global plan are: keeping the robot at a safe distance from obstacles, detection of unexpected obstacles on the track, local corrections of the path such as collision avoidance or compensation of positioning errors, etc. Each requirement should use the local sensor-based map that is created by sensor data fusion module which integrates data from different sensors and robot positions.

The global world map and sensor-based map substantially differ in the level of abstraction of stored information. The global map module includes management of a database, which stores entities describing the environment. These can be stored either in symbolic form or in the form of geometric interpolations of the objects' borders, both of which define objects that exist in the environment. The type of stored information also determines typical operations with the global world model which are: addition and removal of objects and listing of the visible object borders from a given standpoint, etc.

The information stored in the sensor-based map is considered for an intermediate level of abstraction between pure sensor measurements and geometric or symbolic representations contained in the global world map.

2   Sensor Based Maps

The robot's environment is represented by an occupancy grid [4][3] in the local sensor-based map. The data carrier itself is a regular grid, where each cell stores a probability that the corresponding space is occupied (or empty). The probability is updated by accumulated sensor readings. The original updating [4]algorithm has been tested and improved for final implementation. The main improvements were made to the probabilistic model of sonar sensors, which increases robustness of the integration process. The sonar model used also constrains minimal measured distance to suppress specular reflections. These improvements and experiments with real data are described in [8]. Another world-modeling method that uses raw sonar measurements is presented in [1]. The world model there has been created making use of parametric line-segments. An update cycle is applied to detect emerging obstacles. On the other hand Zimmer [2] describes qualitative topologic maps as an alternative to geometric models and builds maps with Kohonen's self-organizing maps.

Our goal is to present methods which enable mutual coupling of contents of various representations of a different nature. Special attention has been paid to the transfer of data between different representations of sensor-based maps. The significance of the proposed solutions can be seen as a substantial support of global world map updating techniques.

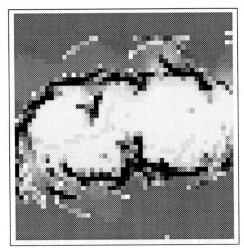

Fig. 1. The occupancy grid. Dark pixels represent high probability of occupancy, light ones stand for high emptiness. Grey pixels denote unknown level.

3 Feature Extraction Using Occupancy Grid

The algorithm is based on computer-vision techniques [5][6] and consists of the following steps:

- Segmentation
- Morphological filtering
- Boundary detection
- Approximation by lines

Segmentation

Firstly, the occupancy grid $G = \{g_{i,j}\}$ obtained from sonar measurements is transferred into a binary image $G^s = \{g^s_{i,j}\}$ by segmentation (see Fig. 2). A simple thresholding for each cell can be used:

$$g^s_{ij} = 1 \equiv g_{ij} > T, \tag{1}$$

where T is a constant parameter defining the desired threshold. Unfortunately, the inequality (1) is applicable only in environments where the sensor error rate is low. The major problem is caused by specular reflections which are accumulated in the probability grid, and this simple thresholding is not capable to recognize these cases. In order to eliminate this problem, an additional condition respecting the value of edge gradient has been added:

$$g^s_{ij} = 1 \equiv g_{ij} > T \wedge |\nabla g_{ij}| > T_{Edge}, \tag{2}$$

where ∇g_{ij} is the value of the edge in the cell g_{ij} and T_{Edge} is a constant defining the edge gradient threshold.

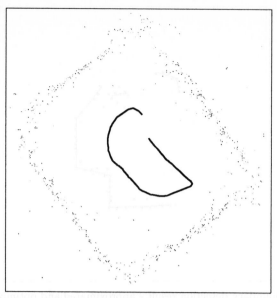

Fig. 9. The first experiment, the robot trajectory (curve) and measured data (dots).

6 Summary and Conclusion

This paper describes two approaches to extracting a geometric description of unknown objects from sonar range measurements. The former method uses an occupancy grid which integrates multiple sonar measurements into a probabilistic representation. The approach used relies heavily on computer vision techniques and morphological operations. The first practical experiments indicate that this method might be suitable for mapping all new entities found in the robot environment. In known environments, this method creates a data structure that can be used to corroborate known robot position with the global world map (e.g., for position refinement, etc.).

The other approach can be used only in cases where the robot follows a particular border of the obstacle. This method can be used to obtain a precise geometric description of the obstacle boundary. Typically, the obtained boundaries are so reliable that the obstacle description can be inserted directly into the global world map when updating.

Acknowledgement

This research has been carried out with the support of VS 96047, FRVŠ 798/1999 and IG 3099070 333 grants.

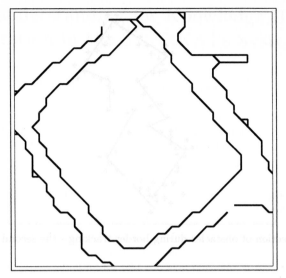

Fig. 10. Obstacles detected by the occupancy grid method - the first experiment.

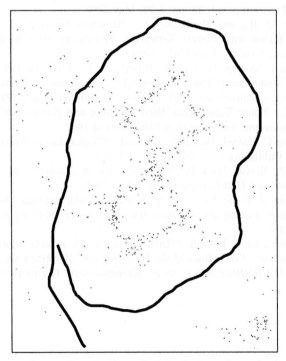

Fig. 11. The second experiment, the robot trajectory (curve) and the measured data (dots).

devices [8]. Thus the information extraction capability of the system is increased in a bootstrapping manner while reading more and more documents. As most of the information extraction systems, we require our parser to be robust to underspecification and ill-formed input, but unlike almost all of them our parsing system is particularly sensitive to the treatment of textual reference relations such as various forms of anaphora. This has immediate consequences on the soundness and validity of the knowledge bases we create as a result of the text understanding process and likewise on the feasibility of sophisticated information system applications based on the acquired text knowledge.

2 System Architecture

The description of the SYNDIKATE text knowledge generator proceeds from two layers. The first one deals with the core elements of any natural language understanding system – grammar, domain knowledge, as well as associated parsing, semantic interpretation, and inferencing routines needed for sentence-level analysis. The second layer of description introduces the mechanisms with which we operate at the text level of analysis, introducing the centering model for discourse memory management. The documents we deal with are currently taken from two domains, *viz.* test reports from the information technology (IT) domain, and finding reports from a medical (MED) subdomain. The overall architecture of SYNDIKATE is summarized in Figure 1 and serves as a frame of reference for the subsequent exposition.

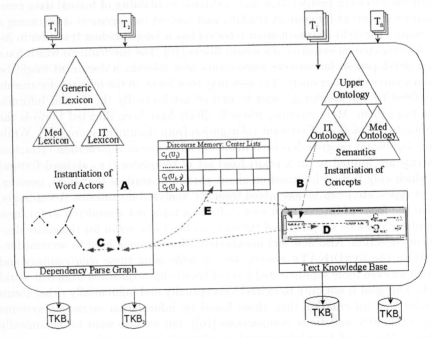

Fig. 1. Architecture of the SYNDIKATE System

2.1 Sentence-Level Understanding

For the basic understanding of clauses and sentences, we supply grammar and domain knowledge, as well as a set of semantic interpretation schemata mediating between these two knowledge sources.

Grammatical knowledge for syntactic analysis is based on a fully lexicalized dependency grammar [7] we refer to in Figure 1 as *Lexicon*. Basic word forms (lexemes) constitute the leaf nodes of the lexicon tree which are further abstracted in terms of word class specifications at different levels of generality. Figure 2 depicts a fragment of the word class hierarchy. Lexemes are given in italics, whereas the inner nodes denote words classes. The *Generic Lexicon* in Figure 1 contains lexical material which is domain-independent (lexemes such as *move*, *with*, or *month*), while domain-specific extensions are kept in separate lexicon partitions serving the needs of particular subdomains, e.g., IT (*hard disk*, *print*, etc.) or MED (*disease*, *surface mucus*, etc.).

A dependency grammar captures binary valency constraints between a syntactic head (e.g., a noun) and possible modifiers (e.g., a determiner or an adjective). In order to establish a dependency relation between a head and a modifier, the corresponding constraints on word order, compatibility of morphosyntactic features, and semantic criteria have to be fulfilled. Figure 4 depicts a sample dependency graph in which word nodes are given in bold face and dependency relations between them are indicated by labeled edges.

Conceptual knowledge is expressed in a KL-ONE-like terminological representation language [18]. A fragment of the IT ontology we use is depicted in Figure 3. Rounded boxes denote concepts, with directed edges indicating specialization relations, e.g., STORAGE is specialized by HARD-DISK. Nonspecialization relations are given by labeled edges between concept nodes and contain restrictions for possible role fillers. For instance, the relation SELL-AGENT (i.e., the one who sells something) defined for SELL has only fillers of the type PERSON.

Corresponding to the partitions at the lexical level, the ontologies we provide (cf. Figure 1) are split up between one that can be used by all applications, the so-called *Upper Ontology*, while several dedicated ontologies account for the conceptual requirements of particular domains, e.g., IT (HARDDISK, PRINT, etc.) or MED (DISEASE, SURFACEMUCUS, etc.).

Semantic knowledge accounts for conceptual linkages between instances of concept types according to those dependency relations that are established between their corresponding lexical items. *Semantic interpretation rules* medi-

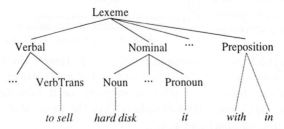

Fig. 2. Fragment of the Word Class Hierarchy

ate between both levels in a way as abstract and general as possible [14]. Their specification and operation share many commonalities with the knowledge representation layer. Hence, the overlapping description in Figure 1.

In order to illustrate how a dependency relation is established computationally, we give a sketch of the basic protocol for *incremental parsing*. The lexicalized grammar and the associated parser we use are embedded in an object-oriented computation model. So, the dependency relations are computed by lexical objects, so-called *word actors*, through strictly local message passing, only involving the lexical items they represent [7]:

- After a word has been read from textual input, its associated lexeme (specified in the lexicon tree) is identified and a corresponding word actor gets initialized (step A in Figure 1). As most lexemes (verbs, nouns and adjectives) are directly linked to the conceptual system, each lexical item w that has a conceptual correlate C in the domain knowledge base gets instantiated in the knowledge base (step B in Figure 1). For example, the lexical item *"Festplatte" (hard disk)* with the conceptual correlate HARD-DISK is instantiated by HARD-DISK.5.
- For integration in the parse tree, the newly created word actor searches its head (or, alternatively, its modifier) by sending a request for dependential government to its left context (step C in Figure 1). The search space is restricted, since this request is propagated upwards only along the "right shoulder" of the dependency graph constructed so far. All word actors addressed this way check, in parallel, whether their valency restrictions are met by the requesting word actor.
- If all grammatical constraints are fulfilled by one of the targeted word actors, a semantic interpretation is immediately performed (step D in Figure 1). If it turns out to produce a valid result, i.e., only if both grammatical and conceptual integrity are guaranteed, the acknowledged syntactic head h sends an acceptance message to the requesting modifier m and the screened dependency relation is finally established.

Semantic interpretation processes operate on so-called *semantically interpretable* subgraphs of the dependency graph. These are subgraphs whose starting and end nodes contain content words (i.e., words with a conceptual correlate), while all intervening nodes contain only non-content words (such as prepositions, articles etc.). Hence, the linkage between content words may be direct (e.g., in Figure 4 the one between *"Compaq"* and *"verkauft"* via the dependency relation *subject*), or it may be indirect (e.g., between *"Computer"* and *"IBM-Festplatte"* via the preposition *"mit"* and the dependency relations *ppatt* and *pobj*).

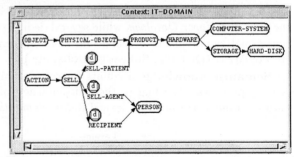

Fig. 3. Fragment of the Ontology

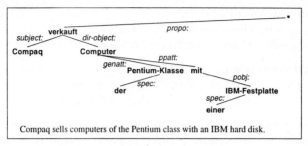

Fig. 4. A Sample Dependency Graph

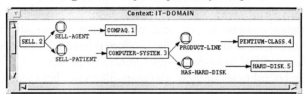

Fig. 5. Corresponding Semantic Interpretation

The semantic interpretation process, in general, consists of finding a relational link between the conceptual correlates of the two content words under consideration. As an example, when the first word in our sample sentence, *"Compaq"*, is read, its conceptual correlate, COMPAQ.1, is instantiated. The next word, *"verkauft" (sells)*, also leads to the creation of an associated instance (SELL.2). Syntactically, the valencies of the transitive verb *"verkauft" (sells)* lead to the check of a *subject* dependency relation for *"Compaq"*. At the conceptual level this syntactic relation always translates into checking AGENT or PATIENT (sub)roles only. In order to infer a valid semantic relation we incorporate knowledge about the concept types of COMPAQ.1 and SELL.2, *viz.* COMPANY and SELL, respectively. Extracting the roles from SELL (cf. Figure 3), only SELL-AGENT and SELL-PATIENT are allowed for interpretation as they are subroles of AGENT and PATIENT. Checking sortal integrity succeeds only for SELL-AGENT (COMPANY is subsumed by LEGAL-PERSON and by PERSON). In an analogous way, the semantically interpretable subgraph < *"verkauft" – dir-object – "Computer"*> is dealt with, while checking a mediated linkage such as the one for (*"Computer", "mit", "IBM-Festplatte"*) requires to incorporate constraints supplied by the intervening nodes (in the example above the conceptual constraints associated with the preposition *"mit" (with)*, viz. limiting the set of allowed relations to HAS-PART, INSTRUMENT or HAS-PROPERTY [14]).

2.2 Text-Level Understanding

The textual phenomena we deal with in SYNDIKATE all have in common that they establish referential links between consecutive utterances in a coherent text. This can be illustrated by two alternative continuations of sentence (1):

(1) Compaq verkauft Computer der Pentium-Klasse mit einer IBM-Festplatte$_{sing,fem}$.
    (Compaq sells computers of the Pentium class with an IBM hard disk$_{sing,fem}$.)

(2) **Pronominal Anaphora:**

$Sie_{sing,fem}$ zeigt eine Zugriffszeit von 6,5 ms.

($It_{sing,fem}$ exhibits an access time of 6.5 ms.)

(3) **Nominal Anaphora:**

$Der\ Speicher_{sing}$ zeigt eine Zugriffszeit von 6,5 ms.

(*The storage$_{sing}$* exhibits an access time of 6.5 ms.)

While pronominal anaphora heavily depend on grammatical conditions – the agreement of the antecedent (*"IBM-Festplatte" (IBM hard disk)*) and the pronoun (*"Sie" (it)*) in number and gender –, the influence of grammatical criteria gradually diminishes for other types of text phenomena. For nominal anaphora, number constraints are still valid, while a generalization relation between the anaphoric noun (*"Speicher" (storage)*) and its proper antecedent (*"IBM-Festplatte" (IBM hard disk)*) must hold, in addition.

From an analytical point of view, the main difference between sentential and textual analysis relates to the fact that at the sentence level dependency relations determine which lexical items, and, hence, which conceptual correlates, are to be related. At the text level, such dependency relations are not available. Hence, complementary structural information has to be supplied. This is achieved via a discourse memory, in which already introduced discourse entities are managed according to centering mechanisms [17] such that they be available for establishing reference relations with upcoming items from the textual input. In this model, each utterance U_i in a discourse segment is assigned a set of *forward-looking centers*, $C_f(U_i)$. The elements of $C_f(U_i)$ are partially ordered to reflect relative prominence in U_i. The ranking imposed on the elements of the C_f (ordering criteria for list items are discussed in [17]) reflects the assumption that the most highly ranked element of $C_f(U_i)$ is the most preferred antecedent of an anaphoric expression in U_{i+1}, while the remaining elements are ordered according to decreasing preference for establishing referential links.

The problems text phenomena cause (unless they are properly accounted for) are of vital importance for the adequacy of the representation structures resulting from natural language processing, and are centered around the notions of incomplete and invalid knowledge bases. *Incomplete* knowledge bases emerge when references to already established discourse entities are simply not recognized, as in the case of *pronominal anaphora*. The occurrence of the pronoun (as in Sentence (2) above) is not reflected at the conceptual level, since pronouns do not have conceptual correlates. Hence, an incomplete concept graph emerges as shown in Figure 6, i.e., the referent for the pronoun *"Sie" (it)*, HARD-DISK.5, is not linked to the access time data. An adequate treatment with a resolved anaphor is shown in Figure 7, where the representation of sentence (1) is linked to the one of sentence (2) by connecting to the proper referent HARD-DISK.5.

Invalid knowledge bases emerge when an entity which has a different denotation at the text surface such as *nominal anaphora* is treated as a formally distinct item at the symbol level, although it refers literally to the same entity. These false referential descriptions appear in Figure 8 treating STORAGE.6 as a new entity in the discourse, whereas Figure 7 shows an adequate conceptual

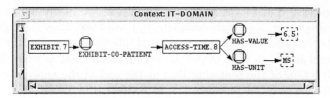

Fig. 6. Sentence (2): Unresolved Pronominal Anaphora

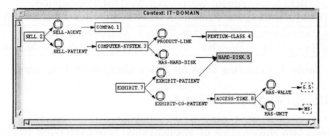

Fig. 7. Sentence (1) and (2)/(3): Resolved Anaphora

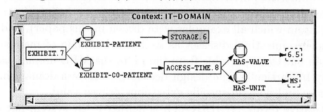

Fig. 8. Sentence (3): Unresolved Nominal Anaphora

representation capturing the intended meaning at the representation level, *viz.* exchanging STORAGE.6 by the proper referent HARD-DISK.5.

We will now focus on nominal anaphor resolution to demonstrate the use of the centered discourse memory. Whenever a definite noun phrase is encountered in the currently analyzed sentence a search in the center-forward list of the previous utterance is started (cf. step E in Figure 1). It proceeds by checking for each discourse unit in the sequence of appearance in this list whether the lexical items agree in number and the conceptual correlate of the anaphoric expression is specialized by one of the antecedents.

Table 1 contains the centering list for the first sentence, $C_f(U_1)$. Grammatically, only nouns and their conceptual correlates are taken into consideration. The tuple notation takes the conceptual correlate of the lexical item in the text knowledge base in the first place, while the lexical surface form appears in second place. Using this centering list for the interpretation of utterance (3) results in a series of queries whether STORAGE is more general than COMPAQ (answer: No), COMPUTER-SYSTEM (answer: No), PENTIUM-CLASS (answer: No), or HARD-DISK (answer: Yes). As the latter relationship obviously holds (cf. Figure 3), in the conceptual representation structure of sentence (3) STORAGE.6, the literal instance for *"Speicher"* (cf. Figure 8), is replaced by HARD-DISK.5, the referentially valid identifier (cf. Figure 7). So, instead of having two unlinked sentence graphs (Figures 8 and 5) the reference resolution for (pro)nominal anaphora leads to joining them in a single complete <u>and</u> valid text knowledge graph. Figure 7 depicts the final result of the conceptual interpretation after the resolution of the nominal anaphora (and of the pronominal anaphora, as well). The subsequent construction of the centering lists at the end of the analysis of sentence (3) (and, alternatively, for sentence (2)) is illustrated in Table 1.

$C_f(U_1)$:	[COMPAQ.1: Compaq, COMPUTER-SYSTEM.3: Computer, PENTIUM-CLASS.4: Pentium-Klasse, HARD-DISK.5: IBM-Festplatte]
$C_f(U_2)$:	[HARD-DISK.5: Sie, ACCESS-TIME.8: Zugriffszeit, MS: ms]
$C_f(U_3)$:	[HARD-DISK.5: Speicher, ACCESS-TIME.8: Zugriffszeit, MS: ms]

Table 1. Centering Data for Three Consecutive Utterances

3 SYNDIKATE Applications

We distinguish two dimensions of applications, those referring to different domains and to different functionalities. With respect to different domains, SYNDIKATE has already been adapted to test reports from the information technology domain (from which all examples were drawn in this paper), and to finding reports on gastro-intestinal diseases as well, a subdomain of medicine [6]. The system turned out to be portable from the IT to the MED domain without major revisions. In particular, the design decisions to have a domain-independent knowledge core and domain-specific extensions proved valid.

In quantitative terms, SYNDIKATE is neither a toy system nor a monster. The generic lexicon currently includes 2,000 entries, the IT lexicon adds 5,000, while the MED lexicon contributes 3,000 entries each. Similarly, at the ontology level, the Upper Ontology contains 1,200 concepts and roles, to which the IT ontology adds 1,000 items and the MED ontology contributes 1,500 concepts and roles. The IT domain was chosen to have a testbed available that can be extended on demand. The MED domain, however, is subject to more serious ontology engineering efforts [9], since we envisage SYNDIKATE's deployment as an experimental hospital information system at our university site. In order to cope with the enormous knowledge engineering requirements, we are currently exploring the import of a high-volume medical terminological server [2] in our system. The vocabulary size of this system ranges on the order of 700,000 terms which are organized in a semantic network.

The second dimension of applications concern different functionalities. In the MED domain several specific medical *classification* services are under development. These require mapping the finding reports to particular disease categories and making the degree of a disease explicit via staging and grading indices. We have made progress here by incorporating the interpretation of comparatives and evaluative assertions based on qualitative metareasoning [16].

While these services still aim at the automation of standard routines in clinical documentation centers, the potential of inferentially based *fact retrieval* considerably exceeds the functionality of today's non-deductive hospital information systems. Given such an application, the validity of the text knowledge bases become a crucial issue. As we have already discussed, disregarding textual phenomena will cause dysfunctional system behavior in terms of incorrect answers. This can be illustrated by a query Q such as

```
Q :  (retrieve ?x (Storage ?x))
A-: (|I| Hard-Disk.5, |I| Storage.6)
A+: (|I| Hard-Disk.5)
```

which triggers a search for all instances in the knowledge base that are of type STORAGE. Given an invalid knowledge base (cf. Fig. 8), the incorrect answer (A-) contains two entities, *viz.* HARD-DISK.5 and STORAGE.6, since both are in the extension of STORAGE (cf. Fig. 3). If, however, a valid knowledge base such as in Fig. 7 is given, only the correct answer, HARD-DISK.5, is inferred (A+).

4 Evaluation

Admittedly, SYNDIKATE has not yet undergone a thorough empirical evaluation at these application levels. We have, however, carefully evaluated its subcomponents. The results can be summarized as follows:

1. **Sentence Parsing.** We compared a standard active chart parser with full backtracking capabilities with the parser of SYNDIKATE, which is characterized by limited memoization and restricted backtracking capabilities, using the same grammar specifications. On average, SYNDIKATE's parser exhibits a linear time complexity the factor of which is dependent on ambiguity rates of the input sentence. The active chart parser runs into exponential time complexity whenever it encounters extragrammatical or ungrammatical input, since then it conducts an exhaustive search of the entire parse space. The loss of structural descriptions due to the parser's incompleteness amounts to 10% compared with the complete, though intractable parser [5].

2. **Text Parsing.** While with respect to resolution capacity (effectiveness) no significant differences could be determined, the functional centering model we propose outperforms the best-known centering algorithms by a rate of 50% with respect to a measure of computation costs which considers "cheap" and "expensive" transitional moves between utterances to assess a text's coherence. Hence, the procedure we propose is more efficient [17].

3. **Semantic Interpretation.** Our group has been pioneering work on the empirical evaluation of meaning representations. In particular, we determined the quality and coverage of semantic interpretation for randomly sampled texts in the two domains we consider. While recall was rather low (57% for MED, 31% for IT), precision was very high (97% and 94%, respectively) [14].

4. **"Heavy" Semantics.** We have also run evaluations for particularly intricate semantic phenomena such as the resolution of metonymies, a variant of figurative language, where we have determined a gain in effectiveness that amounts to 16% compared with the best procedures known so far [11], or comparatives and evaluative assertions, where gains in effectiveness were almost trebled [16].

Evaluating a text knowledge base generator, nevertheless, poses tremendous methodological problems. The main reason being that a gold standard for comparison — what constitutes a canonical interpretation of the content of a text? — is hard to establish, even for expository texts. Even when we assume such a consensus as given, a follow-up problem is constituted by the lack of a significant amount of annotated text knowledge bases on which comparisons might be run.

5   Related Work

The systems most similar to SYNDIKATE's design are geared towards information extraction. In order to have running prototypes quickly available (most notably within the MUC framework [1]), stripped down versions of frame systems providing knowledge templates and finite-state parsers were supplied for shallow analysis and tuned for robustness (e.g., FASTUS [3]). These systems are limited in several ways. They are bounded by an a priori fixed number of domain knowledge frames (i.e., they have no concept learning facilities), they provide no inferencing capabilities which allow reasoning about the template fillers (hence, their understanding depth is low), and their recognition and resolution capabilities concerning textual phenomena are highly constrained, if available at all.

The depth of understanding we provide comes closest to systems such as SCISOR [13] or PUNDIT/KERNEL [12], but SYNDIKATE's concept learning device has no counterpart there. Text understanders as learners are even rarer but, e.g., systems such as SNOWY [4] or WRAP-UP [15] provide no sophisticated handling of text phenomena as we do and, also, have no built-in potential for robust analysis. So, to the best of our knowledge the spectrum of methodologies offered by SYNDIKATE is currently not matched by any other published system.

6   Conclusions

We have introduced SYNDIKATE, a system for automatically acquiring knowledge from real-world expository texts. The system has a robust parsing machinery, incrementally augments its ontological knowledge base, and has a rich repertoire of techniques to deal with textual phenomena. We have focused in this paper on the latter feature in order to demonstrate how vital the proper resolution of referential relationships is for providing usable text knowledge bases.

Two lessons can be learnt from its current development stage. Knowledge-based text understanders can only compete with their knowledge-poorer alternatives, when they provide a reasonable strategy for escaping from the knowledge acquisition bottleneck. We have argued that an online *concept learner* seems a worthwhile approach. Another major key to success was to subscribe to an *object-oriented* way of system design and implementation. In particular, inheritance mechanisms both at the level of grammar and ontology specification have helped to keep it a manageable and extendible system.

Acknowledgment M. Romacker is supported by a grant from DFG (Ha 2097/5-1)

References

1. *MUC-6 – Proceedings of the 6th Message Understanding Conference.* Columbia, Maryland, November 6-8, 1995.
2. *Unified Medical Language System.* Bethesda: National Library of Medicine, 1998.
3. Douglas E. Appelt, Jerry R. Hobbs, John Bear, David Israel, and Mabry Tyson. FASTUS: a finite-state processor for information extraction from real-world text. In *IJCAI'93 – Proceedings of the 13th International Joint Conference on Artificial Intelligence*, pages 1172–1178. Chambery, France, August 28 - Sept. 3, 1993.
4. Fernando Gomez and Carlos Segami. The recognition and classification of concepts in understanding scientific texts. *Journal of Experimental and Theoretical Artificial Intelligence*, 1(1):51–77, 1989.
5. Udo Hahn, Peter Neuhaus, and Norbert Bröker. Message-passing protocols for real-world parsing: an object-oriented model and its preliminary evaluation. In *Proceedings of the 5th International Workshop on Parsing Technologies – IWPT'97*, pages 101–112. M.I.T., Boston, Mass., September 17-20, 1997.
6. Udo Hahn, Martin Romacker, and Stefan Schulz. How knowledge drives understanding – matching medical ontologies with the needs of medical language processing. *Artificial Intelligence in Medicine*, 15(1):25–51, 1999.
7. Udo Hahn, Susanne Schacht, and Norbert Bröker. Concurrent, object-oriented natural language parsing: the PARSETALK model. *International Journal of Human-Computer Studies*, 41(1/2):179–222, 1994.
8. Udo Hahn and Klemens Schnattinger. Towards text knowledge engineering. In *AAAI'98 – Proceedings of the 15th National Conference on Artificial Intelligence*, pages 524–531. Madison, Wisconsin, July 26-30, 1998.
9. Udo Hahn, Stefan Schulz, and Martin Romacker. Partonomic reasoning as taxonomic reasoning in medicine. In *AAAI'99 – Proceedings of the 16th National Conference on Artificial Intelligence*. Orlando, Florida, July 18-22, 1999.
10. Donna Harman, editor. *Proceedings of the 4th Text REtrieval Conference – TREC-4.* Arlington, VA, November 1-3, 1996.
11. Katja Markert and Udo Hahn. On the interaction of metonymies and anaphora. In *IJCAI'97 – Proceedings 15th International Joint Conference on Artificial Intelligence*, pages 1010–1015. Nagoya, Japan, August 23-29, 1997.
12. Martha S. Palmer, Rebecca J. Passonneau, Carl Weir, and Tim Finin. The KERNEL text understanding system. *Artificial Intelligence*, 63(1/2):17–68, 1993.
13. Lisa F. Rau, Paul S. Jacobs, and Uri Zernik. Information extraction and text summarization using linguistic knowledge acquisition. *Information Processing & Management*, 25(4):419–428, 1989.
14. Martin Romacker, Katja Markert, and Udo Hahn. Lean semantic interpretation. In *IJCAI'99 – Proceedings of the 16th International Joint Conference on Artificial Intelligence*. Stockholm, Sweden, August 1-6, 1999.
15. Stephen Soderland and W. Lehnert. Wrap-up: a trainable discourse module for information extraction. *Journal of Artificial Intelligence Research*, 2:131–158, 1994.
16. Steffen Staab and Udo Hahn. "Tall", "good", "high" – compared to what? In *IJCAI'97 – Proceedings of the 15th International Joint Conference on Artificial Intelligence*, pages 996–1001. Nagoya, Japan, August 23-29, 1997.
17. Michael Strube and Udo Hahn. Functional centering. In *ACL'96 – Proceedings of the 34th Annual Meeting of the Association for Computational Linguistics*, pages 270–277. Santa Cruz, Cal., U.S.A., 24-27 June, 1996.
18. William A. Woods and James G. Schmolze. The KL-ONE family. *Computers & Mathematics with Applications*, 23(2/5):133–177, 1992.

Knowledge Discovery
with the Associative Memory Modell Neunet

Josef Küng, Hagmüller Sylvia, Hagmüller Horst

Institute for Applied Knowledge Processing (FAW), University of Linz, Altenberger Str. 69
A-4040 Linz, Austria
e-mail:jkueng@faw.uni-linz.ac.at

Abstract. At the University of Linz a remarkable associative memory model has been developed. A neural network analogous self learning system with the capability of parallel and serial association. But, for data mining tasks it has one shortcoming. It can not reproduce how often it has seen a part of a pattern in its past – it is not able to compute frequencies. In this contribution we introduce an extension of the model with which frequencies, support and confidence are feasible. Besides, all advantages of the model could be retained. Short examples and a comparison with a common data mining tool complete the paper.

1.   Introduction

In the last few years data mining and knowledge discovery have become research topics which promise to be adequate for semi-automatic knowledge acquisition in real world databases. The main goal of the knowledge discovery process is to find interesting patterns or rules which have been unknown so far. But, in spite of the tremendous growth there is still much to explore in this research area. Besides, a good overview of knowledge discovery process and methodology can be found in [6] [7].

One of the big challenges is to find out how artificial intelligence and neuronal networks can be used for knowledge discovery and data mining. It is the universal formulation of neuronal networks which predestine them for solving problems if there is no exact knowledge about the process model. Also if there is no mathematical process model or only small sample surveys are given, neuronal networks are able to resolve and to find very good solutions for such problems [10].

However, for using statistical methods exact knowledge about the data and their dependencies are necessary. Using conventional techniques in non-linear processes always needs a priori assumptions which are sometimes hard to find and moreover, require time, work and last but not least money. In this paper we want to introduce, how the neuronal network analogous associative memory model Neunet which has been developed at the Johannes Kepler University of Linz can be used to find solutions for data mining problems.

The model Neunet (Neural Network) was invented in the late seventies by Reichl [11] [12]. The basic idea was to develop simple neuronal units which do not exactly correspond to a biological neuron with all its complicated aspects. But, the network in its whole still shows a behaviour similar to the biological model. Like all neural networks its consists of nodes (the processing units) and connections between the nodes. Unlike other models it does not make use of weights of connections except for the binary information whether there exists a connection between two units or not.

One of the most important representative of the group of Neunet networks is a version called 'Neunet-3'. Neunet-3 is a self learning system. This means that it gathers perceptions from its environment and constructs the knowledge autonomously. It is also able to reproduce the whole perception after a presentation of any partial data from the original information. A special version – Neunet-3S – allows the perception and reproduction of series of patterns. In that case first a parallel association completes a given pattern and when a sequence of such patterns identifies a former learned series the following outputs are along this series. Another version – Fuzzy Neunet – processes the charges which are normally limited to the values –1, 0 and +1 as probabilities with the result that also similar patterns are identified by the network [2].

This basic example demonstrates the behaviour of a standard Neunet-3-network, which has been taught the digits zero to nine:

input   output

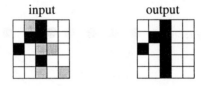

Fig. 1. Example for auto association

After presenting an incomplete pattern to Neunet-3 – grey pixels mean, that its value (its colour) is unknown – it is able to relate the input-pattern to the right output-pattern. In the case of definite input information it is even able to complete inputs with only one known pixel. If the input pattern can be matched to several original patterns, the output is the average of all patterns including this data which means the information is completed as far as possible.

Dale assumed that all artificial and self learning systems can be used for discovering new knowledge: „Almost any technique developed for machine learning can be applied to data mining as well." [4]. So also we faced the challenge to modify Neunet-3 to an extent that knowledge discovery can be done comparable to common systems.

One of the most important data mining techniques to gain new knowledge and draw useful conclusions is the association technique. Associations are used to discover dependant relations between attributes. So you can find out which attribute values seem to be in relation to other attribute values. For instance, one specific method of discovering association rules can be found in [1].

As we already mentioned, Neunet-3 has this special ability to associate attribute dependencies. It returns the original patterns after presenting partial information if it is unambiguous. If not, it completes it as far as possible. Examining the model behaviour one can realise that the major problem of Neunet-3 is its exactness because it only discovers dependencies with a probability of 100 percent. It is not able to complete a pattern with its most probable values. But, it seems to be very reasonable to assume that the Neunet-3 model contains more information in its structure as it in fact exposes. In order to explore this undiscovered information the structure of Neunet-3 will be shown in the following section.

2. The Model Neunet-3

In the beginning Neunet-3 always consists of one single level of nodes. This nodes are called receptors because they are the interface from and to the environment. From the receptors information is flowing into the network where it is stored according to the rules of Reichl. During the storage of new information internal units (nodes and aggregates) are created. So the network is growing with each new pattern. It is important to know that patterns or parts of patterns that are already learned are not stored redundantly.

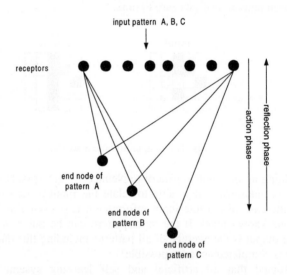

Fig. 2. Pyramidal structure of NEUNET-3

In the first phase, the action phase, the information flows in form of charges from the receptors into the net where it interacts with the experience of the network represented as one stamp in each unit. In the second phase, called the reflection phase, charges come back to the receptors. After some oscillations - a sequence of a perception and reflection phase is called an oscillation - the network comes into a solid state and the output can be seen at the receptors. The rules for the interaction of charges in the units are derived from the trivalent NOR.

When the network is learning a new pattern a new pyramid inside the network will be constructed which can be seen as an exactly representation the input pattern. The figure above shows that the pyramids are overlapping, which means that already known pattern parts are not stored redundantly. Only new aspects result in an extension of the network. Presenting a well known pattern to the network will not expand it, because the corresponding pyramid already exists.

Important components of a Neunet-3 net are the end-nodes. Each information pyramid has one such node. When in such a node a positive charge will be implanted and the network starts with a reflection phase the corresponding pattern will be reproduced after some oscillations. For each learned pattern there is one such end-node which can be seen as the most important representative of this pattern. This property first was introduced by Lehner [9]. Further examinations about the pyramidal structure can be found in [14]. For the next steps we assume the input pattern are not typical images. They shall represent rules.

	A	B	C	D
Pattern 1:	+	-	+	-
Pattern 2:	+	-	-	-
Pattern 3:	-	-	-	-
Pattern 4:	+	+	+	+
Input:	+	-	?	?
Output:	+	-	?	-

Fig. 3. Table showing a first example using rules as input patterns

After giving a partial rule as an input, e.g. the rule $a \wedge \neg b = 1$, Neunet-3 is able to find out all concerned rules, which include this. In the example above rule 1 and 2 are including $a \wedge \neg b = 1$. Furthermore the net is constructing a logical combination with all rules, which can be used again to gain new information. In our example it returns the logical consequence, that, if $a \wedge \neg b = 1 \Rightarrow d = -1$.

$$(\text{rule1} \wedge \text{rule2}) = (a \wedge \neg b \wedge c \wedge \neg d) \wedge (a \wedge \neg b \wedge \neg c \wedge \neg d) = (a \wedge \neg b \wedge \neg d) \qquad (1)$$

If an input-pattern can not be definitely assigned to a well known pattern, the network returns the average of all possible answers. This corresponds to a conjunction of all patterns including the input pattern. With the following example we can realize the problem why the standard Neunet-3 model can be used only to a limited degree as a data mining technique.

	A	B	C	D	E	F
Pattern 1:	+	-	+	-	+	-
pattern 2:	+	-	-	-	+	-
pattern 3:	+	-	-	-	+	+
pattern 4:	+	-	+	+	+	-
pattern 5:	-	-	-	-	-	-
pattern 6:	+	+	+	+	-	+
input:	+	?	?	?	?	?
result:	+	?	?	?	?	?

Fig. 4. Table showing a second example using rules as input patterns

Asking the question ‚A' the network answers only with unknown charges, which results from the conjunction of the patterns 1,2,3,4 and 6. It does not realise that if A has the value +1, variable B in four of five cases (80%) has the value –1. In order to eliminate this disadvantage and to make Neunet-3 usable for data mining the rules and behaviour of the standard algorithm have to be modified.

3. Improving Neunet-3 for calculation frequency, support and confidence

Is the knowledge about dependencies and frequencies implicit included in the Neunet-3 architecture and can questions like the following be asked to the net?

- *'Frequency'*: How often is 'A' included in all patterns?
- *'Frequency on condition of...'*: How often is 'A' included in patterns which also include 'C'?
- *,Relative frequency'* or *,support'*: How is the percentage of the occurrence of ,A'?
- *,Relative frequency on condition of..'* or *,Confidence'*: If 'A' occurs, how is the probability of an occurrence of 'C','D' or 'E'?

Viewing the structure of a Neunet-3 net the overlaps at the base of the information pyramids can be seen. They are the beginning of a pattern which are partial identical with other ones. Therefore, no expansion of the network took place. The charges flew through existing lines. But, at a certain point in the action phase a contradiction happened and new information had to be learned. As a consequence a new information pyramid arose. Does a Neunet-3 contain the frequency of the occurrence of an attribute? In fact the intersections of the information pyramids are relevant for frequency calculations.

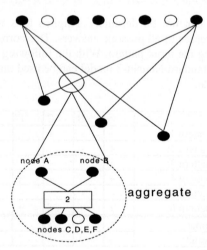

Fig. 5. Information pyramids of Neunet-3

A division into an own pyramid takes place, when a contradiction to already known patterns occurs. At these intersection aggregates at least one of the 'D' or 'E' nodes had executed its memory function. Exactly these aggregates, the so-called contradiction aggregates, are interesting for the frequency calculation. A detailed description of the structure of Neunet-3 can be found in [2]. For a better understanding a short excerpt from the algorithm is listed below. The rules for the reflection phase are:

$$l(A) = \text{sign}(\max(l(C), l(D)) - \max(l(E), l(F)))$$ (2)

$$l(B) = \text{sign}(\max(l(C), l(E)) - \max(l(D), l(F)))$$

In order to bring the result pattern to the receptors in the reflection phase the charges flow through the aggregates in reverse order. From the charges in the C,D,E,F-nodes the charges for the A and B-nodes are calculated according to the rules of (2). To calculate the frequency of the occurrence of all variables in respect to a certain input pattern this rule has to be modified as follows:

$$l(A) = l(C) + l(D) + 1$$ (3)

$$l(B) = l(C) + l(E) + 1$$

From now on charges do not represent a black or white point (or a true or false value) in the receptor field when the net comes into a stable state after oscillating. They represent the frequency of that specific point. Therefore the domain of charges is now not further limited to the values $+1$, 0 and -1 according to the tree valued logic. A charge value can be any positive number.

After this minor change of the processing rules Neunet-3 now can be used for the data mining technique association. The network is able to calculate absolute and relative frequencies of attributes. Furthermore it can compute support and confidence of all other attributes concerning a certain condition.

4. Examples

In this section two examples should demonstrate that the proposed extension of Neunet-3 allows the usage of this associative memory model for data mining tasks. The results will be compared with the output of a standard data mining tool.

Learning of three rules with Neunet-3

Rules		Patterns			
		a	b	c	d
1:	$a \wedge \neg b \wedge c \wedge \neg d = 1$	+	-	+	-
2:	$a \wedge \neg b \wedge c \wedge d = 1$	+	-	+	+
3:	$\neg a \wedge b \wedge c \wedge \neg d = 1$	-	+	+	-

Fig. 6. Rule-to-pattern transformation

The first example is very simple to show both, the input/output behaviour and the flow of the charges in the network itself. For this demonstration three rules are transformed to patterns and given the network as input (see Fig. 6). After these three patterns were presented to the network it now consists of 8 aggregates and 40 nodes. Starting the new algorithm with an empty pattern which means setting all charges to zero can be seen as the following DMQL[1]-query:

```
mine characteristics as "frequency calculation by
Neunet-3"
analyse count, percentage(count)
with respect to a, b, c, d.
```

After the first oscillation (execution of action- and reflection phase) the network has the structure shown in the figure below and returns the following values[2]:

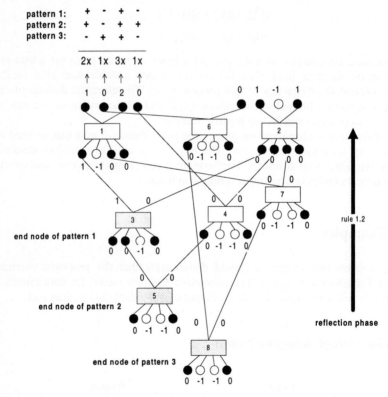

Fig. 7. Example 1 - Structure and charges of a Neunet-3 after the first reflection phase according to rule (**3**)

Using the new formula in the reflection phase the network in fact returns the number of occurrences of each pixel. We now get probable values of the so far unknown

[1] Datamining Query Language [5]
[2] All examples were made with the simulator Simnet [8],[3]

pixels A,B and E. In over 66 percent of all cases, in two of three patterns, variable A had the value of +1. Only once B and E had the value +1 and in 100 percent of all inputs C had a positive charge

Pixel values of result pattern	Count	Relative frequency
+1.00 +0.00 +2.00 +0.00	+2.00 +1.00 +3.00 +1.00	+0.67 +0.33 +1.00 +0.33

Fig. 8. Example 1 - Output of Neunet-3

Sports example

In the following example 18 persons where asked for their favourite sports. They had the choice between swimming, surfing, skateboarding, volleyball, boxing, parasailing and wandering. The persons were divided in three age-groups ([1..25],]25..60[,[60..100]) and according to their sex. We now want to explore, which sports are preferred by people under the age of 25. The corresponding DMQL-query has the following structure:

```
mine associations as "association by Neunet-3"
with respect to swimming,surfing,skateboarding,
        volleyball,boxing,parasailing,wandering,
        male, female
from example XX
where `< 25 years' = +1
set minimum support   0%
set minimum confidence 0 %
```

To get the desired information the answers of the spot check are presented to the network. The information has to be transformed into patterns. Besides, the receptor field has an invisible extension which is used during learning to distinguish same answers from different people.

< 25	**Swimming**	**surfing**
>25 u. <60	**Skateboarding**	**volleyball**
> 60	**Boxing**	**parasailing**
male	**Wandering**	
female		

Fig. 9. Pattern model for sports example

Now the pattern '<25?' is presented to the network. This means that the pixel '<25' is set to 1 and all other to 0 (unknown, in order to be calculated by the network). In the action phase the algorithm works according to the standard rules and in the reflection phase the new rules are applied for calculating the frequencies.

The following figure shows the input and output of the network without pre- and postprocessing.

input		Output
1 0 0		+4.00 **+4.00** **+1.00**
0 0 0	=>	-1.00 **+1.00** **+0.00**
0 0 0	"Show	-1.00 **+0.00** **-1.00**
0 0 0	Freq."	+2.00 **-1.00** -1.00
0 0 0		+1.00 -1.00 -1.00
pattern "<25?"		

Fig. 10. Asking the question "<25"

This output now can be transformed into the tables below.

Result			Support (%)			Confidence (%)		
5	5	2	29.41	**29.41**	**11.76**	100.00	**100.00**	**40.00**
0	2	1	0.00	**11.76**	5.88	0.00	**40.00**	20.00
0	1	0	0.00	**5.88**	**0.00**	0.00	**20.00**	**0.00**
3	0		17.65	**0.00**		60.00	**0.00**	
2			11.76			40.00		

Fig. 11. Example 2 - Result

So the system returns for the question of the preferred sports of persons under the age of 25 the following dependencies. It is the same result as calculated by the data mining tool "DBMiner".

```
,< 25 years'(+1) => ,swimming'(+1) [s=29.41%; c=100%]
,< 25 years'(+1) => ,surfing'(+1) [s=11.76%; c=40%]
,< 25 years'(+1) => ,boxing'(+1) [s=5.88%; c=20%]
,< 25 years'(+1) => ,volleyball'(+1) [s=5.88%; c=20%]
```

5. Conclusion

We introduced a new methodology for knowledge discovery based on the neural network analogous associative memory model Neunet-3. After we showed, that Neunet-3 is able to store rules within its structure and to find dependencies between attributes which correlate with a possibility of 100 percent we introduced a minimal change of the standard Neunet-3 model for calculating frequency, confidence and support. The input/output behaviour corresponds with the common data mining tool "DBMiner".

This result is notable because of following reasons. First, Neunet is in its standard model already remarkable. It is a self learning auto associative system basing only on the three valued NOR-function. There is no application specific semantic background information and therefore, it can be used as a general purpose system. Now it can be also applied with all its advantages for some data mining tasks.

Second, this successful modification of the standard Neunet-3 model is the basis of doing the same with the model 'Fuzzy-Neunet' - a promising approach for automatic knowledge acquisition.

References

1. R. Agrawal, et al.: Fast discovery of association rules. In: Agrawal, H.Mannila, R.Srikant, H.Toivonnen, I. Verkamo (eds.): Advances in Knowledge Discovery and Data Mining, AAAI Press / The MIT Press, 1996 pp. 307-328
2. P. Andlinger: Fuzzy Neunet. Dissertation, Universität Linz 1992
3. S. Burgholzer: Entwurf und Realisierung einer allgemeinen Experimentierumgebung für Neuronale Netze und Implementierung der neuronalen Netze Fuzzy Neunet, Fuzzy Neunet S und Error Backpropagation. Diploma Thesis, Universität Linz 1996
4. L. Dale, T. Bench-Capon: A Datamining Tool for Producing Characteristic Classifications in Legal Domain. In: A. Hameurlain, A Min Tjoa (eds.): Database and Expert Systems Application, Springer 1997, pp.186-191
5. DBMiner E1.0 (Beta), User Manual For Windows NT, Data Mining Research Group, Intelligent Database Systems Research Laboratory, School of Computing Science, Simon Fraser University, British Columbia, Canada V5A 1S6
6. U.M. Fayyad, G. Piatetsky-Shapiro, P. Smyth und R. Uthurusamy: The KDD process for extracting useful knowledge from volumes of data. Communications of the ACM, November 1996, Vol. 39, No. 11. pp. 27-34
7. U.M. Fayyad et al.: From Datamining to Knowledge Discovery: An overview. In: U.M. Fayyad, G. Piatetsky-Shapiro, P. Smyth und R. Uthurusamy (eds.): Advances in Knowledge Discovery and Data Mining", AAAI Press / The MIT Press, 1996. pp. 1-34
8. H. Hagmüller: Entwurf und Implementierung einer Simulationsumgebung für neuronennetzanaloge Modelle und Implementierung der neuronalen Netze Neunet 3, Neunet 3S und Perzeptron. Diploma Thesis, Universität Linz 1996
9. F. Lehner: Erkennen von Ähnlichkeiten im System Neunet. Diploma Thesis, Universität Linz 1984
10. H. Lu, R. Setiono, H. Liu: Effective Data Mining Using Neural Networks. IEEE Transactions on Knowledge and Data Engineering, Vol. 8, No. 6, December 1996 pp.957-961
11. E.R. Reichl: Lernende Systeme. Informatikberichte, Universität Linz 1975
12. E.R.Reichl: Neuronennetz-ähnliche Strukturen als Assoziativspeicher. Applied Computer Science, Bd.8: Datenstrukturen, Graphen, Algorithmen 1978
13. E.R.Reichl: Computermodelle zum menschlichen Gedächtnis. Schriftenreihe der Österreichischen Computergesellschaft, Bd.15: Informatik und Psychologie, 1982
14. F.D.Valach: Parallelen in Struktur und Eigenschaften zwischen einem Assoziativspeichermodell und dem Zentralnervensystem. Dissertation, Universität Linz 1984
15. Y.Show-Jane, A.L.P.Chen: An Efficient Datamining Technique for Discovery Interesting Association Rules. In: A. Hameurlain, A Min Tjoa (eds.): Database and Expert Systems Application, Springer 1997, pp. 664-669

Tracking Mobile Users Utilizing Their Frequently Visited Locations

Chiang Lee *   Chih-Horng Ke   Chao-Chun Chen

Abstract

In wireless computing environment, the explosive growth of demand in communication bandwidth requires new schemes to effectively and efficiently locate users. The Basic HLR/VLR locating scheme does not exploit the fact that many mobile users' moving patterns are likely to be known. In this paper, we propose one locating scheme, the *Frequently Visited Locations First (FVLF)* scheme, to efficiently locate a mobile user. This scheme avoids the high cost of querying the callee's HLR. The cost model of the proposed scheme is derived and the optimal number of prestored RAs is also found.

1 Introduction

In a personal communication serviecs (PCS) network system as shown in Figure 1, geographical region is divided into *cells*, each of which is a radio port coverage area. Each cell is served by one *base station*. Each base station is connected to the PCS network through wire-line links, while it communicates with mobile users within its territory via wireless channels. A *registration area* (RA) is composed of a group of adjacent cells, forming a contiguous geographical region. In a *Common Channel Signaling* (CCS) network using the *Signaling System No. 7* (SS7) protocols [Mod90], each RA is in turn connected via wire-line network to and served by an end-office switch named the *Service Switching Point* (SSP). For simplicity, we assume that the *Mobile Switching Center* (MSC) is collocated with the SSP and a distinct *Visitor Location Register* (VLR) database is associated with each MSC. A number of SSPs of distinct RAs are again connected to a Local Signaling Transfer Point (LSTP), which performs message routing and other SS7 functions, and a number of LSTPs are managed by a Remote STP (RSTP), forming a hierarchy of switching and transferring points. On top of the RSTP is a *Service Control Point* (SCP) that is assumed to contain a *Home Location Register* (HLR).

These HLR and VLR databases are used to store the *user profile information*, including access rights, authentication parameters, user's location, etc. The

---

*Institute of Information Engineering, National Cheng-Kung University, Tainan, Taiwan, R.O.C. leec@dblab.iie.ncku.edu.tw,

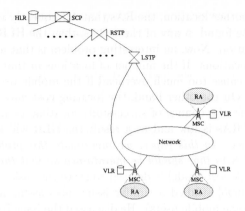

Figure 1: A wireless communication network architecture.

authenticated users' profiles are stored in the HLR. When a user moves out of the region maintained by his HLR, some kind of locating mechanism is needed to find the mobile user. IS-41 [Eia91] in the United States and GSM [Mou92] in Europe are two examples of a standard way of locating a mobile user while he/she travels. The idea of this scheme, also referred to as the *Basic HLR/VLR scheme*, is as follows. When a user travels to a new RA, his HLR is updated and an entry in the VLR database of his new location is created for him. When a call is placed to locate this traveller, the caller's MSC first checks the local VLR for the callee's profile. If the VLR doesn't contain the callee's profile, a message goes to the callee's HLR to ask for the callee's location. The callee's HLR verifies the callee's VLR, and returns it to the MSC which then initiates the connection between the callee and the caller.

However, a major drawback of this scheme is that even though the callee may be physically very close to the caller, the request is still sent across possibly a long distance to the callee's HLR to locate the callee, resulting a high locating cost. Some suggest to alleviate the problem by building a hierarchy of user profile databases [Ana94, Jan96] among the VLRs. A caller's request is first sent to its MSC's local database. If the callee's profile is not found there, then the request is forwarded to the database one level up. The same procedure continues until the callee's location is found. These approaches, however, suffer from another problem that the root or upper nodes become the performance bottleneck when MU's mobility is high.

We propose in this paper a location management strategy which minimizes the time required for locating a mobile user in existing Personal Communications Services (PCS). The idea is as follows. In real world applications, many mobile users have a fixed moving pattern most of the time. For instance, company employee A mostly moves between his home, the building where he is working, and a plant where he participates in a manufacturing project. To locate this type of mobile users, it is useful to keep a list of locations where the user frequently visits. Each of these locations has a corresponding VLR. When A is called by

of HLR and VLR to the hardware of a communication network are simply treated as varying ratios of C_h/C_v in the design of the schemes.

In this section, we present a cost model for deriving the optimal number of prestored RAs. Parameters used in the cost model are summarized in Figure 3. Because of size limitation, the derivation of the equation and the results obtained

Symbol	Meanings
C_{Basic}	The expected cost of the Basic HLR/VLR locating scheme
C_{FVLF}	The expected cost of the FVLF scheme
C_h	The average cost of sending a request from VLR to HLR
C_v	The average cost of sending a request from VLR to another VLR
D_h	The average cost of searching a user profile in an HLR database
D_v	The average cost of searching a user profile in a VLR database
n	The number of a MU's locations that the caller's MSC knows
m	The number of prestored RAs
m_{opt}	The optimal number of prestored RAs
P_i	The probability of finding the callee using the i-th prestored RA in the *PossibleRA* list
π	The total probability that a MSC can locate the MU in n RAs.

Figure 3: Symbols and their meanings.

under various probability distributions are not possibly given here. The reader may refer to [Lee98] for details. We first give the locating cost for the Basic HLR/VLR scheme as follows:

$$C_{Basic} = 4 \cdot C_h + D_h + D_v$$

Then, the expected locating cost using our scheme would be

$$C_{FVLF} = [\sum_{i=1}^{m}(i \cdot P_i)] \cdot (2 \cdot C_v + D_v) + (1 - \sum_{i=1}^{m} P_i) \cdot [m \cdot (2 \cdot C_v + D_v) + (4 \cdot C_h + D_h + D_v)]$$

This is a general formula of locating cost independent of probability distribution. Different optimal length m_{opt} can be found in different probability distributions.

4 Experiments and Results

Experiments were conducted to find the optimal number of prestored RAs. We only present the results obtained under Poisson distribution because it is often used to model human behavior of many aspects. The Poisson distribution has a formula $P_i = e^{-\lambda} \cdot \frac{\lambda^i}{i!}$ for $1 \le i \le n$. Default values of n and π are 10 and 0.8, respectively. λ of the Poisson distribution is set to 2.

4.1 The effect of $\frac{C_h}{C_v}$

Figure 4 shows the benefits obtained for the Poisson distribution. $n = 20$ and $\pi = 0.8$ are the default values used in this experiment. It is seen that a significant benefit is obtained and it rises rapidly with the increase of C_h/C_v. On average, a 10% more benefit than the linear distributions is achieved under the Poisson distribution. In a normal case in which a MU is more likely at several locations than at the others (meeting a Poisson distribution), the location cost becomes dramatically lower than using the Basic HLR/VLR scheme.

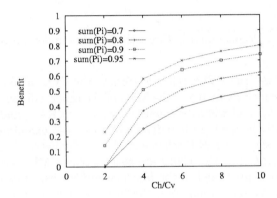

Figure 4: Poisson distribution : the benefit under various $\frac{C_h}{C_v}$.

4.2 The effect of n

Figure 5 shows a dramatic improvement in Poisson distribution. Curves of $C_h/C_v = 4, 6, 8, 10$, respectively, show that the benefit decreases slightly while n increases and then remains a constant for even a rather large n. Curves in this figure indicate that even if C_h/C_v is 2, a notable improvement by using the FVLF scheme is achieved for $n \leq 5$. The improvement increases to about 40% to 80% for higher C_h/C_v.

5 Enhancement – Considering CMR's Effect

In the FVLF scheme, the locating cost is sensitive to the CMR (Call to Mobility Ratio, i.e. C/M) of the callee. When CMR is very high, it may be beneficial not to stickly follow the FVLF scheme. We use an example to illustrate this issue. Assume that the frequently visited locations of MU_i are RA_{i1}, RA_{i2}, RA_{i3}, and RA_{i4}, and the probability of MU_i's being at each of these locations is $P_{i1} > P_{i2} > P_{i3} > P_{i4}$, where P stands for probability. Let the CMR of MU_i be 4 and the calls to MU_i at a certain period of time are shown in Figure 6. Assume that the cost of checking whether a MU is at a prestored list of RAs is 2.

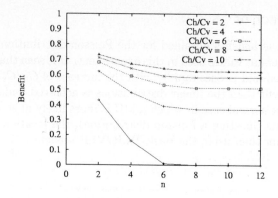

Figure 5: Poisson distribution : the benefits under various n.

When $Call_{i1}$ arrives, the FVLF scheme refers to the FVL table to locate MU_i. Because MU_i is currently at RA_{i4}, the MSC of the caller will fail to locate MU_i using location RA_{i1} and will subsequently try location RA_{i2}, and so on. When MU_i is successfully located, all four RAs will have been examined. Hence, the locating cost of using the FVLF scheme is 4*2=8. Similarly, the locating costs incurred by $Call_{i2}$, $Call_{i3}$, and $Call_{i4}$ are also 8 because MU_i remains at RA_{i4}. If, however, RA_{i4} is promoted to the first place of the list after $Call_{i1}$ is made (even though P_{i4} is lower than P_{i1}), the locating costs of $Call_{i2}$, $Call_{i3}$, and $Call_{i4}$ can all be dropped to 2 because only one probe to the RAs in the list is required.

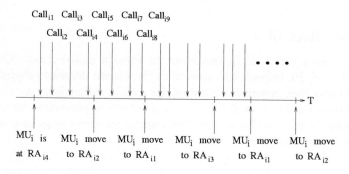

Figure 6: Calls and mobility of MU_i.

Based on this idea, we modified the FVLF scheme and designed a promoted FVLF scheme (denoted as $FVLF_{PROMOTED}$). The $FVLF_{PROMOTED}$ scheme is formally described in the following. In this scheme, we assume that CMR and a threshold θ of each mobile unit can be obtained through analyzing the movement statistical information of the MU, where θ is a CMR below which the FVLF scheme is used and the $FVLF_{PROMOTED}$ version is employed if a MU's CMR is greater than θ.

1. If MU_i is not found in the FVL table, go to step7. Otherwise, do the following.

2. If the list of frequently visited locations of MU_i is empty, go to step 7. Otherwise, denote the list as *PossibleRA$_1$* and copy the list to *PossibleRA$_2$*.

3. Select the first RA, denoted as RA_{if}, in the *PossibleRA$_2$* list.

4. The MSC sends a request to RA_{if} to locate MU_i.

5. If MU_i is not found in RA_{if}, remove RA_{if} from *PossibleRA$_2$* and go to step 3. Otherwise /* MU_i is found in RA_{if} */, the MSC acknowledges to the caller's MSC and establishes the connection.

6. If CMR<= θ, do nothing; /* remain to be FVLF scheme */
   If CMR> θ, move RA_{if} in *PossibleRA$_1$* to the head of the list. Protocol stops.

7. The Basic HLR/VLR scheme is initiated to locate MU_i.

To distinguish this scheme from the FVLF scheme, we hereafter name the FVLF scheme the *pure FVLF scheme* to avoid ambiguity. Experiments were conducted to evaluate this new scheme. The probability of RAs in the prestored list is assumed to follow Poisson distribution in the experiment. $\pi = 0.8$ and $m = 5$. Values of the other parameters are the same as the default values given previously. What we measured is the performance of three schemes, *pure PRO-MOTION, pure FVLF*, and *FVLF$_{PROMOTED}$*. The pure PROMOTION scheme is actually the FVLF$_{PROMOTED}$ scheme without an examination on the CMR value. In other words, the pure PROMOTION always promotes the current RA to the front of a RA list no matter what value of CMR is. The percentage of improvement of the pure PROMOTION scheme and the FVLF$_{PROMOTED}$ scheme over the pure FVLF scheme is measured. The difference of the schemes is the search order of prestored RAs. *In order to understand the effect of search in different orders, we ignore the cost incurred by the situation when a MU is not at any of the prestored RAs.* Figure 7 shows the result under a Poisson distribution. Under the given parameter settings, the threshold θ occurs at 1.6. Below this θ, FVLF$_{PROMOTED}$ is as good as the pure FVLF scheme. Above θ, FVLF$_{PROMOTED}$ is much better. When CMR is as high as 10, the savings of this new scheme can be up to 40% (= 100% − 60%).

6 Conclusions and Future work

Two classes of databases HLR and VLR are often utilized to maintain user location information in a wireless computing system. The Basic HLR/VLR scheme that always sends a request to the callee's HLR has been demonstrated inefficient in locating a callee. As many mobile users have more or less a fixed moving pattern, we propose to utilize this information in locating a callee. A

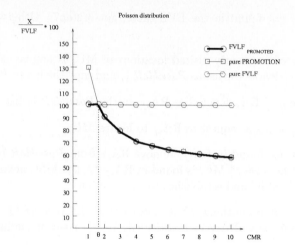

Figure 7: Improvement of the FVLF$_{\text{PROMOTED}}$ scheme versus the others under a Poisson distribution.

scheme based on this concept was proposed and we have demonstrated that under normal conditions this new scheme can provide a significantly better performance than the Basic HLR/VLR scheme. Overall, our scheme provides a way to minimize the cost of locating a callee, while the popular Forwarding Pointers scheme is mainly to reduce the update cost. These two schemes (the proposed scheme and the Forwarding Pointers scheme) can be used together in a system to minimize the total cost (=locating cost + update cost) so as to optimize system performance.

References

[Ana94] V. Anantharam, M.L. Hong, U. Madhow, and V.K. Wei, "Optimization of a database hierarchy for mobility tracking in a personal communications network", *An International Journal of Performance Evaluation*, 1994, pp. 287-300.

[Bar93] Ammotz Bar-Noy and Ilan Kessler, "Tracking Mobile Users in Wireless Communications Networks," *IEEE Transactions on Information Theory*, Vol. 39, No. 6, November 1993, pp. 1877-1886.

[Che97] Ing-Ray Chen, Tsong-Min Chen, and Chiang Lee, "Performance characterization of Forwarding Strategies in Personal Communication Systems", *To appear in IEEE International Computer Software and Applications Conference(COMPSAC'97)*, Washington D.C., 1997.

[Eia91] EIA/TIA IS-41.3, *Cellular Radio telecommunications Intersystem Operations*, Technical Report (RevisionB), July 1991.

[Imi94] T. Imielinski and B. R. Badrinath, "Mobile Wireless Computing : Challenges in Data Management", *Communications of the ACM*, Vol. 37, No. 10, October 1994.

[Jai94] Ravi Jain, Yi-Bing Lin, Charles Lo, and Seshadri Mohan, "A Caching Strategy to Reduce Network Impacts of PCS," *IEEE Journal on Selected Areas in Communications*, Vol. 12, No. 8, October 1994, pp. 1434-1444.

[Jai95] Ravi Jain, Y.B. Lin, C. Lo, and S. Mohan, "A Forwarding Strategy to Reduce Network Impacts of PCS", *14th Annual Joint Conference of the IEEE Computer and Communications Societies, (IEEE INFOCOM'95)*, 1995, pp. 481-489.

[Jan96] Jan Jannink, Derek Lam, Narayanan Shivakumar, Jennifer Widom, and Donald C. Cox, "Efficient and Flexible Location Management Techniques for Wireless Communication Systems," *Second ACM International Conference on Mobile Computing and Networking (MOBICOM '96)*, White Plains, New York, November 1996.

[Lee98] Chiang Lee, Chih-Horng Ke, and Chao-Chun Chen,"Tracking Mobile Users Utilizing Their Frequently Visited Locations," *Technical Report 607-88*, Institute of Information Engineering, National Cheng-Kung University, Taiwan, 1998.

[Mod90] A. R. Modaressi and R. A. Skoog, "Signaling System No. 7: A Tutorial," IEEE Communication Magazine, July 1990, pp. 19-35.

[Mou92] M. Mouly and M.-B Pautet, *The GSM System for Mobile Communications*, Palaiseau, France, 1992.

[Tab95] Sami Tabbane, "An Alternative Strategy for Location Tracking" *IEEE Journal on Selected Areas in Communications*, Vol. 13, No. 5, June 1995, pp. 880-892.

VPSF: A Parallel Signature File Technique Using Vertical Partitioning and Extendable Hashing

Jeong-Ki Kim[1] and Jae-Woo Chang[2]

[1] Real-time Computing Dept., ETRI, Yusong P.O. Box 106, Taejon 305-600, Korea,
jkk@etri.re.kr
[2] Faculty of Electronic and Information Engineering, Chonbuk National University,
Chonju, Chonbuk 560-756, Korea
jwchang@dblab.chonbuk.ac.kr

Abstract. In this paper, we propose a Vertically-partitioned Parallel Signature File (VPSF) method which can partition a signature file vertically. Our VPSF method uses an extendable hashing technique for dynamic environment and uses a frame-sliced signature file technique for efficient retrieval. Our VPSF method also can eliminate the data skew and the execution skew by allocating each frame to a processing node. To prove the efficiency of our VPSF method, we compare its performance with those of the conventional parallel signature file methods, i.e., HPSF and HF, in terms of retrieval time, storage overhead, and insertion time. The experiment runs on several distributions with normal, half, and double standard deviations of the real data. The result shows that our VPSF achieves about 40% better retrieval performance than the HF in all cases. In addition, we show that our VPSF gains about 20~50% improvement in retrieval time, compared with the HF and HPSF on record sets with the half deviation. As a result, our VPSF generally outperforms on retrieval performance when the records of a database are uniform in size.

1 Introduction

As the usage of computer systems is widespread, data management and retrieval has been a major field of computer systems for a long time. This is evident from the rapid development and widespread use of database management systems (DBMS). However, the conventional DBMS has mainly developed to process formatted data. The limitation has hindered the DBMS from dealing with new applications that have a large amount of unformatted multimedia data. Such applications include medical information systems, office information systems, CAD/CAM systems, VOD(video-on-demand) systems, and a variety of multimedia applications[1]. To deal with them, a *signature file method* has been proposed so that it may handle documents (or records) containing multimedia data[2, 3]. The signature file method has been widely advocated as an efficient index scheme to handle applications demanding a large amount of unformatted data as well as formatted data[4]. Here, the *document* is a record or a logical block of the unformatted data.

In order to improve the signature file methods, we can attempt to make a new scheme using the parallel processing architecture, i.e., *a parallel signature file method*. The signature file methods are well suited to the concept of parallelism introduced with the development of a massively parallel machine architecture. Implementing an efficient parallel signature file should obtain real performance gains[5]. For this, the design should avoid not only *data skew* for good data placement, but also *execution skew* for good data retrieval. The data skew means that much more data is placed in one partition than in the others. The execution skew means that execution time in one partition is much higher than in the others.

To overcome the problem, we, in this paper, propose a new parallel signature file method based on an extendable hashing technique and a frame-sliced signature file: *Vertically-partitioned Parallel Signature File* (VPSF) method. According to extendable hashing technique, our new method is a dynamic organization; and based on the frame slicing technique, we can increase a filtering effect of the signature file.

The rest of this paper is organized as follows. In Section 2, we review conventional parallel signature files. In Section 3, we propose a new parallel signature file, called VPSF. In Section 4, we compare the performance of the VPSF with those of the conventional parallel signature files in terms of retrieval time, insertion time, and storage overhead. Finally, Section 5 draws conclusions.

2 Conventional Parallel Signature Files

In a computer processing environment, the speed of the microprocessor has rapidly improved with the development of computer technology while the performance of secondary storages has only been improving at a modest rate. This tendency has yielded a bottleneck of some applications with high I/O activities, such as database management systems and information retrieval systems. To solve the problem, multiprocessor database computers[6] have been designed. There are basically three different structures of the multiprocessor database computers: Shared Everything(SE), Shared Disk(SD), and Shared Nothing(SN). There has been considerable debate about which structure is the most suitable for a database computer implementation. It is generally agreed that the SN is outstanding for achieving good performance because the problem of a data coherency control does not occur. However, the SN may lead to considerable performance degradation due to a *data skew*. In spite of the data skew problem, the SN is the most popular structure for implementing the conventional parallel signature files. In the SN, a set of the processor, memory, and disk is designated as a *processing node*, which is connected with others by a high speed network.

Many studies on parallel signature files have been attempted for parallel database systems, e.g., CAT[7], PBSSF[8], FSF[9], HF[10], and HPSF[11]. Because the CAT and the PBSSF are only suitable for static environments, their insertion time is quite significant for the dynamic environments. Although the FSF, the HF, and the HPSF are efficient for the dynamic environments, the FSF leads to significantly worse retrieval performance than the HF and HPSF as the number of frames is increased[11]. Meanwhile, the HF and HPSF require to uniformly distribute the signatures among parallel processing nodes for the parallel processing. Their distribution schemes are based on key values of hash functions: a linear hashing for the HF and an extendable hashing for the HPSF. However, their good distribution is successful only when the number of words in the records is nearly uniform. Unfortunately, there is no perfect distribution scheme.

3 Vertically-partitioned Parallel Signature File (VPSF)

When parallel signature files using horizontal parallelism, such as HF and HPSF, retrieve a query signature, they must assign uniformly a set of keys to be searched, i.e., *equivalent keys*, into the processing nodes, Here, we define the equivalent keys as a set of descriptor keys which are potentially matched with a hashing key of a query signature. However, they can neither always gain good distribution of equivalent keys in all cases nor predict the distribution well when signatures have various weights due to the records with different lengths. Thus, they yield the degradation of retrieval performance owing to the data skew and the execution skew. In order to overcome the problem, we propose a *Vertically-partitioned Parallel Signature File* (VPSF) method, which can avoid the distribution problem by partitioning a signature vertically.

3.1 Structure of the VPSF

To design a new architecture suitable for a dynamic environment as well as fast retrieval, we construct the VPSF by combining an extendable hashing technique with a frame-sliced signature file scheme as shown in Fig. 1. In order to eliminate the data and the execution skew in the VPSF, we do not store entire signatures into the processing nodes horizontally, but allocate the frames partitioned from a signature into processing nodes respectively and then process the frames in parallel. Thus, we achieve a small insertion time in the VPSF. However, the VPSF has the drawbacks that it cannot utilize the searching order of frames and it yields communication time between processing nodes in order to synchronize the results of searching during the retrieval.

In the VPSF, one processing node accesses only one frame block of a frame group pointed to by an equivalent key, instead of accessing all the frame group in the HPSF. Here, the frame group is a set of frame blocks where frames of a record signature are separately stored. Therefore, after a processing node searches a frame block for a query frame, it should transfer the retrieval result to the next processing node to reconcile the total retrieval results. Nevertheless, the VPSF can obtain a good retrieval performance in the circumstances where HF and HPSF cannot distribute the equivalent keys uniformly. These circumstances are classified into two cases. The first case is where the number of terms per record forms a normal probability distribution with a low *deviation*. The deviation, denoted as σ, is a measure of how widely scattered the number of terms is from a mean of the distribution. In this situation, record signatures are skewed around the mean and keys of the extendable hashing are split more frequently. The second case is where we have a very large number of records in the database. In this case, it is difficult to distribute the equivalent keys uniformly owing to the many keys created from the extendable hashing. While these two cases degrade the retrieval performance of the horizontal parallel signature files, the VPSF gains the good retrieval performance.

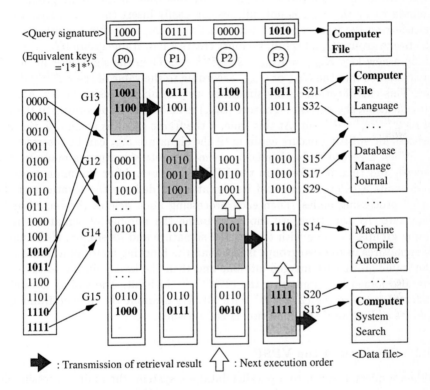

Fig. 1. The VPSF structure

3.2 Insertion and Deletion of the VPSF

In the VPSF, one of the processing nodes is defined as a *main processing node*, which becomes a starting point of parallel processing to operate insertion, deletion, and retrieval. The main processing node may be either one of processing nodes that treat frames in parallel, or a separate processor to play a role of the starting point. When a record is inserted into the VPSF structure, the main processing node makes a signature from the inserted record, and then search the extendable hashing structure to find a location in which the signature will be inserted. In order to store it into the location, we partition the record signature into frames and transfer each of them to a separate processing node, where each frame is stored at the same position of a frame group. That is, all the processing nodes do not make their own extendable hashing structure. There is only one extendable hashing structure in the main processing node.

For example, when we search a location for a record signature (S_{ins}) to be inserted, we first find a key K_{ins} which is a hashing key of the extendable hashing structure in the main processing node. At this time, if the frame group (G_{ins}) pointed to by the K_{ins} is not full, we can easily insert the record signature by transferring the frames partitioned to a processing node. On the other hand, if the frame group (G_{ins}) is full, we must create a new frame group (G_{new}) pointed to by a new key, $K_{new} = K_{ins} + 2^{bitsize(K_{ins})}$. Then the signatures in the G_{ins} are classified into the G_{ins} or G_{new} according to the value of their $2^{bitsize(K_{ins})}$th bit. This classification occurs simultaneously in all processing nodes. After the classification, the current signature (S_{ins}) is also inserted according to the value of its $2^{bitsize(K_{ins})}$th bit. At this time, if the frame group is again full, the above process for splitting occurs again until the signature S_{ins} can be inserted.

When a record to be deleted is given, a delete signature is made from the record, and then it is found in the VPSF structure. After the main processing node finds a delete record and its signature, it delivers the locations of them to all processing nodes. Then each processing node deletes the record and its signature. At this time, we should examine the number of signatures in two frame groups, i.e., one with the deleted signature and its sibling. If the number of signatures in the two groups is less than the blocking factor of a frame group, the frame groups are merged into one and then the keys pointing to the groups are also joined by eliminating the $(2^{keylength-1})$th bit. The sibling keys have a different value in the $(2^{keylength-1})$th bit. We examine the merged frame group and its sibling until the condition is not satisfied.

3.3 Retrieval of the VPSF

When a query is given to a parallel database system, the main processing node extracts a query signature from the given query. Using the query signature, we find a query key from descriptor keys of the extendable hashing. Here, the query key is a seed to obtain the equivalent keys. Dividing the number of equivalent keys by the number of processing nodes, we distribute the same number of equivalent keys into each processing node. When the VPSF retrieves the frame groups pointed to by the equivalent keys, because one processing node accesses only one frame block, we need *searching states* and *matching states* to synchronize the retrieval result of frame groups.

The searching states indicate where the retrieval of the frame groups is performed. Their values are initialized with an index number of the processing node. Thus, the number of searching states is the same as the number of frame groups to be searched. When the number of frame groups is n, the searching states of a processing node, P_i, are defined as:

$$S_{srch}(P_i) = \{S_{FG0}, S_{FG1}, ..., S_{FGn}\} .\tag{1}$$

The matching states inform whether signatures of a frame group are qualified with the query signature or not. Their values are a set of bit string of '0' or '1'. The '0' notifies that a signature of the frame group is not qualified with the query signature, and the '1' notifies that the signature is qualified. When the number of frame groups is n, the matching states of a processing node, P_i, are defined as:

$$S_{mtch}(P_i) = \{STR_0, STR_1, ..., STR_n\} .\tag{2}$$

where the length of the bit string, STR_n, is the same as the number of record signatures in its frame group. The matching states are initialized with a value '1'. If the frame of a record signature is not matched with the frame of a query signature, a bit value of the matching state is changed to '0', and then the record signature including the '0' state is excepted from searching targets. Reversely, if the frame is matched with it, the bit value is originally maintained with '1'.

In order to synchronize the retrieval results of the frame groups, we should transfer the searching states and the matching states to the next processing node after we have finished retrieving current frame blocks of the frame groups in the current processing node. In the next processing node, we continuously retrieve the other frame blocks according to the matching and searching states. If all the bits of a matching state are reset to '0', the frame group need not be searched any longer in the next processing node. In this case, we set its searching state to '-1'. Based on the above processing, we gain the filtering effect of the frame-sliced signature file. Sometimes, the amount of filtered frame groups may not be the same in every processing node. Nevertheless, the execution skew of the VPSF is much less than that of the HPSF.

	After 1st exec.	After 2nd exec.	After 3rd exec.	After 4th exec.
G_{13}	$S_{srch}(P_0) = \{1\}$ $S_{mtch}(P_0) = \{11\}$	$S_{srch}(P_1) = \{2\}$ $S_{mtch}(P_1) = \{10\}$	$S_{srch}(P_2) = \{3\}$ $S_{mtch}(P_2) = \{10\}$	$S_{srch}(P_3) = \{0\}$ $S_{mtch}(P_3) = \{10\}$
G_{12}	$S_{srch}(P_1) = \{-1\}$ $S_{mtch}(P_1) = \{000\}$	$S_{srch}(P_2) = \{-1\}$ $S_{mtch}(P_2) = \{000\}$	$S_{srch}(P_3) = \{-1\}$ $S_{mtch}(P_3) = \{000\}$	$S_{srch}(P_0) = \{-1\}$ $S_{mtch}(P_0) = \{000\}$
G_{14}	$S_{srch}(P_2) = \{3\}$ $S_{mtch}(P_2) = \{1\}$	$S_{srch}(P_3) = \{0\}$ $S_{mtch}(P_3) = \{1\}$	$S_{srch}(P_0) = \{-1\}$ $S_{mtch}(P_0) = \{0\}$	$S_{srch}(P_1) = \{-1\}$ $S_{mtch}(P_1) = \{0\}$
G_{15}	$S_{srch}(P_3) = \{0\}$ $S_{mtch}(P_3) = \{11\}$	$S_{srch}(P_0) = \{1\}$ $S_{mtch}(P_0) = \{01\}$	$S_{srch}(P_1) = \{2\}$ $S_{mtch}(P_1) = \{01\}$	$S_{srch}(P_2) = \{3\}$ $S_{mtch}(P_2) = \{01\}$

Fig. 2. Changing mechanism of searching and matching states in VPSF

For example, when the query key extracted from a query signature would be "1010," in Fig. 1, four equivalent keys are obtained, i.e., $\{1010, 1011, 1110, 1111\}$.

Therefore, we can assign each equivalent key to a processing node. The retrieval starts with their equivalent key in the all processing nodes. In order to process frame groups pointed to by the equivalent keys in parallel, the first processing node loads the first frame block of the frame group, the second processing node loads the second frame block in turn, and so on. In this case, the searching states for the frame groups are initialized with the processing node's number as follows:

$$S_{srch}(P_0) = \{0\}, S_{srch}(P_1) = \{1\}, S_{srch}(P_2) = \{2\}, S_{srch}(P_3) = \{3\}$$

Also, the matching states are initialized with '1' as follows:

$$S_{mtch}(P_0) = \{11\}, S_{mtch}(P_1) = \{111\}, S_{mtch}(P_2) = \{1\}, S_{mtch}(P_3) = \{11\}$$

Based on both states, the steps of the process are illustrated in the Fig. 2. When searching states for all the frame groups are '-1' or they become the initial number of the processing node, we finish searching the signature file. At this time, we regard the signatures whose matching states are left with '1' to be qualified for the query signature in the frame groups. In this example, the first signature S_{21} and the last signature S_{13} are qualified for the query signature. Finally, in order to verify whether the records pointed to by the matched signatures are actually qualified for the query, we should check whether the records actually contain both terms, i.e., "computer" and "file". Because the last signature does not contain the query, it becomes a false match. As a result, only the first signature becomes an actual result for the query.

4   Performance Evaluation

In order to compare the performance of the VPSF with the conventional methods, i.e., HF and HPSF, we implemented the three parallel signature file methods and ran experiments on a set of 200 thousand records under UNIX/SUN Ultra workstation environment. The records used for the experiments, which consist of 12 fields such as title, author, school, degree, date, page, adviser, source, publication, subject, abstract, and keywords, were collected from the library of Chonbuk National University. The number of distinct words per record is 87.7 on an average. We used 16 processing nodes and also 4,000 conjunctive queries so as to make a wide range of experiments. Both HPSF and VPSF used 16 frames owing to achieving the best performance[11]. The VPSF must satisfy the condition that $N_p \leq N_f$ for a balance of data amount when N_p is the number of processing nodes and N_f is the number of frames. It is suitable to delimit the N_f as multiple times of N_p since each processing node must have the same frames. For the experiment, we assume that a communication delay is much shorter than the time for a disk block access because we make use of a high-speed network among the processing nodes.

4.1   Retrieval Performance in terms of Data Distribution

In order to evaluate how uniformly signatures are distributed into processing nodes, we measure the retrieval time in terms of several distributions of records with various lengths. Fig. 3 illustrates normal distributions with several standard deviations. We can know from the figure that the number of terms per record is regarded as an approximately normal distribution whose mean is about 87.7. Others are normal distributions with double and half standard deviations. The double standard deviation means that the number of terms per record is widely distributed, whereas the half standard deviation means it is narrowly distributed. Using these distributions, we evaluate the retrieval times of three parallel signature files, i.e., HF, HPSF, and VPSF.

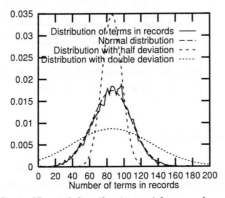

Fig. 3. Normal distributions with several deviations

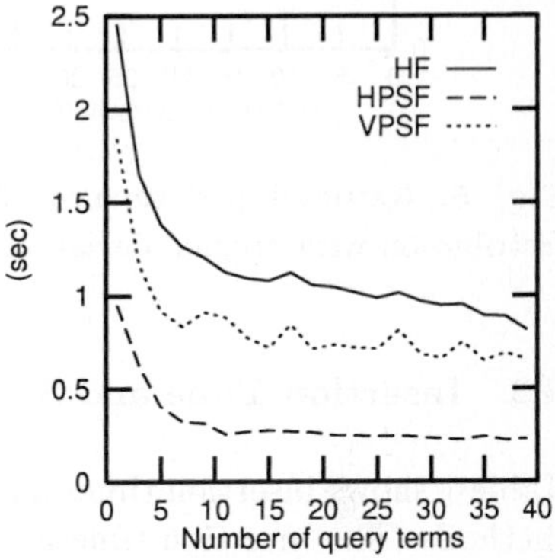

Fig. 4. Retrieval performance of the distribution with double deviation

In case of the normal distribution with the double standard deviation, the order of retrieval performance is HPSF, VPSF, and HF as shown in Fig. 4. Because we gain a wide distribution of the terms per record, thus we will get the wide distribution of record signature weights. Likewise, because we attain a wide distribution of hashing keys made from the extendable hashing or the linear hashing, we can uniformly assign the equivalent keys to processing nodes. Therefore, we obtain a good retrieval performance in the HPSF since the data skew and the execution skew hardly occur.

In case of the normal distribution with the original standard deviation, the order of good retrieval performance is also HPSF, VPSF, and HF as shown in Fig. 5. However, we can find that the graph of the VPSF is lower than that in Fig. 4. Because we obtain the narrower distribution of the hashing keys, the execution skew of the HPSF and the HF occurs more than that in the normal distribution with the double standard deviation.

However, in the distribution with the half standard deviation, we gain a good performance in the order of VPSF, HPSF, then HF as shown in Fig. 6. Because the number of terms per record is distributed near to the mean, the keys of hash functions are frequently split in a narrow range, leading to worse allocation of equivalent keys. Therefore, the VPSF which is not influenced by the equivalent keys attains the best retrieval performance. The reason why retrieval time grows in the order of distributions with the double, original, and half standard deviations is that the amount of block accessed for retrieval increases according to the growth of hashing keys in the distribution with half standard deviation.

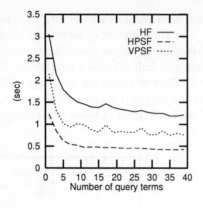

Fig. 5. Retrieval performance of the distribution with original deviation

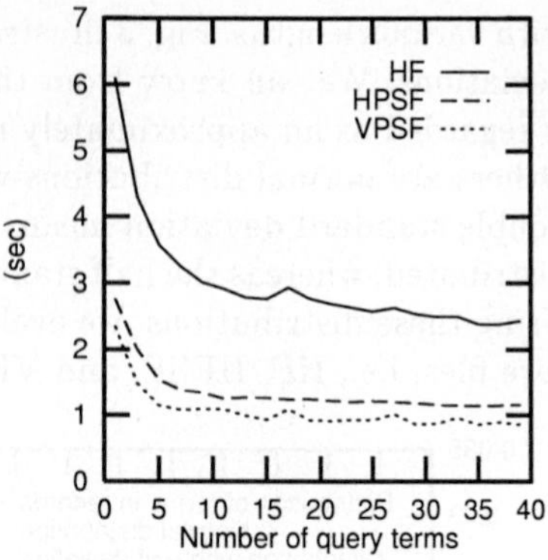

Fig. 6. Retrieval performance of the distribution with half deviation

4.2 Insertion Time and Storage Overhead

Table 1 shows insertion times and storage overheads of the parallel signature file methods. The insertion time is the average of the elapsed time that it takes in order to extract a record signature and store it into the access methods when a record is given for insertion. In the table, the HPSF shows the worst insertion time because one processing node of the HPSF contains all frames of a signature. And, the VPSF is a good insertion time than that of the HF because the number of descriptor keys is increased sharply in the HF without frame-sliced signatures.

Table 1. Insertion times (sec) and storage overhead (%)

Methods	Insertion time	Storage overhead
HF	0.156	18.2
HPSF	0.593	16.9
VPSF	0.105	16.9

Both the HPSF and the VPSF occupy about 16% storage overhead, respectively. However, the processing nodes of the VPSF have almost similar storage space, whereas those of the HPSF yield an unbalance of storage space. The HF shows the worst performance of storage overhead, because its page utilization is about 62~63% in the linear hashing. However, the page utilization of the HPSF and VPSF is about 69% due to the extendable hashing[12]. If all signatures were uniformly distributed, the page utilization would be 75%. Therefore, the storage overhead is mainly determined according to the page utilization.

5 Conclusion

The signature file method has been widely advocated as an efficient index scheme to handle many applications demanding a large amount of multimedia databases. In order to achieve the fast response time for a large amount of database, we proposed a new parallel signature file method using extendable hashing and frame-slicing techniques: a Vertically-partitioned Parallel Signature File (VPSF).

To show the efficiency of our VPSF, we ran experiments in case of a database with 200 thousand records. In our VPSF, when the number of terms per record was arranged with a narrow probability distribution, we gained a good retrieval performance because we partitioned frames into processing nodes instead of difficult equivalent keys to allocate. Therefore, the VPSF can maintain its performance without respect to the record distribution. From the experimental results, we can finally get a guideline according to the specific environment of the databases as follows: when the number of terms per record shows the distribution with a small standard deviation, we make use of the VPSF method; when the distribution has a relatively large standard deviation, the HPSF is suitable; and if the insertion time is important, we utilize the VPSF method.

References

1. Berra, P.B., Chung, S.M., Hachem, N.I.: Architecture for Distributed Multimedia Database Systems. Computer Communications, 13(4) (1990) 217–231
2. Weber, R., Schek, H-J., Blott, S.: A Quantitative Analysis and Performance Study for Similarity-Search Methods in High-Dimensional Spaces. Proc. of VLDB Conf. (1988) 194–205
3. Chang, J.W., Kim, Y.J., Chang, K.J.: A Spatial Match Representation Scheme for Indexing and Querying in Iconic Image Databases. Proc. of ACM CIKM Conf. (1997) 169–176
4. Faloutsos, C., Christodoulakis, S.: Signature Files: An Access Method for Documents and Its Analytical Performance Evaluation. ACM Trans. on Office Information Systems 2(4) (1984) 267–288
5. Stone, H.S.: Parallel Querying of Large Databases: a Case Study. IEEE Computer 1(10) (1987) 133–158
6. Hua, K.A., Lee, C.: Handing Data Skew in Multiprocessor Database Computers Using Partition Tuning. Proc. of VLDB Conf. (1991) 525–535
7. Lin, Z.: Concurrent Frame Signature Files. Distributed and Parallel Databases 1(3) (1993) 231–249
8. Panagopoulos, G., Faloutsos, C.: Bit-Sliced Signature Files for Very Large Text Databases on a Parallel Machine Architecture. Proc. of Conf. on Extending Database Technology (1994) 379-392
9. Grandi, F., Tiberio, P., Zezula P.: Frame-Sliced Partitioned Parallel Signature Files. Proc. of ACM SIGIR (1992) 286–297
10. Zezula, P., Ciaccia, P., Tiberio, P.: Hamming Filter: A Dynamic Signature File Organization for Parallel Stores. Proc. of VLDB Conf. (1993) 314–327
11. Kim, J.K., Chang, J.W.: Horizontally-divided Signature Files on Parallel Machine Architecture. J. of Systems Architecture 44(9) (1998) 723–735
12. Folk, M.J., Zoellick, B.: File Structures. 2nd edition, Addition-Wesley (1992) 503–540

A Case for Deltas in Business-to-Business Electronic Commerce

Shahram Ghandeharizadeh[1] and Frank Sommers[2]

[1] University of Southern California, Los Angeles, California 90089,
shahram@cs.usc.edu
[2] Conceptix, 4751 Wilshire Blvd., Los Angeles, California 90010,
fsommers@nowcom.com

Abstract. At the time of this writing, the electronic commerce market place is dominated by business-to-business transactions. This paper describes one such application and our software prototype in support of this application. Our main contribution is a software solutions (using Java) that employs the concept of deltas to maintain consistency in a replicated, distributed environment. Our proposed solution strives to be independent of the schema of the business objects in order to enhance its portability across different applications.

1 Introduction

With the reduced cost of computer hardware and the growing popularity of the Internet, many small to midsize companies are utilizing database management systems in support of business-to-business electronic commerce. The typical characteristics of this environment are as follows: Multiple office locations must have a unified view of information, and a high-speed reliable network connection between offices is not always an option.

A good example is an insurance company that offers rental car customers liability coverage for accidents. In this environment, the rental car representative acts as an agent of the insurance company to sell the customer a peace of mind. Periodically, the rental car company reports to the insurance company the sold liability policies. The traditional way of conducting business using paper does not work because it has opened the door for fraud. To illustrate, consider a customer who rents a car and buys liability insurance. Upon returning the car without damage, a rental car company may destroy insurance documents in order to increase its profits (without payment to the insurance company). Similarly, the rental car company may find it more economical to sell a customer insurance after the occurrence of an accident, even though the customer did not buy insurance at the time of rental. In both cases, the insurance company loses money.

In this scenario, fraud is prevented if the sales of insurance policies is time stamped and registered in a database management system at the insurance company. However, many rental car offices do not generate enough business for the insurance company to justify installing and maintaining dedicated network connection at each rental car office. The business would benefit from electronic commerce and has the following requirements:

1. Insurance policies are sold at rental car offices, but need to be registered at a remote location (insurance company) without the presence of a reliable network connection.
2. A rental car company might have multiple branches and the customer may rent a car at one branch (say A) and return it at another (say B). If insurance is provided at site A then it must be closed at site B.
3. The system must be highly reliable. If the insurance company does not receive notification of a sold policy, it will not get paid for the premium and may refuse to provide coverage in case of an accident.
4. The application used for issuing the insurance policies must be robust. Customers do not tolerate lengthy delays attributed to either network or database failures.
5. Operational costs must be minimized. Human involvement in database management at the rental offices is too expensive.

In order to address the first two challenges, we envision an environment that consists of (a) satellite servers at each branch of the rental car company, and (b) a master server at the insurance company. The satellite servers communicate with the master server in an asynchronous manner in order to expedite the processing of a transaction. This is accomplished by maintaining a copy of relevant data at each satellite server. To illustrate, consider two rental car companies, say Midway and Allway. Given a city A, Midway might have 10 branches while Allway might have 8 branches. Both companies might purchase insurance from one company, say Knight Insurance. In this environment, there will be one main server at Knight Insurance, and 18 satellite services, one in each branch of the rental car companies. While the data that resides on the Midway and Allway satellite servers are mutually exclusive[1], the data maintained at the 10 satellite servers of midway is replicated and almost identical. Similarly, the data maintained by the 8 branches of Allway are almost identical, pertaining to different customers that might have rented cars from Allway.

In order to simplify the discussion, in the rest of this paper, we focus on the interaction between the satellite servers of one rental car company and the master server. (Extension of the discussion to multiple rental car companies is trivial.) Local updates are performed by each satellite server. They communicate with the master server periodically in order to notify it of local changes. Similarly, the master server periodically connects to the different satellite servers in order to propagate these changes to all satellite servers. We use the concept of deltas[] to represent a change proposed at a satellite server. Moreover, we use a subset of delta operators, e.g., merge, smash, and apply, to maintain consistency between the different replicas and detect conflicting updates proposed by different satellite servers. We foresee the use of the when operator to accommodate hypothetical query processing (in support of decision support) at the master server. The details of this paradigm are still at an evolution stage and described in Section 3.

---

[1] This is because Midway and Allway are competitors, preventing their customers from returning a car at a competitor's branch.

The rest of this paper is organized as follows. Section 2 describes the details of our implementation technique to ensure data consistency between the master and satellite servers. This implementation is novel because it utilizes object-oriented constructs in order to enhance the re-usability of software in support of other applications with similar characteristics. We take special care to ensure serializability of objects to facilitate exchange of information across the network. Section 2 discusses the characteristics of deltas and discusses the use of delta operators. Deltas provide an object-oriented encapsulation of proposed updates to business objects, and their use further enhances to modularity of our software design. Section 3 introduces the challenges of utilizing the when operator in this environment in support of hypothetical query processing. Brief conclusions are offered in Section 4.

2   Data transparency and replicated databases

Our database consists of two kinds of persistent objects: business objects that pertain to insurance certificate, and Delta objects that propose a change to the business objects. Our environment consists of a master server and a collection of satellite servers. The servers are geographically distributed and each maintains a copy of the business objects. The copy maintained at the server is termed a master copy. One of the copies at a satellite server is termed a primary copy while other copies are termed secondary. The satellite server that creates a business object typically contains its primary copy. The master server may demote this copy to secondary and promote another copy to primary in order to enhance system performance (see Section 3).

All updates (Delta objects) proposed by the master copy over-ride those proposed either by a primary or a secondary copy of the object. However, such updates are infrequent and proposed to resolve conflicts. Most often, updates (Delta objects) are proposed by the satellite server that contains the primary copy of an object. Satellite servers containing a secondary copy of an object may pose updates to these objects, however, such updates must be verified by the satellite server containing the primary copy prior to its system wide acceptance.

The software architecture that ensures consistency of the database and implements replication and migration of both business and Delta objects was implemented in a Java class library, or package. In the next section, we describe the software architecture of the system and how it provides for data transparency so that it can support different applications with different schema. Next, Section 2.2 describes how the system propagates updates and detects conflicts. It is worthwhile to note that no conflicts can arise in our environment (conflicts arise under very special circumstances when a satellite server fails). However, we have designed our software for those special applications where conflicts can arise (detailed in Section 3).

2.1 Data transparency

We have an implementation in Java that is flexible and can be tailored to different applications with characteristics similar to our car rental environment. In the following, we introduce the concept of "data transparency" and by this we mean that the constructs used to implement the data schema of a particular application are separate from the mechanisms employed to ensure consistency of the database. When the programmer (or the user) does not have to be concerned much about explicit database management tasks, we approach a more natural programming model required by business-to-businesses electronic commerce applications.

Presently, we focus on one aspect of data transparency: the representation of updates, their propagation across a distributed collection of nodes with replicated data and detection of potential conflicts. The novelty of our approach is that we isolate these mechanisms from the rest of the application in a reusable, object oriented manner. This architecture is applicable to a broad category of applications in support of business-to-business electronic commerce. This class of software is characterized by the semi-nomadic (modem-to-modem) connectivity between the nodes. The primary reason for replicating data is to ensure the availability of *relevant* data at the right nodes in such a way that actions on them can be performed immediately. This results in the third characteristic: data may evolve continuously at each node, i.e., each node is active, independent of whether connected or disconnected to other nodes at a particular time. However, it is important to point out that the possibility of a conflict in this environment is rare. This is because the customer information is mutually exclusive at each site. Even when a customer returns a car to a different branch than the one the car was rented from, there is no possibility of conflict because the update is proposed at one location at a time on behalf of a customer. Incidentally, a number of applications that utilize mobile computing also exhibit the above characteristics and can therefore benefit from the present software architecture.

We wanted to ensure that our environment is general purpose enough to detect conflicts. We utilize what could be termed a "conceptual" approach to conflict management in the sense that it attempts to understand the nature of the conflict itself. This approach is based on the premise that to deal with conflict, we must deal with the differences as entities. This presupposes that differences can be conceptualized in some common forms which can inter-operate among nodes of the system. The common form of such a difference is called a *delta* [GHJ96, GHJ92, DHD96, DHR96, Doh98]. The present system represents a delta as a class. Instances of this class, i.e., Delta objects, are available to the application, and are stored in a database management system. Conflict can be detected using methods defined by delta objects, i.e., performing programmatic operations on them. The design we developed for the imaginary insurance company utilizes Delta objects to ensure data consistency between satellite servers and the master server.

In our environment, business-specific information is stored in the form of persistent objects with the following characteristics: First, they utilize JavaBeans-style property accessor and mutator methods [Sun98] so that the object can utilize the Java reflection mechanism [Sun97]. This is important because it provides for data independence and hence portability of the system (supporting other applications with different schemas for the business objects does not entail a software rewrite). Second, business objects implement the *Updatable* Java interface to ensure that a Delta object can apply itself to the object. This decouples a business object from a Delta object. Third, a business object is typically stored inside a container, or a collection, object that implements the *Updatable-Container* interface, which is subtype of *Updatable*, enabling the container itself to process Delta objects. Fourth, the business objects and their property values need to satisfy the requirements for Java serializability (to support transmission of the object across the network). Finally, a business object must have a unique object ID across the system. The present implementation employs a concatenation of the office code, the teller name, and a time stamp to uniquely identify each business object[2].

Any change *proposed* to a business object is encapsulated in an instance of Delta class (termed Delta object). Our environment supports 3 kinds (specialization) of Delta objects: (1) ADD: proposes to create a new business object created, (2) DELETE: proposes to delete a business object, and (3) EDIT: proposes to modify property values of a business object. These three specializations constitute and define the semantics of change in the system.

Deltaficition is the process by which proposed changes are encapsulated into Delta objects. The creation of an ADD delta involves passing to the delta's constructor a reference to the newly created business object, along with an identifier String regarding the initiator, which could be user ID. The creation of a DELETE delta requires a unique object ID String to be passed to delta's constructor, along with the initiator ID. The creation of an EDIT delta is most interesting and detailed below.

An *EditSession* object constructs an EDIT delta. There is a 1-to-1 relationship between a business object and an EditSession object: the EditSession operates on one, and only one, business object. (However, it is possible to implement this class in a different way.) The EditSession class is a focal point to (1) the business object being modified, (2) the GUI or other property viewing/editing mechanism, (3) the container that stores deltas. Since the EditSession class ties the business object, the editor, and the storage of the Delta together, it is useful not only for creating EDIT Delta objects, but also for creating ADD and DELETE Delta objects. For instance, when the user initiates the creation of a new business object, (1) a new business object is created with its fields set to default values, (2) a GUI is brought up which displays the fields of the business object (default values), (3) the system creates a new EditSession on the business object, and (4) adds the EditSession to the GUI's property change listeners.

---

[2] This means that nodes in the system are **not** completely interchangeable, i.e., we need a priori knowledge of the node (user names and office code). We could not use a global time clock because it is too expensive to synchronize clocks across all satellite servers.

When the edit session is finished, the resulting Delta object is inserted into a container.

In a practical scenario, a user may edit one or more fields of a business object in one editing session. An EditSession bundles the changes made into just one Delta object. This Delta object contains a list of the property names to be modified, along with the old and new values for these properties. One reason we bundle these set of edits together is that they must be applied to a target business object atomically to preserve the object-oriented nature of the system. It is important to note that the EditSession does NOT construct a Delta object if the proposed set of changes are vetoed by the integrity constraints of the business objects. (A business object may implement its constraints using the notion of bound and constrained properties [Sun98] of the JavaBeans programming model.) To illustrate, consider the start and end dates of an insurance certificate. An integrity constraint may specify that the start date must be prior to the end date. A proposed change to either dates is vetoed by the object if this condition is not be satisfied. This is encapsulated at the level of the business object, and the Delta object carrying the proposed updates has no knowledge of this. If the user edits both dates, bundling the two changes in one Delta object ensures that it can be applied atomically to every replica of the business object.

A DeltaContainer is a set of deltas. When a session manager creates a new delta, it is smashed [GHJ96] with those in the delta set in order to localize conflict resolution to each satellite server. The smash operator resolves conflicts in favor of the new delta. Its details are as follows: First, it detects conflicts between the new delta and existing members of the delta sets. Next, it deletes the conflicting member(s) and adds the new delta to the DeltaContainer. To illustrate, assume that a new insurance policy is entered into the system. This update is captured in the form of an ADD Delta object. Shortly thereafter, some one changes the customer name of this policy from John to Peter. This is captured as an EDIT Delta object. The two Delta objects are smashed to result in one Delta object that proposes to add a certificate with Peter as the customer name.

An object that implements the Updatable interface is guaranteed to be able to process a delta object. The Updatable interface requires that a programmer implement a method called *processDelta(Delta delta)*. Business objects that implement this interface are typically stored in a container object. This is similar to the Enterprise JavaBeans architecture which itself is Updatable. It is the responsibility of this container to (1) process a Delta object, and (2) to notify interested parties that the properties of a business object have been modified (i.e., that a Delta object was processed).

Given a Delta object, processing at the satellite server follows the following routine: If it is an ADD Delta object, obtain the business object from the Delta and add it to the internal data structure holding the business objects. If it is a DELETE Delta object, obtain the unique object ID for the to-be-deleted object from the Delta, locate that object, and remove it from the internal object container. If it is an EDIT Delta, obtain the unique target object ID from the Delta, locate the object in the internal container, and pass the Delta itself to this object (since this object must be of type Updatable, it must know how to process Delta objects).

The Java reflection mechanism [Sun98] is used by the Updatable object to perform the changes described by a Delta. This is important because it provides for portability of software to different applications with no software rewrite for the implementation of the Delta class. Using reflection, the environment determines what methods of the business object must be invoked in order to change the property values to their new value.

After processing a Delta object, the container needs to notify its registered listeners of the fact that some data changed. One possible listener might be the GUI. When a Delta object is inserted into the container of pending updates, a notification is sent to the GUI to change the color of the updated fields to green (to imply that the update is under consideration by the insurance company). The business object is not modified as yet. It retains its old values until the Update object is verified by the master server (detailed in Section 2.2). When this happens, the UpdateContainer changes the business object. Once again, the GUI may register an event listener to be notified of this action in order to change the color of the corresponding attribute back to black (to imply that the insurance company has verified the transaction). With this paradigm, the teller by looking at the GUI is aware of what insurance certificates have been approved by the insurance company.

2.2 Conflict detection between proposed updates

A business object has multiple copies distributed across servers. The copy that resides at the master server is termed the master copy. The satellite server that proposes to create this object is termed the primary copy owner of this object. All other copies of this object at the other satellite servers are termed secondaries. All servers may propose to change a copy of this object. The main distinction is when and how the change is made permanent. In our environment, a change proposed by the master copy takes precedence over the changes proposed by the other copies of the object. However, such changes are rare. When a satellite server proposes to change the copy of an object, two possible scenarios arise: either this is a primary or a secondary copy. If it is primary then its change will go into effect as soon as the master server accepts the change (i.e., detects no conflict between the proposed change and its master copy). If it is the secondary then its change will go into effect once: a) the master server is notified of the change, b) the master server propagates the change to the primary copy of the object, and c) both the primary and master accept the change (i.e., detect no conflicts). (The system may change the identity of the server that has the primary copy in order to enhance performance, see Section 3.)

When a satellite server connects and transmits its set of Delta objects to the master server, the master server analyzes each element of this set and performs the following: For each ADD Delta, it obtains the object from the Delta and designates the satellite server as its primary copy owner. With this Delta, there is no possibility of a conflict. Moreover, the master server inserts this Delta object in a queue of deltas (termed Updatecontainer) to be transmitted to other satellite servers (to create secondary copies of this object). This queue is persistent and serves as the means to construct secondary copies of objects along with propagation of updates as detailed below. For each EDIT and DELETE Delta, the master server checks to see if the satellite server is the primary copy owner of the object effected by the update. If so then it tries to apply the proposed change. Otherwise, it inserts the Delta into its local Updatecontainer (for subsequent validation by the primary copy owner of this object). Using a multi-threading environment, the master server performs these operations when the satellite and master are communicating. Given the current speed of CPUs (and the small database size), most often, the master notifies the satellite of the results in the same session. For all those deltas processed, the satellite applies them to its local database and deletes them from its Updatecontainer (that generates events in order to change the GUI).

With those Delta objects that are queued by the master, the master waits until the primary copy owner of these objects connect. Next, it communicates the Delta to the primary copy owner. If the primary copy owner does not detect a conflict then it processes the Delta and notifies the master server of this action. At this point, the master processes the Delta and propagates the update to all other secondary copy owners of this object. The primary copy owner may reject the proposed update at which point the master copy flags the Delta object. Subsequently, when the secondary copy owner that proposed the change connects, the master server informs it of the conflict. At this point, human involvement is necessary to resolve the conflict between the primary copy owner and the secondary copy owner (i.e., two different branches of the rental car company that are manipulating a car rental agreement).

The master server may reject an update proposed by the satellite server. In this case, the UpdateContainer is notified of which element has been rejected. Once again, using the concept of event listeners, the GUI is notified of this event to change the color of the participating objects (and attributes) to red. Moreover, the master server can provide additional information such as why the update was rejected and what its value should be. The GUI can show this information to the teller when the mouse is placed on a red field (using the concept of balloon help).

3 Future directions

In our environment, one may enhance the overall performance of the system by minimizing the number of messages necessary to performed updates. This can be accomplished by minimizing the number of Delta objects constructed by those satellite servers that propose to update the secondary copies of objects. The idea is as follows. At the time of rental, the customer almost always informs the branch if they plan to return the car at a different branch. This information can be communicated to the master server. If the return branch (say B) is different than the branch that the car was rented from (say A) then the master server can change the role of copies at these sites in order to make the copy at site B the primary copy of the business object (and the one at site A as the secondary copy). Of course, if the customer returns the car at a branch different than site B then this would be a wasteful operation that provides no performance enhancements.

With more complex object graphs, if the primary copy of different components of the object reside on different satellite servers then there is a possibility of: a) integrity constraints being satisfied locally at each satellite server, and b) integrity constraints are violated globally at the master server [GHOS96]. The complexity of the problem is exasperated by the fact that the communication between satellite servers and the master server crosses the boundaries of different companies; recall that the master server resides at the insurance company while the satellite servers reside at the branches of a rental car company. One might be tempted to simplify the situation by introducing a server at the head quarters of the rental car company in an attempt to satisfy global constraint violations at the rental car company level prior to their transmission to the master server at the insurance company. However, this may not be acceptable because it opens the door for fraud where the data might be manipulated prior to its transmission to the insurance company (see the discussion of Section 1).

Another interesting research direction is the role of deltas for decision support at the master server. For example, a decision maker might enquire about profit margins if the price of an insurance policy was increased by one dollar per day for those customers whose age is between 25 and 30. The system may process this query in different ways depending on what summary information it has accumulated overtime. One way would be to analyze a log of Delta objects in order to identify those customers whose age is between 25 and 30. Next, it can process a query in a hypothetical database state that has increased the price of these policies by one dollar per day. While this is a straight forward extension of the when operator [GHJ96] to our environment, the situation becomes more complex when a query hypothesize about relationships between objects and deltas themselves [Doh98, DHD96]. We intend to extend our paradigm to support these environments in the near future.

4 Conclusion

In this paper, we describe a geographically distributed, replicated object management system in support of business-to-business e-commerce. This environment utilizes the concept of deltas, primary, secondary and master copies in order to ensure consistency of the database. We use the smash operator in order to minimize the number of Delta objects that are exchanged between a satellite server and the master server. At the master server, we use the merge operator in order to detect potential conflicts that need to be resolved using the assistance of humans. We utilize the concept of reflection provided by Java to maximize the modularity of our software. Indeed, our implementation of the Delta class is independent of the database schema. This minimizes the overhead of porting our implementation to those business-to-business environments with characteristics similar to the one detailed in this paper. We are extending our environment by analyzing the role of the when operator in support of decision support and what-if query processing.

References

[DHD96]   M. Doherty, R. Hull, and J. Durand. On Detecting Conflict Between Proposed Updates. In *Proc. of Intl. Workshop on Database Programming Languages (DBPL)*, 1996.

[DHR96]   M. Doherty, R. Hull, and M. Rupawalla. Structures for Manipulating Proposed Updates in Object-Oriented Databases. In *Proceedings of ACM-SIGMOD*, 1996.

[Doh98]   M. Doherty. *A Multistate Service Based on Deltas and its Application to Support Collaborative Work*. PhD thesis, University of Colorado - Boulder, 1998.

[GHJ92]   S. Ghandeharizadeh, R. Hull, and D. Jacobs. Implementation of Delayed Updates in Heraclitus. In *Proceedings of the 1992 Extending Data Base Technology Conference*, March 1992.

[GHJ96]   S. Ghandeharizadeh, R. Hull, and D. Jacobs. Design, Implementation, and Application of Heraclitus[Alg,C]. *ACM Transactions on Database Systems*, 21(3):370–426, September 1996.

[GHOS96]   J. Gray, P. Helland, P. O'Neil, and D. Shasha. The Dangers of Replication and a Solution. In *Proceedings of ACM-SIGMOD*, 1996.

[Sun97]   Sun Microsystems Inc. *Java Core Reflection API and Specification*, 1997.

[Sun98]   Sun Microsystems Inc. *JavaBeans Specification for Java 2*, 1998.

Flexible Workflow Management Systems: An Approach Based on Generic Process Models

W.M.P. van der Aalst[†]

Department of Mathematics and Computing Science, Eindhoven University of Technology, P.O. Box 513, NL-5600 MB, Eindhoven, The Netherlands , wsinwa@win.tue.nl

Abstract. Today's workflow management systems have problems dealing with change. Since change is a fact of life, this limits the application of these systems. As a result, the workflow management system is not used to support dynamically changing workflow processes or the workflow process is supported in a rigid manner, i.e., changes are not allowed or handled outside of the workflow management system. This paper addresses this problem and tackles it by using generic process models. A generic process model describes a family of variants of the same workflow process. The approach presented in this paper allows for both ad-hoc changes and evolutionary changes. It is a first step in the direction of truly flexible workflow management systems. It turns out that the trade-off between flexibility and support raises challenging questions and that generic processes can answer some of these questions.

1 Introduction

Workflow management promises a new solution to an age-old problem: controlling, monitoring, optimizing and supporting business processes [13,15,16]. What is new about workflow management is the explicit representation of the business process logic which allows for computerized support. At the moment, there are more than 200 workflow products commercially available and many organizations are introducing workflow technology to support their business processes. A critical challenge for workflow management systems is their ability to respond effectively to changes [4,5,6,7,8,12,14,18,21,22,23]. Changes may range from ad-hoc modifications of the process for a single customer to a complete restructuring for the workflow process to improve efficiency. Today's workflow management systems are ill suited to dealing with change. They typically support a more or less idealized version of the preferred process. However, the real run-time process is often much more variable than the process specified at design-time. The only way to handle changes is to go behind the system's back. If users are forced to bypass the workflow management system quite frequently, the system is more a liability than an asset. Therefore, we take up the challenge to find techniques to add flexibility without loosing the support provided by today's systems.

[†] Part of this work was done at AIFB (University of Karlsruhe, Germany) and LSDIS (University of Georgia, USA) during a sabbatical leave.

Typically, there are two types of changes: (1) *ad-hoc changes* and (2) *evolutionary changes*. Ad-hoc changes are handled on a case-by-case basis. In order to provide customer specific solutions or to handle rare events, the process is adapted for a single case or a limited group of cases. Evolutionary change is often the result of reengineering efforts. The process is changed to improve responsiveness to the customer or to improve the efficiency (do more with less). The trend is towards an increasingly dynamic situation where both ad-hoc and evolutionary changes are needed to improve customer service and reduce costs.

This paper presents an approach to tackle the problem of change. This approach is inspired by the techniques used in *product configuration* [19]. As factories have to manufacture more and more customer specific products, the trend is to have a very high number of variants for one product. Products, like a car or a computer, can have millions of variants (e.g., combinations of color, engine, transmission, and options). Also product specifications and their components evolve at an increasing pace. Product configuration deals with these problems and has been a lively area of research for the last decade. Moreover, some solutions have already been implemented in today's enterprise resource planning systems such as SAP R/3 and BaanERP. To deal with changes the traditional *Bill-Of-Material* (BOM) is extended with product families. A product family corresponds to a range of product types and allows for the modeling of generic product structures. The term *generic BOM* [10,11,19,20] is used when generic product structures are described by means of an extension to the traditional BOM. In this paper, we extend traditional process modeling techniques in a similar manner. We adopt the notion of *process families* to construct *generic workflow process models*.

A generic workflow process model is a process model which can be configured to accommodate flexibility and enables both ad-hoc and evolutionary changes. Using generic workflow process models, the workflow management system can support the design and enactment (i.e., execution) of processes subject to change. Moreover, the generic process model introduced in this paper, allows for the navigation through two dimensions: (1) the vertical dimension (is-part-of/contains) and (2) the horizontal dimension (generalizes/specializes). Although the second dimension is absent in today's workflow management systems, it is of the utmost importance for the reusability and adaptability of workflow processes.

2   Generic process models

A generic process model is specified by a set of routing diagrams and inheritance diagrams. Before these two diagram types are presented, we introduce the basic concepts and the relations between these concepts.

2.1   Concepts

Cases are the objects which need to be handled by the workflow (management system). Examples of cases are tax declarations, complaints, job applications, credit card payments, and insurance claims. A *task* is an atomic piece of work. A task is concrete, i.e., it can be specified, but it is not specific for a single case. In principle, a task can be executed for any case. A *non-atomic concrete process* is similar to a task but it is not atomic. A non-atomic concrete process is specified by a routing diagram and corresponds to a case type rather than a specific case. A *concrete process* is either a task or a non-atomic concrete process, i.e., it is a pre-specified piece of work which can be executed for many cases (if needed). A *generic process* is not specified, i.e., it is not concrete but refers to a family of processes. Since it is not concrete, it makes no sense to distinguish between atomic and non-atomic generic processes. In fact, one generic process may refer to both concrete tasks and non-atomic concrete processes at the same time. A *process node* is either a concrete process or a generic process. A routing diagram contains process nodes, i.e., a non-atomic concrete process is specified in terms of both concrete and generic processes. A process node appears in zero of more routing diagrams. In each routing diagram, process nodes are connected by *routing elements* specifying the order in which the process nodes need to be executed. A process node refers to zero or more generic processes. If a process node X refers to a generic process Y, then X belongs to the process family described by Y and we say that X *is a child of* Y. A concrete process can be the child of a generic process, a generic process can be the child of another generic process, but a generic process cannot be the child of a concrete process. Note that a process node can be the child of many generic processes. Each case refers to precisely one non-atomic concrete process. Since the routing diagram describing a non-atomic concrete process may contain generic processes, it is necessary to instantiate generic processes by concrete processes for specific cases, i.e., for a specific case, generic processes in the routing diagram are replaced by concrete processes.

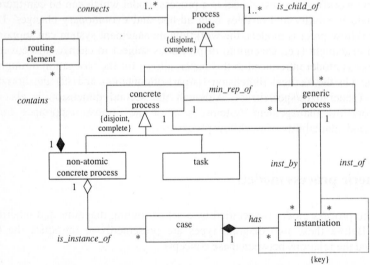

Fig. 1. Class diagram describing the relationships between the main concepts used in this paper.

Fig. 1 shows a class diagram, using the UML notation, relating the essential concepts used in this paper. The diagram shows that non-atomic concrete processes and tasks are specializations of concrete processes, i.e., both the class *non-atomic concrete process* and the class *task* are subclasses of the class *concrete process*. The two subclasses are mutually disjoint and complete. The class *process node* is a generalization of the class *concrete process* and the class *generic process*. The association *is_child_of* relates process nodes and generic processes. If the association relates a process node X and generic process Y, then X belongs to the process family of Y. Since process nodes can be in the process family of generic processes and a generic process can have many children (but at least one), the cardinality constraints are as indicated in the class diagram. A generic process has at least one child because it has a so-called *minimal representative* as indicated by the association *min_rep_of*. The minimal representative of a generic process is a concrete process which captures the essential characteristics of a process family. The minimal representative is needed to enable dynamic change and to generate aggregate management information. The class *routing element* links process nodes to non-atomic concrete processes. A non-atomic concrete process consists of process nodes (i.e., tasks, non-atomic concrete processes, and generic processes) which can be executed in a predefined way. Typical routing elements are the AND-split, AND-join, OR-split, and OR-join. These elements can be used to enable sequential, parallel, conditional, alternative, and iterative routing. In the class diagram, we did not refine the class *routing element* because the approach presented in this paper is independent of the process modeling technique used. The association *contains* specifies the relation between routing elements and non-atomic concrete processes. Note that a routing element is contained in precisely one non-atomic concrete process. The association *connects* specifies which process nodes are connected by each routing element. Note that the associations *contains* and *connects* can be used to derive in which non-atomic concrete processes a process node is used. The class *case* refers to the objects that are handled at run-time using a non-atomic concrete process description. The association *is_instance_of* relates each case to precisely one non-atomic concrete process. It is not possible to execute non-atomic concrete processes containing process nodes which are generic. Before or during the handling of a case, generic processes need to be instantiated by concrete processes. The class *instantiation* is used to bind generic processes to concrete processes for specific cases. Every instantiation corresponds to one case, one generic process, and one concrete process. Note that per case it is not allowed to have multiple instantiations for the same generic process.

There are many constraints not represented in the class diagram. Constraints that are important for the remainder are:

1. The relation given by the association *is_child_of* is acyclic.
2. The relation derived from the composition of association *contains* and association *connects* is acyclic.
3. The relation derived from the composition of the associations *contains*, *connects* and *is_child_of* is acyclic, e.g., a non-concrete process X is not allowed to contain a generic process Y if X is a child of Y.
4. The minimal representative of a generic process is also a child, i.e., the relation specified by the association *min_rep_of* is contained in the relation specified by *is_child_of*.
5. A generic process can only be instantiated by a concrete process if the concrete process is (indirectly) a child of the generic process.

6. For a case it is only possible to instantiate generic processes which are actually contained in the corresponding non-atomic concrete process.

The class diagram shown in Fig. 1 contains three types of information:

1. *Routing information*: The process description of each non-atomic concrete process. It specifies which tasks, non-atomic concrete processes, and generic processes are used and in what order they are executed. The classes *routing element*, *process node*, and *non-atomic concrete process* and the associations *contains* and *connects* constitute the routing information.

2. *Inheritance information*: The relation between a generic process and its children. It specifies possible instantiations of generic processes by concrete processes. The classes *generic process*, *process node*, and *concrete process* and the associations *is_child_of* and *min_rep_of* are involved.

3. *Dynamic information*: Information about the execution of cases and instantiations of generic processes by concrete processes. It involves the classes *case* and *instantiation* and the associations *is_instance_of*, *has*, *inst_by*, and *inst_of*.

Today's workflow management systems do not support the definition of generic processes, i.e., it is only possible to specify concrete processes. In the remainder of this paper we focus on the modeling of generic processes using a combination of routing and inheritance diagrams.

2.2 Routing diagrams

A routing diagram specifies for a non-atomic concrete process the routing of cases along process nodes. Any workflow management system allows for the modeling of such diagrams. Examples of diagramming techniques are Petri-nets (COSA, INCOME, BaaN/DEM, Leu), Event-driven Process Chains (SAP/Workflow), Business Process Maps (ActionWorkflow), Staffware Procedures (Staffware), etc. None of these diagramming techniques supports generic processes. However, each of these diagramming techniques can be extended with generic processes. In this paper, we extend Petri-net-like routing diagrams [1,9] with generic processes.

A routing diagram specifies the contents of a *non-atomic concrete process* and consists of four types of elements:

1. *Tasks*. A task is represented by a square and corresponds to a Petri-net transition.

2. *Non-atomic concrete processes*. A non-atomic concrete process is represented by a double square and corresponds to a link to another Petri-net (i.e., a subnet).

3. *Generic processes*. A generic process is represented by a square containing a diamond and corresponds to a link which can be instantiated by a workflow node.

4. *Routing elements*. Routing elements are added to specify which workflow nodes need to be executed and in what order. Since we use Petri nets, routing elements correspond to places and transitions which are added for routing reasons only.

Fig. 2 shows the four types of elements.

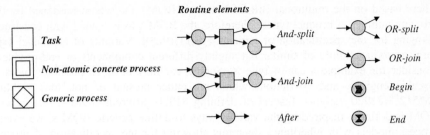

Fig. 2. Symbols used in a routing diagram.

To illustrate the construction of routing diagrams we give an example. Fig. 3 shows the specification of the non-atomic concrete process *handle_insurance_claim*. This process consists of two tasks (*registration* and *pay_damage*), one non-atomic concrete process (*check_policy*), three generic processes (*check_damage*, *evaluate_claim*, and *reject_claim*), and several routing elements. Every insurance claim is first registered, then the policy and the damage are checked, followed by an evaluation which either results in a payment or in a rejection. Note that Fig. 3 contains sequential, parallel, and conditional routing.

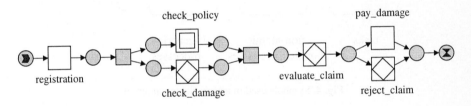

Fig. 3. The non-atomic concrete process *handle_insurance_claim*.

The three generic processes shown in Fig. 3 may refer to several concrete processes. However, this information is not given in the routing diagram but in the corresponding three inheritance diagrams. Since *check_policy* is a concrete process which is not atomic, there is also a routing diagram specifying the contents of this process. The routing diagram shown in Fig. 3 illustrates how a process definition language can be extended with generic processes. In principle, it is possible to use the diagramming technique offered by any workflow management system with a hierarchy concept and extend it with a new type of building block: the generic process.

2.3 Inheritance diagrams

In contrast to routing diagrams, today's products do not allow for inheritance diagrams to specify the process family corresponding to a generic process. The lack of such a concept in today's workflow management systems has many similarities with the absence of product variants in the early MRP/ERP-systems. These systems where based on the traditional Bill-Of-Material (BOM) and where burdened by the growing number of product types. Therefore, the BOM was extended with constructs allowing for the specification of variants [10,11,19,20]. Variants of a product type form a product family of similar but slightly different components or end-products. Consider for example a car of type X. Such a car may have 16 possible colors, 5 possible engines, and 10 options which are either present or not, thus yielding $16*5*2^{10}=81920$ variants. Instead of defining 81920 different BOM's, one generic BOM is defined. Inspired by the various ways to define generic BOM's, we extend process models with inheritance diagrams allowing for the specification of process families.

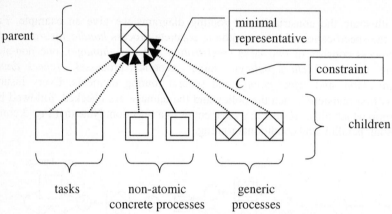

Fig. 4. Symbols used in an inheritance diagram.

Fig. 4 shows an inheritance diagram. The root of an inheritance diagram is a generic process called the *parent*. All other process nodes in the diagram are called the *children* and are connected to this parent. There are three types of children: tasks, non-atomic concrete processes, and generic processes. Each non-atomic concrete process in the inheritance diagram refers to a routing diagram describing the internal routing structure. Each generic child process in an inheritance diagram refers to another inheritance diagram specifying the process family which corresponds to this generic process. Note that the total number of inheritance diagrams equals the total number of generic processes. Every generic process has a child called the *minimal representative* of this task. This child is connected to the parent with a solid arrow. All the other arrows in an inheritance diagram are dashed. The minimal representative has all the attributes which are mandatory for the process family. One can think of this minimal representative as the default choice, as a simplified management version, or as some template object. The actual interpretation of the minimal representative depends on its use. The minimal representative can be considered to be the superclass in an object-oriented sense [3], i.e., all other children in the inheritance diagram should be subclasses of this superclass. For execution, generic processes are instantiated by concrete processes using the relations specified in the inheritance diagram. However, in many cases it is not allowed to instantiate a parent by an arbitrary child. Therefore, it is possible to specify constraints as indicated in Fig. 4.

These constraints may depend on two types of parameters: (1) *case variables* and (2) *configuration parameters*. The case variables are attributes of the case which may change during the execution of the process (cf. [1]). Configuration parameters are used to specify that certain combinations of instantiations are not allowed. These parameters can be dealt with in a way very similar to the parameter concept in [19] for the generic BOM.

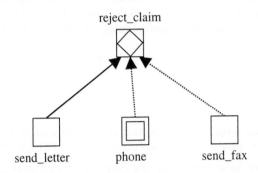

Fig. 5. An inheritance diagram for the generic process *reject_claim*.

Fig. 5 shows an inheritance diagram with parent *reject_claim* and three children (the tasks *send_letter* and *send_fax*, and the non-atomic concrete process *phone*). The task *send_letter* is the minimal representative of *reject_claim*. In this case all children are concrete. Note that the generic process *reject_claim* was used in the process *handle_insurance_claim* (Fig. 2). As Fig. 5 shows, this generic process can be instantiated by the tasks *send_letter* or *send_fax*, or the non-atomic concrete process *phone* defined by some routing diagram.

3   Open problems

Inspired by the generic BOM, we have defined generic workflow process models. A generic process model has two dimensions: (1) the vertical dimension (routing diagrams) and (2) the horizontal dimension (inheritance diagrams). In [17] a similar two-dimensional approach is suggested. The addition of the horizontal dimension, absent in today's workflow management systems, allows for the design and enactment of many variants of a workflow process. However, it is not sufficient to support the design and enactment. There are two additional issues that need to be dealt with: (1) *management information* [21,22], and (2) *dynamic change* [5,7,8]. In spite of the existence of many variants of one process, the manager is interested in information at an aggregate level, i.e., management information which abstracts from small variations. The term dynamic change refers to the problem of handling old cases in a new process, e.g., how to transfer cases to a new, i.e., improved, version of the process. These two issues cause a lot of problems which need to be solved. We think that it is possible to tackle these problems by using the notion of a *minimal representative* of a generic process. By mapping states on this minimal representative it may be possible to generate adequate management information. Moreover, linking states of the members of a process family to the states of a minimal representative seems to be useful for the automated support of dynamic change. Further research is needed to investigate the usefulness of this concept.

The interested reader is referred to [2] where a complete example is given which allows for 75 variants. Moreover, it is shown that the introduction of a minimal representative really simplifies the problem. At the same time, we are working on inheritance notions in the context of workflow flexibility. The first results show that the inheritance preserving transformation rules presented in [3] can be used to avoid the problems related to change.

References

1. W.M.P. van der Aalst. The Application of Petri Nets to Workflow Management. *The Journal of Circuits, Systems and Computers*, 8(1):21-66, 1998.

2. W.M.P. van der Aalst. How to Handle Dynamic Change and Capture Management Information? An Approach Based on Generic Workflow Models. Technical report, UGA-CS-TR-99-01, University of Georgia, Department of Computer Science, Athens, USA, 1999.

3. W.M.P. van der Aalst and T. Basten. Life-cycle Inheritance: A Petri-net-based approach. In P. Azema and G. Balbo, editors, *Application and Theory of Petri Nets 1997*, volume 1248 of *Lecture Notes in Computer Science*, pages 62-81. Springer-Verlag, Berlin, 1997.

4. W.M.P. van der Aalst, G. De Michelis, and C.A. Ellis, editors. *Workflow Management: Net-based Concepts, Models, Techniques and Tools (WFM'98)*. UNINOVA, Lisbon, June 1998.

5. A. Agostini and G. De Michelis. Simple Workflow Models. In W.M.P. van der Aalst, G. De Michelis, and C.A. Ellis, editors, *Workflow Management: Net-based Concepts, Models, Techniques and Tools (WFM'98)*, volume 98/7 of *Computing Science Reports*, pages 146-164. Eindhoven University of Technology, Eindhoven, 1998.

6. F. Casati, S. Ceri, B. Pernici, and G. Pozzi. Workflow Evolution. *Data and Knowledge Engineering*, 24(3):211-238, 1998.

7. C. Ellis, K. Keddara, and G. Rozenberg. Dynamic change within workflow systems. In N. Comstock and C. Ellis, editors, *Conf. on Organizational Computing Systems*, pages 10 - 21. ACM SIGOIS, ACM, Aug 1995. Milpitas, CA.

8. C.A. Ellis, K. Keddara, and J. Wainer. Modeling Workflow Dynamic Changes Using Timed Hybrid Flow Nets. In W.M.P. van der Aalst, G. De Michelis, and C.A. Ellis, editors, *Workflow Management: Net-based Concepts, Models, Techniques and Tools (WFM'98)*, volume 98/7 of *Computing Science Reports*, pages 109-128. Eindhoven University of Technology, Eindhoven, 1998.

9. C.A. Ellis and G.J. Nutt. Modelling and Enactment of Workflow Systems. In M. Ajmone Marsan, editor, *Application and Theory of Petri Nets 1993*, volume 691 of *Lecture Notes in Computer Science*, pages 1-16. Springer-Verlag, Berlin, 1993.

10. F. Erens, A. MacKay, and R. Sulonen. Product modelling using multiple levels of abstraction - instances as types. *Computers in Industry*, 24(1):17-28, 1994.

11. H.M.H. Hegge. Intelligent Product Family Descriptions for Business Applications. PhD thesis, Eindhoven University of Technology, Eindhoven, 1995.

12. P. Heinl, S. Horn, S. Jablonski, J. Neeb, K. Stein, and M. Teschke. A comprehensive approach to flexibility in workflow management systems. Technical report TR-16-1998-6, University of Erlangen-Nuremberg, Erlangen, 1998.

13. S. Jablonski and C. Bussler. *Workflow Management: Modeling Concepts, Architecture, and Implementation* International Thomson Computer Press, 1996.

14. M. Klein, C. Dellarocas, and A. Bernstein, editors. *Proceedings of the CSCW-98 Workshop Towards Adaptive Workflow Systems*, Seattle, Nov. 1998.

15. T.M. Koulopoulos. *The Workflow Imperative*. Van Nostrand Reinhold, New York, 1995.

16. P. Lawrence, editor. *Workflow Handbook 1997, Workflow Management Coalition*. John Wiley and Sons, New York, 1997.

17. T. Malone, W. Crowston, J. Lee, B. Pentland, and et. al. Tools for inventing organizations: Toward a handbook for organizational processes. *Management Science*, 1998 (to appear).

18. A. Sheth. From Contemporary Workflow Process Automation to Dynamic Work Activity Coordination and Collaboration. *Siggroup Bulletin*, 18(3):17-20, 1997.

19. E.A. van Veen and J.C. Wortmann. Generative bill of matarial processing systems. *Production Planning and Control*, 3(3):314-326, 1992.

20. E.A. van Veen and J.C. Wortmann. New developments in generative bom processing systems. *Production Planning and Control*, 3(3):327-335, 1992.

21. M. Voorhoeve and W.M.P. van der Aalst. Conservative Adaptation of Workflow. In M. Wolf and U. Reimer, editors, *Proceedings of the International Conference on Practical Aspects of Knowledge Management (PAKM'96), Workshop on Adaptive Workflow*, pages 1-15, Basel, Switzerland, Oct 1996.

22. M. Voorhoeve and W.M.P. van der Aalst. Ad-hoc Workflow: Problems and Solutions. In R. Wagner, editor, *Proceedings of the 8th DEXA Conference on Database and Expert Systems Applications*, pages 36-41, Toulouse, France, Sept 1997.

23. M. Wolf and U. Reimer, editors. *Proceedings of the International Conference on Practical Aspects of Knowledge Management (PAKM'96), Workshop on Adaptive Workflow*, Basel, Switzerland, Oct 1996.

Object-Based Ordered Delivery of Messages in Object-Based Systems

Katsuya Tanaka, Hiroaki Higaki, and Makoto Takizawa

Department of Computers and Systems Engineering
Tokyo Denki University
e-mail {katsu, hig, taki}@takilab.k.dendai.ac.jp

Abstract. Distributed applications are realized by cooperation of multiple objects. A state of an object depends on in what order the objects exchange request and response messages. In this paper, we newly define an object-based precedent relation of messages based on a conflicting relation among requests. Here, only the messages to be ordered in the object-based system are ordered. We discuss a protocol which supports the object-based ordered delivery of messages. Here, an object vector is newly proposed to order messages.

1 Introduction

Distributed applications are realized by a *group* of multiple application objects. Papers [2, 10] discuss how to support a group of the objects with the causally ordered (CO) and totally ordered (TO) delivery of messages at the network level. Only messages required by the applications have to be causally delivered in order to reduce the overhead. Ravindran *et al.* [11] discuss how to support the ordered delivery of messages based on the message precedence explicitly specified by the application. Agrawal *et al.* [8] define *significant* requests which change the state of the object. Raynal *et al.* [1] discuss a group protocol for replicas of files where write–write semantics of messages are considered. The authors [5] discuss a group protocol where a group is composed of transactions issuing read and write requests to the replicas.

An object is an encapsulation of data and methods. On receipt of a *request message* with a method *op*, an object *o* performs *op* and sends back a *response message* with the result of *op*. Here, *op* may further invoke other methods, i.e. *nested invocation*. States of the objects depend on in what order conflicting methods are performed. If a pair of methods exchanged by the methods conflict in an object, the messages have to be received in the computation order of the methods. Thus, the *object-based ordered (OBO) relation* among request and response messages is defined based on the conflicting relation. In this paper, we present an *Object-based Group (OG) protocol* which supports the *OBO delivery* of messages where only messages to be ordered at the application level are delivered to the application objects in the significant order. We newly propose an *object vector* to order messages, which is independent of the group membership.

In section 2, we discuss the object-based precedence among messages. In sections 3 and 4, the design and evaluation of the OG protocol are discussed.

2 Object-Based Ordered Delivery

2.1 Object-based systems

A *group* G is a collection of objects $o_1, \ldots, o_n$ $(n \geq 1)$ which are cooperating by exchanging request and response messages in a network. We assume that the network is less reliable and is asynchronous, i.e. messages sent by an object are delivered to the destinations with message loss, not in the sending order, and the delay time among objects is not bounded.

Let $op(s)$ denote a state obtained by applying a method op to a state s of an object o_i. A pair of methods op_1 and op_2 of o_i are *compatible* iff $op_1(op_2(s)) = op_2(op_1(s))$ for every state s of o_i. op_1 and op_2 *conflict* iff they are not compatible. The *conflicting relation* among the methods is specified when o_i is defined. The conflicting relation is assumed to be symmetric but not transitive. If op_1 is compatible with every method being performed on o_i, op_1 is started to be performed. Otherwise, op_1 has to wait until op_2 completes.

Each time an object o_i receives a request message of a method op, a thread is created for op. The thread is referred to as an *instance* of op in o_i, which is denoted by op^i. op may further invoke methods of other objects. Thus, the invocation is *nested*.

2.2 Significant precedence

A method instance op_1^i *precedes* op_2^i $(op_1^i \Rightarrow_i op_2^i)$ in an object o_i iff op_2^i is started after op_1^i completes. op_1^i *precedes* op_2^j $(op_1^i \Rightarrow op_2^j)$ iff $op_1^i \Rightarrow_i op_2^j$ for $j = i$, op_1^i invokes op_2^j, or $op_1^i \Rightarrow op_3^k \Rightarrow op_2^j$ for some instance op_3^k. op_1^i and op_2^j are *concurrent* $(op_1^i \| op_2^j)$ iff neither $op_1^i \Rightarrow op_2^j$ nor $op_2^j \Rightarrow op_1^i$. A message m_1 *causally precedes* another message m_2 if the sending event of m_1 precedes the sending event of m_2 [2,7]. In the totally ordered delivery, messages not causally ordered are delivered to the common destinations in the same order in addition to the causal delivery. Suppose an object o_i sends a message m_1 to objects o_j and o_k, and o_j sends m_2 to o_k after receiving m_1. Since m_1 causally precedes m_2, the object o_k has to receive m_1 before m_2. For example, if m_1 is a question and m_2 is the answer for m_1, m_1 has to be received before m_2. However, independent questions m_1 and m_2 can be received in any order.

We define a *significantly precedent relation* "$\rightarrow$" among messages m_1 and m_2, where "$m_1 \rightarrow m_2$" is meaningful for object-based applications. There are the following cases for a pair of messages m_1 and m_2:

S. An object o_i sends m_2 after m_1 [Figure 1].

S1. m_1 and m_2 are sent by op_1^i.

S2. op_1^i sends m_1 and op_2^i sends m_2: **S2.1.** $op_1^i \Rightarrow op_2^i$. **S2.2.** $op_1^i \| op_2^i$.

R. o_i sends m_2 after receiving m_1 [Figure 1].

R1. m_1 and m_2 are received and sent by op_1^i.

R2. op_1^i receives m_1 and op_2^i receives m_2: **R2.1.** $op_1^i \Rightarrow op_2^i$. **R2.2.** $op_1^i \| op_2^i$.

In the case S1, m_1 *significantly precedes* m_2 $(m_1 \rightarrow m_2)$ since m_1 and m_2 are sent by the same instance op_1^i. In S2, m_1 and m_2 are sent by different instances op_1^i and op_2^i in o_i. In S2.1, op_1^i precedes op_2^i $(op_1^i \Rightarrow op_2^i)$. Unless op_1^i and op_2^i conflict, there is no relation between op_1^i and op_2^i, i.e. neither $m_1 \rightarrow m_2$ nor $m_2 \rightarrow m_1$. Here, m_1 and m_2 are *significantly concurrent* $(m_1 \| m_2)$. If op_1^i and op_2^i conflict, the output data carried by m_1 and m_2 depend on a computation order of op_1^i and op_2^i. Thus, if op_1^i and op_2^i conflict, the messages sent by op_1^i have to be delivered before the messages sent by op_2^i, i.e. $m_1 \rightarrow m_2$. In S2.2, $op_1^i \| op_2^i$. Since op_1^i and op_2^i are not related, $m_1 \| m_2$.

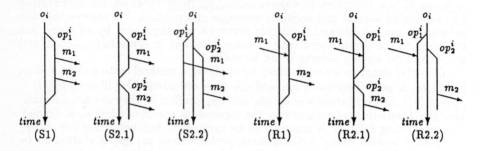

Fig. 1. Send-send and receive-send precedence.

In the case R1, $m_1 \rightarrow m_2$ since the same instance op_1^i receives m_1 and sends m_2. m_1 is received and m_2 is sent by op_1^i. Here, m_1 is the request of op_1^i or a response of a method invoked by op_1^i. m_2 is the response of op_1^i or a request of a method invoked by op_1^i. For example, suppose m_1 is a response of op_2^j invoked by op_1^i and m_2 is a request of op_3^k. The output of op_2 may be the input of op_3^k. In R2, m_1 is received by op_1^i and m_2 is sent by op_2^i ($\neq op_1^i$). In R2.1, $op_1^i \Rightarrow op_2^i$. If op_1^i and op_2^i conflict, $m_1 \rightarrow m_2$. Unless $m_1 \| m_2$. In R2.2, $op_1^i \| op_2^i$ and $m_1 \| m_2$.
[Definition] A message m_1 *significantly precedes* m_2 $(m_1 \rightarrow m_2)$ iff one of the following three conditions holds:
1. An object o_i sends m_1 before m_2 and
    a. a same instance sends m_1 and m_2, or
    b. an instance sending m_1 conflicts with another one sending m_2 in o_i.
2. o_i receives m_1 before sending m_2 and
    a. m_1 and m_2 are received and sent by the same instance, or
    b. an instance receiving m_1 conflicts with another one sending m_2.
3. $m_1 \rightarrow m_3 \rightarrow m_2$ for some message m_3. □
[Theorem 1] A message m_1 causally precedes m_2 if $m_1 \rightarrow m_2$. □
A message m_1 is significantly preceded by only messages related with m_1. m_1 does not necessarily significantly precede m_2 even if m_1 causally precedes m_2.

2.3 Object-based ordered delivery

Suppose an object o_i receives a pair of messages m_1 and m_2. There are the following cases on what instances in o_i receive m_1 and m_2 :

T. o_i receives m_2 before m_1.

T1. m_1 and m_2 are received by an instance op_1^i.

T2. op_1^i receives m_1 and op_2^i receives m_2. T2.1. $op_1^i \Rightarrow op_2^i$. T2.2. $op_1^i \| op_2^i$.

In T1, the message m_1 has to be delivered to the object o_i before m_2 if m_1 significantly precedes m_2 $(m_1 \rightarrow m_2)$. In T2, m_1 and m_2 are received by different instances op_1^i and op_2^i. In T2.1, first suppose op_1^i and op_2^i conflict. If m_1 or m_2 is a request, m_1 has to be delivered before m_2 since $m_1 \rightarrow m_2$. Suppose m_1 and m_2 are responses. Unless m_1 is delivered before m_2, op_1^i waits for m_1

and op_2^i is not performed since op_1^i does not complete. That is, deadlock among op_1^i and op_2^i occurs. Furthermore, suppose m_3 is sent to op_1^i, m_4 is sent to op_2^i, and $m_4 \rightarrow m_3$. Even if op_1^i precedes op_2^i ($op_1^i \Rightarrow op_2^i$) and m_1 is delivered before m_2, deadlock occurs because $m_4 \rightarrow m_3$. Thus, messages destined to different instances cannot be delivered to o_i in the order "$\rightarrow$" unless at least one of the messages is a request. Next, suppose op_1^i and op_2^i do not conflict. The messages m_1 and m_2 can be delivered in any order even if $m_1 \rightarrow m_2$ or $m_2 \rightarrow m_1$. If $op_1^i \| op_2^i$ in T2.2, m_1 and m_2 can be independently delivered to op_1^i and op_2^i.

Suppose an object o_h sends a message m_1 to o_i and o_j, and another o_k sends m_2 to o_i, o_j, and o_h. o_i and o_j are common destinations of m_1 and m_2. There are the following cases on the types of the messages m_1 and m_2:

C. Multiple objects receive messages m_1 and m_2.
C1. m_1 and m_2 are request messages.
C2. One of m_1 and m_2 is a request message and the other is a response one.
C3. m_1 and m_2 are response messages.

In C1, suppose m_1 and m_2 are requests of methods op_1 and op_2, respectively, and op_1 conflicts with op_2 in not only o_i but also o_j. If $m_1 \| m_2$, o_i and o_j may deliver m_1 and m_2 in different orders. However, the state of o_i obtained by performing op_1 and op_2 may be inconsistent with o_j because op_1 and op_2 conflict in o_i and o_j. Therefore, a pair of requests m_1 and m_2 have to be delivered in every pair o_i and o_j of common destination objects in the same order if m_1 and m_2 conflict in o_i and o_j. In C2 and C3, m_1 and m_2 can be delivered in any order.
[Object-based ordered (OBO) delivery] A message m_1 *object-based precedes* (*OB-precedes*) m_2 ($m_1 \preceq m_2$) if

1. m_1 significantly precedes m_2 ($m_1 \rightarrow m_2$),
   1.1 an instance receives both m_1 and m_2, or
   1.2 m_1 and m_2 are received by different instances op_1^i and op_2^i, op_1^i and op_2^i conflict in o_i, and one of m_1 and m_2 is a request.
2. $m_1 \| m_2$, m_1 and m_2 are conflicting requests, and m_1 is delivered before m_2 in every other common destination of m_1 and m_2. $\square$

A message m_1 is *significant* $m_1 \preceq m_2$ or $m_2 \preceq m_1$ for some message m_2. A message m_1 is delivered before m_2 in a common destination object o_i of m_1 and m_2 if $m_1 \prec m_2$.
[Theorem 2] No communication deadlock occurs if every message is delivered by the OBO delivery. $\square$
[Theorem 3] $m_1 \preceq m_2$ if $m_1 \rightarrow m_2$. m_1 totally precedes m_2 if $m_1 \preceq m_2$. $\square$

3 Object-Based Group Protocol

3.1 Object vector

Each object o_i manipulates a *vector clock* $V_i = \langle V_{i1}, \ldots, V_{in} \rangle$ ($i = 1, \ldots, n$) [9], where each V_{ij} is initially 0. o_i increments V_{ii} by one each time o_i sends a message m. The message m carries the vector clock $m.V (= V_i)$. On receipt of a message m', o_i updates V_i as $V_{ij} := max(V_{ij}, m'.V_j)$ for $j = 1, \ldots, n$ and $j \neq i$. m_1 causally precedes m_2 iff $m_1.V < m_2.V$.

It is critical to discuss which instances send messages for ordering only the messages significant in the applications. The OB-precedent relation "$\preceq$" is defined for messages exchanged by the instances invoked in a nested manner while the causality is defined for messages exchanged by objects. Hence, a group is considered to be composed of instances, not objects. If the vector clock composed of instances is used, the group has to be frequently synchronized [2,3,7–9,12] each time an instance is initiated and terminated. The vector clock can be used to causally order messages sent by objects but not by instances. Hence, we newly propose an *object vector* to order only the significant messages in "$\preceq$" which is independent of what instances are being performed.

The object vector V is a tuple $\langle V_1, \ldots, V_n \rangle$ where each element V_i shows an identifier of a method which has been most recently performed. First, we discuss an instance identifier $id(op_t^i)$. o_i manipulates a variable oid, whose value is initially 0, showing the linear clock [7] as follows:

- $oid := oid + 1$ if an instance is initiated in o_i.
- On receipt of a message from an instance op_u^j, $oid := max(oid, oid(op_u^j))$.

When op_t^i is initiated in the object o_i, an identifier $id(op_t^i)$ is a concatenation of the value of oid and the object number $ono(o_i)$ of o_i. Here, let $oid(op_t^i)$ show oid of $id(op_t^i)$. $id(op_t^i) > id(op_u^j)$ if 1) $oid(op_t^i) > oid(op_u^j)$ or 2) $oid(op_t^i) = oid(op_u^j)$ and $ono(o_i) > ono(o_j)$. It is clear that the following properties hold:

I1. If op_t^i is initiated after op_u^i in an object o_i, $id(op_t^i) > id(op_u^i)$.

I2. If o_i receives a request from op_u^j and initiates op_t^i, $id(op_t^i) > id(op_u^j)$.

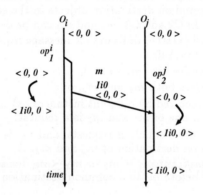

Fig. 2. Object vectors.

Each event e in the instance op_t^i is given an event number $no(e)$. The event number is incremented by one each time op_t^i sends a message. The object o_i manipulates a variable no_i to give the event number to each event e, i.e. $no(e) := no_i$ in o_i as follows:

- Initially, $no_i := 0$.
- $no_i := no_i + 1$ if e is a sending event.

A *global event number* $tno(e)$ is the concatenation of $id(op_t^i)$ and $no(e)$.

An object o_i manipulates a vector $V^i = \langle V_1^i, \ldots, V_n^i \rangle$. Each time an instance op_t^i is initiated in o_i, op_t^i is $V_t^i = \langle V_{t1}^i, \ldots, V_{tn}^i \rangle$ where $V_{tj}^i := V_j^i$ for $j = 1, \ldots, n$. Each element V_t^i is manipulated for op_t^i as follows:

- If op_t^i sends a message m, $no_i := no_i + 1$ and $V_{ti}^i := \langle id(op_t^i), no_i \rangle$. m carries the vector V_t^i as $m.V$ where $m.V_j := V_{tj}^i$ $(j = 1, \ldots, n)$.
- If op_t^i receives a message m from o_j, $V_{tj}^i := max(V_{tj}^i, m.V_j)$ $(j = 1, \ldots, n)$.

- If op_t^i commits, $V_j^i := max(V_j^i, V_{tj}^i)$ $(j = 1, \ldots, n)$.
- If op_t^i aborts, V^i is not changed.

Initially, the object vectors V^i and V^j are $\langle 0, 0 \rangle$ in Figure 2. An instance op_1^i is initiated in o_i where $V_1^i = V^i = \langle 0, 0 \rangle$. The identifier $id(op_1^i)$ is "$1i$". op_1^i sends a message m to another instance op_2^j. The message m carries the vector $V_1^i (= \langle 0, 0 \rangle)$ to o_j. Here, suppose m is a request message of a method op_2. After sending m, V_1^i is changed to $\langle 1i0, 0 \rangle$ where "$1i0$" is the global event number of the sending event of m. On receipt of m, op_2^j is initiated where $id(op_2^j) = 2j$. Here, V_2^j is $\langle 1i0, 0 \rangle$. If op_2^j commits, the vector V^j of o_j is changed to $\langle 1i0, 0 \rangle$.

3.2 Message transmission and receipt

A message m includes the following fields:

$m.src$: sender object of m. $m.dst$: set of destination objects.

$m.typ \in \{request, response, commit, abort\}$

$m.op$: method. $m.dat$: data. $m.tno = \langle m.id, m.no \rangle$: global event number.

$m.V = \langle V_1, \ldots, V_n \rangle$: object vector. $m.SQ = \langle sq_1, \ldots, sq_n \rangle$: sequence numbers.

If m is a request message, $m.tno$ is a global event number of the sending event of m. $m.id$ shows the identifier of the instance which sends m and $m.no$ indicates the event number in the instance. If m is a response of a request m', $m.tno = m'.tno$ and $m.op = m'.op$.

An object o_i manipulates variables $sq_1, \ldots, sq_n$ to detect a message gap, i.e. messages lost or unexpectedly delayed. Each time o_i sends a message to o_j, sq_j is incremented by one. Then, o_i sends a message m to every destination in $m.dst$. o_j manipulates variables $rsq_1, \ldots, rsq_n$. rsq_i shows a sequence number of a message which o_j expects to receive next from o_i. On receipt of m from o_i, o_j receives every message which o_i sends to o_j before m if $m.sq_j = rsq_i$. If $m.sq_j > rsq_i$, there is a gap message m' where $m.sq_j > m'.sq_j \geq rsq_i$. That is, o_j has not yet received m' which o_i sends to o_j. o_j correctly receives m if o_j receives every message m' where $m'.sq_j < m.sq_j$ and $m'.src = m.src(= o_i)$. That is, o_j receives every message which o_i sends to o_j before m. If o_i does not receive a gap message m in some time units after the gap is detected, o_j requires o_i to send m again. The object o_j enqueues m in a receipt queue RQ_j even if a gap is detected on receipt of m.

If an instance op_t^i in an object o_i invokes a method op, o_i constructs a message m as follows:

$m.src := o_i$; $m.dst :=$ set of destination objects;

$m.typ := request$; $m.op := op$; $m.tno = \langle m.id, m.no \rangle := \langle id(op_t^i), no_i \rangle$;

$m.V_j := V_{tj}^i$ for $j = 1, \ldots, n$;

$sq_h := sq_h + 1$ for every object $o_h \in m.dst$; $m.sq_j := sq_j$ for $j = 1, \ldots, n$;

3.3 Message ordering

Let us consider three objects o_i, o_j, and o_k [Figure 3]. An instance op_1^i in o_i sends a message m_1 to o_j and o_k. op_2^i is interleaved with op_1^i in o_i, i.e. op_1^i and op_2^i are concurrent $(op_1^i \| op_2^i)$. op_2^i sends m_3 to o_k. op_3^j sends m_2 to o_k after receiving

m_1. Here, m_1 significantly precedes m_2 ($m_1 \rightarrow m_2$). o_k has to receive m_1 before m_2. However, m_1 and m_3 are significantly concurrent ($m_1 \| m_3$) since $op_1^i \| op_2^i$. Similarly $m_2 \| m_3$. However, since op_3^j is initiated after receiving m_1 from op_1^i and $op_1^i \| op_2^i$, $m_1.V = m_3.V$. Hence, $m_2.V > m_3.V$. Although o_k can receive m_2 and m_3 in any order since $m_2 \| m_3$, "m_2 precedes m_3" because $m_2.V > m_3.V$. In order to resolve this problem, an additional *receipt vector* $RV = \langle RV_1, \ldots, RV_n \rangle$ is given to each message m received from o_i. $m.RV$ shows RV given to m. $m.RV$ is manipulated as follows :

- $m.RV_i := m.tno.$ • $m.RV_h := m.V_h$ for $h = 1, \ldots, n$ ($h \neq i$).

In Figure 3, $id(op_1^i) < id(op_2^i)$ because op_2^i is invoked after op_1^i. Hence, $m_1.RV < m_3.RV$ as shown in Table 1. op_1^i sends m_1 to o_j and o_k where $m.tno = 1i0$ and $m.V = \langle 0, 0, 0 \rangle$. On receipt of m_1, o_j enqueues m_1 into a receipt queue RQ_j. Here, o_j gives RV to m_1, i.e. $m_1.RV = \langle 1i0, 0, 0 \rangle$ while $m_1.V$ is still $\langle 0, 0, 0 \rangle$. Table 1 shows values of tno, V, and RV of the messages. $m_1.V < m_2.V$ and $m_1.RV < m_2.RV$. On the other hand, $m_2.V > m_3.V$ but $m_2.RV$ and $m_3.RV$ are not comparable. Following this example, a pair of messages m_1 and m_2 are ordered by the following rule.

[Ordering rule] A message m_1 *precedes* m_2 ($m_1 \Rightarrow m_2$) if the following condition holds:

1. if $m_1.V < m_2.V$ and $m_1.RV < m_2.RV$, $m_1.op = m_2.op$ or $m_1.op$ conflicts with $m_2.op$,
2. otherwise, m_1 and m_2 are requests, $m_1.op$ conflicts with $m_2.op$, and $m_1.tno < m_2.tno$. $\square$

In Figure 3, op_1^i sends a request m_1 to o_j and o_k where op_3^j and op_4^k are initiated. Then, op_3^j sends a request m_2 to o_k. Here, $m_1.V < m_2.V$ and $m_1.RV < m_2.RV$. Suppose op_4^k conflicts with op_5^k. $m_1 \Rightarrow m_2$ since $m_1.op$ and $m_2.op$ conflict. Next, suppose that m_2 is a data message and op_4^k receives m_2 after op_4^k is initiated by m_1. Here, $m_1 \Rightarrow m_2$ since $m_1.op = m_2.op = op_4^k$. On the other hand, $m_1.V = m_3.V$ but $m_1.RV < m_3.RV$. Accordingly, we check if $m_1.op$ and $m_3.op$ conflict. Since op_1^i and op_2^i are compatible, m_1 and m_3 are not ordered in the precedent relation "$\Rightarrow$". It is clear that $m_1 \Rightarrow m_2$ if $m_1 \preceq m_2$.

Table 1. Object and receipt vectors.

m	$m.tno$	$m.V$	$m.RV$
m_1	$1i0$	$\langle 0, 0, 0 \rangle$	$\langle 1i0, 0, 0 \rangle$
m_2	$2j0$	$\langle 1i0, 0, 0 \rangle$	$\langle 1i0, 2j0, 0 \rangle$
m_3	$2i0$	$\langle 0, 0, 0 \rangle$	$\langle 2i0, 0, 0 \rangle$

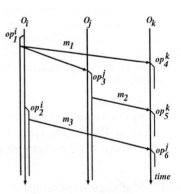

Fig. 3. Receipt vectors.

[Theorem 4] If a message m_1 OB-precedes m_2 ($m_1 \prec m_2$), $m_1 \Rightarrow m_2$. $\square$

"$m_1 \Rightarrow m_2$" is assumed to hold if instances op_1^i and op_2^i are serially performed in Figure 1. In S2.1, if op_2^i conflicts with op_1^i, data carried by m_1 and m_2 depend on the computation order of op_1^i and op_2^i. Hence, "$m_1 \Rightarrow m_2$" has to hold. However, m_1 and m_2 are independent if op_1^i and op_2^i are compatible. Hence, there is no need "$m_1 \Rightarrow m_2$" holds. In the OG protocol, "$m_1 \Rightarrow m_2$" even if op_2^i is compatible with op_1^i. In order not to order m_1 and m_2, each request m sent by an object o_i carries information on what requests conflicting with m precede m. There is a trade off between the complexity and overhead of additional mechanisms and the reduction of delay time of messages obtained by reducing the number of significant messages. Thus, if "$m_1 \Rightarrow m_2$" only for a pair of conflicting requests m_1 and m_2 in S2.1, "$m_1 \prec m_2$ iff $m_1 \Rightarrow m_2$" holds.

3.4 Message delivery

The messages in a receipt queue RQ_i are ordered in the precedent order $\Rightarrow$.
[**Stable message**] Let m be a message which an object o_i sends to another one o_j and is stored in the receipt queue RQ_j. The message m is *stable* in o_j iff one of the following conditions holds:

1. There exists such a message m_1 in RQ_j that $m_1.sq_j = m.sq_j + 1$ and m_1 is sent by o_i.
2. o_j receives at least one message m_1 from every object, where $m \Rightarrow m_1$. $\square$

The top message m in RQ_j can be delivered if m is stable because every message preceding m in $\Rightarrow$ is surely delivered.
[**Ready message**] A message m in a receipt queue RQ_j is *ready* if no method instance conflicting with $m.op$ is being performed in o_j. $\square$

The messages in RQ_j are delivered by the following procedure.
[**Delivery procedure**] If the top message m in RQ_j is stable and ready, m is delivered. $\square$
[**Theorem 5**] The OG protocol delivers m_1 before m_2 if $m_1 \preceq m_2$. $\square$

If an object o_i sends no message to another one o_j, messages in RQ_j cannot be stable. o_i sends every object o_j a message without data if o_i had sent no message to o_j for some predetermined δ time units. δ is proportional to delay time between o_i and o_j. o_j considers that o_j loses a message from o_i if o_j receives no message from o_i for δ or o_j detects a message gap. o_i also considers that o_j loses a message m unless o_i receives a receipt confirmation of m from o_j in 2δ after o_i sends m to o_j. Here, o_i resends m.

4 Evaluation

In the evaluation, three objects o_1, o_2, and o_3 are implemented in Sun Enterprise 450 with 2 CPUs (300MHz) and 512MB memory. Each of o_1 and o_2 supports 8 types of methods and o_3 supports 9 types of methods. Some of the methods invoke other methods. Figure 4 indicates tree structures named *invocation tree* showing invocations of methods. Here, op_i^t shows a method op_t supported by o_i. In this paper, we assume that the methods in the same invocation tree are compatible with each other while every pair of methods in different trees conflict.

Each transaction is initiated on τ[msec] after the first one is initiated. τ is a random number generated among 0 to 9,999. Each transaction randomly selects one method out of 25 methods supported by o_1, o_2, and o_3. For example,

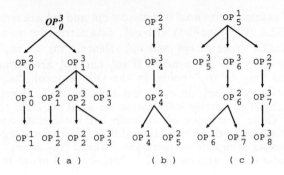

Fig. 4. Invocation trees.

one transaction selects op_0^3 of o_3 which invokes totally ten methods and another transaction selects op_7^2 which totally invokes two methods op_7^3 and op_8^3.

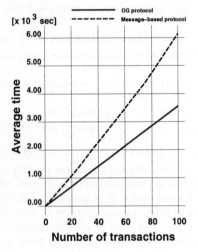

Fig. 5. Average time.

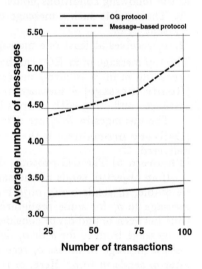

Fig. 6. Average queue length.

The response time and the length of the receipt queue are measured for the OG and the message-based group protocols. The evaluation is iteratively performed until the average value of the response time and the queue length are saturated because each transaction randomly selects one method. The average time for performing all the transactions is measured. Figure 5 shows that the OG protocol is about 50% faster than the message-based protocol because fewer number of messages are required to be waited in the receipt queue in the OG protocol than the message-based one.

In addition, we measure the length of the receipt queue. Figure 6 shows the average queue length for number of transactions. The queue length in the OG protocol is 25-30% shorter than the message-based protocol because messages can be delivered without waiting for messages insignificant for the application. The computation overhead of the OG protocol module is almost the same as the message-based protocol.

5 Concluding Remarks

In this paper, we have discussed how to support the object-based ordered (OBO) delivery of messages. While all messages transmitted in a network are causally or totally ordered in most group protocols, only messages to be causally ordered at the application level are ordered to reduce the delay time. Based on the conflicting relation among methods, we have defined the object-based (OB) precedent relation among request and response messages. We have discussed the object vector to order messages in the object-based systems. The size of the object vector depends on the number of objects, not the number of instances. We have shown how the OG protocol reduces the response time of transactions.

References

1. Ahamad, M., Raynal, M., and Thia-Kime, G., "An Adaptive Protocol for Implementing Causally Consistent Distributed Services," *Proc. of IEEE ICDCS-18*, 1998, pp.86–93.
2. Birman, K., Schiper, A., and Stephenson, P., "Lightweight Causal and Atomic Group Multicast," *ACM Trans. on Computer Systems*, Vol.9, No.3, 1991, pp.272-314.
3. Cheriton, D. R. and Skeen, D., "Understanding the Limitations of Causally and Totally Ordered Communication," *Proc. of ACM SIGOPS'93*, 1993, pp.44–57.
4. Enokido, T., Tachikawa, T., and Takizawa, M., "Transaction-Based Causally Ordered Protocol for Distributed Replicated Objects," *Proc. of IEEE ICPADS'97*, 1997, pp.210–215.
5. Enokido, T., Higaki, H., and Takizawa, M., "Group Protocol for Distributed Replicated Objects," *Proc. of ICPP'98*, 1998, pp.570–577.
6. Enokido, T., Higaki, H., and Takizawa, M., "Protocol for Group of Objects," *Proc. of DEXA'98*, 1998, pp.470–479.
7. Lamport, L., "Time, Clocks, and the Ordering of Events in a Distributed System," *CACM*, Vol.21, No.7, 1978, pp.558–565.
8. Leong, H. V. and Agrawal, D., "Using Message Semantics to Reduce Rollback in Optimistic Message Logging Recovery Schemes," *Proc. of IEEE ICDCS-14*, 1994, pp.227–234.
9. Mattern, F., "Virtual Time and Global States of Distributed Systems," *Parallel and Distributed Algorithms* (Cosnard, M. and Quinton, P. eds.), *North-Holland*, 1989, pp.215–226.
10. Nakamura, A. and Takizawa, M., "Causally Ordering Broadcast Protocol," *Proc. of IEEE ICDCS-14*, 1994, pp.48–55.
11. Ravindran, K. and Shah, K., "Causal Broadcasting and Consistency of Distributed Shared Data," *Proc. of IEEE ICDCS-14*, 1994, pp.40-47.
12. Tachikawa, T., Higaki, H., and Takizawa, M., "Significantly Ordered Delivery of Messages in Group Communication," *Computer Communications Journal*, Vol. 20, No.9, 1997, pp. 724–731.
13. Tanaka, K., Higaki, H., and Takizawa, M., "Object-Based Checkpoints in Distributed Systems," *Journal of Computer Systems Science and Engineering*, Vol. 13, No.3, 1998, pp.125–131.

Storage and Retrieval of XML Documents Using Object-Relational Databases

Takeyuki Shimura, Masatoshi Yoshikawa and Shunsuke Uemura

Graduate School of Information Science Nara Institute of Science and Technology
8916-5 Takayama, Ikoma, Nara 630-0101, Japan
{takeyu-s, yosikawa, uemura}@is.aist-nara.ac.jp

Abstract. This paper describes general storage and retrieval methods for XML documents using object-relational databases. The storage method decomposes tree structure of XML documents into nodes, and stores them in relational tables according to the node types. By using this method, being independent of DTDs or element types, any XML documents can be stored in databases. Also it is possible to utilize index structures(e.g. B^+ trees, R trees, etc.) which are provided in database management systems. As for retrieval, we show the transformation of XQL queries into SQL queries. It is possible to realize the storage method by doing minimal extension to object-relational databases and the retrieval method by adding a preprocessor of a query language. We also performed experiments using XML documents on the plays of Shakespeare, to show the effectiveness of our methods.

1 Introduction

XML (eXtensible Markup Language) [WWWC98a], designed as a subset of SGML[ISO86] and recommended by W3C (World Wide Web Consortium), is a document description metalanguage to represent data and documents on the World Wide Web. The potential of XML is unlimited, and many new applications using XML are currently planned (e.g. [Bos97]). Therefore, efficient storage and retrieval of XML documents in databases is an important research issue. With the increase of sophisticated XML documents, databases managing XML documents are required to support queries on structure, content, and attributes[1].

In this paper, we propose general storage and retrieval methods for XML documents using object-relational databases. As databases managing XML documents, we adopted commonly-used object-relational databases which have functionality of adding abstract data types. Figure 1 shows the logical architecture of our system. The differences between our methods and related work are as follows. Firstly, database schemas for storing XML documents are independent of DTDs or element types. Secondly, in retrieving XML documents, the system rewrites declarative queries for XML into SQL queries which are executed in object-relational databases. Also, it is possible to store XML documents by doing minimal extension to object-relational databases and the retrieval method by adding a preprocessor of a query language.

---

[1] The term 'attribute' is used differently in the context of databases and in XML. We call the former 'database attribute' and the latter 'attribute'.

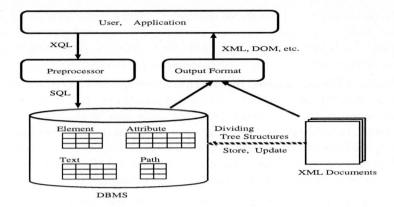

Fig. 1. The logical architecture of our system.

1.1 Related Work

Storage of structured documents There are two major approach to the storage and retrieval of XML documents in databases. XML documents are regarded as structured data in one approach, and as simple character string in another approach.

When structured documents are regarded as structured data, the tree structure representing an XML document is mapped to database schemas. In this approach, database schemas are designed in accordance with the DTD of structured documents. Once such database schema is designed, XML documents stored in databases are guaranteed to conform to the DTD. However, because commonly-used database models (such as relational model and object-oriented model) is not powerful enough to naturally represent the concept of "choice" in element type declarations in the DTD, database schema can not represent the DTD. In [CACS94], a mapping of DTDs to extended database schemas was proposed. However, this approach has a drawback in that (even a small) change of logical structure of XML documents influence on database schemas.

In our approach, since database schemas are independent of DTDs or element types, changes in logical structure do not influence on database schemas. Also, our storage method does not require extended facilities on database models nor database schemas. Also, conformance of XML documents to DTDs, if any, are not guaranteed by DBMSs but by XML processors. Validation check by an XML processor is executed when documents are inserted or modified.

When structured documents are regarded simply as character strings, an XML document is stored in a database attribute. Operations on tree structure are replaced by string operators, and abstract data types which have functions to execute string operators are added to databases. Under this approach, queries on structured documents are described in extended SQL[BCD+95]. Integration engine internally distributes queries to SQL on relational data and to commands on full-text system, and integrates the both query result before they are returned to users or applications. The system provides an interface through which users can view documents as if they were stored in database systems.

Though we also regard structured documents as simple character string, substance of XML documents is stored in databases. We regarded generality as an important design factor. In our approach, we realize storage and retrieval of XML documents using only database management systems.

Index Scheme for structured documents Index schemes for structured documents are described in [SDDTZ97]. The paper presents position-based indexing and path-based indexing to access document collections by content, structure, or attributes. In position-based indexing, queries are processed by manipulating ranges of offsets of words, elements or attributes. In path-based indexing, the paths in tree structures are used. Our storage method of XML documents adopts both of the two indexing schemes and enjoys the advantages of them.

The rest of the paper is organized as follows. Section 2 describes a storage method for XML documents. Section 3 describes a retrieval method for XML documents stored in databases. Section 4 reports the experimental results and demonstrates the effectiveness of our method. We conclude the paper in Section 5.

2 Storage Method of XML Documents

XML processors guarantee that XML documents stored in databases follow tagging rules prescribed in XML or conform to a DTD. Hence, XML documents stored in databases are valid or well-formed.

2.1 A Tree Structure Representing an XML Document

An XML document can be represented as a tree, and node types in the tree are of the following three kinds: Element, Attribute and Text. These node types are equivalent to the node types in XSL[WWWC98b] data model. Though there are other node types such as comment, processing instruction, etc, we do not treat them in this paper.

- Nodes of type **Element** have an element type name as a label. Element nodes have zero or more children. The type of each child node is of one of the three (Element, Attribute and Text).
- Nodes of type **Attribute** have an attribute name and an attribute value as a label. Attribute nodes have no child node. If there are plural attributes, the order of the attributes is not distinguished. This is because there is no order in XML attributes.
- Nodes of type **Text** have character data specified in the XML Recommendation as a label. Text nodes have no child node.

Figure 3 shows the tree structure representing the XML document in Figure 2.

2.2 Design Strategies for Storing XML Documents

We have the following policies for the storage of XML documents:

- Database schemas should not depend on DTDs or element types, and databases shall store any XML documents.
- Index structures which are provided in database management systems shall be used.

209

```
<books>
<book style="textbook">
<title>Designing XML applications</title>
<editor>
  <family>Bob</family> <given>Kraft</given>
</editor>
<author>
  <family>Nick</family> <given>Marcus</given>
  <family>Bob</family>  <given>Pant</given>
</author>
<summary>
This book is the guide to design<keyword>XML</keyword>applications.
</summary>
</book>
</books>
```

Fig. 2. An example of an XML instance.

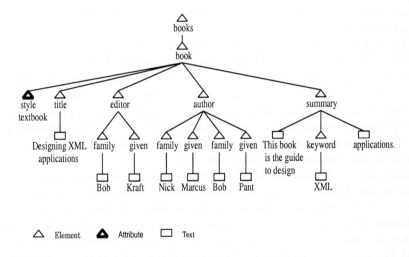

Fig. 3. An example of tree representation.

– Storage method shall be realized by doing minimal extension to object-relational databases.
– Functionalities of XML query languages shall be supported.

As for the storage of XML documents, the key issue is the mapping from the tree structure of an XML document to tuples in relational tables. We decompose the tree structure into relations so that we can easily access and reuse by the unit of logical structure and we can use index structures(e.g. B^+ trees, R trees, etc.) provided in database systems.

Regarding query languages for XML, much discussion have been made on the requirements for languages (e.g. [Wor98]). So far, only a few XML query

- BOOLEAN contain(REGION *pos*)
  This predicate takes an instance *pos* (r_a, s_a) of REGION type as its argument, returns TRUE if and only if (r, s) contains (r_a, s_a).
- BOOLEAN precede(REGION *pos*)
  This predicate takes an instance *pos* (r_a, s_a) of REGION type as its argument, returns TRUE if and only if (r, s) precedes (r_a, s_a).

These predicates are used to decide the inclusion relationship or the order relationship of regions within same document.

2.4 Relational Database Schemas for Storing XML Documents

Relations for storing XML documents are four kinds : Element, Attribute, Text, and Path. The relations Element, Attribute and Text store data about each node type described in Section 2.1. The relation Path stores data about simple paths. Each relation has the following database attributes.

- The relation Element stores data about Element nodes. Database attributes are *docID*, *pathID*, *index*, *reindex* and *pos* to store document identifiers, path identifiers, plus occurrence order, minus occurrence order and regions respectively.
- The relation Attribute stores data about Attribute nodes. Database attribute are *docID*, *pathID*, *attvalue* and *pos* to store document identifiers, path identifiers, attribute values and regions respectively.
- The relation Text stores data about Text nodes. Database attribute are *docID*, *pathID*, *value*, and *pos* to store document identifiers, path identifiers, collections of character data and regions respectively.
- The relation Path stores data about simple paths. Database attribute are *pathexp* and *pathID* to store simple paths and path identifiers respectively.

2.5 Storage of XML Documents to Relational Tables

Data about each node described in Section 2.1 is stored, being based on database schema described in Section 2.4. For example, Figure 6 shows that the tree structure in Figure 3 is stored in relational tables. In many XML documents stored in database, if plural XML documents follow the same DTD, there are many same simple paths. Therefore, by storing the correspondence between pathID and simple path in the relation Path, the number of tuples can be reduced. Each occurrence of database attribute *pathexp* in relation Path is subject to simple path specified in Figure 4.

Element

docID	pathID	index	reindex	pos
1	1	0	-1	0.1, 18.3
1	2	0	-1	0.2, 18.2
1	4	0	-1	0.3, 3.1
1	5	0	-1	3.2, 5.2
1	6	0	-1	3.3, 4.1
1	7	0	-1	4.2, 5.1
1	8	0	-1	5.3, 9.2
1	9	0	-2	5.4, 6.1
1	10	0	-2	6.2, 7.1
1	9	1	-1	7.2, 8.1
1	10	1	-1	8.2, 9.1
1	11	0	-1	9.3, 18.1
1	12	0	-1	16.1, 17.1

Attribute

docID	pathID	attvalue	pos
1	3	textbook	0.2, 0.2

Text

docID	pathID	value	pos
1	4	Designing XML applications	1, 3
1	6	Bob	4, 4
1	7	Kraft	5, 5
1	9	Nick	6, 6
1	10	Marcus	7, 7
1	9	Bob	8, 8
1	10	Pant	9, 9
1	11	This book is ...	10, 16
1	12	XML	17, 17
1	11	applications.	18, 18

Path

pathexp	pathID
/books	1
/books/book	2
/books/book/@style	3
/books/book/title	4
/books/book/editor	5
/books/book/editor/family	6
/books/book/editor/given	7
/books/book/author	8
/books/book/author/family	9
/books/book/author/given	10
/books/book/summary	11
/books/book/summary/keyword	12

Fig. 6. A storage exmple of XML documents.

If tree structures are stored in the relational tables in Figure 6, the source XML documents can be rebuilt because of preserving document identifier and region of each node type.

By dividing tree structures into nodes and storing them according to the node types, we enjoy the following advantages.

- Database schemas to store XML documents do not depend on DTDs or element types. Any XML documents can be managed, being based on the four relational tables.
- Index structures provided in database management systems can be used. B^+ trees on database attributes other than database attributes *pos* and R(or R^*) trees on database attributes *pos* can be constructed. By constructing index structures, queries for XML documents can be efficiently processed.
- It is possible to realize our storage method by doing minimal extension to object-relational databases. The abstract data type which is added to database systems is only REGION type described in Section 2.3. Predicates

of REGION type can decide the inclusion relationship or the order relationship. If this abstract data type is not added, by using simple comparison predicates such as $<$ or $\geq$, we can carry out equivalent operation to predicates of REGION type. Therefore, the described storage method can apply to not only object-relational databases but also relational databases.

3 Retrieval Method of XML Documents

In our architecture, XML documents are decomposed into paths of their tree representation, and stored in the four relations in Figure 6. Their relational tables, in which XML documents are stored, are hidden from users or applications. Users or application consider XML documents as trees, and they specify queries in XML query languages. In this paper, we employ XQL as such an XML query language. In this section, we describe a framework to rewrite XQL queries into SQL queries. However, the query rewriting in detail is omitted due to the limitation of space.

XML documents are decomposed into fragments and they are stored in relational tables. Therefore, identification of sub-documents (i.e. a set of document identifier and region) is expected to be efficient using such tables. However, rebuilding entire documents or large sub-documents from fragments in tables will be inefficient. Hence, when such (sub-)documents are required, we take an approach to scan XML document files.

3.1 Query Rewriting

Using a notation which connects path operators('/' or '//') with element types, etc., XQL can extract sub-documents enclosed with elements. '/' is the child operator which selects from immediate child nodes. '//' is the descendant operator which selects from arbitrary descendant nodes. The '//' can be thought of as a substitute for one or mode levels of hierarchy. Also, in the query, filer clause '[ ]' which is analogous to the SQL WHERE clause, indexing which is easy to find a specific node within a set of nodes, etc. can be specified.

Since data about XML documents such as simple paths are stored as string in databases, functions of pattern matching in SQL-92[DD93] can be used. For example, as basic queries, if XQL queries do not include filer nor indexing, the outline of generating SQL queries is as follows:

(1) Simple paths stored in databases start with path operator '/', and they connect element type with '/'. If XQL queries include path operator '//', every occurrence of '//' in simple paths is replaced with '%/' by using LIKE predicate in the WHERE clause. Then, using the replaced simple paths, pathIDs are selected out from the relation Path.

(2) Pairs of docID and pos in the relation Element are retrieved based on each pathID obtained in (1).

As an example, Query 1 shows that an XQL query which connects element type with path operator can be rewritten into SQL.

Next, Query 2 shows that an XQL query which has a filter is rewritten into SQL. If condition about text is specified in filter, as for rewriting, a query in SQL can be produced by adding relation Text in the FROM clause and condition of text in the WHERE clause. In the WHERE clause, *pos* is REGION type and one of predicates described in Section 2.3 is used.

Furthermore, XQL queries having indexing can also be transformed into SQL queries by using database attribute *index* or *reindex*. We give such an example in Query 3.

```
Query 1:    /books//author          Query 2:    //book[summary/keyword = 'XML']
  SELECT      e1.docID, e1.pos         SELECT      e3.docID, e3.pos
  FROM        Element e1, Path p1      FROM        Element e1, Path p1, Text t2,
  WHERE       e1.pathID = p1.pathID                Path p2, Element e3, Path p3
  AND         p1.pathexp LIKE          WHERE       p1.pathexp LIKE '\%/book
              '/books\%/author'        AND         p2.pathexp LIKE
  ORDER BY    e1.docID, e1.pos                     '\%/book/summary/keyword
                                       AND         p3.pathexp LIKE
Query 3:    //book/author/family[0]                '\%/book/author/family
  SELECT      e1.docID, e1.pos         AND         e1.pathID = p1.pathID
  FROM        Element e1, Path p1      AND         t2.value = 'XML'
  WHERE       e1.pathID = p1.pathID    AND         t2.pathID = p2.pathID
  AND         p1.pathexp LIKE          AND         e3.pathID = p3.pathID
              '%/book/author/family    AND         e1.pos.contain(t2.pos)
  AND         e1.index = 0             AND         e1.docID  = t2.docID
  ORDER BY    e1.docID, e1.pos         AND         e1.pos.contain(e3.pos)
                                       AND         e1.docID  = e3.docID
                                       ORDER BY    e3.docID, e3.pos
```

4 Implementation

We have performed experiments to store XML documents in a database and retrieve them based on the methods described in Sections 2 and 3. This section describes the implementation and shows the experimental results.

We have used PostgreSQL[POS] which is freely available as an object-relational database. PostgreSQL supports B^+ tree and R tree index structures, as well as user-defined types and functions. As an XML processor, we have used XML Parser for Java[IBM98] which is freely available. XML Parser for Java is a validating XML processor, and it supports SAX(The Simple API for XML)[Meg98]. The module to obtain regions of nodes and path expressions is implemented using SAX, which is an interface for event-based XML parsing. Also, the module to rewrite XQL into SQL is coded in C language.

4.1 The Result of Experiments

We ran some experiments using actual XML documents to see executing. The XML documents used for the experiments is the collection of the plays of Shakespeare, documents[2] tagged by Jon Bosak. These data is summarized in Table 1 and 2. The number of tuples in the Relations "Element", "Attribute", "Text" and "Path" is 179,618, 0, 147,525 and 57 respectively. Data size required in storing test data are larger than that of source data(Table 2). However, since the price of disk is sharply decreasing, and

---

[2] <URL:http://sunsite.unc.edu/pub/sun-info/xml/eg/shakespeare.1.10.xml.zip>

Table 1. Details of test data

Item	Number or Data Size
Total XML documents Size	7.65 Mbytes
Number of Documents	37
Average Document Size	206.71 Kbytes

Table 2. Data Size required in storing test data

Item	Data Size	
Relation Element	4.10	Mbytes
Relation Attribute	0	bytes
Relation Text	7.32	Mbytes
Relation Path	1.5	Kbytes
Total	11.42	Mbytes

Table 3. Processing time for sample XQL queries and number of their query results

Sample XML query	Time 1 (sec)	Time 2 (sec)	Time 3 (sec)	Number of results
/PLAY	0.15	0.01	0.26	37
/PLAY/ACT	0.18	0.01	0.29	185
/PLAY/ACT[index() = 2]	0.16	0.01	0.35	37
/PLAY/ACT[-3]	0.18	0.01	0.31	37
/PLAY/ACT/TITLE	0.19	0.01	0.33	185
//SCENE/TITLE	0.34	6.52	0.44	750
/PLAY/ACT//TITLE	0.35	3.15	0.34	951
//ACT//TITLE	0.37	6.38	0.04	951
/PLAY/ACT/SCENE/SPEECH[SPEAKER='CURIO']	1.30	7.04	0.87	4
//ACT[//SPEECH/SPEAKER='CURIO']	1.04	8.96	0.53	4

since documents are much smaller in size than multimedia data such as video and audio, we believe that increase of data size in storing XML documents is not a big problem. The machine we used is Ultra Sparc II 360MHz with 640MB memory. Database-server and client are on this machine, and transmission of data uses socket of UNIX domain.

Table 3 shows the time required for processing some XQL queries using our system and two other systems. Time 1, 2 and 3 indicates the processing time of our system, the XQL module implemented by DataChannel[DM99], and Sgrep[JP98] which can realize similar retrieval functions to XQL, respectively. Time 1 is the total time of connecting database-server from a client, rewriting XQL into SQL, sending the rewritten query, fetching the query results and cutting connection. Measurement of processing time is the average of ten trials. In measuring Time 2, all 37 XML documents are parsed, and then 150MB data is retained on main-memory of the server. As for Time 3, XQL queries are executed after constructing index structure peculiar to Sgrep.

5 Conclusions

We have proposed general storage and retrieval methods for XML documents using object-relational databases. Described storage method can apply to not only object-relational databases but also relational databases, and store XM-L documents having any document structure. As for retrieval, we have shown methods to rewrite XQL into SQL.

Further extensions to the storage and retrieval of XML documents under considerations include storage methods considering data types, corresponding to XQL extensions, integration XML data with other data stored in databases.

References

[BCD+95] G. E. Blake, M. P. Consens, I. J. Davis, P. Kilpeläinen, E. Kuikka, P. -Å. Larson, T. Snider, and F. W. Tompa. Text / relational database management systems: Overview and proposed sql extensions. Technical Report CS-95-25, UW Centre for the New OED and Text Research, Department of Computer Science, University of Waterloo, June 1995.

[Bos97] Jon Bosak. XML, Java, and the future of the Web, March 1997. http://sunsite.unc.edu/pub/sun-info/standards/xml/why/xmlapps.html.

[CACS94] Vassilis Christophides, Serge Abiteboul, Sophie Cluet, and Michel Scholl. From structured documents to novel query facilities. In *Proc. ACM SIGMOD International Conference on Management of Data*, pp. 313–324, May 1994.

[DD93] C. J. Date and Hugh Darwen. *A Guide to The SQL Standard, 3rd ed.* Addison-Wesley, Reading, MA, 1993.

[DM99] DataChannel and Microsoft. DataChannel-Microsoft Java XML Parser (Beta 2) 1. 0. http://www.datachannel.com/xml_resources/developers/, February 1999.

[DFF+98] Alin Deutsch, Mary Fernandez, Daniela Florescu, Alon Levy, and Dan Suciu. XML-QL : A Query Language for XML, Aug 1998. http://www.w3.org/TR/NOTE-xml-ql/.

[IBM98] IBM Corporation. XML Parser for Java. http://www.alphaworks.ibm.com/, Feb 1998.

[ISO86] ISO 8879: 1986. *Information Processing – Text and Office System – Standard Generalized Markup Language (SGML)*, Oct. 15 1986.

[JP98] Jani Jaakkola and Pekka Kilpelainen. sgrep (structured grep) version 1.92a. http://www.cs.helsinki.fi/ jjaakkol/sgrep.html, December 1998.

[Meg98] Megginson Technologies Ltd. SAX 1.0: The Simple API for XML. http://www.megginson.com/SAX/, May 1998.

[POS] Postgresql home page. http://www.postgresql.org/.

[RLS98] Jonathan Robie, Joe Lapp, and David Schach. XML Query Language (XQL), Sep 1998. http://www.w3.org/TandS/QL/QL98/pp/xql.html.

[SDDTZ97] Ron Sacks-Davis, Tuong Dao, James A. Thom, and Justin Zobel. Indexing documents for queries on structure, content and attributes. In *International Symposium on Digital Media Information Base (DMIB'97)*, Nov. 1997.

[SLR98] David Schach, Joe Lapp, and Jonathan Robie. Querying and Transforming XML. In *Position papers for W3C Query Language Workshop*. 1998. http://www.w3.org/TandS/QL/QL98/pp/query-transform.html.

[Wor98] World Wide Web Consortium. QL'98 - The Query Languages Workshop. http://www.w3.org/TandS/QL/QL98/, December 1998.

[WWWC98a] World Wide Web Consortium. Extensible Markup Language (XML) 1.0. http://www.w3.org/TR/1998/REC-xml-19980210, February 1998. W3C Recommendation 10-February-1998.

[WWWC98b] World Wide Web Consortium. Extensible Style Language(XSL) Working Draft, 12 1998. http://www.w3.org/TR/1998/WD-xsl-19981216.

SQL/LPP: A Time Series Extension of SQL Based on Limited Patience Patterns

Chang-Shing Perng and D. Stott Parker

Dept. of Computer Science, University of California, Los Angeles
{perng,stott}@cs.ucla.edu

Abstract. In this paper, we introduce SQL/LPP, a time series extension of SQL. SQL/LPP is based on **Limited Patience Patterns**, a temporal pattern model that is expressive, practical, intuitive, and supports a declarative algebraic syntax permitting query optimization. We illustrate basic features of SQL/LPP, showing the definition and use of popular time series patterns.

1 Introduction

1.1 Motivation

Since 1995, when Schmidt et al[4] observed that time series was a neglected issue in temporal database research, both industrial development and academic research have turned to handle time series data[1]. However, effort has been focused on storage of sequential data and on aggregate computation. As performance of storage and indexing technique[2] have been significantly improved, we believe it is time to offer new functionality by extending query languages in order to answer the call for time series analysis tools.

Our beliefs are quickly illustrated by the following simple example.

Example 1. A user might want to find the periods during which IBM stock price steadily went up. In other words, the user might want to query for an **uptrend** in this stock quote database. An **uptrend** pattern in a daily stock price database is a continuous period which satisfies the following two conditions:

1. The closing price of each day is higher than that of the previous day.
2. The length of the period is at least 5 days.

This example brings three challenges to query languages.

- The expected query result are segments instead of individual records.
- Often users are more interested in local (in time) features instead of global features of the whole time series.

---

[1] Database vendors, including Informix, Oracle, IBM, Fame etc., provide time series modules for their relational database.

– The patterns are defined by users in a totally descriptive way. Users do not provide a sample pattern for similarity searching, and algorithms used in similarity-based pattern searching are not applicable to this problem.

SQL3, the current de facto standard query language, does not respond well to challenges like this. The well-known temporal query language TSQL2[8] does not have the expressive power to define general patterns either. [2] There is a serious lack of adequate languages for expressing time series queries.

1.2 Previous Work

Several languages have been proposed to serve as a query language for 'time series' databases or similar purposes. Examples include the following:

– *TREPL*[5] is a composite event description language which provides strong expressive power in describing time series patterns. TREPL does not provide an incremental execution model for efficient implementation, which we believe is critical for time series applications.
– The Informix TimeSeries DataBlade [3] provides time series types for storage management. It does not extend the SQL language to handle the records in time series tables. Instead, it defines hundreds of time series functions to express queries. Because time series records are accessible only through these functions, it is difficult to develop new functions and this approach is not truly extensible.
– *SEQUIN* [6][7] extends SQL to allow efficient evaluation when database records are sequentially ordered. However, SEQUIN is comparatively weak in expressing pattern queries.
– *SDL*[1] is a shape definition language. It is aimed at numerical (single-quantity) time series only. The other limitation of *SDL* is that symbols (the basic building blocks) of *SDL* describe relationships between two adjacent elements only. So aggregation-related patterns, e.g. moving average, are not expressible in *SDL*.

1.3 Limited Patience Patterns

Figure 1 shows a space of time series segments (intervals in a time series). Any query pattern must search for a matching segment in this space. An important class of queries for which limited patience succeeds is the class of queries that require only *incremental computation*. Queries that rely on many basic feature values of a segment are computable this way. A more general characterization of queries for which this approach succeeds is that they can be implemented with **attributed queues**. Attributed queues not only conceptually capture the

---

[2] TSQL2 does include a RISING aggregate. But it can not capture the exact notion of an uptrend. TSQL2 generally lacks pattern constructs, and was not designed for time series analysis.

searching mechanism well, they also have an advantage in computational efficiency. In Figure 1, we can see that 'adjacent' segments share most of their elements, differing only in the head and tail. This phenomenon conforms readily with the characteristics of queue structure. The idea is to let the queue traverse the search space and update its feature (attribute) values accordingly. When the feature values satisfy the requirements of the query, the queue emits an answer.

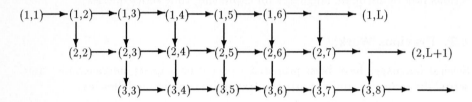

Fig. 1. The segment space as a traversal graph. The length limit is L. A traversal moves through this space by either extending the tail of the segment (moving to the right) or contracting the head of the segment (moving down).

2   Extensional Data Model and Data Definition Language

The data definition language of SQL/LPP and the associated extensional data model are straightforward, as demonstrated by the following example.

Example 2. Consider a daily stock database. The stock symbol serves as the surrogate. Each time series element contains 3 columns: date, closing price and trade volume. The table is declared as:

```
CREATE ROW TYPE quote( date datetime, price  real, volume int )
CREATE TABLE daily_stocks(symbol lvarchar, quotes TimeSeries(quote))
```

Logically, `quotes` is a sequence of time series elements of type `quote`.

In order to define the formal semantics of SQL/LPP later, we give the formal definition of **time series elements**, **time series** and **segments** here.

Definition 1. *A **time series element** is an object of row type $T = \tau_1 \times \cdots \times \tau_n$ where $n > 0$ and $\tau_1, \cdots, \tau_n$ are basic types. The columns of a time series element are named $c_1, \cdots, c_n$. The type of time series elements is written $\{c_1 : \tau_1, \cdots, c_n : \tau_n\}$.*

Definition 2. *A **time series** is a function $ts : integer \to T$ where T is a row type. $ts(i)$ is usually denoted by $ts[i]$.*

Definition 3. *Given a time series ts of type T, a function s is a **time series segment** of length ℓ if there exists a integer $k > 0$ such that for all $1 \leq i \leq \ell$, $s[i] = ts[k + i - 1]$. The set of all segments is denoted by $seg(T)$.*

In the rest of this paper, we simply use **elements** and **segments** for time series elements and time series segments when the context is clear.

Given a time series ts, a segment s can be represented as $ts[u : v]$ which indicates indices of the first and the last elements. That is, $s[1] = ts[u]$ and $s[\ell] = ts[v]$ when s is of length ℓ. We assume the length of a segment is at least 1.

For each time series element $s[i]$, its index is simply the position of the time series element in the time series. That is, given s as a time series or segment, $s[i]$ is an element in s, and $index(s[i]) = i$. In this paper, we assume $index$ starts from 1. We also use $index_s(e)$ to denote the index of e in a time series (or segment) s.

Database queries are usually considered as mappings from one set of data to another. Derived data (views) can be queried. Time series databases are no exception. In order to maintain the connection between the two sets of data, an ordering on segments is required to form derived time series. In the current design of SQL/LPP, the default ordering is **lexicographical ordering** of the index pair of the first and the last elements of segments. The lexicographic ordering detects emerging patterns earlier instead of later, and on length-limited segments it is a linear ordering — which is very useful, as will be discussed in Section 3.3.

With the segment ordering $\ll$, a successor function $succ : seg(\mathcal{T}) \to seg(\mathcal{T})$ is defined as: $succ(s_1) = s_2$ if $s_1 \ll s_2$ and for all s_3, if $s_1 \ll s_3$ then $s_2 \ll s_3$ or $s_2 = s_3$.

3 SQL/LPP: The Language

3.1 Pattern Functions

Pattern functions are the building blocks of SQL/LPP pattern specification. It is our intention to make the function set extensible. The functions we select to introduce in this section are basic but sufficient to define many interesting patterns.

For each segment s of type $seg(\mathcal{T})$ where $\mathcal{T} = \{c_1 : \tau_1, \cdots, c_n : \tau_n\}$, $C = \{c_1, \cdots, c_n\}$, and $|s| = \ell$, we define the following pattern functions:

1. $first : seg(\mathcal{T}) \times int \to \mathcal{T}$, $first(s, k) = e$ iff $index_s(e) = k$ and $k \leq l$.
2. $last : seg(\mathcal{T}) \times int \to \mathcal{T}$, $last(s, k) = e$ iff $1 \leq \ell - k + 1 \leq \ell$ and $index_s(e) = \ell - k + 1$.
3. $length : seg(\mathcal{T}) \to int$, $length(s) = \ell$.
4. $avg : seg(\mathcal{T}) \times C \to \tau_i$, $avg(s, c_i) = t$ iff c_i is of type τ_i, the '+' (plus) and '/' (divide) operators are defined in τ_i, and $t = \sum_{e \in s} \dfrac{e.c_i}{\ell}$.
5. $max : seg(\mathcal{T}) \times C \to \tau_i$, $max(s, c_i) = u$ iff c_i is of type τ_i, the comparison operator '$\leq$' is defined in τ_i, there exists an element e in s such that $e.c_i = u$ and for all e in s, $e.c_i \leq u$.

sum and *min* can be defined in similar ways.

Given a segment s of type $seg(T)$ and an element e of type T, we define the following pattern functions to deal with element reference.

1. $is\_first : T \times int \rightarrow boolean$, $is\_first(e, k) = true$ iff $1 \le k \le \ell$ and $index_s(e) = k$
2. $prev : T \times int \rightarrow T$, $prev(e_1, k) = e_2$ iff $index_s(e_1) = m$, $m - k \ge 1$ and $index_s(e_2) = m - k$.

Also, is_last and $next$ are defined symmetrically to is_first and $prev$.

3.2 Pattern Expressions, Pattern Formulae and Pattern Sentence

Using the functions defined above and usual mathematical operators and functions, we can construct **pattern expressions**. We require pattern expressions to be type-safe. For example, assuming s is a segment of the `quote` type defined in Example 2 and e is a variable, the following expressions are legal pattern expressions: $is\_first(e, 2)$, $last(3).price$, $avg(s, volume) * length(s)$ and $next(first(s, 3), 3).volume - prev(last(s, 2)).volume$.

An **atomic pattern formula** is a pattern expression with resulting type boolean. For example, the following pattern expressions are legal atomic pattern formulae: $is\_first(e)$, $last(s, 3).price > 100$, $avg(s, volume) * length(s) = 3141000$, $next(first(s, 3), 3).price - prev(last(s, 2)).price > last(s, 3).price$ and $last(s, 1).price > e.price$.

Pattern formulae are defined inductively:

1. An atomic pattern formula is a pattern formula.
2. If $\mathcal{P}$, $\mathcal{Q}$ are pattern formulae, then $(NOT\ \mathcal{P})$, $(\mathcal{P}\ AND\ \mathcal{Q})$, $(\mathcal{P}\ OR\ \mathcal{Q})$, $[ALL\ e\ IN\ s](\mathcal{P})$ and $[SOME\ e\ IN\ s](\mathcal{P})$ are all pattern formulae.

A pattern formula $\mathcal{P}$ is a **pattern sentence** if every variable occurrence in $\mathcal{P}$ is quantified.

An interpretation of pattern sentences is a pair (ts, s) where ts is a time series and s is a segment of ts. If a sentence $\mathcal{P}$ evaluates to true in an interpretation (ts, s), we call (ts, s) a model of $\mathcal{P}$ and denote it as $(ts, s) \models \mathcal{P}$. When the context is clear, we simply denote it as $s \models \mathcal{P}$. Pattern formulae are allowed to refer to elements outside s but quantifiers ALL and $SOME$ only quantify the element inside the segment. An atomic pattern formula which refers to non-existing elements always evaluates to false. For example, assume ts is a time series of `quote` type (cf. Section 2) with at least 2 elements, then

- $(ts, ts[1 : 2]) \not\models [ALLe\ IN\ s](e.price > prev(e, 1).price)$ because when $e = ts[1]$, $prev(e, 1)$ refers to a non-existing element. Hence $(ts, ts[1 : 2]) \models NOT\ [ALLe\ IN\ s]\ (e.price > prev(e, 1).price)$.
- $[ALLe\ IN\ s](e.price > prev(e, 1).price)$ can evaluate to true for some $s \subseteq ts$ even though the formula always refers to an element outside the segment.

3.3 Searching Directives

An often encountered problem in pattern searching is that the search engine returns too many segments that overlap with, or properly contain, or are adjacent to one another. Consider the pattern we described in Example 1. Assume there is a 10-day period in which a stock goes up every day. Then there are 21 segments which satisfy the conditions — one of length 10, two of length 9, ..., and six of length 5. In most applications, the number of answers is far more than desired. A pattern query language must provide search directives to reduce the number of matched segments.

Based on the segment ordering, SQL/LPP provides two classes of search directives. **Selection search directives** indicate which segments should be reported before searching the segments in the next row. **Restart search directives** specify where the search process should proceed after a matched segment is reported.

Assume the description of a pattern is a pattern sentence $\mathcal{P}$. The following are SQL/LPP selection search directives:

1. **MAXIMAL**: Given a starting point x, report only those $ts[x : y]$ such that $ts[x : y] \models \mathcal{P}$ and for all $z > y$, $ts[x : z] \not\models \mathcal{P}$. These are the longest matched segments. (Properly contained segments are not reported.) Their length is bounded either by the specification of the pattern or the limit of system resources.
2. **FIRST MAXIMAL**: Given a starting point, report only the shortest segment $ts[x : y]$ such that $ts[x : y] \models \mathcal{P}$ but $ts[x : y + 1] \not\models \mathcal{P}$. No proper sub-segment is reported.
3. **MINIMAL**: Given a starting point, report the shortest matched segment $ts[x : y]$ such that $ts[x : y - 1] \not\models \mathcal{P}$ and $ts[x : y] \models \mathcal{P}$.

These appear to cover the alternatives most useful in practice. Because they conflict mutually, only one of the above directives can be specified in a pattern.

Example 3. Consider a pattern **profitable_period** described by pattern sentence $first(s, 1).price < last(s, 1).price$. As shown in Figure 2, different selection search directives select different segments.

Assume that $s = ts[x : y]$ is the last reported answer and n is a natural number. The following restart search directives indicate the restarting point:

1. **SKIP START** n: $ts[x + n : max(x + n, y)]$.
2. **SKIP END** n: $ts[x : y + n]$.
3. **SKIP** n: $ts[y + n : y + n]$.
4. **MAX-OVERLAPPING** n: $ts[y - n + 1 : y - n + 1]$ if $y - n > x$, $succ(s)$ otherwise.
5. **ALL**: $succ(s)$.

Due to frequent use, we use `NON-OVERLAPPING` for `SKIP 1`. More than one of the restart search directives can be applied to a pattern. If two directives specify

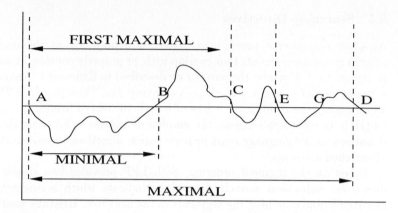

Fig. 2. While searching a pattern specified by formula $first(s).price < last(s).price$ in a time series shown here, for segments start at **A**, **AB,AC** and **AD** are the first segments selected with respect to **MINIMAL**, **FIRST MAXIMAL** and **MAXIMAL** selection directives. Assume no restart directive is specified, **MINIMAL** will report **AB**, **AE** and **AG**. **FIRST MAXIMAL** will report **AC**, **AF** and **AD**.

$ts[x_1 : y_1]$ and $ts[x_2 : y_2]$ as the next starting point, then the search engine will restart at $ts[max(x_1, x_2) : max(y_1, y_2)]$. For example, if the last reported answer is $ts[x : y]$ and the pattern is specified with **SKIP START 3** and **SKIP END 5**, the search will resume at $ts[x + 3 : y + 5]$.

Revisiting the example of monotonic uptrend described in Example 1, if $ts[11 : 20]$ is a long uptrend and the pattern is specified with **FIRST MAXIMAL**, only the segment $ts[11 : 15]$ will be reported. If it is specified with the **MINIMAL** and **NON-OVERLAPPING** directives, two segments $ts[11 : 15]$ and $ts[16 : 20]$ will be reported.

3.4 Defining SQL/LPP Patterns

SQL/LPP patterns, like procedures, functions and triggers, are first-class objects in time series databases. A simple SQL/LPP pattern describes the properties of a single segment. In contrast, a composite SQL/LPP pattern is formed by many defined patterns. The syntax of pattern definition is presented in this subsection.

Simple SQL/LPP Pattern Declaration The main body of a simple SQL/LPP pattern is a segment of a certain element type. A number of public attributes can be defined by the ATTRIBUTE⋯IS clause. Pattern sentences and search directives are placed in the WHERE and WHICH_IS clauses respectively. The following examples demonstrate basic pattern declaration.

Example 4. The pattern *uptrend* described in Example 1 can be expressed as:

```
CREATE PATTERN uptrend AS
```

```
SEGMENT s OF quote  WHICH_IS FIRST MAXIMAL, NON-OVERLAPPING
ATTRIBUTE date IS last(s,1).date
ATTRIBUTE low  IS first(s,1).price
ATTRIBUTE high IS last(s,1).price
WHERE [ALL e IN s]( e.price > prev(e,1).price)
  AND length(s) >= 5
```

This pattern has three publicly accessible attributes, *date*, *low* and *high*. The attributes are the only part of the pattern that other statements can access.

Constants in patterns can also be parameterized.

Example 5. The following pattern takes a period length as a parameter and finds segments of that length with date and moving average as attributes.

```
CREATE PATTERN moving_avg_seg(days int) AS
  SEGMENT s OF quote
  ATTRIBUTE date IS last(s,1).date
  ATTRIBUTE ma IS avg(s,price)
  WHERE length(s)=days
```

Composite Pattern Definition A composite pattern is declared as a concatenation of many patterns which are non-overlapping, or overlapping on edges (having only one element in common). The search directives of sub-patterns can be overridden by specifying new search directives. The syntax of non-overlapping composition is:

```
      {pattern_1 alias_1 WHICH_IS search-directives,
       ...
       pattern_n alias_n WHICH_IS search-directives}
```

Edge-overlapping composition is similar, but the separator ',' is replaced by ';'. In both cases the WHICH_IS phrases are optional. The following example demonstrates the use of composite patterns.

Example 6. Assume the pattern **downtrend** is defined symmetrically to the pattern *uptrend* in Example 4. The pattern *double_bottom* consists of 4 trends as shown in Figure 3. The pattern has following properties:

1. The starting point is 20% higher than the local maximum.
2. The difference of the two bottoms is less than 5% of the first bottom.
3. The ending point is higher than the local maximum.

```
CREATE PATTERN double_bottom AS
  {downtrend p1; uptrend p2; downtrend p3;
   uptrend    p4 WHICH_IS ALL, NON-OVERLAPPING}
  ATTRIBUTE date IS last(p4).date
  ATTRIBUTE price IS last(p4).high
  WHERE (p1.high > p2.high*1.2)
    AND (abs(p1.low-p3.low) < 0.05*p1.low)
    AND (p4.high > p2.high)
```

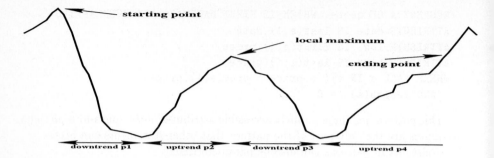

Fig. 3. Double-bottom pattern

3.5 Applying Patterns in Queries

SQL/LPP provides the *BY SEARCHING* clause as an optional part of queries. The syntax is:

```
BY SEARCHING
  pattern1 alias1 IN time-series_1,
  ...
  [ SYNC ON alias1.col_i1,alias2.col_i2,.... ]
```

A query with the `BY SEARCHING` clause collects all patterns found in the corresponding time series. When more than one pattern is under search, the matched segments form multiple streams. The `SYNC ON` clause is used to synchronize these streams and merge them into one.

When there is more than one pattern in the `BY SEARCHING` clause, the matched segments of each pattern are aligned by fields specified in the `SYNC ON` clause. If every pattern finds an instance with an identical value in the fields in the `SYNC ON` clause, these instances form an element of the answer set.

When patterns are used in the `BY SEARCHING` clause, only the attributes defined in their definition are accessible, hence able to be collected into the answers. The content of the segments and local variables are invisible and are discarded after the attributes have been recorded.

The `BY SEARCHING` clause is placed between the `SELECT` and `FROM` clauses. Since usually many matched segments can be found in one time series, the attributes of the matched segments are collected to form a new time series. For example,

```
SELECT ds.symbol,TimeSeries(db.date,db.price)
  BY SEARCHING double_bottom db IN ds.quotes
  FROM daily_stock ds
```

Time series views are created in a fashion very similar to SQL. The following example shows a typical time series view definition.

Example 7. Using the pattern moving_avg_seg defined in Example 5, the following defines a view containing the 20-day moving averages of each stock.

```
CREATE VIEW MovAvg20 (symbol20, ma20(date,ma)) AS
  SELECT ds.symbol,TimeSeries(q.date,q.ma)
  BY SEARCHING moving_avg_seg(20) q IN ds.quotes
  FROM daily_stock ds
```

4 Conclusion

Time series present new challenges for database systems, and existing query languages are not able to respond these challenges well.

In this paper, we have described SQL/LPP, a declarative extension to the standard query language SQL. The essence of SQL/LPP is that it permits descriptive pattern-based query of time series segments (time intervals) instead of individual records. SQL/LPP allows users to define simple and/or composite patterns. Since a given pattern often matches a vast number of time series segments, the pattern language includes time series functions, and directives that optionally restrict query matches to maximal or minimal, separated or overlapping segments.

Complexity is also a critical issue in time series analysis, and SQL/LPP has been designed with complexity in mind. Although the syntax and the semantics of patterns were designed to be declarative, patterns commonly possess properties that permit query optimization. For example the underlying execution model, Limited Patience Patterns, fully utilizes the fact that most pattern queries are incrementally computable and hence complexity can be reduced to an acceptable level.

References

1. R. Agrawal, G. Psaila, E. L. Wimmers, M. Zait. *Querying Shapes of Histories,* Proc. of the 21st Int'l Conference on Very Large Databases, Zurich, Switzerland, September 1995.
2. C. Faloutsos, M. Ranganathan, Y.Manolopoulos. "Fast Subsequence Matching in Time-Series Databases", *Proc. SIGMOD'94.*
3. Informix Software Inc. *Informix TimeSeries DataBlade Module User's Guide* Version 3.1.
4. D. Schmidt et al. *Time Series, a Neglected Issue in Temporal Database Research?* In *Recent Advances in Temporal Databases,* 1995.
5. I. Motakis, C. Zaniolo. *Temporal Aggregation in Active Database Rules* SIGMOD Conference 1997: 440-451
6. P. Seshadri, M. Livny, R. Ramakrishnan. *SEQ: A Model for Sequence Databases.* Proceedings of the IEEE Conference on Data Engineering, March 1995.
7. P. Seshadri, M. Livny, R. Ramakrishnan.*Sequence Query Processing.* Proceedings of the ACM SIGMOD Conference on Data Management,May 1994.
8. R.T. Snodgrass (ed.) *The TSQL2 Temporal Query Language,* New York: Kluwer Academic Publishing, 1995.

A Knowledge Based Approach for Modeling and Querying Multidimensional Databases

Zohra Bellahsene[1] and Mohand-Saïd Hacid[2]

[1] LIRMM, 161 rue ADA
F-34392 Montpellier Cedex 5
bella@lirmm.fr
[2] LISI-INSA Lyon
F-69621 Villeurbanne Cedex
mshacid@lisi.insa-lyon.fr

Abstract. In this paper we address the problem of modeling and querying multidimensional databases by exploiting the possibility of using two different languages. Cubes are described within a description logic and the query language is based on a small set of operators used to build cubes from existing ones.

Keywords: Multidimensional Databases, Intensional Reasoning, Description Logics.

1 Introduction

Recently, much attention has been focused on multidimensional databases. Many commercial systems based on their own data models have been developed. The main strength of multidimensional databases is their ability to view, analyze, and consolidate huge amounts of data. To do so, instead of presenting tables to the user, data can be presented in the shape of so-called *data-cubes* which can be manipulated by using operators to cut out pieces from large cubes, change the granularity of dimensions, pivot cubes, etc. Because of these functionalities, multidimensional databases play an important role in Decision Support Systems, and for On Line Analytical Processing (OLAP). For describing the interdependence of data in a multidimensional database, *data cubes* are regarded as most appropriate data model. In a data cube, each axis is associated with a dimension (e.g., time, location, or products) and its according values. Then, points in the cube (called cells) can be associated with values (called measures) of additional dimensions (like sales volumes). Displaying information to the user as well as navigation in this information are tasks that are well supported by this data model.

In this paper we take a new look at the problem of modeling and querying multidimensional databases. We exploit knowledge representation techniques for concept languages developed in Artificial Intelligence to develop an approach for modeling and querying data in the context of multidimensional databases. Cubes are described within a description logic. The query language is based in part on data cube operators given in [1]. Like [1] operators of the language are defined on cubes and produce cubes. Thus, we can define new cubes from already existing ones using operators like join, restrict, aggregate, etc.

Although, in the basic form that we give here, the query language does not account for all overviewed aspects of cube operators of [1], it constitutes a kernel to be extended.

Paper outline: Section 2 gives an example illustrating the features of a hypercube-based data model. Section 3 presents some definitions. In Section 4, we develop our languages and give their Tarski-style extensional semantics. The schema language allows to describe the structure of cubes and the query language allows to build cubes from other ones. Finally, we conclude anticipating on the necessary extensions.

2 Example

Consider a marketing analyst of a chain of toy stores organizing his/her business data along dimensions like *location, product,* and *time.* This example is drawn from [3] with some modifications. We have sales units for each store (the location), for each item (the product) and for each day (the time). Figure 1 shows a representation of this data in the relational model. These data are called *micro data* or *base data,* since it is supposed to be the most fine-grained data available.

store	item	day	sales
S1	Chess	Jan 10, 97	11
S1	Lego	Jan 10, 97	29
S1	Micado	Jan 10, 97	15
S1	Monopoly	Jan 10, 97	14
S1	Risiko	Jan 10, 97	14
S1	Scrabble	Jan 10, 97	32
S2	Chess	Jan 10, 97	20
S2	Lego	Jan 10, 97	34
S2	Micado	Jan 10, 97	22
S2	Monopoly	Jan 10, 97	18
S2	Risiko	Jan 10, 97	25
S2	Scrabble	Jan 10, 97	40
S3	Chess	Jan 10, 97	35
S3	Lego	Jan 10, 97	28
S3	Micado	Jan 10, 97	10
S3	Monopoly	Jan 10, 97	18
S3	Risiko	Jan 10, 97	26
S3	Scrabble	Jan 10, 97	36
...	...	...	...

Fig. 1. A relational representation of sales

A more concise and clearer way to represent this data is a three-dimensional matrix (Figure 2). This representation is commonly known as a *data cube* (in the multidimensional database jargon). It facilitates navigation. In this representation, each axis is associated with a *dimension*, that is a column of a relational table. Elements within a dimension are called *positions*. A dimension acts as an index for identifying values within a cube. Points in a data cube are called *cells*, and each cell in Figure 2 is associated with the corresponding element of the column *sales*. Then, the cube is said to have dimensions *store*, *item*, and *day*, and to have the measure *sales*. Note that the representation of Figure 2 is only possible because the *sales* is uniquely determined by the *store*, *item* and the *day*.

As multidimensional databases are designed for ease and performance in manipulating and analyzing complex data structures, values of dimensions or measures can be aggregated, decomposed, or combined to new values to form what is commonly known as *macro data* or *summary data*. This corresponds to what is called data *consolidation* [4,5].

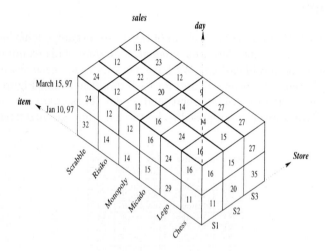

Fig. 2. A cube representation of toy sales

Each dimension has an associated hierarchy of levels of consolidated data. For example, each store rolls up to the city it is located, and each city rolls up to an area. Hierarchies like this one are called *containment hierarchies* in the context of statistical databases [7]. In general, dimensions can have more complex structures. For example, in figure 3, the level day of the dimension *time* rolls up to month and week. While the hierarchy associated with the dimension product has only three levels, the one associated with the dimension location has four levels. Giving names to the levels enables us to drill down or roll-up information to the granularity we have in mind by (possibly) skipping intermediate levels. In the following, we will call the most fine-grained level *base level*. In Figure 3, names of the dimensions are used to denote the lower level of the corresponding dimension.

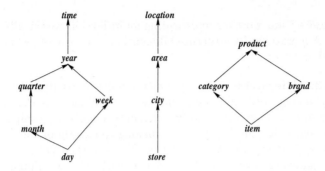

Fig. 3. Multiple hierarchically structured dimensions

3 Preliminaries

We first introduce the notion of *multisets* (or *bags*): In contrast to simple sets, in a multiset an individual may occur more than once, this is to say that, for example, the multiset $\{1\}$ is different from the multiset $\{1, 1\}$.

Definition 1. (Multisets) Let S be a set. A *multiset* M over S is a mapping $M : S \to \mathbf{N}$, where $M(s)$ denotes the number of occurrences of s in M. The set of all multisets of S is denoted $MS(S)$.
    A multiset M is said to be finite iff $\{s \mid M(s) \neq 0\}$ is a finite set.

Next, we define *concrete domains*, which are used to incorporate application-specific domains (i.e., strings, reals, non-negative integers, etc.) into the abstract domain. In the following, the term *abstract individual* means an object of the abstract domain, and the term *concrete individual* means an object of a concrete domain.

Definition 2. (Concrete Domains) A concrete domain
$\mathcal{D} = (\mathsf{dom}(\mathcal{D}), \mathsf{pred}(\mathcal{D}), \mathsf{agg}(\mathcal{D}))$ consists of:

- the domain $\mathsf{dom}(\mathcal{D})$,
- a set of predicate symbols $\mathsf{pred}(\mathcal{D})$, where each predicate symbol $P \in \mathsf{pred}(\mathcal{D})$ is associated with an arity n and an n-ary relation $P^{\mathcal{D}} \subseteq \mathsf{dom}(\mathcal{D})^n$,
- a set of aggregation symbols $\mathsf{agg}(\mathcal{D})$, where each aggregation symbol $\Sigma \in \mathsf{agg}(\mathcal{D})$ is associated with an aggregation function
$\Sigma^{\mathcal{D}} : MS(\mathsf{dom}(\mathcal{D})) \to \mathsf{dom}(\mathcal{D})$.

An example of a concrete domain is the set of (nonnegative) integers with comparisons $(=, <, \leq, \geq, >)$, functions $(+, \cdot)$, and aggregation functions (e.g., *min, max, count, average*).

We propose a framework for representing multi-level hierarchically structured dimensions. A hierarchically structured dimension is a set of objects interrelated by part-whole relations.

Definition 3. (Hierarchies) A *hierarchy* is a finite, partially ordered set $(\mathcal{H}, \succ)$, where $\succ$ is a strict ordering and a unique maximal element $m \in \mathcal{H}$ exists. A *level* is a subset $\ell \subseteq \mathcal{H}$ such that no two elements $x, y \in \ell$ are comparable by $\succ$. Furthermore, each element $h \in \mathcal{H}$ has to belong to exactly one level. If for two levels $\ell \subseteq \mathcal{H}$, $\ell' \subseteq \mathcal{H}$ we have $h \in \ell, i \in \ell'$ with $h \succ i$, then $\forall h' \in \ell \, \exists i' \in \ell'$ such that $h' \succ i'$, and there exist no $h'' \in \ell, i'' \in \ell'$ with $h'' \prec i''$. Finally, if for two levels ℓ, ℓ' we have $h \in \ell, i \in \ell'$ with $h \succ i$, then there exists no $\ell'' \subseteq \mathcal{H}$, different from ℓ and ℓ' such that there exists $i'' \in \ell''$ with $h \succ i''$.

Hierarchies are represented using a concrete domain for each dimension: A hierarchy-concrete domain $\mathcal{H} = (\text{dom}(\mathcal{H}), \text{pred}(\mathcal{H}), \emptyset)$ is a domain where $(\text{dom}(\mathcal{H}), \succ)$ is a hierarchy as defined above, $\succ \in \text{pred}(\mathcal{H})$, and each level ℓ is associated with a unary predicate $\ell^{\mathcal{H}}$, where $\ell^{\mathcal{H}}(x)$ holds for all elements x belonging to the level ℓ.

With this definition, the hierarchy associated with the dimension *product* is split into two hierarchies $\mathcal{H}_1$ and $\mathcal{H}_2$. $\mathcal{H}_1$ is composed of the levels *item, brand*, and *product*, and $\mathcal{H}_2$ is composed of the levels *item, category*, and *product*.

4 The Languages

We introduce two languages: (1) a language for describing the structure of cubes, and for specifying a particular instantiation, and (2) a query language for querying the database and building new cubes from existing ones. They are inspired by description logics and employ a variable free notation. The fact that the measure in a data cube functionally depends upon the other attributes (dimensions) is captured by a specific constructor.

4.1 The Schema Language ($\mathcal{SL}$)

Definition 4. (Syntax) Let N_C, N_f be two disjoint sets of concept and feature (i.e., functional role) names, $\mathcal{D}_1, \ldots, \mathcal{D}_k$ be concrete domains, $P \in \text{pred}(\mathcal{D}_i)$ for some $i \in [1, k]$ be an n-ary predicate name. The set of concepts is the smallest set such that if A is a concept name or a concrete domain name, A' is concept name, C, D are arbitrary concepts, and $f, f_1, \ldots$ are feature names then

$$C \sqcap D, \exists f.A, [fd \; A' \; \{f_1, \ldots, f_m\} \; f], P(f_1, \ldots, f_n)$$

are concepts,

A $\mathcal{SL}$ *schema* $\mathcal{S}$ consists of a finite set of primitive concept specifications, each of the form $A \sqsubseteq C$, where A is a concept name and C denotes an arbitrary concept. This primitive concept specification states that all instances of A are instances of C. Hence, C gives necessary conditions for membership in A.

In the following, we assume the schema *acyclic*. That is, no concept name may occur–neither directly nor indirectly–within its own specification.

Definition 5. (Semantics) The semantics is given by an interpretation $\mathcal{I} = (\Delta^{\mathcal{I}}, \cdot^{\mathcal{I}})$, which consists of an (abstract) interpretation domain $\Delta^{\mathcal{I}}$, and an interpretation function $\cdot^{\mathcal{I}}$. The abstract domain has to be disjoint from any given concrete domain, i.e., $\Delta^{\mathcal{I}} \cap \mathsf{dom}(\mathcal{D}_i) = \emptyset$ for all concrete domain $\mathcal{D}_i$ ($i \in [1, k]$), and the concrete domains are pairwise disjoint. The interpretation function $\cdot^{\mathcal{I}}$ associates each concept C with a subset $C^{\mathcal{I}} \subseteq \Delta^{\mathcal{I}}$ and each feature name with a partial function $f^{\mathcal{I}} : \Delta^{\mathcal{I}} \to (\Delta^{\mathcal{I}} \cup (\bigcup_{i=1}^{k} \mathsf{dom}(\mathcal{D}_i)))$. Intuitively, concepts describe sets and thus correspond to unary predicates. Additionally, $\mathcal{I}$ has to satisfy the following equations:

$$(C \sqcap D)^{\mathcal{I}} = C^{\mathcal{I}} \cap D^{\mathcal{I}}$$
$$(\exists f.A)^{\mathcal{I}} = \{x \in \Delta^{\mathcal{I}} \mid f^{\mathcal{I}}(x) \text{ is defined and } f^{\mathcal{I}}(x) \in A^{\mathcal{I}}\}$$
$$[fd\ A\ \{f_1, \ldots, f_m\}\ f]^{\mathcal{I}} = \{x \in \Delta^{\mathcal{I}} \mid \forall y \in A^{\mathcal{I}}$$
$$\text{if } (f_1^{\mathcal{I}}(x) = f_1^{\mathcal{I}}(y) \text{ and } \ldots \text{ and } f_m^{\mathcal{I}}(x) = f_m^{\mathcal{I}}(y)) \text{ then}$$
$$f^{\mathcal{I}}(x) = f^{\mathcal{I}}(y)\}$$
$$P(f_1, \ldots, f_n)^{\mathcal{I}} = \{x \in \Delta^{\mathcal{I}} \mid (f_1^{\mathcal{I}}(x), \ldots, f_n^{\mathcal{I}}(x)) \in P^{\mathcal{D}}\}$$

An interpretation $\mathcal{I}$ is a model of a schema $\mathcal{S}$ iff it satisfies $A^{\mathcal{I}} \subseteq C^{\mathcal{I}}$ for all axiom $A \sqsubseteq C \in \mathcal{S}$.

Example 6. In our multidimensional data model, *data is organized in cells*. Each cell is identified by a set of feature/value pairs. A cell is considered as an instance of the concept defining the cube the cell belongs to. The cube given in Figure 2 can be described by the following primitive concept specification:

$$cubesales \sqsubseteq \exists store.Stores \sqcap \exists item.Items \sqcap \exists day.\texttt{STRING} \sqcap \exists sales.\texttt{INTEGER} \sqcap$$
$$[fd\ cubesales\ \{store, item, day\}\ sales]$$

where *store*, *item*, *day* and *sales* are feature names. *Stores* and *Items* can be seen as primitive concepts containing the different stores and items respectively. Concrete domains needed here are `INTEGER` and `STRING`. a model $\mathcal{I}$ of *cubesales*, where $\Delta^{\mathcal{I}}$ contains,

The schema language introduced previously allows to describe knowledge about classes of individuals and relationships between these classes. We can now turn our attention to the extensional level, which we call the *ABox*. The *ABox* essentially allows one to specify instance-of relations between individuals and classes (concepts), and between pairs of individuals and features.

Definition 7. Let N_I and N_D be two disjoint alphabets of symbols, called abstract individual names and concrete individual names respectively. Instance-of relationships are expressed in terms of *membership assertions* of the form:

$$a : C, (a, b) : f, (a, z) : f, (z_1, \ldots, z_n) : P$$

In addition, we allow expressions (which we call constraints, or simply assertions) of the form

$$(f_1(a) = f_1(b) \wedge \ldots \wedge f_m(a) = f_m(b)) \rightarrow f(a) = f(b)$$

where a and b are abstract individual names, $z, z_1, \ldots, z_n$ are concrete individual names, C is a concept name or an arbitrary concept, $f, f_1, \ldots$ are feature names, and P is an n-ary predicate name of a concrete domain. Intuitively, the first form states that a is an instance of C, and the second form states that a is related to b by means of the feature f (we also say b is a f-*successor* of a).

In order to assign a meaning to membership assertions, the extension function $\cdot^{\mathcal{I}}$ of an interpretation $\mathcal{I}$ is extended to individuals by mapping them to elements of $\Delta^{\mathcal{I}}$ in such a way that $a^{\mathcal{I}} \neq b^{\mathcal{I}}$ if $a \neq b$ (Unique Name Assumption). *For concrete individuals, the unique name assumption does not hold.*

An interpretation $\mathcal{I}$ satisfies the assertion:

$$a : C \text{ iff } a^{\mathcal{I}} \in C^{\mathcal{I}}, \quad (a, b) : f \text{ iff } f^{\mathcal{I}}(a^{\mathcal{I}}) = b^{\mathcal{I}}$$
$$(a, z) : f \text{ iff } f^{\mathcal{I}}(a^{\mathcal{I}}) = z^{\mathcal{I}}, \quad (z_1, \ldots, z_n) : P \text{ iff } (z_1^{\mathcal{I}}, \ldots, z_n^{\mathcal{I}}) \in P^{\mathcal{D}}$$
$$(f_1(a) = f_1(b) \wedge \ldots \wedge f_m(a) = f_m(b)) \rightarrow f(a) = f(b) \text{ iff}$$
$$(f_1^{\mathcal{I}}(a^{\mathcal{I}}) = f_1^{\mathcal{I}}(b^{\mathcal{I}}) \wedge \ldots \wedge f_m^{\mathcal{I}}(a^{\mathcal{I}}) = f_m^{\mathcal{I}}(b^{\mathcal{I}})) \Rightarrow f^{\mathcal{I}}(a^{\mathcal{I}}) = f^{\mathcal{I}}(b^{\mathcal{I}})$$

An *ABox* is a finite set of membership assertions.

An interpretation $\mathcal{I}$ is a model for an *ABox* $\mathcal{A}$ iff $\mathcal{I}$ satisfies all the assertions in $\mathcal{A}$.

Example 8. Consider the cube of the Example 6. The extensional part which constitutes the *ABox* is specified by using the following assertions:

$$\mathcal{A} = \{ \ c_1 : cubesales, (c_1, S1) : store, (c_1, Chess) : item,$$
$$(c_1, \mathbf{z_1}) : day, (\mathbf{z_1}) : \ =_{"Jan10,97"}, (c_1, \mathbf{z_2}) : sales, (\mathbf{z_2}) : \ =_{11}, c_2 : cubesales$$
$$\ldots \}$$

where $=_{11}$, for example, stands for the unary predicate $\{n \mid n = 11\}$.

4.2 The Query Language ($\mathcal{QL}$)

Querying a database of cubes means retrieving stored individuals (i.e., cells) that satisfy certain conditions. In our framework, concepts (classes) are used to represent sets of individuals and thus it is natural to try to use them also for describing query results. In the multidimensional data model presented here, cube operators may generate new individuals that are deduced as instances of so-called *query classes*.

Definition 9. (Syntax) Let A be a concept name, $f, f_1, \ldots, g$ be feature names, $\mathcal{D}_1, \ldots, \mathcal{D}_k$ be concrete domains, $P \in \mathsf{pred}(\mathcal{D}_i)$ for some $i \in [1, k]$ be an n-ary predicate name, $\Sigma \in \mathsf{agg}(\mathcal{D}_i)$ for some $i \in [1, k]$ be an aggregate function name, and *level* is a name of a level within a hierarchy associated with a dimension. Query concepts are formed inductively by the following rules:

$$
\begin{aligned}
C, D \longrightarrow\; & A \mid \\
& \mathsf{restrict}(C, E) \mid \\
& [fd\ C\ \{f_1, \ldots, f_m\}\ f] \mid \\
& \mathsf{join}(C, D) \mid \\
& \mathsf{aggr}(C, f, \Sigma, g) \mid \\
& \mathsf{roll-up}(C, f, \Sigma, g : level) \\
E \longrightarrow\; & E \sqcap E \mid \\
& P(f_1, \ldots, f_n)
\end{aligned}
$$

Note that in contrast to the schema language, the functional dependency construct applies to complex concepts.

The semantics of the language is now defined in a set-theoretic way.

Definition 10. (Semantics) In addition to the equations in definition 5, $\mathcal{I}$ has to satisfy the following equations:

$$
\begin{aligned}
\mathsf{restrict}(C, E)^{\mathcal{I}} &= \{x \in \Delta^{\mathcal{I}} \mid x \in C^{\mathcal{I}} \text{ and } x \in E^{\mathcal{I}}\} \\
P(f_1, \ldots, f_n)^{\mathcal{I}} &= \{x \in \Delta^{\mathcal{I}} \mid (f_1^{\mathcal{I}}(x), \ldots, f_n^{\mathcal{I}}(x)) \in P^{\mathcal{D}}\} \\
\mathsf{join}(C, D)^{\mathcal{I}} &= \{x \in \Delta^{\mathcal{I}} \mid \exists y \in C^{\mathcal{I}}\ \exists y' \in D^{\mathcal{I}} \text{ and } \mathcal{I} \text{ satisfies} \\
& \qquad x = \mathsf{join}(y, y')\} \\
\mathsf{aggr}(C, f, \Sigma, g)^{\mathcal{I}} &= \{x \in \Delta^{\mathcal{I}} \mid \exists y_1, \ldots, y_n \in C^{\mathcal{I}} : \mathsf{satmax}(\{y_1, \ldots, y_n\}, C, f, g) \\
& \qquad \text{and } \mathcal{I} \text{ satisfies } x = \mathsf{aggr}(y_1, \ldots, y_n, f, \Sigma, g)\} \\
\mathsf{roll-up}(C, f, \Sigma, g : level)^{\mathcal{I}} &= \{x \in \Delta^{\mathcal{I}} \mid \exists y_1, \ldots, y_n \in C^{\mathcal{I}} : \\
& \qquad \mathsf{satmax}(\{y_1, \ldots, y_n\}, C, f, g) \text{ and} \\
& \qquad \mathcal{I} \text{ satisfies } x = \mathsf{roll-up}(y_1, \ldots, y_n, f, \Sigma, g : level)\}
\end{aligned}
$$

Note that the query concept $\mathsf{aggr}(C, f, \Sigma, g)$ is a derived form since it can be rewritten as $\mathsf{roll-up}(C, f, \Sigma, g : ALL)$ where ALL is the maximal element in the hierarchy associated with the dimension g.

The semantics of assertions of the form $x = op(y, \ldots)$ for $op \in \{\mathsf{join}, \mathsf{aggr}, \mathsf{roll-up}\}$ is given as follows:

Let f be a feature name, y, y' be cells (individuals). Let $\mathsf{dom}(f^{\mathcal{I}})$ be the domain of $f^{\mathcal{I}}$, i.e.,

$\mathsf{dom}(f^{\mathcal{I}}) = \{x \in \Delta^{\mathcal{I}} \text{ such that } f^{\mathcal{I}}(x) \text{ is defined }\}$, $N_y = \{f \in N_F \mid y \in \mathsf{dom}(f^{\mathcal{I}})\}$, and ℓ be a name of a level.

The function $\mathsf{satmax}(\{y_1, \ldots, y_n\}, C, f, g)$ returns true if $\{y_1, \ldots, y_n\}$ is a maximal subset of $C^{\mathcal{I}}$ such that f is defined for all the y_i $i \in [1, n]$ and if there is a feature name $h \notin \{f, f\}$ such that h is defined for some y_i, $i \in [1, n]$, then h is also defined for all y_j, $j \in [1, n]$, and all the y_j, $j \in [1, n]$, agree on h. Formally:

1. $\forall i \in [1, n], y_i \in \mathsf{dom}(f^{\mathcal{I}})$;
2. $\forall h \in N_{y_1} \cup \ldots \cup N_{y_n}$, if $h \notin \{f, g\}$ then $\forall i, j \in [1, n], h^{\mathcal{I}}(y_i) = h^{\mathcal{I}}(y_j)$;

3. $\forall y_i \in \{y_1, \ldots, y_n\}, \nexists y_l \in C^{\mathcal{I}}$ such that $y_l \notin \{y_1, \ldots, y_n\}$ and $y_l \in \operatorname{dom}(f^{\mathcal{I}})$ and $\forall i \in [1, n]\, h^{\mathcal{I}}(y_l) = h^{\mathcal{I}}(y_i)\,(h \notin \{f, g\})$

An interpretation $\mathcal{I}$ *satisfies*

- an assertion of the form $x = \operatorname{join}(y, y')$ iff
  1. $N_y \cap N_{y'} \neq \emptyset$;
  2. y and y' agree on all common features. That is, $\forall f \in N_y \cap N_{y'}\, f^{\mathcal{I}}(y) = f^{\mathcal{I}}(y')$;
  3. $\forall g \in N_y \cup N_{y'}, g^{\mathcal{I}}(x) = g^{\mathcal{I}}(y) \cup g^{\mathcal{I}}(y')$.
  Hence, for this join operator, the features on which the two cells are joined are those which occur in both cells. If one wants to use this join in a different way, one may use an operator *rename* on the input cells to change the feature names.
- an assertion of the form $x = \operatorname{aggr}(y_1, \ldots, y_n, f, \Sigma, g)$ iff
  1. $x \notin \operatorname{dom}(g^{\mathcal{I}})$;
  1. $f^{\mathcal{I}}(x) = \Sigma(S)$, where S is the multiset $\{f^{\mathcal{I}}(y_i) \mid 1 \leq i \leq n\}$;
  3. $\forall h \in N_{y_1} \cup \ldots \cup N_{y_n}$, if $h \notin \{f, g\}$ then $h^{\mathcal{I}}(x) = h^{\mathcal{I}}(y_i)$ for some $i \in [1, n]$ (say, for example, $h^{\mathcal{I}}(x) = h^{\mathcal{I}}(y_1)$).
  This operator is used to aggregate the values of the feature f over all those cells coinciding on all their feature-fillers besides their f-fillers and g-fillers. The output cell has no value with respect to the feature g.
- an assertion of the form $x = \operatorname{roll-up}(y_1, \ldots, y_n, f, \Sigma, g : \ell)$ iff
  1. $g^{\mathcal{I}}(x) = d$ with $\ell^{\mathcal{H}}(d)$ and $d \succ g^{\mathcal{I}}(y_i)$ for $i \in [1, n]$;
  2. $f^{\mathcal{I}}(x) = \Sigma(S)$, where S is the multiset $\{f^{\mathcal{I}}(y_i) \mid 1 \leq i \leq n\}$;
  3. $\forall h \in N_{y_1} \cup \ldots \cup N_{y_n}$, if $h \notin \{f, g\}$ then $h^{\mathcal{I}}(x) = h^{\mathcal{I}}(y_i)$ for some $i \in [1, n]$ (say, for example, $h^{\mathcal{I}}(x) = h^{\mathcal{I}}(y_1)$).

Example 11. Using the cube of Example 6, we present simple queries to give a flavor of multidimensional queries.

A query is formulated in terms of a concept Q in $\mathcal{QL}$, with the meaning of asking for the set of all individuals x such that the database logically implies that x is an instance of Q.

- *Select products for which the sales exceed 22 units*

$$\operatorname{restrict}(cubesales, >_{22} (sales))$$

Here $>_{22}$ stands for the unary predicate $\{n \mid n > 22\}$ of all nonnegative integers greater than 22.

- *Select the subset of cubesales limited to stores in Berlin*

$$\operatorname{restrict}(cubesales, city^{\mathcal{H}}(Berlin) \sqcap \succ_{Berlin} (store))$$

Here, the hierarchy concerning the dimension *location* is represented using a concrete domain $\mathcal{H}$. The level *city* is associated with the unary predicate $city^{\mathcal{H}}$, where $city^{\mathcal{H}}(x)$ holds for all objects x belonging to the level *city*. $\succ_{Berlin}$ stands for the unary predicate $\{x \mid Berlin \succ x\}$ of all elements of $\mathcal{H}$.

- *Select products for which the total sales exceeds 1000 units*

$$\operatorname{restrict}(\operatorname{aggr}(cubesales, sales, \operatorname{sum}, day), >_{1000} (sales))$$

5 Conclusion

There has been a deal of research in using techniques from knowledge representation and reasoning in database modeling and querying, and it is reasonable to expect that much of this research will be relevant to new database applications that need advanced features. This paper proposed an approach for modeling and querying multidimensional databases with reasoning capabilities.

Queries in the context of advanced information systems like decision support and on-line-analytical processing systems, datawarehouses, and statistical databases, in particular those issued by end users, involve aggregation. The more the amount of data that are processed by these systems grows, the more important become aggregation functions for summarizing, consolidating, and analyzing these large amounts of data. Hence, reasoning with queries involving aggregation constraints is a crucial task. As for the future work, we want to extend this approach to incorporate aggregation constraints [6,2].

References

1. Rakesh Agrawal, Ashish Gupta, and Sunita Sarawagi. Modeling multidimensional databases. In *Proceedings of the International Conference on Data Engineering (ICDE'97), Birmingham, UK. Also available as Research Report via WWW at http://www.almaden.ibm.com/cs/people/ragrawal/pubs.html#olap*, April 1997.
2. Franz. Baader and Ulrike. Sattler. Description logics with aggregates and concrete domains. In *Proceedings of the ECAI98 Conference, (to appear)*, England, 1998.
3. Luca Cabibbo and Riccardo Torlone. Querying multidimensional databases. In *Proceedings of the 6th International Workshop on Database Programming Languages (DBPL'97), Estes Park, Colorado, USA*, August 1997.
4. E. F. Codd, S. B. Codd, and C. T. Salley. Providing olap (on-line analytical processing) to user-analysts: An it mandate. White paper - http://www.arborsoft.com/essbase/wht_ppr/coddTOC.html, 1993.
5. M. Gyssens, L. V. S. Lakshmanan, and I. N. Subramanian. Tables as a paradigme for querying and restructuring. In *Proceedings of the 1996 Symposium on Principles Of Database Systems (PODS'96), Montreal, PQ, Canada*, June 1996.
6. Kenneth A. Ross, Divesh Srivastava, Peter J. Stuckey, and S. Sudarshan. Foundations of aggregation constraints. In *Proceedings of the Second International Workshop on Principles of Constraint Programming (PPCP'94), Orcas Island, WA (A long version will appear in TCS 190, 1998)*, LNCS 874, pages 193–204. Springer-Verlag, 1994.
7. Arie Shoshani. Olap and statistical databases: Similarities and differences. Technical report, http://www.lbl.gov/ arie (A short version of the paper is published in ACM TODS 1997), 1997.

An Incremental Hypercube Approach for Finding Best Matches for Vague Queries

Josef Küng, Jürgen Palkoska

Institute for Applied Knowledge Processing (FAW), University of Linz, Altenberger Str. 69
A-4040 Linz, Austria
e-mail:{jk,jp}@faw.uni-linz.ac.at

Abstract. In this article we present an extension of the Vague Query System (VQS) which allows the user to efficiently find the best matching record for ad-hoc queries. The VQS operates on top of existing database systems. It maps arbitrary types of attributes to the Euclidean space in order to represent semantic background information. Due to the multi tier concept of the VQS we can not apply conventional multidimensional search methods directly and so we have chosen to use an iterative approach. The concept works on the basis of an incremental extension of the search intervals around the query values which is repeated until the best match is proven to be found. As an indexing method for effectively accessing the semantic background information a slightly modified version of the pyramid technique (Berchtold et. al.) is applied.

1 Introduction

The VQS (Vague Query System, [1]) has been developed in order to support vague query processing in relational databases. The system is able to find similar records on the basis of semantic background information which is stored in the database by the means of a multidimensional representation of the attributes in Euclidean space. A new language, VQL (Vague Query Language), was defined containing the operator "IS" ("similar to") and a data source which can be a conventional table, a view or an SQL-statement as major elements. On the basis of a VQL-statement the system ranks the records of the queried relation according to the query conditions. For this purpose the system specifies for each record a numerical value *TD* (*Total Distance*) which represents a presuming number of goodness.

It has to be taken into account that computing TD for large sets of records can be very time consuming. We have come to the conclusion that in many application areas users do not need a ranked list of all records but it would be sufficient to know only the best matching record. However the original concept of the VQS wouldn't allow to find the best matching record without calculating TD for all the other records too.

Spatial database theory provides many methods for storage and retrieval of multidimensional objects. This kind of databases stores knowledge about objects, their extent and their position in space. Because the VQS stores semantic background information as points in multidimensional space too, we can find some parallels to spatial databases. Within the VQS these methodologies nevertheless can't be applied directly. The reason is that the system accesses multiple high dimensional feature spaces in parallel and so we are facing a more complex task.

In this article we will show the concept for an indexing method that can be applied to efficiently find the nearest neighbor for a specific VQL-query. In order to keep the general usability of the VQS we have tried to realize an indexing concept that is able to use the capabilities of existing DBMSs. For this purpose a mapping of multidimensional points to the one-dimensional space is carried out. With this ability the VQS can still operate on top of conventional database systems and in arbitrary application scenarios.

The remainder of this article is organized as follows: In section 2 we give an overview of multidimensional indexing methods and take a look at some interesting approaches which try to provide semantic based similarity queries. In section 3 we resume the main features of the original VQS which are extended to incremental nearest neighbor search capabilities in section 4. As an conclusion we will summarize our work in section 5 and show our further plans.

2 Related Research

Concepts that are intended to generally extend relational database systems with the capability for vague query processing are in most cases restricted to numerical domains. SQL-extensions of Bosc et. al. [2], the *Fuzzy Database-Query Language* of Wong et. al. [3] as well as *Fuzzy Base* of Gazzotti et. al. [4] are some examples. ARES is one example for a system that tries to enable a flexible interpretation even of non-numeric queries [5]. In ARES the semantic background information is stored in so called *similarity relations*. They hold numerical similarity values for pairs of numerical and non-numerical attribute values. VAGUE presented by Motro in [6] is also a very interesting approach to enhance the query facilities of relational databases. This implementation is based on four types of *data metrics* which are used to store semantics for numerical as well as for alphanumerical domains.

In [1] we have shown that the VQS uses a multidimensional representation of arbitrary attributes as points within the Euclidean space in order to express their semantic meaning. In this respect we can find parallels to the field of spatial databases, where sophisticated search trees and algorithms have been introduced during the past few decades. In [7] Gaede et. al. give an excellent summary of the most important multidimensional access methods. One of the best known structures for storing multidimensional points is the k-d-tree proposed by Bentley [8]. It can be used not only for exact match queries but also for nearest neighbor searches of k-dimensional points. On the basis of this structure many extensions of the k-d-tree (e.g. [9]) and similar search trees have been introduced.

The main reason for the complexity of spatial index structures is the lack of a total order for the objects in multidimensional space. A lot of attempts were made, however, to find mappings to the one-dimensional space in order to apply conventional indexing methods and to provide the possibility to effectively store objects in relational database systems. Nearly all concepts that have been suggested realize some kind of space partitioning and numerate the single partitions according to specific rules. In [7] Gaede et. al. give an overview of the most important of these *space filling curves*. Another very interesting approach is to use dimension reduction mechanisms that work with approximations in specific dimensions [10].

3 Querying with the VQS

When we have defined the original version of the VQS [1] the main intention was to build a system that is able to carry out semantic based similarity searches in relational databases. If a conventional query fails to retrieve any record the VQS should have the capability to find at least a set of approximately matching records.

For this purpose we have defined a query language (VQL) which allows the user to specify what query conditions have to be met exactly and what attributes can differ if no exact match is available. On the basis of the user formulated VQL-statement the VQS carries out a ranking of the records according to the query conditions.

3.1 Representing Semantic Information

Our aim was to find a sophisticated concept for representing semantic background information for non-numeric attributes. We have come to the conclusion that many features of real life objects can be mapped to points in multidimensional Euclidean space. Therefore non-numeric attribute-values are represented as numeric coordinates in a multidimensional feature space. For this purpose we have introduced the *NCR-Tables (Numeric-Coordinate-Representation-Tables)*. The attribute itself is the key of the NCR-Table (*NCR-Key*). Furthermore an NCR-Table contains an arbitrary number of numeric *NCR-Columns* representing the single dimensions of the feature space.

Fig. 1 shows two examples for NCR-Tables, one that represents geographical coordinates of cities and one that shows the numerical representations of the equipment-categories for cars.

City	Name	X	Y
	Salzburg	2500	2000
	Filzmoos	3500	3000
	Munich	500	2500
	Linz	6500	4500

CarCategory	Category	Category_Number
	Basic	1
	Economy	2
	Standard	3
	Comfort Line	4
	S_Class	5

Fig. 1. Examples for NCR-Tables

3.2 Mapping Semantics to Attributes

Users can define the semantic background information for the attributes of arbitrary relations by mapping them to a suitable NCR-Table. Attributes for which a mapping to an NCR-Table exists are called *FuzzyFields*. Fig. 2 shows a simple relation that holds data of hire cars. The attributes *Home Base* and *Category* could for instance be specified as *Fuzzy Fields* of the NCR-Tables *City* and *CarCategory* of Fig. 1.

Furthermore the VQS supports multiple parallel NCR-mappings for the single attributes, in order to express complex semantic definitions.

Hire Cars	ID	Type	Home Base	Category
	1	Volkswagen	Filzmoos	Standard
	2	Mitsubishi	Linz	Standard
	3	Daihatsu	Filzmoos	Economy
	4	Mercedes	Munich	S_Class
	5	Daihatsu	Linz	Economy

Fig. 2. Sample Relation for the Storage of Hire Cars

3.3 Processing the Similarity

The VQS represents similarity between non-numeric attribute values as the Euclidean distance between their NCR-Coordinates. This ability allows the system to find records semantically close to a query. The record having the smallest distance to the query is the best match. If attributes are, however, expressed through the parallel mapping to multiple NCR-Tables or the query spans more than one criterion, the system has to combine multiple distances in order to express the overall record's relevance for the query. For this purpose the VQS carries out a normalization of the single distances. Therefore the distance between a query and a particular record can be defined by the average of the normalized distances calculated for the single query criteria. The result of this computation is called *Total Distance* (*TD*). It is in the interval [0,1] and it can be used as a presuming number of goodness. In order to stress the importance of specific query conditions the user can specify individual weights for the vague query criteria

Example: In the *Hire Cars* relation a user searches for a *standard* car which he would like to hire in *Salzburg*. A crisp query would fail because no car of the specified class is available for Salzburg. However the VQS is able to retrieve records fulfilling the specified query criteria at least to a certain degree.

For this purpose the system arbitrarily starts with the *Home Base* criteria and retrieves the multidimensional representation of *Salzburg* from the associated NCR-Table. On the basis of this information the system is able to calculate the normalized Euclidean distances to all cars in the database:

$$ND_{City} = \frac{D_{City}}{Diameter_{City}} = \frac{\sqrt{(2500-x)^2 + (2000-y)^2}}{\sqrt{(500-6500)^2 + (2000-4500)^2}} \tag{1}$$

In the same manner we can calculate the normalized distances for *Category*. Finally we have to combine the normalized distances to *TD* expressing the entire records' relevance for the query. If we assume that the location criteria was stated twice important than *Category* the system will calculate the *Total Distance* as follows:

$$TD = \frac{2 * ND_{City} + 1 * ND_{Category}}{2 + 1} \tag{2}$$

As we can see in Fig. 3 the best matching record is car number *1* because the attribute *Category* exactly meets the user needs and the home base seems to be rather close to Salzburg. The ranked list is presented to the user as the result of the query.

Hire Cars	ID	Type	Home Base	Category	TD
	1	Volkswagen	Filzmoos	Standard	0.1450
	3	Daihatsu	Filzmoos	Economy	0.3119
	4	Mercedes	Munich	S_Class	0.3781
	2	Mitsubishi	Linz	Standard	0.4838
	5	Daihatsu	Linz	Economy	0.5671

Fig. 3. Ranked Result Relation of the above Query

3.4   Drawbacks

The VQS has been designed for carrying out a ranking of all the records in the database according to the specified query conditions. In large databases, however, calculating the *Total Distance* for every single record can last very long. Therefore it could be useful to enhance the search capabilities of the VQS for the ability to optionally carry out a *k-nearest-neighbor search* or even a *nearest neighbor-search*. If large recordsets have to be processed these search abilities could then be used to achieve performance improvements.

In the following section we will outline a concept that can be used to effectively find the nearest neighbor for an entire record specified by a VQL-statement. In order to avoid the necessity to calculate the *Total Distance* for every single record we will use an indexing mechanism which is able to work on top of relational databases.

4   Multi Space Nearest Neighbor Search

Query processing within the VQS can be described as *three layer multidimensional point search*: In *layer 1* we take into account the multidimensional semantic background information for a specific attribute that is referenced by a query. If a parallel mapping to multiple NCR-Tables exists for an attribute, the system has to combine the single distances in order to represent the similarity to the query value (*layer 2*). Having calculated the numeric similarity measure on attribute level the system has to combine the single similarity distances to the *Total Distance* which represents the entire record's relevance for the query (*layer 3*).

Caused by the three layer architecture indexing methods finding simply the nearest neighbor for a multidimensional point can't be applied directly. The first idea to avoid this problem would be to realize an index structure that spans multiple NCR-Tables. In this context we face, however, the problem that VQL-queries can be formulated "ad-hoc" and therefore no fixed relationship exists between the feature spaces that are combined on *layer 3*.

Therefore we had to find a method for retrieving the best matching record "on the fly" after the user has formulated the query. In the following section we will outline the *incremental hypercube search* concept which is able to find the best matching record for a specific VQL-query.

4.1   Incremental Hypercube Search

The aim of the *incremental hypercube search* is to limit the number of records that have to be retrieved from the database as far as possible. For this purpose the system tries to limit the retrieval of NCR-Values to these ones lying close to the query values. Values lying further away are only retrieved if they are expected to contribute to a better match on record-level. The following incremental method becomes applied:

Step 1: Definition of Initial Search Intervals
The hypercube search starts for each query criteria in the corresponding feature space (represented by an NCR-Table) from the query value and retrieves all NCR-Values within a predefined distance $r0$ to the search value. The extension of $r0$ could be determined by statistical measures or it could simply be a fixed proportion of the feature space's diameter. For determining the NCR-Values lying within the hypersphere specified by $r0$ we would, however, have to calculate the Euclidean distance to the query value for each single record.

Therefore we use the following approximation: With the search value as center point we define a hypercube c_0 with $2*r0$ as length of its sides in each dimension (see Fig. 4). Due to this approximation we do not need to calculate the Euclidean distance from the query value to each NCR-Value because we can decide the membership to the hypercube simply on basis of the single coordinates. Fig. 4 shows the hypercubes $c0$ for the running example in both feature spaces.

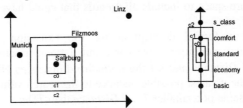

Fig. 4. Hypercubes for the Query Values *Salzburg* and *standard*

Step 2: Regular Extension of Hypercubes
The lengths of sides of the hypercubes $c0$ are extended to $c1$ by a fixed value e_c within all affected feature spaces. The process of expanding the actual hypercubes ca to ca_{+1} is repeated until we have found a tuple of NCR-Values that corresponds to at least one record of the query relation. Referring to the example in Fig. 4 we have chosen to set $e_{c(City)}$ to 1000 and $e_{c(Category)}$ to 1. In practical use the extension of $e_{c(x)}$ could be determined statistically or by a fixed proportion of the feature space's diameter again.

As we can see in Fig. 4 the hypercubes $c1$ are the first that include NCR-Values that are contained in the relation *Hire Cars* of Fig. 2 ((*Filzmoos, Standard*) and (*Filzmoos, Economy*)).

Step 3: Calculating the Actual Nearest Neighbor

We have already outlined that on attribute level (*layer 1*) we can not decide if a found NCR-Value contributes to the best matching record. Therefore the system calculates the *Total Distance* to the query for all records of which the NCR-Values are contained in the actual hypercubes *ca*. For this purpose the concepts of the original VQS become applied. Fig. 5 shows the result of this operation for the running example. Afterwards the preliminary resultset is checked for the actual smallest *Total Distance* *TDa*, which is 0.1450.

Hire Cars	ID	Type	Home Base	Category	TDa
	1	Volkswagen	Filzmoos	Standard	0.1450
	3	Daihatsu	Filzmoos	Economy	0.3119

Fig. 5. Records in the Resultset after the First Iteration

Having finished this step we have found a good match for the query in any case because every contributing *FuzzyField* is a near neighbor to the corresponding query value. However we do not have the guarantee for having found the best matching record for the query. For instance we do not know if a record exists having *Salzburg* as home base and a category just outside the borders of $c1_{Category}$. Therefore we have to extend the hypercubes again with *TDa* as a basis.

Step 4: Dependent Extension of Hypercubes

In this step we do not extend the sides of the hypercubes by a fixed value e_c but by a value that depends on *TDa*. The idea is the following: We look at one specific feature space and assume the worst case what means that we expect the query-values of all other feature spaces to be exact matches. How far do we have to extend the hypercube of the regarded feature space to include all records that could have a smaller distance than the actual *TDa*?

In order to get a formal description for the extension of the hypercube corresponding to query condition i we carry out a transformation of the formula describing the *Total Distance* and set the normalized distances ND_j ($i \neq j$) to 0. With this method we get the greatest possible distance to the search value in feature space i that could cause the same or a smaller *Total Distance* than *TDa*:

$$D_{max(i)} = Diameter_i * (TDa * ws/_{wi}) \qquad (3)$$

where:

$Diameter_i$	Diameter of feature space i
TDa	actual smallest *Total Distance*
w_i	weight of query condition i
w_s	sum of weights over all query conditions

On the basis of this formula we can determine the extensions of the hypercubes of which the sides have the length $2*D_{max(i)}$. For our running example we get the following lengths of the sides for the extended hypercubes $c2$:

$$l(c2_{city}) = 2 * D_{max(city)} = 2827.5 \quad (4) \qquad l(c2_{category}) = 2 * D_{max(category)} = 3.48 \quad (5)$$

Step 5: Rule for Further Hypercube Extension

On the basis of the extended hypercubes the set of the affected NCR-Values becomes extended too. If the system finds new tuples of NCR-Values that cause further records of the query table to become included into the actual resultset a new iteration of the process is initiated: Again the system computes the *Total Distance* for all the records included in the extended hypercube *i+1* and for which the *Total Distance* has not been computed yet. If the process finds a new smallest *Total Distance TDa* the hypercubes become extended and the iteration of steps 4 and 5 starts again.

If we do not find a new smallest *Total Distance* in step 5 we have proven that in the entire database no record exists having a smaller *Total Distance* to the query than the actual smallest *Total Distance TDa*.

In our running example the analysis of the hypercubes *c2* didn't find any new records and so the process terminates. The actual *Total Distance* of 0.1450 (hire car with *ID 1*) is proven to represent the best matching record of the whole database. We have seen that with this method it is possible to retrieve the best matching record for a vague query without calculating the *Total Distance* to every record of the relation.

For simplicity we have neglected the parallel mapping of Fuzzy Fields to multiple NCR-Tables (*layer 2*) in our explanations. The presented concept can, however, be extended straightforward for taking into account *layer 2* aspects too.

4.2 Applying the Pyramid Technique for Handling the Hypercubes

The incremental hypercube search strongly depends on the effective retrieval of the records of which the FuzzyFields lie within the actual hypercubes *ca*. In contrast to the original VQS we can improve the performance because we do not need to calculate *TD* for every record and we can retrieve the affected NCR-Values on the basis of the single NCR-Columns. Therefore conventional indices can be applied.

We expect, however, a further improvement of the performance if we use a multidimensional index for retrieving the NCR-Values lying within the single hypercubes. One of our aims was to guarantee the tight integration of the system into existing database systems. Therefore we have tried to find a concept that is able to use the features of standard DBMSs in order to realize a multidimensional index structure.

We use a slightly modified variant of the *pyramid technique*, an excellent work proposed by Berchtold et. al. in [11]. The original method was defined to work in feature spaces that are normalized into the interval [0,1] in each dimension. However the VQS is defined to work on infinite feature spaces. A simple normalization on the basis of the feature space diameters would not be useful because inserting a new max-value would imply a re-calculation of the index-values for all records in the database. Therefore we have slightly modified the *pyramid technique* to be able to work with infinite feature spaces.

In contrast to the concept of Berchtold et. al. we use a feature space having the multidimensional point (0.0, 0.0, ..., 0.0) as its center. Hence we get the following formula for determining the pyramid p_i holding the d-dimensional point *v*.

$$i = \begin{cases} j_{max} & \text{if } (v_{j_{max}} < 0.0) \\ (j_{max} + d) & \text{if } (v_{j_{max}} \geq 0.0) \end{cases} \qquad (6)$$

$$j_{max} = (j \mid (\forall k, 0 \le (j,k) < d, j \ne k : \mid v_j \mid >= \mid v_k \mid)) \tag{7}$$

In the second step we calculate the height h_v similar to the method presented in [11] with the difference that the height is not normalized into the interval [0,0.5]:

$$h_v = \mid v_{i \, MOD \, d} \mid \tag{8}$$

In the next step we have to combine these two measures to achieve the one-dimensional index-value for point v. Since we want to use an infinite feature space, generating the index-value is more complex than with the original pyramid technique.

In the original concept the number on the left side of the decimal point always represents the number of the pyramid and the digits on the right side of the decimal point show the height within the pyramid. Because the height is always smaller than 1 the order of pyramids and the sort order of heights within the pyramids is guaranteed which is essential for carrying out range queries. In our case, however, for h_v any real number can appear, and so we can not apply this concept directly. Therefore we had to find another representation for the indices.

We have chosen to use an alphanumeric representation for the index-values and to apply lexicographic ordering. In order to guarantee a number like ordering of the index-values we have to apply a special string format model. Therefore we use the following formal definition for calculating the index-values:

On the very left of the index-value $index_{pv}$ we place just as many placeholders as we have digits for expressing the pyramid number i. Then we append the digits representing the pyramid number. As fixed placeholder to force a sort order behind numbers we use "_" (see expression 9). We assume the sort-order of the underlying database to be *binary* so that characters are sorted behind digits.

For expressing the height within the pyramid we use a similar concept: On the left side of the string we place just as many placeholders as we have integer digits for the height. To this string we append h_v (see expression 10).

$$index_{pv} = CONCAT(PH("\_", Len(i)), i) \tag{9}$$

$$index_{hv} = CONCAT(PH("\_", LenI(h_v)), h_v) \tag{10}$$

where

    CONCAT(str1, str2)   concatenates str1 and str2
    PH(c, i) produces a string by placing the character c i times in line
    Len(n)   returns the number of digits for number n
    LenI(n) returns the number of digits for the integer part of number n

Afterwards we simply connect the two strings $index_{pv}$ and $index_{hv}$. For expressing for instance the height 9,834.67 in pyramid 1 we get the index-value _1____9834.67. For another point located in the height 10,230.45 of the same pyramid the index-value is expressed by _1____10230.45 what leads to a ranking of the second point behind the first. With this method we can guarantee the correct alphanumeric ranking of the index-values for arbitrary feature spaces.

On the basis of this mapping-method we can use any one-dimensional index-structure to store and effectively find the index-values. Since we have implemented the VQS on top of an existing DBMS this was one of our major aims for indexing.

Range Queries on the Basis of the Modified Pyramid Technique

Since Berchtold at al. use a transformation of the points to have the coordinates $(0, 0, ..., 0)$ as the center of the feature space for the search process we can use the same search algorithm, in order to retrieve the points within the hypercubes:

Determination of affected pyramids. A pyramid pi is intersected by a search interval $[q0_{min}, q0_{max}],...,[qd-1_{min}, qd-1_{max}]$ if

$$\forall j, 0 \le j < d, j \ne i : qi_{min} \le -MIN(qj) \quad \text{if } i < d \tag{11}$$

$$\forall j, d \le j < 2d, j \ne i : qi \bmod d_{max} \ge MIN(qj \bmod d) \quad \text{if } i \ge d \tag{12}$$

where

$$MIN(r) = \begin{cases} 0 & \text{if } r_{min} \le 0 \le r_{max} \\ \min(|r_{min}|, |r_{max}|) & \text{otherwise} \end{cases}$$

Determining the ranges within the affected pyramids. Having found the affected pyramids the next step is to determine an interval within each pyramid that contributes to the range query. Like in the original pyramid technique we remove all points beyond the center point:

$$\hat{q}i_{min} = qi_{min}, \hat{q}i_{max} = \min(qi_{max}, 0) \quad \text{for } i < d \tag{13}$$

$$\hat{q}i \bmod d_{min} = \max(qi \bmod d_{min}, 0) \quad \hat{q}i \bmod d_{max} = qi \bmod d_{max} \quad \text{for } i \ge d \tag{14}$$

Furthermore we have to distinguish between two types of range queries, depending on the center point of the feature space to be included in the query or not:

$h_{low} = 0$, if center point is included

$h_{low} = \min_{(0 \le j < d, j \ne i)}(\overline{qj}_{min})$, if center point is not included and $i < d$

$h_{low} = \min_{(d \le j < 2d, j \ne i)}(\overline{qj} \bmod d_{min})$, if center point is not included and $i \ge d$

$h_{high} = MAX(qi \bmod d)$

where

$$MAX(r) = \max(|r_{min}|, |r_{max}|)$$

$$\overline{qj}_{min} = \begin{cases} \max(MIN(\hat{q}i), MIN(\hat{q}j)) & \text{if } MAX(\hat{q}j) \ge MIN(\hat{q}i) \\ MIN(\hat{q}i) & \text{otherwise} \end{cases}$$

We can see that the formulas hold although we have expanded the feature space to infinity. The range query necessary for determining the NCR-Values within the hypercubes $c2$ of our running example looks a little different now. Fig. 6 shows the index-values for the NCR-Table *City*. On the basis of the pyramid retrieval method we find the two affected pyramids 2 and 3 and within the pyramids we have to check the ranges [_2____1086.25, _2____3913.75] and [_3____1086.25, _3____3413.75].

I(City)	Name	Index-Value	
	Salzburg	2	2500
	Filzmoos	2	3000
	Munich	3	2500
	Linz	2	4500

Fig. 6. Index-Values for NCR-Table *City*

For the retrieval of the corresponding records the system can use the one-dimensional index structure of the underlying database (e.g. a B-tree). Caused by the approximation through pyramids we can get false hits (*Munich, see* Fig. 7) which have to be filtered after retrieving the recordset from the database.

With the presented method we can effectively retrieve a set of NCR-Values lying within the actual hypercube *ca*. Multidimensional points lying outside the intervals are guaranteed not to be affected by the query and points within the pyramid-ranges will be taken into account when the system calculates the actual nearest neighbor.

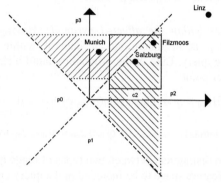

Fig. 7. Feature Space Partitioning by the Modified Pyramid Technique

5. Conclusion

In this article we discussed an extension of the Vague Query System (VQS) which is able to effectively find the best matching record according to ad-hoc formulated VQL-statements. Due to the multi layer query architecture of the VQS an incremental approach is used for finding the nearest neighbor for a query: Spatial sections around the single search values become systematically extended until the best match is shown to be found. In order to improve performance we approximate the spatial partitions by the means of hypercubes that are accessed by a multidimensional indexing-structure. For the realization of the index structure we have used a modified version of the *Pyramid Technique* proposed in [11]. Because the *Pyramid Technique* is able to map the multidimensional points to a one-dimensional index structure the mechanism can be applied on top of existing DBMSs.

Our next step will be to realize the new features of the VQS by the means of a prototype. Since the original VQS has been implemented on top of an Oracle database we will implement the prototype by the means of PL/SQL packages again. The prototype will be used to carry out extensive performance tests. In this context we will pay great attention to the clustering of attribute values. Furthermore the performance tests will bring useful knowledge in question of a proper parameterization of the VQS. Especially concepts for specifying the parameters *r0* and e_c will be essential.

Another topic of interest will be to extend the query facilities of the *incremental hypercube search* in order to retrieve the *k* nearest neighbors for a specified query. Since the pyramid technique is not the only method for realizing a multidimensional indexing concept on top of conventional databases, we would like to evaluate other indexing methods too. Especially the UB-tree proposed by Bayer et. al. is worth a nearer examination [12].

Another task will be to examine the applicability of the incremental hypercube search for the vague joining capabilities we have discussed in [13].

References

1 J. Küng, J. Palkoska: "VQS - A Vague Query System Prototype", *Proceedings of the Eight International Workshop on Database and Expert Systems Applications, DEXA 97*, Toulouse, France, Sep. 1-2, 1997, IEEE Computer Society Press

2 P. Bosc, M. Galibourg, G. Hamon, "Fuzzy Querying with SQL: Extension and Implementation Aspects", *Fuzzy Sets and Systems*, Vol. 28, No.3, 1988, pp. 333-349

3 M.H. Wong, K.S. Leung, "A Fuzzy Database-Query Language", *Information Systems*, Vol. 15, No. 5, 1990, pp. 583-590

4 D. Gazotti, L. Piancastelli, C. Sartori, D. Beneventano, "Fuzzy Base: A Fuzzy Logic Aid for Relational Database Queries", *Database and Expert Systems Applications, 6th International Conference DEXA 1995*, Ed. Norman Revell, A Min Tjoa, Springer-Verlag Berlin Heidelberg New York Barcelona Budapest Hong Kong London Milan Paris Tokyo, London 1995, pp. 385-394

5 T. Ichikawa, M. Hirakawa, "ARES: A Relational Database with the Capability of Performing Flexible Interpretation of Queries", *IEEE Transactions on Software Engineering*, Vol. 12, No. 5, 1986, pp. 624-634.

6 A. Motro, "VAGUE: A User Interface to Relational Databases that Permits Vague Queries", *ACM Transactions on Office Information Systems*, Vol. 6, No. 3, 1988, pp. 187-214

7 V. Gaede, O. Günther, "Multidimensional Access Methods", *ACM Computing Surveys*, Vol. 30, Number 2, June 1998

8 J. L. Bentley, "Multidimensional Binary Search Trees Used for Associative Searching", *Communications of the ACM*, Vol. 18, Number 9, 1975

9 J. H. Friedman, J. L. Bentley, R. A. Finkel, "An Algorithm for Finding Best Matches in Logarithmic Expected Time", *ACM Transactions on Mathematical Software*, Vol. 3, Number 3, 1977

10 K. V. R. Kanth, D. Agrawal, A. Singh, "Dimensionality Reduction for Similarity Searching in Dynamic Databases", *Proceedings of ACM SIGMOD International Conference on Management of Data*, Seattle, Washington, USA, June 2-4, 1998

11 S. Berchtold, C. Böhm, H. P. Kriegel, "The Pyramid Technique: Towards Breaking the Curse of Dimensionality", *Proceedings of ACM SIGMOD International Conference on Management of Data*, Seattle, Washington, USA, June 2-4, 1998

12 R. Bayer, V. Markl, "The Universal B-Tree for multidimensional Indexing", *Technical Report TUM-I9637*, Institut für Informatik, Technische Universität München, Nov. 1996

13 J. Küng, J. Palkoska: "Vague Joins – An Extension of the Vague Query System VQS", *Proceedings of the Ninth International Workshop on Database and Expert Systems Applications, DEXA 98*, Vienna, Austria, Aug. 26-28, 1998, IEEE Computer Society Press

Formalising Ontologies and Their Relations

Trevor Bench-Capon and Grant Malcolm

Department of Computer Science, University of Liverpool
PO Box 147, Liverpool L69 3BX, UK

Abstract. Ontologies allow the abstract conceptualisation of domains, but a given domain can be conceptualised through many different ontologies, which can be problematic when ontologies are used to support knowledge sharing. We present a formal account of ontologies that is intended to support knowledge sharing through precise characterisations of relationships such as compatibility and refinement. We take an algebraic approach, in which ontologies are presented as logical theories. This allows us to characterise relations between ontologies as relations between their classes of models. A major result is *cocompleteness* of specifications, which supports merging of ontologies across shared sub-ontologies.

1 Introduction

Over the last decade ontologies — best characterised as explicit specifications of a conceptualisation of a domain [17] — have become increasingly important in the design and development of knowledge based systems, and for knowledge representations generally. They have been shown to be useful in

- knowledge acquisition (e.g. [23]);
- knowledge reuse (e.g. [19]) and sharing (e.g. [17]); and
- verification and validation of knowledge based systems (e.g. [3]).

It has become recognised that even in a given domain multiple conceptualisations, and hence ontologies, are possible. The conceptualisations will inevitably be oriented to the tasks to be carried out, and are likely to be influenced also by personal tastes, and may even reflect fundamental disagreements as to the nature of the domain. But though they differ, ontologies will be related to one another. Thus knowledge reuse requires that ontologies be refined and extended to tailor them to some new application; sharing knowledge between systems requires that the individual system ontologies be compatible and even, at least in part, common, or capable of being systematically related to some third ontology common to the two systems.

Thus the programme of ontologies requires that we be able to speak of ontologies being consistent, compatible, the result of merging two other ontologies, an extension of some ontology, or a refinement of some ontology. We may even wish to speak of some ontology being closer to a given ontology than some third ontology, to facilitate knowledge sharing, or to inform the choice of an ontology to refine when designing a new knowledge based system. Unfortunately, although intuitions abound, precise characterisations of these relations do not.

We believe that these notions need to be made precise. Therefore in this paper we will set out an abstract and formal way of describing ontologies, so that we can give precise characterisations of these relations in these terms. Accordingly Sect. 2 sets out our formalism for describing ontologies, and Sect. 3 illustrates its use in characterising these relations with some motivating examples.

2 Ontological Specifications

Semantics is of primary importance in designing any language, and a language for formally specifying ontologies should have a clear and precise semantics. In particular, relationships between ontologies are best described in terms of their semantics. We take an algebraic approach, in which ontologies are presented as algebraic theories. This allows us to characterise relations between ontologies as relations between their classes of models. In this section we present an abstract syntax for specifying ontologies and develop the model theory that provides semantics for these specifications. We are much less interested in presenting a concrete syntax; the motivating examples given below are in an *ad hoc* syntax.

For reasons of space, the presentation below assumes some familiarity with algebraic specifications (introductions can be found in [22, 9]) and also with basic category theory (see [20, 1] for introductions). A more detailed presentation, including proofs absent from the present paper, can be found in [2].

Our ontologies specify classes of entities with attributes. These attributes take values in data types such as numbers, booleans, lists and so on. Sometimes it is convenient to make changes in the types of attributes, for example an ontology may be refined by refining the types of some of its attributes, so we consider these types to be a part of ontological specifications. We formalise this part of specifications using the notion of *order-sorted algebraic theory*; [14, 11] give details of order-sorted algebra, the following is an example of a theory for the natural numbers, in the notation of the language OBJ [16, 11].

```
th NAT is
   sorts Nat NonZeroNat .
   subsort NonZeroNat < Nat .
   op 0 : -> Nat .
   op s : Nat -> NonZeroNat .
   op p : NonZeroNat -> Nat .
   var N : Nat .
   eq  p(s(N)) = N .
endth
```

The details of this notation are not essential to the present paper. The main point is that an order-sorted theory presents some sorts, partially ordered by a subsort relation, some typed operations, and some axioms (here just one equation).

Models of such specifications interpret sorts as sets, and operations as functions; these sets and functions should satisfy the axioms in the obvious sense.

The data types in our ontologies are given by an order-sorted theory together with a fixed model interpreting its sorts and operations:

Definition 1. *A* **data domain** *is a pair* (T, D), *where* T *is an order-sorted equational theory* $T = (S, \Sigma, E)$, *where* $S = (S, \leq)$ *is the partially ordered set of sort names,* Σ *is the collection of typed operation symbols, and* E *is the set of equations, and where* D *is a model of* T. *We often write* D *instead of* (T, D).

We do not require that D be an initial model of T [15], although in many cases that would be an obvious choice. Any computable algebra can be specified equationally [4]; even uncomputable algebras, such as the reals, can be used in ontological specifications by fixing an appropriate model D (for example, the reals provide a model of the theory NAT). An important advantage of using order-sorted algebra is that it is implemented in languages such as OBJ [16, 11] and CafeOBJ [8]. This provides support for prototyping and theorem proving.

A *theory morphism*[1] $\phi : T \to T'$ between order-sorted theories induces a functor from models of T' to models of T (see, e.g., [10], though Proposition 7 presents the essential ideas). This means that any model D' of T' gives rise to a model $\phi D'$ of T; this allows us to define morphisms of data domains as follows:

Definition 2. *A* **morphism of data domains** $\psi : (T, D) \to (T', D')$ *is a pair* $\psi = (\phi, h)$, *where* $\phi = (f, g) : T \to T'$ *is an order-sorted theory morphism and* $h : \phi D' \to D$ *is a* T-*homomorphism; We require that if* σ' *in* Σ' *returns values of sort* $f(s)$ *for* $s \in S$, *then* $\sigma' = g(\sigma)$ *for some* σ *in* Σ.

Data morphisms go from coarse to fine structures. For example, one ontology might specify an attribute with values in a data type shade, interpreted in one domain as $\{light, dark\}$, while another ontology may specify values of this attribute in the range $[0, 100)$. A domain morphism might translate values up to 50 as being light, and values between 50 and 100 as being dark. The mapping

$$i \mapsto \begin{cases} \text{light} & \text{if } 0 \leq i < 50 \\ \text{dark} & \text{if } 50 \leq i < 100 \end{cases}$$

describes the homomorphism part of the above definition (i.e., we have h_{shade} mapping i in $\phi D'_{\text{shade}} = (0, 100]$ to $D_{\text{shade}} = \{light, dark\}$).

Definition 3. *An* **ontology signature**, *or just* **signature** *for short, is a triple* $(\mathcal{D}, \mathsf{C}, A)$, *where* $\mathcal{D} = (T, D)$ *is a data domain,* $\mathsf{C} = (C, \leq)$ *is a partial order, called a* **class hierarchy**, *and* A *is a family of sets* $A_{c,e}$ *of* **attribute symbols** *for* $c \in C$ *and* $e \in C + S$, *where* S *is the set of sorts in the order-sorted theory* T. *This family of sets is such that* $A_{c',e} \subseteq A_{c,e'}$ *whenever* $c \leq c'$ *in* C *and* $e \leq e'$ *in* $S + \mathsf{C}$.

---

[1] Order-sorted theory morphisms (see [14]) are pairs (f, g), where f is a monotonic map on sort names, and g maps operation symbols to operation symbols.

For $c \in C$ and $s \in S$, the set $A_{c,s}$ represents attributes of the class c that take values in D_s. Attributes may also take values in classes: for $c, c' \in C$, the set $A_{c,c'}$ represents attributes of the class c that take values in the class c'. The final condition of the above definition states that if $c \leq c'$ then the class c inherits all attributes of the class c'.

Example 4. We give an ontology for different kinds of cars that might be used by a second-hand car dealer, using an *ad hoc* notation that hopefully requires little explanation. There are four classes, Car, Estate-Car, Saloon-Car and Model. Each class is followed by an indented list of its attributes and their result types. We omit the data domain from the specification, but names beginning with a * represent data types, and {white,red,blue} represents a data type with elements white, red, and blue.

```
Car
   colour: {white,red,blue}
   model: Model
   year:   *year
   price: *pounds

Estate-Car < Car
   rear-space:  *square-metres

Saloon-Car < Car
   hatchback: {y, n}

Model
   name: *string
   manufacturer: {maker1, maker2}
   photo: *gif
```

The class Car has four attributes, e.g., model, which takes values in the class Model (i.e., model $\in A_{\text{Car},\text{Model}}$). The class Estate-Car has five attributes: four inherited from Car plus the attribute rear-space, which takes values in a data type *square-meters (we omit the data domain from this specification, but it would be sensible for this data type to consist of some kind of numerical values).

We turn now to the semantics of such specifications:

Definition 5. *A **model** M of an ontology signature $(\mathcal{D}, \mathsf{C}, A)$ consists of:*

- *A C-sorted family of sets M_c for $c \in C$, called the **carriers** of M;*
- *for each attribute symbol $\alpha \in A_{c,e}$, a function $M_{c:\alpha} : M_c \to M_e$, where if $e \in S$ then $M_e = D_e$, subject to the following monotonicity requirement: for $c \leq c' \in C$ and $\alpha \in A_{c',e}$, we have $M_{c':\alpha}|_{M_c} = M_{c:\alpha}$.*

Because of the above monotonicity property, we write simply M_α instead of $M_{c:\alpha}$.

*Given models M and N of (C, A), a **model homomorphism** $h : M \to N$ is a C-sorted family of functions $h_c : M_c \to N_c$ such that for all $\alpha \in A_{c,e}$, $h_c; N_\alpha = M_\alpha; h_e$, where $h_e = 1_{D_e}$ if $e \in S$.*

An ontology consists of a signature and some axioms; its denotation is the class of all models that satisfy the axioms. Before we give the formal definitions, we consider morphisms that relate ontologies:

Definition 6. *An* **ontology signature morphism** $\chi : (\mathcal{D}, \mathsf{C}, A) \to (\mathcal{D}', \mathsf{C}', A')$ *is a tuple* $\chi = (\phi, f, g)$, *where* $\phi : \mathcal{D} \to \mathcal{D}'$ *is a data domain morphism,* $f : \mathsf{C} \to \mathsf{C}'$ *is a morphism of partial orders, and* g *is a family of functions* $g_{c,e} : A_{c,e} \to A'_{f(c),f(e)}$, *where* $f(e) = \phi(e)$ *if* $e \in S$ *(i.e., if* $e \in S$ *then* $g_{c,e}$ *maps attributes that take values in* D_e *to attributes that take values in* $(\phi D')_e$*), such that if* $c \leq c'$ *and* $e \leq e'$ *then* $g_{c',e}(\alpha) = g_{c,e'}(\alpha)$ *for all* $\alpha \in A_{c',e}$.

Signature morphisms give rise to functors on models:

Proposition 7. *A signature morphism* $\chi : (\mathcal{D}, \mathsf{C}, A) \to (\mathcal{D}', \mathsf{C}', A')$ *induces a functor, which we also call* χ, *from the category of* $(\mathcal{D}', \mathsf{C}', A')$-*models to the category of* $(\mathcal{D}, \mathsf{C}, A)$-*models. The functor is defined on objects by*

$$- (\chi M)_c = M_{f(c)} \text{ for } c \in C, \text{ and}$$
$$- (\chi M)_\alpha = M_{g_{c,e}(\alpha)} \text{ for } \alpha \in A_{c,e},$$

where M *is a model of* $(\mathcal{D}', \mathsf{C}', A')$.

The final component in an ontology consists of axioms constraining the possible values of attributes. Here, we consider axioms to be just conditional equations, but other kinds of sentences, such as horn clauses, are also possible.

Definition 8. *An* **ontology** *is a pair* (Σ, Ax) *where* Σ *is a signature and* Ax *a set of axioms. A* **model** *of such an ontology is a model* M *of* Σ *that satisfies each axiom in* Ax, *in which case we write* $M \models Ax$.

An **ontology morphism** $\chi : (\Sigma, Ax) \to (\Sigma', Ax')$ *is a signature morphism* $\chi : \Sigma \to \Sigma'$ *such that* $\chi M \models Ax$ *whenever* $M \models Ax'$.

Example 9. Here is another car ontology that might be used for a buyers' guide:

```
Car
    colour: {white, red, blue}
    model: Model

Model
  name: *string
  type: {estate, saloon}
  hatchback: {y, n, n/a}
  picture: *gif
  rear-space: *square-metres
  manufacturer: Motor-maker
  price: *pounds

Motor-Maker
   name: {maker1, maker2}
   dealer: Dealer
```

```
Dealer
  name: *string
  address: *string

Axioms:
  var M : Model
  hatchback(M) = n/a  if  type(M) = estate
  rear-space(M) = 0   if  type(M) = saloon
```

The axioms in this ontology give specific values of attributes `hatchback` and `rear-space` depending on the `type` of model.

3   Relating Ontologies

Ontology morphisms provide a direct way of relating ontologies; any morphism $\chi : \mathcal{O} \to \mathcal{O}'$ states that the ontology $\mathcal{O}'$ is a *refinement* of the ontology $\mathcal{O}$. This is because any model of $\mathcal{O}'$ gives rise to, by Proposition 7 and Definition 8, a model of $\mathcal{O}$. This approach is standard in algebraic specification (see, e.g., [24]).

A more general way of relating ontologies is through pairs of morphisms:

Definition 10. *A relation between ontologies $\mathcal{O}_1$ and $\mathcal{O}_2$ consists of an ontology $\mathcal{O}$ and a pair of morphisms $\chi_i : \mathcal{O} \to \mathcal{O}_i$ for $i = 1, 2$.*

A morphism $\chi : \mathcal{O}_1 \to \mathcal{O}_2$ is a special case of a relation where $\mathcal{O} = \mathcal{O}_1$.

3.1   Combining and Sharing Ontologies

Ontologies represent knowledge of a given domain from a specific point of view. Examples 4 and 9 specify models of cars, from the points of view of car dealers and buyers' guides, respectively. In order to support knowledge sharing, it is important that ontologies can be merged, as stated in the following theorem:

Theorem 11. *The category of ontologies and their morphisms is cocomplete.*

This is stated in the language of category theory [20], and says that there is a 'best' way (a *colimit*) of combining related ontologies that share some subcomponents. A proof is given in [2]; an example is given below. Colimits are standard in combining algebraic theories (for example [5]; see also [18], whose cocompleteness results for order-sorted theories are used in the proof of Theorem 11).

Example 12. The following is a common subcomponent for the ontologies of Examples 4 and 9.

```
Car                           Model
  colour: {white,red,blue}      name: *string
  model: Model                  manufacturer: {maker1, maker2}
                                photo: *gif
```

There is an inclusion from this ontology (call it $\mathcal{O}$) to the ontology (call it $\mathcal{O}_1$) of Example 4. This gives us $\chi_1 : \mathcal{O} \to \mathcal{O}_1$. To relate $\mathcal{O}_1$ to the ontology (call it $\mathcal{O}_2$) of Example 9, we construct a morphism $\chi_2 : \mathcal{O} \to \mathcal{O}_2$ as follows. The class Car and its attributes are included in $\mathcal{O}_2$. The class Model and its attribute name are likewise included, and the attribute photo is mapped to picture in $\mathcal{O}_2$. The attribute manufacturer is mapped to the *compound* attribute manufacturer;name in $\mathcal{O}_2$, i.e., take the manufacturer attribute, giving a value in the class Motor-Maker, then take the attribute name of that class (this means that this example is not a colimit in the sense of Theorem 11; see [2]).

In the colimit there is just one attribute photo representing both photo from $\mathcal{O}_1$ and picture from $\mathcal{O}_2$. These two attributes are the image of photo in $\mathcal{O}$ under χ_1 and χ_2 respectively, so that this attribute is shared between the two ontologies, just as all the attributes of the class Car are shared. However, there are two manufacturer attributes in the colimit; one representing the attribute of the same name from $\mathcal{O}_1$, and the other (which we call manufacturer2) representing the attribute from $\mathcal{O}_2$. The morphisms χ_i state that manufacturer and manufacturer2;name should be the same, so in the colimit there is an axiom that constrains all models to treat them in the same way; this is the first axiom in the colimit of our two related ontologies, which is given in full below:

```
Car
   colour: {white, red, blue}
   model: Model
   year:  *year
   price: *pounds

Estate-Car < Car
   rear-space:  *square-metres

Saloon-Car < Car
   hatchback: {y, n}

Model
  name: *string
  type: {estate, saloon}
  hatchback: {y, n, n/a}
  picture: *gif
  rear-space: *square-metres
  manufacturer: {maker1, maker2}
  manufacturer2: Motor-maker
  price: *pounds

Motor-Maker
   name: {maker1, maker2}
   dealer: Dealer

Dealer
   name: *string
   address: *string
```

```
Axioms:
  var M : Model
  manufacturer(M) = name(manufacturer2(M))
  hatchback(M) = n/a  if  type(M) = estate
  rear-space(M) = 0    if  type(M) = saloon
```

Note that ontologies can be related in different ways, and the ontology $\mathcal{O}$ does not really correspond to the 'intersection' of two ontologies, but is created in such a way as to state just what is to be shared between ontologies. For example, we might have omitted the manufacturer attribute from $\mathcal{O}$, which would correspond to a judgement that the two attributes of that name in $\mathcal{O}_1$ and $\mathcal{O}_2$ were distinct. We might have included an attribute price in $\mathcal{O}$, mapped to the attribute of the same name in $\mathcal{O}_1$ and to the compound attribute model;price in $\mathcal{O}_2$. This would express the judgement that these two attributes correspond to the same feature. However, in this example, we have not done this because these features are in fact distinct; for the second-hand car dealer, the price is an individual car's saleable value, and for a buyers' guide, the price is the model's new price.

3.2 Compatibility of Ontologies

Our definition of model requires data domains to be interpreted in a fixed way. This means that not all ontologies have models, because the axioms in an ontology might not be satisfiable. That is, the axioms might be inconsistent in the sense that they entail *true = false*, while the fixed data model in the data domain requires that these values be distinct. We say that an ontology is **consistent** iff it has at least one model (so that the axioms are satisfiable).

Definition 13. *Let $\chi_i : \mathcal{O} \to \mathcal{O}_i$ for $i = 1, 2$ be a relation between ontologies. We say that $\mathcal{O}_1$ and $\mathcal{O}_2$ are* **compatible (over** $\mathcal{O}$**)** *iff their colimit is consistent.*

Proposition 14. *Let $\chi_i : \mathcal{O} \to \mathcal{O}_i$ for $i = 1, 2$ and let M_i be a model of $\mathcal{O}_i$ for $i = 1, 2$ such that $\chi_1 M_1 = \chi_2 M_2$; then the colimit of χ_i has a model, and so $\mathcal{O}_1$ and $\mathcal{O}_2$ are compatible over $\mathcal{O}$.*

A proof is given in [2]. Intuitively, this says that if models of $\mathcal{O}_1$ and $\mathcal{O}_2$ agree on their shared parts (i.e., on $\mathcal{O}$), then those models can be 'merged' to provide a model of the colimiting ontology. Similar results in an algebraic setting can be found in [21, 7].

4 Conclusions

We have presented an algebraic approach to formalising ontologies, and used this to capture various relationships between ontologies. Ontologies are specified as classes partially ordered by inheritance, and these classes have attributes that take values either in data types or in other classes. Axioms constrain the values that these attributes can take. The semantics of ontologies is given by classes of models, and this allows us to give precise characterisations of relationships between ontologies at the abstract level of relationships between their classes of models. Refinement corresponds to the existence of a morphism from an 'abstract' ontology to a more 'concrete' one, merging is achieved through colimits, and compatibility refers to the consistency of colimiting ontologies.

The advantages of an algebraic approach include a clean and precise semantics, and the existence of standard tools and techniques that can be used in proving properties such as refinement of ontologies. The main cocompleteness result (Theorem 11), draws on a long tradition of combining algebraic theories through colimits. This also allows us a certain amount of freedom in the logical language used for axioms. In this paper, we opt for equational axioms, because these are simple yet expressive; the study of algebraic theories at the level of institutions [10] shows that many other logics, such as Horn clause logic, are possible, while still retaining cocompleteness.

Our ontologies are similar to 'hidden algebra' [13, 12] in having a fixed data universe (hidden algebra also has a notion of behavioural equivalence that is not relevant to our present purposes). This allows us to reuse some results from hidden algebra. For example, because of the fixed interpretation of data domains, we know that standard equational deduction is sound but not complete for ontologies.

We have concentrated in this paper on developing an algebraic framework for specifying ontologies, rather than giving a concrete syntax for specifications (beyond that used in the examples). The results in Sections 2 and 3 represent a good start to our programme of characterising relations between ontologies, but there is more work to be done. Larger examples would provide validation of the definitions of the various relationships between ontologies, and more importantly suggest new kinds of relationships useful in practice. For instance, the brief examples in this paper use very simple relations between the class hierarchies, and we envisage that real knowledge sharing through ontologies will use rather more sophisticated relationships. It would also be interesting to relate our approach to other possible formalisms for ontologies, such as feature structures [6], which we feel will also prove interesting in relating ontologies to database schemata.

References

[1] Michael Barr and Charles Wells. *Category Theory for Computing Science*. Prentice Hall, 1990.

[2] Trevor Bench-Capon and Grant Malcolm. Relating ontologies. Draft available at http://www.csc.liv.ac.uk/~grant/ps/, 1999.

[3] Trevor Bench-Capon. The role of ontologies in the verification and validation of knowledge based systems. In R. Wagner, editor, *Proceedings of the 9th International Workshop on Database and Expert Systems*, pages 64–69. IEEE Press, Los Alamitos, 1998.

[4] Jan A. Bergstra and John V. Tucker. Algebraic specifications of computable and semicomputable data types. *Theoretical Computer Science*, 50:137–181, 1987.

[5] Rod Burstall and Joseph A. Goguen. The semantics of Clear, a specification language. In Dines Bjorner, editor, *Proceedings, 1979 Copenhagen Winter School on*

Abstract Software Specification, pages 292–332. Springer, 1980. Lecture Notes in Computer Science, Volume 86.

[6] Robert L. Carpenter. *The Logic of Typed Feature Structures*, volume 32 of *Cambridge Tracts in Theoretical Computer Science*. Cambridge, 1992.

[7] Corina Cîrstea. A semantical study of the object paradigm. Transfer thesis, Oxford University Computing Laboratory, 1996.

[8] Răzvan Diaconescu and Kokichi Futatsugi. *CafeOBJ Report*, volume 6 of *AMAST Series in Computing*. World Scientific, 1998.

[9] Hartmut Ehrig and Bernd Mahr. *Fundamentals of Algebraic Specification 1: Equations and Initial Semantics*. Springer, 1985.

[10] Joseph A. Goguen and Rod Burstall. Institutions: Abstract model theory for specification and programming. *Journal of the Association for Computing Machinery*, 39(1):95–146, 1992.

[11] Joseph A. Goguen and Grant Malcolm. *Algebraic Semantics of Imperative Programs*. MIT Press, 1996.

[12] Joseph A. Goguen and Grant Malcolm. A hidden agenda. *Theoretical Computer Science*, 1999. To appear.

[13] Joseph A. Goguen and Grant Malcolm. Hidden coinduction: behavioral correctness proofs for objects. *Mathematical Structures in Computer Science*, 1999. To appear.

[14] Joseph A. Goguen and José Meseguer. Order-sorted algebra I: Equational deduction for multiple inheritance, overloading, exceptions and partial operations. *Theoretical Computer Science*, 105(2):217–273, 1992.

[15] Joseph A. Goguen, James Thatcher, and Eric Wagner. An initial algebra approach to the specification, correctness and implementation of abstract data types. In *Current Trends in Programming Methodology, IV*, Raymond Yeh, editor, Prentice-Hall, 1978, pages 80–149.

[16] Joseph A. Goguen, Timothy Winkler, José Meseguer, Kokichi Futatsugi, and Jean-Pierre Jouannaud. Introducing OBJ. In Joseph A. Goguen and Grant Malcolm, editors, *Software Engineering with OBJ: Algebraic Specification in Practice*. to appear. Also available as a technical report from SRI International.

[17] Thomas R. Gruber. Towards Principles for the Design of Ontologies Used for Knowledge Sharing. In N. Guarino and R. Poli, editors, *Formal Ontology in Conceptual Analysis and Knowledge Representation*. Kluwer Academic Publishers, 1993.

[18] Anne E. Haxthausen and Friederike Nickl. Pushouts of order-sorted algebraic specifications. In *AMAST '96*. Springer-Verlag Lecture Notes in Computer Science 1101, 1996.

[19] Gertjan van Heijst, Guus Schreiber, and Bob J. Wielinga. Using explicit ontologies in KBS development. *International Journal of Human Computer Interaction*, 45:183–192, 1997.

[20] Saunders Mac Lane. *Categories for the Working Mathematician*, volume 5 of *Graduate Texts in Mathematics*. Springer Verlag, 1971.

[21] Grant Malcolm. Interconnection of object specifications. In Stephen Goldsack and Stuart Kent, editors, *Formal Methods and Object Technology*. Springer Workshops in Computing, 1996.

[22] Karl Meinke and John V. Tucker. Universal algebra. In S. Abramsky, D. Gabbay, and T.S.E. Maibaum, editors, *Handbook of Logic in Computer Science*, volume 1, pages 189–411. Oxford University Press, 1993.

[23] Mark A. Musen. *Automated Generation of Model-Based Knowledge-Acquisition Tools*. Research Notes in Artificial Intelligence. Pitman, 1989.

[24] Donald Sannella and Andrzej Tarlecki. Toward formal development of programs from algebraic specifications. *Acta Informatica*, 25:233–281, 1988.

Is This Argument Justified, Overruled or Defensible?

Lambèr Royakkers

Eindhoven University of Technology, Dept. of Philosophy, Technology Management
P.O.box 513, 5600 MB Eindhoven, The Netherlands
L.M.M.Royakkers@tm.tue.nl

Abstract. The purpose of this paper is to develop a theory for argumentation. Its central notion is the determination whether an argument is justified, overruled or defensible in an argumentation framework on the basis of priority. Most approaches are based on a dialectical style, which is also discussed for this approach. I establish a priority hierarchy of rules to solve the problem of conflicts between arguments, and I present a mechanism to reason about nonmonotonicity of rules over the priority hierarchy. The theory presented here is based on default logic, and is a modification and extension of Prakken's argumentation framework, and a fleshing out of the abstract argumentation framework of Dung.

Keywords: Argumentation, nonmonotonic reasoning.

1   Introduction

Logical analysis of reasoning with inconsistent rules is a very relevant area for AI research, since rules are often conflicting, especially, for example, in the legal domain. 'Prioritised' rules received attention in the research on the formalisation of nonmonotonic reasoning, particularly as a way of modelling the choice criterion in dealing with exceptions (cf. [2]; [3]; [8]; [9]).

To deal with the inconsistencies, various sorts of consistency-based approaches have been developed, such as McDermott and Doyle's [6] nonmonotonic logic and Reiter's [11] default logic. As a way of solving the problems of the interactions between arguments with conflicting conclusions, forms of defeasible reasoning (cf. [7]) have been adopted, which provide a mechanism to establish preference hierarchies of rules and to select a more applicable rule from among conflicting ones in a specific situation (cf. [14]).

In this paper, I develop a theory for argumentation[1]; its central notion is whether an argument is justified, overruled or defensible based on an hierarchy of rules (or ordered information). This assumption is probably unrealistic, as in practical reasoning the hierarchy of rules is often itself subject to discussion. However, for convenience, I use this assumption, since otherwise I have to define

---

[1] The theory is besides technical improvements an important revision of [15]. The revision consists, for example, of some new definitions (in particular the definitions of 'defeating' and 'justified argument').

a formal connection between object level and meta level which obscures the central point I want to make in this paper.

The theory can be seen as a fleshing out of and also an extension to Dung's [4] theory, which is an abstract argumentation framework to capture the notion of acceptability of arguments. Further, the theory shows similarity to the argumentation framework in default logic developed in [9] and [10], which is based on dialogue logic, however, the elaboration differs. In these works, the proof theory of the argumentation framework is stated in dialectical style. In contrast to these approaches, I have developed a proof theory in the argumentation framework.

The structure of this paper is as follows. In section 2, I give the representation of rules that are the elements of an argumentation. Section 3 discusses the argumentation framework, based on the four notions argument, defeating, defeasibility chain and justified argument. I end this paper with some conclusions.

2 Rules

The fundamental logical structure of knowledge gives rise to the nonmonotonicity of reasoning: the consequences that may follow from a set of premises can be invalidated by further information. This means that rules can be 'defeated' by other or new rules and facts. The principal idea of this paper, which goes back to Rescher [13], is to allow the rules to be ordered and to use this ordering in such a way that conflicts can be solved in a logical argumentation framework using nonmonotonic logic. The rules are divided along the lines of the hierarchical structure of a system. Rules with a lower rank of priority have to respect the consequences that follow from a higher ranked rule. To describe the ordering between the formulas, I use the following notation. Let x and y be legal rules, then '$x \leq y$' means that y is weakly preferred to x; '$x \sim y$' is an abbreviation of '$x \leq y$ and $y \leq x$'; and '$x < y$' is an abbreviation of '$x \leq y$ and $y \not\leq x$'. The ordering relation $\leq$ is reflexive and transitive.

In this paper I represent rules as conditional statements of the type

$$a_1 \wedge a_2 \wedge \ldots \wedge a_m \Rightarrow a_n,$$

where a_i $(0 \leq i \leq n)$ is a literal.[2] The literal a_n (the consequent of the rule) represents the legal effect and $a_1, a_2, \ldots, a_m$ are the elements of the antecedent of the rule, representing the legal condition.

The statement $A \Rightarrow B$ has to be interpreted as a *normal default* according to Reiter's [11,12] theory, $A : B/B$: 'If A, and it can be consistently assumed B, then we can infer B.' This means that $\Rightarrow$ is *not* interpreted as the material implication, but as an inference rule that can be defeated. From A and $A \Rightarrow B$, we can infer B unless $\neg B$ can be proven. This is called the *default modus ponens*.

The finite set of rules is denoted by Δ. Furthermore, we have a factual set $\mathcal{F}$ representing the factual situation. A set of rules and a factual set is called a default theory.

---

[2] A literal is any atomic propositional formula and any negation of an atomic propositional formula.

Definition 1. *A default theory Γ is a set $(\mathcal{F} \cup \Delta)$, where $\mathcal{F}$ is a consistent subset of a first-order language and Δ a set of defeasible rules.*

3 Arguments and defeasibility chains

The theory of defeasible reasoning for rules is based on four notions:

- the notion of *argument* (definition 5);
- the notion of *defeating* (definition 8);
- the notion of *defeasibility chain* (definition 9);
- the notion of *justified, defensible and overruled arguments* (definition 11).

Before I discuss the notion of argument, I give a definition of explaining derived from Reiter's extension of a default theory (cf. [12]).

Definition 2. *Let $(\mathcal{F} \cup \Delta)$ be a default theory, $M \subseteq \Delta$ and L a literal. Then M explains L $(M \cup \mathcal{F} \models L)$ iff*

$$L \in \bigcup_{i=0}^{\infty} G_i,$$

where

$$G_0 = \mathcal{F} \text{ and}$$

$$G_{i+1} = Th(G_i) \cup \{L \mid \exists_{a_1 \wedge a_2 \wedge \ldots \wedge a_n \Rightarrow L \in M} (\forall_{j \in \{1,2,\ldots,n\}} a_j \in G_i)\},$$

with $Th(G_i)$ denoting the first-order closure of G_i.

Intuitively, *explaining* is the same as logical consequence, except that now we deal with defaults and not with implications.

Definition 3. *Let $(\mathcal{F} \cup \Delta)$ be a default theory and $M \subseteq \Delta$. Then the set of consequents of M is defined as*

$$Cons(M) := \{L \mid M \text{ explains } L\}.$$

Thus, $Cons(M)$ gives the set of all the consequents of the defeasible rules in M and of the formulas in $\mathcal{F}$, that can be derived with default deduction from M and $\mathcal{F}$.

Definition 4. *Let $(\mathcal{F} \cup \Delta)$ be a default theory and $M \subseteq \Delta$. Then M is coherent iff*

$$\neg \exists_{L \text{ is a literal}} (L \in Cons(M) \wedge \neg L \in Cons(M)).$$

The notion of argument can now be defined as follows:

Definition 5. *Let $(\mathcal{F} \cup \Delta)$ be a default theory, $M \subseteq \Delta$, M coherent and L a literal. Then M explains L minimally iff*

- $L \in Cons(M)$ and
- $\neg \exists_{d \in M}(L \in Cons(M \setminus \{d\}))$.

We call M a minimally explaining set *of L or an* argument *for L.*
An argument *(with respect to a default theory $(\mathcal{F} \cup \Delta)$ is any subset M of Δ which is an argument for some literal.*

Further we need the following auxiliary notions.

Definition 6.

- *The set of all arguments with respect to default theory $(\mathcal{F} \cup \Delta)$ is denoted as $\mathcal{M}(\mathcal{F} \cup \Delta)$.*
- *The L-relevant set of Δ, denoted by $[L]\mathcal{M}(\mathcal{F} \cup \Delta)$, is the set of all arguments in $\mathcal{M}(\mathcal{F} \cup \Delta)$ that explain L minimally.*
- *M^* is a* subargument *of M iff $M^* \subset M$ and M^* is an argument.*

Our argumentation framework to reason with inconsistencies is based on an ordering relation $\leq$. Therefore, we need besides a default theory a given ordering of the defeasible rules. Thus, we will use an ordered default theory. The presented ordered default theory is essentially the ordered set of formulas studied, for example, in [5].

Definition 7. *An* ordered default theory *Γ is a pair $(\mathcal{F} \cup \Delta, \leq)$, where $\mathcal{F}$ and Δ are defined as above and $\leq$ an ordering over the defeasible rules of Δ.*

Our definition of 'defeat' is based on the idea that, in order to defeat an argument, a counterargument can point its attack at the argument itself, but also at one of its proper subarguments, since an argument cannot be stronger than its *weakest link* (cf. [10]). The weakest link principle states that an argument cannot be justified unless all its subarguments are justified.

Definition 8. *Let M_1 and M_2 be arguments based on the ordered default theory $(\mathcal{F} \cup \Delta, \leq)^3$. Then, M_1 is* defeated by *M_2 ($M_1 \prec M_2$) iff*

$$\exists_{d_1 \in M_1} \exists_{d_2 \in M_2}\{d_1 < d_2 \text{ and}$$

the set $\{$consequent of $d_1\} \cup \{$consequent of $d_2\} \cup \mathcal{F}$ is inconsistent$\}$.

Thus, an argument M_2 defeats an argument M_1 iff M_1 and M_2 have contradictory consequences L_1 and L_2 with respect to the factual set $\mathcal{F}$, and the rule of M_2 (responsible for the conflict) with consequent L_2 does not have a lower priority than the rule of M_1 with consequent L_1. Note that $\{L_1\} \cup \mathcal{F}$ and $\{L_2\} \cup \mathcal{F}$ are consistent, which directly follows from definition 4.

Proposition 1. *An argument cannot defeat itself.*

---

[3] In the sequel, I will leave the phrase 'based on the ordered default theory $(\mathcal{F} \cup \Delta, \leq)$' and '$(\mathcal{F} \cup \Delta)$' implicit.

This immediately follows from the fact that an argument is coherent.

Relation $\prec$ is not transitive and not asymmetric. It is possible that $M_1 \prec M_2$ and $M_2 \prec M_1$ both hold. The following example illustrates this point:

$$
\begin{array}{lll}
(d_1) & a \Rightarrow b & \\
(d_2) & & c \Rightarrow \neg a \\
\textit{Example 1.} \quad (d_3) & d \Rightarrow a & \\
(d_4) & b \Rightarrow \neg c & \\
(d_5) & & e \Rightarrow c
\end{array}
$$
$\mathcal{F}: \{f, f \to d, e\}$ with $d_5 < d_4 < d_3 < d_2 < d_1$.

Let $M_1 = \{e \Rightarrow c, c \Rightarrow \neg a\}$ and $M_2 = \{d \Rightarrow a, a \Rightarrow b, b \Rightarrow \neg c\}$. Then $M_1 \prec M_2$, since $e \Rightarrow c < b \Rightarrow \neg c$, and $M_2 \prec M_1$, since $d \Rightarrow a < c \Rightarrow \neg a$.

Proposition 2. *Let M and M' be arguments. If M defeats M', then M defeats all arguments M^* which are supersets of M' (thus $M' \subseteq M^*$).*

This immediately follows from definition 8.

Definition 9. *A defeasibility chain is a non-empty sequence of arguments in $\mathcal{M}$:*

$$M_1 \prec M_2 \prec \ldots \prec M_n$$

with the following conditions:

1. $\forall_{k,l \text{ is } odd \wedge k \neq l}(M_k \neq M_l)$;
2. $\neg \exists_{M_{n+1} \in \mathcal{M}} \{(M_1, M_3, \ldots, M_{n-1} \neq M_{n+1}) \to (M_n \prec M_{n+1})\}$ *if n is even;*
3. $\neg \exists_{M_{n+1} \in \mathcal{M}}(M_n \prec M_{n+1})$ *if n is odd.*

We define $Ch(\mathcal{M})$ as the set of all defeasibility chains of arguments in $\mathcal{M}$.

The first condition ensures that cycles in defeasibility chains are avoided. Consider example 1, without this condition the defeasibility chain would be endless: $M_1 \prec M_2 \prec M_1 \prec M_2 \prec M_1 \prec \ldots$. The two other conditions ensure that the length of a defeasibility chain is maximal: the last argument in a defeasibility chain cannot be defeated (with respect to the first condition).

Take the example above, then

$$Ch(\mathcal{M}) = \{\{d \Rightarrow a, a \Rightarrow b\}$$

$$\prec \{e \Rightarrow c, c \Rightarrow \neg a\} \prec \{d \Rightarrow a, a \Rightarrow b, b \Rightarrow \neg c\} \prec \{e \Rightarrow c, c \Rightarrow \neg a\},$$

$$\{d \Rightarrow a, a \Rightarrow b, b \Rightarrow \neg c\} \prec \{e \Rightarrow c, c \Rightarrow \neg a\},$$

$$\{e \Rightarrow c\} \prec \{d \Rightarrow a, a \Rightarrow b, b \Rightarrow \neg c\} \prec \{e \Rightarrow c, c \Rightarrow \neg a\} \prec \{d \Rightarrow a, a \Rightarrow b, b \Rightarrow \neg c\},$$

$$\{d \Rightarrow a\} \prec \{e \Rightarrow c, c \Rightarrow \neg a\} \prec \{d \Rightarrow a, a \Rightarrow b, b \Rightarrow \neg c\} \prec \{e \Rightarrow c, c \Rightarrow \neg a\},$$

$$\{e \Rightarrow c, c \Rightarrow \neg a\} \prec \{d \Rightarrow a, a \Rightarrow b, b \Rightarrow \neg c\}\}.$$

Definition 10. *$Ch(M)$ is the set of all defeasibility chains in $Ch(\mathcal{M})$ starting with M.*

The defeasibility chains in $Ch(\mathcal{M})$ take the set of all possible arguments and their mutual relations of defeat as inputs. They produce a distinction between in three types of argument:[4]

1. *justified* arguments;
2. *overruled* arguments;
3. *defensible* arguments.

A justified argument is a 'winning' argument. Such an argument can be defeated by another argument, but that argument will be overruled. An overruled argument is a 'losing' argument. A defensible argument is an argument that is neither justified nor overruled. In other words, an 'undecided' argument.

Definition 11. *Let* $M, M', M_1, \ldots, M_n \in \mathcal{M}$. *Then*

1. M_1 *is a justified argument iff* $M_1 \in Ch(M_1) \vee$
   $\forall_{M_2}\{M_1 \prec M_2 | \exists_{M_3}\{M_1 \prec M_2 \prec M_3 \in Ch(M_1) \vee$
   $\forall_{M_4}\{M_3 \prec M_4 | \exists_{M_5}\{M_1 \prec M_2 \prec M_3 \prec M_4 \prec M_5 \in Ch(M_1) \vee \ldots \vee$
   $\forall_{M_{n-1}}\{M_{n-2} \prec M_{n-1} | \exists_{M_n}\{M_1 \prec M_2 \prec \ldots \prec M_{n-1} \prec M_n \in$
   $Ch(M_1) \wedge \neg \exists_{M' \in \mathcal{M}} M_n \prec M' \wedge n \text{ is odd}\}\}\}\}\}$.
2. M *is an overruled argument iff there is a justified argument* M' *such that* $M \prec M'$.
3. M *is a defensible argument iff* M *is neither a justified argument nor an overruled argument.*

Note, that all the 'odd' arguments (i.e., $M_1, M_3, M_5, \ldots, M_n$) in definition 11.1 are justified arguments by definition. This definition is a correction of a flaw in [15]. This flaw is that an argument was justified if and only if *all* defeasiblility chains starting with this argument were of even length. In terms of dialogue games: if and only if all dialogues about the argument are won by the proponent. This is clearly incorrect, since it suffices that at each moment there is one possible choice for the proponent that makes him win.

Proposition 3.

1. *A justified argument can only be defeated by an overruled argument.*
2. *If an argument* M *cannot be defeated or can only be defeated by overruled arguments, then* M *is a justified argument.*

Proof.

1. Suppose M_1 is a justified argument. Then by definition 11.1 it holds that for all arguments M_2 which defeat M_1, there is a justified argument, say M_3. Since, all the arguments M_2 can be defeated by a justified argument, the arguments M_2 are all overruled arguments.

---

[4] The terms justified, overruled and defensible arguments were introduced by Prakken and Sartor [10].

2. Suppose M cannot be defeated. Then M is a justified argument by definition 11.1. Suppose now that M can only be defeated by overruled arguments. Consequently, M is not an overruled argument by definition 11.2. Thus, M is a defensible or justified argument. Suppose M is defeated by (chosen at random) overruled argument M^*. This argument can be defeated by a justified argument, say M_1, for which it holds that

$M_1 \in Ch(M_1) \vee$
$\forall_{M_2}\{M_1 \prec M_2 | \exists_{M_3}\{M_1 \prec M_2 \prec M_3 \in Ch(M_1) \vee$
$\quad \forall_{M_4}\{M_3 \prec M_4 | \exists_{M_5}\{M_1 \prec \ldots \prec M_5 \in Ch(M_1) \vee \ldots \vee$
$\quad\quad \forall_{M_{n-1}}\{M_{n-2} \prec M_{n-1} | \exists_{M_n}\{M_1 \prec M_2 \prec \ldots \prec M_{n-1} \prec M_n \in Ch(M_1) \wedge$
$\quad\quad\quad \neg \exists_{M' \in \mathcal{M}} M_n \prec M' \wedge n \text{ is odd}\}\}\}\}\}\}.$

Now we can distinguish two cases:

(a) M is $M_1, M_3, \ldots, M_{n-2}$ or M_n. Then, M is a justified argument, since these arguments are all justified arguments (by definition 11.1).

(b) M is not equal to one of the arguments $M_1, M_3, \ldots, M_n$. Then, for M it holds that

$\forall_{M_2}\{M \prec M^* \prec M_1 \prec M_2 | \exists_{M_3}\{M \prec M^* \prec M_1 \prec M_2 \prec M_3 \in Ch(M) \vee$
$\quad \forall_{M_4}\{M_3 \prec M_4 | \exists_{M_5}\{M \prec M^* \prec M_1 \prec \ldots \prec M_5 \in Ch(M) \vee \ldots \vee$
$\quad\quad \forall_{M_{n-1}}\{M_{n-2} \prec M_{n-1} | \exists_{M_n}\{M \prec M^* \prec M_1 \prec \ldots \prec M_{n-1} \prec M_n \in$
$\quad\quad\quad Ch(M) \wedge \neg \exists_{M' \in \mathcal{M}} M_n \prec M' \wedge n \text{ is odd}\}\}\}\}\}\}.$

Since M^* can be any overruled argument, argument M satisfies the condition of definition 11.1. Thus, M is a justified argument.

From a. en b. it follows that M is a justified argument.

Proposition 4. *Let M be an argument. Then by exclusion it holds that*

- *either M is a justified argument,*
- *or M is an overruled argument,*
- *or M is a defensible argument.*

Proof. We only need to prove that an argument cannot be both overruled and justified, since by definition 11.3 it holds that an argument is defensible if it is not an overruled or a justified argument.

Suppose M is a justified argument. We have to prove that M cannot be an overruled argument. Since M is a justified argument M can only defeated by an overruled argument (proposition 3). Consequently, M cannot be an overruled argument, since by definition 11.2 there has to be a justified argument which defeats an overruled argument.

From definition 11 and propositions 3 and 4 the following statements follow directly:

Corollary 1.

1. *There is no overruled argument, if there is no justified argument;*
2. *There is no justified argument iff all arguments are defensible.*
3. *There is a justified argument iff there is a defeasibility chain with one argument.*

4. *A defensible argument cannot be defeated by a justified argument.*
5. *A defensible argument must at least be defeated by a defensible argument.*

The following example clarifies the above definition:

Example 2.
(d_1) $a \Rightarrow b$
(d_2) $\neg c \wedge e \Rightarrow f$
(d_3) $d \Rightarrow i$
(d_4) $d \Rightarrow \neg b$
(d_5) $\neg b \Rightarrow c$
(d_6) $a \Rightarrow \neg c$
(d_7) $g \Rightarrow \neg e$
(d_8) $d \Rightarrow e$
(d_9) $a \Rightarrow \neg g$
(d_{10}) $d \Rightarrow g$
$\mathcal{F}$: $\{a, d\}$ with $d_{10} < d_9 < \ldots < d_1$.

- Arguments $\{d_1\}$, $\{d_3\}$ and $\{d_9\}$ are justified arguments, since for all these arguments it holds that $Ch(M) = \{M\}$ (see definition 11.1).
- Argument $\{d_2, d_6, d_8\}$ can be defeated by the arguments $\{d_4, d_5\}$ and $\{d_7, d_{10}\}$. These two arguments are overruled arguments, since they are defeated by justified arguments, respectively, $\{d_1\}$ and $\{d_9\}$. Consequently, argument $\{d_2, d_6, d_8\}$ can only be defeated by overruled arguments, thus by proposition 3 this argument is a justified argument.

The following proposition shows that definition 11 satisfies the *weakest link principle*.

Proposition 5.

1. *All subarguments of a justified argument are justified arguments.*
2. *All arguments which are supersets of an overruled argument are overruled arguments.*

Proof.

1. Suppose M is a justified argument and M' is a subargument of M. Suppose M' is defeated by a justified or defensible argument M^*. By proposition 2, M is also defeated by this argument M^* (which is not an overruled argument). Then, by proposition 3, M is not a justified argument, which is in contradiction with the assumption that M is a justified argument. Thus, M' cannot be defeated by a justified or defensible argument. Consequently, M' is a justified argument.
2. Suppose M is an overruled argument. Then M is defeated by a justified argument, say M'. Then, by proposition 2, M' defeats all supersets of argument M. Thus, by definition 11.2, all supersets of argument M are overruled arguments.

Example 3. Consider example 2 There we show that $\{d_2, d_6, d_8\}$ is a justified argument. Thus, by proposition 5 also $\{d_8\}$ and $\{d_6\}$. Argument $\{d_4\}$ is an overruled argument, since this argument can be defeated by justified argument $\{d_1\}$. Thus, by proposition 5.2 also $\{d_4, d_5\}$ is an overruled argument.

The following two examples represent well-known problems in the literature on defeasible arguments. I will show that these problems for defeasible arguments with priorities can be adequately dealt with in the theory as it follows from definition 11.

Example 4. The intermediate conclusion
$(d_1)\ a \Rightarrow b$
$(d_2) \qquad\qquad c \Rightarrow \neg b$
$(d_3)\ d \Rightarrow a$
$\mathcal{F}$: $\{c, d\}$ with $d_3 < d_2 < d_1$.

Here, a conflict arises between rules d_1 and d_2. By definition 3.7, the choice is made between the rules which are certain to be in conflict with each other. Rule d_3 with *intermediate conclusion a*, necessary to derive outcome b, is irrelevant to the conflict.

The minimally explaining sets (arguments) are $\{d_1, d_3\}$, $\{d_3\}$ and $\{d_2\}$. The sets of defeasibility chains are $Ch(\{d_1, d_3\}) = \{\{d_1, d_3\}\}$, $Ch(\{d_3\}) = \{\{d_3\}\}$ and $Ch(\{d_2\}) = \{\{d_2\} \prec \{d_1, d_3\}\}$. Consequently, $\{d_1, d_3\}$ and $\{d_3\}$ are justified, since they cannot be defeated by any argument, and $\{d_2\}$ is overruled, because it is defeated by justified argument $\{d_1, d_3\}$.

Example 5. Iterated conflicts
$(d_1)\ c \Rightarrow a$
$(d_2) \qquad\qquad d \Rightarrow \neg a$
$(d_3) \qquad\qquad \neg a \Rightarrow \neg b$
$(d_4)\ a \Rightarrow b$
$\mathcal{F}$: $\{c, d\}$ with $d_4 < d_3 < d_2 < d_1$.

Here, a conflict arises between rules d_1 and d_2 and between rules d_3 and d_4. Rules d_1 and d_2 have intermediate conclusions a and $\neg a$ for their final conclusions $\neg b$ and b. This type of problem is called *iterated conflicts*: conflicts on both intermediate and final conclusions. The arguments are $\{d_1\}$, $\{d_2\}$, $\{d_2, d_3\}$ and $\{d_1, d_4\}$. The four sets of defeasibility chains are $Ch(\{d_1\}) = \{\{d_1\}\}$, $Ch(\{d_2\}) = \{\{d_2\} \prec \{d_1\}\}$, $Ch(\{d_2, d_3\}) = \{\{d_2, d_3\} \prec \{d_1\}\}$ and $Ch(\{d_1, d_4\}) = \{\{d_1, d_4\} \prec \{d_2, d_3\} \prec \{d_1\}\}$. Thus, $\{d_1\}$ and $\{d_1, d_4\}$ are justified arguments, and $\{d_2\}$ and $\{d_2, d_4\}$ are overruled arguments, because they are defeated by justified argument $\{d_1\}$.

4 Conclusions

In this paper, I have developed an argumentation framework based on an ordering relation of rules to solve the problem of 'conflicting' arguments. In this framework, there is a proof theory that determines whether an argument is justified, overruled or defensible. As noticed by Prakken ([9]), the theory developed in [15] can easily be translated into a dialectical proof theory.

For convenience, we have made some assumptions with respect to the rules which are unrealistic. To remove some of these assumptions, which increase the expressibility of the language and extend the system, we can first introduce symbol ~ for the 'weak negation' in the antecedent of a defeasible rule. Second, we can extend the theory presented here with defeasible conditional norms, which means that a rule can contain a norm (represented in deontic logic) as a consequent (or as legal effect). In particular, the addition of conditional norms is not a trivial extension. This is a challenge for future research, since most consistency-based approaches are based on non-modal logics (cf. [1]). Also the existing formalisations of defeasible deontic reasoning cannot deal with several common forms of deontic logic (cf. [15]).

References

1. Bochman, A., On the relation between default and modal nonmonotonic reasoning, *Artificial Intelligence* 101, pp. 1-34, 1998.
2. Brewka, G., Preferred Subtheories: An Extended Logical Framework for Default Reasoning, in: *Proceedings IJCAI-1991*, pp. 1043-1048, 1991.
3. Delgrande, J., An Approach to Default Reasoning based on a First-Order Conditional Logic, *Artificial Intelligence* 36, pp. 63-90, 1988.
4. Dung, P., On the acceptability of arguments and its fundamental role in nonmonotonic reasoning, logic programming and n-person games, *Artificial Intelligence* 77, 1995.
5. Freund, M., Preferential reasoning in the perspective of Poole default logic, *Artificial Intelligence* 98, pp. 209-235, 1998.
6. McDermott, D.V. and J. Doyle, *Non-monotonic logic I*, Artificial Intelligence 13, pp. 41-72, 1980.
7. Pollock, J.L., Defeasible reasoning, *Cognitive Science* 11(4), pp. 481-518, 1987.
8. Poole, D., A Logical Framework for Default Reasoning, *Artificial Intelligence* 36, pp. 27-47, 1988.
9. Prakken, H., *Logical Tools for Modelling Legal Argument, A study of Defeasible reasoning in law*, Kluwer Academic publishers, Dordrecht, 1997.
10. Prakken, H. and G. Sartor, Argument-based extended logic programming with defeasible priorities, *Journal of Applied Non-classical Logics* 7, pp. 25-75, 1997.
11. Reiter, R., A Logic for Default Reasoning, *Artificial Intelligence* 13, pp. 81-132, 1980.
12. Reiter, R., Nonmonotonic Reasoning, *Annual Review of Computer Science* 2, pp. 147-186, 1987.
13. Rescher, N., *Hypothetical Reasoning*, North-Holland, Amsterdam, 1964.
14. Royakkers, L.M.M., *Extending Deontic Logic for the Formalisation of Legal Rules*, Kluwer Academic Publishers, Dordrecht, 1998.
15. Royakkers, L.M.M. and F. Dignum, Defeasible reasoning with legal rules, in: D. Nute (editor), *Defeasible Deontic Reasoning*, Kluwer Academic Publishers, Dordrecht, pp. 263-286, 1997.

Addressing Efficiency Issues During the Process of Integrity Maintenance

Enric Mayol, Ernest·Teniente

Universitat Politècnica de Catalunya
E-08034 Barcelona - Catalonia
e-mail: [mayol | teniente]@lsi.upc.es

Abstract

We address efficiency issues during the process of integrity maintenance. In this sense, we propose a technique that improves efficiency of existing methods by defining the order in which maintenance of integrity constraints should be performed. Moreover, we integrate view updating into integrity maintenance and we propose a technique for translating view updates efficiently, aimed at reducing the number of alternatives considered during the process of view updating and the EDB accesses required to perform this translation.

1. Introduction

A deductive database is called consistent if it satisfies a set of integrity constraints. When applying a transaction, database consistehcy may be violated. That is, the transaction may falsify some integrity constraint. An approach to deal with this problem is that of *integrity maintenance* [ML91, Wüt93, Ger94, CFPT94, TO95, Maa98, Sch98], which is concerned with trying to repair integrity constraints violations by performing additional updates that restore consistency of the database.

The methods proposed so far for integrity maintenance have been mainly concerned with the generation of a complete set of repairs of integrity constraints violations, but they have paid little attention to efficiency issues. When a constraint is repaired, all other constraints are checked again for consistency, although they were already satisfied prior to the repair and they could not be violated for it.

A database may also contain views, in addition to base predicates and integrity constraints. Views are defined by means of deductive rules that allow deriving new (view) facts from base facts that are explicitly stored in the database.

In the presence of views, the problem of integrity maintenance becomes more complex since a repair of a certain integrity constraint defined in terms of view predicates may consist on a request of updating the view. Therefore, this request must be appropriately translated into correct updates of underlying base facts. Moreover, updates of base facts obtained as a result of view updating could also violate other integrity constraints. For these reasons, it becomes necessary to integrate view updating into the process of integrity maintenance.

Existing methods for view updating [KM90, Wüt93, CST95, TO95, Dec96, LT97] have been mainly concerned with the effective generation of all possible translations that satisfy a view update request. However, they have paid little attention to efficiency issues. Thus, for instance, they do not care about exploring alternatives that do not lead to valid translations or performing unnecessary EDB accesses.

In this paper, we address efficiency issues during the process of integrity maintenance. In this sense, we propose a technique for determining the order in which integrity constraints should be handled. Moreover, we integrate view updating into integrity maintenance and we propose a technique for translating view updates efficiently, aimed at reducing the number of alternatives considered during the process of view updating and the EDB accesses required to perform this translation.

This paper extends our previous work since it provides an efficient implementation of the method specified in [TO95]; and further extends the ideas given in [MT97].

This paper is organized as follows. Sections 2 and 3 review basic concepts needed to define our approach. Section 4 presents the Precedence Graph as a tool for structuring the process of integrity maintenance. Section 5 shows how to translate efficiently repairs on view predicates. Section 6 shows how to use the Precedence Graph to maintain integrity constraints. Section 7 relates our approach to relevant previous work. Finally, section 8 summarizes our conclusions.

2. Deductive Databases

We briefly review the basic concepts related to deductive databases [Llo87]. A *term* is a variable symbol or a constant symbol. If P is an m-ary predicate symbol and t_1, ..., t_m are terms, then $P(t_1, ..., t_m)$ is an *atom*. The atom is *ground* if every t_i (i = 1, ..., m) is a constant. A *literal* is defined as either an atom or a negated atom. A *fact* is a formula of the form: $P(t_1, ..., t_m) \leftarrow$, where $P(t_1, ..., t_m)$ is a ground atom.

A *deductive rule* is a formula of the form: $P(t_1, ..., t_m) \leftarrow L_1 \wedge ... \wedge L_n$, with $n \geq 1$, where $P(t_1, ..., t_m)$ is an atom denoting the conclusion, and $L_1, ..., L_n$ are literals. Any variable in $P(t_1, ..., t_m)$, $L_1, ..., L_n$ is assumed to be universally quantified over the whole formula. A derived predicate P may be defined by means of one or more deductive rules.

An *integrity constraint* is a closed first-order formula that the deductive database is required to satisfy. We deal with constraints in *denial* form[1]: $\leftarrow L_1 \wedge ... \wedge L_m$, with $m \geq 1$, where the L_i are literals and all variables are assumed to be universally quantified over the whole formula. We associate to each integrity constraint an inconsistency predicate Icn. Then, we would rewrite the former denial as: $Icn \leftarrow L_1 \wedge ... \wedge L_m$, with $m \geq 1$. Note that an inconsistency predicate will be true only if the corresponding constraint is violated.

A *deductive database* D is a triple (EDB, IDB, IC), where EDB is a set of base facts, IDB a set of deductive rules and IC a set of integrity constraints. The set EDB of facts is called the *extensional* part of the database and the set of deductive rules and integrity constraints is called the *intensional* part.

Deductive database predicates are partitioned into base and derived (view) predicates. A base predicate appears only in the extensional part and (eventually) in the body of deductive rules. A derived predicate appears only in the intensional part. We deal with *stratified* databases [Llo87] and we require database to be *allowed* [Llo87].

---

[1] More general constraints can be transformed into denials by applying [LT94].

Example 2.1: The following database, which does not contain any fact, will be used throughout the paper.

> PhD(x) ← Has-Thesis(x) ∧ ¬ Fail-exam(x)
> Res-certif(x) ← Has-Thesis(x)
> Ic1(x) ← Res-certif(x) ∧ ¬ Grad(x)
> Ic2(x) ← Prof(x) ∧ ¬ PhD(x)
> Ic3(x) ← Dean(x) ∧ ¬ Prof(x)

Has-Thesis(x) states that x has written his/her PhD-Thesis; Fail-exam(x) states that x has failed the thesis examination; Grad(x) states that x is graduated; Prof(x) states that x is a professor and Dean(x) states that x is a Dean; Res-certif(x) states that x has a research certificate if x has written his/her PhD; PhD(x) states that x has a PhD if x has written his/her PhD-Thesis and has not failed the thesis examination. Integrity constraints state that is not possible to have a research certificate and not be graduated; to be a professor without having a PhD; and to be Dean not being a professor.

3. The Augmented Database [Oli91, UO92]

Our approach is based on taking into account a set of rules that precisely define the difference between two consecutive database states. This set of rules, together with the original database D, form the Augmented Database [Oli91, UO92], denoted by A(D), which explicitly defines the insertions and deletions induced by T.

The concept of Augmented Database is based on the concept of *event*. For each predicate P, a distinguished *insertion event predicate* ιP and a distinguished *deletion event predicate* δP are used to define the precise difference of deducible facts of consecutive database states. Formally, we define them as follows[2]:

> (1) $\forall x\, (\iota P(x) \leftrightarrow P^n(x) \wedge \neg P(x))$
> (2) $\forall x\, (\delta P(x) \leftrightarrow P(x) \wedge \neg P^n(x))$

If P is a base predicate, ιP and δP facts (called *base event facts*) represent insertions and deletions of base facts, respectively. Therefore, we assume that a transaction T consists of a set of base event facts.

Definition 3.1: A *transaction T* is a set of base event facts.

If P is a derived predicate, ιP and δP facts represent induced insertions and induced deletions, respectively. If P is an inconsistency predicate, ιP represents a violation of the corresponding integrity constraint. For inconsistency predicates, δP facts are not defined since we assume that the database is consistent before the update.

For each derived or inconsistency predicate P, the A(D) contains rules about ιP and δP, called *event rules*, which define exactly the insertions and deletions of facts about P that are induced by some transaction T. The definition of ιP and δP depends on the definition of P in D but it is independent of any transaction T_i and of the EDB. The A(D) contains also a set of *transition rules* that define extension in the new state of

---

[2] x is a vector of variables and P^n denotes the evaluation of P in the updated state.

derived and inconsistency predicates in terms of the old state and the events that occur in the transition between both states.

The definition of events, given by rules (1) and (2), determines that an insertion (deletion) of a certain fact may only happen if the fact does not hold (if it holds) in the old state of the database. This is formalized as: $\forall x\ (\iota P(x) \rightarrow \neg P(x))$ and $\forall x\ (\delta P(x) \rightarrow P(x))$. We extend the event rules by explicitly considering these implications:

Example 3.1: The following example shows some relevant event rules of the example 2.1, extended with the corresponding implications.

(C1) $\iota Ic1(x) \leftarrow \text{Res-certif}(x) \wedge \neg\, \delta\, \text{Res-certif}(x) \wedge \text{Grad}(x) \wedge \delta\text{Grad}(x)$

(C2) $\iota Ic1(x) \leftarrow \neg\, \text{Res-certif}(x) \wedge \iota\, \text{Res-certif}(x) \wedge \neg\, \text{Grad}(x) \wedge \neg\, \iota\text{Grad}(x)$

(C3) $\iota Ic1(x) \leftarrow \neg\, \text{Res-certif}(x) \wedge \iota\, \text{Res-certif}(x) \wedge \text{Grad}(x) \wedge \delta\text{Grad}(x)$

(C4) $\iota Ic2(x) \leftarrow \text{Prof}(x) \wedge \neg\, \delta\text{Prof}(x) \wedge \text{PhD}(x) \wedge \delta\text{PhD}(x)$

(C5) $\iota Ic2(x) \leftarrow \neg\, \text{Prof}(x) \wedge \iota\text{Prof}(x) \wedge \neg\, \text{PhD}(x) \wedge \neg\, \iota\text{PhD}(x)$

(C6) $\iota Ic2(x) \leftarrow \neg\, \text{Prof}(x) \wedge \iota\text{Prof}(x) \wedge \text{PhD}(x) \wedge \delta\text{PhD}(x)$

(C7) $\iota Ic3(x) \leftarrow \text{Dean}(x) \wedge \neg\, \delta\text{Dean}(x) \wedge \text{Prof}(x) \wedge \delta\text{Prof}(x)$

(C8) $\iota Ic3(x) \leftarrow \neg\, \text{Dean}(x) \wedge \iota\text{Dean}(x) \wedge \neg\, \text{Prof}(x) \wedge \neg\, \iota\text{Prof}(x)$

(C9) $\iota Ic3(x) \leftarrow \neg\, \text{Dean}(x) \wedge \iota\text{Dean}(x) \wedge \text{Prof}(x) \wedge \delta\text{Prof}(x)$

Rules C_1 to C_9 define all possible ways of inserting facts about predicates Ic1, Ic2 and Ic3. These rules deserve special attention since they define all possible situations in which database consistency is violated by the application of some transaction.

4. Making Explicit an Order for Integrity Maintenance

We achieve efficiency during the process of integrity maintenance by determining the order in which integrity constraints should be handled. This order is provided by the Precedence Graph. To obtain the Precedence Graph we only take into account syntactical information associated to the definition of each integrity constraint.

Violations of database consistency due to a transaction T are only produced because some insertion event rule associated to an integrity constraint becomes true. Moreover, repairs of the constraint are defined by the violated insertion event rule, since a repair corresponds to an additional update that falsifies the effect of T on the corresponding event rule. For this reason, we refer to the insertion event rules of an integrity constraint as the *conditions* of that integrity constraint.

To state precedences more precisely, we consider the conditions associated to an integrity constraint instead of the own integrity constraint definition. Thus, the Precedence Graph will state all relationships between repairs and potential violations of these conditions. First, we need to explicitly state the relationship between base events and their effect on view events and conditions.

Definition 4.1: Let E be an event and C be a condition or a derived event. We say that *C directly depends on E* if there is a rule in A(D) with C as head and such that E appears in its body. A direct dependence is positive (resp. negative) if E is a positive literal (resp. negative).

Definition 4.2: Given an event or a condition C and an event E, we say that:
- *C depends on E* if C directly depends on E.

- *C depends on E* if C depends on a certain event E' and E' directly depends on E.
- *C depends evenly (resp. oddly) on E* if there is an even (resp. odd) number of negative direct dependencies in the dependency path from C to E.

Potential repairs and potential violations can be defined by considering the notion of dependency. A potential violation of a condition C_i is a base event that, when applied to the database, it may induce an insertion of C_i. A potential repair of a condition C_i is a base event that when applied to the database may falsify C_i.

Definition 4.3: Let E be a base event and C_i a condition.

- *E is a potential violation of C_i if C_i depends evenly on E.*
- *E is a potential repair of C_i if C_i depends oddly on E.*

Note that, since a condition C may depend evenly and oddly on a certain event E, E may be a potential violation and a potential repair of C at the same time.

Structuring the process of integrity maintenance is aimed at determining the order of handling conditions to minimize the number of times that each condition is processed. If an event E is a potential repair of a condition C_i and at the same time a potential violation of another condition C_j, then C_i should be handled before C_j because, otherwise, we cannot ensure that C_j will not have to be processed again after C_i's consideration. This is why we talk about precedences among conditions.

Definition 4.4: Let C_i and C_j be conditions and E an event predicate. *C_i precedes C_j due to E* if E is a potential repair of C_i and a potential violation of C_j.

We denote precedences between conditions by, means an arrow. That is, "$C_i \to C_j$ due to E" states that "C_i precedes C_j due to E".

Example 4.1: Precedences between conditions of example 3.1 are the following:

$C_1 \to C_4, C_5, C_6$ due to δHas-Thesis $C_5 \to C_2, C_3$ due to ιHas-Thesis

$C_4 \to C_7, C_9$ due to δProf $C_8 \to C_5, C_6$ due to ιProf

Taking into account all precedences between conditions, we can build the Precedence Graph.

Definition 4.5: A *Precedence Graph* PG for a set C of conditions, is a pair PG=<Nod,Edg> where Nod is a finite number of nodes, Edg $\subseteq$ (Nod x Nod) is a set of directed edges, and such that each node n $\in$ Nod is labeled with a condition identifier and each edge is labeled with an event. There exists a directed edge edg = (n,n'), labeled with event E, if condition of node n precedes condition of node n' due to E.

Example 4.2: The Precedence Graph corresponding to example 4.1 is the following:

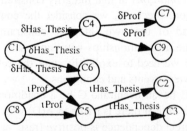

Fig. 1. Precedence Graph of example 4.1

The Precedence Graph provides the information to define an order of handling conditions. Intuitively, conditions without incoming edges should be considered first since they cannot be violated by the maintenance of any other condition. When a condition is processed, it is removed from the Precedence Graph and the integrity maintenance process continues with the rest of the conditions. In fact, there are many possible orders of processing conditions that satisfy this criterion. However, since we always have to process all conditions, none of these orders provides more efficiency than the others do.

Handling conditions in this way we improve efficiency of current methods for integrity maintenance. A good metrics to evaluate this improvement is the number of conditions that a method must consider in each case.

Lemma 1 Let C be the number of conditions associated to the integrity constraints and R the number of repairs needed to obtain the solution. Let the resulting Precedence Graph not contain any cycle. Then, the number of conditions that must be considered by an integrity maintenance process is the following:

- Without the Precedence Graph: number of conditions = (C/2) * R + C
- With the Precedence Graph: number of conditions = C

Therefore, if maintaining integrity requires at least one repair, the integrity maintenance process performs better by considering the conditions in the order provided by the Precedence Graph. This improvement will be much greater whenever a higher number of repairs will be needed.

In some cases, a Precedence Graph could also contain cycles among certain conditions. The existence of cycles means that the conditions inside a cycle may be considered more than once to obtain a solution, but this does not necessarily imply that dealing with conditions of the cycle should be performed forever.

Although cyclic Precedence Graphs are beyond the scope of this paper, the previous metrics could also be generalized in this case. The only difference is that we should to extend the number of conditions visited since conditions in a cycle could be considered several times.

5. Translating a Repair Corresponding to a View Update

When views may appear in an integrity constraint definition, we must also translate efficiently a repair that consists on a view update. Negative events appearing in the body of a condition correspond to possible ways of repairing this condition. In particular, when such a repair involves a negative derived event, it corresponds to a view update request that must be appropriately translated into correct updates of the underlying base facts.

We propose to consider efficiency by performing an analysis of the view update request and of the database contents before obtaining translations. This analysis is made during the Analysis Step, described in section 5.1, and it is aimed at achieving efficiency by considering only those alternatives that are relevant to the request and also by reducing the number of accesses to the EDB. Translations are obtained during the Translation Step, described in section 5.2, by taking into account the results of the analysis step.

5.1 Analysis Step

Event rules associated to a view predicate V define all possible ways of satisfying updates stated on V. Thus, the translation of a view update request into updates of base facts will be performed by taking event rules into account.

Example 5.1: Consider the insertion event rules associated to the view PhD(x).

(I$_1$) ιPhD(x) ← Has-Thesis(x) ∧ ¬ δHas-Thesis(x) ∧ Fail-exam(x) ∧ δFail-exam(x)

(I$_2$) ιPhD(x) ← ¬ Has-Thesis(x) ∧ ιHas-Thesis(x) ∧ ¬ Fail-exam(x) ∧ ¬ ιFail-exam(x)

(I$_3$) ιPhD(x) ← ¬ Has-Thesis(x) ∧ ιHas-Thesis(x) ∧ Fail-exam(x) ∧ δFail-exam(x)

Event rules I$_1$, I$_2$ and I$_3$ define all possible ways of performing insertions on PhD. The applicability of a certain event rule to translate a view update request depends on the contents of the database. Therefore, at execution time, given a view update request U and a database state D, only some of the event rules are relevant for translating U. For instance, the insertion of PhD(Bob) in a database that does not contain Fail-exam(Bob) nor Has-Thesis(Bob) may only be performed by means of I2.

Moreover, not all the facts stored in the EDB are relevant for translating a view update request. For instance, only base facts Fail-exam(Bob) and Has-Thesis(Bob) are relevant for inserting PhD(Bob).

Given an update request U and an Augmented Database A(D), the purpose of the Analysis Step is to determine the event rules in A(D) relevant to translate U and to specialize them so that no additional access to the EDB is needed to perform the translation. This specialization is performed in an "intelligent" way so that relevant base facts are accessed only once.

Definition 5.1: Let E be a derived event on a predicate P(x), defined (directly or indirectly) in terms of a set of base predicates $Q_i(y_i)$. Then, the *relevant extension of E* is the set of all base facts $Q_i(y_i)\theta$, where θ is the m.g.u.(x,y$_i$).

Once we know the relevant extension of the view update request, we can specialize the event rules required to satisfy the request. This specialization is performed by adapting a transformation proposed in [KS90] to split a general rule into two alternative rules: one specific rule to be applied to a concrete instance t' and a general rule to apply to the rest of values t≠t'.

Definition 5.2: Let E(t') be a derived event fact, where t' is a vector of constants and variables, let Ext be its relevant extension. Then, the *Specialized Event Rules R' of E(t')* are, for each event rule E(t) ← L$_1$∧...∧ L$_n$, the following two rules:

(R$_1$') E(t) ← L$_1$ ∧ ... ∧ L$_n$ ∧ t≠t'

(R$_2$') [E(t) ← L$_i$ ∧ ... ∧ L$_j$]θ   with i ≥ 1 and j ≤ n.

where θ is the most general unifier of t and t' and where each literal L$_i$θ of rule R$_2$' that refers to a base predicate is evaluated true with respect to Ext and it has been removed.

This specialization has to be applied also to the event rules associated to the derived event facts that appear in the body of rule R$_2$' to obtain a complete specialization of the event rules defining E(t').

Example 5.2: Given a view update request ιPhD(Bob) and an EDB that does not contain Fail-exam(Bob) nor Has-Thesis(Bob), the Specialized Event Rules of ιPhD(Bob) are:

(I_1) ιPhD(x) $\leftarrow$ Has-Thesis(x) $\land$ ¬ δHas-Thesis(x) $\land$ Fail-exam(x) $\land$ δFail-exam(x) $\land$ x≠Bob

(I_{21}') ιPhD(x) $\leftarrow$ ¬Has-Thesis(x) $\land$ ιHas-Thesis(x) $\land$ ¬Fail-exam(x) $\land$ ¬ιFail-exam(x) $\land$ x≠Bob

(I_{22}') ιPhD(Bob) $\leftarrow$ ιHas-Thesis(Bob) $\land$ ¬ ιFail-exam(Bob)

(I_3) ιPhD(x) $\leftarrow$ ¬ Has-Thesis(x) $\land$ ιHas-Thesis(x) $\land$ Fail-exam(x) $\land$ δFail-exam(x) $\land$ x≠Bob

Previous methods for view updating have paid little attention to efficiency issues since they have been only concerned with the effective generation of all possible translations that satisfy a view update request. So, to the best of our knowledge, ours is the first proposal aimed at dealing with efficiency issues during this process. Two different metrics can be considered to evaluate efficiency of the view updating process: the number of possible alternatives considered and EDB accesses performed.

Given a view P defined by a single rule $P(t_1, ..., t_m) \leftarrow L_1 \land ... \land L_n$, with $n \geq 1$, where $L_1,...,L_n$ are base literals and such that all variables in $L_1,...,L_n$ appear also in t_1, ..., t_m, the following two lemmas hold.

Lemma 2: The number of event rules considered to translate events about P is the following:

- An insertion event fact $\iota P(k_1, ..., k_m)$: 1 event rule.
- A deletion event fact $\delta P(k_1, ..., k_m)$: n event rules

Lemma 3: The number of accesses to the EDB performed to translate events about P is the following:

- An insertion event fact $\iota P(k_1, ..., k_m)$: n EDB accesses.
- A deletion event fact $\delta P(k_1, ..., k_m)$: 1 EDB access

In the case of views defined in terms of other views and of views that may contain existential variables in their rule body, the previous metrics can be easily generalized.

5.2 Translation Step

In the Analysis Step, we have obtained the specialized event rules that allow to perform the translation without accessing the EDB. The purpose of the Translation Step is to translate a given view update request U into all possible translations T_i that satisfy this request. A translation T_i is a transaction that defines a set of base facts to be inserted and/or deleted from the current EDB.

Example 5.3: Consider again the Specialized Event Rules of example 5.2. The only translation that satisfies ιPhD(Bob) is $T_1 = \{\iota$Has-Thesis(Bob)$\}$, which is given by the rule: (I_{22}') ιPhD(Bob) $\leftarrow$ ιHas-Thesis(Bob) $\land$ ¬ ιFail-exam(Bob)

Thus, positive base events in the body of specialized event rules define the updates to be performed to satisfy a view update request. If a view is defined in terms of other views, we must unfold first the positive derived events until we reach a goal where positive literals are only base fact events. Moreover, the resulting goal may contain negative events. Those events correspond to conditions that must be enforced to guarantee that the requested view update remains satisfied when, later on during the process of integrity maintenance, new updates are considered. In the previous example, we need to enforce condition $C_{10} = \{\leftarrow \iota$Fail-exam(Bob)$\}$ to guarantee that ιPhD(Bob) remains satisfied, i.e. a future insertion of Fail-exam(Bob) would cause ιPhD(Bob) to be false.

Definition 5.3: Given a view update U, the *result of the Translation Step* is all possible pairs (T_i, C_i) such that T_i is a translation of U and C_i is a set of conditions to be enforced to guarantee that U will remain satisfied during the process of integrity maintenance.

Conditions resulting from the process of view updating have a clear parallelism with conditions considered during the process of integrity maintenance since both represent requirements that must be enforced to guarantee the correctness of the whole process. Thus, to provide a uniform and more efficient treatment of the whole process of integrity maintenance, conditions resulting from view updating are integrated into the Precedence Graph. This integration is performed dynamically by taken into account information, already determined at definition time, about potential violations and potential repairs of conditions that can be obtained during view updating.

Example 5.4: Consider again example 4.2. The Precedence Graph resulting after the inclusion of the condition $C_{10} \leftarrow \iota$Fail-exam(Bob) is the same of Fig. 3 with an additional node labeled as C_{10}. This node has no incoming nor outgoing edges since condition C_{10} can not be violated by any of the potential repairs of other conditions and, since it does not have any potential repair that could violate other conditions.

6. A Process for Integrity Maintenance

Given a database D and an initial transaction T, the process of integrity maintenance is aimed at obtaining all possible minimal transactions T_i, with $T_i \supseteq T$, that satisfy all integrity constraints in D. New updates in T_i are required to repair the integrity constraint violations induced by T. When a repair is a view update this process must translate it into updates of the underlying base facts.

The Precedence Graph, the Analysis Step and the Translation Step provide the basis for an efficient algorithm for integrity maintenance in the presence of views. The function Maintain_Constraints is used to perform efficiently the process of integrity maintenance.

Definition 6.1: Given a database D, the Precedence Graph PG of conditions in D and an initial transaction T, the *result of the function Maintain_Constraints(T,PG)* is the set of all possible minimal transactions T_i, with $T_i \supseteq T$, that satisfy all integrity constraints in D.

A transaction T_i is *minimal* if there is no transaction T_j, $T_i \supseteq T_j$, that also satisfies the integrity constraints. Note that since $T_i \supseteq T$ the previous definition guarantees that the obtained transactions T_i satisfy the effect of the original transaction T. If the initial transaction T does not violate any integrity constraint, function Maintain_Constraints will provide T as the only solution.

Intuitively, the steps performed by Maintain_Constraints are the following: to consider the conditions in one of the orders provided by the Precedence Graph and, for each condition, to compute all violations and consider a repair of each violation. We mark nodes of the graph to indicate candidate conditions to be processed at each step. A marked node states that its associated condition is potentially violated by the current transaction. Initially, all conditions are marked since they may be violated by T.

We illustrate Maintain_Constraints by means of an example. A complete description of the algorithm implementing this function can be found in [MT99].

Example 6.1: Consider now the database of example 2.1 and the associated Precedence Graph shown in Fig. 1. Assume the initial transaction T={ιDean(Bob)}. Initially, all nodes are marked. Node C_1 is selected first because it does not have any predecessor. Since it is not violated, we unmark it and proceed with following nodes. The same happens with C_4, C_7 and C_9.

In the next step, node C_8 is selected. Since it is violated by T, it is repaired with ιProf(Bob). In following steps, nodes C_6 and C_3 exhibit similar behavior to C_1. Condition C_5 is selected after. The repair ιPhD(Bob) of C_5 must now be translated into base fact updates. As example 5.3 states, the only translation is {ιHas-Thesis(Bob)}. Moreover, condition C_{10} ← ιFail-exam(Bob) is included in the graph.

As a consequence of this update, C_2 is violated (because ιRes-certif(Bob) is induced as a consequence of ιHas-Thesis(Bob)) and it is repaired by ιGrad(Bob). After this repair, condition C_{10} is not violated and all nodes of the graph are unmarked. Therefore, we get a final transaction T'={ιDean(Bob), ιProf(Bob), ιHas-Thesis(Bob), ιGrad(Bob)} that satisfies all integrity constraints.

7. Relation with Previous Work

We compare our proposal with previous work on efficient integrity maintenance [CFPT94, Ger94, FP97, Sch98] and we measure the efficiency improvement of our approach to view updating with respect to that of [TO95].

7.1 Previous Work on Efficient Integrity Maintenance

The most interesting proposals that consider efficiency issues during integrity maintenance are [CFPT94, FP97] and [Ger94], which are based on the automatic generation of active (production) rules for integrity maintenance. As compared to our approach, a first limitation of these proposals is that they do not incorporate view updating during integrity maintenance. They also share two additional drawbacks.

The initial transaction is not always satisfied: Given a transaction requested by the user, [CFPT94, Ger94] maintain the integrity constraints through the execution of active rules that repair the violated constraints. The problem is, as reported in [Sch98], that the resulting database does not always satisfy the transaction originally requested. [Sch98] prevents this problem by detecting dangerous situations. However, it may happen that [Sch98] does not find any solution although there are some, which can be obtained by our method as shown in [MT99].

Not all solutions can be obtained: Efficiency is provided in [CFPT94, Ger94] by defining a graph that expresses whether the execution of a certain active rule that repairs an integrity constraint could violate another integrity constraint. As usual, the presence of cycles indicates that integrity maintenance could not terminate. To guarantee termination, they propose to obtain an acyclic graph by discarding some of the active rules. Thus, they do not consider all possible repairs for an integrity constraint violation.

Instead of restricting the set of possible repairs, our approach is based on defining a more precise graph. This results in a higher number of conditions to take into account but allows to effectively handling a higher number of cases, as shown in [MT99].

[FP97] is devoted to define more clearly an stratified order of handling active rules to avoid infinite loops. Some of the mechanisms proposed in [FT97] could help us to reduce the number of cycles in our Precedence Graph.

7.2 Previous Work on View Updating

Previous work on view updating did not almost care about efficiency issues since it was concerned with proposing effective methods that obtain all possible translations. Our approach is aimed at achieving efficiency by considering only relevant alternatives and by reducing the number of accesses to the EDB, as shown by the metrics considered in Section 5.1. These metrics are directly applicable to the Events Method [TO95].

Given a view P defined by a single rule $P(t_1, ..., t_m) \leftarrow L_1 \wedge ... \wedge L_n$, with $n \geq 1$, where $L_1,...,L_n$ are base literals and such that all variables in $L_1,...,L_n$ appear also in t_1, ..., t_m, the following two lemmas hold.

Lemma 4 The number of event rules considered by the Events Method to translate events about P is:
- An insertion event fact $\iota P(k_1, ..., k_m)$: $2^n - 1$
- A deletion event fact $\delta P(k_1, ..., k_m)$: n

Lemma 5 The number of accesses to the EDB performed by the Events Method to translate events about P is:
- An insertion event fact $\iota P(k_1, ..., k_m)$: $(2^n - 1) * n$
- A deletion event fact $\delta P(k_1, ..., k_m)$: n^2

These results show that we perform better than the Events Method for translating both insertions and deletions. Moreover, this gain of efficiency is further improved in our case by defining the order of handling integrity constraints.

8 Conclusions

We have proposed a technique for improving efficiency of integrity maintenance in the presence of views. This technique is based on making explicit the information required to define an order of handling integrity constraints and on performing some preparatory analysis before translating a view update.

In the first case, we achieve efficiency by reducing the times that an integrity constraint is reconsidered. In the second, efficiency is gained by considering only relevant alternatives to translate a view update request and by reducing the accesses to the EDB required to perform this translation. We have also shown that our results improve those of previous work in the field.

As further work, we are thinking about considering a better marking of the Precedence Graph and on taking into account the information provided by the original transaction to define a better order of handling conditions in this graph.

Acknowledgements

This work is partially supported by the CICYT PRONTIC project TIC97-1157.

References

[CST95] Console, L.; Sapino, M.L.; Theseider,D. "The Role of Abduction in Database View Updating", J. of Intelligent Information Systems, Vol.4, pp. 261-280.

[CFPT94] Ceri, S.; Fraternali, P.; Paraboschi, S.; Tanca, L. "Automatic Generation of Production Rules for Integrity Maintenance" ACM Transactions on Database Systems Vol.19 N°3, Sept. 1994, pp-367-422.

[Dec96] Decker, H. "An Extension of SLD by Abduction and Integrity Maintenance for View Updating in Deductive Databases", Joint International Conference and Symposium on Logic Programming (JICSLP'96), Bonn (Germany), 1996.

[FP97] Fraternali, P.; Paraboschi, S. "Ordering and Selecting Production Rules for Constraint Maintenance: Complexity and Heuristic Solution" IEEE Transactions on Knowledge and Data Engineering, Vol. 9, N° 1, 1997, pp-173-178.

[Ger94] Gertz, M. "Specifying Reactive Integrity Control for Active Databases", Research Issues on Data Engineering:Active Databases(RIDE-ADS'94), Houston, pp.62-70.

[KM90] Kakas, A.; Mancarella, P. "Database Updates through Abduction", Proc. of the 16th VLDB Conference, Brisbane, Australia, 1990, pp. 650-661.

[KS90] Kowalski, R.; Sadri, F. "Logic Programs with Exceptions", Seventh International Conference of Logic Programming (ICLP'90), 1990, pp.598-613.

[Llo87] Lloyd, J.W. "Foundations on Logic Programming", 2nd edition, Springer, 1987.

[LT84] Lloyd, J.W.; Topor, R.W. "Making Prolog More Expressive". Journal of Logic Programming, 1984, No. 3, pp. 225-240.

[LT97] Lobo, J.; Trajcevski, G. "Minimal and consistent evolution in knowledge bases" Journal of Applied Non-Classical Logics. Vol. 7. N° 1-2/1997, pp: 117-146.

[Maa98] Maabout, S. "Maintaining and Restoring Database Consistency with Update Rules", in Proc. DYNAMICS'98 (Workshop of JICSLP'98), Manchester, June 98.

[ML91] Moerkotte, G; Lockemann, P.C. "Reactive Consistency Control in Deductive Databases", ACM Transactions on Database Systems 16(4), 1991, pp. 670-702.

[MT97] Mayol, E.; Teniente, E. "Structuring the Process of Integrity Maintenance", 8th International Conference on Database and Expert Systems Applications (DEXA'97), LNCS-1308, Toulouse, France, September 1997, pp. 262-275.

[MT99] Mayol, E.; Teniente, E. "Addressing Efficiency Issues During the Process of Integrity Maintenance", Technical Report LSI-99-27-R.

[Oli91] Olivé, A. "Integrity Checking in Deductive Databases", Proc. of the 17th VLDB Conference, Barcelona, Catalonia, 1991, pp. 513-523.

[Sch98] Schewe, K.D. "Consistency Enforcement in Entity-Relationship and Object-Oriented Models", Data & Knowledge Engineering Vol 28,1998, pp.121-140

[TO95] Teniente, E.; Olivé, A. "Updating Knowledge Bases while Maintaining their Consistency", The VLDB Journal, Vol. 4, Num. 2, 1995, pp. 193-241.

[UO92] Urpí, T.; Olivé, A. "A Method for Change Computation in Deductive Databases", Proc. of the 18th VLDB Conference, Vancouver, 1992, pp. 225-237.

[Wüt93] Wüthrich, B. "On Updates and Inconsistency Repairing in Deductive databases", Int. Conf. on Data Engineering, Vienna, 1993, pp. 608 - 615.

Quality and Recommendation of Multi-source Data for Assisting Technological Intelligence Applications

Laure Berti

GECT, Systèmes d'Information Multi-Media
University of Toulon, B.P. 132, F-83957 La Garde cedex, FRANCE
berti@univ-tln.fr

Abstract. Due to its costly impact, data quality is becoming an emerging domain of research. Motivated by its stakes and issues, especially in the application domain of Technological Intelligence, we propose a generic methodology for modeling and managing data quality in the context of multiple information sources. Data quality has different categories of quality criteria and their evaluations enable the detection of errors and poor quality data. We introduce the notion of relative data quality when several data describe the same entity in the real world but have contradictory values : *homologous data*. Our approach differs from the general approach for resolving extensional inconsistencies in integration of heterogeneous systems. We cumulatively store *homologous data* and their quality metadata and we recommend dynamically data with the best quality and data which are the most appropriate to a particular user. A value recommendation algorithm is proposed and applied to the Technological Intelligence application domain.

1 Introduction

Accentuated by the Internet phenomenon and the development of Information Technologies, heterogeneity and volume of data flows make economically and humanly difficult the retrieval and the critical analysis of useful information. The user is instantaneously submerged by data which, either do not precisely meet his/her needs, or when relevant, are incomplete, vague and/or contradictory. As a matter of fact, the issues of information searching are moved from the quantitative stakes to the qualitative ones (i.e. from data volume to data quality). Moreover, the validation of information remain difficult. This context requires, not only, a much more active and critical attitude of the user, but also, serious abilities for information interpretation, evaluation, deduction, analysis and synthesis. Although information systems are advantageously used to store, manage and analyze quantitatively information items, few of them propose assistance for examining critically the quality of their information content. When data are stored in the database, they are generally not qualified or certified according to their relative quality and their effective utility. But, it is essential to explicitly evaluate the quality of data stored in databases in order (1) to adapt information quality according to the querying audience, (2) to provide a critical expertise of the quality of the information system content, (3) to enable the user to put into perspective his/her confidence in data and, make him/her change or adapt his/her data usage. Data quality becomes an emerging theme of research and development in various industrial [14, 8], commercial [11], military and scientific [10] application domains. Nowadays, the current approach to measure data quality is statistical by sampling important volumes of data. But, in the profusion of contradictory information, the quality of data can be evaluated by comparison (i.e. by comparing the quality of *homologous data* : data which are extracted from different information sources, which describe the same reality but have contradictory values). Rather than to solve the existing conflicts between the different values of data, our approach is to exploit these conflicts to evaluate the relative quality of data. Because information quality expertise is a necessary daily task in several strategic application domains such as Technological Intelligence, we developed the sQuaL system to assist information quality expertise and to propose an adaptive selection of data with the best quality. Data recommendation is made according to the relative quality of data. As result of a query, the sQuaL system presents the data with the most appropriate quality among the candidate *homologous data*. The user can choose different strategies for recommendation.

The remainder of the article is organized in the following way : Section 2 presents previous works on data quality and introduces our contribution concerning the quality of multi-source data. Section 3 describes a general methodology for integrating the quality expertise of multi-source data in the information processing. Section 4 defines an algorithm for data recommendation. Section 5 illustrates an application example of the sQuaL system in Technological Intelligence. Section 6 concludes and presents our perspectives of research.

2 Data Quality : the multi-source perspective

Data quality aroused an increasing interest since a long time, but, it is now clearly becoming an emerging field of research [13,14,11,10,15]. Globally, the various works on the data quality can be classified in three research avenues according to their objectives : (1) to define each dimension of data quality with a rigorous scientific method (2) to create a universal standard set of operational quality dimensions (3) to let data quality dimensions be defined by users and to propose assistance for data quality evaluation.

Modeling data quality. Since 1980, many propositions have been made for modeling data quality [4,7,14,11,10] but the consensual definition of data quality is still not reached. A very complete analysis [13] presents the vast panorama of research on data quality. Several works completely integrate the modeling and the management of data quality into the design of information systems (by using labels on every element of the conceptual model) [15,12]. The use of metadata for the improvement of data quality is also recommended in many standards of exchange for Geographical Information Systems (ISO 15046-13, CEN 287-008... [5]).

Evaluating data quality. The current approach for measuring data quality is a statistical approach centered on methods such as the inference on missing data and automatic control of data exceptions. Many methods were developed to measure the four essential data quality dimensions : accuracy, completeness, currentness and consistency [9,7,8] in conformance with users' quality specifications. But actually, data quality audits [13,8] are the only practical means for determining data quality in databases.

Relative data quality. In parallel with the frequencist approaches in data quality research, some subjectivist and user-oriented approaches propose assistance to users. In this perspective, we extend the proposition of [15] by modeling the *relative quality of data* which includes three sub-categories of quality criteria [3] : the first sub-category of criteria is related to the context of the application (based on a frame of reference such as time or application), the second sub-category of quality criteria is related to the user (based on the cognitive or emotional frame of reference), and finally, we introduce the multi-source perspective into the characterization of data quality : the quality of one data can be evaluated by comparison with the quality of other *homologous data* : i.e. data from different information sources which represent the same reality but have contradictory values. And we propose recommendation mechanisms based on the relative quality of the *homologous data*. Our problematic joins numerous works on integration of heterogeneous systems, in particular, for what concerns the problems of extensional inconsistencies (problems of tuple identification, conflicts of values...). Although these problems are unanimously admitted, few solutions have been proposed to solve the conflicts between contradictory values of data. Finally, the approaches usually adopted to reconcile heterogeneities between values of data are : (1) to prefer the values of the most reliable sources (2) to mention the source ID for each value (3) to store quality metadata with the data.

3 Methodology for multi-source data quality expertise

In a multi-source information context, users need to be sure about the quality of data they use to make important decisions. This implies the contribution of specialists for examining quality and value-adding data. Here, a particular function of the information system (IS) is to store information quality expertise and to recommend the most appropriate data to the user. Thus, for the same query, different information results may be proposed to various querying users according to their data quality requirements. Consequently, the IS should be able: (1) to cumulate *homologous data* : in the database, the same attribute may have multiple values proposed by different information sources, (2) to assist experts when they cross-check information items and when they evaluate the relative quality of data. In order to present the application context of the sQuaL system, we propose the 7 steps of the following methodology.

Step 1. Detecting needs

In this preliminary step, the needs must be clearly expressed, in particular, the information quality required by the various users (human operators, technological specialists, decision makers...). Requiring a real implication of these actors, the purpose is to specify the vocabulary of the application domain, as well as the vocabulary of the dimensions (criteria) of the information quality concept and to make sure that every body uses the same concepts with the same meaning. The goal of this step is to build an ontology (as a reusable modeling schema) supporting the modeling of intellectual capital resources of the company (information and information quality expertise).

Step 2. Selecting quality criteria

Directly dependent on the first step, the purpose of this second step is to choose several data quality criteria to be measured/evaluated by human specialists for determining the quality of information sources and the quality of their content (as structured data). Two types of quality criteria are to be measured : (1) objective quality criteria (2) subjective quality criteria (authors reputation, credibility...) evaluated by experts.

Step 3. Selecting information sources, collecting and mapping data

The goal of this step is to select relevant information sources, to collect and store their data into the database and finally, to establish correspondences between *homologous data* which describe different versions of the same reality (*mapping*). The selection of information sources is based on the evaluation of selected quality criteria (Step 2). Data flows must be precisely described : actors who can modify data quality and their interventions on the database (creation, update, use, deletion) must be identified. This step underlines attributes that are incomplete or, complete but never used. It raises the question of the effective utility of attributes and it suggests the formalization of decision rules and the distinction between various quality levels for the attributes according to their particular use. The mapping of *homologous data* is supervised by the specialist, expert of the information field. As a result in the multi-source database, attributes have multiple values with the mention of the ID of their information source (Fig. 1).

Step 4. Selecting critical data

The goal of this step is to select the classes, objects and attributes that are *critical* for the application domain. Every data do not have the same importance, they are not equivalent from an strategic point of view : they should not be considered with a uniform way. The concept of criticality is used to compare the importance of data. The *critical* objects and attributes are classified and selected according to their importance with respect to the application objectives. They compose the **subset of critical data**.

Step 5. Evaluating information quality

The goal of this step is the information quality expertise and the storage of information quality metadata for each critical object and attribute. Each quality criteria can be measured by : (1) direct measurements and (2) indirect measurements with objective or subjective quality indicators. Procedures for objective measurement and protocols for subjective evaluation must be explicitly described. In the case of conflicts between contradictory values from various information sources, quality evaluation mainly depends on knowledge and competence of the specialist who supervises data capture, evaluates the quality of the data and affects subjective quality indicators to information items. A tolerance level for data non-quality can be expressed according to the criticality degree of the data. Quality metadata are associated with each critical data (Fig. 1) and stored in the **quality metadatabase**.

Step 6. Identifying non-quality problems and analyzing their causes

The goal of this step is to reveal non-quality problems through the entire information processing (errors or poor quality data) and to analyze their causes. After having identified the actors and the processes which create, maintain, collect, visualize or use each object and attribute, it may appear that a (sub-)process is misused or does not satisfy users. The efforts focus on the identification of problems occurring in the manual or computerized activities. This analysis must identify in particular : who carries out the selection of multi-source data, their mapping, the evaluation of quality ? What is the user satisfaction ?... The purpose of this step is also to search the causes of data non-quality by classifying the events which disturb the information chain.

Step 7. Recommending value-added data and defining new quality objectives

The analysis and the evaluation of data (non-)quality enable recommendation mechanisms. The recommendation must be adaptive, multicriteria and dynamically computed according to each new data arrival and user quality preferences. The company must also lay down objectives for improving its information quality for the mid and long terms, define resources and strategies to be implemented and ensure the support and the improvement of the quality of its data. The strategy of maintenance of the database and the whole information chain must take into account the evolution of the user's needs in terms of data quality.

4 Multicriteria recommendation based on relative data quality

The objective of the methodology was to provide a global vision for the integration of data quality expertise in a multi-source information environment and also to clearly present the application context of our content-quality-based recommender system : the sQuaL system [2,3]. In this section, we describe the structure of data and quality metadata and the recommendation mechanisms used in the sQuaL system.

4.1 Multi-source objects and quality metadata

In the multi-source database, each attribute of a multi-source object has multiple values with the ID of their source and their associated quality expertise (Fig. 1). Quality expertise is represented as metadata associated with each value. Each quality criterion may have a subjective evaluation indicator chosen by the specialist and justified when it's necessary (Fig. 1 : Justificative Comment). The scale of subjective quality evaluation we chose is : 0=very low - 0.25=low - 0.50=medium - 0.75=high - 1=very high.

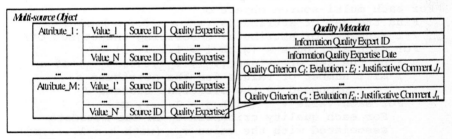

Fig. 1. Multi-source object structure with associated quality metadata.

4.2 Data quality scoring and ranking for recommendation

The objective of the multicriteria recommendation based on the relative quality of data is to propose the *most appropriate* data ; that is, the data which are correct and have the best quality required by the user : for example, he/she may privilege the freshness of the data rather than the credibility of their information source. It is often necessary to take into account the relative importance of the quality criteria and to affect specific weightings on quality criteria for the recommendation. We apply four existing methods in Operational Research [6,1] for data recommendation. For each data value, a score reflects its relative quality according to one of the following quality scoring model :

– *Linear Assignment of Weight (LAW)* which defines a quality score for each data :

$$Qscore(D_i) = \sum_{k=1}^{l} W_k E_{ik} \text{ with } W_k: weight\ of\ the\ k^{th}\ quality\ criterion$$

$$E_{ik}: evaluation\ of\ the\ k^{th}\ quality\ criterion\ for\ the\ i^{th}\ data\ D_i$$

– *Elimination by Aspects (EA)* : this method classifies the quality criteria by importance, then eliminates data that have the worst quality score for the most important criterion. The operation is repeated until there remains only one data for the recommendation.

– *the method of Anderson (AND)* [1] and *the method of Subramanian and Gershon (SG)* : these method uses three matrices (concordance, discordance and magnitude matrices) indicating each one the relative situation of one data compared to its *homologous data*.

4.3 Multicriteria recommendation algorithm

Using the recommendation models, we determine the data with the best quality. For each candidate value in one attribute of one multi-source object, we define a quality score accumulator and propose the following recommendation algorithm :

```
Algorithm Value_Recommendation

Let Vacc[v] be the entry for the value v in the quality
          score accumulator
Init all the accumulator entries to 0
For each multi-source object o
  Find the set of attributes {a₁, a₂,..., a₁} of o
  /*l : number of attributes describing the object o*/
  For each attribute aᵢ (with i = 1,..., l)
    Find the set of values {v_{ai,1}, v_{ai,2},..., v_{ai,mi}} of aᵢ
    /*mi : number of values for the attribute aᵢ
          proposed by the different sources*/
    For each value v_{ai,j} (with j = 1,..., mi)
      For each quality criterion c_k in the metadata
      associated with the value v_{ai,j} (with k = 1,...,nj)
      /*nj : number of quality criteria for v_{ai,j}*/
        Find the set of values {v_{ck,1}, v_{ck,2}... ,v_{ck,ml}} for
        which the criterion c_k has been evaluated
        /*ml : number of values for which the quality
              criterion c_k has been evaluated (mi≤ml)*/
        For each value v_{ck,p} (with p = 1,..., ml)
          Find the source s of the value v_{ck,p}
          Vacc[v_{ck,p}] = Vacc[v_{ck,p}] + Vscore(v_{ck,p}, c_k, s)
Sort the score accumulator by decreasing order
Return the list of values according to score
accumulator value
```

The Vscore($v_{ck,p}$, c_k, s) is the function which gives the score of the value $v_{ck,p}$ for the quality criterion c_k tacking into account the quality score of its source s. This function uses one of the scoring methods previously presented, according to the particular recommendation strategy.

5 Application of sQuaL in Technological Intelligence

In the context of Information Warfare, an Information Service Provider, such as a Technological Intelligence Group (*TIG*), is composed of human experts, specialists whom competencies are used to evaluated the veracity of available contradictory information items. Explicit and tacit knowledge about plausibility of technological information are essential knowledge to be capitalized. In this perspective, the aim of the sQuaL system is to assist the tasks of the *TIG* basically in charge of : (1) selecting information sources (technological patents, technical reports...). The selection of producers is based on objective and subjective quality criteria (e.g. credibility, interest to disclose information...) (2) choosing and collecting dynamically information : the selection of presumed relevant information is based on non-exhaustive information quality criteria : plausibility, accuracy, timeliness, completeness... (3) cross-checking information items (contradictory or partially redundant), evaluating and stamping information quality and information source quality, (4) providing certified relevant information.

The general methodology we proposed in Section 3 is particularly appropriate to the Technological Intelligence application domain [2,3] whose main tasks are : (A) collecting the descriptions of real entities made by various information sources and storing relevant and critical data in the multi-source database (B) evaluating data quality criteria (C) recommending data for consultation. Let's now present a short example of application in the context of Technological Intelligence.

A. Selection of sources and collection of data and quality metadata. For instance, a competitor's product *P* is a real entity which is never entirely and/or precisely known by the *TIG*. To know its characteristics, the *TIG* doesn't have necessarily a direct access to the equipment *P*. Thus, the *TIG* must trust relevant textual information sources. In Fig. 2, three textual information sources S1, S2 and S3 propose characteristics to describe the product *P* : respectively, "*length : 42f*" for S1, "*length = 40 feet*" for S2, and "*long:15.023m*" for S3. Initially, the TIG experts have to collect all the descriptions made on the product *P* by the available information sources. Then, they structure and store these descriptions in the multi-source database of the sQuaL system (Fig. 2). *Homologous data* are stored in *multi-source objects* whose attributes have multiple values with the mention of their source ID. In the example, the product *P* has three values for the attribute *length*.

B. Evaluation of quality criteria. In the example, we suppose that the four quality criteria (selected in Step 1 and 2 of the methodology) are : the plausibility of the data value, its accuracy, the credibility of its source and the freshness of the data. These criteria may be ranked per degree of importance by the TIG expert (Plausibility: 60%, Accuracy: 20%, Source Credibility: 15% and Freshness: 5%). The quality criteria of each value are evaluated by the specialist of the technological field and stored as quality metadata. In the example of Fig. 2, the plausibility of the value "*42 f*" proposed by the source S1 is evaluated *High* by the expert.

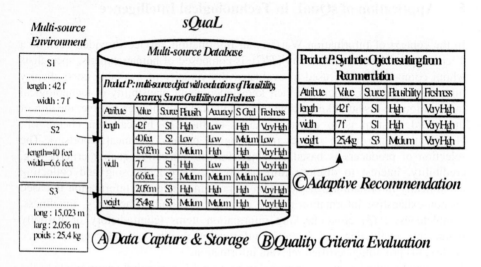

Fig. 2. Application example of sQuaL

C. Adaptive value recommendation. Querying the sQuaL system, the user may have requirements for data quality and may rank the quality criteria he/she considers more important. So, the recommendation results are adapted to his/her data quality needs. The sQuaL system will propose an adaptive value recommendation for each attribute of the multi-source object. For answering the query, a synthetic object is built with the existing values of the multi-source object according to the best quality scores. In the Fig. 2, the user was interested in the plausibility and the freshness of the data (privileging plausibility). A synthetic object is finally proposed to him by the sQuaL system : its attributes are composed of values from heterogeneous sources (S1 and S3) for their optimal plausibility and freshness.

6   Conclusion and perspectives

The objectives of our article are : (1) to briefly present the existing works on data quality and to introduce the notion of multi-source data quality (2) to propose a general methodology for integrating information quality expertise into the information processing (3) to present the sQuaL system for assisting information quality expertise and recommending data according to their relative quality in the specific context of Technological Intelligence. Our current work is now focused on : (1) the assistance for the choice of the best recommendation strategy (2) the anticipation of the sQuaL system for non-intrusive acquisition of user profiles and quality criteria preferences (3) the fuzzy recommendation. The perspectives of research on multi-source data quality and their recommendation are numerous, in particular for extending of the concept of *relevancy-ranking* with the concept of *quality-ranking* for (semi-)structured data.

References

1. Anderson, E., Choice models for evaluation and selection of software packages, J. of Management Information Systems, Vol. 6, (1990) 123-138
2. Berti, L., Out of overinformation by information filtering and information quality weighting, Proc. of the 2nd Information Quality Conf. MIT (1997) 187-193
3. Berti, L., From data source quality to information quality : the relative dimension, Proc. of the 3rd Information Quality Conf. MIT (1998) 247-263
4. Brodie, M.L., Data quality in information systems, Information and Management, Vol. 3 (1980) 245-258
5. Goodchild, M., Jeansoulin, R., (eds), Data quality in geographic information : from error to uncertainty, Hermès (1998)
6. Fritz, C., Carter, B., A classification and summary of software evaluation and selection methodologies, Technical Report, Mississippi State University (1994)
7. Fox, C., Levitin, A., Redman, T., The notion of data and its quality dimensions, Information Processing and Management, Vol. 30, no. 1 (1994)
8. Redman, T., Data quality for the information age, Artech House, (1996)
9. Reddy, M. P., Wang, R., Estimating data accuracy in a federated database environment, Proc. of the 9th Intl. Conf. CISMOD (1995) 115-134
10. Smith, I., Pipino, L., (eds), Proc. of the 3rd Information Quality Conf. MIT (1998)
11. Strong, D., Kahn, B., (eds), Proc. of the 2nd Information Quality Conf. MIT (1997)
12. Wang, R., Kon, H. B., Madnick, S. E., Data quality requirements analysis and modeling, Proc. of the 9th Int. Conf. on Data Engineering (1993) 670-677
13. Wang, R., Storey, V., Firth, C., A framework for analysis of data quality research, IEEE, TKDE, Vol. 7, no. 4 (1995) 623-638
14. Wang, R., (ed), Proc. of the 1st Information Quality Conf. MIT (1996)
15. Wang, R., A product perspective on Total Data Quality Management, Communications of the ACM, Vol. 41, no. 2 (1998) 58-65

On Benchmarking Attribute Cardinality Maps for Database Systems Using the TPC-D Specifications

Murali Thiyagarajah⋆ and **B. John Oommen**⋆⋆

School of Computer Science, Carleton University, Ottawa, Canada K1S 5B6
{murali, oommen}@scs.carleton.ca

Abstract. Current business database systems utilize histograms to approximate frequency distributions of attribute values of relations. These are used to efficiently estimate query result sizes and access plan costs and thus minimize the query response time for database systems. In two recent works [7, 8] we proposed (and thoroughly analyzed) two new forms of histogram-like techniques called the Rectangular and Trapezoidal Attribute Cardinality Maps (ACM) respectively, that give much smaller estimation errors than the traditional equi-width and equi-depth histograms currently being used by many commercial database systems. This paper reports how the benchmarking of the Rectangular-ACM (R-ACM) and the Trapezoidal-ACM (T-ACM) for query optimization can be achieved. By conducting an extensive set of experiments using the acclaimed TPC-D benchmark queries and database [15], we demonstrate that these new ACM schemes are much more accurate than the traditional histograms for query result size estimation.

1 Introduction

Benchmarking is an important step in the developmental cycle of any new software strategy as it validates the functional properties of the new software in a typical real-world environment. It also enables the user to compare the performance of various similar methods against a single standard. But benchmarking is often a challenging and a very complex problem, because it is difficult (if not impossible) to test, validate and verify the results of the various schemes in completely different settings. This is even more true in the case of database systems because the benchmarking also depends on the *types* of queries presented to the databases used in the benchmarking experiments. In this paper, we study the benchmarking of two new query optimization strategies that we recently proposed in [7, 8].

⋆ Supported by the Natural Sciences and Engineering Research Council of Canada
⋆⋆ Senior Member, IEEE. Partially supported by the Natural Sc iences and Engineering Research Council of Canada.

1.1 Query Optimization in Database Systems

One of the important functionalities of the modern-day database management systems (DBMS) is to provide quick determination of answers to user queries. Intensifying competition in the business marketplace continues to increase the sizes of databases as well as sophistication of queries against them. This has resulted in a greater focus (both academically and in the industrial world) to develop systems with superior DBMS functionalities that would, in turn, minimize the response time for business and other queries.

The problem of minimizing query response time is known as Query Optimization, which has been one of the most active research topics in the database and information system fields for the last two decades. Query optimization for relational database systems is a combinatorial optimization problem, which requires estimation of query result sizes to select the most efficient access plan for a query, based on the estimated costs of various query plans. As queries become more complex (such as found in modern-day business systems), the number of alternative query evaluation plans (QEPs) which have to be considered explodes exponentially. For example, for a join of 10 relations, the number of different QEPs is greater than 176 billion!. A typical inquiry that a bank officer runs many times a day, for example, to retrieve the current market value of a customer's mutual fund/stock portfolio, usually transparently carries out a join of many relations (i.e: behind the scene).

Query result sizes are usually estimated using a variety of statistics that are maintained in the database catalogue for relations in the database. Since these statistics approximate the distribution of data values in the attributes of the relations, they represent an inaccurate picture of the **actual** contents of the database. It has been shown in [3] that errors in query result size estimates may increase exponentially with the number of joins. This result, in light of the complexity of present-day queries, shows the the critical importance of accurate result size estimation.

We recently [7, 8] proposed two new catalogue based non-parametric statistical models called the *Rectangular Attribute Cardinality Map* (R-ACM) and *Trapezoidal Attribute Cardinality Map* (T-ACM), that can be used to obtain more accurate estimation results than the currently known estimation techniques. Since they are based on the philosophies of numerical integration, query result size estimations based on these models have been shown to be much more accurate than the traditional equi-width and equi-depth histograms. For a detailed mathematical treatment of these techniques, including their analytic properties, the reader is referred to [7, 8]. The goal of this paper is to demonstrate the power of the R-ACM and the T-ACM for query result size estimation by extensive experiments using the TPC-D benchmark queries and databases [15], and to justify the claim of our analytical results that the R-ACM and the T-ACM are superior to the current state-of-the-art techniques that are being used in the commercial database systems.

1.2 Comparison of the ACMs to the Current State-of-the-Art

Since most of the current commercial DBMSs utilize non-parametric statistical techniques for query result size estimations, we have listed these techniques for some of the popular commercial DBMSs in Table 1. As can be seen from this table, most vendors use equi-depth histograms as it is more accurate than the equi-width histograms for both worst-case and average-case situations.

Table 1. Histograms used in Some Popular Commercial DBMSs.

Vendor	Product	Histogram Type
Oracle	Oracle7	Equidepth
Sybase	System 11	Equidepth
IBM	DB2-MVS	Subclass of End-Biased(F,F)
Tandem	NonStop SQL/MP	Equidepth
Informix	Online Data Server	Equidepth
NCR	Teradata	Equidepth
Microsoft	SQL Server	Equidepth

Having described the properties of the R-ACM and the T-ACM in the previous sections, we shall now provide a comparison of the worst-case and average-case errors of these new techniques to that of the traditional histograms. This is summarized in Table 2. It can be seen from this table that both the R-ACM and the T-ACM are much more accurate for query result size estimation than the traditional equi-width and equi-depth histograms.

Table 2. Comparison of Histogram and ACM Errors. τ is much smaller than l_j.

Histogram	Worst-case Error	Average-case Error
Equi-width	$\max\left(n_j - \frac{n_j}{l}, \frac{n_j}{l}\right)$	$\max\left(n_j - \frac{n_j}{l}, \frac{n_j}{l}\right)$
Equi-depth	$\frac{2n_j}{3l_j}$	$\frac{n_j}{2l_j}$
R-ACM	$\tau\left\|\ln\left(\frac{l_j}{i-1}\right) - 1\right\|$	2τ
T-ACM	$\max\left(a_j + \frac{2(n_j - a_j l)}{l(l-1)}i, n_j - a_j - \frac{2(n_j - a_j l)}{l(l-1)}i\right)$	0

Note that the quantities a_j, n_j, i and l denote the frequency of the first attribute value in a sector, total number of tuples in the sector, location of the attribute value X_i within the sector and the sector width respectively.

2 TPC-D Benchmark Specification

The TPC Benchmark D (TPC-D) has been proposed by the Transaction Processing Performance Council (TPC) as a decision support benchmark. TPC-D models a decision support environment in which complex *ad hoc* business-oriented queries are submitted against a large database. The queries and the data populating the database have been chosen to have broad industry-wide relevance while maintaining a sufficient degree of ease of implementation. We briefly describe the TPC-D benchmark queries and its database model below. A detail description about the complete benchmarking requirements, including auditing can be found in the TPC-D specification document [15].

2.1 TPC-D Benchmark Queries

The TPC-D benchmark queries typically involve, multi-table joins, extensive sorting, grouping and aggregation and sequential scans. The purpose of TPC-D is to assess cost/performance of a particular commercial system which supports the above queries. Since our objective is to study the performance of the ACMs in terms of their estimation accuracy, unlike a commercial DBMS, we do not require a fully functional DBMS for our experiments. Most of the TPC-D queries contain relational operators other than selection and equality join, and thus are not directly suitable for running on ACMs. Consequently, for our testing purposes, we shall use a slightly modified form of TPC-D queries by systematically eliminating the inapplicable operations such as grouping and aggregations etc., which are not supported by our current research work. Eliminating queries containing *views*, and modifying the remaining queries, we obtained a total of 11 query types from the original 17 query types specified in the TPC-D specification.

For each of the relevant query types derived in the above manner, we construct an operator tree and estimate the result size of these operator trees in a bottom-up fashion. This bottom-up query execution strategy works as follows. First, we estimate the result sizes and distributions of leaf-level operators using the ACMs on the base relations. Then we construct the ACMs on the result distributions and use these ACMs for estimating the result size and distributions of the operators in the next level of the tree. This process is repeated until the result size of the root node of the operator tree is estimated. We also compute the exact result size of the query by actually executing the simplified queries on the same data using a simple query processor which we implemented. Using these we compute the error from the result size estimation using the ACMs.

All of the TPC-D benchmark queries involve business oriented questions using standard SQL syntax, conforming to SQL-92 specification. Table 3 describes each query in plain English.

2.2 TPC-D Benchmark Database

The TPC-D database schema consists of eight tables detailed in the TPC-D specification. This schema models a database for a worldwide distributor that

Table 3. Description of the TPC-D Queries

Query No	Name	Description
Q2	Minimum Cost Supplier Query	Find which supplier should be selected to place an order for a given part in a given region
Q3	Shipping Priority Query	Retrieve the 10 unshiped orders with the highest value
Q5	Local Supplier Volume Query	List the revenue volume done through local suppliers
Q6	Forcasting Revenue Change Query	Quantify the amount of revenue increase in a given year
Q7	Volume Shipping Query	Determine the value of goods shipped between certain nations
Q9	Product Type Profit Measure Query	Determine how much profit is made on a given line of parts
Q10	Return Item Reporting Query	Identify customers who might be having problems with parts shipped to them
Q11	Identification of Stock Query	Find the most important subset of suppliers' stock in a given nation
Q12	Shipping Mode Query	Determine whether selecting less expensive modes of shipping affect priority orders
Q14	Promotion Effect Query	Monitor market response to a promotion such as a TV advertisement
Q17	Small-Quantity Order Query	Determine revenue lost if orders where not filled for small quantities of certain parts

purchases parts from suppliers and sells them to customers. The two largest tables are the master-detail pair of Order and LineItem, which together constitute about 85% of the database. The other tables describe the business's parts, suppliers and customers. All tables except the two small Nation and Region tables scale linearly with the size of the database. The TPC-D database can be scaled upto a size of 1000GB in order to support high-end systems. For our experiments, we use a prototype version of this, namely, a test database with a size of approximately 100MB. The TPC-D database itself is generated using the data generation utility, DBGEN, supplied by the TPC. The DBGEN program generates mainly uniformly distributed data. Since, we are interested in modeling skewed data distribution as well, we have opted to populate the database in three different ways listed below.

In the first method we simply use the data from the DBGEN program. This typically results in uniform data.

In the second method, we generate frequencies from a Zipf distribution with an appropriately chosen skew parameter, z, while retaining the original value domain and relation sizes. We combine the attribute values in various attributes in each relation randomly to generate the tuples for that relation, according to the frequencies obtained from the Zipf distribution.

It is claimed that the multi-fractals distributions occur more frequently in the real world data [2]. So in our third method, we generate frequencies using multi-fractal distributions with various bias values for the original value domain from the TPC-D database. The frequency values resulting from the multi-fractal distributions are combined with the values from the TPC-D database to generate the tuples for the new relations.

Zipf distribution is an algebraically decaying function that can be used to describe many real-world data distributions. The multi-fractal distributions are similar to the the "80-20 law" and seem to appear often in the database world. A brief overview of the Zipf and multi-fractal distributions used in the second and third methods of populating the databases of our experiments can be found in [14].

3 Experiments with the TPC-D Benchmark Database

Unlike the prototype validating experiments which were discussed in [10, 9], the TPC-D benchmarking experiments involve arbitrarily large and complex query types. Consequently there are often thousands or more possible query evaluation plans (QEPs) for executing them. Since our objective is to compare the query result size estimation accuracy of various techniques as opposed to choosing the optimal QEP, we randomly selected an arbitrary QEP for a given query type and constructed the corresponding operator tree. The result size of this operator tree was then estimated in a bottom-up fashion from the leaves of the tree to the root of the tree. It is important to note that, unlike the case of a primitive relational operation, with these simulated "real-life" query types, it was necessary to construct the ACMs and histograms for all the resulting intermediate relations. What follows is the details of the results we obtained.

The experiments we conducted with the TPC-D benchmark database involved three distinct groups. In the first set of experiments, we used the uniform distribution data that was generated by the DBGEN program from TPC. We computed the estimation errors from the equi-width, equi-depth histograms, the R-ACM and the T-ACM for the set of TPC-D queries. We conducted ten different set of experiments using the histograms and the ACMs with different build-parameters. The build-parameter for the equi-width histogram and the T-ACM is the sector width, the build-parameter for the equi-depth histogram is the number of tuples per sector and the build parameter for the R-ACM is the tolerance value, τ. For each attribute involved in the query, we generated the equi-width and equi-depth histograms with different sector-widths and different number of tuples/sector respectively. The corresponding T-ACMs were also generated with the same sector widths that were chosen for the equi-width histograms. The T-ACMs were generated using the Implement_T-ACM algorithm, which is a much improved version of the original Generate_T-ACM algorithm given in [8]. Similarly for each attribute involved in the query, we generated the R-ACM with a different value for the tolerance, τ. In order to obtain a fair comparison, the build-parameters for all different techniques were chosen such that the resulting storage requirements were the same, regardless of the method. The result sizes and consequently the computed estimation errors were averaged over these set of experiments. The results are shown in Table 4.

Table 4. Estimation Error with Histograms, R-ACM and T-ACM on Uniform TPC-D Database

TPC-D Query	Actual Result Size	Error with Uniform TPC-D Database			
		Equi-width	Equi-depth	R-ACM	T-ACM
Q2	918	10.94%	9.60%	3.21%	3.72%
Q3	42190	13.62%	11.39%	4.37%	5.73%
Q5	209018	10.05%	9.68%	2.55%	3.61%
Q6	20706	12.33%	10.16%	4.38%	4.27%
Q7	2041	15.20%	10.75%	6.13%	5.99%
Q9	2.71e+06	13.83%	11.42%	5.48%	4.91%
Q10	44823	14.07%	12.93%	5.06%	6.15%
Q11	511	11.39%	10.40%	4.21%	5.03%
Q12	19	25.97%	22.73%	5.81%	5.62%
Q14	36724	14.66%	13.45%	4.77%	5.28%
Q17	523	20.35%	19.73%	5.81%	6.37%

In the second set of experiments, we used Zipf data distributions with three different skew values ($z = 2, z = 4, z = 6$) on the value domains of the various attribute values of the TPC-D database and computed the estimation errors from the equi-width, equi-depth histograms, the R-ACM and the T-ACM. Again we conducted ten different set of experiments using different build-parameters for the equi-width, equi-depth histograms, the R-ACM and the T-ACM. Due to the steep frequency variations of the Zipf distributions used, the R-ACM partitioning resulted in a very large number of sectors. In order to avoid this, we were forced to choose somewhat larger tolerance values for the R-ACM partitioning. As with the first set of experiments, in order to make a fair comparison of the various techniques, the build-parameters were chosen so that the resulting storage requirements were same for the histograms and the ACMs. The experiments were conducted for the set of TPC-D queries described earlier. We averaged the results for the three Zipf distributions and computed the estimation errors. The results are given in Table 5.

The third set of experiments involve using the multi-fractal distributions. A single scan through the data generated by the DBGEN program returns the number of distinct attribute values for each of the attributes involved. We selected three different bias values ($p = 0.1, p = 0.3, p = 0.4$) that resulted in three completely different multi-fractal distributions. The frequencies from these multi-fractal distributions were applied randomly to the value domain of the attributes in the TPC-D database to generate a new set of relations. As before we conducted ten different set of experiments with different build-parameters for the equi-width, equi-depth histograms, the R-ACM and the T-ACM, using the same storage

Table 5. Estimation Error with Histograms, R-ACM and T-ACM on Multi-fractal TPC-D Database

TPC-D Query	Actual Result Size	Error with Zipf-TPC-D Database			
		Equi-width	Equi-depth	R-ACM	T-ACM
Q2	161	27.46%	24.30%	9.62%	11.83%
Q3	26428	29.75%	26.42%	12.87%	12.90%
Q5	38620	19.07%	17.29%	9.46%	10.94%
Q6	16271	17.20%	14.65%	9.33%	6.85%
Q7	263	26.71%	25.80%	13.42%	15.25%
Q9	2.8e+06	19.81%	20.11%	10.66%	11.17%
Q10	22670	26.28%	23.04%	12.37%	8.42%
Q11	395	21.44%	17.59%	9.28%	9.91%
Q12	38	37.46%	31.72%	14.36%	15.11%
Q14	26538	23.81%	21.25%	15.30%	14.65%
Q17	1932	31.63%	29.28%	11.92%	10.87%

requirements. Again the experiments involved applying the TPC-D queries described earlier. We averaged the results for the three multi-fractal distributions and computed the estimation errors. The results are given in Table 6.

4 Analysis of the Experimental Results

Our results from these three set of TPC-D benchmark experiments confirm our theoretical results, summarized in Table 2, and clearly demonstrate that the estimation accuracy of the R-ACM and the T-ACM structures is superior to that of the traditional equi-width and equi-depth histograms.

As we can observe, the estimation errors for the histograms and the ACMs are the lowest for the experiments with the original TPC-D database, which was generated by the TPC supplied DBGEN program. For example, for the TPC-D query $Q2$, the estimation errors for the original TPC-D database from Table 4 are 10.94%, 9.60%, 3.21% and 3.72% for the equi-width, equi-depth, R-ACM and T-ACM respectively. Whereas, as can be seen from Table 5, the estimation errors for query $Q2$ with the multi-fractal TPC-D database are 27.46%, 24.30%, 9.62%, and 11.83% in the same order. The estimation errors for the Zipf TPC-D database, given in Table 6, are even higher. The reason for the lowest error with the original TPC-D database is, that it is uniformly distributed. Similarly the reason for the largest estimation errors with the Zipf TPC-D database is obviously due to the steep frequency changes by virtue of the underlying Zipf distribution. Another reason why the estimation errors for the R-ACM are larger than for the first set of experiments is our choice of comparatively larger tolerance values to avoid generating R-ACMs with large number of sectors. The estimation accuracy of the R-ACM and that of the T-ACM are almost comparable except for range-select queries, where the T-ACM out-performs the R-ACM. This is due to the fact that the trapezoidal rule of numerical integration is more accurate

Table 6. Estimation Error with Histograms, R-ACM and T-ACM on Zipf TPC-D Database

TPC-D Query	Actual Result Size	Error with Multi-fractal-TPC-D Database			
		Equi-width	Equi-depth	R-ACM	T-ACM
Q2	528	30.49%	28.26%	15.42%	17.22%
Q3	26210	29.83%	24.68%	14.58%	16.26%
Q5	132450	40.63%	36.27%	12.72%	10.67%
Q6	19204	30.20%	26.11%	14.32%	11.71%
Q7	3096	34.26%	27.42%	12.33%	15.24%
Q9	3.6e+06	28.39%	25.75%	9.97%	9.29%
Q10	40022	26.92%	24.18%	11.92%	13.33%
Q11	212	28.21%	22.73%	12.07%	13.15%
Q12	86	26.42%	23.12%	10.25%	12.63%
Q14	49270	26.25%	21.49%	13.92%	12.84%
Q17	976	23.46%	21.22%	14.67%	15.90%

than the right-end or the left-end rectangular rule of numerical integration for computing the area under a curve.

The results from all three sets of experiments show that the estimation errors resulting from the R-ACM and the T-ACM are **consistently** much lower than the estimation errors from the equi-depth and equi-depth histograms. This is consequent to the fact the frequency distribution of an attribute value within an R-ACM is guaranteed to be close to the sector mean since the partitioning of the sectors is based on a user-specified tolerance value, and the deviation from the running mean. Similarly, the trapezoidal rule of the numerical integration technique is more accurate than the right-end or left-end histogram approximation techniques. Thus, these set of experiments with the TPC-D benchmark queries and databases demonstrate that the R-ACM and T-ACM strategies exhibit a distinctively superior performance over the traditional equi-width and equi-depth histograms. Such results are typical with both synthetic data and real-world data. The power of the ACM structures is obvious!

5 Conclusion

We recently [7,8] introduced two new histogram-like approximation strategies known as the Rectangular and Trapezoidal Attribute Cardinality Maps, for query result size estimation. Since these techniques are based on the philosophies of numerical integration, they are more accurate than the traditional histograms. Their analytical properties are given in [7,8]. In this paper, we have presented an extensive array of experimental results on these new structures using the industry-popular TPC-D Benchmark specification. These benchmarking experiments included both an arbitrarily large simulated "real-world" database and a set of highly complex simulated "real-world" query patterns. They clearly demonstrate and validate our theoretical analysis of the R-ACM and the T-

ACM and their superiority over the current state-of-the-art estimation techniques based on the traditional equi-width and equi-depth histograms, and augment the prototype validation and testing results from [9, 10].

References

1. Christodoulakis, S.: Estimating selectivities in data bases. Technical Report CSRG-136, Computer Science Dept, University of Toronto, (1981)
2. Christos Faloutsos, Yossi Matias and Avi Silberschatz: Modeling skewed distributions using multifractals and the 80-20 law. Technical Report, Dept. of Computer Science, University of Maryland, (1996)
3. Yannis Ioannidis and S. Christodoulakis: On the propagation of errors in the size of join results. Proceedings of the ACM-SIGMOD Conference, (1991) 268–277
4. R. P. Kooi: The optimization of queries in relational databases. Case Western Reserve University, (1980)
5. Mannino, M.V., Chu, P. and Sager, T.: Statistical profile estimation in database systems. ACM Computing Surveys, (1988) Vol 20 192–221
6. M. Muralikrishna and David J Dewitt: Equi-depth histograms for estimating selectivity factors for multi-dimensional queries. Proceedings of ACM-SIGMOD Conference, (1988) 28–36
7. Oommen, B. John and Thiyagarajah, Murali: The Rectangular Attribute Cardinality Map: A New Histogram-like Technique for Query Optimization. School of Computer Science, Carleton University, Ottawa, Canada, TR-99-01, (1999)
8. Oommen, B. John and Thiyagarajah, Murali: The Trapezoidal Attribute Cardinality Map: A New Histogram-like Technique for Query Optimization. School of Computer Science, Carleton University, Ottawa, Canada, TR-99-04, (1999)
9. Thiyagarajah, Murali and Oommen, B. John: Prototype Validation of the Trapezoidal Attribute Cardinality Map for Query Optimization in Database Systems. International Conference on Enterprise Information Systems - ICEIS'99, Setubal, Portugal, (1999)
10. Thiyagarajah, Murali and Oommen, B. John: Prototype Validation of the Rectangular Attribute Cardinality Map for Query Optimization in Database Systems. International Conference on Business Information Systems - BIS'99, Poznan, Poland, (1999)
11. Oommen, B. John and Thiyagarajah, Murali: Benchmarking Attribute Cardinality Maps for Database Systems Using the TPC-D Specifications. School of Computer Science, Carleton University, Ottawa, Canada, TR-99-07, (1999)
12. Oommen, B. John and Thiyagarajah, Murali: The Rectangular Attribute Cardinality Map: A New Histogram-like Technique for Query Optimization. International Database Engineering and Applications Symposium, IDEAS'99, Montreal, Canada, (1999)
13. Gregory Piatetsky-Shapiro and Charles Connell: Accurate estimation of the number of tuples satisfying a condition. Proceedings of ACM-SIGMOD Conference, 256–276, (1984)
14. Murali Thiyagarajah: Attribute Cardinality Maps: New Query Result Size Estimation Techniques for Database Systems. PhD Thesis, Carleton University, Ottawa, Canada (1999)
15. Transaction Processing Council (TPC): TPC-D Benchmark Specification. (1998)

Using Self-Organizing Maps to Organize Document Archives and to Characterize Subject Matter: How to Make a Map Tell the News of the World

Andreas Rauber and Dieter Merkl

Institut für Softwaretechnik, Technische Universität Wien
Resselgasse 3/188, A–1040 Wien, Austria
www.ifs.tuwien.ac.at/~andi, www.ifs.tuwien.ac.at/~dieter

Abstract. While the focus of research concerning electronic document archives still is on information retrieval, the importance of interactive exploration has been realized and is gaining importance. The map metaphor, where documents are organized on a map according to their contents, has proven particularly useful as an interface to such a collection. The self-organizing map has shown to produce stable topically ordered organizations of documents on such a 2-dimensional map display. However, the characteristics of these topical clusters are not being made explicit. In this paper we present the *LabelSOM* method which takes the applicability of the self-organizing map for document archive organization one step further by automatically labeling the various topical clusters found in the map. This allows the user to get an instant overview of the various topics covered by a document collection.

1 Introduction

Today's information age may be characterized by constant massive production and dissemination of written information. Powerful tools for exploring, searching, and organizing this mass of information are needed. Particularly the aspect of exploration has found only limited attention. While the importance of exploration of document archives has been widely agreed on, current information retrieval technology still relies on systems that retrieve documents based on the similarity between keyword-based document and query representations.

However, the map metaphor for displaying the contents of a document library in a two-dimensional map has gained some interest [1, 2, 5–7]. Maps are used to visualize the similarity between documents in terms of distances within a two-dimensional map display. Hence, similar documents may be found in neighboring regions of the map display, which is comparable to the situation encountered in conventional libraries, where books are organized in topical sections. Finding one book on a desired topic using any of the available information retrieval (IR) techniques then leaves you with several others on the same topic nearby. Apart from interactive retrieval of documents within one topical cluster, a map representation also allows users to browse an unfamiliar library in order to get an overview of the documents found in the repository. Given an enhanced visualization it not only provides information on which topics are covered in a specific collection, but also to which extent they are covered, i.e. how much information is available on a certain topic. Thus, the map serves as a kind of intuitive index to the document repository similar to road signs or overview maps of conventional libraries.

A way for automatically organizing a set of documents on such a map display is provided by the self-organizing map (SOM) [4], a popular unsupervised neural network. It provides a topology preserving mapping from a high-dimensional document space to a two-dimensional output space. On the SOM output space the documents are organized according to their topical cluster structure, i.e. documents on similar topics are grouped together, following the map metaphor of library representation. In spite of these mapping capabilities of the SOM, usage has been limited to some extent by the fact, that the interpretation of the resulting mapping was difficult since it required manual analysis of the trained SOM network. This is because the standard SOM representation provides no justification for a certain mapping and does not reveal the contents or boundaries of the clusters that are present in the map.

To overcome this limitation several enhanced cluster visualization techniques like the *U-Matrix* [17], the *Cluster Connection Technique* [9], *Adaptive Coordinates* [8] were developed to make the cluster structure within the map explicit. But still, none of these methods provide information on the features learned by the map. What we would like to have, is a method to automatically extract that knowledge from a trained map, i.e. to make the cluster structure and the characteristics of each cluster explicit. The *LabelSOM* method presented in this paper automatically extracts this information from a trained SOM by labeling each unit with those features that best describe the data, i.e. the documents mapped onto the respective unit. It thus provides the user with the concepts of the documents represented by the map in an intuitive and readable way. We demonstrate this approach using a real world document archive consisting of an article collection from the *TIME Magazine*.

The remainder of the paper is organized as follows: In Section 2 we give an introduction to the self-organizing map architecture and learning algorithm. Following a brief presentation of the *TIME Magazine* article collection used for the experiments presented in Section 3, we present a standard SOM library map representing the articles on the map display in Section 4. We next identify some of the problems related to the interpretation of such a standard map representation and describe related work addressing them in Section 5. The *LabelSOM* method providing an automatic labeling of the units of a self-organizing map is presented in Section 6, followed by an example showing the results of labeling the previously discussed map of *TIME Magazine* articles in Section 7. We finally present some conclusions on the *LabelSOM* method and the applicability of SOMs for digital library organization in Section 8.

2 Self-Organizing Maps

The *self-organizing map (SOM)* as proposed in [3] and described thoroughly in [4] is one of the most distinguished unsupervised artificial neural network models. It basically provides a form of cluster analysis by producing a mapping of high-dimensional input data $x, x \in \Re^n$ onto a usually 2-dimensional output space while preserving the topological relationships between the input data items as faithfully as possible. This model consists of a set of units, which are arranged in some topology where the most common choice is a 2-dimensional grid. Each of the units i is assigned a weight vector m_i of the same dimension as the input data, $m_i \in \Re^n$. are filled with random values.

During each learning step, the unit c with the highest activity level, the *winner* c with respect to a randomly selected input pattern x is adapted in a way that it will exhibit an even higher activity level at future presentations of that specific input pattern. Commonly, the activity level of a unit is based on the Euclidean distance between the input pattern and that unit's weight vector, i.e. the unit showing the smallest Euclidean distance between it's weight vector and the presented input vector is selected as the winner. Hence, the selection of the winner c may be written as given in Expression (1).

$$c : ||x - m_c|| = \min_i\{||x - m_i||\} \tag{1}$$

Adaptation takes place at each learning iteration and is performed as a gradual reduction of the difference between the respective components of the input vector and the weight vector. The amount of adaptation is guided by a learning-rate α that is gradually decreasing in the course of time. This decreasing nature of adaptation strength ensures large adaptation steps in the beginning of the learning process where the weight vectors have to be tuned from their random initialization towards the actual requirements of the input space. The ever smaller adaptation steps towards the end of the learning process enable a fine-tuned input space representation.

As an extension to standard competitive learning, units in a time-varying and gradually decreasing neighborhood around the winner are adapted, too. Pragmatically speaking, during the learning steps of the self-organizing map a set of units around the winner is tuned towards the currently presented input pattern enabling a spatial arrangement of the input patterns such that alike inputs are mapped onto regions close to each other in the grid of output units. Thus, the training process of the self-organizing map results in a topological ordering of the input patterns.

The neighborhood of units around the winner may be described implicitly by means of a neighborhood-kernel h_{ci} taking into account the distance—in terms of the output space—between unit i under consideration and unit c, the winner of the current learning iteration. This neighborhood-kernel assigns scalars in the range of $[0, 1]$ that are used to determine the amount of adaptation ensuring that nearby units are adapted more strongly than units further away from the winner. A Gaussian may be used to define the neighborhood-kernel as given in

Expression (2) where $||r_c - r_i||$ denotes the distance between units c and i within the output space, with r_i representing the two-dimensional vector pointing to the location of unit i within the grid.

$$h_{ci}(t) = e^{-\frac{||r_c - r_i||}{2 \cdot \delta(t)^2}} \tag{2}$$

It is common practice that in the beginning of the learning process the neighborhood-kernel is selected large enough to cover a wide area of the output space. The spatial width of the neighborhood-kernel is reduced gradually during the learning process such that towards the end of the learning process just the winner itself is adapted. Such a reduction is done by means of the time-varying parameter δ in Expression (2). This strategy enables the formation of large clusters in the beginning and fine-grained input discrimination towards the end of the learning process.

In combining these principles of self-organizing map training, we may write the learning rule as given in Expression (3). Please note that we make use of a discrete time notation with t denoting the current learning iteration.

$$m_i(t + 1) = m_i(t) + \alpha(t) \cdot h_{ci}(t) \cdot [x(t) - m_i(t)] \tag{3}$$

3 Experimental Document Collection

In the experiments presented hereafter we use the *TIME Magazine* article collection available at http://www.ifs.tuwien.ac.at/ifs/research/ir as a reference document archive. The collection comprises 420 documents from the *TIME Magazine* of the early 1960's. The documents can be thought of as forming topical clusters in the high-dimensional feature space spanned by the words that the documents are made up of. The goal is to map and identify those clusters on the 2-dimensional map display. Thus, we use full-text indexing to represent the various documents according to the vector space model of information retrieval. The indexing process identified 5923 content terms, i.e. terms used for document representation, by omitting words that appear in more than 90% or less than 1% of the documents. The terms are roughly stemmed and weighted according to a $tf \times idf$, i.e. term frequency $\times$ inverse document frequency, weighting scheme [16], which assigns high values to terms that are considered important in describing the contents of a document. Following the feature extraction process we end up with 420 vectors describing the documents in the 5923-dimensional document space, which are further used for neural network training.

4 A Map of Time Magazine Articles

Based on the document description as outlined above, we trained a 10×15 self-organizing map to represent the contents of the document archive. Hence, in this particular setup we have 150 neural processing units to represent the contents of the document collection. Figure 1 gives a graphical representation of the training result. Each unit is shown as a rectangular area in the figure containing the document numbers of documents mapped onto that particular unit. Due to space considerations we cannot show the map in full detail in this paper. We therefore have chosen several units for detailed discussion. The document numbers for these units are shown on the sides of the figure.

We find, that the SOM has succeeded in creating a topology preserving mapping of the document collection, i.e. we find documents on similar topics located on the same or neighboring units. For example, all articles mapped onto the units in the lower left corner of the map deal with problems in South Vietnam, with some units representing articles on the Vietnam War and other units covering the government crackdown on buddhist monks. As another example, consider articles *T024, T096, T242, T461*, which are located onto one single unit in the first row of the map, and which all deal with the relationship between India and Pakistan and the Kashmir conflict.

Several further topical clusters can be identified on the map. This capability of organizing free text documents according to their contents, has been demonstrated repeatedly on a number of different document collections using both the self-organizing map as well as variations of its basic architecture for the representation of digital libraries [2, 10–14]. The spatial arrangement of documents on the map provides a very intuitive interface to the text archive similar to manually classified and sorted libraries which also have books on similar topics located next to each other in the shelves.

5 Interpretation of Self-Organizing Maps

The SOM representation of the library suffers somewhat from the fact, that no information on the contents is provided and thus the topical arrangement of the documents cannot be exploited without thorough investigation of the map. There is neither a way to tell from the standard map representation, (1) which clusters are present in the map and where their boundaries are, nor (2) can one tell the characteristics of certain regions within the map. Thus, we cannot learn from the map, which clusters of documents on which topics are located in which place on the map. This renders the map somewhat useless unless one starts to read all articles to determine, which topics are represented by which set of units, which is a rather tiresome process for big maps and huge document collections.

To tackle this problem of map interpretation, several techniques were developed to facilitate intuitive cluster visualization to allow the detection of clusters and cluster boundaries. The *U-Matrix* [17] tries to visualize clusters in the map by creating a kind of 3-dimensional display of the map using the distances between neighboring units as height indicator. Coloring the units similar to conventional map coloring using light colors for high and dark colors for low distances to neighboring units, cluster boundaries become visible as light ridges between darker valleys of units belonging to the same cluster. Similar to this method, *Cluster Connections* [9] allow the interactive analysis of the map based on the distances between neighboring units. Thresholds are interactively adjusted to create a net

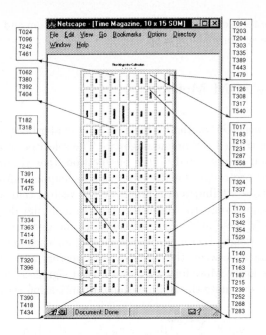

Fig. 1. 10 × 15 map of the *Time Magazine* collection

of connected and disconnected units. A different approach is taken in the *Adaptive Coordinates* method [8], where the movement of the SOM's weight vectors in the high-dimensional input space is mirrored in a two-dimensional output space. This leads to groups of units being located close to each other on the output space making the clusters intuitively visible.

However, while these methods may provide some aid in identifying clusters in the map, no description of the clusters can be derived. Thus, we still have to analyze all clusters manually to be able to tell their characteristics, i.e. to identify the topics of the mapped documents in the case of a self-organizing map representing document collections. Once the clusters are identified, current ways of SOM representation mostly rely on the manual selection of keywords to describe certain areas in the map, similar to the approach used in describing the trained SOM in the previous section. Only when some kind of preclassified information about the various articles is available, an approach for automatic assignment of labels for the clusters identified may be chosen, based on the knowledge about the data. Such a-priori knowledge has been used for example in the WEBSOM project [2]. There, a SOM was trained with articles from various Usenet Newsgroups. The regions in the resulting SOM where then labeled with the newsgroups that the majority of articles on a unit came from.

With the *LabelSOM* [15] method presented thereafter we automatically select those attributes from each weight vector that best describes the input data mapped onto the respective unit, allowing the identification and characterization of clusters in the self-organizing map.

6 The LabelSOM Method

The goal of the *LabelSOM* method is to select a set of attributes to serve as labels for the units of a trained self-organizing map. The selection of attributes in the *LabelSOM* method is motivated by the observation, that the weight vectors of the units serve as prototypes for the input signals mapped onto them. Thus we want to select those attributes of a unit's weight vector, that are shared by all input signals mapped onto the respective unit to a similar degree. In order to be able to identify these attributes, we calculate the quantization error vector q_i of every unit's weight vector m_i by calculating for each vector attribute the cumulative distance between the units' weight vectors and the input vectors mapped onto the units. More formally, for all input signals x_j mapped onto unit i, i.e. $x_j \in C_i$, we calculate the n-dimensional quantization error vector q_i as

$$q_{i_k} = \sum_{x_j \in C_i} \sqrt{(m_{i_k} - x_{j_k})^2}, \qquad k = 1..n \qquad (4)$$

In the resulting quantization error vector, those attributes that are shared by a large number of input signals can be identified as the vector attributes having a low quantization error. Thus we can select those attributes that exhibit the lowest quantization error as labels for the respective unit.

This selection of attributes may suffice in many standard data mining applications, where the shared absence of an attribute in a set of input data is equally important and descriptive as the detection of the shared presence of certain attributes. In the text mining domain we are faced with a somewhat different situation. Here, we typically find a very large number of attributes, i.e. terms, that are *not* present in a group of documents mapped onto a specific unit. These attributes thus usually exhibit a quantization error of close to or actually 0, perfectly qualifying for being selected as labels for the unit in question. Since we are usually not interested in attributes describing what a group of texts is *not* about, we have to use a second criterion to only select those attributes that actually describe the documents mapped onto the very unit in a positive way, i.e. list only those attributes that are strongly present in all documents. This is done by using the weight vector values of the units as a second criterion, eliminating all attributes as potential labels that exhibit weigth vector values below a certain threshold τ. Thus we end up with selecting those attributes with the lowest quantization error but a weight vector value above τ as labels for a unit. Using the threshold τ as well as the maximum number of attributes being selected as labels, we can determine the granularity of the resulting concept descriptions. The lower we set the threshold and the more attributes we allow to be selected as labels, the more details on the units are being revealed.

7   An Index of the Time Magazine Articles

The result of applying this *LabelSOM* method to the map depicted in Figure 1 is given in Figure 2, for which a set of up to 15 labels was selected for every unit. Again, due to space considerations, we can only list the labels for a subset of all units.[1] Based on these automatically selected labels we can now clearly identify the corresponding topic clusters.

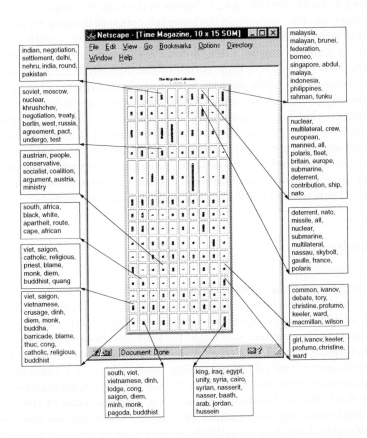

Fig. 2. Automatically assigned labels for the 10 × 15 *TIME Magazine* SOM

For example, the cluster of articles on Vietnam discussed above can be clearly identified in the lower left corner by labels such as *viet, cong, saigon, vietnamese, crusage, dinh, thuc, diem, monk, buddha, barricade, blame, catholic, religious,*

---

[1] However, the listing of all labels as well as the corresponding mapped articles is provided at http://www.ifs.tuwien.ac.at/ifs/research/ir/

buddhist or, for a neighboring node in the same cluster, *viet, saigon, catholic, religious, priest, blame, monk, diem, buddhist, quang*. The unit representing documents on the india-pakistan problem mentioned in Section 4, for example, is labeled with *india, negotiation, settlement, delhi, nehru, india, round, pakistan,* whereas a unit representing two articles on Austrian politics (*T182, T318*) is labeled *austrian, people, conservative, socialist, coalition, argument, austria, ministry*. Thus, simply by considering the automatically created labels for every unit we can determine, articles on which topic can be found in which area of the map.

Furthermore, the results from the automatic assignment of labels to the units can be used to easily identify topical clusters in the map as groups of units having labels in common. For example, in the lower left corner of the map we can identify a number of units sharing the labels *viet, saigon, buddhist* etc., clearly separating the cluster of articles covering Vietnam from neighboring topical clusters e.g. on the Middle East in the lower right corner of the map (with units sharing labels like *egypt, iraq, algeria, syria, nasser, hussein* etc.) or on Africa in the middle-left area of the map (*south, africa, white, black*). Finally, we are easily able to identify topical clusters that are represented by only single units that do not share any labels with neighboring units. Depending on the number of labels to be created for the map and the threshold τ, clusters at differing levels of granularity can be obtained. The more labels we choose to create and the lower we set the threshold, the larger are the clusters we obtain while a lower number of labels and higher setting of τ leads to the identification of more detailed subclusters.

8   Conclusions

The self-organizing map offers itself as an intuitive interface to a document archive, allowing interactive browsing and exploration by organizing documents into topical clusters on the map display. However, the interpretation of the resulting map is not as intuitive as it might be, since the cluster structure as well as the characteristics can not be derived from the resulting map display. To aid in the interpretation of trained self-organizing maps, methods for enhanced cluster visualization were developed supporting the user in identifying clusters of input data in a SOM. But still no information on the characteristics of these clusters are extracted, thus requiring manual labeling. In this paper we presented the *LabelSOM* method which automatically assigns a set of labels to the units of a self-organizing map. It is based on the observation, that the weight vectors of a trained SOM serve as prototypes for the input data mapped onto the respective units. Thus, based on the weight vectors and the input vectors mapped onto the respective units, a set of attributes shared by the input vectors mapped onto a unit can be selected to serve as labels. These labels give the characteristics of the documents mapped onto the respective unit describing the concepts learned by the map. The resulting map can actually be *read* and thus serves as a guide to the document repository, providing an instant and intuitive overview of the contents of a collection.

References

1. M. Hascoët and X. Soinard. Using maps as a user interface to a digital library. In *Proc. Int'l ACM SIGIR Conference on Research and Development in Information Retrieval*, Melbourne, Australia, 1998.
2. T. Honkela, S. Kaski, K. Lagus, and T. Kohonen. WEBSOM - Self-organizing maps of document collections. In *Proc. Workshop on Self-Organizing Maps (WSOM97)*, Espoo, Finland, 1997.
3. T. Kohonen. Self-organized formation of topologically correct feature maps. *Biological Cybernetics*, 43, 1982. Springer Verlag, Berlin, Heidelberg, New York.
4. T. Kohonen. *Self-Organizing Maps*. Springer Verlag, Berlin, Germany, 1995.
5. X. Lin, D. Soergel, and G. Marchionini. A self-organizing semantic map for information retrieval. In *Proc. Int'l ACM SIGIR Conf. on R & D in Information Retrieval*, Chicago, IL, 1991.
6. D. Merkl. A connectionist view on document classification. In *Proceedings of the 6th Australasian Database Conf. (ADC'95)*, Adelaide, SA, 1995.
7. D. Merkl. Exploration of document collections with self-organizing maps: A novel approach to similarity visualization. In *Europ. Symp. on Principles of Data Mining and Knowledge Discovery (PKDD'97)*, Trondheim, Norway, 1997.
8. D. Merkl and A. Rauber. Alternative ways for cluster visualization in self-organizing maps. In *Proc. of the Workshop on Self-Organizing Maps (WSOM97)*, Helsinki, Finland, 1997.
9. D. Merkl and A. Rauber. Cluster connections – a visualization technique to reveal cluster boundaries in self-organizing maps. In *Proc 9th Italian Workshop on Neural Nets (WIRN97)*, Vietri sul Mare, Italy, 1997.
10. D. Merkl and A. Rauber. CIA's view of the world and what neural networks learn from it: A comparison of geographical document space representation metaphors. In *Proc. 9th International Conf. on Database and Expert Systems (DEXA98)*, Vienna, Austria, 1998.
11. D. Merkl and E. Schweighofer. En route to data mining in legal text corpora - Clustering, neural computation, and international treaties. In *Proc. International Workshop on Database and Expert Systems Applications*, Toulouse, France, 1997.
12. A. Rauber. SOMLib: A distributed digital library system based on self-organizing maps. In *Proc. 10th Italian Workshop on Neural Nets (WIRN98)*, Vietri sul Mare, Italy, 1998.
13. A. Rauber and D. Merkl. Creating an order in distributed digital libraries by integrating independent self-organizing maps. In *Proc. Int'l Conf. on Artificial Neural Networks (ICANN'98)*, Skövde, Sweden, 1998.
14. A. Rauber and D. Merkl. Finding structure in text archives. In *Proc. European Symp. on Artificial Neural Networks (ESANN98)*, Bruges, Belgium, 1998.
15. A. Rauber and D. Merkl. Automatic labeling of self-organizing maps: Making a treasure map reveal its secrets. In *Proc. 4th Pacific-Asia Conference on Knowledge Discovery and Data Mining (PAKDD99)*, Beijing, China, 1999.
16. G. Salton. *Automatic Text Processing: The Transformation, Analysis, and Retrieval of Information by Computer*. Addison-Wesley, Reading, MA, 1989.
17. A. Ultsch. Self-organizing neural networks for visualization and classification. In *Information and Classification. Concepts, Methods and Application*. Springer Verlag, 1993.

Combining C-signature with Path Dictionary for Query Processing of Nested Objects in OODBS

Hakgene Shin and Jaewoo Chang

Dept. of Office Automation, Chonju Kijeon Women's College
Chonju, Chonbuk 560-701, Korea
shin@kns.kijeon-c.ac.kr
Dept. of Computer Engineering, Chonbuk National University
Chonju, Chonbuk 560-756, Korea
jwchang@dblab.chonbuk.ac.kr

Abstract. Since an object-oriented database system (OODBS) dealing with composite objects requires expensive traversal costs to process user queries, query processing and indexing have become important issues in the success of object-oriented database systems. In this paper, we propose a new signature-based indexing scheme entitled c-signature. The c-signatures are abstracted from objects in a path in concatenation and are stored in a class-oriented way, so as to reduce search space. By positioning the c-signature file before the path dictionary, we can avoid expensive scanning of the database. Also, the c-signatures pointing to an s-expression in the path dictionary make it possible to avoid the sequential scanning of the path dictionary. Based on the proposed scheme, we develop implement the c-signature and its competitors such as path index, path signature, path dictionary, class unit signature, path dictionary index, and s-signature schemes. Using the experimental results, we compare the c-signature with the competitors under different degrees of reference sharing and in terms of the page I/Os of each scheme. Finally, we show that our c-signature scheme achieves significant improvements in the retrieval operation.

1 Introduction

In general, an object-oriented database system (OODBS) dealing with composite objects requires expensive traversal costs to process queries. Therefore, there are many studies on indexing schemes to support efficient query processing against composite objects in OODBSs. Access Support Relations (ASR) proposed in [1] use a relation containing object identifiers (OIDs) on paths and key fields with the B+tree. Path index, nested index, and multiple index using an inverted file are proposed in [2,3,4]. The path index, which is recommended for an aggregation hierarchy with a long path and is virtually equivalent to the ASR, requires high storage overhead and costly index maintenance to support various key fields. There are several attempts to adopt a signature scheme as an indexing scheme for composite objects. In the first attempt, the path signature scheme[5] creates signatures for each path. This scheme maintains a set of pairs, i.e., path signature and OIDs, where the path signature is generated from objects in the path and OIDs indicate the path along the composite objects. The path signature scheme suffers from redundant object values used in the signature generation and redundant OIDs in the signature file. There is another study using the signature scheme to access set type of data in OODBS[6]. The path dictionary scheme introduced in [7] has shown its lower storage overhead and its universality. In spite of the advantages, the path dictionary lacks in efficient accessing to the databases as well as to the path dictionary itself. To improve the path dictionary, the B+tree is adapted to the path dictionary scheme. The path dictionary index[8] combines the B+tree with the path dictionary, so as to access the path dictionary without scanning of the database. The class unit signature scheme[9] combines object signatures with path information. However the class unit signature rarely considered the reference sharing in composite objects. To resolve the problems of the path dictionary, the s-signature scheme[10] was proposed to provide an efficient filtering mechanism on the path dictionary. The s-signature filters the s-expressions at the initial stage of query processing. However, the s-signature scheme suffers from multiple target OIDs in an s-expression. Therefore, it is necessary to design a new indexing scheme that fully utilizes the advantages of both signature scheme and path dictionary.

In this paper, we propose a new signature-based indexing scheme, entitled *c-signature*, on the path dictionary to efficiently support query processing of different types of queries. Our new c-signature scheme uses path information without any redundant OIDs and also provides an access method for the path information. For this, we generate signatures from all objects in an s-expression of the path dictionary, and concatenate those signatures to form a c-signature for the s-expression. The c-signature provides an efficient filtering mechanism that make it unnecessary to access the database at the initial stage of query processing, which is required in the original path dictionary scheme. The c-signature also provides an efficient filtering mechanism for the path dictionary instead of the sequential scanning. Finally we compare our c-signature scheme with path index, path signature, path dictionary, class unit signature, path dictionary index, and s-signature schemes to show that the c-signature scheme achieves significant improvements in the retrieval operation.

The organization of this paper is as follows. In section 2, we will review some concepts and definitions involved in the query processing of OODBS. In section 3, we propose a new signature scheme for the path dictionary. Section 4 compares the c-signature scheme with the conventional indexing schemes in terms of some database operations and the storage overhead. Section 5 draws our conclusion.

2 Definitions and Concepts

Let us review some definitions and concepts, which follows the lead of [2,3,7]. Figure 1 shows a graphic representation of an *aggregation hierarchy*, and is used to illustrate some key concepts. The class Person has three *primitive attributes*, SSN, age, and residence along with two *composite attributes*, owns and name. The domain of the attribute owns is Vehicle. The class Vehicle has two primitive attributes, model and color along with two composite attributes, manufacturer and drivetrain. The manufacturer's domain is Company and consists of two primitive attributes and a composite attribute. Furthermore, the drivetrain object consists of combinations of primitive and composite attributes. Every object in the database is identified by an unique *object identifier*(OID). By storing the OID of an object O_{i+1} as an attribute value of another object O_i, an aggregation hierarchy is established between two objects. We call O_i the *parent* object of O_{i+1}. A predicate on a non-composite attribute will be called a *simple predicate*, while a predicate defined on a composite attribute will be called a *composite predicate*.

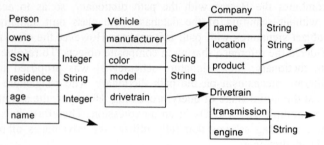

Fig. 1. Aggregation hierarchy

An example query such as "retrieve all vehicles manufactured by Ford and owned by a 50 year old person" can be expressed as follows.

```
select Person.Vehicle
where Person.Vehicle.Company.name="Ford"
and Person.age=50
```

The class from which objects are retrieved is called *target class*, while the class involved in the predicate is called *predicate class*. In the example, Vehicle is the target class and Company and Person classes are the predicate class. To answer the above example query, the traversal between a predicate class and a target class requires a high processing cost. To overcome this cost, we propose c-signature scheme.

3 C-signatures

In this section, we propose a new c-signature scheme and discuss how this new scheme processes a given query. First, we describe a way to combine the c-signature with the path dictionary and then discuss how to generate an efficient c-signature file under the context. Finally, we introduce query processing for the c-signature scheme.

3.1 C-signatures on s-expression

A main bottleneck in the path dictionary scheme is the sequential scanning of the database and the path dictionary. The bottleneck is depicted with dotted lines in Figure 2. To resolve the problem, an efficient access method is needed for the path dictionary and the database. Since the path dictionary only contains the connection information for the objects in the paths, i.e. OIDs, we can not directly compare the predicate given in a query with the path dictionary. However, it provides fast traversal means and processes different types of queries, so we need to develop a new signature scheme on the path dictionary to gain the advantages of the path dictionary as well as provide a means of fast access. The indexing scheme must provide the following requirements:

1. support for different types of queries with predicates on arbitrary attributes
2. support for scanning of the database and the path dictionary
3. support for both forward and backward traversals

In order to fulfill the requirements, we propose our c-signature scheme for the s-expression as shown in Figure 2. By positioning the c-signatures extracted from the database before the path dictionary, we can avoid expensive scanning of the database. The c-signatures pointing to an s-expression in the path dictionary also make it possible to avoid the sequential scanning of the path dictionary.

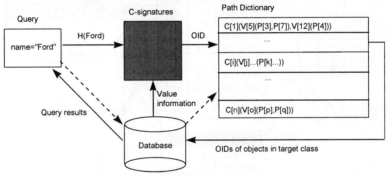

Fig. 2. C-signatures on path dictionary

Let us describe what structure the c-signature has and how to generate it. Figure 3 show how the c-signatures are generated from example s-expressions in Figure 2. Basically an object signature is extracted from attribute values of an object in an s-expression, so that the object signature may represent the object in the database. In other words, for each path terminating at the same object of the aggregation hierarchy, we create an object signature for each object in the path and store the object signature with OID of the object. We call it c-signature because we put the object signatures in concatenation. Whenever a query predicate contains any attribute values from the object, the query signature matches with the c-signature, which is pointing to an s-expression in the path dictionary file. Since we concatenate all the object signatures from an s-expression to form a c-signature, the c-signature represents all the objects in one s-expression. Therefore, the c-signature provides the filtering mechanism of s-expressions in the path dictionary. In other words, once we find whether or not a c-signature matches the query signature generated from the query predicate, we do not have to scan the path dictionary. We use the pointer from the c-signature in the c-signature file to point to the s-expression.

Signature File

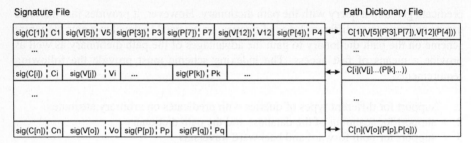

Fig. 3. Generation of c-signature

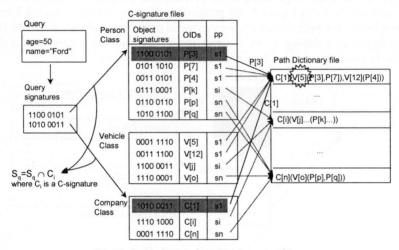

Fig. 4. C-signature scheme on s-expression

The c-signatures generated based on the s-expressions can be stored in several c-signature files to reduce search space. If we store all c-signatures into a file, we have to scan all signatures to find the matching c-signature. But, by separately positioning the c-signatures from each class in different files, like in Figure 4, while keeping the pointers to its s-expression, we can only scan the c-signature file corresponding to a predicate class. In the c-signature file, every signature has an entry *<c-sig(i),OID, pointer_s_expression>* . The *c-sig(i)* is a signature of an object found in the s-expression pointed by the pointer, *pointer_s_expression. OID* is the object identifier of the object that is used to generate the c-signature. The *pointer_s_expression* is the pointer to the corresponding s-expression. This pointer implies the c-signature has been generated from objects in the s-expression.

The c-signature scheme on an s-expression file can filter out a candidate s-expression without a sequential search for the database and can find an OID specified in a query out of the path dictionary. This is considered as the most time consuming task in the conventional path dictionary approach. In the implementation, we sort the entries in a c-signature file over the *pointer_s_expression* and put the entries with the same *pointer_s_expression* into a record. The record has variable length and is stored into storage system.

3.2 Query Processing with C-signature

Suppose there is a query Q that has C_t as the target class and C_p as the predicate class, where $1 \leq t, p \leq n$. Here, n is the number of classes on the path. First, we generate query signatures from the predicates and compare the query signatures with c-signatures for the class. Then, a matched signature will be selected from the c-signature file. Because the matched c-signature has an OID of an object and a pointer to an s-expression, the c-signature scheme avoids searching the database and the path dictionary sequentially. Also, because the s-expression has the OIDs of the predicate and the target objects, the s-expression avoids accessing the objects between C_t and C_p in the database. The retrieval algorithm is described as follows:

Algorithm : c_sig_retrieval
Input : query Q with C_t and C_p
Output : a set of objects
1. Generate the query signature using C_p .
2. Match the query signatures against the c-signatures to select candidate c-signatures, OID(s), and pointers to an s-expression.
3. Read the s-expression pointed by the selected pointers.
4. Based on the qualified OIDs in the s-expression and OID(s) from c-signatures, obtain the OID(s) of C_t.
5. Return a set of OID(s)

Note that the returned set of OIDs may contain false matches. If then, we need so-called 'false drop resolution' step. To reduce the false drop to 0, the size of a signature in the c-signature scheme is dependent upon the false drop probability, which is determined by one over the number of objects.

4 Performance Analysis

In this section, we compare the c-signature scheme with its competitors such as path index, path signature, path dictionary, class unit signature, path dictionary index and s-signature schemes based on our experiments. Because of the limited space, only retrieval operation and storage overhead are covered here. Update operation and analytic performance models are found in [11]

4.1 Experiment design

For the performance comparison, we suppose that a path of 6 classes with the cardinality of N_1 equals 100,000 and the size of an object is between 107 and 154 bytes. The size of a signature in the c-signature scheme, F, depends upon the number of attribute values, D, in an object and upon the false drop probability, Fd. Fd is determined to be $1/N_i$ so that there can be no false drop in theory. For the experiment design, we consider several factors that decide the performance of each indexing scheme. The first factor is the degree of reference sharing. If $k_1 = k_2 = k_3 = k_4 = k_5 = k_6 = $

1, the number of objects in the aggregation hierarchy is the same as the number of classes, that is, 6. Thus, the values of k_i representing the degree of reference sharing decide the number of objects in the path.

Secondly, the queries used in the experiment may have different number of predicate classes. Since we uses the aggregation hierarchy with 6 classes, the number of predicates in a given query can be varied from 1 to 6. In the experiment, we use the queries with a different number of predicate classes from 1 to 5. When we have multiple predicates in the given query, we consider the Boolean operations, "AND" and "OR".

Thirdly, the location of the reference sharing may be at any place in the aggregation hierarchy. The location of target and predicate classes may also affect the performance. So, we consider 6 different locations of the sharing, predicate, and target classes to design the query set used in the experiment as follows:

- STP case has the sharing - target – predicate classes in sequence.
- TSP case has the target - sharing – predicate classes in sequence.
- TPS case has the target - predicate classes and the sharing in sequence.
- SPT case has the sharing - predicate – target classes in sequence.
- PST case has the predicate - sharing – target classes in sequence.
- PTS case has the predicate - target classes and the sharing in sequence.

Finally, we consider whether or not the path index scheme uses the indexed key field to process the given query. Since the path index scheme suggests to implement the path index on every depth 3 class in the aggregation hierarchy, the path index scheme may or may not use the path index to process the given query according to the location of the predicate class. In the experiment, we implement the path index on the 3rd and the 6th classes. So, if the query uses the 3rd class as the predicate class, the path index scheme uses the path index on the 3rd class. However, if the query uses 2nd class as the predicate class, the path index scheme may not use the path index. Based on the above factors, we develop 48 different queries shown in Table 1.

Table 1. Query types used for the retrieval operations

using indexed attribute	degree of reference sharing	Single predicate						Multiple Predicates					
		STP	TSP	TPS	SPT	PST	PTS	STP	TSP	TPS	SPT	PST	PTS
Yes	high	Q_{s1gy}	Q_{s2gy}	Q_{s3gy}	Q_{s4gy}	Q_{s5gy}	Q_{s6gy}	Q_{m1gy}	Q_{m2gy}	Q_{m3gy}	Q_{m4gy}	Q_{m5gy}	Q_{m6gy}
	low	Q_{s1ly}	Q_{s2ly}	Q_{s3ly}	Q_{s4ly}	Q_{s5ly}	Q_{s6ly}	Q_{m1ly}	Q_{m2ly}	Q_{m3ly}	Q_{m4ly}	Q_{m5ly}	Q_{m6ly}
No	high	Q_{s1gn}	Q_{s2gn}	Q_{s3gn}	Q_{s4gn}	Q_{s5gn}	Q_{s6gn}	Q_{m1gn}	Q_{m2gn}	Q_{m3gn}	Q_{m4gn}	Q_{m5gn}	Q_{m6gn}
	low	Q_{s1ln}	Q_{s2ln}	Q_{s3ln}	Q_{s4ln}	Q_{s5ln}	Q_{s6ln}	Q_{m1ln}	Q_{m2ln}	Q_{m3ln}	Q_{m4ln}	Q_{m5ln}	Q_{m6ln}

4.2 Experiment results

To test the various queries, we implemented our c-signature scheme and the competitors by using the storage system proposed in [12]. The storage system can handle the variable-length record with about 90-95% of storage utilization. The data used for the experiments is from yellow page entries of KT&T, the car specifications of Hyundai car company, and registration data from the registrar of Chonbuk National University.

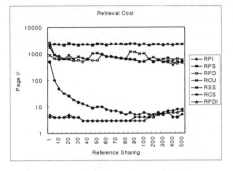

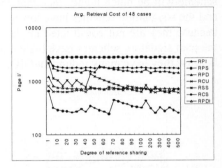

Fig. 5. Retrieval cost   **Fig. 6.** Average retrieval cost

When the query has C_1 as the target class, C_6 as the predicate class, i.e., TSP case, and an attribute of C_6 as the predicate attributes which has an index on it, and also the query has a single predicate, Figure 5 shows the best retrieval costs of the path index, the path dictionary index, and the c-signature schemes. In Figure 5, the x-axis indicates the degree of reference sharing and the y-axis indicates the number of page I/Os. It is shown from the results that the retrieval cost of the path index (*RPI*) and the path dictionary index (*RPDI*) has better overall performance than their competitors, such as c-signature scheme (*RCS*), the path signature (*RPS*), the path dictionary (*RPD*), the class unit signature (*RCU*), and the s-signature (*RSS*). But the c-signature scheme (*RCS*) requires lower cost when the reference sharing increases.

When the 48 different kinds of queries are given as Table 1, Figure 6 shows the average retrieval cost under the varying reference sharing. It is shown from the results that the retrieval cost of our c-signature scheme (*RCS*) has better overall performance than its competitors including the path dictionary index. Based on the average costs, the c-signature scheme only requires about 20% of the cost of the path dictionary to process a given query. In addition, the c-signature scheme is considered as more general approach than the path index and the path dictionary index because the c-signature scheme can be used to process user queries with predicate classes against any attribute in any object on the path. This result means that the c-signature scheme allows user queries in an OODBS to be so flexible that user can give the query against any attribute, which is not key attribute.

Figure 7 and Figure 8 show the storage overhead. It is shown from the results that our c-signature (*SCS*) scheme has higher storage overhead than the path dictionary (*SPD*), and the s-signature(*SSS*) schemes but lower than the path index (*SPI*), the class unit signature(*SCU*), the path signature (*SPS*) and the path dictionary index (*SPDI*) schemes. The c-signature scheme requires about 55% of the storage of the path index and 45% of the class unit signature scheme, but 267% of the path dictionary. Even though the c-signature scheme has high storage overhead, the c-signature files are filtered out based on the given predicate class at the first stage of query processing, so as to reduce the search space. The path index and the path dictionary index schemes have relatively high storage overhead because we suppose there are two indexed attributes, i.e., an attribute in class C_3, and C_6, in the entire aggregation hierarchy. *SPDI* shows the highest storage overhead since it has the identity index for all OIDs in the database besides two attribute indices. If there are as many indexed attributes as the number of classes to support various query patterns, the storage of the path index scheme will be much higher than that shown in Figure 7 and 8. The path dictionary and the s-signature schemes have lower storage overhead than the c-signature scheme because they are not constructed in class-oriented way. The class unit signature and the path signature schemes have higher storage overhead than the c-signature scheme because they have many redundant OIDs.

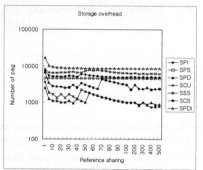 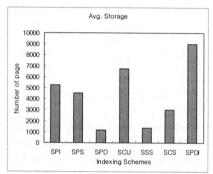

Fig. 7. Storage overhead   **Fig. 8.** Average storage overhead

5 Conclusion

Since user queries in an OODBS can be very flexible, it is difficult to predict which attribute will be used in the queries. The path dictionary scheme encodes the connection information of a class aggregation hierarchy and shows an effective way to process different kinds of queries. However it suffers from the lack of an efficient filtering mechanism for the database and the path dictionary itself. In this paper, we proposed the c-signature scheme on the path dictionary to provide the filtering mechanism. In addition, we developed cost models[11] for retrieval, update operations, and storage overhead and implemented our c-signature scheme and its competitors. Through our experiments, we compared the c-signature with its competitors under different degrees of reference sharing and in terms of the page I/Os of each scheme. Based on the performance results, we showed that our c-signature scheme is appropriate to the efficient retrieval and flexible query processing in OODBSs. We believe our c-signature scheme is applicable to handling the composite relation in extended relational database systems and object-relational database systems.

References

1. A. Kemper and G. Moerkotte, "Advanced query processing in object bases using access support relations", In Proc. of the 16th VLDB Conference, Brisbane, Australia (1990) 290—301
2. E. Bertino and W. Kim, "Indexing technique for queries on nested objects", In IEEE Trans. Knowledge and Data Engineering, 1(2) (1989)196—214
3. W. Kim, K.C. Kim, and A. Dale, "Indexing techniques for object-oriented databases", In Object-Oriented, Concepts, Databases, and Applications, W. Kim and F.H. Lochovsky, eds., Addison-Wesley, Reading, MA (1989) 371--394.
4. E. Bertino and C. Guglielmina, "Path index: An approach to the efficient execution of object-oriented queries", In Data and Knowledge Engineering, North Holland, 10 (1993) 1—27
5. Lee, W.C. and Lee, D.L. "Signature File Methods for Indexing Object-Oriented Database Systems", In Proc. of the 2nd International Computer Science Conference, Hong Kong (1992) 616--622
6. Y. Ishikawa, H. Kitagawa and N. Ohbo, "Evaluation of Signature Files as Set Access Facilities in OODBs", In Proc. of the 1993 SIGMOD Int'l Conf. on Management of Data, Washington D.C. (1993) 247-256
7. D.L. Lee and W.C. Lee, "Using Path Information for Query Processing in Object-Oriented Database Systems", In the Third International Conference on Information and Knowledge Management, Gaitherburg, MD (1994) 64—71
8. W.C. Lee and D.L. Lee, "Combining Indexing Technique with Path Dictionary for Nested Object Queries", In the Proc. of the Fourth International Conference on Database Systems for Advanced Applications, Singapore, April 10-13 (1995) 107-104
9. H. Yong and S. Lee, "Signature File Generation Techniques for Query Processing in Object-Oriented Databases", In Journal of the Korea Information Science Society, Vol. 21, No 5 (1995) 922-930
10. H. Shin and J. Chang, "Signatures of Complex Objects for Query Processing in OODB", In Proc. of the 7th International Conference, DEXA'96, Zurich, Switzerland (1996) 322-332
11. H. Shin, "Efficient Signature-Based Indexing Schemes for Query Processing in Object-Oriented Database Systems", Ph.D. thesis, Dept of Computer Engineering, Chonbuk National University (1999)
12. J. Zobel, A. Moffat, and R. Sacks-Davis, "Storage Management for Files of Dynamic Records", In Proc. of the 4th Australian Database Conference on Advances in Database Research, M.E. Orlowska, M. Papazoglou, eds., Brisbane, Australia (1993) 26-38

A COBRA Object-Based
Caching with Consistency

Zahir Tari[1], Slimane Hammoudi[2], and Stephen Wagner[1]

[1] Royal Melbourne Institute of Technology, Australia
[2] University of Minho, Portugal

Abstract. For many distributed data intensive applications, the default remote invocation of CORBA objects to a server is not acceptable because of performance degradation. Caching can improve performance and scalability of such applications by increasing the locality of data. This paper proposes a caching approach that optimises the default remote invocation behaviour of CORBA clients. Efficient fine-grained access to remote objects requires objects to be shipped to clients and cached across transaction boundaries. This approach is based on cache consistency via backward validation, generic approach for cache storage, object based data shipping and replication management. These features are introduced without changing the object definitions that the client may already depend upon. An implementation of the proposed caching approach is done on Orbix by extending the smart proxies. We have also provided a test with different client workloads. The results demonstrated a significant performance increase, in terms of transactions per second.

1 Motivation

Existing CORBA implementations vary significantly in performance and most of them not yet support latency-sensitive. Whilst CORBA implementations can be optimised[2] along the lines of efficient and data copying, it is the default behaviour of CORBA applications that causes significant latency. Network latency is often the significant component of application invocation latency. By default, a CORBA client application will perform a remote invocation for every method called. For many classes of distributed data intensive applications, such as real-time systems, this is an unacceptable performance overhead. Using client caching it is possible to reduce the number of network invocations during critical client processing. Inter-transaction caching allows clients to retain the contents of the cache across transaction boundaries. Inter-transaction caching requires a cache consistency protocol to ensure that a client's view of the data is globally consistent. Tradeoffs must be made during protocol selection to ensure that the cost of maintaining the cache does not eliminate the gain made by caching. Typically this is dependent upon the workload that the application is expecting.

A very little work is done on the area of CORBA caching. The only work in the area we are aware on is the one proposed by Mowbray in[3]. This approach includes an object caching technique that intercepts any remote invocations within the client if the object is locally available. Objects are migrated to clients via a distributed cache manager (with a single retrieve and single update operation). The cache manager is hand-coded for a specific set of related IDL interface types, which performs coarse-grained shipping using an IDL interface with for a single retrieve operation and a single update operation. One of the major problem of this approach is that it is an "informal one". It does not present an implementation, testing or performance analysis of the approach. Also, this approach does not guarantee one *copy serialisation* of object updates, which is not acceptable for most of the distributed applications.

This paper addresses the problem of including object-based caching aspects into CORBA applications with minimal impact to existing sources. The solution proposed permits inter-transaction caching and performs the necessary validation to ensure that data consistency is maintained. We have designed a CORBA object-based caching with consistency (COCC) model that caches objects across transaction boundaries and significantly reduces the the number of network invocations, thus reducing invocation latency. Filters are used to intercept frequent calls, and the cache manager then uses the information of the filters to keep track of appropriate objects to be cached. The proposed caching model improves scalability of CORBA servers, due to less remote calls from clients.

This paper is organised as follows. Next section summarises the main ideas behind the proposed caching approach for CORBA applications. Section 3 describes the different steps of the caching approach. In Section 4 we present an Orbix implementation of the COCC model, followed by a detailed discussion on the performance of such an implementation. Finally we conclude in Section 5 with the future work.

2   An Overview of the COCC Model

COCC is a transactional-based model. A COCC transaction is defined as a sequence of one or more read operations on one or more objects, followed by an update operation on a single object. Multiple updates in a single transaction are not supported, as this would become an intrusive client source modification, requiring clients to re-partition their application processing into a series of transactions. A sequence consists of an initial object read, followed by any number of object reads, ending with an object update. The client automatically piggybacks validation data to the update request. The process that manages the object implementation performs backward validation. If the transaction is deemed invalid then a system exception is raised and propagated back to the client, without the server satisfying the request. Robust applications should already be built to handle system exceptions. Transaction propagation is implicit, i.e. all object reads and updates implicitly form part of a transaction.

The COCC model performs fine-grained object level data shipping and fine-grained object level replication management. This level of granularity for shipping was increased from attribute to object. This was chosen for the following reasons: (i) decrease the network traffic required to ship an object to a client. This represents an increase in the coarseness of shipping granularity over the CORBA default (attribute shipping). (ii) Decrease algorithm complexity. When multiple levels of granularity are used across shipping and replication management (Orbix smart proxies), algorithm complexity increases. (iii) Page level shipping cannot be implemented as a coarse grained solution, due to CORBA being heterogeneous. Page representations cannot be relied upon as a unit of transfer. (iv) Other coarse grained solutions[3] were not incorporated into this model because they required specific hand coding and knowledge of the application to be more efficient. It is possible to create an artificial grouping analogous to a page or cluster that allows coarser grained shipping and locking management.

The proposed concurrency control is a detection-based. Similar approaches include adaptive optimistic[1] and Cache Locks[5]. No validity information is sent to the server prior to the transaction commit. It is also similar to the protocol used in THOR[1], where cache consistency is performed at the object level. The COCC model supports inter-transaction caching using a *backward validation optimistic* scheme rather than locking at the server or client. It can read locally cached objects without server intervention, however prior to update/commit, the server performs backward validation on the transactional objects. COCC detects invalid access to an object at the client and at the server. Each client based proxy object has a valid flag that can be invalidated by a remote update action. These actions are initiated by the server and occur asynchronously to transaction processing. Before commit the client checks the appropriate flag before attempting to commit. If the object is valid then it attempts to commit. As well as the validation flag, the proxy object stores version information and a timestamp.

3 Cache Design

3.1 Logical Architecture

There are two assumptions in the design of the COCC approach. (1) The transaction granularity is at the object level, therefore any commit requests are automatically propagated to the correct server. The server is then able to validate the transaction unilaterally. i.e. without involving other object servers in a two phase commit protocol. (2) The issue of optimising object creation is not discussed in the description of the COCC model.

Figure 1 shows our proposed logical architecture for CORBA-based caching. LIFR is a generic component that is built from the IFR at process startup. It contains the traversal routines and data structures to index and store the appropriate run time type information. At elaboration the IFR is traversed in full and the information necessary for caching is extracted and stored in the LIFR. The LIFR stores the interface information in volatile memory rather than non-volatile disk. The following aspects of the type information are indexed using hash tables: interfaces, interface methods, interface attributes. DCC also represents a generic and single instance required to be instantiated in the client main program. When the main program is starting this object contacts the Interface

Repository and builds the LIFR. When the client requests an update/commit the dynamic client cache has the responsibility of piggybacking the appropriate validation data to the request. The DCC also maintains the values of the client cache. When an object is shipped to the client, the cached value is updated. CCM checks the piggy-backed validation data against the object implementation version and either raises an exception or allows the transaction to continue. When the server propagates a value the object version information is piggybacked to the response. Finally, the client application which links with appropriate proxies which are invoked rather than the default proxy class. The proxy checks whether the cache is valid. If it is then the value of the cache can be returned, otherwise forward the request onto the default proxy.

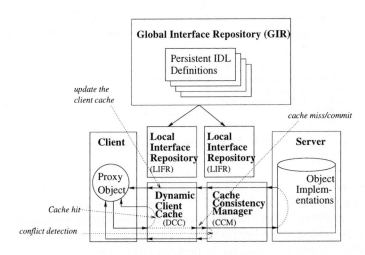

Fig. 1. Logical Caching Architecture

3.2 Example IDL Structure

Figure 2 shows a class diagram of the IDL interfaces for a single caching class - *account*. As mentioned in earlier, this class (or any other class generated from an IDL) does not need to be modified to support caching. In order to add the object shipping and remote update functionality the interface needs to be refined. To increase the data shipping granularity from attribute to object the *ship_account* interface is created and provides an operation that retrieves the entire set of attributes. When an attribute is requested by the client and does not exist in the cache, the *ship_object* method is called in preference to the default attribute shipping method. This action will refresh the attributes for the cache. The benefit of this approach is that the application can be written without concern for how many remote invocations will be made, and can be optimised independently. The *registerProxy* interface allows the client implementation to register for server based remote update actions. It enables the account proxy object to participate in a distributed reference count held at the server. The client registers a distributed callback with the server.

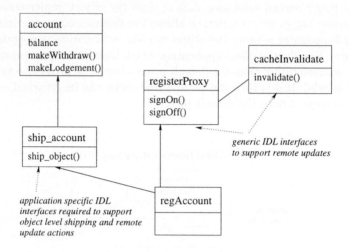

Fig. 2. An example of IDL Interfaces

These two additions - object shipping and distributed reference counting, are the only modifications that need to be made to the IDL definitions. These changes are additive rather than intrusive. The account and *ship_account* interfaces must be added to the Interface Repository in order for the client cache and server cache consistency manager to perform the correct validation and installation actions.

3.3 Scenarios and Design Tradeoffs

The following scenarios illustrate the operation of the client cache: client elaboration, cache hit, cache miss, remote object enters client address space, transaction commit successful and transaction abort.

(A) Client Elaboration. The proposed caching model causes clients to do more work at elaboration and less work during transaction processing. The elaboration phase requires traversal of the non-local interface repository(IFR). The IFR persistently stores IDL interface definitions. These definitions are stored locally in the LIFR. The LIFR is used in subsequent scenarios to perform transaction validation and cache installation. Essentially at elaboration, the client determines the structure of the interfaces that it intends to cache.

(B) Cache Hit - Returning the Contents of the Client Cache. In order to determine if the object has been cached there are three basic techniques that could have been employed: (i) modify default client proxy; (ii) subclass the default client proxy and override methods that cause remote invocations (smart proxy);

and (iii) intercept the call at the process boundary layer (process filters). The first technique, which is discussed in[3], proposed the modification of each generated proxy on a case by case basis.[4] discusses smart proxies, which is an approach that enhances the default proxy without modification to the client stub. The third technique would be the least intrusive of all, and can determine if the cache is valid for any object. It is not possible to return the cache value to the client. Further, in the process of preventing the remote invocation to the target object, an unexpected system exception is generated, which cannot be incorporated into "normal" processing. The philosophy of proposed approach is not to modify the client stubs, therefore the smart proxy mechanism was incorporated. In order to implement this approach the following steps are required: (a) derive a new class from proxy class that overrides the implementation. (b) Derive a new factory that creates the smart proxies instead of the default proxies; and (c) create a single instance of the new factory at client initialisation. The role of the smart proxy is simply to check the validity of the cache upon attribute read and if valid return the cached value. As well as determining if the cache is valid, the smart proxies are part of a distributed reference count. This distributed reference count is used during remote update actions performed by the server. The remote update action in this model is invalidation.

(C) Cache Miss - Maintaining the Cache. Transactions run entirely at clients unless there is a cache miss. When a cache miss occurs the smart proxy is able to invoke an object shipping function rather than an attribute shipping function. The object shipping method returns the set of class attributes as a struct. A trade-off between cache invalidation and propagation has also been made. This model uses invalidation, however some schemes (AOCC) use an adaptive approach. The first approach is used in conjunction with an invalidation remote update action. This approach allows a proxy to override all attribute reads with a call to a method that will return the entire object value. The attribute is then derived from this structure at the client and returned from the method. Transparent to the client and the proxy the entire object value to be stored in the cache. Future reads on this object will not require a remote call. The second approach is used in conjunction with a propagation remote update action and was not chosen for this model. The server piggybacks/propagates the object value to the cache invalidate calls. This protocol was not used for this model. The main reason for not adopting this approach is due to high contention workloads causing large amounts of wasted propagation to clients. i.e. client's data is updated and invalidated before it even uses the data. It has been shown in[6] that propagation can cause up to 3 times the volume of data.

(D) Remote Object Enters Client Address Space. When one of the following events occurs, i.e. _bind, IDL out parameter , string_to_object, or create the re- placement factory creates a smart proxy in the client address space. A separate cache is maintained per client process. If there are multiple client executables on the same machine they will maintain separate caches. This is the simplest approach without introducing shared memory semantics. Clients may have different object caching requirements, for example typical workloads vary from concurrent sharing or sequential sharing (transactions that do not run concurrently access the same data) to completely independent access. The disadvantage of a cache per client, is if the processes do require the same objects then they have to be shipped from the server twice. Further they will have to be maintained. This adds to the workload of the server.

4 Implementation and Performance

The COCC model has been implemented with the Orbix and C++. In this section, we discuss the implementation of COCC model elements, i.e. *object shipping*, *CacheProxy*, *intercepting* remote calls and *traversing* the IFR at elaboration. The Dynamic client cache and the cache consistency manager implemented using Orbix Process filters. Process filters are used as a non-intrusive technique to intercept all method calls propagating to and from application process boundaries. The filters are independent of the client application. The link between the client application and the filters is the cacheProxy class. Once instantiated in the client and server they intercept all method calls in and out of the process. It is important that they only intercept the relevant interface messages. The set of methods that they intercept is determined from the LIFR.

(A) Orbix Smart Proxies. This test adds client based cache invalidation detection prior to committing a value the transaction will check that cache has not already been invalidated by an asynchronous server based remote update action If a conflict is detected then the client aborts the update before the client invokes the remote call. As shown in Table 1, even this simple approach caught up to 80% of the transaction conflicts. This approach reduced the network traffic and therefore increased the total number of conflicts that occurred. This experiment demonstrates that depending upon the level of contention and transaction duration, invalidation callbacks can invalidate client caches during their next transaction. Checking for this prevents more conflicts by early detection. Up to 10% of the total transactions were still conflicting at the server. Without server based detection these cannot be caught. This effect can be attributed to concurrent processes attempting to update the same object.

Table 1. Conflicts generated and detected by OrbixSmart with client detection

Co-located clients	Remote clients	Iteration per client	Total conflicts	Detected conflicts	Un-detected conflicts
	0	10,000	10,433	8,382	2051
0	2	10,000	9,427	8,505	922
2	1	10,000	22,957	19,924	3033

(B) COCC Model - Client Caching with Validation. Backward validation achieves cache consistency even with the highly concurrent access. Table 2 demit demonstrates that there were no undetected conflicts at the server. Once again the bulk of the conflicts were detected at the client, however up to 26% of the conflicts were caught conflicting at the server. This experiment also demonstrated that a small increase in the number of clients caused a significant increase in the number of conflicts with this highly concurrent workload. The next section discusses the workload model and will evaluate the aspects such as number of messages generated per transaction, number of transactions per second for an increasing number of clients. This will be done across different workloads.

Table 2. COCC Model - All conflicts were picked up at either the client or the server

Co-located clients	Remote clients	Iteration per client	Total conflicts	Aborted @client	Aborted @server	Un-detected conflicts
2	0	10,000	11,284	8,252	3,032	0
0	2	10,000	10,060	10,008	52	0
2	1	10,000	16,993	13,625	3,368	0

(C) Experiments and Results. This section documents the results achieved for the model against the PRIVATE, UNIFORM and HICON workloads (see Table 3). The results are measured in transactions per second. Properties of the protocol are also explored using "per commit" metrics including messages per commit and aborts per commit All measurements were carried out using averages over large number of iterations. Figure 3 shows the average number of messages generated on the network as the number of clients increases. Reducing the number of commits per transaction is a key performance optimisation. Reducing the number and content of each message can provide significant reduction in latency.

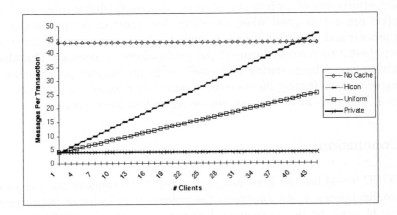

Fig. 3. Messages per transaction

If a client application does not cache, then the number of messages is directly proportional to the number of invocations that it makes. In this case the transaction length is 20 and each object is requested once and delivered once. However the other approaches are dependent upon server based remote update actions. The higher the contention, the greater the number of clients that are caching the same object. This is evident with the HICON workload where every client caches the same set of objects.

Table 3. Workload Parameter Settings

Parameter	PRIVATE	HICON	UNIFORM
TransSize	20	20	20
Objects	2500	2500	2500
HotBounds	500	500	500
Private Data %	100	0	50
Shared Data %	0	100	50
ThinkTime (ms)	30	30	30

When an object is updated the server must invalidate all the client caches, generating a message per client, on top of the standard commit messages. The uniform workload only has 50% of it's objects being shared so it generates less invalidations The private workload is independent of the number of clients because there is no data sharing. Therefore there are no invalidation messages generated. Figure 4 shows the throughput results of the various workload models. Throughput is measured in transactions per second. It shows that for every workload the model outperforms having no cache. The private workload is the most efficient not having to compete with other processes for updating objects. The number of aborts in the private workload is zero. As the degree of data sharing increases the performance decreases due to the number of aborts/conflicts increases.

The performance of each workload increases initially due the demands upon the server are not as great when the client does most of the processing. The server process and network were not initially loaded to capacity. As more clients connect these two resources caused the performance to decrease (Notable in the private case where sharing and conflicts do not impact performance. As the degree of data sharing increases the number of remote update actions also increases. This puts more stress on the server and on the network.

5   Conclusion

The COCC model has not been designed to test ORB implementations or network configurations, it demonstrates the potential performance improvements that can be made by the application developer to an existing CORBA application. It's primary contribution is the reduction of remote network invocations

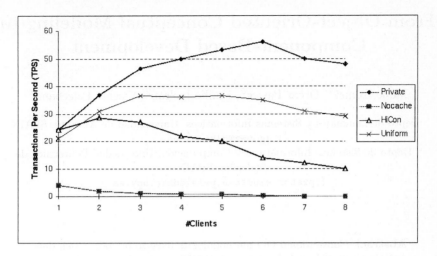

Fig. 4. Workload throughput

during transaction processing. The advantages of the COCC model include object level data shipping, object level replication management, guaranteed cache consistency and reduced hand coding per interface. The performance advantages were presented against multiple workloads and against a non-caching client. It demonstrated significant increase in the number of transactions per second that it was able to perform.

There are a few limitations of the proposed approach and scope for improvement. The current design requires the use of two Orbix extensions to the ORB implementation - smart proxies and filters. Modifying stubs and skeletons was an approach that was avoided for this model due to the complexity and maintenance that be required to update an application However with compiler support this approach has potential to require less hand coding by generating "super-stubs".

References

1. A. Adya, M. Castro, B. Liskov, U. Maheshwari, and L. Srira: *Fragment Reconstruction: Providing Global Cache Coherence in a Transactional Storage Systems.* Proc. of Int. Conf. on Distributed Computing Systems (ICDCS), Baltimore, 1997.
2. A.S. Gokhale and D. Schmidt: *Measuring and Optimising CORBA Latency and Scalability over High-speed Networks.* Technical report, Department of Computer Science, Washington University, 1997.
3. T.J. Mowbray and R.C. Malveau: *CORBA Design Pattern.* Wiley Computer Publishing, 1997.
4. IONA: *Orbix Programmers Guide 2.3c.* Iona Technologies, October 1997.
5. K. Wilkinson and M. Neimat: *Maintaining Consistency of Client-Cached Data.* Proc. of VLDB (Very Large Data Bases), Brisbane, 1990.
6. M. Zaharioudakis, M.J. Carey, and M.J. Franklin: *Adaptive, Fine Grained Sharing in a Client-Server OODBMS: A Callback-Based Approach.* ACM Transactions on Database Systems (TODS), 1997, pp. 570-627.

From Object-Oriented Conceptual Modeling to Component-Based Development

Jaime Gómez[1], Oscar Pastor[2], Emilio Insfrán[2], Vicente Pelechano[2]

[1] Depto de Lenguajes y Sistemas Informáticos, Universidad de Alicante. SPAIN.
jgomez@dlsi.ua.es
[2] Depto de Sistemas Informáticos y Computación, Universidad Politécnica de Valencia. SPAIN.
[opastor,einsfran,pele]@dsic.upv.es

Abstract Conventional OO methodologies have to provide a well-defined Component-based development (CBD) process by which the community of software engineers can properly derive executable software components from requirements in a systematic way. The move toward CBD requires existing OO conceptual modeling approaches to be reconsidered. In this paper, we present a proposal to support CBD in an OO Method based on a formal OO model. The key element of this proposal resides in the concept of execution model. The execution model defines a model and an architecture that provides a pattern to generate software components from OO conceptual models.

Conceptual modeling patterns have a corresponding software representation in the quoted component-based architecture. The implementation of these mappings from problem space concepts to solution space representations opens the door to the generation of executable software components in an automated way.

1 Introduction

Much of the existing work in component-based software technology has concentrated on developing infrastructure capabilities and middleware solutions for connecting independent pieces of system functionality. In this context, where new technologies are continuously emerging, application developers require new additional capabilities that include:

- methods for designing CBD solutions that help the organization focus on the major functional pieces of its domain, and how those pieces will interact.
- tools that support specification of business components using techniques that allow the functionality to be described independently of a particular implementation technology.

* This work has been supported by the CICYT under MENHIR/ESPILL TIC 97-0593-C05-01 Project and by DGEUI under IRGAS GV97-TI-05-34 Project.

In the field of OO methodologies [10,5,1,2], the move toward CBD requires existing approaches to be reconsidered. In particular, any method supporting CBD is required to exhibit at least the following 4 key principles [3]: (1) a clear separation of component specification from its design and implementation, (2) an interface-focused design approach, (3) more formally recorded component semantics, (4) a rigorously recorded refinement process.

Our contribution to this state of the art is the OO-Method approach [7,6], which is basically built on a formal object-oriented model (OASIS [8]) and whose main feature is that developers's efforts are focused on the conceptual modeling step. In this step system requirements are captured according to a predefined, finite set of what we call conceptual modeling patterns because they are a representation of relevant concepts at the problem space level. The full OO implementation is obtained in an automated way following an execution model (including structure and behaviour). This execution model establishes the corresponding mappings between conceptual model constructs and their representation in a particular software development environment. The main contribution of this paper is the proposal of a component-based architecture for the OO-Method execution model. This proposal has two benefits: (1) it provides a pattern for obtaining software components starting from the OO code generated. These components can be dynamically combined to build a software prototype that is functionally equivalent to the specification collected in the conceptual modeling step; (2) it provides a framework for executing the specification in the solution space.

This paper is organized as follows: section 2 describes the main OO-Method features to support CBD. This section also presents a short description of the diagrams that are used to capture the system properties in order to produce what we call a conceptual model. Section 3 introduces the underlying OO OASIS formal specification that is obtained when the conceptual modeling step is finished. This section also describes how to represent this OASIS formal specification in any target software development environment, according to an abstract execution model. The component-based architecture to produce the software components that allow us to link the conceptual model with the abstract execution model in an automated way is presented in detail. Finally, section 4 presents conclusions and further work.

2   Towards CBD

The basic idea in the OO-Method proposal to support CBD resides in clearly separating what we call the conceptual model level and the execution model level. The first one represents the problem space and is centered on what the system is. The second one represents the solution space and is intended to give an implementation in terms of how the system is to be implemented. There are four key steps that make the OO-Method approach suitable for component modeling. These steps are classified as follow: (1) capture a conceptual model, (2) obtain a formal specification of the conceptual model, (3) generate OO code from the formal specification, (4) obtain a component specification of the system in an automated way.

The problem space involves the tasks associated to obtain a formal specification of the requirements that must be accomplished by the system. This is a two-step process; capture a conceptual model and obtain an OASIS formal specification in an automated way. This formal specification acts as a high-level system repository. It is the source for an execution model that must accurately state the implementation-dependent features associated to the selected object society machine representation. In consequence, the execution model establishes a concrete strategy starting from the OASIS formal specification to generate OO code in the solution space. Having generated the code of the application logic, a component specification of the system can be obtained in an automated way.

For reasons of space, in this paper the focus is on the solution space.

3 Solution Space

3.1 An abstract Execution Model

For a complete view of the approach presented here, we are going to illustrate this process using an small example. Consider a conventional library system with readers, books, and loans. A partial OASIS specification for the class reader is specified as follows:

```
class reader                      valuation
 constant_attributes               [loan()] book_count= book_count + 1;
 reader_code : String;             [return()] book_count= book_count - 1;
variable_attributes               preconditions
 book_count : Int;                  destroy_reader () if
private_events                      book_count = 0 ;
 new_reader() new;                 triggers
 destroy_reader() destroy;          Self::punish() if book_count = 10;
 punish();                         process
shared_events                      reader = new_reader() reader0;
 loan() with book;                 reader0= destroy_reader() +
 return() with book;                     loan() reader1;
constraints                        reader1= return() reader0 +
 static book_count < 10;                 loan() reader1;
                                  end_class
```

In accordance with the OASIS class template, for the class reader we have:

The attribute reader_code defined as a constant attribute because its value doesn't change along the entire life of an instance of this class. The attribute book_count defined as a variable attribute; its value represents the number of books that a reader has in a given moment. A set of services including; private events (new_reader(), destroy_reader() and punish()) that participate in the life of instances of a class reader, and shared events (loan() and return()) that participate in the lifes of instances of several classes. This OASIS specification also specifies an integrity constraint which states a condition that must be satisfied (the number of books that a reader has must be lower than 10). The valuations specify the effect of events on attributes. If a loan event occurs the book_count is incremented. If a return event occurs the book_count attribute is decremented. A triggered action is defined for our example; when the value of the book_count attribute is equal to 10 then the event punish must be activated automatically. And finally we have the process definition of a class, where the template for valid object lives is fixed.

This OASIS specification is the source for an execution model that must accurately state the implementation-dependent features associated to the selected object society machine representation. In order to easily implement and animate the specified system, we predefine a way in which users interact with system objects. The process starts by logging the user into the system and providing an object system view determining the set of object attributes and services that it can see or activate. After the user is connected and has a clear object system view, he can then activate any available service in his worldview. Among these services, we will have observations (object queries) or local services or transactions served by other objects. Any service activation has two steps: build the message and execute it (if possible). In order to build the message the user has to provide information to identify the object server[1], and subsequently, he must introduce service arguments of the service being activated (if necessary). Once the message is sent, the service execution is characterized by the occurrence of the following sequence of actions in the server object:

- check state transition which is the process of verifying that a valid transition exists in the OASIS specification for the selected service in the current object state.
- the precondition satisfaction indicates that the precondition associated to the service must hold.

If any of these actions does not hold, an exception will arise and the message is ignored. Otherwise, the process continues with:

- the valuation fulfillment where the induced service modifications take place in the involved object state.
- to assure that the service execution leads the object to a valid state, the integrity constraints are verified in the final state. If the constraint does not hold, an exception will arise and the previous change of state is ignored.
- after a valid change of state, the set of condition-action rules that represents the internal system activity is verified. If any of them hold, the specified service will be triggered.

The previous steps guide the implementation of any program to assure the functional equivalence between the object system specification collected in the

---

[1] The existence of the object server is an implicit condition for executing any service, unless we are dealing with the service *new*

conceptual model and its reification in an imperative programming environment. Now we are going to describe how to link the formal specification captured in the conceptual modeling step with the abstract execution model presented above.

3.2 A tiered component architecture for the execution model

The architecture for the execution model is based on the common three-tiered architecture. We propose a multi-tiered architecture that includes the separation of responsabilities implied by the classic three-tiered architecture. These responsibilities are assigned to software components.

The architecture encompasses the user interface, the application logic and the storage layers. For the purposes of this paper, we are interested in the application logic. This layer is itself composed of the following layers:

- application logic - problem domain: components representing domain concepts that fulfill application requirements according to the OASIS specification.
- application logic - services: non-problem domain components that provide supporting services, such as interfacing with a database (commonly called mediators and/or databasebrokers).

We are going to describe the structure of this layer in detail showing: (1) how to generate OO code from the OASIS formal specification, (2) how to obtain a component specification of the system starting from the code of the domain classes.

3.3 Generating OO code from the formal specification

The responsibilities of the classes that will be generated are to encapsulate the application logic according to the underlying OASIS specification. This translation process has two parts. The first one is about how the domain classes can implement the algorithm to activate a service according to the execution model philosophy. The second one, is about how the OASIS specification is mapped in the code of the domain classes.

Implementing the algorithm to activate services. The design of the domain classes to implement the algorithm to activate a service is based upon the Template method pattern [4]. The most important public method in the OASIS abstract class is activateService, a template method which takes the name of the service as a parameter and returns a boolean value that indicates whether the service has been successfully activated. We illustrate the design of the OASIS abstract class in the Java programming language as follows:

```
public abstract class OASIS {
    // template method
    public abstract boolean activateService(String service,
    String objectIdentifier, Hashtable parameters)
```

```
{
    mediator.materialize(objectIdentifier);
    checkPreconditions(service);
    checkStateTransition(service);
    valuations(service,parameters);
    checkIntegrityConstraints();
    checkTriggers();
    mediator.dematerialize(objectIdentifier);
    return true;
}

//primitive operations
protected abstract void checkPreconditions(String service);
protected abstract void checkStateTransition(String service);
protected abstract void valuations(String service,
                                   Hashtable parameters);
protected abstract void checkIntegrityConstraints();
protected abstract void checkTriggers();


}
```

The activateService template method defines varying parts of the algorithm; specifically, the particulars of how the activation of a service can vary depending on the service that is being activated. These responsibilities are left as primitive operations for subclasses to define. For example, checkPreconditions is a primitive operation for the template method activateService. Consequently, each domain class has to define how to implement the corresponding body of this primitive operation[2]. In this case, the body of this operation must be implemented according to the preconditions associated to the domain class in the OASIS specification for that particular service. Finally, the declaration of the domain class is completed with the services of the class. Having presented the design pattern that implements the algorithm to activate a service, the next step is to describe the design of the domain classes in order to implement every section of the OASIS specification.

Mapping the OASIS specification into the code of the domain classes. We are going to introduce these mappings taking into account the example of the library system presented in section 3.1. The programming language used is Java.

Mapping preconditions. From an object-oriented programming point of view, a precondition is a conditional sentence that must be tested. Therefore, preconditions are mapped using a conditional test. If the condition doesn't hold then an exception will arise. In the library example the precondition is mapped as follows:

---

[2] Obviously, we will declare a primitive operation for every checking process in the execution model

```
protected void checkPreconditions(String serviceName)
throws error {
  if (serviceName.equals("destroy_reader"))
    if (!(book_number == 0))
    throw new error ("Precondition violation.
    The reader has books");}
```

Mapping state transitions. There are basically three different ways for implementing the verification of a valid state transition; conditional logic, the state pattern [4], or a state machine interpreter that runs against a set of state transition rules. It has been recognized that the applicability of the state pattern may not be suitable if there are many states in the system [4]. The implementation of a state machine interpreter is beyond the scope of our proposal. Consequently, we have chosen the use of conditional logic. Particularly, for each concrete state specified in the OASIS specification[3] (in the example of the reader class, these states are nonexistence, reader0, reader1 and post-mortem), we must declare a conditional structure. This structure must ensure that a valid transition exists for the service that is being activated. If this process succeeds, the corresponding change of state is carried out. Otherwise, an exception will arise. For example, let's suppose that the current state of a reader object is reader0 and that the service that is being activated is the service loan(). The checkStateTransition method determines that this is a valid transition and sets the new state of the reader object to reader1. In the example, state transitions are mapped as follows:

```
protected void checkStateTransition(string service)
throws error {
  if (state.equals("nonexistence"))
    { if (service.equals("new_reader"))
        {state="reader0"; return;}}
  else if (state.equals("reader0"))
    { if (service.equals("loan"))
        {state="reader1"; return;}
      else if (service.equals("destroy_reader"))
        {state="post-mortem"; return;}
  else if (state.equals("reader1"))
    { if (service.equals("return"))
        {state="reader0"; return;}
      else if (service.equals("loan"))
        {state="reader1"; return;}}
  throw new error ("State violation. Invalid transition")}
```

Mapping valuations. The valuations are mapped in the solution space as a method of the domain class. This method implements the change of the object attributes values according to valuations specified in the OASIS specification. In the following example, we use conditional logic to check which service has been activated.

---

[3] See the section process in the example of the OASIS specification

```
protected void valuations(String serviceName,
Hashtable parameters) {
if (serviceName.equals("loan"))
    loan(parameters);
if (serviceName.equals("return")
    return(parameters);}
```

The corresponding method will be activated. This method will modify the attribute values according to the OASIS valuations. Let's suppose that the service loan() has been activated for a reader object. The effect of this service activation in the attribute book_count will be an increment in its value.

Mapping integrity constraints. They are mapped using conditional logic. The method constraints will check if the conditional expression book_number < 10 is satisfied.

```
protected void constraints() throws error {
   if (!(book_count < 10))
   throws new error ("Constraint Violation.
   Borrow limit exceeded";}
```

Mapping triggers. Traditionally, the effect of a triggering action has been a topic of interest in the database community, specially in the context of active DBMS. A common proposal of a knowledge model for active systems has been the event-condition-action (ECA) rules mechanism [9]. These rules are composed of an event that triggers the rule, a condition that describes a specific situation, and an action to be performed if the condition is satisfied. In this context, various proposals have been made to include these rule mechanisms in active systems. For our purposes, we only consider a subset of ECA rules. We define an OASIS trigger as an active rule where the event is the current service that is being activated, the condition is the expression that must be evaluated, and the action is the OASIS action that must be activated if the condition is satisfied. We also consider that the effect of the trigger acts in the context of the object society that is being specified. Taking into account these limitations, we propose a simple strategy of implementation. Triggers are mapped as a method, that checks whether the condition associated to the trigger (book_count $= 10$) holds. In this case, the corresponding service (activateService("Punish")), is activated.

```
protected void triggers() throws error
{  if (book_count = 10)
try { activateService("Punish");
} catch (EX_triggers e) {throws e};}
```

This is how starting from the formal OASIS specification, the code of the domain classes is generated following a specific strategy. It is important to note that the use of this strategy to generate code is not attached to any particular programming language. This is possible because the final implementation is obtained in an automated way by programming the corresponding mappings between conceptual model constructs and their representation in a particular software development environment (Java in this paper). Having obtained the full object-oriented implementation, the next step is how to obtain a component specification of the system.

3.4 From problem domain classes to business components

Starting from the code generated for the domain classes, an interface specification of the system can be obtained in an automated way. This interface specification has two benefits: (1) the application generated can be executed in a distributed environment, (2) the components obtained can be reusable for other applications.

An interface definition language (IDL) is used to define the interface of the domain classes in a programming language-neutral form. We are going to illustrate this process for the example of the class reader written in Java. In the context of Java environment, Java RMI can be used. One of the main benefits in the use of RMI to define the interface is that it uses the actual Java interface definition. In consecuence, no external languages are needed to write the interface. We illustrate the interface definition for the class reader:

```
import java.rmi.*;
public interface I_reader extends Remote {
    boolean activateService(String service,
    String objectIdentifier, Hashtable parameters)
    throws RemoteException;}
```

The import statement imports the Java RMI package. The interface I_reader is a normal Java interface with two interesting characteristics: (1) It extends the RMI interface named Remote, which marks the interface as one available for remote invocation. (2) All its methods throw RemoteException, which is used to signal network and messaging failures.

The interface itself supports one method: activateService which returns a boolean value that indicates if a particular service has could been executed. The Java class reader, implements the method of the remote interface I_reader. In this way, clients on remote hosts can use RMI to send messages to reader objects. Following this strategy, a client program, uses a lookup operation consist of an URL string indicating the name under a RMI object is bound in the registry. It results in the stub of the bound RMI object to be shipped to the client. From this moment, the client can make remote calls to the server. In this way, an interface definition serves as a contract between the client of the interface and the provider of an implementation of the interface. Having obtained the interface definition for each domain class, they are grouped in a package to build the component specification of the application logic. Once compiled, this component specification can be deployed in the proposed architecture.

4 Conclusions

Over the past few years, constructing applications by assembling reusable software components has emerged as a highly productive and widely accepted way of developing custom applications. In this paper, we have presented a model as well as a component-based architecture for this model that allow developers to generate software components starting from the conceptual modeling step. These components can be combined to build a software prototype that is functionally equivalent to the specification collected. To achieve this goal, we use a well-defined OO-Method methodological framework, which properly connects OO conceptual modeling and OO software development environments using a component-based model. The most relevant contributions of this paper are the following: (1) A process to support Component-based development in the OO-Method methodological approach, (2) A concrete strategy to generate code based on a clear separation of component specification from component implementation to enable technology-independent application design, (3) A well-defined component-based framework to execute the specification in the solution space.

These ideas are being applied in the context of a CBD tool that has been called JEM. The basic purpose of JEM is to animate conceptual models captured with the OO-Method Conceptual Modeling approach, over distributed internet/intranet environments. JEM fulfills the requirements respect to the model and the architecture proposed in this paper for the execution model.

References

1. G. Booch. *Object Oriented Analysis and Design with Applications. Second Edition.* Addison-Wesley, 1994.
2. G. Booch, J. Rumbaugh, and I. Jacobson. UML v1. Technical report, Rational Software Corporation, 1997.
3. AW. Brown. From Component-based infrastructure to Component-based Development. In AW. Brown and K. Wallnau, editors, *2nd. International Workshop on Component-based Software Engineering*, pages 87–93, 1998.
4. E. Gamma, R. Helm, R. Johnson, and J. Vlissides. *Desing Patterns: Elements of Reusable Object-Oriented Software.* Addison-Wesley, 1994.
5. I. Jacobson, M. Christerson, P. Jonsson, and G. Overgaard. *OO Software Engineering, a Use Case Driven Approach.* Addison-Wesley, 1992.
6. O. Pastor, E. Insfrán, V. Pelechano, and J. Gómez. From Object Oriented Conceptual Modeling to Automated Programming in Java. In Tok Wang Ling, Sudha Ram, and Mong Li Lee, editors, *17th International Conference on Conceptual Modeling*, volume 1507 of *LNCS*, pages 183–196. Springer-Verlag, November 1998.
7. O. Pastor, E. Insfrán, V. Pelechano, J. Merseguer, and J. Romero. OO-Method: An OO Software Production Environment Combining Conventional and Formal Methods. In A. Olivé and JA. Pastor, editors, *Advanced Information Systems Engineering*, volume 1250 of *LNCS*, pages 145–158. Springer-Verlag, June 1997.
8. O. Pastor and I. Ramos. *OASIS 2.1.1: A Class-Definition Language to Model Information Systems Using an Object-Oriented Approach.* Servicio de Publicaciones. Universidad Politécnica de Valencia, 3rd edition, 1995.
9. NW. Paton and O. Díaz. Active Database Systems. *ACM Computing Surveys*, 1998.
10. J. Rumbaugh, M. Blaha, W. Premerlani, F. Eddy, and W. Lorensen. *Object Oriented Modeling and Design.* Prentice-Hall, 1991.

Query Processing in Relationlog

Mengchi Liu

Department of Computer Science, University of Regina
Regina, Saskatchewan, Canada S4S 0A2
mliu@cs.uregina.ca

Abstract. Relationlog is a persistent deductive database system that supports effective storage, efficient access and inference of large amounts of data with complex structures. In this paper, we describe query processing in the Relationlog system. In particular, we illustrate the extended semi-naive and magic-set techniques used in Relationlog.

1   Introduction

During the past decades, the nested relational and complex object models [1, 5, 11, 12, 15, 18, 21, 22] were developed to extend the applicability of the traditional relational model to more complex, non-business applications such as CAD, image processing and text retrieval [2].

Another important direction of intense research has been in using a logic programming based language Datalog [8, 23] as a database query language. Such a language provides a simple and natural way to express queries on a relational database and is more expressive than the traditional relational languages.

In the past several years, there have been some efforts to combine these two approaches, mainly by extending Datalog with set and tuple constructors [3, 7, 6, 9, 13, 14, 19]. Like Datalog, their natural use of fixpoint construct allows to express transitive closure declaratively in polynomial space and time [4, 5], which makes them expressive enough while still practical for real database applications.

However, most of the research on such kind of deductive databases stays at the theoretical level. A few implemented systems such as LDL [10] and CORAL [20] are just memory-based.

In the past few years, we have designed and implemented a persistent deductive database system called Relationlog [16]. The Relationlog system is based on the deductive database language Relationlog [17], which is a typed extension to Datalog with tuples and sets. It provides powerful mechanisms for representing and manipulating nested sets, tuples and relations with a well-defined declarative semantics.

As Relationlog supports nested sets and tuples, the traditional query processing technique for Datalog such as the semi-naive and magic-set rule rewriting techniques cannot be used directly. Therefore, we have extended the semi-naive and magic-set techniques so that queries concerning nested sets and tuples can be answered efficiently. In this paper, we describe the query processing in the Relationlog system. In particular, we illustrate the extended semi-naive and extended magic-set techniques used in Relationlog.

This paper is organized as follows. Section 2 gives a brief overview of the Relationlog data model. Section 3 shows the Relationlog system architecture. Section 4 describes the extended semi-naive technique for evaluating Relationlog rules. Section 5 addresses the extended magic-set strategy. Section 6 summarizes this paper.

2 Relationlog Overview

Datalog [8, 24] is a deductive language for flat relations. Relationlog [17] is a deductive language for nested relations and complex objects. It stands in the same relationship to the nested relational and complex object models as Datalog stands to the relational model. However, Relationlog is typed which is unlike Datalog.

The atomic data type supported in Relationlog includes *String, Token, Integer, Float, Char*, based on which (nested) tuple and set types can be formed. For example, we can have the following set and tuple types:

> {*String*}
> (*Street* : *String, City* : *String*)

In Relationlog, a relation schema is a named tuple type while a relation is a set of tuples that may contain nested sets and tuples. For example, the following are a relation schema called *Robots* and the corresponding relation:

Robots(
  Id :   *String*,
  Arms :{(*Id* :   *String*,
           Axes :{(*Kinematics* :(*Dh_matrix* : {(*Column* : *Integer, Vector* : {*Real*})}
                                  Joint_angle : (*Max* : *Integer, Min* : *Integer*)),
                  Dynamics : (*Mass* : *Real, Accel* : *Real*)
)}
)}
  Grippers : {(*Id* :   *string*(20),
          Function :*string*(20)
)}
)

Id	Arms							Grippers	
	{(Id	Axes)}						{(Id	Function)}
		{(Kinematics			Dynamics)}				
		(Dh_matrix	Joint_angle)		(Mass	Accel)			
		{(Column	{Vector})})	[Max	Min]				
Artoo	Left	1	1, 0, 0, 0	−180	180	50.0	1.0	#100	gripper
		2	0, 1, 0, 0					#200	righthand
	Right	3	0, 1, 0	−90	90	10.0	1.3		
		4	0, 0, 0, 1						
Detoo	Middle	6	1, 1, 1, 0	−270	270	10.0	2.7	#300	lefthand
		8	0, 1, 1, 1						
		9	0, 1, 0, 1						

Relationlog is a rule-based language in which rules can be used to derive complex object relations that are not explicitly stored in the database.

A Relationlog database consists of three parts: a schema, an extensional database (EDB) and an intensional database (IDB). The schema is a set of relational schemas for both extensional and intensional relations. The extensional database is a set of extensional relations stored on disk. The intensional database is a set of rules which define intensional relations.

Example 1. The following is a complete Relationlog database:

> *Schema*
>   *Persons(Name : String,*
>   *Age :   Integer,*
>   *Parents :{String},*
>   *Address :(Street : String, City : String))*
>   *Ancestors(Name: String, Ancestors: {String})*

> *EDB*
>   *Persons*

Name	*Age*	*Parents*	*Address*	
		{ *string* }	(*Street*	*City*)
Mary	25	*LiLy, Sean*	123 *St*	*Toronto*
John	30	*Phil, Pam*	456 *Av*	*Montreal*
Lily	52	*Jim*	321 *St*	*Calgary*
Sean	57	*Sam*	472 *Av*	*Regina*

> *IDB*
>   *Ancestors(X, ⟨Y⟩) :– Persons(X, _, ⟨Y⟩, _)*
>   *Ancestors(X, ⟨Y⟩) :– Persons(X, _, ⟨Z⟩, _), ancestors(Z, ⟨Y⟩)*

where $\_X, \_Y, \_Z$ are variables and $\_$ is an anonymous variable.

In Relationlog, both extensional relations and intensional relations can be queried uniformly. For example, the database in Example 1 can be queried as follows:

> *query Persons(_N, _A, _P, _L), _A > 30*
> *query Persons("John", _A, _P, _)*
> *query Ancestors("Mary", _X)*
> *query Ancestors(_X, _Y)*

3   System Architecture

The Relationlog system has been implemented as a single-user persistent deductive database system. The system architecture of Relationlog is shown in Figure 1.

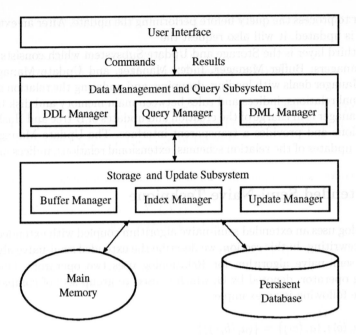

Fig. 1. The Architecture of Relationlog

The system is organized into 3 layers. The first layer is the user interface. Two kinds of user interfaces are provided: textual user interface and graphical user interface. They provide different kinds of environment for the user to define, query, and manipulate databases. The textual user interface accepts, processes user commands and displays results. The graphical user interface allows users to pick operations off menus. Both kinds of interfaces actually send operations in internal form to the lower layer.

The second layer is Data Management and Query Subsystem which consists of three managers: DDL Manager, Query Manager. and DML Manger. They cooperate with each other tightly and direct the lower layer to handle smaller tasks respectively. The DDL Manager is responsible for processing all DDL commands, maintaining system catalogs about domains, relations, indices and rules, and answering all the type checking requests from the DML and Query Managers. It checks if all rules are stratified when a new rule is created.

The Query Manager is responsible for data retrieval and rule evaluation. If the data to be retrieved are in an extensional relation, then it simply uses matching and indices to find the results. If the data to be retrieved are in an intensional relation defined by rules, then it uses the extended magic-set strategy and the extended semi-naive bottom-up fixpoint evaluation technique to find the results to the query.

The DML Manager performs all the updates to the extensional relations. As an update may imply a query, the DML manager may request the Query

$path$	a	$\{b,c,d,e,f\}$
	b	$\{d,e,f,\}$
	c	$\{b,d,e,f\}$
	d	$\{f\}$
	e	$\{f\}$

5   Extended Magic-Set Strategy

The magic-set technique simulates in semi-naive bottom-up evaluation the pushing of selections that occurs in top-down approaches. Its performance can rival the efficiency of the top-down techniques. Here, we assume that readers are familiar with adorned rules and magic-set rewriting and thus only give a brief introduction to the notations applied in Relationlog.

In Relationlog, there is a fixed order of the arguments for each predicate. The arguments can be four kinds: atomic term, complete set term, partial set term, and tuple term. As Relationlog is a typed language, the kinds of arguments allowed for each predicate are in fact known based on the schema.

There are different levels in relations in Relationlog. Each level represent sets or tuples nested in up-level sets or tuples. For the $Robots$ relation in last section, there are four levels. The first is $Robots(Id, Arms, Grippers)$; the second is $Arms : \{[Id, Axes]\}$ and $Grippers : \{[Id, Function]\}$; the third is $Axes : \{[Kinematics, Dynamics]\}$; and the fourth is $Db\_matrix : \{[Column, Vector]\}$ in $Axes$ of $Arms$.

In order to represent the bound or free information to a deeply nested level, an extended adornment for n-ary predicate p in Relationlog is a string of length n on the alphabet $\{b, f, C, P, T\}$, where b is for atomic argument and stands for bound; f is for atomic argument and stands for free; C is for complete set term; P is for partial set term; and T is for tuple term. Moreover, for a complete set term, partial set term or tuple term, we use another string on the alphabet $\{b, f, C, P, T\}$ as a superscript to represent the status of arguments in it.

The following are examples of extended adornments in Relationlog:

Argument	Adornment	Note
a	b	
X	f	X is an atomic variable
$\langle a, b, c \rangle$	P^{bbb}	
$\langle a, b, X \rangle$	P^{bbf}	X is an atomic variable
$\{a, b, c\}$	C^{bbb}	
$\{X, Y, Z\}$	C^{fff}	X, Y, Z are atomic variables
(a, X, Y)	$bC^f T^f$	X is a set variable and Y is a tuple variable
$(a, \{X, Y\})$	bC^{ff}	X, Y are atomic variables
$(a, \langle b, c \rangle, (d, e))$	$bP^{bb}T^{bb}$	

In order to show the extended magic-set strategy in Relationlog, let us consider the rules in Example 2. The typical query patterns for the intensional relation *path* are as follows:

Case 1	bP^b	such as $path(b, \langle f \rangle)$
Case 2	bP^{bb}	such as $path(b, \langle d, f \rangle)$
Case 3	bP^{bf}	such as $path(b, \langle d, X \rangle)$
Case 4	bP^f	such as $path(b, \langle X \rangle)$
Case 5	bC^f	such as $path(b, X)$
Case 6	bC^b	such as $path(b, \{e, f\})$
Case 7	fP^b	such as $path(X, \langle d \rangle)$
Case 8	fP^f	such as $path(X, \langle Y \rangle)$
Case 9	$1fC^f$	such as $path(X, Y)$

We describe how to handle each case in Relationlog below using examples.

Case 1 *query* $path(b, \langle f \rangle)$
The answer to this kind of query is either *true* or *false*. We don't need to evaluate the original rules to answer this query. Instead, we can simply evaluate the following magic-set rewriting rules

$magic(Z) :\!- magic(X), edge(X, \langle Z \rangle)$
$magic(b) :\!-$

and convert the query into the following:

query $magic(f)$

Case 2 *query* $path(b, \langle d, f \rangle)$
The answer to this kind of query is again *true* or *false*. Like Case 1, we don't need to evaluate the original rules. We can simply evaluate the above magic-set rewriting rules and convert the query into the following:

query $magic(d), magic(f)$

Case 3 *query* $path(b, \langle d, X \rangle)$
The answer to this query is either false if there is no path from b to d. Otherwise, it is a possibly empty list of nodes other than d that are reachable from b. Again, we just need to evaluate the magic-set rewriting rules for Case 1 and convert the query into the following:

query $magic(d), magic(X), X \neq d$

Case 4 *query* $path(b, \langle X \rangle)$
The answer to this query is a list of nodes that are reachable from b. We need to evaluate the following magic-set rewritten rules:

$path(X, \langle Y \rangle) :\!- magic(X), edge(X, \langle Y \rangle)$
$path(X, \langle Y \rangle) :\!- magic(X), path(X, \langle Z \rangle), edge(Z, \langle Y \rangle)$
$magic(b) :\!-$

Case 5 *query path(b, X)*
This query is similar to the above one except that the answer to the query is a set of nodes. The exact magic-set rules for Case 4 can be used to find the result.

Case 6 *query path$(d, \{e, f\})$*
This query asks if d can only reach e and f using a complete set $\{e, f\}$. It is similar to Case 5 except that the answer is checked with the set $\{e, f\}$.

Case 7 *query path$(X, \langle d \rangle)$*
The answer to this query is a list of nodes that can reach d. The corresponding magic-set rewritten rules are as follows:

$$path(X, \langle Y \rangle) \; :- \; magic(Y), edge(X, \langle Y \rangle)$$
$$path(X, \langle Y \rangle) \; :- \; magic(Y), edge(Z, \langle Y \rangle), path(X, \langle Z \rangle)$$
$$magic(Y) \qquad :- \; magic(Z), edge(Y, \langle Z \rangle)$$
$$magic(d) \qquad :-$$

Case 8 *query path$(X, \langle Y \rangle)$* and **Case 9** *query path(X, Y)*
There is no magic-set rewritten rule can be used for this query as there is no constant that can be used to reduce the search space. Therefore, the original rules will be evaluated directly.

6 Conclusion

In this paper, we have discussed the query processing mechanism in the Relationlog deductive database system. We have described our extension of the semi-naive and magic-set techniques for evaluating Relationlog programs.

A complete implementation of Relationlog that uses the extended semi-naive and extended magic-set techniques discussed in this paper has been developed. With these new techniques, the Relationlog system achieves reasonable performance for a large volume of data on disk. We have been using this system for various graduate student research projects successfully. After further testing and debugging, we will release the Relationlog system as a new version over the Internet for public access and evaluation at http://www.cs.uregina.ca/~mliu/RLOG.

We are now extending Relationlog into a deductive object-relational database system and providing algebraic and calculus-based query languages.

References

1. S. Abiteboul, P. C. Fischer, and H.J. Schek, editors. *Proceedings of the International Workshop on Theory and Applications of Nested Relations and Complex Objects in Databases*, Darmstadt, Germany, 1987. Springer-Verlag LNCS 361.
2. S. Abiteboul, P.C. Fisher, and H.J. Schek, editors. *Nested Relations and Complex Objects in Databases*. Lecture Notes in Computer Science, vol 361, Springer-Verlag, 1989.
3. S. Abiteboul and S. Grumbach. COL: A Logic-Based Language for Complex Objects. *ACM TODS*, 16(1):1–30, 1991.

4. S. Abiteboul, R. Hull, and V. Vianu. *Foundations of Databases*. Addison Wesley, 1995.

5. Serge Abiteboul and Catriel Beeri. The Power of Languages for the Manipulation of Complex Values. *VLDB Journal*, 4(4):727–794, 1995.

6. F. Bancilhon and S. Khoshafian. A Calculus for Complex Objects. *J. Computer and System Sciences*, 38(2):326–340, 1989.

7. C. Beeri, S. Naqvi, O. Shmueli, and S. Tsur. Set Construction in a Logic Database Language. *J. Logic Programming*, 10(3,4):181–232, 1991.

8. S. Ceri, G. Gottlob, and T. Tanca. *Logic Programming and Databases*. Springer-Verlag, 1990.

9. Q. Chen and W. Chu. HILOG: A High-Order Logic Programming Language for Non-1NF Deductive Databases. In W. Kim, J.M. Nicolas, and S. Nishio, editors, *Proceedings of the International Conference on Deductive and Object-Oriented Databases*, pages 431–452, Kyoto, Japan, 1989. North-Holland.

10. D. Chimenti, R. Gamboa, R. Krishnamurthy, S. Naqvi, S. Tsur, and C. Zaniolo. The LDL System Prototype. *IEEE Transactions on Knowledge and Data Engineering*, 2(1):76–90, 1990.

11. L. Colby. A Recursive Algebra and Query Optimization for Nested Relations. In *Proceedings of the ACM SIGMOD International Conference on Management of Data*, pages 124–138, Portland, Oregon, 1989.

12. R. Hull. A survey of theoretic research on typed complex database objects. In J. Pardaens, editor, *Databases*, pages 193–256. Academic Press, 1987.

13. R. Krishnamurthy and S. Naqvi. Towards a Real Horn Clause Language. In *Proceedings of the International Conference on Very Large Data Bases*, pages 252–263, Los Angeles, California, USA, 1988. Morgan Kaufmann Publishers, Inc.

14. G. M. Kuper. Logic Programming with Sets. *J. Computer and System Sciences*, 41(1):44–64, 1990.

15. Mark Levene and George Loizou. Semantics for Null Extended Nested Relations. *ACM TODS*, 18(3):414–459, 1993.

16. M. Liu and R. Shan. The Design and Implementation of the Relationlog Deductive Database System. In *Proceedings of the 9th International Workshop on Database and Expert System Applications (DEXA Workshop '98)*, pages 856–863, Vienna, Austria, August 24-28 1998. IEEE-CS Press.

17. Mengchi Liu. Relationlog: A Typed Extension to Datalog with Sets and Tuples. *Journal of Logic Programming*, 36(3):271–299, 1998.

18. Z. Meral Ozsoyogly and Li-Yan Yuan. A New Normal Form for Nested Relations. *ACM Trans. on Database Systems*, 12(1):111–136, 1987.

19. R. Ramakrishnan, D. Srivastava, and S. Sudarshan. CORAL: Control, Relations and Logic. In *Proceedings of the International Conference on Very Large Data Bases*, pages 238–250, Vancouver, British Columbia, Canada, 1992. Morgan Kaufmann Publishers, Inc.

20. Raghu Ramakrishnan, Divesh Srivastava, S. Sudarshan, and Praveen Seshadri. The CORAL Deductive System. *VLDB Journal*, 3(2):161–210, 1994.

21. M. A. Roth, H. F. Korth, and D. S. Batory. SQL/NF: A Query Language for ¬1NF Relational Databases. *Information Systems*, 12(1):99–114, 1987.

22. M. A. Roth, H. F. Korth, and A. Silberschatz. Extended Algebra and Calculus for Nested Relational Databases. *ACM TODS*, 13(4):389–417, 1988.

23. J.D. Ullman. *Principles of Database and Knowledge-Base Systems*, volume 1. Computer Science Press, 1988.

24. J.D. Ullman. *Principles of Database and Knowledge-Base Systems*, volume 2. Computer Science Press, 1989.

Rewriting Queries Using Views[*]

Sergio Flesca and Sergio Greco

DEIS
Università della Calabria
87030 Rende, Italy
{ flesca, greco }@si.deis.unical.it

Abstract. In this paper we consider the problem of answering queries using materialized views in the presence of negative goals. The solution is carried out by 'inverting' views and deriving both positive and negative knowledge. In order to derive negative knowledge we invert conjunctive views with negation into a set of (extended) views which may also have, in addition to negation-as-failure, a different form of negation called classical (or strong) negation. Finally, we analyze the problem of inferring knowledge from views based on relations with functional dependencies.

1 Introduction

Recent research on databases has been concerned with the problem of answering queries when only materialized views are available as base relations [3–5, 11, 12, 16, 18]. This problem is becoming more and more important in many database areas such as data warehouse, mobile computing and others.

The problem of finding, given a general query Q and a set of conjunctive views $\mathcal{V}$, a new query $Q_{\mathcal{V}}$ equivalent to Q, which uses only predicates in $\mathcal{V}$ as base relations, has been shown to be undecidable. Therefore, an interesting problem is to find a rewriting which is correct in the sense that only atoms derived from the original query are derived from the rewritten one and, possibly, optimal in the sense that it gives the best approximation of the original query.

Most of the recent research has concentrated on considering the restricted case of positive queries and conjunctive views. In this paper we investigate the problem of finding a rewriting for queries where only materialized views are used as base relations in a more general framework. We extend previous work by considering queries and views with negation whereas due to space limitation disjunctive views will be considered in future work. Furthermore, the techinique proposed here consider also the presence of functional dependencies on the base relations.

Although in this paper we consider only semipositive queries, i.e. queries where negation is applied only to base relation [1], our technique is general and can be applied to general (stratified) queries. We present an algorithm which

---

[*] Work partially supported by a MURST grant under the project "Interdata". The second author is also supported by ISI-CNR.

given a semipositive Datalog program $\mathcal{P}$ and a set of views $\mathcal{V}$ with negation in the bodies, generates a rewritten program $\mathcal{P}_\mathcal{V}$ with the following properties: (i) $\mathcal{P}_\mathcal{V}$ contains only view predicates as base predicates, and (ii) $\mathcal{P}_\mathcal{V}$ is contained in $\mathcal{P}$, i.e. for each database D, the set of tuples derived from the evaluation of $\mathcal{P}_\mathcal{V}$ over D is contained in the set of tuples derived from the evaluation of $\mathcal{P}$ over D. The main difference with respect to previous works is that we allow negation in the rule bodies of both programs and views to derive both positive and negative information. The program generated by our algorithm gives, generally, a 'good' approximation of the original program and for a significant class of queries is optimal. We recall that the case of Datalog queries and conjunctive views was also investigated in [5] whereas [6] also considers the rewriting of positive queries and positive disjunctive views.

2 Preliminaries

Let us assume basic knowledge on logic programming and Datalog [13, 17].

2.1 Program Containment

The set of atoms derived from the application of a *Datalog* program $\mathcal{P}$ to a database D (under a fixed semantics) is denoted $\mathcal{P}(D)$. A program $\mathcal{P}$ is *contained* in a program $\mathcal{P}'$, written $\mathcal{P} \subseteq \mathcal{P}'$, if $\mathcal{P}(D) \subseteq \mathcal{P}'(D)$ for all databases D. If $\mathcal{P} \subseteq \mathcal{P}'$ and $\mathcal{P}' \subseteq \mathcal{P}$ we say that $\mathcal{P}$ and $\mathcal{P}'$ are *equivalent*, written $\mathcal{P} \equiv \mathcal{P}'$. The problem of determining whether a Datalog program $\mathcal{P}$ is contained in a Datalog program $\mathcal{P}'$ is, in general, undecidable [15]. The problem is decidable if one of the two queries is not recursive [14]. Moreover, given a set of literals S and a set of ground terms C, we denote with S_C the set of literals in S which have as arguments only terms in C. We say that $\mathcal{P}$ is *contained* in a program $\mathcal{P}'$ w.r.t. a set of ground terms C, written $\mathcal{P} \subseteq_C \mathcal{P}'$ if $\mathcal{P}(D)_C \subseteq \mathcal{P}'(D)_C$.

2.2 Classical negation

Traditional declarative semantics of Datalog and logic programming uses closed world assumption and each ground atom which does not follow from the database is assumed to be false. *Extended logic programs* extends standard logic programs with a different form of negation, known as *classical* or *strong negation*, which can also appear in the head of rules. Thus, while standard programs provide negative information implicitly, extended programs provide negative information explicitly and we can distinguish queries which fail in the sense that they do not succeed and queries which fail in the stronger sense that negation succeeds [8, 10, 9]. A literal is either an atom, say A or its negation $\neg A$. An extended Datalog program is a set of rules of the form

$$L_0 \leftarrow L_1, ..., L_m, \textbf{not } L_{m+1}, ..., \textbf{not } L_n$$

where $n \geq m \geq 0$, and each L_i is a literal. A (2-valued) interpretation I for an extended program $\mathcal{P}$ is a pair $\langle T, F \rangle$ where T and F define a partition of

$B_P \cup \neg B_P$ and $\neg B_P = \{\neg A | A \in B_P\}$ (B_P is the *Herbrand Base* of P). The truth value of a literal $L \in B_P \cup \neg B_P$ w.r.t. an interpretation I is equal to (i) *true* if $A \in T$ and, (ii) *false* if $A \in F$. The semantics of an extended program P is defined by considering each negated predicate symbol, say $\neg p$, as a new symbol syntactically different from p and $\neg(\neg(A)) = A$. Moreover, we say that an interpretation $I = \langle T, F \rangle$ is *consistent* if there is no atom A such that $A \in T$ and $\neg A \in T$.

The concepts of positive, semipositive and stratified programs also apply to extended Datalog^{not}, denoted Datalog$^\neg$. Generally, the existence of a (2-valued) model for an extended program is not guaranteed, also in the case of negation (as-failure) free programs. For instance, the program consisting of the two facts a and $\neg$a does not admit any (2-valued) model. We recall that different semantics for extended programs, based on well-founded or stable models, have been proposed in the literature [8–10].

3 Rewriting queries

A technique for answering Datalog queries using views restricted to being conjunctive was proposed in [5]. Before presenting the proposed technique we recall the concepts of retrievable program, containment and maximal containment among programs.

Definition 1. Let P be a program and V a set of views. We say P is *retrievable* if the only EDB predicates appearing in P are materialized views of V.

Given two retrievable programs P' and P'', then P' is *contained* in P'', written $P' \sqsubseteq P''$, if for all database D, $P' \cup V \subseteq_C P'' \cup V$ where C is the set of all constants in D.

Given a Datalog program P and a retrievable program P', we say that P' is *maximally contained* in P, if $P' \sqsubseteq P$ and there is no retrievable program P'' such that $P' \sqsubset P'' \sqsubseteq P$. $\qquad\qquad\qquad\square$

In [5] it was shown that given a Datalog program P and a set of conjunctive views V it is undecidable whether there is a retrievable program P_V equivalent to P. Moreover, it was also shown that for Datalog programs and conjunctive views it is possible to generate a retrievable program P_V which is maximally contained in P. The technique consists of building a program that is used to query the database instead of the original one.

This program is essentialy the inversion of rules defining views. Given a view v of the form $v(X) \leftarrow b_1(Y_1), ..., b_n(Y_n)$, the inverse of v, denoted v^{-1}, is a set of n rules of the form $b_i(Y_i') \leftarrow v(X)$ where Y_i' is derived from Y by replacing every variable $y \in (Y_i - X)$ with the function $f_{v/y}(X)$ where v identifies the view and y identifies a distinguished variable in the view. Given a set of views V, V^{-1} denotes the union of all inverses v^{-1} of all view definitions v in V, i.e. $V^{-1} = \bigcup_{v \in V} v^{-1}$.

Example 1. Assume to have three base relations having the following schema supplier(S#, NameS, City), product(P#, NameP, Type, Price) *and* supply(S#, P#). *Consider the views* made *and* price *defined by the following two rules:*

> 1 : made(P, C) ← supplier(S, NS, C), supply(S, P).
> 2 : price(P, Pr) ← product(P, NP, T, Pr).

where a tuple ⟨p, c⟩ *in the materialized view* made *means that the product with code* p *was made by a supplier of city* c *whereas the materialized view* price *consists of the projection of the base relation* product *on the attribute* P# *and* Price. *The inverse of the two views is given by the following set of rules:*

> supplier($f_{1/S}$(P, C), $f_{1/NS}$(P, C), C) ← made(P, C).
> supply($f_{1/S}$(P, C), P)   ← made(P, C).
> product(P, $f_{2/NP}$(P, Pr), $f_{2/T}$(P, Pr), Pr) ← price(P, Pr).

□

Now, given a Datalog program $\mathcal{P}$ and a set of views $\mathcal{V}$, $\mathcal{P}_{\mathcal{V}^{-1}}$ denotes the program derived from the union of $\mathcal{P}$ and $\mathcal{V}^{-1}$. Although $\mathcal{P}_{\mathcal{V}^{-1}}$ contains function symbols it has a unique finite minimal model since function symbols only appear in the body of nonrecursive rules. Therefore, its fixpoint evaluation is guaranteed to terminate.

Essentially, every tuple derived from the inverted views is associated with a tuple of the materialized views which, in turn, can be derived from more than one instance of the view. Thus, a tuple derived from the inverted views has associated a set of tuples in the original definition of the predicate. Consider for instance the definition of made in the above example and the rules defining supplier and supply derived from the inversion of the view made. Assuming that the definition of supply in the database consists of the two tuples supply(s1, p1) and supply(s2, p1), and the definition of supplier consists of the two tuples ⟨s1, ibm, rome⟩ and ⟨s2, sun, rome⟩, the materialized view made contains only the tuple ⟨p1, rome⟩ and, from the inverted view, we derive the two tuples supply($f_{1/S}$(p1, rome), p1) and supplier($f_{1/S}$(p1, rome), $f_{1/NS}$(p1, rome), rome).

Therefore, each tuple with functions symbols has associated a set of database tuples having the same flat terms. In our example the tuple supplier($f_{1/S}$(p1, rome), $f_{1/NS}$(p1, rome), rome) has associated two tuples in the source database, namely ⟨s1, ibm, rome⟩ and ⟨s2, sun, rome⟩. This means that the body of a ground view is satisfied by using database tuples if and only if it is also satisfied by using corresponding tuples with possible function terms. The database built by using materialized views will be called rebuilt database. Moreover, for each tuple t derived from the application of a program $\mathcal{P}$ on the rebuilt database, there is a tuple u derived from the application of $\mathcal{P}$ to the source database coinciding with t on the flat terms of t.

4 Rewriting queries with negation

In this section we present our technique for the rewriting of queries. The main difference with respect to the technique presented in the previous section is that we allow negation in both queries and views and derive, by inverting views, both positive and negative knowledge. We consider here the rewriting of semipositive Datalog queries and conjunctive views with negation whereas the case of disjunctive views is considered in the next section.

Our technique consists of two steps. In the first step, given a set of conjunctive views $\mathcal{V}$, we derive an extended semipositive Datalog program $\mathcal{V}^{-1}$. In the second step we rewrite the rules in the program by generating an extended positive Datalog program, i.e. a program whose rules contain classical negation but not negation-as-failure. Before presenting our algorithm we introduce some notation:

- the extended version of a literal B, denoted $ev(B)$ is derived from B by replacing the negation **not** with $\neg$, i.e. let A be an atom $ev(A) = A$ and $ev(\textbf{not } A) = \neg A$,
- given a set of literals $L_1, ..., L_n$, $var(L_1, ..., L_n)$ denotes the set of variables appearing in $L_1, ..., L_n$,
- given a set of variables Z, $DOM_x(Z)$ denotes the conjunction of atoms $dom_x(z)$ one for each variable z in Z.

Algorithm 1 *Inverting conjunctive view with negation.*
Input: *Conjunctive view v of the form $v(Z) \leftarrow B_1, ..., B_n$;*
Output: *Set of semipositive extended Datalog rules v^{-1};*
begin
    $v^{-1} := \emptyset;$
    For each B_i add to v^{-1} the rule
        $ev(B_i') \leftarrow v(Z)$
        where B_i' is derived from B_i by renaming each variable $x \in var(B_i) - Z$ with
$f_{v/x}(Z);$
    For each B_i add to v^{-1} the rule
        $\neg ev(B_i) \leftarrow ev(B_1), ..., ev(B_{i-1}), ev(B_{i+1}), ..., ev(B_n), \textbf{ not } v(Z),$
                $DOM_c(Z), DOM_f((var(B(v)) \cup Z) - var(B_i)))$
    For each $z \in Z$ **do** add to v^{-1} the rule
        $dom_c(z) \leftarrow v(Z);$
    For each *function symbol f introduced in previous steps* add to v^{-1} the rules
        $dom_f(f(Z)) \leftarrow v(Z);$
        $dom_f(Z) \leftarrow dom_c(Z);$
end.

The algorithm produces four groups of rules. The rules in the first group are used to derive positive information and they coincide with the rules described in the previous section. The idea here is that if the head of the view is true then all literals in the body must also be true since we are considering conjunctive views, i.e. for each view predicate there is only one rule defining it. Variables appearing in the body literals and not appearing in the head have unknown values and they are replaced by functions. The rules in the second group are used to derive negative information. The idea here is that a body literal must be false if the head of the view is false and all other body literals are true. The conjunctions DOM_c and DOM_f are introduced in the body of inverted rules to restrict the range of variables. The rules in the third and fourth groups define the predicates dom_c and dom_f used in the bodies of the rules belonging to the third group; these rules are used to compute all ground terms which can be used as arguments of derived tuples.

Given a set of views $\mathcal{V}$, $\mathcal{V}^{-1}$ denotes the set of rules derived from the application of Algorithm 1 to every rule in $\mathcal{V}$, i.e. $\mathcal{V}^{-1} = \cup_{v \in \mathcal{V}} v^{-1}$. Given a semipositive Datalog program $\mathcal{P}$ we denote with $\mathcal{P}^-$ the set of rules derived from $\mathcal{P}$ by replacing every literal B with $ev(B)$. Thus, we denote with $\mathcal{P}^-_{\mathcal{V}-1}$ the program derived from the union of $\mathcal{P}^-$ and $\mathcal{V}^{-1}$. The following example shows how our algorithm works.

Example 2. Consider the following view v

$\quad$ $v(X) \leftarrow emp(X),\ mgr(X, Y),\ \textbf{not}\ emp(Y).$

The set of rules v^{-1} derived from v is as follows. In the first cycle we derive one rule for each body goal

$\quad$ $emp(X) \qquad\quad \leftarrow v(X).$
$\quad$ $mgr(X, f_{v/Y}(X)) \leftarrow v(X).$
$\quad$ $\neg emp(f_{v/Y}(X)) \leftarrow v(X).$

In the second cycle we also derive one rule for each body goal

$\quad$ $\neg emp(X) \quad \leftarrow mgr(X, Y),\ \neg emp(Y),\ \textbf{not}\ v(X),\ dom_c(X).$
$\quad$ $\neg mgr(X, Y) \leftarrow emp(X),\ \neg emp(Y),\ \textbf{not}\ v(X),\ dom_c(X).$
$\quad$ $emp(Y) \quad\ \leftarrow mgr(X, Y),\ emp(X),\ \textbf{not}\ v(X),\ dom_c(X).$

Finally, we derive the rule

$\quad$ $dom_c(X) \leftarrow v(X).$

Note that the program contains also two rules defining dom_f. These rules are here omitted since they are not used to answer the query. $\qquad\qquad\qquad\qquad\square$

Recall that given a database D and a set of views $\mathcal{V}$, $\mathcal{V}(D)$ denotes the application of the views to the database D which gives the current instance for the materialized views. Moreover, for a given program $\mathcal{P}$, $\mathcal{P}^-_{\mathcal{V}-1}(\mathcal{V}(D))$ denotes the application of $\mathcal{P}^-_{\mathcal{V}-1}$ to the materialized views.

Theorem 1. *Let $\mathcal{P}$ be a semipositive Datalog program, $\mathcal{V}$ be a set of conjunctive views with possible negation in the body and D a database. Then, $\mathcal{P}^-_{\mathcal{V}-1}(\mathcal{V}(D))$ has a perfect minimal model which is finite and consistent.* $\qquad\qquad\square$

Theorem 2. *Let $\mathcal{P}$ be a semipositive Datalog program and $\mathcal{V}$ a set of conjunctive views with possible negation in the body. Then, $\mathcal{P}^-_{\mathcal{V}-1} \cup \mathcal{V} \sqsubseteq \mathcal{P}$.* $\qquad\square$

However, although the program generated by Algorithm 1 gives a good approximation of the original program, generally it is not maximal. The problem is that our algorithm is not able to capture the disjunctive structure of queries. However, maximal containment is guaranteed for a restricted class of programs.

Theorem 3. *Let $\mathcal{P}$ be a positive Datalog program and let $\mathcal{V}$ be a set of conjunctive views with at most one negation for each rule. Then, $\mathcal{P}^-_{\mathcal{V}-1}$ is maximally contained in $\mathcal{P}$.* $\qquad\qquad\qquad\qquad\square$

5 Deriving information by merging rules

One of the drawback of Algorithm 1 is that it consider only one view at time and is not able to capture information which can be derived by considering more than one rule together. Indeed, by using Algorithm 1 it is possible to derive inverted rules containing disjunctive information which is not used to derive additional knowledge. We show this by means of an example. Consider the following views

$$v_1(X) \leftarrow a(X), \ b(X).$$
$$v_2(X) \leftarrow a(X), \ \neg b(X).$$
$$v_3(X) \leftarrow c(X).$$

and assume that the relation a contains the tuples 1 and 2, the relation b contains the tuple 1 and the relation c contains the tuple 3. By inverting the views we derive the following rules defining $\neg a$

$$\neg a(X) \leftarrow \neg b(X), \ \textbf{not } v_1(X), \ dom_c(X).$$
$$\neg a(X) \leftarrow b(X), \ \textbf{not } v_2(X), \ dom_c(X).$$

Since both $b(3)$ and $\neg b(3)$ cannot be derived from the inverted rules also $\neg a(3)$ cannot be derived. However, if $v_1(X)$ and $v_2(X)$ are both false for same value X in the domain, $\neg a(X)$ is true independently of the value of $b(X)$. Therefore we derive the rule

$$\neg a(X) \leftarrow \textbf{not } v_1(X), \ \textbf{not } v_2(X), \ dom_c(X).$$

which permits us to infer $\neg a(3)$. This rule is derived by merging the above two rules defining $\neg a$ and containing in the bodies disjunctive information on the predicate b. To overcome this problem we present an algorithm which generates additional rules which permit us to derive new facts by merging rules derived from the inversion of views. The algorithm receives in input a set of inverted views $\mathcal{V}^{-1}$ and adds to it a supplementary set of rules I.

Algorithm 2 *Merging rules.*
Input: *Set $\mathcal{V}^{-1}$ of inverted rules generated by Algorithm 1;*
Output: *Set $\mathcal{V}^{-1} \cup I$ of inverted rules;*
begin

$\quad I := \emptyset$

$\quad$ **for each** *pair of rules* $r_i = q(X) \leftarrow ...., p(U), ...,$ $r_j = q(Y) \leftarrow ...., \neg p(V), ...$ *in* $\mathcal{V}^{-1}$ **do**

$\quad\quad\quad$ **if** $\exists$ *unifier* θ *such that* $X\theta = Y\theta$ *and* $U\theta = V\theta$ **then**
$\quad\quad\quad\quad$ *add to I* $q(X\theta) \leftarrow (B(r_i) - \{p(U)\})\theta, (B(r_j) - \{\neg p(V)\})\theta, DOM_f(X\theta)$
end.

Observe that in the above algorithm $B(r_i) - \{p(U)\}$ denotes the conjunction of literals in the body of the rule r_i after deletion of the literal $p(U)$. Observe also that, generally, the number of rules generated is combinatorial in the cardinality of the bodies. However, the algorithm generates new rules only when a pair of rules in $\mathcal{V}^{-1}$ admitting a unifier for the heads and for a pair of complementary literals in the bodies is detected. Moreover, since in practical cases, there are only few rules which satisfy these conditions, the number of rules produced is small.

6   Functional Dependencies

Additional information can be derived from information sources by using functional dependencies (FDs). This was first observed by Duschka [6] which proposed an algorithm to infer from functional dependencies conditions on the equality of terms appearing in the rewritten rules. In this section we propose an extension which permit us to infer from functional dependencies also conditions on the inequality of terms. We present first an example to motivate the need for using inequality conditions and next introduce our algorithm.

Example 3. Assume to have two base relations employee(E#, P#) *and* project(P#, S#, D#) *where a fact* employee(e, p) *means that employee e works on the project p and a fact* project(p, s, d) *means that the project p belongs to the sector s and is developed in the department d. Assume also to have the functional dependencies* E# $\rightarrow$ P# *on the relation* employee *and* P# $\rightarrow$ S#D# *on the relation* project. *Consider now the following two views*

> sector(E, S) $\leftarrow$ employee(E, P), project(P, S, D).
> department(E, D) $\leftarrow$ employee(E, P), project(P, S, D).

and the query

> q(E1, E2) $\leftarrow$ employee(E1, P1), project(P1, S, D1),
>   employee(E2, P2), project(P2, S, D2), P1 $\neq$ P2.

computing the pairs of employees working on different projects belonging to the same sector. The above query can be rewritten as

> q(E1, E2) $\leftarrow$ department(E1, D1), department(E1, D2), D1 $\neq$ D2
>   sector(E1, S), sector(E2, S).   □

We assume that the complete scheme for a base relation R is a pair $\langle R, FD_R \rangle$ where R denotes the relation scheme and FD_R denotes the set of functional dependencies on R. A functional dependency $X \rightarrow Y$ is said to be in *standard* form if Y is a singleton and is said to be in *canonical* form if both X and Y are singletons. In the following we assume that functional dependencies are in standard form since every set of FDs can be rewritten in this form.

We use a new predicate, called e, which extend the standard equality predicate =. Further, we use classical negation to define the predicate $\neg e$ which extends the standard inequality predicate $\neq$. Thus, in the rewriting we introduce new rules defining the predicates e and $\neg e$. In particular, we denote with EQ the set of rules

$$e(X, Y) \leftarrow e(X, Z), e(Z, Y)$$
$$e(X, Y) \leftarrow e(Y, X)$$
$$e(X, Y) \leftarrow X = Y, dom_c(X), dom_c(Y)$$

and with NEQ the set of rules

$$\neg e(X, Y) \leftarrow e(X, Z), \neg e(Z, Y)$$
$$\neg e(X, Y) \leftarrow \neg e(X, Z), e(Z, Y)$$
$$\neg e(X, Y) \leftarrow \neg e(Y, X)$$
$$\neg e(X, Y) \leftarrow X \neq Y, dom_c(X), dom_c(Y)$$

where dom_c is used, as usual, to make safe the rules. Further, we introduce additional rules defining both e and $\neg e$ which are inferred from the functional dependencies. This set of rules is generated by the following algorithm.

Algorithm 3 *Extracting information from functional dependencies.*
Input: *Set of base relation S;*
Output: *Set of rules eq(S);*
begin

    $eq(S) := EQ \cup NEQ$

    for each $\langle R, FD_R \rangle \in S$ and for each $X \rightarrow Y \in FD_R$ Add to $eq(S)$ the rule
        $e(Y, Y') \leftarrow r(X, Y, Z), r(X', Y', Z'), E(X, X')$

    for each $\langle R, FD_R \rangle \in S$ and for each $X \rightarrow Y \in FD_R$ **do**
        for each $X_i \in X$ Add to $eq(S)$ the rule
            $\neg e(X_i, X_i') \leftarrow r(X, Y, Z), r(X', Y', Z'), \neg e(Y, Y'), E(X - X_i, X' - X_i')$

end.

In the above algorithm we have denoted i) with $E(X, Y)$, where both X and Y are lists of variables, say $X = (X_1, ..., X_k)$ and $Y = (Y_1, ..., Y_k)$, the conjunction $e(X_1, Y_1), ..., e(X_k, Y_k)$, and ii) with $X - X_i$ the list of variables derived from X by deleting the element X_i.

Since the rules generated by Algorithm 4 extend the definitions of the equality and inequality predicates, we have to replace in the source program and in the inverted views the standard predicates with the extended ones. However, before to replace the standard predicates we rewrite our rules to detect all equality conditions in the rule.

We now present how rules are rewritten. Given a Datalog rule r we denote with r' the rule derived from r by i) replacing every constant c and every variable X occurring more than once in the head or in the body of the rule with a new variable Z and by adding to the body of the rule, respectively, the atoms $e(c, Z)$ and $e(X, Z)$, and ii) replacing all atoms of the form $t_1 = t_2$ (resp. $t_1 \neq t_2$) with $e(t_1, t_2)$ (resp. $\neg e(t_1, t_2)$). The rewritten rule r' is also called the *rectified* version of r. Thus, given a program P, the *rectified* version P' consists of the set of rectified rules r' for all rules r in P. Moreover, we denote with P^r the set of rules derived from P' after replacing of the symbol **not** with the symbol $\neg$, i.e. $P^r = (P')^-$ and with V^{-1r} the rectified version of V^{-1}. Moreover, given a program P, a set of views V and a database schema S we denote with $P^r_{V^{-1}e}$ the set of rules in $P^r_{V^{-1}} \cup eq(S)$ where $eq(S)$ is the set of rules generated by Algorithm 3.

The following result, where Datalog$^{\neq}$ denotes the language Datalog extended with the inequality predicate $\neq$, states that for a restricted set of functional dependencies our technique is optimal.

Theorem 4. *Let $\mathcal{P}$ be a positive Datalog$^{\neq}$ program, let S be a set of relations with canonical functional dependencies FD, and let $\mathcal{V}$ be be a set of conjunctive views. Then, $P^r_{\mathcal{V}^{-1}_e}$ is maximally contained in $\mathcal{P}$.* □

7 Conclusions

In this paper we have considered the problem of answering queries using materialized views. We have extended previous work by also considering negation in both programs and views and we have also considered disjunctive views. Further, we have extended previous techniques for inferring knowledge from views based on relations with functional dependencies.

Future work will be devoted to the identification of more general classes of programs and views. We are currently working on the definition of an algorithm which permits us to extract positive and negative information also from recursive views.

References

1. Abiteboul S., Hull R., and V. Vianu, *Foundations of Databases*, Addison-Wesley, 1994.
2. Abiteboul S., Duschka O., *Proc. PODS Symp.*, 1998.
3. Chaudhuri S., R. Krishnamurty, S. Potamianos, and K. Shim, Optimizing queries with materialized views. *Proc. ICDE Conf.*, 1995, pp. 190-200.
4. Chekuri C., and A. Rajaraman, Conjunctive Query Containment Revisited. *Proc. ICDT Conf.*, 1997, pp. 56-70.
5. Duschka O. M., and M. R. Genesereth, Answering Recursive Queries Using Views. *Proc. PODS Symp.*, 1997, pp. 109-116.
6. Duschka O. M., Query Planning and Optimization in Information Integration. *PhD dissertation*, 1997.
7. Eiter T., G. Gottlob, and H. Mannila, Adding Disjunction to Datalog, *Proc. PODS Symp.*, 1993, pp. 267-278.
8. Gelfond M., and V. Lifschitz, Logic Programming with Classical Negation. *Proc. ICLP Conf.*, 1991, pp. 580-597.
9. Greco S., and D. Sacca', Negative Logic Programming. *Proc. NACLP Conf.*, 1991.
10. Kowalsky R., and F. Sadri, Logic Programming with Exceptions. *Proc. ICLP Conf.*, 1991, pp. 598-613.
11. Levy A., A. Mendelzon, Y. Sagiv, and D. Srivastava, Answering Queries Using views. *Proc. PODS Symp.*, 1995, pp. 95-104.
12. Levy A., A. Rajaraman, and J. Ullman, Answering Queries Using limited external processors. *Proc. PODS Symp.*, 1996.
13. J. Lloyd, *Foundation of Logic Programming*, Second Edition, Spinger-Verlag, 1987.
14. Ramakrinshnan R., Y. Sagiv, J. Ullman, and M. Vardi, Proof-three transformations theorems and their applications. *Proc. PODS Symp.*, 1989, pp. 172-181.
15. Shmueli O., Decidability and expressiveness aspects of logic queries. *Proc. PODS Symp.*, 1987, pp. 237-249.
16. Qian X., Query folding. *Proc. ICDE*, 1996, pp. 48-55.
17. Ullman J.D., *Principles of Database and Knowledge Base Systems*, Computer Science Press, 1988.
18. Ullman J.D., Information integration using logical views. *Proc. ICDT Conf.*, 1997.

A Query Subsumption Technique

S. M. Deen and Mohammad Al-Qasem

DAKE Group, Department of Computer Science, University of Keele,
Keele, Staffs, ST5 5BG, UK.
e-mail: {deen, mohammad}@cs.keele.ac.uk

Abstract. *The paper examines query subsumptions in a relational context and develops a general subsumption technique for queries with function-free first-order predicates. The predicates are compacted (removing redundant terms) and then expressed as of a disjunction of conjunctions without negations, which is then transformed into a canonical form, along with the rest of the query. Queries in this form are then checked for both result and attribute subsumptions. In the process it highlights some of the logical pitfalls and discusses how they are taken into account in the proposed technique. A filter is then used to derive the new query from the old one.*

1 Introduction

In this paper we shall present a technique for query subsumption in a relational framework. Given two queries Q_i and Q_j, Q_i subsumes Q_j if A_j the answer to Q_j exists in A_i the answer to Q_i and that A_j is derivable from A_i at all time from all database states. In distributed applications, particularly in an interoperable environment the use of subsumption techniques is fruitful, not only in reducing communications overheads, but also in minimising query conversions.

The technique we have developed is quite general, comprehensive and easy to follow. As implied above we, check for both result and attribute subsumptions with a minimalist approach, that is if a check is unnecessary we do not carry it out.

The organisation of this paper is as follows: Related work is presented in this section, followed by an exposure to our COAL syntax and the examples to be used. The canonical form is introduced in section 2, followed by a technique on predicate subsumption in section 3. Subsumption between two queries, based on predicate subsumption, is discussed in section 4, followed by some concluding remarks in section 5.

1.1 Related work

The subsumption (containment) problem that the answer of one query contains the answer of another query has been studied by many researchers. Ullman [14] has produced the QinP (Query in Program) algorithm to determine the containment between a conjunctive query and a datalog program. Chan [4] has proposed an algorithm that handles negation in conjunctive queries in the context of restricted object based data and query models. Chan's algorithm focuses on the subsumption between terms, classes and objects. But Staudt and Thadden [13] have proposed an algorithm that covers the negation and the exploitation of semantic knowledge in conjunctive queries.

Hariuarayon and Gupta [10] have proposed an algorithm for deciding efficiently when a tuple subsumes another tuple for queries that use arbitrary mathematical functions. The optimisation of tuple subsumption helps to avoid accessing and checking remote relations. The TSIMMIS project [12] and [3] uses subsumption to check the containment between a description D and a query Q. They have expressed a description D as a datalog program. In [12] they have extended Ullman's QinP algorithm to check if there is a filter query to the existing query in order to return the exact answer without any additional information. They use subsumption to compare a datalog with several query templates and then decide if any of these templates subsume the datalog program and if more than on templates do so, then the algorithm finds the actual maximal supporting templates.

Subsumption also has been used in Boolean queries in digital libraries, but with a query language of very limited features. In Boolean queries a document consists of a set of fields, each representing a particular kind of information such as title, author and abstract [5] and [6].

1.3 Language facility

We use a language notation called COAL (Co-Operating Agent Language). COAL is currently under development in the DAKE Centre, as an extension of an earlier language DEAL which provided a relational facility, fortified with some Prolog like predicates. COAL extends DEAL with additional operations required for inter-agent interactions [8]. In COAL, predicates for every relation are written within square brackets [ ], using what are called link-elements (example elements in QBE). We present below a basic COAL syntax, give some examples and show their equivalence in SQL.

COAL Syntax
```
? [ A1, A2 ...]
 : R1 [tuple-predicates],
   R2 [tuple-predicates],
   Sys [predicates]
```

? implies Retrieve (equivalently Select of SQL), followed by output list which may include attributes and link-elements, and (:) implies the Where clause for what we call tuple-predicates. Commas (,) represents logical AND and vertical bar (|) as logical OR and (~) as NOT. Sys (for System) implies a general relation for all variables not in those defined relations. Thus a tuple-predicate may include attributes (including systems variables), link-elements and values. The above query structure for unconditional retrieval of, say Att_1 and Att_2 from relation R, will look like :

$$? [Att_1, Att_2,] : R[ ].$$

Example : The following relations will be used to illustrate examples in this paper :

pilot   : Pi (p-no, empl-no ,months, hours, flights, salary)
empl   : Em (empl-no, name, city, ...)
pilot-aircraft : Pa (p-no, aircraft-type, hours, flights, ...)
pilot-bonus   : Pb (p-no, bonus)

A Query in COAL	The same query in SQL
? [x1, x2, name]	SELECT Pi.p-no, empl-no, name
: Pi [p-no=x1, empl-no=x2, salary =x3],	FROM Pi, Em, Pa, Pb
Em [empl-no = x2],	WHERE Pi.p-no = Pa.p-no AND
Pa [p-no = x1],	Pi.p-no = Pb.p-no AND
Pb [p-no=x1, (bonus > x3 | x3 > 2000 |	Pi.empl-no = Em.empl-no AND
p-no > 130)]	(bonus > salary OR
	salary > 2000 OR Pb.p-no > 130)

2 The Canonical Form

In this section we classify predicates and explain the transformation rules for their conversion into the canonical form, and then present a description of what we call a canonical query-form.

2.1 Predicate Classification

We begin with the classification of predicates into three hierarchical groups: Atomic predicate (α), conjunction predicate (π), and disjunction predicate (σ). With β standing for any of the above predicates. The term attribute used below can be a system variable, as we treat Sys in a COAL query as a relation.

Atomic predicate (α): An atomic predicate (α) is a single binary predicate of the form $a\theta b$, where a is an attribute and b is another attribute or a value, connected by a comparison operator θ which can be any in the set $\{=, \neq, >, \geq, <, \leq \}$. An α can be of two types as implied by its superscript: (i) α^1 in which the right hand side is a value and (ii) α^2 in which the right hand side is an attribute. For the sake of completeness we shall define an α of a third type, namely α^0, which stands for an empty predicate (i.e. unconditional retrieval). Below an α without a superscript will stand for an α of type α^1 or α^2, except where indicated otherwise.

Conjunction predicate (π): A conjunction predicate (π) is a conjunction of atomic predicates (α's), e.g. a π of n elements: $\pi \equiv \{\alpha_1, \alpha_2, .., \alpha_n\}$. A π of one element reduces to an α. If a π has more than one α^0, they are reduced to a single α^0 and the α^0 is dropped altogether if the π has an α other than α^0.

Disjunction predicate (σ): A disjunction predicate (σ) contains a disjunction of conjunction predicates π's. Thus σ of m elements: $\sigma \equiv \{ \pi_1 \mid \pi_2 \mid .. \mid \pi_m \}$. Again σ of one element is a π, which in turn can be an α. If a π is an α^0, then this σ will reduces to α^0, dropping the other πs if any.

Thus the predicates in a query become a single disjunction predicate σ. Any predicate expressed in the above form will be referred to below as a canonical predicate. From the above classification, it is obvious that α is the basic building block in any predicate. We require the following functions for α :

$T(\alpha)$: returns the type of the α which can be 1 or 2.

$VL(\alpha)$: returns the variable on the left hand side of the α.

$VR(\alpha^2)$: returns the variable on the right hand side of the α^2.

$\theta(\alpha)$: returns the operator of the α.

$V(\alpha^1)$: returns the value on the right hand side of the α^1 .

In addition we need a Boolean function to examine if two α's are literally identical: $I(\alpha_1, \alpha_2)$. This function returns true if both α's (α_1 and α_2) are literally identical and returns false otherwise. Examples are: $\alpha \equiv$ (flights > hours) $\Rightarrow T(\alpha)=2$. $\alpha \equiv$ (flights > hours) $\Rightarrow VL(\alpha)=$flights. $\alpha \equiv$ (flights > hours) $\Rightarrow \theta(\alpha)=">"$. $\alpha_1 \equiv$ (flights > hours) and $\alpha_2 \equiv$ (flights $\geq$ hours) $\Rightarrow I(\alpha_1, \alpha_2)=$False.

2.2 Predicate Transformation

Since the same query can be written in many different form, we need to express our COAL queries in a canonical form so that they can be compared for containment more easily. To achieve this, several transformation rules are needed to be applied to the predicates of the query as discussed in [1]. The effect of these rules are :

(i) In the case of equivalent attribute, e.g. "x=y", x is the lower attribute in alphanumeric order. Therefore x will replace y everywhere except in that equality "x=y". Thus we create sets to include equivalent attribute, called $E(Att_1,Q)$ where Att_1 is the lowest attribute in the set.

(ii) Change each α to ensure that lower attribute is in the left hand side, e.g. change (y>x) to (x<y).

(iii) Remove the negation, using. De Morgan rules.

(iv) Compact predicates, e.g. (a$\geq$b | a>b | ..) becomes (a$\geq$b | ...).

(v) Remove the redundant predicates. e.g. (a>10, a>40,..) becomes (a>40,..), (a$\geq$b | a>b | ..) becomes (a$\geq$b | ...).

(vi) Transform the predicates to the disjunctive normal form and then apply rules (iv and v) again.

2.3 Query transformation

In this phase we transform the query into three lists: (i) relations in the query, (ii) the output attributes and (iii) the canonical predicate, which together constitute the canonical form of the query:

(i). $Rel(Q)$ - all relations used by Q : $Rel(Q) = \{ R_1, R_2, ..,R_n\}$

(ii). $Att(Q)$ - all attributes selected by Q : $Att(Q) = \{ Att_1, Att_2, ..,Att_n \}$

(iii). $P(Q)$ - the disjunction predicate of Q : $P(Q) = \sigma = \{ \pi_1 | \pi_2 \, ... \, | \pi_m \}$

Example of the transformation from a query in COAL to its canonical form :
COAL query: Q ≡ ? [x1, x2, name]

> : Pi [p-no = x1, empl-no = x2, salary = x3, ~(300 ≥ months)],
> Em[empl-no = x2],
> Pa [p-no = x1],
> Pb [p-no = x1, (bonus > x3 | x3>2000 |x1>130)]

The same query in the canonical form:

$\mathcal{R}el$(Q) = { Pi, Em, Pa, Pb }
$\mathcal{A}tt$(Q) = {Pi.p-no, Pi.empl-no, Em.name}
$\mathcal{P}$(Q) = {$\pi_1 | \pi_2 | \pi_3$ }

Where: π_1 = ((Pi.months>300), (Em.empl-no = Pi.empl-no), (Pa.p-no = Pi.p-no) ,
        (Pa.p-no = Pb.p-no), (Pb.bonus > Pi.salary))

   π_2 = ((Pi.months>300) , (Em.empl-no = Pi.empl-no), (Pa.p-no = Pi.p-no) ,
        (Pa.p-no = Pb.p-no), (Pi.salary > 2000))

   π_3 = ((Pi.months>300) , (Em.empl-no = Pi.empl-no), (Pa.p-no = Pi.p-no) ,
        (Pa.p-no = Pb.p-no) , (Pi.p-no > 130))

$\mathcal{E}$(Pa.p-no, Q) = {Pa.p-no, Pb.p-no, Pi.p-no}
$\mathcal{E}$(Em.empl-no, Q) = {Em.empl-no, Pi.empl-no}

In the remainder of the paper all queries will be assumed to be in the canonical form.

3 Subsumption (Containment) between Predicates

As indicated earlier query subsumption has two components; result subsumption, and parameter subsumption. Given two queries Q_i and Q_j with answers in A_i and A_j respectively, if A_i includes A_j then A_i subsumes the result in A_j. However, we may not necessarily be able to derive A_j from A_i as shown in the following example:

Q_i ≡? [empl-no] : Pi [flight > 10, salary > 1000]
Q_j ≡ ? [empl-no] : Pi [flight > 10, salary > 2000]

In the above example the answer A_i will include the answer A_j, but we cannot obtain A_j from A_i, since we cannot find out from A_i the empl-no with salary>2000. Hence Q_i does not subsume Q_j.

However if we also had parameter subsumption, that is if the attribute salary (which is a parameter for restriction) was included in the Select part, then we could have extracted A_j from A_i, and in that case Q_i would have subsumed Q_j. Observe we do not need the parameter flight to be subsumed (in the Select part) since the predicate there is identical in both Qi and Qj. This implies that some parameters do not require subsumption.

In examining subsumption between two queries we need first to check the containment between their predicates. Given a predicate of type β, we define β containment as follows: Predicate β_1 contains predicate β_2 if β_1 is more general than β_2, that is, β_1 subsumes β_2. If both β_1 and β_2 are defined over the attributes of R1, R2 and R3, and if β_1 contains β_2, then all tuples that satisfy β_2 will also satisfy β_1

regardless the values of the tuples. Because of the hierarchy of predicates, we need to check only the predicates of the same type: α containment, π containment, and σ containment.

We use three Boolean functions contain-k (β_1 and β_2) with k=1 for α, k=2 for π and k=3 for σ; each function having two arguments as inputs and returning true if β_1 contains β_2, false otherwise. However, we shall delay the check for parameter subsumption until we consider the σ containment in section 3.3.

3.1 Contain1(α_1, α_2)

Both α_1 and α_2 must of the same type and they must deal with the same attribute(s). For convenience we divide this function into two further parts: Contain1a to check α^1 and Contain1b to check α^2. The containment between two α's of different types returns false.

$$
\begin{aligned}
&\text{Contain1}(\alpha_1, \alpha_2) \Leftrightarrow \\
&\quad T(\alpha_1) = T(\alpha_2) \\
&\qquad \wedge (\, (\, T(\alpha_1) = 1 \wedge \text{Contain1a}(\alpha_1, \alpha_2)\,) \vee (\, T(\alpha_1) = 2 \wedge \text{Contain1b}(\alpha_1, \alpha_2)\,)
\end{aligned}
$$

Contain1a(α_1, α_2): This function first checks that both α_1 and α_2 are of type α^1 (i.e. $T(\alpha_1)=T(\alpha_2)=1$), and the left hand side in both αs has the same attribute. The containment in this case is dependent on the comparison operator θ and the value. The algorithm for the Contain1a can be expressed as:

$$
\begin{aligned}
&\text{Contain1a } (\alpha_1, \alpha_2) \Leftrightarrow \\
&VL(\alpha_1) = VL(\alpha_2) \qquad\quad \{\alpha_1 \,\&\, \alpha_2 \text{ deals with the same attribute}\} \\
&\wedge \quad I(\alpha_1, \alpha_2) \qquad\qquad \{\alpha_1 \,\&\, \alpha_2 \text{ are identical}\} \\
&\quad \vee (\theta(\alpha_1) = "\neq" \\
&\qquad \wedge (\, (\, (\theta(\alpha_2) = "=" \wedge V(\alpha_2) <> V(\alpha_1)) \vee (\theta(\alpha_2) = ">" \wedge V(\alpha_2) \geq V(\alpha_1)) \vee \\
&\qquad\qquad (\theta(\alpha_2) = "\geq" \wedge V(\alpha_2) > V(\alpha_1)) \vee (\theta(\alpha_2) = "<" \wedge V(\alpha_2) \leq V(\alpha_1)) \vee \\
&\qquad\qquad (\theta(\alpha_2) = "\leq" \wedge V(\alpha_2) < V(\alpha_1))) \\
&\quad \vee (\theta(\alpha_1) = ">" \wedge V(\alpha_2) > V(\alpha_1) \wedge (\theta(\alpha_2)="=" \vee \theta(\alpha_2)=">" \vee \theta(\alpha_2)="\geq")) \\
&\quad \vee (\theta(\alpha_1) = "\geq" \wedge V(\alpha_2) \geq V(\alpha_1) \wedge (\theta(\alpha_2) ="=" \vee \theta(\alpha_2)=">" \vee \theta(\alpha_2)= "\geq")) \\
&\quad \vee (\theta(\alpha_1) = "<" \wedge V(\alpha_2) < V(\alpha_1) \wedge (\theta(\alpha_2)="=" \vee \theta(\alpha_2)="<" \vee \theta(\alpha_2)="\leq")) \\
&\quad \vee (\theta(\alpha_1) = "\leq" \wedge V(\alpha_2) \leq V(\alpha_1) \wedge (\theta(\alpha_2)="=" \vee \theta(\alpha_2)="<" \vee \theta(\alpha_2)="\leq"))
\end{aligned}
$$

Examples :
$\alpha_1 \equiv$ (hours > 10), $\alpha_2 \equiv$ (hours > 3), Contain1a(α_1, α_2) is false.
$\alpha_1 \equiv$ (hours > 10), $\alpha_2 \equiv$ (hours > 20), Contain1a(α_1, α_2) is true.

Contain1b(α_1, α_2): This is a subset of Contain1a(α_1, α_2), where $VR(\alpha_1) = VR(\alpha_2)$. For more details see [1].
Examples :
$\alpha_1 \equiv$ (flights $\leq$ hours), $\alpha_2 \equiv$ (flights > hours), Contain1b(α_1, α_2) is false.
$\alpha_1 \equiv$ (flights $\leq$ hours), $\alpha_2 \equiv$ (flights < hours), Contain1b(α_1, α_2) is true.

3.2 Check the Containment Between Two π's. Contain2(π_i, π_j)

In order for π_i to contain π_j, every atomic predicate (α) in π_i must contain at least one atomic predicate (α) in π_j, so we need to check that each α_i in π_i contains at least one α_j in π_j. Observe that π_j can include more α's than in π_i. At this point, recall that we replaced attributes in the predicates by their lowest equivalents (section 2.2), but the lowest attribute in β_i may not be the same in β_j. Consider the following example:

Q_i : a$\geq$b, b=c, b=n, b>t , Q_j : a=b, a=c, a=n, f=t, a>f

E(a, Q_j) = {b, c, n}, E(f, Q_j) = { t }

From the above example we can not compare (b>t) with (a>f) while they are identical. Therefore we need to consult our lists E(Att$_1$,Q_j), E(Att$_2$,Q_j) where Att$_1$ and Att$_2$ are the attributes of α_j. So we get a list ($Same(\alpha_j, Q_j)$) of all possible of α_j from E(Att$_2$,Q_j), with the lower attribute in the left hand side. From the above example:

$Same((a>f),Q_j))$ = {a>f, b>f, c>f, f<n, a>t, b>t, c>t, n>t}

From the above example we can see b>t appear in the list. So in our algorithm we compare with any α equivalent to α_{j1} from the list $Same(\alpha_{j1}, Q)$.

> Contain2(π_i, π_j) $\Leftrightarrow$
> $\forall \alpha_{i1}$ ($\alpha_{i1} \in \pi_i$)
> $\Rightarrow \exists \alpha_{j1}, \alpha_{j2}$ ($\alpha_{j1} \in \pi_j$) $\wedge$ ($\alpha_{j2} \in Same(\alpha_{j1},Q_j)$) $\wedge$Contain1(α_{i1}, α_{j2})

Examples :

$\pi_1 \equiv$ {flights>20, hours>40}, $\pi_2 \equiv$ {flights>30, hours>40}, Contain2(π_1, π_2) is false.

$\pi_1 \equiv$ {flights>20, hours>40}, $\pi_2 \equiv$ {flights>30, hours>60}, Contain2(π_1, π_2) is true.

3.3 Check the Containment Between Two σ's : Contain3(σ_i, σ_j)

In order for σ_i to contain σ_j, each conjunctive predicate (π) in σ_j must be contained in at least one conjunctive predicate (π) in σ_i. Thus σ_i can have more πs than in σ_j. Therefore, we check that all the π 's in σ_j is contained in at least one π in σ_i. As this is the highest predicate, we shall check for parameter containment here. Therefore, we shall define a function (Att-exist (α_{j1},Q_i)) to check if the attributes (i.e. parameters) of α_{j1} exist in the select part of the query Q_i. This function returns true if all variables in α_{j1} exist in $Att(Q_i)$, and returns false otherwise. However if an α is common to each π in a σ, then the parameters in that α will not require subsumption. Consider the following simple example with predicate σ_i of Q_i and predicate σ_j of Q_j with answers A_i and A_j respectively:

$\sigma_i \equiv$ ((a>b, c=10) | (a>b, d$\leq$e)| (a> b, c$\geq$10, f=g) | (a>b, h>t))

$\sigma_j \equiv$ ((a>b, c=10) | (a>b, d=e)| (a> b, c=15, f=g))

In above (a>b) appears in every π in σ_i and in every π in σ_j, and therefore we do not need parameters a and b in A_i to derive A_j from A_i and hence a and b need not be present in A_i (i.e. in $Att(Q_i)$). Observe that the 4th π in σ_i, that is (a>b, h>t) is not needed for σ_j, but nevertheless, it must also have the predicate (a>b) if a and b do not exist in $Att(Q_i)$. All other parameters have to be present in $Att(Q_i)$. For instance if

c, f or g are absent in A_i, we will not be able extract the tuples with $c=10$ or $f=g$ from it. We can now define the function Att-exists and Contain3 as:

$$
\begin{aligned}
&\text{Att-exist}(\alpha_{j1}, Q_i) \Leftrightarrow \\
&\quad T(\alpha_{j1}) = 1 \wedge (\text{VL}(\alpha_{j1}) \in \mathcal{A}tt(Q_i)) \\
&\quad \vee\, T(\alpha_{j1}) = 2 \wedge (\text{VL}(\alpha_{j1}) \in \mathcal{A}tt(Q_i)) \wedge (\text{VR}(\alpha_{j1}) \in \mathcal{A}tt(Q_i))
\end{aligned}
$$

$$
\begin{aligned}
&\text{Contain3}(\sigma_i, \sigma_j) \Leftrightarrow \\
&\quad \forall\, \pi_{j1}\ (\pi_{j1} \subseteq \sigma_j) \\
&\qquad \Rightarrow\ \exists\, \pi_{i1}\ (\pi_{i1} \subseteq \sigma_i) \wedge \text{Contain2}(\pi_{i1}, \pi_{j1}) \\
&\qquad \wedge\, \forall\, \alpha_{j1}\ (\alpha_{j1} \in \pi_{j1}) \\
&\qquad\qquad \Rightarrow (\forall\, \pi_{j2}\ (\pi_{j2} \subseteq \sigma_j) \quad \Rightarrow \exists\, \alpha_{j2}\ (\alpha_{j2} \in \pi_{j2}) \wedge I(\alpha_{j1}, \alpha_{j2}) \\
&\qquad\qquad\qquad \wedge\, \forall\, \pi_{i2}\quad (\pi_{i2} \subseteq \sigma_i) \Rightarrow \exists\, \alpha_{i2}\ (\alpha_{i2} \in \pi_{i2}) \wedge I(\alpha_{j1}, \alpha_{i2})) \\
&\qquad\qquad \vee\, \text{Att-exist}(\alpha_{j1}, Q_i)
\end{aligned}
$$

Examples :

$\sigma_1 \equiv \{\text{flights} \leq \text{hours} \mid \text{hours} = 3 \mid \text{hours} > 20 \mid \text{flights} > 8\}$, $\sigma_j \equiv \{\text{flights} = \text{hours} \mid$ hours $= 5 \mid$ hours $> 30\}$, $\Rightarrow$ Contain3(σ_1, σ_2) is false.
$\sigma_1 \equiv \{\text{flights} \leq \text{hours} \mid \text{hours} = 3 \mid \text{hours} > 20 \mid \text{flights} > 8\}$, $\sigma_j \equiv \{\text{flights} = \text{hours} \mid$ hours $> 30 \}$, $\Rightarrow$ Contain3(σ_1, σ_2) is true.

4 Check Subsumption Between Two Queries

The predicate subsumption techniques developed above can now be applied to establish query subsumption between two queries Q_i and Q_j, and to build a filter to derive A_j from A_i. We present below algorithms for query subsumption and an associated filter.

4.1 Subsumption algorithm

For a query Q_i to subsume Q_j the following statements must hold : All attributes selected by Q_j ($\mathcal{A}tt(Q_j)$) must be in A_i of Q_i ($\mathcal{A}tt(Q_i)$), relations used by both queries ($\mathcal{R}el(Q_i)$ and $\mathcal{R}el(Q_j)$) must be the same, and predicate Q_i must contain the predicate of Q_j, including parameter subsumption in A_i. We can now write the algorithm for query subsumption as:

$$
\begin{aligned}
&\textbf{Subsume}(\mathbf{Q_i}, \mathbf{Q_j}) \Rightarrow \\
&\quad (\mathcal{A}tt(Q_i) \subseteq \mathcal{A}tt(Q_j)) \wedge (\mathcal{R}el(Q_i) = \mathcal{R}el(Q_j)) \wedge \text{Contain3}(\mathcal{P}(Q_i), \mathcal{P}(Q_j))
\end{aligned}
$$

4.2 Building the filter query

To derive A_j from A_i we need to build a filter predicate (Filter(Q_j)), which is constructed from the disjunction predicate $\mathcal{P}(Q_j)$ without the common αs, if any, in the π's of σ_i and σ_j, discussed earlier. The filter algorithm has the following steps :
1. Set filter$(Q_j) = \mathcal{P}(Q_j)$ to start with.
2. Check for all α's in one π, if any of these αs appears in all π's of Q_j and in all π's of Q_i then remove it from all π's of filter(Q_j).
3. Write up the filter query.

$$\text{Filter }(Q_j) = \mathcal{P}(Q_j)$$

For $\pi_f \subseteq$ Filter (Q_j)

$\forall\ \alpha_f\ \ (\alpha_f \in \pi_f)$

if $\forall\ \pi_i\ (\pi_i \subseteq \mathcal{P}(Q_i)) \Rightarrow \exists\ \alpha_i\ (\alpha_i \in \pi_i) \land\ I(\alpha_f, \alpha_i)$

$\land$

$\forall\ \pi_j\ (\pi_j \subseteq \mathcal{P}(Q_j)) \Rightarrow \exists\ \alpha_j\ (\alpha_j \in \pi_j) \land\ I(\alpha_f, \alpha_j)$

$\Rightarrow \forall\ \pi_f\ (\pi_f \subseteq \text{Filter}(Q_j))\ \pi_f = \pi_f - \{\alpha_f\}$

The filter query is : $A_j \equiv$? $[\text{Att}(Q_j)]$
                                            : $A_i\ [\text{Filter}(Q_i)]$

4.3 Examples

In this section we shall give a detailed example to demonstrate our subsumption and filer techniques are applied on queries.

$Q_i \equiv$? [x1, name, salary]
    : Pi   [empl-no = x1, salary > 3000],
    Em   [empl-no = x1]
$\mathcal{R}el(Q_i) = \{$Pi, Em$\}$
$\mathcal{A}tt\ (Q_i) = \{$Pi.empl-no, Em.name, Pi.salary$\}$
$\mathcal{P}(Q_i) = \{$(Em.empl-no=Pi.empl-no, Pi.salary>3000)$\}$

$Q_j \equiv$? [name, salary]
    : Pi   [empl-no = x2, salary > 5000],
    Em   [empl-no = x2]
$\mathcal{R}el(Q_j) = \{$Pi, Em$\}$
$\mathcal{A}tt\ (Q_j) = \{$Em.name, Pi.salary$\}$
$\mathcal{P}(Q_j) = \{$(Em.empl-no=Pi.empl-no, Pi.salary>5000)$\}$

Q_i subsumes Q_j , the filter is: Filter(Q_j) = {(salary > 5000)}
The filter query is : $A_j \equiv$? [name, salary] : A_i [salary > 5000]

If the atomic predicate (salary>5000) in Q_j is changed to (salary>3000) (which is the corresponding predicate in Q_i), then the filter query will reduce to :
        $A_j \equiv$? [name, salary] : A_i [ ]

If the attribute salary is absent in the Select clause of Q_i then Q_i does not subsume Q_j, since A_j is not derivable from A_i without that attribute.

5 Conclusion and Further Work

In this paper we have presented a technique for checking subsumption between two queries and to derive the second query from the first. Although we start from our COAL syntax with tuple-predicates and link-elements, the general algorithm is based on a canonical form of a function-free first-order predicates, and as such it can be generally applied to all relational queries without functions. It can be extended (although we have not considered it here) to partial queries where all the relations used in the second query may not be present in the first query.

We are currently implementing this algorithm for our multi-agent approach to handle interoperability in legacy systems. We intend to extend it to include aggregation functions.

References

1. Al-Qasem, M. and S. Deen. "Query Subsumption" In *Proceedings of the third International Conference of Flexible Query Answering Systems (FQAS'98)*, T. Andreasen et al. (eds), Roskilde University, Denmark, May 1998; Springer, 1998.
2. Beneventano, D. et al, "Using Subsumption in Semantic Query Optimization". IJCAI Workshop on Object-Based Representation System, Chambery , France, August 1993
3. Bergamaschi, S., "Extraction of Informations from Highly Heterogeneous Sources of Textual Data". Proceeding of the First International Workshop of Cooperative Information Agents(CIA'97), Kiel, Germany, February 1997.
4. Chan, Em., "Containment and Minimization of Positive Conjunctive Queries in OODB's". In Proceeding of 11th ACM SIGACT-SIGMOD-SIGART Symposium on Principle of Database Systems. PP 202-211, 1992.
5. Chang, K. et al, "Predicate Rewriting for Translation Boolean Query in a Heterogeneous Information System". available at http://www-db.stanfors.edu/pub/papers/pred_rewriting.ps.
6. Chang, K. et al, "Boolean Query Mapping Across Heterogeneous Information Sources". IEEE Transaction on Knowledge and Data Engineering, Vol. 8, NO. 4, 1996.
7. Chu, W. and Q. Chen, "A Structure Approach for Cooperative Query Answering". IEEE Transaction on Knowledge and Data Engineering, Vol. 6, NO. 5, pp738-749, 1994.
8. Deen, S., "An Architectural Framework For CKBS Applications". IEEE Transaction on Knowledge and Data Engineering, Vol. 8, NO. 4, 1996.
9. Garcia-Molina, H. et al, "The TSIMMIS Approach to Mediation: Data Models and Languages". Journal Of Intelligent Information Systems 8, pp 117-132, 1997.
10. Harinarayan, V. and Ai. Gupta, "Optimization Using Tuple Subsumption". In Database Theory - ICDT'95, 5th International Conference Proceeding, edited by G. Gottlob and M. Vardi. Prague, Czech Republic, January 1995.
11. Mena, Em. et al, "OBSERVER : An Approach for Query Processing in Global Information Systems Based on Interoperation Across Pre-existing Ontologies". Proceedings of the First IFCIS International Conference on Cooperative Information Systems (CoopIS'96), Brusseles, Belgium, June 1996.
12. Papakonstantinou, Y. et al, "A Query Translation Schema for Rapid Implementation of Wrappers". available at : ftp://db.stanford.edu/pub/papakonstantinou/1995/querytran-extended.ps.
13. Staudt, M. and V. Thadden, "A Generic Subsumption Testing Toolkit for Knowledge Base Queries". In 7th International Conference, DEXA'96, Proceeding, edited by R. Wagner and H. Thoma. Zurich, Switzerland, September 1996.
14. Ullman, J., "Principles of Database and Knowledge-Base Systems", Volume 2. Computer Science Press, 1989.

A Conference Key Multicasting Scheme Using Knapsack and Secret Sharing

Shiuh-Jeng Wang * and Jin-Fu Chang

*Department of Information Management
Central Police University
Taoyuan, Taiwan 333
E-mail: sjwang@sun4.cpu.edu.tw

Department of Electrical Engineering
National Taiwan University
Taipei, Taiwan 106

Abstract

In this paper, a conference key multicasting scheme is proposed and analyzed. Each network user U_i is associated with a key pair (x_i, y_i), where x_i is a secret key and y_i is a public key. A sealed lock is constructed from the public keys so that conference key can be enciphered by a chairperson and broadcasted to users in the network system, while only the authorized participants can recover the conference key. The packed sum property aspect of the well known knapsack problem together with the concept of secret sharing is utilized to accomplish the construction of a sealed lock.

I Introduction

With the progress in computer and communication (C&C), a large number of individuals now have personal computer. In order to share resource and to exchange information, these personal computers can be networked together. In network applications, the transmitted messages have the potential of being eavesdropped, altered and even destroyed. Therefore it is necessary to incorporate cryptographic protection into the network. Computer networks of various scales have widely existed. In general, communication within a network can be classified into two types: point-to-point and point-to-multipoint. To achieve secrecy, a message has to be encrypted before sending to the communication channel. Ciphers can be categorized into conventional and public key systems. The concept of public key was first due to Diffie and Hellman [2]. In public key system, each user has two keys: a secret and a public key. To send a secret message, the sender uses the intended receiver's public key to encrypt and the

---

*Correspondence addressee: Dr. Shiuh-Jeng Wang, Department of Information Management, Central Police University, Taoyuan, Taiwan 333

receiver uses his private key to decrypt. In this arrangement a total of $2n$ keys is needed if n denotes the total number of users in the network. In conventional key system, however, a total of $n(n-1)/2$ keys is required. To further strengthen security, when two users wish to communicate with each other, a session key is first created and exchanged. Different session keys are used in different sessions to encrypt and decrypt messages. These session keys can be constructed from the public key system we mentioned in the above.

There are frequent applications where a user wishes to communicate with several other users. The style of point-to-point communication mentioned above would be obviously inefficient. Point-to-multipoint communication or multicasting has to be developed for fast and efficient delivery of a message to a group of recipients. Multicasting is somewhat different from broadcasting. The main feature of broadcasting is that a single transmission from an originating station can be heard simultaneously by, basically, all stations. The transmissions in radio links and local area network bus are both of this nature. In applications such as multicasting only a limited number of users are legitimate to receive a broadcast message. This aim can be achieved through encryption.

In this paper, we develop a new conference key multicasting protocol jointly out of knapsack and secret sharing. In our scheme, we embed the conference key into many sealed keys, pack these sealed keys into the sealed lock and broadcast it to all the intended recipients in the network, while only legal intended recipients can recover the secret conference key. In section II, we review the related works and tell our motivation. In section III, a secure multicasting protocol is presented. Cryptanalysis is done in Section IV. Finally, conclusions are given in Section V.

II Related Works

Secure broadcasting has received considerable attention from researchers [1],[4]-[5]. Ingemarsson et al. [4] proposed a conference key distribution system (CKDS for short) which generalizes the public key distribution system (PKDS for short) to a secure multi-destination communication. The network consists of a group of n users connected into a ring. Each user has to process and send message received from upstream. This undoubtedly increases the threat of acquiring the common conference key by an eavesdropper who may try to intercept the message at each station along the ring. Chiou and Chen [1] proposed a broadcasting scheme in which session keys are packed into a sealed lock using the Chinese remainder theorem (CRT for short). The space requirement in [1] however is formidable. Later, Lin et al. [5] proposed a secret conference key algorithm to reconstruct the sealed lock. Although in comparison with [1] the space requirement in this scheme is reduced, the way that the sealed lock constructed is impractical for a multicasting application.

The well known $0-1$ knapsack problem [6],[7]-[8] examines a sequence v_1, v_2, ..., v_n of integers and a target sum S. It is to find whether a subset of v_1, v_2, ... v_n sums up to S. That is, given a sequence set $V = \{v_1, v_2, \ldots v_n\}$, and

S, find a set $A = \{a_1, a_2, \ldots, a_n\}$ of 0s and 1s such that $\sum_{i=1}^{n} a_i v_i = S$. It is the feature of packing integers up to a specified number, that inspires us to exploit the conference key multicasting scheme.

In 1976, Diffie and Hellman [2] proposed a PKDS which allows each user to place his encryption key in a public file while keeping the decryption key secret. In their basic PKDS, a large prime number p such that $p - 1$ has at least one large prime factor and a generator g of $Z_p - \{0\}$, both public, are used. Consider two users, say U_1 and U_2. Suppose U_1 has a secret key x_1 and U_2 has a secret key x_2. U_1 computes $y_1 = g^{x_1} \bmod p$, and registers it into the public file. U_2 does the same by computing $y_2 = g^{x_2} \bmod p$. U_1 and U_2 base on the following common key K_{12} to communicate

$$
\begin{aligned}
K_{12} &= y_1^{x_2} \bmod p \\
&= y_2^{x_1} \bmod p \\
&= g^{x_1 x_2} \bmod p.
\end{aligned}
\tag{1}
$$

In other words, both U_1 and U_2 are able to compute K_{12} easily only employing the opponent's public key and his own secret key. Although it has not yet been proven that breaking the system is equivalent to computing the discrete logarithm problem, an intruder trying to compute K_{12} appears to be difficult [2].

III Our Protocols

In the network, we assume that users can directly communicate with each other. Consider a network system consisting of $n + 1$ users denoted by $G = \{U_0, U_1, \ldots, U_n\}$ and each U_i has a unique identity number in the range 1 to $n+1$. In our scheme, suppose that a chairperson (or an originator), say, U_0 in G desires to build a secure conference with G', a set of $G' = \{U_{i_1}, U_{i_2}, \ldots, U_{i_k}\}, k \leq n$. Using our proposed mechanism, U_0 generates a common conference key K_c to let only the authorized participant use it. After the conference is set up, they can exchange messages encrypted by K_c to each other. The conference key K_c is embedded into the sealed keys of the authorized participants which are then packed into a sealed lock. U_0 then broadcasts sealed lock to all the other network users, i.e. $G - U_0$. Only the authorized participants in G' can decipher through his own secret key.

In this paper, let p be a large prime number such that $p - 1$ has at least one large prime factor and g be a generator of $Z_p - \{0\}$, both public. Suppose that each U_i in G has a secret key x_i and a public key $y_i = g^{x_i} \bmod p$ for $i = 0, 1, \ldots, n$. The following protocols are designed for U_0 to follow.

Protocol 1: This protocol constructs a sealed lock.

Step 1. Choose a conference key K_c and a random number r such that $gcd(r, p-1) = 1$ and compute a random key $RK^{(1)} = g^r \bmod p$.

Step 2. Find a number s to satisfy

$$T \oplus K_c = (x_0 \times RK^{(1)} + r \times s) \bmod p - 1, \tag{2}$$

where T is the current time and "$\oplus$" denotes the binary exclusive-or operation. The timestamp is used to at least prevent replay and the pair $(RK^{(1)}, s)$ is treated as signature of K_c.

Step 3. Obtain the sealed key

$$S_i = K_c \times y_i^r \bmod p, \tag{3}$$

for U_i in G'.

Step 4. Choose a random number α and compute a random key $RK^{(2)} = y_0^\alpha \bmod p$ and compute the point-pairs $(y_{i_j}^{(1)}, y_{i_j}^{(2)}), j = 1, 2, \ldots, k$ by

$$
\begin{aligned}
y_{i_j}^{(1)} &= (y_{i_j})^r \bmod p \text{ and} \\
y_{i_j}^{(2)} &= (y_{i_j}^{x_0})^\alpha \bmod p,
\end{aligned} \tag{4}
$$

where r is the random number chosen in step 1.

Step 5. Create an interpolating polynomial $f(\beta)$ of degree $k - 1$ over $GF(p)$

$$f(\beta) = w_{k-1}\beta^{k-1} + w_{k-2}\beta^{k-2} + \cdots + w_0 \bmod p \tag{5}$$

which passes through the point-pairs $(y_{i_j}^{(1)}, y_{i_j}^{(2)})$ of the k authorized participants $U_{i_j}, j = 1, 2, \ldots, k$. (Here, we require that all of coefficients of $f(\beta)$ be nozero, otherwise go to step 1 and restart).

2). Select $k - 1$ other point-pairs $(\beta_j, \gamma_j), 1 \leq j \leq k - 1$, on the curve of polynomial $f(\beta)$.

Step 6. Choose an initial vector $V_1 = (v_{11}, v_{12}, \ldots, v_{1j}, \ldots, v_{1k})$, where $v_{1j} \in [1, n]$ is the identity of the jth intended recipient U_{i_j} in G' for $j = 1, 2, \ldots, k$. Next select a prime number θ_1 that satisfies the inequality

$$\theta_1 > \sum_{l=1}^{k} v_{1,l} \times \mu_k \tag{6}$$

where $\mu_k = \max\{S_{i_j}\}_{1 \leq j \leq k}$ and S_{i_j} is the sealed key of U_{i_j} in G'. Then generate V_j for $j = 2, 3, \ldots, k$ as follows.

1). Let

$$
\begin{aligned}
\hat{V}_j &= V_{j-1} \bullet w_{j-1} \bmod \theta_{j-1} \\
&= (\hat{v}_{j,1}, \hat{v}_{j,2}, \ldots, \hat{v}_{j,j-1}, \hat{v}_{j,j}, \hat{v}_{j,j+1}, \ldots, \hat{v}_{j,k}),
\end{aligned} \tag{7}
$$

where "$\bullet$" denotes a scalar multiplication between a vector and a scalar.

2). Use Gaussian elimination method, to transform the row vectors $V_1, V_2, \ldots, V_l, \ldots, V_{j-1}$ and $\hat{V}_j$ to vectors $E_1, E_2, \ldots, E_l, \ldots, E_{j-1}$, and

$\hat{E}_j$, where E_l, $1 \le l \le j - 1$, is a vector in which the first $(l - 1)$ elements are zero and the lth element is nonzero and $\hat{E}_j$ is a vector in which the first $(j - 1)$ elements are zero. If the jth element of $\hat{E}_j$ is zero, let

$$V_j = (\hat{v}_{j,1}, \hat{v}_{j,2}, \ldots, \hat{v}_{j,j-1}, \hat{v}_{j,j} + \theta_{j-1}, \hat{v}_{j,j+1}, \ldots, \hat{v}_{j,k}), \tag{8}$$

otherwise

$$V_j = (\hat{v}_{j,1}, \hat{v}_{j,2}, \ldots, \hat{v}_{j,j-1}, \hat{v}_{j,j}, \hat{v}_{j,j+1}, \ldots, \hat{v}_{j,k}). \tag{9}$$

Next, select a new prime number θ_j that satisfies

$$\theta_j > \sum_{l=1}^{k} v_{j,l} \times \mu_k \tag{10}$$

3). Return to 1) till the vector V_k is generated.
4). Construct a sealed lock Z_k by

$$Z_k = \sum_{l=1}^{k} v_{k,l} \times S_{i_l}. \tag{11}$$

Step 7: U_0 writes information such as $\{(RK^{(1)}, s), RK^{(2)}, V_k, \theta_j, (\beta_j, \gamma_j) | 1 \le j \le k - 1\}$, into the network database and broadcasts T, Z_k to G'.

$\square$

Once the above steps are accomplished, the authorized participants in the network can rapidly decompose the sealed lock Z_k using some of the public information generated in the above protocol. For an authorized participant U_i in G', deciphering can be done by the following protocol.

Protocol 2: This protocol enables U_i in G' to obtain a secret K_c sent from U_0.

Step 1. Check if the received time T^* is too much later than the T in (2). If the difference between T^* and T is less than a reasonable delay time then accept the broadcast message, otherwise reject.

Step 2. Compute the point-pair $(y_i^{(1)}, y_i^{(2)})$ by

$$y_i^{(1)} = (RK^{(1)})^{x_i} \bmod p \text{ and}$$
$$y_i^{(2)} = (RK^{(2)})^{x_i} \bmod p.$$

and then construct the interpolating polynomial $f(\beta) = w_{k-1}\beta^{k-1} + w_{k-2}\beta^{k-2} + \cdots + w_0$ of degree $k - 1$ over $GF(p)$ via the just generated point-pair $(y_i^{(1)}, y_i^{(2)})$ and the $k - 1$ known point-pairs (β_j, γ_j), $1 \le j \le k - 1$.

Step 3. Obtain V_j and Z_j recursively, $k - 1 \ge j \ge 1$, as follows.

1).

$$V_j = V_{j+1} \bullet w_j^{-1} \bmod \theta_j, \tag{12}$$

and

$$Z_j = Z_{j+1} \times w_j^{-1} \bmod \theta_j. \tag{13}$$

2). Obtain the seled key S_{i_j} of U_{i_j} according to the order of the entry v_{1j} in vector V_1.

$$\begin{pmatrix} S_{i_1} \\ S_{i_2} \\ \vdots \\ S_{i_j} \\ \vdots \\ S_{i_k} \end{pmatrix} = \begin{pmatrix} v_{11} & v_{12} & \cdots & v_{1j} & \cdots & v_{1k} \\ v_{21} & v_{22} & \cdots & v_{2j} & \cdots & v_{2k} \\ \vdots & \vdots & \ddots & \vdots & \ddots & \vdots \\ v_{j1} & v_{j2} & \cdots & v_{jj} & \cdots & v_{jk} \\ \vdots & \vdots & \ddots & \vdots & \ddots & \vdots \\ v_{k1} & v_{k2} & \cdots & v_{kj} & \cdots & v_{kk} \end{pmatrix}^{-1} \times \begin{pmatrix} Z_1 \\ Z_2 \\ \vdots \\ Z_j \\ \vdots \\ Z_k \end{pmatrix}. \tag{14}$$

Step 4. Obtain the conference key by

$$K_c = S_i \times ((RK^{(1)})^{x_i})^{-1} \bmod p. \tag{15}$$

Step 5. Check if the following equation is satisfied

$$(g)^{T \oplus K_c} = (y_0)^{RK^{(1)}} \times (RK^{(1)})^s \bmod p. \tag{16}$$

If the equation holds then it is guaranteed that K_c is sent from U_0 in this conference, otherwise the conference key is invalid.

$\square$

Lemma 1. The polynomial constructed in Protocol 2 by an authorized participant U_i in G' is the same as that constructed by U_0 in Prototol 1.

Proof. We describe the fact as follows. Consider a polynomial $f(\beta)$ of degree $k-1$ which is constructed by interpolating on k distinct coordinate points. If U_0 chooses other $k-1$ distinct coordinate points (β_j, γ_j), $j = 1, 2, \ldots, k-1$ from the loci of $f(\beta)$. U_i in G' interpolates on the $k-1$ coordinate points (β_j, γ_j)s with his own coordinate pair (a, b) to obtain a polynomial $\hat{f}(\beta)$. Examine the coordinate pair (a, b) used by U_i, we observe that

$$
\begin{aligned}
a &= (RK^{(1)})^{x_i} \bmod p \\
&= y_i^r \bmod p \\
&= y_i^{(1)} \quad \text{and}
\end{aligned}
$$

$$
\begin{aligned}
b &= (RK^{(2)})^{x_i} \bmod p \\
&= (y_0^\alpha)^{x_i} \bmod p \\
&= (y_0^{x_i})^\alpha \bmod p \\
&= (y_i^{x_0})^\alpha \bmod p \\
&= y_i^{(2)}.
\end{aligned}
$$

That is $(a, b) = (y_i^{(1)}, y_i^{(2)})$. Then $\hat{f}(\beta)$ is identical to $f(\beta)$.

Q.E.D.

Lemma 2. The k vectors $\{V_1, V_2, \ldots, V_k\}$ in Protocol 1 are linearly independent.

Proof. Let E_j be a k-dimensional row vector of which the first $(j-1)$ elements are zero and the jth element is nonzero and V_j be a k-dimensional row vector, for $1 \leq j \leq k$. Clearly, V_1 does satisfy the form of E_1. When the row vector $\hat{V}_j$ is generated from (7), the vectors $V_1, V_2, \ldots, V_{j-1}$, and $\hat{V}_j$ for $2 \leq j \leq k$, can be sequentially transformed into $E_1, E_2, \ldots, E_{j-1}$, and $\hat{E}_j$ such that the first $(j-1)$ elements of $\hat{E}_j$ are zero using Gaussian elimination method. Inspect the jth element of $\hat{E}_j$, if it is nonzero V_j can be directly detrmined from (9), otherwise V_j would have to be constructed from $\hat{V}_j$ using (8). Repeat this process, all the vectors V_j can thus be generated and transformed into E_j for $2 \leq j \leq k$.

Let matrix $V = \begin{pmatrix} V_1 \\ V_2 \\ \vdots \\ V_k \end{pmatrix}$. As constructed above, V can be transformed into a

matrix $E = \begin{pmatrix} E_1 \\ E_2 \\ \vdots \\ E_k \end{pmatrix}$. Clearly, the matrix E is an upper triangular matrix which

is nonsingular. Since E is transformed from V via Gaussian elimination, we conclude that V is also invertible. In other words, the row vectors $\{V_1, V_2, \ldots, V_k\}$ must be linearly independent.

Q.E.D.

Theorem 1. The sealed key can be correctly recovered in Protocol 2 if the recipient is legal.

Proof. We have proven in Lemma 1 that an authorized user U_{i_j} in G' can uniquely and correctly recover the polynomial $f(\beta) = w_{k-1}\beta^{k-1} + w_{k-2}\beta^{k-2} + \cdots + w_0$ of degree $k-1$. U_{i_j} can further collect numbers θ_j, $j = 1, 2, k-1$, vector V_k from the network database and the sealed lock Z_k. Then U_{i_j} computes

$$
\begin{aligned}
Z_k \times w_{k-1}^{-1} \bmod \theta_{k-1} &= \sum_{j=1}^{k} (v_{k,j} \times S_{i_j}) \times w_{k-1}^{-1} \bmod \theta_{k-1} \\
&= \sum_{j=1}^{k} (v_{k-1,j} \times w_{k-1} \times S_{i_j}) \times w_{k-1}^{-1} \bmod \theta_{k-1} \\
&= \sum_{j=1}^{k} v_{k-1,j} \times S_{i_j} \bmod \theta_{k-1} \\
&= \sum_{j=1}^{k} v_{k-1,j} \times S_{i_j}
\end{aligned}
$$

$$= Z_{k-1},$$

and $V_{k-1} = V_k \bullet w_{k-1}^{-1} \bmod \theta_{k-1}$. Repeat this procedure, one can obtain Z_j and V_j, $j = k-2, k-3, \ldots, 1$ and construct (14). In Lemma 2 we have shown that the k vectors V_j are linearly independent. Thus we conclude that (14) is valid and the sealed key is correctly recovered.

$$Q.E.D.$$

Example. Consider a network of twelve users, i.e. $G = \{U_0, U_1, U_2, \ldots, U_{11}\}$. Suppose that U_0 is the originator who desires to setup a conference and communicate to, say, $G' = \{U_{6_1}, U_{10_2}, U_{11_3}\}$. We further assume that the sealed keys to U_{6_1}, U_{10_2}, and U_{11_3} that U_0 computes, are $S_{6_1} = 2, S_{10_2} = 4$, and $U_{11_3} = 1$ and the interpolating polynomial that U_0 acquires is $f(\beta) = w_2\beta^2 + w_1\beta + w_0 \bmod p = 2\beta^2 + 14\beta + 5 \bmod 17$. In Protocol 1, clearly, the initial vector $V_1 = (6, 10, 11)$ and the prime number $\theta_1 = 109$ can be decided with $\theta_1 > \sum_{l=1}^{k} v_{1,l} \times \mu_k$, where $\mu_k = \max\{S_{6_1}, S_{10_2}, S_{11_3}\} = 4$. The vector $V_2 = (84, 31, 45)$, $\theta_2 = 641$ and $V_3 = (v'_{31}, v'_{32}, v'_{33} + \theta_2) = (v_{31}, v_{32}, v_{33}) = (168, 62, 731)$ are thus obtained by execcuting Protocol 1. Finally the sealed lock is constructed as

$$\begin{aligned}
Z_3 &= \sum_{j=1}^{3} v_{3j} \times S_{i_j} \\
&= (168 \times 2 + 62 \times 4 + 731 \times 1) \\
&= 1315.
\end{aligned}$$

Next, consider the recovery of the sealed keys in Protocol 2. The sealed lock $Z_3 = 1315$, the vector $V_3 = (168, 62, 731)$ and $\theta_1 = 109, \theta_2 = 641$ are acquired from the network database. An authorized participant U_{i_j} in G' can correctly reconstruct the polynomial $f(\beta) = 2\beta^2 + 14\beta + 5 \bmod 17$. Furthermore

$$\begin{aligned}
V_2 &= V_3 \times w_2^{-1} \bmod \theta_2 \\
&= (168, 62, 731) \times (2)^{-1} \bmod 641 \\
&= (84, 31, 45), \text{ and}
\end{aligned}$$

$$\begin{aligned}
Z_2 &= Z_3 \times w_2^{-1} \bmod \theta_2 \\
&= 1315 \times (2)^{-1} \bmod 641 \\
&= 337.
\end{aligned}$$

Similarly,

$$\begin{aligned}
V_1 &= V_2 \times w_1^{-1} \bmod \theta_1 \\
&= (84, 31, 45) \times (14)^{-1} \bmod 109 \\
&= (6, 10, 11), \text{ and}
\end{aligned}$$

$$Z_1 = Z_2 \times w_1^{-1} \bmod \theta_1$$
$$= 337 \times (14)^{-1} \bmod 109$$
$$= 63.$$

Since the vectors V_1, V_2 and V_3 are linearly independent, the sealed key S_{i_j} of $U_{i_j}, j = 1, 2, 3$ can be correctly derived from

$$
\begin{pmatrix} S_{6_1} \\ S_{10_2} \\ S_{11_3} \end{pmatrix} = \begin{pmatrix} 6 & 10 & 11 \\ 84 & 31 & 45 \\ 168 & 62 & 731 \end{pmatrix}^{-1} \times \begin{pmatrix} 63 \\ 337 \\ 1315 \end{pmatrix}
$$
$$
= \begin{pmatrix} 2 \\ 4 \\ 1 \end{pmatrix}
$$

Finally, the sealed keys of U_{6_1}, U_{10_2} and U_{11_3} are, $S_{6_1} = 2, S_{10_2} = 4$ and $S_{11_3} = 1$, respectively.

□

IV Cryptanalysis

Since the sealed lock is broadcasted in the network, it can be heard by any one no matter it is legal or not. In other words, an intruder may derive the conference key K_c or the secret key x_i of an authorized participant U_i in G' and even to forge. Clearly K_c in (3) is protected from illegal invasion because the random number r is unknow to intruders, it is difficult to break discrete logarithm problem [2]. To acquire the secret key x_i of U_i is also not easy. There are two such attacks. The first attack comes from some illegal recipient. In this case, the intruder tries to obtain the secret key x_i by solving $y_i = g^{x_i} \bmod p$ which is a hard discrete logarithm problem. The second attack comes from some authorized participants, say $U_l, l \neq i$. Although U_l can derive S_l, K_c and U_i's sealed key S_i from (14), he still has no information of getting x_i based on the difficulty of discrete logarithm problem. If an intruder wishes to impersonate the originator, it is easy to decide the validity from (16) [3].

Since the identity of an authorized participant in G' is embeded into our sealed lock. Except the originator any outsider does not know who participates in the conference. Of course, if he wishes to know, equations (5), (12) and (13) must be solved. But as metioned in Lemma 1, the outsider would fail in such attack.

Lastly, let us address the attack of replaying K_c by the authorized participant U_i. In this case, U_i in G' has derived the conference key K_c, he might pretend to be the originator U_0 some other time by changing the intercepted time $\hat{T}$ instead of T in (2) in order to eliminate the delay time. But the attack would fail because T has been altered, (16) of Protocol 2 would not hold.

V Conclusions

We have proposed a new integrated mechanism for solving multicast problem in distributed network environment. Our scheme has the following features.

1. The knapsack is successfully used to pack arbitrary messages into a sealed lock. On the contrary, the messages is able to be correctly extracted from the sealed lock.

2. The conference key under the protection of hard discrete logarithm problem is secure.

3. The digital signature is performed to prevent forgery.

4. Our scheme eliminates the extra transmission of authorized participants' identity by using sealed lock in network systems. In particular, when these participants in G' are needed to be known with each other but prevented from exposing their identity to outsiders.

5. The complexity in computing the sealed keys is somewhat time consuming when the number of authorized participants is not small. How to reduce such complexity remains to be studied.

References

[1] G. H. Chiou and W. T. Chen, "Secure Broadcasting Using the Secure Lock," IEEE Trans. Software Engineering, Vol. 15, No. 8, 1989, pp. 929-934.

[2] W. Diffie and M. E. Hellman, "New Directions in Cryptography," IEEE Trans. Information Theory, Vol. 22, No. 6, 1976, pp. 644-654.

[3] T. Elgamal, "A Public Key Cryptosystem and a Signature Scheme Based on Discrete Logarithms," IEEE Trans. Information Theory, Vol. 31, No. 4, 1985, pp. 469-472.

[4] I. Ingemarsson, D. T. Tang and C. K. Wang, "A Conference Key Distribution System," IEEE Trans. Information Theory, Vol. 28, No. 5, 1982, pp. 714-720.

[5] C. H. Lin, C. C. Chang and R. C. T. Lee, "A Conference Key Broadcasting System Using Sealed Locks," Information Systems. Vol. 17, No. 4, 1992, pp. 323-328.

[6] S. Martello and P. Toth, Knapsack Problem: Algorithms and Computer Implementations, John Wiley & Sons, England, 1990.

[7] R. C. Merkle and M. E. Hellman, "Hiding Information and Signatures in Trapdoor Knapsacks," IEEE Trans. Information Theory, Vol. 24, No. 5, 1978, pp. 525-530.

[8] A. Shamir, "Embedding Cryptography Trapdoors in Arbitrary Knapsack Systems," Information Processing Letters, Vol. 17, No. 2, 1983, pp. 77-79.

Verify Updating Trigger Correctness

Sin-Yeung Lee and Tok-Wang Ling
School of Computing, National University of Singapore,
Lower Kent Ridge Road, Singapore 119260
email: jlee@comp.nus.edu.sg, lingtw@comp.nus.edu.sg

Abstract. One of the major applications of trigger rules is to maintain database integrity. However, since trigger rules, like computer programs, may not be written correctly, it is important to have tools to verify the correctness. Generally, this is an undecidable problem. Only few works exist on this problem. However, most of these works either depend on human inspection, or incur a run-time overhead. In this paper, we introduce a new approach which does not depend on any human judgment nor any run-time monitoring. The trigger rules we are checking are those trigger rules which update object properties but do not insert any new object nor destroy an existing object. The constraints in our paper do not have any existential quantifier. If our method returns "yes", we can guarantee that the set of trigger rules are written correctly to enforce the given constraint.

1   Introduction

Active rules can be used to enforce integrity checking [9]. For example, triggers are often used to impose business rules such as bonds marketing. When an update is submitted, certain trigger rules respond to the update event to check if the update violates any constraint. If so, some remedial actions will be executed to restore the database integrity. Trigger rules, like computer programs, may not be written correctly, thus fail to enforce a constraint. Patently, we need to have a rule verifier.

However, active rules are quite difficult to monitor and verify due to their subtle behaviors. Indeed, just to decide whether the rules can terminate is an undecidable problem. Hence, it is not surprising that many trigger rules are manually debugged and very few partial rule verifiers exist nowadays. A trigger rule verifier needs to handle at least two issues: The trigger rules can terminate, and the resultant database obeys the intended constraint.

Until now, there are many works $[1, 4, 12, 2, 5, 7, 11]$ on termination detection. However, little works have been done to address the second issue. Most existing methods such as good design methodology [3], prototype testing tool [4] eventually require the experience of trigger-rule writers. Without the experts, these methods cannot really verify the rule correctness. For this reason, we shall propose an automatic rule verification method that does not need any human judgment. Furthermore, our method needs to be done only once for a set of trigger rules, hence it does not affect the run-time performance.

2 Basic Setting

2.1 The database and trigger rules

The underlying database is an object-oriented active database. Each object has a set of *properties* which can be updated. The trigger rules are the standard ECA (Event-Condition-Action) rules. In this paper, we will only study the trigger rules that are triggered by updates of an object property. Trigger condition is a boolean expression. It can be a simple (:new.salary < 0), but it can also be a complex SQL queries. Trigger rules can be further classified as either *BEFORE-rules* or *AFTER-rules*. For a BEFORE-rule, the trigger condition is checked using the database before the trigger event. For an AFTER-rule, the checking uses the database after the trigger event. For the uniformity of the discussion, we assume all rules are AFTER-rules.

2.2 Rule selection method

When two rules can respond to the same event, we need to decide which rule should be tested first. Some systems, such as Oracle, choose according to the order of the rule specification, some other use rule priority so that higher priority rules are chosen first. In this paper, we introduce a more general *rule selection method*: Each trigger rule r is associated with a rule sequence $r_1, \cdots, r_m$ where r_i's are all the rules that can be triggered by r directly. This sequence can either be explicitly declared in the DML, or be implicitly implied by factors such as the rule priority. Whenever the trigger condition of r is satisfied, $r_1, \cdots, r_m$ will be fired in the given order. In other words, the trigger rule r_1 will always be evaluated first and r_m will be evaluated last.

2.3 Trigger execution order

In this paper, we assume the trigger rules are executed immediately. Furthermore, outstanding trigger rules are queued in a LIFO manner. For example, assume r1 is currently evaluated, and r2 is in the evaluation queue. If r1 triggers r3, then r3 will be evaluated first before r2 according to LIFO manner. This is also the model which Oracle adopts.

2.4 Constraint

Constraints in this paper are conjunctions/disjunctions of comparison predicate on object properties. Furthermore, the whole expression is universally quantified. For example, "$\forall E_{\in emp} \ E.salary \leq E.mgr.salary$" is a constraint which states that "every employee's salary cannot be more than that of his manager." If we label the property $E.salary$ as A, and the property $E.mgr.salary$ as B, we can express this constraint as

$$A \leq B$$

We will also parameterize a constraint with variables to distinguish different database states. For example, $IC(\prec A, B \succ)$ denotes that the constraint IC are evaluated under the properties (will be defined in next section) $\prec A, B \succ$.

3   State Transform Predicate

Definition 1. *A property, Θ, denotes an attribute of a particular object instance. For example, emp.salary as well as emp.mgr.salary are two different properties. We will use $\prec \Theta_1, \cdots, \Theta_m \succ$ to denote the set of the properties of all the active objects, where Θ_i represents a particular property.*

Definition 2. *An* update trigger rule *is a trigger rule which is triggered by an update of a property Θ. It is written in the form,*

$$\ll name \gg :: \Delta_\Theta \ \ll condition \gg \rightarrow \ll updates \gg$$

where $\ll name \gg$ represents the name of the rule. The event Δ_Θ indicates that the trigger is fired only when properties Θ are updated. $\ll condition \gg$ represents the trigger condition. Finally, the trigger action $\ll updates \gg$ is a list of database update, each takes the form $\theta_0 := f(\theta_1, \cdots, \theta_n)$. θ_k is a variable that denotes an object property. f is an evaluable function that returns an object property.

This rule will be fired whenever an update of the property Θ occurs. During its evaluation, the $\ll condition \gg$ is checked against the updated database. If it is satisfied, the $\ll updatelists \gg$ will be executed immediately.

Example 1. Consider an OODBMS which stores images, if R represents the property *image.rank* and C represents the content of the image *image.content*, then the following trigger rule will decompress the image object if the rank of the access is updated to be within the top ten:

$$r :: \Delta_R \ (R \leq 10) \rightarrow C := decompress(C)$$

Definition 3. *Given a trigger system with a rule selection method RSM, a state transform predicate with respect to a trigger rule r, denoted as $\wp_r(\xi, \xi')$, is a predicate that takes two property sets as parameters. It returns true if and only if when the database after the trigger event update but before the trigger action has a set of properties denoted in ξ, then this set of properties is updated to ξ' after rule r and all the subsequent trigger rules that r triggers are executed in the order given by RSM.*

Example 2. Assume that the database instance has only two properties: A and B, and the only trigger rule on this object in the trigger system is

$$r1 :: \Delta_A \ A < 1 \rightarrow B := 2$$

Now when A is updated to a new value a. Since no trigger rule further updates A, the final value of A remains to be a. Moreover, if a is not less than 1, then the trigger condition of $r1$ is false, B will not be updated. Otherwise, B will be updated to 2. From this, we conclude that both $\wp_{r1}(\prec 1, 5 \succ, \prec 1, 5 \succ)$ and $\wp_{r1}(\prec 0, 5 \succ, \prec 0, 2 \succ)$ are true, but $\wp_{r1}(\prec 1, 5 \succ, \prec 0, 2 \succ)$ is false.

Consider now a new trigger rule is inserted:

$$r2 :: \Delta_B \ A \neq B \rightarrow A := B$$

When $r1$ is fired, if A is not less than 1, no other updates occur. Otherwise, B is updated to 2, which triggers $r2$. Since the value of A is different from the value of B, $r2$ will update A to be equal to B, which is 2. This update of A

further triggers rule $r1$ again, but since the new value of A, 2, is not less than 1, the trigger condition fails and the trigger sequence terminates. The final value of $\prec A, B \succ$ is now $\prec 2, 2 \succ$. In other words, $\wp_{r1}(\prec A, B \succ, \prec 2, 2 \succ)$ is true whenever A is less than 1. Otherwise, when $A \not< 1$, $\wp_{r1}(\prec A, B \succ, \prec A, B \succ)$ is true. Written in Prolog, $\wp_{r1}$ can be expressed as:

$$\wp_{r1}(\prec A, B \succ, \prec A', B' \succ) \leftarrow \neg(A < 1) \wedge (A' = A) \wedge (B' = B)$$
$$\wp_{r1}(\prec A, B \succ, \prec A', B' \succ) \leftarrow (A < 1) \wedge (A' = 2) \wedge (B' = 2)$$

From the previous example, we can see that to formulate a state transform predicate, we need to trace the trigger rule execution in the system. The following algorithm summarizes how a state transform predicate can be formulated:

Algorithm 1. Given a trigger system, a rule r and a rule selection method RSM, the state transform predicate $\wp_r(\xi, \xi')$ can be computed as follows,

1. Assume r is in the form,
   $$r :: \Delta_\Theta \ C_r(\xi) \to \xi := f_r(\xi)$$
   And we assume the update of ξ may trigger trigger rules in the order of $r_1, \cdots, r_n$ according to the given RSM,
2. We now add two deductive definitions of $\wp_r$ as follows,,
   $$\wp_r(\xi, \xi') \leftarrow \neg C_r(\xi) \wedge (\xi' = \xi)$$
   to denote that no other update occurs if the trigger condition fails, and
   $$\wp_r(\xi, \xi') \leftarrow C_r(\xi) \wedge (\xi_1 = f_r(\xi)) \wedge \wp_{r_1}(\xi_1, \xi_2) \wedge \cdots \wedge \wp_{r_n}(\xi_n, \xi')$$
   to denote that if the trigger condition succeeds, the property set ξ is updated to $f_r(\xi)$. This further triggers rules $r_1, \cdots, r_n$ subsequently. Note that if r does not trigger any rule, then ξ_1 is the same as ξ'.

Example 3. Recall in Example 2, there are two trigger rules,
   $$r1 :: \Delta_A \ A < 1 \to B := 2$$
   $$r2 :: \Delta_B \ A \neq B \to A := B$$
To construct $\wp_{r1}$, according to Algorithm 1, we add two deductive definitions:
   $$\wp_{r1}(\prec A, B \succ, \prec A', B' \succ) \leftarrow \neg(A < 1) \wedge (A' = A) \wedge (B' = B)$$
to indicate that if the trigger condition of $r1$ is not satisfied, then the trigger actions of $r1$ will not be executed, and
   $$\wp_{r1}(\prec A, B \succ, \prec A', B' \succ) \leftarrow (A < 1) \wedge (A_1 = A) \wedge$$
   $$(B_1 = 2) \wedge \wp_{r2}(\prec A_1, B_1 \succ, \prec A', B' \succ)$$
to indicate that if the trigger condition of $r1$ succeeds, then the value of B is updated to 2, and rule $r2$ will be fired which may further update A and B.

3.1 Verification of non-indefinitely-recursive trigger rules

If the given trigger rule does not indefinitely trigger itself recursively, which can be proven by [4, 2, 10], then any deductive definition $\wp_r$ can be unfolded so that the body does not contain any state transform predicate. In this case, to verify if an integrity constraint IC holds after an update, we just need to assume IC holds before the update, and using rule unfolding technique to evaluate the new updated database states after the trigger system completes its execution. Finally, we prove that IC remains satisfied at the new updated database.

Example 4. Given the following trigger rules:

$r1 :: \Delta_A$ TRUE $\rightarrow B := 2$

$r2 :: \Delta_B \; B \neq A \rightarrow B := A$

Now, we want to verify if the constraint "$B \neq 2$" holds after A is updated. Note that although the update of A alone will not violate the constraint, however, this update can trigger $r1$, which alters the value of B. Thus update of A can violate the constraint. According to Algorithm 1, we first construct $\wp_{r1}$ and $\wp_{r2}$,

$$\wp_{r1}(\prec A, B \succ, \prec A', B' \succ) \leftarrow \neg(\text{TRUE}) \wedge (A' = A) \wedge (B' = B)$$
$$\wp_{r1}(\prec A, B \succ, \prec A', B' \succ) \leftarrow (\text{TRUE}) \wedge (A_1 = A) \wedge$$
$$(B_1 = 2) \wedge \wp_{r2}(\prec A_1, B_1 \succ, \prec A', B' \succ)$$
$$\wp_{r2}(\prec A, B \succ, \prec A', B' \succ) \leftarrow \neg(B \neq A) \wedge (A' = A) \wedge (B' = B)$$
$$\wp_{r2}(\prec A, B \succ, \prec A', B' \succ) \leftarrow (B \neq A) \wedge (A_1 = A) \wedge$$
$$(B_1 = A) \wedge \wp_{r2}(\prec A_1, B_1 \succ, \prec A', B' \succ)$$

[4] shows that $r2$ is a deactivating rule, and can always terminate. Hence, $\wp_{r2}$ can be rewritten without recursion. The unfolded definition of $\wp_{r2}$ is as follows,

$$\wp_{r2}(\prec A, B \succ, \prec A', B' \succ) \leftarrow \neg(B \neq A) \wedge (A' = A) \wedge (B' = B)$$
$$\wp_{r2}(\prec A, B \succ, \prec A', B' \succ) \leftarrow (B \neq A) \wedge (A' = A) \wedge (B' = A)$$

Finally, $\wp_{r1}$ can now be unfolded into,

$$\wp_{r1}(\prec A, B \succ, \prec A', B' \succ) \leftarrow \neg(\text{TRUE}) \wedge (A' = A) \wedge (B' = B)$$
$$\wp_{r1}(\prec A, B \succ, \prec A', B' \succ) \leftarrow (\text{TRUE}) \wedge (A_1 = A) \wedge (B_1 = 2) \wedge$$
$$\neg(B_1 \neq A_1) \wedge (A' = A_1) \wedge (B' = B_1)$$
$$\wp_{r1}(\prec A, B \succ, \prec A', B' \succ) \leftarrow (\text{TRUE}) \wedge (A_1 = A) \wedge (B_1 = 2) \wedge$$
$$(B_1 \neq A_1) \wedge (A' = A_1) \wedge (B' = A_1)$$

To prove that IC remains satisfied, we only need to prove that for the final value B', the constraint $B' \neq 2$ holds. Moreover, as the constraint is not violated directly by the update of A, we can assume $B \neq 2$ holds before the evaluation of $r1$. In other words, IC is enforced if the following is satisfied,

$$IC(\prec A, B \succ) \wedge \wp_{r1}(\prec A, B \succ, \prec A', B' \succ) \rightarrow IC(\prec A', B' \succ)$$

After unfolding and simplification, the condition becomes,

$$[\text{FALSE} \rightarrow (B = 2)] \wedge [(B = 2) \wedge \neg(A \neq 2) \rightarrow (2 = 2)] \wedge$$
$$[(B = 2) \wedge (A \neq 2) \rightarrow (A = 2)]$$

It is easy to verify that the first and second conjunctions are always true. However, the third conjunction is not always satisfiable. In other words, if the updated A is not 2, then the integrity constraint $B = 2$ may not hold.

The following algorithm summarizes the above idea:

Algorithm 2. Given an update u, a constraint IC, a set of non-indefinitely recursive trigger rules, and a rule selection method RSM, the following constructs the condition such that IC remains satisfied after the update u:

1. Construct the state transform predicate p_r for each rule r with respect to the given RSM according to Algorithm 1.
2. Insert a new predicate $final_u$ as
$$final_u(\xi, \xi') \leftarrow \wp_{r_1}(\xi, \xi_1), \cdots, \wp_{r_m}(\xi_{m-1}, \xi')$$
where r_i's are rules that can be triggered by the update u in the sequence according to the given RSM.

3. Unfold all predicates $\wp_i$ in $final_u$ so that $final_u$ does not make use of any predicate $\wp_j$. This can always be done if the set of trigger rules are non-indefinitely recursive.

4. Assume after unfolding, the predicate $final_u$ is expressed in disjunction normal form as
$$final_u(\xi,\xi') \leftarrow W_1(\xi,\xi') \vee \cdots \vee W_k(\xi,\xi')$$
where each expression $W_i(\xi,\xi')$ are conjunctive of evaluable predicates or functions using only the property sets ξ and ξ'.

5. Let C be $IC(\xi)$ if the update u does not immediately violate IC. Otherwise, let C simply be TRUE.

6. The condition where IC remains satisfied after rule r is executed is now,
$$(C \wedge W_1(\xi,\xi') \to IC(\xi')) \wedge \cdots \wedge (C \wedge W_k(\xi,\xi') \to IC(\xi'))$$

3.2 Verification of purely indefinitely-recursive trigger rules

In this section, we shall due with another subset of trigger system, which contains only rules that form indefinite cycles. For example,
$$r1 :: \Delta_A \ A > 2 \to A := A - 1$$
This trigger rule does not necessarily terminate after a fixed number of execution. Indeed, it will trigger itself for an indefinite number of times. We call this type of trigger rules as *indefinitely-recursive trigger rules*. Since termination problem itself is undecidable, trigger correctness problem cannot be solved completely. Despite this, we can still have a partial solution. If our method answers "yes", then we can conclude that the trigger system are written correctly if the system terminates. However, for some correctly written trigger rules, our algorithm can only answer "don't know".

Let's reconsider the above mentioned rule,
$$r1 :: \Delta_A \ A > 2 \to A := A - 1$$
since $r1$ cycles indefinitely, we cannot use Algorithm 2 as the rule cannot be unfolded within a fixed number of steps. However, if $r1$ terminates, then its trigger condition must be false. Hence, $\neg(A > 2)$ must hold at the last execution of $r1$. It is also the condition for the final value of A if there is no other further update on A. This condition can now be used to verify trigger correctness. If the given constraint is $A \leq 0$, clearly the terminating condition $\neg(A > 2)$ logically implies this constraint. Thus, if the trigger system terminates, the constraint is enforced. This idea can be generalized to the cases of mutually recursive rules. The following gives the full algorithm to handle indefinitely-recursive rules,

Algorithm 3. Given a set of indefinitely-recursive trigger rules, an integrity constraint IC, a rule selection method RSM, and an update u. which can trigger rules $r_1^u, \cdots, r_m^u$ in this order. We now construct the final condition C as follows:

1. Designate the variable ξ' as the final set of properties when all the trigger rules terminate. Let the initial termination condition $TC(\xi')$ be false, and let r_{cur} be r_m^u.

2. Loop the followings until C has no more change:

- Rename all the variables in r_{cur} by the corresponding variables in ξ'. Disjunct into $TC(\xi')$ the negation of the new trigger condition of r_{cur}.
- Set the new r_{cur} to be the last predicate that can be triggered by the current r_{cur} according to the rule selection method.

3. return $TC(\xi') \rightarrow IC(\xi')$ as the condition that the integrity constraint remains satisfied after the update.

Example 5. Consider the following mutually recursive rules:

$r1 :: \Delta_A \;\; A < 10 \rightarrow B := B - 1$
$r2 :: \Delta_B \;\; B < 10 \rightarrow A := A \times 2$

We want to verify if the constraint $IC(\prec A, B \succ)$

$$(A \geq 10) \wedge (B \geq 10)$$

holds after an update of the property A. We follow Algorithm 3. In step 1, we let $\prec A', B' \succ$ to represent the final property and $TC(\prec A', B' \succ)$ to be *false*. Since only $r1$ can be triggered by the update of A, we let r_{cur} to be $r1$. In step 2, we rename all the variables in $r1$ by substituting A by A' and B by B'. TC is now disjuncted with the negation of the new trigger condition of $r1$ and is updated to be $\neg(A' < 10)$ and r_{cur} is updated to be $r2$ as it is the last rule that can be triggered by $r1$. Repeat step 2. When the algorithm terminates, the final expression of $TC(\prec A', B' \succ)$ will be,

$$\neg(A' < 10) \vee \neg(B' < 10)$$

To verify the constraint, we just need to prove

$$(\neg(A' < 10) \vee \neg(B' < 10)) \rightarrow ((A' \geq 10) \wedge (B' \geq 10))$$

Since the formula may not be satisfied, we conclude that the given trigger rules may not enforce the given constraint.

3.3 Verification of general trigger rules

The situation becomes more complex when rules contain both non-indefinitely and indefinitely recursive rules. Consider the following three rules:

$r1 :: \Delta_A \;\; A < B \rightarrow A := A - 1$
$r2 :: \Delta_A \;\; A < B \rightarrow A := A - B$
$r3 :: \Delta_A \;\; A = 1 \rightarrow B := 2$

Rule $r1$ and $r2$ are indefinitely recursive rules while $r3$ updates property B without triggering other rules. We also assume the rule selection method is to choose $r1$, then $r2$ and finally $r3$. When an update of A is submitted, we can apply Algorithm 3 to know that $\neg(A < B)$ is true immediately after the two recursion rules terminate. However, these A and B are not of the final database state yet. In this example, $r3$ will still be executed and it may set the value of B to be 2 if A is 1. In this case, the final property is $\prec 1, 2 \succ$. Clearly, $\neg(A < B)$ no longer holds. A correct post-condition should be

$$(\neg(A = 1) \wedge \neg(A < B)) \vee ((A = 1) \wedge (B = 2))$$

To cater for this situation, we need to combine both Algorithm 2 and 3. The following algorithm describes this:

Algorithm 4. Given a set of trigger system, an integrity constraint IC, a rule selection method RSM, and an update u, which can trigger rules $r_1^u, \cdots, r_m^u$ in this order, we decide if IC are correctly enforced after the update u as follows,

1. Construct the state transform predicate p_r for each rule r wrt RSM.
2. Insert a new predicate
$$final_u(\xi, \xi') \leftarrow \wp_{r_1^u}(\xi, \xi_1) \wedge \cdots \wedge \wp_{r_m^u}(\xi_{m-1}, \xi')$$
3. Loop for $j = m$ back to 1 the following,
   - if rule r_j^u can be terminated in a fixed number of steps, then $\wp_{r_j^u}(\xi_{j-1}, \xi_j)$ can be unfolded so that its deductive body does not need to use any $\wp_{r_k}$ at all. Replace $\wp_{r_j^u}(\xi_{j-1}, \xi_j)$ by the unfolded expression.
   - if $\wp_{r_j^u}(\xi_{j-1}, \xi_j)$ cannot be unfolded, then apply Algorithm 3 to find the termination condition $TC(\xi_j)$. Replace the remaining expression
   $$\wp_{r_1^u}(\xi, \xi_1) \wedge ... \wedge \wp_{r_j^u}(\xi_{j-1}, \xi_j)$$
   by $TC(\xi_j)$. Exit the loop.
4. If the constraint is not immediately violated by the update u, then let C be $IC(\xi)$, otherwise simply let it be TRUE.
5. if $C \wedge final_u(\xi, \xi') \rightarrow IC(\xi')$ is always true, then conclude that "the constraint will not be violated by the given update u if it terminates." Otherwise, conclude that "the constraint may be violated by the given update u."

Example 6. Consider the object COURSE has two properties: the max_intake and the cur_intake. Two constraints are given:

1. ($IC1$) For each course, the cur_intake cannot be more than the max_intake.
2. ($IC2$) For each course, a non-zero cur_intake cannot be less than two.

In order to enforce $IC1$, a trigger writer may have a trigger rule to recursively reduce the value of cur_intake once it is greater than max_intake after an update of the cur_intake. For $IC2$, another trigger rule is written to reset the max_intake to be zero whenever the cur_intake is less than two so that the cur_intake is reset to zero via the first trigger rule. However, if $r1$ is always selected before $r2$, then our method can show that the two trigger rules may not enforce $IC1$ after an update of cur_intake.

We shall use the symbol A to represent cur_intake, and B to represent max_intake, now the two trigger rules can be written as,
$$r1 :: \Delta_A \ A > B \rightarrow A := A - 1$$
$$r2 :: \Delta_A \ A < 2 \rightarrow B := 0$$
The constraint can now be represented as,
$$A \leq B$$

According to Algorithm 4, we first construct all the state transform predicates and insert a new predicate $final_A$ as:
$$final_A(\prec A, B \succ, \prec A', B' \succ) \leftarrow \wp_{r1}(\prec A, B \succ, \prec A_1, B_1 \succ) \wedge$$
$$\wp_{r2}(\prec A_1, B_1 \succ, \prec A', B' \succ)$$
Step 3 of Algorithm 4 requires us to replace $\wp_{r1}$ and $\wp_{r2}$ in $final_A$ by a suitable expression. $\wp_{r2}$ can be unfolded into

$$\wp_{r2}(\prec A, B \succ, \cdots, \prec A', B' \succ) \leftarrow \neg(A < 2) \wedge (A' = A) \wedge (B' = B)$$
$$\wp_{r2}(\prec A, B \succ, \cdots, \prec A', B' \succ) \leftarrow (A < 2) \wedge (A' = A) \wedge (B' = 0)$$

$\wp_{r1}$ cannot be unfolded, and hence we apply Algorithm 3 to decide its terminate condition, which is $\neg(A_1 > B_1)$. The final $final_A$ is

$$final_A(\prec A, B \succ, \prec A', B' \succ) \leftarrow \neg(A_1 \succ B_1) \wedge$$
$$((\neg(A_1 < 2) \wedge (A' = A_1) \wedge (B' = B_1)) \vee$$
$$((A_1 < 2) \wedge (A' = A_1) \wedge (B' = 0)))$$

To prove that the constraint is satisfied, we need only to prove that

$$final_A(\prec A, B \succ, \prec A', B' \succ) \rightarrow (A' \leq B')$$

After simplification to retain only the final values A' and B', the above formula is further simplified to be,

$$[\neg(A' > B') \wedge \neg(A' < 2) \rightarrow (A' \leq B')] \wedge [(B' = 0) \wedge (A' < 2) \rightarrow (A' \leq B')]$$

Since the second conjunctive may not always be satisfiable, we conclude that the integrity constraint may not be enforced after an update of cur_intake. The trigger system therefore may not be written correctly.

Note that if $r2$ is replaced by

$$r2' :: \Delta_A \ A < 2 \rightarrow B := 2$$

Then the second conjunctive of the above analysis becomes,

$$[(B' = 2) \wedge (A' < 2) \rightarrow (A' \leq B')]$$

which is always true. In this case, our method proves that the trigger system can enforce the given constraint after the change of property A.

Note that rule selection method is important. If the rule selection method instead chooses rule $r2$ first before rule $r1$, then $final_A$ now becomes,

$$final_A(\prec A, B \succ, \prec A', B' \succ) \leftarrow \neg(A' > B')$$

Clearly, $\neg(A' > B') \rightarrow (A' \leq B')$, thus, $IC1$ is enforced under the new rule selection method.

3.4 Correctness of the entire system

After we prove the trigger correctness for a single update, we can proceed to prove correctness for any update. The main idea is to ensure that for each update that may violate the given constraint, there is a trigger rule that restores it:

Algorithm 5. Given a constraint IC, and a set of trigger rule $r_1, \cdots, r_m$ we verify if these rules are written correctly to enforce IC by the follows,

1. Using [6,8] or other methods, emulate all the possible update operations $u_1, \cdots, u_n$ that can violate IC.
2. For each update u_j do,
   (a) if there is no rule among $r_1, \cdots, r_m$ that is triggered by u_j, then conclude
      "IC may not be enforced. There is no rule for u_j."
      Exit the algorithm.
   (b) Apply Algorithm 4 to test if IC is satisfied after u_j. If we cannot prove that IC will definitely satisfied after u_j, then conclude
      "IC may not be correctly enforced after update u_j."
      Exit the algorithm.
3. Conclude that the set of rules enforces IC against all atomic updates.

4   Conclusion

We have proposed a new method to verify whether a given set of updating trigger rules is written correctly to enforce a given constraint. Our method differs from existing approaches in that,

1. Our method does not depend on human knowledge, and needs no extra input knowledge from any expert. This allows full-automation of the verification process.
2. Our approach does not incur any run-time overhead. Some existing systems need to monitor the database during run-time to detect any incorrectly written rule. Our approach, however, is a preventive method. The rules are tested at the design phrase before the actual execution.

Although the correctness problem itself is not decidable, our method can still help trigger writers to focus only the suspicious subsets, and greatly ease the verification process. For further work, we can extend this method to handle a more general trigger rules with object creation/destruction as well as a more general constraint type.

References

1. J.Widom A.Aiken and J.M.Hellerstein. Behavior of database production rules: Termination, confluence, and observable determinism. In *SIGMOD*, pages 59–68, June 1992. San Diego.
2. S.D.Urban A.P.Karadimce. Refined trigger graphs: A logic-based approach to termination analysis in an active object-oriented database. In *ICDE*, pages 384–391, 1996. New Orleans.
3. S.Ceri E.Baralis and S.Paraboschi. Improved rule analysis by means of triggering and activation graphs. In *RIDS*, pages 165–181, 1995.
4. S.Ceri E.Baralis and S.Paraboschi. Run-time detection of non-terminating active rule systems. In *DOOD*, pages 38–54, 1995. Singapore.
5. S.Ceri E.Baralis and S.Paraboschi. Compile-time and runtime analysis of active behaviors. In *IEEE Transactions on Knowledge and Data Engineering*, pages 353–370, May/June 1998.
6. S.Y. Lee and T.W. Ling. Further improvements on integrity constraint checking for stratifiable deductive databases. In *VLDB*, pages 495–505, 1996. Bombay.
7. S.Y. Lee and T.W. Ling. A path removing technique for detecting trigger termination. In *EDBT*, pages 341–355, 1998. Valencia, Spain.
8. T.W. Ling. The prolog not-predicate and negation as failure rule. In *New Generation Computing*, 1990.
9. S.Ceri and J.Widom. Deriving production rules for constraint maintenance. In *Proc 16th VLDB Conf*, pages 566–577, 1990. Brisbane, Australia.
10. S.Y.Lee and T.W.Ling. Refined termination decision in active databases. In *DEXA*, pages 182–191, 1997. Toulouse.
11. S.Y.Lee and T.W.Ling. Unrolling cycle to decide trigger termination. In *VLDB*, 1999. Edinburgh, UK. Accepted to be published.
12. T.Weik and A.Heuer. An algorithm for the analysis of termination of large trigger sets in an oodbms. In *Proceedings of the International Workshop on Active and Real-Time Databases Systems*, June 1995. Skovde, Sweden.

A Flexible Weighting Scheme for Multimedia Documents

Iadh Ounis

School of Computing, National University of Singapore
Phone: (65) 874 2911; Fax: (65) 779 4580
E-mail: ounis@comp.nus.edu.sg

Abstract. In information retrieval systems, it is common practice to rank the retrieved documents in decreasing order of their estimated relevance to the user's
query. Information retrieval models, such as the vector-space model (see Salton's
work), provide weighting schemes and matching functions that follow this necessity. However, they were mainly developed in the context of textual document
retrieval. The contribution of this paper is twofold. Firstly, it takes a look at the
challenges involved in the ordering of the results in image retrieval, while using the expressive conceptual graphs formalism as the indexing language. New
parameters appear to be useful in the vector-space weighting schemes, that take
into account the richness and complexity of documents such as images. We inspect such parameters and give a flexible weighting scheme. Secondly, this paper
gives a general weighting scheme, applied for the conceptual graphs formalism.
The matching function of this formalism, which otherwise gives only a boolean
yes or no decision on a document's relevance to a user's query, is refined so that
to obtain ranked results.

1 Introduction

One of the criteria that have to be considered when building an information retrieval
(IR) system is that the documents it retrieves should be ordered with respect to their
relevance to the user's information need [1–3]. Indeed, the users's cognitive effort is
diminished if the documents that cope most with their need are at the beginning of the
retrieved list of documents. Most of the efforts to find a solution to this necessity were
concentrated on text retrieval [4]. In this case, the indexing language most frequently
used are the keywords or, in some cases, combinations of keywords or noun phrases [5,
6]. In the case of multimedia documents, it is more difficult to capture the important
parts of the document content in the form of keywords [7, 8]. The indexing language
has to be a rich and expressive formalism, so that to support accurate indexing. Conceptual graphs were proposed as such a language, as they allow to represent complex
and highly structured documents [9]. On the other side, the task of understanding the
system results gets more complex for documents such as an image, as the passage from
the signal level to the semantic level involves a more important cognitive effort. Indeed,
we think that the matching performed in the user's mind between groups of letters and
the semantics of the compounding word is less demanding than the matching between
an image area and possibly different interpretations, according to shape, colour, user

knowledge etc. While keywords offer multiple solutions for obtaining a flexible matching function, which returns an ordered list of documents [10, 6], conceptual graphs, like other expressive formalisms, do not provide such a ranking. This paper focuses on two aspects. Firstly, we are concerned about finding a weighting scheme for the conceptual graph formalism. Secondly, we are interested in the particular characteristics of multimedia documents, especially images, that should be captured in an extended weighting scheme. We combine these two aspects into an IR-oriented solution, which offers a weighting scheme for image retrieval when the indexing language is the conceptual graphs formalism. Our claim, here, is that the proposed weighting scheme is general enough to accommodate all kinds of media indexed by relational formalisms. Such formalisms allow to represent not only terms, but also relationships between terms [11, 12].

The rest of this paper is organized as follows. In section 2, we review some of the parameters that distinguish images from texts, and have to be considered in an efficient weighting scheme. In section 3, we present an outline of a general approach for weighting multimedia documents, when expressive formalisms are used for indexing. After having identified in section 4 the impact of a formalism like conceptual graphs on the general weighting scheme, we apply it in the case of images in section 5. The implementation of the approach is presented in section 6. Section 7 gives the impact of the application of our weighting scheme on an image retrieval system called RELIEF [13].

2   Images versus Text: New Weighting Parameters

Each media type has different characteristics, which may have an influence on the weighting criteria. A widely used weighting scheme is $tf \times idf$, which models both the importance of a term within the document, and its importance with respect to the document collection [1, 2, 14]. The first kind of term importance is approximated by tf. Here we find a first text weighting parameter, which is the number of occurrences of a given keyword [1]. Other parameters include text length [15], text layout and keyword position in the text [16]. Generally, they are taken into account only as a normalization of the tf factor, for practical reasons. While they give satisfying results, they do not apply for different types of media, such as images. Moreover, the within-document term weight can depend more on parameters different from term frequency, and simple normalization may not suffice.

Weighting parameters are generally approximations used in the computation of the relevance value of a document for a given query. Relevance is related to the user's perception. Our basic hypothesis is that an image is more relevant if the users can locate easier the objects that they requested in their queries. This follows the model presented in [17], where it is argued that, in the design of user interfaces, there are various factors affecting the user's perception. We give more importance within the image to objects that appear more clearly or, in other words, are more obvious. This leads to new parameters, that are related to images only and do not apply for text. We identify the following parameters for modeling object importance:

---

[1] Keywords are sometimes replaced by more complex structures, such as noun phrases.

- p_1: *area*. Objects that are larger generally seem to be closer and attract more the user's attention [18]. In figure 1, the boat in the middle image is large and seems to be dominant.

- p_2: *contrast*. For instance, in the image on the left in the same figure, the boats on shore are relatively small but still clear, as they are black objects on the white background given by the sand. It is not the case for the objects on the right hand of the same image.

- p_3: *composition level*. Objects that are higher in the image composition hierarchy are given more importance. For instance, for the second image in figure 1, the importance of the boat is higher than that of the man, if the composition hierarchy is that in figure 2.

- p_4: *coverage*. Objects that are covered by others are given less importance than completely visible objects.

- p_5: *position*. Objects appearing in the middle of the image are given more importance than those occurring in the corners.

- *tf*: *frequency of occurrence*. Objects that occur several times in the same image are given more importance. For instance, in figure 1, there are several boats in the image on the left.

Fig. 1. Three sample images

The reader may note that this list is not exhaustive. However, in the first version of our implementation, these parameters seem to be more interesting. Many other parameters could be identified. They may be related, for instance, to physical aspects such as colour or texture, or may be more abstract and hard to capture parameters, e.g. the user's background knowledge. With the parameters listed above, the *term importance* of an object is computed by the following formula, where i identifies the occurrence of the object in the image (it can occur several times) and j is the parameter number (p_{ij} is the parameter j of the object i):

$$ti = \sum_{i=1}^{tf} \frac{\sum_{j=1}^{5}(a_{ij} \times p_{ij})}{5} \qquad (1)$$

The parameters a_{ij}, $a_{ij} \in [0.1]$ modify the impact of each parameter p_{ij}. The parameters p_{ij} are normalized in the $[0,1]$ interval, by taking not absolute, but relative values. For instance, p_1 is not the area of the object in the image, but the area computed relatively to the maximum area of the indexed objects in the image. We divide the inner sum by 5 for normalization, to keep the overall value in the interval $[0,1]$.

We note that the formula above is a generalization of the *tf* factor for the case of images. Indeed, if none of the parameters p_{ij} are considered, it is clear that *ti* will only depend on the *tf* factor.

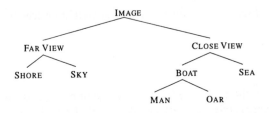

Fig. 2. A possible composition hierarchy for the second image in figure 1

In the case of images, the vector-space *tf × idf* formula becomes *ti × idf*. More specifically, the overall weight of a term l in a document k is given by:

$$w_{kl} = ti_{kl} \times idf_{kl}. \tag{2}$$

We note that the semantics of the *idf* factor does not change with respect to text documents and it is computed using the known formula $\log \frac{N}{n}$, where N is the number of documents in the collection and n the number of documents that contain the term [5, 15].

3   An Outline of Weighting Rich Formalisms

Multimedia information retrieval requires an expressive indexing language, allowing to represent not only terms, but also relationships between them [11, 8]. There are various kinds of relationships, depending on the media type. The indexing language associates the real terms occurring in the document to more abstract entities, such as concepts giving their semantics. For instance, in the case of text, the passage "the boat floats on the sea" may result in the concepts BOAT and SEA, together with the relationship *floats on* between them. For images, two different regions can be also identified as the concepts BOAT and SEA, with the same relationship between them (see the second image in figure 1).

Our approach is general and does not depend on the formalism used for indexing, nor on the media type. As shown in figure 3, any formalism can be used, as well as different media types or combinations of them in multimedia documents. Indeed, we have to consider not only the media characteristics, but also the indexing language used to represent the semantic content of the document. As a consequence, a general formula is to be used. In the following, we specify how such a formula can be introduced.

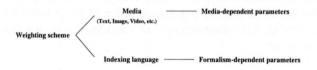

Fig. 3. The outline of a general weighting scheme

As one can see, there are two levels of abstraction, the first for the terms as they occur in the documents (signal level), and the second for their associated concepts (semantic content level) as they are related to the chosen formalism. Each of these levels introduces its own weighting parameters, which have to be taken into account together in the overall weighting scheme, as shown in figure 3. As an illustration, in the previous section, we associated the first abstraction level to objects, in the case of images. The parameters depending on the formalism are dealt with in the next section, for the case of conceptual graphs.

In fact, a multimedia document is a set of sub-documents, each of them being text, image, video and the like. For instance, it may contain text parts (e.g. the document title) and some images. For the weighting of the corresponding indexing terms, the features (parameters) of the media in which a sub-document is expressed are taken into consideration. For example, if it is an image, the parameters presented in section 2 are considered. In the case of text, the position, the frequency or the layout (italic, bold, underlined, etc.) of a given word are captured (see figure 4). Furthermore, each sub-document is indexed by a specific indexing language. The formalism-dependent parameters are relative to this indexing language. Hence, we propose the following formula for a given sub-document:

Definition 1 (Weighting Sub-documents). $w_{sub-document} = b \times w_{media-dependent} + (1 - b) \times w_{formalism-dependent}$

We use the adjustment parameter $b \in [0,1]$ to modify the relative importance of the media-dependent parameters or, conversely, of the formalism-dependent parameters, in the sub-document weight.

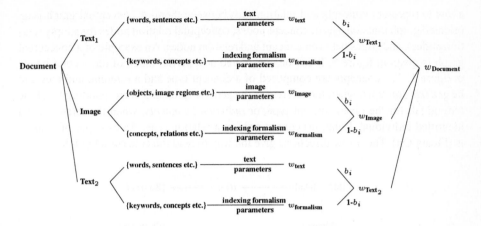

Fig. 4. The weight of a multimedia document depends on the weights of its sub-documents

The media-dependent weight is computed from the weights associated to each indexing term matched to the query terms. More precisely, these terms are the terms of the index which are put in correspondence, by the matching function, with at least a term occurring in the user's query. If we have n indexing terms in a document index matched to the user's query terms, then the weight associated to the document is the following:

Definition 2 (Media-dependent Weighting). $w_{media\text{-}dependent} =$
$\sum_{i=1}^{n} w_{media\text{-}dependent\,matched\,indexing\,term,i}$

The formalism-dependent weight can be computed, once the indexing formalism is chosen. The next section illustrates how this weight can be computed in the case of conceptual graphs.

Now, the weight of a multimedia document can be introduced, as a combination the weights of its sub-documents. If s is the number of sub-documents, by using the definition 1, we have (see figure 4):

Definition 3 (Weighting Multimedia Documents). $w_{document} = \bigoplus_{i=1}^{s} w_{sub\text{-}document_i} = \bigoplus_{i=1}^{s} b_i \times w_{media\text{-}dependent_i} + (1 - b_i) \times w_{formalism\text{-}dependent_i}$

The operator $\bigoplus$ can be specified according to the practical needs. For instance, it can be the sum operator.

In the following, we illustrate our general approach for documents consisting in images only and indexed by conceptual graphs. Applying the general scheme for other media types is straight-forward.

4 Weighting a Conceptual Graph

Conceptual graphs were introduced in [19] as an expressive and intuitive formalism for knowledge representation and reasoning. As other rich formalisms, conceptual graphs allow to represent concepts and relationships between them. A conceptual graph is an oriented graph that consists of concept nodes, conceptual relation nodes (or simply relation nodes), and edges between concept and relation nodes. An example of a conceptual graph is given in figure 5. It can be considered as a partial index of the second image in figure 1. The concepts are composed of a concept type and a referent, and they can be *generic concepts*, when the referent is the generic referent ⋆ corresponding to all the individuals for the given concept type, or *individual concepts*, when the referent is an identified individual. Relations consist only in a relation type. An example of relation is (Floats-On). The arrow directions give the way to read the conceptual graph.

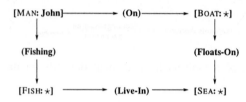

Fig. 5. An example of index in conceptual graphs

Concept types are organized in a concept type lattice, according to a partial order IsA relation $\leq$. For instance, we say that FISH is a subtype of ANIMAL or that FISH is a specialization of ANIMAL, and we note FISH $\leq$ ANIMAL. We introduce a weighting on the concept type lattice. There are different ways to weigh concept types: either the weight is proportional to the probability of occurrence of a certain concept type, or the weight favours the more specific concept types. The first approach would associate a larger weight to ANIMAL than to FISH. Indeed, each occurrence of FISH in the graph implicitly involves the occurrence of ANIMAL (FISH IsA ANIMAL in the lattice). Therefore, the probability of occurrence of ANIMAL is greater than or equal to that of FISH. More specifically, there is an initial probability for each concept type C, given by the number of occurrences in all the indexes: $p(C_i) = tf(C_i)$. Then the probability of the children nodes are added to the probabilities of their parents, from the leaves of the lattice up to the top: $p(C_i) = tf(C_i) + \sum_{C_j \leq C_i} p(C_j)$.

We follow here the second approach, which is more specific to knowledge representation formalisms. Indeed, for the evaluation of the information carried by an index, the conceptual graphs community seems to favour the more specific graphs [2]. Thus we measure in our weights the information content. There is more information in the occurrence of FISH than in that of ANIMAL, because FISH is a refined information, obtained from ANIMAL.

Hypothesis 1 (Weighting a concept type) *The weight of a concept type C_i is the information content of C_i. It is the inverse of the probability of occurrence of C_i: $w_{C_i} = \frac{1}{p(C_i)}$, where the probability $p(C_i)$ is computed from the concept type lattice.*

---

[2] This issue was discussed on the conceptual graphs mailing-list (cg@cs.uah.edu)

For obvious reasons, we refine the probability and the weight of a concept type. To this effect, we divide both of them by the maximum probability, and by the maximum weight respectively. From the weight of a concept type, we derive the weight of a generic concept; we assume that, for a concept type C_i, we have $w_{[C_i:\star]} = w_{C_i}$. The weights of individual concepts are computed by taking into account the relation $\leq$ between individual and generic concepts. For instance, [MAN: John]$\leq$[MAN: $\star$]. The probability of occurrence of the individual concept is less than that of the generic concept. Indeed, we may consider that each time we have an occurrence of an individual concept, we implicitly have an occurrence of the generic concept. If we have $r_1 \ldots r_n$ as possible referents for a concept type C, and we assume that the occurrences of these referents are equally probable (let this probability be p), then $p([C : \star]) = \sum_{i=1}^{n} p([C : r_i]) = n \times p$. Following the hypothesis 1, the weight is the inverse of the probability: $w_{[C_i:r_j]} = \frac{w_{C_i}}{n}$.

Relation types are also organized in a similar relation type lattice. Every relation links certain concepts, and the information content of the relation is determined by the information content of the concepts that it links [20, 8]. Therefore, the weight of a relation is a completely determined function of the weights of its concepts. The hypothesis here is that the information content of a relation is the product of the information contents of the concepts that it links, so the weight of a relation is the product of the weights of its component concepts.

Hypothesis 2 (Weighting a relation type) *If an n-ary relation R links a set of concepts $C_1 \ldots C_n$, then its weight is given as follows: $w_R = \prod_{i=1}^{n} w_{C_i}$.*

As a relation consists in a relation type only, the weight of a relation is equal to the weight of its relation type. In the same light, the weight of a conceptual graph is the information content of its component relations, which in turn capture the weight of their component concepts. A conceptual graph is a set of relations which are linked together on some particular concepts (see figure 5). Assuming independence between the occurrences of these relations, we have a product in terms of both probabilities and information content. In particular, the weight of a conceptual graph is given by the following definition:

Definition 4 (Weighting a conceptual graph). *If R_i, i=1,n are the component relations of a graph, then the weight of a conceptual graph is: $w_{cg} = \log \prod_{i=1}^{n} (w_{R_i} + 1)$.*

We apply log for normalization reasons, after having added 1 to each relation weight so that to attenuate the impact on w_{cg}. In information retrieval, this is a very usual approach [6, 15]. In fact, we adopt it for practical reasons, so that the impact of the formalism-dependent weight be comparable to that of media-dependent weight in the applications of definition 1.

5 Related Work and Discussion

Previous research on conceptual graphs that focused on weighting include a relatively low number of approaches. They were either limited solutions for particular problems in domains such as recognition systems [21], or general frameworks, providing sound extensions of the formalism [22]. A common characteristic is that these works are too distant from our needs in information retrieval. In particular, no clear method is given to compute the proposed theoretic parameters, nor any real application is shown. Therefore, this paper aims to overcome this limitation.

As we mentioned in section 3, our weighting scheme is general and takes into account both media and formalism dependent weighting parameters. We consider here that our document is an image. We already presented the parameters that are specific to the conceptual graphs formalism. We also presented a media-dependent weighting scheme for images. As we consider that documents consist in one media type, i.e. an image, their weights are given by their sub-documents, one for each of them (the images themselves). Hence, the final weight of a document is computed according to definition 1, when the image is indexed by a conceptual graph:

$$w_{\text{image}} = b \times w_{\text{image-dependent}} + (1 - b) \times w_{\text{cg}} \tag{3}$$

The term w_{cg} is computed as we presented in definition 4. By "cg", we mean the conceptual graph used to index the image. On the other side, $w_{\text{image-dependent}}$ takes benefit from the parameters specific to images, which we gave in section 2. These parameters correspond to the real objects of the image. We already saw how to compute the weight for each object appearing in the image.

Now, by applying the definition 2 in the case of images and introducing the weights of the objects, as given in formula 2, we obtain:

$$w_{\text{image-dependent}} = \sum_{k=1}^{n} w_{\text{image-dependent matched indexing term},k} = \sum_{k=1}^{n} ti_k \times idf_k$$
$$= \sum_{k=1}^{n} \sum_{i=1}^{tf_k} \frac{\sum_{j=1}^{5} (a_{ijk} \times p_{ijk})}{5} \times idf_k$$

This formula applies for images. It allows to rank all images indexed by conceptual graphs. In the next section, we will show how this formula can be integrated in a logic-based indexing approach.

6   Implementation of the Approach

In information retrieval, if conceptual graphs are used as the indexing language, each document in the collection is indexed by a conceptual graph $\chi(d)$. The information need is also formulated in the form of a conceptual graph $\chi(q)$. The retrieval process is implemented through the so-called projection operator [19]. The projection operator allows to logically derive one graph u from another v. Hence, it constitutes a way to implement logical inferences, which makes it a matching function for the logical IR model [23].

There is a convergence in the IR community with respect to the various ways in which a multimedia document can be considered. Depending on the point of view, some information is extracted from the document, and this information is captured by the notion of *facet*. For instance, the extracted information is different if the point of view concerns the layout of the image or its semantical content. The notion of facet can be either very specific and static [7, 24] or abstract and related to logic [25, 8]. The latter approach has the advantage that it may be applied to the conceptual graphs formalism, while being dedicated to IR and preserving the semantics of the formalism.

We share here the opinion that a multimedia document must be indexed by a set of facets, each one corresponding to a particular logical point of view on the document. More precisely, each sub-document of a multimedia document, such as an image or a text, must be indexed by a set of facets. The facet inherits the properties of the sub-document to which it is associated. In particular, this means that the media-dependent parameters of a facet are those of the sub-document. This is illustrated in figure 6. The index of a sub-document is the set of its facets, hence the weight of the sub-document is a combination of the weights of its facets. In our implementation, we choose the conceptual graphs formalism as logic. In this case, each facet is represented by a conceptual graph. If an indexing model is associated to a particular media, for example the image model in [24], or the model for structured textual documents in [26], there is an easy way to detect these facets according to the indexing model.

Accordingly, the query $\chi(q)$ is also divided into facets. The model presented in [25] offers a way to evaluate the relevance degree of a document for a query from a logical point of view. The relevance degree of a document is based on the logical correspondence between the query facets and the document facets. Each of these correspondences is related to the application of the projection operator. However, the computation of the relevance degree is not detailed, in particular there is no method to give a weight to a facet. Indeed, the method assumes that a weight for each facet is already computed, without specifying this computation. Hence, the importance of our work is that it applies this general logical model for real IR needs, by computing the weights of the facets. Thus we obtain a ranking for documents of any type of media, that are indexed with the conceptual graphs formalism, while preserving the semantics of the formalism.

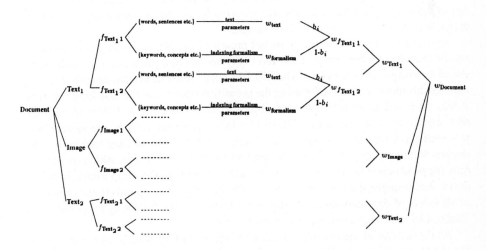

Fig. 6. Considering facets in the weighting scheme

In the previous sections, we showed how to associate a weight to a sub-graph or, in the light of the model in [25], to a facet of the indexes, while taking into account media-dependent parameters. The facets of the query are each weighted by an adjustment parameter $w_{f_j q}$, according to the user's interest in that facet. Let n be the number of facets in the query which can be projected in a facet of the document index. The relevance degree of a document d_i for a given query q is computed as follows:

$$\text{RELEVANCE VALUE}(d_i, q) = \oplus_{j=1}^{n} w_{f_j d_i} \times w_{f_j q}$$

In [25], it is mentioned that the operator $\oplus$ is either the sum or the product. We note that, as it is the last step of our weighting scheme, this operator always increases the relevance value, so choosing one or another is just a matter of normalization. In our next section, we apply the sum.

We note that our approach not only supports the projection operator, as defined by Sowa, but it implicitly introduces a more flexible projection operator. The idea is to remove certain facets of the query, for which there is no projection in an index facet, and then apply the general approach for the rest of the query. Thus soundness is preserved, as the logical constraints must still be satisfied by the query, after the removal of the "offending" query facets that do not have a projection in the index facets. Moreover, the relevance calculus complies with this idea, as the value computed by the above formula will be lower for the new, reduced query, because removal of facets implies removal of terms in the computed sum $\oplus$.

7 Application to an Image Test Collection

The weighting scheme presented in this paper is applied to an image test collection. It consists of 650 images [27], indexed in the form of conceptual graphs. The indexing process is computer-assisted, and it includes the contour-based identification of the image objects, as polygons drawn by the human indexer. The indexer associates to each object a concept. Then the concepts are organized by the indexer in a composition hierarchy, according to the structure of the image.

Indexing is based on the image model presented in [24]. Accordingly, three facets can be detected in each image. Each facet corresponds to a particular subgraph, introduced by using a specific syntax. The RELIEF image retrieval system described in [13] handles this image collection by using the projection operator as the matching function. It was proposed as an integration of object-oriented modeling and Web technology, and implemented on top of the DBMS O_2. In the previous version, the system only provided classification of images into relevance classes, without finer ranking for the images within a class. The classes correspond to the model in [25], which means that only the presence of the facets is taken into account, without their importance in the indexes. Accordingly, there are three classes. The first class corresponds to the projection of all facets of the query in the document indexes, and the following two classes are obtained by removing a certain facet from the query.

As the number of images in a class can be big, the lack of within-class ranking may constitute a major drawback for the user. Images have to be ranked not only with respect to facets, but also with respect to the importance of facets in the images. By using the approach described in this paper, this problem is solved, and the images within a class can be ranked (see figure 7).

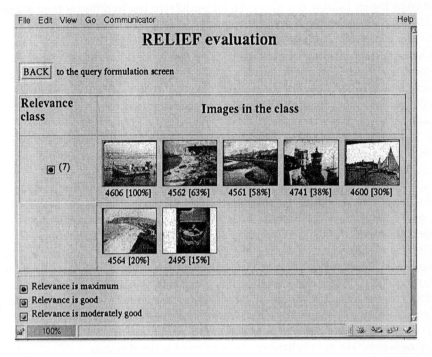

Fig. 7. The system retrieves 7 images, for a query formulated by a conceptual graph and corresponding to "boats and sea".

If we look at the retrieved images, we can see that they are indeed ordered according to the area parameter. For instance, the areas of the boat and the sea in the first image are the greatest, hence this image is the first to be retrieved. An interesting point is related to the image 2495. It is the last in the ranking, due to the composition parameter. Indeed, the composition hierarchy of this image places the objects boat and sea deeper, as compared to the other images: to get to the objects by starting from the top of the hierarchy, we pass by image (the top), church (the context of the image, not seen explicitly), sculpture, picture (which is drawn on the sculpture), to finally arrive at the objects boat and sea. The current status of the system includes the area and composition image parameters. We are presently implementing the other parameters identified in section 2. Therefore, the ranking of the retrieved images may change accordingly.

8   Conclusion

The weighting scheme presented in this paper was implemented on an image retrieval system based on conceptual graphs. However, we argue that the approach is general and can be applied for any relational indexing language [8]: the proposed scheme does not depend on how the indexing terms are made, and these terms could be not only conceptual graphs or keywords, but also any element of a complex language, i.e. terminological logics, Datalog etc. Moreover, the media type can be different from images, without any change of the core of our approach.

This paper is a challenge, as it provides a weighting scheme for complex media using expressive indexing languages. We hope that it opens fruitful developments in information retrieval, as we believe that it may be extended and applied not only as a research proposition, but also as a possible direction to provide better services for the millions of users that access the Web search engines every day, in search of multimedia documents.

The next step is to perform more elaborate experimentations, to study the effectiveness of the weighting scheme introduced in this paper. In particular, we would like to include the user as a salient part of the ranking method. This leads to a kind of relevance feedback where relevance not only concerns *"how relevant the documents are for the user"* but also *"what the user thinks of the preferences (parameters) suggested by the system between documents"*. Indeed, it is important to know whether the media dependent parameters and the weighting functions that we proposed capture well the relevance of objects from the user point of view, or whether other measures and features would be better. For instance, the parameters we used here for images have tried to capture some of their characteristics; others certainly remain to be included, such as colour [18] and texture [28], and still others have to be detected. Extending the ranking method with approaches for this sort of feedback is in the scope of our future work. Our first step toward a user-centered image retrieval system was presented in [29]. Our final purpose is to build a personalized precision oriented retrieval system.

References

1. G. Salton and M.J. McGill. *Introduction to Modern Information Retrieval*. Mcgraw Hill Book Company, New York, 1983.
2. C.J. van Rijsbergen. *Information Retrieval*. Butterworths, London, 1979.
3. K. Sparck Jones. A statistical interpretation of term specificity and its application in retrieval. *Journal of Documentation*, 28(3):289–299, 1972.
4. G. Salton. *Automatic Text Processing: the transformation, analysis, and retrieval of information by computer*. Addison-Wesley Publishing Company, 1989.
5. G. Salton and C. Buckley. Term-weighting approaches in automatic text retrieval. *Information Processing & Management*, 24(5):513–523, 1988.
6. C. Buckley, J. Allan, and G. Salton. Automatic routing and retrieval using SMART: TREC-2. *Information Processing & Management*, 31(3):315–326, 1995.
7. C. Meghini, F. Sebastiani, U. Straccia, and C. Thanos. A model of information retrieval based on a terminological logic. In R. Korfhage, E. Rassmussen, and P. Willet, editors, *Proceedings of the 16th Annual International ACM SIGIR Conference on Research and Development in Information Retrieval, Pittsburgh, PA*, pages 298–307. ACM, ACM Press, June 1993.
8. I. Ounis. *Un modèle d'indexation relationnel pour les graphes conceptuels fondé sur une interprétation logique*. PhD thesis, Université Joseph Fourier, Grenoble, February 1998.

9. T.W.C. Huibers, I. Ounis, and J.P. Chevallet. Conceptual graphs aboutness. In P.W. Eklund, G. Ellis, and G. Mann, editors, *Proceedings of the 4th International Conference on Conceptual Structures, ICCS'96*, volume 1115 of *Lecture Notes in Artificial Intelligence*, pages 130–144, Sydney, August 1996. Springer-Verlag, Berlin.

10. J.P. Callan, W.B. Croft, and J. Broglio. TREC and TIPSTER experiments with INQUERY. *Information Processing & Management*, 31(3):327–343, 1995.

11. I. Ounis and T.W.C. Huibers. A logical relational approach for information retrieval indexing. In *19th Annual BCS-IRSG Colloquium on IR Research, Aberdeen, Scotland*. EWIC, Springer-Verlag, 8–9 April 1997.

12. J. Farradane. Relational indexing Part I. *Journal of Information Science*, 1(5):267–276, 1980.

13. I. Ounis and M. Pasca. RELIEF: Combining expressiveness and rapidity into a single system. In *The ACM SIGIR'98 conference, Melbourne, Australia*, 1998.

14. G. Salton, C.S. Yang, and C.T. Yu. A theory of term importance in automatic text analysis. *Journal of the ASIS*, 26(1):33–44, 1975.

15. A. Singhal, G. Salton, M. Mitra, and C. Buckley. Document length normalization. *Information Processing & Management*, 32(5):619–633, 1996.

16. O. Andrieu. *Trouver l'info sur l'internet*. Eyrolles, Paris, France, 1998.

17. J. May and P. Barnard. Modelling multimodal interaction: A theory-based technique for design analysis and support. In *Human-Computer Interaction (INTERACT '97)*, pages 667–668, London. Also in www.shef.ac.uk/ pc1jm/guide.html, 1997. Chapman & Hall.

18. A. Plante, S. Tanaka, and S. Inoue. Evaluating the location of hot spots in interactive scenes using the 3R toolbox. In *Proceedings of the ACM SIGCHI Conference on Human Factors in Computing Systems (CHI'98)*, pages 117–123, Los Angeles, USA, 1998. ACM Press.

19. J.F. Sowa. *Conceptual Structures : Information Processing in Mind and Machine*. Addison-Wesley Publishing Company, 1984.

20. H. van den Berg. *Knowledge Graphs and Logic*. PhD thesis, September 1993.

21. P.E. Maher. A similarity measure for conceptual graphs. *International Journal of Intelligent Systems*, 8:819–837, 1993.

22. V. Wuwongse and M. Manzano. Fuzzy conceptual graphs. In *In ICCS' 93 International Conference on Conceptual Structures, Quebec City, Canada*, pages 430–449, August 1993.

23. C. J. van Rijsbergen. A new theoretical framework for information retrieval. In *ACM Conference on Research and development in Information Retrieval, Pisa*, pages 194–200, 1986.

24. M. Mechkour. EMIR2. An extended model for image representation and retrieval. In *DEXA'95. Database and EXpert system Applications, London.*, pages 395–404, September 1995.

25. I. Ounis and J.P. Chevallet. Using conceptual graphs in a multifaceted logical model for information retrieval. In R.R. Wagner and H. Thoma, editors, *Proceedings of the 7th International Conference on Database and EXpert Systems Applications, DEXA'96*, volume 1134 of *Lecture Notes in Computer Science*, pages 812–823, Zurich, Switzerland, September 1996. Springer.

26. F. Paradis. *Un modèle d'indexation pour les documents textuels structurés*. PhD thesis, Université Joseph Fourier, Novembre 1996.

27. Y. Chiaramella and M. Mechkour. Indexing an image test collection. Technical report, FERMI BRA 8134, April 1997.

28. J. May, S. Scott, and P. Barnard. *Structuring Displays: a psychological guide*. Eurographics Tutorial Notes Series, EACG: Geneva, 1995.

29. I. Ounis and M. Pasca. Finding the best parameters for image ranking: a user-oriented approach. In *The IEEE Knowledge and Data Engineering Exchange Workshop (KDEX-98), Taipei, Taiwan, November, 1998*.

A Fast Method for Ensuring the Consistency of Integrity Constraints

Barry G. T. Lowden and Jerome Robinson

Department of Computer Science, The University of Essex,
Wivenhoe Park, Colchester CO4 3SQ, Essex,
United Kingdom

Abstract. The last few years have seen an increasing trend to use database technology in more innovative and diverse application domains which places even greater demands on DBMS for accuracy of information. The provision of correct and reliable data is therefore of vital importance and systems for integrity enforcement crucial. At the same time, as systems become more sophisticated, the sheer number and complexity of integrity constraints, associated with applications, is steadily increasing together with the rate at which changes are made to the constraint base itself. In this paper we examine the problem of constraint maintenance and propose a fast method for validating additional and modified constraints. The method is based on the construction of *Modal Records* to determine if a newly defined constraint is consistent with an existing constraint set.

1. Introduction

Integrity constraints, or rules, are used to specify database semantics relating to the correctness, or legality, of data residing in the database. Any attempted change, to the database, which violates one or more integrity constraints would therefore result in rejection by the DBMS integrity control system. In addition, however, to their conventional use in validating update transactions, integrity constraints are seen as an increasingly valuable information source in their own right. Thus recent developments in query optimisation [1,9,10,11,14] make use of the semantic information inherent in integrity constraints, together with rules derived from the data itself, to transform user queries into semantically equivalent alternatives which execute in far less time. Also many systems, such as taxation and social security, now incorporate facilities for interrogating the constraint base to provide answers to hypothetical *'what if'* questions, e.g. *'what criteria must X meet if s/he is to be eligible for disability allowance?'*.

These new forms of application demand more sophistication in the way constraints may be expressed over and above the standard 'range and domain' types which are a feature of most current database systems. Increased constraint complexity, however, must of necessity place a greater burden on the constraint management system to ensure that the constraint set is consistent within itself.

In this paper we address the specific issue of constraint consistency and propose a fast technique for validating new and modified constraints against an existing constraint base. Section 2 reviews the different types of constraint with which we are concerned and in section 3 we briefly describe a traditional approach to consistency checking. section 4 introduces our new method based on the formulation of hypothetical modal records and illustrates the algorithm's effectiveness with respect to several examples. Finally in section 5 we present our conclusions.

2. Constraint Definition

A typical database system will have associated with it a number of constraints which are intended to ensure the accuracy and correctness of the data in the database. These are known as integrity constraints, and are dealt with more fully in the literature [3,4,6]. We will assume a relational model and operate under the assumption that constraints are expressed in some variation of first-order logic or predicate calculus language [5,12,13]. In order not to restrict ourselves to any particular database system, our system uses a version of the Tuple Relational Calculus (TRC) as defined below.

Tuple Relational Calculus:

Constraints: Φ

$$\Phi ::= A \mid (\sim\Phi) \mid (\Phi\wedge\Phi) \mid (\Phi\vee\Phi) \mid (\Phi\rightarrow\Phi) \mid (\Phi\leftrightarrow\wedge\Phi) \mid (\forall v\in\tau\Phi) \mid (\exists v\in\tau\Phi)$$

$$A ::= (\alpha=\beta) \mid (\alpha<\beta) \mid (\alpha>\beta) \mid (\alpha\leq\beta) \mid (\alpha\geq\beta)$$

$$\alpha ::= \kappa \mid (v.\alpha)$$

Constraints are constructed from the usual logical connectives, plus equality and the inequalities, terms α, β comprise constants and tuple variables dotted with an appropriate attribute.

The constraints themselves can typically be divided into several classes. Firstly, there are *domain* and *range* constraints which place restrictions upon the values which an attribute may take. For example, if we assume the following relations:

EMP(emp#, name, sex, department, commission, basic-salary).
DEPARTMENT(name, location, budget)

and we wish to restrict, say, the salary range of all employees, in the EMP relation, to between 10000 and 40000, then the following TRC formula would be specified:

$$\forall x\in EMP(x.basic\text{-}salary > 10000 \wedge x.basic\text{-}salary < 40000)$$

Conditional constraints are those which limit the values certain attributes may take based on the values of other attributes. A typical example of such a constraint might be:

$$\forall x \in EMP((x.commission > 0.03) \rightarrow (x.basic\text{-}salary >= 20000))$$

which states that if the commission is greater than 0.03 then the basic salary for this EMP record must be greater than 20,000.

Constraints associated with the key fields of the various database relations include *primary key* constraints and *foreign key* constraints. Primary key constraints require the relations have unique, non-null primary keys. With respect to the relation EMP, we can easily specify the non-null requirement by:

$$\forall x \in EMP \sim (emp\# = NULL)$$

It is also possible to specify the *uniqueness* constraint as a TRC expression. For example, if we wish to assert that only one name is associated with each EMP, then the constraint would be:

$$\forall x \in EMP(\forall y \in EMP(x.emp\# = y.emp\#) \rightarrow (x.name = y.name))$$

Primary key constraints are actually a special case of functional dependency where the primary key attribute(s) of a relation functionally determine(s) the values of all other attributes in that relation. Of course in order for a uniqueness constraint specified in this way, to have its desired effect, the underlying database system must be able to ensure that stored relations do not contain duplicate tuples, While this is specified in the underlying relational model [3], this is not actually implemented in many existing systems.

Finally, foreign key constraints are to ensure that any attributes within a relation that are pointers into other relations take on meaningful values. For example, if we assume in our EMP relation that the attribute department is required to match the key field 'name' of *DEPARTMENT*, then the appropriate foreign key constraint would be:

$$\forall x \in EMP(\exists y \in DEPARTMENT(x.department = y.name))$$

These then are the general types of constraint which are likely to be associated with a database. Whilst other classifications are discussed in the literature, they tend to be some variation of those described above.

3. Constraint Maintenance

Maintaining the consistency of a complex constraint base, containing the classes described above, is a non-trivial task involving the checking of new or modified constraints to ensure they do not violate the existing constraint set. Maintenance is particularly complex where *conditional* constraints are involved, ie. those specifying implication, since these may *imply* further constraints which are not explicitly defined in the constraint set and yet are part of database integrity. A simple example might be that, from $(A \rightarrow B)$ and $(B \rightarrow C)$ we may infer $(A \rightarrow C)$ even though the latter is not explicit. Any attempt then to introduce a new constraint $((A \rightarrow (\sim C))$ should be rejected even though it does not violate either of the original constraints individually.

A traditional *theorem proving* approach would indeed require all the interactions between constraints, in the modified set, to be expressed explicitly. By viewing the constraints as a set of logical axioms and the database relations as forming the relational structure against which these axioms are evaluated, the constraints could be turned into a set of 'compiled' or derived constraints [7]. To generate this, the constraints would normally first be converted to clausal form [2]. It is then a case of using repeated resolution and subsumption [8] until a fixed point is reached.

Take for example:

Initial Rules:

$\forall x \in EMP(x.status = 'M') \rightarrow (x.basic\text{-}salary > 15000)$
$\forall x \in EMP(x.sex = male) \rightarrow (x.basic\text{-}salary < 15001)$
$\forall x \in EMP(x.basic\text{-}salary > 15000) \leftrightarrow \sim(x.basic\text{-}salary < 15001)$
$\forall x \in EMP(x.sex = female) \leftrightarrow \sim (x.sex = male)$

using the process referred to above, these would lead to the following closure:

$\forall x \in EMP(x.basic\text{-}salary > 15000) \rightarrow (x.sex = female)$
$\forall x \in EMP(x.status = 'M') \rightarrow (x.sex = female)$
$\forall x \in EMP(x.status = 'M') \leftrightarrow \sim (x.basic\text{-}salary < 15001)$
$\forall x \in EMP(x.status = 'M') \leftrightarrow \sim (x.sex = male)$
$\forall x \in EMP(x.basic\text{-}salary < 15001) \leftrightarrow \sim (x.sex = male)$
$\forall x \in EMP(x.sex = female) \vee (x.basic\text{-}salary < 15001)$
$\forall x \in EMP(x.sex = female) \leftrightarrow \sim (x.sex = male)$
$\forall x \in EMP(x.sex = female) \vee (x.sex = male)$
$\forall x \in EMP(x.basic\text{-}salary < 15001) \leftrightarrow \sim (x.basic\text{-}salary > 15000)$
$\forall x \in EMP(x.basic\text{-}salary < 15001) \vee (x.basic\text{-}salary > 15000)$
$\forall x \in EMP(x.sex = male) \rightarrow (x.basic\text{-}salary < 15001)$
$\forall x \in EMP(x.status = 'M') \rightarrow (x.basic\text{-}salary > 15000)$

To generate the closure of the theorems of the constraints, it is necessary for all the relevant axioms regarding relations to be available as constraints. Thus, for example,
Rule 4:

$$\forall x \in EMP(x.sex = female) \leftrightarrow \sim (x.sex = male)$$

would need to be explicitly stated by the system user.

The completeness of resolution depends, therefore, on how the axioms are expressed and the presence of transitive axioms can prevent the existence of a finite fixed point. If the full set of axioms were use then there might be problems in controlling over-generation, deciding what constitutes a fixed point and consequently of detecting termination.

4. An Alternative Approach to Checking Rule Consistency

Reliance on a theorem prover then is problematic and impractical for ensuring constraint consistency in systems, particularly those with large and volatile constraint sets. In this section we present a new approach whereby we find some hypothetical modification to the database such that the TRC expression Φ associated with the new or changed constraint is true and then evaluate the existing constraint set with respect to this modified state using a constraint checking algorithm Ω. If there are no constraint violations, then the modified state is legal and the proposed constraint update is consistent.

Generating hypothetical database modifications is a two stage process. We begin by considering the case of constraint addition. The first stage involves building a representation of the basic requirements of the new constraint, while the second stage involves instantiating this representation further with respect to information currently held in the constraint base. The output from the first stage is a set of initial *modal* record(s) R which encode the requirements of the new constraint. We will illustrate this process by example and assume a database containing a variation of the relation defined earlier:

$$EMP(name, department, sex, status, commission, basic\text{-}salary)$$

We will also assume that we wish to check the following new constraint Φ

$$\Phi1[\;\forall x \in EMP((x.sex = female \land x.status = \text{'}M\text{'} \land x.commission > 0.01))$$
$$\rightarrow (x.basic\text{-}salary > 15000)]$$

against an existing constraint set.

First we create a tuple template for the relation in which each attribute value is unknown. We represent this by associating with each attribute a unique, uninstantiated variable U :

$$\{name = u1, department = u2, sex = u3, status = u4, commission = u5,$$
$$basic\text{-}salary = u6\}$$

and then instantiate these variables according to the values contained in $\Phi1$ to yield the initial modal record:

$$R0\{name = u1, department = u2, sex = female, status = \text{'}M\text{'},$$
$$commission = (> 0.01), basic\text{-}salary = (> 15000)\}$$

It is important to note that, in a modal record, attributes (including keys) can remain uninstantiated and attribute values may be specified as equal to constants, sets or ranges. Instantiated values must be consistent with domain/range constraints specified for the associated attribute, if not the algorithm terminates and the new constraint is rejected immediately.

Constraints containing disjunction are *normalised* and so may give rise to more than one initial modal record, for example:

$$\Phi2[\ \forall x \in EMP((x.status = \text{`}M\text{'}) \vee (x.sex = male \wedge x.commission > 0.01)) \\ \rightarrow (x.basic\text{-}salary > 15000)]$$

would be expressed as:

$$\Phi3[\ \forall x \in EMP(x.status = \text{`}M\text{'} \rightarrow (x.basic\text{-}salary > 15000)]$$
$$\Phi4[\ \forall x \in EMP(x.sex = male \wedge x.commission > 0.01)) \\ \rightarrow (x.basic\text{-}salary > 15000)]$$

generating records:

$R1\{name = u1, department = u2, sex = u3,\ status = \text{`}M\text{'},\ commission = u5,\\ basic\text{-}salary > 15000\}$

$R2\{name = u1, department = u2, sex = male,\ status = u4, commission > 0.01,\\ basic\text{-}salary > 15000\ \}$

each being a valid representation with respect to $\Phi2$.

Having encoded the initial modal record(s), we may now attempt a hypothetical update of the database to see whether any of the existing constraints are violated. In doing so, however, the possibility of unknown values occurring in the transaction must be taken into account by the constraint checking algorithm. If it is possible to find a consistent set of assumptions about all the values introduced by the new constraint, then we can report that the modified constraint set is consistent. If no such set of assumptions can be found, then the modified constraint set is not consistent. The algorithm is best illustrated by example. In what follows we assume that the usual preliminary checks will already have been made confirming that any proposed constraint change is consistent with the current state (data contents) of the database and that the existing constraints are consistent with each other.

Assume an existing constraint set Ψ in which, to preserve uniformity, domain/range constraints are represented as the instantiation of NULL values.

Domain/Range
$\Psi1[\ \forall\ x \in EMP((x.sex = NULL) \rightarrow (x.sex = female \vee x.sex = male))]$
$\Psi2[\ \forall\ x \in EMP((\ x.status = NULL)\\ \qquad\qquad \rightarrow (\ x.status = \text{`}M\text{'} \vee x.status = \text{`}S\text{'} \vee x.status = \text{`}D\text{'}))]$
$\Psi3[\ \forall\ x \in EMP((x.basic\text{-}salary = NULL)\\ \qquad\qquad \rightarrow (x.basic\text{-}salary > 10000 \wedge x.basic\text{-}salary < 40000))]$

Conditional

$\Psi 4[\ \forall\ x \in EMP(x.sex =\ male \rightarrow x.basic\text{-}salary < 25000)]$

$\Psi 5\ \forall\ x \in EMP((x.sex =\ female \wedge x.status =\ 'M') \rightarrow (x.basic\text{-}salary > 15000))]$

$\Psi 6[\ \forall\ x \in EMP((x.sex =\ male \wedge x.commission > 0.01) \rightarrow (x.status =\ 'M'))]$

$\Psi 7[\ \forall\ x \in EMP((x.sex =\ female \wedge x.commission > 0.03)$

$\rightarrow (x.basic\text{-}salary >= 20000))]$

We first take the simple case of attempting to add a new range constraint:

$$\Phi 1\ (\ \forall\ x \in EMP(x.commission >= 0.03 \wedge x.commission < 0.2))$$

which generates the initial state of the modal record:

$R\{name = u1,\ department = u2,\ sex = u3,\ status = u4,$

$commission = (\geq 0.03 \wedge < 0.2),\ basic\text{-}salary = u6\}$

The constraint checking algorithm now begins the validation of this record by processing through the constraint base, instantiating or updating attribute values as implied by each individual constraint.

During this process, two situations may arise:

(i) the implied record attribute value is currently NULL, in which case it is simply instantiated.

(ii) the record attribute value is not NULL, in which case the algorithm decides whether the implied value is consistent with the existing value. If so, then the value is updated, if not the constraint modification fails and the algorithm terminates. Updating (restricting) an existing value, however, may invalidate the modal record with respect to earlier constraint(s) requiring the validation process to be repeated. This condition is registered by the setting of a *restriction* flag.

In our example, instantiating attribute values with respect to each constraint, in turn, transforms ($\Rightarrow$) the modal record as follows:

$\Psi 1$ *through* $\Psi 5$

$\Rightarrow R5\{name = u1,\ department = u2,\ sex = (male, female),\ status = ('M','S','D'),$

$commission = (\geq 0.03 \wedge < 0.2),\ basic\text{-}salary = (>10000 \wedge < 40000\}$

continuing the validation process, we see that:

$\Psi 6[\ \forall\ x \in EMP((x.sex =\ male \wedge x.commission > 0.01) \rightarrow (x.status =\ 'M'))]$

$\Rightarrow R6\{name = u1,\ department = u2,\ sex = (male, female),\ status = ('M'),$

$commission = (\geq 0.03 \wedge < 0.2),\ basic\text{-}salary = (>10000 \wedge < 40000\}$

the instantiation of *x.status* = *'M'* causing the restriction flag to be set. A further cycle of the algorithm reveals no violations and the new constraint is shown, therefore, to be consistent with Ψ. Note that the domain/range constraints in Ψ need not be checked again, in subsequent cycles, since the attributes referred to are no longer *NULL*.

As a second example we consider the introduction of a new conditional constraint:

$$\Phi2(\forall\ x\in EMP(x.status = \text{'}M\text{'} \land x.commission > 0.01)$$
$$\rightarrow (x.basic\_salary >= 25000))$$

which translates into the initial modal record:

R0{name = u1, department = u2, sex = u3, status = ('M')), commission = (>0.01), basic-salary = (>= 25000)}

Processing through the constraint base:

Ψ1 through Ψ3
$\Rightarrow$ *R3{name = u1, department = u2, sex = (male, female), status = 'M', commission = (>0.01), basic-salary = (>= 25000}*

however the algorithm terminates on attempting to validate the record against:

Ψ4[$\forall$ x$\in$EMP((x.sex = male) $\rightarrow$ (x.basic-salary < 25000))]

since the implied value is inconsistent. The system responds by identifying *Ψ4* as the constraint violated, and presents the user with a proposal to modify *Φ2 to:*

$$\Phi2\text{'}(\forall\ x\in EMP(sex = female \land x.status = \text{'}M\text{'} \land x.commission > 0.01)$$
$$\rightarrow (x.basic\text{-}salary >= 25000))$$

The discussion so far has related only to insertion of new constraints, however *modification* of existing constraints may be expressed simply as the deletion of the original followed by attempted insertion of the revised constraint.

As a final example, therefore, suppose the original constraint set Ψ is extended by:

Ψ8[$\forall$ x$\in$EMP(x.basic-salary < 25000) $\rightarrow$ (x.department = 'computing')]
Ψ9[$\forall$ x$\in$EMP(x.department = 'computing') $\rightarrow$ (x.status = 'M' $\lor$ x.status = 'S')]

and we wish to modify constraint:

Ψ6[$\forall$ x$\in$EMP((x.sex = male $\land$ x.commission > 0.01) $\rightarrow$ (x.status = 'M'))]
to: *Ψ6'[$\forall$ x$\in$EMP((x.sex = male $\land$ x.commission > 0.02)*
$\rightarrow (x.status = \text{'}M\text{'} \lor x.status = \text{'}D\text{'}))]$

The modified constraint is first encoded as initial modal record:

$$R0\{name = u1, department = u2, sex = male, \ status = (`M', `D'))$$
$$commission = (>0.02), \ basic\text{-}salary = u5\}$$

and validation against the existing constraints yields:

$\Psi1$ *through* $\Psi3$

$\Rightarrow R3\{name = u1, department = u2, sex = male, \ status = (`M', `D')),$
   commission $= (>0.02), basic\text{-}salary = (>10000 \wedge < 40000)\}$

$\Psi4$ *through* $\Psi5$

$\Rightarrow R5\{name = u1, department = u2, sex = male, \ status = (`M', `D')),$
   commission $= (>0.02), basic\text{-}salary = (< 25000)\}$ *(with restriction flag set)*
$\Psi6$

$\Rightarrow$ *not enforced. (replaced by updated version).*

$\Psi7$ *through* $\Psi8$

$\Rightarrow R2\{name = u1, department = `computing', sex = male, status = (`M', `D')),$
   commission $= (>0.02), \ basic\text{-}salary = (< 25000)\}$

$\Psi9 \Rightarrow$ *algorithm terminates on attempting to update status to (`M', `S').*

Feedback, to the user, is that the constraint modification was rejected, by reference to $\Psi9$, on the grounds of status 'D' being an invalid option.

The constraint checking algorithm, described above, has a worst time complexity of $O(n)^2$ where n is the number of conditional constraints. This is because, potentially, each of these constraints could restrict a domain value requiring the validation cycle to be repeated. However, $O(n)^2$ is still a considerable time saving over the theorem proving approach in which the number of derived constraints generated may increase exponentially with the number of original constraints.

5 Conclusions

We have explained how it is possible to construct a system which allows the simple checking of new or modified constraints against an existing constraint base. Firstly we reviewed the different classes of constraint which may be encountered in database systems and subsequently discussed the traditional theorem proving approach for determining constraint consistency.

A new method was then introduced, involving the construction of modal records which are representations of the constraint changes to be effected. During this process, unknown values in the modal records are instantiated or updated, where appropriate, by reference to existing constraints. The algorithm attempts a hypothetical update of the database, which involves checking the validity of these modal record(s) against the original constraint set. If a new or modified constraint is found to be inconsistent, the user is provided with concise, helpful information concerning the reasons for the violation and suggested revisions to ensure consistency.

Bibliography

[1] Chakravarthy U.S., Grant J. and Minker J., *'Logic-based approach to semantic query optimisation'*, ACM Transactions on Database Systems, Vol. 15, No.2, 162-207, June 1990.

[2] Clocksin W.F. and Mellish C.S., *'Programming in Prolog'*, Springer, Berlin, 1987.

[3] Codd E.F., *'Domains, keys and referential integrity in relational databases'*, Info DB3, No.1, 1988

[4] Elmasri R. and Navathe S.B., 'Fundamentals of database systems', 2nd Edition, Addison-Wesley, 1994.

[5] Freytag J. and Goodman N., 'On the translation of relational queries into iterative programs', ACM Trans. Database Syst. Vol.14, No.1, 1 – 27, 1989.

[6] Godfrey P., Grant J., Gryz J. and Minker J., 'Integrity Constraints: Semantics and applications', Logics for Databases and Information Systems, Kluwer, Ch.9, 1998.

[7] Henschen L. and McCune W., 'Compiling constraint-checking programs from first-order formulas', Advances in Database Theory, Vol.2, Gallaire, Minker, and Nicolas, Eds., Plenum Press, New York, 145 – 169, 1984.

[8] Kowalski R., 'Logic for problem solving', North Holland, Amsterdam, 1979

[9] Lowden B.G.T. and Robinson J., 'A semantic query optimiser using automatic rule derivation', Proc. Fifth Annual Workshop on Information Technologies and Systems, Netherlands, 68-76, December 1995.

[10] Lowden B.G.T. and Robinson J., 'A statistical approach to rule selection in semantic query optimisation', to appear in Proc. ISMIS'99, Warsaw, June 1999.

[11] Siegel M., et. al., 'A method for automatic rule derivation to support semantic query optimisation', ACM, TODs, Vol.17, No.4, 563-600, December 1992.

[12] Qian X., 'The expressive power of the bounded-iteration construct', Acta Inf. 28, 631 – 656, October 1991.

[13] Qian X., 'The deductive synthesis of database transactions', ACM Trans. Database Syst. 18, 4, 626 – 677, December 1993.

[14] Sayli A.and Lowden B.G.T., 'A fast transformation method for semantic query optimisation', Proc. IDEAS'97, IEEE, Montreal, 319-326, 1997.

A Mechanism for Deriving Specifications of Security Functions in the CC Framework

Jussipekka Leiwo

Vrije University
Division of Mathematics and Computer Science, Faculty of Sciences
De Boelelaan 1081a, 1081 HV Amsterdam, The Netherlands
leiwo@cc.vu.nl

Abstract. At the first stage of the Common Criteria process for evaluating the security of information systems, organizational objectives for information security are translated into the specification of all relevant security functions of a becoming system. These specifications are then assessed to specify the subset to be implemented, and further evaluated. The second stage involves risk analysis or related technologies, and the evaluation phase is the major contribution of the common criteria. The derivation of security function specifications from security objectives is the area where further research is needed to provide pragmatic tools for supporting the task. This paper describes a mechanism, harmonization of information security requirements, that aids in this process.

1 Introduction

Early criteria for security evaluation, such as TCSEC [1] and ITSEC [2] focused on the correctness of the specification and implementation of a computer security policy model, mostly in multilevel security (MLS) environments. These criteria were heavily based on early formal models for computer security, dealing with formal security policy models that can be proven to prevent access violations. Models for computer security have proven efficient in designing secure computer systems, and with the aid of cryptography, formal models have been successfully applied in networked environments [6]. A system can be composed of potentially recursive partitions, where each partition has consists of a trusted computing base (TCB) that implements the access control facility. Assuming each partition is secure, it can be shown that under certain conditions, the set of partitions is also secure. At early research, this was called a hook-up property [13] and was further generalized to the theory of composability [14].

Security requirements for distributed systems are of much broader range than only access control. Confidentiality, authenticity, integrity and non-repudiation of messages and communications must also be protected. Security evaluation methods based on access control models do not adequately take into consideration these types of security requirements. The Common Criteria (CC) for the evaluation of information security [3] is a different approach. In CC, the scope of security requirements is expanded to cover also typical security requirements of distributed systems, and it therefore provides a promising alternative for estimating security of information systems. The major difficulty in the pragmatic application of CC framework is the lack of tools for deriving secifications of security functions from organizational security objectives. The contribution of this paper is a mechanism to aid in this derivation.

The CC based Kruger-Eloff process [11] for the evaluation of information security is illustrated in Fig. 1. Tasks in the development and evaluation of information security are illustrated as rectangles. Round cornered rectangles represent deliverables of tasks, and ellipses input from participants. In first stage, all possible security relevant functions are determined. Security objectives are formulated, and security requirements derived from the objectives. The security foundation consists of elements to be protected against expected threats, and high level strategies according to which counter measures are determined. In the second stage, various risk/importance ratings are applied to security relevant functions, and together with the predicted impact of security functions, a decision matrix or other decision support structure is generated to aid in the decision of the subset of functions to be implemented. Third stage is then the actual evaluation of the target of evaluation (TOE).

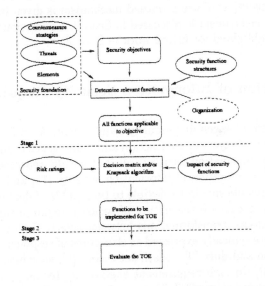

Fig. 1. CC Framework for the evaluation of information security

As neither the Kruger-Eloff framework nor the CC provides concrete means for carrying out the task, the importance of the proposed mechanism for deriving specifications of security functions emerges. Illustrated as a dotted ellipse, the organization in which information security is developed is added as an input to the specification of security functions. Security development organization refers to the structure of responsibility in security, not to the business structure in which security work is orgnized. The role of the organization becomes important, and it has been shown that both dependencies and groupings of information security requirements can be achieved through organizational modeling [10].

It is assumed that organizational security objectives are known. The proposed mechanism contributes to expressing, organizing and further processing the organizational knowledge of information systems security. Security objectives are business-oriented informal statements by managerial personnel and must first be formulated into a suitable notation for being processed by automated harmonization tools. This task is typically delegated to security analysts, those with detailed knowledge of security enforcement technologies and experience with formal statements and security development tools. Since managerial personnel is responsible for making decisions under business risks and organizing resources to meet various business objectives, dealing with formal security development frameworks is not within their interests. Therefore, objectives are assumed to found the basis for the work of security analysts. Once the security specifications are derived, business decisions are made to select those to be implemented. This is mostly carried out by risk analysis, that is a well established area of professional practise.

This paper first surveys mechanisms for expressing information security requirements. An overview of the proposed mechanism is given in Sect. 3. Implementation of the mechanism is discussed in Sect. 4. Conclusions shall be drawn and directions highlighted for future work in Sect. 5.

2 Specification of Information Security Requirements

The major problem of specifying security requirements for information systems is the large number of layers of abstraction and many types of information security requirements. Information security policies typically represent various layers of organizational coordination of information security [15] and mechanisms for expressing requirements should be flexible to be capable of dealing with all these layers, expressive to capture the nature of security requirements at each layer and to provide smooth transformations between layers. High level information security policies are typically expressed as structures of responsibility [5], expressions of permission and duty [9], speech act theory [8], as valued probabilities of various threats [4], through requirement engineering techniques [7], or even as natural language descriptions [16]. The transformation of these descriptions into the actual specifications of information security functions is not very smooth and a different approache is required.

In dependable computing, security is usually seen as a quality of service (QOS) attribute alongside with safety, accuracy, performance and correctness. A specific notation is needed for information security requirements. The notation must also bind protection requirements into criteria that are needed from automated or human subjects to access specific tangible resources, such as communication subsystems. This may sound undesirable from the system holistic point of view, but is essential to differentiate security requirements from generic QOS requirements, usually expressed as constraints in system design.

The problem of transition of security policy objectives into technical information security policies is approached by loosening the semantics of statements used for expressing security requirements. Once the notation is made flexible, various requirements are processed by harmonization functions. Harmonization function is a statement used for transforming requirements into lower levels of abstraction and for solving internal inconsistencies of a requirement base. Merging of requirements is supported to transform requirements into lower levels of abstraction in a formal and, as in the Harmonizer software, automated manner.

3 Overview and Concepts of Harmonization

Harmonization of information security requirements [12] is a process of transforming formally expressed information security requirements into lower levels of abstraction, represented as lower levels in the formally specified information security development organization. Requirements can be partially defined, but harmonization can be applied to incomplete requirements to assure from details being added in a systematic and comprehensive manner. This is believed to lead to a more optimized collection of security requirements, and higher assurance of the consistency of security enforcement. As the notation for expressing information security requirements is consistent throughout the levels of abstraction, the transition path from abstract information security objectives (stated as highly incomplete requirements with generic security enforcement methodologies) into technical security policies (with exact specifications of mechanisms and configurations) is smooth and verifiable.

The organization in which requirements are harmonized is a hierarchy consisting of a number of organizational layers, each consisting of a number of organizational units. The organization is characterized by *Child* and *Parent* relationships, that specify the ways which requirements are refined throughout the organization. Formal specification is available at [12]. As *Child* units belong to lower layers than their *Parent* units, the mapping implements information security meta-policies that coordinate the specification of actual information security policies, required for coordinating communication between processes under different administrative domains.

Harmonization of requirements is a process where a requirement base or a subset of a requirement base is modified by enforcing harmonization functions, expressed as statements *[precond : postcond]* that can be informally interpreted as "For each requirement of the chosen subset of all requirement bases that matches *precond*, the alteration must be carried out as specified in *postcond*".

Merging of requirements occurs when either layer specific requirements are enforced for each unit at that layer or when requirements are enforced through *Child*-relationship. If certain conditions are satisfied, requirements of the unit into which requirement base higher priority requirements are altered or new requirements are generated to align the requirements into the upper level coordination. Theoretically, Merging is just a special case of harmonization. However, as the Harmonizer software deals with them separately, they shall also be discussed separately.

Requirements of units belonging to lower layers are formulated according to the coordination of units at upper layers. Layer specific requirements are requirements that are specific to each unit at a specific layer. Unit specific requirements are those specific only to the particular unit. Requirements of a unit are formulated by merging upper layer requirements, layer specific requirements, and unit specific requirements of a particular unit.

4 Implementation of Harmonization

4.1 Expression of Information Security Requirements

Information security requirements within the harmonization model are expressed as tuples $A;P;Q;Pr;Alg;PV$ where A is an association used for communication between processes P and Q. Association A is used to carry data according to protocol Pr and is required to be protected by algorithm Alg as coordinated by a parameter vector PV. For example, a requirement

Internet;Site1; Site2; SMTP; PGP; kl = 1024

is an requirement stating that E-mail (SMTP protocol) communication over the Internet between *Site1* and *Site2* must be protected by PGP with the encryption key length (parameter *kl*) being 1024 bits. This requirement does not contain adequate detail for implementation but highlights the nature of the way information security requirements are expressed. Further refinements to the notation can be made by describing the Alg as a pair (λ, Alg) that states that the communication is allowed at maximum to the data with security label λ. Absence of a protocol in a requirement base should be interpreted as a statement that no communication of that type is allowed.

Because of the loose semantics of requirement descriptions, generic names of various components can be used at higher levels of abstraction, and details can be added during the harmonization of requirements. Since personnel at different levels of the organization have different technical and managerial duties, it is logical to assume that details are added by various personnel according to various duties.

The limitation of the notation is that it is mostly concerned with specific requirements. Specific security requirements improve security of a specific system component, whereas pervasive requirements are concerned with issues such as assurance of implementation, the level of evidence required of the correctness of design and implementation of security functionality. Non-technical requirements state issues that are required for adequate administration and operation of trusted systems, as well as user education needed to improve security awareness and understanding of specific products. As the model and software discussed is a tool for dealing with security requirements, it is part of pervasive requirements, as it can be used to provide assurance of correctness of a requirement base. User education, operation and administration are strongly implementation dependent requirements. It is possible to have generic security management and education, but that will remain on a highly abstract and conceptual level, and specific system dependent issues can not be specified until a system design is complete.

4.2 Specification and Enforcement of Harmonization Functions

Harmonization functions are expressed as conditional statements where a specific transformation in a requirement base is enforced when a certain pre-condition is satisfied. A harmonization function is expressed as a statement *Precond : Transformation* where *Precond* is formulated using the syntax given in Fig. 2. Form example, *Precond*

$$Algorithm = PGP \ AND \ NOT \ kl > 768$$

matches with each requirement in a given harmonization scope where protection algorithm is PGP and key length is less than or equal to 768. Harmonization scope is the subset of requirement bases to which harmonization is to be applied to. The harmonizer software specifies four different scope. Transformation specifies one of the three types of harmonization: Requirement modifying harmonization, requirement generating harmonization or requirement removing harmonization.

```
Precond      ::= atom_cond | atom_cond log-op Precond
log-op       ::= AND | OR
atom_cond    ::= atom | NOT atom
atom         ::= num-field num-op num-value | str-field str-op str-value
num-field    ::= param-name
str-field    ::= Association | Process1 | Process2 | Protocol | Algorithm
field        ::= str-field | num-field
num-op       ::= = | < | >
str-op       ::= =
op           ::= str-op | num-op
value        ::= str-value | num-value
str-value    ::= String
num-value    ::= [0..9]*
```

Fig. 2. Syntax for harmonization functions

Requirement modifying harmonization is the basic case of harmonization. The syntax of *Transformation* statement is

$$A \ field = value$$

where *field* is any component of a requirement string and *value* is either either a string or a numeric value to which *field* is to be set for each matching requirement in the harmonization scope. The *A* letter just indicates the type of harmonization. For example, the harmonization function

$$Algorithm = PGP : A \; kl = 1024$$

alters parameter *kl* of each requirement within the current scope to be exactly 1024 for each requirement where *Algorithm* field equals to PGP. If the parameter *kl* does not exist for any of those requirements, it is created and added to the parameter vector. Requirement modifying harmonization is used for removing inconsistencies of requirement bases and for reducing abstraction of requirements. Since each unit in the organization may specify requirements independently, the probability of highly inconsistent application of protection measures and their configurations is high. As part of efficient management of information security is to reduce these inconsistencies, requirement modifying harmonization is a suitable tool.

Requirement generating harmonization is indicated by *G req* statement as a *Transformation* field of a harmonization function. Character *G* is only to indicate the type of harmonization and *req* is the specification of a requirement to be added to a requirement base of each layer and unit where the *Precond* is true. Requirement removing harmonization is simply indicated by specifying *Transformation* to be *R*. As a result, each requirement that matches *Precond* is removed from the requirement base. For example, the following pair of harmonization functions

$$Protocol = SMTP \; AND \; NOT \; Algorithm = PGP : G \; A;P;Q;SMTP;PGP;kl = unspec$$
$$Protocol = SMTP \; AND \; NOT \; Algorithm = PGP : R$$

first causes an examination of requirement bases for each requirement where protocol is SMTP but the protection algorithm something else than PGP. A new requirement isgenerated to to fix Algorithm to be PGP, leaving key length unspecified. The second function then removes each requirement that matches the original condition. This is, however, not a recommended way to use generating and removing harmonization since the abstraction of generated requirements is not necessarily reduced. This is because harmonization functions can not examine specifications of fields and specify the new requirement accordingly. It is recommended, instead, that requirement generating harmonization being used for situation where there are clear dependencies between requirements. For example, when an encryption specifying requirement also requires key exchange and key generation to be specified.

4.3 Merging of Requirements

The core of harmonization of information security requirements is to support transformation of requirement primitives to *Child* units and to enforce layer-specific requirements to various units. This is implemented by two types of requirement merging: Merging of layer-specific requirements into all units at that layer and merging of requirements of a unit to all its *Child* units. The essential function in merging is conflict identifying. The requirements to be merged (layer-specific or upper layer requirements) override requirements of target unit whenever they are in conflict. The *r* be a requirement to be merger into requirement *r'*. Three types of conflicts are identified:

1. *Association* and *Protocol* fields of r equal to those of r' but the *Algorithm* fields are different. This is fixed by altering the *Algorithm* field of r' to be that of the corresponding field of r.
2. Value v of any parameter *param* in r is different from the value of *param* in r'. This is fixed by forcing the *param* of r' to get the value v.
3. Exists parameter p in r such that there is no corresponding p in r'. This is fixed by adding a parameter $p = v$ into r' where v is the value of parameter p in r.

In practise, merging is enforced by identifying the above conflicts for each requirement to which upper level requirements are to be merged. If a conflict exists, a corresponding harmonization function is generated and enforced to the specific unit that is the target of harmonization.

As there are two types of merging involved, it is left to the user of harmonizer software in which order they re to be applied. It would be in most cases that layer-specific requirements are merged first to each unit at that layer, and the upper layer requirements after this. This order would indicate the higher priority of upper layer requirements than layer specific requirements. As the order depends on the environment on which the requirements are processed, exact guide lines can not be given out of a specific application context.

5   Conclusions and Future Work

Harmonizer software, including source code, scientific material, technical documentation and user manual is available at

http://www.pscit.monash.edu.au/links/harm

for evaluation. The software is implemented using Java 1.1 language, and both stand alone and applet version are available. A case study has also been conducted with the harmonization of information security requirements. FIndings are summarized in [10].

The major contribution of this paper falls into two major categories: Provision of a proof of concept for harmonization functions and to provide a tool to be used in the development of information security in organizations. It is also hoped that the model examined is a step towards modeling of information security in organizations. The major concern of the development of trusted systems is specification, validation and implementation of a security policy model of the system being developed. As the modeling approach has proven to be effective in the construction of secure computer systems, it provides only little support for constructing secure information systems. Parameterization of security measures and step by step refinements help on the next generation of information security management. Current models, based on risk analysis and extensive check lists, provide only limited support for layers of abstraction. The proposed approach offers more flexibility. A case study has been conducted in the medical informatics domain. Details can be found in [10].

Opportunities for further research are numerous. The software is subject to further versioning in case a commercial tool is to be developed, but the model itself can be extended by including various levels of security in a more integrated manner. Also the deduction of a requirement base from a component might provide with an improved reusability of requirements. The success of various baseline criteria as a basis for information security in organizations suggests that many systems share roughly the same requirements. If the requirement-organization dependency could be loosened, increased support could be provided for organizations where security requirements change frequently, or to any organizations under same business domain.

References

1. Trusted computer systems evaluation criteria. U.S. Department of Defence, 1983.
2. Information technology security evaluation criteria (ITSEC). provisional harmonized criteria, version 1.2. Commossion of the European Communities COM(92) 298 final, Brussels, Belgium, Sept. 1992.
3. International standard ISO/IEC 15408 common criteria for information technology security evaluation (parts 1-3), version 2.0, CCIB-98-026, May 1998.
4. A. Anderson, D. Longley, and L. F.K. Security modelling for organizations. In *Proceedings of the 2nd ACM Conference on Computer and Communications Security*, pages 241 – 250. ACM Press, 1994.
5. J. Backhouse and G. Dhillon. Structures of responsibility and security of information systems. *European Journal of Information Systems*, 5(1):2 – 9, 1996.
6. D. L. Brinkley and R. R. Schell. Concepts and terminology for computer security. In M. D. Abrams, S. Jajodia, and H. J. Podell, editors, *Information Security, An Integrated Collection of Essays*, pages 40 – 97. IEEE Computer Society Press, 1995.
7. E. Dubois and S. Wu. A framework for dealing with and specifying security requirements in information systems. In *Proceedings of the IFIP TC11 11th International Conference on Information Systems Security*. Chapmann & Hall, 1996.
8. R. Grimm. A model of security in open telecooperation. In *Upper Layers, Protocols, Architectures and Applications, Proceedings of the IFIP TC6/WG6.5 International Conference*, IFIP Transactions C: Communication Systems, pages 425 – 440. North–Holland, 1992.
9. A. J. I. Jones and M. Sergot. Formal specification of security requirements using the theory of normative positions. In *Computer Security – ESORICS'92*, number 648 in Lecture Notes in Computer Science, pages 103 – 121. Springer–Verlag, 1992.
10. C. G. Jussipekka Leiwo and Y. Zheng. Organizational modeling for efficient specification of information security requirements. In *Advancaes in Databases and Information Systems, Proceedings of the 3rd East-European Conference*, Lecture Notes in Computer Science, Maribor, Slovenia, September 1999. Springer–Verlag.
11. R. Kruger and J. H. P. Eloff. A common criteria framework for the evaluation of information technology systems security. In *Information Security in Research and Business, Proceedings of the IFIP TC11 13th International Conference on Information Systems Security (SEC'97)*, pages 197–209, Copenhagen, Denmark, May 14-16 1997. Chapmann & Hall.
12. J. Leiwo, C. Gamage, and Y. Zheng. Harmonization of information security requirements. *Informatica*, 17, 1999. accepted, to appear.

13. D. McCullough. Specifications for multi-level security and a hook-up property. In *Proceedings of the 1987 IEEE Symposium on Security and Privacy*, pages 161–166, 1987.
14. C. Meadows. Using traces based on procedure calls to reason about composability. In *Proceedings of the 1992 IEEE Symposium on Security and Privacy*, pages 177–188, 1992.
15. D. F. Sterne. On the buzzword "security policy". In *1991 IEEE Symposium on Research in Security and Privacy*, pages 219 – 230. IEEE Computer Society Press, 1991.
16. M. J. Warren, S. M. Furnell, and P. W. Sanders. ODESSA – a new approach to healthcare risk analysis. In *Information Security in Research and Business, Proceedings of the IFIP TC11 13th International Conference on Information Systems Security (SEC'97)*, pages 391–402, Copenhagen, Denmark, May 14-16 1997. Chapmann & Hall.

Efficient Retrieval of Structured Documents from Object-Relational Databases*

Rafael Berlanga, María José Aramburu and Salvador García

Universitat Jaume I, Departamento de Informática, Castellón, Spain
{berlanga, aramburu, garcia}@inf.uji.es

Abstract. This paper proposes a new and efficient method to represent, store and retrieve structured documents from object-relational databases. Its main contribution consists of a codification scheme for document structures that assigns codes to documents as an additional attribute. Thus, retrieval conditions on the structure of documents can be evaluated by applying these codes, avoiding traversing object references. The paper also gives some clues to the construction of a repository of structured documents over object-relational tables, so that query conditions regarding the contents, structure and metadata of documents are executed by the underlying database system.

1. Introduction

The risen of Internet based digital libraries has led to a general request for efficient tools to store and retrieve documents. Although information retrieval techniques have shown very useful when applied to centralised document repositories, some of the most important requirements of digital libraries cannot be supported by them. Given that object-relational database systems can satisfy many of these requirements, a valid approach to the development of future digital libraries consists of integrating object-relational databases technology with information retrieval techniques.

The main contribution of this paper is a new codification scheme for document structures that assigns codes to documents as an additional attribute. Retrieval conditions on the structure of documents can be evaluated by applying these codes, thus avoiding traversing object references. Assuming that an information retrieval module is provided, query conditions regarding the contents, structure and metadata of documents, can be executed by the underlying object-relational database system without any further extensions.

The rest of the paper is organised as follows. In Section 2 we describe the adopted document model and its implementation in an object-relational database. Section 3 analyses the document retrieval language and section 4 describes the new codification scheme. The translation of the document retrieval language into the object-relational query language is analysed in Section 5. Finally, Section 6 gives some conclusions.

* This work has been partially funded by the CICYT project TEL97-1119 and the Fundación Caixa Castelló.

2. TOODOR Document Model

TOODOR (Temporal Object-Oriented Document Organisation and Retrieval) is a document model intended to represent and query structured documents with temporal behaviour. In previous works [1-2], we have shown its utility for the construction of digital libraries. This section summarises some of its main features.

The document model of TOODOR relies on a type system denoted $\mathcal{DTS}$ whose constructors are similar to those defined by SGML [3]. This type system starts from a set of attribute names *Att*, a set of class names *Class*, and a set of multimedia data types *RawData*, to construct document types as follows [4-5]:

$$\mathcal{DTS} := RawData \mid Class \mid (T_1 \mid ... \mid T_m) \mid T+ \mid T^* \mid T? \mid [a_1 : T_1, ..., a_m : T_m]$$

By using TOODOR, the schema of a digital library consists of a group of document classes whose definitions can evolve along time. Each class is expressed as a 3-tuple (*C-name, C-span, C-history*). Here, *C-name* is a class name from *Class*, *C-span* is the lifespan of the class, and *C-history* contains a sequence of type definitions for the class. The history of a class is represented as a series of 3-tuples (*T, Pop, I*), where *T* is a valid type from $\mathcal{DTS}$, *Pop* groups the set of class instances created with that type, and *I* is a time interval that indicates when instances are inserted according to that class definition. The integrity constraints of this data model were described in [2, 4].

An important property of this data model is that the schema of a TOODOR digital library cannot contain recursive definitions and therefore, in its hierarchies of composition cycles never appear. Thus, the schema can be always represented as a directed acyclic graph (DAG), whose nodes set comprises the names of its attributes and classes, and the edges set represents the composition relationships between classes and attributes. Given that classes can be redefined, edges are labelled with time periods. Additionally, the label "SET" is assigned to denote multi-valued composition relationships (i.e. attributes with + and * type constructors). Figure 1 shows an example with two historical definitions and its corresponding DAG.

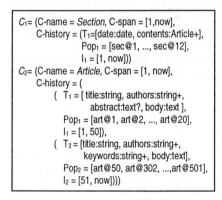
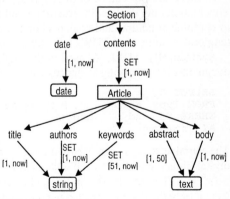

Fig. 1. Example of Schema and Graph

2.1. Some Implementation Issues

When representing the schema of a digital library in an object-relational database, the following two relational tables can be used to store the schema graph:

```
node_table(Node_name, Type, Code)
edge_table(Node_name1, Node_name2, Span, Set_valued)
```

The first table describes the nodes in the schema graph, where *Type* indicates if the node denotes a class, an attribute or a raw data type. The column *Code* represents a unique identifier for each node that will serve us to codify the schema. The second table describes the composition relationships, where *Node_name*1 and *Node_name*2 are two nodes connected by an edge during the period *Span*, and *Set_valued* indicates whether the relationship is multi or single valued. These two tables take part of the digital library data dictionary, so that can be used to consult the schema, to validate the consistency of document structures or to parse path expressions.

Concerning the instance documents of a possible Internet-based digital library, they could be expressed in either HTML or XML format. However, the management of HTML documents in this application is not optimal because the logical structure of the documents has to be inferred from its formatting tags [6], which cannot always be made automatically. In the other case, supposing that the XML tag names correspond to the names of the attributes and classes in the schema, documents can be directly inserted into the database. Section 4 presents a format of storage for XML documents that allows for their efficient retrieval in an object-relational database.

3. Document Retrieval Language

This section is dedicated to describe the main features of the retrieval language of TOODOR, named TDRL (Temporal Document Retrieval Language). In this language, retrieval conditions can be of three types: structural, contents and temporal conditions. This section only deals with structural conditions, whereas Section 5.3. discusses how to combine structural and contents conditions during query processing. The range of temporal conditions of TDRL was already presented in [7].

Syntactically, TDRL is based in the OQL standard [8], and allows the retrieval of documents by specifying sentences with the following format:

SELECT O_{target}
FROM $Type_1$ **as** $O_1,$ ... , $Type_k$ **as** O_k
WHERE Cd_1 **and** ... **and** Cd_n
AT $TimeSpan$

The variable O_{target} represents the set of documents included in the portion of the digital library specified by the object variables $O_1,$ ..., O_k and the conditions $Cd_1,$ ..., Cd_n. The **AT** clause can be used to make a temporal projection of the database, so that only the documents inserted during the specified time interval are retrieved.

3.1 Path Expressions

Like in other object query languages, in TDRL path expressions are used to generate the set of objects that can be accessed through the corresponding schema trajectory. The syntax of path expressions is as follows:

```
<Path>   ::= Class <Path'>
<Path'>::= <Elem> <Path'> | ε
<Elem>   ::= .Att | .Att(Num) | .#
```

Notice that when a path expression includes multi-valued references, it is possible to specify a number between brackets that indicates the exact position of the intended component. Furthermore, TDRL allows for generalised path expressions [9] by using the symbol '#', which matches to any valid path of any length. The following sentences are examples of queries with path expressions:

SELECT The_Times.contents.sections(3).articles(2).title;

SELECT O **FROM** The_Times.contens.#.title **as** O;

SELECT O **FROM** News.data.place **as** O;

Path expressions must always terminate in a single class, in the other case they are said ambiguous. There happen two possible cases of path expression ambiguity: when the type of a component of the path is a union of types, and when a component of the path has several historical definitions. In both cases the reached objects can belong to different types. To avoid this ambiguity, before execution queries with ambiguous path expressions must be rewritten into several sub-queries in the following way:

1. The query "**SELECT** O **FROM** C.#.att **as** O;" where the type of att is $(C_1 | C_2)$, contains an ambiguous path expression (C.#.att) must be rewritten into:

   SELECT O **FROM** C.#.att{C_1} **as** O; **SELECT** O **FROM** C.#.att{C_2} **as** O;

   In this case, when generating the domain of the variable O, only the objects of the specified class will be considered.

2. The query "**SELECT** O **FROM** C.#.att **as** O;" with att of type C_1 during I_1 and of type C_2 during the period I_2, must be translated into the following sub-queries:

   SELECT O **FROM** C.#.att O **AT** I_1; **SELECT** O **FROM** C.#.att O **AT** I_2;

Another matter caused by ambiguity is that query conditions may be inconsistent for some of the objects in the query. At this respect, in TDRL when a condition cannot be evaluated over certain object the result is always false.

3.2 Structural Conditions

Apart from generating the values of object variables by means of path expressions, TDRL also allows the evaluation of structural conditions on documents. With this purpose the following predicates are defined:

- $in(o_1, o_2)$ is true if there exists a path expression of any length that goes from o_1 to o_2. For instance, the following query retrieves all the articles within the fourth section of a newspaper:

```
SELECT A FROM Article A, The_Times.#.sections(4) as S
WHERE in(S, A);
```

- *child*(o_1, o_2, i) is true if o_1 is the i-th child of o_2. The parameter i is optional.
- *same-parent*(o_1, o_2, d) is true if o_1 and o_2 are siblings of the same parent and there are d elements that separate o_1 from o_2. As an example, the following query looks for news talking about 'Brasil' which have a contiguous news talking about 'IMF'.

```
SELECT N1 FROM News as N1, N2 WHERE same-parent(N1, N2, 1)
and contains(N1,'Brasil') and contains(N2,'IMF');
```

- *common-ancestor*(o_1, o_2, l) is true if o_1 and o_2 have a common ancestor which it is located in the composition tree at least l levels above the less deep of both objects.

Previous works have defined some algebra operators with similar semantics (see [10, 11] for reviews). In the next section we propose a new scheme of codification for document structures that allows the evaluation of structural conditions with a new approach that reduces their computational cost.

4. Representing Documents with the Object-Relational Data Model

With the model of TOODOR, documents are represented as objects with the format (*Oid*, *It*, *Vt*, *Contents*) where *Oid* denotes the unique identifier of the document, *It* is its time of publication, *Vt* is the time interval during which its contents are valid, and the multimedia contents of the document are represented in the last component. Furthermore, given the object-oriented data model of TOODOR, the *Contents* component also stores the references that represent the relationships of composition.

However, object references mean some important drawbacks. By one hand, although references are typed, the union of types is not supported by most data models of current solutions [9, 12]. This is an issue that increases the complexity of query processing tasks. On the other hand, evaluating structural conditions requires navigating through object references, which in the case of large volumes of documents is too expensive.

In this section we propose a scheme of codification for storing structured documents with object references but with the advantage of allowing the evaluation of structural conditions in an efficient way. With this scheme the problem of the union of types is also avoided. As a result, documents can be stored into object-relational tables and queried by following the same model.

4.1 Document Representation

Starting from a TOODOR digital library schema, in this section we explain how to match documents into object-relational tables. Firstly, each document class in the initial schema is associated to a table whose rows contains its instances. The format of each table depends on the metadata defined for the corresponding document class (i.e.: attributes such as author, data, etc.). They follow the format:

```
class-name(Oid, Scode, It, Vt, Metadata, Contents)
```

Here *Oid* is a unique identifier, *SCode* is an especial code relating to the document structure, *Metadata* is a record of attributes describing the metadata, and the document contents are stored in the last column as multimedia values with references.

The idea of a code for representing the structure of documents was taken from the work presented by [13] for evaluating recursive-relàtional queries. The objective is to define a codification schema for expressing the position of each instance document inside the global schema of classes. In order to build codes that can be efficiently processed, a codification scheme must satisfy the following two properties:

1. Codes must induce a clustering of each document and its components. In this way, each tree of composition corresponds to a single cluster.
2. Codes must facilitate the evaluation of structural conditions and path expressions, avoiding as much as possible navigating through object references.

4.2 Codifying Document Structures

The code of a document object represents its position inside the logical organisation of the whole repository. This position is determined by the path followed through the digital library schema before inserting it in its corresponding class. Given that the schema of a digital library in TOODOR coincides with a directed acyclic graph and the structure of a document is a tree, this path is unique for each inserted object. Consequently, by codifying these paths it is possible to assign a different code to each object, which also indicates its exact position.

Given that each code, here denoted *SCode*, must be unique for each inserted document object, it is also necessary to ensure a different code for each object at the end of a multi-valued reference. Thus, for all the siblings of an ordered sequence, it is their relative position into the sequence what distinguish them.

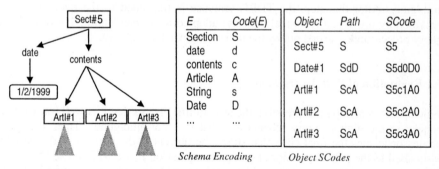

E	Code(E)
Section	S
date	d
contents	c
Article	A
String	s
Date	D
...	...

Schema Encoding

Object	Path	SCode
Sect#5	S	S5
Date#1	SdD	S5d0D0
Artl#1	ScA	S5c1A0
Artl#2	ScA	S5c2A0
Artl#3	ScA	S5c3A0

Object SCodes

Fig. 2. Schema Encoding and its *SCodes*

Each document in HTML or XML format can be considered as a tree whose internal nodes correspond to instances of the classes in the schema and whose leaves are instances of multimedia raw data types that store the contents of the document. In this way, we denote with *parent(N)* the parent of the node N, being N_{root} the root of the composition tree. For repetitive components, *pos(N)* expresses the position of the node N with respect to its siblings. Finally, each *SCode* is build by concatenating the codes associated to the elements E of the schema (see Section 2), these are denoted

$code(E)$. Therefore, to obtain the *SCode* of a node, the following recursive function can be applied:

$$\text{SCode}(N_{root}) \quad = \quad \text{code}(N_{root}) \; \bullet \; \text{Root\_Id}$$
$$\text{SCode}(N) \quad = \quad \text{SCode}(\text{parent}(N)) \; \bullet \; (\text{code}(N) \; \bullet \; \text{pos}(N))$$

The operator $\bullet$ is applied to concatenate codes that depending on the size of the application, can be represented as strings of either characters or bits. Each separated pair of codes ($\text{code}(N) \; \bullet \; \text{pos}(N)$) obtained for each node is named a *segment*. Thus, the number of segments in a *SCode* coincides with the level of the node in its composition tree. Furthermore, *Root_Id* denotes a unique identifier associated to the root node, which is inherited as a prefix by all the *SCodes* of the tree nodes. Thus, it constitutes the identifier of the whole composition tree.

It can be proved that this codification scheme defines a partial order between document elements by means of the prefix relationship. By this reason the objects in a composition tree representing certain document can be clustered and indexed by a conventional B^+-tree. Therefore, the first property of an efficient codification scheme is satisfied. In the next section, the advantages of this codification for the evaluation of path expressions and structural conditions are analysed.

5. Query Processing in TOODOR

Under this representation, query processing in TOODOR can be summarised in the following steps. Firstly, the TDRL sentence is analysed in order to find ambiguous path expressions and inconsistent conditions. As a result, some query elements can be simplified and the initial sentence may be divided into several queries without ambiguity. After this step, the TDRL sentence is translated to the query language provided by the object-relational database adopted for implementing TOODOR. Thus, query processing is carried out by the underlying database system.

5.1 Evaluation of Path Expressions

When processing a path expression, the system first checks that it is well formed with respect to the digital library schema and that it is not ambiguous. Then, the query processor locates the final class that stores the objects in the domain of the variable associated to the path expression. For a path expression P, we will denoted this class and its associated table as $goal(P)$. Afterwards the path expression is codified with the same scheme used for assigning the *SCode* to each inserted document (see Section 4.2). *SCode(Path)* is the resulting *SCode* and its evaluation is made by applying the interpreted grammar below:

```
<Path>::= Class <Path'> {CodePath = Code(Class) •'%'• CodePath'}
<Path'>::= <Elem> <Path'2> {CodePath' = CodeElem • CodePath'2} |
    ε {CodePath' = ''}
<Elem>::= (.Att {CodeElem = Code(Att)•'_'•Code(type(Att))•'_'}|
    .Att(Num) {CodeElem = Code(Att)•[Num]•Code(type(Att))•'_'}|
    .# {CodeElem = '%'} )
```

In this grammar, we assume that *Scodes* are represented as strings of chars, and each code segment comprises two chars (except for the code of the root). Here, we use two wildcards: '_' to denote one anonymous char, and '%' to denote one anonymous substring of any length. Additionally, we use the operator [N] to denote the conversion of the number N to a string.

Once the path expression is codified and its final class identified, the objects of its domain are generated by a select operation and the standard SQL *like* operator for evaluating string matching conditions as follows:

table(Path) = SEL $_{like(SCode, SCode(Path))}$ (goal(Path))

The need for the *like* operator is due to the inclusion of wildcards into the codes of path expressions. One limitation of this approach is that the wildcard '%' does not indicate the length of the intermediate sub-strings that can appear in path expression codes. In our case, the size of segments is fixed and therefore the length of these sub-strings is a multiple of that size. As a consequence, the operator *like* can produce some false drops in the answer, which need to be removed. It is worth mentioning that the inclusion of regular expressions in the *like* operator would solve this drawback.

5.2 Evaluation of Structural Conditions

After this process, each variable in a TDRL sentence has its initial domain restricted to the objects in a table. The table associated to the variable O is here denoted *table(O)*. Among the conditions of a query can only appear unary and binary conditions, these are conditions on a single variable and conditions relating two variables of the query. Thus, the evaluation of unary conditions can be made with a select, whereas binary conditions require a join over the corresponding tables.

In the special case of the structural predicates, the required join operation can be evaluated in terms of the *SCodes* associated to the implicated objects. Supposing that X and Y are two tables with the domains of two object variables involved in an structural condition, this can be evaluated as follows:

structural_condition(X, Y) $\Rightarrow$ JOIN$_{join\_condition}$ (X, Y)

The evaluation of each structural predicate of Section 3.2 needs a different join-condition. As these are conditions over the strings that represent the *SCodes* of the objects, their definition requires the following string operators:
- *prefix(code$_1$, code$_2$)* indicates whether the first *code* string is a prefix of the second.
- *length(code)* says the number of segments that constitute the string *code*.
- *codel$_p$* returns the left part of the *code* string truncated after its *p-th* segment.
- *codel^p* returns the right part of the *code* string truncated after its *p-th* segment.
- *code[p]* returns the *p-th* segment of *code*.
- *code[p].i* returns the first or second (*i*) component of the *p-th* segment of *code*.

Table 1 specifies the process of evaluating the structural predicates of Section 3.2 by means of the previous string operators. In this table, consider *code$_1$* as the *SCode* of the object o_1 and *code$_2$* as the *SCode* of o_2.

Table 1. Join Conditions to Evaluate Structural Conditions on Documents

Predicate	Join Condition
$in(o_1, o_2)$	$prefix(code_1, code_2)$
$child(o_1, o_2, i)$	$code_1|_{length(code1)-2} = code_2 \wedge code_1 [length(code_1)-1].2 = i$
$same\_parent(o_1, o_2, d)$	$code_1|_{length(code1)-2} = code_2|_{length(code2)-2} \wedge$ $code_1 [length(code_1)-1].1 = code_2 [length(code_2)-1].1 \wedge$ $abs(code_1 [length(code_1)-1].2 - code_2 [length(code_2)-1].2) = d$
$common\_ancestor(o_1, o_2, l)$	$\exists p / code_1|_p = code_2|_p \wedge length(code_1|^p) \geq l \wedge length(code_1|^p) \geq l$

5.3 Combining Structural and Contents Conditions

Given that the *SCode* of a document distinguishes it from the rest of instances in the repository, these codes could be used as document identifiers in an information retrieval system. As a result, structural conditions could be evaluated with the same mechanisms as contents conditions. These mechanisms would first extract from an inverted index the *SCode* codes of the documents that satisfy the contents conditions. Afterwards, the retrieved *SCodes* would serve to evaluate the structural conditions before retrieving the documents from the repository.

Additionally, *SCodes* can be used to improve the precision and recall of the information retrieval system. The idea is to assign to each *SCode* a level of relevance depending on its relative position in the schema. In other words, those topics that appear in a relevant position of the document such as the title would have a higher level of relevance than those that appear in another section. Thus, starting from the following function to assign a relevance to each *SCode*:

$$structure\_relevance : SCode \rightarrow [0, 1]$$

and after processing the conditions on contents and structure, the resulting documents could be ordered by their relevance in terms of both the frequency of topics (*IDF* [17]) and the position of topics. In general, the relevance of a document could be evaluated as follows:

$$relevance(D) = f(IDF_D, structure\_relevance(SCode(D)))$$

With the purpose of improving the precision and recall of the system, at the moment we are analysing some possible linear functions to rank answers.

6. Conclusions

Traditionally, the problem of storing and retrieving structured documents has been approached from two separate perspectives: databases and information retrieval systems. The work presented in this paper is an attempt to join both areas with the purpose of integrating conditions on the structure and contents of documents. By one hand, queries are specified by means of an object-oriented language that also supports conditions on metadata and path expressions. On the other hand, the proposed language consists of some operators similar to those provided by information retrieval systems to specify conditions on the contents and structure of documents. In Section 5.3 we showed how to combine both types of conditions when assigning a level of relevance to each document.

TOODOR has been implemented on the top of a commercial object-relational database system with good information retrieval capabilities [14]. In the current version, structure codes have been represented as strings of characters so that they are queried by using the string matching operators of the database system. Text queries are performed by an information retrieval server, which is fully maintained by the database management system. This first version of TOODOR is being tested on a national newspaper document database. The schema of this database has about 30 elements (types and attributes) and the number of stored documents is about 10,000 documents. In this context, the size of the structure codes is at most 20 characters. Preliminary results show a good performance for this approach, and typical queries on the structure and contents of newspapers are evaluated in the order of seconds.

Future work is mainly focused on applying TOODOR to distributed digital libraries. Additionally, further work is being carried out in defining document relevance functions that relate contents and structure.

References

1. M. Aramburu and R. Berlanga. "An Approach to a Digital Library of Newspapers". In Information Processing & Management, Vol. 33(5), pp. 645-661, 1997.
2. M. Aramburu. "TOODOR: A Temporal Database Model for Historical Documents". PhD Thesis, The University of Birmingham, UK, 1998.
3. ISO 8879. I.P.T.O.S., Standard Generalized Markup Language, 1996.
4. M. Aramburu and R. Berlanga. "Temporal Object-Oriented Document Organisation and Retrieval". In Proc.of the Third Biennial World Conference on Integrated Design and Process Technology: Issues and Applications of Database Technology, pp. 368-375, 1998.
5. M. Aramburu and R. Berlanga. "Metadata for a Digital Library of Historical Documents". In Proc. 8th DEXA Conference, pp. 409-418, 1997.
6. I. Sanz, R. Berlanga and M. Aramburu. "Gathering Metadata from Web-based Repositories of Historical Publications". In Proc. 9th DEXA Workshop, pp. 473-478, 1998.
7. M. Aramburu and R. Berlanga. "A Retrieval Language for Historical Documents". In Proc. of 9th DEXA Conference, pp. 216-225, 1998.
8. R. Cattell (ed.). "The Object Database Standard: ODMG-93 Release 1.2". Morgan Kaufmann, 1996.
9. V. Christophides, et al. "From Structured Documents to Novel Query Facilities". In Proc. of the ACM SIGMOD International Conference on Management of Data, pp. 313-324, 1994.
10. R. Baeza-Yates and G. Navarro. "Integrating Contents and Structure in Text Retrieval". In SIGMOD Record, Vol. 25, No.1, pp. 67-79, 1996.
11. G. Navarro and R.A. Baeza-Yates. "Proximal Nodes: A Model to Query Document Databases by Content and Structure". In ACM Transactions on Information Systems, Vol. 15, No. 4, pp. 400-435, 1997.
12. S. Cluet. "Modelling and Querying Semi-Structured Data". In Lecture Notes in Computer Science, Vol. 1299, Springer-Verlag, pp. 192-213, 1997.
13. J. Teuhola. "Path Signatures: A Way to Speed Up Recursion in Relational Databases". In IEEE Transactions on Knowledge and Data Engineering, Vol. 8(3), 1996.
14. Oracle 8.0.4, User and Administrator Guides, 1998.

Analysis of Active Database Rules Behaviour Using Rewriting Logic

Yahia Rabih and Michel Schneider

LIMOS - Université Clermont-Ferrand II, Complexe Scientifique des Cézeaux
63177 Aubière, France
rabih@libd1.univ-bpclermont.fr
schneider@cicsun.univ-bpclermont.fr

Abstract. Integration *of activity in object-oriented database systems, through the support of active rules, requires to guarantee certain properties such as termination and confluence. It is necessary in particular to be able to take into account various dimensions of the execution model since these dimensions directly influence termination and confluence. Few studies relating to termination and confluence consider these dimensions. In this paper, we suggest using a formalism based on the rewriting logic to describe an active object-oriented system. We show that the main dimensions of the active rule execution model can be expressed by adding three strategies: activate all the solutions of a subset, choice at more one solution of a subset, reiterate a solution as many times as possible. The problem is then to model the behaviour of a whole system. We suggest distributing the rules into strata. The interest of such a process is that the global strategy which models the behaviour of the system is the concatenation of the local strategies which model the behaviour of the different strata. Three different stratification algorithms are given. The analysis of termination and confluence then rests on the simulation of the global strategy.*
Keywords. object-oriented databases, active rules, termination, confluence, rewriting logic.

1 Introduction

A database management system is known as active (in opposition to a passive one) when it enables users to specify actions which will be automatically carried out. In fact, the occurrence of some events when certain conditions are satisfying will start the execution of these actions without any intervention of the user. The taking into account of the activity is made, generally, through active rules (ECA rules). Automatic triggering and non-determinism of these rules make the analysis of their dynamics complex. It is thus important to ensure that a given set of rules verifies properties such as *termination* and *confluence*. Termination ensures that the triggering process of the rules is finished, while confluence ensures that the final state is independent of the execution order of the rules.

Termination and confluence for a set of rules are, in general, undecidable problems. They can be approached using different ways: by considering special situations, by exhibiting sufficient (and restrictive) termination conditions, by detecting loops in active programs at run time.

Various works in the field of databases have addressed termination and confluence of active rules. They can be classified into four main categories: debuggers ([7], [8]), simulators ([5], [6], [9], [25]), methods using graph models ([1], [2], [3], [4], [12], [16]), and other approaches ([11], [14], [18]). Debuggers are used at run time while other approaches permit a priori analysis. The study of termination in debuggers and simulators is based on the detection of cycles during the execution or during the simulation. With methods using graph models, termination analysis generally rests on the detection of cycle in the triggering graph. Some of them also introduce an activation graph and are able to consider the influence of rule conditions.

Except debuggers, these various tools or methods do not explicitly take account of the various dimensions of the active rule execution model [10], [19]. In fact, these dimensions as we have shown in [21], influence directly the termination property and also the confluence property.

To design an "a priori" approach, able to consider the influence of rule dimensions, we have explored the possibilities of the rewriting logic (RL) [17]. In [20], it is shown how the RL can provide a suitable formalism to model active databases. In fact, this formalism is not sufficient to describe rule dimensions. We show in this paper that the main dimensions of active rules can be expressed by adding three strategies: explore all the solutions of a subset, choice at more one solution of a subset, reiterate a solution as many times as possible. Our approach consists to model the behaviour of a rule set by a combination of strategies. The problem is determining a correct combination which satisfies the active application requirements. We suggest separating the whole rule set into strata. The behaviour of each stratum is modelled through a local strategy and the behaviour of the whole rule set is modelled through a global strategy which is the concatenation of the local strategies. The analysis of termination and confluence then rests on the simulation of the global strategy.

The paper is structured as follows: section 2 shows through a simple example the influence of one active rule dimension on the termination property, section 3 presents the modelling framework of a system with the Rewriting Logic, section 4 introduces the three basic strategies, section 5 specifies the way in which active rule dimensions can be taken into account with the RL and the basic strategies, section 6 clarifies the stratification process, section 7 presents the elaboration of a local strategy, section 8 described our overall process for analysing the termination and confluence properties and section 9 illustrates its application on an example.

For the following, an ECA rule will be said triggerable as soon as its triggering event E is present in the system.

2 Influence of the Dimensions of Active Rule Execution Model on the Termination Property

It is not possible in this paper to show how the various dimensions of the execution model of the active rules influence the termination and confluence properties. A complete presentation can be found in [21]. We will illustrate only the influence of the net effect on the termination property by means of a simple example.

The example is based on a set of three rules R1, R2 and R3 (described in a SQL like form):

```
define rule R1
on insert to Employee where Employee.function = "Director"
then do default_salary = select(avg(salary) from Employee
     where Employee.function = "Director")- 50
replace Employee (salary = default_salary) where
            Employee.number = New.number and Employee.salary = Null

define rule R2
on insert to Employee where Employee.function = "Director" and
                           Employee.department = "Computer"
then do replace Employee (salary = 1,1 * Employee.salary)
     where Employee.number = New.number

define rule R3
on replace to Employee.salary where Employee.name = "Simon" and
                              Employee.function = "Director"
then do replace Employee (salary = 1,15 * Employee.salary)
     where Employee.number = New.number and Employee.salary < 20000
```

We consider that the inserted employee is Director Simon of the computer department whose salary is not initialised, that the events are locally consumed, that rule R1 has priority on rule R2, and that rules R1, R2 and R3 have immediate E-C and C-A couplings.

First situation: Net Effect is Taken into Account

Following the insertion of Director Simon of the Computer Department, rules R1 and R2 become triggerable. Since R1 has priority on R2 and R1 and R2 have immediate E-C and C-A couplings, we have first an execution of rule R1. At the end of this execution, the salary of Director Simon is equal to the average of the Directors salaries decreased by 50. Rule R2 is triggerable with salary for Simon equal to the default salary (because the net effect is taken into account). At the end of the execution of R2, the salary of Director Simon will be higher 10% than the default salary. Rule R3 is now triggerable with salary for Simon different from Null. This rule R3 is triggered recursively since each execution modifies the salary of Director Simon by increasing it of 15%. This recursive execution is finished because after N executions (N is finite) the R3 condition becomes false. The termination is thus guaranteed.

Second situation: Net Effect is not Taken into Account

Following the insertion of the Director Simon of the Computer Department, rules R1 and R2 become triggerable. Since R1 has priority on R2 and R1 and R2 have immediate E-C and C-A couplings, we have first an execution of rule R1. At the end of this execution, the salary of Director Simon is equal to the average of the Directors salaries decreased by 50. Rule R2 is triggerable with salary for Simon equal to Null because the net effect is not taken into account. At the end of the execution of rule R2, the salary of Director Simon is also equal to Null because its initial value was equal to Null. Rule R3 is triggered recursively since the salary of Director Simon remains equal to Null after each execution. This recursion is infinite. Termination is thus not obtained.

3   Specification of an Active Object-Oriented System with the Rewriting Logic

In the rewriting logic (RL) [17], a system is described through a signature (static part) and a set of rewriting rules (dynamic part). In [20] we have shown how the RL can provide a suitable formalism to model active object-oriented databases. Thus, the signature (Fig. 1) gives the basic syntax for the objects, the events, and the configurations. In this signature, Oid, Cid and Aid are respectively the object identifier, class identifier and attribute identifier. The special character @ reserves a position for every argument.

module Signature		
import global Oid Cid Aid Value;		(1)
sort Attribute ListAttributes Event Object Configuration;		(2)
op global		
Tuple(@':'@I@) :	(Oid Cid ListAttributes) Object;	(3)
@':'@ :	(Aid Value) Attribute;	(4)
@':'Tuple(@) :	(Aid ListAttributes) Attribute;	(5)
@ :	(Attribute) ListAttributes;	(6)
@,@ :	(ListAttributes ListAttributes) ListAttributes (AC);	(7)
@ :	(Object) Configuration;	(8)
@ :	(Event) Configuration;	(9)
@ @ :	(Configuration Configuration) Configuration (AC);	(10)
endop		
end of module		

Fig. 1. Signature of an active object-oriented system with the rewriting logic

The rewriting rules (RR) in the RL describe the communication between the various components of the system. This behaviour corresponds to the notion of logical deduction. This deduction is accomplished by some non-deterministic and concurrent rewritings modulo structural axioms which are Associativity, Commutativity and Identity (ACI). Thus, the RR execution is a non-deterministic and concurrent execution modulo ACI. The general form of a RR is illustrated by Fig. 2.

$E\ O_1\ ...\ O_m => O'_1...O'_m\ E_1\ ...\ E_k$ [Cond]
or more explicitly
E Tuple(Oid_1 : Cid_1 I ListAttributes$_1$) ... Tuple(Oid_m : Cid_m I ListAttributes$_m$) =>
Tuple(Oid_1 : Cid_1 I ListAttributes'$_1$) ... Tuple(Oid_m : Cid_m I ListAttributes'$_m$) E_1 ... E_k [Cond]

Fig. 2. General form of a RR in the rewriting logic

In this form, E is a simple or composite event, Oid_i is an object of the class Cid_i, [Cond] is a condition which expresses the triggering condition of the rule, ListAttributes$_i$ specifies the state of the object Oid_i (assignment of a value to each attribute of the list ListAttributes$_i$) at triggering time, and ListAttributes'$_i$ specifies the new state of the object Oid_i after the triggering of the rule.

To trigger such a rule, it is necessary that the event E is present, that the objects Oid_1... Oid_m are in the specified state, and that condition [Cond] is evaluated as true.

The result of this triggering is as follows: the event E disappears; the state of the objects $Oid_1...$ Oid_m may change ; new events E_1 ... E_k are sent.

As indicated in [20], the matching between an ECA rule and a RR is the following: the event of the ECA rule corresponds to the event E of RR; the condition of ECA corresponds to the objects states Oid_i (represented by $ListAttributes_i$) and to the condition [Cond] of RR; the action of ECA corresponds to the rewriting of the objects Oid_i (the states of these objects are changed) and the sending of the events E_1 ... E_k.

4   The Three Basic Strategies

As the RR are carried out in a concurrent and non-deterministic way, some strategies are useful to express constraints on the execution of this concurrent rewriting. It is then possible to control the application of the RR to conform to the needs for an application. Dimensions of the active rules execution model are kinds of constraints and can thus be expressed with strategies.

These strategies can be three. The strategy *don't know(action_list)* (abbreviated as *dk*) makes it possible to activate all the actions of a list (an action is either a rule or a strategy). The strategy *don't care(action_list)* (abbreviated as *dc*) consists in choosing no more than one of the actions of a list. The strategy *while <strategy> endwhile* iterates a strategy <strategy> until it fails and returns just the result of the last unfailing call.

These strategies can be expressed in different programming languages such as BeBOP [15] and ELAN [13]. The BeBOP language combines the features of the parallel logic programming and object oriented programming. It is implemented by translation down to NU-Prolog and its parallel extension PNU-Prolog. The ELAN language is a specification language based on the RL.

These three basic strategies can be combined between them to form more complex strategies.

5   Taking into Account the Active Rule Dimensions

Benefiting from the semantics of the RR and the strategies, the various active rules dimensions can be taken into account, in our approach. Unfortunately, it is not possible in this paper to present them. A complete presentation can be found in [23]. These various dimensions and their formalisation are summarised in Table 1.

6   Stratification Algorithms

Since a rule can produce several events which trigger other rules, the problem is posed to schedule the global execution of all these rules. This global execution is modelled through a global strategy. We can distinguish three different kinds of global strategies depending on the way the triggering tree is browsed: flat (or uniform) browsing, in-depth browsing, in-width browsing.

Table 1. Summary of the various active rules dimensions taken into account in our approach

Dimensions	Values	Corresponding basic strategies or other construct
Granularity of event processing	1 Instance-oriented 2 Set-oriented	Implicit -
Event consumption mode	1 Consumption 2 Preservation	No regeneration Regeneration
Time of event consumption	1 Evaluation 2 Execution	- Implicit
Scope of event consumption	1 Local 2 Global	Parallel execution No parallel execution
Rule execution mode	1 Atomic 2 Interruptible	Implicit -
Rule triggering mode	1 Simple (Single) 2 Multiple (Perpetual)	dk(r1) while dk(r1) endwhile
Coupling mode	1 Immediate 2 Deferred 3 Separate	Implicit Through stratification -
Local strategy	1 Random sequential 2 Ordered sequential 3 Parallel Execution 4 Choice of a rule	dk(dk(r1) dk(r2) ‖ dk(r2) dk(r1)) dk(dk(r1) dk(r2)) dk(r1 r2) dc(r1 r2)
Net effect	Boolean	Yes or not
Global strategy	1 Flat 2 In-depth 3 In-width	Stratification (algorithm 1) Stratification (algorithm 2) Stratification (algorithm 3)

We suggest specific algorithms for processing each of these kinds of global strategies. The principle of these algorithms is to organise the rules in strata, so we named them stratification algorithms. The stratification process is presented in the next paragraph.

The idea behind the stratification process is decomposing the initial rule set into smaller subsets such that the behaviour of the whole set can be easily derived from the behaviour of the subsets. Thus the global strategy which models the global behaviour of the system can be obtained from the different local strategies which model the behaviour of the different strata.

This stratification process must respect some criteria. First, it must be able to produce the different kinds of global strategies we have identified in the previous section. Elsewhere, it is necessary to take into account a possible ordering between rules. Often there are priorities between rules and this ordering must respect priorities. However, not all the rules are necessarily ordered strictly because we want to preserve some non-determinism in their execution. It is necessary also to be able to manage recursive triggering. It is the case when there is a cycle in the triggering graph. The existence of a cycle is not contradictory with termination: the execution of rules in a cycle can be terminating or non-terminating according to the evaluation of the condition in each rule.

To take into account these different cases, the stratification is processed such that :

– a stratum brings together rules which can be triggered at the same time in a non-deterministic way and having the same priority or no priority between them,
– all the rules of a cycle are placed in a same stratum.

We have elaborated three different stratification algorithms: one for each kind of global strategy. These algorithms use three lists of strata : LSI, LSD and LS. List LSI will contain the immediate rules to trigger. List LSD will contain the deferred rules to trigger. List LS will contain the stratification result. We use two orderings: an ordering on the rules, noted $>_r$ (r1 $>_r$ r2 if rule r1 has priority on rule r2) and an ordering on the strata, noted $>_s$ (S1 $>_s$ S2 if there is a rule r1 $\in$ S1 and a rule r2 $\in$ S2 such as r1 $>_r$ r2).

As an example, the stratification algorithm corresponding to the global strategy with an in-depth browsing of the triggering tree is given in Fig. 3. The two other algorithms have a similar structure.

Stage 1:
Determine the initial stratum SInt corresponding to the rules which are the first triggerable rules.
Divide SInt into two substrata: the stratum of immediate rules SI and the stratum of deferred rules SD.
Divide each stratum SI and SD into substrata according to the priorities between rules (order $>_r$).
Initialise list LSI with the substrata of SI by respecting the order $>_s$.
Initialise list LSD with the substrata of SD by respecting the order $>_s$.
Initialise list LS to empty.

Stage 2:
Let SH be the stratum at the head of list LSI.
Determine a new stratum SN containing all the triggerable rules from rules of SH.
Remove SH from LSI and insert it in tail of LS.
If a rule r of SN appears in a stratum S of LS and if there is a cycle containing this rule r
Then
    Move all the rules of the cycle in the stratum S of LS;
    Remove r from SN;
    Reiterate for all cases.
Endif
If SN is not empty Then
    Divide SN into two substrata: the stratum of immediate rules SI and the stratum of deferred rules SD;
    Divide each stratum SI and SD in substrata according to the priorities between rules (order $>_r$);
    Transfer each substratum from SI at the head of LSI by respecting the order $>_s$;
    Transfer each substratum from SD at the tail of LSD by respecting the order $>_s$.
Endif
If LSI is empty Then / * treatment of the deferred rules * /
    Initialise list LSI with LSD;
    Initialise list LSD to empty.
Endif
Reiterate stage 2 until list LSI becomes empty

Fig. 3. Stratification algorithm with in-depth browsing of the triggering tree

7 Elaboration of the Local Strategy for a Stratum

A local strategy is used to model the behaviour of a stratum. The dimensions of each rule are taken into account at this moment.

Since several rules can be triggered at same time, the system must decide which rules will be triggered and in which order. There are different possibilities: random or ordered sequential execution, parallel execution, mixed execution, choice of a rule. In our approach, each of these situations is modelled through a local strategy which is itself a combination of the basic strategies shown below.

To choice the appropriate form it is necessary to separate the rules of a stratum into three disjoined subsets: the subset S1 of the rules which are in mutual exclusion, the subset S2 of the rules belonging to a cycle, and the subset S3 of the other rules [24]. Two rules are in mutual exclusion if their respective conditions or if their respective triggering events are in mutual exclusion. Two events E1 and E2 are in mutual exclusion if E1 occurs then E2 does not occur, and reciprocally.

8 Overall Process for Analysing the Termination and Confluence Properties

Fig. 4 gives an overview of our approach to check the termination and confluence properties for a set of active rules.

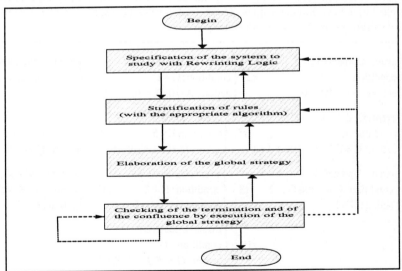

Fig. 4. General overview of our approach

Checking of the termination and the confluence properties requires the simulation of the global strategy. Elaboration of the global strategy results directly from the stratification. It consists to concatenate the local strategies of the different strata. This concatenation must respect the ordering of the strata (>s) in the list LS. This global strategy is executed on an initial configuration which corresponds to an initial state of the database. We note that ELAN provides the execution trace. This trace includes the triggered rules, the states obtained at each step, etc.

If the execution stops, then we have termination for this initial state. Checking the confluence is then based on the analysis of the final configurations. If there is a unique final configuration, hence there is confluence for this initial state. If there are several final configurations two cases are possible: either these final configurations are equivalent modulo the AC properties, thus there is confluence for this initial state; or these final configurations are not equivalent and there is non-confluence for this initial state.

If the execution doesn't stop, then termination is not obtained for this initial state. This situation occurs when a loop appears in the execution trace (i.e. a same sequence – with the same rules associated with the same states – occurs several times).

Note: Instead of carrying out this process in a global way on all the strata of the list LS, we can do it in an incremental way on each stratum separately. Indeed, if for each stratum we have termination and confluence, we can say that we have also termination and confluence for the entire strata set.

9 Application Example

The example we consider (Fig. 5) is partially taken from [2]. The active database is composed of a single class Thing having attributes A, B, C, D, E, F, G, H, I, J, K. All these attributes have integer values. There are ten rules r1, r2, r3, ..., r10. Events are update operations on the above attributes.

r1 : $\begin{cases} \text{event}: \text{Update(F)} \\ \text{condition}: G = 2 \\ \text{action}: B = 0, G = 0 \end{cases}$	r2 : $\begin{cases} \text{event}: \text{Update(F)} \\ \text{condition}: G = 1 \\ \text{action}: A = 0, D = 0, G = 2 \end{cases}$	r3 : $\begin{cases} \text{event}: \text{Update(B)} \\ \text{condition}: H \neq 1 \\ \text{action}: H = 1 \end{cases}$
r4 : $\begin{cases} \text{event}: \text{Update(A)} \\ \text{condition}: G = 2 \\ \text{action}: C = 1, G = 1, H = 2, J = 1 \end{cases}$	r5 : $\begin{cases} \text{event}: \text{Update(E)} \\ \text{condition } K = 5 \\ \text{action}: D = 0, G = 3, K = 3 \end{cases}$	r6 : $\begin{cases} \text{event}: \text{Update(J)} \\ \text{condition}: K \neq 0 \\ \text{action}: G = 3, K = 0 \end{cases}$
r7 : $\begin{cases} \text{event}: \text{Update(F)} \\ \text{condition}: G \neq 1 \text{ and } G \neq 2 \\ \text{action}: G = 1 \end{cases}$	r8 : $\begin{cases} \text{event}: \text{Update(C)} \\ \text{condition}: H = 2 \\ \text{action}: H = 1, I = 2 \end{cases}$	r9 : $\begin{cases} \text{event}: \text{Update(I)} \\ \text{condition}: K \neq 5 \\ \text{action}: K = 5 \end{cases}$
	r10 : $\begin{cases} \text{event}: \text{Update(D)} \\ \text{condition}: G = 3 \\ \text{action}: G = 5, E = 1, K = 1 \end{cases}$	

Fig. 5. A small active database

The triggering tree for this rule set is given in Fig. 6.

We consider the following assumptions : rules r1, r2, and r7 are first triggerable; rules r2 and r7 have the same priority as rule r1; rule r8 has the same priority as rule r6; for all other rules, ri >$_r$ rj if i < j; all the rules except r4 are of immediate type.

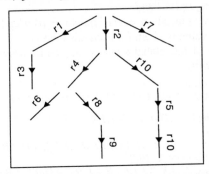

Fig. 6: Triggering tree for the rules of our example

Case 1: r4 is of Immediate Type (Immediate E-C and C-A Couplings)

With the preceding assumptions, the in-depth stratification algorithm gives the list LS presented in Fig. 7.

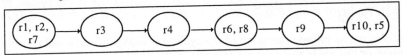

Fig. 7. List LS obtained with the in-depth stratification algorithm (case 1)

To elaborate the local strategies we made the supplementary following assumptions : rule r3 has a multiple triggering; all other rules have a simple triggering; events are consumed; the net effect is taken into account.

As rules r1, r2 and r7 are in mutual exclusion, then we execute r1, or r2, or r7. As rules r6 and r8 have the same priority, we insert them in a random sequential execution. Rules r10 and r5 form a cycle. As this cycle may be triggered many time, it is inserted into a *while endwhile* strategy.

Thus, the global strategy GS_Thing corresponding to this list LS is given in Fig. 8. This strategy is a concatenation of the different local strategies corresponding to each stratum. For example, the local strategy *dk(dk(r1) || dk(r2) || dk(r7))* models the behaviour of the first stratum (r1,r2,r7) of LS.

```
Strategy GS_Thing
    dk(dk(r1) || dk(r2) || dk(r7))
    while dk(r3) endwhile
    dk(r4)
    dk(dk(r6) dk(r8) || dk(r8) dk(r6))
    dk(r9)
    while dk(r5 r10) endwhile
end of strategy
```

Fig. 8: Global strategy GS_Thing

To simulate this global strategy, we have coded it with ELAN [13]. To execute the code, we must input an initial state (i.e. initial configuration) of the database. An example of such an initial state is: *Tuple(100:Thing | A:1,B:0,C:0,D:5,E:4,F:9,G:1, H:1,I:3,J:2,K:1) Update_F(100) end*

In this state, we have placed an event Update_F(100) and an instance (with Oid 100) of class Thing. A value is given for each attribute.

The execution trace of the global strategy GS_Thing provided by ELAN for this initial state is the following :

[] start with configuration :
Tuple(100:Thing | A:1,B:0,C:0,D:5,E:4,F:9,G:1,H:1,I:3,J:2,K:1) Update_F(100)

'r2' : Tuple(100:Thing | A:0,D:0,G:2,K:1,J:2,I:3,H:1,F:9,E:4,C:0,B:0) Update_A(100) Update_D(100)
'r4' : Tuple(100:Thing | C:1,G:1,H:2,J:1,K:1,I:3,F:9,E:4,D:0,B:0,A:0) Update_D(100) Update_J(100) Update_C(100)
'r6' : Tuple(100:Thing |G:3,K:0,J:1,I:3,H:2,F:9,E:4,D:0,C:1,B:0,A:0) Update_D(100) Update_C(100)
'r8' : Tuple(100:Thing | H:1,I:2,K:0,J:1,G:3,F:9,E:4,D:0,C:1,B:0,A:0) Update_D(100) Update_I(100)
'r9' : Tuple(100:Thing | K:5,J:1,I:2,H:1,G:3,F:9,E:4,D:0,C:1,B:0,A:0) Update_D(100)
'r10' : Tuple(100:Thing | E:1,G:5,K:5,J:1,I:2,H:1,F:9,D:0,C:1,B:0,A:0) Update_E(100)
'r5' : Tuple(100:Thing | D:0,G:3,K:3,J:1,I:2,H:1,F:9,E:1,C:1,B:0,A:0) Update_D(100)
'r10' : Tuple(100:Thing | E:1,G:5,K:5,J:1,I:2,H:1,F:9,D:0,C:1,B:0,A:0) Update_E(100)
'r5' : Tuple(100:Thing | D:0,G:3,K:3,J:1,I:2,H:1,F:9,E:1,C:1,B:0,A:0) Update_D(100)
...

We observe an infinite execution of the cycle containing rules r10 and r5 (for each execution of this cycle the database remains in the same state). Thus, for this initial state, the termination is not obtained.

Case 2: r4 is of Deferred Type (Deferred E-C Coupling and Immediate C-A Coupling)

With the preceding assumptions, the in-depth stratification algorithm gives the list LS presented in Fig. 9.

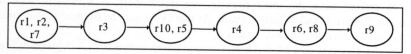

Fig. 9. List LS obtained with the in-depth stratification algorithm (case 2)

We consider the same complementary assumptions as in case 1. Thus, the global strategy GS_ThingBis corresponding to this list LS is given in Fig. 10.

> Strategy GS_ThingBis
> dk(dk(r1) ‖ dk (r2) ‖ dk(r7))
> while dk(r3) endwhile
> while dk(r5 r10) endwhile
> dk(r4)
> dk(dk(r6) dk(r8) ‖ dk(r8) dk(r6))
> dk(r9)
> end of strategy

Fig. 10. Global strategy GS_ThingBis

The execution trace for GS_ThingBis with the same initial state as in case 1 is now

[] start with configuration :
Tuple(100:Thing \ A:1,B:0,C:0,D:5,E:4,F:9,G:1,H:1,I:3,J:2,K:1) Update_F(100)

'r2' : Tuple(100:Thing \A:0,D:0,G:2,K:1,J:2,I:3,H:1,F:9,E:4,C:0,B:0) Update_A(100)
Update_D(100)
'r4' : Tuple(100:Thing \ C:1,G:1,H:2,J:1,K:1,I:3,F:9,E:4,D:0,B:0,A:0) Update_J(100)
Update_C(100) Update_D(100)
'r6' : Tuple(100:Thing\ G:3,K:0,J:1,I:3,H:2,F:9,E:4,D:0,C:1,B:0,A:0) Update_D(100)
Update_C(100)
'r8' : Tuple(100:Thing \ H:1,I:2,K:0,J:1,G:3,F:9,E:4,D:0,C:1,B:0,A:0) Update_D(100)
Update_I(100)
'r9' : Tuple(100:Thing \ K:5,J:1,I:2,H:1,G:3,F:9,E:4,D:0,C:1,B:0,A:0) Update_D(100)

[] final configuration :
Tuple(100:Thing \ K:5,J:1,I:2,H:1,G:3,F:9,E:4,D:0,C:1,B:0,A:0) Update_D(100)

'r2' : Tuple(100:Thing \ A:0,D:0,G:2,K:1,J:2,I:3,H:1,F:9,E:4,C:0,B:0) Update_A(100)
Update_D(100)
'r4' : Tuple(100:Thing \ C:1,G:1,H:2,J:1,K:1,I:3,F:9,E:4,D:0,B:0,A:0) Update_J(100)
Update_D(100) Update_C(100)
'r8' : Tuple(100:Thing \ H:1,I:2,K:1,J:1,G:1,F:9,E:4,D:0,C:1,B:0,A:0) Update_I(100)
Update_J(100) Update_D(100)
'r6' : Tuple(100:Thing \ G:3,K:0,J:1,I:2,H:1,F:9,E:4,D:0,C:1,B:0,A:0) Update_I(100)
Update_D(100)
'r9' : Tuple(100:Thing \ K:5,J:1,I:2,H:1,G:3,F:9,E:4,D:0,C:1,B:0,A:0) Update_D(100)

[] final configuration :
Tuple(100:Thing \ K:5,J:1,I:2,H:1,G:3,F:9,E:4,D:0,C:1,B:0,A:0) Update_D(100)

[] end

We observe two paths in the execution. The first path gives the final configuration *Tuple(100:Thing \ K:5,J:1,I:2,H:1,G:3,F:9,E:4,D:0,C:1,B:0,A:0) Update_D(100)* and the second one gives the final configuration *Tuple(100:Thing \ K:5,J:1,I:2,H:1,G: 3,F:9,E:4,D:0,C:1,B:0,A:0) Update_D(100)*. In the two paths, the cycle containing rules r10 and r5 was not executed because the condition of rule r10 is false.

The execution of the global strategy GS_ThingBis stops. Thus, for this initial state, we have termination. The two final configurations are equivalent modulo the AC properties and we have also confluence. Note that the final configuration represents the new state of the database.

This is a small example and its manual analysis would not be very difficult. For this example, we can note that the behaviour analysis becomes relatively straightforward as soon as the strata are drawn. Of course, the interest of such a method appears in fact for more complex systems. A more significant illustration is completely developed in [22].

10 Conclusion

In this paper we suggested an approach based on the rewriting logic to study "a priori" the termination and the confluence of active rules in an object oriented context. Its main feature is to make it possible to consider dimensions of the active rule execution model. This approach also takes into account the rule conditions and the effects of the rule actions on the conditions.

The rules' behaviour, including their dimensions, are described thanks to three main features: rewriting logic, strategies and stratification. Rules are first partitioned into strata, the behaviour of each stratum is then captured through a local strategy, the behaviour of the whole set of rules is lastly modelled through a global strategy which is the concatenation of the different local strategies. The study of termination and confluence then rests on the simulation of this global strategy.

The practical interest of such a proposal comes from the possibility of checking the behaviour of the system soon during the design process. It is important to note that the stratification process allows an incremental design of the active application. Many active object-oriented applications, the behaviour of which are naturally modelled through rule paradigms, can take advantage of such an approach: workflow, groupware, ...

The concept of strategy plays an important role in our approach. Languages such as ELAN, BeBOP or PNU-Prolog incorporate this concept and can be used to put this approach into practice. Non-specialist users can find difficult to translate the result of the stratification process into one of these languages. Fortunately, this translation can be made partly automatic. Often, the first specifications of an object-oriented system are expressed in semi-formal languages like UML. It is not difficult to elaborate a package which helps the translation of UML specifications. This package can be designed as a stand alone tool or can be integrated into a CASE tool.

We think that this approach can be useful for other purposes. It can be extended to permit the analysis of other rule properties (inconsistencies, useless rules, ...). It can help also to design more efficient tools for visualising the behaviour of active rules.

In this paper we have focused on object-oriented systems. Our approach can be arranged to consider other of active systems.

Bibliography

1. Aiken A., Hellerstein J.M. and Widom J. Static Analysis Techniques for Predicting the Behaviour of Active Database Rules. ACM Transaction on Database Systems, Vol. 20, No 1, March 1995, pp. 3-41.
2. Baralis E., Ceri S., and Paraboschi S. Improved Rule Analysis by Means of Triggering and Activation Graphs. In Proc. of RIDS'95, Sep. 25-27 1995, Athens, Greece, pp. 165-181.
3. Baralis E., Ceri S., and Paraboschi S. Compile-Time and Runtime Analysis of Active Behaviors. IEEE Transactions on Knowledge and Data Engineering, Vol. 10, No. 3, May/June 1998, pp. 353-370.
4. Baralis E. and Widom J. An Algebraic Approach to Rules Analysis in Expert Database Systems. In Proc. of VLDB'94, Sep. 12-15 1994, Santiago de Chile, Chile, pp. 475-486.
5. Behrends H. Simulation-based Debugging of Active Databases. In Proc. of RIDE-ADS'94, Houston, Texas, February 14-15 1994, pp. 172-180.
6. Benazet E., Guehl H. and Bouzeghoub M. VITAL : a Visual Tool for Analysis of Rules Behaviour in Active Databases. In Proc. of RIDS'95, Sep. 25-27 1995, Athens, Greece, pp. 182-196.
7. Chakravarthy S., Tamizuddin Z., and Zhou J. A Visualisation and Explanation Tool for Debugging ECA Rules in Active Databases. Technical Report UF-CIS-TR-95-028, University of Florida, November 1995.

8. Diaz O., Jaine A. and Paton N. DEAR : a DEbugger for Active Rules in an object-oriented context. In Proc. of RIDS'93, August 30 - Sep. 1 1993, Edinburgh, Scotland, pp. 180-193.

9. Fors T. Visualisation of rule behaviour in active databases. In Proc. of VDB'95, March 27-29 1995, Lausanne, Switzerland, pp. 215-231.

10 Fraternali P. and Tanca L. A Structured Approach for the Definition of the Semantics of Active Databases. ACM Transactions on Database Systems, Vol. 20, No.4, December 1995, pp. 414-471.

11. Karadimce A.P. and Urban S.D. Conditional Term Rewriting as a Formal Basis for Analysis of Active Databases Rules. In Proc. of RIDE-ADS'94, IEEE-CS 1994, February 14-15 1994, Houston, Texas, USA, pp. 156-162.

12. Karadimce A.P. and Urban S. D. Refined Triggering Graphs: A Logic-Based Approach to Termination Analysis in an Active Object-oriented Database. In Proc. of ICDE'96, February 26 - March 1 1996, New Orleans, Louisiana, USA, pp. 384-391.

13. Kirchner C., Kirchner H., and Vittek M. ELAN : user manual. Novembre 1995.

14. Kokkinaki A.I. On Using Multiple Abstractions Models to Analyze Active Database Behavior. In Proc. of IDPT-IADT'98, July 6-9 1998, Berlin, Germany, pp. 136-143.

15. Lee J. and Davison A. The BeBOP System. Department of Computer Science, University of Melbourne, August 1993, Australia.

16. Lee S.Y. and Ling T. W. A Path Removing Technique for Detecting Trigger Termination. In Proc. of EDBT'98, March 23-27 1998, Valencia, Spain, pp. 341-355.

17. Meseguer J. A Logical Theory of Concurrent Objects. In Proc. of ECOOP-OOPSLA'90, Ottawa, Canada, October 1990, pp. 101-115.

18. Montesi D. and Torlone R. A Transaction Transformation Approach to Active Rule Processing. In Proc. ICDE'95, March 1995, Taipei, Taiwan, pp. 109-116.

19. Paton N.W., Diaz, O., Williams M.H., Campin J., Dinn A. and Jaime A. Dimensions of Active Behaviour. In Proc. of RIDS'93, August 30 - September 1 1993, Edinburgh, Scotland, pp. 40-57.

20. Rabih Y. La Logique de Réécriture: un formalisme pour modéliser les bases de données actives. INFORSID'96, Bordeaux, France, Juin 1996, pp. 351-367.

21. Rabih Y. and Schneider M. Influence of the dimensions of active rule execution model on the termination property. Technical Report, LIMOS-98-06, Université Clermont II, June 1998.

22. Rabih Y. and Schneider M. Specification of an object-oriented system with ELAN. Technical Report, LIMOS-98-07, Université Clermont II, July 1998.

23. Rabih Y., Schneider M.: The strategies : a support for model the dimensions of the active rules execution model. Technical Report, LIMOS-98-08, Université Clermont II, August 1998, France.

24. Rabih Y., Schneider M.: Behaviour study of active object-oriented systems. Technical Report, LIMOS-99-01, Université Clermont II, January 1999, France.

25. Tomas I.S. and Jones A.C. OLAF : The GOAD Active Database Event/Rule Tracer. In Proc. of DEXA '96, September 9-13 1996, Zurich, Switzerland, pp. 436-445.

Parallel Object Server
Architecture and Performance

Petr Kroha and Joerg Lindner

Fakultät für Informatik, TU Chemnitz
09107 Chemnitz, Germany
kroha@informatik.tu-chemnitz.de

Abstract. In this paper we describe the architecture and the performance of an implemented prototype of a parallel object server that we developed for storing fine grained objects. Finally, we present results of our experiments that concern the question how the speedup depends on the number of processors involved and the number of users working simultaneously.

1 Introduction

Sequential computers that are currently used as servers have their physical limits of performance. It is difficult to estimate the time point when their limits will be reached, but the usage of parallelism in parallel and distributed systems may be the only possibility to increase the performance of servers in the future.

Some applications, especially in engineering, use servers for management and storing fine grained objects. For storing and processing complex, fine grained data, the object-oriented DBMSs seem to be in principle more suitable than the relational DBMSs [2]. The normalization of tables in the relational model can cause the splitting of fine structured objects into many tables. During the phase of fetching objects, many tables are to be joined for getting the parts of objects together again [5]. This is paid by less performance.

The problem is that currently there are in principle no object-oriented DBMSs for parallel computers available as commercial products which could be used and tested. Because of the lack of standard, large variety of parallel computers, and a small demand, their arrival cannot be expected in the near future. Well, there is an object-relational ORACLE implementation on nCUBE, but object-relational is not object-oriented and nCUBE is only one of hundreds of types of parallel computers.

In this paper we describe our prototype of an object-oriented server OPAS (Object-oriented PArallel Server) running on a parallel computer (shared disk, distributed memory) as a data repository for a CASE tool. For our experiments, we have used data of two CASE tool applications and have measured speedup by changing the number of processors, the number of users, and other parameters.

The rest of this paper is organized as follows. Related work will be described in Section 2. In Section 3 we explain what advantages hierarchical data structures may have for parallel processing. Section 4 briefly describes the software architecture designed for the parallel object server. In Section 5, we discuss the implementation of the prototype on a parallel computer having shared-disk and distributed memory architecture. The results achieved and future work are discussed in Section 6.

2 Related work

The research of OODBMSs in a parallel environment seems to be at its very beginning. Until now, the OODBMS producers have paid very little attention to the parallel environment until now because of the small market.

In [8] we described how data have been stored in our first prototype, how buffers are organised, and how efficiently the object manager, the lock manager, and the disk manager have been working. Specific questions concerning properties of data repositories of CASE tools used in a multi-user environment in software engineering have been discussed in [9].

We did not find any papers discussing object-oriented parallel servers. Thus, we cannot compare our results with other results achieved by other researchers. The key contribution of this paper is that this is the very first attempt in this research direction.

3 Data structures and parallel processing

For the first attempt we simplified and focused our considerations on two groups of hierarchical data structures stored in the data repository:

- Structured data representing more levels of abstraction, e.g. stored in trees, are naturally hierarchically organized. They are typical in top-down analysis and bottom-up synthesis.
- Structured data representing only one level of abstraction, e.g. stored in lists and graphs, can be seen for purposes of parallel processing as hierarchical structures having a root (containing the name of the whole structure and OIDs of elements of the structure) and only one level of nodes which are leaves. Such structures will be used e.g. for representing ER-diagrams, finite state machines, Petri nets, etc.

From the point of view of data structures (objects), there are the following sources of parallelism:

- Object components which have a common father can be searched in parallel. This kind of parallelism will be called intra-object parallelism.
- Objects of different users can be searched in parallel. This kind of parallelism will be called inter-object parallelism.

To get data for our experiments we considered the development of two applications (hotel, warehouse). The top-down method of stepwise refinement via decomposition delivered hierarchically organized data.

In contrast to multimedia applications, large objects in CASE tools data repositories are usually aggregated and contain OID's of their components. Basic components contain their type, some parameters, and some OID's of related basic components if any. Our test applications generated objects of size between 50 and 500 bytes having the following statistical distribution: 48 % of objects of size 50-100 bytes, 30 % of objects of size 101-150 bytes, 11 % of objects of size 151-200 bytes, and 10 % of objects of size 201-500 bytes.

In our test examples, data representing data flow diagrams have been used, but we believe that similar results could be achieved for other hierarchically structured data, e.g. for relations Is-A (inheritance) and Is-Part-Of (aggregation) used in object-oriented modeling. As stated above, frequently used ER-diagrams can be processed as one-level hierarchical structures.

4   Hardware and software architecture

The parallel computer we used has the shared-disk architecture and a distributed memory. All accesses of its 128 processors to its shared permanent memory must be synchronized for using 8 access channels. Although it was originally bought for another purpose, we tested its features in our project and we found it being suitable for the given purpose as we describe in conclusions.

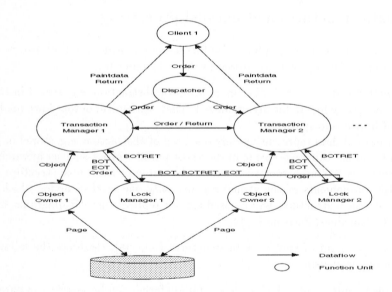

Fig. 1. Architecture of parallel server

The software architecture of the parallel server can be seen in Figure 1. The interface between the object server and its environment will be represented by a dispatcher. It communicates with clients, accepts their queries, and asks some of transaction managers to execute the corresponding tasks. The load of transaction managers will be planned to be evenly distributed.

The transaction manager concept has been designed as distributed, i.e. as a set of transaction managers. This makes possible the parallel processing of transactions (Fig. 2).

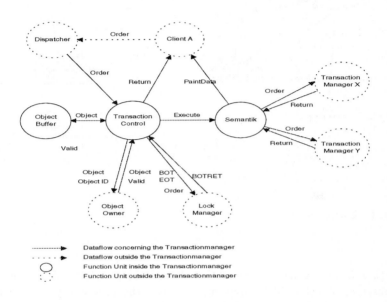

Fig. 2. Transaction manager

Because of possible problems of redundancy, the concept of an object owner has been designed. An object owner is responsible for the consistency of some subset of objects, i.e. there is a set of object owners responsible for the consistency of all data. Each object owner has available its own page-oriented disk manager for accessing data on files. The disk manager has its own page buffer. Because of the dynamic assignment between objects and transaction managers, replication of objects in the buffer can exist. The object owners get information about current values of object attributes from the transaction managers and check the consistency of their objects, i.e. of objects they are responsible for. Object owners represent an interface between transaction managers and disk managers.

We used a distributed lock manager, i.e. a set of lock managers. They are responsible for the synchronization of parallel transactions. Each lock manager is assigned a subset of objects. The distributed locking process concerns all corresponding lock managers. The simple 2-phase protocol has been used for locking to avoid deadlocks in the locking phases. Each lock manager uses a lock

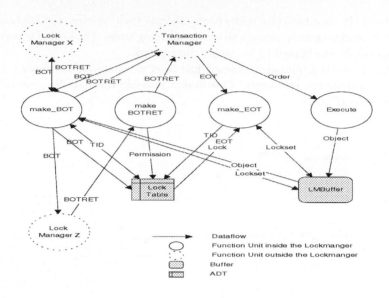

Fig. 3. Lock manager

table (Fig. 3) into which all information about locking and unlocking concerning its subset of objects will be written. However, the probability of such access conflicts seems to be very small, because software development team members normally work on disjunct objects. If not, versioning should be used.

Each transaction manager checks the consistency of objects by means of the corresponding object owner (Fig. 4) and controls the synchronisation by means of the lock managers.

The processing of a client's contract is done as follows. The dispatcher accepts the contract (query), which has the form of a message that is to be sent to an object Obj. According to the load distribution of transaction managers, the dispatcher finds a suitable transaction manager and delegates the contract to it. This transaction manager starts a new transaction by asking the lock manager (responsible for the object Obj) to start the locking process. Then, it tries to lock all involved objects of the intended transaction. While the lock manager is running, the transaction manager looks for the object Obj. If it is in its object buffer, the object owner will be asked for its validity. If the object Obj is not in the object buffer or if its value is obsolete, the transaction manager asks the object owner for an updated copy. Having fetched the object, the transaction manager asks the corresponding lock manager about the result of the locking process. If at least one object has just been locked by another transaction, later, the access attempt will several times be repeated until the desired object Obj is locked for the planned transaction.

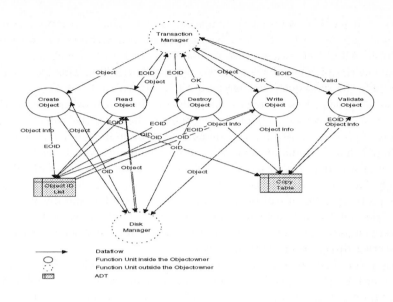

Fig. 4. Object owner

Now the message can be delivered to the object Obj which can cause some subtransactions to be started. After a transaction has been successfully finished, the lock managers unlock the objects involved. If some values of attributes have changed, the corresponding object owners will obtain the updated versions of these objects.

Transactions will be constructed using concepts of intra-object parallelism and inter-object-parallelism. As long as there are no synchronization conflicts in processing transactions and as longs as there are enough nodes, transactions are running fully in parallel. Synchronization conflicts occur, if some transactions ask for the same objects. Lock managers will solve them, but this will reduce the degree of overlapping of different queries, of course. However, on real conditions, although users are working on the same project using the same data repository, they are usually not working simultaneously on the same object in software engineering. If they exceptionally would, the process would slow down. In our test data, sets of objects involved in each transaction were disjunct. Thus, restricting factors in this sense are the number of processors and the accesses (read/write conflicts) to the shared disk.

5 Implemented prototype OPAS

In the first step, we simulated the logical concepts of the software architecture and the functionality of the server. We used Ada95 on a Sun machine for writing the first version of OPAS as a running design specification. We implemented clients, a dispatcher, transaction managers, object owners, lock managers, and disk managers as tasks. To describe the shared-disk architecture, we wrote a disk task. All object owners have to share this disk task, which has exclusive access. Queries of clients have been written into batch files. This has been done to simplify the subsequent debugging of the prototype in C++.

This step helped us to solve some problems. Besides proving the algorithms we obtained an overview about the dependence between the speedup and the number of processors used for a single-user and for a multi-user environment. We also found that the dynamic allocation of functional units which has been implemented as a part of the dispatcher in the first version does not work efficiently enough. Therefore, we have used the static allocation in the further development of the prototype. The use of the dynamic strategy would be suitable if the methods of the data model enclosed a large amount of instructions. CASE tools for software engineering seldom have such methods, but CAD tools used in other engineering disciplines have them very often.

After this first phase, the prototype was written in C++ for the parallel computer PARSYTEC/GC Power Plus - 128 with operating system PARIX. Our configuration of this computer consists of 64 nodes organized into 2D lattice.

The transfer unit of our server is one page and the optimal possibility for data transfer would be the one-to-one mapping between objects and pages. This is not always possible because some objects are (or can become) bigger than one page. We used a mapping between one object and one or more pages. After experiments with data used in CASE tools [8], the page size was defined 800 bytes because our objects mostly fit to this size.

We have placed the transaction manager and object owner on one processor and the lock manager on the next processor in the node. Under PARIX, more than one thread can be started in one node in the context of the node's program. If more than two threads are used in one node, time-sharing will be used.

6 Results, conclusions, future work

As a conclusion, we present some speculative results concerning the used hardware architecture and some experimental results concerning the behavior of our prototype in response to the experimental data.

First, we argue that the shared-disk hardware architecture used in our project does not bring significant disadvantages when used as hardware background for parallel object-oriented databases as data repositories for fine grained objects.

Usually, the shared-nothing hardware architecture will be recommended as the more suitable one for relational database systems [1], but when using it for our purposes in client/server environment, an important question is where the common data repository should be stored:

- If the common data repository is stored distributed and non- replicated on many disks then the responsible processor has to ask other processors to access and send data while processing the query. This increases the overhead.

- If the common data repository is stored distributed and replicated on many disks then it would bring an overhead (because of the checking of consistency) depending very strongly on how often the data will be used and changed.
- If the common data repository is stored on one disk then we have the same problem as in the shared-disk architecture.

When using the shared-disk architecture users are competing for the disk. In a trivial case, there can be only one disk connected. Usually, there are more channels in the switch which can work in parallel and support more disks. The query GET OBJECT will be processed by one processor which does not have sole access to the data, i.e. sometimes it has to wait for a free channel, but it can access to the data directly, i.e. without asking other procesors for help. It seems to be a good solution that the shared, common data repository is stored on the shared disk.

Second, in our experiments with the implemented prototype we investigated at first how the speedup depends on the intra-object parallelism in a single-user environment.

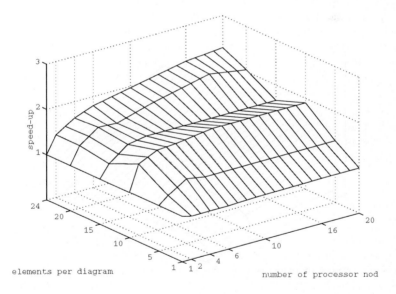

Fig. 5. speedup = f1(elements, nodes)

The function f1 (Fig. 5) shows the influence of the data structure of our objects on the speedup for increasing number of processor nodes involved. The number of elements per diagram (components of an aggregated object) represents the degree of the intra-object parallelism of the investigated data model. If an object is to be fetched and shown, its data structure has to be synthesized using pointers to its components that will be searched in parallel. We can see that the use of a parallel machine in this direction would not bring too much (factor 2.5 for 24 elements in diagram and 20 nodes used), at least not too much for objects composed from 1 to 24 components which we have tested. Of course, it depends strongly on the cardinality of aggregation used in classes which are typical for the specific application. For some CAD tools this kind of parallelism can bring perhaps much more speedup.

In the multi-user environment we investigated the dependence of the speedup on the number of clients and number of nodes. However, as shown above, there are some additional dimensions expressing the properties of data namely the size of methods and the number of components. Thus, it can be drawn in 3D only using some specific cuts, i.e. additional conditions. Fig. 6 represents the function f3 in the situation when all clients want to paint an object (not the same) consisting of 20 components 10 times (properties of the painting method). The situation when all clients want to process disjoint objects is a typical situation for using CASE tools and we used it in our tests.

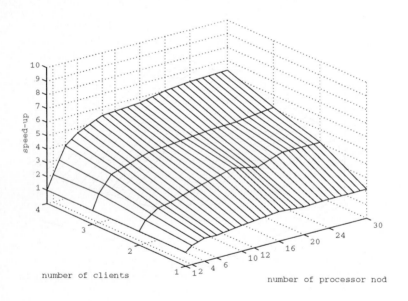

Fig. 6. speedup = f3(clients, nodes) for the painting method

Our main goals for the future research will concern the extension of test data and the usage of alternative concepts. Using extended test data, the implemented prototype will be tested in the future with the goal to investigate other dimensions of this problem given by improved strategies of parallel and distributed processing, e.g. optimistic locking.

References

1. De Witt, D., Naughton, J.F. et al: ParSets for Parallelizing OODBMS Traversal: Implementation and Performance. In: Proc. 3rd International Conference on Parallel and Distributed Information Systems, pp. 111-120, Austin, September 1994.
2. Emmerich, W., Kroha, P., Schäfer, W.: Object-Oriented Database Management Systems for Construction of CASE Environments. In: Marik, V. et al. (Eds.): Proceedings of the 4th Int. Conference DEXA'93, Lecture Notes in Computer Science, No. 720, Springer, 1993.
3. Freitag, B., Jones, C.B., Lengauer, Ch. Schek, H.-J.: (Eds.): Object Orientation with Parallelism and Persistence. Kluwer Academic Publishers, 1996.
4. Kroha, P.: Translation of a Query in OODBMS into a System of Parallel Tasks. EUROMICRO'92, Microprocessing and Microprogramming 37 (1993), North- Holland.
5. Kroha, P.: Objects and Databases. McGraw-Hill, 1993.
6. Kroha, P.: Shortcoming and Extensions of Relational DBMS. In: Adelsberger,H. et al. (Eds.): Information Management in Computer Integrated Manufacturing. Lecture Notes in Computer Science, No. 973, Springer, 1995.
7. Kroha, P.: Softwaretechnologie. Prentice Hall, 1997. (In German)
8. Kroha, P., Rosenbaum, S.: Object Server on a Parallel Computer. In: Wagner, R.R. (Ed.): Proceedings of the 8th International Workshop on Database and Expert Systems Applications DEXA'97, IEEE Computer Society, Toulouse 1997.
9. Kroha, P., Lindner, J.: Parallel Object Server as a Data Repository for CASE Tools. In: Croll, P., El-Rewini, H.(Eds.): Proceedings of International Symposium on Software Engineering for Parallel and Distributed Systems PDSE'99, Workshop of ICSE'99, pp. 148-156, IEEE Computer Society, Los Angeles, May 1999.
10. Lindner, J.: Properties of a Parallel Object Server as a Data Repository for CASE-Tools. M.Sc. Thesis, Faculty of Informatics, TU Chemnitz, 1998. (In German).
11. Maier, D.: Making Database Systems Fast Enough For CAD. In: Kim, W., Lochovsky, F. (Eds.): Object-oriented Concepts, Databases and Applications, pp. 573-582, ACM Press 1989.
12. Radestock, M., Eisenbach, S.: An Object Model for Distributed and Concurrent Programming Based on Decomposition. In: [3].
13. Stonebraker, M.: The case for shared nothing. Database Engineering, Vol. 9, No. 1, 1986.
14. Valduriez, P.: Parallel database systems: the case for shared nothing. In: Proc. of the 9th Int. Conf. On Data Engineering, pp. 460-465, Vienna 1993.

Using Contextual Fuzzy Views to Query Imprecise Data

P. Buche[1], S. Loiseau[2]

[1]INAPG, UER d'informatique/INRA BIA
16, rue Claude Bernard 75231 Paris Cédex 5, France
Tel 331 44 08 16 75, Fax 331 44 08 16 66
Buche@inapg.inra.fr
[2]LERIA, Université d'Angers
2, Boulevard Lavoisier 49045 ANGERS Cedex 1, France
Tel 332 41 73 50 77, Fax 332 41 73 53 52
loiseau@info.univ-angers.fr

Abstract. This work is concerned with the expression of querying using fuzzy values and with the storage and handling of imprecise information. This article introduces the concept of contextual fuzzy view based on the fuzzy logic theory and on case based reasoning system. The concept of contextual fuzzy view provides *(i)* a way to encapsulate the flexibility management induced by fuzzy querying, *(ii)* an optimisation of fuzzy filtering processing time, *(iii)* an enlargement of users' preferences, *(iv)*, in addition to the nearest data, an estimation of values that may be computed thanks to statistical models incorporated in case based reasoning system. The concept of contextual fuzzy view has been implemented in a prototype called CFQ written in Java language. This research takes place within a project to build a tool for the analysis of microbial risks in food products. An example of an application using CFQ is presented in the field of microbial risk assessment.

1 Introduction

An important aim for each actor of firms and government institutions is to be able to retrieve easily the most relevant information for his activity. Our research takes place in a national project which brings together government institutions and industry to build a tool for the analysis of microbial risks in food products. In this field of application, information can be qualitative or quantitative. The information is in general imprecise due to the complexity of the biological processes involved. Therefore, in this paper, we are concerned on one hand with the expression of querying using fuzzy values and on the other hand with the storage and handling of imprecise information.

The bibliography covers two types of problems. In a first category of papers, the fuzzy set framework has been shown to be a sound scientific choice to model such queries [2]. It is a natural way to represent the notion of preference using a gradual scale. In [3], the semantic of a language called SQLf has been proposed to extend the well-known SQL language by introducing fuzzy predicates processed on crisp information. In this framework, prototypes have been realised. We have tested the

FQUERY97 system described in [22]. This system has been designed in the Microsoft Access graphical environment; a special toolbar allows the user to define graphically and use fuzzy predicates in Access queries. The answers belong to a fuzzy relation: answers are ordered according to a matching degree which is a result of the comparison between fuzzy predicates and crisp values. In the second category of papers, the fuzzy set framework has also been proposed to represent imprecise values by means of possibility distributions [21]. Several authors have developed this approach in the context of databases [14], [16], [20], [23]. We have tested the FSQL system prototype presented in [11]. This system has been developed in the Oracle 7 DBMS environment. The imprecise information represented as possibility distribution is stored in standard tables. The user has to write a fuzzy query using the FSQL language. This query is then translated once only into a standard SQL query calling upon functions provided by the FSQL package to compute the degrees of matching.

In the previous works which propose querying systems such as FSQL or FQUERY97, the user is associated to the building of the query flexibility; for instance, in FSQL, the user has to specify in his query wether he is using a fuzzy join or a standard one. Those systems are more or less aimed at computer science specialists. The central point of our work is to propose a way to assist a standard user to make a fuzzy query. It is realised by the concept of **contextual fuzzy view.** This notion is an extension of the classical view concept in databases, e.g. a virtual table in which all the information needed by the user is brought together. This view is **fuzzy** because on one hand the selection criteria are expressed as fuzzy predicates as in [11], [22] and on the other hand the query associated to the view may be expressed in a fuzzy extension of the SQL language. This view is **contextual** because it associates the users' preferences expressed in his query to a category of queried information. Three advantages are provided by this contextual fuzzy view. First, the view engine enlarges queries if they are too restrictive due to the real content of the database: it provides an additional degree of flexibility not available in the previous systems. Second, the view engine is able to propose, in addition to the nearest information retrieved from the database, an estimation of the data sought. For this purpose, statistical models have to be defined in the categories. Third, the view engine optimises the fuzzy matching processing because the users' preferences are only compared to the information associated to the category selected: in the previous systems, all the information stored in the queried tables are compared to the users' preferences.

To provide this contextual querying, we have designed a knowledge base expressed in a case-based reasoning framework [13]. In this problem-solving approach, a set of reference cases is available. The problem to solve, called the target, is first compared to the set of cases to find the nearest one. Second, the most similar case is adapted to the target to provide a solution. Third, optionally, the adapted case may be stored in the set of reference cases to be reused. In [19], the set of cases is structured in categories. The comparison step of the processing is then divided in two: *(i)* the target is associated to the nearest category, *(ii)* the selected category provides a way to compare the target to the set of cases belonging to the category. In our system, we drew upon the comparison step replacing the target by the fuzzy query and the set of cases by the set of information stored in the database. We have implemented the concept of **contextual fuzzy view** in a prototype called CFQ (for contextual fuzzy querying). This software is written in Java language. The information is stored in an Oracle 7 DBMS using the representation model of FSQL [11].

This paper is organised as follows. In section 2, we present in the preliminary section the imprecise data representation used. The main steps of the view processing are described in section 3. An example of application is given in section 4.

2 Preliminary

Data stored in the database may be crisp or imprecise values. Imprecise data are represented using the usual possibility theory-based approach. The value associated to an attribute A for a tuple t is defined as a possibility distribution $\pi_{A(t)}$ on the underlying domain D. The possibility distribution $\pi_{A(t)}$ can be viewed as a fuzzy restriction of the possible value of $A(t)$ by a fuzzy subset F. Given χ the membership function associated to F :

$$\begin{cases} \forall d \in D, \chi_F(d) \in [0,1] \\ \pi_{A(t)}(d) = \chi_F(d). \end{cases} \tag{1}$$

For instance, the information « *thermisation t has a high duration* » will be represented by: $\pi_{Duration(t)}(d) = \chi_{HighDuration}(d)$. Here, $\chi_{HighDuration}$ is a membership function which represents the vague predicate *HighDuration* defined as a fuzzy subset. This approach proposes a unified framework for representing precise and imprecise values of attributes. We consider two kinds of membership functions depending on the domain: *(i)* on an ordered and continuous underlying domain, a trapezoidal fuzzy subset is associated to each value (see Fig. 1), *(ii)* on a discrete and non ordered domain, a standard fuzzy subset is associated to each value (see Fig. 2).

3 Contextual fuzzy view processing

The contextual fuzzy view can be considered from structural and processing points of view. In the structural point of view, we distinguish that of the user (section 3.1) and the internal one of the knowledge base (section 3.2). The user selects a fuzzy view in the set of available views stored in the knowledge base and expresses in this view an input query, i.e. the characteristics of the data he wants to retrieve. The knowledge base contains resemblance relations and fuzzy views descriptions. The resemblance relations are used for attribute values comparison. For each fuzzy view, the knowledge base contains the set of data categories descriptions. Each category is composed of *(i)* a characterisation filter used to determine which category corresponds to the input query, *(ii)* a fuzzy SQL query to retrieve data associated to the selected category, *(iii)* information to build a filter which enlarges the input query, *(iv)* statistical models that can provide estimated data in addition to the closest data matching the input query. From the processing point of view, four steps are performed (section 3.3) to execute a query in the fuzzy view. The first step determines the best category relative to the input query. The second one builds the fuzzy filter adapted to the selected category. In the third step, estimated values are computed using statistical models. The last step uses the fuzzy filter to retrieve and sort the closest data. The first and third steps use a similarity measure to compare fuzzy values (section 3.4). Finally, we briefly present the software architecture (section 3.5) of this mechanism implementation.

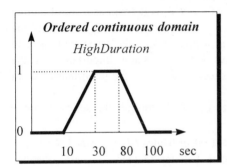
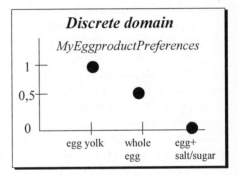

Fig. 1. a trapezoidal fuzzy subset   **Fig. 2.** a standard fuzzy subset

3.1 The user point of view

The user point of view is characterised by the input and the output. An input query in the view is described as follows. If we call *AS*, the set of all the attributes available through the considered view, we define *QAS* as an *AS* subset composed of all the attributes which can be queried through this view. A query in the view is defined by a set, called *IP*, of atomic fuzzy predicates P_i defined as triples $<QA_i, L_i, B_i>$ where:

(i) QA_i is an attribute which belongs to *QAS*. All these attributes are fuzzy attributes. This means that values associated to these attributes are fuzzy values and comparison between these attributes are fuzzy comparisons.

(ii) L_i is a linguistic label defining the value associated to the queried attribute QA_i. L_i is a fuzzy set on the underlying domain *D*. Its membership function χ is defined by $\chi_{L_i}: D \rightarrow [0,1]$. We distinguish two kinds of labels depending on the underlying domain of the attribute as we mentioned for the imprecise data stored in the database.

(iii) $\boldsymbol{B_i}$ is a Boolean value specifying to the view engine whether the users' preferences expressed in the linguistic labels may be modified or not.

An example of *IP* set query input is given in section 4.3.

The output view is a fuzzy relation, e.g. a fuzzy set defined on the Cartesian product of *AS* belonging to the view. Tuples *t* are ordered according to a matching degree *md* which will be defined in the following sections. An example of output is given in section 4.4.

3.2 Knowledge base structure

First, the main element of the knowledge base is the description of information categories associated to each fuzzy view. For a given view, each category, denoted C_j, is defined as a quadruplet $<CF_j, Q_j, FBA_j, SEM_j>$ where:

(i) CF_j is the fuzzy characterisation filter of C_j. CF_j is defined as a set of atomic fuzzy predicates P_k defined as triples $<QA_{jk}, L_{jk}, I_{jk}>$. QA_{jk} is an attribute which belongs to *QAS*. L_{jk}, defined as a fuzzy set, is the associated value to QA_{jk}. The attributes do not always have the same importance in the characterisation filter. The aggregate is weighted. I_{jk} is the importance weight associated to QA_{jk} in CF_j.

(ii) Q_j is a fuzzy SQL query associated to C_j. It determines the set of database tuples associated to C_j.

(iii) FBA_j is the filter building array. It is a set of triples $<QA_{jk}, \lambda_{jk}, I'_{jk}>$ ($\lambda_{jk} \in$ R, $I'_{jk} \in$ R). QA_{jk} is an attribute which belongs to *QAS*. λ_{jk} are tolerance coefficient values. They are introduced to modify the user preferences specified in the *IP* set. They express expert knowledge about the real content of the database relaxing preferences concerning specific attributes. I'_{jk} is the importance weight associated to QA_{jk} in the constructed filter.

(iv) SEM_j is a set of statistical estimation models of the following form:
$$\hat{A}_{jk} = f\left(A_1,\ldots,A_i,\ldots,A_n\right) \text{ with } \hat{A}_{jk} \in AS \text{ and } A_i \in QAS$$
We assume that A_i attributes are defined on continuous and ordered domain D_i. It is possible to estimate the $\hat{A}_{jk}$ values if all the attributes involved in the estimation model belong to the *IP* set (e.g. are queried and valued in the view input query).

Examples of categories are given in section 4.2.

Second, for underlying application needs, resemblance relations res_i are defined on the domain D_i of each attribute which belongs to *QAS*. Given a distance *d* on the domain D_i, the resemblance relations are defined as follows:

$$\begin{cases} res_i: D_i \times D_i \to [0,1] \\ \forall(x,y) \in D_i \times D_i, res_i(x,y) = \dfrac{1}{1+d(x,y)} \end{cases} \qquad (2)$$

Some examples of distances are given in section 4.1.

3.3 Main steps of the processing

Starting from the *IP* set, the view engine acts in four steps to deliver the fuzzy relation and possibly estimated values, resulting from the querying.

First, the *IP* set is compared to the characterisation filter of each *Cj* category. The set of fuzzy predicates P_i (e.g. triples $<QA_i, L_i, B_i>$) must be satisfied together. Therefore, the similarity measures between corresponding attributes belonging to *CFj* and *IP* (resp. QA_{jk} and QA_i), noted $\mu_{rep}(L_{jk}, L_i)$, are aggregated using a *min* operator. As the attributes QA_{jk} do not always have the same importance, the aggregate is weighted using the I_{jk} value defined in *CFj*. For that, we use the method proposed by [9]. The user query is associated to the C_j category which maximises the following similarity measure *sm*:

$$sm(IP, CF_j) = \min_{\substack{QA_i = QA_{jk} \\ QA_i \in IP \\ QA_{jk} \in CF_j}} \max(\mu_{rep}(L_{jk}, L_i), 1 - I_{jk}). \tag{3}$$

Second, as in [19], the user preferences expressed in the *IP* set (e.g. triples $<QA_i, L_i, B_i>$) are modified giving *IP'* according to the tolerance coefficients defined in the FBA_j array belonging to the selected C_j. If λ_{jk} is the tolerance coefficient associated to the QA_{jk} attribute corresponding to QA_i in FBA_j, *IP'* is defined as follows:

$$IP' = \left\{ P'_i \; / \; if \; \neg B_i \; then \; P'_i = P_i \; else \; P'_i = \, < QA_i, f\left(L_i, \lambda_{jk}\right), B_i > \right\}. \tag{4}$$

The membership function associated to the fuzzy subset $f(L_i, \lambda_{jk})$ is defined by:

$$\begin{cases} \mu_{f(L_i, \lambda_{jk})}(d) = \sup_{d_1 \in D} \min\left(\mu_{L_i}(d_1), \mu_R(d_1, d)\right) \\ with \; \mu_R(u, v) = \max\left(0, 1 - \left(d(u, v) / \lambda_{jk}\right)\right). \end{cases} \tag{5}$$

Application of such a fuzzy tolerance is possible only if a distance relation has been defined on the domain *D* corresponding to the attribute considered. In CFQ, such a distance is defined for each attribute belonging to *QAS*.

Third, if SEM_j, a set of statistical estimation models, has been defined for the selected category C_j, $\hat{A}_j$ values are calculated if all the attributes involved in the estimation models belong to *IP*. As the values L_i associated to A_i in the *IP* set are fuzzy values defined on continuous and ordered domains, L_i are represented by trapezoidal functions. Therefore, we compute an estimated value for each of the four control points of L_i.

Fourth, the fuzzy filter *IP'* is compared to each tuple associated to the selected category C_j. The set of tuples attached to the category is updated from time to time executing the fuzzy SQL query Q_j associated to C_j. The set of fuzzy predicates P'_i belonging to *IP'* (e.g. triples $<QA_i, f(L_i, \lambda_{jk}), B_i>$) must be satisfied together. Therefore, the similarity measures obtained for each tuple *t*, noted

$\mu_{rep}(QA_i(t), f(L_i, \lambda_{jk}))$, are aggregated using a *min* operator. As the attributes have not always the same importance, the aggregate is weighted using the I'_{jk} coefficient defined for the attribute QA_{jk} corresponding to QA_i in the FBA_j of the selected category C_j. Tuples t are ordered according to a matching degree *md* defined as follows:

$$md(t) = \min_{QA_i \in IP'} \max(\mu_{rep}(QA_i(t), f(L_i, \lambda_{jk})), 1 - I'_{jk}). \quad (6)$$

3.4 Similarity measure between fuzzy values

In this section, we present the similarity criterion used in CFQ to compare fuzzy values. CFQ uses it twice: *(i)* for the comparison between *IP* set and CF_j characterisation filter of C_j categories in order to determine the closest information category, *(ii)* for the comparison between *IP'* set and $QA_i(t)$ values to determine the closest tuples. We can distinguish two families of approaches to compare fuzzy values. In the first one, a measure is used to evaluate the possibility degree of equality between two fuzzy values [7], [8], [15]. They are suitable when strict equality is the only way to compare domain values. In CFQ, resemblance relations are defined on the domain for each attribute belonging to *QAS*. For this reason, the measure proposed in the second family of approach ([4], [5], [6]) is more appropriate because it evaluates the extent to which two representations are close to each other taking into account resemblance relations. More precisely, if we consider two fuzzy value representations A and B defined on the same domain D, the degree of closeness between $<d/\pi_A(d)>$ and $<d'/\pi_B(d')>$ is defined as an aggregation of the degree of closeness between d and d' (according to the resemblance relation *res* defined on D) on one hand and the degree of closeness between $\pi_A(d)$ and $\pi_B(d')$ on the other hand. The contribution of a particular value d on the global measure depends on the degree $\pi_A(d)$ acting as a weight. The overall measure $\mu_{rep}(A, B)$ is:

$$\begin{cases} \mu_{rep}(A,B) = \inf_{d \in Support(A)} \max\left(1 - \pi_A(d), \sup_{d' \in Support(B)} \min\left(\mu_{res}(d,d'), \mu_\theta(\pi_A(d), \pi_B(d'))\right)\right) \\ \text{with } \mu_\theta(x,y) = 1 - |x - y|. \end{cases} \quad (7)$$

3.5 Software architecture

We are engaged in a national project which brings together government institutions and industry to build a tool for the analysis of microbial risks in food products. This tool will include databases and a *suitable* information retrieval system available on the Internet. Our implementation shows that in this context, a fuzzy logic based information retrieval system is well adapted. We have built a prototype, called CFQ, written in Java language which interacts with Oracle. The choice of using Oracle is justified by the fact that firstly it is the DBMS used by our industrial partners and secondly the FSQL fuzzy query server [11] that we use has been developed on this DBMS. A CFQ query is executed using a three tier process architecture: *(i)* the CFQ Java client applet running under a usual Web browser, *(ii)* a database connectivity middleware (running on the Web server due to security checking on applet execution), *(iii)* an Oracle/FSQL database server. In the following, we will summarize the two main steps to execute a contextual fuzzy view using CFQ engine. The knowledge bases (described in section 3.2) containing the fuzzy views are stored in the database as the crisp or imprecise information accessible from the views. The information is stored according to the imprecise information representation format proposed in [11]. First, using the graphical interface (see Fig. 6), the user has to select a particular knowledge base. The CFQ engine loads it from the database. Second, the user selects a fuzzy view belonging to the knowledge base. Again, the CFQ engine loads this view from the database. Third, the user expresses his preferences creating the *IP* set and asks for information scanning. The CFQ engine analyses *IP* set to select the closest category of data C_j associated to this view and accesses the database to retrieve the tuples associated to C_j.

4 An example of application

The first aim of our information retrieval system is to select the most relevant information published in the recent scientific bibliography for an engineer who wants to analyse the microbial risks in food products. As a first example of fuzzy view, we have worked on information concerning the resistance of Listeria monocytogenes bacterium (dangerous for human health) to heat processing [1]. For a given bacterium, at a given temperature, Listeria bacterium destruction is considered to be an exponential curve [18]. The curve slope is the elapsed time (in minutes) to destroy 90% of the living Listeria population at a given temperature. This elapsed time is called *decimal reduction time*. The information is in general an imprecise value due to the complexity of the underlying biological process. For instance, in whole milk, the decimal reduction time is between 0.33' and 0.58' at 63.3°C. In his paper [1], Augustin has studied different categories of food products: dairy products, meat products and egg products. He has shown that decimal reduction times are homogeneous in dairy and meat products inside each group, but not homogeneous in egg product group. As a consequence, in CFQ knowledge base, it is possible to propose a relevant statistical estimation of the decimal reduction time given the temperature only for dairy and meat products; but it is not possible for the egg product group. For this latest category, in CFQ knowledge base, it is interesting to set a fuzzy tolerance parameter λ large enough to take into account the intragroup variability. We show respectively in section 4.1 distance relations we have used and in section 4.2 categories we have defined for this fuzzy view.

4.1 Distance relations

Distance relations d_i have been defined on the domain D_i of each attribute belonging to the QAS set. More precisely, we have defined two kinds of relations:

(i) for biological qualitative information (as, for instance, substrates or serotypes), called concepts in the following, we have defined a semantic distance computed in generalisation/specialisation trees, called GS trees. A GS tree is defined as follows: concept C_1 is the father of C_2 if C_1 is more general than C_2 (C_2 is more specific than C_1). An example of GS tree is given in Fig. 3. We drew upon the work of [10] to build a distance function on GS trees. Given two concepts C_1 and C_2, we consider C_3, the more specific concept which generalises C_1 and C_2. The semantic distance d between C_1 and C_2 is the sum of distances from C_1 to C_3 and C_2 to C_3.

(ii) for information defined on an ordered domain, we have used a distance d defined as follows: given an increasing series of pairs of values (x_i, x_{i+1}) (with $x_i \prec x_{i+1} \forall i$) associated to a value d_i on the domain D:.

$$\forall (x,y) \in D_i^2, d(x,y) = d_i \ if \ x_i \leq |x - y| \prec x_{i+1} . \tag{8}$$

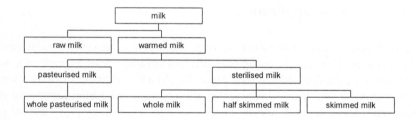

Fig. 3. Example of GS tree for milk products

4.2 Categories

We have defined 3 categories of data in the fuzzy view: C_1 for dairy products, C_2 for meat products and C_3 for egg products. We give the description of C_1 and C_3 in the following. A statistical estimation model is defined in C_1 because information is homogeneous in this category. No model is defined for C_3 however, because of the information heterogeneity in this category. A high λ value is associated to Duration attribute in C_3 to take into account the high variability in this category.

Category C_1:

Fuzzy characterisation filter CF_1 = <Substrate, ((Milk,1.0)), 1.0>

Filter building array FBA_1 = {< Substrate, 0, 1.0>, <Serotype, 0, 0.7>, <Temperature, 0, 1.0>, <Duration, 0, 0.9>}

Statistical estimation models SEM_1 = {($\log_{10}$Duration=11.72-0.19*Temperature)}

Fuzzy FSQL query Q_1 = select IdResult, cdeg(*) from Results where
SUBSTRAT FEQ $MILK .1 order by 2 desc

Category C₃:

Fuzzy characterisation filter CF3 = <Substrate, ((Eggproduct,1.0)), 1.0>
Filter building array FBA3 = {< Substrate, 0, 1.0>, <Serotype, 0, 0.7>,
<Temperature, 0, 1.0>, <Duration, 6, 0.9>}
Statistical estimation models SEM3 = {}
Fuzzy FSQL query Q3 = select IdResult, cdeg(*) from Results where
SUBSTRAT FEQ $EGGPRODUCT .1 order by 2 desc

4.3 Example of querying

We show in this paragraph two examples of CFQ query. Let Q1 be the following query whose *IP* set is the following: {<Temperature, *LowTemperature*, true>, <Substrate, *MyEggproductPreferences*, true>, <Serotype, *MySerotypePreferences*, true>, <Duration, *HighDuration, false>*}. The fuzzy subsets *HighDuration* and *MyEggproductPreferences* are defined in Fig. 1 and Fig. 2. The fuzzy subsets *LowTemperature* and *MySerotypePreferences* are defined in Fig. 4 and Fig. 5. The CFQ graphical interface corresponding to query Q1 is given in Fig. 6.

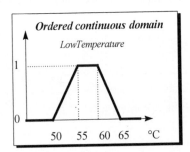

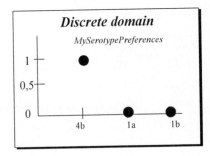

Fig. 4. Fuzzy subset *LowTemperature*

Fig. 5. Fuzzy subset *MySerotypePreferences*

4.4 Result of the querying

The result given by the CFQ engine to this query (with a threshold equal to 0.3 on the *md* matching degree) is the following (DurationFormat=5 means that Duration is an imprecise value represented by an interval defined by the 2 control points D1 and D4 [11]):

Id	md	Substrate	Bacterium	Serotype	Temp (°C)	Dura-tion Format	D1	D2	D3	D4
80	0.9	egg yolk	Scott A	4b	60	5	55.2	0	0	101.4
81	0.33	whole egg	Scott A	4b	60	5	90	0	0	126
85	0.33	egg yolk	5 strains	NULL	64.4	5	26.4	0	0	26.4
78	0.3	whole egg	3 strains	1	60	5	78	0	0	84

The IdResult 80 matches all the criteria, except the duration which is a little bit different to the predicate *HighDuration*. It explains the matching degree equal to 0.9. IdResult 81 (resp. 85 and 78) has a worse matching degree because of the Substrate criterion (resp. Serotype). Query Q2 is the same as query Q1 except the boolean value associated to the attribute Duration which is set now on true. It means that CFQ may modify the preferences for this attribute expressed in the predicate *HighDuration*. The new results are the following:

Id	md	Substrate	Bacterium	Serotype	Temp (°C)	Dura-tion Format	D1	D2	D3	D4
80	0.961	egg yolk	Scott A	4b	60	5	55.2	0	0	101.4
81	0.333	*whole egg*	Scott A	4b	60	5	90	0	0	126
85	0.333	egg yolk	5 strains	*NULL*	64.4	5	26.4	0	0	26.4
86	**0.333**	egg + salt or sugar	5 strains	*NULL*	64.4	5	*366.6*	*0*	*0*	*366.6*
78	0.3	*whole egg*	3 strains	1	60	5	78	0	0	84

The answer is quite similar. But the CFQ system gives **very relevant** new information to the engineer who asked this question. If, in his process, he mixes salt or sugar with the egg, he can obtain a decimal reduction time very different from his preferences which correspond to his processing conditions (366.6 sec compared to the interval [26.4, 126]).

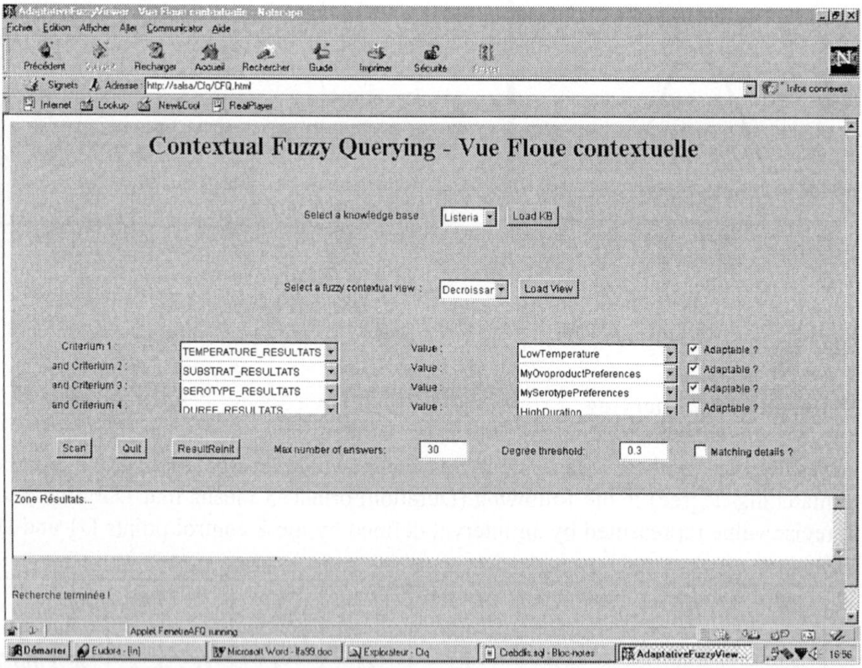

Fig. 6. CFQ graphical interface

5 Conclusion

In this paper, we have introduced the concept of contextual fuzzy view. Using this view, the user has only to specify his fuzzy preferences: he eliminates the need to explain *how* the system will process the fuzzyness. The CFQ engine builds a fuzzy filter with the user preferences *adapted to the category* of queried data - thanks to contextual knowledge. It brings three benefits: *(i)* The CFQ engine *optimizes* the processing time of the filtering because it only scans the data associated to the selected category ; *(ii)* the CFQ engine can deliver an *estimate* of the queried data if an estimation method has been defined for the selected category of data ; *(iii)* the CFQ engine can *enlarge* users' preferences to adapt them to the real content of the database. The CFQ engine has been developed in Java language. It has been coupled to Oracle extended for fuzzy SQL [11]. A first real application has been successfully implemented and concerns microbial risk assessment in food products. Immediate prospects are the following: *(i)* we are developing deeper links between the CFQ engine and statistical models. This is a natural addition to information retrieval systems which try to deliver the most relevant information for the user. In particular, we will study links with new models proposed in microbiology [17] and fuzzy statistical models [12]. *(ii)* We want to propose a convenient method to help the knowledge base administrator to determine the fuzzy characterisation filters of the categories. *(iii)* We are studying the extension of CFQ engine for querying numerical images.

Acknowledgments

Research and preparation of this manuscript were partially supported by head offices of the French Ministry of Agriculture, DGAL (Food Head Office) and DGER (Research and Education Head Office).

References

1. Augustin J.C. Résistance de Listeria monocytogenes aux traitements physiques. Pathologie-Biologie, vol 44, N°9, pp 790-807, November 1996.
2. Bosc P., Lietard L., Pivert O. Soft querying, a new feature for database management system. DEXA'94 LNCS 856, 1994 pp 631-640.
3. Bosc P., Pivert O. SQLf: a relational database language for fuzzy querying. IEEE Transactions on fuzzy systems, vol 3, no 1, February 1995, pp 1-17.
4. Bosc P., Pivert O. On the comparison of imprecise values in fuzzy databases. Proceedings of FUZZ-IEEE'97, pp 707-712. Barcelona, 1997.

5. Bosc P., Pivert O. On representation-based querying of databases containing ill-known values. Proceedings of ISMIS'97, Charlotte, USA, pp 477-486, 1997.

6. Bosc P., Pivert O. A new approach to the filtering of ill-known data. Proceedings of FUZZ-IEEE'98, pp 1308-1313. Anchorage, 1998.

7. Chen G.Q., Kerre E.E., Vandenbulcke, J. *A general treatment of data redundancy in a fuzzy relational data model.* Journal of the American Society for Information Science, 43: pp 304-311, 1992.

8. Cubero J.C., Vila M.A. A new definition of fuzzy functional dependency in fuzzy relational databases. Journal of Intelligent Systems, 9: pp 441-448, 1994.

9. D. Dubois, H. Prade, C. Testemale. *Weighted fuzzy pattern matching.* Fuzzy Sets and Systems, vol. 28, pp 313-331. 1988.

10. Foo N., Garner B.J., Rao A., Tsui E. *Semantic distance in conceptual graphs.* Proceeding of the 4th annual workshop on conceptual structures, pp 1-9. 1989.

11. Galindo J., Cubero J.C., Pons O., Medina J.M. *A server for fuzzy SQL queries.* Proceedings of the 1998 workshop FQAS'98 (Flexible Query-Answering Systems), Roskilde, Denmark, pp 161-171, May 1998.

12. Gil M. A. Modelling and analysing fuzzy elements in statistics. Proceedings of LFA 98 (Rencontres françaises sur la Logique Floue et ses Applications), Rennes, France, pp 187-200. November 1998.

13. Mille A., Napoli A. *Aspects du raisonnement à partir de cas.* PRC-GDR IA'97, pp 261-284.

14. Prade H. Lipski's approach to incomplete information data bases restated and generalized in the setting of Zadeh's possibility theory. Information Systems. Vol. 9, N°1, pp. 27-42, 1984.

15. Prade H., Testemale C. *Generalizing database relational algebra for the treatment of incomplete or uncertain information and vague queries.* Information Sciences, 34: pp 115-143, 1984.

16. Prade H., Testemale C. Fuzzy relational databases: representational issues and reduction using similarity measures. Journal of the American Society for Information Science. 38(2): pp118-126, 1987.

17. Rosso L. *Convenient model to describe the combined effects of temperature and pH on microbial growth.* Applied and Environmental Microbiology, 61(2), pp. 610-616.

18. Rozier, Larlier, Bolnot. *Bases microbiologiques de l'hygiène des aliments.* Séporic Edition, pp 55-63.

19. Salotti S., *Filtrage flou et représentation centrée-objet pour raisonner par analogie: le système FLORAN.* Thèse de l'Université Paris XI Orsay. December 1992.

20. Umano M. *FREEDOM-0: a fuzzy database system.* Fuzzy Information and Decision Processes. Eds M. Gupta and E. Sanchez (Amsterdam: North-Holland). pp 339-347, 1982.

21. Zadeh L.A. *Fuzzy sets as basis for a theory of possibility.* Fuzzy Sets and Systems, vol. 1, pp 3-28. 1978.

22. Zadrozny S., Kacprzyk J. *Implementing fuzzy querying via the internet/WWW: Java applets, activeX controls and cookies.* Proceedings of the 1998 workshop FQAS'98 (Flexible Query-Answering Systems), Roskilde, Denmark, pp 358-369, May 1998.

23. Zemankova-Leech M., Kandel A. *Fuzzy relation databases - a key to expert systems,* (Köln: Verlag TÜV Rheinland), 1984.

Combining Pat-Trees and Signature Files for Query Evaluation in Document Databases

Yangjun Chen and Karl Aberer

IPSI Institute, GMD GmbH, Dolivostr. 15,
64293 Darmstadt, Germany

Abstract. In this paper, a new indexing technique to support the query evaluation in document databases is proposed. The key idea of the method is the combination of the technique of pat-trees with signature files. While the signature files are built to expedite the traversal of object hierarchies, the pat-trees are constructed to speed up both the signature file searching and the text scanning. In this way, high performance can be achieved.

1 Introduction

We consider the combination of two different indexing techniques: signature files and pat-trees for optimizing query evaluation in document databases. Signature files can be feasibly organized into a hierarchical structure and therefore suitable for indexing documents stored structurally (in an object-oriented database). Concretely, it can be used to speed up the traversal along object hierarchies by filtering non-relevant objects as early as possible. The drawback of the signature file is that it is an inexact filter. A key word (appearing in the query) surviving the checking may be not in the text. Therefore, a scanning of the text has to be carried out to see whether the text really contains it. Furthermore, if many texts should be checked or a text is long, much time will be spent to do this task if no index is available. On the other hand, for a large document database, a signature file may be very large by itself and therefore the overhead caused by the sequential search of such files become significant. To make the matter worse, since the signature file works only as an inexact filter, it can not be sorted and thus the binary search can not be applied (see 5.3). To this end, we combine the technique of the pat-tree with the technique of the signature file to make both the searching of a signature file and the scanning of a text more efficient. As we can see later, the processes of the tree traversal and the signature file searching (also text scanning) supported by the pat-trees will be interleaved, leading to an efficient method.

The rest of this paper is organized as follows. In Section 2, we survey related work. In Section 3, we describe the basic features of a document database and discuss the approaches to query processing. Section 4 is devoted to hierarchies of representative words. In Section 5, we discuss different indexing techniques as well as their combination. In Section 6, we present our algorithms for evaluating queries with signature file hierarchies and pat-trees used. Finally, Section 7 is a short conclusion.

2 Related work

Index techniques have been extensively investigated in both information retrieval and database research area and a lot of methods have been developed within the past three decades.

To index large files in information retrieval systems, different tree indexing approaches have been proposed, such as binary trees [Kn73], suffix trees [CR94] and their variants, position trees [AHU74, We73] built over flat files as well as pat-trees [Mo68] using individual bits of keys. Equipped with these mechanisms, the system performance can be improved by one order of magnitude or more. Signature file [CF84, DGL98, Fa92] is a method quite different from the tree indexing techniques, by which each key word is assigned a signature and a set of key words is assigned a "super" signature constructed by superimposing the signatures in the set. It works as an inexact filter. Another interesting approach is the inverted index that is a set of postings lists [HEBL92, WMB94], each of which maps one keyword to a list of links to the documents containing that keyword. Inverted indices can be implemented as sorted arrays, tries and various hashing structures [HFBL92]. The drawback of this approach is that much space is required for indices and not suitable for the implementation of a layered index structure as the signature file does (see 5.2).

Some of the techniques mentioned above have been modified or extended to support the query evaluation in databases. A notable example is B-tree [BU77] and its variants such as B^+-tree and B*-tree [EN89] which were developed based on the balancing mechanism of binary trees with some special features augmented to ease the tree balance or to minimize the accesses to data files. In addition, the signature files have been proved to be useful in object-oriented databases and many researches have been done to integrate this technique into the object-oriented databases to improve the response time of a query [YA94, LL92].

One may notice that there is no application of pat-trees or position trees in the database area. It is due to the essential distinction between the key structures of a relation and the key words in a text. In this paper, we explore a way to use the pat-tree in document databases indirectly - we build the pat-trees over signature files (therefore, it is a method of indexing over indexes.) Obviously, if an object-oriented database system uses signature files as the indexing mechanism, our method can also be used to improve the query evaluation. Additionally, in a document database, texts stored as attribute values may be long and it is necessary to index them if the space overhead for indexes remains low.

3 Queries in document databases

In document database systems, an element is represented as an object, which consists of methods and attributes. Methods are procedures and functions associated with an object defining the actions taken by the object in response to messages received. Attributes represent the state of the object. Objects having the same set of attributes and methods are grouped into the same class. A class is either a *primitive* class or a *complex* class. Objects in the respective classes are called primitive objects and complex objects. A primitive class, such as integer and string, is not further broken down into attributes or substructures. A complex class is defined by a set of attributes which may be primitive or complex with user-defined classes as their domains. Since a class C may have a complex attribute with domain C', a relationship can be established between C and C'. The relationship is called aggregation relationship. Using arrows connecting classes to represent aggregation relationship, an aggregation hierarchy can be constructed to show the nested structure of the classes.

Fig. 1(a) shows a possible DTD for *letter* documents (SGML/XML documents). The class definition for the corresponding elements and the resulting aggregation hierarchy are shown in Fig. 1(b).

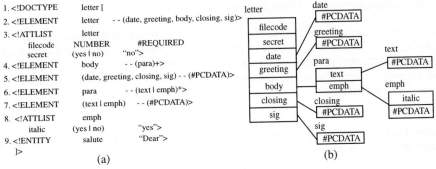

Fig. 1. DTD and hierarchy structure

To show the application of our indexing method and to provide a background for discussion, here we consider a kind of simple queries: key word queries (but with the path concept involved) which are most frequently utilized in practice. In such queries, a search condition is expressed as conjunction of predicates of the form: *<path operator value>*. The *path* is of the form: $p_1.p_2 \ldots .p_n$, where each p_i ($i = 1, 2, \ldots, n$-1) represents a class name and p_n is an attribute name. In general, an *operator* represents a (set) relation operation $\{\supseteq, =\}$ and a *value* is a set of individual (representative) words connected with "∧" or "∨".

As an example, consider the query: retrieve all letters received in 1993, which contain strings "SGML" and "database", which can be expressed as follows:

> select *
> where *Letter.Date* $\supseteq$ "1993"
> and *Letter.Body.Para.text* $\supseteq$ "SGML" ∧ "database"

The search condition against the classes *Letter*, *Date* and *Para* consists of two predicates, one involving the nested attribute *Date* and the other involving the nested attribute *text* of *Para*.

A top-down approach will search all of the objects in class *Letter* and those whose *date* attribute contains "1993" will be singled out. Then, the system retrieves the *Body* objects referred by the *Letter* objects found in the previous scan and checks their *para* attribute, which leads to retrieving part of *Para* objects referred by the found *Body* objects. Finally, those *Para* objects containing both "SGML" and "database" are returned.

From the above description, we can see that two processes are involved to evaluate a query. They are

(1) traversing along object hierarchies and

(2) scanning texts to see whether the key words appearing in the query are contained.

What we want is to optimize these two processes by building indexes over both the object hierarchies and the texts stored as attribute values. For this purpose, we first introduce an important concept: *representative word hierarchy* in the next section, which is useful to specify the key idea of our method.

4 Representative word hierarchies

As is well-known, in a traditional document system, it is important to assign *representative words* to documents, capable of representing document contents and used to obtain access whenever documents are wanted. Then, signature files can be built over them and organized into a hierarchy, corresponding to the hierarchical structure of a document stored in databases.

- Representative words

Given a set of documents doc_i $(i = 1, ..., n)$, we can identify a set of (representative) words W_i for each doc_i to discriminate it from others by computing *weight* for each word:

$$weight_{ik} = f_{ik} \cdot signal_k, \tag{1}$$

where f_{ik} represents the frequency of word k appearing in doc_i and $signal_k$ is the signal value of word k, which can be computed as shown in [SM83]. For example, the representative words of a *letter* document may be a set (denoted W_{letter}) like {January, 27, 1993, Jean, SGML, databases, information, regards, Genise}, determined by applying the above formula to the actual document set. In some cases, we can use almost all words in the document only with high-frequency words (called *stop list*) removed. The words appearing in the stop list are poor discriminators and cannot possibly be used by themselves to identify document content.

- Representative word hierarchy

As mentioned above, the representative word hierarchy is built in terms of the storage structure of the documents, which can be illustrated as shown in Fig. 2.

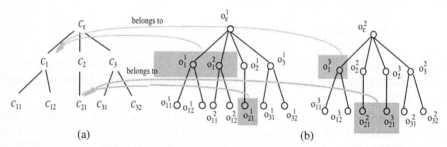

Fig. 2. Class hierarchy and object hierarchy

For exposition, we assume that the database is of the schema as shown in Fig. 2(a), containing two documents which are organized into two object hierarchies as shown in Fig. 2(b). In the figure, the objects are subscripted in such a way that the objects with the same subscript belong to the same class. The superscripts are used to number the objects of a class. For example, o_1^1, o_1^2 and o_1^3 belong to C_1 and superscribed with 1, 2, and 3, respectively.

Complying with such an storage structure of documents, the representative word hierarchy can be constructed in a recursive way as follows.

(i) First, each o_ε^i is associated with a set of representative words (representing doc_i) determined using formula (1).

(ii) Let o be an object and W be the set of representative words associated with o. Let $o_1, ..., o_n$ be the sub-objects of o, which are partitioned into several groups $g_1, ...,$

g_m ($m \le n$) such that each group g_j belongs to the same class. Then, W is partitioned into W_1, ..., W_m by regarding each g_j as a single document with the following two rules observed:

(1)　If $w \in W$ and w appears in g_j, but $w \notin W_j$, then add w to W_j: $W_j \leftarrow W_j \cup \{w\}$.

(2)　If $w \notin W$, but $w \in W_j$, then delete w from W_j: $W_j \leftarrow W_j - \{w\}$.

(iii) For each g_j, its W_j is further partitioned into W_{j1}, ..., W_{jk} such that each $o_{jl} \in g_j$ is associated with W_{jl}, which is made in the same way as step (ii).

(iv) For each o_{jl} and its W_{jl}, do step (ii).

For example, W_{letter} may be partitioned into {January, 27, 1993}, {Jean}, {SGML, databases, information}, {regards}, {Genise} for those texts accommodated at classes *Date*, *Greeting*, *Body*, *Closing* and *Sig*, respectively (see Fig. 3).

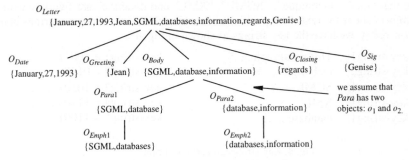

Fig. 3. Representative word hierarchy

For each W, its signature can be calculated as discussed in 5.2, based on which we construct signature files for each class (subclass) by collecting the relevant signatures together.

5　Pat trees and signature files

Now we discuss our indexing technique. The main idea of it can be summarized as follows:

(i)　construct the signature file hierarchies to support the traversal of the object hierarchies;

(ii)　build the pat trees over the texts to expedite the text scanning; and

(iii)　build the pat tree over the signature files to avoid the sequential search of them.

In the following, we first discuss the technique of the pat trees in 5.1. Then, in 5.2, the signature file hierarchies are addressed. We motivate the combination of the pat trees and signature files in 5.3. (The discussion on the application of such a combination is shifted to Section 6.)

5.1　Pat-tree built over representative words

Pat-tree is a digital (binary) tree, by which the key words (or representative words) is represented as a sequence of digits (in our case, the ASCII codes of characters are used.) During a traversal of a pat-tree, the individual bits of the key words are used to decide on the branching.

Given a text containing key words kw_1, kw_2, ..., kw_n. We define the corresponding key strings as the strings, each starting from the place where the corresponding key word first appears to the end of the text. To make each key string not be a prefix of another, we add a special symbol, say $, to the end of the text, which appears nowhere else. If a key word appears several times in the text, only the first appearance is used. The following example helps for illustration.

	1	30	51	57	65
text:	This paragraph describes the technique concerning SGML, XML and databases.$				

Each position in the text indicates a *suffix* or *semi-infinite string* (sistring), which goes to the end of the text. There are about 70 characters in the example; therefore, there are about 70 semi-infinite strings. We look at only semi-infinite strings that start at the beginning of key words. There are 5 such strings ("This ....", "technique ...", etc.) Here we assume that "this", "technique", "SGML", "XML" and database" are five key words. The numbers above the text show positions of starting characters of these sistrings in the text. Concretely, we have the key strings as shown in Fig. 4(a).

key-string1:	This paragraph ... .$	key-string1 = 10011 ... ...
key-string2:	technique ... .$	key-string2 = 01000 ... ...
key-string1:	SGML ... .$	key-string3 = 10101 ... ...
key-string1:	XML ... .$	key-string4 = 11100 ... ...
key-string1:	database ... .$	key-string5 = 11001 ... ...
(a)		(b)

Fig. 4. Key strings and arrays of bits

Note that we take the text as an array of bits and assume that they are of the form as shown in Fig. 4(b).

Using *patricia* algorithm [Mo68], a graph shown in Fig. 5(a) can be constructed. (Due to space limitation, a complete description of this algorithm can not be given here.)

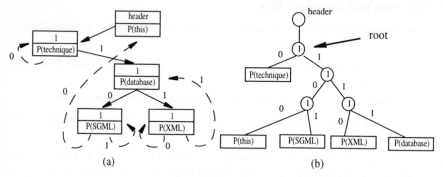

(a)   (b)

Fig. 5. Pat-tree

It consists of a header and $n - 1 = 5 - 1 = 4$ nodes. Each node contains six fields:

- Pointer to the text. In Fig. 5(a), P(x) (where x is a word) shown within each node is a pointer to the text, e.g., P(SGML) is the number 51, the starting place of key-string3 in the text.

- LLINK and RLINK: pointers within the graph. (LLINK is always labeled with 0 and RLINK is always labeled with 1.)

- LTAG and RTAG: one-bit fields which tell whether or not LLINK and RLINK, respectively, are pointers to sons or to ancestors of the node. The dotted arcs in Fig. 4(a) correspond to pointers whose TAG bit is 1.

- SKIP: a number which tells how many bits to skip when searching, as explained below. The SKIP fields are shown as numbers within each node of Fig. 5(a).

The graph shown in Fig. 5(a) can be represented as a tree by splitting each node into two ones as shown in Fig. 5(b). That is, each pointer to the text is separated from the corresponding node. There is an arc from a node v to a separated pointer node u (corresponding to a pointer to the text) if there is an ancestor link (dotted arc) from v to a node containing u in the original graph.

A search in Pat-tree is carried out as follows. Suppose we are looking up the word SGML (assume that its bit pattern is 10101 11100 11000 10001). We start by looking at the SKIP field of the root node (see Fig. 5(b)), which tells us to examine the first bit of the argument (the bit pattern of SGML). It is 1, so we move to the right. The SKIP field in the next node tells us to look at the $1 + 1 = $ 2nd bit of the argument. It is 0, so we move to the left. The SKIP field of the next node tells us to look at the $2 + 1 = $ 3rd bit, which is 1; now we reach a leaf node which refer us to the text at position P(SGML). The search path we have taken would occur for any argument whose bit pattern is 010x ... x (where "x" represents "don't care), and we must check to see if it matches the unique key which begins with that pattern. If it matches, we know that the text contains SGML. Otherwise, SGML does not appears in the text since the path leading to the leaf node with P(SGML) is unique and nowhere else through a path matches the pattern 010x ... x.

From Fig. 5(b) we see that the size of a pat-tree is very small. Its space complexity is bounded by $O(num_w)$, where num_w is the number of the representative words of a text. If the text is long, it is worth while building a pat-tree to make the text scanning quickly.

5.2 Signature File Hierarchy

Signature files are based on the inexact filter. They provide a quick test, which discards many of the nonqualifying elements. But the qualifying elements definitely pass the test although some elements which actually do not satisfy the search requirement may also pass it accidentally. Such elements are called "false hits" or "false drops". In a document database, an element is stored as an object and represented by a set of representative words assigned to the text stored in it. The signature of a representative word is a hash-coded bit string of length k with m bit set to "1", stored in the "signature file" (see [Fa85]). An object signature is formed by superimposing the signatures of its representative words. Object signatures of a class will be stored sequentially in another signature file. Fig. 6 depicts the signature generation and comparison process of an object having a text attribute value which is represented by three words, say "SGML", "database", and "information".

text: ... SGML ... databases ... information ...

representative word signature:		queries:	query signatures:	matchin results:
SGML	010 000 100 110	SGML	010 000 100 110	match with OS
database	100 010 010 100	XML	011 000 100 100	no match with OS
information	∨ 010 100 011 000	informatik	110 100 100 000	false drop
object signature (OS)	110 110 111 110			

Fig. 6. Signature generation and comparison

When a query arrives, the object signatures are scanned and many nonqualifying objects are discarded. The rest are either checked (so that the "false drops" are discarded) or they are returned to the user as they are. Concretely, a query specifying certain values to be searched for will be transformed into a query signature s_q in the same way as for representative words. The query signature is then compared to every object signature in the signature file. Three possible outcomes of the comparison are exemplified in Fig. 6: (1) the object matches the query; that is, for every bit set in s_q, the corresponding bit in the object signature s is also set (i.e., $s \wedge s_q = s_q$) and the object contains really the query word; (2) the object doesn't match the query (i.e., $s \wedge s_q \neq s_q$); and (3) the signature comparison indicates a match but the object in fact doesn't match the search criteria (false drop). In order to eliminate false drops, the object must be examined after the object signature signifies a successful match.

The purpose of using a signature file is to screen out most of the nonqualifying objects. A signature failing to match the query signature guarantees that the corresponding object can be ignored. Therefore, unnecessary object accesses are prevented. Signature files have a much lower storage overhead and a simpler file structure than inverted indexes.

In terms of the representative word hierarchy, a signature file hierarchy can be constructed as follows:

(i) For every representative word w, assign it a signature $wsig$. (How to construct a signature for a representative word can be found in [DGL98].)

(ii) Let o be an object and $W = \{w_1, ..., w_k\}$ be the set of representative words associated with it. There exists an entry $<osig, oid>$, where $osig$ is the signature of o and oid is the object identifier of o. $osig$ is obtained by superimposing the signatures of w_i ($i = 1, ..., k$).

(iii) Let C be a class and $o_1, ..., o_l$ be its objects, there exists a signature file S such that each o_i ($i = 1, ..., l$) has an entry $<osig, oid>$ in S.

(iv) Let S_i and S_j be two signature files associated with classes C_i and C_j, respectively. If there exists an arrow from C_i to C_j, then there is implicitly an arrow from S_i to S_j.

As an example, see the signature file hierarchy shown in Fig. 7, which is constructed in terms of the representative word hierarchy shown in Fig. 3.

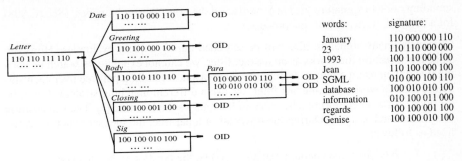

Fig. 7. Signature file hierarchy

5.3 Combining pat trees and signature files

In a large document database, a signature file itself may be long. Therefore, the time elapsed for searching such a file becomes significant. A first idea to improve the performance is to sort the signature file and then employ a binary searching. Unfortunately, this does not work due to the fact that a signature file is only an inexact filter. The following example helps for illustration.

Consider a sorted signature file containing only three signatures:

$$010\ 000\ 100\ 110$$
$$010\ 100\ 011\ 000$$
$$100\ 010\ 010\ 100$$

Assume that the query signature s_q is equal to 000010010100. It matches 100 010 010 100. However, if we use a binary search, 100 010 010 100 can not be found.

For this reason, we try another method and construct a pat-tree over a signature file by considering each signature as a word code; but use a different matching strategy. That is, for the pat-tree built for a text, the exact matching is used (i.e., 1 matches 1 and 0 matches 0) while for the pat-tree built for a signature file the inexact matching will be utilized to work as an inexact filter. Concretely, it works as follow. Let $s_q(i)$ be a bit checked when a node v is met during a traversal of the pat-tree. If $s_q(i) = 0$, then the entire subtree rooted at v will be further searched. If $s_q(i) = 1$, we move to the right child of v. That is, only the subtree rooted at the right child of v will be further traversed.

How to control this process is discussed in detail in the following section.

6 Retrieval

In this section, we first briefly sketch how to use the signature files to cut branches. Then, we discuss how to use the pat-tree to speed up this process in great detail. During the traversal of a pat-tree, an inexact matching is carried out, which is quiet different from the method shown in 5.1.

The signature file can be utilized to expedite the query evaluation by constructing a query signature tree for the submitted (simple) query, in which each node is a signature. To evaluate the query, the corresponding signature file hierarchy S_f will be searched against the query signature tree Q_T and at each step, a node in Q_T is checked against the corresponding node (a signature file) in S_f to discard the non-relevant branches. (See [CA98] for a detailed discussion of this process.)

Obviously, many signature files will be searched during a query evaluation. However, since the signature file works as an inexact filter, we can not expedite its search by sorting it and then using a binary search. For this reason, we build a pat-tree over each signature file. To work as an inexact filter, we use a different matching strategy. Let s_q be the node encountered during a traversal of the query signature tree Q_T. The i-th position of s_q is denoted as $s_q(i)$. During the traversal of a pat-tree, the inexact matching is defined as follows:

(i)   Let b be the node encountered and $s_q(i)$ be the position to be checked.

(ii) If $s_q(i) = 1$, we move to the right child of b.

(iii) If $s_q(i) = 0$, both the right and left child of b will be visited.

In fact, this definition just corresponds to the signature matching criterion.

To implement this inexact matching strategy during a traversal of a pat-tree, we search the pat-tree in the depth-first manner and maintain a stack structure $stack_p$ during the process.

Algorithm *pat-tree-search*

input: a node in Q_T;

output: set of object OIDS whose signatures survive the checking;

1. Let s_q be the node encountered during a traversal of the query signature hierarchy Q_T. The i-th position of s_q is denoted as $s_q(i)$. $S \leftarrow \varnothing$.

2. Push the root of the pat-tree into $stack_p$.

3. If $stack_p$ is not empty, $b \leftarrow$ pop $stack_p$; else return(S).

4. If b is not a leaf node, $i \leftarrow$ skip(b);
   If $s_q(i) = 0$, push c_r and c_l into $stack_p$; (where c_r and c_l are b's right and left child, respectively.) otherwise, push only c_r into $stack_p$.

5. Compare s_q with the substring beginning from position pointed by b.
   If s_q matches, $S \leftarrow S \cup \{OID\}$, where OID is the object identifier associated with the substring (signature).

The following example helps for illustrating the main idea of the algorithm.

Example 3 Consider the signature file shown in Fig. 8(a). The pat-tree built over it is shown in Fig. 8(b).

Assume $s_q = 010\ 000\ 000\ 000$. Then, only part of the pat-tree (marked with thick edges) will be searched. On reaching a leaf node, the bit substring from the position pointed by the leaf node will be checked against s_q. Obviously, this process is much more efficient than a sequential searching. If the signature file contains N signatures, this method requires only $O(N/2^l)$ comparisons in the worst case, where l represents the number of bits set in s_q, since each bit set in s_q will prohibit half of a subtree from being visited.

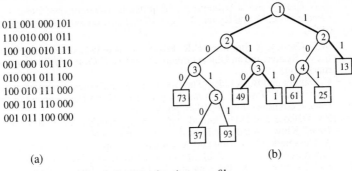

```
011 001 000 101
110 010 001 011
100 100 010 111
001 000 101 110
010 001 011 100
100 010 111 000
000 101 110 000
001 011 100 000
```

(a)   (b)

Fig. 8. Pat-tree for signature file

7 Conclusion

In this paper, a new indexing technique has been proposed. The main idea of this approach consists in the combination of pat-trees and signature files. To optimize the traversal of object hierarchies, we build signature file hierarchies to cut off non-relevant branches as early as possible. However, since the signature file works only as an inexact filter, it can not be sorted and thus the binary search can not be utilized to improve the efficiency. To this end, we construct a pat-tree over each signature file which appears as a node in the signature file hierarchy. In this way, the sequential search can be avoided. In addition, we may build a pat-tree over a text stored as an attribute value if it is very long. At last, we notice that a pat-tree itself is small and therefore no much space overhead is assumed. On the other hand, since each sequential search (of a signature file or a text) is replaced with a small tree search along one or several paths (see Subsection 5.1 and Section 6), the time complexities of both the traversal of a signature file hierarchy and the text search can be reduced by one order of magnitude or more.

References

ACCM96   S. Abiteboul, S. Cluet, V. Christophides, T. Milo, G. Moerkotte and J. Simeon, "Querying documents in object databases," *Int. J. on Digital Libraries*, Vol. 1, No. 1, Jan. 1997, pp. 5-19.

ACM93   S. Abiteboul, S. Cluet and T. Milo, "Querying and Uodating the File," *Proc. of the 9th VLDB Conference*, Dublin, Ireland, 1993, pp. 386-397.

AHU74   Aho, A.V., Hopcroft, J.E. and Ullman, J.D., *The Design and Analysis of Computer Algorithms*, Addison-Wesley Publishing Com., London, 1969.

BA94   K. Böhm and K. Aberer, "Storing HyTime Documents in an Obeject-Oriented Database," *Proc. of 3th Int. Conf. on Information and Knowledge Management*, Gaithersburg, Maryland, ACM, Nov. 1994, pp. 26-33.

BDK92   F. Bancihon, C. Delobel and P. Kanellakis, "*Building an Object-oriented Database System: The Story of O_2*," San Mateo, California, Morgan Kaufman, 1992.

BANY97   K. Böhm, K. Aberer, E.J. Neuhold and X. Yang, "Structured Document Storage and Refined Declarative and NAvigational Access Mechanism in HyperStorm," *Int. J of VLDB*, 1997.

BU77   R. Bayer and K. Unterrauer, "Prefix B-tree," ACM Transaction on Database Systems, 2(1), 11-26.

CA98   Y. Chen, K. Aberer, Layered Index Structures in Document Database Systems, *Proc. 7th Int. Conference on Information and Knowledge Management (CIKM)*, Bethesda, MD, USA: ACM, 1998, pp. 406-413.

CF84   S. Christodoulakis and C. Faloutsos, "Design consideration for a message file server," *IEEE Trans. Software Engineering*, 10(2) (1984) 201-210.

Cr86   D.A. Cruse, *Lexical Semantics*, Cambridge University Press, 1986.

CR94   Crochemore, M. and Rytter, W., *Text Algorithms*. Oxford University Press, New York, 1994.

CST92   W.B. Croft, L.A. Smith and H.R. Turtle, "A Loosely Coupled Integration of a Text Retrieval System and an Object Oriented Database," *Proc. of 15th Ann. Int. SIGIR*, Denmark, June 1992.

DaD88   C. Damier and B. Defude, "The Document Management Component of a Multimedia Data Model," *Proc. of 11th Int. Conf. on Research&Development in Information Retrieval*, Grenoble, France, 1988, pp. 451-464.

DD94   S.J. DeRose and D.D. Durand, "*Making Hypermedia Work: A User's Guide to HyTime*," Kluwer Academic Publishers, London, 1994.

DGL98   A. Dessmark, O. Garrido and A. Lingas, "Comparison of signature file models with superimposed coding," *J. of Information Processing Letter* 65 (1998) 101 - 106.

DWL92   S.C. Deerwester, K. Waclena and M. Lamar, "A Textual Object Management System," *Proc. of 15th Ann. Int. SIGIR*, Denmark, 1992.

EN89   R. Elmasri and S. B. Navathe, *Fundamantals of Database Systems*, Benjamin Cumming, California, 1989.

Fa85   C. Faloutsos, "Access Methods for Text," *ACM Computing Surveys*, 17(1), 1985, pp. 49-74.

Fa92   C. Faloutsos, "Signature Files," in: *Information Retrieval: Data Structures & Algorithms*, edited by W.B. Frakes and R. Baeza-Yates, Prentice Hall, New Jersey, 1992, pp. 44-65.

GBS92   G.H. Gonnet, R.A. Baeza-Yates, "New Indices for Text: Pat Trees and Pat Arrays," in: *Information Retrieval: Data Structures & Algorithms*, edited by W.B. Frakes and R. Baeza-Yates, Prentice Hall, New Jersey, 1992, pp. 66-82.

Hew92   Hewlett-Packard, *OpenODB Reference Manual B3185A*, 1992.

HFBL92   D. Harman, E. Fox, R. and Baeza-Yates, "Inverted Files," in: *Information Retrieval: Data Structures & Algorithms*, edited by W.B. Frakes and R. Baeza-Yates, Prentice Hall, New Jersey, 1992, pp. 28-43.

Kn73   D.E. Knuth, *The Art of Computer Programming: Sorting and Searching*, Addison-Wesley Pub. London, 1973.

LL92   W. Lee and D.L. Lee, "Signature File Methods for Indexing Object-Oriented Database Systems," *Proc. ICIC'92 - 2nd Int. Conf. on Data and Knowledge Engineering: Theory and Application*, Hongkong, Dec. 1992, pp. 616-622.

Ma90   I.A. Macleod, "Storage and Retrieval of Structured Documents," *J. of Information Processing & Management*, Vol. 26, No. 2, 1990, pp. 197-208.

[Mo68]   Morrison, D.R., PATRICIA - Practical Algorithm To Retrieve Information Coded in Alphanumeric. *Journal of Association for Computing Machinary*, Vol. 15, No. 4, Oct. 1968, pp. 514-534.

Sch93   P. Schäuble, "SPIDER: A MultiMedia Forum - An Interactive Online Journal," *Proc. of Conf. on Electronic Publishing*, John Wiley & Sons, Ltd, 1994, pp. 413-422.

SM83   G. Salton and M.J. McGill, "*Introduction to Modern Information Retrieval*," McGray-Hill Int. Book Com., Hamburg, 1983.

VAB96   M. Volz, K. Aberer and K. Böhm, "Applying a Flexible OODBMS-IRS_Coupling to Structured Document Handling," *Proc. of 12th Int. Conf. on Data Engineering*, New Orleans, 1996, pp. 10-19.

VML95   VODAK V 4.0 User Manual. *Technical Report 910*, GMD-IPSI, St. Augustin, April 1995.

WMB94   I.H. Witten, A. Moffat and T.C. Bell, *Managing Gigabytes*, Van Nostrand Reinhold, 1992.

YA94   T.W. Yan and J. Annevelink, "Integrating a Structural-Text Retrieval System with an Object-Oriented Database System," *Proc. of 20th VLDB Conf.*, Santiago, Chile, 1994, pp. 740-749.

YLK94   H.S. Yong, S. Lee and H.J. Kim, "Applying Signatures for Forward Traversal Query Processing in Object-Oriented Databases," *Proc. of 10th Int. Conf. on Data Engineering*, Houston, Texas, Feb. 1994, pp. 518-525.

Answering Queries by Semantic Caches

Parke Godfrey and Jarek Gryz

York University
Toronto ON M3J 1P3, Canada
{godfrey,jarek}@cs.yorku.ca
URL: http://www.cs.yorku.ca/{~godfrey,~jarek}

Abstract. There has been growing interest in *semantic query caches* to aid in query evaluation. Semantic caches are simply the results of previously asked queries, or selected relational information chosen by an evaluation strategy, that have been cached locally. For complex environments such as distributed, heterogeneous databases and data warehousing, the use of semantic caches promises to help optimize query evaluation, increase turnaround for users, and reduce network load and other resource usage. We present a general logical framework for semantic caches. We consider the use of all relational operations across the caches for answering queries, and we consider the various ways to answer, and to partially answer, a query by cache. We address when answers are in cache, when answers in cache can be recovered, and the notions of *semantic overlaps*, *semantic independence*, and *semantic query remainder*.

While there has been much work relevant to the use of semantic caches, no one has addressed in conjunction the issues pertinent to the effective use of semantic caches to evaluate queries. In some cases, this is due to overly simplified assumptions, and in other cases to the lack of a formal framework. We attempt to establish some of that framework here. Within that framework, we illustrate the issues involved in using semantic caches for query evaluation. We show various applications for semantic caches, and relate the work to relevant areas.

1 Introduction

There has been growing interest in *semantic query caches* to aid in query evaluation. Semantic caches are simply the results of previously asked queries cached locally, or selected relational information chosen by some strategy to be cached locally. In complex information environments as mediation over distributed, heterogeneous databases and data warehousing, the use of semantic caches promises to help optimize query evaluation, increase turnaround for users, and reduce network load and other resource usage.

The concept of caching is basic in computer science. Integrated circuits for CPU's now have built-in high speed memory caches to reduce fetches to main memory. Operating systems employ complex cache strategies to decide which virtual pages to keep in main memory, to reduce fetches to secondary memory. Relational database management systems employ buffer management strategies to reduce I/O, reusing previously fetched data pages.

In distributed database environments, another layer of caching is possible: to cache information between servers and clients. Two caching approaches, *page caching* and *tuple caching* in which memory pages or tuples are cached, respectively, have been studied in this context [4, 10]. Semantic query caching (SQC) offers a third approach. In [4], it is shown that semantic caching may outperform the page and tuple caching due to *semantic locality*: subsequent queries often are related conceptually with previous queries, so ultimately will be pulling data from the same logical sources. Thus semantic caches will often contain some of the answers of the current query. In heterogeneous, distributed environments, it is unclear how page or tuple caching might be adapted. SQC, however, can be well applied in these environments.

We present a general logical foundation for semantic query caching. We explore in what ways queries can be answered by semantic caches, and within this framework, we elucidate issues to be addressed in implementing SQC. We extend the paradigm of SQC to consider the use of the caches in composite to answer queries; thus we allow any relational operations across the caches which are stored locally as relational tables. We call any relational expression across the caches a *cache expression.*

While the notion of a semantic cache itself is quite simple (it is an answer set stored as a relational table, labeled by the query that resulted in the answer set), the use of semantic caches to answer queries can be complex. This is because it requires reasoning over the query and cache formulas to determine how they are related semantically. Current database systems have limited facilities to *reason* about the queries that they process.[1] To use SQC, specific tools to reason over cache and query expressions are needed to determine when caches can be used to answer the query. Specifically, we address the topics of

1. deciding when answers are in cache,
2. extracting answers from cache,
3. semantic overlap and semantic independence, and
4. semantic remainder.

It is interesting to note that there are cases when it is possible to determine that the answers of the query are in cache, but there is not enough information locally so that the answers can be recovered. Under topics 1 and 2, we consider when a query is contained in the caches, and conversely, when a cache expression is contained by the query. Under topic 3, we generalize to the case when the query and a cache expression "overlap" somehow, but there is not containment in either direction. Under topic 4, we consider how *remainder queries* might be found that represent the "rest" of the query not answered by cache. This topic is challenging and not yet well defined. We attempt to provide some insights.

In Section 2, we provide an overview of semantic caches and discuss its possible applications. In Section 3, we provide a logical formalism (based on Datalog and the logic model [26]) for SQC, and address each of the topics enumerated

---

[1] They do *evaluate* queries well, and this does involve certain types of reasoning over the queries. However, by *reasoning* here, we mean the ability to compare queries, and to employ information about what the queries "mean" in support of applications.

above, in turn. In Section 4, we discuss related work and topics, and topics to be addressed. There is much work relevant to SQC. We are only able to provide a brief summary. We relate what issues in semantic caching have been addressed, and which remain open. In Section 5, we conclude.

2 Semantic Query Caching

2.1 Overview

We start with an informal description of the possible relationships between a query's answer set and the tuples stored explicitly in, or computable from, the caches. The boxes in Figure 1 abstractly represent relational tables. The clear boxes represent the answer tuples of a cached query; the shaded boxes, the answer tuples of a query. The boxes represent relational tables: "rows" (the horizontal) represent tuples; "columns" (the vertical), attributes. Assume initially the only operations performed on the queries were selects and projects. The current query may overlap with a cached query in several possible ways. The query may be computable entirely from a cache (case 1) or only partially (cases 2 through 5). Case 3 represents a *vertical* partition of a query: only some of the attributes-of-interest (a projection of the query) are available in cache. If the cache contains the key columns of the relation, the missing columns could be imported from the server, to be joined with the cache locally. Case 4 represents the situation when *some* of the answers to the query are available from cache, a *horizontal* partition of a query. Case 5 represents a mixed partition of a query.

The scenario above can be generalized allowing both caches and queries to involve joins. The clear boxes in Figure 1 then may represent the result of an arbitrary join of *several* caches stored locally. Even in the simplest case (1), it may be impossible to compute the answer set to the query without more information from the servers. For example, if a cached query C resulted from the join $R_1 \bowtie ... \bowtie R_n$ and the current query Q is the join $R_1 \bowtie ... \bowtie R_n \bowtie R_{n+1}$, we would at least need to compute the values from a join column of the relation R_{n+1} to evaluate Q by cache. Cases 2 through 5 introduce yet another complication: the need to *modify* the query so that only the parts that cannot be evaluated by cache are evaluated subsequently.[2] Whether this should be done depends on one's objective: answer set pipelining generally benefits from heavier use of caches than is the case for optimizing the overall query response time.

One should not be misled by Figure 1. We are not interested in how the *answer sets* of queries and caches overlap *syntactically*; that is, the actual tuples they share in common. Instead, we are interested in discovering subsets of answers that the query and cache *must* share. This happens when the query and the cache are *semantically* related. If they are semantically unrelated, then one cannot use the cache to answer any of the query. For instance, consider the two relations *employee*(X) and *stock_holder*(X). Assume these are base relations (not views). Then the contents of the *employee* table in no way affects the *stock_holder*

---

[2] Such a query is called a *remainder query* in [9] or a *trimmed query* in [15].

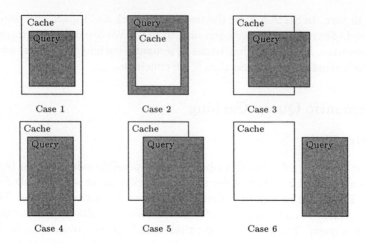

Fig. 1. Possible relations between cached and current queries.

table, nor vice versa.[3] The two tables may still share values by happenstance (for instance, *employee (john)* and *stock_holder (john)*).

Two views may be defined in part over the same base relations. If the query employs one of the views and the cache, the other, one may be able to determine semantically that they must share answers. Furthermore, we might be able to determine a query expression that is evaluable against the cache that retrieves these answers. This is the topic of this paper.

By expressing queries and caches in a logical formalism, we can employ analytical tools developed for logic databases to decide when a cache, or combination thereof, answers, or partially answers, the query [27]. The basic inference needed is *containment* determination for extensional, conjunctive queries (called *conjunctive query containment* in [26]): we say the query $\mathcal{F}$ is contained in the query $\mathcal{G}$, if all answers to $\mathcal{F}$ are also answers to $\mathcal{G}$. The containment test alone is sufficient for the simplest case, when a single cache which is extensional (one that does not refer to views) partially answers the query. SQC with joins, or with queries and caches composed over views, requires more sophisticated inferencing.

2.2 Applications

SQC is critical for optimization in heterogeneous, multi-database environments. It helps to address many issues that arise in mediated, distributed environments.

- *Query optimization.*
  - *Improvement in overall query response time (traditional optimization).* Since part of query processing is done by the client via caches, the workload at the database servers is reduced. If the answer set of a query is

---

[3] In truth, even though these are base relations, there may exist integrity constraint relationships between them. In such cases, one might be able to determine that *employee* semantically affects *stock_holder*. This is beyond the scope of this paper.

large, computing some of it locally provides savings in network communication. As some of the query is evaluated at the client and the rest at the server(s), this can be done in parallel.

- *Saving money.* In environments with monetary charges for information, such as in electronic commerce, caching techniques can be used to optimize over these costs.
- *Optimization of queries with few answers.* If the cardinality of the query's answer set can be determined in advance (for example, there is only *one* answer) and the number of answers in cache is equivalent to the known cardinality, then one knows it is complete with no further work.
- *Optimization of queries in batch (multiple query optimization).* If a request is for the union of answers of a collection of queries, and if the queries are evaluated sequentially, any part of a subsequent query that can be answered *by cache* need not be re-evaluated. Only the parts of subsequent queries that are *semantically independent* of the previous queries need be evaluated.
- *Data Security.* One can limit the sending of sensitive data over the network by storing it as caches locally.
- *Fault tolerance.* Some databases may not always be accessible. If a query can be partially answered from caches, at least those answers can be returned.
- *Approximate answering.* Sometimes a good approximation of aggregate values such as *average* can be obtained from caches. If it is determined that a cache contains a representative sample over which the aggregate function is to be computed, then it can be evaluated over just the cache.
- *Better user interaction.*
  - *Answer set pipelining.* The subset of the answers derivable from cache can be returned *promptly*, while remaining answers are evaluated.
  - *Indirect answering.* The information that a query is contained in cache may be all that the user requires. This happens when the next query in a sequence does not add any new tuples to those already seen.
  - *Limiting the size of the answer set.* A user may not be interested in retrieving all answers, but may be satisfied with just some answers. Or the user might want to terminate the query evaluation, if the answer set is larger than expected. In either case, query processing can be possibly terminated after retrieving just the answers from cache.

3 Evaluating Queries by Caches

3.1 Logical Notation

We employ the terminology of logic databases and Datalog [21, 26]. A database DB consists of two parts: the *extensional database*, EDB, and the *intensional database*, IDB. The EDB is the database's collection of *facts*. The IDB is the database's collection of *rules* (relational views).[4] A predicate is either defined

---

[4] The IDB may also include *integrity constraints*. We do not consider integrity constraints, however, in this paper.

via rules in the IDB (an *intensional* predicate) or is defined via facts in the EDB (an *extensional* predicate). A *Horn clause* is a logical sentence of the form:

$$\forall. \ A \vee \neg B_1 \vee \ldots \vee \neg B_n \tag{1}$$

in which A, and each B_i, is an atomic formula. The '$\forall$.' states that all free variables in the formula are universally quantified. The notation '$\exists$.' is likewise for existential quantification. A Horn clause can be interpreted as a *rule* in the form of an implication. In Datalog, the Horn clause (1) written as a rule, $\mathcal{R}$, is:

$$\mathcal{R}: A \leftarrow B_1, \ldots, B_n. \tag{2}$$

The '$\forall$.' is now implicit. A *query clause* in Datalog is a Horn clause as in (1), but with no positive atom. It is written as:

$$\mathcal{C}: \leftarrow Q_1, \ldots, Q_k. \tag{3}$$

Again, the Q_i's are atomic formula. This is convenient in logic programming systems, such as Prolog, and in deductive database systems which find answers to a query by means of refutation proofs [21, 26]. Given a query clause $\mathcal{C}$, if $\mathrm{DB} \cup \{\mathcal{C}\}$ is inconsistent, then $\mathcal{C}$ has answers.

We find it more convenient to work with queries as conjunctive formulas, not in "negated" form as with query clauses. Define *query formula* Q to be an existentially quantified, conjunctive formula of the form:

$$Q: \exists \vec{e}. \ Q_1 \wedge \ldots \wedge Q_k. \tag{4}$$

We call a query formula simply a query, when understood in context. In Q, $\vec{e}$ denotes a list of variables that appear in the B_i atoms, called the *existential variables* of Q. The free variables of Q, those not in $\vec{e}$, are called the *distinguished variables* of Q. Let query formula Q' be syntactically equivalent to Q except that $\vec{e}'$ replaces $\vec{e}$, and $\vec{e}' \supset \vec{e}$. Thus Q' has fewer distinguished variables than Q (and, conversely, more existential variables). We call Q' an *abbreviated query formula*—or an *abbreviation* for short—of Q.

Define an *unfolded* query—or *unfolding* for short—of Q with respect to the IDB as follows. Given atom A from rule $\mathcal{R}$ in Formula (2) and atom Q_i from query Q in Formula (4), assume that $A\theta = Q_i\theta$ with most general unifier θ. Let $\vec{f}$ be the variables that appear in $\mathcal{R}\theta$, but not in $A\theta$. Then

$$Q': \ \exists \vec{e}, \vec{f}. \ Q_1\theta \wedge \ldots \wedge Q_{i-1}\theta, B_1\theta \wedge \ldots \wedge B_n\theta, Q_{i+1}\theta \wedge \ldots \wedge Q_k\theta. \tag{5}$$

is an *immediate* unfolding of Q. An unfolding of Q is any immediate unfolding of Q, or any unfolding of an immediate unfolding of Q, *ad recursion.*[5]

Define an *answer* of Q with respect to database DB to be a ground substitution θ over the free variables of Q, such that

$$\mathrm{DB} \models Q\theta$$

The *answer set* of Q is the set of all Q's answers, to be denoted as $[\![Q]\!]_{\mathrm{DB}}$, or simply as $[\![Q]\!]$ when the DB is understood. A relational *table* is synonymous for us with an answer set.

A *semantic query cache*—or just *semantic cache* for short—is the pair of a query formula with its answer set, $\langle Q, [\![Q]\!] \rangle$. We presume that the query's answer set $[\![Q]\!]$ has been stored locally as a relational table, and the table is labeled by the query Q. A query formula which has been cached is refered to as a *cache*

---

[5] This is simply equivalent to top-down evaluation by resolution, as in Prolog.

formula, and the cached answer set as the *cache table*. We use the term *cache* to refer to just the cache formula, when understood in context.

3.2 Determining when Answers are in Cache

We describe the conditions that need to be satisfied for the query Q to be *answerable* from the collection of caches $\mathcal{C} = \{\mathcal{C}_1, \ldots, \mathcal{C}_m\}$. We first consider cases 1, 2, and 3 depicted in Figure 1. Let Q be a query and $\mathcal{E}$ be any select-project-join expression—called a *cache expression*—over any subset of the cache collection, $\mathcal{C}$. A cache expression $\mathcal{E}_i$ can be expressed as an existentially quantified, conjunctive formula too.

$$\mathcal{E}_i\colon \exists \vec{y}.\ C_{i,1} \wedge \ldots \wedge C_{i,k_i}.$$

where each $C_{i,j} \in \mathcal{C}$, the variables and constants of the $C_{i,j}$'s represent the appropriate selects and joins, and the variables are appropriately named.

- *Containment: All answers to a query Q are in cache.* There is a finite collection of cache expressions $\mathcal{E}_1, \ldots, \mathcal{E}_n$ such that

$$\text{IDB} \models \forall.\ Q \rightarrow (\mathcal{E}_1 \vee \ldots \vee \mathcal{E}_n) \tag{6}$$

- *Abbreviated containment: All answers of an abbreviation Q' of Q are in cache, by the containment definition in Formula (6).*

Note that IDB is on the left-hand side of the entailment operator. Thus inference over the rules in the IDB is allowed; the right-hand side is *not* at tautology, but holds only with respect to the IDB. The following examples illustrate the two cases from above.

Example 1. Consider a database DB, with two tables: **Employee**[Name, SSN, Age] and **Benefits**[SSN, Provider].

1. Consider query Q which asks for names of employees with benefits:

$$Q\colon q(N) \leftarrow employee(N,S,A),\ benefits(S,P).$$

and the caches C_1 and C_2 which store names of employees younger than 50 and older than 20 respectively:

$$C_2\colon c_1(N) \leftarrow employee(N,S,A),\ A < 50.$$
$$C_2\colon c_2(N) \leftarrow employee(N,S,A),\ A > 20.$$

Clearly, all answers to Q are contained in the union of answer sets for C_1 and C_2. Note, however, that without knowing the values of S in $benefits(S,P)$ it is impossible to *distinguish* the tuples that are answers to Q from among all of the tuples in $[\![C_1]\!] \cup [\![C_2]\!]$.

2. Let the caches C_1 and C_2 be as defined above and the query Q now ask for names and SSN's of employees with benefits:

$$Q\colon q(N,S) \leftarrow employee(N,S,A),\ benefits(S,P).$$

This query cannot be answered by any combination of C_1 and C_2. However, all sub-tuples projected for N—tuples with just the names of employees—are contained in $[\![C_1]\!] \cup [\![C_2]\!]$.

3.3 Finding the Answers in Cache

The test describing the query-cache containment is not sufficient to guarantee that any answers to a query can actually be *retrieved* from cache. We state another condition that provides this guarantee.

- *Answerability: Some answers to Q can be retrieved from cache.* There exists a cache expression $\mathcal{E}$ such that:
$$\text{IDB} \models \forall. \; \mathcal{E} \to \mathcal{Q} \tag{7}$$
- *Some answers of an abbreviation Q' of Q can be retrieved from cache.*

The case of when the query can be completely answered from cache can now be stated. It is a combination of conditions (6) and (7): all answers to $\mathcal{Q}$ can be retrieved from cache *if and only if* there is a finite collection of cache expressions $\mathcal{E}_1, \ldots, \mathcal{E}_n$, such that

$$\text{IDB} \models \forall \vec{x}. \; \mathcal{Q} \to (\mathcal{E}_1 \vee \ldots \vee \mathcal{E}_n) \text{ and}$$
$$\text{IDB} \models \forall \vec{x}. \; \mathcal{E}_i \to \mathcal{Q}, \text{ for each } i \in \{1, \ldots, n\}. \tag{8}$$

Condition (8) establishes an equivalence between $\mathcal{Q}$ and the union of $\mathcal{E}_1, \ldots, \mathcal{E}_n$. The only known general procedure for establishing equivalence between two queries is testing for containment in both directions [27]. The ultimate goal of SQC for many applications is to answer a query entirely from caches, thus Formula (8). Often, however, only one "half" of (8)—that is, either Formula (6) or (7)—will be satisfied.

3.4 Semantic Overlap and Semantic Independence

We next consider cases 4, 5, and 6 from Figure 1, in which the query and a cache expression *overlap* somehow, but without being contained in either direction. There are two different ways in which they may overlap. First, it may be that the query $\mathcal{Q}$ itself is not contained by the cache expression $\mathcal{E}$, but an unfolded query $\mathcal{U}$ of $\mathcal{Q}$ is. If $\mathcal{U}$ is answerable by $\mathcal{E}$, then $\mathcal{Q}$ is partially answerable by $\mathcal{E}$. As seen in Formula (4), it can be determined whether a collection of cache expressions in composite completely answers the query. It is possible that one can only partially answer $\mathcal{Q}$ with the cache expressions. This is possible when certain unfoldings of $\mathcal{Q}$ are not answerable by cache, even while the rest of $\mathcal{Q}$'s unfoldings are. Second, a query $\mathcal{Q}$ and a cache expression $\mathcal{E}$ may *semantically overlap*, yet *no* unfolding of $\mathcal{Q}$ is *completely* contained by $\mathcal{E}$. The sharing between $\mathcal{Q}$ and $\mathcal{E}$ may be finer grained. Consider the following example.

Example 2. Consider that the views *employee* and *taxed* are defined as:
$$employee\,(X) \leftarrow payroll\,(X), position\,(X).$$
$$taxed\,(X) \leftarrow payroll\,(X), national\,(X).$$

An employee is someone on the payroll with an official position. The company sets aside taxes for anyone on the payroll who is a national. People may be on the payroll who are not employees. (Retirees could be handled this way.) Likewise, people may be on the payroll who are not nationals. The company does not handle their taxes.

Let $taxed\,(X)$ be cached and $employee\,(X)$ be the current query. Clearly, the query is not contained in the cache, nor vice versa. However, it is also clear they are semantically related, since they mutually rely on the same table *payroll.* Some answers to the query are potentially in the cache (case 3 in Figure 1).

In essence, queries (and caches) overlap whenever they mutually rely on the same sources. We can capture logically when two query and cache formulas semantically overlap. Queries Q and $\mathcal{E}$ *extensionally overlap iff* there exists a query formula $\mathcal{F}$ such that[6]

$$\models \forall. (Q \rightarrow \mathcal{F}) \wedge (\mathcal{E} \rightarrow \mathcal{F}) \tag{9}$$

(call $\mathcal{F}$ an *overlap witness*) and, there exists a query formula $\mathcal{G}$ such that[7]

$$\models \forall. (\mathcal{G} \rightarrow Q) \wedge (\mathcal{G} \rightarrow \mathcal{E}) \tag{10}$$

(call $\mathcal{G}$ an *overlap formula*). Neither (9) nor (10) alone are sufficient to guarantee that Q and $\mathcal{E}$ overlap. Condition (9) states that Q and $\mathcal{E}$ share a common resource, namely $\mathcal{F}$. This indicates they must share some sources, ultimately tables, in their evaluation. However, Q and $\mathcal{E}$ may be queries on the same table, yet have incompatible select conditions. Condition (10) guarantees that there is an overlap formula $\mathcal{G}$ (but does not guarantee that Q and $\mathcal{E}$ share resources). In the degenerate case, $\mathcal{G}$ could be constructed as $Q \wedge \mathcal{E}$. The two conditions together *do* ensure that there is a meaningful overlap. In Example 2, $payroll(X) \wedge position(X)$ and $payroll(X) \wedge national(X)$ extensionally overlap. The overlap witness is $payroll(X)$, and the overlap formula is $payroll(X) \wedge position(X) \wedge national(X)$.

We define a *most general overlap formula* as an overlap formula $\mathcal{G}$ such that there does not exist another overlap formula $\mathcal{G}'$ such that

$$\models \forall. (\mathcal{G} \rightarrow \mathcal{G}') \quad \text{but} \quad \not\models \forall. (\mathcal{G}' \rightarrow \mathcal{G}) \tag{11}$$

The answers of an overlap formula are answers of both the query and cache. If one could evaluate the overlap formula, one can partially answer the query. A most general overlap formula determines a maximal set of mutual answers.

For the intensional case, the definition of an overlap is more complex. To test whether Q and $\mathcal{E}$ overlap, we must examine whether any of their unfoldings overlap. Queries Q and $\mathcal{E}$ *intensionally overlap* with respect to IDB *iff* any of their respective unfoldings overlap. This may be stated as follows. For any $\mathcal{U}_Q$ and $\mathcal{U}_\mathcal{E}$ such that

$$\mathsf{IDB} \models \forall. (\mathcal{U}_Q \rightarrow Q) \wedge (\mathcal{U}_\mathcal{E} \rightarrow \mathcal{E}) \tag{12}$$

and $\mathcal{U}_Q$ and $\mathcal{U}_\mathcal{E}$ extensionally overlap, then Q and $\mathcal{E}$ intensionally overlap.

Call overlap formula $\mathcal{G}$ *horizontally-complete iff* all free variables of $\mathcal{G}$ are also free variables of Q. (This is case 2 of Figure 1.) Call it an abbreviated overlap if there is an abbreviation Q' of Q, and $\mathcal{G}$ is horizontally-complete for Q' but not Q. (This is case 4 of Figure 1.) Abbreviated overlaps are only useful if one is willing to answer in part a query without all the attributes-of-interest [22].

Call queries Q and $\mathcal{E}$ *semantically independent* (with respect to IDB) *iff* Q and $\mathcal{E}$ do not intensionally overlap (with respect to IDB) in any way. This is case 6 in Figure 1. Note that is necessary to have semantic overlap well defined before we can introduce the notion of semantic independence.

---

[6] Note that our definition of a query formula (4) does not allow disjunction nor negation, thus $\mathcal{F}$ cannot be a tautology and it cannot be a contradiction.

[7] Likewise for $\mathcal{G}$.

Determining overlap is a generalization of containment. If no cache expression can be found that is contained by the query, then we cannot partially answer the query locally. However, overlap expressions tell us what can *almost* be evaluated locally. Some of the tables and views in the overlap expression are apparently not available locally (else, we would have discovered a containment). If these are inexpensive to import, this might be worthwhile. Thus, overlaps offer more choices to an evaluation strategy that employs semantic caches.

3.5   Semantic Remainder

Even if we can partially answer the query by cache, we still have the responsibility to evaluate the *rest* of the query's answers. The simplest action would be to evaluate the entire query anyway. For pipelining answers to the user, this is sufficient. The user receives the answers from cache quickly, while the query is being evaluated. This strategy does little to optimize the overall evaluation effort, however. It is also unacceptable when caches are kept for security reasons. On the other hand, computing the query that would return just the remaining answers may be too expensive too. Consider the following example.

Example 3. Let the query Q be:
$$Q: q(N) \leftarrow employee(N,S,A).$$
and the cache C be:
$$C: c(N) \leftarrow employee(N,S,A), \; benefits(S,P).$$
Clearly, C partially answers Q. To save in network bandwidth, one could compute $Q \wedge$ **not** C at the server and only ship those results back.[8] This would require computing the join **Employee** $\bowtie$ **Benefits** at the server again.

The notation $Q \backslash \mathcal{E}$ represents the remainder query that results from Q when $\mathcal{E}$ has been removed.[9] We introduced this notation in [12] and call it a *discounted query*. The discounted query should satisfy the following conditions with respect to the query Q and the cache expression $\mathcal{E}$ that partially answers Q.
- *Soundness.* All answers to $Q \backslash \mathcal{E}$ should be correct; that is, for any Q and $\mathcal{E}$,
$$[Q \backslash \mathcal{E}] \subseteq [Q]$$
  This condition should hold uniformly for all applications of semantic caching.
- *Completeness.* The answers to $Q \backslash \mathcal{E}$, with those retrieved from cache, should provide the complete answer set of Q; that is, for any Q and $\mathcal{E}$,
$$[Q] - [\mathcal{E}] \subseteq [Q \backslash \mathcal{E}]$$
  As with soundness, this condition should hold for all applications.
- *Independence.* $Q \backslash \mathcal{E}$ and $\mathcal{E}$ should be semantically independent. If $Q \backslash \mathcal{E}$ and $\mathcal{E}$ are *not* semantically independent, then some of the answers already retrieved from cache may be recomputed at the server. For some applications, such as

---

[8] We have not considered negation in this paper. We introduce it here for discussion in this section. The query $Q \wedge$ **not** C should evaluate to all answers of Q *minus* those of C, or $[Q] - [C]$, in which '$-$' is the standard relational *set minus* operator.

[9] This general concept has been called a *remainder query* [9]. We usurp the use of '$\backslash$' to mean "discounting", so it does not mean the same as '$-$' here.

caching secure data, semantic independence should be enforced at *all* costs. For other applications, (in particular, query optimization) cost effectiveness is most important, and we may be willing to recompute some answers if this is a more efficient use of resources. One extreme to enforce semantic independence is to define $Q \backslash \mathcal{E}$ as $Q \wedge \mathbf{not} \ \mathcal{E}$. This, however, may make $Q \backslash \mathcal{E}$ more expensive to evaluate (as shown in Example 3) than Q. Also, this does not capture what $Q \backslash \mathcal{E}$ is intended to mean: query Q with all the overlaps with cache $\mathcal{E}$ "removed".

- *Uniformity.* The following condition should hold:

$$[Q \backslash \mathcal{E}] - [\mathcal{E} \backslash Q] = [Q] - [\mathcal{E}] \tag{13}$$

If $\mathcal{A} \backslash \mathcal{B}$ is defined degenerately just as $\mathcal{A}$, this trivially holds. If $\mathcal{A} \backslash \mathcal{B}$ is defined degenerately as $\mathcal{A} - \mathcal{B}$ then this again trivially holds. If $\mathcal{A} \backslash \mathcal{B}$ randomly evaluates to something between $[\mathcal{A}]$ and $[\mathcal{A}] - [\mathcal{B}]$, this does not always hold. It would be possible for $Q \backslash \mathcal{E}$ to evaluate to $[Q]$, but for $\mathcal{E} \backslash Q$ to evaluate to $[\mathcal{E}] - [Q]$, thus resulting in $[Q]$. However, if $\mathcal{A} \backslash \mathcal{B}$ is defined meaningfully, it should be possible to ensure uniformity.

- *Cost effectiveness.* Evaluating $Q \backslash \mathcal{E}$ plus $\mathcal{E}$ should cost less than evaluating Q. This condition can vary depending on the application and computing environment. If the cost is measured by the processing time until all answers are retrieved and $Q \backslash \mathcal{E}$ and $\mathcal{E}$ can be computed in parallel, then it is sufficient that Q costs more to evaluate that the more expensive of $Q \backslash \mathcal{E}$ and $\mathcal{E}$. If the cost is measured by the money paid for answers, defining $Q \backslash \mathcal{E}$ as $Q \wedge \mathbf{not} \ \mathcal{E}$ is always more cost effective than Q (as long as $\mathcal{E}$ is nonempty).

We are interested to define a semantics for $Q \backslash \mathcal{E}$, and ways to evaluate $Q \backslash \mathcal{E}$ efficiently. In [12], we introduce *intensional query optimization* (IQO). The idea behind IQO is to "remove" certain unfoldings from a view query that, say, may be known to evaluate empty, or which can be evaluated inexpensively locally. For IQO, we introduced and defined a weaker version of discounting: given query Q and a collection of some of its unfoldings $\mathcal{U}_1, \ldots, \mathcal{U}_k$, then $Q \backslash \{\mathcal{U}_1, \ldots, \mathcal{U}_k\}$ denotes Q with those unfoldings "removed".[10]

We have explored various approaches to evaluate $Q \backslash \{\mathcal{U}_1, \ldots, \mathcal{U}_k\}$. One method is to rewrite the query Q algebraically in a way that the resulting query evaluates to $[Q \backslash \{\mathcal{U}_1, \ldots, \mathcal{U}_k\}]$. We explore the complexity issues of such rewrite techniques in [13]. Another approach is to develop a specialized evaluation strategy that can evaluate discounted queries directly. We have introduced such a method which we call *tuple tagging*. The method is an optimization as, in general, the discounted query is less expensive to evaluate than the query itself.

We can already define a limited notion of $Q \backslash \mathcal{E}$ via $Q \backslash \{\mathcal{U}_1, \ldots, \mathcal{U}_k\}$: find the collection of unfoldings of Q for which each is answerable by $\mathcal{E}$. However, we want to capture a stronger notion, and "remove" all overlaps with $\mathcal{E}$ instead. If we had an evaluation strategy to generally evaluate $Q \backslash \mathcal{E}$ less expensively than Q itself—and we do have such a strategy for $Q \backslash \{\mathcal{U}_1, \ldots, \mathcal{U}_k\}$—then condition (13) above means we would have a method to optimize *set minus*. Since *set*

---

[10] $Q \backslash \{\mathcal{U}_1, \ldots, \mathcal{U}_k\}$ might be called *syntactic discounting*, while $Q \backslash \mathcal{E}$ might be called *semantic discounting*.

minus is an increasingly important relational operator in OLAP queries, such an optimization technique might be beneficial.

4 Related Work

Similar problems have been addressed in two contexts: theoretically, as a *query containment* problem; and practically, as a *query optimization* problem. One query can be useful for answering another query when there is a semantic "overlap" between them. A special case of overlap is known as *query containment*; that is, when it can be shown that the answer set of one query is a subset of the answer set of another. Containment between *extensional, conjunctive queries* was first studied in [5], and the problem was shown to be NP-complete.[11] Several sub-classes of extensional, conjunctive queries have been identified to have polynomial-time algorithms [2, 3, 14]. Containment tests for extensional, conjunctive queries that permit negation have been presented in [18], and for those that involve arithmetic comparisons in [16]. Containment between intensional queries with respect to a Datalog program is computationally harder: the containment question is undecidable [25]. Whether a Datalog program is contained by a extensional, conjunctive query is doubly exponential [7].

An extension of the query containment problem is the problem of rewriting a given query by means of other queries. This is known as *query folding*. This problem has been considered in the context of heterogeneous database systems [20, 23] and query rewriting using materialized views [6, 19]. In each of these cases, however, only extensional, conjunctive queries have been considered.

Practical issues of query overlaps have been considered in the context of *multiple query optimization* [24]. Its goal is to optimize evaluation in batch of a set of queries. The developed techniques are geared towards finding and reusing common sub-expressions in the set of queries and are heuristics-based.

The idea of the caching of query results to optimize the processing of subsequent queries was first studied in [11] and [17]. The developed techniques are restricted to a subset of extensional, conjunctive queries. (No self-joins are permitted.) The techniques do not, however, find queries that are contained by the original query. In [8], the ADMS system is described, which includes a query caching system based on [11]. Both [9] and [15] extend the paradigm of query caching to use caches to provide partial answers to the query. They assume, however, that a semantic cache is only useful when some of the query's answers can be obtained from a single cache via project and select operations. Although this framework allows for an efficient implementation of semantic caching, it does not guarantee that all of the query's answers available from caches will be found. Moreover, these semantic caching strategies have been designed explicitly for the purpose of query optimization. Other applications have not been considered. Query caching in heterogeneous environments has been investigated in [1]. This approach also does not consider joins over cached queries.

---

[11] In [5], extensional, conjunctive queries are simply called conjunctive queries.

5 Conclusions

We have presented a general logical framework for SQC. We specified conditions to determine when answers to a query are *present* in, and whether they can be *retrieved* from, cache. Our framework extends on previous work in several ways.

1. Our criteria to check whether caches are useful in answering a query are complete in that all answers that *can* be retrieved through any relational combination of cache expressions *can*, in fact, be discovered.
2. Our criteria work for intensional queries and caches (queries and caches over views), which is pertinent for data warehousing and mediated environments.
3. We extend the notion of a partial answer to account for the case when only a subset of requested attributes is returned. This has been shown useful in heterogeneous environments [22] when data sources are not always available.
4. We introduce a new concept of *semantic overlap* between queries and caches. Previously, only *containment* has been considered. Semantic overlap allows for more possibilities to exploit caches for answering queries.
5. We introduce a richer formalism for remainder queries, called *discounted queries*, and outline the issues in defining a formal semantics.

Acknowledgement
This research was supported in part by NSERC (Grant 203218-98).

References

1. S. Adalı, S. Candan, Y. Papakonstantinou, and V. S. Subrahmanian. Query caching and optimization in distributed mediator systems. In *Proc. SIGMOD*, pages 137–148, Montreal, Canada, June 1996.
2. A. Aho, Y. Sagiv, and J. Ullman. Efficient optimization of a class of relational expressions. *TODS*, 4(3):434–454, 1979.
3. A. Aho, Y. Sagiv, and J. Ullman. Equivalence of relational expressions. *SIAM Journal of COmputing*, 8(2):218–246, 1979.
4. M. Carey, M. Franklin, and M. Zaharioudakis. Fine-grained sharing in page server database system. In *Proceedings of Sigmod*, 1994.
5. A. Chandra and P. Merlin. Optimal implementation of conjunctive queries in relational databases. In *Proc. Ninth ACM Symposium on the Theory of Computing*, pages 77–90, 1977.
6. S. Chaudhuri, R. Krishnamurthy, S. Potamianos, and K. Shim. Optimizing queries with materialized views. In *Proceedings of the 11th ICDE*, pages 190–200, 1995.
7. S. Chaudhuri and M. Vardi. On the equivalence of datalog programs. In *Proceedings of PODS*, pages 55–66, 1992.
8. C. M. Chen and N. Roussopoulos. The implementation and performance evaluation of the ADMS query optimizer: Integrating query result caching and matching. In *Proc. of the 4th EDBT Conference*, Cambridge, UK, 1994.
9. S. Dar, M. Franklin, B. Jónsson, D. Srivastava, and M. Tan. Semantic data caching and replacement. In *Proceedings of VLDB*, 1996.
10. D. DeWitt, P. Futtersack, D. Maier, and F. Velez. A study of three alternative workstation-server architectures for object-oriented database systems. In *Proceedings of VLDB*, 1990.

11. S. Finkelstein. Common expression analysis in database application. In *Proceedings of SIGMOD*, pages 235–245, 1982.

12. P. Godfrey and J. Gryz. Overview of dynamic query evaluation in intensional query optimization. In *Proceedings of Fifth DOOD*, pages 425–426, Montreux, Switzerland, Dec. 1997.

13. P. Godfrey and J. Gryz. View disassembly. In C. Beeri and P. Buneman, editors, *Proceedings of the Seventh International Conference on Database Theory (ICDT'99)*, Lecture Notes in Computer Science, Vol. 1540, pages 417–434, Jerusalem, Israel, Jan. 1999. Springer.

14. D. S. Johnson and A. Klug. Optimizing conjunctive queries that contain untyped variables. *SIAM Journal of Computing*, 12(4):616–640, 1983.

15. A. M. Keller and J. Basu. A predicate-based caching scheme for client-server database architectures. *The VLDB Journal*, 5(2):35–47, Apr. 1996.

16. A. Klug. On conjunctive queries containing inequalities. *Journal of the ACM*, 35(1):146–160, 1988.

17. P.-A. Larson and H. Yang. Computing queries from derived relations. In *Proc. of 11th VLDB*, pages 259–269, 1985.

18. A. Levy and Y. Sagiv. Queries independent of updates. In *Proc. of VLDB*, pages 171–181, 1993.

19. A. Y. Levy, A. O. Mendelzon, Y. Sagiv, and D. Srivastava. Answering queries using views. In *Proc. PODS*, pages 95–104, 1995.

20. A. Y. Levy, A. Rajaraman, and J. Ordille. Querying heterogeneous information sources using source descriptions. In *Proc. 22nd VLDB*, 1996.

21. J. W. Lloyd. *Foundations of Logic Programming*. Symbolic Computation—Artificial Intelligence. Springer-Verlag, Berlin, second edition, 1987.

22. H. Naacke, G. Gardarin, and A. Tomasic. Leveraging mediator cost models with heterogeneous data sources. In *Proceedings of the Fourteenth International Conference on Data Engineereing (ICDE'98)*, pages 351–360, Orlando, Florida, Feb. 1998.

23. X. Qian. Query folding. In *Proceedings of the 12th International Conference on Data Engineering*, pages 48–55, 1996.

24. T. Sellis and S. Ghosh. On the multiple-query optimization problem. *TKDE*, 2(2):262–266, June 1990.

25. O. Shmueli. Decidability and expressiveness aspects of logic queries. In *Proc. 6th ACM Symposium on Principles of Database Systems*, pages 237–249, 1987.

26. J. D. Ullman. *Principles of Database and Knowledge-Base Systems, Volumes I & II*. Principles of Computer Science Series. Computer Science Press, Incorporated, Rockville, Maryland, 1988/1989.

27. J. D. Ullman. Information integration using logical views. In *Proceedings of the Sixth International Conference on Database Theory (ICDT'97)*, Delphi, Greece, Jan. 1997.

Simulating the Interaction of Database Agents

Angelo E. M. Ciarlini and Antonio L. Furtado

Departamento de Informática
Pontifícia Universidade Católica do R.J.
22.453-900 Rio de Janeiro, Brasil
angelo@inf.puc-rio.br, furtado@inf.puc-rio.br

Abstract. An environment is described for using behavioural patterns, extracted from past actions of different collaborating or competing agents, in order to predict through simulation their possible future interactions. The architecture and functioning of the environment are outlined and illustrated via an example involving a simplified database application. The underlying machinery comprises plan recognition and generation methods, as well as the use of rules to infer new goals in response to problems and opportunities arising at successive states. A prototype implementation in Prolog augmented with constraint programming features is operational.

1. Introduction

Databases are primarily repositories of *facts* describing a mini-world of interest. But the facts holding in a state of the mini-world change as a consequence of *actions* performed by different *agents*. Sequences of actions involving certain related entities can be interpreted as coherent *narratives*, which one should be able to retrieve in databases extended to also somehow record each action performed. On the other hand, finding *patterns* in past narratives is a promising knowledge discovery task, since such patterns, together with models of each class of agents, should help to predict, through simulation, the future action of the agents, and thus provide assistance to *decision-making*. The agents we model are human beings and corporations in general. They may be *collaborating agents*, comparable to what is provided by *Multi-Agent Systems* [6], wherein separate modules cooperate with each other during the execution of their respective complex tasks. Alternatively, we may handle *competing agents*, since our approach also covers conflict situations and the possible consequences they can originate.

In [9] we showed how *plan-recognition* and *plan-generation* algorithms can be used in the context of database narratives, in order to detect, from a few observations, what plan an agent is pursuing and, in case obstacles are found, how to adapt the intended plan or to generate an alternative plan aiming at the same goal; only the current state and a single goal state were considered. We now work with a richer and more realistic scenario, in which, in view of the interactions between agents, further goals can be induced whilst different reachable states are successively examined. Our work stems from Propp's seminal work on the structure of a specific genre of narratives [16], namely folktales, and incorporates contributions from previous work on goal taxonomies [21] and on Cognitive Science [18,19,20,7]. A prototype implementation in Prolog, augmented with constraint programming features [14], has been developed in order to perform simulation experiments; the project makes provision for the future addition of modules to support the preparatory knowledge discovery tasks.

The thrust of the present paper is the architecture and functioning of our simulation environment. Section 2 reviews the basic foundations of our approach. Section 3 introduces the criteria and methods used to model and then simulate, throughout a multistage process where new goals are generated in response to an evolving context, the interactive behaviour of collaborating and competing agents. Section 4 describes the simulation environment and its prototype implementation, a running example being included to illustrate the actual use of the environment. Section 5 contains concluding remarks.

2. Database Narratives

Database *facts* can be conveniently denoted by *predicates*. A database *state* is the set of all predicate instances holding at a given instant. A state provides a *description* of the mini-world underlying the database. *Actions* performed in this mini-world can be denoted, always at the conceptual level, by *operations*. If the set of predicate instances before an operation constitutes a state S_i, then when the operation is executed, a transition from S_i to a new state S_j occurs. An operation can be specified, in a STRIPS-like formalism [10], by declaring its pre-conditions and post-conditions, which characterize the states before and after the operation is executed.

Temporal databases [15] enable the keeping of descriptions of all states reached, without making explicit, however, what actions caused the transitions. If, in addition to the records of facts, a *log* registering the (time-stamped) executions of operations is maintained [8], we can say that, besides static descriptions, databases thus enhanced now contain *narratives* represented by *plots* [9], i.e. sequences of events (executions) of operations). Plots should suffice to capture (here, in easy-to-process standard notation) the essential *structure* of some meaningful succession of events. Narratives contained in a database log, far from being fortuitous, usually reflect the *goals* of the several agents who promote the execution of operations. It is therefore useful to distinguish, from amongst the many possible effects of an operation, those that correspond to achieving a recognized goal of an agent; intuitively, they are the reason for executing the operation – which justifies calling them the *primary effects* of the operation. Sometimes a goal corresponds to the combination of the primary effects of more than a single operation. Even when only one operation would seem to be enough, it may happen that its pre-conditions do not currently hold, but might be achieved by the preliminary execution of another operation. In all such cases, a partially ordered set of operations is required, the execution of which in some sequence leads from an initial state S_0, through an arbitrary number of intermediate states, to a final state S_f where the goal holds. On the other hand, there are cases in which one finds more than one set of (one or more) operations as alternative ways of reaching a given goal.

Such partially ordered sets (posets) constitute *plans*. The characterization of plots as sets of plans enables us to use planning techniques for the simulation of possible future database states.

Frequently occurring *plot patterns* correspond to *typical plans*, in that they reflect how agents have been proceeding in practice towards their goals. The detection of such patterns enables us to build a *library of typical plans* for future use by plan recognition algorithms. We can also examine the log to try to formulate rules relating database states to the goals the agents will pursue. In this paper, we discuss neither the construction of libraries nor the formulation of rules. Instead, we explore the results that can be achieved by the integration of planning techniques and the progressive inference of new goals.

3. Modelling the behaviour of agents

Our model uses plan-recognition and plan-generation as complementary processes in the generation and understanding of interactions of database agents. For a complete model, we basically need four kinds of transformations:

1. Plan recognition: observations → possible plans. Observations about database states and operations thus far attempted or actually executed are matched against a library of typical plans, to predict which known typical plans might be intended by the agents.
2. Goal recognition: plan → goal. Once a plan is recognized, through the matching process above, its corresponding goal is determined as a by-product of the process, since each typical plan kept in the library is a complex operation the main effect of which is registered as part of its definition.
3. Plan generation: goal → plan. Given a goal, a planner is applied for the generation of partially-ordered sets of operations able to achieve the goal.
4. Goal generation: database state → goal. The execution of a plan changes the current database state, and, as a result, further goals can be inferred by activating appropriate rules relating the new situation with the needs and motivations of the various agents.

All these transformations are provided by our system. In this paper, however, we are interested mainly in transformations 3 and 4 and the connections between them, because they are the activities directly related to the simulation of the interaction among database agents.

Most sequences of events occurring in the mini-world modelled by a database are **not** motivated by a single ultimate goal initially formulated. When an agent executes operations to achieve one of his goals, he changes the current database state. New goals, both of the original agent and of others, may arise as a result of the modification. Further executions of operations, corresponding to new plans, are necessary to achieve the newly identified goals. Thus, we have a progressive process, in which a plot (denoting, as explained, a database narrative) is generated on the fly by the alternation between generating goals and planning additional executions of operations. It is important to notice that new goals are motivated not only by past events but also by operations already scheduled for future execution and by the beliefs of each agent about the future behaviour of the others.

The actions performed for the achievement of a goal may help to achieve other goals, establishing a positive relationship among all of them. But, often leading to intriguing problematic situations, goals may have a negative interaction, requiring their mutual conciliation or the abandonment of certain goals.

Imagine, in a corporate context example, that an employee was promoted. Seeing this, his co-workers may want to be promoted too. In order to achieve their goal, they may decide to take a course and improve their skills. If no more than two employees are allowed to take a course at the same time, we have a negative interaction, which demands a solution. The simulation of the agents' behaviour should handle such situations and simulate all possible outcomes.

This section explains how we propose to model the behaviour of database agents. We first discuss the relationship among goals, which delimits the kind of situations we intend to work on. Next, we describe how we can use interactive planning to simulate the interaction of database agents when there are many goals to be fulfilled. Then the notion of progressive generation of new goals is introduced.

3.1. Goal Relationships

Wilensky [22], dealing with plan recognition and generation in everyday life situations, classified the interactions among goals of one or more agents into two distinguishable types:

- positive interactions, where reaching a goal can help to achieve other goals;
- negative interactions, where reaching a goal can interfere, and even render impossible (totally or partially) the satisfaction of other goals.

Negative interactions comprise *conflicts* (referring to goals of the same agent) and *competitions* (related to goals of diverse agents).

Studying the mental act of understanding stories, Wilensky [21], argued that, to raise the reader's interest, stories must have *points*. Points are mostly negative goal interactions which precipitate a series of events in a not too obvious fashion. Thus, plot generation must include mechanisms supporting not only positive but, more importantly, also negative interactions. This creates the need to handle cases of *abandonment of goals* (often necessary to solve conflicts) and of *competitive plan execution*, wherein goals of one agent may be frustrated in the benefit of those of another (to solve competitions). Notice that it is not only in literary composition that negative interactions play a fundamental role. Simulations for decision support tend to prove more useful in situations involving critical conflicts among agents.

3.2. Interactive Planning

Aiming at the simulation of database agent interactions, we use planning methods to discover possible operations that the agents can execute to achieve their goals. Planners implementing a simple backward-chaining strategy are not enough to solve our problem because they do not cover the case in which many goals of many different competing or collaborating agents are to be achieved and they neither support abandonment of goals nor competitive plan execution, which usually entail the need to force one agent to give up one of his goals. Moreover, they introduce constraints that are not imposed by the satisfaction of goals but by the algorithm itself. In such planners, plans are treated as totally ordered sequences, so that, for all pairs of operations, one must precede the other for execution, even when there is no causal connection between them.

Because of these reasons, and also in the benefit of efficiency, we looked at *non-linear planners* in the Tweak [3] category. A non-linear plan consists of a set of partially ordered operations. In order to check whether a pre-condition of an operation is satisfied, non-linear planners apply the *Modal Truth Criterion* (MTC). They use a least commitment strategy, according to which a constraint (on the order of execution of operations or prescribing codesignations and non-codesignations of variables) is activated during the generation of a plan only when necessary. This then happens when the constraint must be applied to consider the insertion of an operation for establishing a pre-condition of another operation, or to resolve conflicts between operations.

According to MTC, a condition C is *necessarily true* at the execution time t1 of an operation (*user*) if C was necessarily established by another operation (*establisher*) at time t2, before t1, and there is no operation (*clobberer*) that can establish the negation of C at a time t3 between t2 and t1. A condition is *possibly true*, at a given time t1, if it is either necessarily true or can be made true by the addition of constraints on time and on the values of variables.

In conventional planners, there is no priority for the resolution of goals. In order to be able to assign priorities for the resolution of certain goals, and also to enhance the performance of our simulation environment, we adapted a non-linear planner (AbTweak [23,24]) that is also a hierarchical planner. It tries to resolve all pre-conditions of all operations at a certain level before taking into account lower level pre-conditions. It is a useful mechanism, particularly when we envisage forcing an agent to give up one of his goals. Being inserted first, operations for solving a high priority goal may prevent the insertion of operations aiming at conflicting lower priority goals. That will be the case if we establish in a corporate context that "corporate goals are more important than employees' goals".

The planner performs a heuristic search for good plans. This function obtains the estimated total cost of each partial plan by summing the current cost to an estimated cost for the solution of the lower level pre-conditions (which were not solved so far). The planner works on many plans in parallel and each time selects the candidate with minimal estimated total cost. Then, it selects a pre-condition of an operation that is not necessarily true and tries to make it true. While doing that, the planner generates all possible successors of the current plan. It considers the possibility of using establishers already included in the plan as well as the insertion of new operations. All possibilities of resolving conflicts caused by clobberers are also considered.

We use two main mechanisms to simulate goal abandonment and competitive plan execution: *conditional goals* and *limited goals*.

Conditional goals have a *survival* condition attached to them, which the planner must check to determine whether the goal should be pursued or not. Operations added for the fulfilment of conditional goals are also conditional. They are kept as part of the plan only if their survival conditions are valid at the appointed execution time. However, even in case of failure, the planner keeps the operations preceding the instant when the failing survival conditions ceased to hold. Survival conditions and pre-conditions must be handled in a consistent way: the planner begins by trying to solve all pre-conditions of all operations at least once; if a survival condition of an operation fails, the planner determines that its pre-conditions will not be considered for a second time.

Limited goals are those that are tried once only, and have an associated *limit* (expressed as a natural number). The limit restricts the number of new operations that can be inserted to achieve the goal. An operation inserted for the establishment of limited goals is termed a limited operation. A limited operation tentatively inserted in a plan can be kept only if all its pre-conditions are true. In addition, all its pre-conditions are in turn limited subgoals, the limit of which is that of the original goal minus one. A goal with limit 0 can only be satisfied by an operation already present in the plan. We use limited goals to model situations in which agents are willing to invest no more than a certain measure of effort, not necessarily the same for each agent, towards the fulfilment of their goals.

In order to adapt planning methods to the database context, we implemented two additional features: We modified MTC to cope with the *Closed World Assumption* [17]. All facts not belonging to the database are considered (initially) false. So, we had to provide a special treatment for the evaluation of negative conditions, because they can be established simply by observing the absence of the corresponding positive facts in the database. We used *Constraint Logic Programming* [14] to deal with pre-conditions that involve arithmetic constraints, frequently involved in database updates. The added features enable the handling of such pre-conditions even in the presence of free variables, since Constraint Logic Programming leaves a goal frozen until the moment it can be evaluated. In order to process numbers, it provides a solver of systems of equations and inequations able to run in parallel with the planning procedure. The solver tries as early as possible to find out whether a frozen goal can no longer be fulfilled, in which case it immediately cuts the current branch of the search tree, thus causing an improvement in the performance of the overall system.

3.3. Progressive Goal Generation

In order to generate the goals that the agents will pursue in specific situations, one needs to establish a relation between database states, specified by plots generated so far, and goals. To characterize modification of states by means of operations, a Temporal Logic notation, e.g. Event Calculus [12], would seem to be an obvious choice. However, because we are working with database events, we decided to also borrow from Multi-Sorted Database Logic [1]. Accordingly, our logic is a Multi-Sorted Database Logic in which a special status is conferred on the sort *time-stamp*. Our truth model is based on the MTC criterion, which is fully compatible with Event Calculus with Preconditions [2]. We do not formalize our logic here, because of space considerations. Instead, we describe informally the meta-predicates used for speaking about database facts and operations associated with time. Then, we indicate how to write rules, using these meta-predicates, aiming at the specification of the behaviour of agents.

The order of execution of operations being merely partial, two different criteria for truth evaluation are needed. We should be able to verify whether a fact associated with a certain time-stamp is either necessarily or possibly true. In addition, it must be possible to speak about the time when a fact was established by an operation, because a condition is valid only **after** (but not **at**) its establishment. We should also be able to mention the time when a specific operation happened (i.e. was executed). Accordingly, we have four temporal meta-predicates, noting that *LITERAL* stands for a positive or negative fact:

- *h(T,LITERAL)*: *LITERAL* is necessarily true at *T*;
- *p(T,LITERAL)*: *LITERAL* is possibly true at *T*;
- *e(T,LITERAL)*: *LITERAL* is established at *T*; and
- *o(T,OPERATION)*: *OPERATION* happened at *T*.

In order to express constraints relating variables of specific sorts, we have two additional meta-predicates:

- *h(CONSTRAINT)*: *CONSTRAINT* is necessarily true; and
- *p(CONSTRAINT)*: *CONSTRAINT* is possibly true.

The atomic formulae are meta-predicates and negations thereof. The rules are formulated as implications, in which the antecedent is a conjunction of atomic formulae and the consequent is a conjunction of meta-predicates of types *h(T,LITERAL)* and *h(LITERAL)* only. Furthermore, whenever conditional or limited goals are involved, their associated conditions or limits, respectively, must be included in the rule definition. If the antecedent holds, then the consequent will correspond to a goal to be pursued (unless it already holds). By assumption, all variables in the antecedent are universally quantified, whereas those appearing only in the consequent are existentially quantified. For consistency with the Closed World Assumption, variables that appear only in negated meta-predicates or facts are regarded as existentially quantified within the negation. Variables are represented by capital letters. "_" stands, as in Prolog, for anonymous variables.

To express in a corporate example the rule: "If C became a client at T1 and, at time T2 (after T1), no one serves C and there is a person E who is not serving any client, *then the company will try to arrange that,* at a time T3, after T2, E will be serving C" we write:

$$e(T1,is\_client(C)) \land h(T2>T1) \land \neg e(T2,serves(\_,C)) \land e(T2,person(E)) \land$$
$$h(T2, \neg serves(\_,C)) \land \neg e(T2,serves(E,\_)) \rightarrow h(T3>T2) \land h(T3,serves(E,C))$$

When there is a set of goals to be achieved, by potentially different agents at potentially different times, the simulation proceeds as described in 3.2. When all these currently active goals have been either fulfilled or discarded, the planning process completes one stage. Then, the set of existing rules is exhaustively evaluated, over the initial database state and the alternative future states resulting from the set of partially ordered operations generated thus far. If the consequent of a rule does not already hold and the corresponding goals have not previously been tried, these new goals will be pursued in the next stage of the planning process. The cycle ends when no new goal can be generated.

This progressive generation of goals can be compared to the triggering process in *Active Databases* [5]. A trigger is usually a rule defined by a triple *<Event, Condition, Action>*. When an event happens, a condition is evaluated and, if the condition is true, the corresponding action is performed automatically. Trigger events and conditions are semantically equivalent to the antecedents of our rules. The consequent of a trigger, however, is an action, whereas the consequent of our rules simply corresponds to goals.

4. The Interactive Plot Generator

In order to try out the model described in section 3, a prototype system — *Interactive Plot Generator (IPG)* — was designed and implemented. In this section we first outline the overall structure and function of IPG, and then demonstrate its use with an example related to the simple database of a company called Alpha.

4.1. A short description of IPG

IPG mainly consists of two modules, which can be used either separately or in combination, to handle plots of narratives: one composes plots (the *Simulator*) whereas the other performs plan and plot recognition (the *Recognizer*). They are complemented by three auxiliary modules: the *Goal Evaluator*, the *Temporal Logic Processor* and the *Query Interface* (whereby users can retrieve information about plots generated by the Simulator). The implementation of two additional modules is planned as part of the continuation of the project, with the purpose of automating the construction of the library of typical plans and the discovery of agent behaviour rules. Figure 1 displays the architecture of the system. Rectangles represent modules, ellipses correspond to data repositories, and arrows to the flow of data. Dashed rectangles indicate modules to be incorporated in future versions.

The user can enter *observations*, which are taken by the system as hints about the plot to be obtained by simulation or plan-recognition (some of the operations to be executed, a few assertions about the situation of agents at intermediate states and goals to be finally reached, etc.), and the system looks for a plot that may fit the observations supplied.

The Recognizer uses a plan-recognition algorithm adapted from the algorithm defined by Kautz [11]. The adaptations extend it to handle pre- and post-conditions of operations and establish its connection with the Simulator. The user·enters his observations and the system fills in what is missing in the characterization of agents, taking into consideration the pertinent facts found in the initial state of the database. The plots recognized are communicated to the user, together with the indication that its pre-conditions can (or cannot) be satisfied. According to the user's choice, the Simulator can be activated to adapt or extend plots, or else to generate plots with the same primary effects identified. The Recognizer explores all alternatives recognizable and displays them to the user, as requested.

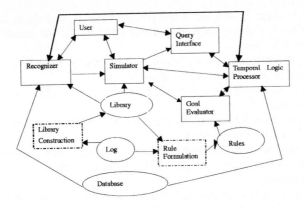

Fig. 1. General architecture of IPG

The Simulator executes planning tasks, as described in 3.2, supported when necessary by the Temporal Logic Processor. To obtain new goals, the Simulator calls the Goal Evaluator, which performs their evaluation as explained in 3.3. Differently from the Recognizer, the Simulator can generate plotes even when no observation is provided by the user, because new goals can arise from the facts stored in the initial database. During simulation, the selection, from the set of partially generated plots, of those still deserving examination is made by interacting with the user. When a partial plot is exhibited, the system signals to the user that the Query Interface is available. The Query Interface enables the user to formulate queries about the situation of agents at diverse states along the plot. For this purpose, the Query Interface can also access the Temporal Logic Processor. After consulting, the user can return normally to the Simulator and decide whether or not to proceed with the current plot.

In our example databases, the construction of the libraries of typical plans was done systematically but manually. The same happened with behaviour rules, in the formulation of which we were guided by previous work on goal relationships (3.1) and interconnections of events [18,19,20,7]. We are currently investigating methods to support these processes, to turn part, respectively, of the future *Library Construction* and *Rule Formulation* modules.

The IPG prototype was implemented in SICSTUS Prolog [4], and extensively employs its constraint programming features to express arithmetic relationships and non-codesignations among variables, as well as to evaluate temporal logic expressions.

4.2. Running Example

Our running example corresponds to the context of a company called Alpha. There are three different classes of agents: employees, clients and company Alpha itself. In order to model their behaviour, we defined in the logic notation described at 3.3 — here transcribed informally for easier reading — the following rules:

1. Whenever a client C has no employee to serve it, and there are people still unassigned to any client, such people *will compete* for the position until one of them achieves the goal.
2. Whenever an employee is not content with his salary, *he will try, in accordance with his persistence,* to increase his status by one.
3. Whenever an employee has a status higher than what his salary indicates, his salary level will be raised by one.
4. Whenever the salary of an employee E goes beyond the budget of client C, whom E is serving, E will stop serving C.
5. Whenever an employee E is not associated with any client and there are neither clients without employee nor potential clients to conquer, E will cease to be Alpha's employee.
6. Whenever a client C is dissatisfied with an employee E at its service, some action will be undertaken to remedy the situation.

```
        assign(john,beta)
                Goal(Stage 1): serves(john,beta)
        work_hard(david)
                Goal(Stage 1): status(david,2.0)
        work_hard(leonard)
                Goal(Stage 1): status(leonard,2.0)
        hire(mary) -CANCELLED
        assign(mary,beta) - CANCELLED
                Goal(Stage 1): serves(mary,beta) - CANCELLED
        raise_level(leonard)
                Goal(Stage 2): has_level(leonard,2.0)
        raise_level(david)
                Goal(Stage 2): has_level(david,2.0)
        train(david,c135)
        train(david,c136)
                Goal(Stage 3): status(david,3.0)
        train(leonard,c136) - CANCELLED
                Goal(Stage 3): status(leonard,3.0) - CANCELLED
        raise_level(david)
                Goal(Stage 4): has_level(david,3.0)
        hire(mary)
        replace(david,mary,epsilon)
                Goal(Stage 5): not(serves(david,epsilon))
        fire(david)
                Goal(Stage 6): not(is_employee(david))
```

Fig. 2. Plot after six stages

Rules 1 and 2 give origin, respectively, to conditional and limited goals.

An initial database is given with 3 employees (David, Leonard and John), one unemployed person (Mary) and three clients (Beta, Epsilon and Lambda). David is serving Epsilon and Leonard is serving Lambda. All employees have salary level 1 and the budget of every client company can afford, at most, salary level 2. Both David and Leonard have the ambition of reaching salary level 3, but David's persistence is stronger than Leonard's.

After iterating across 6 stages, the system generates the narrative described below, transcribing into natural language the actions belonging to each stage:

"David and Leonard work hard and their status is raised to 2. John and Mary compete for client Beta. John wins and Mary's actions towards this objective are cancelled. David and Leonard have their salary raised. David and Leonard try to increase their status again. But now this requires that two courses be taken. David takes them, whereas Leonard abandons his attempts to reach a higher status. David's salary is raised again. Since David's salary now exceeds Epsilon's budget, Mary is hired and replaces David at the service of Epsilon. Since David is no longer serving any client, and there is no current client to which he might be appointed, nor even potential clients to bring in, David is fired".

Notice the looping structure generated, whereby David's repeated initiatives seem to improve his situation as far as status and salary are concerned, but their cumulative impact on Epsilon's expenditures end up compromising the stability of David's assignment. Figure 2 shows the plot obtained at the conclusion of the sixth stage in one of its possible orders. Both the constituent operations and the goals successively inferred are displayed. Goals and planned operations later abandoned are marked as "cancelled".

5. Concluding Remarks

Simulation offers answers to "what if" questions, so crucially relevant to decision-making. A user conducting simulation experiments has thus an opportunity to anticipate and compare the favourable and unfavourable results of different lines of action, some of which conforming to the traditional attitudes and policies adopted in the past, and others exploiting valid but still untried alternatives. Our environment leaves room to the user's interference, so that his personal knowledge can guide the choice among options. Besides helping to decide with respect to specific situations, its continued use may disclose shortcomings in how agents and operations are currently modelled, thus leading to the revision of the inadequate models.

Planning algorithms are known to be, in the unrestricted cases, semi-decidable and exponential, and, therefore, good heuristics are indispensable to speed-up convergence towards the achievement of goals marked with highest precedence. We have been looking at this topic in the context of our prototype system, but more work is still needed. Even with the present version, however, promising results have already been obtained in very diverse domains, enabling the treatment of considerably more complex plots of narratives than commonplace database applications. Folktales are providing a nontrivial benchmark, and the example in section 4.2 suggests that phenomena involving "circular causality", with positive and negative feedback effects, such as the unstabilizing effect of government efforts to control economic crises [13], can also be handled. Further research will involve gaining experience with our interactive multistage planning paradigm, as well as investigating methods to be applied in the enhancement of the system, with particular emphasis on the automatic construction of libraries of typical plans and formulation of behaviour rules.

analysis of objects' structure (i.e., objects' attributes) but also on the analysis of object contexts, of object semantic relevance [4] and of objects' inter-relations within schemes [3]. A major limit of manual methods relies in the difficulty of applying them with large applications since, in such contexts, it is needed to face integration problems involving hundreds of scheme objects.

To face large integration/abstraction problems, a number of semi-automatic methods has been also proposed. In the past, they were based on considering only structural similarities among objects belonging to different schemes [5]. However, *"purely structural considerations do not suffice to determine the semantic similarities of classes"* [4]. Therefore, more recently, techniques for deriving inter-scheme properties taking into account also scheme semantics have been proposed [3, 4, 6, 7, 9]; these new algorithms, however, still require a significant intervention of the human expert.

As far as the scheme abstraction is concerned, in the literature, proposed approaches are completely manual and, therefore, they are difficult to apply when the scheme to be abstracted has been obtained from the integration of a large number of schemes (such as in Central Public Administration contexts).

The purpose of this paper is the presentation of two *automatic* and *semantic* algorithms realizing the integration and the abstraction of database schemes. Our methods are largely *automatic* since human intervention is limited to special cases. Both algorithms are also *semantic* in that they consider object contexts and semantic relevance and, in addition, they exploit semantic relations holding among scheme objects as encoded in a set of *interscheme properties* [1]. Interscheme properties are assumed to be given, but they can be extracted from input schemes using methods presented in the literature (e.g. [3, 9, 6, 7]).

Generally, each transformation operated on schemes for the purpose of integration/abstraction can be described by providing either the input and the output or the input and the set of operations performed during the transformation itself. However, it is difficult to obtain the description of performed operations if the former representation is adopted. Similarly, it is expensive to derive the output if the latter representation is assumed. In the literature, almost all scheme integration and abstraction approaches describe transformations using input and output schemes. An important characteristic of our approach consists in describing scheme integrations and abstractions using both input and output schemes and the set of operations which led to output schemes from input ones. In our case maintaining both representations is cheap, automatic and does not need a great amount of storing resources, as shown in the following.

The techniques we are presenting here work as follows. All information about schemes and their objects are stored in a *metascheme M*. Insertions, deletions and modifications of objects and properties among them, which will be often referred to in the following, are realized by modifying the content of the metascheme. Besides information traditionally stored in the metascheme, M stores also a *set of mappings* (hereafter denoted by $M.SoM$) and *a set of views*, hereafter called $M.SoV$. $M.SoM$ describes the way an object belonging to output schemes has been obtained from one or more objects belonging to input schemes. *M.SoV* allows to obtain instances of objects of the output schemes from instances at the input scheme level.

Given a set of input database schemes and an associated set of interscheme properties, the first algorithm we present produces an integrated global scheme; all information about the global scheme, the objects belonging to it and properties relating them is stored in *M*; in addition, each operation performed during the scheme integration is stored in *M.SoM*; views corresponding to *M.SoM* entries are stored in *M.SoV*. The abstraction algorithm works analogously.

The plan of the paper is as follows. In Section 2 we discuss preliminary concepts. In Section 3, the integration algorithm is presented. Section 4 is devoted to illustrating the abstraction algorithm.

2   Preliminaries

2.1   Interscheme Property Derivation

As explained above, our algorithms assume that a set of interscheme properties, describing relationships holding among input scheme objects, is given. In the literature, several techniques have been proposed for extracting interscheme properties [3, 4, 6, 7, 9].

We assume to have at disposal a dictionary *LSPD* of lexicographic synonymy properties and a dictionary *IPD* of interscheme properties. The *LSPD* stores lexical synonymies; they are assumed to be derived from a standard thesaurus, but may be also application specific and provided by database experts. Lexicographic synonymies are stored in the *LSPD* as triplets $[A, B, f]$, where A and B are database objects and f is a fuzzy coefficient, in the real interval $[0, 1]$, denoting the plausibility of the property.

The *IPD* is a collection of dictionaries; more in particular we shall refer to the following components: *(i) IPD.SD*, the *Synonymy Dictionary* storing triplets of the form $\lfloor A, B, f \rfloor$, where A and B are the involved objects and f is a fuzzy coefficient expressing the strength of the property; *(ii) IPD.HD*, the *Homonymy Dictionary* storing triplets of the form $\|A, B, f\|$, where A and B are the involved objects and f is a fuzzy coefficient expressing the strength of the property; *(iii) IPD.ID*, the *Inclusion Dictionary*, storing inclusion properties between objects; inclusion properties are denoted as triplets $\langle A, B, f \rangle$, where A is the included object, B is the including object and f is a fuzzy coefficient expressing the plausibility of the property; *(iv) IPD.TCD*, the *Type Conflict Dictionary*, storing type conflicts; a type conflict holds between two objects belonging to two schemes if they represent the same concept, yet having different types[1]; type conflicts are stored as triplets of the form $\lceil A, B, f \rceil$, where A and B are the involved objects and f is a fuzzy coefficient expressing the plausibility of the property.

---

[1] The type of an object indicates if it is an entity, an attribute or a relationship.

2.2 The set of mappings and the set of views

$M.SoM$ can be looked at as to store the way a scheme object has been obtained from other objects through integration/abstraction steps. $M.SoM$ includes an entry for each new object obtained along the application of integration and abstraction algorithms. As we shall see, $M.SoM$ entries are used to define views belonging to $M.SoV$.

Thus, a set of mappings can be assumed to consist of a set of tuples, each of which must have one of the following forms: *(i)* $\langle E_1, E_2, E_{12}, EMerge \rangle$ indicating that entities E_1 and E_2 are merged into the entity E_{12} (note that E_{12} can coincide either with E_1 or with E_2); *(ii)* $\langle A_1, A_2, A_{12}, AMerge \rangle$ and $\langle R_1, R_2, R_{12}, RMerge \rangle$, which are the analogous, for attributes and relationships, of the tuple $\langle E_1, E_2, E_{12}, EMerge \rangle$; *(iii)* $\langle E_1, E_2, R, Isa \rangle$ denoting the creation of an *is-a* relationship R from E_1 to E_2; *(iv)* $\langle R, E_1, E_2, RDelToE \rangle$ indicating the abstraction of the relationship R (between E_1 and E_2) and of the entity E_1, into the entity E_2; *(v)* $\langle R, -, E, CRDelToE \rangle$ denoting the abstraction of the cyclic relationship R into the corresponding entity E; *(vi)* $\langle R, E_1, E_2, RCreate \rangle$ indicating the creation of a relationship R between E_1 and E_2; *(vii)* $\langle R, E_1, E_2, RToE \rangle$ denoting the transformation of the relationship R (between E_1 and E_2) into an entity having the same name; *(viii)* $\langle A, E, R, AToE \rangle$ indicating the transformation of the attribute A, belonging to the entity E, into an entity linked to E by the relationship R.

Tuples of the first four formats will be generated during the integration process; tuples of the fifth and the sixth type are produced during the execution of the abstraction algorithm; tuples of the last three formats derive from the resolution of type conflicts (see below).

The set of views $M.SoV$ stores a view for each object belonging to schemes obtained by the execution of integration and abstraction algorithms (and, therefore, a view for each tuple of $M.SoM$). Views allow to obtain instances of a new object from instances of objects it derives from. Views are defined by a metalanguage, independent from conceptual and logic scheme models, whose basic operators are parametric procedures that, once instantiated, compute derived data instances from input data instances. Each basic operation of our metalanguage can be easily translated into an operation valid for the DBMS storing data a certain view operates upon.

2.3 Structures and contexts of objects

Definition 1. Given an entity E, the *structure* of E consists of the set of its attributes; the *context* of E consists of relationships it takes part into and all other entities linked by these relationships.

Given a relationship R, the *internal structure* of R consists of its attributes; the *structure* of R consists of its internal structure plus the entities involved in R and their attributes; the *context* of R consists of entities linked (through some other relationship different from R) to entities belonging to the structure of R.

□

2.4 Metascheme

Our algorithms use a metascheme, which is represented in Figure 1.

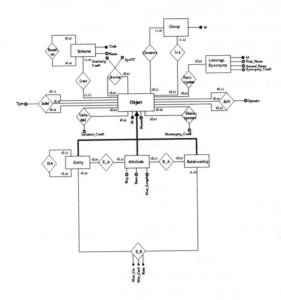

Fig. 1. The metascheme

In the metascheme, the central entity is the *Object*. An object can be similar to other objects: this similarity is represented by the relationship *Similar*; this relationship owns an attribute *Similarity_Coeff*, indicating the strength of the similarity itself, and an attribute *Syn/TC*, indicating if the similarity represents a synonymy or a type conflict. Once translated in a suitable logic model, this relationship stores the Synonymy and the Type Conflict Dictionaries. In an analogous way, the metascheme contains the relationship *Included*, which stores the Inclusion Dictionary, and the relationship *Homonymous*, which stores the Homonymy Dictionary. The entity *Lexicographic Synonymy* denotes lexical synonymies between two names.

The entity *Group* allows to represent the concept of object abstraction; indeed, a group contains more than one object of a scheme; all objects belonging to a group are abstracted, by the abstraction algorithm, and represented by only one object in the abstracted scheme. An *attribute* can be a primary key, a secondary key or a non-key; the attribute *Key* is used for representing this information. A *scheme* can be based on one or more schemes (this happens when it is obtained by integrating or abstracting other schemes).

The ternary relationship *SoM* is used for storing the set of mappings; the attribute *Type* indicates the kind of the transformation. Similarly, the ternary relationship *SoV* is used for storing the set of views. For each entry, the attribute *Operator* indicates the parametric procedure which the view corresponding to the entry is an instance of.

3 Integration Algorithm

The algorithm for scheme integration can be encoded as follows:

Algorithm for scheme integration

Input: a dictionary $LSPD$ of lexicographic synonymy properties, a dictionary
IPD of interscheme properties; a set SS of schemes; a metascheme M;
Output: a global scheme GS;
type
$\quad VarToBeIncluded = (First, Second, None);$
const
$\quad th_{ls} = 0.25; \ th_{us} = 0.75; \ th_{li} = 0.25; \ th_{ui} = 0.75;$
var
$\quad TSS$: a (temporary) set of schemes;
$\quad g : real \in [0..1]; \ which : VarToBeIncluded;$
begin
$\quad NBR\_Normalization(IPD, SS, M, TSS);$
$\quad TC\_Normalization(IPD, M, TSS);$
$\quad Union(TSS, GS);$
$\quad$**for each** $\lfloor E_1, E_2, f_{E_1 E_2} \rfloor \in IPD.SD$ such that E_1 and E_2 are entities
$\quad$**do**
$\qquad$**if** $f_{E_1 E_2} > th_{us}$ **then**
$\qquad\quad E\_Merge(LSPD, E_1, E_2, GS, M);$
$\qquad$**else if** $th_{ls} < f_{E_1 E_2} \leq th_{us}$ **then begin**
$\qquad\quad EvaluateSubset(E_1, E_2, IPD, which, g);$
$\qquad\quad$**if** $(which = None)$ **or** $(g \leq f_{E_1 E_2})$ **then**
$\qquad\qquad E\_Merge(LSPD, E_1, E_2, GS, M)$
$\qquad\quad$**else if** $(which = First)$ **then**
$\qquad\qquad E\_Include(LSPD, E_1, E_2, GS, M)$
$\qquad\quad$**else**
$\qquad\qquad E\_Include(LSPD, E_2, E_1, GS, M)$
$\qquad$**end**;
$\quad$**for each** $\langle E_1, E_2, g_{E_1 E_2} \rangle \in IPD.ID$ such that E_1 and E_2 are entities
$\quad$**and not** $ProbablyCoincident(E_1, E_2, IPD)$ **then begin**
$\qquad EvaluateSubset(E_1, E_2, IPD, which, g);$
$\qquad$**if** $(which = First)$ **then** $E\_Include(LSPD, E_1, E_2, GS, M)$
$\qquad$**else** $E\_Include(LSPD, E_2, E_1, GS, M)$
$\quad$**end**;
$\quad$**for each** $\lfloor R_1, R_2, f_{R_1 R_2} \rfloor \in IPD.SD$ such that R_1 and R_2 are
$\quad$relationships **do**
$\qquad$**if** $f_{R_1 R_2} > th_{ls}$ **then** $R\_Relate(LSPD, IPD, R_1, R_2, GS, M);$
end

Procedures called within the algorithm have the following meaning:

- *NBR_Normalization* takes in input a set SS of schemes, a dictionary IPD of
  interscheme properties and a metascheme M; it performs a scheme normalization by transforming each non binary relationship into a set of binary ones;
  in addition it updates the metascheme accordingly; the procedure yields a
  set TSS of normalized schemes and the modified metascheme as the outputs.

- *TC_Normalization* takes in input a set TSS of schemes, a dictionary IPD of interscheme properties and the metascheme M; it normalizes the set of schemes by solving type conflicts. More details about the algorithms underlying this procedure can be found in [10].
- *Union* takes in input a group of schemes TSS; it computes the juxtaposition of schemes of TSS to obtain the global scheme GS and yields this scheme in output;
- *EvaluateSubset* is a procedure which takes in input two entities E_1 and E_2 and a dictionary IPD of interscheme properties; if $g_{E_1 E_2} > g_{E_2 E_1}$ and $g_{E_1 E_2} > th_{li}$ the procedure assigns the value *First* to *which* and sets $g = g_{E_1 E_2}$; otherwise, if $g_{E_2 E_1} > g_{E_1 E_2}$ and $g_{E_2 E_1} > th_{li}$ then *which = Second* and $g = g_{E_2 E_1}$; finally, if neither $\langle E_1, E_2, g_{E_1 E_2}, \rangle$ nor $\langle E_2, E_1, g_{E_2 E_1} \rangle$ belong to the IPD or both their coefficients are less than or equal to th_{li}, *which = None* and $g = 0$.
- *ProbablyCoincident* is a function that takes two entities E_1 and E_2 and a dictionary IPD of interscheme properties as inputs and returns *True* if a synonymy between E_1 and E_2 exists with plausibility coefficient greater than th_{ls}, *False* otherwise.
- *E_Merge* takes entities E_1 and E_2 belonging to GS in input and merges them for obtaining a unique entity.
- *E_Include* takes entities E_1 and E_2 belonging to GS in input and connects them through an *is-a* relationship.
- *R_Relate* considers relationships R_1 and R_2 and decides if either both of them must be merged into a third relationship or if one of them must be merged into the other one or finally, if they must be kept distinct in the global scheme.

As an example consider the procedure *E_Merge*. It receives a dictionary of Lexicographic Synonymy Properties $LSPD$, two entities E_1 and E_2, a global scheme GS and the metascheme M; it merges entities E_1 and E_2 into one entity and updates $M.SoM$ accordingly. The procedure is as follows:

Procedure *E_Merge*($LSPD$: a Lexicographic Synonymy Property Dictionary; E_1, E_2: Entity; **var** GS: a global scheme; **var** M: a metascheme);
var
    E_{12}: Entity; A: a set of attributes;
begin
    $S\_EMerge(GS, E_1, E_2, E_{12}, M)$;
    $M.SoM := M.SoM \cup \langle E_1, E_2, E_{12}, EMerge \rangle$;
    $M.SoV := M.SoV \cup \{D\_EMerge(E_1, E_2, E_{12})\}$;
    for each $A_i, A_j \in EStructure(E)$ such that $\langle A_i, A_j, f \rangle \in LSPD$ and
    $f > th_{us}$ **then begin**
        $S\_AMerge(GS, A_i, A_j, A_{ij}, M)$;
        $M.SoM := M.SoM \cup \langle A_i, A_j, A_{ij}, AMerge \rangle$;
        $M.SoV := M.SoV \cup \{D\_AMerge(A_i, A_j, A_{ij})\}$
    end
end

The function *(i)* *EStructure(E)* takes in input an entity E and returns the set of attributes belonging to its structure.

The procedure *S_EMerge* substitutes, in the scheme GS, entities E_1 and E_2 with the entity E_{12}. Attributes of the new entity are obtained as the union of attributes of entities which the new entity is derived from. As previously pointed out, all changes in a scheme are obviously implemented as changes in the metascheme. The procedure is as follows:

Procedure *S_EMerge*(**var** GS: a scheme; **var** E_1, E_2, E_{12}: Entity; **var** M: a metascheme);
begin
    $E\_Add(GS, E_{12}, M)$;
    $E_{12}.Att := EStructure(E_1) \cup EStructure(E_2)$;
    $Transfer\_Relationships(GS, E_1, E_{12}, M)$;
    $Transfer\_Relationships(GS, E_2, E_{12}, M)$;
    $E\_Delete(GS, E_1, M)$; $E\_Delete(GS, E_2, M)$;
end

The procedure *E_Add* adds the entity E_{12} to the scheme GS. The procedure *Transfer_Relationships* takes in input two entities E_i and E_j and transforms relationships of E_i so that they become relationships of E_j; in our case the procedure is called twice for transferring relationships of E_1 and E_2 to E_{12}. If some of these relationships are similar, they will be merged by the procedure *R_Relate* when this is activated. The procedure *E_Delete* eliminates the entity E from the scheme GS.

The procedure *S_AMerge* is analogous of *S_EMerge* but for attributes.

4 Scheme abstraction

The abstraction algorithm takes in input a scheme S and abstracts it. To this end it uses an abstraction dictionary AD, consisting of three components: *(i)* $AD.EE$, storing triplets of the form $((E_i, E_j, p_{E_i E_j}))$, where E_i is an entity linked by a relationship, different from the *is-a* one, to E_j and $p_{E_i E_j}$ is a fuzzy coefficient representing the plausibility that E_i can be abstracted into E_j; *(ii)* $AD.ISA$, storing triplets of the form $\langle\langle E_i, E_j, q_{E_i E_j}\rangle\rangle$, where E_i is an entity linked by an *is-a* relationship to E_j and $q_{E_i E_j}$ is a fuzzy coefficient representing the plausibility that E_i can be abstracted into E_j; *(iii)* $AD.CR$, storing triplets of the form $[[E, R, s_{ER}]]$, where R is a cyclic relationship linking the entity E twice (e.g., a relationship *Parent* and the entity *Person*) and s_{ER} is a fuzzy coefficient indicating the plausibility that R can be abstracted into E.

The abstraction algorithm is given next:

Algorithm for scheme abstraction
Input: a dictionary IPD of interscheme properties; a scheme S; a metascheme M;
Output: an abstracted scheme AS;
var

AD: an abstraction dictionary;
begin
  NBR_Normalization(IPD, S, M, AS);
  TC_Normalization(IPD, M, AS);
  Construct_AD.EE(AS, M, AD);
  Construct_AD.ISA(AS, M, AD);
  Construct_AD.CR(AS, M, AD);
  for each entity $E_i \in S$ **do begin**
    Compute_Max$(E_i, E_m, p_{E_i E_m}, p_{E_m E_i}, AD.EE)$;
    if $p_{E_i E_m} > th_a$ **then**
      if $p_{E_i E_m} > p_{E_m E_i}$ **or** $(p_{E_i E_m} = p_{E_m E_i}$ **and**
      MustBeAbstracted$(E_i, E_m))$ **then**
        EE_Abstract(E_i, E_m, AS, M)
  end;
  for each entity $E_s \in S$ linked to an entity E_f by an *is-a* relationship R_k
  do begin
    let $\langle\langle E_s, E_f, q_{E_s E_f}\rangle\rangle$ the corresponding tuple belonging to *AD.ISA*;
    if $q_{E_s E_f} > th_a$ **then** *ISA_Abstract*(E_s, E_f, R_k, AS, M)
  end;
  for each cyclic relationship $R_j \in S$ **do begin**
    let $[[E_k, R_j, s_{E_k R_j}]]$ the corresponding tuple belonging to *AD.CR*
    if $s_{E_k R_j} > th_a$ **then** *CR_Abstract*(R_j, E_k, AS, M)
  end
end

Procedures called within the algorithm have the following meaning:

- The function *Compute_Max* takes an entity E_i and computes the most plausible entity which E_i must be abstracted into. If more than one entity exists with the same maximum plausibility coefficient value, then the final decision on which of these must be assumed as E_m is left to the human expert. The function returns also $p_{E_i E_m}$ and $p_{E_m E_i}$.

- The function *MustBeAbstracted* returns *True* if E_i must be abstracted into E_m, *False* otherwise; the procedure requires the support of human expert for taking this decision.

- Functions *Construct_AD.EE*, *Construct_AD.ISA* and *Construct_AD.CR* take in input a scheme AS, a metascheme M and adds suitable tuples to *AD.EE*, *AD.ISA* and *AD.CR*. More details about the computation of abstraction coefficients can be found in [6].

- The procedure *EE_Abstract* takes in input entities E_i and E_m, linked by a relationship different from an *is-a*, and abstracts E_i into E_m. *M.SoM* and *M.SoV* are consequently updated.

- The procedure *ISA_Abstract* takes in input two entities E_s and E_f, such that E_s is linked to E_f by an *is-a* relationship R_k, and abstracts E_s into E_f.

- The procedure *CR_Abstract* takes in input a cyclic relationship R_j and the corresponding entity E_k, which it links twice, and abstracts R_j into E_k. *M.SoM* and *M.SoV* are correspondingly updated.

As an example consider the procedure *ISA_Abstract*; it takes in input two entities E_s and E_f, such that E_s is linked to E_f by an *is-a* relationship R_k, and abstracts E_s into E_f. The procedure calls *S_RDelToE* for merging E_s and R_k into E_f (or into the entity which E_f has been abstracted to) and correspondingly updates *M.SoM* and *M.SoV*. This procedure is as follows:

Procedure *ISA_Abstract* (**var** E_s, E_f: Entity; **var** R_k: Relationship; **var** AS: a scheme; **var** M: a metascheme);
var
    E_{ff}: Entity;
begin
    $E_{ff} := Astr(E_f, M)$;
    $S\_RDelToE(AS, R_k, E_s, E_{ff}, M)$;
    $M.SoM := M.SoM \cup \langle R_k, E_s, E_{ff}, RDelToE \rangle$;
    $M.SoV := M.SoV \cup \{D\_RDelToE(R_k, E_s, E_{ff})\}$
end

References

1. C. Batini, M. Lenzerini, A methodology for data schema integration in the entity relationship model, *IEEE TSE* 10(6), 650-664, 1984.
2. C. Batini, M. Lenzerini, S.B. Navathe, A comparative analysis of methodologies for database scheme integration, *ACM Computing Surveys*, 15(4), 323-364, 1986.
3. S. Castano, V. De Antonellis, Semantic Dictionary Design for Database Interoperability, *Proceedings of ICDE'97*, Birmingham, United Kingdom, 1997.
4. P. Fankhauser, M. Kracker, E.J.Neuhold, Semantic vs. Structural Resemblance of Classes, *SIGMOD RECORD*, 20(4), 59-63, 1991.
5. S.B. Navathe, R. Elmasri, J.A. Larson, Integrating user views in database design, *IEEE Comput.* 19(1), 50-62, 1986.
6. L. Palopoli, D. Saccà, D. Ursino, Semi-automatic, semantic discovery of properties from database schemes, *Proc. IDEAS'98*, 244-253, IEEE Press, Cardiff, United Kingdom, 1998.
7. L. Palopoli, D. Saccà, D. Ursino, An Automatic Technique for Detecting Type Conflicts in Database Schemes, *Proc. ACM CIKM'98*, 306-313, Bethesda (Maryland), USA, 1998.
8. A. Sheth, J. Larson, A. Cornelio, S.B. Navathe, A tool for integrating conceptual schemata and user views, *Proceedings ICDE '88*, Los Angeles (California), USA, 176-183, 1988.
9. S.Spaccapietra, C.Parent, View Integration: A Step Forward in Solving Structural Conflicts, *IEEE TKDE* 6(2), 258-274, 1994.
10. G. Terracina, D. Ursino, A study on the interaction between interscheme property extraction and type conflict resolution. Submitted for publication. Available from the authors.
11. J. Widom, Research Problems in Data Warehousing, *Proc. CIKM '95, Proc. ACM CIKM '95*, 25-30, Baltimore (Maryland), USA, 1995.
12. G. Wiederhold, Mediators in the architecture of future information systems, *IEEE Computer*, 25(3), 38-49, 1992.

Dialogue Management in a Virtual College

Martin D. Beer[1], Trevor J. M. Bench-Capon[1], and Andrew Sixsmith[2]

[1] Department of Computer Science, University of Liverpool,
Chadwick Tower, Peach Street, LIVERPOOL. L69 7ZF United Kingdom.
mdb@csc.liv.ac.uk and tbc@csc.liv.ac.uk
[2] Institute of Human Ageing, University of Liverpool,
PO Box 147, LIVERPOOL. L69 3BX United Kingdom.

Abstract. The development of distributed high-bandwidth data networks at the home and business level allows many new distributed information services to be developed, based on the co-operation of autonomous agents and distributed information sources. Agents collaborate by passing messages in an agent communication language, such as KQML. The validity and meaning of these messages depends critically on the context of the communication of which they form a part. The conversation class to which the communication belongs determines this context.

This paper describes some of the problems associated with conversation classes derived from a distance learning application. We discuss the mechanisms necessary to satisfy a number of complex scenarios within the application domain, and show how these conditions need to be specified in terms of the policies and strategies of particular agents.

1 Introduction

Many new applications are being considered which rely on effective high capacity communication between stakeholders of various types. One architectural model that is being considered for such applications is that of co-operative agents. The fundamental requirement of an information system for widespread non-technical use is ease of use. While the use of a Web browser such as Internet Explorer or Netscape is acceptable for relatively sophisticated users, it is far from ideal for large-scale general use. In particular, problems have been identified with navigation when the information space becomes large and complex, and when World Wide Web servers become overloaded. This has led to a relatively passive environment, in which users seeking information have to collate and apply it themselves. We are currently investigating the use of intelligent agent based Internet technology to provide a much more flexible level of response than is currently possible. Example applications have been developed for both Distance Learning [1] and Community Care [2]. The basic architecture is that of Wiederhold [3], and is based on communication using performatives specified in KQML (Knowledge Query and Manipulation Language) [4].

The intention of this paper is to show how current research in distributed knowledge sharing and intelligent agents can be used to provide effective distributed services using agent-based techniques. The particular application considered is that of a 'Virtual College' environment [5]. The motivation for this study has been the design of an Occupational Therapy Internet School (OTIS), funded by the European Union [6]. If a single Internet School is to be developed over such a large geographical spread, effective communication mechanisms must be devised and implemented. Fortunately, for the pilot, the language of operation will be English, so that multi-lingual issues can be addressed at a later stage.

2 The 'Virtual College' Scenario

A basic Use-Case diagram is given in Figure 1, showing the principal actors involved, and some of the activities in which they are involved in the running of a course. In our model, a Course Director, who is responsible for ensuring its proper running and monitoring student activity, manages the course. Student support and assessment is undertaken by a number of Course Tutors, who each have a number of students assigned to them.

Courses are organised across institutions so the Course Director and the Course Tutors may well be in separate Institutions, using very different communications infrastructures. Our architecture allows them to use the systems with which they are most familiar, and to manage the necessary conversations through the use of wrappers. Wrappers provide the conversion facilities necessary to allow processing within the agent to be undertaken in whatever internal format is most appropriate, while communication between agents is in a common format (in our case KQML). Students will wish to communicate not only with the staff, but also with other students studying the same course.

3 System Architecture

All resource agents are required to *advertise* to the facilitator before they can accept communications of a particular type from other agents. This advertisement remains in force until the agent issues a corresponding *unadvertise*. For the purposes of this study, the message can be considered to be routed directly from the requesting to the responding agent. The facilitator simply acts as a name service. The User Agent acts as the interface for all actors, providing a common interface to all activities, no matter how and where they are provided.

A facilitator is first contacted to obtain the address of a suitable service mediator, to which an appropriate message is sent. This mediator directs the message to a suitable service provider after possibly adding additional information from the service database. Examples of information that may be added at this stage, are the validity of the student's registration, or the Course Tutor to whom the student is assigned. The service provider's mediator determines the appropriate course of action and forwards the message.

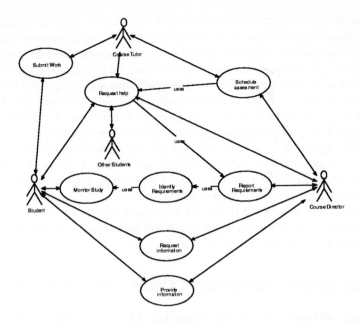

Fig. 1. A Basic Use-Case Analysis of managing a Virtual College Course

The facilitator therefore manages the routing of messages depending on the capability of the responding agent, whereas the mediator manipulates messages using its 'application domain knowledge' to decompose the problem and determine the most appropriate service to provide the necessary information. Once the requested information has been collected, the appropriate reply is formulated and the conversation is completed by its receipt by the requesting agent.

One of the main features of the work described is the specification of the conversational abilities of agents. In line with KQML [4], these are determined by a set of speech acts which that agent can perform, and another set to which it can respond. A speech act comprises a performative, indicating the illocutionary and intended perlocutionary force of the act, together with an argument, typically a proposition [7].

The semantics for the speech acts are as follows, following Labrou [8]:

1. a set of preconditions for the performance of the act,
2. a set of post-conditions to be enforced immediately on performance of the act, and
3. a set of completion conditions which are to apply when all the intentions associated with the act have been finally satisfied.

This means that the completion conditions may be achieved at some time after the communication being described has taken place, following some further conversation. Acts with such conditions can provide a context for later utterances.

Although performatives provide the building blocks for conversations between agents, they must be co-ordinated in a way that is appropriate to the particular conversation. The need for this co-ordination is shown by Barbuceanu et al [9]. It is possible to extend Labrou's method by representing the conversation rules as additional preconditions, postconditions and completion conditions on the speech acts they use. Experimental use of this approach has been reported in [10], which describes the specification of conversation rules for several dialogue games. In our particular application it is necessary to customise the act to particular agents. It is possible, for example, for confidentiality reasons, for an agent to be required not to respond to questions from some class of agents with a particular content. It may be that there is a rule that work for assessment can only be submitted to the appropriate course tutor, and the results returned only to the student who submitted it. We therefore need to impose further conditions on the performatives of a given agent which will be individual to the agent rather than derived from the conversation class.

4 Some Specific Instances of Conversation Classes

This section will show some of the situations that may be used to give preconditions, postconditions and completion conditions for the tell performative. We choose to express these conditions in terms made explicit within the context of the conversation itself.

4.1 Conditions Derived from the Conversation Classes

Within the context of a distance learning application, the conversations maintained between the agents in Figere 2 would be typical and fit well with the model that we have adopted. The student asks a question, which is to be answered by a Course Tutor. It is routed via a Mediator, which uses the information in a Student Registration Database to determine a list of appropriate Course Tutors to contact. This may be controlled by a number of factors known to the Mediator, for example:

1. Pass the query to the Course Tutor allocated to that student if the tutor is available
2. Otherwise it is passed to an appropriate Course Tutor, who is currently available to answer the query.

The Course Tutor receives the query and answers it. The answer is then passed back to the student along its original route. It is an implicit condition that the Course Tutor will only answer queries only from a student. This means that a course tutor can issue a in reply to an *ask* in this conversation class.

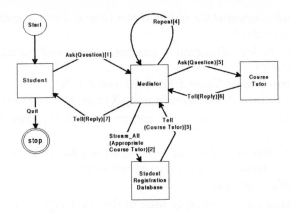

Fig. 2. The Conversation initiated by a Student Asking a Question

A set of preconditions and postconditions for each major stage (those in square brackets in Figure 2) in the conversation can be established as follows:

Once registered, a student can *ask* a question at any time. The student's Interface Agent passes the question to an appropriate Mediator, which will forward it to an appropriate Course Tutor [1]:

Precondition: X is a registered student?
Postcondition: create conversational instance and update records
Completion: Help request has been sent (*tell* [5] issued)

The Mediator obtains the names of appropriate Course Tutors from the student Registration Database [2]. Additional information, such as the identity of the tutor to whom the student is allocated can also be included, so that the question can be directed to the most appropriate tutor. The conditions for initiating this request are:

Precondition: A Question has been *ask*ed and no appropriate Tutor is known
Postcondition: Tutor I is appropriate to answer this question
Completion: Tutor I has answered the question satisfactorily[5]

And for the *tells* giving appropriate tutors [3]:

Precondition: A list of appropriate tutors has been requested
Postcondition: An appropriate Tutor I has been found
Completion: none

The database provides the identities of different course tutors singly, in an appropriate order of priority until a suitable Tutor is contacted, and the communication is terminated, or the list is exhausted [4]:

Precondition: No replies from a previous *ask* with same content
  There is a suitable Course Tutor available
Postcondition: Records updated
Completion: Reply [6] received

The Mediator forwards the question to a Course Tutor, starting with the most appropriate [5]:

Precondition: Question *q* has been *ask*ed and no *tell(q)* received

Postcondition: Tutor *I* has been *ask*ed *q* [5]

Completion: A satisfactory reply [6] has been received

The Course Tutor replies to the question, which is passed back to the Mediator [6]:

Precondition: Tutor has received an *ask* from the mediator

Postcondition: Tutor is committed to the reply

Completion: none

The Mediator passes the reply back to the student [7]:

Precondition: Mediator has received an *ask* from the student [1] and tutor is committed to the reply[6]

Postcondition: The mediator is committed to the reply

Completion: A reply is transmitted.

The query will often raise questions which the tutor considers to be of a wider interest, and which are best answered by telling all appropriate students the information given in the reply. An appropriate description of such a conversation is given in Figure 3. Here the problem is that the reply is being sent to a number of students who have not asked the appropriate question. This is handled by using the insert performative, which does not require the responding agent to have been asked before it can provide information to another agent.

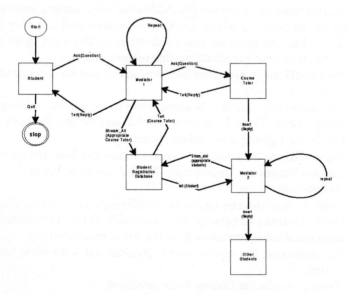

Fig. 3. Replying to a Student and Informing all Others of the Reply

The difficulty remains that the other students have not *asked* for the information being given, and have no basis on which to base their belief in the efficacy of the information included in it. Both inserts have the same properties:

Preconditions: A question has been *asked* and a *tell* has been issued
Postconditions: The sender is committed to the information contained in the message
Completion conditions: none

It will be seen that since the message is unsolicited, no preconditions or completion conditions apply to the receiving agent, and it is therefore always able to receive them. In this case, there are no difficulties with the other students believing the information as the students can be expected to believe implicitly any information provided by Course Tutors.

Another Conversation Class that poses interesting problems is that which controls the assessment process. The scenario in Figure 4 is that the Assessor provides model answers to Course Tutors who compare these with the answers submitted by the students, and enter their assessments in the appropriate database. Students have access to this database in some form, and can use this knowledge to allow them to progress to another module, or repeat the assessment if they have failed. If we follow the direction of the conversation, it will be seen to flow through a number of stages, with no agent replying directly to messages sent to it from another agent. This is because the Tutor is attempting to determine what the student believes to be the correct answer to the assessment. The Tutor, when marking the student's work, believes the Course Director's model answer is correct and assesses the student's work accordingly.

4.2 Conditions Derived From Policies and Heuristics

It is now necessary to consider the issues raised by the imposition of additional conditions required to customise the behaviour of agents in a given conversation class.

Preconditions Consider first a precondition for *tell*, found in Labrou's specification believes(S,X) If this is strictly imposed, an agent will only be able to commit to a proposition that it believes to be true. Adding this precondition thus gives an honest agent.

Take the case of the assessment scenario previously discussed. The course Director Agent sets an assignment to discover what the Student Agent 'believes'. The Course Tutor Agent, which could be a person or some form of automated agent (for example [11]), then compares the student's work against a model answer 'believing' that the model answer is the closest to the ideal. An assessment mark is determined by some measure of 'closeness' to this ideal, and this is entered into the result depository. The Student Agent 'believes' the accuracy of the results once they are stored in the Student Record. This relies on a number of specific 'beliefs' which are determined by the actions specified by the conversation class, rather than the form of the performatives used.

Another situation to be considered is where the agent has sensitive information, which can only be issued to a restricted group. A good example of this is the transmission of the model answer from the Course Director agent to the various Course Tutor agents. It is essential that this communication is received by the agents to whom it is addressed, and not intercepted by Student Agents. They could then subvert the assessment process by using this knowledge to provide an answer that does not represent what the agent 'believes' to be the correct answer, but what it 'believes' the assessment agent will accept as the correct answer.

Postconditions Postconditions help us to specify the effect of a performative. This will very often depend on the stance of the recipient. For example, a strongly credulous agent can be defined similarly, by adding the postcondition `believes(R,X)` This would cause the receiver to be permanently updated and any previously held beliefs of this form are discarded. This is very similar to committing the result at the end of a database transaction. Final reporting of the assessment mark is an activity of this type. It should be noted that these postconditions are entirely independent of the conversation class. The other agent need not be aware of what use is being made of the information, and only the receiving agent can be in a position to know what use is appropriate.

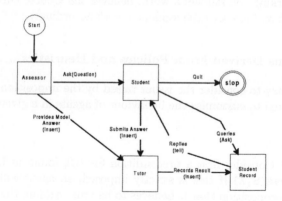

Fig. 4. The Assessment Conversation

Completion Conditions Policies and heuristics are less fruitful as a source of completion conditions, since a performative is complete once something has been agreed between the participants in the conversation. It should therefore be expected that these conditions derive always from the conversation class, and cannot, unlike preconditions and postconditions, be personal to an agent.

In our case completion conditions for the conversation not the acts, would be in the form:

For the student query scenario - that the query has been successfully answered (possibly after several supplementary questions), and that all other students have been informed, if necessary.

For the assessment scenario - that the work to be assessed has been received and the results to the student.

In the first case it may take several supplementary queries to ensure that a satisfactory reply has been given. Further communication with all other relevant students may also be required before completion can be achieved. In the second case, there may well be a rule that no assessments can be accepted after the first result has been returned. This may be enforced either by setting a latest hand-in date, or by waiting until all assessments expected have been received.

5 Discussion

The motivation for the analysis described here was to show that the communication between agents is characterised by the nature of the conversation between them, rather than the properties of the agents themselves or individual performatives consider out of context [12]. In the context of the distance learning scenario, the 'agents' include people, databases and expert systems. It does not matter which are to communicate, just the mode in which this communication is to take place. This is defined by the conversation class, within which performatives are defined to meet the overall requirements. In the context of different conversations a given performative may have different conditions associated with it. The conversation class says how a performative can be used, and sharing the conversation class harmonises the use of the particular set of performatives across agents. In order for effective communication to be possible, the communicators must operate within the same conversation class, so that they can share the conventions governing the use of the performatives.

6 Conclusions

This paper shows that by the adoption of appropriate conversation classes, it is possible to provide a wide range of services robustly and securely. One of the most important of these is ongoing educational activities, as it is increasingly required to update skills on a regular basis throughout life. It is an area where current Web based technology has been used effectively, but has proved not to be scalable when the number of students involved grows beyond certain limits. Simply adding additional servers is not a full answer, as effective distance learning systems require access to certain major information pools. These contain information on:

1. The course materials to be delivered
2. The students registered to take the course
3. Staff responsibilities and availability in the roles that they are expected to undertake
4. Student progress and assessment records

The definition of conversation classes between multiple agents allows these information sets to be separated. Adequate resources can then be allocated to the management and delivery of each. When a single agent is unable to handle the traffic directed to it, it can be replicated. The new agent needs to commit to the same conversation classes in order to perform all the necessary tasks, but does not need to be a clone of the original agent. This is because it does not have to commit to the policies and heuristics of the original to join the same conversation classes. The highly distributed nature of information delivery reduces the likelihood of bottlenecks as any agent that becomes overloaded can be replicated quite simply, without disturbing the stability of the rest of the system.

References

1. Wabi, J. (1998), Communication Requirements in Distance Learning Environments, MSc Dissertation, University of Liverpool.
2. Shin, A. P.J. (1998), INAS - Intelligent Alarm System for the Elderly, Honours Project Dissertation, University of Liverpool.
3. Wiederhold, G., (1992), Mediators in the Architecture of Future Computing Systems, IEEE Computer, 25(3), 38-49, March 1992.
4. Finnin, T., Labrou, Y. and Mayfield, J. (1997), KQML as an Agent Communication Language, MIT Press, Cambridge MA
5. Beer, M. D. (1997), Developing Distributed Learning Environments for the Workplace, ECSCW'97 Workshop on Network Communities: Supporting Community on the Net, Lancaster, UK, September 1997.
6. University of Liverpool, (1998) Occupational Therapy Internet School - OTIS, Submission to the European Union TEN Telecom Programme, June 1998.
7. Searle, J. R., (1969), Speech Acts: An Essay in the Philosophy of Language, Cambridge University Press
8. Labrou, Y., (1996), Semantics for an Agent Communication Language, PhD Thesis, University of Maryland, Baltimore.
9. Barbuceanu M and Fox M.S., (1995) COOL: A language for co-ordination in multi-agent systems. Procedings, 1st International Conference on Multi-Agent Systems, MIT Press, Cambridge. Mass.
10. Bench-Capon, T.J.M., (1998) Specification of Communication between Information Sources, Proceedings of DEXA98, Lecture Notes in Computer Science, 1460, Springer.
11. Benford, S. D., Burke, E. K., Foxley, E., Gutteridge, N. H. and Zin, A. M. (1994), Ceilidh as a Course Management Support System, The Journal of Educational Technology Systems, 22 (3) pp 235-250.
12. Carlson L. (1983), Dialogue Games: an approach to discourse analysis, Reidel, Dordrecht.

Meta Data Based EDI for Small Enterprises

Wolfram Wöß

Institute for Applied Knowledge Processing (FAW)
Johannes Kepler University Linz, Austria
e-mail: wwoess@faw.uni-linz.ac.at

Abstract. Today in many cases electronic data interchange is limited to large scale industry connected to their own value added networks. Small-scale enterprises are not yet integrated in the communication flow, because actual EDI solutions are to complex, to inflexible or to expensive.
The approach presented in this paper separates the knowledge about data structures and data formats from the process of the generation of destination files. This knowledge is transformed into a meta data structure which is stored within a database system. If any changes of the data interchange specification are necessary, it is sufficient to update the corresponding meta data information. The implementation of the data interchange processor remains unchanged. This type of adaptation does not require a software specialist and therefore it meets an important requirement of small-scale enterprises. Data transmission is done by using Internet technology.

1 Introduction

Electronic data interchange (EDI) is not a very new topic in computer science and computer technology. The basic idea of EDI is interchange of structured data between applications of participating communication partners without human intervention based on electronic transport media [1], [5].

Today Internet technology offers a medium for low-cost EDI. The following statement takes the importance of Internet technology as basic medium for EDI into account: EDI is the electronic exchange of business documents, business data and information using a public standard format. Increasingly the medium for sending and receiving EDI documents is the Internet [...]. In practice, EDI is an application-to-application system, where two EDI systems (applications) are communicating with each other without human intervention [2].

An important aspect of EDI is the standardization of data structures and protocols [3]. But in the last years many different standards have been developed, most of them suitable for a special business sector. Examples are: ODETTE (Organization for Data Exchange by TeleTransmission in Europe), VDAFS (Verband der Automobilindustrie Flächenschnittstelle) specialized for automobile industry, SEDAS specialized for trade companies, IGES (Initial Graphics Exchange Specification) and STEP (Standart d'Échange et de Transfert) specialized for producing enterprises. Some of these standards are in addition characterized by national restrictions.

This scenario of a large number of concurrent EDI standards leaded to the specification of ANSI X12 [2] and UN/EDIFACT (United Nations / Electronic Data Exchange For Administration, Commerce and Transport).

Both standards meet the demands for independence from manufacturer, hardware, software, national aspects and business area.

By exemplary discussing the EDIFACT standard, the following EDI scenario can be found out [1], [4]:

- Several versions of the EDIFACT specification have been developed.
- Incompatible standard-versions of EDIFACT are used.
- The result are several subsets (sub-standards) of EDIFACT which are only suitable for special applications. This is in contrast to the original idea of a common standard.
- The specification of the EDIFACT standard is complicated and therefore introduction and application of EDIFACT is time and cost intensive.
- EDIFACT was defined for machine processing and therefore EDIFACT messages are difficult to read for humans.

The mentioned drawbacks can be categorized into four problem areas:

- *Standards:* complicate standards that are characterized by an inflexible standardization procedure and which are suitable only for a few application scenarios.
- *Message-orientation:* classic EDI focuses only messages without consideration of the corresponding business processes and interactions.
- *Interpretation:* complex interpretation processes because EDI messages are defined for machine processing.
- *Costs:* the introduction of EDI is very time and cost intensive (hardware, software and network resources).

Due to the discussed problems, today EDI is limited to large-scale industry characterized by large and powerful EDP departments which are connected to VANs (value added networks).

Small-scale enterprises are not yet integrated in these communication possibilities, because actual EDI solutions are to complex, to inflexible or to expensive.

In this paper a configurable interface for EDI based on meta data is introduced, which allows to administrate several interfaces for data interchange with other business partners. The basic concept of this approach is to transform information about data interchange formats and data structures in the form of meta data into a database system. After a request, the data interchange processor transforms the required information into the destination format which depends on the corresponding meta data. Data interchange is possible in both directions, to and from a communication partner.

This approach focuses the special requirements of small-scale enterprises:

- high flexibility,
- lean administration and
- low costs.

The paper proceeds as follows: Section 2 starts with a discussion of general problems with EDI in small-scale enterprises, which are characterized by lean organizations and low EDP budgets. In Section 3 the concept of the meta data based data interchange processor is introduced. This section includes a description of the system architecture and an example of the required meta data. Section 4 concludes and gives an outlook on future research.

2. Problems with EDI in Small-scale Enterprises

Today the EDIFACT standard dominates wide areas of business to business EDI. The basic components of EDIFACT are a vocabulary (specified in directories), character sets and its grammar. EDIFACT is based on pre-defined separation signs which separate single data elements from each other.

The vocabulary of EDIFACT consists of data elements, data element groups, segments, messages and message groups. These components are organized in a hierarchical order. Figure 1 shows this hierarchy up to data element groups.

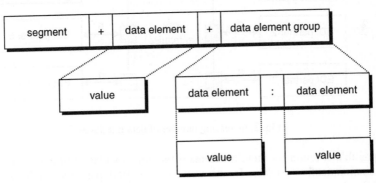

Fig. 1. Structure of an EDIFACT segment.

The set of segments which is necessary to describe a business transaction is called message. Single messages are itself combined to message groups. In general an EDIFACT communication consists of a set of messages groups which are integrated to a single EDIFACT file. The communication between two EDIFACT partners is asynchronous.

The components of an EDIFACT file are specified in "directories", which are updated periodically to fulfill industrial demands. A correct EDIFACT communication requires identical versions of EDIFACT components at both communication partners [1]. This demand significantly increases the administration effort which is necessary to establish a correct and efficient EDIFACT communication.

In general, large-scale enterprises have powerful organizations including an EDP department. Though the application of EDIFACT results in additional administration tasks, enterprises of this type make use of the rationalization potential in this field. Today in many cases the following scenario can be found out: a large-scale enterprise dominates a group of smaller suppliers by giving detailed specifications of the communication operations, including the physical network, the communication protocol and the data structures. In this case the consequence is that the advantages of EDI are only for the benefit of the large enterprise [5].

To overcome some of the discussed problems EDI clearing centers have been established. The main functionality of an EDI clearing center is the conversion of plain data into the requested EDIFACT data format in both conversion directions. The consequence is that the administration effort to establish EDIFACT data interchange is transferred from a small enterprise to the EDI clearing center. But at the same time a third communication partner, the EDI clearing center, is involved with the data interchange process. On the one hand this approach decreases the administration costs of the smaller enterprise on the other hand the EDI process is more inflexible. As a second aspect the EDIFACT overhead has to be considered. The question is: Why put up with the whole EDIFACT overhead if only a very simple data structure has to be transferred?

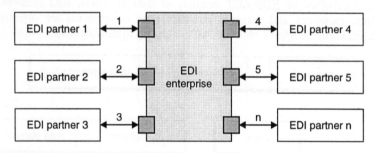

Fig. 2. Increasing number of data interfaces.

One possible solution for these problems is the implementation of a data interface per EDI communication partner. In the worst case n EDI partners require n different interfaces (Figure 2). In this situation the implementation and maintenance of the whole set of interfaces is very time and cost intensive.

The approach presented in this paper stores the information about data structures and data formats in the form of meta data within a central database. After a request, the data interchange processor transforms the required information into the destination format which depends on the corresponding meta data. Then data files are ready for electronic transmission. If changes of the specification of the destination data format are necessary it is sufficient to update the corresponding meta data information within the database. The implementation of the data interchange processor remains unchanged. This type of adaptation requires neither a database administrator nor a software engineer. Therefore this concept meets the special requirements of small-scale enterprises.

Section 3 introduces the concept of the meta data based data interchange processor in detail.

3. The Meta Data Based Data Interchange Processor

As discussed in Section 1 and Section 2 there are two contrary ways to solve the data interchange problem:

- Definition of a common standard which covers nearly all possible data interchange scenarios. This approach results in a complex interface specification with a more or less great overhead.
- Implementation of a data interface per EDI communication partner. In the worst case *n* EDI partners require *n* different interfaces.

In contrast to many existing systems the approach presented in this paper separates the knowledge about data structures and data formats from the processes of the generation of destination files and electronic transmission.
To establish such a system three components are necessary (Figure 3):

- *Meta data* about data structures and data formats is stored within a central database.
- The *interface management module* is necessary to administrate the meta data information which represents an individual data interface to a communication partner.
- The *data interchange processor* in the first step receives input data which has to be transformed into the required destination format. In the next step the processor reads the meta data information corresponding to the required destination format. Based on this meta data the destination data file is generated dynamically.

The data interchange processor does not determine the type of electronic transmission of the destination files. Especially for small-scale enterprises Internet technology offers a medium for low-cost file transmission. Beside low costs the advantages of an Internet solution in this context are its availability, flexibility and the standard protocol TCP/IP. Moreover, a number of additional features like WWW and e-mail are available.

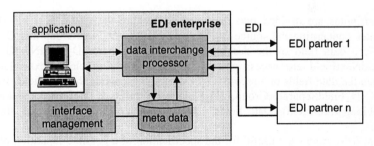

Fig. 3. Components of meta data based EDI.

To realize the introduced concept of a configurable data interface the knowledge about each destination file format is transformed into a meta data structure which is stored within a relational database system. The following tables are simplified representations of these meta data tables.

The table *destination_file* contains a reference to the first data field of a record of the destination file. Moreover, it includes information about the EDI partner, the corresponding application, the name of the destination file and the name of the source file. The attribute "direction" specifies the data interchange direction. *Construction* means data interchange to an EDI partner and *translation* means data interchange from an EDI partner.

destination_file								
EDI_partner	Application	D_File	D_FileNo	D_FieldGroup	D_FieldNo	S_File	Direction
Miller	order	order.new	1	1	1	ord.txt	construct

The table *destination_file_field_order* contains the data field specification of a record of the destination file. In this example a column of the table is equivalent to a tuple of the database table.

destination_file_field_order						
D_FileNo	1	1	1	1	1	1
D_FieldGroup	1	2	3	3	3	4
D_FieldNo	1	1	1	2	3	1
D_FieldStartsGroup	-	-	1	1	1	-
D_FieldStart	1	10	21	30	37	41
D_FieldLength	8	10	8	6	3	6
D_FieldType	char	char	char	num	num	int
D_FieldSeparatorGroup			:	:	:	
D_FieldSeparatorField	;	;	;	;	;	;
D_FieldName	Customer	Town	Product	Price	Quantity	OrderNo
D_FieldNextGroup	2	3	3	3	4	
D_FieldNextField	1	1	2	3	1	
S_FieldStart	17	6	33	42	49	57
S_FieldLength	8	10	8	6	3	4
S_FieldType	char	char	char	num	num	int
S_FieldSeparatorGroup			+	+	+	
S_FieldSeparatorField	;	;	;	;	;	;
S_FieldName	Customer	Place	Part	Price	Quantity	Order

The attributes are divided into attributes concerning the destination file (D_) and attributes concerning the source file (S_). D_FileNo, D_FieldGroup and D_FieldNo identify a data field of the destination file. The attributes D_FieldNextGroup and D_FieldNextField are necessary for the specification of clear next relationships between the data fields of a record. Field separators separate the data fields from each other (D_FieldSeparatorGroup, D_FieldSeparatorField, S_FieldSeparator-Group, S_FieldSeparatorField). Data fields may be organized in groups or as single data fields.

Data field groups are useful for the specification of a possible repetition of a set of data fields. For example, part number, quantity and price are combined to a customer order position within a customer order, which itself may consist of a set of customer order positions. D_FieldStartsGroup specifies the first data field within a data field group. In case of a repetition of the data field group this information is necessary for data interchange processor to generate the data field sequence in correct order.

D_FieldStart, D_FieldLength, D_FieldType and D_FieldName are well known attributes of a data field specifying the starting position, the length of the data field, its data type and its name.

The main advantage of the presented approach is that the knowledge about data structures and data formats is separated from the processes of the generation of destination files and electronic transmission. The consequence is that if changes of the data interchange specification to or from an EDI partner are necessary, it is sufficient to update the meta data information (knowledge). The implementation of the data interchange processor remains unchanged. This type of adaptation requires neither a database administrator nor a software engineer.

A second important advantage of the introduced concept is, that the form of data transmission is not pre-defined. The Internet offers a low-cost medium for flexible data interchange with excellent availability. Internet technology in combination with the introduced concept of meta data based EDI meets the special requirements of small-scale enterprises characterized by a low number of data interchange transactions.

A prototype of the meta data based data interchange processor is almost finished. In the next step we will focus on

- the integration of customers and
- the cooperation between departments.

Both aspects require improved and easy to use EDI features. The World Wide Web (WWW) provides a unified platform in combination with an easy-to-use user interface. The implementation of a customer order form on a WWW client demonstrates the wide spectrum of EDI possibilities. It reaches from a simple transmission of data in one direction from the customer to the enterprise up to bi-directional transmission of data based on Java technology [6]. In this case the Web-browser is not only a own-way data presentation interface but a real two-way application. In addition the introduction of VRML 2.0 (Virtual Reality Modeling Language) makes the presentation of 3-dimensional data (pictures) on a WWW client possible [7]. VRML is not a programming language but a modeling language which allows to model 3D objects. The main advantage of VRML is that the visualization of data is independent from the generating system (for example a CAD system). But VRML is not only useful for visualization of data. It also allows to define behavior of objects and therefore VRML makes process simulations possible [6]. VRML is a powerful extension of conventional WWW applications, especially for EDI between several departments of an enterprise (CAD data) as well as between the customer an the enterprise. For example, the customer specification of a final product may be generated and immediately visualized on a WWW client.

Conventional Web applications are based on HTML (HyperText Markup Language). In contrast to HTML which aims at the *presentation* of information the new meta language XML (eXtensible Markup Language) focuses on *structuring* of information. Structuring of data is also the most important process of an EDI application. Therefore XML seems to be a flexible concept for the specification of an EDI message. For example, it is possible to model existing message types of EDIFACT as XML messages. The main advantages of XML based EDI are high flexibility and low implementation costs. In combination with XSL (eXtensible Style Language) XML is a tool for structuring information and for its presentation. EDI messages are not longer specialized for machine-processing but also easy to ready for humans [8].

4 Conclusions

As discussed in Section 1 and Section 2, today in many cases EDI is limited to large-scale industry characterized by great and powerful EDP departments which are connected to VANs (value added networks). Small-scale enterprises are not yet integrated in these communication possibilities, because actual EDI solutions are to complex, to inflexible or to expensive.

In this paper a configurable interface for EDI based on meta data is introduced, which allows to administrate a number of interfaces for data interchange with other business partners efficiently. The special requirements of small-scale enterprises are the focus of interest: high flexibility, lean administration processes and low costs.

In contrast to many existing systems the presented approach separates the knowledge about data structures and data formats from the processes of the generation of destination files and electronic transmission. The knowledge about each destination file format is transformed into a meta data structure which is stored within a relational database system. After a request, the data interchange processor transforms the required information into the destination format which depends on the corresponding meta data. The main advantage of this concept is that if changes of the data interchange specification to or from an EDI partner are necessary, it is sufficient to update the corresponding meta data information. The implementation of the data interchange processor remains unchanged. This type of adaptation requires neither a database administrator nor a software engineer and therefore it meets the special requirements of small-scale enterprises.

Further work will be concentrated on additional integration of WWW and Internet technology. Focus of interest will be EDI between customers and the enterprise as well as cooperation between departments of an enterprise.

The advantages of EDI based on Internet and WWW are [9]:

- a uniform and standardized protocol (TCP/IP),
- availability of several kinds of services based on the same platform and user interface,
- ease-to-use services,
- multi-media presentation of data,
- linked information and
- low costs in comparison to many VANs.

Additionally, new concepts and technologies like VRML and XML in combination with XSL open new possibilities for the implementation of Web based EDI.

References

1. Schmoll, Thomas: Handelsverkehr elektronisch, weltweit: Nachrichtenaustausch mit EDI/EDIFACT. Markt & Technik Verlag, München (1994)
2. Netscape: Electronic Data Interchange (EDI) Fundamentals. Netscape Communications Inc., California, USA (1998)
3. Picot, Arnold: Strategische, organisatorische und wirtschaftliche Perspektiven von EDI. In: Software AG (ed.): EDI Congress, Wiesbaden, BRD (1991)
4. Kalakota, R., Whinston, A.: Frontiers of Electronic Commerce. Addison-Wesley Publishing, USA (1996)
5. Alpar, P., Pickerodt, S.: Electronic Commerce im Internet – ein Überblick. Industrie Management 14 (1998), No. 1, GITO-Verlag Berlin (1998)
6. Knechtel, Ulrich: Produktdatenmanagement im Intranet/Extranet. Industrie Management 14 (1998), No. 1, GITO-Verlag Berlin (1998)
7. Hartmann, J., Wernecke, J.: The VRML 2.0 Handbook. Addison-Wesley Publishing USA (1996)
8. Ebner, Winfried: Mit XML in die Zukunft. AustriaPro Nachrichten 16 (1999), No. 1, Austria
9. Lackes, Richard: Intranets als Teil betrieblicher Informationssysteme. Industrie Management 14 (1998), No. 1, GITO-Verlag Berlin (1998)

Database Challenges for Genome Information in the Post Sequencing Phase

Fouzia Moussouni[1], Norman W. Paton[1], Andy Hayes[2], Steve Oliver[2]
Carole A. Goble[1] and Andy Brass[2]

[1] Department of Computer Science, University of Manchester,
Oxford Road, Manchester M13 9PL, UK
(fouzia,norm,carole)@cs.man.ac.uk,
`http://img.cs.man.ac.uk`
[2] School of Biological Sciences, University of Manchester,
Oxford Road, Manchester M13 9PL, UK
abrass@man.ac.uk
`http://bioinf.man.ac.uk`

Abstract. Genome sequencing projects are making available to scientists complete records of the genetic make-up of organisms. The resulting data sets, along with the results of experiments that seek systematically to find new information on the functions of genes, will present numerous opportunities and challenges to biologists. However, the complexity and variety of both the data and the analyses required over such data sets also pose significant challenges to computer scientists charged with providing effective information management systems for use with genome data. This paper presents models for the sorts of information that are being produced on genomes and genome-wide experiments, and outlines a project developing an information management system aimed at supporting analyses over genomic data. This information management system replicates data from other sources, with a view to providing an integrated environment for performing complex analyses.

1 Introduction

The recent availability to biologists of the sequences of complete genomes provides new opportunities for identifying and understanding properties of the genome that have hitherto been out of reach, and for conducting comparisons of genomes. The exploitation of this new information resource is, however, dependent upon the provision of effective tools for the management, integration and presentation of genome and related information.

This paper provides an overview of the current information management challenges posed by the presence of an increasing number of complete genome sequences. Genome sequencing has presented information management challenges throughout the '90s, but most attention to date has been focused on supporting the sequencing effort [DTM92,Goo95], rather than on tools for underpinning analysis over the completed sequence. These tasks are significantly different. For example, much of the data gathered and stored during sequencing is used principally during the construction of the complete sequence, and is of less interest after the genome has been fully sequenced. In addition, analysis of genomes requires access to data sets that are not relevant to the sequencing process, and some of which cannot be constructed until much of the genome is in place.

It is well known that the sequencing of the human genome is well underway; the complete human genome can be expected to have been sequenced by around 2003. However, having access to the complete sequence and making sense of the complete sequence are two quite different things, as the function of many of the genes discovered in a genome will not be known. As a result, a range of model organisms are being sequenced with a view to allowing comparisons to be made between the genomes of these organisms and the human genome. These organisms, of which *Saccharomyces cerevisiae* (a yeast) and *C. elegans* (a nematode) are two examples, generally have much smaller genomes than the human genome, and can be experimented on more easily than human subjects.

As well as having access to fully sequenced organisms for the first time, various new experimental techniques promise to provide large, important, and challenging to analyse data sets. For example, DNA chips (or arrays) [Dav98] allow experiments to be carried out that enable the levels of expression of different genes in the cell to be measured under different conditions. The level of expression of a gene is related to the amount of the gene being produced in the cell. Relating the levels of expression of the genes to the behaviour of the cell can provide insights into the purpose of the genes. It is now the case that changes in the levels of expression of genes across the whole genome across a range of conditions can be detected in a single experiment. In yeast, for example, there are around 6000 genes, and a single experiment could identify gene expression levels for each of these genes as many as 20 times, thereby providing an indication of how levels of gene activity fluctuate. This one form of experiment is of great interest to researchers seeking to understand what genes do and how cells work, but promises to deliver huge amounts of data over the next few years.

This paper discusses the information management challenges presented by recent advances in genomics, and presents ongoing work in the Genome Information Management System (GIMS) project. GIMS is a collaborative research project involving computer scientists, bioinformaticians and yeast genome researchers, which is using object database technology to support the storage and analysis of genomic and related data. The paper is structured as follows. Section 2 presents the schema used to model core genome data. Section 3 outlines some of the novel data sets that are associated with genomic data, and shows how they can be modelled. Section 4 provides an overview of the GIMS database being used to support genome data storage and analysis. Section 5 presents some conclusions.

2   Modelling Genomic Data

This section describes the basic information that must be stored to describe a fully sequenced genome. The schema diagram for the core data set is presented in figure 1. The schema designs in this and subsequent sections are presented using object modelling techniques because our target implementation platform, as described in Section 4, is an ODMG compliant object database. Furthermore, as the initial focus of the GIMS project is on the *Saccharomyces cerevisiae* (yeast) genome, the models presented must be understood in this context. Although we have sought to design generic models that will be usable with other species, we only have experience populating the model with Yeast data.

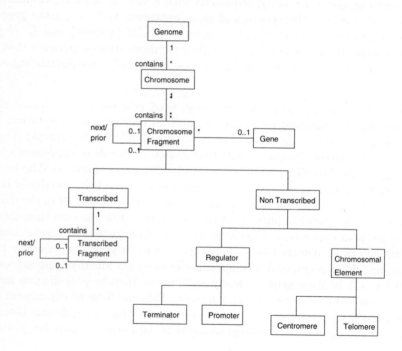

Fig. 1. Basic schema diagram for genomic data.

The model in figure 1 describes the basic components of a genome. The complete *genome* consists of a collection of chromosomes. Each *chromosome* can be considered to be a long sequence of DNA, which in turn consists of a sequence of fragments of DNA. These fragments are either *transcribed* regions of DNA or *non transcribed* regions. The transcription of DNA is the conversion of DNA into RNA, which is a preliminary step in the production of proteins. Proteins do most of the work in a cell. The non transcribed chromosome fragments often have some function relating to the replication of the cell or control of the production of proteins.

The *transcribed* chromosome fragments are illustrated more fully in figure 2. Each *transcribed* region contains a collection of *transcribed fragments*. Each of the transcribed fragments is either an *intron* or a *spliced transcript component*. Basically, a length of sequence from a DNA molecule is translated into a protein sequence, but some parts of the DNA are omitted – these are the introns.

The *spliced transcript components* are then assembled (with the *introns* removed) to form spliced transcripts. Each *spliced transcript* is associated with a length of RNA, which may serve some functional purpose in the translation process (*tRNA*) or be translated into a protein by way of an *open reading frame* (or *ORF*).

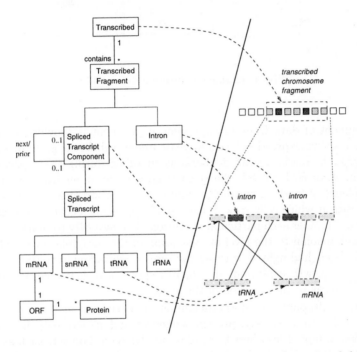

Fig. 2. Fragment of schema diagram with illustration of associated data.

3 Managing Expression Data

Expression data across all the genes in a cell (the transcriptome), as mentioned in Section 1, is an important new category of information about levels of gene activity in a cell [Dav98]. In essence, in yeast, expression data provides a measure of the amount of every gene in the organism that is present in a cell at different points in time. Given that the points in time may be associated with some sort of condition, it is possible to identify what genes become more or less active in response to, for example, the introduction of a drug, or a change in environmental conditions.

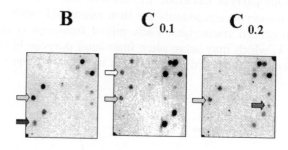

Fig. 3. Example expression data results.

A fragment of data from an expression experiment is provided in figure 3. This figure shows expression levels in yeast under 3 different growth conditions – these growth conditions are deliberately modified during the experiment. In essence, in state B, for *batch*, the yeast is growing in an environment in which there is plenty of food. In states $C_{0.1}$ and $C_{0.2}$, there are nutrients present that limit the rate at which cells grow. Each "spot" represents a gene that is expressed ("turned on") under each particular condition. The intensity (or darkness) of the spot is proportional to the level of expression of the particular gene. The spots that have been highlighted with arrows are potentially interesting, since the context (i.e. growth condition) in which a spot, or rather gene, is turned on provides clues as to the function of the gene.

However, although bioinformaticians are experienced in interpreting some forms of biological data (e.g. protein sequences and structures), there is much less understanding of how best to conduct analyses on data sets such as the one shown. It is clear, though, that there will certainly be lessons to be learned from relating the expression data to other data sets. For example, the relationship between the levels of expression and the location of genes within the genome could lead to lessons being drawn about the nature of genome organisation. This means that there is a need for the expression data to be fully integrated with the core genome data.

A conceptual model for describing gene expression data is provided in figure 4. The *mRNA* class is common to this schema diagram and that in figure 1. Each *experiment* has a collection of *measurement points*, each of which is at some *time* from the start of the experiment. Each *measurement point* associates a collection of *expression events* with a description of the *conditions* at which the events were recorded. Each *expression event* captures the quantity of a particular gene expressed at the time of the *measurement point*. To relate this model with the experimental values in figure 3: each *mRNA* fragment represents a position in the array; the *level* of each *expression event* represents the intensity of the "spot" at a specific position; there is a separate image of the array for each *measurement point*, and the *condition* and *condition degree* classes represent the labels on the images of the arrays, such as B and $C_{0.1}$.

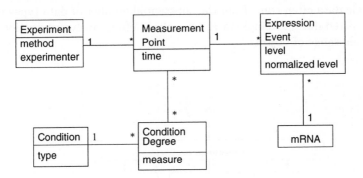

Fig. 4. Schema for gene expression data.

4 The Genome Information Management System

This section presents an overview of the GIMS project. In particular, an outline is given of the architecture of the system, and examples are given to illustrate the sorts of analyses that are being carried out.

4.1 Architecture

GIMS can be seen as a scientific data warehouse, in a problem domain that is characteristic of the sorts of application in which the warehousing approach is relevant. In [Wid95], it is stated that the warehousing approach is appropriate in applications in which:

- Clients require specific, predictable portions of the available information.
- Clients require high performance.
- Native applications at the information sources require high performance.
- Clients want access to private copies of the information so that it can be modified, annotated and summarised.

All of these points are applicable to genome information management. However, there are a number of ways in which genome information management differs from classical business data warehousing applications:

- The core data set is much more complex (i.e. the core data set is that of the genome, rather than, for example, a collection of sales transactions).

- The data sets that "surround" the core data set in *star schemas* are themselves likely to be complex, containing experimental results (e.g. expression data, protein-protein interaction data), rather than more straightforward product or supplier information.
- The role of aggregation in analyses is currently seen as less central to genome information management. Instead, the complexities in the analysis of genomic data often come from the substantial number of data types that may be visited during a single task, as analyses often involve navigation through a wide range of objects.

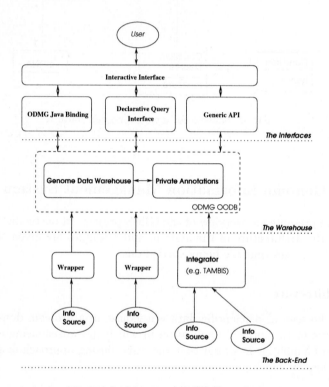

Fig. 5. Architecture of GIMS system.

The architecture of the GIMS system is outlined in figure 5. The core warehouse is an ODMG compliant object database [C+97], in our case POET. This is accessed by the user interface through the standard ODMG Java binding, declarative query languages (both OQL and the deductive language DOQL [PS98] are supported), and a generic application programming interface. The latter is necessary because some features of the user interface require access to the database in a manner that is data type independent. For example, the classes used to implement forms in the browser illustrated in figure 6 are generic in the sense that their implementation contains no domain specific code – the same user interface classes could be used to browse instances from any database.

At present the core warehouse is populated principally using data from MIPS [MAH⁺97], and associated information is generally drawn via wrappers from remote sites.

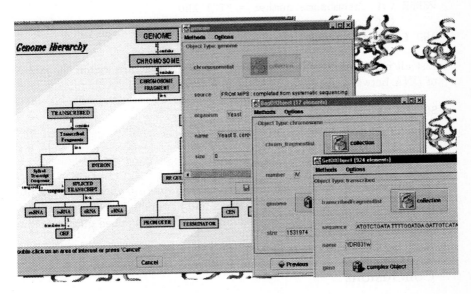

Fig. 6. Schema based genome browser.

4.2 Queries and Analyses

There are three principal means of access to the GIMS database – an interactive browser, textual queries, and canned queries. The interactive browser, is illustrated in figure 6. This allows users to browse class extents, and navigate along relationships between classes. The browser makes the schema of the database explicit to the users – users of some other genome databases report that they get lost when navigating around the database. We have thus sought to produce a model that is biologically intuitive to the users, so that it can be used as a way of explaining what information is available. It is anticipated that eventually a range of visualisations will be used for presenting information within the browser. However, most users are interested in performing queries or analyses over the database, and a substantial list of analysis tasks has been identified in a requirements analysis activity.

Analyses and retrieval requests can be phrased against the GIMS database using OQL, or by way of canned queries. The following are example OQL queries:

- List all transcribed chromosome fragments of size greater than 3500, which are within the stretch of DNA between position 20000 and position 210000 of chromosome I.

```
SELECT cf
FROM cf IN transcribedExtent
WHERE (cf.chromosome.number = "I") AND
      (cf.position >= 20000 OR cf.position >= 210000)
AND (cf.size > 3500)
```

- List all non transcribed chromosome fragments that are within the stretch of DNA between position and 250000 of chromosome I.

```
SELECT nt
FROM nt IN non_transcribedExtent
WHERE (nt.chromosome.number = "I") AND
      (cf.position >= 1 OR cf.position >= 250000)
```

The database can be also queried with canned queries, which are Java programs that allow users interactively to select and parameterise common requests over the database. The searches carried out in support of canned queries are implemented using the ODMG Java binding.

5 Conclusions

Novel applications have long been seen as effective drivers for the development of new information management technologies. When object databases were first proposed, it was often with design or environmental applications in mind. However, although object databases are now being applied to a wide range of applications, there has not been widespread attention given to the use of object databases in distinctive warehousing applications.

This paper has described a category of scientific data warehousing application that we believe will become extremely important in the near future. The sequencing of the human genome will provide among the most important information resources in science. However, it is clear that the information storage and analysis challenges of genomics are extremely great. Effective analysis of genomes will require high performance access to a diverse collection of complex information resources, which are typically developed at a range of sites. These information resources are made available in a wide range of formats, and generally in a form that allows the data to be browsed or downloaded, but not necessarily analysed effectively in conjunction with other information sources.

A range of researchers have investigated tools for distributed querying of biological sequence information sources (e.g. [BDH+95,CKMS97,BBB+98]), but although some of the authors are involved in one such activity, we believe that the warehousing approach will be at least as relevant in the genomic area. The key difference in genomics is that typical analyses are likely to be much more complex than in non genomic bioinformatics. In genomics, value is added through the close association of specific data resources, so that genomes can be compared with each other, and information from large scale experiments, such as those relating to gene expression and protein-protein interactions, is easily associated and displayed.

The GIMS project is using object database technology to support storage and analysis of genomic data. This paper has presented models of some of the information of relevance to GIMS, and has indicated how the GIMS system is being used to support querying and analysis of this data. Current activities are extending the range of different types of experimental data within the GIMS system, and developing single and multiple genome analyses.

Acknowledgements: This work is supported by the BBSRC/EPSRC Bioinformatics Programme, whose support we are pleased to acknowledge. We have also benefited from input from a number of colleagues, including Simon Hubbard and Robert Stevens.

References

[BBB+98] P.G. Baker, A. Brass, S. Bechhofer, C.A. Goble, N.W. Paton, and R. Stevens. TAMBIS - Transparent Access to Multiple Biological Information Sources. In *Proc. Int. Conf. on Intelligent Systems for Molecular Biology*, pages 25–34. AAAI Press, 1998.

[BDH+95] P. Buneman, S.B. Davidson, K. Hart, C. Overton, and L. Wong. A Data Transformation System for Biological Data Sources. In *Proc. 21st VLDB*, pages 158–169. Morgan Kaufmann, 1995.

[C+97] R.G.G. Cattell et al. *The Object Database Standard: ODMG 2.0*. Morgan Kaufmann, 1997.

[CKMS97] I-Min A. Chen, A.S. Kosky, V.M. Markowitz, and E. Szeto. Constructing and Maintaining Scientific Database Views in the Framework of the Object Protocol Model. In *Proc. SSDBM*. IEEE Press, 1997.

[Dav98] B. Daviss. What silicon chips have done for computers, DNA chips may do for biological research. *New Scientist*, November:47–50, 1998.

[DTM92] R. Durbin and J. Thierry-Mieg. ACeDB – A C.elegans Database. Technical report, December 1992. Available at http://probe.nalusda.gov:8000/acedocs/index.html.

[Goo95] N. Goodman. An Object-Oriented DBMW War Story: Developing a Genome Mapping Database in C++. In *Modern Database Systems*. Addison-Wesley, 1995.

[MAH+97] H.W. Mewes, K. Albermann, K. Heumann, S. Liebl, and F. Pfeiffer. MIPS: a database for protein sequences, homology data and yeast genome information. *Nucleic Acids Research*, 25(1):28–30, 1997.

[PS98] N.W. Paton and P.R. Sampaio. Extending the ODMG Architecture with a Deductive Object Query Language. In S.M. Embury et al., editors, *Proc. 16th British National Conference on Databases*, pages 149–164. Springer-Verlag, 1998.

[Wid95] J. Widom. Research Problems in Data Warehousing. In *Proc. 4th Int. Conf. on Information and Knowledge Management*, pages 25–30, November 1995.

Supporting Teams in Virtual Organizations

I.T. Hawryszkiewycz
School of Computing Sciences
University of Technology, Sydney
PO Box 123, Broadway, NSW 2007, Australia
(e-mail: igorh@socs.uts.edu.au)

Abstract. Virtual organizations are characterized by their dynamic nature and transient work arrangements. This in turn requires computer toolkits that go beyond workflow systems to provide support for process emergence and continually varying team members. Such toolkits must allow users to quickly form teams, allocate responsibilities, and set up support services. The paper describes requirements placed on such toolkits by the nature of collaborative work and describes the feasibility of meeting them by illustrating a prototype toolkit that meets such requirements.

1 Introduction

Globalization of organizations is placing new requirements on computer support for their information systems. One aspect is such support are ways to bring together teams of people separated by distance, to carry out organizational goals, which usually call for the creation of new services or products. Ways to progress to these goals, while using the best available expertise, must also be found. In virtual environments such teams may include participants, who may join teams for short periods of time to contribute expertise whenever it is needed. Generically, processes followed by such teams are emergent and can be characterized as innovation (Kuczmarski, 1997) processes, or processes that support personalized and varying client needs. The ability to support emergent and rapidly changing processes places a number of requirements on computer support toolkits, which are provided to distributed users. These toolkits must be able to set up systems that provide users with easy access to specialized knowledge (Grant, 1995), both explicit and tacit, and to combine such knowledge to create new knowledge forms. They must enable individuals to participate in many teams and to easily move between the teams. This in turn requires flexible governance structures (Jones, et.al. 1997) and awareness mechanisms to ensure that distributed workspace activities converge to a common aim.

The flexible nature of virtual work thus has an impact on both the design methods to model it, and the technologies to implement the models. Different modeling methods than those used with predefined processes are needed. Similarly, technologies to support virtual work no longer emphasize the more defined workflows that characterize traditional processes but must support emergent processes. These technologies must allow flexible combinations of modules to support a variety of ever changing personal interactions. What is needed are flexible groupware systems and toolkits that can be used to compose workspaces dynamically. Toolkits themselves must be based on terms that can be used to express a wide variety of activities. This results in modeling taking a new goal. It is to identify the generic terms to describe emergent processes. Such terms are then directly implemented as components in groupware toolkits, and are used to dynamically specify new work units and collaboration between them.

This paper describes a toolkit called LiveNet, which is being developed to satisfy these requirements and which is bases on tested modeling terms (Hawryszkiewycz, 1997). The toolkit provides the support through shared workspace systems. Before doing so the paper will describe requirements in more detail. It will then outline a way to model the emergent processes found in virtual work. This will define a set of modeling terms, which are directly implemented by the toolkit.

2 Toolkit Requirements for Virtual Teams

We see requirements falling into a number of categories, namely:

Establishment of a context for collaborative work, which includes **bringing together** all the objects and people in a collaborative context into the one workspace, and the **ability to quickly locate needed information.** This requires the ability to quickly find the explicit information needed by a newly established task as well people who possess the tacit information.

Support for emergent processes, which characterize work in virtual organizations. Emergent processes are a direct opposite of the commonly found predefined production workflows, which are made up of a number of predefined tasks that are executed in some defined sequence. Emergent processes, on the other hand, are opportunistic in nature and are often characterized by parallel and disconnected activities that must be coordinated to meet global goals (Dourish, 1998). They not only imply that the process steps can be carried out in different sequences but even that new tasks can be created dynamically as unexpected situations and consequent goals emerge.

Support for flexible team formation and governance, including the **redefinition of and dynamic creation of tasks** and support for **dynamic team structures**. In addition **evolving governance** must be supported as cooperative work must provide a balance of sharing and open access while at the same time providing governance structures to ensure consistency with the organizational culture. **Interaction support** so that team members must constantly keep in touch, both synchronously and asynchronously, and quickly build meaningful relationships oriented to system goals.

Provision of status support through awareness and common understanding of goals, so that team members are kept aware of the goal of their work, how their work fits in with other people, and what milestones must be maintained. Furthermore, in emergent processes these goals and milestones themselves change and team members must be kept aware of any such changes. Awareness can be classed in two ways. One is *awareness of current status*, which includes obvious features such as news items, but also ways to allow newcomers to quickly become aware of the current situation, the ability to deal with unusual events. Additional class of features center on *support for organizational memory*, so that people can quickly find out how similar situations were treated in the past.

Generic modules, which include **greater emphasis on knowledge sharing** work. Work is now departing from well defined tasks, such as setting up a spreadshhet, to more knowledge oriented work requiring people to quickly make sense of situations in related domains, and interpret them in their own context. There is the need to analyze increasingly specialized knowledge and to bring together explicitly stored knowledge and tacit knowledge possessed by individuals (Nonaka, 1996). Team members from different backgrounds must be able to quickly arrive at common terminologies so that they for example describe the need to form perspectives (Boland and Tensaki, 1995) within different frames of reference. Dougherty (1992) describes the kinds of problems that arise when knowledge must be interpreted in different frameworks.

Provision of generic modules for process management by combining checklists with milestones to expedite review processes across distance. Ultimately such support can include software agents to expedite process flows.

This paper proposes that one way to support such environments is to use shared workspaces that can dynamically evolve. Flexibility is achieved through the ability to create a new workspace, invite people into it, and provide them with the support needed to carry out their work in a collaborative manner.

2.1 Workspace requirements

We see virtual work as proceeding in any number of workspaces that can be connected into networks as work expands and new opportunities are identified. The idea of workspace is not new - it has been used most commonly to describe shared workspaces for usually small groups working towards relatively defined goals, such as joint editing. Our goal is to extend shared workspaces into enterprise wide operations that can involve large numbers of people. This in turn requires extension to workspace networks, where each workspace in the networks supports one collaborative knowledge sharing activity, while activities are coordinated through project support.

Most toolkits to date have concentrated on only some of these major requirements. For example, shared editing tools emphasize awareness primarily through synchronous work. There are also tools that maintain awareness in predefined systems based on workflow management. Examples include LinkWorks (http://www.digital.com/linkworks/) or Livelink (http://www.opentext.com/livelink/), which primarily concentrate on concrete operations concerned with documents.

Our goal is to combine the major requirements into the one toolkit, called LiveNet. LiveNet, can be used to create workspaces to support a particular work activity, and allows processes to emerge by dynamically allowing new workspace to be created. It supports collaboration between the workspaces by providing a variety of ways to maintain awareness across them. To do this each workspace is made up of the major components illustrated in Figure 1.

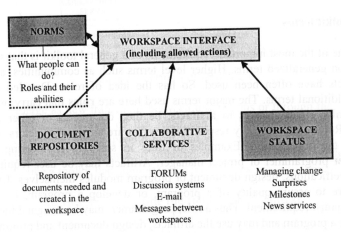

Figure 1 - A Collaborative Workspace

The major components are chosen to satisfy requirements as follows:

An interface and **document repository**, including documents needed to carry out the needed work. This will include reference to any background material needed for the workspace task, as well as any documents produced within the workspace.

A set of norms to create team structures and **governance structures**. They describe responsibilities within the workspace, including the actions allowed for each participant. These allow **new participants to be added to workspaces**, and roles assigned to them within workspaces, with responsibilities assigned to roles.

Workspace status reporting to **report progress and maintain awareness** between workspaces. These include aspects such as dealing with surprises, monitoring milestones, keeping track of goals and so on.

Collaborative services that support **interactions between people**, including exchange of messages between them. This will include both synchronous and asynchronous communication between workspace participants. These can be discussion databases, chatboxes and so on.

An overriding requirement of emerging processes is that the components must be dynamically changed, that is they can be created or changed during system execution, not only at definition time. Workspace commands are provided in LiveNet to **allow processes to emerge** through the creation of new workspaces or

The top level menu includes selections for:

> Documents – brings up a window displaying the documents accessible to the user through the workspace. The user can then select the documents.
> People – brings up role and participant windows. An authorized user can then create new roles, and assign participants to roles.
> ThingsToDo – brings up windows that describe the actions and collaborations within the workspace.

Menu selections bring up the windows, some of which are shown in Figure 3, to display the objects in the workspace. These include roles, documents, background, participants, discussions and actions. Users are then free to add or delete such objects as needed. Additional features are provided to ensure that any changes are consistent with enterprise governance and to maintain awareness across workspaces.Governance is defined in two ways. One are the specific actions and discussions in which selected roles can participate. Access to documents and actions is defined through the assign command found in the documents and actions boxes in Figure 3. The other way is to restrict roles to a subset of menu selections. Figure 4 illustrates the interface provided to assign menu selections to roles. This interface is initially available to the workspace owner but can be made available to the selected role. It shows the role 'product-specialist' being given the ability to open documents.

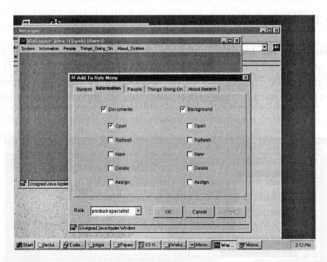

Figure 4 – Creating a role menu

In general most roles are only allowed to participate in carrying out actions and discussions and creation of documents. Abilities to create new roles, actions or discussions are often restricted to few selected roles. Teams are created by first setting up roles and then assigning people to these roles.

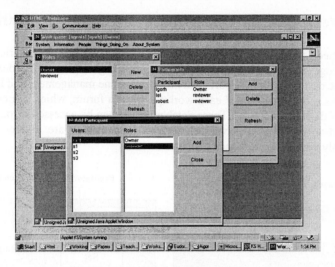

Figure 5 – Adding Participants

Additional menu selections are also available for maintaining awareness and growing the network. The status databases are accessible and displayed through the ThingsToDo/AboutWorkspace selection shown in Figure 6. Awareness itself is an on going process involving collaboration and becomes part of our discourse system.

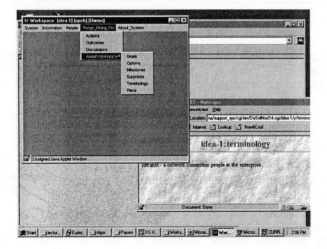

Figure 6 – Displaying Status

This selection provides access about the current status of work. This includes news items and FAQs, surprises and problems reported in the workspace, agreed upon terminology shared between workspaces, and goals and milestones, and check points to monitor progress towards them. Abilities to change these elements are part of the governance structure and can be customized to the workspace.

4   General Tools for Collaboration and Knowledge Sharing

LiveNet meets the requirement of a generalized toolkit to support generic operation in knowledge sharing and process management through a general discourse system that can be customized to support awareness, milestone management and knowledge sharing. As shown in Figure 7 each workspace has a forum, which can contain any number of discussion blocks. These databases can then be accessed through actions in the action menu of a LiveNet interface. The actions are assigned to roles consistently with the governance structures.

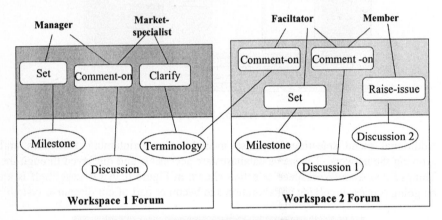

Figure 7 - FORUMs and Discussion Blocks

Figure 7 illustrates the way of organizing the forums. There is a separate forum for each workspace. The forum is made up of a number of discussion blocks, as for example, 'Milestones', 'Discussion'; and 'Terminology' in workspace 1. A number of actions are created in the forum to operate on each block. These actions are assigned to roles consistently with the governance structure. Thus 'Manager' can comment on discussion and set milestones. The 'Market-analyst' can comment on discussion and clarify terminology. Other actions can restrict some roles to only view particular blocks or act on selected statement types in the block. Access to blocks in one forum can be shared between workspaces to support collaboration between them. Thus access to terminology is shared between workspaces 1 and 2 in Figure 7.

Our goal is to extend the forum structure to support awareness and knowledge sharing by providing flexible structures to customize blocks to a variety of requirements. For this reason, the discourse system will support a range of statement types that can be combined and for different kinds of discourse. Examples include:

Using blocks for awareness – examples here are the simple structure to keep track of status information such as news items, surprises and workspace goals. Moderation can be used to give different roles different abilities to raise status items or comment on them. Discussion blocks can be used to transmit news items, record questions or problems and surprises and can be adapted to maintain milestones. Each statement is a milestone, with amendments made to milestones as new workspaces are created.

Using blocks for knowledge sharing - Knowledge sharing imposes other requirements in that users can be provided with evaluation screens on which to analyze documents and to assist users to maintain a consistent terminology.

4.1 Extending To Agents

Our current research is towards using agents to support work within the network. The agents have the knowledge of how to maintain awareness and milestones and can assist users in a variety of ways to set up workspaces. Perhaps the simplest is to locate team members and selection of collaborative services. Agents can also support coordination of parallel and disconnected processes through monitoring the activities in those workspaces.

5 Summary

The paper first described requirements of workspaces within collaborative environments, stressing the importance of supporting emergent processes. It then outlined a set of requirements that must be met by toolkits that support such requirements and illustrated the feasibility of building such a toolkit.

6 References

Boland, R.J. and Tenkasi, R.V. (1995): "Perspective Making and Perspective Taking in Communities of Knowing" in Fulk, J. and DeSanctis, G., (editors) (1995): *Focused Issue on Electronic Communication and Changing Organizational Forms, Organizational Scienc*e, Vol. 6, No. 4, July-August, 1995..

Dougherty, D. (1992): "Interpretive Barriers to Successful Product Innovation" in Large Firms" *Organizational Science*, Vol. 3, No. 2, May, 1992, pp.179-202.

Dourish, P. (1998): "Using Metalevel Techniques in a Flexible Toolkit for CSCW Applications" ACM Transactions on Computer-Human Interaction, Vol. 8, No.2, June 1998, pp. 109-155.

Grant, R.M. (1996): "Prospering in Dynamically-competitive Environments: Organizational Capability as Knowledge Integration" *Organization Science*, Vol. 7, No. 4, July, 1996, pp. 375-387.

Hawryszkiewycz, I.T. (1997): *Designing the Networked Enterprise*, Artech House, Boston.

Jones, C.T., Hesterly, W.S., and S.P. Borgatti (1997): A General Theory of Network Governance: Exchange Conditions and Social Mechanisms. *Academy of Management Review*, Vol. 22, No. 4, October, 1997, pp. 911-945.

Nonaka, I. (1994): "A Dynamic Theory of Organizational Knowledge Creation" *Organizational Science*, Vol. 5, No. 1, February, 1994, pp. 14-37.

If We Refuse the Inheritance ...

Lina Al-Jadir[1], Michel Léonard[2]

[1] Department of Mathematics, American University of Beirut
P.O. Box 11-0236, Beirut, Lebanon
lina.al-jadir@aub.edu.lb
[2] Centre Universitaire d'Informatique, Université de Genève
24, rue Général-Dufour, 1211 Genève 4, Switzerland
michel.leonard@cui.unige.ch

Abstract. Specialization is an abstract concept which expresses the IS-A relationship while inheritance is a mechanism which implements specialization. Our experiences in extended entity-relationship DBMSs and object-oriented DBMSs have shown that specialization can be implemented by several mechanisms. We propose in this paper a mechanism which is more flexible than inheritance with respect to object dynamics and schema evolution. In our "hologram" approach, an object is implemented by multiple instances which represent its many faceted nature. Those instances are linked together through aggregation links in a specialization hierarchy. Objects are dynamic since they can migrate between the classes of a hierarchy. Attributes and methods are not inherited but reached by navigating in a specialization hierarchy. Class views provide customized interfaces of classes. Our approach makes schema changes more pertinent and easier to understand.

1 Introduction

Inheritance in object-oriented database management systems (OODBMSs) is defined in [8] as "a powerful modeling tool, because it gives a concise and precise description of the world and it helps in factoring out shared specifications and implementations in applications". We distinguish the notions of specialization and inheritance. *Specialization* is an abstract concept which expresses the IS-A relationship. It is used in many fields other than computer science, for example in botany [34]. *Inheritance* is a mechanism which implements specialization. We think that these two notions are often confused together in the literature. Our experiences in extended entity-relationship DBMSs [17] and object-oriented DBMSs [4] [3] have shown that specialization can be implemented by several mechanisms. We propose in this paper a mechanism which is more flexible than inheritance with respect to object dynamics and schema evolution.

Implementing specialization by inheritance has several shortcomings:
- *static nature of objects*: once an object is created in a class C, it stays in that class until it is deleted from it. It is a serious problem, since one is forced to model real-world entities that *evolve* dynamically with objects that cannot [28] [30] [26]. As an example in [30], the class *Person* has two subclasses *Student* and *Alumnus*. Existing systems may capture the notion that a student *is* a person, they do not support the

notion that a given person may *become* a student and that after graduation, that person *ceases* to be a student, and becomes an alumnus.

- *single instantiation of objects*: an object is an instance of only *one* class. In most OODBMSs, one must use multiple inheritance to model objects that play many roles at once. This approach can lead to a combinatorial explosion of sparsely populated classes [30] [25] [26]. For example, to create an object that is both a student and an employee, one would first define a new class, *StudentEmployee*, that is a subclass of both *Student* and *Employee*. This intersection class adds no new state or behaviour.
- *name conflicts*: conflicts of attribute and method names may arise between a class C and its superclasses or between the superclasses of a class C. In the first case, existing systems give precedence to the name used in class C. In the second case, each system has a policy to resolve the conflict by default. For example, in Orion [19], there is a precedence ordering between the superclasses of a class. In O_2 [1] and Goose [24], attributes/methods are renamed by the system. In both cases, which attribute/method is inherited is automatically decided by the system and may be not the effect desired by the user [12].
- *scope of inheritance*: should a class inherit *all* the properties from *all* its superclasses except those involved in name conflicts (*full inheritance*) or *some* of them (*selective inheritance*) [19] ? Almost all commercial systems adopted full inheritance. It is sometimes convenient to have selective inheritance but it is difficult for both the user and the system to keep track of it. As an example in [16], the class *Square* is a subclass of class *Rectangle*, since one could say: a square is a rectangle with all four sides equal. However this class hierarchy results in two problems: (i) each square instance contains two data components for the side lengths (width and height), where one would be sufficient (e.g. width); (ii) the subclass *Square* inherits methods from *Rectangle* that are not applicable to a square (e.g. setHeight).
- *schema evolution*: class modification becomes complex with inheritance. Orion [9] requires twelve rules in order to disambiguate the effects of class modification. They include conflict resolution rules and propagation rules. Gemstone [27] does not support some schema changes, such as change the superclass of a class, because one of their motivation is to provide modifications that are "well understood".

We propose the "hologram" approach to implement specialization in an object-oriented DBMS and to overcome the shortcomings we discussed. An object is implemented by multiple instances which represent its many faceted nature. Those instances are linked together through aggregation links in a specialization hierarchy. Objects are dynamic since they can migrate between the classes of a hierarchy. Attributes and methods are not inherited but reached by navigating in a specialization hierarchy. Class views provide customized interfaces of classes. Our approach makes schema changes more pertinent and easier to understand.

The remainder of the paper is organized as follows. Section 2 introduces the hologram approach. Section 3 describes objects manipulation in this approach. Section 4 shows how our approach makes schema evolution more flexible. Section 5 compares our work with other approaches. Section 6 provides concluding remarks.

2 Hologram Approach: Implementing Specialization

The IS-A relationship may be implemented with [19]: (i) the *strong interpretation,* which states that an instance of a class C also belongs to the superclasses of C (and the superclasses of these superclasses and so on); or (ii) the *weak interpretation,* which states that an instance of class C belongs to only C. The strong interpretation presents more difficulties with the deletion of instances. In fact, if an instance of a class is deleted, it must continue to exist as an instance of the superclasses of that class. Almost all commercial OODBMSs implement the weak interpretation.

Classes are usually related by two types of relationships: *aggregation* and *specialization.* Although these notions are conceptually different, they can be implemented by the same mechanism [15]. The hologram approach implements an IS-A link between the subclass C and its superclass S by two attributes:

- the attribute *sub* links S to its subclass C and has zero as minimal cardinality and one as maximal cardinality. An instance of S *may* be linked to at most *one* instance of C.
- the attribute *super* links C to its superclass S and has one as minimal cardinality and one as maximal cardinality. An instance of C *is* linked to at most *one* instance of S.

It implements then the strong interpretation of the IS-A relationship. For example, the class *Student* is a subclass of *Person* (see fig. 1). A person who is a student is modelled by an instance p of *Person* and an instance s of *Student* that are linked through the attributes *super* and *sub* ($p.sub=s, s.super=p$).

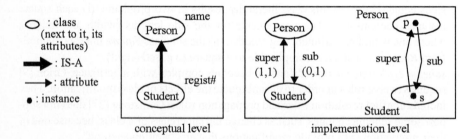

Fig. 1. Specialization link at conceptual level and implementation level

In the hologram approach, an object is implemented by multiple instances in a specialization hierarchy. For example, let the class *Person* have another subclass *Employee.* A person who is a student and an employee is modelled by an object which is implemented by three instances: p in *Person,* s in *Student* and e in *Employee.* Each instance has an oid $<C, I>$ where C is the class identifier and I the instance identifier within C. Since an object is multi-instantiated, it has multiple oids. There are two operators for checking the identity of object references: "==" checks if two instances are identical, while "@=" checks if two instances implement the same object.
For example, in figure 1:

```
(p == s)  = FALSE,
(p @= s)  = TRUE,
correspond(p, Student) = s.
```

Thus, our approach overcomes the "single instantiation of objects" shortcoming we mentioned in the introduction.

In the hologram approach, attributes and methods are no more inherited in the classical sense of inheritance; they are *reached* by navigating in a specialization hierarchy. This contrasts with traditional inheritance. For an instance of a subclass C, only the values of attributes locally defined at C are stored. The values on attributes defined at the superclass S of C are not stored with C instances but with their corresponding S instances. For example, in figure 1, if *p.name="Dupont"* and *s.super=p* then *s.name="Dupont"*, because *s.super.name="Dupont"*. The name values are stored with *Person* instances.

The hologram approach allows *multiple inheritance* by the same mechanism. A subclass C that has n superclasses $S_1, ..., S_n$ will have n attributes $super\_S_1, ..., super\_S_n$, and each of its superclasses will have an attribute sub_C. For example, teaching assistants are both students and employees, and they do research in some field. In this case, it is useful to create a subclass *Assistant* which has two superclasses *Student* and *Employee* and a specific attribute *research-field* (see fig. 2). An assistant is modelled by four instances (p, s, e, a, such that $a.super\_S=s$, $a.super\_E=e$, $s.super\_P=p$, $e.super\_P=p$ and $p.sub\_S=s$, $p.sub\_E=e$, $s.sub\_A=a$, $e.sub\_A=a$).

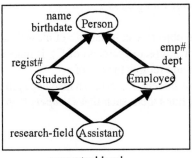 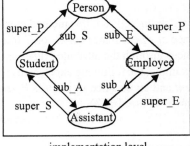

| conceptual level | implementation level |

Fig. 2. Multiple inheritance

We can define *class-views* on a class. A class-view is a simplification of contexts [13] [6] which can include several classes. A class-view allows to show some of the accessible (local and reachable) attributes/methods and hide the others. For example, the view V_{Emp} on *Employee* shows the attributes *emp#* and *dept* (local) and *name* (reached) while hiding *birthdate* (see fig. 2).

```
view V_Emp on Employee (emp#, dept, Person.name)
```
One can use different views of the same class in different applications according to her/his needs. Thus a class-view is a customized interface of a class. When a name conflict occurs, the DB designer resolves it explicitly by choosing which attribute/method to access. Moreover, this choice may be different in two different applications. Thus, our approach overcomes the "name conflicts" shortcoming we mentioned in the introduction. Using a class-view is interesting for the case of squares discussed in the introduction, since now we can define the class *Square* as a subclass of *Rectangle* and define a view

V_{Square} on it which shows only the attribute *width* and the method *SetWidth* from *Rectangle*. With traditional inheritance, one would have modelled a rectangle as a specialization of square! Thus, our approach overcomes the "scope of inheritance" shortcoming.

3 Hologram Approach: Manipulating Objects

In the hologram approach, the set of classes related by IS-A links forms a graph with several disjoint components called specialization hierarchies. Each of them is a rooted and connected directed acyclic graph (DAG). It differs with systems that have a system-defined OBJECT class and consequently one DAG. To each specialization hierarchy is associated a view called *DAG-view* which contains *all* the classes of the hierarchy with all their attributes and methods. The objects of a class C are manipulated inside the DAG-view containing C with four primitive methods: create, extend, delete and modify.

3.1 Primitive Methods

In the following, DV denotes the DAG-view containing class C.

Create. *create (DV, C)*: this method creates an object as an instance c of class C and an instance c_k of each ancestor C_k of C (direct or indirect superclass of C). It links these instances through the attributes *super* and *sub* and returns the oid of c.

For example, the following expression creates a student. It creates an instance s_1 in class *Student* and an instance p_1 in class *Person*. It links them such that $s_1.super\_P=p_1$ and $p_1.sub\_S=s_1$ (see fig. 3).

```
s1 := create (DV, Student);
```

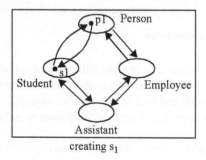 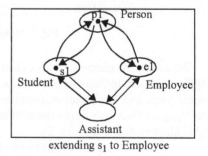

creating s_1 extending s_1 to Employee

Fig. 3. Object creation and extension

Extend. *extend (DV, c, F)* with c an instance of class C and both classes C and F belong to DV. Let R be the root class of the DAG-view and r the instance of R which corresponds to c. This method extends the instance c by creating an instance f in class F and linking it to r. The classes F and R may be linked by several paths composed of the *sub* attributes (called sub-paths). The extend method links the instances *f* and *r* through *all* these sub-paths, which may create instances in intermediate classes. It returns the oid of *f*. Note that class *F* is not necessarily a descendant of *C* (direct or indirect subclass of *C*); it may be a sibling class of *C*.

For example, the following first expression states that student s_1 becomes an employee (see fig. 3). It creates an instance e_1 in *Employee* and links it to p_1 (instance of the root class *Person* that corresponds to s_1) by setting $p_1.sub\_E=e_1$ and $e_1.super\_P=p_1$. The third expression states that student s_2 becomes an assistant (see fig. 4). It creates an instance *a* in *Assistant* and links it to p_2. *Person* and *Assistant* are linked by 2 sub-paths forming a cycle: 1) *Person-Student-Assistant*, 2) *Person-Employee-Assistant*. On the first path, since p_2 is already connected to s_2, it connects s_2 to *a* (sets $a.super\_S=s_2$ and $s_2.sub\_A=a$). On the second one, it creates an instance e_2 in *Employee*, connects it to p_2 and then to *a* (sets $e_2.super\_P=p_2$ and $p_2.sub\_E=e_2$; sets $a.super\_E=e_2$ and $e_2.sub\_A=a$).

```
e1 := extend (DV, s1, Employee);
s2 := create (DV, Student);
a  := extend (DV, s2, Assistant);
```

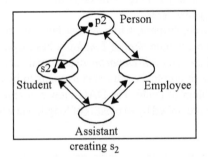 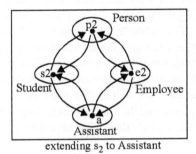

creating s_2 extending s_2 to Assistant

Fig. 4. Object extension with several *sub*-paths

Delete. *delete (DV, c)*: this method deletes the instance *c* of class *C*, which consequently deletes its corresponding instances in the descendants of *C* thanks to the existential dependencies expressed on the *super* attributes (minimal cardinality 1). When one deletes an object from *C*, it remains in the superclasses of *C*. To delete an object as a whole, one has to delete it from the root class of the DAG-view.

For example, the following first expression states that s_1 ceases to be a student. It deletes the instance s_1 from *Student*. The object remains as a person (p_1 in *Person*) and an employee (e_1 in *Employee*). The second expression states that p_2 ceases to exist because p_2 is an instance of *Person* which is the root class of the DAG-view. It deletes the instance p_2 from *Person*, which recursively deletes the instances s_2, e_2 and *a*.

```
delete(DV, s1);
delete(DV, p2);
```

As we saw, the extend and delete methods allow objects to migrate between the classes of a specialization hierarchy. Thus, our approach overcomes the "static nature of objects" shortcoming we mentioned in the introduction.

Modify. *modify (DV, c, [A:v])* with *A* an attribute of class *D* in *DV*, *D* being an ancestor, a descendant or a sibling class of *C*. This method assigns the value *v* on the attribute *A* to the instance *d* of class *D* which corresponds to the instance *c* of class C.
For example, the following expression updates the name of the employee e_2, by setting $p_2.name = "Bonjour"$.

```
modify(DV, e₂, [name: "Bonjour"]);
```

3.2 Attribute and Method Redefinition

Multiple instantiation and object dynamics raise new questions about the redefinition of attributes and methods.

Redefining Attributes. In classical OO approach, one can constrain the domain of an inherited attribute. The underlying assumption is that an object is stored in only one class and values on an inherited attribute are stored with the objects of the subclass inheriting it. This assumption is no more true in our approach. Thus assigning an attribute value to an object belonging to classes C_1 and C_2, which have both the same attribute *A*, may be inconsistent, since the value may belong to the domain of $C_1.A$ and not $C_2.A$. We call it the *attribute inconsistency problem*.

For example, an employee works in any department, while an assistant can work only in a research department (see fig. 5). The attribute *dept* of *Employee* has *Department* as domain class while *dept* of *Assistant* has *Research-Department* as domain class. Can one assign a non-research department to an employee who also happens to be an assistant ? We address this question as a problem of cycle. The DAG-view containing *Employee* and the one containing *Department* are linked by two paths of length one with the same label "dept". We have then a cycle.

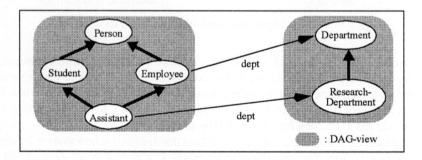

Fig. 5. Redefining an attribute

We make the following assumption: two attributes with the same name represent the same information. Our approach is to say that a multi-instantiated object *o* is linked to the *same* object *o'* through *all* the attributes of a DAG-view having the *same* name. In the given example, if *e* in *Employee* and *a* in *Assistant* implement the same object, and the instance *e* is assigned to a department *d* and the instance *a* to a research-department *rd* then *d* and *rd* must implement the same object. This has consequences on the semantics of the methods modify and extend.

Overloading Methods. In classical OO approach, when a message is sent to an object of class C, the definition of class C is searched to see if it has a method that matches the signature of the message. If found, the method is executed. Otherwise, a search up the class hierarchy is initiated until either a method is found or failure is returned. The underlying assumption is that only one class is associated with an object and it is its most specific class. This assumption is no more true in our approach. Thus a message sent to an object becomes potentially ambiguous, since it can be for any of the classes that the object belongs to. This is called the *message ambiguity problem* [23].

For example, *fees()* is a method in both *Student* and *Assistant* such that the implementation of *fees()* of *Assistant* overrides the implementation of *fees()* of *Student*. When a *fees()* message is sent to an instance of *Student* who also happens to be an assistant, which method should be executed ? Our approach is to say that two methods with the same name (in a DAG-view) executed on two instances of the same object must return the same result. It is the responsibility of the database designer to ensure this condition when writing methods. Our choice is the same as for attributes: the values on two same named attributes (in a DAG-view) of two instances of the same object are the same. The motivation of our choice is to have uniformity between attributes and methods. In our example, executing the method *fees()* of *Assistant* or *fees()* of *Student* on a student instance returns the same result.

4   Schema Evolution and Specialization

Schema evolution is the ability to update the schema of a populated database. Inheritance in OO models makes schema evolution complex, because schema changes do not affect only one class but a class hierarchy. Thus, one needs to define the semantics of these changes with complex rules as in [9] to preserve the model invariants. But the question is: do users understand the semantics of schema changes ? As we will see, the hologram approach makes schema changes easier to understand and more pertinent. We will consider the taxonomy of schema evolution used in Orion [9] (see fig. 6) and discuss some of these schema changes.

Add a New Attribute/Method to a Class (1.1). Since an attribute/method is not inherited in our approach, adding a new attribute/method to a class C does not need to be propagated to C descendants. Orion [9] and Gemstone [27] propagate it and block the propagation of this change when it implies a name conflict in subclasses. The resulting schema may be confusing for users.

Drop an Existing Attribute/Method from a Class (1.2). In our approach, deleting an attribute/method does not need to be propagated to the descendants since it is not inherited. If this attribute/method was defined in some view, it is automatically removed

---

(1) Changes to a class
    (1.1) Add a new attribute/method to a class
    (1.2) Drop an existing attribute/method from a class
    (1.3) Rename an attribute/method
    (1.4) Change the inheritance of an attribute/method
    (1.5) Change the domain of an attribute
    (1.6) Change the code of a method
    (1.7) Rename a class
(2) Changes to the superclass/subclass relationship
    (2.1) Add a new class
    (2.2) Drop an existing class
    (2.3) Add a class S to the superclass list of a class C
    (2.4) Remove a class S from the superclass list of a class C
    (2.5) Change the order of superclasses of a class C

Note: we omit the operations on default value, shared value and composite property of an attribute because they are specific to the Orion model.

Fig. 6. Orion taxonomy of schema evolution

from it thanks to existential dependency. Orion removes recursively the attribute/method from subclasses inheriting it while Gemstone does not.

Change the Inheritance of an Attribute/Method (1.4). In our approach, we do not need this schema change. Instead of it, we show or hide an attribute/method in class-views.

Change the Domain Class of an Attribute A from C to C' (C and C' in Same Hierarchy) (1.5). Orion allows only to generalize a domain while Gemstone can generalize and specialize it. The choice of Orion was to avoid losing values. In our approach C' can be either a superclass, or a subclass, or a sibling class of C. Only values on A that have no correspondent in C' are replaced by null: for each instance o in the origin class of A, $A(o)$ is set to $correspond(A(o), C')$.
Note that changing the domain of an attribute to a class C' outside the specialization hierarchy of C is equivalent to dropping the attribute and adding a new one.

Change the Origin Class of an Attribute A from C to C' (C and C' in Same Hierarchy). This schema change misses in Orion and Gemstone taxonomy, but is supported in Goose [24]. It is useful and not equivalent to dropping the attribute from C and adding it to class C' because in this case values taken on the attribute are lost. In our approach information is kept: for each instance o in C': $A(o)$ is set to $A(correspond(o, C))$ (note that $A(null)$ returns null). Due to this change, some classes may no more reach the modified attribute. If the attribute was included in views defined on these classes, it is removed from the views definition.

Add a New Class (2.1). In our approach, one can add a class C as a leaf in a specialization hierarchy with classes S_1, S_2, ..., S_n as superclasses. N attributes super_S_i are added to C and an attribute sub_C is added to each superclass S_i in a transparent way to users. Objects may be now created in or extended to this new class.

Drop an Existing Class (2.2). In our approach, deleting a class C deletes the attributes whose origin or domain class is C. It deletes C instances and also C descendants. It differs from Orion where the subclasses of C have one less superclass. Views defined on C are automatically deleted thanks to existential dependency.

Add a Class S to the Superclass List of a Class C (2.3). In our approach, an attribute super_S is added to C and an attribute sub_C to class S. There is no need to recompute the inheritance of attributes/methods in C as in Orion. Set inclusion has to be checked:
- if S and C are in the same hierarchy: for each instance c of C, $r := correspond(c, R)$ where R is the root class of the specialization hierarchy of C, and $sc := correspond(r, S)$. If sc is not null, then $c.super\_S$ is set to sc and $sc.sub\_C$ to c, else delete(c);
- if S and C are in different hierarchies: this is allowed if the specialization hierarchy of C remains a rooted DAG (for example, C a non-subclass becomes a subclass of S). The DB designer decides which instance in S corresponds to each instance in C. An interesting schema change is to merge two specialization hierarchies which have C_1 and C_2 as root classes by creating a new class SC and making C_1 and C_2 subclasses of SC. If an instance c_1 in C_1 and an instance c_2 in C_2 implement the same object (an attribute from C_1 to C_2 can be used to express these correspondences), then only one instance will be created in SC and linked to c_1 and c_2 through the sub and super attributes (we say that c_1 and c_2 are unified).

Remove a Class S from the Superclass List of a Class C (2.4). In our approach, the attribute super_S is deleted from C and the attribute sub_C from S. There are no repercussions on the instances of C. There is no need to recompute the inheritance of attributes/methods in C as in Orion. If S was the only superclass of C, then C is detached from the specialization hierarchy and is no more a subclass.

5 Related Work

[31] [11] [15] [23] [20] use the aggregation mechanism to implement a single object by several connected instances. In [31] an object is implemented by a set of instances arranged in an object hierarchy and linked through the attribute "parent". [11] uses aggregation links for security purpose. [15] proposes to use aggregation relationships (variable "super") instead of inheritance in an object-oriented programming language. In [23] the authors propose an approach where an object is linked to its superclass instances and subclass instances via the oids of these instances. An object belongs to one most specific class. In [20] an object is implemented by a single conceptual object (instance of a system class) and a set of implementation objects (instances of user-defined

classes). There is a bi-directional link between a conceptual object and its implementation objects.

[28] [30] [2] [26] [18] represent the many faceted nature of objects. In [28] a class has several roles. Each role is composed of: attributes, messages, states and rules which define the allowed state transitions. An object is created as an instance of a given class. Role instances may be added to or removed from an object. In [30] an aspect may add state, define new behaviour, and export selected parts of a base class. An object is an instance of a class. Aspect instances may be added to or removed from an object (they share the same oid). Aspects [30] and roles [28] do not integrate with the class hierarchy. In [2] [26] an object may belong to several classes in a specialization hierarchy (called roles). An object with several roles has a single oid. In [26] the author notices the problem of virtual binding and thinks that "a more natural solution, may be to have virtual method implementations take into consideration which subclasses the (persistent) object is an instance of, and perform a computation based on this knowledge". In [18] a deputy object is introduced to play a role of its source object. An object can have multiple deputy objects which have their own identifiers. They inherit attributes and methods of the source object and may have additional ones. Inheritance of attributes/methods can be selective by using switch operations.

[12] introduces the *point of view* notion to resolve conflicts in case of multiple inheritance. When sending a message to an object o (an object belongs to only one class), one specifies a class C. The point of view of class C on object o is computed as the intersection of (C union its ancestors union its descendants) and (instantiation class of o union its ancestors). It returns a set of classes where to search the method. [16] proposes *abstract classes* to avoid the problem of full inheritance. The addition of these artificial classes makes a specialization hierarchy more complex.

In [3] we proposed the multiobject mechanism which differs from the hologram approach: (i) the instances implementing a single object are not linked through sub and super attributes but have the same oid; (ii) the mechanism supports automatic classification; (iii) it does not support class-views. The multiobject mechanism has two shortcomings. The first is that it does not allow to have two attributes/methods with the same name in a specialization hierarchy. The second is that it makes difficult the operation of merging two specialization hierarchies and unifying some of their objects since the instances of a single object must have the same oid. The hologram approach overcomes these shortcomings.

6 Conclusion

If we refuse the inheritance, we could have a much more flexible implementation of specialization. In fact, we presented the hologram approach which:
- allows objects to be multi-instantiated and play many roles at once,
- allows objects to be dynamic and migrate between classes of a specialization hierarchy,
- makes attributes/methods reachable by traversing a specialization hierarchy,

- removes name conflicts since two same named attributes/methods of an object return the same result,
- allows selective inheritance by using class-views,
- eases the understanding of schema changes.

We made a first simplified implementation of this approach in our F2 object-oriented database system [4]. We are currently working on extending it to support the features described in this paper.

References

1. Adiba M., Collet C., *Objets et bases de données: le SGBD O2*, Hermès, 1993.
2. Albano A., Bergamini R., Ghelli G., Orsini R., *An object Data Model with Roles*, Proc. Int. Conf. on Very Large Data Bases, VLDB, Dublin 1993.
3. Al-Jadir L., Léonard M., *Multiobjects to Ease Schema Evolution in an OODBMS*, Proc. Int. Conf. on Conceptual Modeling, ER, Singapore 1998.
4. Al-Jadir L., Estier T., Falquet G., Léonard M., *Evolution Features of the F2 OODBMS*, Proc. Int. Conf. on Database Systems for Advanced Applications, DASFAA, Singapore 1995.
5. Al-Jadir L., Le Grand A., Léonard M., Parchet O., *Contribution to the Evolution of Information Systems*, in: Methods and Associated Tools for the Information Systems Lifecycle, A.A. Verrijn-Stuart & T.W. Olle (eds), IFIP, Elsevier, 1994.
6. Al-Jadir L., Falquet G. , Léonard M., *Context Versions in an Object-Oriented Model*, Proc. Int. Conf. on Database and Expert Systems Applications, DEXA, Prague 1993.
7. Andany J., Léonard M., Palisser C., *Management of Evolution in Databases*, Proc. Int. Conf. on Very Large Data Bases, VLDB, Barcelona 1991.
8. Atkinson M., Bancilhon F., De Witt D., Dittrich K., Maier D., Zdonik S., *The Object-Oriented Database System Manifesto*, Proc. Int. Conf. on Deductive and Object-Oriented Databases, DOOD, Kyoto 1989.
9. Banerjee J., Kim W., Kim H-J., Korth H.F., *Semantics and Implementation of Schema Evolution in Object-Oriented Databases*, Proc. Int. Conf. on Management Of Data, ACM SIGMOD, San Francisco 1987.
10. Bertino E., *A View Mechanism for Object-Oriented Databases*, Proc. Int. Conf. on Extending Database Technology, EDBT, Vienna 1992.
11. Bertino E., Jajodia S., *Modeling Multilevel Entities Using Single Level Objects*, Proc. Int. Conf. on Deductive and Object-Oriented Databases, DOOD, Phoenix 1993.
12. Carré B., Geib J-M., *The Point of View Notion for Multiple Inheritance*, Proc. Conf. on Object-Oriented Programming Systems, Languages and Applications, OOPSLA, Ottawa 1990.
13. Falquet G., *Interrogation de bases de données à l'aide d'un modèle sémantique*, Ph.D. thesis, Faculty of Sciences, University of Geneva, 1989.
14. Ferrandina F., Meyer T., Zicari R., Ferran G., Madec J., *Schema and Database Evolution in the O2 Object Database System*, Proc. Int. Conf. on Very Large Data Bases, VLDB, Zürich 1995.
15. Hauck F.J., *Inheritance Modeled with Explicit Bindings: An Approach to Typed Inheritance*, Proc. Conf. on Object-Oriented Programming Systems, Languages and Applications, OOPSLA, Washington 1993.
16. Hürsch W.L., *Should Superclasses be Abstract ?*, Proc. European Conf. on Object-Oriented Programming, ECOOP, Bologna 1994.

17. Junet M., Falquet G., Léonard M., *ECRINS/86: An Extended Entity-Relationship Data Base Management System and its Semantic Query Language*, Proc. Int. Conf. on Very Large Data Bases, VLDB, Kyoto 1986.
18. Kambayashi Y., Peng Z., *Object Deputy Model and Its Applications*, Proc. Int. Conf. on Database Systems for Advanced Applications, DASFAA, Singapore 1995.
19. Kim W., *Introduction to Object-Oriented Databases*, MIT Press, 1990.
20. Kuno H.A., Ra Y-G., Rundensteiner E.A., *The Object-Slicing Technique: A Flexible Object Representation and Its Evaluation*, Technical Report, CSE-TR-241-95, University of Michigan, 1995.
21. Kuno H.A., Rundensteiner E.A., *Implementation Experience with Building an Object-Oriented View Management System*, Technical Report, University of Michigan, 1993.
22. Lerner B.S., Habermann A.N., *Beyond Schema Evolution to Database Reorganization*, Proc. Conf. on Object-Oriented Programming Systems, Languages and Applications, OOPSLA, Ottawa 1990.
23. Ling T.W., Teo P.K., *Object Migration in ISA Hierarchies*, Proc. Int. Conf. on Database Systems for Advanced Applications, DASFAA, Singapore 1995.
24. Morsi M.M.A., Navathe S.B., Kim H-J., *A Schema Management and Prototyping Interface for an Object-Oriented Database Environment*, in: Object Oriented Approach in I.S., F. Van Assche & B. Moulin & C. Rolland (eds), IFIP, North-Holland, 1991.
25. Nguyen G.T., Rieu D., Escamilla J., *An Object Model for Engineering Design*, Proc. European Conf. on Object-Oriented Programming, ECOOP, Utrecht 1992.
26. Odberg E., *Category Classes: Flexible Classification and Evolution in Object-Oriented Databases*, Proc. Int. Conf. on Advanced Information Systems Engineering, CAISE, Utrecht 1994.
27. Penney D.J., Stein J., *Class Modification in the GemStone Object-Oriented DBMS*, Proc. Conf. on Object-Oriented Programming Systems, Languages and Applications, OOPSLA, Orlando 1987.
28. Pernici B., *Objects with Roles*, Proc. IEEE Conf. on Office Information Systems, 1990.
29. Peters R.J., Özsu M.T., *An Axiomatic Model of Dynamic Schema Evolution in Objectbase Systems*, ACM Transactions on Database Systems, vol. 22, no 1, march 1997.
30. Richardson J., Schwarz P., *Aspects: Extending Objects to Support Multiple, Independent Roles*, Proc. Int. Conf. on Management Of Data, ACM SIGMOD, Denver 1991.
31. Sciore E., *Object Specialization*, ACM Transactions on Information Systems, vol. 7, no 2, april 1989.
32. Skarra A.H., Zdonik S.B., *Type Evolution in an Object-Oriented Database*, in: Research Directions in OO Programming, B. Shriver & P. Wegner (eds), MIT Press, 1987.
33. Smith J.M., Smith D.C.P., *Database Abstractions: Aggregation and Generalization*, ACM Transactions on Database Systems, vol. 2, no 2, june 1977.
34. Stace C., *Plant taxonomy and biosystematics*, 2nd edition, Edward Arnold, 1989.
35. Tresch M., *A Framework for Schema Evolution by Meta Object Manipulation*, Proc. Int. Workshop on Foundations of Models and Languages for Data and Objects, Aigen 1991.

Viewpoints Handling in an Object Model with Criterium-Based Classes

Stéphane Coulondre and Thérèse Libourel

L.I.R.M.M. (U.M.R. 5506 Université Montpellier II / C.N.R.S.)
161 rue Ada, 34392 Montpellier Cedex 5, France
{coulondre,libourel}@lirmm.fr

Abstract. Traditional class-based object-oriented data models and programming languages do not allow an object to have several types or to play different roles while keeping the same identity. Therefore, the modeling of persistent evolving entities is a difficult task. Some specific models and languages exist, but do not support some of the features of traditional OODB models such as inheritance, late binding or common implementation through the notion of class. In this paper, we propose an object model that extends the one proposed by the ODMG while keeping the statical strong type-checking property of the programming language. The model is based on the novel concept of *criterium-based class*, from which instance objects have an immutable identity and several viewpoints which are accessible through a single interface. The model allows to consider new features such as property sharing and viewpoints merging, unconsidered so far, in a clean and homogeneous way.

1 Introduction

In traditional object-oriented databases, evolution of objects is a considerable issue. A lot of work has been carried out on schema evolution and correlated instances [13, 17, 7, 1, 4, 5]. The database schema represents a common structure and behaviour for instances of classes. However, the concept of class is too restrictive to support evolution of structure or behaviour dynamically. Moreover, these modifications should not, because of persistence, require recompilation of existing code, nor creation of new objects. Indeed, the OID should stay the same during the lifetime of an object, regardless of its evolution. These requirements are highly incompatible with traditional object-oriented languages. However evolution seems more and more inevitable and relevant mechanisms are needed.

These issues have been considered in the past by many authors. Comparison with our work is done in section 4. In this paper, we propose a model that extends the one proposed by the ODMG [10], and its associated programming language while keeping the statical strong type-checking property. The model is based on the novel concept of *criterium-based class (CBC)*. This concept allows to add new features such as multiple viewpoints[1] handling, property sharing

---

[1] Note that the notion of *viewpoint* is not related to that of database view, but to that of object role.

and viewpoint merging. The two latter points represent a novelty in OODB, as different roles are so far always accessed independently, and a property can not be shared by several roles unless the user creates a common superclass. These new features will be detailed later on.

For sake of clarity, various concepts of the model are introduced progressively. Therefore, the paper in organized as follows: in section 2, we present the notion of CBC, object instanciation and attributes access, and how to model object viewpoints. Then we detail in section 3 all the features presented above such as property sharing and viewpoints merging, and some considerations on inheritance. Section 4 compares our approach with some previous work, and finally section 5 concludes the paper.

2 The model

2.1 Classes and objects

As stated before, the traditional class notion usually associated to OODB models does not fit the requirements of modern databases. Therefore we propose an extended notion of class based on *criteria*. Let us consider the following definition of the class Person :

```
create class Person() {
private:
    string name;
    date birth;
public:
    string name() {return name;};
    int age() {return (DaysToYears(now()-birth));};
    Person(string n, date b) {name=n; birth=b;};
};
```

The class Person is defined with the empty criterium *()* and has two private attributes *name* and *birth*, three public methods *name()*, *age()* and a constructor *Person(string,date)*. Note that encapsulation is supported. This class is so far associated to a unique role, and therefore a unique type, as usual in OODB models, and its definition presents no specificity.

Once the class *Person* has been defined, we can create instance objects of this class. For example, a new person *henry* is created, and values are assigned to its attributes by `Person henry()('Henry',1975);`. To perform an access to the method *age* of the object *henry*, we use for example `print henry().age();` that displays 24.

2.2 Criteria

Let us now suppose that a person can also be a student, and therefore can have new attributes and behaviour in that context. The novelty of our model is that it does not require creation of another class in order to model this new type. Indeed, conceptually speaking, we think that if a person can have many viewpoints, then this is part of its inherent type, and the class to which it is linked must be able to model that feature. Therefore, we consider that *student* is part of the class *person* and represents only a viewpoint of that class.

Definition 1 (Criterium.). *A criterium is a formula of First-Order Logic under the disjonctive normal form (a disjunction of conjunction of atoms) : $C_1 \vee \ldots \vee C_n$, where each C_i, $i \in [1..n]$ is of the form $A_{i1} \wedge \ldots \wedge A_{in_i}$. Atoms do not contain variables nor function symbols.*

Examples of criteria syntax are : *(), (context(student)), ((user(john) and town(london)) or (user(henry) and priority(high)))*. Criteria are used in two complementary ways :

- Definition of a viewpoint in a class is made by specifying a criterium, that reflects the semantic of the viewpoint.
- An access to an object is made through an access criterium e. An access criterium is only a conjunction of atoms ($n = 1$). The criterium determines the composition of the object by logical implication: the object accessed is composed by all viewpoints from which criterium is logically implied by e.

To illustrate the notion of criterium, consider the simple situation in which we would like to take into account that a person can also be a student: we alter the class schema as follows :

```
alter class Person(context(student)) add {
private:
    string university;
    int studentnumber;
public:
    string university() {return university;};
    int studentnumber() {return studentnumber;};
    extPerson(string univ, int Stno)
        {university=univ; studentnumber=Stno;};
    Person(string n, date b, string univ, int Stno)
        {self().Person(n,b); extPerson(univ, Stno)};
};
```

Note that, instead of defining the methods inline, we can also define them outside the class definition. Once the student viewpoint[2] has been added to the schema definition, there are two ways of instancing an object to that viewpoint. The first one is to instance it from scratch.
`Person henry(context(student))('Henry',1975,'Jussieu',1045);`, for example, calls the constructor of the viewpoint *(context(student))* because the

---

[2] The choice of predicate names (context, etc.) is not constrained by the model. They are simply choosen by the user according to the semantic of the viewpoints.

access criterium is $c = (context(student))$ and thus $c \models context(student)$. Each viewpoint can implement its own constructor. Note that there was already a constructor in the viewpoint with an empty criterium. The conflict of message intepretation is investigated next.

Another way is to extend an already existing object (as it is actually for *henry*) by adding the viewpoint *(context(student))*. This is performed by the *extend* keyword that adds a new viewpoint to the list associated to henry, that will contain two elements, an empty one *()* for the main viewpoint, and *(context(student))* for the student viewpoint. A special constructor, defined by *extPerson*, is called only when an extension is performed by specifying values, e.g. `extend henry(context(student))('Jussieu',1045);`. If the values are not specified, the constructor is not called. An access to the method *age* of the newly extended object *henry* is performed, for example in the viewpoint *(context(student))*, by `print henry(context(student)).age();`

Viewpoint specialization. Methods defined in the viewpoint *()* are available in the the new viewpoint *(context(student))*, but, for example, the message *student-number* raises a static error if sent to *henry* with no criterium. Therefore:

Definition 2 (Viewpoint Specialization.). *A viewpoint indentified by a criterium c_1 is* more specialized *that another viewpoint indentified by a criterium c_2 if and only if $c_2 \models c_1$.*

The viewpoint specialization corresponds to subtyping. Therefore, if $c_2 \models c_1$, then an object with a viewpoint criterium c_2 can be used in every place where an object with a viewpoint criterium c_1 is expected. In order to keep type safety, the model use contravariant specialization. Indeed, covariant specialization, such as is O_2, can lead to runtime error, even if the program has passed static type-checking [8].

A call to the constructor of *henry(context(student))* has two possible implementations: that with the empty criterium (the original one), and that with the criterium *(context(student))*.

Therefore, the last one is chosen, because $context(student) \models \square$. This corresponds to the late binding mechanism. Another issue arises when many viewpoints come into play and are merged. These issues are adressed in section 3. The model also support strict binding by specifying the desired viewpoint criterium. For example, in the viewpoint *(context(student))*, the new constructor is defined by calling the constructor of *Person* with an empty criterium by specifying an empty criterium to the keyword *self*.

Viewpoints querying. Instance of objects viewpoints can be dynamically created. Therefore, it is not possible to know statically all the viewpoints of an objects. However, the class definition provides the user with the maximum set of viewpoints an object may have. In order to test for the presence of viewpoints within a given object, we use the *listvp* keyword that gives all the available viewpoints from which criterium logically imply the parameter. For example listvp henry(); displays () and (context(student)), because $\Box \models \Box$ and *context(student)* $\models \Box$.

3   Use of CBCs

The previous section has illustrated the main features of the model. We now focus on the novel possibilities allowed by CBCs. Let us consider a new viewpoint :

```
alter class Person(context(employee)) add {
private:
    string company;
    int salary;
public:
    string company() {return company;};
    int salary() {return salary();};
    void raiseSal(int percent) {salary+=(salary*percent)/100;};
    extPerson(string comp, int sal) {company=comp; salary=sal;};
    Person(string n, date b, string comp, int sal)
        {self().Person(n,b); extPerson(comp, sal)};
};
```

3.1   Viewpoints merging

Suppose that we extend *henry* to the new viewpoint *(context(student))*. We can access the two viewpoints *(context(employee))* and *(context(student))* with only one syntactic form, by constructing a new criterium that is the *conjunction* of the criteria of these two viewpoints.

Therefore, the user does not have to differenciate the accessed viewpoint according to the property he wants. For example henry(context(student) and context(employee)).raiseSal(15); accesses the method *raiseSal* of the viewpoint *(context(employee))*. A call to the method *studentnumber* is also possible in the same way, although these methods are defined in two different viewpoints. It is possible to combine all the wanted viewpoints by this mechanism. This allows to virtually build a new object by choosing the sets of properties the user wants to access. All accesses and modification are of course made on the original object *henry*. This ability to merge viewpoints leads to some possible conflicts. Indeed, two viewpoints can define an attribute or a method with the same name or signature. In this case, unless syntactically specified (see previous section), the compiler will raise an error. Indeed, there is no priority order between viewpoints, so it would be a semantic mistake to choose arbitrarily one og them. Another conflict is when a method accesses an attribute that has two definitions because of the merging. In this case, the method will access the attribute defined in the same viewpoint or in one of the viewpoints from which it inherits (by logical implication).

3.2 Property sharing

Another interesting possibility of CBCs is the ability to share properties between them. For example, consider the National Health Service number, that is usually the same when a person is a student an an employee. In this case, we could have defined it in the way that these two viewpoints inherit it, without another viewpoint inheriting it. In most of the approaches (see section 4), the only way is to create a common viewpoint from which the student and employee viewpoints inherit, in which we define this property. This is highly unconvenient, from a conceptual point of view, because it leads to the creation of many classes that are used only to solve technical problems. Criteria can solve this issue in a clean way. If a property is common in two or more viewpoints, the class is then extended with it, by combining the criteria with the *or* keyword[3]:

```
alter class Person(context(employee) or context(student))
    add {int NHSnumber;}
```

3.3 Viewpoint specialization and inheritance

So far, viewpoints are only a simple extension of the 'main' class, that is the part of the class defined with an empty criterium. For example, *(context(student))* and *(context(employee))* are simple extensions of Person. The specialization of a viewpoint is obtained by defining a new viewpoint from which criterium is built by conjunction of the criterium of the specialized viewpoint and of a new criterium describing the semantic of the specialization.

As stated before, inheritance between viewpoints is defined by *logical implication* on criteria. Therefore, assume the definition of a viewpoint with the criterium *(context(student) and context(employee))*. Therefore, the properties are valid only if the two subcriteria are valid at the same time. In this case, a new set of attributes and methods are available. Note the difference between viewpoints merging in which no new attribute or method was defined, but they were only made accessible in one operation. With this new class extension, a supplementary set of attributes and method will be available if the two viewpoints are merged. This corresponds to the traditional notion of multiple inheritance. The relations between viewpoints by logical implication of their criteria corresponds to inheritance. The notion of superclass is replaced by that of superviewpoint.

As in classical object models, multiple inheritance leads to conflicts. If there is not a more specialized implementation, then, as no order exists on the set of methods defined in the superviewpoint, none of them has a priority. In this case, the conflict is solved by taking into account the order of creation of viewpoints for the object. Implementation is searched in the older one first, and then towards the last one, if it is relevant (i.e. if the property is defined in it or in its ancestors).

---

[3] The NHS number is intentionally left public because otherwise, the example would require definition of an accessor. For sake of clarity, we avoid it.

3.4 Access rights

CBCs can be used to handle access rights for users, very common in DBMSs. Consider confidential information such as medical treatments, mind troubles, etc. Let us suppose that one of the users is a doctor. In this case, he might have an access to this information granted. Assume the existence of a viewpoint with the criterium *(context(sport))*. Then we could define some medical information as a specialization of this viewpoint, for example with the criterium *(context(sport) and user(doctor))*. Therefore the access would be forbidden if the access criteria does not meet these requirements:

```
print henry(context(sport) and user(secretary)).medicalcomment();
-> method not available with this criterium
```

3.5 Inheritance between classes

We intentionally allow inheritance from a class having only a viewpoint defined with the empty criterium. The latter is equivalent to traditional classes. Classes with several viewpoints are leaves in the inheritance hierarchy. There are two major reasons:

- Conceptually speaking, if a class has several viewpoints, then a subclass of it can be considered as another viewpoint and modeled as such. Creating a subclass that can handle all the viewpoints of its superclass plus one seems useless.
- An alternative is creating subclasses that inherit only from a viewpoint (that can be a complex one - i.e. the result of viewpoint merging). There are two major drawbacks: the first one is that it is simply equivalent to creating a new viewpoint in the superclass, the second one is that if the subclass inherits only from a viewpoint, then its type cannot be considered as a subtype of its superclass, and this is not inheritance.

Inherently, our model provides therefore a way to differenciate the different specialization links, and, as such, is very close to the willings of conceptual models [11] that make a sharp distinction between them.

4 Related Work

In this section, we compare the features of our model with some of the closest work in the object context. We shall divide our comparison in two main threads: with object-oriented database programming languages, and with object-oriented knowledge representation, where evolution and roles have also been studied. There has been a lot of work carried out, including Fibonacci [3], Iris [14], Clovers [19], Views [18], Aspects [16], IQL(2) [2]. Each of them include roles handling, dynamic evolution, unique OID, and encapsulation. The closest work are Fibonacci and IQL(2). Therefore we shall position our work relatively to these two latter. [3] provides a quick survey of other work, except for IQL(2), as well as their shortcomings. In a few words, they do not support late binding and multiple inheritance, together with multiple roles handling and dynamic object extension.

4.1 Fibonacci

Fibonacci is an object-oriented database programming language, that supports static and strong type-checking. It is based on the notion of roles. Each object has its own attributes and behaviour. Therefore the notion of class is different from our, in the sense that it only describes the type of objects but not their implementation. Each object keep an immutable OID and can gain new roles dynamically. However, attribute sharing and viewpoint merging is not supported. Each object is accessed through a specified role and each role within an object has a different name. There is a total independance between *cousin* roles (not ancestors nor descendants from each other, but having a common ancestor). Therefore, there is not a unique interface for the user as it is here. Moreover, Fibonacci does not support directly the modeling of access rights.

4.2 IQL(2)

IQL(2) is a model with classes, objects and inheritance as defined by ODMG. From this point of view, it is closer to our work than Fibonacci. IQL(2) aim at unifying many concepts that have been considered separately in the past. Therefore, some of its features, as view specification, are out of the scope of this paper, and we shall compare only the notion of roles. IQL(2) is based on the concept of context, used to parametrize class and relation names. Therefore, a class and a relation can have different definitions according to the context they are in. Each object has a unique OID and multiple inheritance and late binding are supported. Roles are modeled by classes, therefore, there can be inheritance between roles. This issue has been intentionally forbidden here (see previous section). Access rights are modeled through the use of contexts. IQL(2) provides contexts not only for classes but also for relations. This features can also be added in our model in a straightforward way. However, viewpoint merging and attribute sharing is not provided.

5 Concluding remarks and future work

We have presented a new model that introduces the notion of CBCs in order to model many features such as multiple viewpoints handling, property sharing and viewpoint merging. There two latter represent a novelty in OODB languages and allow also the modeling of access rights, in a clean and homogeneous way. We are currently extending the model in the following directions:

- The ability to handle exclusive classes is made by restricting the use of classes only to the empty viewpoint, as shown in section 3.5. However, handling of exclusive viewpoints is so far not provided. It would consist, for example, in defining a viewpoint with the criterium $(context(employed))$ and another one with the criterium $(\neg context(employed))$, that can never coexist within an object.
- Viewpoints dropping is a very interesting issue, that unfortunately can not be solved without giving up static type-checking.
- Dynamic specification of criteria. So far, criteria must be known at compile time, in order to keep the static type-checking property. But it may be very powerful to perform viewpoint access by specifying a variable as the criterium, instead of a compile-time known constant.
- Criteria allow modeling of evolution of the database. However we would like to make a distinction between objects evolution that can gain new viewpoints, by modifying the schema, thus reflecting it on the set of all instances, and a discrete evolution of *one* particular object, that may gain some new properties and behaviour in the real world, which are not shared by the other instances. This kind of evolution concerns only one object and the instanciation mechanism forbids that differentiation. We have already proposed a model to handle such objects, that we call *variable objects* [12], based on the notion of semi-structured data [15][9]. We are working on the integration of these features in the CBCs model, at the price of static type-checking, thus yielding to the merging of a statically strongly-typed object model *à la* ODMG, and a dynamically typed object model as for semistructured data, giving a unified model for objects with variability (of structure, in time, in space, of roles). We think this unified model fits into the proposed research agenda of the Asilomar Report on Database Research [6]. We are currently developping a prototype of DBMS for variable objects, including the notion of CBCs, called VOR (Variable Object Repository).

References

[1] S. Abiteboul and A. Bonner. Objects and Views. In *Proceedings of the ACM/SIGMOD International Conference on the Management of Data*, 1991.

[2] S. Abiteboul and C. Souza dos Santos. IQL(2): A model with ubiquitous objects. In *Database Programming Languages (DBPL-5), Proceedings of the Fifth International Workshop on Database Programming Languages Gubbio, Umbria, Italy, 6-8 September, 1995*, 1995.

[3] A. Albano, R. Bergamini, G. Ghelli, and R. Orsini. An object data model with roles. In Rakesh Agrawal, Sean Baker, and David Bell, editors, *VLDB '93: proceedings of the 19th International Conference on Very Large Data Bases, August 24-27, 1993, Dublin, Ireland*, pages 39–51, Palo Alto, Calif., USA, 1993. Morgan Kaufmann Publishers.

[4] J. Andany, M. Leonard, and C. Palisser. Management of schema evolution in databases. In *Proceedings of International Conference on Very Large Data Bases (VLDB'91), Barcelona, Spain*, 1991.

[5] J. Banerjee, W. Kim, K.J. Kim, and H. Korth. Semantics and Implementation of Schema Evolution Object-Oriented Databases. In *Proceedings of the ACM SIGMOD Conference, San Francisco, California*, pages 311–322, 1987.

[6] P. A. Bernstein, M. L. Brodie, S. Ceri, D. J. DeWitt, M. J. Franklin, H. Garcia-Molina, J. Gray, G. Held, J. M. Hellerstein, H. V. Jagadish, M. Lesk, D. Maier, J. F. Naughton, H. Pirahesh, M. Stonebraker, and J. D. Ullman. The asilomar report on database research. *SIGMOD Record (ACM Special Interest Group on Management of Data)*, 27(4), 1998.

[7] E. Bertino. A view mechanism for object-oriented databases. In *Proceedings of International Conference on Extensive Data Base Technology (EDBT'92)*, pages 136–151, 1992.

[8] J. Boyland and G. Castagna. Type-safe compilation of covariant specialization: A practical case. In P. Cointe, editor, *Proceedings ECOOP '96*, LNCS 1098, pages 3–25, Linz, Austria, July 1996. Springer-Verlag.

[9] P. Buneman, S. Davidson, G. Hillebrand, and D. Suciu. A query language and optimization techniques for unstructured data. *SIGMOD Record*, 25(2):505–516, 1996.

[10] R. G. G. Cattell. ODMG-93: A standard for object-oriented DBMSs. *SIGMOD Record (ACM Special Interest Group on Management of Data)*, 23(2):480–480, June 1994.

[11] P. Coad. Object-oriented patterns. *Communications of the ACM*, 35(9):153–159, September 1993.

[12] S. Coulondre, T. Libourel, and L. Spéry. Variable objects: An alternative to "strong" structure. In Jacques Malenfant and Roger Rousseau, editors, *Proceedings of the 5th International Conference on Languages and Models with Objects (LMO'99)*, pages 261–276, 1999, in french.

[13] F. Ferrandina, T. Meyer, R. Zicari, G. Ferran, and J. Madec. Schema and Database Evolution in the O2 Object Database System. In *Proceedings of International Conference on Very Large Data Bases (VLDB'95), Zurich, Switzerland*, 1995.

[14] D. H. Fishman et al. Iris: An object-oriented DBMS. *ACM Transactions on Office Automation Systems*, 5(1), January 1987.

[15] Y. Papakonstantinou, H. Garcia-Molina, and J. Widom. Object exchange across heterogeneous information sources. In *Proceedings of the 11th International Conference on Data Engineering*, pages 251–260, Los Alamitos, CA, USA, 1995.

[16] J. Richardson and P. Schwarz. Aspects: extending objects to support multiple, independent roles. *SIGMOD Record (ACM Special Interest Group on Management of Data)*, 20(2):298–307, June 1991.

[17] M. H. Scholl and M. Tresch. Evolution towards, in, and beyond object databases. *Lecture Notes in Computer Science*, 777, 1994.

[18] J. J. Shilling and P. F. Sweeney. Three Steps to Views: Extending the Object-Oriented Paradigm. In *Proceedings of the OOPSLA '89 Conference on Object-oriented Programming Systems, Languages and Applications*, pages 353–361, October 1989.

[19] L. A. Stein and S. B. Zdonik. Clovers: The dynamic behavior of types and instances. Technical Report CS-89-42, Department of Computer Science, Brown University, November 1989.

The Constructive Method for Query Containment Checking

Carles Farré, Ernest Teniente, Toni Urpí

Universitat Politècnica de Catalunya
E-08034 Barcelona -- Catalonia
[farre | teniente | urpi]@lsi.upc.es

Abstract. We present a new method that checks Query Containment for queries with negated derived atoms and/or integrity constraints. Existing methods for Query Containment checking that deal with these cases do not check actually containment but another related property called Uniform Containment, which is a sufficient but not necessary condition for containment. Our method can be seen as an extension of the canonical databases approach beyond the class of conjunctive queries.

1   Introduction

Query Containment (QC) [Ull89] is the problem concerned with checking whether the answers that a query obtains on a database are a subset of the answers obtained by another query on the same database, for every possible content of the database.

In this paper, we present a new method that checks QC for queries with safe stratified negation on derived (view) predicates. Previous methods that deal with negation can be classified into two different approaches. The first one is taken by those methods that check QC for query classes where negation is used in a restrictive way [LMSS93 LS95, Ull99]. The second approach is represented by those methods that do not check actually QC but another related property called *Uniform* QC [LS93, ST96], which is a sufficient but not necessary condition for QC.

The following example illustrates the limitations of these methods. Consider a deductive database consisting of two base predicates. $Emp(x)$ indicates that x is an employee. $Works\_for(x, y)$ indicates that x works for y. There are also two derived predicates. $Boss(x)$ when x has someone else working for him/her. $Chief(x)$ when x has some boss working for him/her.

$Boss(x) \leftarrow Works\_for(z, x)$
$Chief(x) \leftarrow Works\_for(y, x) \land Boss(y)$

Then we define two different queries with the same predicate query $Sub(x)$ to retrieve those x that are subordinates:

Q_1: $Sub(x) \leftarrow Emp(x) \land \neg Chief(x)$.
Q_2: $Sub(x) \leftarrow Emp(x) \land \neg Boss(x)$

Intuitively, Q_1 retrieves employees that are not *Chief*, that is, those employees that do not have any boss working for them. Instead, Q_2 retrieves employees that are not bosses, that is, those employees that have nobody working for them. In this sense, Q_1 is less restrictive than Q_2 because Q_2 does not allow anyone to work for x, while Q_1 only applies this restriction to the ones that are *Boss*. Hence, we can find a database, like {*Emp*(joan), *Works_for*(ann, joan)}, showing that the answers that Q_1 obtains, i.e. *Sub*(joan), are not always answers to Q_2. Therefore, Q_1 is not contained in Q_2 ($Q_1 \not\sqsubseteq Q_2$).We will see how our method reaches the same conclusion in Section 3.1 below. Conversely, if Q_1 is less restrictive than Q_2 then all the answers to Q_2 will be also answers to Q_1. Therefore, Q_2 is contained in Q_1 ($Q_2 \sqsubseteq Q_1$).

This example cannot be handled in a satisfactory way by the methods proposed in the literature. On one hand, this example does not fall into the classes of queries covered by [LMSS93, LS95, Ull99]. On the other hand, the methods of [LS93, ST96] would prove that Q_1 is not uniform contained in Q_2 and Q_2 is not uniform contained in Q_1, but these results do not help to determine whether $Q_1 \sqsubseteq Q_2$ or $Q_2 \sqsubseteq Q_1$ hold.

When considering the integrity constraints defined in a database, the containment relationship between two queries does not need to hold for any state of the database but only for those that satisfy the integrity constraints. This idea is captured by the notion of **IC**-compliant Query Containment. Again, current methods that handle **IC**-compliant QC [Sag88, ST96, DS96] take the uniform containment approach. Our method checks both "true" **IC**-compliant QC and QC in a uniform and integrated way.

Roughly, the main idea of our Constructive Method for Query Containment Checking is to construct a *counterexample* that proves the opposite [**IC**-compliant] QC relationship that we want to check. That is, our method is intended to construct a counterexample that shows that a query is not [**IC**-compliant] contained in another one. The facts added to this counterexample are instantiated according to the same *patterns* that are applied when constructing the set of canonical databases used for conjunctive query containment checking in [Klu88, Ull89, LS93, BH97, Ull99]. If this constructive procedure fails, then [**IC**-compliant] QC holds.

The Constructive Method for Query Containment Checking is based on the reduction of the QC problem to the view-updating problem [FTU98]. In particular, our method specializes the Events Method for view updating [TO95] to focus more on the characteristic aspects of QC checking.

This paper is organized as follows. Section 2 reviews base concepts needed in the rest of the paper. Section 3 presents, informally, the Constructive Method for [**IC**-compliant] Query Containment Checking with safe stratified negated negation. In Section 4, we present the correctness and completeness results of our method. The proofs of these results as well as the formalization of the method are stated in [FTU99]. Section 5 discusses some decidability issues. Section 6 reviews the related work. Finally, we present conclusions and point out further work in Section 7.

2 Base Concepts

In this Section, we briefly review some definitions related to Deductive Databases, Queries and QC.

A *deductive database* D is a triple $D = (EDB, DR, IC)$ where EDB is a finite set of facts, DR a finite set of deductive rules, and IC a finite set of integrity constraints.

Base predicates appear only in EDB and (eventually) in the body of deductive rules in DR. *Derived* (view) predicates appear only in DR. *Evaluable* (built-in) predicates, like arithmetic comparisons, can be evaluated without accessing the database.

We require that variables appearing in negated or evaluable atoms must appear in a positive derived or base literal in the same rule body (*safeness*). We demand also that there must not be negative literals about recursively defined derived predicates (*stratified negation*).

An *integrity constraint* is a formula that every EDB is required to satisfy. We deal with constraints in *denial* form[1]: $\leftarrow L_1 \wedge \ldots \wedge L_m$ with $m \geq 1$. For the sake of uniformity, we associate to each integrity constraint an inconsistency predicate Icn. Then, we would rewrite the former denial as an *integrity rule* $Ic1 \leftarrow L_1 \wedge \ldots \wedge L_m$. We also define an standard auxiliary predicate Ic with the following rules: $Ic \leftarrow Ic1$, $\ldots$, $Ic \leftarrow Icn$, one for each integrity constraint of the database. A fact Ic will indicate that there is an integrity constraint that is violated.

A *query* Q for a deductive database D is a finite set of deductive rules that defines a dedicated n-ary *query predicate* Q. Without loss of generality, we assume that all predicates other than Q appearing in Q belong to D.

The *answer* to the query is the set of all ground facts about Q obtained as a result of evaluating the deductive rules from both Q and DR on EDB: $\{Q(a^i_1,\ldots, a^i_n) \mid Q(a^i_1,\ldots, a^i_n) \in (Q \cup DR)(EDB)\}$. Therefore, a query Q_1 is *contained* in an another query Q_2 when the set of ground facts answering Q_1 is a subset of the set of ground facts answering Q_2, regardless of the underlying EDB.

Definition 2.1. Let Q_1 and Q_2 be two queries defining the same n-ary query predicate Q on a deductive database $D = (EDB, DR, IC)$. Q_1 *is contained in* Q_2, written $Q_1 \subseteq Q_2$, if $\{Q(a^i_1,\ldots, a^i_n) \mid Q(a^i_1,\ldots, a^i_n) \in (Q_1 \cup DR)(EDB)\} \subseteq \{Q(a^k_1,\ldots,a^k_n) \mid Q(a^k_1,\ldots,a^k_n) \in (Q_2 \cup DR)(EDB)\}$ for any EDB.

When considering integrity constraints, the containment relationship between two queries must not hold for any EDB but only for consistent EDB's, i.e. those that satisfy the integrity constraints. As stated before, we assume that the database defines the inconsistency predicate Ic that holds whenever some integrity constraint is violated. Thus, consistent EDB's are those where the fact Ic does not hold.

Definition 2.2. Let Q_1 and Q_2 be two queries defining the same n-ary query predicate Q on a deductive database $D = (EDB, DR, IC)$. Q_1 *is IC-compliant contained in* Q_2, written $Q_1 \subseteq_{IC} Q_2$, if $\{Q(a^i_1,\ldots, a^i_n) \mid Q(a^i_1,\ldots, a^i_n) \in (Q_1 \cup DR)(EDB)\} \subseteq \{Q(a^k_1,\ldots,a^k_n) \mid Q(a^k_1,\ldots,a^k_n) \in (Q_2 \cup DR)(EDB)\}$ for any EDB such that $Ic \notin (IC \cup DR)(EDB)$.

---

[1] More general constraints can be transformed into this form [LT84]

3   The Constructive Method for QC Checking

As we have just seen, the containment relationship between two queries must hold for the whole set of possible databases in the general case, or for those that satisfy the integrity constraints in the **IC**-compliant case. A suitable way of checking QC is to check the lack of containment, that is, to find just one EDB where the containment relationship that we want to check does not hold.

Given Q_1 and Q_2 two queries defining the same n-ary query predicate Q on a deductive database $D = (EDB, DR, IC)$, the Constructive method for QC Checking, CQC method for shorthand, is addressed to construct one EDB T where the presumed containment relationship does not hold. If the method succeeds, noncontainment is proved. Otherwise, i.e. no EDB may be built, the containment relationship holds.

The first step of the method is to define the *noncontainment goal* expressing the noncontainment relationship between Q_1 and Q_2, which should be satisfied by a certain EDB T. The noncontainment goal is $NC = \leftarrow Q_1(x_1,...,x_n) \wedge \neg Q_2(x_1,...,x_n)$ when trying to prove that $Q_1 \sqsubseteq Q_2$ does not hold. $NC = \leftarrow Q_1(x_1,...,x_n) \wedge \neg Q_2(x_1,...,x_n) \wedge \neg Ic$ when trying to determine whether $Q_1 \sqsubseteq_{IC} Q_2$ is false. $\neg Ic$ is added to NC to ensure that the target EDB does not violate any integrity constraint.

It is also stated the set R that contains the deductive rules defining the query and derived predicates that may appear during the CQC procedure. $R = Q_1 \cup Q_2 \cup DR$ when checking $Q_1 \not\sqsubseteq Q_2$. $R = Q_1 \cup Q_2 \cup DR \cup IC$ when checking $Q_1 \not\sqsubseteq_{IC} Q_2$.

Positive literals in the noncontainment goal NC define information that must be made true by the target EDB. Since some of these literals, e.g. $Q_1(x_1,...,x_n)$, are defined in terms of other, base and/or derived, literals, they will be unfolded, using their defining rules in R, until a goal with only base atoms will be reached. These base atoms will determine the information to be included in the EDB T to satisfy NC.

Moreover, the intermediate goals resulting from this unfolding process could contain negative literals, $\neg Q_2(x_1,...,x_n)$ for instance. Such literals correspond to conditions that must be enforced to guarantee that the noncontainment goal NC remains satisfied. In the particular case of $\neg Q_2(x_1,...,x_n)$, we have to guarantee that base facts required for making $Q_1(x_1,...,x_n)$ true do not make also $Q_2(x_1,...,x_n)$ true at the same time. When one of such conditions is violated, we have to look for additional facts to be included in T to make it succeed again.

Therefore, we can see the work performed by the CQC method as an interleaving of two activities: 1) including base facts in the ongoing target EDB T (constructive derivation); and 2) enforcing that negative literals found during 1) are not satisfied by the current T (consistency derivation). Such activities (derivations) are performed along the way depending on whether the considered literal is positive or negative.

In the remaining of this Section, we illustrate in Section 3.1 how our method works by recapturing the example presented in the introduction. In Section 3.2 we explain in a more detailed way how the method instantiates nonground base atoms before including them to the target EDB T. The formalization of the CQC method as well as execution examples of a concrete implementation are found in [FTU99].

3.1 Example

Let us review the example presented in the introduction. As we saw there, Q_1 was less restrictive than Q_2, so we said that Q_1 was not contained in Q_2. Now, let the CQC method prove that $Q_1 \sqsubseteq Q_2$ does not hold by constructing an EDB **T** satisfying the noncontainment goal $NC = \leftarrow Sub_1(x) \wedge \neg Sub_2(x)$. Such a **T** is built by performing a constructive derivation for NC with **R** as initial input set, where

$$\mathbf{R} = \{ \ Sub_1(x) \leftarrow Emp(x) \wedge \neg Chief(x)$$
$$Sub_2(x) \leftarrow Emp(x) \wedge \neg Boss(x)$$
$$Boss(x) \leftarrow Works\_for(z, x)$$
$$Chief(x) \leftarrow Works\_for(y, x) \wedge Boss(y)\}$$

This constructive derivation is partially shown in figure 3.1. (circled labels appearing at each derivation step are references to the rules of the method as they are defined in [FTU99]). For the sake of simplicity, we suppose left-to-right selection of literals. Note that **T** is initially empty.

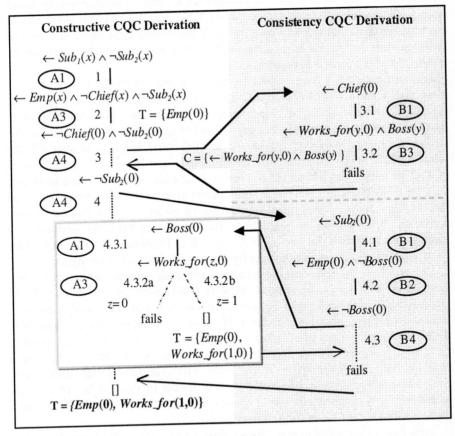

Fig. 3.1.

The first step unfolds the selected literal, the derived atom $Sub_1(x)$, by substituting it with the body of its defining rule in **R**. At step 2, the selected literal is $Emp(x)$, which is a positive base literal. To get a successful derivation, i.e. to obtain an EDB **T** satisfying *NC*, $Emp(x)$ must be true on **T**. For this reason, the method should instantiate x with a constant and include the new ground base fact in **T**. The procedure assigns an arbitrary constant to x, say 0 for instance. So $Emp(0)$ is added to **T**.

At step 3, the selected literal is $\neg Chief(0)$. To get success for this constructive derivation, $Chief(0)$ must not be true by **T**. This is guaranteed by enforcing a consistency derivation for $\{\leftarrow Chief(0)\}$ to fail using $\mathbf{R} \cup (\mathbf{T}=\{Emp(0)\})$ as input set. This consistency derivation is shown in the shaded right half of figure 3.1.

Step 3.1 in this consistency derivation unfolds the selected derived atom $Chief(0)$. At step 3.2 the selected base atom, $Works\_for(y, 0)$, cannot be *unified* with $\mathbf{T}=\{Emp(0)\}$. This means that the current content of **T** does not make $Works\_for(y, 0)$ true, and thus $Chief(0)$ can not be true either. In this case, we say that the consistency derivation fails. However, we must take into account that facts satisfying $\leftarrow Works\_for(y, 0) \wedge Boss(y)$ could be added to **T** in later constructive steps. To prevent these situations, our method uses an auxiliary set **C**, called *condition set*, to record those goals that fail with respect to the current **T** but that could succeed afterwards. In this way, before including a new base fact in **T** the method must check that such an inclusion does not satisfy any condition of **C**. For this reason, the condition $\leftarrow Works\_for(y, 0) \wedge Boss(y)$ is added to **C**.

Since the consistency derivation for $\{\leftarrow Chief(0)\}$ fails, $\neg Chief(0)$ is true at step 3 in the main constructive derivation. At step 4, the selected literal is $\neg Sub_2(0)$. Hence, the CQC method calls a consistency derivation for $\{\leftarrow Sub_2(0)\}$ with $\mathbf{R} \cup (\mathbf{T}=\{Emp(0)\})$, to guarantee that $Sub_2(0)$ is not satisfied by **T**. Step 4.1 in this second consistency derivation unfolds the selected literal $Sub_2(0)$. At step 4.2 the selected literal, the positive base atom $Emp(0)$, can be unified with the current content of **T**. This means that the current content of **T** satisfies the selected base atom and, thus, the method discards this literal in its attempt to make the consistency derivation fail. At step 4.3, the selected literal is $\neg Boss(0)$. To ensure failure of this consistency derivation, $Boss(0)$ must be made true. This is accomplished by performing a constructive derivation for $\leftarrow Boss(0)$ with $\mathbf{R} \cup \left(\mathbf{T}=\{Emp(0)\}\right)$. This subsidiary constructive derivation is shown in the light box on the left half of the figure 3.1

Step 4.3.1 in the subsidiary constructive derivation unfolds the selected literal $Boss(0)$. At step 4.3.2a the selected literal is $Works\_for(z, 0)$. As at step 2, the method should instantiate z with a constant, e.g. the previously introduced constant 0, and include the new ground base fact in **T**. However, before adding $Works\_for(0, 0)$ to **T**, the CQC method must enforce that this inclusion does not violate any condition of **C**. This is done by calling a consistency derivation for $\{\leftarrow Works\_for(y, 0) \wedge Boss(y)\}$ with $\mathbf{R} \cup (\mathbf{T}=\{Emp(0), Works\_for(0, 0)\})$. The fact is that such a new consistency derivation cannot be failed as it is shown in figure 3.2a. That is, the inclusion of $Works\_for(0, 0)$ would violate the condition $\leftarrow Works\_for(y, 0) \wedge Boss(y)$ added at step 3.2, making $\neg Chief(0)$ false.

After this failed attempt to make $Works\_for(z, 0)$ true, the method considers a new constant value, e.g. 1, at step 4.3.2b. Therefore, the current goal is to add

Works_for(1,0) to **T**. Again, we must enforce that such a inclusion does not violate any condition of **C** by calling a consistency derivation for $\{\leftarrow$ *Works_for*(y,0) $\wedge$ *Boss*(y)$\}$ with **R**$\cup$(**T**=$\{Emp(0), Works\_for(1,0)\}$) This is done in steps 4.3.2b.1 to 4.3.2b.3 in figure 3.2b. In this case, the consistency derivation fails and then the method can include *Works_for*(1,0) in **T**. Note that, at step 4.3.2b.3, a new condition $\{\leftarrow$ *Works_for*(z,1)$\}$ has been included in **C** to prevent 1 from becoming a *Boss*. After performing step 4.3.2b, the subsidiary constructive derivation gets the empty clause and, so, it ends successfully. Therefore *Boss*(0) becomes true and the consistency derivation for $\{\leftarrow Sub_2(0)\}$ fails at step 4.3.

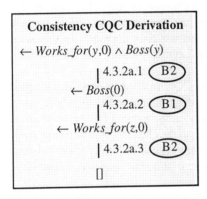

Consistency CQC Derivation	**Consistency CQC Derivation**

Fig. 3.2a   Fig. 3.2b

Returning to the main constructive derivation, these last subsidiary derivations have allowed the method to make $\neg Sub_2(0)$ true at step 4. After this successful step, there are no more literals to be satisfied and CQC method gets the empty clause in the main constructive derivation. Hence, the constructive derivation for $NC = \leftarrow Sub_1(x) \wedge \neg Sub_2(x)$ is over successfully. The constructed EDB **T** is $\{Emp(0), Works\_for(1,0)\}$, proving that $\mathbf{Q_1} \not\subseteq \mathbf{Q_2}$.

3.2 Variable Instantiation Patterns

In the previous example, the CQC has considered the variable instantiations $x = 0$ and $z = 0$ in a first failed attempt (step 4.3.2a), and $z = 1$, as a successful alternative (step 4.3.2b). If this latter instantiation had also failed, the CQC would have considered no other variable instantiation and the subsidiary as well as the main constructive derivation would have failed definitively. The reason is that, in this example, any other constant assignation to x and y would be *isomorphic* with respect to the ones considered previously. That is, any other possible instantiation of the two variables would produce the same result as either $\{x = z = 0\}$ or $\{x = 0, z = 1\}$.

Therefore, the aim of the CQC method is just to check the variable instantiations that are *relevant* to the derivations that it performs, but enforcing at the same time that all the possible relevant alternatives have been checked before accepting the failure of a constructive derivation.

This strategy for instantiating the base facts that the CQC method adds to the target EDB **T** is connected to, indeed it is inspired by, the concept of *canonical databases* [Klu88, Ull89, LS93, BH97, Ull99]. This concept is based on the idea that it is not necessary to check the whole (infinite) set of possible EDBs to prove containment but only a (finite) subset of them, the set of canonical EDBs.

The canonical databases-based approach for QC checking has been applied for the class of conjunctive queries, where queries are expressed in terms of base and/or evaluable atoms. In this case, the whole set of canonical databases is bounded a priori and it is generated easily before performing the containment tests. In contrast, the CQC method is intended to construct dynamically just one "canonical" EDB, the one that proves that QC does not hold, following a test-and-error approach. In this way, the method fails to prove noncontainment after having discarded all the relevant, "canonical", instantiations.

This "dynamic canonical" approach allows the CQC method to deal with negated derived atoms, since it is not always possible to determine a priori the whole set of relevant EDBs to be tested in these cases. Therefore, our method can be seen as an extension of the canonical databases-approach beyond the class of conjunctive queries.

Since the canonical databases to take into account depend on the concrete subclass of queries that are considered, we distinguish two different *variable instantiation patterns*, VIPs for shorthand.

In our running example, with negation but without any arithmetic comparison, the method applied the *Negation VIP* to instantiate facts. The EDBs generated and tested with this VIP correspond to the canonical EDBs considered in [LS93, Ull99] for the conjunctive query case with negation[2] and to the canonical EDBs defined in [BH97] for conjunctive query checking over bag semantics. The intuition behind this VIP is clear: Eeach new variable appearing in a base fact to be grounded is instantiated with either some constant previously used or a constant never used before. In this way, for each pair of variables appearing during the CQC procedure there is an equality relationship: either they are equal and then they" share" the same constant; or they are different and then they are instantiated with distinct constants. In the example, this is manifested by the two variable intantiations $\{x = y = 0\}$ and $\{x = 0, y = 1\}$, respectively

The other VIP, the *General VIP*, is applied when there are arithmetic comparisons, with or without negation. The EDBs generated and tested with this VIP correspond to the canonical EDBs considered in [Klu88, LS93, Ull99] for the conjunctive query case. See [FTU99] for more details on this VIP.

---

[2] That is, conjunctive queries with negated base atoms in their rule bodies.

4 Soundness and Completeness of the Constructive Query Containment Method

In this Section, we summarize the main results concerning the soundness and completeness results of the CQC method.

Theorem 4.1: (Soundness of the CQC Method)
Let Q_1 and Q_2 be two queries defining the same n-ary query predicate Q on a deductive database $D = (EDB, DR, IC)$. If T is an EDB obtained by the CQC Method on the noncontainment goal $NC = \leftarrow Q_1(x_1,...,x_n) \wedge \neg Q_2(x_1,...,x_n) [\wedge \neg Ic]$, then $Q_1 \not\sqsubseteq Q_2$ ($Q_1 \not\sqsubseteq_{IC} Q_2$).

Theorem 4.2: (Completeness of the CQC Method)
Let Q_1 and Q_2 be two queries defining the same n-ary query predicate Q on a deductive database $D = (EDB, DR, IC)$ such that $R = DR \cup Q_1 \cup Q_2 [\cup IC]$ is allowed, strict[3] and stratified. If $Q_1 \not\sqsubseteq Q_2$ (or $Q_1 \not\sqsubseteq_{IC} Q_2$) then the CQC Method obtains an EDB T that satisfies the noncontainment goal $NC = \leftarrow Q_1(x_1,...,x_n) \wedge \neg Q_2(x_1,...,x_n) [\wedge \neg Ic]$.

The detailed proofs of these theorems are given in [FTU99]. Such proofs rely on the soundness and completeness of the SLNDF resolution. In this way, if the SLDNF resolution is sound and complete in the deductive framework that we consider, then the CQC method is also sound and complete for that framework.

5 Decidability issues

The QC problem for the general case of queries and databases that the CQC method covers is undecidable [Shm87, AHV95]. One possible source of undecidability is the presence of recursive derived predicates that could make our method build and test an infinite number of EDBs. Another reason for undecidability is the presence of "axioms of infinity" [BM86] or "embedded TGD's" [Sag88]. In this case, the noncontainment goal could only be satisfied on an EDB with an infinite number of base facts because each new addition of a fact to target EDB T triggers a condition to be *repaired* with another insertion on T and so on.

In any case, the CQC method is semidecidable in the sense that if there exist one or more finite solutions satisfying a noncontainment goal, our method finds/constructs one and terminates. In terms of the concrete behavior of the CQC method, the two sources of undecidability seen before manifest the same "symptom": an inflationary introduction of new variables to be instantiated with the consequent unlimited increment of the set of constants assigned to them. Therefore, to ensure the termination of CQC procedures we could set the maximum number of different constants. In this case, this maximum number of constants would correspond to the *k-degree* of the databases that we would be considering, according to [IS97].

---

[3] See [CL89] for more details.

6   Related Work

We refer to [LMSS92, LS95, Ull99] to find other QC Checking methods that deal with negation. All of them are intended to solve QC for special decidable subclasses of queries, where negation are used in a restrictive way. Besides their differences, these subclasses have in common that negation is only allowed to appear on base atoms.

The inherent undecidability of the QC problem when considering unrestricted negation is bypassed by those methods in [LS93, ST96] that check Uniform QC instead of "true" QC. [LS93] provides an algorithm to check Uniform Query Equivalence, that is whether $Q_1 \subseteq^u Q_2$ and $Q_2 \subseteq^u Q_1$ hold at a time, for datalog queries with safe stratified negation and built-in predicates. In addition, [ST96] proposes a more efficient but incomplete algorithm to perform also uniform query containment.

As pointed out in [Sag88, LS93], uniform QC provides a sufficient but not necessary decidable condition for QC. Hence, if the uniform query containment test fails nothing can be said about whether $Q_1 \subseteq Q_2$ holds. See [FTU98] for a more detailed discussion on this subject.

Finally, there are several works that also take integrity constraints into account when checking QC. As the so called tuple generating dependencies, they were already considered in [Sag88] to check **IC**-compliant QC for datalog queries. Moreover, [ST96] extends [Sag88] by taking also equality generating dependencies into account and [DS96] provides a method to check **IC**-compliant QC for conjunctive queries and disjunctive-datalog integrity rules. However, all these proposals also tackle this problem from the uniform containment approach.

7   Conclusions and Further Work

In this paper we have presented the Constructive Method for QC Checking, which performs QC tests for queries and databases with safe stratified negation and/or integrity constraints. As far as we know, this is the first method that tackles broadly "true" [**IC**-compliant] QC, instead of uniform query containment, for these cases.

The CQC method is sound and complete for those queries and databases for which the SLDNF resolution is sound and complete.

If there exist one or more finite EDBs satisfying a noncontainment goal, the method obtains one and terminates. However, the QC problem in stratified databases is undecidable in the general case. Therefore, to ensure termination for our method, we propose to bound the number of constants to be considered as a possible solution. As a further work we plan to characterize those nontrivial classes of queries and deductive rules for which our method always terminates.

Other possible extensions of our work would be to consider QC in the presence of aggregate functions, queries over bags, or in object oriented databases as addressed in [LS97, CV93, BH97, BJNS94], to mention some previous work.

Acknowledgements

This work has been partially supported by Spanish CICYT (project TIC97-1157).

References

[AHV95]   S. Abiteboul, R. Hull, V. Vianu: *Foundations of Databases*. Addison-Wesley, 1995.

[BH97]   N.R. Brisaboa, H.J. Hernández: "Testing Bag-Containment of Conjunctive Queries". *Acta Informatica*, Vol. 34, No.7, 1997, pp. 557-578.

[BJNS94] M. Buchheit, M.A. Jeusfeld, W. Nutt, M. Staudt: "Subsumption of queries in object-oriented databases". *Information Systems*, Vol. 19, No. 1, 1994.

[CL89]   L. Cavedon, J. Lloyd: "A Completeness Theorem for SLDNF Resolution", Journal of Logic Programming, vol. 7, 1989, pp. 177-191.

[CV93]   S. Chaudhuri, M. Vardi: "Optimizing real conjunctive queries". *Proceedings of the PoDS'93*. ACM Press, 1993, pp. 59-70.

[DS96]   G. Dong, J. Su: "Conjunctive QC with respect to views and constraints". *Information Processing Letters*, No. 57 1996, pp. 95-102.

[FTU98]   C. Farré, E. Teniente, T. Urpí: "Query Containment as a View Updating Problem". *Proceedings of the DEXA'98*. Springer, 1998, pp. 310-321.

[FTU99]   C. Farré, E. Teniente, T. Urpí: *The Constructive Method for Query Containment Checking (extended version)*. Research Report LSI-99-23-R, Universitat Politècnica de Catalunya, 1999.

[IS97]   O.H. Ibarra, J. Su: "On the Containment and Equivalence of Database Queries with Linear Constraints". *Proceedings of the PoDS'97*. 1997, pp. 32-43

[Klu88]   A. Klug: "On Conjunctive Queries Containing Inequalities". *Journal of the ACM*, Vol. 35, No. 1, 1988, pp. 146-160.

[LMSS93] A. Levy, I.S. Mumick, Y. Sagiv, O. Shmueli: "Equivalence, query-reachability and satisfiability in Datalog extensions". *PoDS'93*. pp. 109-122.

[LS93]   A. Levy, Y. Sagiv: "Queries Independent of Updates". *Proceedings of the VLDB'93*. Morgan Kaufmann, 1993, pp. 171-181.

[LS95]   A. Levy, Y. Sagiv: "Semantic Query Optimization in Datalog Programs". *Proceedings of the PoDS'95*. ACM Press, 1995, pp. 163-173.

[LS97]   A. Levy, D. Suciu: "Deciding Containment for Queries with Complex Objects". *Proceedings of the PoDS'97*. ACM Press, 1995, pp. 20-31

[LT84]   J.W. Lloyd, R.W. Topor: "Making Prolog More Expressive". *Journal of Logic Programming*, 1984, No. 3, pp. 225-240.

[Sag88]   Y. Sagiv: "Optimizing Datalog Programs". J. Minker (Ed.): *Foundations of Deductive Databases and Logic Programming*. Morgan Kaufmann, 1988, pp. 659-698.

[Shm87]   O. Shmueli: "Decidability and expressiveness aspects of logic queries". *Proceedings of the PoDS'87*, 1987, pp. 237-249.

[ST96]   M. Staudt, K.v. Thadden: "A Generic Subsumption Testing Toolkit for Knowledge Base Queries". *Proc. of DEXA'96.*, Springer, 1996, pp. 834-844.

[TO95]   E. Teniente, A. Olivé: "Updating Knowledge Bases while Maintaining their Consistency". *The VLDB Journal*, Vol. 4, No. 2, 1995, pp. 193-241.

[Ull89]   J.D. Ullman: *Principles of Database an Knowledge-Base Systems, Volume 2: The New Technologies*. Computer Science Press, Rockville, MD, 1989.

[Ull99]   J.D. Ullman: *Principles of Databases*. Lecture notes of the course. http://www-db.stanford.edu/~ullman/cs345-notes.html

On the Specification of Representation-Based Conditions in a Context of Incomplete Databases

Patrick Bosc, Olivier Pivert

IRISA/ENSSAT
Technopole Anticipa BP 447
22305 Lannion Cedex France
{bosc, pivert}@enssat.fr

Abstract. In this paper, we are concerned with the querying of databases containing imperfect attribute values. In the usual querying approach, a condition compares a variable (associated with an attribute) and a value, which leads to an answer pervaded with uncertainty. In the approach we propose (described as representation-based), a condition concerns the representation of an ill-known attribute value, and, as such, induces no uncertainty in the answers. The idea is to exploit at the querying level some concepts which are part of the model used for representing ill-known data, and which concern the qualification of imprecision/uncertainty. A formal framework suited to the expression of this new type of query is presented and a typology of representation-based queries is given, with the corresponding expressions in that framework.

1 Introduction

For many years, database management systems have been used almost exclusively for applications (mainly business applications) where data were perfectly known. However, in real life, information is often imperfect in several ways. Giving a precise characterization of imperfectness is not easy, but several different situations can be pointed out, notably the two following ones.

First, attribute values can be ill-known. Indeed, the attribute value of an item may be completely unknown, partially known (i.e. known as belonging to a proper subset of the attribute domain), or somewhat uncertain. This latter case can be dealt with through different formalisms (probability [1], [8], and possibility theory [16, 17], in particular; see [21] for a survey). Besides, an attribute may be irrelevant for some of the considered items; moreover we may not know whether the value does not exist or is simply unknown.

Second, the information relating to a fact can be uncertain. In this case, weighted relations may be handled, and the information in a tuple is qualified with a certainty (or a possibility, or a probability, depending on the type of knowledge available) equal to its weight.

In this paper, we only consider the case where attribute values may be ill-known. Besides the representation issue, an important aspect is the handling of such data. Up to now, the querying of databases containing imperfect values has been considered to relate to the same general principle as usual database querying: the conditions allowed concern the *value* that a variable (associated with a given attribute) can take. When attribute values are ill-known, this querying approach leads to uncertainty in the answers. For instance, let us suppose that an image I1 represents an airplane whose (ill-known) type is represented by the disjunctive set {Mig-31, Mig-23, Su-33}. An example of a usual filtering (i.e., value-based) criterion is: "find the images representing a Mig" (in this case, I1 belongs to the set of possible answers, but not to the set of certain answers because of the candidate Su-33). This querying philosophy corresponds to an important type of information need, but another kind of approach can be thought of. An example is the filtering criterion: "find the images for which at least three candidate values are possible for the airplane type". In this case, I1 belongs to the result, which is no longer uncertain. In this type of querying approach (described as representation-based in the following), a condition concerns the *set of candidates* for a given attribute value, i.e., the *representation* of this attribute value. The approach we propose goes beyond the handling of simple disjunctions; it is also intended to deal with weighted disjunctions in order to allow the querying of possibilistic or probabilistic data. Then, the information concerning the underlying levels of imprecision and/or uncertainty has to be taken into account too. An important point is that representation-based conditions cannot be expressed using the same constructs as value-based conditions. Therefore, there is a need for a specific framework suitable for this new type of query, and the main contribution of this paper consists in the introduction of such a framework.

The remainder of this paper is structured as follows. Section 2 is devoted to the modeling of ill-known atomic values. We point out the fact that imperfect data can be represented in terms of different kinds of disjunctions. In Section 3, we present the basic principles of a formal framework for the expression of representation-based conditions. Section 4 illustrates the use of this framework, through several examples of queries.

2 Representing Imperfect Values: a Brief Survey

Hereafter, we present several approaches that have been proposed to handle imperfect data values in the framework of the relational model of data.

2.1 Null Values

For databases under the closed world assumption, two notable types of null values have been proposed [7] [2]: i) existential value (denoted ω): the value exists, but it is not known, ii) inexistent value (denoted $\perp$): the value does not exists (in other words, it is not applicable). Imielinsky and Lipski [12] introduced several unknown values for obtaining a richer modeling power, and they generalized the relational algebra operators.

2.2 Disjunctive Sets

Or-sets (or disjunctive sets) [14] generalize existential null values. An existential value represents an attribute whose actual value is in a database domain. An or-set represents an attribute whose value is in an explicit, smaller set. An ordinary atomic value can be viewed as a singleton. An existential value corresponds to an or-set containing the entire attribute domain (it is indeed a disjunction of all the values of the domain).

2.3 Weighted Disjunctive Sets

Probability theory and possibility theory are two possible frameworks for managing uncertainty. In both frameworks, an uncertain value is represented by a weighted disjunction, the difference residing in the meaning of the weights and in the nature of the uncertainty modeled.

A probabilistic database (see for instance [1]) contains probabilistic information about data values in the following way. Probabilistic relations have key attributes that are deterministic, as in classical relations. The other attributes may be deterministic or stochastic. The latter are described with the help of probabilistic sets. An example of such a probabilistic relation is shown hereafter:

Takes	Student	Course
	John	{Algebra/0.5, Calculus/0.4}
	Ann	{Physics/0.5, Calculus/0.5}

The relation above has six possible worlds (because John can also take no course), and a probability degree can be computed for each world.

On the other hand, the possibility theory [20] provides a purely ordinal model for uncertainty where imprecision is represented by means of a preference relation coded by a total order over the possible situations. The concept of a possibility distribution in a universe X refers to an application π of X to [0, 1] which is interpreted as a restriction of the possible values of a variable taking its values in X. We denote by $\pi(a)$ the degree of possibility that the effective value of x is a. The possibilitic approach can be applied for representing uncertain values in a relational database in the following way (see [16, 17]). The available information about the value of a single-valued attribute A for a tuple x is represented by a possibility distribution $\pi_{A(x)}$ on $D \cup \{e\}$ where D denotes the domain of attribute A and e is an extra-element which stands for the case when the attribute does not apply to x. If information is consistent, there should exist a value in $D \cup \{e\}$ for A(x), which leads to the normalization condition $\max_d \pi_{A(x)}(d) = 1$ (i.e., at least one value in $D \cup \{e\}$ is completely possible). This approach proposes a unified framework for representing precise values, as well as imprecise ones (regular sets) or vague ones (fuzzy sets), and various null value situations.

3 A New Type of Conditions: Representation-Based Conditions

3.1 Principles of Representation-Based Querying

Representation-based querying [3, 5] consists in exploiting at a query level some concepts of the data model which concern the representation of imprecision and/or uncertainty. In order to illustrate this approach, let us consider a military database containing aerial images of aircrafts (each image is supposed to represent a single aircraft), described by the set of attributes: (#id, location, date, type). The attributes #id, location, and date are supposed to take precise values whereas the attribute "type" describing the type of aircraft present in the picture will generally take imperfect values (in many cases, during the scene interpretation process, uncertainty will result from ambiguities in interpretations).

Let us assume that imperfect values are represented by possibility distributions. An example of such a description is: (7, Dolon, 02-03-96, { 1/Mig-31, .8/Mig-29, .6/Mig-23, .4/Su-33}). Now let us consider the query: "find the images for which the set of type candidates contains at least two elements whose possibility degree is over .7". In this querying approach, a condition concerns the *representation* of a given attribute value, i.e., the *set of candidates* for that attribute value. In this sense, there is a certain similarity between representation-based querying and the querying of databases containing multivalued attributes. In both cases, a condition may refer explicitly to a set of values, the difference being that in the first case, the elements are seen as candidate values whereas in the latter case, they are all supposed to be actual values.

It is important to notice that representation-based queries are not just value-based queries expressed another way, but that they are queries of a different nature. A value-based criterion applying to an ill-known value has to be evaluated on each possible world associated with the attribute value (even though the explicit computation of those worlds is not always necessary). On the other hand, the evaluation of a representation-based query does not rest on a concept of possibility of matching and thus does not induce any uncertainty. We have shown in [3] that representation-based queries in general cannot be formulated in a value-based querying framework.

An important remark concerns the assumption underlying the representation-based approach, i.e., the assumption that the queries do not produce uncertain results inasmuch as the conditions involved apply to precise information (i.e., the descriptions of ill-known data). As soon as the descriptions are no longer precise, some representation-based criteria must be dismissed since they would introduce uncertainty in the answers (it can be the case, for instance, in a probabilistic context where some distributions are allowed to be incomplete, cf. [1]).

3.2 Motivations

The main motivation underlying the representation-based querying approach is to be able to exploit *at a query level* all the information available concerning the qualification of imperfectness in the data. In other words, we want to be able to express conditions on the descriptions of ill-known data. The concept of a representation-based query is somewhat similar to that of a structural query introduced in [13] in a slightly different context (the authors consider complex objects represented as unweighted sets (disjunctive or conjunctive) whose elements can be themselves regular or disjunctive sets). Representation-based queries can notably be used to:

i) express conditions on specified sets of candidates (the specified set being a subset of a given distribution representing an ill-known attribute value). The corresponding generic query is: "find the tuples such that all the elements of a specified subset of the candidate values (for a certain attribute) satisfy a given condition".

ii) compute aggregates on the weighted sets corresponding to the representations of ill-known data (e.g., the cardinality of a specified subset of candidate values for a given attribute) and to use these aggregates inside conditions.

iii) compare a piece of data with a given pattern in a context where the data are ill-known and the user cannot express his information needs precisely but rather uses linguistic descriptions. Let us consider for instance the case of a database system containing facial images such as described in [11]. Such images can be described by various facial features such as length of hair, size of eyes, length of nose, etc. It is not quite easy to determine a precise value for each of these attributes, and a more convenient way of describing the images (and of formulating queries) consists in using linguistic labels (interpreted as possibility distributions) such as "short", "narrow", "fairly long", etc. In the representation-based querying framework, the comparison is based on the notion of synonymy of representations, contrary to what is done, for instance, in the (value-based) possibilistic framework where the comparison is based on the notion of possibility/necessity of matching.

4 A Language for Representation-Based Querying

A common point to the probabilistic and the possibilistic data models is the notion of set which is used to represent the different candidates for a given attribute value. We will thus define a formal framework, based on the concept of a weighted set, allowing to express representation-based conditions.

4.1 Conditions Involving One Representation

Two kinds of constructs are necessary in order to express conditions on sets of values. On the one hand, one must have some functions extracting a set from another one. On the other hand, aggregate functions must be available.

A weighted set is assumed to be a set of pairs (v_i, d_i) defined on $V \times D$ where V denotes the domain of the attribute and D is the unit interval. As noted before, at least two meanings are possible for d_i: probability degree or possibility degree. Let us notice that or-sets are a special case of a possibility distribution where all the elements have the degree 1.

In this context, an extraction function f is defined on $V \times D$ and it consists of a conjunction of two conditions: one used to filter the values, the other one to filter the degrees:

$$f = [f_v, f_d] \text{ with } f_v: V \to \{\text{true, false}\} \text{ and } f_d: D \to \{\text{true, false}\}.$$

A condition $f_v(x)$ is of the form:

$$f_v(x) = x \; \theta_1 \; v_1 \; \textbf{and/or} \; ... \; \textbf{and/or} \; x \; \theta_n \; v_n$$

where the θ_i's are comparators ($\{=, \neq, >, \geq, <, \leq\}$ for numerical attributes, $\{=, \neq,$ contains, etc$\}$ for character strings and so on), and the v_i's are elements of V (either literals or aggregate expressions, this latter case corresponding to a nested query). Similarly, a condition $f_d(y)$ is of the form:

$$f_d(y) = y \; \theta_1 \; d_1 \; \textbf{and/or} \; ... \; \textbf{and/or} \; y \; \theta_n \; d_n$$

where the θ_i's are comparators ($=, \neq, >, \geq, <, \leq$), and the d_i's are elements of D (either literals or aggregate expressions, this latter case corresponding again to a nested query).

As far as aggregates are concerned, one needs to consider functions aggregating values of V and functions aggregating degrees. In other terms, one needs to have available two sets of standard aggregate functions:

$$G_v = \{v\text{-count, v-id, v-min, v-max, v-avg, v-sum}\}$$
$$G_d = \{d\text{-count, d-id, d-min, d-max, d-avg, d-sum}\}.$$

The aggregate function v-id (resp. d-id) is assumed to return the value of a singleton given as an argument (and d-id returns 0 if its argument is the empty set). Depending on V, only a subset of G_v may make sense. Similarly, depending on the framework used (probabilistic or possibilistic), not all the functions from G_d will be available (for instance, sum appears useful only in a probabilistic framework). In addition to these standard functions, some user-defined aggregate functions may also appear in a query (cf. example iii in the next section).

Finally, the general form of a representation-based condition C: $W \rightarrow \{\text{true, false}\}$ (where W is the set of all the weighted sets defined on $V \times D$) will be:

$$C(A) = g_1(f_1(A)) \; \theta_1 \; \alpha_1 \; \text{and/or} \; ... \; \text{and/or} \; g_n(f_n(A)) \; \theta_n \; \alpha_n$$

where $g_i \in G_v \cup G_d$, the f_i's are extraction functions as defined above, the θ_i's are comparators and the α_i's are either literals or aggregate expressions.

4.2 Some Examples in the Context of a Database Describing Images

Hereafter, we consider different types of representation-based conditions involving one attribute and give some examples of such conditions expressed in the framework proposed above. Let A be a weighted set corresponding to an attribute value, and V the domain of A. Let v (resp. d) denote a variable on V (resp. on D = [0, 1]). Again, we consider as an example a military database containing aerial images of aircrafts.

i) Conditions referring to the degrees of some values of the domain:

- find the images which represent more likely a Mig-29 than a Mig-23

$$C(A) = (d\text{-id}([v = \text{'Mig-29', true}](A)) \geq d\text{-id}([v = \text{'Mig-23', true}](A)))$$

- find the images such that all the candidates which are possible (or probable) over .3 are of the type Mig

$$C(A) = (v\text{-count}([true, d > .3](A)) = v\text{-count}([v = 'Mig\text{-}*', d > .3](A))).$$

ii) Conditions referring to the cardinality of a given α-cut (i.e., set of values whose grades are not less than α):

- find the images for which at most 2 types of airplane are considered possible (or probable) over degree .3

$$C(A) = (v\text{-count}([true, d \geq .3](A)) \leq 2)$$

- find the images for which the only best candidate is 'Mig-29'

$$C(A) = (d\text{-id}([v = 'Mig\text{-}29', true](A) = 1 \text{ and}$$
$$v\text{-count}([true, d = pmax(A)](A) = 1)$$

where $pmax(A)$ returns the highest degree in the distribution A (in the possibilistic framework, this degree is necessarily equal to 1 because of the normalization condition).

iii) Conditions on the imprecision of an attribute value.

- find the images representing airplanes whose type is not precisely known (i.e., there are more than one candidate)

$$C(A) = (v\text{-count}([true, true](A)) > 1)$$

If one wants to qualify more accurately the amount of imprecision attached to an attribute value, one can use a specific measure indicating the extent to which a value is imprecise. Such measures are studied in [19]. Let us denote by d-spec such a function. It can play the role of a user-defined aggregate in a query, which allows to express a filtering predicate such as:

- the amount of imprecision associated to A is less than α

$$C(A) = (d\text{-spec}([true, true](A)) < \alpha.$$

iv) Conditions on the uncertainty level attached to a given attribute value (possibilistic framework): it is the largest value α in [0, 1] such that $\forall x \in V$, the degree associated to x in the considered distribution is not less than α. In order to express such queries, it is necessary to have available the cardinality of the related domain (denoted $|domain(A)|$ hereafter).

- the uncertainty level associated to A is less than λ

$$C(A) = (v\text{-count}([true, d \geq \lambda](A) < |domain(A)|)$$

Example. Let us consider an item I from the part of the database where images of helicopters are stored: I = (17, Arkhangelsk, 09-27-96, {1/Ka-52, .7/Ka-50, .4/Mi-26T}), and let us assume that the underlying domain is D = {Ka-50, Ka-52, Mi-26T}. The uncertainty level associated to the attribute "type" of image I is equal to .4 ♦

These conditions being Boolean, the result of a query will be a usual relation (i.e., a relation containing non-weighted tuples). However, in the possibilistic framework, such criteria may also take a fuzzy form. For example, one can imagine to use gradual representation-based conditions such as "all the candidate values $\{v_1, ..., v_n\}$ have a *high* degree of possibility", "*many* candidate values are possible over a degree λ", the attribute value A is *very* imprecise, etc. Then, the result would be a fuzzy relation i.e., a relation where a membership degree is assigned to each tuple.

4.3 Conditions Involving Two Representations

The idea, here, is to perform a kind of "syntactic" comparison of two weighted sets. This comparison can check for equality, inclusion, etc. of two representations. For the sake of brevity, let us focus on equality checking. Let us consider an attribute A and two items x and y whose A-values are ill-known. Let us denote by $\pi_{A(x)}$ and $\pi_{A(y)}$ the (possibility or probability) distributions that we want to compare. Let V be the domain of attribute A. Straightforwardly, the expression of strict equality is:

$$\forall v \in V, \pi_{A(x)}(v) = \pi_{A(y)}(v).$$

However, it seems particularly interesting to have available a measure of approximate equality in order to take fully into account the ambiguities in interpretations. In the possibilistic framework, several representation-based measures of approximate equality have been proposed. In [18], Raju and Majumdar define such a measure, denoted by EQ, in the following way:

$$\mu_{EQ}(\pi_{A(x)}, \pi_{A(y)}) = \min_{u \in V} \psi(\pi_{A(x)}(u), \pi_{A(y)}(u))$$

where ψ is a resemblance relation (i.e., reflexive and symmetric) over [0, 1]. Similar methods have also been advocated in [15] and [17]. An alternative approach consists in defining the similarity of two fuzzy sets (two possibility distributions in our case) A and B as a function of A $\cap$ B, B − A and A − B. This approach is studied in particular in [6]. In [9] and [11], another method founded on a so-called fuzziness dependent matching measure [10] is proposed.

The approach defined in [4] deals with the case where a resemblance relation on domains is available. Then, the comparison consists in estimating the extent to which the respective representations of A(x) and A(y) are interchangeable with respect to the considered resemblance relation. The corresponding measure of interchangeability defined in [4] generalizes Raju and Majumdar's measure of fuzzy equality.

On the one hand, such representation-based measures can be used to define selection or join conditions aimed at comparing two ill-known attribute values. An example is: "find the images taken over Krasnoyarsk that represent the same (or similar) airplane(s)" (meaning: airplanes described the same way). On the other hand, these measures can be used to compare an ill-known attribute value with a linguistic value acting as a constant. The basic idea is the same: one evaluates the extent to which the predicate and the linguistic value represent the same concept. In other words, one measures the synonymy of their representations, contrary to what is done in the possibilistic value-based querying framework where one evaluates a possibility/necessity of matching. This approach is especially useful in the context of applications where user queries can be conveniently expressed by means of linguistic terms defined on continuous domains. This is the case for instance in the application described in [11] which deals with the retrieval of facial images, and where a user can submit a query such as "find the images of persons with fairly long hair, a slender face and a high forehead".

Lastly, the concept of representation-based comparison can be used to define the notions of representation-based intersection, union and difference in a straightforward manner.

5 Conclusion

In this paper, we have proposed a querying framework allowing to handle ill-known data at a representation level. This framework, based on the notion of a weighted set, involves three types of constructs (extraction function, aggregate, comparison operator), and reveals itself simple and powerful. Future works should concern the definition of a higher level query language integrating the functionalities described here.

References

1. Barbará, D., Garcia-Molina, H., Porter, D.: The Management of Probabilistic Data. IEEE Transactions on Knowledge and Data Engineering **4** (1992) 487-502
2. Biskup, J.: A Formal Approach to Null Values in Database Relations. In: Gallaire, H., Nicolas, J.M. (eds.): Advances in Data Base Theory, Vol. 1. Plenum Press (1981) 299-341
3. Bosc, P., Pivert, O.: On Representation-Based Querying of Databases Containing Ill-Known Values. Lecture Notes in Artificial Intelligence, Vol. 1325. Springer Verlag, Berlin Heidelberg New York (1997) 477-486
4. Bosc, P., Pivert, O.: On the Comparison of Imprecise Values in Fuzzy Databases. Proc. of the 6th IEEE Int. Conf. on Fuzzy Systems, Barcelona, Spain (1997) 707-712
5. Bosc, P., Pivert, O.: A New Approach to the Filtering of Ill-Known Data. Proc. of the 7th IEEE Int. Conf. on Fuzzy Systems, Anchorage, USA (1998) 1302-1307
6. Bouchon-Meunier, B., Rifqi, M., Bothorel, S.: Towards General Measures of Comparison of Objects. Fuzzy Sets and Systems **84** (1996) 143-153
7. Codd, E.F.: Extending the Database Relational Model to Capture More Meaning. ACM Transactions on Database Systems **4** (1979) 397-434
8. Dey, D., Sarkar, S.: A Probabilistic Relational Model and Algebra. ACM Transactions on Database Systems **21** (1996) 339-369

9. Fukushima, S., Ralescu, A.: Improved Retrieval in a Fuzzy Database from Adjusted User Input. J. of Intelligent Information Systems **5** (1995) 183-210

10. Gasos, J., Ralescu, A.: Fuzziness Dependent Matching of Fuzzy Sets. Proc. of the First Asian Fuzzy Systems Symposium, Singapore (1993)

11. Gasos, J., Ralescu, A.: Adapting Query Representation to Improve Retrieval in a Fuzzy Database. Int. J. of Uncertainty, Fuzziness and Knowledge-Based Systems **3** (1995) 57-77

12. Imielinski, T., Lipski, W.: Incomplete Information in Relational Databases. J. of the ACM **31** (1984) 761-791

13. Libkin, L., Wong, L.: Semantic Representations and Query Languages for Or-Sets. Proc. of the 12th PODS Conf. (1993) 37-48

14. Lipski, W.: On Semantic Issues Connected with Incomplete Information Databases. ACM Transactions on Database Systems **4** (1979) 262-296

15. Liu, W.: The Fuzzy Functional Dependency on the Basis of the Semantic Distance. Fuzzy Sets and Systems **59** (1993) 173-179

16. Prade, H.: Lipski's Approach to Incomplete Information Data Bases Restated and Generalized in the Setting of Zadeh's Possibility Theory. Information Systems **9** (1984) 27-42

17. Prade, H., Testemale, C.: Generalizing Database Relational Algebra for the Treatment of Incomplete/Uncertain Information and Vague Queries. Information Sciences **34** (1984) 115-143

18. Raju, K.V.S.V.N., Majumdar, A.K.: Fuzzy Functional Dependencies and Lossless Join Decomposition of Fuzzy Relational Database Systems. ACM Transactions on Database Systems **13** (1988) 129-166

19. Yager, R.R.: On the Specificity of a Possibility Distribution. In: Dubois, D., Prade, H., Yager, R.R. (eds.): Readings in Fuzzy Sets for Intelligent Systems. Morgan Kaufmann Publishers (1993) 203-216

20. Zadeh, L.A.: Fuzzy Sets as a Basis for a Theory of Possibility. Fuzzy Sets and Systems **1** (1978) 3-28

21. Zimanyi, E., Pirotte, A.: Imperfect Information in Relational Databases. In: Motro, A., Smets, P. (eds.): Uncertainty Management in Information Systems, Kluwer Academic Publishers (1997) 35-87

Methods and Interpretation of Database Summarisation

John F. Roddick[1], Mukesh K. Mohania[1] and Sanjay Kumar Madria[2]

[1] School of Computer and Information Science, University of South Australia,
The Levels Campus, Mawson Lakes, South Australia 5095, Australia.
Email: {roddick, mohania}@cis.unisa.edu.au
[2] Department of Computer Science, Purdue University,
West Lafayette, Indiana, IN 47907, USA
Email: skm@cs.purdue.edu

Abstract. The summarisation of large quantities of linear, tabular and multi-dimensional data to a more manageable quantity has found application in a number of areas including mobile databases, data warehouses, executive reporting and summary (commonly main memory) databases. The method of summarisation used has a significant bearing on the manner in which the resultant data can be employed and the way in which the information content can be subsequently interpreted. This paper surveys various summarisation procedures and provides a categorisation of the mechanisms by which information can be summarised and the nature and conditions under which valid interpretation of the summarised data can be made.

Keywords: Data Summarisation, Inference, Information Capacity, Existential Domain Values, Relation Decomposition.

1 Introduction

The summarisation of data is becoming increasingly important for a number of reasons. Firstly, the increasing quantities of data being collected demands efficient methods for storing and analysing that data. This demand is resulting *inter alia* in the development of more or less autonomous data mining techniques, which aim to extract useful knowledge from structured and semi-structured data. Secondly, Moore's Law is continuing to apply to the affordability of disk space but is not currently applicable to I/O channel speed improvements, resulting in a greater proportion of processes involving large datasets becoming I/O-bound. Offline analysis of data and data summarisation are thus being offered as solutions to reduce the volume of data needed to be read in real-time. Thirdly, increasing business competitiveness is requiring an information-based industry to make more use of its accumulated data and thus techniques of presenting useful data to decision makers in a timely manner is becoming crucial.

However, while data summarisation is becoming increasingly used in data mining, data warehouses, data visualisation and main memory databases, to date the mechanisms for data summarisation have been designed for each specific task and this has frequently led to a summarisation procedure producing data which cannot be reused for other purposes. For example, a summarisation procedure that provides synoptic data for management decision-making may or may not be able to be used for query optimisation or data distribution. While the costs of summarisation remains low this is not a problem but as the volume of data increases, summaries that can be used for a number of purposes become extremely useful. Moreover, applications such as mobile databases (which have limited and intermittent access to data on the main server) increasingly rely on making the most of transportable summaries.

This work builds on some earlier work which outlined a process for utilising summary data as an alternative to main database access [10]. The concept was to decompose a query such that some of the fine-grained segments of that query might be able to be answered by the summary. The query segments are executed in parallel with the faster, local database either providing an answer in a shorter time or failing, in which case the main database was used, if available. The advantage of this method is that on the occasions that both summary and main database failed to provide an answer, an *over-complete* answer is often possible. For further details please refer to the previous paper.

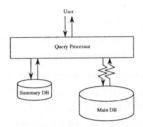

Fig. 1. Parallel Summary and Main DB Access

This paper thus investigates the ways in which databases can be summarised with a view to providing *maximal* support for such architectures given the space restrictions. Summarisation techniques discussed include horizontal and vertical decomposition, domain lattices and existential and statistical attributes. Section 2 provides a discussion on the scope of the techniques available while Section 3 discusses in more depth the semantics of concepts as domain values in a summary database. Section 4 provides a formal categorisation of these techniques and Section 5 provides a further discussion of the field including some ideas for future research.

Other previous work in this area includes studies towards the development of induction in databases which included some discussion on the ways of summarising data [8, 9] and a discussion of the effects of accommodating hierarchical domains on a query language is provided in [11]. Other early work in this area includes [2, 6, 12].

2 Data Summarisation Techniques - Discussion and Scope

The various methods of summarisation can be categorised in many different ways. For example, as data summarisation is rarely lossless[1], summarisation techniques could be

---

[1] in that there is normally some inference that could have been made from the original data that cannot be made from the summary.

categorised by the information lost during the process (both explicitly and implicitly) or the structural manner in which the data is eliminated. Alternatively, since inference will be applied to the resultant data, techniques could be categorised by the classes of inference that can be performed, perhaps weighting the classes according to business criteria.

The manner in which the method of summarisation is chosen is highly application dependent and can be complex but includes factors such as the space available, the query hit rate required, the ability to update the summary, the expected or historical query profile, etc. In its simplest form, given a query Q on a database D composed of relations $R_1, R_2 \ldots R_n$ and a series of summarisation functions $S_1, S_2 \ldots S_n$, the ideal summarisation process is such that

$$Q(D) = Q(S_1(R_1), S_2(R_2), \ldots S_n(R_n)) \tag{1}$$

That is, the answer provided by the summarised relation is identical with that that would have been obtained from the original database. For this to happen the summarisation techniques must be chosen carefully.

In all of the following examples, we assume that, together with the resultant summary relation, the mechanism used for its construction (and therefore its relationship with the source relation) is known and available. As an example of summarisation for discussion, consider the example below which shows an original Employee relation and four successive summarisations.

Employee	Name	Id	Position	Level	PositionType	Salary
	Smith, Jane	872	Full Professor	1	Academic	$80,500
	Brown, Len	773	Associate Professor	2	Academic	$65,000
	Wong, Anne	876	Associate Professor	3	Academic	$68,000
	Black, John	992	Senior Lecturer	1	Academic	$55,000
	Grey, Kim	090	Senior Lecturer	1	Academic	$55,000
	Green, Mike	138	Lecturer	2	Academic	$43,000
	Long, Angela	094	Lecturer	2	Academic	$43,000
	Brittain, Jack	138	Lecturer	3	Academic	$45,500
	Tan, Jim	873	Programmer	1	Non-Academic	$36,000
	Lee, Leslie	590	Administrative Officer	2	Non-Academic	$27,500

Employee2	Position	Level	PositionType	Salary
	Full Professor	1	Academic	$80,500
	Associate Professor	2	Academic	$65,000
	Associate Professor	3	Academic	$68,000
	Senior Lecturer	1	Academic	$55,000
	Lecturer	2	Academic	$43,000
	Lecturer	3	Academic	$45,500
	Programmer	1	Non-Academic	$36,000
	Administrative Officer	2	Non-Academic	$27,500

Employee3	Position	Level	Salary
	Full Professor	1	$80,500
	Associate Professor	2	$65,000
	Associate Professor	3	$68,000
	Senior Lecturer	1	$55,000
	Lecturer	2	$43,000
	Lecturer	3	$45,500

Employee4	Position	Salary Range
	Full Professor	$80,500
	Associate Professor	$65,000 - $68,000
	Senior Lecturer	$55,000
	Lecturer	$43,000 - $45,000

Employee5	Position	Salary Range
	Senior Academic Staff	$65,000 - $80,500
	Junior Academic Staff	$43,000 - $55,000

Each of these summarisations has reduced the size of the previous relation and represents a different method of summarisation. Moreover, at each point a number of alternative steps in the summarisation process were available. Employee2 is constructed from Employee by deleting the two attributes with the largest spread of domain values and eliminating duplicates. Employee3 is constructed by retaining only tuples with a PositionType of Academic and removing the attribute PositionType. Employee4 then introduces range values into the Salary domain and collapses a number of tuples as a consequence, and Employee5 then utilises concept hierarchies (qv. section 3) to reduce the Position field to fewer values.

Each type of reduction also results in a different semantic interpretation. For example, a query that requires merely the attributes that remain can be answered from Employee2 as easily as it can from Employee (and possibly more quickly if Employee2 is able to be stored on a faster access device or at a local site or in main memory). The same query of Employee3 can only be answered if it was known that only those tuples with a PositionType of Academic were to be included, for instance, by an explicit reference in the query or by virtue of an interim result. By the time summarisation reduces to Employee5 the available information is restricted severely, particularly if the rules by which the data has been summarised are not available. Consider the following five queries:

- *What is Professor Smith's Salary?*
- *Given that Leslie Lee is an Administrative Officer, what is her salary?*
- *Given that Jane Smith is a Professor, what is her salary?*
- *Does the Department employee any Associate Professors?*
- *What is the minimum salary paid to a Senior Academic Staff member?*

Assuming we know the summarisation mechanisms, Employee can provide answers to all five of these questions, Employee2 to all but the first question, Employee3 to all but the first two, etc.[2]

---

[2] In some circumstances, the ability to answer a closely related question or provide an answer which is a generalisation of the correct answer (for instance in real-time applications, mobile

There is an important issue here – note that not only the answer, but also the *ability* to answer is as dependent on the data as on the construction of the relation. This differs from unsummarised relations in which the ability to answer the question is dependent wholly on the database structure. For example, the question *Given that Mike Green is a Lecturer, what is his salary?* cannot be answered by reference to `Employee2` (unlike the example regarding Leslie Lee's salary above).

The *interpretation* of the absence of information in an unsummarised (ie. a source) relation is commonly governed by the closed world assumption – put simply, if it is not recorded, it is considered false. For summary relations a tri-state logic approach is necessary and this must be incorporated into the mechanism for interpreting summarised relations. For example, again used `Employee2` consider the following questions:

– *Given that Jane Smith is a Full Professor, what is her Salary?*
– *Given that Anne Wong is an Associate Professor, what is her Salary?*
– *Given that Chris Trent is an Assistant Professor, what is his Salary?*

The first can be answered, the second and third cannot. However, the second cannot because some ambiguity between the salary level of an Associate Professor has been introduced by the summarisation process. The third cannot answer as `Employee2` shows that there are no Assistant Professors recorded. Moreover, assuming we know the summarisation method, `Employee2` can also state the that main database will not be able to answer the query either.

2.1 Augmenting the Summary Relation

Note that some augmentation, in the form of additional attributes, could also be performed during summarisation. For example, the number of original tuples represented by the summarised tuple might be held which could assist in answering some questions. For example, `Employee` might be reduced to `Employee2B` as below.

Employee2B	Position	Level	PositionType	Salary	Source Cardinality
	Full Professor	1	Academic	$80,500	1
	Associate Professor	2	Academic	$65,000	1
	Associate Professor	3	Academic	$68,000	1
	Senior Lecturer	1	Academic	$55,000	2
	Lecturer	2	Academic	$43,000	2
	Lecturer	3	Academic	$45,500	1
	Programmer	1	Non-Academic	$36,000	1
	Administrative Officer	2	Non-Academic	$27,500	1

A question such as *How many Senior Lecturers are in the Department?* could then be answered.

Furthermore, if we were to impose the rule that all source tuples were to be represented *in some form* in the summarised relation, perhaps through the introduction of additional existential domain values (such as *Other values*, *Many values*, etc.), then further

databases, etc.) may be useful and could be performed. This aspect is not covered here and readers are directed to other work, such as [5, 10], for further details.

questions still could continue to be answered. Consider the reduction of `Employee2B` to `Employee3B` as below.

Employee3B	Position	Level	Salary	Source Cardinality
	Full Professor	1	$80,500	1
	Associate Professor	2	$65,000	1
	Associate Professor	3	$68,000	1
	Senior Lecturer	1	$55,000	2
	Lecturer	2	$43,000	2
	Lecturer	3	$45,500	1
	OTHER	MANY	OTHER	2

In this example, a question such as *How many members of the Department are there?* could continue to be answered. Note that the space taken for a source cardinality attribute or the existential domain values would normally be relatively small. The semantics of existential domain values is considered formally in section 4.5.

Clearly, it is important if we are to reuse summarised data for a number of purposes that there is a general understanding of the semantics of generalised data and of the rules of reduction, particularly if summarised data is to be shared between systems.

3 Concepts as Domain Values

3.1 Semantics

It is essential to define carefully the semantics of summarised data including the use of any higher level concepts that will be used as domain values. The definition of null, for example, in classical relational database theory had a number of meanings, the two most significant being [15]:

- The attribute value was unknown;
- The attribute was inapplicable.

The misinterpretation of this value has led, on occasions, to problems[3]. The definition of concepts as domain values must be similarly carefully defined (indeed, perhaps more so) particularly if range queries are to be processed correctly. There are at least three possible interpretations when a concept is used as a domain value such as in `Employee5` (remembering that a tuple in a summary database may represent a number of instances):

- The attribute takes zero or more of the values represented by the concept;
- The attribute takes one or more of the values represented by the concept;
- The attribute takes all of the values represented by the concept.

---

[3] Note that as well as the misinterpretation of null, the use of other special purpose values has also been problematic. Consider, for example, the oft used code of 99 which has contributed to problems of non-year 2000 compliance when used in date fields.

Summary database construction and query language processing depends critically on which of these definitions are adopted. For example, take the following two queries of Employee5 earlier:

- Do we employ any Senior Academic Staff members?
- Do we employ any Associate Professors?

Each interpretation of *Senior Academic Staff* would yield different answers to these questions. To the first question, the first interpretation would have to answer *Unknown* while the latter interpretations would be able to answer *Yes*. To the second question, the first two interpretations would have to answer *Unknown* while the last interpretations would answer *Yes*. We take the pragmatic view that the second interpretation is the most useful for three reasons:

- The method of summary database construction leads naturally to this interpretation;
- The utility of the first interpretation is limited;
- The chances of a successful summarisation (including the maintenance of those summaries) with the third interpretation is small.

4 A Formal Categorisation of Summarisation Strategies

As stated at the start of Section 2, the categorisation of summarisation methods can be performed in a variety of ways. In the taxonomy below, we adopt the following metric of utility for a summarisation technique:

$$W = \frac{\zeta(R)}{\zeta(S)} \cdot \frac{\Upsilon(S)}{\Upsilon(R)} \tag{2}$$

Where ζ returns the space requirements of a relation, in this case either the complete relation, R or the summary relation S,

Υ returns the Information Capacity of a relation (see Section 4.1 below).

Thus, using various summarisation strategies, a summarisation weighting W can be determined which estimates the advantages of the space saving with the disadvantages the loss of information capacity of the resultant relation. As these are constructed using the same elements, they can be directly compared and the most beneficial strategies adopted.

A number of summarisation techniques are identified below. On top of these, compression techniques can be adopted to reduce space usage; as they do not affect the information capacity of the resulting dataset and will not be investigated here (although interestingly, the space saving can be directly compared with the summarisation techniques here through equation 2).

4.1 Information Capacity

Information Capacity (as a measure of the usefulness or inferencing capability) of relations has been discussed in other research and will not be explored in depth here [7].

However, it is important to note that the calculation of the function Υ is likely to be highly context sensitive and may depend on the historical use of the attributes or the participation of attributes in foreign key dependencies and constraints. Moreover, while the first term in the calculation of W above is fairly accurate in terms of the space saving, the second term is highly dependent on the data actually held and will be, in many cases, an estimated value. Note that while a value for $\Upsilon(S)$ or $\Upsilon(R)$ may be hard to determine, a value for their ratio (ie. $\Upsilon(S)/\Upsilon(R)$) will be easier.

4.2 Vertical Reduction by Attribute Projection

This method involves the selection and deletion of one or more attributes and the subsequent elimination of duplicate tuples. It is a commonly adopted method of summarisation. For each attribute, the summarisation weighting W is determined as follows:

$$W(t) = \frac{\zeta(R)}{\zeta(R-t)} \cdot \frac{K(R)}{K(\pi_t R)} \cdot \frac{\Upsilon(R-t)}{\Upsilon(R)} \tag{3}$$

Where ζ returns the space requirements of a tuple, in this case either the complete tuple of the relation, R or a tuple without attribute t,

K returns the cardinality of a relation, in this case the cardinality of R projected over attribute t and of R itself, and

Υ returns the Information Capacity of a relation.

For semantic query optimisation purposes, the summary relation S ($= R - A$ where A is the set of attributes removed) can be used whenever no attributes in A will be used directly or indirectly (through use as a foreign key, for example) in the query process[4].

4.3 Horizontal Reduction by Tuple Selection

This method involves the retention or deletion of tuples according to one or more selection criteria. As with vertical reduction, it is a commonly adopted method of summarisation. For each selection criteria, the summarisation weighting W can be determined as follows:

$$W(c) = \frac{K(R)}{K(\sigma_c R)} \cdot \frac{\Upsilon(\sigma_c R)}{\Upsilon(R)} \tag{4}$$

Where K returns the cardinality of a relation, in this case the cardinality of R over selection criterion c and of R itself, and

Υ returns the information capacity of a relation as for vertical reduction.

For semantic query optimisation purposes, the summary relation $S(= \sigma_c R$ where c is the conjunction of the selection criteria applied to either remove/retain tuples) can be used instead of R whenever c is exclusive of/subsumes the selection criterion specified in the query process. For example, if S only contains details of the staff in Science and the query applies only to Computer Science staff, then the query can be executed on S instead of R with no loss of accuracy.

---

[4] Note that in practice, the use of S may result in the suppression of duplicate lines due to the elimination of duplicate tuples. In pure relational databases this should happen anyway but few implementations adhere to this.

4.4 Concept Ascension and Ranges

Horizontal Reduction by Concept Ascension. The last two methods are relatively simply understood and accommodated but suffer from the problem that the information capacity reduces rapidly as attributes and tuples are removed. The idea of accommodating hierarchical domains has been discussed elsewhere [3–5, 10] and provides a mechanism whereby the information capacity of a summary dataset may degrade more slowly for a similar reduction in space.

Briefly, the idea is to provide, commonly through user-supplied hierarchies although they may also be generated *a priori* by autonomous procedures, higher level concepts (which in earlier work [5] we referred to as Domain-Value Hierarchies or DVH), which when applied to one or more attributes may result in duplicate tuples that may then be coalesced. This method can be especially useful for use with temporal, spatio-temporal and other implicitly hierarchical data. The summarisation weighting calculation is similar as that for horizontal reduction:

$$W(c) = \frac{K(R)}{K(A(R))} \cdot \frac{\varUpsilon(A(R))}{\varUpsilon(R)} \tag{5}$$

Where $A(R)$ returns the relation after applying various concept ascension procedures.

The definition of the information capacity function is difficult to determine and depends largely on the manner in which hierarchies are used in query optimisation and query processing. Clearly, if the query processor is able (and is allowed) to provide sound but possibly overcomplete answers[5], the information capacity will be higher. Nevertheless, it has been shown elsewhere that summarised data can sometimes produce (knowingly) correct answers [10], and thus even in this limited case, the information capacity may be higher.

Vertical Reduction by Concept Ascension. In rarer cases, a concept hierarchy may exist between attributes (or an Inter-Attribute Hierarchy or IAH). (It should be noted that these will only occur if the relation is deliberately unnormalised (such as commonly occurs in a data warehouse) or if an induced dependency exists.) In this case, either the attribute with the higher or lower concept can be deleted. Deletion of the attribute with the higher concept would result in no information loss (assuming the hierarchy is held elsewhere) but would generally result in a lower space saving. Deletion of the attribute with the higher concept would result in some information loss but would generally allow greater compression of the relation. See, for example, the example below in which EmplId is removed followed by either Faculty (as in EmplDept2A) or Department (EmplDept2B):

---

[5] ie. an answer which contains all of the requested tuples but may also contain additional answers. For example, the return of a range within which all answers lay might also include other answers which do not fit the criteria.

EmplDept	EmplId	Rank	Department	Faculty
	091	Assoc. Professor	Computer Science	Science
	100	Professor	History	Humanities
	114	Senior Lecturer	Languages	Humanities
	117	Professor	Mathematics	Science
	134	Senior Lecturer	Computer Science	Science
	383	Professor	Languages	Humanities
	763	Assoc. Professor	Electronic Engineering	Engineering
	873	Professor	Computer Science	Science
	889	Assoc. Professor	Computer Science	Science
	927	Senior Lecturer	History	Humanities

EmplDept2A	Rank	Department
	Professor	Computer Science
	Professor	History
	Professor	Languages
	Professor	Mathematics
	Assoc. Professor	Computer Science
	Assoc. Professor	Electronic Engineering
	Senior Lecturer	Computer Science
	Senior Lecturer	History
	Senior Lecturer	Languages

EmplDept2B	Rank	Faculty
	Professor	Humanities
	Professor	Science
	Assoc. Professor	Engineering
	Assoc. Professor	Science
	Senior Lecturer	Humanities
	Senior Lecturer	Science

The summarisation weighting calculation can be calculated in the same way as for Vertical Reduction by Attribute Projection. For the purposes of summarisation and the summarisation weighting calculation, the introduction of ranges can be considered a special case of concept ascension. For example, the reduction of Employee3 to Employee4 resulted in the same form of tuple aggregation as would have happened if concepts equivalent to each range had existed instead.

4.5 Existential Domain Values

Some Existential Domain Values (ESDs) can be considered a special case of the definition of concepts, notably the root nodes, however even in these cases it remains important to define carefully the semantics of such a value. Three ESDs are considered and defined here:

- MANY - The attribute can take one or more of the allowable values from the domain. Note that this is effectively the root node of the concept hierarchy for the domain. Note also that the term MANY is used in preference to ANY or ALL due to the semantics described in section 3.1.

- OTHER - The attribute can take one or more of the allowable values from the domain except those already used by that attribute in other explicitly enumerated tuples. This attribute was termed REST in some earlier work [8] but that term has been discarded for the same reasons as for ANY and ALL.
- NULL - The attribute is inapplicable or the value is unknown.

Other ESDs could, of course, be defined and while much research remains to be done, these are considered the most useful at this stage. Consider the early example, Employee3B. The advantage of the additional tuples becomes clear when questions such as:

- Which ranks are paid $80,500? and
- How many staff are recorded in the database?

In the first case, the OTHER indicates that whatever tuples there were that were deleted, none had a salary of $80,500 and thus the question can be answered exactly. In the second case, the source cardinalities can be totalled to give the correct answer.

Note that one of the significant benefits from the introduction of ESDs is in improvements in query language optimisation, a field that has increasingly encountered problems with the introduction of data mining and warehousing technology. For example, using ESDs, a complete mapping can be enforced between tuples in a relation and its summarised counterpart, as follows. Given a Source Relation R with tuples $r_1, r_2, \ldots r_n$, and a summarised relation S with tuples $s_1, s_2, \ldots s_n$, we have a complete mapping:

$$\exists i, j : \forall r_i \in R \to \Psi(s_j \in S) \tag{6}$$

where Ψ is a function that takes each attribute value and translates it to itself or to a higher level concept of the same concept (including ESDs).

A converse mapping also exists. Note that this indicates that if a fact is not represented in the summary relation in some form, it will also be absent from the source relation and thus some query processing may be completed using summary relations (qv. [10]).

4.6 Source Cardinality, Statistical Summarisation and other Summarisation Techniques

The introduction of additional attributes, such as the cardinality of the number of original tuples, is another strategy to improve the information capacity of the resultant, summarised relation. Source cardinality, for example, could be used to answer questions requiring the count of tuples (although care must be taken with averages if ranges have also been introduced). However, the source cardinality is also of use in summary database maintenance as an addition, amendment or deletion from the main database may, or may not, result in a corresponding change to the summarised data.

5 Further Discussion and Future Research

This research was originally conceived to handle the increasing disparity between the fast decreasing costs of disk storage and main memory and the slower improvements in the performance of I/O access [9]. However, we have also applied these ideas to mobile databases [5] and we believe they may also find applicability in distributed systems including internet based distributed data sources.

Interest in the development of models for semi-structured data [13] has suggested both the embedding of the structural component of the schema and the introduction of (largely structural) Document Type Descriptors [14]. Both remove the domain descriptions that have traditionally resided in the database schema and which are useful for data integration. It is thus necessary for any integration mechanism to be moved to the mediator [1] however, it is not yet clear how this might be achieved.

While this paper does not discuss the details of relational operations on summary relations, it is clear that some forms of induction are being introduced into the normally "deductively" correct area of query language processing and it should be expected that a change in the interpretation of answers may be required. In [10] we discussed knowingly correct answers and a mechanism for providing a graceful degradation of responses was outlined. This becomes more significant when complex operations are performed over a number of relations, some of them summaries.

References

1. Cluet, S., Delobel, C., Simeon, J. and Smaga, K.: Your mediators need data conversion! In Proc. *ACM SIGMOD International Conference on the Management of Data*, 177-188. 1998.
2. Chen, M.C. and McNamee, L.P.: On the data model and access method of summary data management. *IEEE Trans. Knowl. and Data Eng.*, 1(4):519-529. 1989.
3. Han, J. and Fu, Y. Dynamic Generation and Refinement of Concept Hierarchies for Knowledge Discovery in Databases. In Proc. *AAAI'94 Workshop on Knowledge Discovery in Databases*, 157-168. 1994.
4. Hu, X. Conceptual Clustering and Concept Hierarchies in Knowledge Discovery. Masters Thesis, Simon Fraser University, 1993.
5. Madria, S.K., Mohania, M.K. and Roddick, J.F. A query processing model for mobile computing. In Proc. *Foundations of Database Organisation*, 147-157. 1998.
6. Malvestuto, F. The derivation problem for summary data. *SIGMOD Rec.*, 17(3):82-89. 1988.
7. Miller, R.J., Ioannidis, Y.E. and Ramakrishnan, R. The use of information capacity in schema integration and translation. In Proc. *Nineteenth International Conference on Very Large Databases*, 120-133. 1993.
8. Roddick, J.F. A model for temporal inductive inference and schema evolution in relational database systems. Ph.D. Thesis, Department of Computer Science and Computer Engineering, La Trobe University, 1994.
9. Roddick, J.F., Craske, N.G. and Richards, T.J. Handling discovered structure in database systems. *IEEE Trans. Knowl. and Data Eng.*, 8(2 (April)):227-240. 1996.
10. Roddick, J.F. The use of overcomplete logics in summary data management. In Proc. *Eighth Australasian Conference on Information Systems*, 288-298. 1997.
11. Roddick, J.F. and Rice, S. Towards induction in databases. In Proc. *Ninth Australasian Information Systems Conference*, 2, 534-542. 1998.
12. Sato, H. Handling summary information in a database. *SIGMOD Rec.*, 1981.
13. Suciu, D. Semistructured Data and XML. In Proc. *5th International Conference on Foundations of Data Organisation*, 1-12. 1998.
14. World Wide Web Consortium Extensible Markup Language (xml). Version 1.0. 1998.
15. Zaniolo, C. Database relations with null values. *J. Comput. Syst. Sci.*, 28(1):142-166. 1984.

An Efficient Scalable Parallel View Maintenance Algorithm for Shared Nothing Multi-processor Machines

M. Bamha, F. Bentayeb and G. Hains

LIFO, Université d'Orléans, B.P. 6759, 45067 Orléans Cedex 2, France
{bamha,bentayeb,ghains}@lifo.univ-orleans.fr

Abstract. The problem of maintenance of materialized views has been the object of increased research activity recently mainly because of applications related to data warehousing. Many sequential view maintenance algorithms are developed in the literature. If the view is defined by a relational expression involving join operators, the cost of re-evaluating the view even incrementally may be unacceptable. Moreover, when views are *materialized*, parallelism can greatly increase processing power as necessary for view maintenance.

In this paper, we present a new parallel join algorithm by partial duplication of data and a new parallel view maintenance algorithm where views can involve multi-joins. The performances of these algorithms are analyzed using the scalable and portable BSP^1 cost model which predicts a near-linear speedup.

Key words: $PDBMS^2$, *materialized view maintenance, parallel incremental algorithm, data-warehouse, multi-joins, data skew, dynamic load balancing.*

1 Introduction

Data warehousing has become increasingly visible as a research issue following enormous market activity in the past few years [1]. Similarly, materialized views are finding increased research activity, with applications in decision support, OLAP[3], query optimization and replication, all of which are relevant for data warehousing. A view can be materialized by storing the tuples of the view in the database. A materialized view provides fast access to data. The speed difference is critical in applications where the query rate is high and the views are complex, so that it is not feasible to recompute the view of every query. If some of the base relations are changed, materialized views must be updated to ensure correctness of answers to queries. The problem of finding such changes has come to be known as the *view maintenance problem* and has been studied extensively [6, 5, 8]. Many sequential incremental algorithms are developed to this end. Note that if the view is defined by a relational expression containing join operators, the cost involved when reevaluating the view even incrementally may be unacceptable. Parallelism can greatly increase processing power. However, the effectiveness of parallel processing depends on ability to evenly divide

---

[1] BSP : Bulk Synchronous Parallelism.
[2] PDBMS : Parallel Database Management Systems.
[3] OLAP : On Line Analytical Processing.

load among processors while minimizing local computation and communication costs inherent to multi-processors machines. *Data skew* can have a disastrous effect on parallel performance [4, 13, 2, 9, 7] and parallelism can only maintain acceptable performance through efficient algorithms realizing complex queries on dynamic, irregular and distributed data. Such algorithms must dynamically reduce or eliminate data skew at the lowest possible cost. Our contributions to materialized view maintenance are:

1. a new parallel join algorithm called *duplicating_join*. This algorithm guarantees a near-linear speed-up and is based on:
   (a) a partial duplication of data allowing to reduce the communications' costs inherent to multi-processor machines.
   (b) the redistribution algorithm of *fa-join* [4] which efficiently avoids the problem of attribute value and join product skews.
2. a parallel incremental algorithm to maintain materialized views. This algorithm is based on a new incremental approach. This model has near-perfect balancing properties and supports flexible control of communications.
3. We use the scalable and portable BSP cost model to predict the performances of these algorithms.

2 PDBMS, join operations and the BSP cost model

2.1 The BSP cost model

Bulk-Synchronous Parallelism (BSP) is a parallel programming model introduced by Valiant [14] to offer a high degree of abstraction like PRAM models and yet allow portable and predictable performance on a wide variety of architectures. A BSP computer contains a set of processor-memory pairs, a communication network allowing inter-processor delivery of messages and a global synchronization unit which executes collective requests for a synchronization barrier. Its performance is characterized by 3 parameters expressed as multiples of the local processing speed: the number of processor-memory pairs p, the time l required for a global synchronization and the time g for collectively delivering a 1-relation (communication phase where every processor receives/sends at most one word). The network can deliver an h-relation in time $g * h$ for any arity h.

A BSP program is executed as a sequence of *supersteps*, each one divided into three successive and logically disjoint phases. In the first phase each processor uses its local data (only) to perform sequential computations and to request data transfers to/from other nodes. In the second phase the network delivers the requested data transfers and in the third phase a global synchronization barrier occurs, making the transferred data available for the next superstep. The execution time of a superstep s is thus the sum of the maximal local processing time, of the data delivery time and of the global synchronization time:

$$\text{Time}(s) = \max_{i:processor} w_i^{(s)} + \max_{i:processor} h_i^{(s)} * g + l,$$

where $w_i^{(s)}$ = local processing time on processor i during superstep s and $h_i^{(s)} = \max\{h_{i+}^{(s)}, h_{i-}^{(s)}\}$ where $h_{i+}^{(s)}$ (resp. $h_{i-}^{(s)}$) is the number of words transmitted (resp. received) by processor i during superstep s.

2.2 Load balancing in parallel join operations

Join is an expensive and frequently used operation and parallelization of this operation is highly desirable. In PDBMS, relations are generally partitioned among processors by *horizontal fragmentation* with respect to the values of a chosen attribute. Parallel join usually proceeds in two phases: a redistribution phase by join attribute hashing and then sequential join of local fragments. Many algorithms have been proposed. The principal ones are: *Sort-merge join, Simple-hash join, Grace-hash join* and *Hybrid-hash join* [12]. All of them (called hashing algorithms) are based on hashing functions which redistribute relations so that tuples having the same attribute value are forwarded to the same node. Local joins are then computed and their union is the output relation. Their major disadvantage is to be vulnerable to both *attribute value skew* (imbalance of the output of the first phase) and *join product skew* (imbalance of the output of local joins) [13, 11, 10]. The former affects immediate performance and the latter affects the efficiency of output or pipelined operations in the case of a multi-join.

Research has shown that the join is parallelizable with near-linear speed-up on scalable SN architectures but only under ideal balancing conditions. Many algorithms have been proposed to handle data skew for a simple join operation, but little is known for the case of complex queries leading to multi-joins [10, 7, 2, 11]. In particular, the performance of PDBMS has generally been estimated on queries involving one or two join operations only [15]. However the problem of data skew is more acute with multi-joins because the imbalance of intermediate results is unknown during static query optimization.

To address this problem, we introduced in [4] a data-redistribution algorithm with near-perfect balancing properties. It is adaptable to θ-join and efficient for multi-joins. It computes *exact* frequency histograms to avoid *join product skew* (JPS). A scalable and portable cost analysis was made with the BSP model. The analysis suggests a hybrid *frequency-adaptive* algorithm (*fa_join* algorithm)[4], dynamically combining histogram-based balancing with standard hashing methods. The *fa_join* algorithm avoids the slowdown usually caused by attribute value skew (AVS) and the imbalance of the size of local joins processed by standard algorithms. It avoids AVS and JPS at the cost of extra processing time. We analyzed this overhead both theoretically and experimentally and concluded that it does not penalize overall performance.

Moreover, *fa_join*'s performance can be slightly improved when computing the join of two relations R and Δ where $\|\Delta\| \ll \|R\|$ by reducing communication cost. We therefore introduce a new parallel algorithm called *duplicating join* to perform such joins. Its performance is analyzed using the BSP cost model which also predicts a near-linear speedup for this case.

3 Duplicating join algorithm

In this section we describe our new algorithm for SN machines, adapted to the treatment of the join of two relations R and Δ where $\|\Delta\| \ll \|R\|$. This algorithm is called *duplicating_join* and is based on :(1) a partial duplication of data allowing to reduce the communication costs between different processors and (2) the redistribution algorithm of *fa_join* algorithm which allows to avoid efficiently both attribute value and join product skews.

In the rest of this paper we use the following terminology for each relation T:

- T_i denotes the fragment of relation T placed on processor i,
- $Hist(T)$ denotes the histogram of T with respect to the join attribute,
- $\|T\|$ denotes the size of relation T.

We first assume that relation R (resp. Δ) is partitioned among processors by horizontal fragmentation and the fragments R_i for $i = 1 \ldots p$ are almost of the same size on every processor, i.e. $\|R_i\| \simeq \frac{\|R\|}{p}$ where p is the number of processors.

We will describe the *duplicating_join* algorithm while giving an upper bound on the *BSP* execution of each phase. This algorithm proceeds in 4 phases :

Phase 1 : Partial data duplication

To minimize the communication costs, each processor i broadcasts the fragment Δ_i to the other processors in time: $time_{phase1} = O(g * \|\Delta\|)$, where g is the time to send/receive a message of one word (cf. 2.1).

At the end of phase 1, each processor has a local access to the whole relation Δ (note that $\|\Delta\| \ll \|R\|$). Due to the identities : $R \bowtie \Delta = (R_1 \cup R_2 \cup \ldots \cup R_p) \bowtie \Delta = \cup_i (R_i \bowtie \Delta)$, broadcasting the fragments Δ_i allows us to perform (in parallel) local joins: $R_i \bowtie \Delta$ without extra communication costs.

Phase 2 : Processing local semi-joins

To reduce the redistribution cost, we compute the local semi-joins : $\widetilde{R_i} = R_i \ltimes \Delta$ by a sequential scan of the hash table, on each processor, in time:

$$time_{phase2} = O\left(\max_{i=1\ldots p} \|R_i\| + \|\Delta\| \right) = O\left(\frac{\|R\|}{p} + \|\Delta\| \right).$$

We mention that, unlike the hash-based algorithms where both the *build* and the *probe* relations are redistributed, and contrary to the *fa_join* algorithm where only the build relation is redistributed, in the *duplicating_join*, we only redistribute $R \ltimes \Delta$ to perform $R \bowtie \Delta$. Thus we reduce to the minimum, the communication cost.

Phase 3 : Data redistribution

To avoid data skew and thus evenly divide load among processors, the semi-joins $\widetilde{R_i} = R_i \ltimes \Delta$ are redistributed using the redistribution algorithm of the *frequency-adaptive* algorithm [4]: On each processor i, the relation $\widetilde{R_i} = R_i \ltimes \Delta$ is divided into the two sub-relations $\widetilde{R_i'}$ and $\widetilde{R_i''}$ in the following manner: $\widetilde{R_i} = R_i \ltimes \Delta = \widetilde{R_i'} \cup \widetilde{R_i''}$ where :

- All the tuples of relation $\widetilde{R_i'}$ occur more than a threshold frequency f_0,
- All the tuples of relation $\widetilde{R_i''}$ occur less than the threshold frequency f_0 [4].

---

[4] In this paper, we assume $f_0 = p * log(p)$.

To avoid *JPS*, the relations $\widetilde{R_i'}$ are redistributed using the redistribution algorithm of the *fa_join* [4] in time:

$$time_{a1} = O\left(g * (\max_{i=1...p} \|\widetilde{R_i'}\| + \|Hist(\widetilde{R'})\|) + \|Hist(\widetilde{R'})\| * \log(p) + (g+l) * \log(p)\right),$$

where $\|Hist(\widetilde{R'})\|$ denotes the size of the histogram, of $\widetilde{R'}$, based on the join attribute and l the time to achieve a synchronization barrier (cf. 2.1). Due to $\|Hist(\widetilde{R'})\| \leq \frac{\|\widetilde{R'}\|}{f_0} = \frac{\|\widetilde{R'}\|}{p*\log(p)}$, we have :

$$time_{a1} \leq O\left(g * \max_{i=1...p} \|\widetilde{R_i'}\| + (g+l) * \log(p)\right).$$

Relations $\widetilde{R_i''}$ are also redistributed using a hash function in time : $time_{a2} = O\left(g * \max_{i=1...p} \|\widetilde{R_i''}\|\right)$. Hence, the global redistribution of the relations $\widetilde{R_i}$ has therefore taken the sum of the above two redistribution times :

$$time_{phase3} = time_{a1} + time_{a2} \leq O\left(g * \max_{i=1...p} \|\widetilde{R_i}\| + (g+l) * \log(p)\right).$$

Redistribution of $\widetilde{R_i}$ is performed to avoid JPS because the values which could lead to AVS (those having high frequencies) are those which often cause the join product skew. It avoids thus, the slowdown usually caused by attribute value skew and the imbalance of the size of local joins processed by the standard algorithms. Local joins $\widetilde{R_i} \bowtie \Delta$ will have therefore almost the same size on each processor (i.e. $\|\widetilde{R_i} \bowtie \Delta\| \simeq \frac{\|R \bowtie \Delta\|}{p}$, for $i = 1 \ldots p$).

Phase 4 : Processing local joins

Once the redistribution of $\widetilde{R_i}$ is achieved, local joins could be computed in time :

$$time_{phase4} = O\left(\max_{i=1...p} (\|\widetilde{R_i}\| + \|\Delta\| + \|\widetilde{R_i} \bowtie \Delta\|)\right) \leq O\left(\frac{\|R\|}{p} + \|\Delta\| + \frac{\|R \bowtie \Delta\|}{p}\right).$$

The global cost of the *duplicating_join* algorithm has therefore taken the sum of the costs of the 4 phases above :

$$time_{duplicating-join} = time_{phase1} + time_{phase2} + time_{phase3} + time_{phase4}$$

$$\leq O\left((1+g) * (\frac{\|R\|}{p} + \|\Delta\|) + \frac{\|R \bowtie \Delta\|}{p} + (g+l) * \log(p)\right).$$

Remark : Observe that sequential join processing of two relations R and S would require at least time : $bound_1 = \Omega(\|R\|+\|S\|+\|R \bowtie S\|)$. Parallel processing with p processors requires therefore $bound_p = \frac{1}{p} * bound_1$, and the *duplicating_join* algorithm has optimal asymptotic complexity when :

$$\|\Delta\| \leq \frac{1}{p} * \max\left(\|R\|, \|R \bowtie \Delta\|\right).$$

4   Incremental view maintenance : A new approach

In relational database systems, a derived relation or *view* is defined by a relational expression (i.e. a query evaluated over the base relations). A view may be virtual, which corresponds to the traditional concept of a view; or materialized, which means that the resulting relation is actually stored. As the database changes because of updates applied to the base relations, the materialized views involving the updated relations may also require change. The incremental method to evaluate the materialized view consists to identify the set of tuples to be inserted or deleted in the views avoiding the whole evaluation of the view [6, 5, 8].

In this paper, we are interested in SPJ^5 views. As in [6], we suppose that the duplicates are kept in the view, either explicitly, or using a counter (necessary to the delete operations when the materialized view involves project operators [6]). Let $v = R^1 \bowtie R^2 \bowtie \ldots \bowtie R^n$ where R^i are base relations. Assume that we insert the sets of tuples $Ins(R^i)$ in relations R^i, $i = 1, \ldots, n$, respectively. Then the new state of the view is $v' = (R^1 \cup Ins(R^1)) \bowtie \ldots \bowtie (R^n \cup Ins(R^n))$.

By distributivity of join over union, the updated view v denoted by v' is equal to the union of 2^n multi-joins called *partial multi-joins*. For $n = 3$, the [6]'s (resp. the following new approach's) partial multi-joins are shown in table Tab. 1.(a) (resp. Tab. 1.(b)). The multi-join $R^1 \bowtie R^2 \bowtie R^3$ corresponds to the materialized view v.

$R^1 \bowtie R^2 \bowtie R^3$
$R^1 \bowtie R^2 \bowtie Ins(R^3)$
$R^1 \bowtie Ins(R^2) \bowtie R^3$
$R^1 \bowtie Ins(R^2) \bowtie Ins(R^3)$
$Ins(R^1) \bowtie R^2 \bowtie R^3$
$Ins(R^1) \bowtie R^2 \bowtie Ins(R^3)$
$Ins(R^1) \bowtie Ins(R^2) \bowtie R^3$
$Ins(R^1) \bowtie Ins(R^2) \bowtie Ins(R^3)$

$R^1 \bowtie R^2 \bowtie R^3$
$Ins(R^1) \bowtie R^2 \bowtie R^3$
$(R^1 \cup Ins(R^1)) \bowtie Ins(R^2) \bowtie R^3$
$(R^1 \cup Ins(R^1)) \bowtie (R^2 \cup Ins(R^2)) \bowtie Ins(R^3)$

(a) (b)

Tab.1 : [6]'s and new approach's partial multi-joins for n=3.

Using the [6] approach, For a given view $v = R^1 \bowtie \ldots \bowtie R^n$, we must perform $2^k - 1$ multi-joins where k is the number of the updated relations involved in v.

In this paper, to reduce the number of the necessary partial multi-joins to be performed to maintain v incrementally, we use a variant of the [6] approach using only k partial multi-joins. To capture these k partial multi-joins, we associate to $v = R^1 \bowtie \ldots \bowtie R^n$ a matrix T with n rows and n columns in such away that every row of T corresponds to one partial multi-join PMJ_i of v :

$$PMJ_i = T_{i,1} \bowtie T_{i,2} \ldots \bowtie T_{i,n} \quad \text{where :} \quad T_{i,j} = \begin{cases} R^j \cup Ins(R^j) & \text{if } j < i \\ Ins(R^j) & \text{if } i = j \\ R^j & \text{if } j > i \end{cases}$$

Note that, if a relation R^j is not updated, the corresponding partial multi-join PMJ_j is a null relation. We generalize this result to SPJ views and show that for every materialized view, $v = \sigma_C \pi_X (R^1 \bowtie R^2 \bowtie \ldots \bowtie R^n)$, if we insert the sets of tuples $Ins(R^i)$ in the relations R^i, $i = 1, \ldots, n$, respectively, the set of tuples v_{Ins} to be inserted in the view v is :

---

5 SPJ : Select, Project and Join.

$$v_{Ins} \;=\; \sigma_C \pi_\chi \, (Ins(R^1) \bowtie R^2 \bowtie R^3 \bowtie \ldots \bowtie R^n) \;\cup$$
$$\sigma_C \pi_\chi \, ((R^1 \cup Ins(R^1)) \bowtie Ins(R^2) \bowtie R^3 \bowtie \ldots \bowtie R^n) \;\cup$$
$$\sigma_C \pi_\chi \, ((R^1 \cup Ins(R^1)) \bowtie (R^2 \cup Ins(R^2)) \bowtie Ins(R^3) \bowtie R^4 \bowtie \ldots \bowtie R^n) \;\cup$$
$$\vdots$$
$$\sigma_C \pi_\chi \, ((R^1 \cup Ins(R^1)) \bowtie \ldots \bowtie (R^{n-1} \cup Ins(R^{n-1})) \bowtie Ins(R^n)).$$

Tab. 2 : Insertion into base relations.

The same idea may be applied when we delete the sets of tuples $Del(R^i)$ from the relations R^i [3]. Thus, the set of tuples v_{Del} to be deleted from the view v is the set v_{Ins} defined before in which $Ins(R^i)$ are replaced by $Del(R^i)$ and the union symbol $\cup$ is replaced by the set difference symbol $-$.

5 Parallel incremental evaluation

An update of a base relation of a materialized view v can be decomposed into two phases: insertion phase in base relations followed by deletion phase from base relations. After insertion phase (or deletion phase) of sets of tuples in base relations, we evaluate the set of tuples v_{Ins} (or v_{Del}) to be inserted (or deleted) in (from) v using the appropriate parallel incremental algorithm, then we use the appropriate parallel maintenance algorithm to perform the view update.

We present our parallel algorithm in the case of the insertion into base relations, the deletion update is detailed in [3].

5.1 Case of simple join

Let $R \bowtie S$ be the join expression defining the view v. Assume we insert the sets of tuples $Ins(R)$ and $Ins(S)$ in relations R and S respectively. To maintain v incrementally, according to the [6] approach, it is sufficient to compute the set v_{Ins} of tuples to be inserted in v :

$$v_{Ins} = (Ins(R) \bowtie S) \cup (R \bowtie Ins(S)) \cup (Ins(R) \bowtie Ins(S)). \qquad (1)$$

Now we present a parallel incremental evaluation algorithm of v based on the [6] approach. The sequential maintenance of the view v (cf. equation 1) requires the following lower bound :

$$bound_{inf_1} = \Omega\Big(\, \|Ins(R)\| + \|S\| + \|Ins(R) \bowtie S\| + \|R\| + \|Ins(S)\| +$$

$$\|R \bowtie Ins(S)\| + \|Ins(R)\| + \|Ins(S)\| + \|Ins(R) \bowtie Ins(S)\| \Big). (2)$$

Therefore, the processing time using p processors requires at least :

$$bound_{inf_p} = \frac{1}{p} * bound_{inf_1}. \qquad (3)$$

We first assume that relations R (resp. S) is evenly partitioned among different processors using horizontal fragmentation. And when the base relations are updated, each processor holds a fragment of relations $Ins(R)$ and $Ins(S)$.

The view update of v according to the [6] approach, is performed by computing the view v_{Ins} which corresponds to the three joins $Ins(R) \bowtie S$, $R \bowtie Ins(S)$ and $Ins(R) \bowtie Ins(S)$ in the following manner:

a: when $\|Ins(R)\| \ll \|S\|$, the (*duplicating_join algorithm*) can be used efficiently to process the join $Ins(R) \bowtie S$ in time:

$$time_{step_a} = O\Big((1+g)*(\max_{i=1...p}\|S_i\|+\|Ins(R)\|)+\frac{\|Ins(R)\bowtie S\|}{p}+(g+l)*\log(p)\Big),$$

b: when $\|Ins(S)\| \ll \|R\|$, the (*duplicating_join algorithm*) can be used efficiently to process the join $R \bowtie Ins(S)$ is in time:

$$time_{step_b} = O\Big((1+g)*(\max_{i=1...p}\|R_i\|+\|Ins(S)\|)+\frac{\|R\bowtie Ins(S)\|}{p}+(g+l)*\log(p)\Big),$$

c: To compute the join $Ins(R) \bowtie Ins(S)$, we compute one of the following local joins: $Ins(R) \bowtie Ins(S)_i$ or $Ins(R)_i \bowtie Ins(S)$. If we choose to compute $Ins(R)_i \bowtie Ins(S)$, the join $Ins(R) \bowtie Ins(S)$ is processed at most in time:

$$time_{step_c} = O\Big(\max_{i=1...p}\|Ins(R)_i\| + \|Ins(S)\| + \max_{i=1...p}\|Ins(R)_i \bowtie Ins(S)\|\Big).$$

Hence, the global view maintenance cost is:
$$time_{v_{Ins}} = time_{step_a} + time_{step_b} + time_{step_c}.$$

$$= O\Big((1+g)*(\|Ins(R)\|+\|Ins(S)\|+\max_{i=1...p}\|R_i\|+\max_{i=1...p}\|S_i\|)+\frac{\|Ins(R)\bowtie S\|}{p}$$

$$+\frac{\|R\bowtie Ins(S)\|}{p}+\max_{i=1...p}\|Ins(R)_i \bowtie Ins(S)\|+(g+l)*\log(p)\Big). \quad (4)$$

The view maintenance algorithm is optimal when:

$$\max\Big(\|Ins(R)\|,\|Ins(S)\|,\max_{i=1...p}\|Ins(R)_i \bowtie Ins(S)\|\Big)$$

$$\leq \frac{1}{p}*\max\Big(\|R\|,\|S\|,\|R\bowtie Ins(S)\|,\|Ins(R)\bowtie Ins(S)\|\Big), \quad (5)$$

this is due to the fact that all the terms in $time_{v_{Ins}}$ are bounded by those of $bound_{inf_p}$ (cf. équation : 3).

Observe that unlike the [6] approach, in our incremental algorithm, the two joins $R \bowtie Ins(S)$ and $Ins(R) \bowtie Ins(S)$ are implicitly evaluated by computing the join $(R \cup Ins(R)) \bowtie Ins(S)$ (cf. section 4). Using the *duplicating_join* algorithm, the computation of $(R\cup Ins(R)) \bowtie Ins(S)$ is done in time: $O\Big((1+g)*(\max_{i=1...p}(\|R_i\|+\|Ins(R)_i\|)+\|Ins(S)\|)+\frac{\|Ins(R)\bowtie Ins(S)\|}{p}+\frac{\|R\bowtie Ins(S)\|}{p}+(g+l)*\log(p)\Big)$, which is slightly better than the sum of the times of the steps b and c, i.e. $time_{step_b} + time_{step_c}$. This reduces to two the number of the joins to be evaluated. In general (cf. section 4), the number of the joins to be evaluated is reduced from $2^k - 1$ to k (where k is the number of the updated relations). Therefore, the incremental evaluation's cost for multi-joins views is greatly reduced.

The equation 5 is generally verified when $\|Ins(R)\| \ll \|S\|$ and $\|Ins(S)\| \ll \|R\|$. However, when $\|Ins(R)\| \simeq \|S\|$ (resp. $\|Ins(S)\| \simeq \|R\|$), the join $Ins(R) \bowtie S$ (resp. $R \bowtie Ins(S)$) can be efficiently evaluated using the *fa_join* [4] algorithm with near-linear speedup. We recall that the two algorithms *fa_join* and *duplicating_join* guaranty a near-perfect balance of join results. Hence, these algorithms are well adapted for multi-joins operations. Due to the fact that all the multi-joins are evaluated with near-linear speedups, the incremental view maintenance is then evaluated in a near-linear speedup too.

5.2 Case of SPJ views

We consider in this section materialized views defined by relational SPJ expressions of the form $v = \sigma_C \pi_X (R^1 \bowtie R^2 \bowtie \ldots \bowtie R^n)$ where R^i are relations, C a select condition and π_X is the projection over the set of attributes X. Assume we insert the sets of tuples $Ins(R^i)$ in the base relations R^i, $i = 1, \ldots, n$, respectively.

To optimize the incremental evaluation cost, the partial views are evaluated from the top to the bottom (cf. table Tab.2). Hence, the first partial view to evaluate is $\sigma_C \pi_X (Ins(R^1) \bowtie R^2 \bowtie R^3 \bowtie \ldots \bowtie \mathcal{R}^n)$. As the rest of the partial views to evaluate involve the relation $R^1 \cup Ins(R^1)$, we definitely update the relation R^1 by computing $R^1 \cup Ins(R^1)$, we compute then the partial view $\sigma_C \pi_X ((R^1 \cup Ins(R^1)) \bowtie Ins(R^2) \bowtie R^3 \bowtie \ldots \bowtie R^n)$. After that, we definitely update the relation $\mathcal{R}^2$ by computing $R^2 \cup Ins(R^2)$ in time $\max_{i=1\ldots p} \|(Ins(R^2))_i\|$. Then, we compute the partial view $\sigma_C \pi_X ((R^1 \cup Ins(R^1)) \bowtie (R^2 \cup Ins(R^2)) \bowtie Ins(R^3) \bowtie \mathcal{R}^4 \bowtie \ldots \bowtie R^n)$. Note that when we compute the above partial view, we do not evaluate $R^1 \cup Ins(\mathcal{R}^1)$ since it is already done in the previous step. The rest of partial views to be evaluated is computed with the same manner so that, during every partial view evaluation, one and only one base relation is updated.

The fa_join and duplicating_join algorithms avoid the problem of AVS and JPS. Therefore, the local joins results sizes are almost the same in each processor. The select and project operations could be done with a near-linear speedup.

We have shown that, in the insertion (resp. deletion[3]) updates over base relations, the parallel incremental evaluation algorithm of the materialized view v, has a near-linear speedup since all the partial views of v_{Ins} (resp. v_{Del}) have near-linear speedups. Hence, our parallel algorithm for evaluating views incrementally has a near-linear speedup.

6 Parallelizing materialized view updates

The evaluation algorithm of the view v_{Ins} (resp. v_{Del}) has near-linear speedup. For the incremental view maintenance, we must insert (resp. delete) the tuples of the view v_{Ins} (resp. v_{Del}) in (resp. from) the materialized view.

To this end, local fragments $(v_{Ins})_i$ (resp. $(v_{Del})_i$) are redistributed using the same placement function as for the materialized view. The global redistribution cost (and thus the materialized view update cost) depends generally on the placement function used to store the materialized view on different processors. The average cost of the redistribution is $g * \max_{i=1,\ldots,p}(v_{Ins})_i$ (resp. $g * \max_{i=1,\ldots,p}(v_{Del})_i$). Note that in the worst case, when all the blocs $(v_{Ins})_i$ (resp. $(v_{Del})_i$) are sent to same processor, the redistribution cost would not exceed $g * \|v_{Ins}\|$ (resp. $g * \|v_{Del}\|$). This algorithm is detailed in [3].

7 Conclusion

In this paper we have presented a new parallel join algorithm called duplicating_join based on partial duplication of data with near perfect balancing properties. We have shown that this algorithm combined with the fa_join[4] algorithm can greatly increase processing power in the case of materialized views and thus data-warehousing applications by the design of a new parallel view maintenance algorithm for Shared Nothing machines.

The performances of these algorithms are analyzed using the BSP cost model which predicts a linear speedup. The $O(\ldots)$ notation only hides small constant factors: they depend only on the implementation but neither on data nor on the the BSP machine. Our experience with the join operation [4] is evidence that the above theoretical analysis is accurate in practice.

References

1. B. Moon A. Datta and H. Thomas. A case for Parallelism in Datawarehousing and OLAP. In *Ninth International Workshop on Database and Expert Systems Applications, DEXA 98*, IEEE Computer Society, Vienna, 1998.
2. Kien A.Hua and Chieng Lee. Handling Data Skew in Multiprocessor Database Computers Using Partition Tuning. *in Proc. 17th international conf. on very Large Data Bases, pp 525-535,*, 1991.
3. M. Bamha, F. Bentayeb, and G. Hains. Un algorithme incrémental parallèle pour la maintenance des vues matérialisées. Technical Report RR99-3, LIFO, Université d'Orléans, 1999.
4. M. Bamha and G. Hains. A self-balancing join algorithm for Shared Nothing machines. *In the Proc of the 10th International Conference on Parallel and Distributed Computing Systems, Las Vegas, Nevada*, October 1998.
5. José A. Blakeley, Neil Coburn, and Per-Ake Larson. Updating derived relations: Detecting irrelevant and autonomously computable updates. *ACM TODS*, 14(3):369–400, September 1989.
6. José A. Blakeley, Per-Ake Larson, and Frank Wm. Tompa. Efficiently Updating Materialized Views. *ACM SIGMOD*, 1986.
7. David J. DeWitt, Jeffrey F. Naughton, Donovan A. Schneider, and S. Seshrdri. Practical Skew Handling in Parallel Joins. In *Proceedings of the 18th VLDB Conference, Vancouver, British Columbia, Canada*, 1992.
8. Timothy Griffin and Leonid Libkin. Incremental maintenance of views with duplicates. In *Proc. of ACM SIGMOD Int. Conf. on Management of Data*, 1995.
9. K. A. Hua, W. Tavanapong, and H. C. Young. A Performance Evaluation of Load Balancing Techniques for Join Operations on Multicomputer Database systems. In *Proc. of the 11th International Conference on Data Engineering, CA, USA*, 1995.
10. Hongjun Lu, Beng-Chin Ooi, and Kian-Lee Tan. *Query Processing in Parallel Relational Database Systems*. IEEE Computer Society Press, California, 1994.
11. Viswanath Poosala and Yannis E. Ioannidis. Estimation of query-result distribution and its application in parallel-join load balancing. *In: Proc. 22th Int. Conf. on Very Large Database Systems, VLDB'96, Bombay, India*, 1996.
12. Donovan A. Schneider and David J. DeWitt. A performance of four parallel join algorithms in a shared-nothing multiprocessor environment. *in the Proc ACM SIGMOD, pp. 110-121*, 1989.
13. M. Seetha and Philip S. Yu. Effectiveness of Parallel Joins. *published in the IEEE, Trans. Knowledge and Data Enginneerings, Vol. 2, No 4, pp 410-424*, 1990.
14. Leslie Valiant. A Bridging Model for Parallel Computation,. *Communication of the ACM, Vol 33, No. 8.*, August 1990.
15. Annita N. Wilschut, Jan Flokstra, and Peter M.G. Apers. Parallel Evaluation of Multi-join Queries. *In the Proc. Of the ACM-SIGMOD, California*, 1995.

Using Back Propagation Algorithm and Genetic Algorithm to Train and Refine Neural Networks for Object Detection

Mengjie Zhang and Victor Ciesielski

Department of Computer Science
Royal Melbourne Institute of Technology
GPO Box 2476V, Melbourne Victoria 3001, Australia
{mengjie,vc}@cs.rmit.edu.au
http://www.cs.rmit.edu.au/~{mengjie,vc}

Abstract. We introduce a two stage approach to the use of pixel based neural networks for finding relatively small objects in large pictures. In the first stage the network is trained by using a back propagation algorithm and a genetic algorithm on sample objects which have been cut out from the large pictures. In the second stage the weights of the two trained networks are refined on the full training images using a second genetic algorithm. Four methods are formed by the two training algorithms in stage one and combining them with the genetic algorithm in stage two. We have tested these methods on three object detection problems of increasing difficulty. In all cases the methods with the refined genetic algorithm resulted in improved detection performance over those without the refinement. The method with the best performance is the use of the back propagation algorithm for the network training and the genetic algorithm for the network refinement.

Keywords. Pixel based neural network; Target recognition; Target detection; Image mining; Network refinement.

1 Introduction

As more and more images are captured in electronic form the need for programs which can find objects of interest in a database of images is increasing. For example, it may be necessary to find all tumours in a database of x-ray images, all cyclones in a database of satellite images or a particular face in a database of photographs. The common characteristic of such problems can be phrased as "Given $subpicture_1, subpicture_2...subpicture_n$ which are examples of the object of interest, find all pictures which contain this object and the locations of all of the objects of interest". Figure 2c shows an example of a problem of this kind, which presents a human retina. We are required to find all of the micro aneurisms and haemorrhages, as indicated by the white squares. (Note: The picture is presented at too coarse a level of resolution for the difference between micro aneurisms and haemorrhages to be evident). Examples of other problems of this kind include target detection problems [5, 14] where the task is to find, say, all tanks, trucks or helicopters in a picture. Unlike most of the current work in the object recognition area, where the task is to recognise only one object of only one class or to find multi-objects of only one class in a large picture [5, 9, 10] , the goal of this approach is to detect a image database with a number of large pictures each of which contains multi-objects of multi-classes.

Two main approaches have been used in neural network systems for these kinds of problems – feature based and pixel based. In feature based approaches various features such as brightness, colour, size and perimeter are extracted from the sub-images of the objects of interest and used as inputs to the networks, as in [2, 9, 16]. In pixel based approaches [3, 7, 12] the pixel values are used directly as inputs. The approach described in this paper is pixel based. The paper suggests an improvement to a current approach and describes an investigation of its effect on pictures of increasing difficulty.

There are a number of reports in the literature on the use of the genetic paradigm in object recognition and feature extraction. Typically genetic programming is used rather than genetic algorithms (GAs), such as [13] and [15]. This approach aims to use GAs to train and refine pixel based networks for the object detection problems.

It is important to note that finding objects in pictures with very cluttered backgrounds is an extremely difficult problem and that false detection rates of 200-2,000% (that is the detection system suggests that there are 20 times as many objects as there really are) are common [10, 12].

1.1 Goals

In the first stage of the approach, we used a back propagation algorithm(BP) and a genetic algorithm(GA) to train pixel based neural networks on the object examples cut out from the full training image set. A second genetic algorithm was used to refine the above two trained networks on the full training images set itself in the second stage. The architecture of the approach is shown in Figure 1. Conveniently, we use *BP-train*, *GA-train* and *GA-refine* to represent the BP algorithm, GA in stage one and the GA in stage two respectively. Directly applied to the full test image set, the *BP-train* and *GA-train* can be used as two independent methods for object detection. Combining *BP-train* and *GA-train* with *GA-refine*, two additional detection methods, *BP-train + GA-refine* and *GA-train + GA-refine*, are created.

We have applied the *BP-train* method to object detection in [17, 18]. In this paper, we investigate:

1. Whether the first genetic algorithm, *GA-train*, can lead to better detection performance, compared with the back propagation algorithm, *BP-train*.
2. Whether the second genetic algorithm, *GA-refine*, can refine the weights of networks trained by *GA-train* and *BP-train* in the first stage.
3. Which of the four methods has the best detection performance.

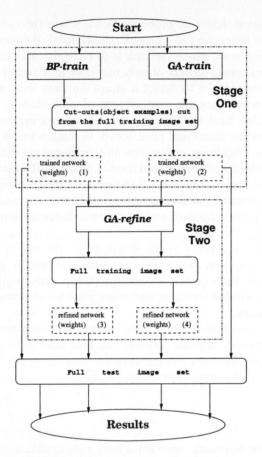

Fig. 1. The Architecture of the two-stage approach: Four methods – *BP-train, GA-train, BP-train + GA-refine* and *GA-train + GA-refine*.

2 Back Propagation Algorithm and Genetic Algorithm for Network Training

The first stage of our approach requires generating a number of networks trained on cut-outs of the objects of interest. In this approach, we use two algorithms, a back propagation algorithm and a genetic algorithm, to train the networks.

2.1 Back Propagation Algorithm for Network training

The details of the back propagation algorithm can be seen from [11]. We have used this algorithm (*BP-train* here) for object detection[17, 18]. A brief outline of the method of directly using *BP-train* or *GA-train* for object detection is as follows:

1. Assemble a database of pictures in which the locations and classes of all of the objects of interest are manually determined. Reserve some of the pictures as 'unknowns' for measuring detection performance.
2. Determine an appropriate size (n) of a square which will cover all objects of interest and form the input field of the networks.
3. Build training and test sets by cutting out squares of size n. The $n \times n$ pixel values form the inputs of a training pattern and the classification is the output.
4. Choose a hidden layer size and train a three layer feed forward network by the *BP-train* or the *GA-train*.
5. Use the trained network as a moving window template [1] across the full pictures from which the training data was extracted. If the correlation (i.e neural network output) between the image and the template is high enough at any point, an occurrence of the object should be registered at that point. Determine thresholds for each class.
6. Use the trained network as a moving window template on the pictures reserved with step 1. If the output for a class exceeds the threshold then report an object of that type at the current location.
7. Determine the detection rate, and the false alarm rate. In the usual case trying to improve the detection rate results in a increase in false alarm rate.

2.2 Genetic Algorithm for Network Training

We use the *2DELTA-GANN* [8] as the first genetic algorithm (*GA-train*), which has been used to train small neural networks such as the *xor* network and the *4-2-4 encoder* network. In this approach, we apply this algorithm to training the relatively large networks with the raw image data.

Rather than have the genetic algorithm evolve the actual weights and biases themselves, only the way in which the rules are to be applied and the changes of them are evolved. Accordingly, while the chromosomes being modified by the genetic algorithm do not represent the weights or biases of the network, only the method by which the rules are to be applied and the *delta* values are represented. A gene in the genetic algorithm is a composite structure:

- There are three rule bits, called $x1, x2$ and $x3$.
- There are two floating point values called *delta1* and *delta2*.

The commonly used "roulette wheel" [6] mechanism is used for parent selection. The crossover operator is based on parameterised uniform crossover [4]. The mutation operator consists of standard bit flipping of the rule bits followed by the generation of new random values of *delta1* and *delta2*.

The fitness of a chromosome is obtained by realizing a network from the weights and the changes of the weights (*delta values*) encoded in the chromosome, passing all cases in the training set through this network and calculating the total sum squared error. The network training will be terminated when the fitness becomes reasonably small or after enough training generations.

3 Genetic Algorithm for Network Refinement

Directly applying the trained networks obtained in the first stage to detecting full large pictures containing the small objects often results in some false positives, particularly when the large pictures have highly cluttered background [17, 18]. To decrease the false alarm rate, the second stage is developed for refining the networks found in stage one. This is done by another genetic algorithm (*GA-refine*).

3.1 Characteristics of GA-refine

Compared with the first one (*GA-train*), the second genetic algorithm (*GA-refine*) has the following new features:

- Initialise the weights of the networks with the trained weights in the first stage instead of totally random initial weights;
- Directly utilise the full large pictures rather than the cut-outs of them as input for the network refinement (training);
- Use a new fitness function based on the detection rate and false alarm rate for full training images instead of the total sum squared error on the cut-outs.

3.2 Fitness Function

To improve the detection performance, we develop a new fitness function for evaluating the networks based on the detection rate and false alarm rate themselves. The fitness of a chromosome is calculated as follows:

1. Realise the network from the weights and the changes of the weights encoded in the chromosome.
2. Apply the network as a moving n×n window template across the full training images and obtain the locations of all the objects detected.
3. Compare them with known locations of the desired objects and determine the detection rate and false alarm rate of this network.
4. Compute the fitness as:

$$fitness(Fr, Dr) = A * Fr/(Fr + Dr) + B * (1 - Dr) \tag{1}$$

where Dr and Fr represent the detection rate and false alarm rate of the network, and A and B are constants which reflect the relative importance of false alarm rate *vs* detection rate.

Under this design, it is clear that the smaller the fitness, the better the detection performance. The best case is zero fitness when the detection rates for all classes are 100% and the false alarm rates are zero, that is, all the objects of interest were found out by the network without any false alarms.

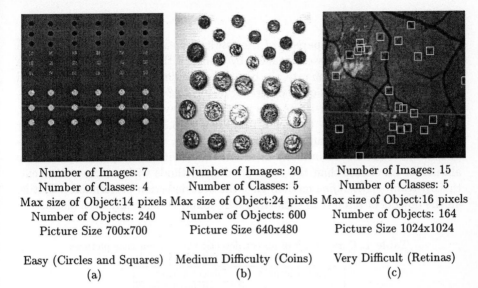

Number of Images: 7	Number of Images: 20	Number of Images: 15
Number of Classes: 4	Number of Classes: 5	Number of Classes: 5
Max size of Object:14 pixels	Max size of Object:24 pixels	Max size of Object:16 pixels
Number of Objects: 240	Number of Objects: 600	Number of Objects: 164
Picture Size 700x700	Picture Size 640x480	Picture Size 1024x1024
Easy (Circles and Squares)	Medium Difficulty (Coins)	Very Difficult (Retinas)
(a)	(b)	(c)

Fig. 2. Object Detection Problems of Increasing Difficulty

4   The Image Databases

We used three different databases in the experiments. Example pictures and key characteristics are given in Figure 2. The pictures were selected to provide problems of increasing difficulty. Database 1 (Easy) was generated to give well defined objects against a uniform background. The pixels of the objects were generated using a Gaussian generator with different means and variances for each class. The coin pictures (Database 2) were intended to be somewhat harder and were taken with a CCD camera over a number of days with relatively similar illumination. In these pictures the background varies slightly in different areas of the image and between images and the objects to be detected are more complex, but still regular. The retina pictures (Database 3) were taken by a professional photographer with special apparatus at a clinic and contain very irregular objects on a very cluttered background. Note that in each of the databases the background counts as a class.

5   Results

This section describes a series of comparisons of the object detection performance among the four methods. For the easy and coin databases the averages of 15 runs are presented. For the retina pictures, due to the high computational cost, the averages of 5 are presented.

5.1 Easy Pictures

Table 5.1 shows the comparison of the results for easy pictures. The detection rate for all the three classes obtained by using all the four methods can reach 100%. Under this detection rate, the best corresponding false alarm rate achieved for each class, however, is quite different. Take *class2* (grey squares) as an example, while *BP-train + GA-refine* does not produce any 'hallucinations', *BP-train*, *GA-train* and *GA-train + GA-refine* result in 0.92, 8.39 and 6.63 false alarms per object respectively. As can be seen from Table 5.1, *GA-train* led to more 'hallucinations' than *BP-train* method; the methods with *GA-refine* had less false alarms for all classes than the corresponding methods without the refinement; the *BP-train + GA-refine* method gave the best detection performance, that is, all the objects of interest in each class were found without any false alarms.

Table 1. Comparison of object detection results on *easy* pictures

Easy Pictures		Object Classes		
		Class1	Class2	Class3
Detection Rate(%)		100	100	100
Best False Alarm Rate	BP-train	0	0.92	0
	GA-train	0.80	8.39	2.73
	BP-train + GA-refine	0	0	0
	GA-train + GA-refine	0	6.63	1.44

5.2 Coin Pictures

Experiments with the coin images give similar results. The best false alarm rates for all the four classes *head005, tail005, head020 and tail020* under the detection rate of 100% obtained by the four methods are shown in Table 5.2. Of all the four methods, *BP-train + GA-refine* gave the best results, where the detection rate for all the four object classes reached 100% without any false alarms. The methods with *GA-refine* always result in less false alarms than the corresponding basic methods without the refinement for all classes. However, *GA-train* produced more false alarms than *BP-train*.

According to Table 5.2, detecting heads and tails of the 5 cent coins turned out to be relatively straight forward, while detecting the heads and tails of the 20 cent coins was a difficult problem. To give a clear view of the comparison of the four methods, we present the detail (ROC curves) of detecting the heads and tails of the 20 cent coins, which are shown in Figure 3.

5.3 Retina Pictures

The results for the retina pictures are summarised in Figure 4. Compared with the results for the other two image databases, these results are disappointing.

Table 2. Comparison of object detection results on *coin* pictures

Coin Pictures		Object Classes			
		head005	tail005	head020	tail020
Detection Rate (%)		100	100	100	100
Best False Alarm Rate	BP-train	0	0	1.82	0.375
	GA-train	3.57	0.19	3.33	7.78
	BP-train + GA-refine	0	0	0	0
	GA-train + GA-refine	1.25	0	0.375	2.15

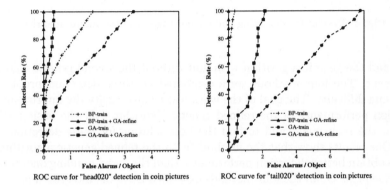

ROC curve for "head020" detection in coin pictures   ROC curve for "tail020" detection in coin pictures

Fig. 3. Results for detecting the heads and tails of the 20 cent coins

However, the results show similar trends: Regarding either the detection rate or false alarm rate obtained, the methods with the refined genetic algorithm are clearly superior to the corresponding basic methods without the refinement, and the *BP-train + GA-refine* method gave the best results among the four methods. Unlike the results of detecting other objects, *GA-train* produces less false alarms than *BP-train* for detecting *micro aneurisms* in the retina pictures.

6   Conclusions

This paper introduced a two stage approach to the use of pixel based neural networks trained and refined by the back propagation and genetic algorithms on the problems of detecting small objects in large pictures. In stage one, the networks are trained by a back propagation algorithm and a genetic algorithm with the fitness of total sum squared error on cut-outs of the objects of interest. In stage two, the best networks found in stage one are refined by applying a second genetic algorithm which uses a linear combination of false alarm rate and detection rate on a training set of full images as the fitness function. The two stage approach covers four detection methods: the back propagation algo-

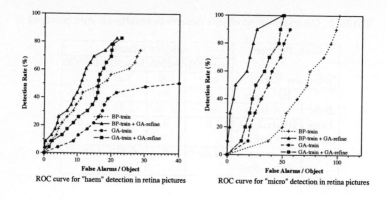

Fig. 4. Results for detecting the haemorrages and the micro aneurisms

rithm and the genetic algorithm with and without the second genetic algorithm refinement. The four methods were compared on three detection problems of increasing difficulty. The goal of the work was to investigate the improvement in detection performance of the refined genetic algorithm over the basic methods without the refinement, and to find the best solution for these detection problems. Our results show that the methods with the refined genetic algorithm can always obtain better detection performance than the corresponding ones without the refinement. Of all the four methods described here, the integrated method of the back propagation algorithm in stage one and the refined genetic algorithm in stage two always produces the best detection performance. The genetic algorithm without the network refinement does not give better performance in most cases compared with the back propagation algorithm.

7   Future Work

The training times for the network refinement are quite long. Some of the runs took longer than 48 hours on a SPARC station. We are investigating ways of shortening the training times.

Overall, the method of the BP algorithm with refined GA produces pixel based networks that work well on objects on a relatively uniform background. However more work is needed for objects on non-uniform and cluttered backgrounds such as our retina pictures.

The best method described here is a two-stage one. The investigation of a single stage with only one GA for the network training on the full images needs to be carried out.

References

1. Ballard, D.H., Brown, C.M.: Computer Vision. Englewood Cliffs, N.J: Prentice-Hall, Inc. (1982)

635

2. Casasent, D.P., Neiberg, L.M.: Classifier and Shift-invariant Automatic Target Recognition Neural networks. Neural Networks, Vol.8. **7/8** (1995) 1117–1129
3. Ciesielski,V., Zhu, J.: A very reliable method for detecting bacterial growths using neural networks. In:Proceedings of the International Joint Conference on Neural Networks, Beijing (1992) 62–67
4. DeJong,K.A., Spears,W.M.: On the virtues of parameterized uniform crossover. In: Belew, R.K., Booker, L.B. (eds.): Proceedings of the Fourth International Conference on Genetic Algorithms. Morgan Kaufman, San Mateo (1991) 230–236
5. Gader, P.D., Miramonti, J.R., Won Y., Coffield P.: Segmentation Free Shared Weight Neural Networks for Automatic Vehicle Detection. Neural Networks, Vol. 8. **9** (1995) 1457-1473
6. Goldberg, D.E.: Genetic Algorithms in Search, Optimization and Machine learning. Addison Wesley, Reading, Ma (1988)
7. Jean, J., Wang, J.: Weight smoothing to improve network generalization. IEEE Transactions on neural networks, Vol. 5. **5** (1994) 752-763
8. Krishnan, R., Ciesielski, V.: 2DELTA-GANN:A New Approach to Using Genetic Algorithms to Train Neural Networks. In: Tsoi, A.C. (ed.): Proceedings of the Fifth Australian Neural Networks Conference, Brisbane (1994) 38–41
9. Roitblat, H.L., Au, W.W.L., Nachtigall, P.E., Shizumura,R., Moons, G.: Sonar Recognition of Targets Embedded in Sediment. Neural Networks, Vol. 8. **7-8** (1995) 1263–1273
10. Roth, M.W.,: Survey of neural network technology for automatic target recognition. IEEE Transactions on neural networks, Vol. 1. **1** (1990) 28–43
11. Rumelhart, D.E., Hinton, G.E., Williams, R.J.,: Learning internal representations by error propagation. In: Rumelhart, D.E., McClelland J.L., and the PDP research group: Parallel distributed Processing, Explorations in the Microstructure of Cognition, Vol. 1:Foundations, Chap. 8. The MIT Press, London (1986)
12. Shirvaikar, M., Trivedi, M.,: A network Filter to detect small targets in high Clutter backgrounds. IEEE Transactions on Neural Networks, Vol. 6. **1** (1995) 252–257
13. Tackett, W.A.: Genetic Programming for Feature Discovery and Image Discrimination. In: Forrest S. (ed.): Proceedings of the 5th International Conference on Genetic Algorithms(ICGA-93), Morgan Kaufmann, University of Illinois at Urbana-Champaign(1993) 303–309
14. Waxman, A.M., Seibert, M.C., Gove, A., Fay, D.A., Bernandon, A.M., Lazott, C., Steele, W.R., Cunningham, R.K.: Neural Processing of Targets in Visible, Multispectral IR and SAR Imagery. Neural Networks, Vol. 8. **7-8** (1995)1029-1051
15. Winkeler, J.F., Manjunath, B.S.: Genetic Programming for Object Detection. In: Koza, J.R., Deb, K., Dorigo, M., Fogel, D.B., Garzon, M., Iba, H., Riolo, R.L. (eds.): Genetic Programming 1997: Proceedings of the Second Annual Conference, Morgan Kaufmann, Stanford University, (1997) 330–335
16. Winter, P., Sokhansanj, S., Wood, H.C., Crerar, W.: Quality assessment and grading of lentils using machine vision. In: Agricultural Institute of Canada Annual Conference, Saskatoon (1996)
17. Zhang, M.: A pixel-based approach to recognising small objects in large pictures using neural networks. In: Proceedings of the Annual RMIT Computer Science Postgraduate Students' Conference, Department of computer science, RMIT. TR 97-51, Melbourne (1997) 57-68
18. Zhang, M., Ciesielski, V.: Centred Weight Initialization in Neural Networks for Object Detection. In: Proceedings of the Twenty Second Australasian Computer Science Conference, Auckland (1999)

An Adaptive, Maintainable, Extensible Process Agent

John Debenham

University of Technology, Sydney,
School of Computing Sciences,
PO Box 123, NSW 2007, Australia
debenham@socs.uts.edu.au

Abstract. Intelligent agents should be autonomous, cooperative and adaptive. An intelligent multi-agent architecture for business process applications also supports maintenance and extensibility. Agent adaptivity is based on observations of the agent's environment, of the results of previous agent decisions, and of estimated reasons for those results being what they were. Maintainability enables agents to do things that are both correct and politically astute. Extensibility enables the agents to develop ways for doing new things. Agent autonomy and cooperation are achieved by building the architecture on a three-layer BDI, hybrid, multi-agent architecture.

1. Introduction

An intelligent multi-agent system is a society of autonomous cooperating components each of which maintains an ongoing interaction with its environment. Intelligent agents should be autonomous, cooperative and adaptive. For business process applications intelligent agents should also support maintenance and extensibility. An approach to process agent adaptivity, maintainability and extensibility is described here. Adaptivity should ensure that agents react to their changing environment intelligently. Maintainability enables agents to do things that are both correct and politically astute. Extensibility enables the agents to develop ways for doing new things.

The growth of activity in agent research [1] and of industrial interest in the applications of agent technology is well documented [2]. A profusion of simple information agents is available on the World Wide Web, and agent-building tools are appearing on the market in increasing numbers. The majority of those tools are intended for comparatively simple, internet-based agents, but the appearance of these tools is an indication that agent technology is beginning to mature. Compared with the number of these information agents, the number of deployed multi-agent systems as reported in the serious research literature is comparatively low [3]. A reason for this low number is the immaturity of intelligent, multi-agent technology; systems worthy of the description "intelligent, multi-agent system" are presently expensive both to build and to maintain. The work described here makes a contribution to the performance, maintenance and extension of intelligent multi-agent systems.

The term 'agent' has a wide range of meaning [4] in the research literature. The term 'agent' is used here, following [3] in the sense that "an agent is a computer system, *situated* in some environment, that is capable of *flexible autonomous* action in order to meet its design objectives" and "the term 'multi-agent systems' ... is now used to refer to all types of systems composed of multiple (semi-)autonomous components".

Business process management is an established application area for agent research [6] [7]. The term *business process* is taken here to refer to processes that are not pre-defined, that are usually not of a routine nature and that may rely on some level of initiative from the system to bring them to a conclusion [8] [9]. One valuable feature of business process management as an application area is that 'real' experiments may be performed with the cooperation of local administrators; a business process management system for postgraduate enrolment [10] was trialed in this way. The architecture described here has been trialed on a local business process application.

2. Active Component

The *active component* of the process agent is responsible for actually handling the process instances. The process agent contains two other component the *maintenance assistant* and the *extension assistant*; they are described in Secs. 4 and 5.

A variety of architectures have been described for autonomous agents [3]. A fundamental distinction in intelligent agent architectures is the extent to which an architecture exhibits deliberative (feed forward, planning) reasoning and reactive (feed back) reasoning. Agent architectures that combine these two forms of reasoning are called *hybrid architectures*. One well reported class of hybrid architectures is the three-layer, BDI agent architectures. One member of this class is the INTERRAP architecture [11] which has its origins in the work of [12]. The INTERRAP architecture was designed to control forklifts in a warehouse environment. An architecture similar to INTERRAP has been applied successfully to business process management [10]. The architecture described here extends that architecture.

As a hybrid architecture this architecture exhibits both deliberative and reactive reasoning [4]. Deliberative reasoning is described in Sec. 2.1. Reactive reasoning is realised by a set of "procedure triggers" that respond with specified priority to the arrival of an observation in the agent's world model. This mechanism supports simple reactive behaviour such as, for example, "if I say 'stop' then stop what you are doing no matter what that is"; this example of reactive reasoning could be vital in a safety-critical application. This is an example of *strong reactivity* for which procedure triggers fire without question. Procedure triggers can be more complicated and so they may support more subtle forms of reactivity. In applications that are not safety-critical a procedure trigger may be interpreted with respect to a model of its context no matter what the context-independent intention of a particular procedure trigger is. So an agent may not "quite" do as it is told. For example, if I say "stop" it may respond by saying "give me a minute and I'll finish what I'm doing" provided that the current context of "stop" allows for this flexibility. This is an example of *weak reactivity* for which procedure triggers are interpreted in the agent's context. In its present form this model of context is a simple case-base to which examples are added by the user when an agent responds in an inappropriate way.

The basis of the inter-agent communication protocol for the generic business process agent is that the sender of a message is responsible for the life of that message

reasons are translated into probabilities and are combined with the "blind" estimates to give an *informed* estimate of agent performance that takes into account the *reasons why* an agent behaved the way it did.

3.1 Blind adaptivity

Agent performance is measured to enable good choices to be made during execution. The availability of different plans for a goal gives flexibility to the choice of plan for that goal. The presence of disjunctive nodes in a plan gives flexibility to the choice of path through that plan. The performance of plans, sub-plans and paths through a plan is measured. To avoid unnecessary repetition, the following description refers only to the measurement of paths, but the method applies equally to plans and sub-plans.

The successful execution of a path only guarantees the success of the plan if the success condition is satisfied. Plans that do not succeed are to be avoided if possible; they waste time and resources and may annoy those who use the system. The meaning of "best" path may be related to: the likelihood that each path will lead to success, the *cost* of achieving each path, the *time* taken to achieve each path and the *value* added to the process by achieving each path.

The following parameters are estimated. "p" is the probability that the path will succeed the next time it executes. "t" is the expected time that the path will take to execute. "c" is the expected cost of executing the path. "v" is the expected value added to the process by executing that path. Suppose that the n events $\{e_i\}_{i=1}^{n}$ are the n previous terminations of a path in order of occurrence, where e_1 is the most recent termination. For each termination of a path e_i the following measurements are made. $Pr(e_i)$ has value "1" for "success", and "0" otherwise. $Ti(e_i)$ is the observed time for path execution. $Co(e_i)$ is the observed cost of path execution. $Va(e_i)$ is the observed added value.

The parameter p is binomially distributed, and is approximately normally distributed under the standard conditions. The parameters t and c are assumed to be normally distributed. The shape of the distribution for the parameter v depends on the precise meaning of "value" chosen; this distribution is also assumed to be normal.

The statistic:

$$P = \frac{\sum_{i=1}^{n} \beta^{i-1} \times Pr(e_i)}{\sum_{i=1}^{n} \beta^{i-1}}$$

where β lies in the range $(0, 1)$ is a point estimate for $\hat{p}$. The extent to which this estimate gives more emphasis to recent behaviour is determined by the value of β. The value of β is chosen to reflect the expected pattern of behaviour for each path. An estimate of this geometric mean is given by the iterative formula:

$$\phi A_{new} = (1 - \beta) \times Pr(e_1) + \beta \times \phi A_{old}$$

which is used to update the ϕ_A values on each occasion that path A is executed. ϕ_A is used as a point estimate for $\hat{p}$. To commence this iteration some initial value $\phi_{A\,init}$ is required; a value of say 0.6 represents a cautiously optimistic starting point.

If the same assumptions hold that were required to estimate $\hat{p}$ above then:

$$\sqrt{\frac{\pi}{2}} \times \frac{\sum_{i=1}^{n} \beta^{i-1} \times |\Pr(e_i) - \hat{\mu}_P|}{\sum_{i=1}^{n} \beta^{i-1}} = \sqrt{\frac{\pi}{2}} \times \Phi_A$$

is a point estimate for the standard deviation $\hat{\sigma}_P$. [This distribution is the "folded distribution".] Φ_A is estimated by:

$\Phi_{A\,new} = (1 - \beta) \times |\Pr(e_1) - \hat{\mu}_P| + \beta \times \Phi_{A\,old}$

where e_1 is the most recently observed behaviour of path A. To commence this iteration some initial value $\Phi_{A\,init}$ is required; a value of say 0.3 represents a cautiously optimistic starting point. This method for updating the Φ_A values requires a point estimate for $\hat{\mu}_P$ the mean of the P statistic for path A. There are two choices for this estimate, either $\phi_{A\,old}$ or $\phi_{A\,new}$. As $\Pr(e_1)$ contributes to the $\phi_{A\,new}$ value there seems little virtue in using it. So the formulae for updating the ϕ_A and the Φ_A values are:

$\Phi_{A\,new} = (1 - \beta) \times |\Pr(e_1) - \phi_{A\,old}| + \beta \times \Phi_{A\,old}$

$\phi_{A\,new} = (1 - \beta) \times \Pr(e_1) + \beta \times \phi_{A\,old}$

These values are expressed in terms of a "path behaviour stability" factor β. For example, if $\beta = 0.85$ then "everything more than twenty trials ago" contributes less than 5% to the weighted mean; if $\beta = 0.70$ then "everything more than ten trials ago" contributes less than 5% to the weighted mean, and if $\beta = 0.50$ then "everything more than five trials ago" contributes less than 5% to the weighted mean.

The method above estimates the probability distribution of a sub-plan, path and whole plan leading to success. In the same way the *time, cost* and *value* associated with a sub-plan, path and plan may be estimated. The precise sense given to "time", "cost" and "value" is not important; measurements can be any real number, and are usually non-negative. Using an argument similar to the estimates of the p distribution:

$(\Omega_{A\,new}, \omega_{A\,new})$, $(\Psi_{A\,new}, \psi_{A\,new})$ and $(\Theta_{A\,new}, \theta_{A\,new})$

are used to estimate the means and standard deviations of the distributions for the parameters t, c and v respectively. The performance measurements available to support the choice of the "best" path through a plan are shown in Fig. 2.

The process agent is adaptive in that it adjusts its behaviour on the basis of the observed performance of chosen paths. The probability that a path is chosen by the agent is the probability that that path is the "best" path. Suppose that the "best" path is to be selected with the criterion "choose the path most likely to succeed". The probability that path A is "more likely to succeed" than path B is the probability that $(p_A - p_B) > 0$. An estimate for this probability is given by the area under the normal distribution with:

Feature	Likelihood of success	Time	Cost	Value
Parameter λ	p	t	c	v
Statistic Σ	P	T	C	V
Measurement	$\Pr(e_i)$	$Ti(e_i)$	$Co(e_i)$	$Va(e_i)$
$\hat{\mu}$ Σ for A	ϕ_A	ω_A	ψ_A	θ_A
$\hat{\sigma}$ Σ for A	$\Phi_A \times \sqrt{\dfrac{\pi}{2}}$	$\Omega_A \times \sqrt{\dfrac{\pi}{2}}$	$\Psi_A \times \sqrt{\dfrac{\pi}{2}}$	$\Theta_A \times \sqrt{\dfrac{\pi}{2}}$
Weighting factor	β_A	γ_A	δ_A	ε_A

Fig. 2. Performance measurements

$$\text{mean} = \phi_A - \phi_B$$

$$\text{standard deviation} = \sqrt{\frac{\pi}{2} \times (\Phi_A^2 + \Phi_B^2)}$$

for $x > 0$. This method estimates the probability that one path is more likely to succeed than another. It may be extended to estimate the probability that one path is more likely to succeed than a number of other paths.

3.2 Informed adaptivity

The "blind" method for path selection described in §3.1 takes account of *what* happened when a path was selected, but does not take account of *why* that former selection behaved the way that it did. Inferred explanations of *why* a selected path through a plan behaved as it did may sometimes be extracted from observing the interactions with the users and other agents involved in that path. For example, a "blind" agent may note that "Person X" was very slow in attending to a certain process instance yesterday" and that the path failed; an observation of Person X's interactions may reveal that "Person X was working on another process instance concerned with the company's annual report yesterday; that instance is scheduled for completion within six days" and that that appeared to be a reason for path failure. Inferred knowledge such as this gives *one possible cause* for the observed behaviour; so such knowledge enables us to *refine*, but *not* to *replace*, the blind estimates of path parameters.

Suppose that e is the event that a selected path A has terminated. Then given:
- a particular observed value $M(e)$ for some parameter λ for which the expected value was $E(\lambda)$ (ie. the "what");
- an inferred explanation Γ for the observation $M(e)$ (ie. one possible "why");
- an estimate of the expected value for λ given Γ: $E(\lambda \mid \Gamma)$;
- an estimate of the effect that Γ will have on expected values for λ at a future time τ: $E(\lambda \mid \Gamma)_\tau$.

In the above example consider ϕ_A. Suppose that the expected value was $\phi_{A_{old}}$, then path A failed, and on the basis of that observed failure the blind estimate for parameter p is $\phi_{A_{blind}} < \phi_{A_{old}}$. Then suppose that the above explanation (involving the company's annual report) was inferred and that it was seen to be largely responsible for the observed behaviour. The refined expected value for parameter p given that explanation could be: $\phi A_{blind} + (\phi A_{old} - \phi A_{blind}) \times 0.2$. Further suppose that the above explanation was seen to be of decreasing relevance up to time $\tau = 6$ days. Then:

$$\phi A_{new} = \phi A_{blind} + (\phi A_{old} - \phi A_{blind}) \times f(\tau), \quad \text{where:}$$

$$f(\tau) = \begin{cases} undefined & if \ \tau < 0 \\ 0.2 + 0.1 \times \tau & if \ 0 \leq \tau \leq 6 \\ 0.8 & if \ \tau > 6 \end{cases}$$

This mechanism provides a way of refining the blind estimates by taking *a reason* for path performance into account. Unlike the blind estimates, the informed estimates are temporal.

4. Maintenance Assistant

A multi-agent process system must adapt to both changes in corporate procedures and in corporate culture. *Corporate procedures* are the way that things should be done. *Corporate culture* is knowledge of "how to make the system work" or "how to be politically astute". Procedures are represented within the multi-agent system as agent plans. Culture is represented as interpretations of those plans. The *currency* of a system is the extent to which it represents current corporate regulations and is politically astute. A plan can be "valid" and "acceptable" whilst not being "astute". Agents choose from the available plans; that choice, and the interpretation of plans chosen, reflects the current corporate culture.

A method for building maintainable knowledge bases is described in [15]. That method is adapted to the maintenance of the currency of plans. If a business process instance goes wrong then a high level trace assists users to identify the particular plan(s) that require maintenance. A deep problem in knowledge maintenance (op. cit.) is the problem of ensuring that a maintenance operation has been completely carried out. This problem is not computable. For example, a change to one part of a knowledge base may require that another part be modified if consistency is to be persevered. The same is true of maintaining the currency of plans. In (op. cit.) a method is described in detail that establishes "links" between two things if modification of one of them could in general require that the other should be modified to preserve consistency. The issue here is the representation of processes [16] rather than rule-related knowledge. The process representation used is "state-activity charts" (op. cit.). Links between plans are determined by decomposing each plan into atomic components (op. cit.). So maintainability is provided in the form a "maintenance assistant" that helps the user to re-establish the currency of the system in the event that a business process goes wrong. One major issue is how changes in the corporate procedures and culture should be applied, if at all, to process instances that are presently being executed [17].

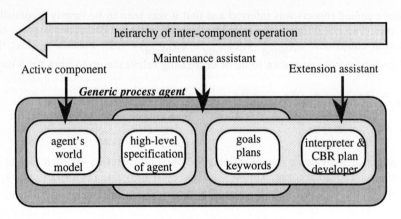

Fig. 3. Extensions to the architecture

5. Extension Assistant

To be extensible a system must be able to develop ways of doing new things that it can not presently do. A request to do something new may originate from outside the system, or, for example, from within the system if an existing plan fails to reach its goal. At one extreme, requests from outside the system could be in natural language, alternatively they could be in a formal language representing a new goal and plan. A middle option is to interactively develop goal and plan descriptions; this is the role of the extension assistant. The extension assistant has two separate components:
• an interactive request interpreter, and
• an interactive plan developer.
A request for an agent to do something that it can not presently do may originate externally to the multi-agent system. The interactive request interpreter assists the user to relate their request to a process representation through a standard dictionary of keywords. For example, does the new process involve "purchasing" something? The standard dictionary of keywords may thus be extended or modified. Then, using a metric based on any related keywords, the interactive plan developer employs case-based reasoning to suggest possible plan structures that could be re-used or modified to achieve the given goal. All that has to be achieved is a plan to describe the process in so far as it interacts with that agent. Once a plan has been developed for one agent, requests to other agents to develop plans for their share of the process are expressed as messages in KQML [13]; natural language understanding is not included [4].

6. Conclusion

The process agent described above is implemented in Java. The 3-layer BDI part is called the active component. It is implemented as an interpreter of high-level agent specifications. This interpreter enables agents to be built quickly. It also simplifies the work of the maintenance assistant which only has to deal with high level specifications of goals and plans. So the maintenance assistant feeds directly into the active component. The maintenance assistant contains representations of goals and plans, and a keyword dictionary to index those goals and plans. The extension assistant uses those representations and that dictionary to drive the case-based reasoning involved in developing new plans for doing new things. So the extension assistant feeds directly into the maintenance assistant. The hierarchy of the active component, maintenance assistant and extension assistant is shown in Fig. 3.

7. References

1. Jennings, N.R., and Wooldridge, M.J. (eds) (1998), "Agent Technology: Foundations, Applications and Markets." Springer-Verlag: Berlin, Germany, 1998.
2. PAAM'96, PAAM'97, PAAM'98, PAAM'99: International Conference and Exhibition on the Practical Application of Intelligent Agents and Multi-Agents.
3. Jennings, N.R., Sycara, K. and Wooldridge, M.J. (1998) "A Roadmap of Agent Research and Development" in Autonomous Agents and Multi-Agent Systems, 1, 7–38 (1998) Kluwer Academic Publishers.
4. Weiss, G. (ed) (1999) "Multi-Agent Systems." The MIT Press: Cambridge, MA.
5. Brenner, W., Zarnekow, R. and Wittig, H. (1998) "Intelligent Software Agents: Foundations and Applications", (July 1998), Springer Verlag.
6. Merz, M., Lieberman, B. and Lamersdorf, W. (1997) "Using mobile agents to support inter-organizational workflow management." Applied Artificial Intelligence, vol. 11(6) pp. 551–572, 1997.
7. Huhns, M.N. and Singh, M.P. (1998) "Managing heterogeneous transaction workflows with cooperating agents." in N.R. Jennings and M. Wooldridge, (eds), "Agent Technology: Foundations, Applications and Markets." Springer-Verlag: Berlin, Germany, 1998, pp. 219-239.
8. O'Brien, P.D. and Wiegand, M.E. (1997). Agents of Change in Business Process Management. In H.S. Nwana & N. Azarmi (Eds.) Software Agents and Soft Computing: Towards Enhancing Machine Intelligence. Springer-Verlag (1997).
9. Norman, T.J., Jennings, N.R., Faratin, P., Mamdani, E.H. (1997). "Designing and Implementing a Multi-Agent Architecture for Business Process Management". In J.P Müller, M.J. Wooldridge & N.R. Jennings (Eds) Intelligent Agents III, Springer-Verlag (1997).
10. Debenham, J.K. (1998a). An Experimental Agent-based Workflow System. In proceedings Third International Conference on The Practical Application of Intelligent Agents and Multi-Agents PAAM'98, London, March 1998, pp101—110.
11. Muller, J.P. (1997): "The Design of Intelligent Agents: A Layered Approach (Lecture Notes in Computer Science, 1177)" (May 1997), Springer Verlag
12. Rao, A.S. and Georgeff, M.P. (1995). BDI Agents: From Theory to Practice. In Proc 1st Int Conf on Multi-Agent Systems (ICMAS-95), San Francisco, USA, pp 312—319 (June 1995)
13. Finin, F. Labrou, Y., and Mayfield, J. (1997): "KQML as an agent communication language", in Jeff Bradshaw (Ed.), "Software Agents", MIT Press (1997).
14. Sutton, R.S. and Barto, A.G. (1998) "Reinforcement Learning" (MIT Press)
15. Debenham, J.K. (1998b) "Knowledge Engineering: Unifying Knowledge Base and Database Design", Springer-Verlag, 1998
16. Scholz-Reiter, B. and Stickel, E. (Eds) (1996) "Business Process Modelling" Springer-Verlag
17. Riempp, G. (1998). "Wide Area Workflow Management." Springer-Verlag 1998.

Metadata, a 'Semantic' Approach

Gian Piero Zarri

Centre National de la Recherche Scientifique
EHESS - CAMS
54, boulevard Raspail
75270 Paris Cedex 06, France
zarri@ehess.fr, zarri@msh-paris.fr

Abstract. In this paper, we describe the data structures proper to NKRL (Narrative Knowledge Representation Language), a language expressly designed for representing, in a standardised way ('metadata'), the semantic content (the 'meaning') of complex multimedia documents. For example, NKRL is actually used in the CONCERTO project (Esprit P29159) to encode the 'conceptual annotations' that will be added to Web documents in order to facilitate their 'intelligent' retrieval, processing, displaying, etc.

1 Introduction

The term 'metadata' — i.e., data about data — denotes, in general, any piece of knowledge that can be used in order to get information about the structure and the contents of a (usually huge) collection of documents. A traditional library catalogue is, therefore, metadata. Recently, metadata has become synonymous of machine understandable knowledge describing Web 'resources', where a resource may concern all sorts of multimedia documents, texts, videos, images, and sounds.

Even if several types of metadata exist, only the content-specific metadata allow to achieve a sufficient degree of generality. Independent of media type and media processing, they "reflect the semantics of the media object in a given context" [1] : they are then related to the 'meaning' that a given document or document component can assume for its potential users. In the world of digital media, expressions like 'semantic approach', 'semantic indexing', 'extraction of semantic features' etc. are, in fact, especially popular.

This indiscriminate use of the label 'semantic' seems, however, to be at least partly unjustified. Most of the 'semantic' features now used as metadata seem to concern only, in reality, the 'external identification framework' (the 'physical structure') of the digital documents considered, more then a description of their true 'meaning'. This is particularly well-evident for non-textual documents like images and videos, where the use of some external, physical characteristics of the media, such as colour, shape, texture, motion patterns, scene breaks, pauses in the audio, camera pans and zooms, etc. is often traded for the use of true semantic techniques. As remarked in [1], "... color distribution feature values of an image for red, black, and yellow still do not allow the conclusion that the image shows a sunset". But even if we stick to textual data, the use of an approach to metadata that is still fundamentally structure-based is also well evident see, e.g., the 15 metadata elements (title, subject, description, source, language, creator, publisher, date, type, format etc.) defined in the framework of the Dublin Core initiative [2].

A traditional — and semantically very poor – way of supplying metadata has typically consisted in the use of keywords ; keywords can be assimilated, to a certain extent, to low-level 'concepts' considered in isolation. Accordingly, several researchers have recently proposed to make use of concepts structured according to an 'ontology' to describe in some depth ('annotate') the information content of the WWW objects to retrieve, see projects like Web-At-a-Glance [3] or Ontobroker [4].

Making use of ontologies constitutes, undoubtedly, an important step towards true semantic-grounded utilisation ; ontologies may not be sufficient, however, to fully render the semantic content of digital documents. For example, the textual documents that are of any industrial and economic interest (news stories, telex reports, corporate documents, normative and legal texts, intelligence messages, etc.) consist often of 'narratives' about 'actions', 'facts', 'events', 'states' etc. that relate the real or intended behaviour of some 'actors' (characters, personages, etc.). In this case, the simple description of concepts is not enough, and must be integrated by the description of the mutual relationships between concepts — or, in other terms, the description of the 'role' the different concepts and their instances have in the framework of the global actions, facts, events etc., see the following Sections about NKRL. Ontologies normally supply, on the contrary, only a static, rigid vision of the world, a taxonomy of pinned up, 'dead' concepts.

From the point of view of the *specific semantic categories* proposed until now as examples of possible metadata (i.e., what is sometimes called the 'vocabulary' of metadata, see the 15 categories of Dublin Core) the situation seems then far from being satisfactory. With respect on the contrary to the *general interoperability mechanisms* for building up metadata systems, the situation is rapidly evolving.

RDF (Resource Description Format) is a proposal for defining and processing WWW metadata, see [5], that is developed by a specific W3C Working Group (WRC = World Wide Web Consortium). The model, implemented in XML (eXtensible Markup Language), makes use of Directed Labelled Graphs (DLGs) where the nodes, that represent any possible Web resource (documents, parts of documents, collections of documents etc.) are described basically by using attributes that give the named properties of the resources. No predefined 'vocabulary' (ontologies, keywords, proposals in the Dublin Core style etc.) is in itself a part of the proposal. The values of the attributes may be text strings, numbers, or other resources. Initially, the model bore a striking resemblance to some early work on semantic networks ; in the last versions of the RDF Model and Syntax Specifications, however, new, very interesting constructs have been added. Among them, of particular interest are the 'containers', i.e., tools for describing 'collections' of resources. RDF can then be considered, now, as an interesting proposal which could be used as a basic environment (basic set of tools) to set up real 'semantic' metadata systems, see, below, Section 4.

In the following, we describe some of the main data structures proper to NKRL ('Narrative Knowledge Representation Language'), see [6, 7], a language expressly designed for representing, in a standardised way ('metadata'), the 'meaning' of complex multimedia documents. NKRL has been used in European projects like Nomos (Esprit P5330), Cobalt (LRE P61011), and WebLearning (GALILEO Actions). It is now employed in the new CONCERTO project (Esprit P29159) to encode the 'conceptual annotations' that will be added to Web documents to facilitate their 'intelligent' retrieval, processing, displaying, etc.

2   The architecture of NKRL

NKRL is structured according to a two-layer approach.

2.1   The lower layer

The lower layer of NKRL consists of a set of general representation tools that are structured into several integrated components, four in our case.

The 'definitional' component of NKRL supplies the tools for representing the important notions (concepts) of a given domain ; in NKRL, a concept is, therefore, a definitional data structure associated with a symbolic label like *physical_entity*, *human_being*, *city_*, etc. These definitional data structures are, substantially, frame-like structures ; moreover, all the NKRL concepts are inserted into a generalisation/specialisation (tangled) hierarchy that, for historical reasons, is called H_CLASS(es), and which corresponds well to the usual 'ontologies' of terms.

A fundamental assumption about the organisation of H_CLASS concerns the differentiation between 'notions which can be instantiated directly into enumerable specimens', like 'chair' (a physical object) and 'notions which cannot be instantiated directly into specimens', like 'gold' (a substance). The two high-level branches of H_CLASS stem, therefore, from two concepts labelled as *sortal_concepts* and *non_sortal_concepts*, see [8] and Fig. 4 below. The specialisations of the former, like *chair_*, *city_* or *european_city*, can have direct instances (chair_27, paris_), whereas the specialisations of the latter, like *gold_*, or *colour_*, can admit further specialisations, see *white_gold* or *red_*, but do not have direct instances.

The enumerative component of NKRL concerns then the formal representation of the instances (lucy_, wardrobe_1, taxi_53, paris_) of the sortal concepts of H_CLASS. In NKRL, their formal representations take the name of 'individuals'. Throughout this paper, we will use the italic type style to represent a *concept_*, the roman style to represent an individual_.

The 'events' proper to a given domain — i.e., the dynamic processes describing the interactions among the concepts and individuals that play a 'role' in the contest of these events — are represented by making use of the 'descriptive' and 'factual' tools.

The descriptive component concerns the tools used to produce the formal representations (predicative templates) of general classes of narrative events, like 'moving a generic object', 'formulate a need', 'be present somewhere'. In contrast to the binary structures used for concepts and individuals, templates are characterised by a threefold format where the central piece is a predicate, i.e., a named relation that exists among one or more arguments introduced by means of roles :

$$(P_i (R_1 \, a_1) (R_2 \, a_2) \dots (R_n \, a_n)) \, ,$$

see the examples in subsection 3.1. Presently, the predicates pertain to the set {BEHAVE, EXIST, EXPERIENCE, MOVE, OWN, PRODUCE, RECEIVE}, and the roles to the set {SUBJ(ect), OBJ(ect), SOURCE, DEST(ination), MODAL(ity), TOPIC, CONTEXT}. Templates are structured into an inheritance hierarchy, H_TEMP(lates), which corresponds, therefore, to a taxonomy (ontology) of events.

The instances ('predicative occurrences') of the predicative templates, i.e., the representation of single, specific events like 'Tomorrow, I will move the wardrobe' or 'Lucy was looking for a taxi' are, eventually, in the domain of the factual component.

2.2 The upper layer

The upper layer of NKRL consists of two parts. The first is a catalogue describing the formal characteristics and the modalities of use of the well formed, 'basic templates' (like 'moving a generic object' mentioned above), built up using the lower layer tools and permanently associated with the language. Presently, the basic templates are more than 150, pertaining mainly to a (very broad) socio-economico-political context where the main characters are human beings or social bodies. By means of proper specialisation operations it is then possible to obtain from the basic templates the 'derived' templates that could be concretely needed to implement a particular application. The second part of the layer is given by the general concepts (general notions) that belong to the upper levels of H_CLASS, such as *sortal_concepts*, *non_sortal_concepts*, *physical_entity*, *modality_*, *event_*, etc., see Fig. 4. They are, as the basic templates, invariable.

3 A brief survey of some important NKRL features

3.1 Descriptive and factual components

Fig. 1 reproduces the NKRL representation of a 'semantic' annotation like "Three nice girls are lying on the beach" that could be associated with a WWW image.

```
c1) EXIST  SUBJ   (SPECIF girl_1 nice_ (SPECIF cardinality_ 3)):
                                             (beach_1)
          MODAL lying_position

     [ girl_1
            InstanceOf :   girl_
            HasMember :   3 ]
```

Fig. 1. Annotation of a WWW image represented according to the NKRL syntax.

The 'predicative occurrence' c1, instance of a basic NKRL template, brings along the main features of the event to be represented. EXIST is a predicate, SUBJ(ect) and MODAL(ity) are roles. In the complex argument ('expansion') introduced by the SUBJ role, girl_1 is an individual (an instance of an NKRL concept) ; nice_ and cardinality_ are concepts, like the argument, lying_position, introduced by MODAL. A 'location attribute' (a list that contains here the individual beach_1) is linked with the SUBJ argument by using the colon code, ':'.

The 'attributive operator', SPECIF(ication), is one of the NKRL operators used to build up structured arguments, see [7] (and Section 4 below). The SPECIF lists, with syntax (SPECIF e_1 p_1 ... p_n), are used to represent some of the properties which can be asserted about the first element e_1, concept or individual, of the list — i.e., in c1, the properties associated with girl_1 are nice_ and (cardinality...), the property associated with cardinality_ is '3'.

The non-empty HasMember slot in the data structure explicitly associated with the individual girl_1, instance of an NKRL concept (girl_), makes it clear that this individual is referring in reality to several instances of girl_ ('plural situation'). In Fig. 1, we have supposed, in fact, that the three girls were, *a priori*, not sufficiently important *per se* in the context of the caption to justify their explicit representation as specific individuals, i.e., girl_1, girl_2, girl_3 ; note that, if not expressly required by the characteristics of the application, a basic NKRL principle suggests that we should try to avoid any unnecessary proliferation of individuals.

A conceptual annotation like that of Fig. 1 can be used for posing queries in the style of : "Find all pictures of multiple, recumbent girls", with all the possible, even very different, variants ; the queries must be expressed in NKRL terms giving then rise to data structures called 'search patterns'. Search patterns are NKRL data structures that represent the general framework of information to be searched for, by filtering or unification, within a metadocument (annotations etc.) repository, see also Fig. 2 below and, for the technical details, [6].

We reproduce now in Fig. 2 the NKRL coding of an information like : "On June 12, 1997, John was admitted to hospital" (upper part of the Figure). This occurrence can be successfully unified with a search pattern (lower part of the Figure) in the style of : "Was John at the hospital in July/August 1997?" (in the absence of explicit, negative evidence, a given situation is assumed to persists within the immediate temporal environment of the originating event, see [9]).

```
c2)   EXIST   SUBJ      john_: (hospital_1)
                [ begin ]
                date-1:   (2-june-97)
                date-2:

( ?w   IS-PRED-OCCURRENCE
                :predicate    EXIST
                :SUBJ         john_
                (1-july-1997, 31-august-1997))
```

Fig. 2. NKRL coding of temporal information, and a simple example of search pattern.

From Figure 2 (upper part), we see that temporal information in NKRL is represented through two 'temporal attributes', date-1 and date-2. They define the time interval in which a predicative occurrence (the 'meaning' represented by the occurrence) 'holds'. In c2, this interval is reduced to a point on the time axis, as indicated by the single value, the timestamp 2-july-93, associated with the temporal attribute date-1 ; this point represents the 'beginning of an event' because of the presence of 'begin' (a 'temporal modulator'). The temporal attribute date-1 is then represented 'in subsequence' (category of dating) ; see [9] for the full details. The two timestamps of the search pattern in the lower part of Figure 2 constitute the 'search interval' linked with this pattern, to be used to limit the search for unification to the slice of time that it is considered appropriate to explore. Examples of complex, high-level querying (and inferencing) procedures that are characteristic of the NKRL approach are the so-called 'transformation rules', see [6].

As a last example of descriptive/factual structures, we give now, Fig. 3, an NKRL interpretation of the sentence : "We have to make orange juice" which, according to Hwang and Schubert [10], exemplifies several interesting semantic phenomena. To translate then the general idea of "acting to obtain a given result", we use :

- A predicative occurrence (c3 in Fig. 3), instance of a basic template pertaining to the BEHAVE branch of the template hierarchy (H_TEMP), and corresponding to the general meaning of 'focusing on a result'. This occurrence is used to express the 'acting' component, i.e., it allows us to identify the SUBJ of the action, the temporal co-ordinates, possibly the MODAL(ity) or the instigator (SOURCE), etc.
- A second predicative occurrence, c4 in Fig. 3, with a different NKRL predicate and which is used to express the 'intended result' component. This second occurrence, which happens 'in the future', is marked as hypothetical, i.e., it is always characterised by the presence of a 'uncertainty validity attribute', code '*'.
- A 'binding occurrence', c5, linking together the previous predicative occurrences and labelled with GOAL, an operator pertaining to the 'taxonomy of causality' of NKRL. Binding structures — i.e., lists where the elements are symbolic labels, c3

and c4 in Fig. 3 — are second-order structures used to represent the logico-semantic links that can exist between (predicative) templates or occurrences.

```
c3)  BEHAVE  SUBJ  (SPECIF human_being (SPECIF cardinality_
                                                several_ ))
                [oblig, ment]
                date1:  observed date
                date2:

c4)  *PRODUCE  SUBJ  (SPECIF human_being (SPECIF cardinality_
                                                several_ ))
                OBJ   (SPECIF orange_juice (SPECIF amount_ ))
                date1: observed date + i
                date2:

c5)  (GOAL  c3  c4)
```

Fig. 3. Representation in NKRL of 'wishes and intentions'.

The general schema for representing the 'focusing on an intended result' domain in NKRL is then :

```
c_α)     BEHAVE   SUBJ  <human_being_or_social_body>
c_β)     *<predicative_occurrence>, with any syntax
c_γ)     (GOAL c_α c_β)
```

In Fig. 3, oblig and ment are 'modulators', see [7]. ment(al) pertains to the 'modality' modulators. oblig(atory) suggests that 'someone is obliged to do or to endure something, e.g., by authority', and pertains to the 'deontic modulators' series. Other modulators are the 'temporal modulators', begin, end, obs(erve), see Fig. 2 and, again, [9]. In the constructions for expressing 'focus on ...', the absence of the ment(al) modulator in the BEHAVE occurrence means that the SUBJ(ect) of BEHAVE takes some concrete initiative (acts explicitly) in order to fulfil the result ; if ment(al) is present, as in Fig. 3, no concrete action is undertaken, and the 'result' reflects only the wishes and desires of the SUBJ(ect).

3.2   Definitional and enumerative components

Fig. 4 gives an extremely simplified representation of the upper level of H_CLASS (hierarchy of concepts, definitional component). We can note, from this figure, that *substance_* and *colour_* are regarded in NKRL as examples of non-sortal concepts. For their generic terms, *pseudo_sortal_concepts* and *characterising_concepts*, we have adopted again the terminology of [8]. For a discussion about *substance_*, see, e.g., [7].

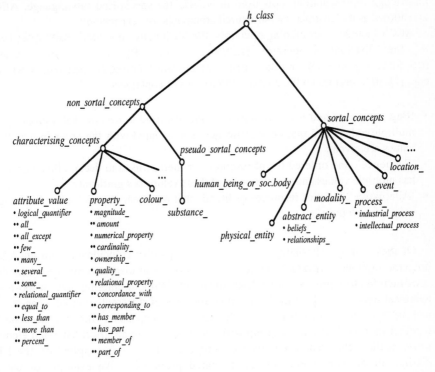

Fig. 4. An abridged view of the 'upper level' of H_CLASS.

Concepts (definitional component) and individuals (enumerative component) are represented essentially as frame-based structures ; their design is, then, relatively traditional. These structures are composed of an OID (object identifier), and of a set of characteristic features (slots). Three different types of slots are used, 'relations', 'attributes', and 'procedures', see again [7].

4   Implementation notes : NKRL and RDF

The usual way of implementing NKRL has been until now that of making use of a three-layered approach : Common Lisp + a frame/object oriented (commercial) environment (e.g., CRL, Carnegie Representation Language) + NKRL.

In the framework of the new CONCERTO project, the partners have decided that a new version of NKRL, RDF-compliant, should be realised. In this context, RDF has then the function of a 'general tool box' for implementing a specific (semantic) 'vocabulary', NKRL in this case. The recent developments of RDF already offer a basis for realising some of the most complex data structures present in NKRL : e.g., the RDF 'containers' correspond, at least roughly, to one of the most important knowledge representation tools used in NKRL, the specialised sublanguage, AECS, that allows us to construct the 'structured arguments' or 'expansion'.

AECS includes four binding operators, the 'disjunctive operator' (ALTERNative = A), the 'distributive operator' (ENUMeration = E), the 'collective operator' (COORDination = C), and the 'attributive operator' (SPECIFication = S), see, e.g., [7]. RDF defines on the contrary three types of containers :

- 'Bag', an unordered list of resources or literals, used to declare that a property has multiple values and that no significance is associated with the order in which the values are given ;
- 'Sequence', and ordered list of resources or literals, used to declare that a property has multiple values and that the order of these values is significant ;
- 'Alternative', a list of resources or literals that represent alternative for the (single) value of a property.

Of these, only 'Alternative' presents a very precise coincidence with an AECS operator, obviously, ALTERN ; moreover, we have at our disposal only *three* container constructions to represent *four* NKRL operators. Without entering now in too many technical details, see [11] in this context, the way of differentiating between COORD and ENUM — in a COORD list, all the elements of the expansion take part (necessarily) together in a particular relationship with the predicate, in an ENUM list, each element satisfies this relationship, but they do this separately — is supplied by the RDF distinction of 'containers' versus 'repeated properties'. An example of use of 'repeated properties' given in [5] is the following : "Sue has written 'Anthology of Time', 'Zoological Reasoning', and 'Gravitational Reflections'". Given that each of the three books has been written independently by the same writer, at different moments, this situation corresponds then to a typical ENUM situation in NKRL terms. An example of the use of Bag is associated, on the contrary, with the representation of the sentence : "The committee of Fred, Wilma and Dino approved the relation", see [5], where, as Lassila and Swick themselves say, "…the three committee members *as a whole* voted in a certain manner…". This situation corresponds certainly in NKRL to a COORD situation. This had led us to implement ENUM making use of the RDF 'repeated properties', and to reserve Bag for the representation of COORD lists.

Using the previous solutions, we are now left with Sequence in order to represent SPECIF. Even if this solution can appear as less natural than the previous ones, it is not totally senseless for the following two reasons, see again, for more details, [11] :

- generally speaking, no specific need exists, in the AECS constructions, for operators based on order constraints ;
- more important, there is a specific order relation that concerns the first element of an NKRL SPECIF list, and that is used to informs us that this first element is,

necessarily, the 'main' element of the list, i.e., the elements whose properties are related by the other elements, see again the example of Fig. 1.

5 Conclusion

In this paper, we have described some of the main data structures proper to NKRL, a language expressly designed for representing, in a standardised way ('metadata'), the semantic content (the 'meaning') of multimedia documents. Our aim was to show that the use of this language can present some advantages, from the point of view of an in-depth indexing of digital documents, with respect to the current metadata techniques.

References

1. Boll, S., Klas, W., Sheth, A.: Overview on Using Metadata to Manage Multimedia Data. In: Sheth, A., Klas, W. (eds.): Multimedia Data Management - Using Metadata to Integrate and Apply Digital Media. McGraw Hill, New York (1998).
2. Weibel, S., Hakala, J.: DC-5 : The Helsinki Metadata Workshop - A Report on the Workshop and Subsequent Developments. D-Lib Magazine (February 1998).
3. Catarci, T., Iocchi, L., Nardi, D., Santucci, G.: Conceptual Views over the Web. In: Intelligent Access to Heterogeneous Information - Proc. of the 4th Knowledge Representation Meets Databases Workshop (Athens, August 1997).
4. Fensel, D., Decker, S., Erdmann, M., Studer, R.: Ontobrocker : Or How to Enable Intelligent Access to the WWW. In: Proc. of the 11th Banff Knowledge Acquisition for KBSs Workshop, KAW'98. Dept. of CS of the University, Calgary (1998).
5. Lassila, O., Swick, R.R. (eds.): Resource Description Framework (RDF) Model and Syntax Specification. W3C (1999).
6. Zarri, G.P., Azzam, S.: Building up and Making Use of Corporate Knowledge Repositories. In: Plaza, E., Benjamins, R. (eds.): Knowledge Acquisition, Modeling and Management - Proc. of EKAW'97. Springer-Verlag, Berlin (1997).
7. Zarri, G.P.: NKRL, a Knowledge Representation Tool for Encoding the 'Meaning' of Complex Narrative Texts. Natural Language Engineering 3 (1997) 231-253.
8. Guarino, N., Carrara, M., Giaretta, P.: An Ontology of Meta-Level Categories. In: Proc. of the 4th Int. Conference on Principles of Knowledge Representation and Reasoning. Morgan Kaufmann, San Francisco (1994).
9. Zarri, G.P. : Representation of Temporal Knowledge in Events : The Formalism, and Its Potential for Legal Narratives. Information & Communications Technology Law 7 (1998) 213-241.
10. Hwang, C.H., Schubert, L.K.: Meeting the Interlocking Needs of LF-Computation, Deindexing and Inference : An Organic Approach to General NLU. In: Proc. of the 13th Int. Joint Conf. on Artificial Intelligence. Morgan Kaufmann, San Francisco (1993).
11. Jacqmin, S., Zarri, G.P.: Preliminary Specifications of the Template Manager (CONCERTO NRC-TR-4). CNRS-CAMS, Paris (1999).

HEROS^{fw}: A Framework for Heterogeneous Database Systems Integration

Elvira Maria Antunes Uchôa, and Rubens Nascimento Melo

Departamento de Informática, Pontifícia Universidade Católica do Rio de Janeiro
Rua Marquês de São Vicente, 225 - Rio de Janeiro - RJ - 22453-900 - Brazil
{elvira, rubens}@ inf.puc-rio.br

Abstract. HEROS^{fw} is an object-oriented framework that allows the construction of heterogeneous database management systems. This work provides an overview of HEROS^{fw} framework, with emphasis on its components and hot spots. A detailed discussion of its implementation is also given.

1 Introduction

Heterogeneous database systems (HDBSs) have been considered one of the most feasible solutions for the integration of existing systems, both autonomous and different, without the need of alterations. A heterogeneous database management system (HDBMS) must be able to integrate new types of component database systems (DBSs), new hardware and software platforms, and new forms of communication, without having to restructure its existing implementation code and design.

The framework technique provides the adequate infrastructure to meet this requirement, since a framework is a software (sub)system of a particular domain that can be tailored for individual applications. A framework consists of a large structure that can be reused as a whole for the construction of a new system, which represents a new federation in the heterogeneous database systems context.

This work proposes a framework for integrating heterogeneous database systems, based on the experience acquired through developing HEROS - Heterogeneous Database Management System [1], currently under research at PUC-Rio Computer Sciences Department.

The remaining sections are organized as follows. In section 2, the motivation for the development of this framework is described. In sections 3, 4 and 5, the HEROS^{fw} framework, its main components and hot spots and its implementation are detailed. In section 6, some related projects are mentioned. To conclude the paper, in section 7, the current status of the work and its continuation are commented upon.

2 An Overview of the HEROS Project

HEROS - HEteRogeneous Object System is a tightly coupled object oriented HDBMS, which has been built in PUC-Rio Computer Sciences Department. HEROS DBSs components may differ in their database management system (DBMS), data model computational environment and physical location. The main issues in the HEROS project [1] were the global data model, the scheme integration mechanisms, the global transaction model and the management and treatment of heterogeneity. A comparative analysis between HEROS and some HDBMS is presented in [2], [3] and [4].

In HEROS first version [3], the transaction manager was developed using a set of functional modules, communicating through RPC mechanisms. In [4], we presented a short summary of this previous HEROS version and studied the feasibility of HEROS architecture based on restructuring object classes, with its remote components communicating using a CORBA implementation. Its implementation details are available at http://www.inf.puc-rio.br/~tecbd/heros.

Several federations were developed, each one requiring a new extension of HEROS architecture: the first [3] incorporated three types of DBS component: the Oracle DBMS (vs. 6.0), the Postgres DBMS (vs. 4.0) and the native HEROS database. The second one [5] integrated Oracle DBMS (vs. 7.3.2) and metadata of heterogeneous information available in Intranets. The third federation [6] incorporated *Legacy System* DBS components.

The development of these many applications, using HEROS HDBMS, showed some limitations and challenges in its architecture:

- By definition, HEROS HDBMS may be extended to integrate any DBS component but the information of which components of its architecture should be extended/adapted is not clearly stated in the project documentation. It needs real hard reading to find this information.
- If someone wishes to switch the communication system, e.g., DCOM instead of CORBA, it becomes necessary to restructure the whole system, as it happened when RPC was replaced by CORBA. This is not coherent since the core of HEROS HDBMS remains the same, undergoing alterations only in the communication system.
- The documentation of HEROS project is organized using object classes and this implies in a high degree of details in its models. For the instantiation of federations, this depth of knowledge should not be a requirement. In fact, it would be enough to visualize its components and the information that the points may be extended/adapted/shaped to build a new federation. In this context, a component is the encapsulated part of a software system, which disposes services, and it is used as building blocks in the making of systems, in a transparent manner to its implementation [7].

Ultimately the main detected problem is the need of reutilization of HEROS architecture (as code and design) to build different federations. This reutilization must allow the choice or redefinition of certain components of the architecture to serve particularities of each federation. The framework technique is a proposal to solve this challenge.

3 HEROS^fw Framework

Bushmann et al. [7] define framework as a partially complete software (sub)system (implemented in a programming language) that is intended to be instantiated. A framework defines the architecture for a family of (sub)systems and provides the basic building blocks to create them. It also defines the parts of itself that must be adapted to achieve a specific functionality. In an object-oriented environment a framework consists of *abstract* and *concrete* classes. Instantiation of such a framework consists of composing and subclassing the existing classes. Concrete classes should usually be invisible to the framework user.

According to [8] a framework consists of *frozen spots* and *hot spots*. Frozen spots define the overall architecture of a software system - its basic components and the relationships between them. These remain unchanged in any instantiation of the framework. Hot spots represent those parts of the framework that are specific to individual software systems. Hot spots are designed to be generic - they can be adapted to the needs of the application under development. When creating a concrete software system with a framework, its hot spots are specialized according to the specific needs and requirements of the system.

The aim of HEROS^{fw} framework [9] is to enable the instantiation of software (HDBMSs) which, in turn, will allow such a integration in a federation of a set of heterogeneous database systems, co-operative but autonomous, where queries and updates can be made, with transparency in relation to the location of data, access paths and any possible heterogeneity or redundancy.

HEROS^{fw} framework consists of six frameworks, i.e., its components are other frameworks (Fig. 1). HEROS^{fw} framework is divided in two parts: global and local. The global part is unique and corresponds to the HEROS^{fw} segment that interacts with global users of the federation. The local part represents HEROS^{fw} segment that interacts with the DBS components - there must be one of these segments to each local where a DBS component is located.

The *User interface* framework is responsible for HEROS communication with the final user, allowing the creation and utilization of new federations. One HEROS federation may be used - through direct call of procedures pertinent to the (global or

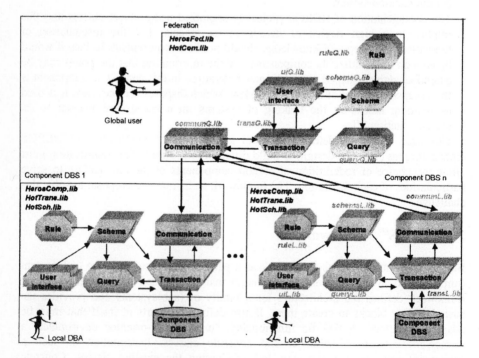

Fig. 1. Components of HEROS^{fw} framework.

external) schema or through global query in HEROS query language (SQL-like). Global queries are derived from the interaction process with the user, through the *User interface* framework, which returns the data and messages resulting from the HEROS processing to the global user. This framework also makes syntactical analysis of requests, detecting semantic mistakes or invalid references to (global or external) schema objects.

The *Schema* framework [2] accounts for the management of HEROS schemas. HEROS uses a four-level schema architecture composed of local schemas, export schemas, global schema and external schemas. Each local schema has a description of its objects that will be shared with the federation, according to the data model used by the respective DBMS. The export schema of each local database contains the description of the local shared objects, expressed in terms of the HEROS global data model. The global schema contains the integrated description of the objects shared by the DBS components. Each external schema represents an application view of the global schema.

The *Query* framework accounts for:

- deriving, from a received global query and global schema, the subqueries that should be submitted to several DBS components. The subqueries are part of an execution query plan.
- producing an alternative optimized execution plan, based on the execution plan and further data about HEROS DBS components.

The *Transaction* framework [3] submits queries or execution requests of global procedures to respective locations. This framework implements database operations fundamental to the composition of the partial results and temporary storage of results. This framework is also responsible for the atomicity control of a transaction and the detection and treatment of global deadlocks. Additionally this framework is liable for submission and execution control of local subtransactions as well as the generation of the "prepared" state necessary for synchronism protocol which implements global transaction atomicity.

The *Communication* framework [9] is responsible for the physical accomplishment of communication between the federation and the DBS components, i.e., it is responsible for the connection with the distributed servers - representing integrated DBS component - detecting and reporting to the *Transaction* framework any troubles related to access to remote data.

The *Rule* framework is responsible for the supply of an active behavior to HEROS, i.e., the ability to automatically answer to the occurrence of certain events. This characteristic is used in HEROS, mainly, to map the local schema concepts into HEROS data model elements, generating automatically the export schemas, when the DBS component and its local schema are included in a HEROS federation. The use of active behavior during the process of executing transactions, although quite interesting, is beyond the scope of this work, being still a research issue, although foreseen [2] in the HEROS data model.

The dynamic aspect of HEROS^{fw} framework [9] was represented using Jacobson's Use Case Model and Interaction Diagram and its static aspect was represented using Rumbaugh's Class Diagram. CASE Select Enterprise helped modeling, and C++ programming language was used for implementation.

4 Hot spots of HEROS[fw] Framework

HEROS[fw] framework may be extended in relation to three issues - the so-called hot spots:

- *Data model of DBS component* – in order to allow automatic translation from the local schema of DBS component to HEROS data model (export schema) through triggering of mapping rules.
- *Type of communication between federation and DBS component* - the framework already offers RPC, ORB and direct call as result of previous experiments with HEROS HDBMS, although other communication modalities (e.g., Microsoft's DCOM) may still be defined.
- *Local transaction management* – in order to allow updating, from the federation, DBS components related to different types of DBMSs, preserving global operation integrity, i.e., the integrity of operations that include various DBS components.
  Each one of these issues is discussed in detail next.

4. 1 Data Model Hot Spot

In order to integrate a new type of data model to HEROS architecture it is necessary to adapt *Schema* framework as follows:
1. define a new class that is a specialization of the *Local schema* class, describing the characteristics [2] of the data model to be integrated (Fig. 2). The local schemas of this kind of DBS component will correspond to objects of these classes.

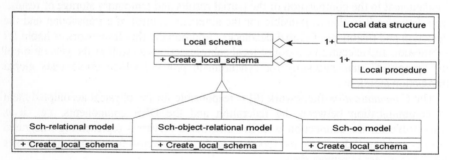

Fig. 2. Class Diagram – Data model Hot spot

2. create an object of *Data model type* class which represents the new data model. Associations between this object and mapping rules (*Rule* framework) must be defined in order to convert concepts of a new data model into a HEROS data model (Fig. 3).
3. define mapping rules (*Rule* framework) between a new data model and the HEROS object-oriented data model (Fig. 3). When this new component system is included as an object of the *Component system* class, it should be associated to a type that corresponds to its data model (*Component data model type* class). Therefore, when its local schema is included, mapping rules are automatically triggered and the export schema is created.

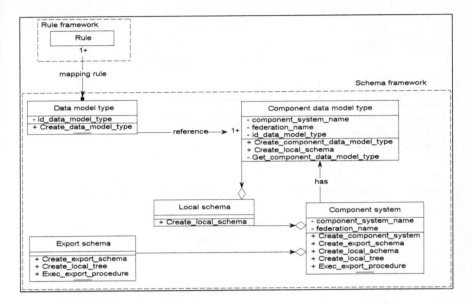

Fig. 3. Class Diagram – Data model type

4. 2 Communication Hot Spot

To integrate a new type of communication to HEROS architecture (Fig. 4), it is necessary to adjust the *Communication* framework as follows:

1. define a specialized class from *Communication client* class to play the role of client in communication between federation and the component system. The *Exec_remote_service* method, requested by the global management of the federation, has to be redefined to establish communication to the remote component (server).

2. create an object of the *Communication* type class, which represents the new kind of communication.

3. add to Request_*remote_service* method, that belongs to the *Component communication type* class, an invocation of the *Exec_remote_service* procedure relative to an object of the new specialized class from *Communication client* class (Fig. 5). The *Component communication type* class is responsible for identifying which specialization of *Communication client* class should be used for communication with each component system. When a new component system is included as an object of the *Component system* class, it must be associated with a type corresponding to its communication (*Component communication type* class) so that an adequate class can be invoked, through *Exec_remote_service* procedure.

4. define a new class that is a specialization of the *Communication server* class to act as a server during communication between federation and component system. The redefinition of *Exec_local_management* method, invoked by *Communication client* class, is crucial. The *Exec_local_management* method, belonging to the new class, should invoke the *Exec_local_management* service of the generic *Communication server* class, responsible for communication to local frozen spots.

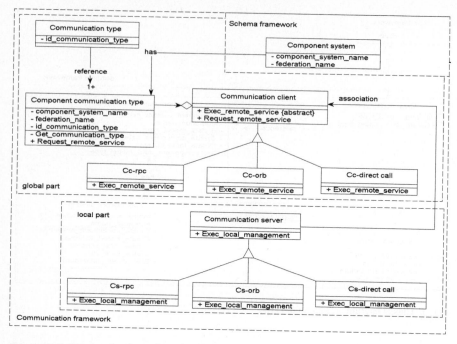

Fig. 4. Class Diagram – Communication Hot spot

4. 3 Transaction Hot Spot

If a new type of local transaction management is to be integrated to HEROS[fw] architecture (Fig. 6), *Transaction* framework should be adapted as follows:

1. define a new class that is a specialization of the *Transaction server* class, and implement the three basic operations for it: {*Exec_oper, Exec_commit, Exec_abort*}. These operations are responsible for formatting operations such as: submit a command (*Exec_oper*), commit (*Exec_commit*) and abort (*Exec_abort*) a

```
type_out_msg
Component_communication_type::Request_remote_service
( type_in_msg in_par)
{
    type_out_msg    out_par;
    int             com_tp;

    Get_communication_type ( in_par.local, &com_tp );

    switch ( com_tp ) {
    case 1 :
        Cc_direct_call  ocomcli_1;
        out_par = ocomcli_1.Exec_remote_service ( in_par );
        break;
    case 2:
        Cc_orb          ocomcli_2;
        out_par = ocomcli_2.Exec_remote_service ( in_par );
        break;
    case 3:
        Cc_rpc          ocomcli_3;
        out_par = ocomcli_3.Exec_remote_service ( in_par );
        break;
    }
    return out_par; }
```

Fig. 5. Request_remote_service implementation

transaction, so that they are accepted by local DBMS, submitting derived

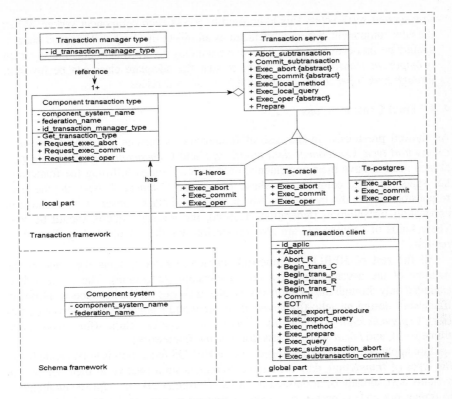

Fig. 6. Class Diagram – Transaction Hot spot

commands to execution and getting corresponding answers. If there are any differences in the data representing form between local DBMS and HEROS, they are also responsible for making the necessary conversions.

2. create an object of *Transaction manager type* class that represents the new type of local transaction management.

3. add to *Request_exec_oper*, *Request_exec_commit* and *Request_exec_abort* methods (Fig. 7) of Component *transaction type* class, invocations of *Exec_oper*, *Exec_commit* and *Exec_abort* procedures, respectively, relative to an object of the new specialized class from *Transaction server* class. The *Component transaction type* class is responsible for identifying which specialization of *Transaction server* class should be used to access

```
int
Component_transaction_type::Request_exec_abort
( type_local local )
{
    int    trans_tp;

    Get_transaction_type ( local, &trans_tp );

    switch ( trans_tp ) {
    case 1:
        Ts_heros            otranserv_1;
        otranserv_1.Exec_abort ();
        break;
    case 2:
        Ts_oracle           otranserv_2;
        otranserv_2.Exec_abort ( );
        break;
    case 3:
        Ts_postgres         otranserv_3;
        otranserv_3.Exec_abort ( );
        break;
    }
    return 1;}
```

Fig. 7. Request_exec_abort implementation

Transaction server class should be used to access each component system. When the new component system is included as an object of *Component system* class, it should be associated with a type corresponding to its transaction management (*Component transaction type* class) so that the adequate class can be invoked, through *Exec_oper*, *Exec_commit* and *Exec_abort* services.

4. 4   Final Considerations

As showed previously, in the case of framework extensions, only the *Component transaction type*, *Component data model type* and *Component communication type* classes need to have their implementation adjusted through fulfilling the framework hot spots. In fact, components whose names are *Component...type* are the ones responsible for the discovery of to which specialized class, chosen at the moment of application instantiation (federation creation), the service requests should be sent. These kinds of components are also responsible for the act of sending the service requests.

All the rest of HEROS^{fw} framework implementation remains the same at the moment of the development of a new application (federation). The framework is extended only through the creation of specialized classes for the hot spots identified in framework design namely: *Communication client* and *Communication server* classes (for *Communication* framework); *Transaction server* class (for *Transaction* framework), and *Local schema* class (for *Schema* framework).

If an application will be developed (i.e., a HEROS federation is to be created) and the types of transaction, data model and communication relative to their component systems have already been defined in HEROS^{fw} framework, no adjustment/alteration in framework code is necessary. When component systems of the new federation are instantiated, they should be associated to the respective types through the creation of objects of the preexistent classes. In this case, the HEROS^{fw} framework works as a "black box" framework [10].

5   Implementation of HEROS^{fw} Framework

HEROS^{fw} framework was implemented in C++ programming language. *Query*, *Rule* and *User interface* frameworks were not totally implemented, however, they were included as abstract classes in an attempt to mark their place of incorporation when they are developed. Details of this implementation are available at http://www.inf.puc-rio.br/~tecbd/heros.

The HEROS^{fw} implementation was organized in two libraries (Fig. 1):

- HerosFed.lib (Global management) - This library represents HEROS^{fw} global component, i.e., the federation point of view. Its header file is: *Heros.h*. This library should be used in global user applications that should request services for *Heros* class. If a graphic interface is developed for query submission and federation creation, then it also must use this library. This library comprises global segment of *User interface*, *Schema*, *Query* and *Rule* frameworks, and the client (or global) segment of *Transaction* and *Communication* frameworks; each one was implemented as a library. The client (or global) part of *Transaction* framework (*transG.lib* library) corresponds to the following classes: {*Transaction client*, *Root transaction*, *Subtransaction*, *Compensating command*, *Compensating process*,

Concurrency control, Global log}. The client (or global) part of *Communication* framework (*communG.lib* library) comprises classes: {*Communication client, Cc-direct call, Cc-orb, Cc-rpc}.* The global part of *Schema* framework (*schemaG.lib* library) comprises the classes: {*Federation, External schema, Global schema, Global class, Global attribute, Global procedure, Global tree, Data dictionary}.* The *User interface* (*uiG.lib* library), *Query* (*queryG.lib* library) and *Rule* (*ruleG.lib* library) frameworks are still to be developed so it is not possible to list their component classes.

- HerosComp.lib (Local management) - This library represents HEROS[fw] local component, i.e., the segment of HEROS[fw] framework that must be present in each local where there is a component system to be integrated to a federation. Its header file is: *Heros,h.* This library should be used by the communication server which requests services to the *Communication server* class. A local application, preferably with a graphic interface, is necessary for the creation of local schema. This application will also use this same library, requesting services for *Heros* class. This library comprises local segment of *User interface, Schema, Query* and *Rule* frameworks and server (or local) segment of *Transaction* and *Communication* frameworks; each one was implemented as a library. The server (or local) part of *Transaction* framework (*transL.lib* library) corresponds to classes: {*Transaction server, Ts-heros, Ts-oracle, Ts-postgres, Local log, Local transaction}.* The server (or local) part of *Communication* framework (*communL.lib* library) comprises the following classes: {*Communication server, Cs-direct call, Cs-orb, Cs-rpc}.* The local part of *Schema* framework (*schemaL.lib* library) comprises the classes: {*Component system, Export schema, Local schema, Data model type, Sch-relational model, Sch-oo model, Sch-object relational model, Export class, Export attribute, Export procedure, Local tree, Local data structure, Local data element, Local procedure}.* The *User interface* (*uiL.lib* library), *Query* (*queryL.lib* library) and *Rule* (*ruleL.lib* library) frameworks will be developed. Therefore, it is not possible to list their component classes.

Besides these two, other three libraries were created but they are provided with their source code (in C++) and they need to be altered at each framework extension. Here they are:

- HotCom.lib (*Communication* hot spot) - This library is altered only when a new kind of communication appears between global and local components of HEROS[fw] framework. It only comprises the class: {*Component communication type}.* This class is responsible for invoking services of specialized class from *Communication client* class. The latter is in charge of establishing the communication with a certain component system. This library should be used in global user applications and in the graphic interface to submit queries and create federations.

- HotTrans.lib (*Transaction* hot spot) - This library is altered only when a component system with a new type of transaction management is to be integrated into a federation. Its only element is the following class: {*Component transaction type}.* This class is responsible for invoking services of specialized *Transaction server* class. The latter is, in turn, liable for submitting transactions to a certain kind of component system. Communication server and the application, which creates the local schemas, should use this library.

- HotEsq.lib (*Schema* hot spot) - This library is altered only when a new kind of data model will be integrated into HEROS[fw] framework. Its only element is the following class: {*Component data model type*}. This class is responsible for invoking services of specialized *Local schema* class. The latter deals with the local schema representation of a certain kind of component system. Communication server and the application, which creates the local schemas, should use this library.

In Fig. 1, the *Rule* framework is used locally for the translation of DBS components data models into the HEROS data model, automatically generating export schemas when the component system and its corresponding local schema are included. In global level, rules are used by global schema to manage some semantic heterogeneity [2].

Arrows reaching the *Schema* framework - at global component level - depict federation creation and - at local component level - depict local and export schema creation. *User interface* framework is used for this very purpose in local module and is the reason why (in Fig. 1) local DBA is interacting with HEROS^fw.

6 Related Work

In literature, there is a large amount of framework reports. The purposes of these works are very different (user-interface - MVC [11]; operational systems - Choices [12]; banking systems - Gebos [13]; broadcast planning for television stations [14], among others). Nevertheless it was not found any description about a framework for integration of heterogeneous database systems.

Although related HDBMS projects (Jupiter [15], VODAK [16], IRO-DB [17] and MIND [18], among others) examine extensibility, they do not employ the framework reuse technique in their architecture. This technique is advantageous because it offers a whole group of concepts that permits a clear identification of extension/adaptation points in its architecture, at both project and code level. Besides that, the technique supports the fulfilling of these points, through definition/choice of specific components to each case of framework instantiation, i.e., definition of a federation in the HDBS context.

7 Final Comments

Three characteristics may be stressed in the architecture of HDBMSs: interoperability, since the component systems of HDBS typically run in heterogeneous hardware and software platforms; distribution, because component systems of HDBS usually are physically distributed; and extensibility, since a HDBMS should be able to integrate new types of component systems with no alteration of the code already made.

Recently, in PUC-Rio Computer Science Department, a HDBMS - HEROS - has been developed. Interoperability and distribution are issues already solved using an object-oriented interoperability standard. Nevertheless, extensibility had remained as one of the greatest challenges because of the ability to generate new federations, reusing the existing project and implementation. A possible solution to this problem - examined in this work - is the use of the reuse technique called *framework*. The HEROS^fw framework was used in the development of an application for a holding company that deals with transportation, storage of containers (warehouse) and storehouses. Oracle vs. 7.3.2 and Informix were used as integrated DBMSs, while Visibroker (Borland) was the communication system used between HEROS^fw global and local parts.

Now the following questions are being investigated: development of *User interface*, *Query* and *Rule* frameworks; development of rule mechanisms to provide for HEROS active ability; integration of new types of component systems including some that are not database systems; development of *design patterns* to describe systematic for instantiation of HEROS^{fw} framework.

References

1. Uchôa, E.M.A., Lifschitz, S., Melo, R.N.: HEROS: a Heterogeneous Object Oriented Database System. In: Proc of the 9th Intl Conf. on Database and Expert Systems Applications (DEXA'98), Lecture Notes in Computer Science, n. 1460, Springer-Verlag, Vienna, Austria (1998) 223-230.
2. Uchôa, E.M.A.: HEROS - A Heterogeneous Database System: Scheme Integration (in Portuguese). M.Sc. Thesis, Pontifícia Universidade Católica do Rio de Janeiro (1994).
3. Silva, S.D.: Heterogeneous Database Systems: a Transactions Management Execution Model (in Portuguese). Ph.D. Thesis, Pontifícia Universidade Católica do Rio de Janeiro (1994).
4. Uchôa, E.M.A., Melo R.N, Lifschitz S.: Object Interoperability in Heterogeneous Database Systems (in Portuguese). Tech. Rep. MCC45/96, Pontifícia Universidade Católica do Rio de Janeiro (1996).
5. Piccinini, H.S.: Integrating Internet/Intranet data for Heterogeneous Database System (in Portuguese). M.Sc. Thesis, Pontifícia Universidade Católica do Rio de Janeiro (1998).
6. Castro, C.E.P.S.: Integrating Legacy Systems for Heterogeneous Database System (in Portuguese). M.Sc. Thesis, Pontifícia Universidade Católica do Rio de Janeiro (1998).
7. Bushmann, F., Meunier, R., Rohnert, H., Sommerlad, P., Stal, M.: Pattern-Oriented Software Architecture: A System of Patterns. John Wiley & Sons, Chichester, West Sussex, England (1996).
8. Pree, W.: Meta-Patterns - a means for capturing the essentials of reusable object-oriented design. In: Proc of European Conf. on Object-Oriented Programming (ECOOP'94), Bologna, Italy (1994) 150-162.
9. Uchôa, E.M.A.: Framework for Integrating Heterogeneous Database Systems (in Portuguese). Ph.D. Thesis, Pontifícia Universidade Católica do Rio de Janeiro (1999).
10. Pree, W.: Framework Patterns. SIGS Books & Multimedia (1996).
11. LaLonde, W.R., Pugh, J.R.: Inside Smalltalk, Volume II. Prentice Hall (1991).
12. Russo, V.F.: An Object-Oriented Operating System. Ph.D. Thesis, University of Illinois at Urbana-Champaign (1990).
13. Bäumer, D., Gryczan, G., Knoll, R., Lilienthal, C., Riehle, D., Züllighoven, H.: Framework Development for Large Systems. In: Comm. of the ACM, vol. 40, n. 10 (1997) 52-59.
14. Codenie, W., Hondt, K.D., Steyaert, P., Vercammen, A.: From Custom Applications to Domain-Specific Frameworks. In: Comm. of the ACM, vol. 40, n. 10 (1997) 71-77.
15. Murphy J., Grimson J.: The Jupiter System: an Environment for Multidatabase Interoperability. Tech.Rep. Dublin City University and Trinity College Dublin (1994).
16. Gesellschaft fuer Mathematik und Datenverarbeitung mbH: "VODAK V4.0 User Manual". Arbeitspapiere der GMD - GMD Tech. Rep. 910, German National Research Center for Information Technology, Darmstadt, Germany (1995).
17. Kapsammer E., Wagner R.R.: The IRO-DB Approach Processing Queries in Federated Database Systems. In: Proc of 8th Intl Workshop on Database and Expert Systems Applications (DEXA'97), Toulouse, France (1997) 713-718.
18. Kilic E., Özhan G., Dengi C., Kesim N., Koksal P., Dogac A.: Experiences in Using CORBA for a Multidatabase Implementation. In: Proc of the 6th Intl Workshop and Conf. on Database and Expert Systems Applications (DEXA'95), London, UK (1995) 223-230.

Resolving Ontological Heterogeneity in the KRAFT Project

P.R.S. Visser, D.M. Jones, M.D. Beer, T.J.M. Bench-Capon, B.M. Diaz and M.J.R. Shave

CORAL - Conceptualisation and Ontology Research at Liverpool
Department of Computer Science, University of Liverpool
PO Box 147, Liverpool, L69 7ZF
United Kingdom
dean@csc.liv.ac.uk

Abstract. KRAFT is an agent architecture for the integration of heterogeneous information systems. The focus in KRAFT is on the integration of knowledge in the form of constraints. In this article we describe the architecture from an ontological perspective. We start by introducing the agent architecture and illustrate its application in the telecommunication-network design. We then describe how we assess the ontological heterogeneity in the domain, which problems the integration of constraint knowledge pose, and how we construct a shared ontology. Also, we describe the mapping functions that are used to translate information between the shared and the local ontologies. Finally, we look at the direction our research is taking hereafter.

1 Introduction

KRAFT is a research project on the integration of heterogeneous information using an agent architecture [1]. The project differs from many other integration projects, such as OBSERVER [2], SIMS [3], Carnot [4], and COIN [5], in that knowledge (in the form of constraints) is integrated rather than just data or enriched data. The project is a collaboration between the Universities of Aberdeen, Cardiff and Liverpool in conjunction with BT and began in May 1996. At present the KRAFT architecture has been evaluated in the area of student-admission policies and the in the design of a router configuration in the telecommunications domain.

Information sources in the KRAFT architecture are heterogeneous with respect to their ontologies, or, domain conceptualisations, and before information can be integrated this heterogeneity has to be reconciled (here referred to as *ontological mediation*). In this article we report on the application of ontologies and ontological mediation as it is done in the KRAFT architecture. Also, we will briefly address our ideas on future generation of KRAFT architectures. It is intended as an overview article of the techniques applied. More details on each of the techniques can be found in other papers.

Section 2 discusses the KRAFT architecture and its application in the router-configuration domain. Section 3 contains an assessment of the communication needs and the heterogeneity between the various ontologies in terms of their ontology mismatches. This assessment is then used to develop a shared ontology on the basis of the local ontologies and WordNet. This is described in section 4. Section 5 addresses the issues involved in the mapping of expressions between local ontologies and the shared ontology. Finally, section 6 contains the conclusions.

2 The KRAFT architecture in the Router-Configuration domain

In essence, the KRAFT architecture allows the combination of information from a set of legacy systems, here referred to as resources. Examples of resources are databases, knowledge systems, constraint solvers, and web pages. The user interacts with the middleware architecture via the a user agent which allows him to formulate his queries and which also presents the results obtained. The agent-middleware architecture has three types of agents:

Wrapper (W)   Links the external resources onto the KRAFT middleware. To do so it resolves language, protocol and ontology heterogeneity as these have to be translated into the KRAFT application internal 'standards'.

Facilitator (F)   White and Yellow page facility. Consulted by the other agents to 'recommend' services that match their required functionality.

Mediator (M)   KRAFT-internal problem solvers. Mediators analyse and decompose information request and arrange for the required information to be gathered from the resources. Thereafter, information is combined if necessary and passed back to the agent that consulted the mediator.

Communication between the agents is done using our Constraint Command and Query Language (CCQL, based on KQML [6]). A typical session starts with the mediators and resources making themselves known to the facilitator (performative: register). After registration the mediator and resources advertise their capabilities (performative: advertise), also to the facilitator. The user agent, aiming to have a query answered, will contact the facilitator via his wrapper with the request to recommend an agent who can deal with his query (performative: recommend-one or recommend-all). The facilitator then consults his internal database of advertised capabilities and replies by forwarding (performative: forward) the appropriate advertisement(s) to the user agent. This advertisement allows the wrapper (or user agent) to communicate directly with the agent that made this advertisement. The latter agent will then be sent the query (performatives: ask-one, ask-all). By contacting the facilitator every time an agent needs the service of another agent the network can adopt to situations in which resources are (temporarily) out of service, or, select the most appropriate agent to deal with the query.

As mentioned earlier, KRAFT differs from other DB integration projects in that not only data is integrated but also constraints. To express constraints we have defined a Constraint Interchange Format (CIF), based on the constraint language CoLan [7].

The router-configuration prototype supports a network designer in his task of selecting a router that can be used to connect a customer site with a so-called point-of-presence (POP). The latter is the WAN entry point that the customer site will be connected to. An example of a typical user query is 'configure a network connection

indication for the hardness of resolving these mismatches and finally gives us a stepping stone for defining mapping functions (see section 5). It thus allows us to focus in an early stage on the integration difficulties that can be expected. The basic idea of the refinement is to classify the type of semantic correspondence, or rather the type of semantic mismatch. The mismatch framework distinguishes three components of a formal definition: the concept to be defined (C), the term to refer to it (T), and the *definiens* or body of definition (D). Two definitions can in principle fail to match in all combinations of these three components, which implies that the semantic correspondence between two entity definitions falls in one of seven different categories (if non of three matches then there is no correspondence). How the entity and attribute comparison is used in the construction of a shared ontology is described in the next section.

4   The Construction of the Shared Ontology[1]

In the KRAFT architecture the resource ontologies are not mapped directly onto each other. Instead, KRAFT uses shared ontologies which serve as the ontology counterpart of a lingua franca. Resource ontologies are mapped onto the shared ontology thus avoiding the potentially large number of individual resource mappings that may have to be defined. Although not used in the router-configuration domain the KRAFT architecture allows for multiple shared ontologies, organised in clusters. The idea behind ontology clusters is that resources do not have to commit to one over-arching standardised ontology but they can from groups (clusters) of resources that all want to commit to some standard.

In the router configuration domain there is one shared ontology. The local schemas in the resources are based on local ontologies. Ideally, the schemas are derived from their local ontology but this is - in the context of legacy system integration - usually not achievable. Rather, the ontology will be created after the schema, with the aim of clarifying the semantics of the entities (objects) used. Here, we will not address the relation between schemas and ontologies in any more detail. This issue is addressed in a separate - forthcoming - paper. The mapping functions bridge the gap between the concepts defined in the local ontologies and the concepts defined in the shared ontology (see section 5). This situation is depicted in Fig. 2 (the open arrows denote relation between schema and local ontology, the solid arrows denote mapping functions). There is not necessarily a one-to-one mapping between concepts in the local ontology and concepts in the shared ontology. Which concepts are mapped onto which shared concepts depends on whether a set of preconditions is satisfied. More on mapping functions in the next section. Before we can map the local ontologies onto the shared ontology we construct the shared ontology so as to support the definition of mapping functions.

---

[1] More details on this can be found in [9].

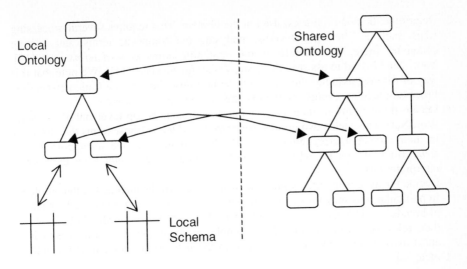

Fig. 2. Mappings between Local Schema and Local and Shared Ontologies

Besides supporting the mapping functions there are other design criteria for the shared ontology. How the shared ontology will be designed also depends on the communication needs. On the one hand, one would like the shared ontology to have the full expressiveness of the 'union' of the resource ontologies. The conclusion is of course that in the design of the shared ontology it is desirable to know what kind of queries and constraints have to be communicated. Also, the intensity of the communication plays a role in the design. Ignoring the optimal degree of expressiveness of the shared ontology we have chosen to make the shared ontology as expressive as the 'union' of the resource ontologies, thus anticipating future information requests.

The approach taken is the result of an ongoing research effort into conceptualisation and ontology design [10]. In short, we create the ontology by linking the required concepts onto the concept structure of an existing top-level ontology. The required concepts are determined by a text-based analysis of the router domain together with the results of the analysis that was described in the previous section. The ontology is thus more a *differential theory* derived from a corpus of natural language texts rather than a theory of concepts that are defined as extensions of a set of individuals in the domain [11]. The top-level ontology we use is WordNet [12]. In addition to this, we use text-analysis techniques to conceptualise domains [13] and techniques for the linking of our ontology into the top-level ontology [14]. The approach, which we here describe in condensed form, consists of three phases: (a) the domain analysis phase, (b) the ontology definition phase, and (c) the resource tuning phase.

A. Domain Analysis Phase
1. Determine a corpus of text material, such as brochures and technical manuals, that describe the domain. The advantage of using these documents as basis material is that we are sure to adopt the vocabulary that is used in the domain.

2. Determine the noun (phrases) used in the domain. This requires several processing steps, such as filtering out verbs, analysing the composite terms, and relating synonym (here, we will refer to the remaining terms as *seed terms* after [14]. Tools can be used to assist in these steps (see, for instance [11]). We note that this way of filtering assumes the domain to be best described from a static perspective. Processes, actions, events and the like are - as yet - not considered.

3. Locate these terms in their correct interpretation in a top-level ontology (here: WordNet). This yields two groups: *supported seed terms* (those terms that do occur in their correct interpretation in the top-level ontology), and *unsupported seed terms* (those terms for which the top-level ontology does not have the correct interpretation).

4. Decide for the unsupported seed terms which ones will be included in the ontology. In particular, this may imply filtering out less relevant proper nouns such as names of brands etc. The decision to include or exclude a proper noun should be based on their relevance to the domain. For example, protocol names such as Token Ring and Ethernet are likely to be important in the networking domain and should be included.

All terms that are selected in step 4 of the analysis phase will be modelled in the domain ontology during the ontology definition phase. To do this, we need a specification language. Most ontology-specification languages support entities, attributes, and values. ONTOLINGUA, LOOM and Classic are examples of such languages.

For each term determined in the previous phase, it has to be decided whether it will be modelled as an entity, an attribute, or as a value (or indeed as a combination of these). For instance, given the terms 'name' and 'customer', it is common to model 'name' as an attribute of entity 'customer'. This is done during the next phase.

B. *Ontology Definition Phase*

1. Define a concept for each of the supported seed terms using only terms that occur in the top-level ontology. The definition should have a unique concept identifier and the seed term itself should be kept as an attribute. In this stage, the concepts will not have any other attributes.

2. Define in a similar way concepts for all terms that are used to define the concepts in steps 1 and 2 and repeat this process until all terms are defined (or until a primitive term has been reached). If WordNet is used as a top-level ontology this means that all concepts on the path from the term to be defined until the root node(s) are modelled.

3. Define in a similar way as above the unsupported seed terms by linking them to the existing definitions. This may imply defining intermediate concepts. For instance, if the terms 'X.21' and 'FDDI' (denoting router interfaces) are to be defined and the term 'router interface' has been defined already, then it might be desirable to introduce intermediate classes representing LAN and WAN router interface.

4. Extend the ontology by assigning attributes to the defined concepts. This may involve the definition of additional concepts.

5. Complete the ontology by defining constraints over the defined concepts and their attributes. Define the constraints so that they exclude incorrect data, but do not use them to exclude unanticipated (unlikely) data.

The ontology as it stands covers the concepts that are relevant for application domain but it is not yet tailored to the specific resources. The last phase in the development of the shared ontology allows for the definition of additional concepts and attributes that enable a more convenient mapping onto the resources. This means that we extend the ontology with concepts required for the interoperation but not yet supported in the shared ontology.

C. *Resource Tuning Phase*
1. Extend the shared ontology with more specialised concepts that resemble the concepts defined each of the local ontologies.
2. Extend the shared ontology concepts with attributes and constraints so as to capture their intended meaning.

After this step, the shared ontology is completed and can be linked onto the resources via mapping functions. This is addressed in the next section.

5   Ontology Mappings

To overcome the mismatches between a resource and a shared ontology, an *ontology mapping* is defined. An ontology mapping is a partial function that specifies mappings between terms and expressions defined in a source ontology to terms and expressions defined in a target ontology. To enable bi-directional translation between a KRAFT network and a resource, two such ontology mappings must be defined. Here we describe the format that we use to specify ontology mappings.

In defining an ontology mapping, we begin by specifying a set of ordered pairs or *ontological correspondences*. An ontological correspondence specifies the term or expression in the target ontology that represents as closely as possible the meaning of the source ontology term or expression. For each term in the source ontology, we try to identify a corresponding term in the target ontology. It may not be possible to directly map all of the source ontology terms to a corresponding target ontology term. For some of the terms in the source ontology that cannot be mapped in this way, it may be possible to include them in the ontology mapping by defining correspondences between compound expressions. This leads us to the following classification of ontological correspondences:

class mapping: maps a source ontology class name to a target ontology class name;

attribute mapping: maps the set of values of a source ontology attribute to a set of values of a target ontology attribute;

attribute mapping: maps a source ontology attribute name to a target ontology attribute name;

relation mapping: maps a source ontology relation name to a target ontology relation name, and

compound mapping: maps compound source ontology expressions to compound target ontology expressions.

There are many subtypes for each of these types (more details on this can be found in [14]).

As the local and shared ontologies are not represented in the same format as that which is used for the CIF, the semantic transformation of CIF expressions by wrappers is not done by directly interpreting the ontology mappings. Rather, the relevant ontology mappings are used as part of the specification of a wrapper. Consequently, developers have complete autonomy in the implementation of wrappers.

A pair of terms and/or expressions in an ontological correspondence are not necessarily semantically equivalent. However, when a wrapper translates a CIF expression, we need to ensure that the target CIF expression is semantically equivalent to the source CIF expression. If this were not the case, constraints passed to the CPE-mediator using terms defined in the shared ontology could express very different knowledge about a vendor's products than the original constraints expressed in terms defined in the local ontology. We ensure that the semantics of CIF expressions are maintained by defining *pre-* and *post-conditions* for each ontological correspondence. A wrapper that implements an ontology mapping must ensure that these conditions are satisfied when translating CIF expressions from the source to the target ontology.

6   Conclusions

KRAFT is an agent architecture that integrates knowledge rather than merely data. This is different from other resource integration projects such as OBSERVER [2], SIMS [3], and Carnot [4] in which merely data is interchanged. In the COIN project [5] the interchanged information consists of semantic values rather than pure data. Semantic values in COIN consist of a piece of data plus semantic information about the correct interpretation of the data. The expressiveness of this semantic information is limited. KRAFT uses the more expressive CIF constraint language to specify the exchanged knowledge. By translating local constraints into the shared ontology the design problem space can be reduced before the actual information retrieval. The aim is to provide the designer with a reduced problem space and to make the information retrieval itself more efficient.

Acknowledgements

The KRAFT project is funded by the Engineering and Physical Sciences Research Council (EPSRC) and BT. More information on the KRAFT project can be obtained from: http://www.csc.liv.ac.uk/~kraft/. The authors wish to express their gratitude to their colleagues of the KRAFT project and to Valentina Tamma.

References

1. Gray, P.D.M., A. Preece, N.J. Fiddian, W.A. Gray, T.J.M. Bench-Capon, M.J.R. Shave, N. Azarmi, M.Wiegand, M. Ashwell, M. Beer, Z. Cui, B. Diaz, S.M. Embury, K. Hui, A.C. Jones, D.M. Jones, G.J.L. Kemp, E.W. Lawson, K. Lunn, P. Marti, J. Shao, and P.R.S. Visser (1997) "KRAFT: Knowledge Fusion from Distributed Databases and Knowledge Bases", *Database and Expert System Applications (DEXA' 97)*, Toulouse, France.

2. Mena, E., V. Kashyap, A. Sheth, A. Illarramendi (1996) "OBSERVER: An Approach for Query Processing in Global Information Systems based on Interoperation across Pre-existing Ontologies", *Proceedings of 1ˢᵗ IFCIS International Conference on Cooperative Information Systems* (CoopIS'96), Brussels, Belgium.

3. Arens, Y., C.A. Knoblock, and W. Shen (1996) "Query Reformulation for Dynamic Information Integration", *Journal of Intelligent Information Systems*, **6**, 99-130.

4. Woelk, D., W. Shen, M. Huhns and P. Cannata (1992) "Model Driven Enterprise Information Management in Carnot", in C.J. Petrie Jr., (ed.), *Enterprise Integration Modelling, Proceedings of the First International Conference*, MIT Press, Cambridge, MA, USA.

5. Daruwala, A., C.H. Goh, S. Hofmeister, K. Hussein, S. Madnick and M. Siegel. (1995) "The Context Interchange Network", *IFIP WG2.6 Sixth Working Conference on Database Semantics (DS-6)*, Atlanta, Georgia.

6. Finin, T., Y. Labrou, and J. Mayfield (1997) "KQML as an agent communication language", in Jeff Bradshaw (ed.) *Software Agents*, MIT Press, Cambridge, MA.

7. Bassiliades, N., and P.M.D. Gray (1994) "CoLan: A Functional Constraint Language and its Implementation", *Data & Knowledge Engineering*, **14**, 203-249.

8. Visser, P.R.S., D.M. Jones, T.J.M. Bench-Capon and M.J.R. Shave (1998) "Assessing Heterogeneity by Classifying Ontology Mismatches", in N. Guarino (*ed.*) *Formal Ontology in Information Systems*, (Proceedings FOIS'98, Trento, Italy), IOS Press, Amsterdam, p.148-162.

9. Jones, D.M. (1998) "Developing Shared Ontologies in Multi-agent Systems", *ECAI'98 Workshop on Intelligent Information Integration*, Brighton, U.K., August 25ᵗʰ.

10. Jones, D.M., T.J.M. Bench-Capon and P.R.S. Visser, (1998) "Methodologies for Ontology Development", *Proceedings IT&KNOWS Conference of the 15th IFIP World Computer Congress*, Budapest, Hungary.

11. Assadi, H. (1998) "Construction of a Regional Ontology from Text and its Use within a Documentary System", in N. Guarino (ed.) *Formal Ontology in Information Systems*, (Proceedings FOIS'98, Trento, Italy), IOS Press, Amsterdam, The Netherlands, p.236-249.

12. Miller, G.A., R. Beckwith, C. Fellbaum, D. Gross, and K.J. Miller (1990) "Introduction to WordNet; An On-line Lexical Database", *International Journal of Lexicography*, **3**(4), 235-244.

13. Bench-Capon, T.J.M., and F.P. Coenen (1992) "Isomorphism and Legal Knowledge Based Systems", *Artificial Intelligence and Law*, **1**(1), 65-86.

14. Swartout, B., R. Patil, K. Knight, and T. Russ (1997) "Toward Distributed Use of Large-Scale Ontologies", *Working notes AAAI-1997 Spring Symposium on Ontological Engineering*, Stanford University, Palo Alto, CA, USA.

15. Jones, D.M. (*forthcoming*) "Ontology Mappings", KRAFT Working Paper KPW55.

Generation of Conceptual Wrappers for Legacy Databases

Ph. Thiran, A. Chougrani, J-M. Hick, J-L. Hainaut

Institut d'Informatique, University of Namur
rue Grandgagnage, 21, 5000 Namur, Belgium
{pth, ach, jmh, jlh}@info.fundp.ac.be

Abstract. One way to solve the heterogeneity problem of distributed legacy databases consists in wrapping them as objects that can be queried for retrieval and updating. This paper presents the InterDB approach for the generation of conceptual wrappers for legacy databases. The generated wrapper is a software layer that offers a conceptual interface based on the conceptual schema of the wrapped database. The InterDB approach provides a complete methodology for conceptual schema recovery (through reverse engineering) and mapping building. The methodology is supported by the DB-MAIN CASE tool that helps generate the wrapper.

1   Introduction

The most popular way to solve the heterogeneity problem of distributed legacy databases consists in wrapping them as objects that can be queried for retrieval and updating (e.g. [11], [2]). In this way, they can be given a standard interface, such as ODBC, JDBC or CORBA IDL, that allows system builders to federate old databases with newly developed ones in a uniform way [2]. The problem of developing these wrappers is manifold. For instance, one has to solve the following questions: how to extract the conceptual schema of an existing, and generally undocumented, physical database, how to map this conceptual schema onto the physical data structures and how to describe this mapping, how to write the wrapper in a systematic way?

The paper concentrates on building the conceptual/physical mapping of legacy databases and on deriving wrappers from them. This is being developed as part of the InterDB project[1] [10]. The paper is organized as follows. Section 2 presents the main aspects of the conceptual wrapper architecture for a legacy database. Section 3 defines the concept of schema transformation. Section 4 proposes a methodology for wrapper generation. In section 5, we present the role of CASE technology in order to support this methodology. Section 6 concludes the paper.

---

[1] The InterDB project [1995-2000] is supported by the Belgian Région Wallonne.

2 Architecture

2.1 Hierarchy architecture

To describe legacy databases, we adopt the standard three levels representation of a database or of a consistent collection of files, materialized into its physical, its logical and its conceptual schema. The *Physical Schema* (PS) describes the physical data structure of the database as they are implemented by the Data Manager. The *Logical Schema* (LS), is the description of the data structures perceived by users and programmers. For instance, the logical schema of a relational database describes its tables, columns, primary and foreign keys as well as all the constraints to which the data are submitted. In this approach, the logical schema also includes implicit constraints, that is, data properties that have not been explicitly declared, but that are managed by, say, application programs. Finally, the *Conceptual Schema* (CS) is the semantic, technology-independent description of the database.

Due to the multiple levels of abstraction involved in this approach, it has been found essential to base it on a unique wide spectrum specification model, namely the *generic model*. This object-relationship formalism is intended to express physical, logical and conceptual data structures, as well as mappings between them

2.2 Component architecture

The component architecture comprises two main components, namely the conceptual wrapper and the conceptual middelware, both dedicated to a database. The conceptual wrapper offers a unique conceptual interface to the applications whereas the conceptual middleware provides a transparent distribution across the network.

Conceptual wrapper

Such a wrapper is developed on top of a legacy database to give it a specific interface. In the InterDB approach, conceptual wrappers offer a conceptual interface based on the conceptual schema of the wrapped database. The queries are expressed into CQL (Conceptual Query Language), a variant of the SQL language which uses the semantics defined in the conceptual schema. That allows writing queries addressing the data independently of the specific aspects of a family of models as well as of the technical constructs of the actual database [11].

Functionally, the conceptual wrapper translates the CQL queries expressed on conceptual schema objects into commands expressed on physical schema constructs. It also assembles the extracted physical data (records and rows) into objects. For instance, a conceptual wrapper associated with a set of COBOL files translates the CQL queries into COBOL program codes and assembles the COBOL records into objects. The conceptual wrapper is based on the mapping between the physical schema and the conceptual schema. It is a program component dedicated to a particular database (i.e. the logical/physical and conceptual/physical mapping rules are hardcoded in the modules).

The conceptual wrapper can be complex if the physical/conceptual mapping is complex, that is, if the physical schema includes many technical and optimization constructs that obscure the source conceptual data structures. Hence the need for systematic building rules based on the formal mapping definition (Section 3), a methodology for its generation (Section 4) and a CASE tool that supports this methodology (Section 5).

Conceptual Middleware

The conceptual middelware manages the communications between the conceptual wrapper and client applications. It offers the object distribution across the network. CORBA [7] and RMI [8] can be used as middleware in our architecture. CORBA and RMI are two distributed object standards supported by the OMG (Object Management Group). CORBA is an architecture standard for building heterogeneous distributed systems. RMI supports distributed objects written entirely and only in the JAVA programming language. For the future, enabling RMI to use the IIOP protocol to communicate with CORBA-compliant remote objects is expected.

A JDBC interface implementation

The current implementation of the architecture concentrates on building a conceptual middleware as a JDBC driver [8] to provide a JDBC-like interface to a JAVA application (Cf. Fig. 1).

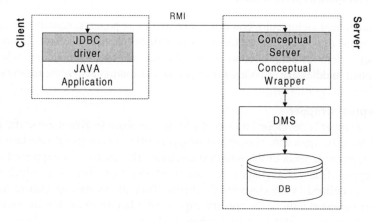

Fig. 1. CQL/JDBC architecture. The architecture provides a conceptual JDBC-like interface for a JAVA application.

The conceptual middelware is made up of a conceptual server and a JDBC-like driver. The conceptual server establishes the TCP/IP connection between the driver and the conceptual wrapper: it receives the queries sent by the driver and sends the result objects from the conceptual wrapper. We use the RMI system to manage the communications between the conceptual server and the driver. The JDBC-like driver is a JAVA API for executing CQL statements. Connected to the conceptual server, it provides JAVA applications with the JDBC-compliant classes and interface. The driver offers a standard API for heterogeneous databases based on a pure JAVA API and a common conceptual query language. Such an architecture provides an adequate way for solving the DMS and platform heterogeneity that appears when one wants to build a multidatabase or federated system. DMS independence is guaranteed by the conceptual wrapper. The wrapper provides an equivalent conceptual schema and a unique query language interface whatever the DMS wrapped. Platform independence is ensured by both the conceptual wrapper and JAVA.

3 Schema Transformations

The conceptual wrapper is based on the mapping between the Physical Schema (PS) and the Conceptual Schema (CS). To formally define the physical/conceptual mapping, we adopt the transformational approach described in [4]. According to this approach, we hypothesize that producing the CS from the PS can be formalized as a schema transformation (T) and that this transformation has an inverse (T') such as: CS=T(PS) and PS=T'(CS).

In this way, schema transformations are essential to formally define forward and backward mappings between the physical schema and the conceptual schema. In addition, they can be stored in a history log that provides a trace of them. The notion can be summarized as follows.

3.1 Definition

A schema transformation consists in deriving a target schema S' from a source S by replacing construct C (possibly empty) in S with a new construct C' (possibly empty). A transformation T can be completely defined by a couple of mappings <T,t> where T is called the structural mapping and t the instance mapping: C' = T(C) and c' = t (c). T explains how to replace construct C with construct C' while t states how to compute instance c' of C' from instance c of C.

Another equivalent way to describe mapping T consists of a pair of predicates <P,Q>, where P is the weakest precondition that C must satisfy for T being applicable, and Q is the strongest postcondition specifying the properties of C'. So we can write T = <P,Q,t>.

3.2 Semantics-preserving transformations

A transformation T can be associated with an inverse transformation T', such that, for any construct C: $P(C) \Rightarrow C= T'(T(C))$. T is declared *semantics-preserving* if the following property is preserved for any construct C and any instance c of C: $P(C) \Rightarrow C= T'(T(C)) \wedge c= t'(t(c))$. Structural mapping T explains how to modify the schema while instance mapping t states how to compute the instance set of C.

3.3 Semantics-preserving transformation sequence

A *transformation sequence* $T_{12} = T_2 \circ T_1$ is obtained by applying T_2 on the schema that results from the application of T_1. This concept is analyzed in [4] and [1]. As an illustration, Fig. 2 shows a sequence of two transformations usually used in database engineering process. The first one (T_1) replaces a foreign key with a relationship type and the second one (T_2) expresses a multiple attribute as an external entity type.

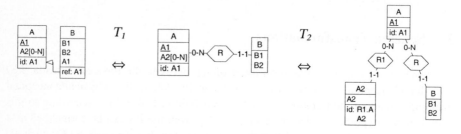

Fig. 2. Sequence of two common semantics-preserving schema transformations: a foreign key transformation followed by an attribute transformation into an entity type

4 Methodology

Building the conceptual wrapper for a legacy database is a complex engineering activity. It requires to recover the physical and conceptual schemas of the legacy database. It also requires to define the physical/conceptual mapping modeled through compound semantics-preserving transformations. Recovering the physical and conceptual schemas of an existing local database is the main goal of the **database reverse engineering** process (DBRE). A general DBRE methodology has been developed in [3].

4.1 Physical schema recovery

The *physical extraction process* aims at building a physical schema (PS) in which only the explicit (i.e., declared) constructs and properties are documented. This process consists in analyzing the data structures declaration statements included in the schema scripts, in DDL schema declaration, in data dictionaries and in application programs. It produces the PS that is the physical view of the legacy database. This process is more complex for file systems, since the only formal descriptions available are declaration fragments spread in the application programs.

4.2. Conceptual schema recovery

Conceptual schema recovery aims to build the conceptual schema of an existing database. It is made up of two processes, namely schema refinement and the Data Structure (DS) conceptualization (cf. Fig. 3). These processes are carried out by transforming the physical schema (PS) successively into the logical (LS) and conceptual schemas (CS). Conceptual schema recovery is performed through compound semantics-preserving transformations that guarantee that the physical and conceptual schemas bear the same semantics.

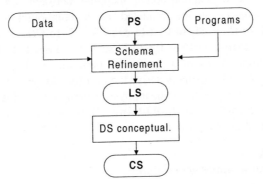

Fig. 3. Conceptual schema recovery. The main processes refine the physical schema (PS) to produce the logical schema (LS) and interpret the latter as a conceptual schema (CS).

Schema refinement process

Unfortunately, many data structures and constraints have been left undeclared in the physical schema. The *schema refinement process* is a complex task through which the PS is refined mainly through analysis of the data and the application programs, but also by analyzing other components of the applications (views, subschemas, screen and report layouts, programs, fragments of documentation, program execution, data, etc.). Through this process, the initial physical schema is enriched with implicit constructs elicited through specific analysis techniques [5] that search non declarative sources of information for evidences of implicit data structures and constraints. This schema is finally cleaned from its non-logical structures. The names are translated to make them more meaningful. The end product of this phase is the logical schema (LS).

Data Structure Conceptualization

The Data Structure Conceptualization Process addresses the semantic interpretation of the LS. It consists for instance in detecting and transforming, or discarding, non-conceptual structures. The main objective is to extract all the relevant semantic concepts underlying the logical schema. Two different problems have to be solved through specific techniques and reasoning: the identification and the replacement of DMS constructs with the conceptual constructs they are intended to translate and the elimination of optimized structures. The result of this process is the conceptual schema (CS). This process has been described in, e.g., [5].

4.3 Building the Mappings

The mappings are modeled through semantics-preserving transformation history [4]. By processing the latter, it is possible to derive functional mappings that explain how each conceptual construct is expressed into physical constructs.

For instance, the logical/conceptual mapping between *logical constructs* and *conceptual constructs* can be modeled as a compound semantics-preserving transformation **L-to-C** = <L-to-C, l-to-c>: CS = **L-to-C**(LS). This transformation admits an inverse: **C-to-L** = <C-to-L,c-to-l> such that: LS = **C-to-L**(CS).

Finally, the logical/conceptual mappings between the logical data *ld* and the conceptual data *cd* can be formally derived: cd = **l-to-c**(ld) and ld = **c-to-l**(cd).

In addition, we consider the logical/physical mappings **P-to-L** = <P-to-L,p-to-l> and its inverse **L-to-P** = <L-to-P,l-to-p>. Now, we are able to describe the physical/conceptual mapping for databases.

4.4 Conceptual wrapper generation

The conceptual wrapper relies on the conceptual schema description and the compound mapping [**C-to-L o L-to-P**] to translate queries and depends on the physical data description and the compound mapping [**p-to-l o l-to-c**] to form the result instances (cf. Fig. 4). The mappings are pure transformational functions that cannot be immediately translated into executable procedures in 3GL. However, it is fairly easy to produce procedural data conversion programs as shown in [5].

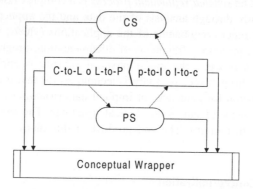

Fig. 4. Conceptual wrapper generation. It is based on the structural mapping and the conceptual schema (CS) constructs for the queries translation. It depends also on the data mapping and the physical schema (PS) data for the results formation.

5   Computer-aided design of wrappers

Manually developing wrappers can be considered for small databases only. Indeed, recovering the physical and conceptual schema, elaborating the functional mapping and writing the wrapping code are complex and tedious tasks. On the other hand, completely automating these processes is unrealistic for real world systems. Hence the need for computer-based assistance tools for each of these processes.

5.1   The DB-MAIN Case environment

The DB-MAIN CASE[2] environment is a complete set of tools dedicated to database applications engineering. This graphical, repository-based, software engineering environment is dedicated to *database applications engineering*. Besides standard functions such as specification entry, examination and management, it includes advanced processors such as transformation toolboxes, reverse engineering processors and schema analysis tools. In particular, DB-MAIN offers a rich set of *semantics-preserving transformational operators* that allow developers to carry out in a systematic way the physical/conceptual mapping. Another interesting feature of DB-MAIN is the *Meta-CASE layer*, which allows method engineers to customize the tool and to add new concepts, functions, models and even new methods. In particular, DB-MAIN offers a complete development language, Voyager 2, through which new functions and processors can be developed and seamlessly integrated into the tool.

5.2   Physical extraction support

The *physical extraction* process is carried out by a series of processors that automatically extract the data structures declared into a source text. These processors identify and parse the declaration part of the source texts, or analyze catalog tables, and create corresponding abstractions in the repository.   Extractors have been developed for SQL, COBOL, CODASYL, IMS and RPG data structures. Additional extractors can be developed easily thanks to the Voyager 2 environment.

5.3   Conceptual schema recovery

The *logical extraction* process, through which implicit constructs are elicited, is supported by a collection of processors that help analyze program code, schemas and data in order to find evidence of these constructs [6] (e.g. a *variable dependency analyzer* that detects and displays the dependencies between the objects (variables,

---

[2] An Education version of the DB-MAIN CASE environment as well as various materials of the DB-MAIN laboratory, e.g. [6], can be obtained at http://www.info.fundp.ac.be/~dbm

constants, records) of a program ; a *foreign key assistant* that help find the possible foreign keys of a schema). The *conceptualization* process can be performed in a reliable way thanks to the semantics-preserving transformation toolset. Transformation scripts that implement specific heuristics can be quickly developed.

5.4 Mapping building

DB-MAIN can automatically generate and maintain a history log (say **h**) of all the transformations that are applied when the developer carries out any engineering process such as database analysis, optimization, implementation or reverse engineering. This history is completely formalized in such a way that it can be replayed, analyzed and transformed. For example, any history **h** can be inverted into history **h'**. Histories must be normalized to remove useless sequences and dead-end exploratory branches. History **h** of the reverse engineering process that produces the conceptual schema of a legacy database from its physical schema PS can be considered as a *structural mapping*. In other words, **h** ≡ [P-to-L o L-to-C], according to the notation of the Section 4.3.

5.5 Conceptual Wrapper generation

If **h'** ≡ [C-to-L o L-to-P], and if **t** is the *instance mapping* of **h**, that is, **t** ≡ [p-to-l o l-to-c], then {**h'**, **t**} is the functional specification of the conceptual wrapper. **h'** explains how to translate queries while **t** explains how to form the result instances. Therefore, history **h** can be used to generate the wrapper. As suggested in Section 4.4, the generator needs the description of the physical and conceptual schemas as well as the history of their derivation. For simplicity, the wrapper generation is performed in two steps, namely the *history analysis* and the *wrapper encoding*. They have been developed in Voyager 2. A history basically is a procedural description of inter-schema mapping. This form does not provide a good support for reasoning and processing, for which a functional expression is better suited. The history analyzer analyses **h** in order to transform it into functional specifications from which the conceptual schema is enriched with conceptual/physical semantics correspondences. The end product of this phase is an *enriched* conceptual schema that includes, for each construct, the way it has been mapped onto physical constructs. In this way, this schema holds all the information required for the generator (cf. Section 4.4). From the enriched CS, the wrapper encoder produces the procedural code of the specific wrapper and a documentation for the programmers.

6 Conclusions

In this paper, we have described the InterDB approach for wrapper generation of legacy databases. A wrapper is defined as a software layer that offers a conceptual interface based on the conceptual schema of the wrapped database. The wrapper plays an important role in building multidatabases and federated databases. It provides an adequate way for solving the data model heterogeneity that appears when one integrates existing, independently developed, files and databases. This paper reports on two original aspects of the approach.

First, it proposes a strong formal basis for a generic methodology of wrapper generation. This methodology is based on a formal transformational approach to schema engineering. This approach formally defines the mappings between the physical schema of the legacy data component and its conceptual schema, so that, it is possible to derive the wrapper from them in a systematic way.

The second original aspect is that the methodology is supported by a CASE tool, i.e., DB-MAIN, that gives the user an integrated toolset for reverse engineering and inter-schema mappings definition and processing. Besides standard functions to represent and manage abstract and concrete specifications, this tool provides a powerful environment, such as Voyager 2 meta-language, to develop domain-specific processors. For instance, mapping analyzers and transformers, schema analyzers and wrapper generators have been written as seamless add-ons to the standard CASE engine.

References

1. Batini, C., Ceri, S., Navathe, S., Structuring Primitives for a Dictionary of Entity Relationship Data Schemas, *IEEE TSE*, 19(4) (1993)
2. Bouguettaya, A., Benattallah, B., Elmagarmid, A., *Interconnecting Heterogeneous Information Systems*, Kluwer Academic Publishers, USA (1998)
3. Hainaut, J-L., Chandelon, M., Tonneau, C., Joris, M. Contribution to a Theory of Database Reverse Engineering, in *Proc. of the IEEE Working Conf. on Reverse Engineering*, IEEE Computer Society Press, Baltimore (1993)
4. Hainaut, J-L. Specification preservation in schema transformations - Application to semantics and statistics, *Data & Knowledge Engineering*, Elsevier Science Publish, 16(1) (1996)
5. Hainaut J-L., Henrard J., Hick J-M., Roland D., Englebert V., Database Design Recovery, in *Proc. of the 8th Conf. on Advanced Information Systems Engineering* (CAISE'96), Springer-Verlag (1996)
6. Hick J-M., Englebert V., Henrard, J.,Roland, D., Hainaut, J-L. The DB-MAIN Database Engineering CASE Tool (version 4) - Functions Overview, *DB-MAIN Technical manual*, Institut d'informatique, University of Namur (1998)
7. Mowbray, T., and Zahavi, R., *The Essential CORBA: Systems Integration Using Distributed Objects*, Wiley, New-York (1995)
8. Reese, *Database Programming with JDBC and JAVA*, O'Reilly, Sebastopol (1997)
9. Sheth, A.P., Larson, J.A., Federated Database Systems for Managing Distributed, Heterogeneous, and Autonomous Databases, *ACM Computing Surveys*, 22(3) (1993)
10. Thiran, Ph., Hainaut, J-L., Hick, J-M., Bodart, S., Deflorenne A., Interoperation of Independent, Heterogeneous and Distributed Databases. Methodology and CASE Support: the InterDB Approach, in *Proc. of the Coopis'98 Conference*, New-York (1998)
11. Wiederhold, G., "Mediators in the Architecture of Future Information Systems", *IEEE Computers*, pages 38-49 (1992)

Design and Implementation of Linear Hash Algorithm in a Nested Transaction Environment[1]

Sanjay Kumar Madria[1]   Malik Ayed Tubaishat[2]   Bharat Bhargava[1]

Department of Computer Science[1]
Purdue University
West Lafayette, IN 47907, USA
{skm, bb}@cs.purdue.edu

School of Computer Science[2]
Universiti Sains Malaysia
11800 Penang, Malaysia
malik@cs.usm.my

Abstract. In this paper, we present a design and implementation of a linear hashing algorithm in nested transaction environment to handle large amount of data. Nested transactions allow parallel execution of transactions, and handle transaction aborts, thus provides more concurrency and efficient recovery. We design a client/server model using layered system architecture. We have used object-oriented methodology in our system implementation that helps in designing and implementing the programming components independently. In our model, buckets are modeled as objects and linear hash operations are modeled as methods. These methods correspond to nested transactions and are implemented using multithreading paradigm.

1 Introduction

Nested transaction processing and concurrency control [1,13] issues play a major role in providing higher concurrency and better handling of transaction's abort and hence have been an important area of research in database systems. The motivation for using nested transactions is to allow transactions to exploit parallelism that might naturally occur within themselves. The benefits of parallel execution of transactions include performance improvements and better control over recovery.

Attention is being given to the designing of concurrency control algorithms which take advantage of the knowledge of particular data structures and the semantics of operations such as insert, delete, find, etc. to improve availability and expedite accesses. Data structures that have been studied with above in mind are B-trees ([2], [3]) and hashing techniques ([4], [5], [6], [7]). Among various hashing techniques, Linear Hashing ([8], [9]) is interested because of its simplicity, ability to handle large amount of data with increased concurrency, and very fast in retrieving data.

Current database applications are increasingly using object-oriented techniques, which necessitate the revaluation of the traditional concurrency control methods that are in use for more efficiency. When combining database functionality with object-oriented concepts, object-oriented databases become the ideal repository of the information that is shared by multiple users and multiple applications on different platforms. Nested transaction is one of the important concepts associated with object-oriented database. In object-oriented databases, if the execution of methods is seen as a transaction then the execution of methods generates a hierarchy that correspond to

---

[1] This research is partially supported by NSF under grant number 9805693-EIA.

nested transactions. While it is essential that object-oriented database systems must support multiple concurrent users, to our knowledge, no implementation of nested transactions accessing linear hash structure has been available in literature. In [10], B-tree algorithm in nested transaction environment has been presented to show its correctness but no implementation issues have been discussed. In one of the author's earlier work [11], linear hashing using nested transactions has been studied only with the aim of proving the correctness of the algorithm using I/O automaton model [12]. In [14], we examined how linear hash structures behave in multi-level transaction [16] environment to exploit the semantics of operations at various levels.

In this paper, we present a system design and implementation of a nested transaction version of the linear hash structure algorithm using object-oriented concepts and multithreading paradigm. In our implementation, we model buckets as objects and linear hash operations find, insert, delete, split, and merge as methods. These methods correspond to nested transactions and are implemented as multithreads. Multithreading is a programming paradigm that allows the application processes to run concurrently. When the process performs multiple tasks at the same time, multithreading split themselves into separate threads that run concurrently and independently. Each thread performs one atomic action. The threads execute individually and are unaware of the other threads in a process. Thus, multithreading can be used very efficiently to implement the behavior of nested transactions. Finally, We have designed and implemented our system using layered system architecture in a client/server environment, which allows more flexibility in term of decomposing of application programs whose modules may be designed and implemented independently.

2 Linear Hash Structures in Nested Transaction Environment

The nested transaction tree of our model is shown in Figure 1. In the nested transaction tree, we have a level of transaction managers. Each transaction manager (TM) corresponds to an operation. The agent, as shown in Figure 1, will send the user-transaction to the appropriate operation (find, insert, or delete). The requested operation then will pass user-transaction to the appropriate TM. The TMs can be thought of as separate, concurrently running processes. Each TM handles transaction-related processing requests like when transactions are created, when they are to be committed or aborted. The find operation is performed logically by an equivalent read-TM whereas insert and delete are performed by write-TM. The search-read (for find) and search-write (for insert/delete) access subtransactions are situated at the leaf level. Search-read accesses read the keys present in a bucket whereas search-write accesses physically modify or delete the key present in a bucket. For split and merge, a split-TM and a merge-TM are provided respectively. During an insert operation, an overflow means a split is required whereas a delete operation may account for an underflow, which signals the need for merging. If the root transaction T intercepts an "overflow" message, it triggers a split-TM whereas if it intercepts an "underflow" message, it invokes a merge-TM. These TMs invoke access subtransactions of the type split-write and merge-write respectively, to physically accomplish the split and merge operations.

On the system building side, when a user requests for an operation to be performed, the agent initiates the corresponding TM. TM can further initiate various subtransactions, which are passed to the appropriate bucket containing the needed data. TM receives the data from the subtransaction and processes the collected data, and may initiate some more subtransactions if required. The scheduler as shown in Figure 1 determines the order in which subtransactions are to be executed. The scheduler receives two types of request; to create a transaction (*request-create*) or request for committing a transaction (*request-commit*). In return, scheduler responds by creating, committing, or aborting the transaction (Figure 2). The scheduler will control operations of the subtransactions, makes a decision about the completion of subtransaction and reports back to their parent (a *report-commit* or *report-abort*), and informs objects the fate of transactions. Transactions situated at one level above the leaf level hold lock on the *root* variable (i.e., *level* and *next*) that is managed by the scheduler. More details can be found in [11,17].

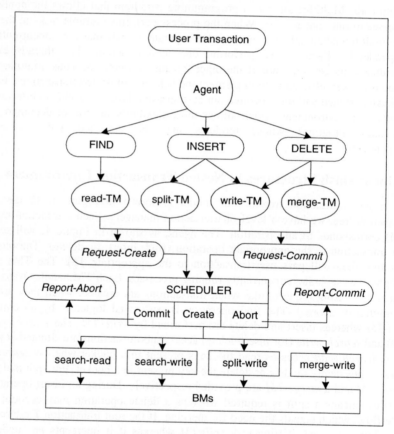

Figure 1. Nested transaction tree with schedulers

To synchronize the leaf node of the transaction tree accessing the buckets we use a bucket manager (BM). In our model, each BM handles one bucket and all its overflow buckets. A BM provides the status and the lock type of each subtransaction accessing the bucket. BM receives the subtransactions, and determines the appropriate time to execute each one, and whether to execute one subtransaction or more depending on each subtransaction's lock mode. Further, BM provides the lock management on keys present in a bucket and in its overflow buckets to control accessing the keys within the same bucket chain. Since a key k in the linear hash structure is a resilient object (A resilient object has no capabilities for managing concurrency, rather it assumes that concurrency control is handled externally by bucket managers. Also, a resilient object has additional capabilities to undo operations of transactions that it discovers have aborted), different transactions may see different versions of the same key. However, there is only one version of each linear hash structure. Therefore, at any time, the set of all keys contained in a linear hash structure is partitioned among the buckets, and each key in a bucket has a set of versions associated with it. When keys move from a bucket to another as a result of split or merge, all its versions move with it.

In our model, transactions situated at one level above the leaf level also hold locks on the *root* variable being provided by the scheduler. The value of the *root* variable would be returned to the scheduler when a lock is granted to a transaction. Lock management on the *root* variable and on buckets is done using Moss's two phase locking algorithm [1] and locking algorithm using lock-coupling protocols given in [8]. The locks on the keys are according to general read/write lock algorithm.

3 Layered System Architecture

In this section, we discuss the layered system architecture of our model as shown in Figure 2. It consists of six layers distributed between the clients and the server. Each client site has one layer called user interface (UI) layer. The other layers are implemented at the server site. These layers are ordered as operations layer, transaction manager (TM) layer, scheduler layer, bucket manager (BM) layer, and finally file manager (FM) layer respectively. All layers at the client and server site work in chronological order to achieve the transaction's computation.

The purpose of this layering system is to partition each transaction into nested transactions which can operate concurrently. A very important feature of our layered system architecture is that if a subtransaction fails at any level; the parent at a higher layer level can initiate another subtransaction without aborting the entire transaction.

➢ **User Interface (UI) Layer**
UI layer's task is to receive an operation request from the user and pass it to the operations layer at the server. In UI layer, two components exist; user interface operations (i.e., find, insert, and delete) and the agent. When the user initiates one of the operations, the agent will pass the message, containing the key requested by the user, to the appropriate operation at the server site. At the end of computations at the server site, the agent will receive a message from the server site, which could be either *"record is found"*, *"record does not exist"*, or confirmation messages.

➢ **Operations Layer**
It creates the transactions, depending on the operation required, and pass them to the appropriate TMs in the next layer. It contains find, insert, and delete operations. These operations will receive response from the TM layer and in turn will pass the

appropriate message to the client. In case the message received from the TM layer is an "overflow" or "underflow" as a result for insert or delete, split and merge will be called. If the message is "overflow", insert operation will initiate *split-TM* to complete the operation. Whereas, if the message is "underflow", delete operation will initiate *merge-TM* to complete the operation.

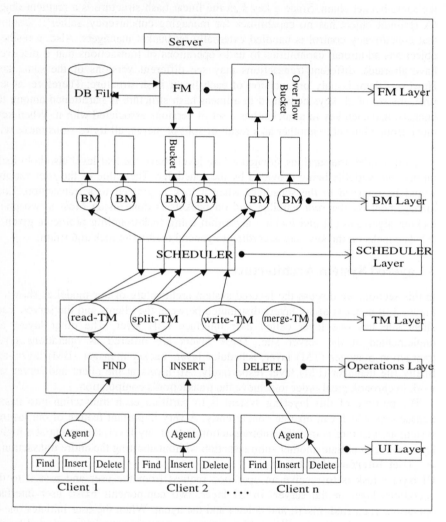

Figure 2. Layered architecture for client/server model

➢ Transaction Manager (TM) Layer

TM layer contains the four TMs; *read-TM*, *write-TM*, *split-TM*, and *merge-TM* explained before. Each TM creates subtransactions to complete the required operation. TMs will work concurrently and independently. After a TM completes its execution, it reports back to the main operation, in the previous layer, the result of the operation. Transactions created at this layer will be passed to the scheduler at the next layer to synchronize various subtransactions created by TMs. Subtransactions created by TMs can also work concurrently and only leaf level subtransactions will access the buckets directly.

> **Scheduler Layer**

At this layer we have a scheduler that synchronize all transactions. Scheduler will determine when to create, commit, and abort a transaction. Scheduler will send the synchronized subtransactions to the BM layer to access the buckets. When a transaction completes, the scheduler will report back to the TMs the state of each transaction; whether it is successfully created, committed or aborted.

> **Bucket Manager (BM) Layer**

At this layer, each BM handles a bucket and all its overflow buckets. Before a transaction accesses any bucket, the corresponding BM will determine whether to permit the transaction to access the bucket or suspend it with the help of the lock compatibility-matrix shown in Table 1. If two transactions accessing the same bucket interfere with each other, BM will permit one of the transactions to access the bucket while suspending the other until previous transaction finishes. Thus, BMs will restrict accesses to the buckets that lead to an inconsistent database state. To insure serializability, BM also handles the keys' locks within the bucket chain. The subtransactions, which access the BMs, are called decisive subtransactions as they are the only subtransactions that access the buckets directly and any interference between transactions at this layer will lead to an inconsistency. BMs work independently of each other.

> **File Manager (FM) Layer**

FM layer will insure the durability of the transaction. Any updates on the buckets will be stored in the database file (i.e., DB File in Figure 2) which resides on a permanent disk space. Updating of the database file will be performed after the commit of a top-level transaction to insure the consistency of our database file. FM is also responsible for loading the keys from the database file to the memory pages (i.e., buckets). It can also restore the current database state in case of a system crash.

4 Object-Oriented Design

We have implemented our layered system architecture discussed in the previous section using object-oriented methodology in the client-server environment The server side in our implementation consists of eight components namely, server, agent, server socket, file manger (FM), user operations, socket file, bucket manager (BM), and linear hash operations (LH). The client side in our implementation consists of four main components (classes), namely, client, client socket, agent, and socket file. These components are implemented as classes using Microsoft Foundation Classes [MFC]. Below, we discuss the scenario of some of the classes from the server side only. Client side classes are similar to the server side so we omit the details from here. More details on the implementation of transaction managers, bucket managers and the classes can be found in [17].

> **Agent**

Agent class is responsible for creating a new thread for each operation received from the client through the socket file. Agent starts by calling FM class to load the DB file before enabling windows sockets. After loading the DB file, agent will call server socket class to create windows sockets. When connecting client to the server, agent will be ready to receive a user request, and then, to create the thread that will be passed to the user operations class to perform this operation.

➢ **File Manager (FM)**

When instantiating this class, the DB file will be loaded into memory so that data can be accessible any time. Three main member functions exist in this class. These functions are: Store, Load, and Update. Store function stores a key from memory to the DB file. Load function fetches a key from the DB file to memory. Update function is called whenever an update is occurred to the DB file. FM sends and receives messages, containing the target key, to the TM class as this class is directly connected to the buckets.

➢ **User Operations**

User operations class contains the three main operations for database information retrieval. These operations are: insert, delete and find. These operations initiated when the user operations class receives a thread from the agent. Multithreads work concurrently at this class. Each thread is responsible for performing an atomic task. Before the three operations insert, find, and delete pass the message to the TM to perform the required operation, they will call the BM class to set a lock on the target bucket before accessing it. When reading or writing the key, BM will be called again to set a lock for the key.

If insert operation is initiated, it will pass a message to the TM class to perform an insert operation. If after the insertion, user operation class receives an "overflow" message from the TM class, insert function will send another message to the TM class to perform the split operation. In case an "underflow" message is received, delete function will send a message to the TM class to perform a merge operation. Each time user operations class call TM it will call BM first to set a lock depending on the operation required.

➢ **Bucket Manager**

BM is responsible for locking and unlocking the buckets and the keys. BM receives a message from the user operations class to set a lock depending on the operation to be performed. After the operation is finish, BM will be called again to unlock the bucket or the key. Locking the bucket and the key afterwards will insure the serializability. Locking the key is implemented using read/write lock technique in which a key is granted a *read-lock* while being read and a *write-lock* while updating it. The *read-lock*, *selective-lock*, and *exclusive-lock* variables, for locking the buckets, are also declared in this class.

OODBMS may provide locking at the object and/or page level. We choose a physical page; a bucket in our design. As each LH object has two buckets, holding lock on the object level will decrease the concurrency among transactions that access the buckets.

➢ **Transaction Managers (TM)**

TMs are implemented using methods. ReadTM method will search for a key in bucket. WriteTM method will either insert a key or delete a key depends on the message received. SplitTM method will split the *next* bucket and will send a message to the user operations class to create a new object if needed for the new bucket. MergeTM method will merge the two buckets involved in the merge operation (*next* and *partner* buckets), and will send a message to the user operations class to delete the object if it has empty buckets.

TMs' methods will communicate with the FM class to load or store keys and to update file after a write operation. Also, TM class will send messages to the socket file to serialize data. That is, sending data to the clients.

In our model, each LH object contains two buckets. We have considered two buckets in each object rather than one to reduce the system's overhead during split and merge operations. This is due to the fact that when the first bucket of any object say O1 needs to be split, a new object say O2 will be created with two buckets. However, when the second bucket from the object O1 splits, no new object (bucket) has to be created as the keys from this bucket can move to the second bucket of the object O2. Similarly, no object needs to be deleted when one of the buckets becomes empty after a merge operation as the other bucket may contain some data. An object will be deleted to free memory space, only if both the buckets become empty. On the other hand, having more buckets in each object will waste memory space. Thus, having two buckets in an object is a compromise between speediness and space utilization.

Whenever split operation is called, the agent will read the *local-level* of the last bucket of the last object. If the *local-level* is *0* (which indicates that this bucket has not been accessed yet), the keys of the split bucket will move to this bucket. Otherwise, a new object will be created and the keys will move to the first bucket of this object in this object. At each level of the hash function, we have a maximum of 2^{level} objects. We find an object id (*OID*) using the following:

$$bucket\ no. = key\ mod\ (2^{level} * N)$$
$$OID = bucket\ no.\ /\ N.$$

Where N is the number of buckets contained in each LH object (In our model, N = 2)

5 Nested Transactions as Multithreads

Multithreads have been used to implement nested transactions in our system. Multithreads are managed in such a way that they do not interfere with each other. Life cycle of the thread is hidden from clients. During a thread's life cycle, many multithreads may be created. A thread may be halted, or an inconsistency may occur, however, these situations will not affect clients. For the clients, a creation and a commit of the top-level thread is important. As clients operate concurrently, many multithreads will be created. To control these threads from interfering, a locking scheme [17] is implemented. The operations in our model will require multithreads to complete their jobs such as searching for the object, inserting, deleting, etc.

5.1 User Interface Operations

➢ **Find**

Find operation searches for a record in the DB file. This operation is handled by *read-TM*. When a user initiates the find operation, a request for creating a thread to search for a key will be sent to the *read-TM*. *Read-TM* will create a *search-read* thread to perform a search for the key. *Search-read's* thread will acquire a *read-lock* on *root* variable and on the bucket being accessed. Further, before accessing the target key a *read-lock* is granted to it to insure that other transactions can not update it. Holding a *read-lock* permits other multithreads to perform simultaneously a search, insert, delete, or split operations. When the search process finishes, a report *"transaction-commit"* will be issued to inform *read-TM* that the thread is committed along with a message which is either *"key is found"* or *"key does not exists"*.

➢ **Insert**

Insert operation inserts a record into the DB file. This operation is handled by *Write-TM*. *Write-TM* will create a *search* thread to search for the requested key. If the key does not exist, another subthread *write* will be created to insert the key into its appropriate bucket. In the searching phase, the *search* thread will be granted a *read-lock* on the *root* variable so that other threads can also execute concurrently. After finding the bucket, a new *write* thread will be created and will be granted a *selective-lock* on this bucket, so that no other operations can access the same bucket. Another type of locks also granted to the requested key, while reading the key a *read-lock* is granted and while writing it a *write-lock* is granted.

If an overflow occurs after insertion, agent will send a message to the *split-TM* to create a subthread *split-write* that will perform the split operation. *Split-write* thread will hold a *selective-lock* on the *root* variable and on the bucket to be split so other operations can work concurrently with split but on different buckets. Before splitting the bucket a *read-lock* is granted to all the keys in the primary and in its overflow buckets as split will not update the keys.

➢ **Delete**

Delete operation is called to delete a record from the DB file. It is handled by *Write-TM*. As before, *write-TM* will create a *search* thread to search for the requested key. If the key exists, another *write* thread will be created to delete the key from the bucket. In the searching phase, the subthread *search* will grant a *read-lock* to the *root* variable so that other threads can work concurrently. In the second phase, the write thread will hold a *selective-lock* on the bucket being accessed so no other insert and delete operations can access the same bucket.

If the bucket becomes empty after deletion, the agent will send a message to the *merge-TM* to create a subthread that will perform the merge operation. *Merge-write* thread will hold an *exclusive-lock* on the *root* variable and on both buckets to be merged. No other operations can work concurrently with merge operation. As merge operation will not permit any other operation to execute concurrently, there will be no need to lock the keys in the buckets involved in the merge operation (*next* and *partner* bucket).

6 Conclusions

In this paper, we have presented the linear hash structure algorithm [8] in nested transaction environment to expedite concurrency and to handle transaction aborts. We have presented an object-oriented client/server model for the implementation of nested transactions that access linear hash structures. We have exploited nested transactions in concurrent linear hash structure to robust the concurrency and handle transaction aborts. We have used object-oriented technology, which is suitable for client/server systems for its speediness in accessing data at the server site, and the property to encapsulate communications from the user. In our model, buckets are modeled as objects whereas linear hash operations find, insert, delete, split, and merge are considered as methods. These methods correspond to nested transactions in their behavior and are implemented as threads and multithreads. More details on our work can be found in [17]. As a future work, we would like to do the conduct various experiments to evaluate the performance of our algorithm and to measure the overheads associated with our system. Another direction of research is to study the model in a distributed environment [15] where a linear hash structure can be spread over a number of machines.

References

[1] Moss, J. E., Nested Transactions: An Approach to Reliable Distributed Computing, MIT Press Cambridge, Massachusetts, 1985.

[2] Sagiv, Y., Concurrent Operations on B-trees with Overtaking, in Proceedings of the 3rd ACM SIGACT-SIGMOD Symposium on Principles of Database Systems, pp. 28-37, Mar. 1985.

[3] Lehman, P. L., Yao, S. B., Efficient Locking for Concurrent Operations on B-trees, ACM Transaction on Database Systems, 6(4): 650-670, Dec. 1981.

[4] Enbody, R. J., Du, H. C., Dynamic Hashing Schemes, ACM Computing Surveys, 20(2): 85-113, Jun. 1988.

[5] Kumar, V., Concurrency Control on Extendible Hashing, Information Processing Letters, 31(1): 35-41, April 1989.

[6] Larson, P. A., Linear Hashing with Separator: A Dynamic Hashing Scheme Achieving One-Access Retrieval, ACM Transaction on Database Systems, 13(3): 366-388, Sep. 1988.

[7] Mohan, C., Aries/LHS: A Concurrency Control and Recovery Method Using Write-Ahead logging for Hashing With Separators, in Proceedings of the 9th IEEE International Conference on Data Engineering, Vienna, Austria, Apr. 1993.

[8] Ellis, C. S., Concurrency in Linear Hashing, ACM Transactions on Database Systems, 12(2): 195-217, Jun. 1987.

[9] Hsu, M., Tung, S. S., Yang, W.P., Concurrent Operations in Linear Hashing, Information Sciences, 51(2): 193-211, 1990.

[10] Fu, A., Kameda, T., Concurrency Control of Nested Transactions Accessing B-Trees, in Proceedings of the 8th ACM Symposium on Principles of Database Systems, pp. 270-285, 1989.

[11] Madria, S. K., Maheshwari, S. N., Chandra, B., Formalization of a Concurrent Linear Hash Structure Algorithm Using Nested Transactions and I/O Automation Model, in Proceedings of International Workshop on Issues and Applications of Database Technology (IADT'98), Germany, July 1998.

[12] Lynch, N., Merrit, M., Weihl, W., Fekete, A., Atomic Transactions, Morgan Kaufman Publishers, San Mateo, California, 1994.

[13] Madria, S. K., A Study of the Concurrency Control and Recovery Algorithms in Nested Transaction Environment, The Computer Journal, 40(10), 1998.

[14] Madria, S. K., Tubaishat M. A., An Overview of Semantic Concurrency Control in Linear Hash Structures, in Proceedings of 13th Int. Symposium on Computer and Information Systems (ISCIS'98), Turkey, Oct.1998.

[15] Litwin, W., Neimat, M., Schneider, D., LH* - A Scalable, Distributed Data Structure, ACM Transactions on Database Systems, 21(4): 480-525, Dec. 1996.

[16] Weikum, G., Principles and Realization Strategies of Multi-level Transaction Management, ACM Transactions on Database Systems, 16(1): 132-180, 1991.

[17] Madria, S. K., Tubaishat M. A. Design and Implementation of Linear Hash Structures in Nested Transaction Environment, Technical Report, CAIS-TR-98-17, CAIS, School of Applied Science, Nanyang Technological University, Singapore, Oct. 1998.

Supporting Partial Isolation in Flat Transactions

Randi Karlsen

Department of Computer Science,
University of Tromsø, 9037 Tromsø, Norway
randi@cs.uit.no

Abstract. This paper describes a new adaptable correctness criterion, called ACC^{tr}, that allows correctness requirements to be attached to each individual transaction. Correctness requirements may vary both between transactions and within a single transaction. ACC^{tr} allows partial isolation, where isolation may be required for some parts of a transaction T, while interleaving is allowed for other parts of T. To support ACC^{tr}, we describe a concurrency control mechanism, called *Two-dimensional locking*. Through early release of locks, Two-dimensional locking allows controlled access to a partially updated database. This is offered as a new type of isolation level which is available for both read and update transactions. The paper briefly considers the recovery mechanism needed to support Two-dimensional locking. Here we suggest using a combination of compensation and rollback to undo flat transactions.

1 Introduction

It is widely recognized that advanced database applications stresses the limits of functionality and performance of traditional transaction management, and that advanced transaction management is needed for these applications [1–6]. One particular problem in many advanced applications, is a need to support long-lasting transactions. The length of duration of a long-lasting transaction may cause serious performance problems if it is allowed to lock resources until it commits. This may either force other transactions to wait for resources for an unacceptable long time, or it may increase the likelihood of transaction abort [1, 6].

By studying consistency and correctness for concurrent transactions, we find that there may be different correctness requirements both between transactions and within a single transaction. (Examples are found in chapter 2). To reflect these differences and possibly allow a more flexible execution of transactions, we propose a new adaptable correctness criterion, called ACC^{tr}, which allows correctness requirements to be attached to each individual transaction. A correctness requirement for a transaction T may specify that isolation is required for some parts of T, while a higher degree of interleaving is allowed for other parts. We do not assume any decomposition of transactions, but use semantic information in *flat transactions* to allow non-serializable executions.

To support ACC^{tr}, we describe a concurrency control mechanism, called *Two-dimensional locking*. This method offers a new type of isolation level, called

'Interleave', which allows controlled access to a partially updated database. To support the new isolation level, each lock in Two-dimensional locking includes information about the transactions correctness requirements.

We believe that our approach may be used as an alternative to decomposing transactions. It may e.g. be used in environments where it is difficult to find suitable decompositions. It may also be used in combination with decomposition, especially in situations where steps or sub-transactions are in themselves long lasting.

This paper is organized as follows. Section 2 motivates for the use of ACC^{tr} and Two-dimensional locking. Section 3 presents some related work. Correctness requirements and ACC^{tr} are described in sections 4 and 5. Section 6 presents Two-dimensional locking, while section 7 briefly describes the need for a new recovery mechanism. Section 8 concludes.

2 Motivation

When two or more transactions execute concurrently, their operations execute in an interleaved fashion that may cause concurrency problems. These problems have traditionally been avoided by guaranteeing serializable executions of transactions. However, there are in many applications a need for more concurrency and thereby non-serializable executions.

We will in the following distinguish between internal and external consistency for an object. *Internal consistency* describes consistency for the object itself and ignores the relationship to other objects. *External consistency* considers the relationship between objects and describes mutual consistency for a group of objects. An external consistency requirement may e.g. be an integrity constraint stating for example that $(x < y)$ or $(a = b)$. Concurrent executions of (individually consistent) transactions, may cause both internal and external inconsistency. Situations causing problems like 'lost update', 'dirty read', and 'unrepeatable read' (as described in [7]) may all lead to internal inconsistency, while 'inconsistent retrieval' (see [8]) may cause external inconsistency.

We find that the notion of consistency is situation dependent. In particular, we find that a so-called 'inconsistent retrieval' may, under certain circumstances, reflect a consistent execution. This depends on the transaction semantics and on the environment where the transaction is executed. Consequently, two different transactions, executing in the same environment, may well have different correctness requirements. Additionally, we also argue that there may be different correctness requirements within the same transaction. The following examples illustrate such differences.

Example 1:
Assume the following history including operations from transaction T_1 and T_2.

$H : write_1(x) \prec write_2(x) \prec write_2(y) \prec write_1(y)$

$write_1(x)$ denotes that T_1 performs a write operation on object x.

In history H, transaction T_2 sees a database state which reflects a partial update of x and y. If traditional serializability is required, this history is considered inconsistent and therefore not allowed. Inconsistencies will typically occur if e.g. x and y are both modules of the same program P, and P can not be compiled and run unless both modules are updated. Under such assumptions, history H illustrates the 'inconsistent retrieval' problem.

However, there are situations where traditional serializability is not required. If T_2 does not compile and run the program modules, a partial update of x and y need not be considered inconsistent. This is also the situation if x and y are modules of two different programs. If we allow T_2 to succeed after seeing a partial update of x and y, the non-serializable history H represents a consistent execution of T_1 and T_2.

In addition to having different correctness requirements between transactions, we also argue that there may be different correctness requirement within the same transaction. There may well be situations where a transaction may access some objects using a weak requirement, while other objects are accessed using a strong requirement. This is a situation which existing database systems does not support. Example 2 illustrates such a situation.

Example 2:
Assume that a group of people is working on a project where several different programs are written. Assume also that some design decision taken during the course of the work will effect a number of those programs. Different modules from these programs must be changed, and to implement these changes, a transaction is specified.

$$T_3 : Update(A_1), Update(A_2), Update(C_1), Update(D_1)$$

The Update operation involves both reading of a program module, and updating according to the new design. Transaction T_3 updates modules from three different programs, i.e. modules A_1 and A_2 from program A, and modules C_1 and D_1 from program C and D respectively. To have a correct execution, T_3 should access each program in isolation. This means that modules A_1 and A_2 must be used in isolation, while there are no such requirement between any other modules accessed by T_3.

As described in the above examples, different correctness requirements may be needed both between transactions and within a single transaction. This situation is to some extent recognized in SQL-92 (in the following called SQL), where the user may choose between 4 different isolation levels (called 'Read Uncommitted', 'Read Committed', 'Repeatable Read', and 'Serializable'). By using an appropriate isolation level, a transaction may be allowed to read a partially updated database. However, the SQL approach does not fully provide the functionality we are seeking. Firstly, if a weak isolation level is applied, concurrency problems like 'dirty read', and 'unrepeatable read' may occur. This may lead to inconsistent use of single objects. Secondly, SQL will not allow a history like H (from example 1), where an update-transaction is legally given access to a partially updated database. Also, SQL allows different correctness requirements between transactions, but does not allow different correctness requirements within a single transaction.

In the following we describe an approach to concurrency control where non-serializable executions are allowed through the use of a new type of isolation level, called 'Interleave'. Based on the transaction semantics, the user may relax the consistency requirement through declaring the whole transaction or parts of the transaction as 'Interleave'. When 'Interleave' is declared, 'inconsistent retrieval' is not considered a concurrency problem. 'Interleave' may be chosen for both read and write transactions. With respect to internal consistency, this approach gives full correctness guarantees for single objects. This means that it protects against both 'lost update', 'dirty read', and 'unrepeatable read'.

3 Related work

This work describes how we can use transaction semantics to allow early release of objects and thereby allow non-serializable transaction executions. Related research, where transaction semantics is used for determining legal interleaving of transactions, is found in [9–15]. These papers describe how transaction semantics are used to decompose transactions into atomic steps, and how interleaving of transactions are allowed between steps.

In [10, 12, 13] the application designer will explicitly specify breakpoint for each transaction and determine the allowed interleaving at these points. This requires detailed knowledge about concurrent transactions.

In [11, 14, 9, 15] transactions are decomposed into subtransactions or steps, and interleaving is allowed between steps. Both [11, 14] requires that the decomposition is done so that subtransactions may interleave freely. In [9] decomposition can result in steps that may interfere, but this interference is controlled by providing high-level concurrency control. When decomposing transactions in [14, 9], information about the set of concurrent transactions is needed. In [15] a semantic-based decomposition of transaction is described, and allowable interleavings identified. The paper focuses on developing a model for transaction decomposition, and properties to ensure the developer as to the soundness of a given decomposition.

In contrast to the work described above, our approach does not assume any decomposition of transactions. We do on the contrary use transaction semantics to provide early release of locks in flat transactions. This makes it possible to release a lock on an object without delaying this until commit of some step. Also, we do not assume any detailed knowledge of concurrent transactions. The correctness requirement of a transaction T is in our approach determined only by considering the needs of T.

4 Partial isolation and isolation units

We will in the following describe correctness for concurrently executed transactions based on the notion of *partial isolation*. Partial isolation is a property that generally does not apply to the whole transaction, but rather to a *unit of isolation*. An isolation unit is a set of objects, $U = \{o_1, \ldots, o_n\}$ (where $n \geq 1$), which makes it possible to specify a correctness requirement that effects only some operations within a transaction. This will further make it possible to have different correctness requirements both within a single transaction, and between different transactions.

Partial isolation: It must appear to each transaction T requiring isolation for U, that other transactions executed on U either before or after T.

We distinguish between two types of partial isolation, which is handled somewhat differently. If the isolation unit includes only a single object, the correctness requirement is called object isolation, otherwise it is called group isolation.

Object isolation: describes correctness for a single object. Object isolation is a basic and compulsory requirement, and every transaction will automatically require object isolation for each object it accesses.

Group isolation: describes correctness for a group of objects where mutual consistency requirements exist. Group isolation is an optional requirement. We assume this requirements to be explicitly specified as part of the transaction specification. The requirement will only apply to the transaction(s) that specified the unit.

In our approach, we need an explicit specification for each isolation unit containing two or more objects. We assume that this specification is done by the users as a part of the transaction specification. The singleton isolation units are compulsory for each transaction, and will therefore not need an explicit specification. In this work, isolation units have the following properties:

- There exists one singleton isolation unit for each object in the database.
- Group isolation units are explicitly specified and include a number of objects where mutual consistency requirements exist.
- An isolation unit specified for a transaction T, indicates a correctness requirement for T only, and need not be required by any other transaction.
- Two isolation unit, specified either in different transactions or in the same transaction, may well intersect. As long as isolation is guaranteed for each unit, correctness is also guaranteed.

We continue example 2 by assuming that transaction T_3 is specified as follows:

BEGIN_TRANSACTION,
BEGIN_ISOLATE, Update(A_1), Update(A_2), END_ISOLATE,
Update(C_1), Update(D_1), END_TRANSACTION

A new type of construct, called $BEGIN\_ISOLATE \ldots END\_ISOLATE$, is assumed. This construct encloses an *isolate region*, and every object accessed within this region belong to the same (non-singleton) isolation unit. Singleton isolation units is not explicitly specified. Each object accessed by the transaction is automatically identified as a singleton unit. For transaction T_3, the following isolation units can be identified.

- Four singleton units, one unit for each object accessed by T_3. These units are: $U_1 = \{A_1\}$, $U_2 = \{A_2\}$, $U_3 = \{C_1\}$, and $U_4 = \{D_1\}$.
- One unit reflecting a group isolation requirement, i.e. $U_5 = \{A_1, A_2\}$.

From this example, we see that both objects A_1 and A_2 are included in two isolation unit. A correct execution on object A_1 requires isolation for both U_1 and U_5.

5 An adaptable correctness criterion

In this section, we define an *adaptable correctness criterion*, called ACC^{tr}, which allows correctness requirements to be attached to individual transactions. A correctness requirement for a transaction T may specify that isolation is required for some parts of T, while interleaving is allowed for other parts of T.

The definition of ACC^{tr} correct histories is based on the notions of ACC^{tr} serial history and conflict equivalence between histories. ACC^{tr} is essentially a correctness criterion where serializability is required with respect to units of isolation. It is worth noting that the following definitions introduce a form of asymmetry, where isolation units may effect transactions differently. As an example, take an isolation unit U which includes two or more objects. U is normally specified by one specific transaction T (say), and isolation with respect to U must therefore only be guaranteed for T. Another transaction T', not specifying U as an isolation unit, may well see a partially update of objects in U as long as this does not cause inconsistencies for T.

Concurrent execution of a set of transactions is represented by a history H as a partially ordered set of operations. The correctness of history H is guaranteed by controlling the ordering of conflicting operations. Since correctness is described for a unit of isolation, we only need to control the ordering of conflicting operations accessing objects within the unit. We therefore specify a set of history projections on H, denoted $\Pi(H)$, which includes one projection for each unit of isolation represented in H. We describe the projection as follows.

History projection (for an isolation unit U): Let $H^{(U)}$ denote a projection of history H with respect to operations on objects in isolation unit U. Projection $H^{(U)}$ is the history obtained from H by deleting all operations that do not access objects in U.

Isolation is guaranteed by enforcing legal ordering of conflicting operations in each history projection in $\Pi(H)$. To do this, we need to identify conflicting operations.

Definition 1 (Conflicting operations in U). *Let p_i and p_j be operations of two different transactions in a history projection $H^{(U)}$. Operation p_i and p_j conflict in $H^{(U)}$ if p_i and/or p_j belongs to a transaction requiring isolation for U, they both access the same object, and their order of execution effects either the state of the database or the return value from the transaction(s) that require an isolated U.*

Our approach to correctness of histories is based on the concept of serial histories. Every serial execution of transactions is correct since each transaction is (by assumption) individually correct. Below we first define an ACC^{tr} serial history, secondly an ACC^{tr} correct history.

Definition 2 (ACC^{tr} serial). *A history H_S is ACC^{tr} serial iff there for each history projection in $\Pi(H_S)$ exists a total order of all transactions.*
A history projection $H_S^{(U)}$ is serial iff for every two transactions T_i and T_j in $H_S^{(U)}$, either all operations of T_i appear before all operations of T_j or vice versa.

It can be shown that all serial histories are correct. Every history that can be shown equivalent to a serial history is consequently also correct.

Definition 3 (ACC^{tr} correct). *Assume two histories H and H_S, where H_S is ACC^{tr} serial. Let $\Pi(H)$ and $\Pi(H_S)$ denote the set of history projections over H and H_S respectively.*
A history H is ACC^{tr} correct iff each projection $H^{(U)}$ in $\Pi(H)$ is conflict equivalent to the corresponding projection $H_S^{(U)}$ in $\Pi(H_S)$. Conflicts are determiner based on the definition of 'Conflicting operations in U'.

The correctness theorem can be found in [16].

6 Two-dimensional locking

Two-dimensional locking is a concurrency control method supporting ACC^{tr}. This method guarantees object isolation for every object in the database, and additionally, group isolation where this is explicitly requested. A description of Two-dimensional locking is given below. The locking rules and correctness proof can be studied in [16].

Two-dimensional locking allows for a flexible and customized execution of transactions. The user can either choose 'isolation' for the whole transaction, or she can choose to give the transaction a customized correctness requirement which is weaker then the 'isolation' requirement. A relaxed correctness requirement may increase concurrency. We are currently doing a simulation study that investigates the possible performance gains obtained through the use of Two-dimensional locking. The results of this work is not available at the moment, but will be reported later.

The costs of using Two-dimensional locking is, at least compared to traditional Two-phase locking, more complex locking and recovery methods. Also,

	req_lock modes			exec_lock modes	
lock mode	set by	set when	lock mode	set by	set when
int	Interleave-transaction	before use of o	read	Read-transaction	before read of o
isol	Isolate-transaction	before use of o	write	Write-transaction	before write of o
–	both types of transactions	in second lock stage	–	Write-transaction	in second lock stage

Table 1. Lock modes for the requirement and execution lock component

by allowing the users to specify correctness requirements for the transaction, we make the user (partly) responsible for database consistency and correctness. The user must especially take care if she weakens the correctness requirements of a transaction that updates the database. If the transaction is allowed to start executing on a partially updated database, the user must be capable of determining that updates will not violate database consistency.

6.1 Isolation levels and lock components

Two-dimensional locking presents some novel features. Firstly, it introduces a *new isolation level*, called *'Interleave'*. Secondly, each lock consist of two separate *lock components*, which describes different transaction properties. Both properties are used to determine whether transactions conflict or not. These features are described below.

Isolation levels
Two-dimensional locking identifies two different isolation levels, called 'Interleave' and 'Isolate'.

'Interleave' is an isolation level, used for (parts of) a transaction to indicate that the transaction is allowed to see a partially updated database during execution (i.e. group isolation is not required). 'Interleave' is a new type of isolation level that can be chosen for both read and write transactions.

'Isolate' is a stronger isolation level, which is used when both object and group isolation must be guaranteed.

In this work we assume the ability to specify isolation levels, and the ability to identify isolation units based on this specification. To do so, we need a language construct that makes it possible to choose between isolation levels.

In the following, assume a transaction T for which a set of non-singleton isolation units, $\mathcal{U} = \{U_1, \ldots, U_n\}$, is explicitly specified. Each unit in $\mathcal{U}$ includes two or more objects and reflects a group isolation requirement. (Additionally, a set of singleton isolation units are associated with T, one unit for each object accessed by T.) Having an isolation unit $U_i \in \mathcal{U}$, implies that 'Isolate' is chosen for the execution of all operations in T that accesses objects in U_i. If $o \in U_i$ and

$U_i \in \mathcal{U}$, we say that transaction T is an Isolate-transaction on o, otherwise T is an *Interleave*-transaction on o.

Lock components

In Two-dimensional locking, each lock consists of two separate lock components. A lock on the form $lock^T(req\_lock, exec\_lock, o)$ is a two-dimensional lock, that includes a requirement-lock (req_lock) and an execution-lock ($exec\_lock$) component set on object o by transaction T. Each lock component is associated with a transaction property, where both properties are needed to determine whether two operations conflict or not.

The req_lock component reflects $T's$ isolation level on o, by identifying T as either an *Isolate-* or an *Interleave*-transaction with respect to o.

The exec_lock component describes the effect T has on o. Here we distinguish between *read-* and *write*-transactions.

Both the req_lock and the $exec\_lock$ component have three different lock modes. The req_lock modes are: *'int'*, *'isol'*, and *'-'*, while the $exec\_lock$ modes are: *'read'*, *'write'*, and *'-'*. These lock modes are all described in table 1. There we see e.g. that mode *int* is a req_lock, set by an *Interleave*-transaction before access to o, and it indicates that the transaction requires object isolation only. The possible combinations of lock modes are shown in the compatibility matrix in table 2.

From table 1 we can see that the *'-'* lock modes are somewhat special. These locks are never used initially. The *'-'* locks are used later in the execution, after the transaction has completed its execution on o.

6.2 Lock stages

Transaction T will hold a lock on object o for as long as necessary in order to guarantee both object isolation and group isolation. The period in which o is locked by T can be divided into two lock stages.

First lock stage starts when T first obtain a lock on o (before the first access to o), and ends when T completes its last operation on o. Locks held during this period must guarantee both object isolation and group isolation requirements.

Second lock stage starts when the first lock stage ends, and lasts until $T's$ unlock operation on o. Since T has completed every operation on o, object isolation can no longer be violated. Locking in the second lock stage must therefore guarantee group isolation.

We will now describe how locks are used during these two stages. This description is summarized in table 3. We are in the following assuming a transaction T accessing object o.

Locking in the first lock stage: Before transaction T can access o for the first time, one of the following locks will be requested (depending on transaction properties): $lock^T(int, read, o)$, $lock^T(isol, read, o)$, $lock^T(int, write, o)$,

	(int,read)	(isol,read)	(int,write)	(isol,write)	(isol,-)	(-,-)
(int,read)	yes	yes	no	no	yes	yes
(isol,read)	yes	yes	no	no	no	no
(int,write)	no	no	no	no	no	yes
(isol,write)	no	no	no	no	no	no

Table 2. Compatibility matrix for Two-dimensional locking

or $lock^T(isol, write, o)$. The lock set at the beginning of the first lock stage is held until T has completed all its operations on o.

From first to second lock stage: The task in the second lock stage is to guarantee group isolation where this is required. However, fewer operations are now potentially conflicting, since not every transaction require isolation for a unit U (say). Therefore, to release the object to non-conflicting transactions, we allow both lock switching and unlocking. These lock changes are shown in table 3. (For lock switching see the next section.)

Locking in the second lock stage: A transaction T locks an object during the second stage for two reasons: Firstly, if T is an *Isolate*-transaction, to protect T from seeing a possibly inconsistent state produced by another transaction. Secondly, if T is an *Write*-transactions, to shield the update(s) so that this does not cause inconsistency for other transactions. The lock is released as soon as there are no risk of violating group isolation.

6.3 Lock switching and unlocking

In Two-dimensional we seek to allow increased concurrency through early release of lock. Objects are released through both lock switching and execution of unlock operations.

Lock switching

Lock switching is used in situations where object isolation is already guaranteed, but where group isolation can still be violated. The $lock^T(isol, -, o)$ lock is held by an *Isolate*- transaction, for which group isolation may still be violated. The '-'-component indicates that the transaction has updated o and may therefore conflict with other *Isolate*-transactions.

The $lock^T(-, -, o)$ lock is held by a transaction where both object isolation and group isolation (for each isolation unit where o is a member) is already guaranteed. The second '-'-component (i.e. the $exec\_lock$ component) has the same meaning as in $lock^T(isol, -, o)$.

By studying the compatibility matrix in table 2, we see that lock switching represents a downgrade for *Interleave*-transactions only. *Isolate*-transactions handle the locks held on o before and after a switch as equivalent locks. An

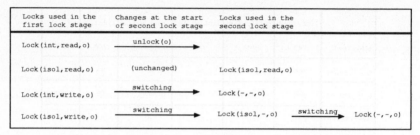

Locks used in the first lock stage	Changes at the start of second lock stage	Locks used in the second lock stage
Lock(int,read,o)	unlock(o) →	
Lock(isol,read,o)	(unchanged)	Lock(isol,read,o)
Lock(int,write,o)	switching →	Lock(-,-,o)
Lock(isol,write,o)	switching →	Lock(isol,-,o) switching→ Lock(-,-,o)

Table 3. Locks used during the first and second lock stage

Interleave- transaction may be given access to an object after a switch, while the same object can not be accessed by *Isolate*-transactions.

Unlocking

To unlock an object, certain conditions must hold. For *Isolate*-transactions and *Write*-transactions there are different unlock conditions, which are described below.

1. An *Isolate*-transaction (where $o \in U_i$ and $U_i \in \mathcal{U}$) can unlock o as soon as it has obtained a lock on every object in U_i.
2. A *Write*-transaction (updating a set of objects G, where $o \in G$) can unlock o as soon as it has obtained a lock on every object in G.

We will now describe, for each of the lock types used in the second lock stage, when the lock can be released.

$Lock^T(int, read, o)$ is unlocked when the first locking stage ends. The reason for this is that T is here neither an *Isolate*-transaction, that needs to protect its execution so that group isolation is guaranteed, nor an *Write*-transaction, that may cause inconsistency for other transactions.

$Lock^T(isol, read, o)$ can be unlocked when unlock condition 1 holds.

$Lock^T(-, -, o)$ can be unlocked when condition 2 holds.

$Lock^T(isol, -, o)$ can be unlocked when both condition 1 and 2 hold.

If condition 1 is first satisfied, this means that group isolation is guaranteed. The lock is switched to $Lock^T(-, -, o)$, and is released when condition 2 holds.

If condition 2 is first satisfied, this means that T holds a lock on every object that is/will be updated. However, T must still protect the objects in U_i so that group isolation is satisfied. The lock is therefore kept until condition 1 also holds, at which time the lock can be released.

Early release of locks will make objects updated by a transaction T available to other transactions (through an unlock or switch operation) before commit of T. An abort of T may then influence other transactions, and this must be handled by the recovery mechanism.

7 Recovery

There is a close relationship between concurrency control and recovery, in that the chosen concurrency control mechanism must always be supported by a suitable recovery mechanism. Recovery is not treated in full detail here. This section points out a problem connected with allowing early release of locks, and suggests an approach to the problem. We are currently working on this topic, and the results will be reported elsewhere.

By using Two-dimensional locking, objects updated by a transaction T can be made available to other transactions (through an unlock or switch operation) before commit of T. Allowing early release of locks does, however, cause problems in case of an abort of T. Take for example history H in example 1 (see chapter 2). Assume a situation where T_2 has committed after a successful execution, while T_1 is still executing. If T_1 now aborts, the recovery mechanism must have a way of undoing T_1 without undoing the (committed) T_2 transaction. Traditional rollback can not be used in this situation. In order to allow early release of locks, we need a new type of recovery mechanism.

To guarantee recoverability of transactions, one could *delay commit* of transactions so that each transaction using an object updated by T, commits after commit of T. Rollback is possible in this situation, since the transactions using uncommitted results have themselves not committed. A main problem with this approach is that the recovery mechanism rely on cascading abort, and that the number of aborted transactions may be huge. Another problem is that commit of transactions may be postponed for a long time.

To avoid these problems, we will consider using compensation [17] for undoing uncommitted flat transactions. We need a recovery mechanism that uses *compensating actions* to undo update operations where the results have been released before commit. Compensation has previously been used for undoing committed subtransactions [4, 11, 18]. Compensating actions are viewed as actions with some special characteristics. A compensation does not exist in its own right, but is always connected to the subtransaction which it undoes. It is executed only under certain circumstances in order to restore consistency, and it must always complete.

Using compensation requires the ability to attach a compensating action to some unit of work within the transaction (such as a subtransaction). It is also necessary to have some knowledge about the state of the transaction execution at the time of the failure. We will view every operation on o executed by a single transaction as a unit of work, and we will consider the possibility of defining a compensation action for this unit.

Two-dimensional locking is based on the assumption that it is possible to determine when a transaction has completed its use of an object. When a transaction has completed its last operation on o, the second lock stage is reached, and the object is partly released through a switch or unlock operation. To be able to use compensation in the recovery of a transaction T, we must be able to specify a compensating action for each object that has reached the second lock stage. A compensating action for object o will semantically undo every operation transaction T executed on o. Rollback will be used for every object which is still in the first lock stage. This may be possible since these objects have not been released, and the results of T have consequently not been seen by other transactions. The state of the objects at the time of the failure, will be known by the scheduler.

It is normally not possible to compensate in every situation. This can in our environment be dealt with by for example postponing the release of locks in uncompensatable transactions. In doing so we may have to introduce a new type of transaction, for which locks are released at commit time. This will of cause not improve concurrency, but it will make it possible to execute uncompensatable transactions in this environment.

8 Conclusions

We have in this paper presented a new *adaptable correctness criterion*, called ACC^{tr}, which allows correctness requirements to be attached to each individual transaction. Correctness requirements may vary both between transactions and within a single transaction. ACC^{tr} allows partial isolation, where isolation may be required for some parts of a transaction T, while interleaving is allowed for other parts of T.

To support ACC^{tr}, we describe a concurrency control mechanism, called *Two-dimensional locking*. This method offers a new type of isolation level, called 'Interleave', which allows a controlled access to a partially updated database. Each lock in Two-dimensional locking consists of two separate lock components; one component indicates the correctness requirement for the execution of T, the other component indicates the effect T has on o. The use of two lock components represents, as far as we know, a new approach for controlling concurrent transactions. By introducing a new dimension to the locking mechanism, we include more information about the transaction which we utilize to allow early release of locks and possibly a higher degree of concurrency.

This work is part of an ongoing project and is a continuation of work presented in [19]. Another and important part of this project is the study of a suitable recovery mechanism. This paper briefly considers the type of recovery mechanism needed to support Two-dimensional locking. We suggest using a combination of compensation and rollback to undo flat transactions. Compensation in flat transactions is not fully described here. The work on this issue will continue and will be reported elsewhere.

We believe that Two-dimensional locking together with a supporting recovery mechanism can increase concurrency in environments where some of the transactions are allowed to access a partially updated database. It has been argued that traditional transaction management is not applicable to long-lasting transactions since the length of duration of these transaction can cause serious performance problems [1, 6]. We believe that these problems can be reduced if the long-lasting transactions are allowed to execute on a partially updated database. We further believe that our approach may be used as an alternative to decomposing transactions. It may e.g. be used in environments where it is difficult to find suitable decompositions. It may also be used in combination with decomposition, especially in situations where subtransactions are in themselves long lasting.

References

1. Barghouti, N.S., Kaiser, G.E., Concurrency Control in Advanced Database Applications, ACM Computing Surveys, vol. 23, no. 3, September 1991.
2. Breitbart, Y., Garcia-Molina, H., Silberschatz, A., Overview of Multidatabase Transaction Management, VLDB Journal, Vol. 2, 1992, pp. 181-239.
3. Bukhres, O.A., Elmagarmid, A.K. (eds.), Object-Oriented Multidatabase Systems, A Solution for Advanced Applications, Prentice Hall, 1996.
4. Elmagarmid, A.K. (ed.), Database Transaction Models for Advanced Applications, Morgan Kaufmann, 1992.
5. Jajodia, R., Kerschberg, L. (eds.), Advanced Transaction Models and Architectures, Kluwer Academic Publishers, 1997.
6. Kim, W. (ed.), Modern Database Systems, The Object Model, Interoperability, and Beyond, Addison Wesley, 1995.
7. Gray, J., Reuter, A., Transaction Processing: Concepts and Techniques, Morgan Kaufmann Publishers, 1993.
8. Bernstein, P.A., Hadzilacos, V., Goodman, N., Concurrency Control and Recovery in Database Systems, Addison-Wesley, 1987.
9. Bernstein, A.J., Lewis, P.M., Transaction Decomposition Using Transaction Semantics, Distributed and Parallel Databases, vol. 4, no. 1, 1996.
10. Garcia-Molina, H., Using Semantic Knowledge for Transaction Processing in a Distributed Database, ACM Transactions on Database Systems, vol. 8, no. 2, June 1983.
11. Garcia-Molina, H., Salem, K., SAGAS, Proc. of the ACM SIGMOD Int. Conf. on Management of Data, 1987.
12. Lynch, N., Multilevel Atomicity - A New Correctness Criterion for Database Concurrency Control, ACM Transactions on Database Systems, Vol. 8, No. 4, 1983.
13. Farrag, A.A., Ozsu, M.T., Using Semantic Knowledge of Transactions to Increase Concurrency, ACM Transactions on Database Systems, Vol. 14, No. 4, 1989.
14. Shasha, D., Simon, E., Valduriez, P., Simple Rational Guidance for Chopping Up Transactions, Proc. of the 1992 ACM SIGMOD Int. Conf. on Management of Data, San Diego, California, June 2-5, 1992.
15. Ammann, P., Jajodia, S., Ray, I., Semantic-Based Decomposition of Transactions, in Advanced Transaction Models and Architectures, R. Jajodia and L. Kerschberg (eds.), Kluwer Academic Publishers, 1997.
16. Karlsen, R., Correctness for Partially Isolated Transactions, CS Research Report, Dept. of Computer Science, University of Troms, 1999.
17. Gray, J., The transaction Concept: Virtues and Limitations, Proc. of the Int. Conf. on Very Large Data Bases, Cannes, France, 1981.
18. Korth, H.F., Levy, E., Silberschatz, A., A Formal Approach to Recovery by Compensating Transactions, Proc. of the 16th VLDB Conf., Brisbane, Australia, 1990.
19. Karlsen, R., Adaptable Correctness through Two-dimensional locking, Proc. of the 8th Int. Workshop on Database and Expert Systems Application (DEXA), Toulouse, France, September 1-2, 1997.

- *Partial overriding:* A child concept inherits some values and overrides (refines) other values of the relationship. In Fig. 2 (c), B inherits the target D from A. However, the target C is overridden by the new target E, which is a child of C.
- *Full overriding:* A child concept overrides (refines) all values of the relationship. In Fig. 2 (d), all targets of the relationship r of A are overridden. B refers to E and F instead of their respective parents, C and D.

We will now introduce a similarity formula that takes the possibilities listed above into account. Consider a child having m relationships and its parent having n relationships. The number of fully overridden relationships is f, the number of partially overridden relationships is p, and the number of additive inheritance relationships is d. Then the similarity of the child/parent pair is:

$$\sigma = \frac{n - f - p - d}{m} \tag{2}$$

When the child has the same number of relationships as its parent ($m = n$) and no relationships are overridden, the similarity of the child/parent pair will be 1. On the other hand, if there is no full inheritance for any relationship, the similarity for the child/parent pair will be 0.

Using Formula 2, we can compute the property similarities for all child/parent pairs. Then, we can remove IS-A links between child concepts and their parents for pairs with low similarities. Ideally, the network will be partitioned into several smaller sub-networks, within each of which all concepts are quite similar.

Unfortunately, due to multiple inheritance, this is not always true. Because the InterMED is a DAG, cutting "random edges" gives us little control over partitioning into components. For example, if after cutting, each child is still connected to at least one parent, the original network will not be partitioned at all. If we can first reduce the graph to a tree, then removing links from the tree will result in a forest. There are additional advantages to working with a tree. It is generally easier to comprehend a tree than a DAG consisting of the same concepts, because in a tree upward paths are not branching. Therefore, we reduce the DAG to a tree as follows. We call this step *tree identification*.

Assume that a child concept C has q parent concepts ($q > 1$). The property similarities of child/parent pairs are $\sigma_1, \sigma_2, \ldots, \sigma_q$ respectively. If there is only one maximum number, call it σ_{max}, among $\sigma_1, \sigma_2, \ldots, \sigma_q$, then all links with similarities σ_i ($i \neq max$) will be removed. If there are two or more maximum numbers among $\sigma_1, \sigma_2, \ldots, \sigma_q$, one IS-A link with maximum similarity σ_{max} will be retained randomly, and all others will be removed.

Because *tree identification* will produce a tree, removing any links in the tree will result in a forest of more than one tree. Now the question is: Which links of the tree should be removed to create a useful partitioning result? Because the purpose of partitioning is to help users comprehend the concept network, each subtree produced by the partitioning scheme should be meaningful and have a manageable size. After we compute the similarities for all child/parent pairs, the distribution of property similarities can be calculated (Table 1). According to

Table 1, there are n_1 child/parent pairs that have property similarities between 0 and k_1, etc. Table 1 gives us the similarity distribution for the whole network and helps us decide which concepts should reside in the same context. We can choose a numeric parameter K and remove all the IS-A connections between child concepts and their parent concepts for which the similarity $\sigma < K$. The result will be several trees. All child/parent pairs in each tree have similarities greater than K. By varying K, we have some control over the number of links that are cut. With that, we get some control over the size of the contexts that are generated.

Table 1. Distribution of similarities

Property Similarities	Number of child/parent pairs
0	n_0
$(0, k_1)$	n_1
$[k_1, k_2)$	n_2
$\vdots$	$\vdots$
$[k_i, 1)$	n_{i+1}
1	n_{i+2}

$0 < k_1 < k_2 < ... < k_i < 1$

Table 2. Similarities of the InterMED

Property Similarities	Number of child/parent pairs
0	855
$(0, 0.1)$	0
$[0.1, 0.2)$	0
$[0.2, 0.3)$	1
$[0.3, 0.4)$	17
$[0.4, 0.5)$	0
$[0.5, 0.6)$	72
$[0.6, 0.7)$	775
$[0.7, 0.8)$	22
$[0.8, 0.9)$	212
$[0.9, 1.0)$	1
1	864

Table 3. Similarities of complex network MED

Property Similarities	Number of child/parent pairs
0	0
$(0, 0.1)$	0
$[0.1, 0.2)$	0
$[0.2, 0.3)$	0
$[0.3, 0.4)$	0
$[0.4, 0.5)$	1
$[0.5, 0.6)$	2
$[0.6, 0.7)$	4
$[0.7, 0.8)$	2
$[0.8, 0.9)$	3
$[0.9, 1.0)$	0
1	26

An interesting question is whether we gain anything if we combine similarity by property introduction with similarity by relationship overriding. The answer is "no," because the contribution of relationship introduction is already contained in Formula 2. For example, if a child has more relationships than its parent due to relationship introduction, the link will not be assigned a similarity of 1, even if the child has full inheritance for all relationships. The contribution of attribute introduction is negligible because there are only 12 attributes in a vocabulary of 2,820 concepts, most of which are introduced at the root.

2.3 Partitioning the InterMED

Now let us use the approach described above to partition the InterMED. The InterMED contains 2,820 medical concepts. The number of child/parent pairs is 4,687. After *tree identification*, the distribution of property similarities can be computed (Table 2). Based on this distribution figure, we can choose a K to partition the InterMED by removing all links with similarities less than K. We can vary K to obtain alternative partitioning results.

First, let us choose $K = 1.0$. This means that each subtree resulting from the partitioning will contain concept pairs with similarities 1. The number of subtrees created by this partitioning is 1,955; the biggest subtree contains 519 concepts; there are 1,868 subtrees with only one concept. Fig. 3 shows the number of trees for each size of the trees.

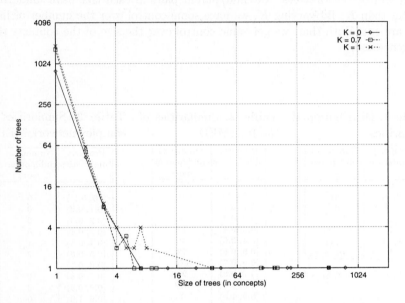

Fig. 3. Size of trees vs. number of trees for different values of K

For $K = 0.7$, the partitioning gives us 1,720 subtrees, containing the child/parent pairs with similarities greater than 0.7 (Fig. 3). The biggest tree consists of 519 concepts. The number of trees consisting of a single concept is 1,646. Compared with $K = 1.0$, this result is better because even though the biggest tree is still of the same size, the number of small trees is reduced. However, there are still too many trees with small numbers of concepts. With $K = 0$, the partitioning will produce a forest, with trees containing child/parent pairs with similarities greater than 0. The number of trees is 855. The largest contains 758 concepts. There are 795 trees which consist of only one concept (Fig. 3).

As we have seen, different values of K can be chosen to partition the InterMED differently. Unfortunately, we do not get ideal partitioning results. Some of trees contain large numbers of concepts, which cannot be displayed neatly on one screen. There are also many trees consisting of only a single concept or very few concepts; such trees do not capture much meaning.

The appearance of a large number of single-concept trees or trees with very few concepts is due to the incompleteness of the the InterMED; among the 2,820 concepts of the InterMED, 2,186 are leaves. Most of the single-concept trees are derived from the leaves of the original network. If more concepts were added to the InterMED, some of these leaves would become parents and the trees would turn into contexts with significant numbers of concepts. The remaining large trees would need to be partitioned by a human. Our partitioning algorithm still improves the situation, because there are few large trees left. In addition, even the largest of those trees is considerably smaller than the original vocabulary.

3   Structural Partitioning vs. Expert Partitioning

In this section, we will compare our partitioning results with the results obtained by semantic partitioning [14]. We apply these two methods to the most complex subnetwork of the MED. The results turn out to be quite similar.

In the MED, the concept **Cortisporin Opthalmic Ointment** has the most ancestors: 39. We will focus on the subnetwork containing this concept and all its ancestors. The subnetwork contains 62 IS-A relationships and 157 other relationships. For 62 child/parent pairs, we use Formula 2 to compute their similarities. After applying *tree identification*, we compute the similarity distribution of the tree (Table 3). If we want only child/parent pairs with maximum similarity to reside in the same tree, we can choose $K = 1$. After removing all IS-A links with $\sigma < 1$, we obtain a forest with 13 trees (Fig. 4).

In [14], we described a methodology to partition a network into several trees. There, a domain expert is required to make a judgment about whether a child concept and its parent concept are similar. Using that approach, the complex subnetwork was partitioned into 18 trees (Fig. 5).

Comparing the results obtained from the two approaches (Fig. 4 and Fig. 5), we find that our "structural" approach gives results that are similar to the results of the semantic approach in [14]. The results of the structural approach also appear semantically plausible. There are 10 tree roots out of 13 that are the same as for the semantic partitioning obtained from a domain expert's knowledge.

4   Related Literature

The issue of grouping concepts together in a "reasonable" manner has long been known as "conceptual clustering" in AI. "Clustering is usually viewed as a process of grouping physical or abstract objects into classes of similar objects. One needs to define a measure of similarity between the objects and then apply it to determine classes" [21]. A "goodness measure" is usually defined for the overall partitioning of objects [7]. Note that these are not classes in the sense of object-oriented programming, but classes in the sense of conceptual categories. On the other hand, in statistical clustering [11] and numerical taxonomy [27], most similarities are defined between pairs of objects. Our formula considers child/parent pair similarity and is applied to all concepts in order to partition an entire network into a collection of trees.

In [16], we find one of the oldest AI approaches to this problem, which partitions networks into "net spaces." These net spaces delimit the scopes of quantified variables. The partitioning into net spaces is done by experts and it cannot

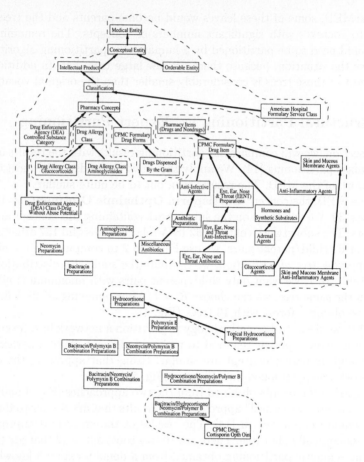

Fig. 4. Partitioning result based on structural partitioning

be carried out by checking the similarity among concepts. Different from our vocabulary networks, in SNePS [25] the IS-A relation is treated in the same way as all other relations. In [18], Levinson presents the principle of pattern-associativity by indexing objects into multi-levels. This approach allows one to organize conceptual graphs into a multi-level partial order by subgraph-isomorphism.

In [30], Woods describes the taxonomies of structured conceptual descriptions following work of the KL-ONE family [5]. Such taxonomies were generated by the subsumption relationship that relates each pair of concepts [13]. Our formula provides an approach to break the IS-A hierarchy in a reasonable way to generate a collection of trees.

To answer queries using different knowledge representations at different abstraction levels, Chu [6, 20] proposed the "Type Abstraction Hierarchy" which characterizes the instance values differently at different knowledge levels. However, the instances have neither subsumption relationships nor attributes among

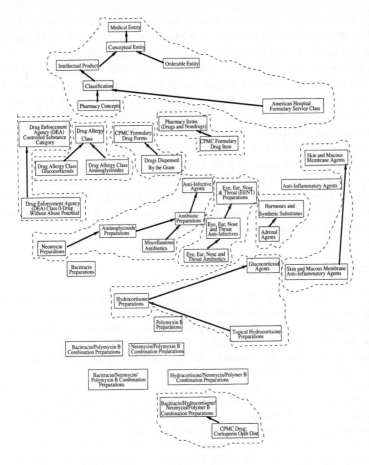

Fig. 5. Partitioning result based on expert partitioning

them. For the purpose of generating a concept hierarchy, the method cannot be applied to a complicated network with attributes and subsumption relationships. In OODB approaches, objects with common properties are grouped into classes. The class hierarchy is also used to capture generalization and specialization information [4]. However, the similarity among instance values is not considered in the creation of the class hierarchy.

5 Conclusions and Future Work

In this paper, we have presented a technique for "structurally" partitioning a large network of medical concepts. The technique has as its basis a similarity measure which is assigned to child/parent pairs in the vocabulary. We have shown the results of applying the approach to a large vocabulary, breaking it into meaningful subnets for the purpose of graphical display and comprehension.

We have obtained an important result, namely, that the outcome of a human expert-based partitioning of a large vocabulary is quite similar to the partitioning which is the result of applying our purely structural method.

In future work, we will further refine our similarity measures by in turn computing the similarity of every single partially overridden relationship. Another interesting idea is to combine the structural and expert-based approaches. The task of partitioning a vocabulary of thousands or tens of thousands of concepts into manageable groups can be overwhelming and by far too time consuming. As an expert is needed for the semantic partitioning, this can be very expensive! In short, the semantic approach by itself is not realistic for large vocabularies, and large vocabularies are the only interesting ones. We can use our structural approach to help a domain expert. The results of the structural partitioning method can be given to a domain expert who can then work on partitioning the remaining large trees into smaller subtrees.

References

1. Agasi, E., Becker, R. I., Perl, Y.: A shifting algorithm for constrained min-max partition on trees. Discrete Applied Mathematics **45** (1993) 1–28
2. Becker, R. I., Perl, Y.: The shifting algorithm technique for the partitioning of trees. Discrete Applied Mathematics **62** (1995) 15–34
3. Becker, R. I., Perl, Y., Schach, S.: A shifting algorithm for min-max tree-partitioning. J. ACM **29** (1982) 56–67
4. Bertino, E., Martino, L.: Object-Oriented Database Systems: Concepts and Architectures. Addison-Wesley Publishing Company, New York (1993)
5. Brachman, R. J., Schmolze, J.: An overview of the KL-ONE knowledge representation system. Cognitive Science **9** (1985) 171–216
6. Chu, W. W., Chen, Q., Lee, R.: Cooperative query answering via type abstraction hierarchy. In: Proc. Int'l Working Conference on Cooperating Knowledge Based Systems. Univerity of Keele, UK (1990) 271–290
7. Chu, W. W., Chiang, K.: Abstraction of high level concepts from numerical values in databases. In: Proc. AAAI Workshop on Knowledge Discovery in Databases. Seattle, WA (1994) 133–144
8. Cimino, J. J., Barnett, G. O.: Automated translation between medical terminologies using semantic definitions. MD Comput. **7** (1990) 104–109
9. Cimino, J. J., Clayton, P. D., Hripcsak, G., Johnson, S.: Knowledge-based approaches to the maintenance of a large controlled medical terminology. JAMIA **1** (1994) 35–50
10. College of American Pathologists: The Systematized Nomenclature of Medicine. Skokie, IL (1982)
11. Everitt, B.: Cluster Analysis. Heinemann Educational Books, London (1980)
12. Gary, M. R., Johnson, D. S.: Computers and Intractability. Freeman, New York (1979)
13. Gregor, R. M.: The evolving technology of classification-based knowledge representation systems. In: Lehman, F. (ed.): Semantic Networks in Artificial Intelligence. Pergamon Press, Oxford, UK (1992) 385–400
14. Gu, H., Perl, Y., Geller, J., Halper, M., Singh, M.: A methodology for partitioning a vocabulary hierarchy into trees. Artificial Intelligence in Medicine **15** (1999) 77–98

15. Health Care Financing Administration: International Classification of Diseases: 9th Revision, Clinical Modification: ICD-9-CM. 4th edn. Washington, DC (1991)

16. Hendrix, G. G.: Encoding knowledge in partitioned networks. In: Findler, N. V. (ed.): Associative Networks: Representation and Use of Knowledge by Computers. Academic Press, Inc., New York (1979) 51–92

17. Kundu, S., Misra, J.: A linear tree-partitioning algorithm. SIAM J. Comput. **6** (1977) 131–134

18. Levinson, R.: Pattern associativity and the retrieval of semantic networks. In: Lehman, F. (ed.): Semantic Networks in Artificial Intelligence. Pergamon Press, Oxford, UK (1992) 573–600

19. Liu, L., Halper, M., Geller, J., Perl, Y.: Controlled vocabularies in OODBs: Modeling issues and implementation. Distributed and Parallel Databases **7** (1999) 37–65

20. Merzbacher, M., Chu, W. W.: Pattern-based clustering for database attribute values. In: Proc. AAAI Workshop on Knowledge Discovery in Databases. Washington, DC (1993) 291–298

21. Michalski, R. S., Stepp, R. E.: Clustering. In Shapiro, S. C. (ed.): The Encyclopedia of Artificial Intelligence. 2nd edn. John Wiley & Sons, New York (1992)

22. National Library of Medicine: Medical Subject Headings. Bethesda, MD (1997; updated annually)

23. Oliver, D., Shortliffe, E.: Collaborative model development for vocabulary and guidelines. In: Cimino, J. J. (ed.): Proc. '96 AMIA Annual Fall Symposium. Washington, DC (1996) 826

24. Perl, Y., Geller, J., Gu, H.: Identifying a forest hierarchy in an OODB specialization hierarchy satisfying disciplined modeling. In: Proc. CoopIS'96. Brussels, Belgium (1996) 182–195

25. Shapiro, S. C., Rapaport, W. J.: The SNePS family. In: Lehman, F. (ed.): Semantic Networks in Artificial Intelligence. Pergamon Press, Oxford, UK (1992) 243–275

26. Shortliffe, E., Barnett, G., Cimino, J. J., Greenes, R., Huff, S., Patel, V.: Collaborative medical informatics research using the Internet and the World Wide Web. In: Proc. '96 AMIA Annual Fall Symposium. Washington, DC (1996) 125–129

27. Sneath, P. H. A., Sokal, R. R.: Numerical Taxonomy: The Principles and Practice of Numerical Classification. W. H. Freeman and Co., San Francisco, CA (1973)

28. Sowa, J. F. (ed.): Principles of Semantic Networks. Morgan Kaufmann Publishers, Inc., San Mateo, CA (1991)

29. US Dept. of Health and Human Services, NIH, National Library of Medicine: Unified Medical Language System (1998)

30. Woods, W. A.: Understanding subsumption and taxonomy: A framework for progress. In Sowa, J. F. (ed.): Principles of Semantic Networks. Morgan Kaufmann Publishers, Inc., San Mateo, CA (1991) 45–94

A Study on Musical Features for Melody Databases

葉志立 YIP Chi Lap and Ben KAO

Dept. of Computer Science and Information Systems, The University of Hong Kong
{clyip,kao}@csis.hku.hk   http://www.csis.hku.hk/~{clyip,kao}/

Abstract. The design of content-based music retrieval systems on the Web is a challenge, since music is auditory, temporal, and multidimensional — the same piece can be interpreted in multiple ways. Most literatures on music retrieval simply map the problem to existing information retrieval paradigms, mainly that of text, by modeling music as a sequence of features. However, this mapping raises questions to be answered. Through the study of the statistical properties of six features, namely Profile, Note Duration Ratio Sequence, Interval Sequence and their variants, we answer four of these questions in this paper. They are: the number of musical "alphabets" and "words" in musical features, whether Zipf's law holds for musical features, whether there are any musical "stopwords", and the range of n for n-gram based music indices.

1 Introduction

The widespread use of multimedia on the Web renders media data management important. Archival and indexing are needed to handle large amounts of media data so that retrieval and reuse is possible. In recent years, we witnessed a rapid growth of research and development of systems that handle images [11], digital video [1], geographical information [9], or sound effects [4]. However, only a few considered specifically the retrieval of music, and few of the relevant ones considered the unique characteristics of music in the design of retrieval systems. What is so special about music?

Music is auditory and temporal. Musical expression depends heavily on the temporal relationship between musical elements. Rhythmic patterns, chords and musical ornaments such as trills all depend on the temporal relationships between elements of music. In contrast, text, image, animation and video are all visual media, and only the latter two are temporal. Multiple instances of these media forms can be displayed by using thumbnail or filmstrip images. However, the auditory nature makes simultaneous playback of multiple pieces of music annoying at best, and the temporal nature would make the playback from the middle of a piece confusing because of the lack of musical context. Visualization of music is one possibility; a system can display the printed score or use specially-designed visualization techniques [8]. Yet, a level of musical literacy or familiarity with the visualization technique is required to use these systems. Thus, it is not suitable for Web-based systems whose users are from every walk of life.

In music, patterns are abound. These patterns are often described by ordinary languages, such as "the piece is in common meter", but no complete formalism has been established to describe these patterns precisely. Music is also multidimensional; the same piece can be simultaneously interpreted in multiple, and often unrelated, ways. Translated to information retrieval terms, this means multiple indices are needed. Reduction of index size is thus important in music retrieval systems. Moreover, music cannot be fully represented. Every music representation has its limitations. None of them, digital, written or otherwise, can capture all the aspects of music. In short, no single feature can capture the essence of music.

To study how we should design a Web-based music retrieval system in face of the unique characteristics of music, we choose to investigate statistical properties of some commonly-used musical features on our music collection introduced in Sect. 3. These features, introduced in Sect. 2, are Profile, Note Duration Ratio Sequence, Interval Sequence and their variants. In particular, we are going to answer four questions in Sect. 4 to 7. They are: the number of feature "alphabets" and possible musical "words", whether Zipf's law holds for musical features, whether there are any musical "stopwords", and the value of n for n-gram indices of musical features. A short summary and discussion on future works ends the paper in Sect. 8.

2 Features

Music can be analyzed in a number of dimensions, such as melody, harmony, rhythm, form and dynamics. It is only possible to introduce some features useful for music retrieval in this paper. As in most music retrieval literatures, we limit ourselves to features pertaining to the monophonic melodic lines of the pieces, and choose the most commonly used ones for analysis. They are:

Interval Sequence is a sequence of numbers each denoting the musical interval size, in number of semitones, between two temporally consecutive notes. An example of the interval sequence for an excerpt of the "Happy Birthday" tune is shown in Fig. 1(a). It gained popularity because it can be easily computed from computer music representations. Also, its independence of the key of the piece makes support of key-independent queries much easier.

Profile shows the ups and downs in the pitch of a piece. Since each note of a piece can only be of higher, lower, or the same pitch as another note temporally preceding it, the profile is writen as a sequence of $\nearrow$, $\rightarrow$, and $\searrow$. Profile has been shown to be related to human melody memory [3]. Some "fake books", such as [10], uses Profile for indexing.

Coarse Interval Sequence, like Profile, are also quantized interval sequences. Grouping intervals of three, five or seven together with the unison interval at the center, we obtain three features CI3, CI5, and CI7. Mathematically, an interval of x is mapped to $sgn(x) \left\lfloor \frac{|x|+n}{2n+1} \right\rfloor$ for the feature CI$\{2n + 1\}$.

Fig. 1. Excerpt of "Happy Birthday"
(a) Interval Sequence, (b) Profile, (c) Note Duration Ratio Sequence

Note Duration Ratio Sequence is a sequence of duration ratios for each temporally consecutive note pair. Fig. 1 shows an example. In some literatures, this sequence is called "rhythm", which is a misnomer because other characteristics of rhythm, such as accent, are ignored in the construction of Note Duration Ratio Sequence.

3   Music collection

Our music collection consists of 1003 MIDI files of music popular in Hong Kong, Taiwan, or Japan. As opposed to most literature on music retrieval (one notable work includes [5]), we obtained these MIDI files from the Web, rather than using sets of well-quantized and well-tagged folk or classical pieces for experiments. Since popular music is always on the vogue, this parallels the situation of our target music retrieval application: content-based retrieval of music on the Web. The tracks of the MIDI files containing the melody are manually extracted and automatic onset quantization [2] is done on the melodies before feature extaction. Six features, namely Interval Sequence, CI3, CI5, CI7, Profile and Note Duration Ratio Sequence, are used for analysis.

4   Feature "alphabets" and "words" — how many?

The number of "alphabets" for music features affect music retrieval system parameters, such as the maximum branching factor of suffix tree indices [12] and the maximum possible number of length-n feature sequence (n-gram) combinations. Figure 2(a) gives the number of n-grams on Interval Sequence for the 1003 melodies of our music collection. Only 117, that is, about 45.9 percent, of all the 255 possible interval sizes make up the 357657 intervals (count of n-gram for $n = 1$) in our collection. A closer examination of the feature files revealed that the range of interval sizes varied only from -74 to $+72$. Indeed, the human hearing range of 20Hz to 20kHz covers a range of $12\log_2(20000/20) \approx 120$ semitones. Thus, allowing interval sizes from -120 to $+120$ semitones would be more than adequate for Interval Sequences. Similarly, the ranges for the features CI3, CI5 and CI7 would be from -40 to $+40$, -24 to $+24$, and -17 to $+17$ respectively. Profile, of course, has only three "alphabets", $\nearrow$, $\searrow$ and $\rightarrow$.

Len n	nComb theory a	nComb actual b	Count of n-grams k	Value of k/b
1	255^1	117	357657	3056.89
2	255^2	3484	356654	102.36
3	255^3	20073	355651	17.71
4	255^4	45417	354648	7.80
5	255^5	76399	353645	4.62
6	255^6	110828	352642	3.18
7	255^7	141424	351639	2.48
8	255^8	162531	350636	2.15
9	255^9	174979	349633	1.99
10	255^{10}	182460	348630	1.91
11	255^{11}	187729	347627	1.85
12	255^{12}	191875	346624	1.80
13	255^{13}	195409	345621	1.76
14	255^{14}	198553	344618	1.73
15	255^{15}	201430	343615	1.70
16	255^{16}	204050	342612	1.67
17	255^{17}	206478	341609	1.65
18	255^{18}	208747	340606	1.63

a: Theoretical max. no. of combinations
b: Actual no. of distinct combinations
k: Total no. of n-grams, distinct or not
(a) Interval Sequence statistics

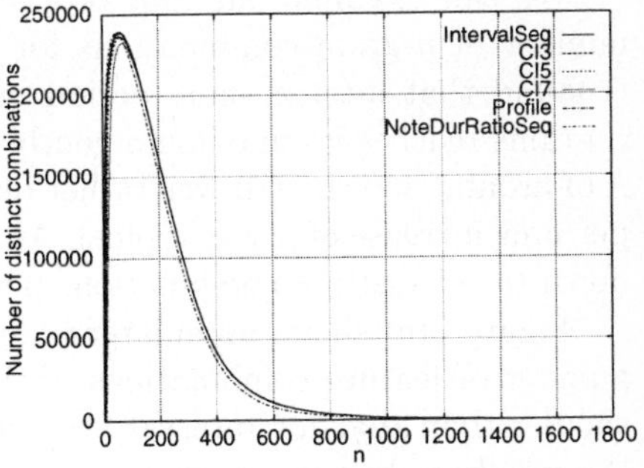

(b) Number of distinct n-grams vs. n

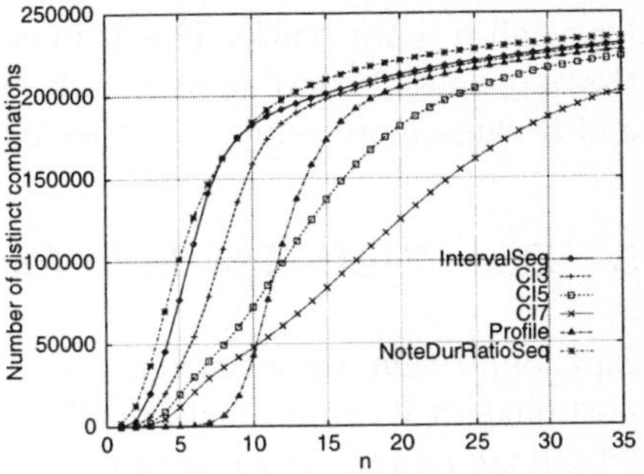

(c) Curves zoomed in for $n \leq 35$

Fig. 2. Feature statistics

Since note lengths can be arbitrary, we do not have a bound on the number of "alphabets" for Note Duration Ratio Sequences. For our collection, there are 2046 note duration ratio combinations. However, these combinations are rather skewed in distribution; the most frequent 24, 68 and 146 combinations appear 80, 90 and 95 percent of the time respectively. We will investigate their n-gram distributions in Sect. 5 by studying whether they obey Zipf's law.

As n increases, a few observations were made. First, the actual number of n-gram combinations (b in Fig. 2(a)) increase slower than exponential (a in the figure). This indicates that interval sequences in music is not completely independent of each other. Second, the total count of n-grams decrease linearly. It is a simple consequence of n-gram usage: a sequence of length k has $(k - n + 1)$ n-grams, so an increase of n corresponds to a decrease in $(k - n + 1)$. Third, the ratio of the count of n-grams to the actual number of n-gram combinations approaches one. This reflects that for any given n-gram, on average, fewer exact matches to the song sequences are possible as n increases. Long n-grams, which are mostly distinct, will almost uniquely identify the section of music. For example, an n of 4 would give 7.8 Interval Sequence pattern matches in our database on average if the n-grams were uniformly distributed.

We can examine our first observation closer by plotting, in Fig. 2(b), the number of n-gram combinations for each feature (b of Fig. 2(a)) against n. It is found that after a short period of exponential-like increase, the number of n-grams reaches its maximum gently at $n \approx 60$ and falls afterwards. At smaller n of around 200 the fall was rather quick; a slope of -700 distinct combinations per unit increase of n was typical. As n increases, the rate of fall gradually slows down to -1 distinct combinations per unit increase of n.

Figure 2(c) shows an enlarged view of Fig. 2(b) for $n \leq 35$. Expectedly, the number of feature combinations of the coarse interval sequences are in general smaller than that for Interval Sequences. However, for n larger than about 25, the numbers become more or less the same. Quantization by grouping more interval sizes together in general makes the increase of number of combinations for small n more gentle. This is in contrast of the feature Profile, which follows the exponential curve quite closely until $n \approx 10$, after which it is slowed down and became more similar to other interval sequence-related curves.

5 Does Zipf's law hold for musical features?

Zipf found that the occurrence probability of English words is inversely proportional to its rank in descending occurrence frequency order [14]. Since the "resolving power" of terms in text retrieval peaks in the middle occurrence frequency range [6], if musical features obey Zipf's law, musical index sizes can be reduced effectively by ignoring frequently-occuring features sequences, since they consitute a major proportion of features with low resolving power.

To investigate whether this is the case, we count the occurrence frequency of all feature sequences of length 2 (bigrams), 3 (trigrams), no more than 7, and no more than 20, rank them according to their occurence frequency, and plot the graphs of the logarithm of their relative occurence probability, $\log_{10} P(r)$, against the rank r in log scale. Figure 3 shows the graphs. Data obeying Zipf's law should form straight lines on the graphs. It is found that for bigrams and trigrams, the curves are not straight but convex upwards. This convex behaviour means that the occurrence probabilities fall slower than expected when r is small but faster when r is large. Interestingly, this convex behaviour is also found in the distribution of alphabets (not words) for natural languages such as English, Chinese and Hebrew, as well as those of amino acids, which are building blocks of proteins [7]. Bigrams and trigrams thus seem to be more alphabet-like than word-like.

In Fig. 3(c), the Profile curve still shows convex behaviour, while all other curves approximate straight lines well. Figure 3(d), which includes the statistics for feature sequences of length no more than 20, shows that all features obey Zipf's law. Thus, music feature sources can be modelled as stochastic processes [14], and techniques such as co-occurrence analysis can be applied for the analysis, clustering and indexing of musical features. Profile, because of its small alphabet size, require longer "word length" to make them behave statistically like musical "words". Whether this is the case will be investigated in Sect. 7.

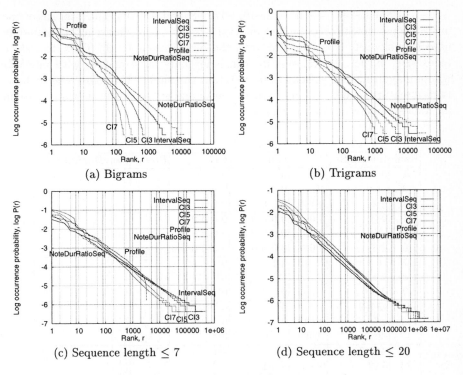

Fig. 3. log occurrence probability versus rank

6 Are there any musical "stopwords"?

Text retrieval systems ignore words that appear often in many documents, called "stopwords", in queries. Although musical features do not have "word boundaries", the question of whether there are any "stopwords" is still significant. By knowing what the frequently-occurring sequences are, music analysis can be sped up by the use of heuristics. Music retrieval systems can also use them for query refinement, and index sizes can be reduced by excluding musical stopwords.

Table 1 shows the most frequent sequences for the features under consideration. Short sequences of small intervals or repeats (-3 to $+3$ semitones) are common in our melody collection. A closer look at the raw data shows that intervals of ± 5 and ± 7 semitones, which correspond to musically significant intervals of perfect fourth and perfect fifth, are among the top 25 as well. For coarse interval sequence CI3, zero or size one jumps, which correspond to intervals between -4 to $+4$ semitones, are most common. For CI5 and CI7, top-ranked sequences consist of consecutive zeros or short sequences of zeros or small jumps. These indicate that intervals with large magnitudes are less commonly used, and thus give more "surprises".

If we consider interval unigrams alone, the most frequently occurring ones, in descending order of their occurrence frequency, are $0, -2, +2, -3, +3, -1, +1,$

$+5, -5, +7, +4, -4, -7, +9, +12, -9, -12, +8$, and -8. Diatonic intervals of one or two steps, which correspond to interval sizes of -4 to $+4$, are most commonly used in melodies. This is in line with the observations in [3]. Thus, to reduce index size, music retrieval systems can index only on sequences with intervals whose magnitude are greater than a certain threshold. Also, since the highest-ranked feature sequences tend to be of length one or two, musical "words" useful for indices should usually be longer.

Rank	IntervalSeq	CI3	CI5	CI7	Profile	NoteDurRatioSeq
1	0	0	0	0	↘	$\frac{1}{1}$
2	-2	-1	0 0	0 0	↗	$\frac{1}{1}\frac{1}{1}$
3	+2	+1	0 0 0	0 0 0	→	$\frac{1}{1}\frac{1}{1}\frac{1}{1}$
4	0 0	0 0	0 0 0 0	0 0 0 0	↘↗	$\frac{1}{1}\frac{1}{1}\frac{1}{1}\frac{1}{1}$
5	-3	0 -1	0 0 0 0 0	0 0 0 0 0	↗↘	$\frac{2}{1}$
6	+3	0 0 0	0 0 0 0 0 0	0 0 0 0 0 0	↘↘	$\frac{1}{2}$
7	-1	-1 +1	+1	0^7	↗↗	$(\frac{1}{1})^5$
8	+1	-1 -1	-1	0^8	→→	$(\frac{1}{1})^6$
9	0 0 0	+1 -1	0^7	0^9	↘↗↘	$(\frac{1}{1})^7$
10	-2 +2	+2	0^8	0^{10}	↗↘↗	$\frac{1}{1}\frac{2}{1}$
11	+5	+1 0	0 -1	0^{11}	→↘	$(\frac{1}{1})^8$
12	-2 -2	-1 0	+1 0	0^{12}	↘↘↗	$\frac{2}{1}\frac{1}{2}$
13	+2 -2	+1 +1	0^9	+1	↗↘↘	$\frac{1}{2}\frac{1}{1}$
14	0 -2	0 +1	0 +1	0^{13}	↘↗↗	$(\frac{1}{1})^9$
15	-2 0	-2	-1 0	0^{14}	↗→	$\frac{3}{1}$

Table 1. Most frequent sequences. x^n means x repeated n times.

For Profile, raw data shows that → is only about sixty percent as frequent as either ↘ or ↗. This is in contrast with the case for Interval Sequence and coarse interval sequences where the unison interval appears rather frequently and make poor features. One of the reasons is that while coarse interval sequences are uniformly quantized Interval Sequences, Profiles are nonuniformly quantized ones. Only the unison interval is mapped to →; all pitch upleaps and downleaps are mapped to ↗ and ↘ respectively. Thus, the flat profile becomes an important feature. Indeed, the first Profile feature sequence with nonconsecutive flat profiles ranked 54th in the table, with an occurrence probability of less than 0.04 percent, infrequent enough to be useful index sequences.

For Note Duration Ratio Sequence, the predominance of the ratio $\frac{1}{1}$ as components of the sequences implies that pieces without rhythmic variation do not distinguish themselves. Some pieces, such as Mozart's K.525 *Eine Kleine Nachtmusik* (Fig. 4), are especially recognizable even by rhythm only. The ten most frequently-occurring note duration ratio unigrams, in decreasing order of frequency, are $\frac{1}{1}, \frac{2}{1}, \frac{1}{2}, \frac{3}{1}, \frac{1}{3}, \frac{2}{3}, \frac{3}{2}, \frac{4}{1}, \frac{1}{4}$ and $\frac{1}{6}$, and they are all among the top 35 of all Duration Ratio Sequences whose lengths are no more than 20.

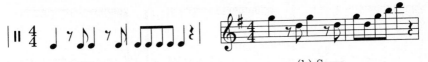

(a) Note duration only   (b) Score

Fig. 4. Excerpt of Mozart's K.525 *Eine Kleine Nachtmusik*

7   What should n be for n-gram indices?

Documents in languages without word separators, such as Chinese, are often indexed using n-grams so that computationally expensive or inaccurate text analysis routines are not needed. Yet, we have to choose a value for n. As discussed in Sect. 4, n controls the maximum number of n-grams. Since this number is exponential to n, a small n is preferred. However, a larger n would often better fit language characteristics and provide better precision. Given that n-gram indexing works for those natural languages, we can use the technique for indexing music, since there is no "word separator" in music feature sequences too.

To study what n should be, we want to know, for every feature and for each $n < 30$, how the accumulated fraction of feature n-grams vary with the maximum number of songs they can match. First, we fix an n. Then, we match each of the n-grams in our database with our collection of 1003 songs to obtain the number of songs that match each n-gram. We then invert the statistics and obtain the number of n-grams that match a given number of songs. With that, we can calculate the fraction of all n-grams in the collection that matches no more than a given number of songs. The pattern matching is then repeated for other values of n.

Figure 5 shows the graphs for the six features. The lowest (bottom rightmost) curves in the graphs are the ones for $n = 1$, the next lowest for $n = 2$, and so on. A more detailed set of graphs can be found in [13]. From these graphs, it is found that for the same n, Note Duration Ratio Sequence matches a smaller number of songs than Profile does in general. Hence, for the same feature sequence length, Note Duration Ratio Sequence is most discriminating, and Profile is the least discriminating, if every feature sequence of the same type is selected with the same probability.

Suppose we want to design an n-gram-based music retrieval system that, in 80 percent of the time, retrieves no more than 20 of the 1003 songs when an n-gram in the database is randomly chosen. The minimum n should thus correspond to that for the line above the point $(20, 0.8)$ on the graphs. If Interval Sequence is used, we found that n should be no less than 2. For CI3 and CI5, n should be no less than 3, and for CI7 no less than 4. Profile, because of its small alphabet size, requires a longer sequence length of 9 or more, but for Note Duration Ratio Sequence, a length of 1 would do the work. Yet, since it was shown in Sect. 6 that the most frequent Note Duration Ratio Sequences are all among the top 35 of Duration Ratio Sequences of length no more than 20, a larger n should be chosen and a minimum of 2 is needed.

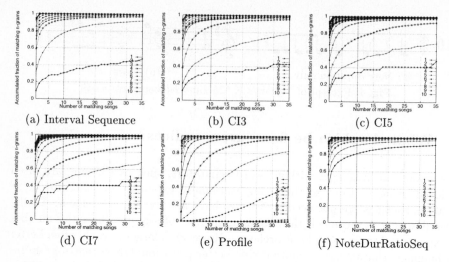

Fig. 5. Feature matching graphs, zoomed in for number of matching song ≤ 35

Note that in this set of experiments, it is assumed that every length-n feature sequence would be selected with equal probability. The distribution of n-grams has not been taken into account, and this is one of the reasons for the small n found for Note Duration Ratio Sequence. Because of the skewed distribution of features n-grams, system designers should take the above results as a minimum value for n and be liberal to choose a larger value whenever practical.

8 Summary and future work

Music retrieval is a largely unexplored domain. The auditory, temporal and multidimensional nature of music, together with the limitations of its representations, pose challenges on the design of content-based music retrieval systems on the Web. Through the study of six features, we tried to answer four important questions that arise from the mapping of music retrieval to other information retrieval paradigms. These include the number of musical "alphabets" and "words", whether Zipf's law holds for musical features, whether there is any musical "stopword", and the range of n for n-gram indices on musical pieces.

The authors are also currently working on six aspects of music retrieval. One, to investigate features, such as chord progressions, that are suitable for handling polyphonic music and their queries. Two, to carry out experiments that use information retrieval notions other than occurrence frequency, such as "term frequency × inverse document frequency", to elaborate the results on musical "alphabets" and "stopwords". Three, as discussed in Sect. 7, to find n for n-grams by taking their distribution into account. Four, to investigate how musical "distance" should be defined so that traditional string or multidimensional matching methods to handle inexact or nearest-neighbour queries can be used. Five, to study how musical feature combined can improve music retrieval performance such as recall and precision. And finally six, to study how different genre of music affects the effectiveness of music retrival systems.

Acknowledgements

Special acknowledgements are given to Ms. CHENG Man Yee, Mr. HO Wai Shing, Mr. TANG Fung Michael, and Mr. YUEN Kin Wai for their painstaking melodic line extraction effort that made the experiments possible.

References

[1] M. Christel, T. Kanade, M. Mauldin, R. Reddy, and M. Sirbu. Informedia digital video library. *Communications of the ACM*, 38(4):57–58, April 1995.

[2] Peter Desain and Henkjan Honing. The quantization problem: Traditional and connectionist approaches. In Mira Balaban, Kemal Ebcioğlu, and Otto Laske, editors, *Understanding Music with AI: Perspecives on Music Cognition*. The AAAI Press and The MIT Press, 1992. ISBN 0-262-52170-9.

[3] W. Jay Dowling. Scale and contour: Two components of a theory of memory for melodies. *Psychological Review*, 85(4):341–354, July 1978.

[4] Douglas Keislar, Thom Blum, James Wheaton, and Erling Wold. Audio analysis for content-based retrieval. In *Proceedings of International Computer Music Conference*, pages 199–202, 1995.

[5] Rodger J. McNab, Lloyd A. Smith, Ian H. Witten, Clare L. Henderson, and Sally Jo Cunningham. Towards the digital music library: Tune retrieval from acoustic input. In *Proceedings of the 1st ACM international conference on Digital libraries*, pages 11–18. The Association for Computing Machinery, 1996.

[6] Gerald Salton and Michael J. McGill. *Introduction to Modern Information Retrieval*. McGraw-Hill, 1983. ISBN 0-07-Y66256-5.

[7] S. Shtrikman. Some comments on Zipf's law for the Chinese language. *Journal of Information Science*, 20(2):142–143, 1994.

[8] Sean M. Smith and Glen N. Williams. A visualization of music. In *Proceedings of the conference on Visualization '97*, pages 499–503, 1997.

[9] Terence R. Smith. A digital library for geographically referenced materials. *IEEE Computer*, 29(5):54–60, May 1996.

[10] *The Ultimate Fake Book*. Hal Leonard Publishing Corporation, "C" instruments edition, 1981. ISBN 0-9607350-0-3.

[11] Robert Wilensky. Toward work-centered digital information services. *IEEE Computer*, 29(5):37–44, May 1996.

[12] Chi Lap Yip and Ben Kao. Indexing multilingual documents on the web. In *COMPSAC 1998, Proceedings of the twenty-second annual international Computer Software and Applications Conference*, pages 576–581. IEEE Computer Society, August 1998. ISBN 0-8186-8585-9; ISSN 0730-3157.

[13] Chi Lap Yip and Ben Kao. A study on musical features for melody databases. Technical Report TR-99-05, Department of Computer Science and Information Systems, The University of Hong Kong, 1999.

[14] George Kingsley Zipf. *The Psycho-Biology of Langauge*. The MIT Press, first MIT paperback edition, August 1965.

Using Multimedia in Aeronautical Technical Documentation

Franck DULUC

Aerospatiale-Matra Airbus/IRIT, Service BISU/A, BP D0611
316, route de Bayonne 31060 TOULOUSE Cedex 03 France
franck.duluc@avions.aerospatiale.fr

Abstract. This paper addresses the management of a multimedia and hypermedia documentary repository within the framework of aeronautical documentation, whose the most important features are its high volume and its high revision frequency. The requirements of such a documentation are recalled, needs are listed and a state-of-the-art on multimedia document works is presented. At the end, the paper proposes some modelling to manage the issues raised by the needs analysis, in particular about multimedia and hypermedia documents management within a documentary repository.

Introduction

Are the new means provided by multimedia and hypermedia for conveying information, adapted to the aircraft operations technical documentation context? Today, this question comes up against not only the characterisation of the semantics brought about by these new means but also by the feasibility of managing these new characteristics in this context. Indeed, the introduction of all innovations must be controlled, complying with the specific production constraints for such documentation: life-cycle of the documents and automated process. This paper briefly recalls these constraints and the temporal features induced by the use of new media. After that it gives the issues that are extended or created by their combination, before presenting hypermedia and multimedia research results. It ends by making proposals for managing the use of multimedia documents within the aeronautical technical documentation production framework, which is complex and automated.

1 Study Background

1.1 Technical Documentation Framework

Aeronautical technical documentation data are bulky, complex and regulated. For instance, for an Airbus A320, the documentation represents 1.2 gigabytes of data in

39 different manuals. These are inter-referenced to a high extent and contain technical data, text and illustrations. In addition, they are revised on average every three months. The regulations drawn up by the ATA[1] impose the use of standards as SGML [21]. The choice of using standards is guided by the wish to ensure the longevity of the data, their interchangeability and their processing by airlines and manufacturers (for instance, creation of job cards from the maintenance documentation), by making them independent of the tool vendors. The evolution of the technical documentation towards hypermedia documentation must be considered within this context. The use of standards, such as XML [31], SMIL [32], etc., is a stringent constraint.

The technical documentation is also produced in a very exacting context:

- The technical documentation produced for each aircraft is different and depends both on the aircraft and on the airline concerned.
- The duplication of information existing in the various manuals must be created when the manuals are produced, in order to ensure consistency of the information.
- The documentary volume regularly increases because of the increase in the aircraft population.

These three constraints have been met by automating the production of the technical documentation. This is based on the use of a documentary repository containing the information required to produce the documentation. The information is stored and managed in the form of documentary units within a database system. Production processes collate these units for producing the final documents.

Using this repository allows separating contents (documentary units) from documents, running configuration management, eliminating data redundancy by managing reuse of data and automating production processes.

Lastly, the technical documentation information is used for maintenance, training and for the operation of the aircraft by the pilots. Its content and meaning are very important in terms of operating costs and safety and it is mandatory to ensure that they are correct and pertinent.

1.2 Multimedia Documents

Today, numerous works address issues related to multimedia. Therefore, before going further, we give in the following lines the definitions of the terms we use

- The term media designates the different means to deliver information. such as videos, audios, text, graphics, photos, virtual reality and generated speech.
- Multimedia documents are a combination of different media and temporal relationships between them. This combination creates a stand-alone document presenting the different media sequentially or simultaneously.
- Hypermedia documents are hypertext [6] documents in which the data can be on different media. Temporal relationships are not necessarily defined in hypermedia documents. However when we speak of hypermedia documents we mean

---

[1] Air Transport Association

documents that contain the both aspects, hypertext capabilities and temporal relationships.

The essential characteristic of these documents is the new dimension that they introduce: the temporal dimension. The documents become dynamic, their meaning depends on time. In addition, the simultaneous use of media coupled with the interaction and navigation possibilities contributes towards making this temporal dimension more complex. This simultaneous use of media is made possible by multimedia synchronisation techniques which we present in the next section.

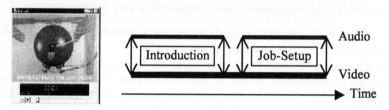

Fig. 1. The basic synchronisation goal: creating a meaning by combining different media. The introduction part of the video must be presented in the same time as the audio corresponding to introduction, etc

This goal is also the base problematic of multimedia documents related works. Indeed many problems occur within the different stages of the multimedia document life-cycle; creation, presentation and management.

2 Needs Analysis in the Environment of Technical Documentation Production

Multimedia can only be integrated into aeronautical technical documentation by taking into account and controlling the difficulties added to the conventional technical documentation production problems. It appears that most of the issues are already known. Indeed, they have already been solved for the previous production of conventional text and graphic documentation.

The current production processes equal to, within the multimedia framework, defining synchronisation and navigation relationships between documentary units. This extends existing issues by the emerging need to take into account the temporal dimension within the repository. The final goal is to make the new multimedia documents repository offer the same level of services as the repository currently used.

2.1 Extension of Existing Problems

Configuration Management Process. The technical documentation reflects the technical state of each aircraft and therefore it evolves at the same time. The synchronisation mechanisms required to make up multimedia documents and documentary units imply the implementation of specific version management mechanisms. For example, a documentary units defines the synchronisation of a video and an audio; for the aircraft 823 video and audio have the same duration, but for aircraft 827, the audio is twice as long as the video. In this case configuration management rules will have to identify this difference and create a version of the documentary unit for both configurations.

Data Evolution Process. Information reuse is built on documentary unit management rules and on models of final documents. It allows separating the respective changes of the document structure (i.e. models) and of the document content (i.e. data). Changes to the data stored in the repository are achieved in a transparent way. Their modifications are taken into account at the time of a new publishing of the impacted documents. It is not mandatory that the writer of the initial document, that collated and created whole parts of this document, re-edits it.

Within the multimedia documentation framework, this level of automation may be reached. But the same process as of today is not sufficient to handle multimedia document. Indeed the correctness of the temporal relationships has to be checked within the repository. For instance, an audio presented at the same time as a video whose duration is 40 seconds evolves from a duration of 20 seconds to a duration of 80 seconds. The repository has to check that the documentary unit is still valid before the document is presented. Besides, reuse of data makes that such a change could imply changes on many documents that are reusing the evolving data.

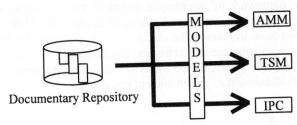

Fig. 2. Reuse process: the repository holds the documentary unit that are incorporated within the models of the final documents.

Furthermore, reusability may be applied to the multimedia documents created because they may be reused by new documents as documentary units. That means the definition given to a documentary unit within the repository has to evolve.

2.2 New Issues

Comparing multimedia documents problematics with our context lead us to identify two new types of issues.

On-line Access and Interaction Management. Multimedia and hypermedia documents give the possibility to navigate within the different documentary units of which they are comprised of. This capability is inherited from hypertext system and allows accessing information in a non-linear-way, which is more intuitive [6]. Besides, by using interaction capabilities, the user is able to control and select the informations he wants to be displayed.

On the other hand, technical documentation has some critical features induced by the type of information and products it deals with. For instance «Warnings» have specific contents and must be read by the mechanics that are working on the aircraft.

With these statements we identified the need to manage consultation scenarios and interactive capabilities within the technical documentation repository. Mandatory presentation of a document or prerequisite documentary unit consultation management are a good example of what we are thinking about.

Control of Document Quality. Multimedia state-of-the-art on multimedia and presentation systems emphasises the following needs:

- Respecting the author's intents: when an author places a relationship between two different media, he wants to add meaning to the semantic contained in each of the separate media.
- Guaranteeing that presentation systems deliver documents in compliance with author specifications.

Within the framework of aeronautical technical documentation, these two needs raise issues related to consistency and quality of documents. While we think that an author does not have to manage the changes of the document he created, we assert that it is necessary to manage some characteristics added to the documents at the time of their creation, and describing the limits in which his document could evolve: for instance, minimal duration of presentation of one graphic

2.3 Summary

This section identifies the problems raised by introducing multimedia/hypermedia documents into the technical documentation. The list given below is probably not exhaustive.

They can be summarised as follows:

- Integrating multimedia data into configuration management.
- Enabling the reusability of multimedia data.
- Defining controls required for on-line access to the mass of technical documentation information.
- Automating the multimedia document processing operations.
- Allowing quality checks of the new multimedia documents.

As our final goal is the definition of a multimedia document repository built on a database, we have chosen to tackle these problems by looking at the definition of a data model. In the next section, we will put forward the problematics common to multimedia and hypermedia and some «data model» approaches already developed, before presenting in the last section how we are trying to reach our goal.

3 Multimedia and Hypermedia: Analysis and Conclusions

3.1 Multimedia Synchronisation

The aim of multimedia synchronisation is simultaneous presentation of varied documents to a user [5]. It specifies and makes the temporal relations existing between the various documents. The specifications are drawn up by the author of the document and execution is accomplished by document presentation applications. The synchronisation problematic consists in the modelling, the specification and the compliance with temporal relations between two different entities [13], for example «train 1954 will leave 10 minutes after the arrival of train 6302».

In addition, the computerised consultation stations consist of peripherals, which may or may not be shared. The sharing of these resources must be managed and this extends the temporal synchronisation problem to the spatial and temporal synchronisation [23].

Previous works first addressed network issues related to multimedia. This works focused on how to reduce overhead, etc. [12] and guarantee a level of QOS[2].

Other studies dealt with multimedia synchronisation from the document viewpoint. We focused on these approaches which are the most similar to ours.

According to [14], there are two media synchronisation categories. The first, «continuous synchronisation» consists in guaranteeing the synchronisation of the two media at each moment. The aim of the second synchronisation, called «point synchronisation», is to make the synchronisation points (instant defined in a media) coincide. The goal is to guarantee synchronisation for each of these points. This synchronisation is used extensively for presenting multimedia documents where continuous synchronisation is not required [9]. Therefore we focused on this one.

Time is modelled in two different ways depending on the approaches developed. The first one models time as a sequence of time-ordered events [22]. The second one models time using basic units, the intervals [2], and identifies thirteen possible synchronisation relations between intervals. As it is possible to represent an interval by two points (start and end), it is easy to pass from one representation to the other [30].

Many time models have been studied. The first one is the Time-line model [15], [8] and [23]. The Time-line model consists in representing time along a line flagged with points. The various documents are placed on it to describe the expected behaviour of the presentation. The rigidity of its specifications limits the creator of the documents. [17] has developed the «Temporal glue» approach, which enables the duration of certain media to be contracted or extended, and these specifications to be relaxed. This type of model cannot be used to manage the users' interactions.

---

[2] Quality Of Service.

[4] describes the possible use of «Temporal points network» and [20] the use of «path expressions». Little and Ghafoor [25] studied the use of Timed Petri Networks in order to define and manage synchronisation relationships between media. The INRIA[3] describes the synchronisation relationships by using acyclic graph models. Their multimedia documents editor, MADEUS [23], uses this description and solves synchronisation specification by using decomposition into STP[4] [7].

Generally, spatial synchronisation is managed by means of channels [18]. A channel is a logical representation of a system resource (loudspeaker, screen area, etc.). Within the synchronisation models defined by the previous models, a Time-Line representation of the documents that must appear is generated for each channel.

3.2 Hypermedia

In the hypermedia document research field, issues are different depending on whether they appear during the authoring or the consultation of the documents.

At creation time three issues are raised, they consist in

- ensuring document readability within heterogeneous platforms [28],
- describing the temporal constraints and relationships of the documents [19],
- expressing navigation links through the different documents [18] [23].

At consultation time, three new issues appear:

- delivering a document compliant with the author specifications,
- accessing the data contained in a distributed database,
- managing navigation and interaction capabilities [5].

The Amsterdam Hypermedia Model (AHM) [18] is the result of the combination of DEXTER hypertext model [16] and of the CMIF work [28]. Most synchronisation relationships are managed through the hierarchical structure of the AHM model. The others are managed by the use of «synchronisation arcs». Besides AHM propose the «context» notion: «the part of the document which is changed when a link is browsed».

The INRIA has developed a hypermedia and multimedia structured documents model for the realisation of their MADEUS editor [23]. The power of the MADEUS model lies on the use of direct acyclic graphs, which allows efficiently managing temporal constraints. Finally, temporal formatting capability (stretching or contraction of media duration) allows a better compliance with the temporal constraints defined by the authors, as envisaged in the Temporal Glue approach [17].

[29] formalises hypermedia by using Petri Network and defines the HTPSN[5]. This proposal is based on the use of TSPN[6] which are derived from the OCPN[7] [25].

---

[3] Institut National de Recherche en Informatique et Automatique, Grenoble, France.
[4] Simple Temporal Problem.
[5] Hierarchical Time Stream Petri Nets.
[6] Time Stream Petri Nets.
[7] Object Composition Petri Networks.

3.3 Database Approaches

The hypermedia documents and their temporal characteristics, have not really been considered within the database framework. Certain approaches [3] have tried to make the use of hypermedia documents contained in a database possible. In the same way [26] proposes a model for the management of multimedia presentations. This work defines, by using the STORM model [1], the different objects which can be found within a multimedia database, then it models the 13 Allen relationships and give management rules for multimedia presentations. However it does not address the life-cycle of the document within the repository for mass production as it is needed in our context. [27] underscores the need to integrate synchronisation at data model level and at request language level and the need to enable requests on the content of the multimedia elements.

3.4 Analysis Result

The multimedia and hypermedia models presented above have enabled the semantics of the time constraints and hyperlinks to be captured and managed at presentation and creation time. Their study reveals the complexity of the management of temporal relationships between documents. For the production of aeronautical technical documentation, database issues have not yet been entirely tackled, at least in a context equivalent to our. The approaches presented before are needed for our works; in particular the AHM [18] and MADEUS [23], but they are not sufficient. The last section presents the approach we are developing to meet our needs.

4 Definition of a Multimedia and Hypermedia Repository

Our state-of-the-art revealed that many approaches tried to manage multimedia and hypermedia documents as a set of structured data and documents [23] [26] [29] [18].

These approaches describe a kind of tree-structure intended to simplify the issues encountered. Indeed, they offer means for handling issues at a given level of the structure without having to deal with the other levels. In our work, we think this structured approach is justified by the three assertions below:

- Aeronautical technical documents are complicated but structured in a very strict way. a maintenance task contains many actions which contains many steps.
- Reuse of data and documents implies that they could be used as atomic elements by «client» documents [11].
- Most of the synchronisation relationships can be handled by the structure of the documents [18].

The following parts describes how we are proceeding to obtain this structuring. Currently, our work only answers to two of the problems we identified in section 2, the description of multimedia documentary units within a repository; the reuse and structuring capability.

4.1 Solving the Basic Issue: Multimedia Document Synchronisation Modelling

Figure 2 shows how final documents are built from the documentary repository. This process allows separating data changes from documents structure models changes. We propose to keep this boundary by the definition of two separate data models:

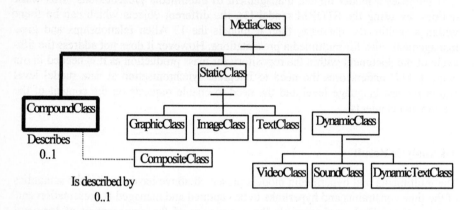

Fig. 3. Media Model: a data model representing the documentary units contained in the documents. This model, presented with an object-oriented notation, describes these different media through a hierarchy of classes identifying the features proper to each type of media, as well as the information for their management.

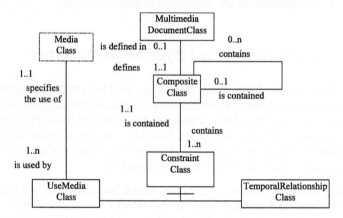

Fig. 4. Temporal Model: a data model representing the organisation of the different media which are composing a multimedia document. It describes the different classes and the synchronisation and composition relationships existing between them.

The critical point of such a separation is the relationship that must exist between these two models. Indeed, they are not completely independent from each other, the documentary units (i.e. the different media) are in fact used as atomic components for the composition of multimedia documents.

That is why we propose to identify the concept of *MediaClass* and the concept of *UseMediaClass*:

- The first one is the more intuitive. It describes the properties of a real media, for instance a video. The properties could be the duration of the media, its display dimension...
- The second one fits with the use of such a media within a multimedia document. Therefore, it describes properties - such as the duration of its presentation, its configuration and version data – which are depends of the document context.

The two classes are linked by the «*specifies the use of*» relationship. A *MediaClass* can be used many times while a *UseMediaClass* specifies the use of only one *MediaClass*.

[10] highlights the needed separation of these two types of information. Besides, this approach is compliant with our needs of configuration management and of reuse of information. Indeed, the same media may be used many times in many documents in an independent way.

4.2 Integration of Structuring Capability

The previous part describes how we intend to implement multimedia documents. At this stage, we have only addressed the definition of a model allowing creation of documents from basic media. However, we previously mentioned the needed capability of reuse of the multimedia documentary units already created, and our wish to obtain a structured model.

We propose to add to the Media Model a class for taking into account the existing multimedia documents. This class is the *CompositeClass* and specialises the *MediaClass*. In fact, it represents in the Media Model a new media whose description is given by the Temporal Model classes (see figure 3).

By adding this class, we enable the structuring of our documents. This way, a multimedia document (described by the *MultimediaDocumentClass*) can be built with already defined documents.

4.3 Synchronisation Unit

While our work consists in automating the production of multimedia documents, we are aware of the fact that complete automation cannot be achieved. Indeed, temporal constraints expressed in a document may not be met [24].

Besides, in our context of information reuse, the evolution of a document, either a media or a document, may have such a large impact on the document that it may be decided to manage its change under human-control, in order to keep its temporal characteristics constant. Acting like this, this will prevent the modification of too many documents.

That is why we propose to define the notion of «synchronisation unit», by the following rule: «All objects of class MediaClass and its sub-classes are a synchronisation unit». This means that its temporal characteristics cannot be modified except under human control and agreement. By inheritance mechanism, the CompoundClass is also a synchronisation unit: temporal constraints expressed in it have to be resolved within it.

Therefore, within our repository all reusable units are synchronisation units. At the time of the creation of an instance of CompositeClass, the author will have to choose between reusability or evolving capability of it.

Conclusion

This paper allowed us to identify the preliminary steps to the integration of multimedia and hypermedia within the aeronautical technical documentation framework. Although it does not question the better readability of such documents, it emphasises the point that their features must be managed in a large and complicated documentation production environment.

To sum up, it could be highlighted that:

- multimedia and hypermedia documents presentation and creation have already been studied. Issues are identified and mostly solved.
- Management of a multimedia repository has not been fully tackled yet, even less in our specific field (the aeronautical technical documentation), where documents have a life-cycle.

This last point is a new research area that we are addressing. The state-of-the-art we have presented in this paper allowed us to make our first proposals in order to meet our needs.

References

1. Adiba M., "STORM: Structural and Temporal Object-oRiented Multimedia database system", IEEE International Workshop on Multimedia DBMS, New-York, pp 10-15, 1995.
2. Allen James F., "Maintaining Knowledge about Temporal Intervals", Communications of the ACM, Vol. 26(11), November 1983.
3. Bapat Ajit, Wäsch Jürgen, Aberer Karl, Haake Jörg M., "HyperStorM: An Extensible Object-Oriented Hypermedia Engine", Proceedings of the 7th ACM Conference on Hypertext (HYPERTEXT'96), Washington DC, March 1996.
4. Buchanan Cecilia M. Zellweger Polle T., "Automatic Temporal Layout Mechanisms", Proceedings of the 1st ACM international conference on Multimedia, Anaheim (CA), pp 341-350, 1993
5. Buford J. F. K., "Multimedia Systems", Addisson-Wesley, New-York, 1994.
6. Conklin, Jeff, "Hypertext: An introduction and survey", IEEE Computer, Septembre 1987.
7. Dechter, R., Meiri, I., Pearl, J., "Temporal constraints networks ", 1st International Conference on Principles of Knowledge Representation and Resoning, Toronto, pp 83-93, May 1989.

8. Drapeau George D., Greenfield Howard, "MAEstro-A Distributed Multimedia Authoring Environment", Proceedings of Usenix Summer 1991, June 1991.

9. Drapeau George D., "Synchronisation in the MAEstro Multimedia Authoring Environment", Proceedings of the 1st ACM international conference on Multimedia, Anaheim (CA), pp 331-339, 1993.

10. Duluc Franck, "Multimédia, Hypermédia et documentation technique aéronautique", 1° journées sur la Ré-ingénierie des Systèmes d'Informations, papier court et poster, 1-2 Avril 1998.

11. Duluc Franck, "Multimedia and aeronautical technical documentation: new challenge..., and new issues", Markup Technologies'98 Conference proceedings, Chicago(IL), pp 135-143, Novembre 1998.

12. Ehley Lynnae, Furht Borko, Ilyas Mohammad, "Evaluation of Multimedia Synchronization techniques", Proceedings of IEEE International Conference on Multimedia Computing and Systems, ICMS'94, pp 514-519, 1994

13. "Specifications of temporal constraints in multimedia documents using HyTime", Electronic Publishing, Vol. 6(4), pp 397-411, December 1993.

14. Furht Borko, "Multimedia Systems: An overview", IEEE Multimedia, vol. 1, NR1, 1994.

15. Gibbs Simon, "Composite Multimedia and Active Objects", Proceedings of OOPSLA'91, pp 97-112, 1991.

16. Halasz F., Schwartz M., "The Dexter Hypertext Reference Model", communications of the ACM, Vol. 37(2), pp 30-39, February 1994.

17. Hamakawa Rei, Rekimoto Jun, "Object Composition and Playback Models for Handling Multimedia Data", Proceedings of the 1st ACM international conference on Multimedia, Anaheim (CA), pp 273-281, 1993.

18. Hardman Lynda, Bulterman Dick C. A., van Rossum Guido, "The Amsterdam Hypermedia Model: extending hypertext to support real multimedia, CWI Amsterdam, Report CS-R9306, The Netherlands, 1993.

19. Hardman Lynda, van Rossum Guido, Bulterman Dick C. A., "Structured Multimedia Authoring", Proceedings of the 1st ACM international conference on Multimedia, Anaheim (CA), pp 283-289, 1993.

20. Hoepner Petra, "Synchronizing the presentation of multimedia objects", Computer Communications, Vol 15(9), pp 557-563, November 1992.

21. "Standard Generalized Markup Language", ISO/IEC 8879:1986.

22. Lamport Leslie, " Time, Clocks and the ordering of events in a distributed system ", Coommunication of the ACM, Volume 21, number 7, pp 558-565, July 1978.

23. Layaïda Nabil, Sabbry-Ismaïl Loay, "MADEUS : un modèle de documents structurés", Techniques et science informatiques, Vol. 15, n°9/1996, pp 1227-1257, 1996.

24. Layaïda Nabil, "Madeus : système d'édition et de présentation de documents structurés multimédia", Thèse de l'Université Joseph Fourier - Grenoble1, 1997.

25. Little Thomas D. C., Ghaffor Arif, "Synchronization and Storage Models for Multimedia Objects", IEEE Journal on selected areas in communications, Vol. 8(3), April 1990.

26. Mocellin Françoise, "Gestion de données et de présentation multimédia par un SGBD à objets", rapport de thèse, Université Joseph Fourier Grenoble I, LLSR-IMAG, 1997.

27. Rakow Thomas C., Neuhold Erich J., Löhr Michael, "Multimedia Database Systems, The Notions and the Issues", Tagungsband GI-Fachtagung Datenbanksysteme in Büro, Technik und Wissenschaft (BTW), Dresden März 1995, Springer Informatik Aktuell, Berlin 1995.

28. van Rossum Guido, Jansen Jack, Mullender Sjoerd K., Bulterman Dick C. A., "CMIFed: A Presentation Environment for Portable Hypermedia Documents", , CWI Amsterdam, Report CS-R9305, The Netherlands, 1993.

29. Sénac Patrick, Diaz Michel, Léger Alain, de Saqui-Sannes Pierre, "Modeling Logical and Temporal Synchronization in Hypermedia Systems", IEEE Journal on selected areas in communications, Vol. 14(1), January 1996.

30. Wahl Thomas, Rothermel Kurt, "representing Time in Multimedia Systems", Proceedings of IEEE International Conference on Multimedia Computing and Systems, ICMS'94, Boston (MA), pp 538-545, 1994
31. World Wide Consortium, "Extensible Markup Language (XML) 1.0", World Wide Web Consortium Recommendation February 10 th 1998.
32. World Wide Consortium, "Synchronized Multimedia Integration Language (SMIL) 1.0 Specification", World Wide Web Consortium Recommendation June 15 th 1998.

Data Warehouse Design and Maintenance through View Normalization

Mukesh Mohania[1], Kamalakar Karlapalem[2] and Yahiko Kambayashi[3]

[1] Advanced Computing Research Centre,
School of Computer and Information Science,
University of South Australia,
The Levels 5095, Australia
Email: mohania@cis.unisa.edu.au
[2] Department of Computer Science,
Hong Kong University of Science and Technology,
Clear Water Bay, Kowloon, Hong Kong, China
Email: kamal@cs.ust.hk
[3] Department of Social informatics,
Kyoto University, Kyoto, Japan
Email: yahiko@kuis.kyoto-u.ac.jp

Abstract. Database design has always been a challenging problem, more so if the performance of queries is the prime goal. Thus, data warehouse design driven by queries is lot more difficult because of the materialized view selection and maintenance problems. Since user queries change over time, data warehouse design becomes a dynamic problem, that has to contain frequent changes to data warehouse design. In this paper, we advocate the applicability of view normalization technique to facilitate robust data warehouse design and facilitate efficient maintenance of materialized views.

Keywords: Databases, Normalization, Data Warehousing, Incremental View Maintenance

1 Introduction

A data warehouse has two specific properties which makes efficient application processing very challenging. The first property is that most of the applications are decision support oriented applications which need to summarize huge amounts of data. This is typically supported by a set of views which are materialized [3] for fast retrieval of data integrated from several distributed data sources, but there views tend to be very complicated [11], and many a times summarize tuples by joining more than two tables [12]. The second property is currency of the data, since data warehouses are snap shots of the real data, data warehouse views need to be periodically, adaptively or incrementally maintained to retain the currency of the data warehouse. This requires maintenance of complicated views which is an exceedingly costly problem. The maintenance of view is often done, for reasons of efficiency, using incremental techniques rather than recomputing the view from scratch. There has been some work [1, 2, 4, 5, 9, 13] in maintenance of views and most of the current work revolves around direct manipulation (incrementally) of auxiliary relations [5, 7, 8] in order to improve the efficiency of view maintenance. These auxiliary relations are derived from the intermediate results of the view computation.

In this paper, we advocate *view normalization* driven data warehouse design and maintenance. In the following, we portray the utility of this technique.

2 Data Warehouse Design by View Normalization

A major component of data warehouse design consists of selecting views that need to be materialized. In [12], we presented a query driven approach for view selection problem. Such an approach is not only very complex, but requires constant fine tuning for every change in queries or query processing plans. Thus, additional methodological steps need to be provided to handle these changes to views selected.

In view normalization, we look at the problem at a higher level, without going into the detail of query processing plans. From a given set of queries we consolidate the query results to form a set of views. Since these views encompass multiple query results, they are lot more robust to changes in the queries. Each query result can be treated as a view with its own set of functional dependencies (FDs), and by using these FDs one can restructure the views to an initial set of materialized views. From these set of views, based on the functional dependencies valid on the views, we decompose these views into a set of materialized views that either facilitate maintenance of materialized views or processing of queries.

Since most views in data warehouse environments involve aggregates and group-by clauses, the theory of functional dependencies needs to be enhanced to work with FDs on aggregate and group-by values. In this context, the concepts and properties of aggregate FDs are developed. The concepts of aggregate FDs are shown to be useful in not only helping design data warehouses but as a concept on their own to provide insight on the primary key/foreign key dependencies and aggregate values. Thus, at a higher level semantics oriented data warehouse design approach is facilitated.

3 Data Warehouse Maintenance by View Normalization

Though view selection aims to facilitate efficient processing of queries, in order to provide most accurate results for the queries these materialized views need to be maintained with respect to the changes to the base relations. View maintenance is a very costly problem and many techniques have been proposed for facilitating efficient view maintenance. One of the techniques is based on the concept of auxiliary relations that feed the materialized views. By having a layered approach, with boot layer being base relations (i.e. source data), middle layer being auxiliary relations and top layer being materialized views, the whole process of view maintenance can be pipelined. Such a pipe line not only stream lines the view maintenance but also does incremental changes that are efficient.

The main problem with auxiliary relations is to select them for a set of materialized views that benefit the efficient execution of a set of queries. Existing solutions advocate a tight coupling between query processing plans and selection of auxiliary relations [5, 7, 8, 10]. This requires frequent changes to both auxiliary relations and materialized views when query processing plans or queries change. Therefore, we advocate auxiliary relation design by view decomposition through normalization [6] for SPJ views. We have shown that such an approach facilitates robust and yet quite beneficial auxiliary relations that efficiently maintain materialized views.

We developed a methodology, wherein the auxiliary relations are derived from the materialized views, and the base relations by considering the functional dependencies valid on the view. The basic premise is that the auxiliary relations are much closer to base relations in terms of being vertical or horizontal fragments on the base relations, and hence much easier to maintain by applying query data localization rules developed for distributed relational databases. Further, instead of processing much larger base relations, the materialized views deal with with much smaller auxiliary views. Also, the techniques developed for maintaining such materialized views from base relations, will work more efficiently for maintaining materialized views since these auxiliary relations can be maintained directly without much computation. The main drawback of this approach is two level maintenance of both auxiliary relations and materialized views. This incurs extra storage overhead. One way to redeem this drawback is to only maintain auxiliary relations (which is quite cheap) and compute views as and when required, and use multiple query optimization or caching for improving the efficiency.

4 Challenges and Open Issues

In order to design auxiliary relations and to maintain these auxiliary relations and materialized views, one needs to address following main issues.

1. Concepts and Principles
   - Define Aggregate functional dependencies and properties of Aggregate FDs on views.
   - Determine functional dependencies (also aggregate FDs) on views from functional dependencies hold in base relations.
2. Normalization
   - Develop algorithms for normalization of a view using the primary key of the view and aggregate and normal FDs to generate the schema of auxiliary relations,
   - Develop algorithms for determining the relationship between the schema of the normalized views and the schema of the base relations. Define these in terms of relational algebraic expressions.
   - Determine the contents of each normalized view from the base relations.
3. Query Processing and Maintenance

- Develop algorithms for maintaining auxiliary relations and materialized views. Can we still use existing view maintenance algorithms?
- Develop algorithms for query processing using auxiliary relations, views and base relations.

References

1. J. Bailey, G. Dong, M. Mohania, and X. Sean Wang. Distributed view maintenance by incremental semijoin and tagging. *Distributed and Parallel Databases*, 6(3):287–309, 1998.
2. T. Griffin and L. Libkin. Incremental maintenance of views with duplicates. In *Proc. ACM SIGMOD Int. Conf. on Management of Data*, 1995.
3. A. Gupta and I. S. Mumick. Maintenance of materialized views: problems, techniques, and applications. *IEEE Data Engineering Bulletin, Special Issue on Materialized Views and Warehousing*, 18(2), 1995.
4. A. Gupta, I. S. Mumick, and V. S. Subrahmanian. Maintaining views incrementally. In *Proc. ACM SIGMOD Int. Conf. on Management of Data*, pages 157–166, 1993.
5. R. Hull and G. Zhou. A framework for supporting data integration using the materialized and virtual approaches. In *Proc. ACM SIGMOD Conf. On Management of Data*, pages 481–492, 1996.
6. Mohania M. K., Karlapalem Kamal, and Vincent Millist. Maintenance of data warehouse views using normalisation. In *Proc. of 8th International Conference on Management of Data, Madras, India*, pages 32–50, 1997.
7. Mukesh Mohania and Yahiko Kambayashi. Making aggregate views self-maintainable. *Journal of Data and Knowledge Engineering*, to appear.
8. Dallan Quass, Ashish Gupta, Inderpal Singh Mumick, and Jennifer Widom. Making views self-maintainable for data warehousing. In *Proc. of International Conference on Parallel and Database Information Systems*, 1996.
9. R. Ramakrishnan, K. A. Ross, D. Srivastava, and S. Sudarshan. Efficient incremental evaluation of queries with aggregation. In *Int. Logic Programming Symp.*, 1994.
10. K.A. Ross, D. Srivastava, and Sudarshan S. Materialized view maintenance and integrity constraint checking: Trading space for time. In *Proc. ACM SIGMOD International Conference on Management of Data, Montreal, Canada*, 1996.
11. Jennifer Widom. Research problems in data warehousing. In *Proc. Fourth Intl. Conference on Information and Knowledge Management*, 1995.
12. J. Yang, K. Karlapalem, and Q. Li. Algorithms for materialized view design in data warehousing environment. In *Proc. of International conference on Very Large Databases*, 1997.
13. Y. Zhuge, H. Garcia-Molina, J. Hammer, and J. Widom. View maintenance in a warehousing environment. In *Proc. ACM SIGMOD Int. Conf. on Management of Data*, pages 316–327, 1995.

Cleansing Data for Mining and Warehousing

Mong Li Lee   Hongjun Lu   Tok Wang Ling   Yee Teng Ko

School of Computing
National University of Singapore
{leeml, luhj, lingtw}@comp.nus.edu.sg

Abstract. Given the rapid growth of data, it is important to extract, mine and discover useful information from databases and data warehouses. The process of data cleansing is crucial because of the "garbage in, garbage out" principle. "Dirty" data files are prevalent because of incorrect or missing data values, inconsistent value naming conventions, and incomplete information. Hence, we may have multiple records refering to the same real world entity. In this paper, we examine the problem of detecting and removing duplicating records. We present several efficient techniques to pre-process the records before sorting them so that potentially matching records will be brought to a close neighbourhood. Based on these techniques, we implement a data cleansing system which can detect and remove more duplicate records than existing methods.

1 Introduction

Organizations today are confronted with the challenge of handling an ever-increasing amount of data. In order to respond quickly to changes and make logical decisions, the management needs rapid access to information in order to research the past and identify relevant trends. These information is usually kept in very large operational databases and the easiest way to gain access to this data and facilitate strategic decision making is to set up a data warehouse. Data mining techniques can then be used to find "optimal" clusterings, or interesting irregularities in the data warehouse because these techniques are able to zoom in on interesting sub-parts of the warehouse.

Prior to the process of mining information in a data warehouse, **data cleansing** or **data scrubbing** is crucial because of the "garbage in, garbage out" principle. One important task in data cleansing is to **de-duplicate** records. In a normal client database, some clients may be represented by several records for various reasons: (1) incorrect or missing data values because of data entry errors, (2) inconsistent value naming conventions because of different entry formats and use of abbreviations such as 'ONE' vs '1', (3) incomplete information because data is not captured or available, (4) clients do not notify change of address, and (5) clients mis-spell their names or give false address (incorrect information about themselves). As a result, we encounter situations where several records may refer to the same real world entity while not being syntactically equivalent. We can treat a set of records that refer to the same entity in two ways. We can view one of the records as correct and the rest of the records as duplicates containing erroneous information. Then the objective is to cleanse the database of the duplicate records [6, 2]. Alternatively, we can view each matching record as a partial source of information. Then the objective is to merge the duplicate records to obtain one record with more complete information.

In this paper we hold the latter view when we examine the problem of detecting and removing duplicating records. We present several novel techniques to pre-process the records before sorting them so that potentially matching records will be brought to a close neighbourhood subsequently. This will enable more matching records to be detected and removed. The pre-processing techniques include scrubbing data fields using external source files to remove typographical errors and the use of abbreviations, tokenizing data fields and then sorting the tokens in the data fields to solve the different field entry format problem which always exists in dirty data files but has been neglected by existing methods. We also introduce the use of field weightage to compute similarity among records. Accuracy is further improved with the help of external source files. Based on these techniques, we implement a data cleansing system which is able to detect and remove duplicate records than existing methods.

The rest of the paper is organized as follows. Section 2 gives a motivating example and surveys related works. Section 3 describes our proposed data cleansing methodology. Section 4 discusses the implementation and time complexity of our system, and finally we conclude in Section 5.

2   Motivation

To remove duplicated records from a dataset, the main consideration is how to decide that two records are duplicate? We need to compare records to determine their degree of similarity, which implies that corresponding fields in the records has to be compared. The comparison of fields to determine whether or not two syntactic values are alternative representations of the same semantic entity is also known as the **field matching problem** [5].

Record	EmpNo	Name	Address
1	142625M	Liu Hang Xiang	1020 Jalan Bandar Lamma, Industrial Park 3, West Malaysia
2	142725M	Mr. Liu H.X.	Ind Park 3, 1020 Jalan Bandar Lama, Malaysia

Table 1. Example of two duplicate records.

Table 1 shows two records, Record 1 and Record 2. At first glance, all the field values in both records look different. On closer examination, we note that the EmpNo in Record 1 and Record 2 are very similar except for a digit difference. We observe that "Liu" is common in the Name field of Record 1 and Record 2 and "H.X." in Record 2 seems to be an abbreviation of "Hang Xiang" in Record 1. If the address of Record 2 is reorganized as { *1020 Jalan Bandar Lamma,*

Ind Park 3, Malaysia}, we find that the Address of Record 1 and Record 2 are actually the same except for a typographical error {*Lamma*} in Record 1 and a missing word {*West*} in Record 2. Moreover, abbreviation {*Ind*} has been used in Record 2 instead of {*Industrial*}. Since the EmpNo, Name and Address field values of Record 1 and 2 are very similar to each other, we may conclude that Record 1 and Record 2 are most likely to be duplicates and they refer to the same employee in the real world. The differences in the Name and Address field values in Record 1 and 2 are typical of **different field entry format** problem.

There has been little research on the field matching problem although it has been recognized as important in the industry. Published work deals with domain-specific cases such as the Smith-Waterman algorithm for comparing DNA and protein sequences [7], and variant entries in a lexicon [4]. [2] use domain specific equational axioms to determine if two tuples are equivalent. [5] gives a basic field matching algorithm based on matching strings and a recursive algorithm to handle abbreviations. However, the former algorithm does not handle abbreviation while the latter has quadratic time complexity.

The standard method of detecting **exact** duplicates in a database is to sort the database and check if neighbouring records are identical [1]. The most reliable way to detect approximate duplicates is to compare every record with every other record in the database. But this is a very slow process which requires N(N-1)/2 record comparisions, where N is the number of records in the database. [2] proposed a **Sorted Neigbourhood Method (SNM)** to detect approximate duplicates by first sorting the database on a chosen application-specific key such as {Name, Address} to bring "potentially matching" records to within a close neighbourhood. This key is a sequence of a subset of attributes, or substrings within the attributes, which has sufficient discriminating power in identifying likely candidates for matching. There is no rule specifying how the key should be designed. We can design a key which concatenates the first 3 digits in EmpNo and the first 5 consonants in Name. Next, pairwise comparisons of nearby records are made by sliding a window of fixed size over the sorted database. Suppose the size of the window is w records, then every new record entering the window is compared with the previous w-1 records to find "matching records". The first record in the window slides out of the window.

SNM is obviously faster since it requires only wN comparisons. However, the effectiveness of this approach depends on the quality of the chosen keys which may fail to bring possible duplicate records near to each other for subsequent comparison. For example, if we choose the Address field in Table 1 to be the key to sort the database, then Record 1 and Record 2 will be very far apart after sorting because the address field value of Record 1 starts with "1020" while that of Record 2 starts with "Ind". If we choose the Name field to be the sort key, then Record 1 and Record 2 will be very close after sorting since both their name field values start with "Liu".

The **Duplication Elimination SNM (DE-SNM)** [3] improves the results of SNM by first sorting the records on a chosen key and then dividing the sorted records into two lists: a duplicate list and a no-duplicate list. The duplicate list contains all records with exact duplicate keys. All the other records are put into the no-duplicate list. A small window scan is performed on the duplicate list to find the lists of matched and unmatched records. The list of unmatched records is merged with the original no-duplicate list and a second window scan is performed. But the drawback of SNM still persists in DE-SNM.

In general, the duplicates elimination problem is difficult to handle both in scale and accuracy. Our proposed approach aims to increase the accuracy by first pre-processing the records so that subsequent sorting will bring potentially matching records to a close neighbourhood. In this way, the window size can be reduced which improves processing time. Finally, we note that while there are a few data cleansing software in the industry, most companies do not disclose the details of how it's done.

3 Proposed Cleansing Methodology

Our approach to cleansing a database comprises of several steps.

1. **Scrub dirty data fields.** This step attempts to remove typographical errors and abbreviations in data fields. This will increase the probability that potentially matching records be brought closer after sorting which uses keys extracted directly from the data fields.
2. **Sort tokens in data fields.** Characters in a string can be grouped into meaningful pieces. String values in data fields such as Name and Address can be split into meaningful groups, called **tokens**, which are then sorted.
3. **Sort records.**
4. **Comparison of records.** A window of fixed size is moved through the sorted records to limit the comparisons for matching records. Field weightage is used to compute the degree of similarity between two records.
5. **Merge matching records.** Matching record are treated as a partial source of information and merged to obtain a record with more complete information.

Steps 1 and 2 are not found in existing cleansing methods. These additional steps enhance the possibility that matching records will be brought closer during the sorting. The following subsections elaborates on steps 1, 2 and 4.

3.1 Scrubbing Dirty Data Fields

Existing data cleansing techniques such as the SNM and the DE-SNM are highly dependent on the key chosen to sort the database. Since the data is dirty and the keys are extracted directly from the data, then the keys for sorting will also be dirty. Therefore, the process of sorting the records to bring matching records together will not as effective. A substantial number of matching records may not be detected in the subsequent window scan.

Data in records are "dirtied" in various ways. It is common to find data entry errors or typing mistakes in name and address fields. Such **typographical**

errors causes the data to be incorrect or contain missing values. These fields may have different **entry format** as illustrated in Table 1. **Abbreviations** are often used to speed up data entry. The effectiveness of any de-duplicating method is to first remove such dirty data in the record fields.

Suppose we have a record with entry *ACER TECHNOOLGY PTE LTD* in its Company Name Field. There may be some typographical error in this field which cannot be corrected by a spelling checker because special names such as the name of a person or a company cannot be found in any dictionaries. For example, *ACER* is not spelled wrongly because it is a company name but *TECHNOOLGY* has a typographical error. Abbreviations such as *TECH.* for *TECHNOLOGY* may also be used. To ensure the correctness of data in the database, we use **external source files** to validate the data and resolve any data conflicts. The external source files contain information in record format. each record will have fields as shown in Table 2. Such external source files can be obtained from National Registries such as the Registry of Birth, Registry of Companies etc, which would contain more accurate and complete information on a person or company.

In Table 2, a particular person's information is contained in only one record. This external source file can be used to format and correct the information in a "dirty" database. We note that there exists a functional dependency $SSNO \rightarrow Name, Age, Sex$ in our example external source file. $SSNO$ is unique and is called the **key** field. This feature in the external source file may be used to enforce any functional dependencies between the fields in the database. Fields in the source files should correspond to fields in the database and this correspondence have to be provided by users. Formatting of the fields in the "dirty" database will be carried out according to key field in the external source file. Table 3 shows an example "dirty" record in the database. During the scrubbing process, the system will find the SSNO of this record in the external source file (Table 2). It will then change the values of the Name and Age fields of of the "dirty" record (Table 3) to the corresponding field values of the equivalent record in the external source file (Table 2). Table 4 shows the cleansed record with the Name field value re-formatted and the Age value corrected. With this step, we can guarantee the correctness of data as well as standardize the entry format in the database.

There are two possible scenarios for errors in the SSNO of the dirty database:

1. The wrong SSNO does not exist in external source file.
   In this case, the system would inform the user of the error.
2. The SSNO is the SSNO of another person.
   Here, the system should calculate the similarity between the record in the database and those in the external source file. We develop a method to compute the similarity between two records by using field weightage. This method (details in section 3.3) can be used to calculate the similarity between a record in the database and a matching record in the external file. The field values in the database record will only be re-formatted or corrected if

the computed similarity exceed certain value. Otherwise, the system would prompt the user whether or not to format the record in the database.

SSNO	Name	Age	Sex
0273632T	Koh Yiak Heng	43	M
3635290Y	Tan Kah Seng	16	M
5927356K	Vivian Chua	25	F

Table 2. Example of an external source file.

SSNO	Name	Age	Sex
0273632T	Koh Y.H.	42	M

Table 3. "Dirty" record in the database.

SSNO	Name	Age	Sex
0273632T	Koh Yiak Heng	43	M

Table 4. "Cleaned" record in the database.

3.2 Tokenizing and Sorting Data Fields

We have seen how a key chosen for sorting the database records plays an important role in bringing potentially matching records to within a window. This key can also cause the matching records to become further apart and hence reduce the effectiveness of the subsequent comparison phase. Table 5 shows three records in a database. If we choose the Address field in Table 5 to be the key to sort the database, then Record 1 and Record 2 will be very far apart after sorting because the address field value of Record 1 starts with a numeric string "1020" while that of Record 2 starts with "Industrial".

We observe that characters in a string can be grouped into meaningful pieces. We can often identify important components or **tokens** within a Name or Address field by using a set of delimiters such as space and punctuations. Hence, we can first tokenize these fields and then sort the tokens within these fields. For example, we obtain the tokens {Liu Kok Hong} in the Name field of Record 1 in Table 5. After sorting these tokens, we will obtain {Hong Kok Liu}. Table 6 shows the resulting database.

Records will now be sorted based on the sorted tokens in the selected key field. If the user chooses to use the Address field to sort the database, then the order of the records in the database will be 3, 2, 1. However, if the user selects the Name field to sort the database, then the order of the records in the database will be 2, 1, 3. Users can also choose to use {Name, Address} to sort the database. In this case, the system will make two pass on the database. It will first sort the records according to the Name field and remove any duplicate records. Then it will sort the database according to the Address field and remove any duplicate records. Information in the duplicate records are merged to obtain a record with more complete information. Note that if a field contains digits and character strings, then we need to separate the character string tokens and digit tokens. Otherwise, a record containing an address with a house number will never be close to another record with the same address but without the house number. Furthermore, users should choose fields which contains representative information of the record. For example, using the Sex field to sort the database will not be able to bring matching records close to each other since there are a lot of records containing same value in this field.

Record	Name	Address	Sex
1	Liu Kok Hong	1020 Jalan Bandar Lama, Industrial Park 3, Malaysia	M
2	Liu K.H.	Industrial Park 3, 1020 Jalan Bandar Lama, Selangor Darul Ehsan, Malaysia	M
3	Yap Kooi Shan	Blk 33 Marsiling Ind. Estate, #07-03, Singapore 130037	F

Table 5. Unsorted database

Record	Name	Address	Sex
1	Hong Kok Liu	3 1020 Bandar Industrial Jalan Lama Malaysia Park	M
2	H K Liu	3 1020 Bandar Darul Ehsan Ind. Jalan Lama Selangor	M
3	Kooi Shan Yap	03 07 33 130037 Blk Estate Ind. Marsiling Singapore	F

Table 6. Database with fields tokenised and sorted

3.3 Comparing Records

After the records in the database has been sorted, a window of fixed size w is moved through the records to limit comparisons of potentially matching records to those records in the window. Every new record entering the window is compared with the previous $w - 1$ records to find matching records. The first record in the window slides out of the window.

An efficient method is required to compare two records to determine their degree of similarity. We introduce the concept of **field weightage** which indicates the relative importance of a field to compute the **degree of similarity** between two records. The Name field obviously have a higher weightage than Sex field since because name is more representative of a record than sex. The field weightage is provided by users and the sum of all field weightages should be equal to 1. For example, if the user want to eliminate duplicate records based on the Name and Address fields equally, then they should assign a weightage of 0.5 to each of these two fields and 0 for the other fields in the record. Thus, records with same Name field and Address field will be considered as duplicates.

The process of computing the similarity between two records starts with comparing the sorted tokens of the corresponding fields. The tokens are compared using exact string matching, single-error matching, abbreviation matching and prefix matching. Based on the field token comparison results, the similarity between the entire field is computed. Finally, the record similarity can be computed from the fields similarity and the fields weightage. This is given in the following two propositions.

Proposition: Field Similarity

Suppose a field in Record X has tokens $t_{x_1}, t_{x_2}, ..., t_{x_n}$ and a corresponding field in Record Y has tokens $t_{y_1}, t_{y_2}, ..., t_{y_m}$. Each token $t_{x_i}, 1 \leq i \leq n$ is compared with tokens $t_{y_j}, 1 \leq j \leq m$. Let $DoS_{x_1}, ..., DoS_{x_n}, DoS_{y_1}, ..., DoS_{y_m}$ be the maximum of the degree of similarities computed for tokens $t_{x_1}, ..., t_{x_n}, t_{y_1}, ..., t_{y_m}$ respectively. Then field similarity for Record X and Y $Sim_F(X, Y)$ is given by $(\sum_{i=1}^{n} t_{x_i} + \sum_{i=1}^{m} t_{y_i})/(n + m)$.

Proposition: Record Similarity

Suppose a database has fields $F_1, F_2, ..., F_n$ with field weightages $W_1, W_2, ..., W_n$ respectively. Given records X and Y, let $Sim_{F_1}(X, Y), ..., Sim_{F_n}(X, Y)$ be the field similarities computed. Then record similarity for X and Y is given by the expression $\sum_{i=1}^{n} Sim_{F_i}(X, Y) * W_i$

We can have a rule that two records with record similarity exceeding a certain threshold such as 0.8 are duplicates and therefore, should be merged. While it is straightforward to check whether two tokens are exactly the same, it is not sufficient because of the existence of typographical errors, use of abbreviations etc. We need to consider single-error matching, abbreviation matching and substring matching when comparing tokens to calculate the degree of similarity. If two tokens are an exact match, then they have a degree of similarity of 1. Otherwise, if there is a total of x characters in the token, then we deduct $\frac{1}{x}$ from the maximum degree of similarity of 1 for each character that is not found in the other token. For example, if we are comparing tokens "cat" and "late", then $DoS_{cat} = 1 - \frac{1}{3} = 0.67$ since the character c in "cat" is not found in "late" and $DoS_{late} = 1 - \frac{2}{3} = 0.33$ since the characters l and e are not found in "cat". We shall now elaborate on the various matching techniques and how the degree of similarity of tokens are obtained.

1. **Exact string matching**

   The standard *strcmp()* function will return 1 if two tokens are exactly the same, else return 0.

2. **Single-error matching**

   Single-error checking includes checking for additional characters, missing characters, substituted characters and transposition of adjacent characters. Table 7 shows resulting degree of similarities when we compare the tokens "COMPUPTER", "COMPTER", "COMPUTOR", "COMPUTRE" to the token "COMPUTER".

3. **Abbreviation matching**

   An external source file containing the abbreviations of words is needed. Table 8 shows an example abbreviation file. A token A is a possible abbreviation of token B only if all the characters in A are contained in B and these characters in A appear in the same order as in B. If a token is found to be an abbreviation of another, then they have a similarity of degree 1.

4. **Prefix substring matching**

Here, we look for two similar tokens where one is a leading substring of the other. For example, "Tech." and "Technology", or "Int." and "International". Note that $DoS_{Tech} = 1$ since all the characters in "Tech." are found in "Technology" while $DoS_{Technology} = 0.4$ since there are 6 characters in "Technology" that are not found in "Tech". If a substring does not occur at the beginning of a token, then the two token may not be too similar. For example, "national" and "international" and we assign a similarity of degree of 0.0 for both these tokens.

Token 1	Token 2	DoS_{Token1}	DoS_{Token2}
COMPUTER	COMPUPTER	1.0	0.89
COMPUTER	COMPTER	0.88	1.0
COMPUTER	COMPUTOR	0.88	0.88
COMPUTER	COMPUTRE	1.0	1.0

Table 7. Single-error matching

Abbreviation	Word
SVCS	Services
PTE	Private
LTD	Limited

Table 8. Example of an abbreviation file

4 Data Cleansing System - Implementation and Performance

We implemented a data cleansing system in C on the UNIX and tested our system with an actual company dataset of 856 records. Each record has seven fields: Company Code, Company Name, First Address, Second Address, Currency Used, Telephone Number and Fax Number. Manual inspection of the dataset reveals 40 duplicate records. Typical problems in this dataset include records with empty Company Code or Address, matching records with different Company Code, typographical errors and abbreviations. The fields which contains representative information of a record and are most likely able to distinguish the records are Company Name, First Address and Second Address. We merged the First Address and Second Address fields because almost half the number of records have empty First Address.

It is possible that duplicate records are not detected and similar records which do not represent the same real world entity are treated as duplicates. These incorrectly paired records are known as **false-positives**. We obtain the following results when we run our system on the company dataset with a window size of 10:

1. **Misses.** The system failed to detect 5 individual records. That is, it has 12.5 % misses or 87.5 % true-positives.
2. **False-positives.** The system incorrectly matched 1 record. That is, it has 0.12 % false-positives.

The results show that our system is able to detect and remove the majority of the duplicate records with minimal false-positives. The additional pre-processing steps of scrubbing the data fields using external source files, tokenizing and sorting the data fields enables the subsequent sorting step to bring more potentially matching records to a close neighbourhood. An mathematical analysis of our system's time complexity shows that although these pre-processing steps may take extra time, they are not exponential.

5 Conclusion

We have examined the problem of detecting and removing duplicating records. We presented several efficient techniques to pre-process the records before sorting them so that potentially matching records will be brought to a close neighbourhood subsequently. These techniques include scrubbing data fields using external source files to remove typographical errors and the use of abbreviations, tokenizing data fields and then sorting the tokens in the data fields. These pre-processing steps, which have been neglected by existing methods, are necessary if we want to detect and remove more duplicate records. We also proposed a method to determine the degree of similarity between two records by using field weightage. We implemented a data cleansing system and the preliminary results obtained has been encouraging. Ongoing work involves testing the system's scalability and accuracy with real-world large data set.

References

1. D. Bitton and D.J. DeWitt. Duplicate record elimination in large data files. *ACM Transactions on Database Systems*, 1995.
2. M. Hernandez and S. Stolfo. The merge/purge problem for large databases. *Proc. of ACM SIGMOD Int. Conference on Management of Data* pages 127-138, 1995.
3. M. Hernandez. A generation of band joins and the merge/purge problem. *Technical report CUCS-005-1995*, Department of Computer Science, Columbia University, 1995.
4. C. Jacquemin and J. Royaute. Retrieving terms and their variants in a lexicalized unification-based framework. *Proc. of the ACM-SIGIR Conference on Research and Development in Information Retrieval* pages 132-141, 1994.
5. A.E. Monge and C.P. Elkan. The field matching problem: Algorithms and applications. *Proc. of the 2nd Int. Conference on Knowledge Discovery and Data Mining* pages 267-270, 1996.
6. A. Siberschatz, M. Stonebraker, and J.D. Ullman. Database research: achievements and opportunities into the 21st century. A report of an NSF workshop on the future of database research. *SIGMOD RECORD*, March 1996.
7. T.F. Smith and M.S. Waterman. Identification of common molecular subsequences. *Journal of Molecular Biology* 147:195-197, 1981.

DROLAP – A Dense-Region Based Approach to On-Line Analytical Processing

David W. Cheung[1], Bo Zhou[2], Ben Kao[1], Kan Hu[3], and Sau Dan Lee[1]

[1] Department of Computer Science, The University of Hong Kong, Hong Kong
{dcheung, bzhou, kao, hukan, sdlee}@csis.hku.hk
[2] Dept. of Computer Science and Engineering, Zhèjīang University, Hángzhōu, China
[3] Department of Automation, Tsinghua University, Běijīng, China

Abstract. ROLAP (Relational OLAP) and MOLAP (Multidimensional OLAP) are two opposing techniques for building On-line Analytical Processing (OLAP) systems. MOLAP has good query performance while ROLAP is based on mature RDBMS technologies. Many data warehouses contain sparse but clustered multidimensional data which neither ROLAP or MOLAP handles efficiently and scalably. We propose a dense-region-based OLAP (DROLAP) approach which surpasses both ROLAP and MOLAP in space efficiency and query performance. DROLAP takes the bests of ROLAP and MOLAP and combines them to support fast queries and high storage utilization. The core of building a DROLAP system lies in the mining of dense regions in a data cube, for which we have developed an efficient index-based algorithm EDEM to handle. Extensive performance studies consistently show that the DROLAP approach is superior to both MOLAP and ROLAP in handling sparse but clustered multidimensional data. Moreover, our EDEM algorithm is efficient and effective in identifying dense regions.

1 Introduction

On-Line Analytical Processing (OLAP) has emerged recently as an important decision support technology. [4, 8, 10, 12] It supports queries and data analysis on aggregated databases built from data warehouses. Recently, Jim Gray et al. has introduced the *data cube* model for OLAP systems, and the Data Cube operator to support multiple aggregates. [6] The Cube operator is an n-dimensional generalization of the group-by operator which computes all possible group-bys on n given attributes.

Currently, there are two dominant approaches to implement data cube: Relational OLAP (ROLAP) and Multidimensional OLAP (MOLAP). [1, 13, 15] ROLAP stores aggregates in relation tables in traditional RDBMS. MOLAP, on the other hand, stores the aggregates in multidimensional arrays. Due to the direct access nature of arrays, MOLAP is more efficient in processing queries. [9] On the other hand, ROLAP is more space efficient for a large database if its aggregates have a very sparse distribution in the data cube. [16] However, being unable to take advantage of the multidimensional nature of the data, ROLAP cannot process data-cube queries efficiently.

It has been recognized widely that the data cubes in many business applications exhibit the dense-regions-in-sparse-cube property. In other words, the cubes are sparse but not uniformly so. They are often "lumpy", i.e., their data points are not distributed evenly throughout the multidimensional space, but are mostly clustered in some *dense regions*. For instance, a supplier might be selling to stores that are mostly located in a particular city. Hence, there are few records with other city names in the supplier's customer table. With this type of distributions, most data points are gathered together to form some dense regions, while the remaining small percentage of data points are distributed sparsely in the cube space.

We propose the Dense-Region-based OLAP (DROLAP) approach for this type of data cubes to deliver efficient query and storage utilization. It takes the bests of MOLAP and ROLAP and combines them wisely to deliver fast query response and efficient space utilization. We first identify the dense regions in a data cube. Then, we can build a DROLAP system as follows: (1) store each dense region in a multidimensional array (small MOLAP); (2) build an R-tree index on the small MOLAPs; (3) store all the sparse points not in any dense region in a ROLAP. Figure 1 illustrates such a structure. To answer a query, the R-tree index is searched to locate the relevant dense regions. The corresponding small MOLAPs are retrieved on which the query is applied as in a traditional MOLAP system. Also, the ROLAP for sparse points is searched via the supporting indices. We remark that for a data cube with a small sparse point population, the ROLAP table and the R-tree index can possibly be stored in main memory for efficient query processing. A fast query response time and small I/O cost thus ensues.

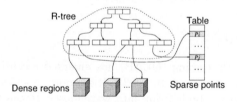

Fig. 1. Dense regions and sparse points indexed by an R-tree like structure

DROLAP thus inherits the merit of being space efficient from ROLAP because data in sparse regions are stored in a relational table. It also inherits the merit of high query performance because it uses small MOLAPS and R-tree to store the data in dense region, thus exploiting the multidimensional nature of the data. We note that the DROLAP data organization is based on three well-studied structures, namely, MOLAP, ROLAP, and index trees. Realization is thus straight-forward once the dense regions are identified. Our contributions are in the study of three fundamental issues which make DROLAP possible. First, what constitutes a dense region? Secondly, given a data cube, how one could efficiently and effectively identify the dense regions? Thirdly, how much performance gain (in terms of storage space and query response time) DROLAP can achieve over MOLAP and ROLAP?

The dense-region mining problem is defined formally in Section 2. A solution to it, our EDEM algorithm (**E**fficient **DE**nse region **M**ining) is described in Section 3. Extensive studies, brief results given in Section 4, demonstrate that the DROLAP approach is superior to MOLAP and ROLAP, and EDEM is efficient. We conclude this paper in Section 5 with some discussions.

2 Problem Definition and Related Works

To simplify our discussion, we first define some terms. We assume that each dimension (corresponding to an attribute) of a data cube is discrete, so that it covers only a finite set of values. If the attribute is continuous we quantize its range into discrete buckets. We consider the whole data cube space to be partitioned into equal-sized *cells*. A cell is a *small rectangular* sub-cube. A cell that contains at least one data point is called a *valid cell*. The *volume* of a cell is the number of possible distinct tuples in the cell. A *region* consists of a number of cells. The volume of a region is the sum of the volume of its cells. The density of a region is equal to the number of data points it contains divided by its volume.

2.1 Problem Statement

The dense region mining problem is formulated as the following optimization problem. Let $S = D_1 \times D_2 \times \cdots \times D_d$ be a d-dimension data cube such that, for $1 \leq i \leq d$, $D_i = \{x | x \in A_i, L_i \leq x < H_i\}$ is a range in a totally ordered domain A_i, bounded above and below by H_i and L_i respectively. The data cube contains a set of data points $D = \{v_1, v_2, ..., v_n\}$, where $D \subseteq S$. The data cube S is partitioned into equal size cells such that the *cell length* on the i-th dimension is c_i. That is, the i-th dimension is divided into $n_i = (H_i - L_i)/c_i$ equal intervals. The volume of a region r, denoted by V_r, is the total number of data points that can be filled into the region. The density of a region r, denoted by ρ_r, is the number of data points that fall in r divided by the volume of r.

Given a data cube S, a set of data points D in S, a cell based partition on S, together with three input thresholds $\rho_{\min}$, ρ_{low} and $V_{\min}$, computing the dense regions in S is to solve optimization problem stated in Table 1. The problem

Objective:	Maximize $\sum_{i=1}^{m} V_{dr_i}$, for any set of non-overlapping rectangular regions dr_i, $(i = 1, \cdots, m)$, in the cube S
Constraints:	$\rho_{dr_i} \geq \rho_{\min}$, $\forall i = 1, \cdots, m$;
	$V_{dr_i} \geq V_{\min}$, $\forall i = 1, \cdots, m$;
	$\forall i = 1, \cdots, m$ for each cell cl in dr_i, $\rho_{cl} \geq \rho_{\text{low}}$.

Table 1. Problem statement of dense region computing

of mining dense regions is to find a maximal set of non-overlapping rectangular regions such that the density of each of them is larger than ρ_{min}, volume larger than V_{min}, and the density of each cell in the regions is at least ρ_{low}. Here, ρ_{min} is a user specified minimum density threshold a region must have to be considered "dense". The parameter ρ_{low} is specified to avoid the inclusion of empty and low density cells into a dense region. The parameter V_{min} is introduced to avoid generating too many dense regions of very small sizes. For a detailed discussion of why these thresholds are introduced, please refer to [3].

2.2 Related Works

We have evaluated a number of existing techniques for mining dense regions in a data cube. These include image analysis, decision tree classifiers, clusterization, CLARANS [11], BIRCH [14], CURE [7], CLIQUE [2] and DBSCAN [5]. However, none of them are suitable for this task because they have one or more of the following shortcomings: They 1) do not handle the density requirement; or 2) do not generate rectangular regions; or 3) are distance based; or 4) do not scale well with more than 3 dimensions; or 5) produce highly fragmented regions; or 6) have to scan all the data multiple times. Moreover, the shortcomings are not easy to overcome with these algorithms. See [3] for an in-depth discussion.

Our contribution, besides proposing the DROLAP approach to integrate the merits of MOLAP and ROLAP, is the development of an efficient algorithm for mining dense regions in a data cube.

3 The EDEM Algorithm for Mining Dense Regions

A dense region is a connected set of cells each of which has a density higher than ρ_{low}. We call this type of cells *admissible cells*. Among the admissible cells, those that have density higher than ρ_{min} are called *dense cells*. Any cell which is not empty is called a *valid cell*. Hence, a dense region must be a connected set of admissible cells. Because of space limitations, we can only give a brief descriptions of the EDEM algorithms in this paper. See [3] for details.

The EDEM algorithm is divided into three main steps. We will briefly go through these steps in the following subsections. This algorithm has two important merits: (a) it can identify very efficiently a set of small subspaces, the covers, for finding the dense regions; (b) the searching is limited within each cover separately and there is no need to traverse between covers.

3.1 Building a k-d Tree to Store the Valid Cells

We first build a k-d tree to store the valid cells in the data cube S. For every point in the set of data point D, the cell which it belongs to is inserted into the tree. The number of points in each cell is also kept. The resulting nodes in the k-d tree are in fact rectangular regions in the cube space such that the union of all the leaf nodes covers the whole space. The following theorem defines the node-splitting criteria of our k-d tree.

Theorem 1. *Let $V_{\min}$ be the minimum volume of a dense region, and V_{cl} be the volume of a cell. Let R be a rectangular subspace in the data cube S. If the number of admissible cells in R is less than $V_{\min}/V_{cl}$, then no dense region can be completely contained in R.*

Proof. Since the volume of a dense region must be larger than $V_{\min}$, it must contain at least $V_{\min}/V_{cl}$ admissible cells. Hence no dense region can be completely contained in R. □

Thus, we split a leaf node in the k-d tree whenever it has more than $V_{\min}/V_{cl}$ admissible cells. By doing that, we can guarantee that a dense region will always touch some boundary of some leaf node, i.e., it can never be contained in a single node without touching any boundary. Figure 2 shows the case that a dense region is split across four nodes on a k-d tree.

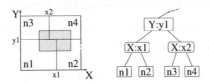

Fig. 2. Dense regions split across boundary

3.2 Growing Dense Region Covers along Boundaries

Let R be the region associated with a leaf node of the k-d tree. Let A be the set of admissible cells in R. If the minimum bounding box $MBR(A)$ of A does not touch any boundary of R, then according to Theorem 1, R cannot contain any dense region, and hence can be ignored in the mining of dense regions. On the other hand, if this is not the case, then we will grow covers from the boundary to contain the dense regions in R.

Suppose $MBR(A)$ does interest with some boundary of R. Let k be a boundary (a $(d-1)$-dimensional hyperplane) of R. Let $B \subseteq A$ be the set of admissible cells touching k. Let P be the projection of $MBR(B)$ on k. It is straight-forward to see that the projection on k of any dense region in R which touches k will be contained in P. Let X be the axis perpendicular to k. (Note that X has been divided into intervals by the cell partition.) Let $F = \{I \mid I$ is an interval on $X, \exists$ a cell $c \in A - B$ such that the projection of c on X is $I\}$. Let T be the maximal connected set of intervals in F which touches the boundary k. (The existence of T is guaranteed by B since it touches k.) The region $P \times T$ is called the *dense region cover* (DRC) grown from k in R. The following theorem follows immediately from these definitions.

Theorem 2. *Let C be a dense region cover grown from a boundary k in a region R. If r is a dense region in R which touches k, then $r \cap R \subseteq C$.*

Therefore, the set of all DRC's contains all the dense regions of the cube. We find out all the DRC's by examining every leaf node in the k-d tree built from the previous step. For each node, we find out the boundaries for which MBR(A) touches the R, the region associated with the leaf node. For each such boundary, we find out the DRC. Some prunings can be done here; see [3] for details.

Since the k-d tree may split a dense region across several nodes, the DRC's of the leaf nodes found need to be merged at the split boundary. For example, in Figure 2, the dense region has been separated into 4 pieces among the leaf nodes of the k-d tree. Merging combines DRC's n_1 and n_2 into a larger DRC, which is attached to the non-leaf node (X:x_1). Similarly, n_3 merges with n_4 to form a larger DRC for the node (X:x_2). Further merging combines them into a single DRC at node (Y:y_1). The details of the merging algorithm are presented in [3]. After the merging, no dense region will be divided up into different covers.

3.3 Searching Dense Regions among the Covers

Suppose C is a DRC discovered in the previous step. We store all the cells in C, (including cells with no data point), in a multi-dimensional array so that we can scan the cells in C to search for dense regions. The order of scanning in C is determined by a pre-selected dimension order $O(D'_1, D'_2, \cdots, D'_d)$, i.e., first on dimension D'_1, then on D'_2, etc. During the scanning, we first find a dense cell as the *seed cell*, and then use the seed to grow a maximal dense region along each dimension according to the dimension order. After a dense region is found, we search another dense region in the reminding cells of C until all cells have been scanned. [3]

3.4 Complexity of EDEM

Let N be the number of data points and C_a be the number of admissible cells. Let the number of leaf nodes on the k-d tree be N_d, and C_p be the average number of valid cells in a leaf node. According to the splitting criterion and Theorem 1, $C_p \leq V_{\min}/V_{\text{cl}}$. Also note that $C_a = O(N)$ and $N_d \times C_p = O(N)$.

The complexity of building the k-d tree (step 1) is $O(N \times (\log N_d + d \log C_p))$. Since C_p is bounded above by the constant $\frac{V_{\min}}{V_{\text{cl}}}$ and $N_d = O(N)$, this cost is $O(N(\log N + d))$. The complexity of generating the DRC's is $O(N_d \times d \times C_p) = O(d \times N)$ and the cost of merging them is $O(N_d \times d \times N_C \log N_C) = O(N \times d)$ where N_C is the total number of DRC's, which is on the order of the number of dense regions, which is bounded by a small constant. So, step 2 consumes $O(d \times N)$ time. Finding the dense regions from the covers (step 3) requires examining every admissible cell along every dimension, thus taking $O(d \times C_a) = O(d \times N)$ since the $C_a = O(N)$.

In summary, the complexities for the second and third steps of EDEM are both linear to N and d. The dominating cost is in the building of the k-d tree, which is $O(N(\log N + d))$. The cost is linear to d, the number of dimensions and sub-quadratic to N, the number of data points. This shows that EDEM is a very efficient and scalable algorithm. Please see [3] for a detailed analysis.

3.5 Environments with Limited Memory

In general, because we only record cell information, not the data points, on the k-d tree, the memory space required to store the tree should not be too big. This would depends on the cell size, though. If there is not enough memory, the tree can be stored on disk, and the computing of DRC's can be performed separately on different branches. Covers from different branches can be merged afterwards.

In the last step of finding dense regions from their covers, since dense regions have high density and their covers have same order of capacity, the array built from a cover in general should not be too big to fit in the memory. If it happens that a cover cannot be fully contained in the available memory, then chunking can be used to partition the cover. Dense regions can be computed in each chunk separately. [16] In the end, an additional step of merging the dense regions found from the chunks is required.

4 Performance Studies

We have carried out extensive performance studies on a Sun Sparc 5 workstation running Solaris 2.6 with 64M main memory. Our first goal is to study the space efficiency and query performance of the DROLAP system by comparing it with both the MOLAP and ROLAP. The second goal is to study the performance of the EDEM algorithm. Owing to limited space, we can only briefly present the most important results here. Please refer to [3] for a thorough discussion.

4.1 System Implementation and Data Generation

We implemented a MOLAP system using chunking with chunk-offset compression. The ROLAP system is implemented by inserting the data points in a table randomly to build a disk-based B+ tree index on each dimension. The DROLAP system uses an in-memory R-tree index to manage the dense regions, each of which is stored as an array on disk, and the sparse points are organized like our ROLAP implementation. In the performance studies, we use synthetic databases to do the comparison. The generation methods are described in [3].

The queries in our experiments are range queries generated randomly. Each query is corresponding to a rectangular region in the cube. Since we assume that the distribution of the dense regions in the cube reflects the distribution of the data, substantial percentage of the queries can be answered by a single dense region. To simulate this query distribution, we generate two types of queries: those that fall randomly into one dense region; and those that appear randomly anywhere in the cube space. We call the first type of queries *region query*, and the second type of queries *space query*.

4.2 Performance Results of DROLAP

We have compared the space efficiency and query performance of the DROLAP system with those of the MOLAP and ROLAP systems. Query performance is measured by total response time and number of pages accessed. In each experiment, we took the measurement over the execution of 100 range queries. Space efficiency is measured by the *expansion ratio* of each OLAP system, which is is the storage required divided by the size of original data set.

Effect of the Database Size In this test, we varied the number of data points from 0.25 to 2.5 million, (5% of sparse point in each case), in a 3-dimensional data cube. Figure 3 shows the result. DROLAP is consistently better than MOLAP and ROLAP; and ROLAP's performance deteriorates much faster than MOLAP. Once the data size becomes rather big, processing queries on the indices becomes very slow for ROLAP. Therefore, MOLAP is more efficient than ROLAP if the data cube has a very high data density. Overall, DROLAP is consistently the winner with very efficient performance and storage utilization.

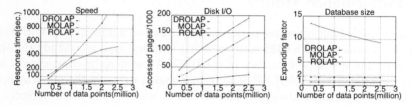

Fig. 3. Effect of the database size

Effect of Number of Dimensions In this experiment, we fixed the size of the data cube and increased the number of dimensions from 2 to 6. To be fair, we also have fixed the total volume of dense regions involved in the queries. The I/O activities of MOLAP increase rapidly, because the number of chunks that a range query may need to retrieve increases with the dimension. On the other hand, ROLAP needs to perform searches on more indices when the number of dimensions increases. Overall, ROLAP is faster than MOLAP with a lower number of dimensions, but MOLAP outperforms ROLAP with more dimensions. In all cases, DROLAP outperforms both of them.

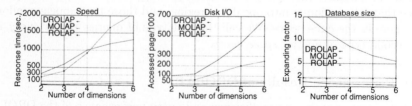

Fig. 4. Effect of number of dimensions

Summary In addition, we also studied the effect of the percentage of sparse points in the data cube. As sparsity increases, MOLAP deteriorates severely, while ROLAP and DROLAP slow down linearly. After all, DROLAP performs 10–20 times faster than OLAP and the amount of I/O it does is only $\frac{1}{4}$ to $\frac{1}{3}$ of that of ROLAP. In a nutshell, we found that DROLAP performs much better than MOLAP and ROLAP in both space efficiency and query performance. In particular, it is superior in the case that the dimension is high, the data set is large and there is certain level of sparsity.

4.3 Performance of EDEM

We have also done some studies on the performance EDEM, our dense region mining algorithm. We varied the number of dimensions, number of data points as well as number of dense regions in the synthesized database, and ran EDEM to find out the dense regions in it. Our finding is that EDEM scales linearly with the number of data points and number of dimensions, and it is relatively insensitive to the number of dense regions.

5   Discussion and Conclusion

Many data cubes have data distributions which contain some dense regions and a small percentage of sparse points. DROLAP is a much more efficient approach for building an OLAP system on these cubes than ROLAP and MOLAP.

In this paper, we have made the following contributions: (1) proposed the DROLAP approach and a data structure to support the processing of queries on a DROLAP system; (2) defined the problem of mining dense regions; (3) discussed that conventional clustering technique is not suitable for finding dense regions; (4) proposed a cell-based algorithm EDEM to compute dense regions; (5) performed performance study which shows that DROLAP is in fact superior to both MOLAP and ROLAP.

EDEM first scans the data base to build up a k-d tree to store the valid cells in the cube. It then uses a bottom up approach to compute the dense regions from the tree. The complexity of finding the dense regions is linear to both the database size and the number of dimensions, which gives the algorithm good scalability. In fact, EDEM combines the top-down, bottom-up, and greedy approaches in one algorithm. It builds up the k-d tree top down from the database. Then it uses a bottom-up approach to grow the DRC's. Finally, it uses a greedy algorithm to compute the dense regions in each cover.

Performance studies demonstrate that DROLAP is superior to both ROLAP and MOLAP if the data distribution has the assumed characteristics, i.e. being overall sparse but locally dense in certain regions of the data cube. We also have shown that EDEM has good scalability. As for future works, we observe that the dense region mining problem is, in a certain sense, a data mining problem. Its techniques may have important applications in the mining of multidimensional data. Indeed, the dense regions discovered may represent some useful, interesting, previously unknown knowledge that we desire to mine.

References

[1] S. Agrawal, R. Agrawal, P.M. Deshpande, A. Gupta, J.F. Naughton, R. Ramakrishnan, and S. Sarawagi. On the computation of multidimensional aggregates. In *Proceedings of VLDB*, pages 506-521, Bombay, India, September 1996.

[2] R. Agrawal, J. Gehrke, and D. Gunopulos. Automatic Subspace Clustering of High Dimensional Data for Data Mining Applications. In *Proceedings of the ACM SIGMOD Conference on Management of Data*, Seattle, Washington, May 1998.

[3] David W. Cheung, Bo Zhou, Ben Kao, Kan Hu and Sau Dan Lee. DROLAP—A Dense-Region Based Approach to On-line Analytical Processing. Technical Report (TR-99-02), Dept. of Computer Science & I.S., the University of Hong Kong, 1999. http://www.csis.hku.hk/publications/techreps/document/TR-99-02.ps

[4] G. Colliat. OLAP, relational, and multidimensional database systems. *SIGMOD Record*, pages 64-69, Vol.25, No.3, September 1996.

[5] M. Ester, H. Kriegel, J. Sander, and X. Xu. A Density-Based Algorithm for Discovering Clusters in Large Spatial Databases with Noise. In *Proceedings of KDD*, pages 226-231, Portland, Oregon, August 1996.

[6] J. Gray, A. Bosworth, A. Layman, and H. Piramish. Data cube: A relational aggregation operator generalizing group-by, cross-tab, and sub-total. In *Proceeding of ICDE*, pages 152-159, New Orleans, February 1996.

[7] S. Guha, R. Ratogi, and K. Shim. CURE: An Efficient Clustering Algorithm for Large Databases. In *Proceedings of the ACM SIGMOD Conference on Management of Data*, Seattle, Washington, May 1998.

[8] H. Gupta, V. Harinarayan, A. Rajaraman, and J. Ullman. Index selection for OLAP. In *Proceedings of the 13th Intl. Conference on Data Engineering*, pages 208-219, Burmingham, UK, April 1997.

[9] C.T. Ho, R. Agrawal, N. Megiddo and R. Srikant. Range Queries in OLAP Data Cubes. In *Proceedings of the ACM SIGMOD Conference on Management of Data*, pages 73-88, Tucson, Arizona, May 1997.

[10] V. Harinarayan, A. Rajaraman, and J. D. Ullman. Implementing data cubes efficiently. In *Proceedings of the ACM SIGMOD Conference on Management of Data*, pages 205-216, Montreal, Quebec, June 1996.

[11] R.T. Ng, and J. Han. Efficient and Effective Clustering Methods for Spatial Data Mining. In *Proc. of VLDB*, pages 144-155, Santiago, Chile, 1994.

[12] N. Roussopoulos, Y. Kotidis, and M. Roussopoulos. Cubetree: organization of and bulk incremental updates on the data cube. In *Proceedings of the ACM SIGMOD Conference on Management of Data*, pages 89-99, Tucso, Arizona, May 1997.

[13] K.A. Ross and D. Srivastava. Fast computation of sparse datacube. In *Proc. of VLDB*, pages 116-125, Athens, Greece, August 1997.

[14] T. Zhang, R. Ramakrishnan, and M. Livny. BIRCH : An Efficient Data Clustering Method for Very Large Databases In *Proceedings of the ACM SIGMOD Conference on Management of Data*, pages 103-114, Montreal, Quebec, June 1996.

[15] Y.H. Zhao, P.M. Deshpande, and J.F. Naughton. An array-based algorithm for simultaneous multidimensional aggregates. In *Proceedings of the ACM SIGMOD Conference on Management of Data*, pages 159-170, Tucson, Arizona, May 1997.

[16] Y.H. Zhao, K. Tufte, and J.F. Naughton. On the Performance of an Array-Based ADT for OLAP Workloads. Technical Report CS-TR-96-1313, University of Wisconsin-Madison, CS Department, May 1996.

Availability and Reliability Issues in Distributed Databases Using Optimal Horizontal Fragmentation

Khalil N., Eid D., Khair M.

Department of Computer Science
Faculty of Natural and Applied Sciences,
Notre Dame University, Louaize, Lebanon
nazo@iname.com, doryeid@iname.com, mkhair@ndu.edu.lb, mariekhair@yahoo.com

Abstract. In this paper, a horizontal fragmentation algorithm and a replication protocol that increases the availability and reliability are proposed and proven for a distributed database system. The first implements a previously proven vertical transaction-based algorithm that yields to an optimal number of fragments. The proposed horizontal algorithm substitutes the concept of attributes in the vertical problem by the predicates. The second algorithm, increases the availability and reliability by using a matrix log replicated at each site. Further, the system is fully maintained even during network partitioning and it remains operational as long as there is one available replica of an object. The latter algorithm minimizes the number of object replicas using an adaptive algorithm, and hence reduces the costs of message transfer, updates and storage.

Keywords: Distributed Database Design, Optimal Horizontal Fragmentation, Distributed Database Availability and Reliability.

I-Introduction

A distributed database is a collection of multiple databases logically interrelated but physically spread over several sites. The natural geographical distribution of institutions such as banks, government organizations and large companies lead to the distribution of the centralized database. Its purpose is to increase the locality of reference in comparison to a centralized database during transaction and query processing in order to reduce the overall processing time due to communication overhead. The distributed database concept evolved from the centralized database to achieve also goals such as availability, data independence and ease of expendability. The distributed database design is processed similarly to the centralized database for the requirement analysis and the conceptual design phases. It is a complex optimization task that requires solutions to several interrelated subproblems including data fragmentation, data allocation and data replication [4][5][6][7][16][18].

Data fragmentation is a process of subdividing global relations into subsets to be distributed over sites. It has three types: vertical, horizontal and mixed. The vertical fragmentation is the process of projecting a global relation over subsets of attributes called vertical fragments [3][18]. Horizontal partitioning is the process of selecting from global relation subsets of tuples called horizontal fragments, each of which is identified by a unique predicate [1][2][6]. The mixed fragmentation is the implementation of a vertical fragmentation on each of the horizontal fragments or vice versa. The resulting fragments need to be allocated and replicated to different sites.

Even though Apers in [6] considers data fragmentation and data allocation as a single problem, in this paper, they are dealt as two separate issues. In brief, data allocation is an undergoing task to store fragments at dispersed sites. This process is heavily depending on the transactions: their types (retrieval and/or update), their frequencies and the site where the results are to be performed. Allocation should be achieved in a way that the cost transfer function is minimized with a general reduction of the execution time. Several algorithms were proposed and can be found in [4][6][22].

Data replication is a necessity to enhance data availability and reliability especially during site failure, link failure, communication and network partitioning. Communication costs are generally reduced since the probability of having a local replicated data increases.

In this work, we deal on the fragmentation and replication issues. For the allocation, we adopt the hill-climbing allocation algorithm of [22]. Section 2-a of this paper reviews horizontal partitioning algorithms and section 2-b reviews with replication algorithms. Section 3 presents a proposed horizontal fragmentation algorithm and section 4 presents an enhanced replication control protocol. Conclusion and future research are summarized in section 5.

II-Previous Related Work

II-a. Fragmentation

Each horizontal fragment is associated with a predicate. A predicate is a Boolean function of type <domain><operator><value> implemented on a relation [1][2][14]. Several algorithms are suggested as solutions to the horizontal partitioning problem. The minterm algorithm uses the conjunction of all simple predicates taken either in their natural or negated form [1]. The graphical algorithm is developed based on the affinity values grouped in a matrix form. Affinity is a bond showing the togetherness among two predicates only. The latter algorithm transforms the affinity matrix into an affinity graph. While constructing a spanning tree, each cycle represents a fragment [9][14]. A third algorithm clusters the predicates of the affinity matrix constructing a semi block diagram. Then a fixed point is selected dividing the matrix in two sets of predicates. The same routine is recursively applied on each fragment to obtain the complementary fragments [3][16].

The last two algorithms are generated based on the affinity matrix. This matrix is by itself generated from a predicate usage matrix where the rows represent the transactions and the columns the predicates. The elements of the matrix represent the frequencies showing which transactions using which predicates [3][9][14][16]. The use of the affinity matrix does not consider the transaction on the database when creating the fragments. To solve the problem, we introduce a horizontal transaction-based partitioning algorithm in section 3.

II-b. Replication

The produced fragments need to be replicated to increase availability and reliability of the system [7]. The production of replication uses two matrices. The first is an $S \times T$ matrix known as the Issue Matrix where S represents at the row level the sites and T represents at the column level the transactions. The elements of the Issue Matrix are the number of occurrences of each transaction from each site. The second is a $T \times O$ matrix known the Access Matrix where T identifies at the row level the transactions and O at the column level the objects involved. The elements of the Access Matrix are 1 if T_i uses $[x]$ ($[x] \in O$) otherwise it is set to 0. The multiplication of these two matrices results an $S \times O$ Replica Matrix. Its elements represent the need to place an object $[x]$ on site S_i. The final replication of all objects occurs upon a predefined designer threshold. This threshold is evaluated depending on the user needs, the application, the cost, storage and/or other constraints [13][22].

The problem of maintaining high availability and reliability has been dealt from different perspectives. This Single Replica Control Protocol (known as full replication) and Available Copy Protocol achieve extreme availability at the expense of transfer cost and storage cost in case of no partitioning [4][8][13]. The view concept preserves the availability and reliability during partitioning by alternating the view [5][7][8][11][20]. Even though many algorithms are implemented to determine the locality of objects in order to reduce the communication and transfer cost, they also decrease at a certain degree the availability of the system [5][12][19][21]. Others consider the concurrency control protocol to render the system One Copy Equivalent at the expense of the message transfer cost [17]. Agrawal et. al. reduce the storage cost of replicas in the system at the expense of read/write operations [10]. This study proposes the replica control protocol that aim to a high availability and reliability while lowering message transmission cost detailed in section 4.

III- A Proposed Horizontal Fragmentation Algorithm

The proposed horizontal fragmentation algorithm is developed using the vertical transaction-based algorithm [15]. Recall from [15], the purpose of a vertical partitioning is to minimize the total number of disk accesses by partitioning relations into several fragments, i.e.,

$$\text{Minimize total costs} = \sum_{i=1}^{n} \sum_{j=1}^{d} f_i\left(l\left(I + F_j\right)\right) \tag{1}$$

where n is the number of transactions, d is the number of fragments generated by the partitioning algorithm. I is the primary key (or tuple identifier), $l(I+F_j)$ is the sum of the length of the attributes of F_j and I, and $f_j(l(I+F_j))$ is the cost of accessing a given fragment F_j by a transaction i. However, in the horizontal partitioning, the access of a transaction is a subset of tuples in a relation and not a subset of attributes as it is the case in vertical partitioning. Therefore the parameter $l(I+F_j)$ of (1) becomes irrelevant because the length of the vertical fragmentation is constant. As the purpose of the horizontal fragmentation is also to minimize the total number of disk accesses by partitioning relation into several fragments, i.e.,

$$\text{Minimize total cost} = \sum_{i=1}^{n} \sum_{j=1}^{d} f_i(c_j) \tag{2}$$

Where c_j is the cardinality of fragment j, $f_i(c_j)$ is the cost of accessing c_j tuples of fragment j by transaction i, n is the number of transactions and d is the number of fragments generated by the partitioning algorithm. The variable parameter for the horizontal fragmentation is the cardinality of the fragment and the variable parameter for the vertical fragmentation is the length of the schema fragments.

A reasonable cut is then applied on the vertical usage matrix known as the access pattern matrix in [15]. The reasonable cut is defined in [15] as: A *self-contained fragment* is the set of attributes that a transaction accesses. A *contained fragment* is the union of such self-contained fragments. A *reasonable cut* divides a relation to two parts having one of the fragments as being a contained fragment. All binary cuts that are not reasonable are called unreasonable cuts. In a relation of n transactions, there are $2^n - 1$ possible reasonable cuts grouped according to $\binom{n}{i}$ for $i=1\ldots n$.

It is clear from the definition that reasonable and unreasonable cuts are used on a relation. As the optimal binary partitioning for the vertical fragments of [15] can be only used in an environment where there are only reasonable cuts, and thus eliminating the unreasonable cuts, a proved theorem 1 is supplied. Wesley *et. al.* states: "let x be the length of the tuple and $f_i(x)$ be the access cost function for transaction i. If the second derivative of $f_i(x)$, $f_i''(x) < 0$ (concave downward), then for a given unreasonable cut of a relation, there exists at least one reasonable cut that yields less or equal cost than that of the unreasonable cut".

The same reasonable cut concept is implemented using the predicate usage matrix. In order for the binary partitioning algorithm to be implemented using the horizontal fragmentation, the theorem 1 must be proved using equation (2). Thus similarly to theorem 1, our theorem 2 regarding the horizontal partitioning states: let c_j be the cardinality of fragment j and let $f_i(c_j)$ be the cost of accessing c_j tuples of fragment j by transaction i. If the second derivative of $f_i(c_j)$, $f_i''(c_j) < 0$ (concave downward) for all i, then for a given unreasonable cut of a relation, there exists at least one reasonable cut that yields less or equal than that of the reasonable cut.

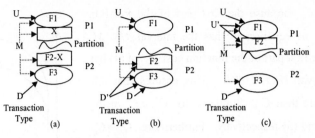

Fig. 1. Reasonable and unreasonable cuts of a relation

Proof: An unreasonable cut divides a relation in two parts as shown in fig. 1(a). Afterwards, the tuples are divided into two sets *P1* and *P2*. Let types *U* (Up) and *D* (Down) transactions access the tuples only in *P1* and *P2* respectively. Let *F1* be the set of tuples accessed by *U* and *F3* be the set of tuples accessed by *D*. Let *X* be the set of tuples not accessed by *U* transactions in *P1* and *F2-X* the ones not accessed by *D* transactions in *P2*. Transactions of type *M* (Middle) access both partitions *P1* and *P2*. Consider the fig. 1(b) where the cut is moved to the boundary of *F1*. The cost of accessing a fragment of type *U* transactions is not affected. But the cost of type *M* transactions may decrease since some tuples are moved from *P1* to *P2*. Those transactions of type *M* that only access *X* no longer need to access tuples in *P1* after the partition is moved to the boundary *F1*. We call these transactions type *D'*. Similarly transactions of type *U'* in fig. 1(c) represent the transactions of type *M* that only access *F2-X* which no longer access *P2* after the partition has been moved to the boundary of *F3* fragment.

Let C_u be the cost of the unreasonable cut Cut_u. Let C_{r_1} be the cost of the reasonable cut Cut_{r_1} deduced from Cut_u by moving the partition to the boundary of *F1* (fig. 1(b)); and let C_{r_2} be the cost of the reasonable cut Cut_{r_2} deduced from Cut_u by moving the partition to the boundary of *F3* of (fig. 1(c)). From (2), we deduce:

$$C_u(x) = \sum_{i \in U \cup M} f_i(c_1 + x) + \sum_{i \in M \cup D}(c_3 + (c_2 - x)) \tag{3}$$

such that $x \in [0..F2]$

$$C_{r_1} = \sum_{i \in U \cup M - U'} f_i(c_1) + \sum_{i \in M \cup D}(c_3 + c_2), \tag{4}$$

$$C_{r_2} = \sum_{i \in U \cup M} f_i(c_1 + c_2) + \sum_{i \in M - D' \cup D}(c_3) \tag{5}$$

Let $C_{r_1}^*$ represents the cost of $C_u(x)$ at the point 0 of the interval $[0..F2]$ and $C_{r_2}^*$ represents the costs for $C_u(x)$ at the point F2 of the boundary of $[0..F2]$ (fig. 2). Therefore,

$$C_{r_1}^* = \sum_{i \in U \cup M} f_i(c_1) + \sum_{i \in M \cup D} f_i(c_3 + c_2) \geq C_{r_1}, \tag{6}$$

$$C_{r_2}^* = \sum_{i \in U \cup M} f_i(c_1 + c_2) + \sum_{i \in M \cup D} f_i(c_3) \geq C_{r_2} \tag{7}$$

$C_{r_1}^* \geq C_{r_1}$ because the first part of the function cost $C_{r_1}^*$ of equation (6) has the interval $U \cup M$ while the first part of the function cost C_{r_1} of (4) has the interval $U \cup M - U'$. This ensures that $C_{r_1}^*$ costs more than C_{r_1}. Similarly, for $C_{r_2}^* \geq C_{r_2}$ using the (7) and (5) respectively. Furthermore, $C_{r_1}^* - C_{r_1}$ is the reduction in access cost by transactions type U' which do not require the access of $P1$; $C_{r_2}^* - C_{r_2}$ is the reduction in access cost by transactions type D' which do not require the access of $P2$ (Fig. 1). Due to concavity downward of $f_i(c_j)$,

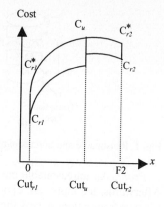

Fig. 2. Cost region for unreasonable cut

$$\frac{d^2 C_u(x)}{dx^2} = C_u''(x) = \sum_{i \in U \cup M} f_i''(c_1 + x) + \sum_{i \in M \cup D} f_i''(c_3 + (c_2 - x)) < 0 \qquad (8)$$

Therefore, $C_u(x)$ $C_u(x) \geq \min(C_{r_1}^*, C_{r_2}^*)$. As $C_{r_1}^* \geq C_{r_1}$ (6) and $C_{r_2}^* \geq C_{r_2}$ (7) then $C_u(x) \geq \min(C_{r_1}, C_{r_2})$. This result shows that there is a reasonable cut having a cost smaller or equal to the unreasonable cut for the horizontal partitioning.

The optimal binary partitioning algorithm of [15] can be applied because the work space area can be reduced to the reasonable cuts only thus reducing the unreasonable cuts. It is based on the branch and bound algorithm.

The optimal binary partitioning algorithm for the vertical fragmentation can be implemented exactly in the same manner with the horizontal partitioning (by substituting the attribute usage matrix by the predicate usage matrix) with a complexity of $O(2^n)$. Trivially, the optimal binary horizontal partitioning produces two fragments. The same algorithm is implemented recursively on each two sub-fragments separately to obtain the desired fragments.

In case there is a large number of fragments, the optimal binary partitioning can be implemented on each group of the reasonable cuts. Its complexity varies from $O(n)$ to $O(2^n)$ where n is the number of transactions.

IV- A Proposed Replication Algorithm

Redundancy is a concept introduced to a distributed database to increase the presence of data in the system. Replication becomes a necessity to improve data availability and system reliability during site failure and network partitioning. This essential improvement brings with it its own problems, mainly inconsistency among replicas of the same objects (fragments). Any system is considered valid if it is a One-Copy-Equivalent, i.e., replicas should hold the same version number as far as the user can tell. The latter condition is verified by a concurrency control protocol. Several proposed protocols tried to remedy inconstancy among replicas due to sites and link failures. Protocols takes advantage of the remaining operational links and sites in the network to render the system functional [2][4][5][7][8]. In this paper, we present an enhancement over the Replica Control Protocol in [8]. The enhancement reduces the number of replicas, minimizes the storage costs and reduces message and transfer cost by using a matrix log replicated at each site, while keeping the system available to the user during crashes and failures. Also, the protocol uses an adaptive algorithm to select the view corresponding to each site. The Enhanced Replicated Control Protocol is the conjunction of three parts: (a) setting the work space area and quorums, (b) applying the adaptive algorithm and (c) replicating a matrix log.

The first part considers sites in partitions intercommunicate with each other but never with sites in another partition. Sites are connected by bi-directional links. A unique identifier is assigned to each site. A distributed database consists of sets of objects (fragments) represented by $[x]$ residing at different site locations. A transaction T_i is an ordered set $(S_i <_i)$ where S_i is the set of all operations executed by T_i, $<_i$ reflects the order in which the transactions should be executed. Also a transaction reads and writes $[x]$ at most once and T_i reads $[x]$ before writing $[x]$. $R_i[x]$ is a read operation executed by T_i on $[x]$. $W_i[x]$ is write operation executed by T_i on $[x]$. Let *initiator* be the site where a transaction is issued. An operation is atomic if it commits or aborts all its operations to the database. Partitions may prevent some transactions from terminating the operations. Let $T=\{T_{init},T_1,T_2,...,T_i,...,T_n,T_{final}\}$ a set of transactions where T_{init} is a write transaction that initiates the database and T_{final} is a read operation that reads the final state of the database. The transaction execution is modeled by log file L, which is usually initiated with the execution of T_{init} and ends with T_{final}. Two operations conflict if they both operate on the same object and one of them is a $W_i[x]$. Let x_p represents object $[x]$ residing on site p. Each x_p·has a version number and is initialized by T_{init} applied on all replicas of object $[x]$. Let *copies*$[x]$ be the set of all copies of object $[x]$. Let *sites*$[x]$ be the set of site where object $[x]$ resides. The cardinality of *copies*$[x]$ is C. The logical write $W_i[x]$ is executed by:
1. selecting a set of *copies*$[x]$
2. determining V_{nmax} (version maximum number of situated copies) and
3. writing all the selected copies with a version number greater than V_{nmax}
   The logical read $R_i[x]$ is executed by:
1. selecting a set of *copies*$[x]$
2. accessing all the selected copies to find the one with the highest version number and
4. reading V_{nmax}.

Let $R_i[x_p]$, $A_i[x_p]$, $W_i[x_p]$ be the read, access and write operations executed on a copy x_p by transaction T_i respectively. Concerning for the read operation, it will read the needed replica associated to each view. The concurrency control protocol is performed during a write operation [8].

Definition 1: A view is a set of sites accessed by transactions from the initiator. Each view has a unique view id. Each initiator independently decides which sites to include in its current view and which replica of $[x]$, T can access using the adaptive algorithm.

Let $Ar[x]$ be the read accessibility of an object $[x]$. Let $Aw[x]$ be the write accessibility of an object $[x]$. In a view, the initiator view site accesses an object $[x]$ if it is $Ar[x]$ and/or $Aw[x]$. Accessibility satisfies that $Ar[x]+Aw[x]>C$, i.e., copies related to $Aw[x]$ should at least have one copy in common with $Ar[x]$ [8]. Since $Ar[x]$ and $Aw[x]$ in this study are occurring on the same object replica, the accessibility function becomes $2Ar[x] > C$ or $2Aw[x] > C$.

Definition 2: A quorum is the number of $Ar[x](.Aw[x])$ that identifies the way the accessibility threshold is achieved in view V.

Let $Qr[x,v]$ be a read quorum assigned to every $[x]$ in V, let $Qw[x,v]$ be write quorum assigned to every $[x]$ in V. Let C_v be the number of *copies*$[x]$ that reside on sites in a view V. In each view V, quorums of object $[x]$ satisfies the following relations:

☐ $Qr[x,v] + Qw[x,v] > C_v$ where $Qw[x,v]$ is executed after $Qr[x,v]$ in a given view V.

☐ $2Qw[x,v] > C_v$ the write quorum should write at least more than the half of replicas included in view V.

☐ $1 < Qr[x,v] < C_v$ that means at least one read quorum is required.

The second part of the Enhanced Replica Control Protocol is the Adaptive Algorithm leading each site to choose the optimal path to every required object in its view and is processed as follows:

Step 1: Initial determination of the best view

1. define the location of replicas replicated in the system according to

$$B_{ij} = \sum_k f_{kj} r_{kj} - C \times \sum_k \sum_{j' \neq j} f_{kj} u_{kj} \tag{9}$$

2. Initiate m transactions to replicas.

3. Put in an ascending order the average cost function taking into consideration transaction frequencies, response delays, storage costs, transfer constraints and other constraints.

Step 2: Creating and handling the matrix log.

1. uses the Initiate-New-View procedure [8] to create the create the matrix log where the results of average costs is stored

2. insures that the matrix log at each site is periodically updated by triggering 1.2

Step 3:

3. If a transaction is aborted (the site is down or there is a link failure) then the algorithm will refer to the matrix log to install Install-View procedure [8] using the next best link. This procedure will establish links with preferences to sites holding replicas of $[x]$

4. Repeat 3.1 until a view is established.

The system will remain operational until the last site holding a replica of object O_i is down.

The third part of the Enhanced Replica Control protocol is the installation of the matrix log that reduce the communication and message transfer cost in the read and write states from $2k+1$ messages to even one message in case of network partitioning. The $2k+1$ messages is the result of the following procedure used in [8]: (1) read the version number of the entire objects in the view with permissible $Ar[x]$, i.e., k messages broadcast for k accessible read object. (2) another k messages feedback, propagated backward to the initiator, notifying the version number of each replica with $Ar[x]$ in current view. Then 1 transfer message of the original read request is issued to the site holding the object with V_{nmax}. Since each $W_i[x]$ needs to read the latest version number of any $[x]$ before applying any changes, $W_i[x]$ will inquire the

$R_i[x]$, except in the absolute write case where no read prior to the $W_i[x]$ is required. However, instead of updating the whole transaction, only the version number is updated in the same manner, where as the updating of object occurs as a background process.

The improvement to reduce the $2k+1$ messages to 1 message, is as follows:
1. Each site adaptively chooses its view (refer to step 1).
2. Each view of the initiator site holds all the needed objects. Either the objects are stored on the initiator or on the assigned by current *View-id* sites. In other words, all fragments needed by the transaction T_i issued from S_1 must be located for example, in group of 8 sites, on (S_1,S_4,S_5,S_7,S_8). This group represents the view of S_1, in a manner that the most frequently used object is located at the view initiator (e.g. S_1,) to minimize the access, transfer and communication cost.
3. Each site has a *matrix log*. The matrix log contains information regarding the objects showing the sites they are replicated, their version number the ordering of cost function (refer to table 1).

Object Name	Replicated Site	Version Number	Order Cost function
O_1	$[S_1,S_3,S_5,S_7]$	$\{[S_1,13],[S_3,12],[S_5,13],[S_7,14]\}$	$\{[S_1,5],[S_3,7],[S_5,20],[S_7,26]\}$
O_2	$[S_2,S_5,S_8]$	$\{[S_2,25],[S_5,26],[S_8,25]\}$	$\{[S_2,20],[S_5,26],[S_8,45]\}$

Table 1. An example of a matrix log

Every time a site S_1 performs a local update in view V_1, only the *matrix logs* located at sites S_1, S_3, S_5, S_7 are updated. In this manner if transaction T_i, issued at site S_1, wants to read an object in a fragment. It will simply consult locally its *matrix log* and addresses itself to the designated site reducing the $2k+1$ message propagation protocol to a direct request for the site having the highest version number.

V-Conclusion and Future Work

In this paper we have presented an optimal horizontal partitioning algorithm and a replication protocol that increases the availability and reliability of a distributed database. The horizontal algorithm uses the optimal vertical transaction-based algorithm by replacing the vertical usage matrix with predicate usage matrix. To achieve this usage and adapting the notion of reasonable and unreasonable cuts, we have proved that there exists a reasonable cut that cost $\leq$ to the unreasonable cut.

The replication protocol enhances the availability and reliability of the system with a general reduction of communication cost. The protocol is achieved in three steps. First define the work area including setting the constraints and conditions. Second run an adaptive algorithm functional according to a user define cost function and third replicating a matrix log showing the storing places of replicas, their version numbers and the ordered cost function to update and retrieve data.

Further research can be accomplished to check if the mixed fragmentation using the optimal vertical fragmentation and the optimal horizontal fragmentation is also optimal, and evolving the adaptive algorithm to decide how to optimally replicate the resulted fragments during view installation.

References

[1] S. Ceri, M. Negri, G. Pelagatti, "Horizontal Data Partitioning in Database Design," *ACM*, pp. 128-136, 1982.

[2] S. Ceri, S. Navathe, G. Wiederhold, "Distribution Design of Logical Database Schemas," *IEEE Transactions on Software Engineering*, vol. SE-9, no. 4, pp. 487-503, Jul. 1983.

[3] S. Navathe, S. Ceri, G. Wiederhold, J. Dou, "Vertical Partitioning Algorithms for Database Design," *ACM Transactions on Database Systems*, vol. 9, no. 4, pp. 680-710, Dec. 1984.

[4] S. Ceri, G. Pelagetti, *Distributed Databases: Principles and Systems*, McGraw-Hill, 1984.

[5] M. Herlihy, "Dynamic Quorum Adjustment for Partitioned Data", *ACM Transaction on Database Systems*, vol. 12, no. 2, pp. 170-194, Jun 1987.

[6] P. M. G. Apers, "Data Allocation in Distributed Database Systems", *ACM Transaction on Database System*, vol. 13, no. 3, pp. 263-304, Sept. 1988.

[7] H. M. Gladney, "Data Replicas in Distributed Information Services", *ACM Transaction on Database Systems*, vol. 14, no. 1, pp. 75-97, Mar. 1989.

[8] A. E. Abbadi, S. Toueg, "Maintaining Availability in Partitioned Replicated Databases", *ACM Transaction on Database Systems*, vol. 14, no. 2, pp. 246-290, Jun. 1989.

[9] S. B. Navathe, M. Ra, "Vertical Partitioning for database Design: a Graphical Algorithm," *ACM SIGMOD*, pp. 440-450, Jun. 1989.

[10] D. Agrawal, A. El Abbadi, "Storage Efficient Replicated Databases", *IEEE Transactions on Knowledge and Data Engineering*, vol. 2, no.3, pp. 342-352, Sept. 1990.

[11] P. Triantafilou, D. TAYLOR, "Efficiently Maintaining Availability in the Presence of Partitionings in Distributed Systems", *IEEE*, 1991.

[12] D. Agrawal, A. El Abbadi, "The Generalized Tree Quorum Protocol: An Efficient Approach for Managing Replicated Data", *ACM Transactions on Database Systems,* vol. 17, no. 4, pp. 689-717, Dec. 1992.

[13] D. Bell, J. Grimson, *Distributed Database Systems*, Addison-Wesley Pub, 1992.

[14] M. Ra, "Horizontal Partitioning for Distributed Database Design: a Graph-Based Approach", *Australasian Database Conference: Brisbane*, pp. 101-120, 1993.

[15] W. W. Chu, I. T. Ieong, "A Transaction-Based Approach to Vertical Partitioning for Relational Database Systems," *IEEE Transactions on Software Engineering*, vol. 19, no. 8, pp. 804-812, Aug. 1993.

[16] Y. Zhang, "On Horizontal Fragmentation of Distributed Database Design," *Australian Database Conference: Brisbane*, pp. 121-130, 1993.

[17] M. L .Liu, D. Agrawal, A. El Abbadi, "What Price Replication?", *Technical Report TRCS94-14,* Computer Science Department, University of California, Santa Barbara, Jul. 1994.

[18] S. Chakravarthy, J. Muthuraj, R. Varadarajian, S. B. Navathe, "An Objective Function for Vertically Partitioned Relations in Distributed Database and Its Analysis", *Distributed and Parallel Databases*, vol. 2, pp. 183-207, 1994.

[19] P. Triantafilou, D. J. Taylor, "The Location-Based Paradigm for Replication: Achieving Efficiency and Availability in Distributed Systems", *IEEE Transaction on Software Engineering*, vol. 21, no. 1, pp. 1-17, Jan. 1995.

[20] P. Triantafilou, D. J. Taylor, "VELOS: A New Approach for Efficiently Achieving High Availability in Partitioned Distributed Systems", *IEEE Transactions on Knowledge and Data Engineering,* vol. 8, no. 2, pp. 305-321, Apr. 1996.

[21] M. Nicola, M. Jarkej, "Integration Replication and Communication in Performance Models of Distributed Databases", *Technical Report–Technical University of Aachen, Informatik V (Information Systems)*, Germany 1997.

[22] K. Karlapalem, N. M. Pun, "Query Driven Data Allocation Algorithms for Distributed Database Systems", *Proceedings of the 8th Int'l Conference on Data and Expert Systems Application (DEXA)*, pp. 347-356, Sept. 1997.

Object Clustering Methods and a Query Decomposition Strategy for Distributed Object-Based Information Systems

Eric Leclercq, Marinette Savonnet,
Marie-Noëlle Terrasse, and Kokou Yétongnon

Université de Bourgogne
Laboratoire Ld'Electronique Informatique et Image (LE2I)
B.P. 47870 - 21078 Dijon Cedex - France
{savonnet,terrasse,kokou}@khali.u-bourgogne.fr

Abstract. Emerging developments and advances in distributed processing have created a need for tools and methods to partition and distribute information systems across interconnected processors. In particular, distribution approaches which take into account the key characteristics of OO concepts are required to extend traditional fragmentation results to object oriented database systems. To fulfill the above requirements, we propose a methodology for the distribution design of object-based information systems. The underlying approach consists of techniques and heuristics that can be used to create clusters of inter-related object classes that can be fragmented interdependently, producing distribution units called tree-fragments. We define a corresponding tree-fragment based approach to query decomposition and execution. Several method activation flow metrics are used to support allocation of tree-fragments to network sites.

1 Introduction

In recent years, object oriented development and distributed processing have become increasingly popular. The OO paradigm is becoming a de facto design tool 1)for capturing both structural and behavioral properties of complex information systems via object classes, and 2) for organizing classes in relationship hierarchies (including inheritance, aggregation or composition). Distributed processing ranging from parallel architecture and client-server computing to internet and intranet computing provide frameworks for exploiting the benefits of the inherent parallelism and distribution of object based applications.

Database distribution design has been the focus of a number of investigations. The primary goal is to 1) partition a database into appropriate distribution units, and 2) allocate the distribution units to interconnected processors in a way that minimizes processing costs. Previous work in distribution design has focused to a large extent on traditional file-based and relational-based information systems. The primary concern of this research effort has been on what fragmentation techniques are, how these techniques fit into conceptual design methodologies, how to optimize file allocation among systems, and what tools and protocols are needed to allow inter-system communication and remote execution of applications. Recently, there have been attempts to extend the results of these initial research efforts to distributed object computing. For example, at the middle architecture level, OMG's CORBA standards provide various protocols and environment to create, distribute and process objects across the boundaries of a collection of independents systems or machines. At a conceptual level, relational partitioning methods have been extended for distribution design of OO applications [1, 3, 6].

To use distributed object computing effectively requires appropriate distribution strategies to provide guidelines on how to model application and how to evaluate distribution costs. In [5] Karlapalem has discussed several issues of distribution design and has pointed out the lack of fragmentation and allocation methods for OO systems. In this paper we will focus on the definition of a methodology for partitioning and distributing object-based information systems. The approach is based on techniques and heuristics 1) for creating clusters of inter-related object classes which can be fragmented interdependently and 2) for an allocation method and query decomposition based on a cost model which uses a variety of flow measures.

The remainder of the paper is organized as follows. We present an overview of the OO distribution methodology in the next section. A strategy for query decomposition is detailed in section 3 while section 4 presents the bases for allocation. Section 5 concludes the paper and presents the on-going work.

2 Fragtique: An OO distribution design methodology

In this section we present an overview of the OO distribution approach. First we briefly present the key components of the distribution design approach. Then we discuss the properties of local sufficiency, semantically natural methods, queries and relevant issues of distributed object computing.

2.1 An overview of the steps of the Fragtique OO distribution design

Figure 1 presents the different steps and concepts used by the methodology. A brief description of the steps is given below. A more detailed description of the first two (fragmentation) steps can be found in [2].

•**Pre-fragmentation:** Defining an appropriate level of granularity for partitioning a database is an essential step in the distribution methodology. Several fragmentation granularities can be identified including individual objects, classes of objects or groups of classes. In Fragtique, fragmentation units are groups of inter-related classes, called partition-trees. The primary goal of this step is to determine these units and the related key concept of "cut-links". As depicted in figure 2.a, the input of the step is an OO application specification consisting of a conceptual graph (figure 2.b) and methods' navigation paths (2.c). The output of the step are sets of partition-trees and cut-links. Partition-trees are

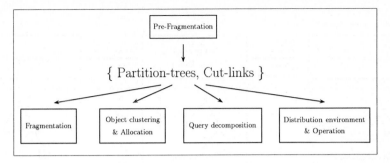

Fig. 1. Distribution design

constructed by using heuristics to maintain strong inter-relationships that exist among classes. Cut-links represent edges that are removed from the conceptual graph when it is broken into a set of partition-trees. Thus, these edges are not included in any partition-tree, and can be used to evaluate methods activities among class-fragments.

•**Main fragmentation step:** This step creates for each partition-tree one or more distribution units called tree-fragments. This is done by substituting extensions (set of object instances) for the conceptual classes of the partition-tree. The resulting instantiated classes are fragmented interdependently to determine the class-fragments for classes directly linked to the root class. This process is repeated by considering each added class-fragment as the root of a tree. The fragmentation derivation method aims at maintaining in a tree-fragment the inter-class relationships of the corresponding partition-tree.

•**Object clustering and allocation:** This step consists of two phases. First, an object cluster-graph is created to evaluate method activation and data flows among tree-fragments. The nodes of a cluster-graph are object-clusters consisting of instances which behave similarly with respect to method activations. Next, the allocation process is based on method activation flow metrics. The main objective is to create allocation groups in which each tree-fragment exhibits strong inter-communication with other members of the group.

•**Query decomposition:** This step defines a query processing method which takes into account key characteristics of the proposed distribution methodology. In particular decomposition is based on the property of local sufficiency which aims to break up a query in such a way that subqueries can execute independently on their corresponding sites.

2.2 OO distribution design: modeling methods and queries

Besides the semantic properties (structural, behavioral and inter-relations descriptions), quantitative information related to methods and query processing play an important role in the construction of partition-trees, class-fragments and allocation blocks. To take into account quantitative information in the distribution design, we need a model to represent method activation and usage patterns

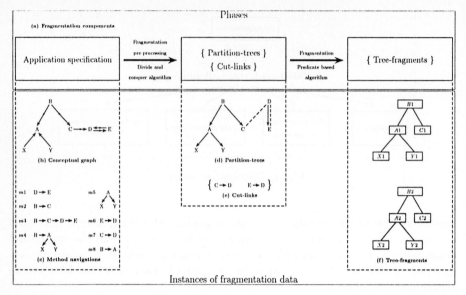

Fig. 2. Fragmentation phases

and properties. This is achieved by two concepts: a method navigation-model and the property of local sufficiency of method.

Method navigation-model: The model of a method m is a path expression and related concepts which are formally described by the following navigation-model

$$Navig(m) = (Def(m), SPaths(m), SPreds(m))$$

where the components of $Navig(m)$ are as follows:

• $Def(m)$ determines the set of classes, called *entry points* of m, which can be starting classes for method m. This includes the class C and all classes which can be substituted for C using subclass relationships. Other classes traversed by a path of m are called internal classes. For example, in figure 2.c, the entry classes of method $m5$ of class A are classes A, X and Y.

• $SPaths(m)$ is a set of navigation paths used by m to traverse and access object classes. Consider a navigation path of a method m denoted by $P = (C_1, \ldots, C_n)$ where C_1 is the entry point. Each navigation step $(C_i, C_{i+1})_{(i=1..n-1)}$ must satisfy OO semantic navigation requirements. That is $(C_i, C_{i+1})_{(i=1..n-1)}$ is a valid navigation step if 1) link (C_i, C_{i+1}) is a generalization or a composition link in the conceptual schema or 2) link (C_{i+1}, C_i) is a specialization link of the conceptual schema.

• $SPreds(m)$ is a set of predicates associated with the navigation paths of m. For each navigation path P of $SPreds(m)$, a selection predicate denoted by $Pred(m, P, C)$ is associated with each class C comprising P to specify the objects of C retrieved by the traversal of the path.

Method navigation-model are used to guarantee that navigation steps are consistent with the semantics of the database schema. We use this property to define the property of semantically natural queries which extends to OO database the definition proposed by Wong et al in [9] who define the concept of "natural" relations as a restriction of relational queries to contain only equijoin operations along referential constraint paths.

Local sufficiency properties: Local sufficiency properties are used to guarantee that queries can be decomposed into two or more independent sub-queries which can be executed on a set of tree-fragments assigned to interconnected sites. Formally, local sufficiency is characterized by:

- A navigation-path $P = (C_1, \ldots, C_n)$ is *locally sufficient* with respect to a fragmentation result if it contains no navigation step that corresponds to a cut-link. Thus, all navigation steps of P access data in classes contained in the same tree-fragment.
- A navigation-path $P = (C_1, \ldots, C_n)$ is *piece-wise locally sufficient* with respect to a fragmentation result if P can be decomposed into two consecutive sub-paths $P1$ and $P2$ such that 1) $P1$ is locally sufficient, 2) the link from the end node of $P1$ to the start node of $P2$ is a cut-link and 3) $P2$ is locally sufficient or piece-wise locally sufficient.

A method m is locally sufficient if it consists of locally sufficient navigation-paths. Similarly, m is piece-wise locally sufficient if it contains only locally sufficient paths and piece-wise locally sufficient paths.

3   Query decomposition based on tree-fragments

The object distribution methodology of Fragtique is defined to capture and maintain strong semantic bond among the component class-fragments of tree-fragments. In addition, to satisfy the local sufficiency requirements, the elements of a tree-fragment are allocated as a single unit to a process site. In order to meet the above requirement, we propose a new approach to query decomposition and execution. The query decomposition methodology must deal with several problems including locating and processing data; moving a query or subquery to remote site if the requested data is not at the local site; and providing the required operations for combining the partial results of subqueries. We describe the query decomposition and show how local sufficiency requirements can be satisfied by a query.

Selecting the candidate partition-trees Query submission and execution is based on the following schema. A query m is submitted to the distributed object by a user at a site S_{query} which becomes the home site responsible for breaking the query and processing the final result. The effective execution and evaluation of data transfer cost incurred by the query m requires 1) the identification of the tree-fragments and 2) the selection of the sites that contained the data accessed by m. To achieve this, the navigation-graph $Navig(m)$ of m is determined. $Navig(m)$ is used to select the candidate tree-fragments required by method m. This is done by mapping the navigation-paths of m onto the partition-trees of the distributed database to determine the set $PT(m) = \{pt_i\}_{i \in 1...n}$ consisting of partition-trees that are relevant to the execution of m. The classes of the navigation-graph $Navig(m)$ are covered by the set $PT(m)$, that is each class of $Navig(m)$ is included in one and only one partition-tree of $PT(m)$. However, because the navigation-graph $Navig(m)$ may contain one or more cut-links, some of its edges may not be covered by $PT(m)$. Let denote by $Missing(m)$ the edges of $Navig(m)$ which are not covered by $PT(m)$. The execution of method m consists of the following steps.

– This step tests if method m satisfies local sufficiency properties. Depending on whether the set $Missing(m)$ is empty or not and on where the missing edges are located in navigation paths, three cases can be distinguished:

• If $Missing(m) = \emptyset$, $PT(m)$ contains a single partition-tree which necessarily covers both the classes and the directed edges of $Navig(m)$. So m is locally sufficient.

• If $Missing(m)$ contains one or more links which are internal links in some navigation-paths of m, the set $PT(m)$ contains one or more partition-trees. The execution of m can be decomposed into two parts. In the first part, the sub-methods of m are executed in parallel on several partition-trees until a link (cut-link) of $Missing(m)$ is reached. This partial execution satisfies the property of local sufficiency. The execution of the second part involves the traversal of a cut-link followed by the remote execution of some sub-methods of m. This remote execution can be carried out in parallel over several tree-fragments. So method m is piece-wise locally sufficient. To illustrate this case, consider a method m consisting of the execution of sub-method $m2$ followed by sub-method $m7$. The navigation path (B, C, D, E) of m comprises a cut-link (C, D). The first partial execution involves a navigation from B to C, which can be executed in parallel. The second partial execution consists in traversing the cut-link (C, D). Finally, a partial execution corresponding to the navigation link (D, E) is carried out.

• If the missing links of the set $Missing(m)$ represent a sub-path which starts from the entry point of the method, the property of local sufficiency can not be verified by method m. The results of the decomposition of method m depends on cut-links whose end nodes may not be root classes. Thus, the decomposition may not correspond to any tree-fragment.

– This step is devoted to the identification of the set *matched tree-fragments* of tree-fragments relevant to the execution of a method. The identification of the sites corresponding to the tree-fragments is based on the fragmentation and allocation schema. Let $TF(pt)$ denotes the set of tree-fragments of a partition-tree pt. Denote by $Pred(tf)$ the selectivity predicate associated with each tree-fragment tf.

To determine the set of matched tree-fragments of a method m, we distinguish the following cases:

- If method m is locally sufficient, let pt be the single partition-tree in $PT(m)$, E the entry point of m and $Pred(m, P, E)$ the selectivity predicate of E in $Navig(m)$. By comparing $Pred(m, P, E)$ and predicates $Pred(tf)_{tf \in TF(pt)}$, the set $MatchedTF(m, pt)$ consisting of the tree-fragments referenced by the execution of m can be determined and used to compute the set of matched sites.

- If method m is piece-wise locally sufficient, denote by $pt_1 \ldots pt_n$ partition-trees of $PT(m)$. By a construction similar to first case above, the set *matched tree-fragments* is given by the set of tree-fragments used by partial executions that do not involve cut-links:
$$\bigcup_{pt_i \in PT(m)} MatchedTF(m, pt_i).$$

- This case corresponds to a method which is not locally sufficient. The set of matched tree-fragments is determined by the tree-fragments corresponding to all partition-trees of $PT(m)$. It is defined by:
$$\bigcup_{pt_i \in PT(m)} TF(pt_i).$$

4 Allocation

The allocation of distribution units (tree-fragments) to sites is based on a set of metrics which are used to evaluate method activation flows through tree-fragments. To define the metrics we construct *cluster-graph* to allow efficient flow evaluation by avoiding costly calculations on large number of individual objects. The metrics are used to determine distribution units called *virtual-blocks*.

4.1 Modeling method activity

Distribution design can be done at different granularities. The *object graph* level is a fine-grain level based on inter-object references. Object distribution and placement algorithms used at this level are high cost graph partitioning techniques [4]. Fragtique is based on a medium-grain level consisting of clusters composed of objects that exhibit the same behavior with respect to method activations. Abstraction mapping functions are used to associate nodes and edges of object graph, cluster-graph and conceptual schema. At the cluster-graph level, incident paths that are medium-grain weighted instantiations of navigation paths are used to model method activities.

A *Cluster-graph* is a multi-graph consisting of nodes (object-clusters) and directed edges corresponding to flows of method activations among the nodes. it includes two types of nodes: Starting cluster nodes (entry point from which method activation flows are propagated) and internal nodes. The nodes and edges of the cluster-graph are derived from a set of components (classes and navigation-paths) related to cut-links. These components from a cluster-domain. A detailed description of cluster-domain can be found in [8]. The *Object-clusters* are constructed as follows:

1) object-clusters partition a class into several non empty disjoint subsets,

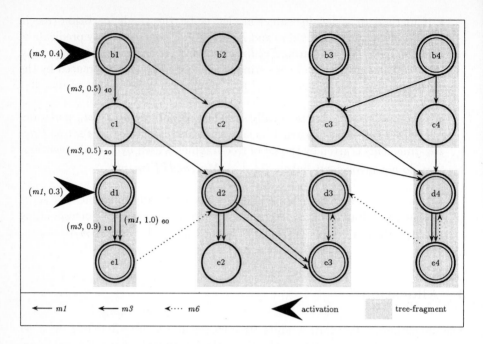

Fig. 3. Cluster Graph & corresponding tree-fragments

2) a method induces subsets, which are determined by using and propagating the predicates associated with the navigation-paths, on the classes it traverses. The objects of a class which are not selected by any predicates of the methods are regrouped in an extra subset,

3) given a class C and a set S of subsets of C, a partition of C (in a mathematical sense) over S is a set of pairwise disjoint subsets of C, computed by the usual set operators, whose union equals C.

4.2   Quantifying method activity

The quantification of method activation is represented by two types information. The first corresponds to method usage pattern and the second indicates how method activity span the classes of OO schema. These information are represented in the cluster-graph by labels associated with edges and nodes.

- Labels: Each starting cluster is associated with label of the form (m_i, f_i) where m_i is a method and f_i is the fraction of m_i's global activation that is addressed to the considered object-cluster.

The label of an edge e_i is defined by $(m_i, f_i)_{n_i}$ where m_i identifies the method, f_i is a coefficient representing the fraction of times an activation of m_i traverses e_i and n_i is the input activation of the source node of the edge.

Figure 3 shows an example of label assignments. The starting cluster $b1$ is associated a label $(m3, 0.4)$ and edge $(b1, c1)$ is associated a label $(m3, 0.5)_x$. If the global input activation for $m3$ is set to 100, starting cluster $b1$ will be activated by 40, edge $(b1, c1)$'s label will be instantiated in $(m3, 0.5)_{40}$ and edge $(b1, c1)$'s flow is quantified by 20.

- *Incident-path* are used to compute the weight of an edge. An incident-path into an edge e of the cluster-graph instantiates the navigation of a method from a starting cluster to the cluster e. The computation of the cumulative weights n_i along an incident path is carried out by propagating method activation flow counts along the edges of a path and by multiplying the corresponding weights by the coefficient of the edge. A cumulative weight is associated to an edge e depending of the set $SetIPath(e)$ of all incidence paths whose e is the last edge. For example, in Figure 3 labels are instantiated for a global input activation of 100 for $m3$ on $b1$ and 200 for $m1$ on $d1$. The $Weight((d1, e1))$ associated with the edge $(d1, e1)$ is given by the following:

$Weight((d1, e1), m1) = 200 * 0.3 * 1.0 = 60$,

$Weight((d1, e1), m3) = 100 * 0.4 * 0.5 * 0.5 * 0.9 = 9$.

Thus $Weight((d1, e1)) = 69$.

Flow measures that quantify remaining activity between tree-fragments are deduced by trivial summations from quantification of the cluster-graph. For example in Figure 3 remaining activity between the tree-fragments containing clusters $b1$ and $d2$ respectively is given by the sum of $Weight((c1, d2))$ and $Weight((c2, d2))$. Both tree-fragment flow measures and work load measures are detailed in [8].

4.3   Virtual-blocks

Allocation pre-processing consists in constructing virtual-blocks by grouping tree-fragments. It is based on the two phases of K-nearest-neighbours algorithm: First, for each tree-fragment a distance string is constructed with others tree-fragments in decreasing order of tree-fragment flow measures. In contrast to classical algorithm, here tree-fragment flow measures are not a distance but a pre-order. Second, each distance string is used to produce a sub-string adapted to maximum work load of virtual sites. We assume virtual sites not dedicated to specific application which have uniform work load. See [8] for more details about list construction. Each selected list is called a virtual-block and there is an associated external flow value which represents the sum of method invocation flows going out of the block. To determine the set of allocation units, a covering set of the tree-fragments is extracted from the union of virtual-blocks. The cost model used for allocating virtual-blocks is detailed in [7]

5   Conclusion

In this paper, we have focused on fundamental issues of OO distribution design. A major goal of our work is that OO distribution design must be carried out at both the conceptual level where the structural relationships of a system are defined and the instance level where method and query access patterns and inter-object references can be evaluated. We have presented the Fragtique OO distribution methodology that achieves the above goal by using partition-trees to capture strong inter-relation among groups of classes and by fragmenting them interdependently to preserve the relationships among class-fragments. In addition, we define a query decomposition strategy to allow effective parallel execution over the distributed class-fragments.

Our on-going work is directed at two levels. First,we are investigating how the issues involved in the allocation phase can be formalized to define analysis method to allow a designer to monitor the impact of distribution on an application, refine the partition of OO database and respond to changes in the usage characteristics of queries. Second, we are defining an environment of tools to support the distribution methodology. The tools can be used to achieve semi-automated distribution design and can be included in the life cycle of an application.

References

1. Ladjel BELLATRECHE, Kamalakar KARLAPALEM, and Ana SIMONET. Horizontal Class Partitioning in Object-Oriented Databases. In *Lecture Notes in Computer Science*, volume 1308, pages 58–67, Toulouse – France, September 1997.
2. Djamal BENSLIMANE, Eric LECLERCQ, Marinette SAVONNET, Marie-Noëlle TERRASSE, and Kokou YÉTONGNON. Distributing Object-Oriented Databases. *Journal of Computing Information*, 1999.
3. C.I. EZEIFE and Ken BARKER. A Comprehensive Approach to Horizontal Class Fragmentation in a Distributed Object Based System. *Distributed and Parallel Databases*, 3(3):247–272, July 1995.
4. Shahram GHANDEHARIZADEH and David WILHITE. Placement of Objects in Parallel Object-Based Systems. Technical Report 94-589, Department of Computer Science – University of Southern California, 1994.
5. Kamalakar KARLAPALEM, Shamkant B. NAVATHE, and Magdi M.A. MORSI. Issues in Distribution Design of Object-Oriented Databases. In Valduriez Özsu, Dayal, editor, *Distributed Object Management*, pages 149–164. Morgan Kaufmann, 1994.
6. Franck RAVAT. La fragmentation d'un schéma conceptuel orienté objet. *Ingénierie des systèmes d'information (ISI)*, 4(2):161–193, 1996.
7. Marinette SAVONNET, Marie-Noëlle TERRASSE, and Kokou YÉTONGNON. Object Clustering Methods and a Cost Model for the Design of Distributed Object-Oriented Databases. In *Proceedings of the ISCA International Conference on Parallel and Distributed Computing Systems (PDCS'99)*, 1999.
8. Marinette SAVONNET, Marie-Noëlle TERRASSE, and Kokou YÉTONGNON. Partitioning and Allocating Object-Oriented Databases. In *Proceedings of the International Conference on Database Systems for Advanced Applications (DASFAA'99)*, Hsinchu – Taiwan, April 1999.
9. E. WONG and R. H. KATZ. Distributing a Database for Parallelism. *Proceedings ACM SIGMOD International Conference on Management of Data*, 13(4):23–29, May 1983. San Jose C.A.

Dynamic Adjustment of Localized Constraints

Mateusz Pietrzyk, Subhasish Mazumdar, and Robert Cline

Department of Computer Science
New Mexico Institute of Mining and Technology
Socorro, NM 87801, USA

Abstract. Distributed integrity constraints are costly to check; they may also conflict with site autonomy for multidatabases. It has been shown that simple distributed linear inequality constraints can be broken up into independent local constraints that can be dynamically adjusted. Earlier, we have given a framework for generalizing this approach and shown that more complex constraints can be handled on its basis. In this paper, we focus on dynamic adjustment of the local constraints. Special care is needed for constraints that are more complex than linear inequalities since simultaneous requests for constraint adjustment can lead to inconsistency. We have explored various issues including the problem of simultaneity, and have tested our solutions using an implementation. Our experimental results show that simultaneity is important, that our solutions are effective, and the overall strategy of localization is successful.

1 Introduction

While database integrity is an important guarantee provided by Database Management Systems, the cost of integrity checking for complex constraints limits the guarantee in practice. Several methods of simplification of the constraints have been suggested [2], [4], [5], [11], [13], for centralized databases. In particular, it was pointed out that sufficient tests are also useful [14]. Distributed databases exacerbate the problem of constraint maintenance [9]; there are a lot more constraints to maintain when databases are distributed: fragmentation and replication both generate integrity constraints. Verifying a distributed constraint at the end of a transaction, even one that is local, could involve the expenses associated with distributed transactions: network communication, commit protocols, distributed concurrency control for synchronization of remote data. Further, in case the constraint is not satisfied, the penalty is more severe, since rollback and recovery must occur at all participating sites. In multidatabases, aborting a local transaction simply for a violation of a distributed constraint may not be acceptable because this may conflict with local autonomy. Simply adapting some of the strategies of centralized databases [12] is clearly not enough.

An interesting idea is that simple linear numeric inequality constraints of the form $x_1 \leq x_2$ (where x_1 and x_2 reside at different sites, hence distributed) can be broken up into a pair of *local* inequalities $x_1 \leq L_1$ and $x_2 \geq L_2$ where L_1, L_2 are quotas assigned such that $L_1 \leq L_2$. These quotas are dynamically adjustable:

in case the quota is violated, communication needs to be is established between the sites and a new quota set up at one or both sites. The Demarcation Protocol [1] is a development of this idea. But it works only for linear inequalities.

We have broadened its limited scope by observing that the key idea is that for some distributed constraints, it is possible to find a conjunction of entirely *local* constraints that forms a *sufficient condition* for the original constraint [7,8,15]. A geometric interpretation allows us to find such local sufficient conditions. We focus here on the dynamic changes of these localized constraints. Unfortunately, the algorithms of the Demarcation Protocol are not enough when the constraints get complex. The reason is that for very simple constraints like linear inequalities, requests for adjustment of local constraints that are sent concurrently by more than one node do not pose a problem. But for more complex constraints, such concurrent requests for constraint changes may result in inconsistencies.

The paper is structured as follows. First, we survey related work. Next, we review the framework of localization, give an introduction to the geometric method, and present an initial algorithm for dynamic adjustment of constraints which ensures that simultaneous requests are detected. In the following section, we explore issues related to the implementation of the algorithm. In the subsequent section, we report experiments with the implementation that give us insight regarding the performance of the algorithm and the effectiveness of the basic strategy. Finally, we make concluding remarks.

2 Related Work

Reformulation of distributed constraints was suggested for finding the optimal among a set of semantically equivalent alternatives of the original constraint [10] and also for finding alternatives that were local [9]. Our approach explores sufficient, instead of equivalent, conditions, and thus has a broader scope.

The Demarcation Protocol [1] can be used to maintain distributed linear arithmetic inequality constraints. We have broadened its range of constraints and have a more elaborate algorithm with the necessary concurrency control.

In [3], local sufficient conditions of the distributed constraint are generated exploiting the fact that the constraint is satisfied by the database before state change. However, it does not update the local conditions dynamically.

The basis for a design-time tool was outlined in [6] to analyze constraints as well as transactions, derive sufficient conditions using a metric for constraint locality. It was shown that predicates based on binary relations such as total and partial orders and equivalence relations are amenable to this approach.

3 Dynamic Localization

We assume that data is distributed among nodes $1, 2, ..., N$. A constraint C is *local* if it involves data at only one node and *distributed* otherwise. A distributed constraint C is *localizable* if there is a rule $C_1 \wedge C_2 \wedge ... \wedge C_N \rightarrow C$, where C_i is a local constraint at node i (for variables and quantifier scope, the rules of Horn clauses apply). We denote the left side of the rule by SC, a sufficient condition for C, and say that C is *localizable through* SC. The simultaneous enforcement of the local C_i's at each node i implies the distributed constraint C.

Since SC is only sufficient for C, some local update at j may violate C_j, and hence SC, while still satisfying C. In this case, we would like SC to be changeable to, say, $SC' = C'_1 \wedge C'_2 \wedge ... \wedge C'_N$ that would accommodate the updated value. However, the change of SC to SC' must not require a distributed transaction.

SC is said to be *incrementally changeable to* SC' *through a sequence of constraints* $W_0(= SC), ..., W_i, ..., W_N(= SC')$ if, for $1 \leq i \leq N$, $W_i \rightarrow C$ and the difference between W_{i-1} and W_i is that exactly *one* conjunct C_j (for some j) in W_{i-1} is replaced by C'_j in W_i. Such a change of SC to SC' is referred to as *Incremental Update*.

By *Dynamic Localization*, we mean the substitution of C by SC, and its dynamic adjustment through Incremental Update. Thus, for a local transaction at i that satisfies the local C_i, no global constraint is checked and no network communication costs are incurred. Incremental Update can be done one node at a time, i.e., without a distributed transaction thus avoiding expensive commit protocols and distributed concurrency control.

3.1 A Geometric Method for Localization

Any constraint $C(x_1, ..., x_N)$ with $\mathcal{R}$ being the domain of $x_1, ..., x_N$ defines a domain $Dom(C)$ in the N-dimensional Cartesian space, with the i-th coordinate for x_i. Geometrically, the datum $(x_1, ..., x_N)$ satisfies C if and only if $(x_1, ..., x_N) \in Dom(C)$. Suppose we can find $R_1, ..., R_N$, each a range of $\mathcal{R}$, such that

$$(x_1 \in R_1) \wedge ... \wedge (x_N \in R_N) \rightarrow [(x_1, ..., x_N) \in Dom(C)]. \qquad (1)$$

Then C is localizable. From a geometric viewpoint, the left hand side of (1) defines a *rectangular subset* of $Dom(C)$. All we need to do for localization therefore is to find and maintain a (N-dimensional) rectangle that is contained within $Dom(C)$. Each node i needs to maintain x_i within the projection of the rectangle on the axis x_i. Incremental update allows the change of one rectangle into another making sure that all intermediate rectangles are contained within $Dom(C)$. Thus, the geometric approach reduces to rectangle management.

For example, let $C = \sum_{i=1}^m a_i x_1^{b_i} x_2^{c_i} \leq 0$, where b_i and c_i are non-negative integers whose $Dom(C)$ is the interior of an ellipse (Figure 1). Initially, let $x_1 = u, x_2 = v$. The data is the point P for which we construct the rectangle AB (diagonal) which encloses P, is within the ellipse, and is maximal. The local constraints are $(p < x_1 < q)$ and $(r < x_2 < s)$ for 1 and 2 respectively. Now let a local transaction at node 1 attempt to change x_1 from u to u', i.e., move P to P', which is not in rectangle AB but still inside the ellipse. Node 2 then computes a new rectangle (shown dashed) with diagonal CD, computes the new projections on x_1, x_2 which then become the new local constraints. The intermediate rectangle is the intersection of AB and CD; it too is inside the ellipse. The algorithms for rectangle computation is given in [8, 7].

As an aside, referring to Figure 1, note that both nodes may concurrently send requests to each other effectively desiring to move point P to Q: such a change is a legal since Q is inside the ellipse. However, with a linear inequality constraint (and a maximal rectangle), such concurrent requests always imply an illegal change. Here we are dealing with more complex constraints and we accommodate such legal concurrent requests by processing them in a sequence.

3.2   Initial Algorithm for Incremental Update

There are three processes [8] at node i: Req_i, Con_i, Acc_i (the subscript is dropped when the node is obvious) that sleep and awake periodically. Also, there is a flag F_i which is set when a constraint change request is pending and a queue $RequestQueue_i$ containing those pending requests.

Assume that $N = 2$ and data x_1, x_2 are at nodes 1 and 2 respectively and a transaction at 1 attempting to update x_1 to x_1' is aborted because it would violate C_1. Node 1 then enqueues x_1' and initiates a change of constraints. Req_1 wakes up, finds x_1' enqueued, sends a message to node 2 passing C_1 and x_1'. This message invokes Con_2.

Con_2 first locks x_2 (in some way, the data is prevented from changing while the constraint is revised; locking need not be the concurrency control technique) and then invokes an algorithm CSEARCH which searches for an appropriate C_1', C_2'. If this search is successful, then C_2 is changed to C_2', x_2 is unlocked, and a message is sent to node 1 with C_1'. If unsuccessful, a "no" message is sent instead and x_2 is unlocked. This message invokes Acc_1.

If the message is "no", Acc_1 just dequeues x_1'. Otherwise, it also updates C_1 to C_1', and arranges for the re-execution of the problematic transaction.

The algorithms are designed to recognize simultaneous (more correctly, concurrent) initiations of constraint change. This case is important since Con_1 and Con_2 may decide on different SC'''s and inconsistency could result. Both Con's detect this situation by checking their F's. The requests are ignored and re-sent after a random delay. Eventually they will be processed sequentially.

4   Implementing the Algorithm

While implementing the algorithm outlined in the previous section, we made three modifications. First, if the global constraint is more complex than a single convex region, a single rectangle provides limited coverage of the global constraint and therefore less transactions remain local. So, we added support for a union of rectangles (i.e., multiple intervals at nodes). Second, we introduced *independent* and *invalid intervals* to further enhance local processing: an local update falling into such intervals can be executed or rejected respectively. An *independent (invalid) interval* at node i as a range such that if the local data value at i is within it, the global constraint is (never) satisfied regardless of the data values at other nodes. Third, to eliminate inefficiencies when the user throughput is high, the processes were driven by interrupts rather than periodic sleep-wakeup cycles.

Also, in order to mimic a transaction environment and allow variation of parameters for experimentation, we have introduced three additional processes, *Usr*, *Trn*, and *Del* at each node. *Usr*, a *user* process generates updates, *Trn*, a *transaction* process executes user updates; in case of local constraint violation, it enqueues the offending user update in *RequestQueue*, and *Del*, *delay* processes simulate network delay; they buffer and delay every inter-node message.

When processes that handle messages are asynchronous, messages transmitted by the network in order may not be *processed* by the destination node in order. This can cause incorrect simultaneity detection, and even an infinite loop.

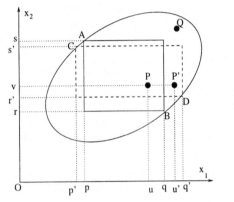

Fig. 1. Rectangle AB is incrementally updated to CD as P moves to P'.

Fig. 2. Messages received in order can be processed out of order.

Consider the scenario in Figure 2 (the numbers in parentheses denote events depicted in the figure). (1) Req_1 sends a request r_1 for constraint change; (2) Con_2 sends a reply l_1; (3) then Req_2 sends its request r_2 for constraint change; (4) Con_1 finds r_2 before Acc_1 finds l_1 (possible because these processes are asynchronous); so, Con_1 detects simultaneity and ignores r_2 while resetting F_1. (5) Acc_1 receives l_1, resets flag F_1, and (6) Req_1 is free to send the next request r_3. (7) But Con_2 detects simultaneity since flag F_2 is still set; it ignores r_3, and resets F_2; (8) Then Req_2 re-sends r_2 (ignored earlier). At this point, we have a non-terminating loop: simultaneity would be detected at node 1 which would re-send its request r_3 and 2 would detect simultaneity, ad infinitum. The cause is a single message processed out of order.

To cope with this problem, two additional data items were introduced at each node: a *local message counter* (LC) which is incremented and appended to every sent out message, and a *remote message counter* (RC), that is the "expected" LC of the next message to be received from the other node. Before a message is processed its appended LC is synchronized with RC at processing node, i.e., in case of mismatch a process handling the message sleeps until $LC = RC$.

4.1 Handling Simultaneity

Our earlier solution of ignoring and re-sending requests after a random interval in case of simultaneity is adequate when network delays are reasonably well-bounded and user transactions are infrequent or violate local constraints infrequently. But when this is not the case, network delays often compensate for the random sleep interval and when simultaneous requests are ignored and re-sent, it is likely that the re-sent messages are found to be simultaneous too.

We require that (a) simultaneity should be correctly observed by *both* nodes; (b) when simultaneity is observed, an asymmetric delay must be enforced; (c) asymmetric delays should be fairly distributed, i.e., no node suffers. Condition (a) is ensured by in-order message handling as outlined in the previous section. To achieve (b), a node detecting simultaneity no longer ignores the request at hand; instead, it sends a *SIMUL* (*simultaneity*) reply. When a *SIMUL* reply is received, a node decides whether to wait for the other node's request or to immediately re-send its own request. The node that decides to wait sets a special flag (G) which blocks its own *Req* process from sending out requests. After the node has received, considered, and sent a reply for the other node's immediately re-sent request, G is reset, and the node goes back to normal behavior. Condition (c) is achieved by using a toggling boolean variable at each node so that the assignment of the asymmetric delay alternates between the two nodes.

Since the implications of a divergence in the value of that variable in the two nodes are very serious: a node could wait forever for the other's re-sent request, we have, for robustness, introduced an asymmetric override procedure: one designated node compares both decisions and makes an adjustment in the case of disagreement.

4.2 Categorizing User Transactions

To understand the behavior of the system and the results, we found it useful to categorize the transactions as follows:

	C_i violated	C violated	# Msgs
type A	no	no	0
type B	yes	yes	0
type C	yes	yes/no	0, 1, 2, or 3

C-Subtype	summary	# Msgs
type C1	Constraint change request is made and resolved	1
type C2	Update is valid owing to recent constraint change	0
type C3	Simultaneity	see below
type C3a	Re-sent after delay	see below
type C3a1	Resolved	2
type C3a2	Simultaneity; Re-sent immediately and resolved	3
type C3b	Re-sent immediately and resolved	2

Types A and B are accepted and rejected respectively — locally. Type C represents those requests that are enqueued. We divide type C into 3 sub-types. For C1, a request is sent and receives a decisive reply ((YES, $new\_constraint$) or NO). For C2, the update now satisfies the local constraint owing to some beneficial constraint change (in the interim period when the user update was enqueued). For C3, a request is sent but receives a $SIMUL$ reply. There are two subcases. In C3a, the first subcase, this node waits and re-sends the request. There are now two possibilities; either (C3a1), the reply is decisive, or (C3a2) it is $SIMUL$; in the latter case, the request is re-sent immediately but this time it must receive a decisive reply because it is the other node's turn to wait. Similarly, in the second subcase C3b, the request is re-sent immediately. The reply will be decisive since it is the other node's turn to wait.

Thus, in addition to types A and B, updates of type C2 are also processed locally. Note that not only is starvation avoided but there is an upper bound of *three* on the number of network messages needed by a single user update.

5 The Experiment

We report on an experiment in which $N = 2, C = x_1^2 + x_2^2 < 4$, and initially $(x_1, x_2) = (0, 0)$. Multiple rectangles were avoided to explore the basic issues. We observed the outcomes of transactions containing random user updates, and measured actual times on a simulated network. We relied on the operating system to handle buffering. This closely approximated the relative timings involved in a typical database operation (i.e., delays due to context switches, locks, sending/receiving messages, etc. are taken care of). However, since delays from/to actual user transaction were missing, we added a compensating adjustment of 0.2 ms to all timing results. Two parameters were chosen to explore the algorithm's performance.

1. the time between successive user transactions submitted by the *Usr* process: a random value within a *user sleep interval* specified by (*minsleep, maxsleep*). Five such sleep intervals (or 5 users) were assigned from (0.05 s, 1 s), the *slowest* User 1, to (0.1 ms, 5 ms), the *fastest* User 5.
2. the degree of restraint exercised by the user in selecting the updated data value, i.e., how close the updated value is to the current value. The user attempts to update the current data value v to a new value given by $v + wg/r$, where w is a random value ($-1 \leq w \leq 1$), g is a constant range computed from the global constraint, and r, the *user restraint*, acts as an inverse weight. The bigger the r value, the smaller the difference between the current data value and the user update request.

In this experiment $g = 4$ (the diameter of the constraint circle). We varied the value of r from 0.5 to 10 in increments of 0.5, and then to 15 in increments of 1. For each of the 5 users and each of the 25 restraint values, a 15 minute-long simulation was run. We summarize our observations in Figures 3 through 7.

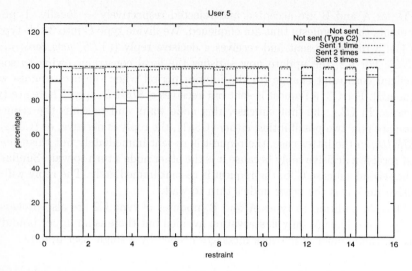

Fig. 3. We categorize the user updates based on the number of network messages needed. For each restraint, we show the percentages of the transactions that require 0, 1, 2, or 3 messages for User 5. Over 80% of update requests do not need a message; the figure changes to 75% for User 1 since type C2 is non-existent for that slow user.

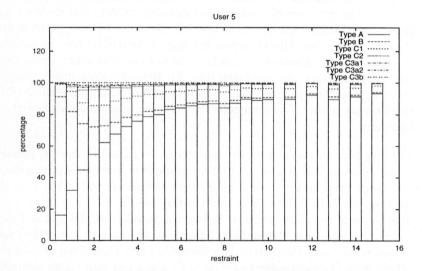

Fig. 4. A distribution similar to the previous figure but based on types. The majority of the update requests need zero messages, i.e., are processed locally. For large user restraints, most user updates are executed locally; for small user restraints, they are rejected locally. For a certain value of user restraint close to 2, there is a maximum of user update requests needing messages to be sent.

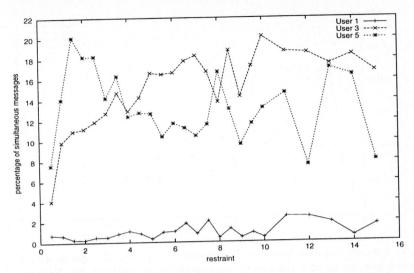

Fig. 5. Percentage of simultaneous messages versus restraint. Up to 20% of network messages are simultaneous when user is fast. This shows that simultaneity is a non-trivial factor when user update requests are frequent.

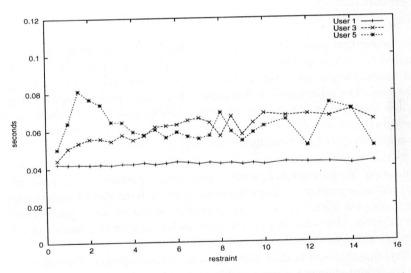

Fig. 6. Average response time for type C requests versus restraint. Response time is the elapsed time between enqueueing a request and the moment it either has been re-executed following a *YES* reply or is eliminated after a *NO* reply. Slow user has a reasonably constant response time of roughly the network delay (20 ms each way). For a fast user, it can be up to twice longer — owing to simultaneity and the need to re-send a request.

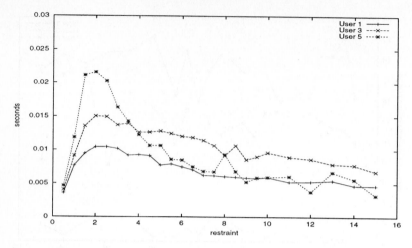

Fig. 7. Average response time for all requests; Comparing this graph with that in Figure 6, one can see that the overall response times are much smaller. This reduction has occurred because a majority of user updates are processed locally (see Figure 3).

6 Conclusion

The localization approach is to compute local sufficient conditions for a distributed constraint and *incrementally update* these local constraints at the various nodes when a user transaction violates one without violating the global constraint. The advantages of this approach are that update requests that satisfy the localized constraint are processed locally and remote synchronization is avoided. Further, database sites preserve autonomy, this method is equally applicable to distributed databases and multidatabases.

In this paper, we have focused on the dynamic behavior associated with localization. We have studied, implemented, and experimented on this approach. The most important problem we found was that of simultaneous update requests, which, coupled with the fact that algorithm processes are asynchronous, can lead to errors. Our solution puts an upper bound of 3 on the number of network messages per constraint update and avoids starvation.

Experimental results show that our solutions are effective. The response time of a constraint change request roughly equals the network delay for a slow user and increases for faster users due to simultaneity. Regardless of the user restraint, the majority (over 75%) of transactions are processed locally. Owing to transactions of type C2, the faster users have a somewhat higher percentage of locally processed transactions. On the other hand, owing to simultaneity, some of the faster user's updates need more than one (but at most 3) network messages.

In summary, the experimental results demonstrate that simultaneity is an important factor and that our solutions to this and other problems are effective. Further, the strategy of localization is successful.

Acknowledgements The work was supported by a grant from the National Science Foundation under contract IRI-9509789.

References

1. D. Barbará and H. Garcia-Molina. The Demarcation Protocol: A Technique for Maintaining Linear Arithmetic Constraints in Distributed Database Systems. In *Proc. EDBT'92.*, pages 373–388, 1992.
2. P. A. Bernstein and B. T. Blaustein. A Simplification Algorithm for Integrity Assertions and Concrete Views. In *Proc. COMPSAC-81*, pages 90–99, 1981.
3. A. Gupta and J. Widom. Local Verification of Global Integrity Constraints in Distributed Databases. In *Proc. SIGMOD'93*, pages 49–58, 1993.
4. L. Henschen, W. McCune, and S. Naqvi. Compiling Constraint Checking Programs from First-Order Formulas. In H. Gallaire, J. Minker, and J. Nicolas, editors, *Advances in Database Theory*, volume 2, pages 145–169. Plenum Press, 1984.
5. S. Koenig and R. Paige. A Transformational Framework for the Automatic Control of Derived Data. In *Proc. VLDB'81*, pages 306–318, 1981.
6. S. Mazumdar. Optimizing Distributed Integrity Constraints. In *Proc. DASFAA-93*, pages 327–334, 1993.
7. S. Mazumdar and G. Yuan. Localizing A Class of Distributed Constraints: A Geometric Approach. *Journal of Computing and Information*. To Appear.
8. S. Mazumdar and G. Yuan. Localizing Global Constraints: A Geometric Approach. In *Proc. ICCI'98*, 1998.
9. X. Qian. Distribution Design of Integrity Constraints. In L. Kerschberg, editor, *Proc. Expert Database Systems*, pages 205–226. Benjamin Cummings, 1989.
10. X. Qian and D. Smith. Constraint Reformulation for Efficient Validation. In *Proc. VLDB'87*, pages 417–425, 1987.
11. T. Sheard and D. Stemple. Automatic Verification of Database Transaction Safety. *ACM TODS*, 12(3):322–368, September 1989.
12. E. Simon and P. Valduriez. Integrity Control in Distributed Database Systems. In *Proc. Hawaii Intl. Conf, on System Sciences*, pages 622–632, 1986.
13. D. Stemple, S. Mazumdar, and T. Sheard. On the Modes and Meaning of Feedback to Transaction Designers. In *Proc. SIGMOD'87*, pages 374–386, 1987.
14. D. Stemple, E. Simon, S. Mazumdar, and M. Jarke. Assuring Database Integrity. *Journal of Database Administration*, 1(1):12–26, Summer 1990.
15. Z. Yuan. Dynamic Localization of Global constraints in Distributed Databases. Master's thesis, New Mexico Institute of Mining and Technology, 1997.

Solent – A Platform for Distributed Open Hypermedia Applications

Siegfried Reich[1], Jon Griffiths[1], David E. Millard[1], and Hugh C. Davis[1]

Multimedia Research Group
University of Southampton
SO17 1BJ, UK
E-Mail: {sr, jpg96r, dem97r, hcd}@ecs.soton.ac.uk

Abstract. Today's open hypermedia systems (OHS) provide middleware services for a range of hypertext applications. However, configuration and adaptation to specific applications' requirements is a tedious task. Research has been conducted into further splitting hypermedia middleware systems up into sets of interacting components that can be combined, extended and configured dynamically. These component-based open hypermedia systems (CB-OHS) allow for better adaptability, configurability and also interoperability amongst hypermedia middleware systems themselves.

Described is the *Solent* component-based open hypermedia system. In particular, we focus on architecture, dynamic service discovery and invocation as well as the storage interface, which allows for storage and retrieval of arbitrary hierarchical structures encoded in XML.

Authoring and managing links are without doubt essential issues in hypertext systems. Thus, research has been conducted into separating link data from content, i.e. the documents, which results in link services being available to *all* applications on the user's desktop. These third generation hypertext systems are called *open* and are referred to as open hypermedia systems (OHS) [18].

There are several consequences of designing a system with separate links [10]: documents can still be managed and edited by those applications that created them and more links can be applied to documents that are read-only, such as documents on a CD-ROM or documents owned by another user. In addition to this, multiple users can use their own link bases at the same time, thus there are different views on the same information space. One of the most important features lies in the possibility of link maintenance: when updating links only the link bases have to be updated, the documents themselves remain unchanged. This clearly has great advantages in contrast to systems with embedded links — the WWW serving as a very prominent example — because these systems demand all relevant documents to be changed.

While the development from the early monolithic and closed hypertext systems to today's open and distributed hypermedia systems with support for collaboration has resulted in increased openness and flexibility [13, 20], integrating or adapting various different tools as client applications has remained a tedious task. Many developers found themselves implementing essentially similar components, simply for the benefit of having their own platform on which to experiment with hypertexts.

At the Second Workshop on open hypermedia systems (OHS) held in conjunction with the '96 ACM Hypertext Conference [19] the open hypermedia systems working group (OHSWG) was formed, with its main focus being interoperability between OHSs [18]. The group felt that the community had reached a level of maturity and stability such that it was possible to abstract the common features of the various systems, and to propose to move towards one of the major goals of any open system: interoperability.

This goal resulted in the hypermedia middleware, i.e. the link servers, being split up into several components with well defined interfaces [2, 20]. Some of these interfaces, e.g. for navigational hypertext, have been standardised by the open hypermedia systems Working Group (OHSWG) and therefore allow interoperability amongst components [7].

This paper describes the design and implementation of the Southampton component-based open hypermedia system (CB-OHS) which we refer to as the "Solent" system, named after the waters around Southampton. The system has been developed to address the many issues posed to hypermedia middleware and serves as a platform for the development of advanced multmedia applications such as content-based retrieval [4], content-based navigation [12], or navigation in audio [3].

1 Requirements

The objective of efficiently supporting a diverse range of advanced open hypermedia applications by a set of middleware components leads to a number of requirements that have to be met. Besides the more technical requirements, there are goals that we as a research group would like to address, such as building a framework that could serve as a research vehicle with which we could further experiment.

Dynamic Setup of Components (Requirement 1, R1). This precondition arises from our experience in providing middleware services for various open hypermedia applications. Configuring these applications is often a quite complex task, additionally it may require updates to components at runtime with minimal impact on other components, dynamic lookup of services, and more [8]. Besides, within the context of the research undertaken towards interoperability amongst open hypermedia systems, there is the need to support multiple hypermedia link models at the same time and allow dynamic exchange and adaptation of these. Often components run on various platforms and therefore the communicaion mechanism between components should be platform independent.

Support for Navigational Hypertext (R2). Various forms of navigation still build the core features of many hypertext systems. Thus, it has been a requirement to support the standardised navigational interface as promoted by the OHSWG [7].

Support for Storage of Arbitrary Structured Data (R3). The data being dealt with in hypermedia applications is often highly structured. Hence it is a requirement to support such structures, e.g. encoded in eXtensible Markup Language (XML) we believe that support of this standard is necessary. XML has an interesting property in that it allows a mode whereby no document-type-definition is required to form an XML document (hence approaches such as [5] cannot be directly applied). This implies that the storage system has to support storage and retrieval of structures that it does not "know" about. Besides encoding of data in documents, XML is also often used for communicating messages between components. This further strengthens the need for support of XML (see also Section 2.2).

Support for Computations (R4). In particular for supporting content-based retrieval [4] and navigation in multimedia documents [12], it is necessary to support the abstract notion of a computational service as a "black-box" which takes defined parameters as input and produces a fixed output. A computation stores the information about a service in the same way that a node represents a wrapper to a document, it is a meta-information object.

Open, Extensible Framework (R5). It was a requirement to build a framework which can be used as a research vehicle in a number of research projects. By *Framework* we refer to a software environment that is designed to simplify the development and management of hypermedia applications [2] by supporting re-use of existing components [11]. In particular, we want to research issues such as streaming content data and its synchronisation with link data, the use of computations for content-based retrieval and navigation, and adjust the architecture to different configurations in order to e.g. address scalability [1].

2 Description of the Architecture

The architecture of the *Solent* system builds on the experience gained in developing the open hypermedia systems Microcosm [6], Microcosm TNG [9], MEMOIR [8] and others. Figure 1 depicts the conceptual architecture.

The Figure shows the separation of components into front-end components (i.e. the applications), middleware services, and the storage backend. This is in agreement with both other CB-OHSs such as Microcosm TNG [9] or Construct [20] and also the requirements mentioned above (R1, R5).

Solent is designed to support the standardised interfaces being developed within the OHSWG [7], distributing that support over many communicating components. Key to the system is the notion of an "engine" which is a software process managing a certain functionality within the system. The most essential

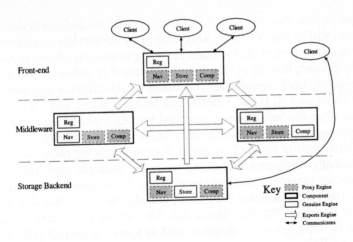

Fig. 1. The Component Architecture of the *Solent* System

engine, present in every component, is the *registration engine* ("Reg" in Figure 1). The purpose of this engine can be compared to that of an information broker, e.g. in Corba. This engine is tightly coupled to the hosting component. Its job is to receive registration requests from other components in the system. When one component registers with any other it sends its connection details (the protocol and version it speaks as well as the host and other location information that it resides on). The registration engine then creates a *proxy engine* (see grey boxes in Figure 1) in its own component and sends its own registration information back. Registration and de-registration can be truly dynamic (R1, R5).

A proxy engine appears to the outside world as would any other engine but in actual fact proxies all requests to the real engine in a separate component. This has several advantages:

1. When a component registers it sends details not only of its own genuine engines but also to all of the proxy engines.
2. Because the proxy engine retains the connection information of the genuine engine, when it registers it sends this information rather then that of the proxy. This means that messages are only ever re-directed once (client to proxy to engine).
3. Any component can be treated as if it contained an appropriate engine as long as it knows the location of such an engine in another component.

The communication objects are currently configured to work using messages represented in XML over plain TCP/IP sockets as "on-the-wire" protocol. Other communication mechanisms such as Corba's IIOP or Java's RMI have been investigated as well; however, due to reasons of platform independence and standardisation within the OHSWG, XML over plain Sockets has remained the communicatin mechanism of choice. Each incoming message is offered to each engine in the component, it is up to the engine to decide if it wishes to deal with a particular request. Each engine does this based on the protocol and version of the message being sent (if it can differentiate between them) and also the name of the engine that the message was intended for. As a result, concurrent support of multiple versions of a particular interface is possible (R1, R5).

This architecture results in a group of communicating components that can be dynamically configured and distributed over multiple platforms and at the same time act together cohesively as a whole. Even though currently only two core hypertext interfaces are supported, namely the navigational and the computational interface (R2, R4), the architecture allows for an easy integration of interfaces to other hypertext domains such as spatial hypertext [14] or workflow applications [17].

In the following subsections we will describe two components in more detail, the computation and storage components.

2.1 Dynamic Service Discovery and Execution

Hypermedia systems often allow their proprietary clients access to advanced functionality, in particular for supporting retrieval [4] and navigation within multimedia documents [12]. To enable this functionality to be accessed by generic clients it is necessary to support the abstract notion of a *computational service* (R4). A computation is a black box of functionality, known to a client only by its name as well as its input and output parameters, that can be invoked and its results understood, even though its workings are completely opaque. In this way a generalised client gains access to complex functionality that would otherwise be unavailable (see also Section 3).

The OHSWG has been working on a standard interface for accessing these computations. The *Solent* system contains a computation engine that understands what computations are and the interface that deals with them.

Often computations may actually take a long time to complete resulting in the obvious problem of giving feedback to the user. The definition of the computation interface therefore includes a mechanism which lets the calling component know the time that a service takes and allows the called component to send progress messages back to give explicit feedback. This can be compared to the notion of "Quality-of-service" (QoS).

Sometimes a single computation cannot effectively represent a facility. For instance, for content-based navigation in audio [3], a computation might analyse a section of music and produce a *contour*; it would then check that contour against the ones in a database to produce a list of nodes representing musical scores similar to the selection. The issue here is that although the input and output parameters of this complex computation are well defined the computation itself needs to be split up into several sub-computations for scalability and performance reasons. Clearly, the analysis of a huge audio file should take place at the file's location, however, matching the resulting contour against a database could be performed elsewhere. We have therefore come up with the definition of a composite computation.

Composite computations represent a way for components to "impart knowledge" to the rest of the system about how computations can be combined (in serial or in parallel). This leaves plenty of scope for the development of more sophisticated systems which learn about particular combinations of computations and also provides a framework for the exploration of mobile code and agents within a CB-OHS environment.

2.2 A Storage Engine for XML

The *Solent* CB-OHS contains a storage component which corresponds to the *storage engine* of Figure 1 (R3). Its role is to manage the storage of arbitrary structured data encoded in XML. The storage engine comprises a relational database which other components of the *Solent* system can access via a Java application, called the *storage manager*.

We have found that being able to store arbitrary structured data has afforded some benefits.

- It encourages rapid prototyping of protocols which describe meta-data about components of the system, such as the navigational or the computational interfaces. This is because different versions of the same protocol can be stored in the same database at the same time, without having to create a new database or alter the schema of existing database tables.
- The ability to store arbitrary structured data enables the installation of new components within the system without having to consider the protocol that is being used to manipulate the meta-data representation of its objects, the only factor being that the meta-data must be able to be represented in XML.

Due to the fact that all (structured) objects are stored as flat relations in the database, retrieving objects from the database involves building XML elements which are composed of smaller entities: sub-elements and values. The XML elements used to represent the arbitrary structured data in the storage engine take the form of n-ary trees; i.e., each XML sub-element can be considered to be a branch and XML values represent leaves of a branch.

The implementation of the storage engine comprised of several steps, these were particularly necessary due to performance issues. We will now briefly describe these steps.

Firstly, data was retrieved using a *breadth-first* approach. This method begins at the element root and works its way down the tree. A typical retrieval operation using this technique took 121 seconds.[1] The problem with this approach is that

---

[1] The data was calculated with the following configuration: Pentium P75, 32 MB Ram, Windows 95, JDK 1.1, MS-Access 95. Our test data consisted of around 80 high-level objects which resulted in approximately 2500 XML objects stored in the database overall. Times given are for a typical query with a single user.

when storing similarly structured objects in the database, the difference between objects meant for retrieval and ones that are not, may only be perceivable when examining the values of the leaves of the retrieved XML structure. Therefore there may be a lot of retrieval activity within the database, which is retrieving structure that is not associated with the database objects meant for retrieval, but this is not discovered till late into the retrieval process. This is an inherent flaw when retrieving XML structure using a top-down approach, where the discerning information is located at the bottom of the structure.

In a next step, data was retrieved using a *depth-first* approach. This involved retrieving the value at the botton of the branch for each unexplored sub-element of an element. A typical retrieval operation using this method took 28 seconds. A major problem concerned with this approach is when there are lots of objects in the database which match the object meant for retrieval. By retrieving objects from the bottom-up, the retrieval algorithm may begin constructing objects which comprise the same structure as one of those objects meant for retrieval, but may actually contain the values and/or sub-elements which belong to different objects. Therefore such objects should not be retrieved after all.

Thirdly, we investigated a *combination* of depth-first and breadth-first retrieval methods. It follows the same steps as the depth-first retrieval technique until the first branch is encountered within the template object. Then instead of searching the database for the value at the end of that branch, it performs the breadth-first technique for retrieving database entries down that branch. The performance measured 24 seconds on average for a typical retrieval operation.

In a final step, we employed *caching* of objects in main memory to further increase the efficiency of retrieving objects from the database. On system start-up, each object stored in the database was built into its corresponding XML structure. Then when an object was requested, a breadth-first retrieval algorithm was employed for object retrieval on the database cache. Although breadth-first retrieval had proven to be the most inefficient retrieval method earlier, caching easily compensated for this inefficiency. A typical retrieval operation took 5 seconds.

We also investigated query optimisation at the application level [16]. This involved modifying the client application which sent database retrieval requests. The order of the elements which the storage engine would use as a basis for searching the database was changed in order to optimise the retrieval operation.

In general, our approach towards flexibility by supporting storage and retrieval of arbitrary structures encoded in XML meant that we needed to investigate various tuning techniques to achieve the performance needed for our applications.

3 Sample Applications: Generic Media Player and Car Stereo

A number of hypermedia applications have been built using the *Solent* system. We will briefly describe two examples, a software Car Stereo and a generic Media

Player. The Car Stereo Viewer replicates a car CD system which can play files encoded in the MP3 standard and it was built specially for use within the *Solent* system. The second application, a generic media player, is an adapted client of the windows media player which has been developed for content based navigation in audio [3]; it demonstrates how services can be dynamically discovered using the compu

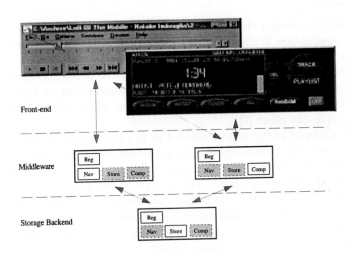

Fig. 2. Media Player and Car Stereo as Sample Applications of *Solent*

As can be seen in the Figure, the adapted generic Media Player (see top left) communicates using two interfaces, the navigational and computational interfaces, whereas the purpose-built Car Stereo client only uses the computational interface. The Car Stereo has a built-in set of requests it understands, those can be instantiated by users through pressing a button. E.g., users might want to ask for "similar songs" to the one that they are currently listening to.

The Media Player on the other hand, is a generic application that, besides others, supports the computational interface. Hence, this application is able to negotiate with a computational engine the set of services it is offered. The Media Player understands the basic mechanisms on how to call a computation and how to parse its results, i.e. it knows how to deal with input and output parameters. In doing so it can dynamically discover the set of computations available, offer them to the user, perhaps ask the user to provide it with some additional parameters and finally execute the computation. By supporting the navigational interface the Media Player not only allows users to retrieve tracks by executing a computation, but also to navigate from e.g. a track to some description in form of an HTML file on the Web, etc. This clearly demonstrates the advantage of component-based open hypermedia systems in that specific parts of functionality can be supported and combined if feasible.

4 Summary and Conclusions

In this paper we have considered the evolution of open hypermedia systems to component-based open hypermedia systems. In particular, we have described the design and development of the *Solent* CB-OHS which have been driven by the requirements being set by today's advanced hypermedia applications.

The experiences we gained during the design, implementation and prototyping are manifold.

- The modular design clearly helped in restructuring the system to the different application areas and allowed us to better select the components to support various functionalities [15].
- Furthermore, the flexibility helped to address the problems encountered in serving different versions of protocols and interfaces that we needed to support during the development of standardised interfaces within the OHSWG's interoperability effort [7].
- The modularity of the system allowed us to run different interfaces simultaneously assisting interoperability, in particular at the front-end [20].
- The trade offs between flexibility and performance have been shown by the example of the storage layer. The feature of being able to support arbitrary structures proved useful during the development phase with structures changing constantly and also, often being undefined (i.e., no document-type-definition existed). On the other hand, for demonstrating the system as described above it was necessary to tune the performance of the retrieval operations.

In summarising we believe that the current system provides us with a platform which allows us to exploit research issues of open hypermedia systems. In particular, we are interested in addressing scalability aspects of our architecture not only with respect to data [1] but also with respect to number of users, number of concurrent computations, etc. Additionally, we are currently investigating the feasibility of a standardised interface to access documents within open hypermedia systems. This includes issues such as streaming document content, synchronising content data with link data and more.

Acknowledgements

The authors would like to thank the members of the multimedia research group at Southampton, in particular Steve Blackburn, Dave DeRoure, Ian Heath, and Wendy Hall. We would also like to acknowledge the members of the open hypermedia systems community, in particular Ken Anderson, Pete Nürnberg and Uffe Wiil.

References

1. Kenneth M. Anderson. Data scalability in open hypermedia systems. In *Hypertext '99, Darmstadt, Germany*, pages 27–36, February 1999.

2. Philip A. Bernstein. Middleware: A model for distributed system services. *Communications of the ACM*, 39(2):86–98, February 1996.
3. Steven G. Blackburn and David C. DeRoure. A tool for content based navigation of music. In *Multimedia '98, Bristol, UK*, pages 361–368, September 1998.
4. Stavros Christodoulakis and Peter Triantafillou. Research and development issues for large-scale multimedia information systems. *ACM Computing Surveys*, 27(4):576–579, December 1995.
5. Vassilis Christophides, Serge Abiteboul, Sophie Cluet, and Michel Scholl. From structured documents to novel query facilities. In *SIGMOD '94, Minneapolis, Minnesota*, pages 313–324. ACM, 1994.
6. Hugh C. Davis, Wendy Hall, Ian Heath, Gary J. Hill, and Robert J. Wilkins. Towards an integrated information environment with open hypermedia systems. In *Hypertext '92, Milan, Italy*, pages 181–190, 1992.
7. Hugh C. Davis, David E. Millard, Siegfried Reich, Niels Olof Bouvin, Kaj Grønbæk, Peter J. Nürnberg, Lennert Sloth, Uffe Kock Wiil, and Kenneth M. Anderson. Interoperability between hypermedia systems: The standardisation work of the OHSWG (technical briefing). In *Hypertext '99, Darmstadt, Germany*, pages 201–202, February 1999.
8. Dave C. DeRoure, Wendy Hall, Siegfried Reich, Aggelos Pikrakis, Gary J. Hill, and Mark Stairmand. An open architecture for supporting collaboration on the web. In *IEEE WET ICE 98, Stanford University, California*, pages 90–95, 1998.
9. Stuart Goose, Jonathan Dale, Gary J. Hill, Dave C. DeRoure, and Wendy Hall. An open framework for integrating widely distributed hypermedia resources. In *Multimedia '96, Hiroshima*, pages 364–371, June 1996.
10. Wendy Hall. Ending the tyranny of the button. *IEEE Multimedia*, 1(1):60–69, 1994.
11. Ralph E. Johnson. Frameworks = (components + patterns). *Communications of the ACM*, 40(10):39–42, October 1997.
12. Paul H. Lewis, Hugh C. Davis, Steve R. Griffiths, Wendy Hall, and Robert J. Wilkins. Media-based navigation with generic links. In *Hypertext '96, Washington, D.C.*, pages 215–223, March 1996.
13. Peter J. Nürnberg, John J. Leggett, and Uffe K. Wiil. An agenda for open hypermedia research. In *Hypertext '98, Pittsburgh, PA*, pages 198–206, 1998.
14. Olav Reinert, Dirk Bucka-Lassen, Claus A. Pedersen, and Peter J. Nürnberg. CAOS: A collaborative and open spatial structure service component with incremental spatial parsing. In *Hypertext '99, Darmstadt, Germany*, pages 49–50, February 1999.
15. Douglas E. Shackelford, John B. Smith, and F. Donelson Smith. The architecture and implementation of a distributed hypermedia storage system. In *Hypertext '93, Seattle, WA*, pages 1–13, 1993.
16. Dennis E. Shasha, *Database Tuning: A Principled Approach*. Prentice Hall, 1992.
17. Weigang Wang and Jörg M. Haake. Implementation issues on ohs-based workflow services. In Uffe Kock Wiil, editor, *5th Workshop on Open Hypermedia Systems, Hypertext '99, Darmstadt, Germany.*, pages 52–56, 1999.
18. Uffe Kock Wiil. Open hypermedia: Systems, interoperability and standards. *Journal of Digital Information (JoDI). Special Issue on Open Hypermedia*, 1(2), 1997.
19. Uffe Kock Wiil and Serge Demeyer, editors. *Proceedings of the 2nd Workshop on Open Hypermedia Systems, Hypertext '96, Washington, D.C.*, 1996.
20. Uffe Kock Wiil and Peter J. Nürnberg. Evolving hypermedia middleware services: Lessons and observations. In *ACM Symposium on Applied Computing (SAC '99), San Antonio, TX*, pages 427–436, February 1999.

Concurrency Control for Global Transaction Management in MDBSs

Kyu-Woong Lee[1] and Seog Park[2] and Gil-Rok Oh[1]

[1] Computer & Software Tech. Lab., ETRI,
Yusong P.O. Box 106, Taejon, 305-600, KOREA
{leekw, groh}@etri.re.kr
[2] Dept. of Computer Science, Sogang University,
C.P.O. Box 1142, Seoul, 100-611, KOREA
spark@dblab.sogang.ac.kr

Abstract. The objectives of global transaction management in multidatabase systems(MDBS) are to avoid the inconsistent retrievals and guarantee the global serializability under the existence of *indirect conflict* which is unknown to to the global transaction manager(GTM). Many researches have shown that it is difficult to design the global concurrency control method because of local autonomy. In these method global transactions have a few opportunities to be executed concurrently. We concentrate our attention on 1) investigation into the more accurate indirect conflict situation and 2) supporting the higher concurrency degree by using the concept of global integrity constraints. We define the multidatabase transaction model and then propose the concurrency control protocols. In our method the more global transaction can be concurrently executed, since the refined boundary of possibility of indirect conflict is offered.

1 Introduction

The GTM has the responsibility for maintaining the global consistency of MDBS. The GTM however cannot take any kind of helpful information from local database systems to adjust the global serialization order. Many techniques in managing transactions for MDBS environments have been researched. These vary in degree to which they violate local autonomy and also in the degree of concurrency that they provide to users. The major difficulties addressed in these researches are to serialize the global transaction under the existence of indirect conflicts which is unknown to the GTM. Traditional concurrency control methods are not directly applicable in MDBS because of these indirect conflict. We briefly examine the definition of indirect conflict.

Definition 1. The global transaction G_i and G_j are in indirect conflict in global schedule S if and only if there is a local transaction sequence $L_1, L_2, \ldots, L_r$, such that G_i is in direct conflict with L_1 , L_1 is in direct conflict with L_2, $\ldots$, finally, L_r is in direct conflict with G_j. $\square$

In order to resolve these indirect conflicts, previous researches provide global concurrency control methods with the lower degree of concurrency by using forced data conflicts between global transactions. They did not figure actual indirect conflict situation. In this paper we adopt the characteristics of *global integrity constraints* to achieve the higher degree of concurrency. A consistent global database state is fragile if a local transaction can be executed by the LDBS that is unaware of inter-site integrity constraints. Thus we investigate the more accurate indirect conflict cases and present the multidatabase transaction model by using the property of global integrity constraints.

The rest of paper is organized as follows. In next section, we describe the related works on transaction management of MDBS and their problems. In Section 3, we propose *site-locking* method that guarantees the global serializability of MDBS. We define the new kinds of lock type for acquiring a site and explain its protocol. Section 4 concludes the paper.

2 Research Backgrounds

2.1 Previous Works

Several researches have been proposed in order to ensure the serializability in MDBS environment [BST90, DELO89, GRS93, MRKS91]. These methods are classified into three groups depending on their strategies and assumptions as follows:

- Violation of local autonomy
  These methods violates local autonomy in some degree in order to control local transaction [AGMS87, EH88]. These methods have impractical assumptions. It has proved that the global serializability is not ensured in these methods [DELO89].
- Relaxation of correctness criteria
  The solutions in this category introduce the notion of *quasi serializability* by using the hierarchical nature of global concurrency control scheme [DEK91] and *two level serializability* [MRKS91, MRKS92]. These methods assume that there is no value dependency between subtransactions within a global transaction or there is weaker form of value dependency. Under these assumption, they guarantee the relaxed criteria rather than the conflict serializability(CSR). *Two level serializability* especially can be ensured in the specific transaction model, and moreover, there is no value dependency between local and global data items.
- Forcing some restriction on LDBS
  The techniques in this category force the each participating LDBS to be restricted on execution of transaction. [WV90] proposes the *2PC agent method* in which each LDBS uses *strict two phase locking*. The fact that local schedule has the strictness is not sufficient to preserve the global serializability. [BGRS91] requires that each LDBS produce the *rigorous schedule*. Rigorousness has all the properties of *strictness* and the extra property that no data

Table 1. Summary of Previous Works

related works	violation of local autonomy	correctness criteria	ensuring global serializability	restriction on global transaction	preserving global IC
[AGMS87]	√	CSR		√	
[EH88]	√	CSR		√	
[DEK91]		QSR	△	√	△
[MRKS91] [MRKS92]		2 Level SR	△	√	△
[WV90]		CSR		√	
[BGRS91]		CSR	√	√	
[BST90]		CSR	√	√	
[GRS93]		CSR	√		

√ : positive   △ : neutral

item may be written until the transaction, which previously read it, either commits or aborts. The rigorous schedule is the smaller subset of serializable schedule than one of traditional concurrency control scheme. In other words, the global transaction is restricted to access some data items that may cause the indirect conflict [WV90, BST90, BST92]. In practical cases, however, the major purpose of MDBS is to freely access the distributed data. [GRS93] proposed *optimistic ticket method(OTM)* which requires extra data item, called *ticket* per a LDBS. The conflicting order for the ticket reflects relative serialization order of global transactions. The global serializability is ensured by the forced data conflict on ticket, but concurrency degree of OTM is lower than conventional distributed concurrency control method.

Table 1 shows the summary of previous works for the global transaction management in MDBS. Previous researches for global concurrency control have the following difficulties.

- They did not figure the actual indirect conflict cases. They suppose that the global transaction is indirect conflict if any other global transaction is concurrently executed in the same site.
- They provide lower concurrency degree that is similar to the performance of a serial execution.
- They have non-realistic assumptions such that there is no inter-site constraints or value dependency between local and global data items.

2.2 Research Motivation

Each LDBS in MDBS is designed and implemented independently and also defines certain local integrity constraints(LIC) among data items within a single site. However, as a number of various DBMSs are integrated into an MDBS, global inter-site constraints are introduced. These distributed integrity constraints arise naturally whenever the data that is semantically related is stored in different local database systems. Each LDBS is unaware of these global integrity constraints. The most fundamental issue of global integrity constraints in MDBS are how and where the global integrity constraints is maintained without the violation of local autonomy.

A logically consistent global database state may become inconsistent if the data is modified without maintaining the global integrity constraint. For example, if a data item is defined in global integrity constraints, the update on it through the interface of *LDBS* may cause an inconsistent database state. The data item especially may be replicated at different sites. In this case, the consistency of its replicated versions cannot be maintained by LDBS, because LDBS is unaware of replicated version at different site. Since the LDBS does not have the capability to maintain the global integrity constraint, the data item which is defined in the global integrity constraint should be managed by the GTM. Hence, restriction on the local transaction is necessitated in MDBS.

3 Site-Locking Protocol for Global Concurrency Control

3.1 Integrity Constraints and Transaction Model

In MDBS environment, the integrity constraints are classified into local and global integrity constraint. The local integrity constraints are pre-existing integrity constraints which are maintained by LDBS, and the global integrity constraints are newly defined by MDBS according to the integration process.

The introduction of inter-site constraints enable us to partition the set of data item at a site i, D_i, into local data items, LD_i, and global data items, GD_i, such that $LD_i \cap GD_i = \phi$ and $D_i = LD_i \cup GD_i$[MRKS91]. Furthermore, if there is an integrity constraints between the data item $d_i \in D_i$ and $d_j \in D_j$,$i \neq j$, then data items d_i and d_j are global data items in GD_i and GD_j, respectively. Therefore, we partition the data items of MDBS in two groups, as follows [LP97].

- *Global Data Item :*
  the set of data items which is defined in the global integrity constraints
- *Local Data Item :*
  the set of data items which is defined in the local integrity constraints

In our work, we prohibit the local transaction from updating on global data item without the knowledge of global integrity constraints. This restriction enables us to easily maintain global integrity constraints and reduce cost of verifying the global consistency. The local transaction, however, is not restricted to read the data item. The local transaction can read both local and global data items. Some researches propose the method that the global transaction is restricted to read and update the data item and they assume that there are no inter-site constraints [DEK91, MRKS91]. As described in Section 2, some approaches propose the transaction model in which the data set that can be updated by global or local transaction is completely separated [BGRS91, BS92, BST92]. In practical cases, the global transaction cannot be imposed on updating the data item. These restrictions cannot be adopted in general MDBS system, because the global transaction must be free to access the data item. Hence, in our work, global transaction is free to access data items.

We define our multidatabase transaction model called *Global-Free Transaction Model* for maintaining global integrity constraints as described in Table 2.

Table 2. Global-Free Transaction Model for MDBS

Data Transaction		Data Item	
		Local Data	Global Data
Local Transaction	Read Operation	◯	◯
	Write Operation	◯	×
Global Transaction	Read Operation	◯	◯
	Write Operation	◯	◯

◯ : possible × : impossible

3.2 Ensuring the Global Serializability

We describe the situation that the global transaction G_i cannot be serialized with respect to other global transaction G_j. If there is a direct conflict between global transactions and at least one indirect conflict between them(Figure 1 (a)), the global serializability cannot be ensured. Similarly, if there exists the indirect conflict at two or more sites(Figure 1 (b)), the global serializability cannot be ensured. An indirect conflict consists of at least two direct conflicts between local and global transaction as shown the Figure 1. Thus, we need to investigate the accurate situation of direct conflict between global and local transaction.

In our *Global-Free* transaction model, we can easily find the situation that there is no direct conflict between the local and global transaction. The Table 3 shows all cases of direct conflicts between the local and global transaction, by classifying the operation of transaction. In Table 3, "◯" means that the direct conflict cannot occur between corresponding two operations. In these cases, two operations are both read operations or they are executed on the distinct data group. On the other hand, "×" denotes that the direct conflict may exist. Such a direct conflict between local and global transaction may cause the indirect conflict between global transactions. The indirect conflict consists of at least

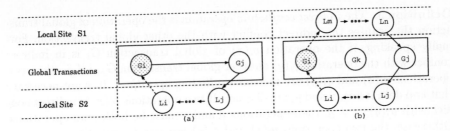

Fig. 1. Globally Non-serializable Schedule

Table 3. Direct Conflict between the Local and Global Transaction

			Global Transaction			
			Read Operation		Write Operation	
			Global data	Local data	Global data	Local data
Local Transaction	Read Operation	Global data	◯	◯	×	◯
		Local data	◯	◯	◯	×
	Write Operation	Local data	◯	×	◯	×

◯ : no direct conflict × : direct conflict

two direct conflicts between local and global transaction. Therefore, if one of the direct conflicts can be resolved or prevented, the global serializability is ensured in multidatabase transaction management.

3.3 Lock Operation for Accessing the Site

In this section, we propose a *site-locking* global concurrency control method that use the lock operation for accessing the site. The basic idea of site-locking method is that a global transaction cannot execute concurrently with other global transactions if it has the possibility of indirect conflict. We enhance the degree of concurrency by investigating the more actual indirect conflict situations.

In Table 3, we list all possible cases of direct conflict between the local and global transaction. However, MDBS cannot know which type of local transaction is executed in the site, when the global subtransaction is submitted to the LDBS in that site. Hence, The GTM must guarantee global serializability by controlling only the global transaction.

Definition 2. The *indirect conflicting operation* is the operation of global transaction that causes the indirect conflict with the other global transaction. Formally speaking, if the operation $p_i(x)$ of global transaction G_i is in indirect conflict with the operation $q_j(y)$ of other global transaction G_j, $i \neq j$, then two operations $p_i(x)$ and $q_j(y)$ are *indirect conflicting operations*. It is not necessary that two data items, x and y, are distinct. If two operations $p_i(x)$ is indirect conflict with $q_j(y)$, $x = y$, then operations p and q must be both read operations. Otherwise, the two operations $p_i(x)$ and $q_j(y)$ are *direct conflicting operations*. □

If we can determine the serialization order of *indirect conflicting operations* of global transactions, the global serializability is guaranteed.

Our global concurrency control method uses the lock operation for indirect and direct conflicting operations, like basic 2PL[BHG87]. In Table 3, we can easily find that the read operation of global transaction that is executed on the global data item is not in direct conflict with any local transactions. Therefore, the read operation of global transaction for global data item cannot be the *indirect conflicting operations*. The remainder operations of Table 3 may cause the indirect conflict with other global transactions because it may be in direct conflict with the local transaction.

To present our *site-locking* method, we need some notations. Locking granularity is a site, rather than a data item. An operation of global transaction is submitted to a site either for *reading* or *writing* a data. Moreover, a read operation is submitted to a site for reading either the *global* or *local data item*. We associate three types of locks with sites : *Read_Global(RGL)*, *Read_Local(RLL)*, and *Write(WL)* locks. We use $RGL_{Gi}(S_x)$ (or $RLL_{Gi}(S_x)$) to indicate that the global transaction G_i has obtained a read lock for global(or local) data item on site S_x. Similarly, we use $WL_{Gi}(S_x)$ to indicate that the global transaction G_i has obtained a write lock on site S_x. We use $RGU_{Gi}(S_x)$(or $RLU_{Gi}(S_x)$) to denote the operation by which G_i releases its read lock for global(or local) data item on the site S_x, and similarly, $WU_{Gi}(S_x)$ to denote the operation by which G_i releases its write lock on the site S_x. A global transaction must acquire one of corresponding lock before its operation is submitted to the site.

Let the P and Q be an arbitrary type of lock operation and G_i and G_j are global transactions which access the same site S_x. P and Q are of conflicting types if one of following conditions are satisfied.

i) Either P or Q is a *Write* lock(WL), and the other is *Read_Local* lock(RLL), or *Write* Lock(WL).

ii) Either P or Q is a *Write* lock(WL), and the other is *Read_Global* lock(RGL), and also G_i and G_j access the same data item.

We define the *site-conflict* between global transactions.

Definition 3. Two locks $P_{Gi}(S_x)$ and $Q_{Gj}(S_x)$ are *site-conflict* if $G_i \neq G_j$ and P and Q are of conflicting types. □

By Definition 3, we present the *site-lock compatibility matrix* for controlling indirect conflicts, as shown in Table 4. Two locks are *site-conflict* if there may be

Table 4. Site-Lock Compatibility Matrix for MDBS

G_i (owner)		Read Lock		Write Lock
G_j (requester)		RGL (Global Data)	RLL (Local Data)	WL
Read Lock	RGL (Global Data)	◯	◯	⊗
Read Lock	RLL (Local Data)	◯	×	×
Write Lock WL		⊗	×	×

◯ : shared mode   × : *Site-Conflict* mode   ⊗ : shared or *Site-Conflict* mode

indirect conflict between two global transactions or there is a direct data conflict between them.

3.4 Protocol of Site-Locking

We illustrate the more detailed rules and site-locking protocol. To maintain global serializability, *site-locking protocol* must ensure that the subtransactions of each global transaction have the same relative serialization order in their corresponding LDBS. It is the basic idea of site-locking protocol that the relative serialization order of the subtransactions at each LDBS is reflected in the order of acquiring the site lock operation.

Site-locking protocol processes a global transaction G_i as follows. Before an operation of global subtransaction G_{ix} is submitted into a site S_x, the GTM must acquire the associated site-lock of site S_x. The site-lock which is once acquired by the global transaction G_i is released only after the G_i has been globally committed. Our site-locking protocol is almost the same as basic two phase locking, except that the three types of site-lock is used and the locking granularity is a site rather than a data item. We present our rules according to which the GTM manipulates its site-locks.

Rule 1 : When GTM receives an operation of global subtransaction G_{ix} for the site S_x, the GTM determines the corresponding the site-lock type and tests if the requesting site-lock operation is *site-conflict* with some site-lock operations that are already set at a site S_x, according to Table 4. If so, the requesting operation is delayed until the owner releases the site-lock. If not, then the GTM sets the associated site-lock and sends the operation of global transaction to the LDBS at the site S_x.

Rule 2 : Once the GTM has set a site-lock on the site S_x for the transaction G_i, it may not release that site-lock at least until the global transaction G_i has globally been committed.

Rule 3 : Once the GTM has released a site-lock for a global transaction, it may not acquire any more site-locks for that global transaction.

Rule 1 prevents two global subtransactions from concurrently accessing the same site in *site-conflict* mode. Therefore, the site-conflicting operations of global transactions are scheduled in the same order in which the corresponding site-locks are acquired for the site. As illustrated in Section 2, the basic problem of MDBS is that the GTM cannot determine the serialization order of global transactions at local sites. However, by the *Rule 1*, we can determine the serialization order of indirect conflicting global transactions. *Rule 2* and *Rule 3* are for the growing phase and shrinking phase of basic two phase locking method, respectively.

Our *site-locking* protocol is summarized as follows.

Decomposing the global transaction : The global transaction G_i is decomposed into several global subtransactions.

Requesting site-lock : Before the global subtransaction G_{in} is sent to the local site, it requests the corresponding *site-lock*.

Sending the subtransaction : If G_{in} acquire the *site-lock*, it is sent to the local site. Otherwise, it waits until the corresponding *site-lock* is acquired.

Processing in LDBS : G_{in} that is sent to the local site is controlled and executed by LDBS as a general local transaction.

Releasing the site-lock : If all global subtransactions enter their *prepared-to-commit* state, G_i commit and all of their *site-lock* is released.

According to our proposed *site-locking protocol*, a global transaction that may have an indirect conflict with other global transaction can be serialized and global serializability is guaranteed.

4 Conclusion

Our goal in this paper has been to propose the global concurrency control in MDBS which provides the higher concurrency degree. Primary difficulties in previous researches are 1) the lack of concurrency control protocol that ensure the global consistency in the presence of unknown updates by the local transaction, and 2) the insufficient investigation of indirect conflict cases. These problems introduce numerous unnecessary data conflict between global transactions as well as inconsistent global database state. In this paper, by using the characteristics of global integrity constraints, *site-locking protocol* is proposed to guarantee the global consistency and enable the more global transactions to execute concurrently. We have a plan to prove and analyze our proposed method and have the more detail comparative experiments on simulation model. Our work can be extended to various concurrency protocol in order to adapt to diverse distributed applications.

References

[AGMS87] Rafael Alonso, Hector Garcia-Molina, and Kenneth Salem. "concurrency control and recovery for global procedures in federated database systems ". *A quarterly bulletin of the IEEE Technical Committee on Data Engineering*, 10(3):5–11, 1987.

[BGRS91] Yuri Breitbart, Dimitrios Georgakopolous, Marek Rusinkiewicz, and Abraham Silberschatz. "on rigorous transaction scheduling ". *IEEE Transactions on Software Engineering*, 17(9):954–960, 1991.

[BHG87] Philip A. Bernstein, Vassos Hadzilacos, and Nathan Goodman. " *Concurrency Control and Recovery in Database Systems*". Addison-Wesley Publishing Company, 1987.

[BS92] Yuri Breitbart and Avi Silberschatz. "strong recoverability in multidatabase systems ". In *Proceedings of the Research Issues in Data Engineering*, pages 170–175, 1992.

[BST90] Yuri Breitbart, Avi Silberschatz, and Glenn R. Thompson. "reliable transaction management in a multidatabase system". In *Proceedings of the 1990 ACM SIGMOD International Conference on Management of Data*, pages 215–224, 1990.

[BST92] Yuri Breitbart, Avi Silberschatz, and Glenn R. Thompson. "transaction management issues in a failure-prone multidatabase system environment ". *The International Journal on Very Large Data Bases*, 1(1):1–39, 1992.

[DEK91] Weimin Du, Ahmed K. Elmagarmid, and Won Kim. "maintaining quasi serializability in multidatabase systems ". In *Proceedings of the Research Issues in Data Engineering*, pages 360–367, 1991.

[DELO89] Weimin Du, Ahmed K. Elmagarmid, Y. Leu, and S. Osterman. "effects of autonomy on maintaining global serializability in heterogeneous distributed database systems ". In *Proceedings of the 2nd International Conference on Data and Knowledge Systems for Manafacturing and Engineering*, pages 113–120, 1989.

[EH88] Ahmed K. Elmargarmid and A.A. Heral. "supporting updates in heterogeneous distributed database systems". In *IEEE Proceedings of the 4th International Conference on Data Engineering*, pages 564–569, 1988.

[GRS93] Dimitrios Georgakopoulos, Marek Rusinkiwicz, and Amit P. Sheth. "using tickets to enforce the serializability of multidatabase transactions". *IEEE Transactions on Knowledge and Data Engineering*, 6(1):166–180, 1993.

[LP97] Kyuwoong Lee and Seog Park. " *Chapter 7 : Optimistic Concurrency Control for Maintaining the Global Integrity Constraints in MDBSs, IFIP TC11 WG11.5 Integrity and Internal Control in Information Systems, Volume 1*". Chapman & Hall, 1997.

[MRKS91] Sharad Mehrotra, Rajeev Rastogi, Henry F. Korth, and Abraham Silberschatz. "non-serializable execution in heterogeneous distributed database systems". In *Proceedings of the 2nd International Conference on Parallel and Distributed Information Systems*, pages 245–252, 1991.

[MRKS92] Sharad Mehrotra, Rajeev Rastogi, Henry F. Korth, and Avi Silberschatz. "relaxing serializability in multidatabase systems ". In *Proceedings of the Research Issues in Data Engineering*, pages 205–212, 1992.

[WV90] A. Wolski and J. Veijalainen. "2pc agent method : Achieving serializability in presence of failures in a heterogeneous multidatabase ". In *Proceedings of PARBASE-90 Conference*, pages 268–287, 1990.

Transactional Computation

Alfs Berztiss[1,2]

[1] University of Pittsburgh, Pittsburgh PA 15260, USA
[2] SYSLAB, University of Stockholm, Sweden

Abstract. The concept of transaction is highly significant in the context of data bases. We broaden this concept by making it refer to any atomic operation that changes the state of a software system or its environment. This allows us to consider software systems as composed of transactional and procedural computations. We discuss the specification of transactional computations in some detail. However, our primary aim is to identify procedural and transactional computation as two well-defined foci for research, and to consider transactional computation as a common foundation of information systems and data base management.

1 Introduction

For some time there has been a realization that some computations are fundamentally different from others. For example, Harel [1] talks of reactive systems and transformational systems, where reactive systems are driven, at least to some extent, by external events, and transformational systems under his interpretation include data-processing systems. We agree with a two-way classification, but would not place the boundary quite where Harel puts it. Moreover, it is also being understood that different modes of computation may be needed for the one application. Thus, Stonebraker *et al* [2] suggested quite a while back that procedures should be introduced into data bases. This suggestion has evolved into the active data base concept (see, e.g., [3]). The role that transactions play in information systems is studied in [4, 5]. Our purpose here is to explore these developments. We shall not deal with the so-called advanced transaction models [6].

We propose to group computations into two classes, *transactional* and *procedural*, where a software system is likely to contain components belonging to both classes. In so doing we shall arrive at an interpretation of a transaction that is both broader and narrower than the one given to it by the data base community. Our primary purpose for introducing the two-way partition is to identify two distinct foci for research. and thus help reduce the fragmentation that currently characterizes much of the research in computer science and software engineering. In particular, we hope that this investigation will lead to a closer interaction and cooperation of researchers in information systems and data bases.

Section 2 is an examination of the differences between transactional and procedural computation. In Section 3 we introduce our interpretation of a transaction, and discuss how queries fit into our framework. Sections 4 and 5 describe an approach to the specification of transactions. In Section 6 we summarize our work and identify several research issues.

2   Two Modes of Computation

Throughout computer science and software engineering we can observe different modes of computation. Looking back at the history of the field, the earliest computations were simple transformations of inputs into outputs. Soon there arose the realization that data files could be preserved from one instance of a computation to another, and that different applications could make us of the same file. Operating systems were soon providing file management systems, and separate data base management systems arose. What characterizes this trend is the evolution of persistent memory: from no persistent memory at all, to rather rigid data files, to highly complex data bases. Persistent memory is one characteristic of transactional computation, but the more important characteristic is that transactional computation brings about changes in this persistent memory.

Persistent memory is irrelevant for procedural computation. Here the concern is with a transformation of an input into an output. Let the transformation be effected by a device F that accepts an input x and produces an output $f(x)$. One example is the cosine function, which, given angle x, produces $cos(x)$. Of course, both x and $f(x)$ can be composite data elements. Now, quite often the input x will be picked up from a data base, and the result $f(x)$ deposited in a data base, but as concerns F, it is immaterial where the inputs come from, or what happens to outputs.

A procedural computation does not change system states; its reference to data bases is in a read-only mode. It may refer to a type of persistent memory, and make changes in it, but this memory is persistent in a very limited sense. Whereas under conventional block-structured computation all local data are lost on exit from a block, devices such as generators or iterators preserve local memory in a block between entries to the block (see, e.g., [7]). However, once the computation has been completed, all local data become inaccessible. Transactional computation differs radically from this: transactions operate on truly persistent memory, and almost invariably they bring about changes in this memory.

Procedural computation obeys what we shall call I/O semantics, i.e., the specification of such a computation has to describe the output, and indicate how the output is related to the input. Time is irrelevant. Transactional computation obeys state-transition semantics. Invariants describe valid states of a system. They may also indicate impermissible state transitions. For example, we may have a situation in which borrowers are not permitted to borrow books from a library if they owe money to the library. Then a state in which a borrower holds four books and owes money is valid, and so is the state in which the borrower holds five books and owes money, but not a transition from the first state to the second. In such a case the borrowing transaction can be equipped with a precondition that stops further borrowing. Alternatively, an invariant is defined in terms of temporal logic, which introduces a further difference between the two modes of computation: time can be important in transactional computation.

3 Transactions Redefined

In traditional data base applications a transaction is a data base update or a query evaluation. We shall both broaden this interpretation and make it narrower. The broadening will allow "updates" to relate not just to a data base, but also to the environment in which a software system may be embedded. The narrowing will exclude query processing.

We regard the processing of a query as a typical procedural task. First, it does not bring about a state change of the system. Second, it obeys I/O semantics as we defined them above — the input is a data base and a predicate defining a result the user is interested in, the output is the result, and the computation consists of operations applied to the data base to produce the result.

Moreover, at a sufficiently high level of abstraction, there are cases in which it is immaterial whether a query will refer to a data base or be evaluated by an algorithmic procedure. Suppose one is interested in the times of sunrise for Pittsburgh in the year 2000. One approach would be to list the 366 entries in a table, and to look up the table. The other would be to evaluate the sunrises by means of an algorithm.

The difference between updates and queries is quite fundamental. In updating, i.e., changing the state of a system, there must be a system to update, and it must be possible to describe states of the system. Thus, if I am adding sunrises for the year 2001 to my year-2000 system, I must point to a specific system that is to be augmented, and I must be aware of how this system determines its responses. However, when a user puts a query to this system, there should be no need for the user to know whether the response is obtained by means of look-up or algorithm. Indeed, if I need the sunrise time for Pittsburgh for September 18, 2000, I do not necessarily have to go to my system. I could also try to get this information by means of internet search. Of course, with existing query systems, such as SQL, a detailed knowledge of a data base is needed.

At a conceptual level, then, query evaluation follows precisely our model of input x (the query), processed by device F (the query processing system), resulting in $f(x)$ (the answer to the query). Conceptually this seems no different from a control action: the system receives an input x from a sensor, a device F determines a response $f(x)$, which is conveyed to an actuator. The point here is that a dynamic response, i.e., a change imposed on a controlled system, is to be made only if F detects a change in the controlled system. This means that F must be able to refer to earlier sensor readings, which means in turn that some kind of data base, however rudimentary, must be maintained, and that the data in this data base undergo changes.

So the model underlying a control system is not as simple as that underlying a query system. There is still the x (now it is a sensor input), but F consults also a data base db, and there are two outcomes, a control response $f(x, db)$, and an updated data base *db'*, but, in order to obtain *f(x, db)*, the transaction may have to invoke a procedure. Moreover, the control response may be subject to a timing constraint. Let us determine the nature of another operation. While an "update" of an algorithm is essentially different from changing the state of a transaction system, a repository of procedural software, e.g., a reuse library, can be regarded as subject to transactions that update this repository.

A problem can in general be addressed in different ways. The simplest solution is usually purely transactional, from which we can advance to solutions in which there is an increasing dependence on procedures. We illustrate this by a simple example: a date and place are to be selected for a meeting, and participants are to be registered for the meeting.

At the lowest level a steering committee selects a date and place for the meeting, and an information system merely performs registration transactions. At the next higher level the steering committee selects a date, but now considers several places for the meeting. A procedure selects the place for which the travel costs of the participants are minimized. A third solution is obtained in stages. In the first stage the steering committee polls prospective participants, asking for preferred dates and places, with the preferences ranked or given numerical weights. An algorithm then selects a time and place that maximizes an objective function.

Our example shows that an information system may have to allow both transactional and procedural computations. It should also be kept in mind that differences between information systems and control systems are vanishing — in which category would one put programmed stock market trading by a mutual fund? Also, research on active data bases deals with the introduction of aspects of information systems into data bases, thus reducing the distinction between the two. There remain concerns that relate purely to data bases, such as query optimization and data base locking, and concerns that relate purely to information systems, such as enterprise analysis. However, the two fields have much in common, and an in-depth study of the two modes of computation should be a joint undertaking of data base and information systems researchers and developers. In order to provide an initial direction, we look in the next two sections at the specification of transactional software.

4 Specification of Transactions

Specification languages fall into several categories. Some are concerned with program correctness, some with abstract data types, but the most widely known specification languages today, namely VDM [8] and Z [9], have a transactional orientation (although they can specify procedural transactions as well, Z in particular). For example, the VDM-specification of an e-mail system described in [10] consists of specifications of the various transactions that define such a system.

It has been argued that specifications should be implicit [11]. Under an implicit specification, predicates define valid states, but there is no explicit defini-

5 Transactions and Processes

Nearly every computer program implements some process, but there is great variety in the interpretation of what is meant by a process. A fairly extensive search through software engineering textbooks revealed that most did not have *process* in the index. Where they did, process was interpreted as something that converts an input into an output, or as a bubble in a data flow diagram, or as something that results in a software system. In [13] we define a business process as an ordered collection of tasks that is to achieve a value-adding objective within a finite time interval. To allow for control processes as well, particularly continuous processes, this definition should be generalized: a process is an ordered collection of tasks that is to achieve some objective.

A definition is important because organizations such as business enterprises are increasingly being defined in terms of processes rather than their organizational structures. Davenport [14], among others, considers this a basic characteristic of business reengineering. Moreover, Davenport argues convincingly that the management of the data on which a process is based should be the responsibility of the manager of the process. This seems to go against the philosophy of enterprise-wide data bases, but does not really do so. There can still be a central data base, but the transactions that effect changes in this data base are to be defined by the designers of the software systems supporting the individual business processes.

A very simple instance of a process arises with the telephone network discussed earlier. Whenever a connection terminates (the first transaction), an attempt is made to establish new connections (the second transaction of this rudimentary process). Recall that the second transaction is only implicit in the specification of [12]. The first transaction is to remove $\{A, B\}$ from the collection *Conn*, but it also sends out the signal *TryToConnect*, which will be explained below.

> TRANSACTION *CallTermination*(A, B);
>   DATACONDITIONS $Conn' = Conn - \{A, B\}$;
>   SIGCONDITIONS $(TryToConnect(A, B))$ON;
> ENDTRANSACTION;

> TRANSACTION *ConnectionTry*(A, B);
>   PRECONDITIONS $\exists\, x \in Req: x \cap \{A, B\} \neq$ null;
>   DATACONDITIONS
> $\exists\, x \in Req: A \in x \wedge \exists\, y \in Req: B \in y \wedge x \cap y =$ null $\rightarrow$
> $Req' = (Req - x) - y \wedge Conn' = Conn \cup x \cup y \vee$
> $\exists\, x \in Req: A \in x \wedge \not\exists\, y \in Req: B \in y \rightarrow$
> $Req' = (Req - x) \wedge Conn' = Conn \cup x \vee$
> $\not\exists\, x \in Req: A \in x \wedge \exists\, y \in Req: B \in y \rightarrow$
> $Req' = (Req - y) \wedge Conn' = Conn \cup y;$
> ENDTRANSACTION;

The second transaction takes place only if there exists some pair in collection *Req* such that either A or B belongs to this pair. Actually the precondition is redundant because if this condition is false, then also the three disjuncts of the data condition will be false. Our semantics require the minimal activity to take place that makes a data condition true. Hence, if the antecedents are false, all three disjuncts are automatically true, and nothing happens. Our specification philosophy is to allow redundancy because it tends to improve the readability of a specification. The connection criterion is the simplest possible that is consistent with the predicates of the implicit specification. The problem that complicates even this simple specification is the possibility that set *Req* contains requests { *C, A*} and { *C, B*}, which cannot both be turned into connections. Explicit specification makes one consider such situations early in the software development process, which may avoid complex rework later on.

There has to be a way for the first transaction to initiate the second. We call the specification component that effects this an action. The particular action that we require here picks up the signal *TryToConnect*, and initiates *ConnectionTry*:

> ACTION;
> ON(*TryToConnect(A,B)*)OFF:: *ConnectionTry(A, B)*;
> ENDACTION;

The action here is particularly simple. Actions can be started by a signal, or by a calendar or clock, and the initiation of a transaction by an action may be delayed. It is also possible to perform periodic monitoring of a system, and to initiate a transaction when the system is found to be in a particular state. The reason why we insert actions between transactions instead of allowing a transaction to initiate another transaction directly has a formal reason. An entire process composed of our transactions and actions can be represented by a Petri net (actually a slightly modified time Petri net — for time Petri nets see [15]). In this net a transaction is represented by a place, a signal by a token, and an action by a subnet composed of places and transitions. This provides actions with formal semantics.

Many formalisms for connecting transactions have been devised; two based on finite state machines are discussed in [1, 5]. However, the partitioning of transactions into user, system, and prompted transactions, where system and prompted transactions are the responsibility of actions, is unique to our approach. So is the introduction of time constraints and delays, which can be expressed as time intervals rather than sharp values, with this feature having sound semantics based on time Petri nets. Our transaction-action model was first introduced in our specification language SF — for a brief introduction and earlier references see [13], but there a transaction is called an event, and the actions of this paper are called transactions. The Petri-net based semantics are discussed in [16].

6 Conclusions and Research Issues

By identifying transactional and procedural computing as the two principal modes of computation we have tried to give a basis for the examination of some recent trends in information systems and data base research. For example, active data bases can be regarded as transactional systems in which the triggers

Database Versions to Represent Bitemporal Databases

Stéphane Gançarski

LIP6 - Université P. et M. Curie
Case 169 - 4, place Jussieu - 75252 Paris cedex 5, France
Stephane.Gancarski@lip6.fr

Abstract. We present a new approach to implement an object bitemporal database where both valid-time and transaction-time are represented. It is based on the DataBase Version model, which allows an efficient management of object versions. This facilitates the manipulation of past events and allows a straightforward representation of branching evolution in valid-time.

Keywords : bitemporal database, valid-time, transaction time, versions.

Introduction

In many applications time must be considered and introduced as an information stored in the database, as it has been pointed out in a huge literature (see for instance [Cen]). Among the various temporal dimensions that have been studied in databases, two of them appear particularly important, useful and moreover complementary: the *valid-time* of a fact which expresses the time when this fact is true in the real world, and the *transaction-time* which is the time of storing the fact in the database. They gave birth to *bitemporal* data models, such as, among the most recent ones [KTF98,Ste98]. In a bitemporal database, a fact is stored associated with: 1) its valid-time domain which is generally represented as an interval where a special value 'now' may be used, meaning that the fact is still valid, 2) its transaction-time domain, also usually represented by an interval which begins when the fact is stored in the database and ends when its value is replaced by another one; a special value 'until change' may be used to express that the value has not been changed by a more recent transaction.

Those two time dimensions are not structurally equivalent. Transaction time is *read-only*, a transaction never erase a fact produced by a former transaction, but creates a new one that is 'more recent' than the former one, and *linear*, following the order among transactions that successively update the value of a given item. On the opposite, valid time should not have those restrictions. We may have to *modify a fact even when it is past*, in order to correct a previous error (John's shirt was not green but blue in 1972). A transaction produces and stores a new –corrected– history of the real world while keeping the former one, to keep a trace of errors which were done. As the reality may have alternatives

(John's shirt may be green or white), valid time may have to be *branching*, as suggests the following example represented in Figure 1[1].

Paula Smith is working for a company since November 95, in Sales department. Her monthly salary has been increased from 1900 to 2000 in March 96. In July 96, the company decides to give an extra money of 200 to each employee with a PhD degree, starting from January of the same year. If Paula Smith has a PhD degree, it is necessary to update not only her last salary (from 2000 to 2200 for the period March96-July96) but also the former one (from 1900 to 2100 for the period January 96-February 96). For valid time, past events have to be modified, even if they are not the most recent ones. Paula actually defended her PhD in another country before being hired by the company. It needs some time before she can get a certification that her PhD is valid here. Until she will obtain it, two alternatives must be stored (Fig. 1) for transaction time 7/96: the 'real' one, where her salary is not yet increased with the extra-money, and the 'optimistic' one (assuming she will obtain the certification) with the extra money since January 96. Those two alternatives must be maintained in the database until we will know whether she will get or not the certification. For instance, the fact that, in August 96, Paula is promoted to the newly created Account department, with her salary increased of 10% is recorded in both alternatives. Finally, Paula gets her certification in December 96. To fix things up, it is sufficient to compare the two alternatives to calculate how much money has to be paid to Paula (the difference between what she actually earned and what she should have earned since January 1st.). Then the optimistic alternative becomes the real one. Managing branching time in a bitemporal database is very useful.

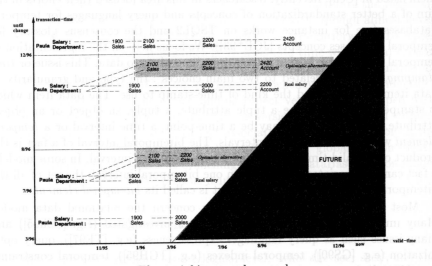

Fig. 1. A bitemporal example

---

[1] We do not consider the problems raised by representing the future and consider only past or present facts.

At the logical level, the multiversion database is seen as a set of database versions, identified by a database version identifier (dbvid). Each DBV represents a context, a possible state of the modeled world. It is composed of one logical version of each object, identified by a pair (object identifier, database version identifier). If object o does not exist in DBV d, the value of its logical version (o, d) is $\perp$. DBVs are created by logical copy, or *derivation*, from an existing DBV. Thus, at the creation of the multiversion database, a *root DBV* is generated but is hidden from users. Users always manipulate logical versions of objects within their context (the DBV they belong to), and a new object version cannot be created outside an existing DBV. The modification or the deletion of a logical object version has no side effect on the object in other DBVs.

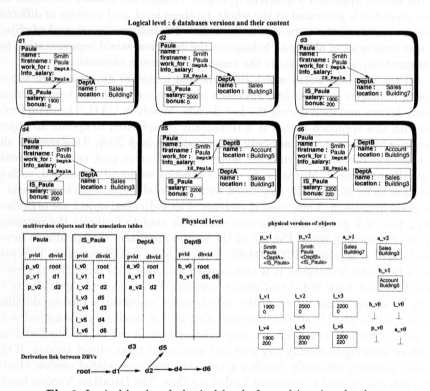

Fig. 2. Logical level and physical level of a multiversion database

At the physical level, each multiversion object is composed of its set of physical versions, identified by physical version identifiers (pvid), and of a table, called *association table*, mapping dbvid to pvid. This mapping allows to retrieve the physical version of an object, and thus the value associated with a given logical version of this object. When a DBV d_2 is created by logical copy of d_1, d_2 shares all the physical versions of object with d_1. To avoid the updating of the association table of all the multiversion objects, the system stores the derivation link between DBVs and uses the following rule: *the physical version associated with a given logical version (o, d) is the physical version associated with (o, d') in the association table of o, d' being the nearest ascendant of d, relatively to the derivation link.* This rule allows an efficient version management, particularly in case of a tree structure among DBVs.

Figure 2 gives a simplified example of a company multiversion database. The object Paula represents the employee Paula Smith. The objects DeptA and DeptB respectively represent the Sales department and the Account department, the object IS_Paula contains information about Paula's salary. The database is composed of six database versions, d1, d2, d3, d4, d5, d6. The object DeptB does not appear in d1, d2, d3 and d4 because the value of its version in those DBVs is $\perp$. Note that the logical versions (DeptB, d5) and (DeptB, d6) are both associated with the physical version b_v1 (i.e. they both correspond to location in building5). d5, derived from d2, does not appear in the association table of DeptA: the logical version (DeptA, d5) shares the physical version a_v2 of DeptA with (DeptA, d2). The versions value of complex object Paula contains object identifiers and not object version identifiers. For a logical version of Paula in a given DBV d, these object identifiers refer to the logical version of the specified objects in DBV d.

The DBV approach is a very general approach. It can be adapted to any data model identifying objects independently from their value, and is efficient to represent and manipulate complex object version, provided that the data model allows values containing object identifiers. Manipulation operations for DBVs [GJ94] have been implemented in the Modesty prototype on top of the O_2 DBMS. Operations can be performed efficiently thanks to the mechanisms used to implement the DBV approach. They represent the framework we used to develop bitemporal databases using database versions, as shown below.

3   Bitemporal database using DBVs

We discuss the issues raised by the implementation of a bitemporal database using database versions. We first do not take alternative into considerations. We show in 3.2, how our solution can be extended to manage branching time.

3.1   Associating time dimensions to DBVs

As mentioned in Section 1, associating time to globally identified versions is straightforward and is completely independent from the way object versions are managed by the system. A database version represents a possible state of the universe, where every object has a single possible value (possibly $\perp$). It is thus well adapted to represent the part of a bitemporal database where no object changed its value. To represent the whole bitemporal database, we must map each bitemporal couple (valid-time, transaction-time), which identifies a possible state of the 'bitemporal reality', to a given DBV identifier. The value of an object for the given (valid-time, transaction-time) couple is the value of its logical version in the corresponding DBV.

The diagram of Figure 3 extends Figure 1 by adding rectangles, each rectangle covering the *bitemporal interval*, i.e. the couple (transaction-time interval, valid-time interval), associated with a DBV. The DBV identifier is in the left-up corner of the rectangle. The association between a DBV and its bitemporal domain is stored in a *mapping table* between DBVs and time intervals, as shown in the bottom of the figure. For instance, DBV d1 is associated with a valid-time interval [11/95, 3/96] and a transaction-time interval [3/96, 12/96]. The transaction at date 8/96 updated both current salary and current department of Paula. As, at date 8/96, the current state was represented by DBV d2, a new DBV was created by deriving d2, updated with the new salary and department of Paula, and associated with transaction-time [8/96, until_change] and valid-time [8/96, until_change]. Of course, d2 previously associated with valid-time [3/96, now] was associated then with valid-time [3/96, 8/96].

To minimize the creation of DBVs, we must ensure that when no object changed its value, in both valid-time and transaction-time, the same DBV is used. This is straightforward if no update in the past valid-time are allowed, i.e. if each update made in a transaction is valid for interval [t, now], where t is the transaction-time of the transaction[2]. In this case, the transaction generates a new DBV, corresponding to valid-time [t, now] and to transaction time [t, until_change]. This is the case on Figure 3, for all transactions except the one performed at date 12/96. It is obvious that, in this case, every DBV is associated with a single bitemporal domain.

When updates in the past are allowed, the situation is a little bit more complex. If a transaction can perform updates for any valid time interval $[t_1, t_2]$, it may happen that a DBV d is associated with transaction time [t, until_change] and with valid-time $[t_x, t_y]$ intersecting with $[t_1, t_2]$, i.e. such as $t_x < t_1 < t_y$ (or $t_x < t_2 < t_y$). In this case, a new DBV associated with valid-time $[t_1, t_y]$ must be created by deriving d, to represent the new state induced by the update on this interval. But the former state, stored in d, must now be associated with two valid-time intervals: $[t_x, t_y]$ 'before' the transaction and $[t_x, t_1]$ 'after' the transaction. Thus we create a new DBV by deriving again d, and associate it with valid-time interval $[t_x, t_1]$. This is shown in Figure 3, where DBV d7 is created to be associated with valid-time [11/95, 1/96] and transaction-time [12/96, until_change]. This solution is very simple but generates a DBV with the same content as d1. However, we must keep in mind that deriving a DBV is neither time nor space consuming since it simply consists of adding a DBV identifier in the DBV derivation tree. Moreover, an object can be updated with the same value in many DBVs by a one-pass algorithm we implemented.

Note that we investigated two possibilities to avoid to create a DBV with the same content as the one it has been derived from: timestamping DBVs with bitemporal elements or handling overlapping bitemporal intervals. We finally rejected them to keep our solution simple and efficient.

---

[2] this situation is usually called a *degenerated bitemporal database* [ÖS95]

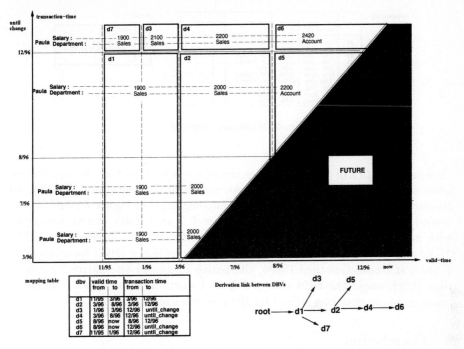

Fig. 3. Mapping time dimensions to DBV identifiers

When an update within a transaction stamped by t is stored in a DBV, this DBV is associated with the transaction-time interval [t, until_change], as the new value entered the database at transaction time t and will remain the most recent ones until a new transaction will eventually replace them. As a consequence, all the DBVs created during the same will be associated with the same transaction-time interval [t, until_change]. The updating procedure takes into account the DBVs already created by previous updates within the same transaction. New DBVs are only be created for a valid-time not associated to one of those DBVs.

The facts stored for a past transaction-time cannot be removed. Thus, an object cannot be removed from the database as soon as it has at least one possible value for a past transaction-time. Therefore, the deleting procedure only updates a given object with a ⊥ value for the valid-time interval [vt_min, now], where vt_min is the minimal valid-time date represented in the database. As the identifier of the object is not removed from the database, we may mark it with a special flag to prevent it to 'revive' through a subsequent update.

3.2 Managing branching evolution

To manage branching evolution is very straightforward in our approach: we associate DBVs not only with valid-time and transaction-time, but also with alternative identifier.

mapping table

dbv	valid time from	valid time to	transaction time from	transaction time to	alternative
d1	11/95	3/96	3/96	12/96	1
d2	3/96	8/96	3/96	12/96	1
d3	1/96	3/96	12/96	until_change	1
d4	3/96	8/96	12/96	until_change	1
d5	8/96	now	8/96	12/96	1
d6	8/96	now	12/96	until_change	1
d7	11/95	1/96	12/96	until_change	1
d3	1/96	3/96	7/96	12/96	2
d4	3/96	8/96	7/96	12/96	2
d6	8/96	now	7/96	12/96	2

alternatives

id	semantics
1	"real salary"
2	"optimistic alternative"

Fig. 4. Managing alternatives

The semantics of the alternative identifiers is managed at the application level: simple characters strings or more complicated annotations [GJZ95]. To represent the example of Figure 1, the mapping table of Figure 3 could be extended as suggested in the left side of Figure 4. A same DBV can be associated with more than one alternative, for possibly different time intervals (as DBVs d3, d4 and d6). Actually, it was not necessary to create new DBVs for alternative 2 since, at transaction time 12/96, alternative 1 replaced alternative 2 for valid time [1/96, now]. The right side of Figure 4 shows how the application could manage simple character strings for the semantics of alternatives.

4 Conclusion

This paper presents a new approach to implement bitemporal object databases. It is based on the DataBase Version model which allows an efficient version management in any object database system and allows branching valid-time. As opposed to other approaches, time is attached to possible states of the whole real world, represented by a database version (DBV), not to possible states of individual objects. This makes the implementation of the bitemporal database very straightforward and renders the management of branching valid time much easier. Moreover, as in the DBV model any existing version can be modified, it is possible to modify any past fact, which is necessary in a bitemporal database used to correct and keep traces of errors made on the history of real world entities. The prototype Modesty_2T, which implements the present work is based on the the Modesty prototype (cf 2), itself built on top of the O_2 OODBMS.

To go further, we first investigate the possibilities of indexing temporal data in our framework, with respect to the numerous existing solutions [Sal94,TGH95]. The mapping between DBVs and bitemporal intervals may be indexed by a two-dimensional spatial index, associated with any index developed for the version manager, such as a versioned B^+-Tree. We also want to integrate in our time manager various phenomena found in temporal databases, such as the future or periodic events. Finally, we aim to optimize our system for applications which requires 'partial transaction-time', i.e. applications where the changes made to the database are only stored sometimes, to keep regular traces.

Acknowledgment The author is grateful to Sylvain Rozenberg who co-designed and developed the MODESTY_2T prototype, and to Anne Doucet for her helpful comments on the paper.

References

[Böh95] M.H. Böhlen. Temporal database system implementations. *SIGMOD Record*, 24(4):53–60, 1995.

[Cen] The Time Center. A ftp-able bibliography on temporal databases. ftp://FTP.cs.arizona.edu/bib/time.bib.

[CJ90] W. Cellary and G. Jomier. Consistency of versions in object-oriented databases. In *VLDB International Conference*, Brisbane (Australia), 1990.

[CK86] H.-T. Chou and W. Kim. A unifying framework for version control in a cad environment. In *Proc. VLDB*, pages 336–344, 1986.

[CN93] J. Chomicki and D. Niwinski. On the feasibility of checking temporal integrity constraints. In *Proc. ACM PODS*, pages 202–213, 1993.

[DGJM96] A. Doucet, S. Gançarski, G. Jomier, and S. Monties. Using database versions to implement temporal integrity constraints. In *Workshop "Constraints and Databases"*, Boston (USA), Aout 1996.

[GJ94] S. Gançarski and G. Jomier. Managing entity versions within their context : a formal approach. In *Proc. DEXA*, pages 400–409. LNCS 856, 1994.

[GJZ95] S. Gançarski, G. Jomier, and M. Zamfiroïu. A framework for the manipulation of a multiversion database. In *DEXA'95 Workshop proc.*, pages 247–256, London (U.K.), 1995. ISBN 3-901653-00-7.

[GS90] H. Gunadhi and A. Segev. A framework for query optimization in temporal databases. In *5th International Conf. on Statistical and Scientific Database Mgt.*, pages 131–147, Charlotte, NC, 1990.

[JCE+93] C. S. Jensen, J. Clifford, R. Elmasri, S. K. Gadia, P. Hayes, and S. Jajodia (eds.). A consensus glossary of temporal database concepts. Technical Report R 93-2035, Department of Mathematics and Computer, Institute for Electronic Systems, Denmark, nov 1993.

[KL91] J. Kimball and A. Larson. Epochs, configuration schema, and version cursors in the kbsa framework ccm model. In *Proc. 3rd Int. Worksh. on Software Configuration Mgt.*, pages 33–42, Trondheim (Norway), 1991.

[KS92] W. Käfer and H. Schöning. Mapping a version model to a complex-object data model. In *IEEE Conference on Data Engineering*, Tempe (Arizona), February 1992.

[KTF98] Anil Kumar, Vassilis J. Tsotras, and Christos Faloutsos. Designing access methods for bitemporal databases. *IEEE Transactions on Knowledge and Data Engineering*, 10(1):1–20, January 1998.

[OPS+95] M. T. Ozsu, R. Peters, D. Szafron, B. Irani, A. Lipka, and A. Munoz. Tigukat: A uniform behavioral objectbase management system. *VLDB Journal*, page 37, jan 1995.

[ÖS95] G. Özsoyoğlu and R. Snodgrass. Temporal and real-time databases: A survey. *tkde*, 7(4), aug 1995.

[Sal94] Betty Salzberg. On indexing spatial and temporal data. *Information Systems*, 19(6):447–465, 1994.

[Sci91] E. Sciore. Using annotations to support multiple kinds of versioning in an object-oriented database system. *tods*, 16(3):417–438, sep 1991.

[Ste98] A. Steiner. *A generalisation approach to temporal data models and their implementations*. PhD thesis, Swiss Fed. Instit. of Technology, Zürich, 1998.

[TE97] A. Tansel and Tin. E. The expressive power of temporal relational query languages. *IEEE Tr. on Knowledge & Data Engineering*, 9(1):120–134, 1997.

[TGH95] V. J. Tsotras, B. Gopinath, and G. W. Hart. Efficient management of time-evolving databases. *tkde*, 7(4):591–608, aug 1995.

A Case Study in Information Delivery to Mass Retail Markets

Vladimir Kotlyar, Marisa Viveros, Sastry S. Duri, Richard D. Lawrence, and
George S. Almasi

IBM T.J. Watson Research Center
30 Saw Mill River Road
Hawthorne, NY 10532, USA
vkotlyar@us.ibm.com

Abstract. The growth in the capabilities of hand-held computers coupled with improvements in database systems and communication infrastructure have brought us closer to enabling truly ubiquitous access to information. In this paper, we describe the SmartPad system, a software solution in the consumer space, providing consumers with ubiquitous access to interactive shopping. This solution enables end-users to shop remotely using personalized content, searching and selecting in incremental mode and disconnected from the network. This is achieved by combining in-store and on-line transactions, by leveraging current efforts in data mining, and by delivering information through hand-held devices. SmartPad is currently used by several hundred consumers with very encouraging initial feedback.

1 Introduction

The growth in the capabilities of hand-held computers coupled with improvements in database systems and communication infrastructure have brought us closer to enabling truly ubiquitous access to information. Technologies for low-power high-density microprocessors, storage devices and communication hardware combined with advances in handwriting and speech recognition technologies enable new uses for hand-held devices - well beyond simple address-book or calendar applications. Improvements in database and networking technologies have the potential of providing mobile users with access to vast corporate and consumer information resources.

Despite the large and comprehensive databases maintained by retailers, only a fraction of this data is transformed into actionable knowledge that could be used for facilitating consumers shopping experience; an experience which is considered uninteresting and time consuming. Recent developments in electronic commerce require consumers to be equipped with a computer infrastructure that is costly and difficult to maintain. Therefore, it becomes necessary to provide a solution that enhances consumers' experience by combining their in-store and on-line purchases, wherein consumers can shop remotely using small and inexpensive devices and retailers can deliver relevant information in a timely manner.

The requirements placed on the capabilities and the cost of hand-held devices and associated information infrastructure vary significantly between different applications. In some cases, sophisticated and expensive technology can be deployed enabling *thousands* of employees to connect instantly to the company's information systems; for example, an employee of an insurance company can access a claims database via a generic Web browser. In other cases, inexpensive mobile technology can be deployed enabling *millions* of consumers to shop remotely. In either case, database systems are needed to manage deployment of devices and to deliver information, taking into account the following characteristics of hand-held systems:

- Due to the combination of small screen size, slow CPU and small memory, the information delivered to the device must be *customized* according to the interests of the user and capabilities of the hardware. For example, a product catalog in a super-market can contain thousands of products. Since only a small subset of the catalog can be stored on a hand-held device and presented to a shopper, it is necessary to analyze past shopping behavior in order to present each shopper with a *personalized catalog*.
- Small portable devices are subject to loss of battery power that can lead to loss of information in flash memory. Wireless devices can sporadically loose connectivity to the base station. And wired devices (e.g. PalmOS-based with a modem) are designed to be connected for only short periods of time. To deal with this combination of *unreliable operation* and *weak connectivity* we need to develop information infrastructure that can support disconnected operation and recovery on connection. For example, in a retail shopping application a consumer should be able to download his personalized catalog and special offers during periods of connected operation, then browse the catalog and prepare a shopping order while disconnected. At the same time the server should mirror the information delivered to the device in order to help in recovering from failure.

In this paper we describe *SmartPad*, a system which provides ubiquitous access to electronic grocery shopping through hand-held devices. Specifically, it allows consumers to shop from anywhere, anytime, and build their shopping list over time. This project is carried-out in cooperation with Safeway Stores plc, who is a major retailer in the UK. The system serves as a test-bed for research into the design of large scale mobile information systems in mass retail markets. Ours is an interdisciplinary project, with interest in three areas:

- Data analysis and transformation for delivery of personalized information to the devices.
- Data management for the support of weakly connected, unreliable mobile devices.
- Design of scalable and extensible application software.

In this paper we report our initial experiences with the SmartPad system, with a focus on data management and analysis. We start by describing in Section 2

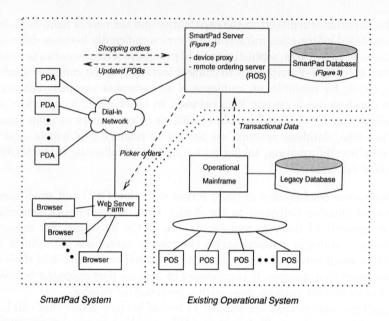

Fig. 1. System overview

the overall system operation. The software design of the major components is described in Section 3. Section 4 discusses the organization and management of data across various stages in information processing. Section 5 describes our experience with the initial installation and presents performance measurements of the main data processing steps.

Although there are other projects attempting to create a similar infrastructure for travel services [6], to the best of our knowledge, SmartPad is the first research project dealing with issues of supporting mass retail on-line commerce from hand-held devices. We hope that our experience with the system proves useful to both researchers and applications designers.

2   System overview

As illustrated in Figure 1, the system consists of a network of mobile devices (PDAs) connected to the SmartPad server through a dial-in service. Each device runs a *consumer application*. The application allows the user to build a shopping order and send it to the server. Products in the order are chosen from three *personal databases* (PDBs) stored on the PDAs: *personal catalog, recommendations* and *promotions*. Together, the PDBs serve as a surrogate for the store catalog that is too large to be stored on the device or presented to the user.

The *personal catalog database* consists of the products which the user has bought within a recent time window. The time window is chosen to (a) account for the seasonal changes in consumer behavior, (b) avoid presenting products that are no longer in use and (c) still keep data sufficient for data analysis. We have experimented with various sizes for this window. The experiments reported in Section 5 were done for a window of one month.

The *promotions database* contains store-wide offers of the "buy-one-get-one-free" variety that usually appear as inserts in weekend newspapers. Promotions are prepared by the marketing personnel and are not personalized at this time.

The *recommendations database* introduces the shopper to new products – those that do not appear in the personal catalog or the set of promotions. The system attempts to recommend those products that are most likely to be bought by the shopper. Details of the recommender algorithm are beyond the scope of this paper and will appear in [4]. We outline the main computational and data processing steps in Section 4.4.

Communication and data processing tasks in the SmartPad server are divided among two components (see [5], Section 2.1.1):

- The *device proxy server* handles device-specific details of communication. It performs authentication and exchanges personal databases with mobile devices. The capability to recover from device failures (such as loss of battery power) is achieved by mirroring the contents of the personal databases on the server.
- The remote ordering server (ROS) generates PDBs based on operational data and processes orders received from mobile devices (via the proxy). Each shopping order is formatted by the ROS into an HTML document that is published on the *Web server farm* in order to be viewed and printed at the store that fills the order. Personal databases are generated by analyzing and transforming historical transaction data.

In summary, the information in the SmartPad system flows in two directions:

- A shopping order is originated at the client device and is communicated through the proxy server to ROS, where it is formatted for presentation to store pickers.
- Transactional data, both from on-line and in-store sales, is sent to ROS in order to generate product recommendations and personal catalogs for transition back to the client device.

3 Software Architecture

SmartPad is structured using widely known extensions to the client/server model for mobile applications, wherein a proxy server acts as an agent for the mobile device in order to service requests for resources. Scalability and availability of the application services are achieved by replicating the proxy across multiple physical systems (see [5], section 2.1.1).

Figure 2 depicts the main components of the SmartPad server. *Proxy Server* exchanges personal databases with the PDAs. *Order Processor* formats shopping orders into HTML documents that are published to the stores. *Promotions Processor* handles generic store promotions. *Personalized Catalog Processor* creates personalized shopping lists. And the *Recommender* generates product recommendations.

The components communicate via *events*. For example, on the arrival of a new shopping order the proxy sends a "new order" event to the order processor. The

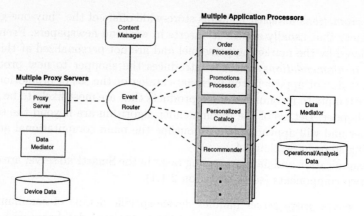

Fig. 2. Software Architecture

routing and generation of events is controlled by the *Content Manager* according to business rules. For example, a typical rule says that new recommendations should be generated weekly on Sunday night. In accordance with this rule an event is sent to the recommender at that time.

Data Mediators separate application processors from the details of data storage. For example, the order processor is concerned with abstract lists of ordered products which can be either stored in a "flat" file or in a relational database. The data mediator translates a request to fetch the shopping list for a particular customer into either a sequence of file accesses of an SQL query.

The division of software into application processors, data mediators and events provides for both scalability and extensibility. The application processors can be replicated across multiple physical systems. New processors can be added and old processors updated with new logic with no changes to the rest of the system, except for the content manager.

4 Data management

SmartPad system operates by transforming data between three sets of data structures: *operational* data, *analysis* data and *personal device* data (Figure 3). The main steps involve (a) aggregating and normalizing the raw operational data into a form suitable for data analysis and (b) transforming the result of the data analysis together with some operational data into personal databases. We start by describing the characteristics of the data structures and conclude this Section by outlining the major computations.

4.1 Operational data

Operational data is generated by in-store and on-line sales, as well as supply and marketing operations. It is stored on a mainframe and is transferred to the SmartPad ordering server as needed. Six main tables are used by the SmartPad server: **Customer, Product, Spending, Transactions, CategoryMap** and **DisplayCategory**. The **Customer** table contains typical information about frequent shoppers in the store (name, address, shopper card number, etc.). The

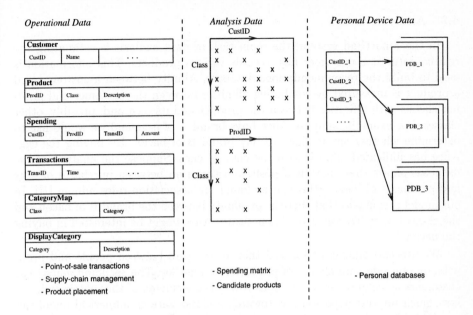

Fig. 3. Data organization

Product table stores the classification of products and other information, such as supply sources or brand names. The **Spending** table records sales of products to customers. The **Transaction** table stores information about each transaction (i.e. basket of products bought at once): day, time and possibly other attributes. The **CategoryMap** and **DisplayCategory** tables relate fine-grain classes of products, such as "Milk/Low Fat" or "Cheese/Swiss", to broad display categories, such as "Dairy Products". The categories correspond roughly to super-market aisles and are used in product placement. There are about 20 categories in all. In the SmartPad system, categories are used to group products in the personal catalog.

A single store serves about 20K customers, with about 5M customers served chain-wide. There are about 250K products divided into about 2000 classes and 20 display categories. On average, each month a customer (more precisely a shopper card) generates about 100 records in the **Spending** table. Given that the retail chain has approximately 5 million active customers, this translates into 400M records generated each month. Two years worth of spending data are kept on-line in the data warehouse – roughly 9.6 billion records in the **Spending** table. Each record in the **Transaction** table corresponds to a shopping trip. The average customer makes 5 trips a month, which translates into 600M records kept on-line in the warehouse.

4.2 Analysis data

In the SmartPad system, the main task of data analysis is estimating the relative interest a customer has towards various products. This information is used to build the recommendations database. Affinity between a customer and a product is measured by combining affinities between the customer and product classes with affinities between the product and its own and, possibly, other classes. For example, suppose Alice buys brand A of eggs and we would like to determine whether she is likely to buy brand B of bacon. By buying the eggs Alice has indicated affinity with the class of eggs. Suppose the analysis of the database shows that there is a positive association between purchases of eggs and purchases of bacon (this can be found via association rules mining [1]). In our model this means that there is an affinity between the brand B of bacon and the class of eggs. Transitively, this indicates Alice might be interested in buying the bacon.

We use two matrices to model this relationship between people and products, on one side, and classes of products, on another. The *spending matrix* has customers as columns and classes as rows. The elements of the matrix indicate how much interest a person has towards a class. Various numerical quantities can be used to express the interest quantitatively. For example, we can use the total spending of a person within a class, or fraction of the budget that a person has spent within a class. Details of the computation of the matrix appear in [4]. Observe, that the matrix is sparse, since a person does not usually buy within every class of products. There are about 50 non-zeros in each column, on average. The matrix is also large, as it can have up to 5 million columns corresponding to all customers of the super-market chain.

Products to be evaluated are arranged into the *candidate product matrix* whose elements reflect affinities between products in classes. In this simplest case, we can set to 1.0 each entry $\langle i, j \rangle$ corresponding to a class i and its member product j. This captures the affinity between different products in a class. For example, two brands of low fat milk will be represented by exactly the same vector that has 1.0 in the position corresponding to the class of low fat milk. Unfortunately, this assignment still ignores associations between classes of products. For example, if the use of bacon strongly implies the use of eggs, then the vector for a particular brand of bacon should have a non-zero entry for the class "Eggs". Associations between classes are used to add non-zero entries to product vectors.

The columns of the matrices represent vectors in the space of product classes: person-vectors in the spending matrix and product-vectors in the product matrix. By computing some distance measure between these vectors we can estimate the relative affinities between people and products. Details of this computation appear in [4].

4.3 Personal device data

Personal databases: personal catalog, recommendations and promotions – are stored in the database as *binary large objects* (BLOBs). BLOBs enable introduction of user-defined data types into a relational database by providing storage for arbitrary binary data in database tables [2]. We use BLOBs to store the representation of the PDBs as they are written to or read from the network. Since the PDBs are usually precomputed prior a client/server session, this speeds up communication by removing the need to format the data in real-time.

The BLOBs are generated by formatting, for each customer, the current shopping order, the personal catalog, recommendations and promotions into text buffers. In this process each record is formatted by comma-separating its fields. A collection of records is formatted by separating the record with newlines. Typical personal catalog occupies about 20Kbytes of storage. Promotions occupy about 40Kbytes and recommendations (currently limited to 10 products) take about 500 bytes.

4.4 Main data processing steps

The most time consuming data processing steps are the transformation of business and analysis data into personal databases and the computation of recommendations.

Transformation of business and analysis data into personal databases (i.e. personal catalog, recommendations and promotions) consists of formatting the appropriate collections of records into BLOBs. Here the most expensive step is computation of personal catalogs. While promotions and recommendations contain only a few (≈ 10) products, a personal catalog can grow to a few hundred products. As a result, this step involves large amounts of I/O, namely, reading all spending records for each customer within the time window, then formatting and writing them back (as BLOBs) into the database.

Recommendations are generated by computing a numerical estimate of how much interest a customer has to each of the pre-selected candidate products. In the initial prototype we use 4000 most frequently bought products and choose the 10 most interesting products for each customer. The interest of customers to products is estimated by computing a measure of distance between customer and product vectors.

5 Initial experience and performance

In the current phase of the system we use Palm III hand-held organizer with 2Mbytes of RAM as the client device [3]. Both the proxy and remote ordering components of the SmartPad server reside on a single IBM RS6000 model F40 with a 233MHz PowerPC processor and 896Mbytes of RAM. The database is stored in IBM DB2 version 5.2.

During the initial trial period about 200 customers in an individual store are supported with the goal of evaluating the system. The initial version of the system is written in Java and uses JDBC for database connectivity. We are using IBM's implementation of JDK 1.1.6. We have chosen Java primarily for its portability, since we eventually plan to move the server code to the operational mainframe. Unfortunately, the performance of Java and JDBC for large scale computational and data processing tasks still lags behind more mature alternatives, such as C with embedded SQL.

Number of Customers	Personal Catalog (sec/customer)	Recommendations (sec/customer)
Unoptimized Java code in the trial prototype:		
150	19	12.08
Optimized C with embedded SQL:		
20K	0.055	0.059
40K	0.056	0.061
60K	0.062	0.061
80K	*	0.064

(Times are in seconds)

* – out of disk space

Table 1. Performance of data processing

We have experimented with scalability of the main processing kernels of the system. We have re-implemented personal catalog generator and recommender in C with embedded SQL. In addition to using statically compiled code, we have optimized some of the data structures. In the Java version of the system the spending matrix is stored in a database table. Due to the overhead of logging, we found it too expensive to update the large matrix for 20K and more customers in the database. Instead, the C version of the recommender maintains the matrix in a file.

We have experimented with the resulting code on the data sets for large numbers of customers. We started out with a month worth of spending data for about 20K customers and have "cloned" the transactions for each customer 1, 2 and 3 times in order to measure how processing times scale as the workload scales from 20K to 80K customers. The size of the **Spending** table ranges from 2M records to 8M records.

Table 1 shows the performance of personal catalog generator and the recommender written in Java and in C. C code with optimized data accesses is two to three hundred times faster (per customer). However, this difference should not be read as an indictment of Java for large scale data processing. Improvements in Just-in-time compilation combined with faster implementation of JDBC should reduce this gap. Additionally, we need to perform careful profiling of the code in order to establish the relative contribution of such factors as data structure implementation, data copies and conversions in JDBC, and guarded array and string access in Java.

The performance of the C code indicates that personalization processing scales virtually linearly with the number of customers. This is to be expected since the time complexity of the main steps is proportional to the number of customers multiplied by various factors which can be considered constant, such as the number of candidate products or the average number of product classes that a person buys into in a month.

6 Conclusions

We have described the design and initial experience with SmartPad system, a software solution in the consumer space, providing consumers with ubiquitous access to interactive shopping through hand-held devices. This system is currently used, in a trial study, by a set of customers of Safeway Stores plc – a major retailer in the UK. The initial feedback is very encouraging since the system enhances shoppers experience, an experience which is considered uninteresting and time consuming. The SmartPad system enables end-users to shop remotely using personalized content, searching and selecting in incremental mode and disconnected from the network. This is achieved by combining in-store and on-line transactions, by leveraging current efforts in data mining, and by delivering information through hand-held devices.

We have experimented with the main processing kernels and their implementation demonstrating scalability as the number of customers increase. In addition, a set of data structures were designed for storing personal databases which can be expediently accessed and transmitted to a mobile device.

Our future work focuses on four areas:

- Performance tuning of the main application processes.
- Reduction in communication between the mobile device and the device proxy server by using compression and incremental updates to personal databases.
- Evaluation of emerging standards for mobile computing, such as Wireless Markup Language (WML) and Wireless Access protocol (WAP).
- Finally, evaluation of various algorithms for recommending new products.

Acknowledgements

We would like to thank Jeeva Nadesan, Neal Bircher, and Jeremy Wyman, who work at Safeway Information Systems, for their continuous support in providing business knowledge and data.

References

1. R. Agrawal, T. Imielinski, and A. Swami. Mining associations between sets of items in massive databases. In *Proc. of the ACM SIGMOD Int'l Conference on Management of Data*, Washington D.C., May 1993.
2. Don Chamberlin. *Using the new DB2: IBM's Object-Relational database system.* Morgan Kaufmann Publishers, Inc., 1996.
3. Palm Computing. Palm III organizer technical specifications. http://www.palm.com/products/palmiii-details.html.
4. Richard D. Lawrence, Marisa S. Viveros, George S. Almasi, Sastri S. Duri, and Vladimir Kotlyar. Personalization of product recommendations in mass retail markets. (in preparation).
5. Evaggelia Pitoura and George Samaras. *Data management for mobile computing.* Kluwer Academic Publishers, 1998.
6. SABRE Group Press Release. The SABRE Group, IBM and Nokia team to create traveler service for enhanced mobile phone. http://www.sabre.com/news/pr031899a.htm, March 1999.

Towards a Scalable System Architecture in Digital Libraries

H. Haddouti[1], W. Wohner[1], R. Bayer[2]

[1]FORWISS (Bavarian Research Center For Knowledge-based Systems)
[2]Technische Universität München, Institut für Informatik
Orleansstr. 34, 81667 Munich, Germany
{haddouti, wohner}@forwiss.de
bayer@in.tum.de

Abstract. In this paper we will present the digital library system developed in the framework of the VD17 Project, in which all prints of the 17th Century published in the German-speaking area are being cataloged and partially digitized. The intensive use of this system showed that the current architecture suffers from performance problems. Therefore, scalability is of great importance, and in particular the question arises, in which way and through which measures efficiency can be increased. We will describe some principles, which can generally lead to an increase in performance. Subsequently, we will present our scalable system architecture which improves the performance drastically and allows additional partners to join this project.

1 Introduction

Digital libraries (DL) are widely used in practically every field of scientific as well as in a vast variety of business applications, providing rich repositories of online information. The universal acceptance and use of digital libraries among natural and engineering scientists as well as among humanities scholars can be attributed to the chief advantage of digital information retrieval: instantaneous online availability of the requested information, in combination with optimized (full text) search facilities that guarantee fast access to the digitally stored and well-organized data.

On the other hand, the quantity of data being held within digital libraries is steadily increasing in order to serve the demand of the scientific community. The designers and maintainers of digital library systems are thus challenged with performance issues concerning efficient transaction management in very large databases, i.e. scalability.

In this paper we will present a scalable DL architecture that allows efficient data retrieval and maintenance even in large-scale databases. Section 2 introduces the currently used architecture of the VD17 digital library system and its scalability problem. In Section 3 we discuss various solutions addressing performance issues and then we suggest our approach to solving the scalability problem as described in Section 4. The last Section closes with perspectives for future work.

2 VD17: An example of a Digital Library Project

The VD17[1] (German National Bibliography of 17th Century Prints) project involves cooperative and simultaneous cataloging in several libraries aiming at building the bibliographic core of the 17th Century prints published in the German-speaking area, digitizing a part of them, and making them accessible worldwide [5]. Currently, 100,000 of an estimated number of 300,000 prints have been cataloged and 190,000 key pages have been digitized. The whole collection is available on the Internet[2].

Six of the largest German state and university libraries are participating in the VD17 project. They are contributing their valuable stock of 17th Century prints to the VD17 database, while the Bavarian Research Center for Knowledge-Based Systems (FOR-WISS) has been commissioned to design and implement an adequate software solution. About 30 librarians working at the six registration centers spread over Germany are cooperating to build the catalog of the VD17 prints via remote connections to the VD17 database.

Considering the high frequency of both update and retrieval requests, a system architecture has been chosen that provides fast response times for all the required database functions (see Section 2.1). Nevertheless, this architecture cannot prevent from slower response times as the database grows in size. Having already augmented to a size of about 780 MB, the VD17 database is expected to reach 2.5 GB by the end of the project. Thus, high reliability of the involved computer systems and special performance issues due to latency and bandwidth of the Internet are crucial.

2.1 System Architecture

The VD17 database is internally divided into two separate logical databases, called MAB-DB and OMNIS-DB (see Fig. 1). This architecture has been chosen to optimize database access, namely update and retrieval operations. Data retrieval is solely handled by the OMNIS-DB while the MAB-DB supports data manipulation.

In more detail, the MAB-DB is used to store the complete bibliographical data according to MAB, an electronic exchange format (similar to MARC). An import and an export component (*mabim* and *mabex*; see Fig. 1) are provided enabling designated users to insert, alter and delete records of the MAB-DB.

In contrast to the MAB-compliant hierarchical data structure of the MAB-DB, the structure of the OMNIS-DB is optimized in respect of retrieval functions. It serves as a document view of the whole VD17 database and is as such designed to meet the human user's need for a clear layout of the supplied information. A subset of the MAB-DB's data is stored here in easy-to-access structure fields, such as 'Author' or 'Title'. The OMNIS-DB also offers text BLOBs that contain all essential bibliographic information for each document, pre-formatted in HTML. This allows direct and very fast access to document data instead of navigating through the hierarchical

---

[1] Funded by the German Research Foundation (DFG)
[2] http://www.forwiss.de/~vd17

and complex structure of the MAB-DB. Additionally, the user can search the OMNIS-DB's full text vocabulary containing keywords of all VD17 documents.

As all update operations only refer to the MAB-DB, a separate update component, called Update Manager, is needed for gradually adapting the OMNIS-DB to the current state of the MAB-DB. The specific actions of the update component are determined by an easily adjustable configuration file which allows adequate and flexible data presentation.

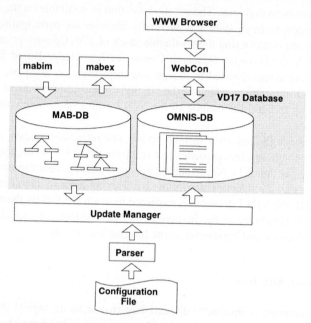

Fig. 1. Current System Architecture

Import Component. Bibliographical data is inserted into the MAB-DB via the import component *mabim*. *Mabim* accepts files in MAB format, parses them and extracts the values of the different MAB fields. Import files may contain one or more bibliographic records of the 17th Century prints. The hierarchical structure of each cataloged document is then analyzed and stored in the MAB-DB. All data field records are inserted into this structure.

Mabim offers the complete update functionality, i.e. inserting new documents and altering or deleting existing documents. In any case, *mabim* has to search the MAB-DB for the document that has to be updated. This is done via a unique record identifier (RID) that is also part of MAB. If the database contains no RID as specified in the import file, a new document will be created. Otherwise, the already existing document will be altered according to the MAB data of the import file.

Export Component. The export component *mabex* is used for exporting data from the MAB-DB. *Mabex* collects the complete hierarchy and all data fields of a given document and writes this bibliographical information to a MAB file which is being stored on the client machine. Thus, any document stored inside the VD17 database may easily be extracted, again, by specifying the record's unique identifier RID.

Having exported the MAB file containing a particular document the cataloger is able to edit its data fields. The altered document can then be re-imported into the database using *mabim*, or simply be passed to another library for internal use.

Update Manager. Whenever data is imported into the VD17 database, only the MAB-DB is affected, i.e. the OMNIS-DB will stay unchanged until an intermediate system component, the Update Manager, balances the two logical databases. Since changes to the database are very common and frequent due to the constant cataloging process, the Update Manager is run periodically at fixed time intervals.

The Update Manager analyzes the MAB-DB and filters data records which have been changed since its last iteration. Newly created or updated documents can therefore be easily identified and analyzed. Their data will be inserted into the structure fields of the OMNIS-DB. Additionally, text BLOBs pre-formatted in HTML and entries for the VD17 full text vocabulary are generated and also stored in the OMNIS-DB.

In order to maintain a maximum of flexibility the Update Manager's behavior depends on a separate configuration file. This file defines where and how data entries will be stored in the OMNIS-DB.

User Interface. To profit from the advantages and universal acceptance of Web browsers, FORWISS developed a Web-based user interface. The platform independence of this solution enables users to search the VD17 database without any specific requirements to the client machine. The VD17 database supports full text search and so-called attribute queries that offer a pre-structured form for accessing the structure fields, such as 'author' or 'publisher'. Catalogers, however, who have to update the database are equipped with an additional interface that allows them to make use of the functionality provided by the import and export components.

3 Performance Issues

The first design, as described in Section 2, was based on a centralized solution, because we could not fully anticipate how intensively our system would be used. The crucial issue, though, is that many other libraries and institutions outside Germany showed their interest in collaboration. In practice, this means that the number of catalogers will rise by a factor of 2 or 3. Furthermore, we have learned many lessons from the three years of the VD17 system operation which will also be considered in the forthcoming new architecture.

The new system architecture is addressing two drawbacks: synchronization over the Internet and the growing volume of the database. Synchronizing the system´s components over the Internet is the more challenging problem. On the one hand the latency and network bandwidth must be used in an optimized way, on the other hand the resource and time-intensive multi-user update operations are in such centralized solution no longer manageable.

3.1 User and log Studies

The following statistics are based on user assessments and a database log file. For gaining a better understanding of the user side we distributed questionnaires to be answered by catalogers. By examining the log file on the other hand we can observe all events occurred in the database. Examples of such events are errors, logins in a database, queries, begin and end of a transaction, etc. The resulted log file has been spooled into a database for a better analysis and evaluation.

The data considered was recorded from October 1998 to December 1998 (3 months). Since the users and their hosts (IP numbers) are recorded, we can incorporate the geographic location into the transaction log analysis. Moreover, we can analyze the queries and database operations in more detail according to the specific needs of each library.

About 4 million events have been registered and analyzed. More than 192,446 database connection errors have occurred. Subsequently, 141,414 locking errors (75%) have been observed. This confirms our assumption, that the central system strongly suffers from a concurrency bottleneck. On the other hand, approximately 2.126,312 DML operations (e.g. select, insert, delete, update), 285,936 DDL operations (such as create table, create index, drop table, drop index, create view, etc.) and 133,512 database sessions have been recorded.

Table 1. The Current Cataloged Holdings

Library	Library ID	Number of Roots	Percentage
Berlin	1:*	12,283	17,9
Dresden	14:*	7,439	10,8
Gotha	39:*	9,405	13,7
Halle	3:*	6,575	9,6
München	12:*	17,940	26,1
Wolfenbüttel	23:*	15,077	21,9

There are six library partners, however 3 of them (Berlin, München and Wolfenbüttel) are the main contributors, whereas the other three libraries are associate partners. In other words, the main partners and their associate partners are mainly working on their respective holdings, but cross working on other library data can be not excluded. According to the partners´ feedback 70 % of their cataloging are based on their own holdings and the rest on "foreign" data.

Table 1 depicts the actual state of the VD17 database sorted by library record ID. For instance, records belonging to the State Library of Berlin begin with "1:" ("*" stands for truncation). A data record is hierarchically structured according to the MAB format (e.g. multi-volume, volume, issue, article) and is identified by the root record ID (top hierarchy). Hence, at the moment about 12,283 roots from Berlin have been cataloged. This means that 17,9 % of the already cataloged holdings belong to the State Library of Berlin.

3.2 Discussion of Possible Solutions

It is clear that the main issue of our system is scalability. Hence, the transaction concept and locking procedures play the key role. It is important to hold locks only as long as necessary; to keep the transactions short; to hold only a few locks during a transaction. Basic principles and solutions are briefly presented in the following.

Synchronization by object versioning. Here, an object which is to be changed, is split into two versions, an old and a just newly created one [1]. The administration of versions makes it possible that several obtained database states are accessible. A version administration can be realized on different levels, such as database versioning, node versioning, and object versioning. The disadvantage of this procedure is the increased memory and read expenditure [6]. Furthermore, maintaining relationships between different versions is quite challenging.

Optimistic Concurrency Control. Optimistic concurrency control (OCC) is an interesting alternative to locking strategies [7]. One can save the time for the generation and administration of locks, if the transaction conflicts are exceptions. In case of conflicts, the conflicting transaction can be backed up. Contrary to locking procedures conflicts will be recognized very late, which may leads to high-overhead.

Hierarchical locks. The hierarchical locking strategy permits choosing different granularities for different transactions. The granularity can be based on a table, a page or a record. The granularity size depends strongly on the type of a given transaction (see ARIES/IM in [8]).

We believe that hierarchical locking will yield acceptable results in the VD17 system. However, since the used DBMS TransBase [11] supports only page or table locking, we have implemented the fine-grained locking strategy which allows reducing the lock granularity to the record level.

4 A Suitable Solution

4.1 Description

During the past years, a large attention has been paid to research on developing high performance DBMS. A few examples of such efforts have been presented in [3], [10], [9], and [2] by developing the multiprocessor database machines Gamma, Tandem, Oracle Parallel Server and DB2 parallel edition, respectively. Databases are partitioned horizontally and distributed across multiple processors.

There are three partitioning strategies: *range*, *round-robin* and *hashing* partitioning [4]. When using the *round-robin* technique records are assigned to n partitions, so that the *i-th* record is placed in the (*i mod n*) partition. This is ideal for applications with sequential access to data. The hashing method requires the distribution of records to partitions due to a hash function. This method is suitable for applications with sequential and associative access. Range partitioning can be performed, for instance, based on lexicographic order. Bubba, Gamma, Oracle and Tandem provide range partitioning. The risk of range partitioning is data skew. However, this problem is less susceptible to the VD17 system, because range partitioning is based on very detailed user studies and long-term experiences gained in the first phase of the system operation. However, a combination of such methods is also conceivable.

Considering our observations based on user studies and the log file analysis we decided to partition the VD17 database into three independent partitions horizontally. Technically, each partition corresponds to our previous architecture. This means that for each partition there is an import component, an export component and an update manager (see Section 2). Hence, this approach cannot lead to a communication overhead.

4.2 Scalable System Architecture

The architecture depicted below has the following features:

- Scalability: Adding a new node is possible without any new software development. Additionally, the existing nodes could also be divided into further partitions, once the node is growing increasingly.
- Transparency: Partitions are invisible to the user.
- Reliability: A fault-tolerance component is not yet considered in our system. But, a moderate option has been developed. The catalogers of each library can work locally on their own data, so that no conflicts with other libraries occur. The data is being stored locally and can be spooled to the database partition, once it is available again.

The MAB database has been divided into three partitions according to the statistic studies. The MAB database partitions are disjoint and can be distributed on different machines and different locations. Each partition is built similarly to the former architecture as a standalone VD17 database with its own import, export and update manager component. It will yield a high performance if a location factor and the network topology is taken into consideration. For instance, related libraries regarding their holdings and location can host and maintain their partition strategically located. But this does not mean that cross cataloging processes are excluded. On the contrary, such processes exist and will still exist. That is why we emphasize on the term "Cooperative Cataloging".

We also decided to partition the OMNIS-DB in order to increase the VD17 performance substantially. Many partitions of the OMNIS database will make the newly built document displayable to the user rapidly. Additionally, building a document in very small partitions requires less time than in a huge database. In other words, the Update Manager now locks MAB database partitions very short. Moreover, this approach also allows distributing the OMNIS database partitions on many machines with their appropriate system resources and Update Managers.

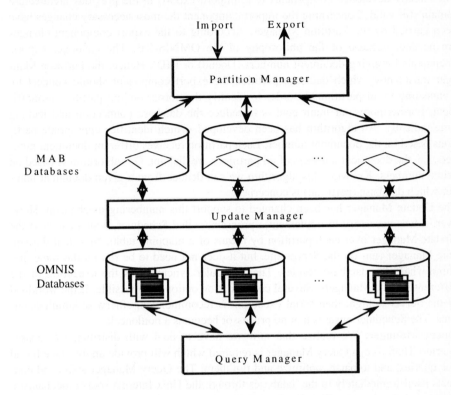

Fig. 2. A Scalable System Architecture

Partition Manager. This is a very powerful component which is responsible for routing client requests to the appropriate node (database partition). The partitioning has been based on library record identifiers (RID). We assume that cataloger A is sending a data record R_i to the Partition Manager. The parser tool included in the Partition Manager will analyze the exchange file containing MAB data and look for the library record identifier by means of the MAB syntax. Some verification procedures are necessary to be sure that a given data record is belonging to a certain partition, because R_i could be a cross data record which means that the super title belongs to library L1; the sub title to library L2 and copies to many other libraries. Therefore, the identification must be done at the root level (top level of data record hierarchy). Once the root identifier is recognized, the Partition Manager will route the exchange file to the import component by indicating the appropriate database partition.

Adding new partitions or re-organizing the partitions does not require new software development. There is a configuration file in which the system operator can configure a number of partitions, their features and further options. The purpose of the configuration file is to make our solution flexible and general.

The already developed components (e.g. import, export) in the previous architecture remain still valid. Concerning the import component the most necessary changes have been carried by the Partition Manager. According to the export component changes are needed, because of the philosophy of the OMNIS-DB. The cataloger exports documents by giving document numbers (Docno) or RID[3]. Hence, the Partition Manager must know which database partition the export component should connect to. Connecting to all partitions in order to identify the corresponding partition is inefficient. Furthermore, our main goal is to reduce the database connection and locking time radically. An algorithm has been developed, which identifies appropriate partitions based on the document number. Each partition receives different document numbers, i.e. the document numbers of all partitions are disjoint. Our algorithm is based on prime numbers. Knowing this algorithm we can deduce from a given document number which database (partition) is concerned.

The Update Manager has been changed to support this numbering mechanism. However, it was necessary to implement a program, called Scheduler, which can start the Update Manager over each partition by means of a mapping table. Note that the Update Manager runs on the Server site, but it does not need to be run on the same machine where the database resides. The Scheduler synchronizes the execution of the different Update Managers. Several configuration options are possible. If the workload of the Server is high, then serial execution is recommended, otherwise simultaneous runs. The Scheduler ensures that no processor becomes a bottleneck.

Query Manager. We realize that now we have to deal with distributed databases queries. Therefore, a Query Manager is required which will provide an interface for ad hoc queries, and to parse, optimize and run them. The Query Manager starts and connects itself immediately to the databases through the Unix Internet socket mechanism. Otherwise, the system will suffer from delayed response times.

The statistics gained from the analysis of the database log file show that in most cases the queries of the catalogers are based on the record identifier and/or the document number. Therefore, the Query Manager can recognize by means of given rules that certain queries can be routed to one node only instead of overloading other nodes unnecessarily. For instance, queries using document numbers and/or record identifiers can be directed immediately to appropriate partitions. Hence, the unnecessary connect and SQL requests to other databases are saved. The deduction takes place on the client site without any connection to databases. This is thanks to the number assigning algorithm.

5 Conclusion

In this work we investigated optimization strategies in order to improve the scalability of the VD17 system. Subsequently, we presented our scalability approach which is

---

[3] Docno is the internal ID of OMNIS-DB documents, while RID is the identifier of MAB-DB entries.

currently in testing phase. The first evaluation showed that this new architecture has achieved in inserting, updating or deleting data records an improvement of 45 %. Even the retrieval time remains more or less unchanged in comparison to the central architecture.

However, we think that further improvements will be the agenda of our next work packages. For instance, balancing the workload upon system resources (I/O operations, CPU, memory, network traffic) dynamically. According to the Query Manager, a variety of heuristics can be used to route queries to different database partitions. These heuristics include data record identifying conventions or special features within the data itself.

Acknowledgements

We would like to thank Pavel Vogel, Liselotte Steinherr-Isen for helpful comments. We are grateful to Marianne Dörr for the great cooperation in the VD17 project. Special thank is owed to Otto Krischer for his support in the implementation work.

References

[1]   Bayer R., Heller H., Reiser A. Parallelism and Recovery in Database Systems. In ACM Transactions on Database Systems, 5 (2) , pp. 139-156, June 1980

[2]   Chitanya K. B. DB2 Parallel Edition, IBM Systems Journal, 34 (2), pp. 292-322, April 1995

[3]   DeWitt D. J. et al. The Gamma Database Machine Project. IEEE Transactions on Knowledge on Data Enginnering, 2(1), pp. 44-62, March 1990

[4]   DeWitt D. J, Gray J. Parallel Database Systems: The Future of High Performance Database Systems. In Communication of the ACM, 35(6), pp. 85-98, June 1992

[5]   Dörr M., H. Haddouti, S. Wiesener, The German National Bibliography 1601 - 1700, Proceedings of ADL'97, Washington, DC, May 7-9, 1997, IEEE Computer Society, Press, Los Alamitos, 1997

[6]   Härder T., Reuter A. Principles of Transaction-Oriented Database Recovery. In ACM Computer Surveys, Vol. 15 No. 4, pp.287-317, December 1983

[7]   Kun H. T., Robinson J. T. On optimistic Methods for Concurrency Control. In ACM Transaction on Database Systems, 6(2), pp. 213-226, 1981

[8]   Mohan C., Levine F. ARIES/IM: An Efficient and High Concurrency Index Management Method Using Write-ahead Logging. In Proceedings of the 1992 ACM SIGMOD, San Diego, pp. 371-380, June 1992

[9]   Oracle & Digital. Oracle Parallel Server in the Digital Environment. Technical Report, Oracle, June 1994

[10]   The Tandem Performance Group. A Benchmark of Nonstop SQL on the Debit Credit Transaction. In Proceedings of the ACM SIGMOD Conference, Chicago, IL, pp. 337-341, June 1988

[11]   TransAction Software GmbH: TransBase Relational Database System Version 4.2.2 System and Installation Guide. München, 1996

MOSAIC: A Multi-feature Access Method for Large Image Databases

Shen-Tat Goh   Kian-Lee Tan

Department of Computer Science, National University of Singapore

Abstract. In this paper, we present an image retrieval system that made used of an index structure, called *MOSAIC* to facilitate speedy retrieval of images. MOSIAC is a multi-tier structure that indexes multiple features of an image, with each tier dealing with one feature. Our current implementation of MOSAIC organizes images based on color, size and spatial location of *clusters* extracted from the images. We evaluated MOSAIC, and our results show that it is able to prune the search space and retrieve relevant images quickly.

1   Introduction

The management of a large number of images in a multimedia database has received much attention in recent years. Most of the earlier works are largely focused on techniques to extract useful information (such as the color, texture or shape features) that represents the content of images. It is only recently when this extraction technology is more mature, that researchers are becoming more concern about assisting structures or indexes that will help to retrieve the relevant images quickly. Rapid retrieval is becoming an important issue as image databases continue to grow in size and a slow system will no longer be acceptable to the user community.

Traditionally, an image is represented by its features such as color, texture and shape of objects. It has been observed that a single feature is insufficient to fully represent the content of an image [10]. For example, the effectiveness (in terms of recall and precision) of retrieving images based on color alone or texture alone is found to be much lower than if both the color and texture features are integrated. And recently, there have been an increasing interest in studies relating in an integrated color-spatial retrieval approach [2, 6, 7, 9, 3]. Moreover, the set of relevant images for each feature can be very different if they are used separately.

One straightforward approach to facilitate fast retrievals in an image system that supports multiple features is to build an index structure for each feature. The set of relevant images can then be obtained by intersecting candidate images from all features. This approach, though simple, has two disadvantages. First, the system must manage multiple indexes. Second, each feature can contribute a large number of candidate images, and combining the results from these features can be expensive.

In this paper, we present an image system that supports multiple features. In our system, an image is represented by a set of *clusters* that are extracted. For each cluster, we maintain information on three features: color, size and spatial location within the image. During the retrieval process, the query image's clusters and features information are also extracted and compared against those stored in the database. The retrieved images are ranked and returned to the users. In particular, we propose an index structure, called *MOSAIC* to facilitate speedy retrieval of images. We have also evaluated MOSAIC, and our results show that it is able to prune the search space and retrieve relevant images quickly.

Due to space constraint, we have omitted details of the algorithms, and presented only representative experimental results. For further details, see [4].

2 Multi-feature Cluster-Based Image Retrieval

Ideally, a retrieval system should be both effective and efficient. For an effective retrieval, a good representation for each image is a necessary requirement. Together with the representation, we will also need an accurate way of measuring the similarity between any two images. The effectiveness of a retrieval system depends on how well the system is able to retrieve all the wanted images and at the same time not retrieving too many unwanted ones. On the other hand, we also want such retrieval to be fast and efficient. With this in mind, we shall first present our representation of the image in this section. In the next section, we shall discuss the issue of speedy retrieval.

Inclining towards an automatic content-based retrieval system, we have chosen to represent an image by a set of *clusters* that are extracted from the image. Moreover, for each cluster we maintain information on three features: color, size and the spatial location within the image. We note that all these features can be automatically extracted from an image. Here, we will look at the representation of the multi-feature cluster, their extraction, and the similarity function.

2.1 Color Representation

We have chosen the CIEL*u*v* color space since the linearity of this space allows the perceptual differences between the colors to be determined by the Euclidean distance measure. In other words, two different pixels in an image (or from different images) are perceptually similar in terms of color if their colors are close to one another in the 3D-space.

2.2 Representation of Cluster Information

Humans are particularly sensitive to large clusters of colors [1]. Two images appear to be similar to one another if they both have regions of similar colors at roughly the same locations in the images. Thus, we felt that a set of such clusters extracted from an image will serve as a good representation of an image. However, since clusters come in all forms of irregular shapes, storing them may be costly in terms of storage as well as when we need to assess the similarity between two shapes. We adopted a simple approach: instead of storing the exact cluster shape, we store its bounding rectangle (which requires only two points). Our approach thus captures three features of an image:

- **Color.** Each cluster contains pixels that are similar in color.
- **Spatial Location.** From the bounding rectangle, we essentially have the spatial location of the cluster in the image space. Since a cluster contains pixels with similar colors, to some extent, the spatial location of the cluster also provides an indication of the spatial distribution of colors in the image.
- **Size of cluster.** As the cluster is not physically stored, we would like to at least know its size. As such, in this work, we have also maintained the size of the cluster.

2.3 Extraction of Multi-feature Clusters

To extract the cluster information from an image, we employ a two-phase heuristics. Our technique works as follows. In the first phase, we extract a set of *dominant* clusters. To achieve this, we employ a two-step segmentation process. Step 1 is done to "smoothen" the image. It allows more gradual change in color from a pixel to all its adjacent pixels. In step 2, we use a merging threshold value to combine pixels in an image into clusters. This merging threshold is set at a p percentile of the color Euclidean distances between all adjacent pairs in an image. At the end of phase one, we have a large set of distinct color clusters.

In phase two, we rank the clusters in descending order of their sizes (i.e., number of pixels). The $Cl_{dominant}$ largest clusters will be picked as the dominant clusters to represent the image. For these $Cl_{dominant}$ clusters, we keep track of their sizes, and their spatial location within the image.

Before leaving this section, we note that the number of clusters can affect performance. A small number of clusters can speed up the retrieval process and lower the storage cost at the expense of the retrieval accuracy. Adding more clusters may increase the retrieval accuracy since these clusters are likely to lead to more retrievals. However, having too large a number of clusters will eventually lead to poor performance. This is because the set will contain small clusters which may contribute to the retrieval of irrelevant images. Further, the storage of these large number of spatial rectangles, and retrieval and comparison cost are likely to become high too. Therefore, it is important to fine-tune $Cl_{dominant}$ so that a compromise between retrieval effectiveness and retrieval efficiency can be obtained.

2.4 Similarity Function

This function determines the matching criterion between two comparing images. As our interest lies in comparing large clusters between the images, we will only consider the similarity between these clusters. Any two clusters are considered similar when their colors are perceptually similar, approximately equal in size and positioned within close range. The similarity function is then derived from a function of the compounded similarity values for all the matching clusters, where each cluster's similarity value follows the contribution from all the cluster features.

2.5 Image Retrieval Process

The image database is initially preprocessed to determine the clusters (color, size and spatial information) of the images. Given a sample query image, *at most* Cl_{query} clusters are extracted, where Cl_{query} is a predetermined value. Note that it is possible to have fewer than Cl_{query} clusters because a painted query may contain just a single-colored object such as an orange sun. The color, size and spatial information of each image in the database is then compared with those of the query image using the similarity function described above. The images can then be ranked, retrieved and displayed in that order.

3 MOSAIC: A Multi-feature Index Structure

Having described the basic retrieval technique, there remains the problem of speedy image retrieval. With tens of thousand of images, it is not practical to sequentially test each image in the database against the sample image. Even though we restrict the number of clusters to $Cl_{dominant}$, the number of cluster comparisons to be performed remains very large. Consider a database with N images and each is represented by $Cl_{dominant}$ clusters. If Cl_{query} clusters are extracted from the query image, there will be about $N \cdot Cl_{dominant} \cdot Cl_{query}$ comparisons. Since only a small number of images is likely to match the sample image, a large number of unnecessary comparisons are being performed. As the comparison is expensive, we propose an index structure, called MOSAIC, to provide an efficient means to reduce the number of comparisons.

3.1 The MOSAIC structure

MOSAIC is a multi-tier index structure where each tier handles an image feature. For example, the top tier can be based on color, the second is based on size of the cluster, and the last is based on spatial property. Each layer can be constructed using any indexing mechanism. For example, the "color" and "spatial" layers can be implemented using a multidimensional single dimensional indexing structure such as the R-tree [5]. On the other hand, the "size" layer can employ a single-dimensional array. Except for the lowest level, entries in the leaf nodes of all levels point to the roots of the trees in the next level. Only the leaf nodes of the lowest level tree contain pointers to the image data. Thus, MOSAIC essentially consists of multiple trees integrated together in a hierarchical manner. Such a structure can facilitate speedy retrieval of images. To reach to the lowest layer of MOSAIC where the actual images are pointed to, the query must satisfy the conditions relating to the discriminating keys in all the higher layers. Any condition violated in any layer will terminate the search path prematurely. Thus, MOSAIC can reduce the search space by pruning off redundant paths early.

While MOSAIC is a general structure, we have implemented a three-tier MOSAIC structure. Figure 1 shows the MOSAIC structure implemented. The first layer discriminates clusters based on color. In our work, we have represented the color of a cluster by the mean L, U and V values of its pixels. For simplicity, we chose to implement this layer as 3 sub-layers serving as filters for the L, U and V values. Each sub-layer is essentially a single-dimensional vector that directs the search to the next sub-layer (or layer for the V filter) so that only those clusters with the relevant L, U, V values need to be searched. Each entry in the L and U sub-layers contain a range and a pointer to the next sub-layer. The V sub-layer contain a range and a pointer to the second layer. The second

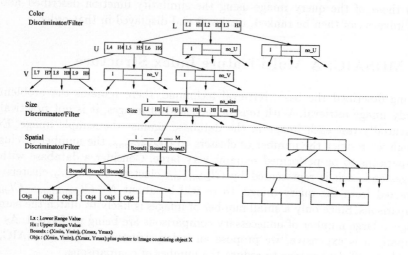

Fig. 1. The MOSAIC indexing structure.

layer is the size layer. that acts as a filter to prune away those clusters whose sizes do not match those of the query clusters. Like the V sub-layer of tier 1, entries in this layer contain a range (on the sizes of clusters) and a pointer to the next tier.

Finally, the last layer is based on the spatial information of the clusters, which is adequately handled by the R-tree structure. Each entry of the internal node contains a rectangle that defines its child node's data space and a pointer pointing to the subtree. For the leaf nodes, entries contain the bounding rectangles of the clusters and a pointer to the image containing that cluster.

We adopted a *static* strategy to evenly distribute clusters across the pointers to the last layer. This is done by first preprocessing the image database and determine the best values to set for the various filter vectors in the first two tiers of MOSAIC. In this way, equal number of data clusters will be placed along all paths and all the R-trees will be of equal depth at the last tier. Hence, we will have a balanced indexing structure on the whole.

3.2 Matching and Searching a MOSAIC structure

Figure 2 shows the algorithm for retrieving the images that are similar to a sample image. Given a sample image, the algorithm extracts Cl_{query} dominant clusters together with information on color, size and spatial location (line 1). For each of the clusters extracted, it determines the set of images that are similar to it (lines 2-7). This is done by traversing MOSAIC to determine the clusters that match those of the sample image. It suffices to know that the *search* algorithm returns a list of pointers to potential matching images. Since different clusters of the query image may have the same resultant matching images, the similarity measure has to be cumulated (line 5). Finally, the set of potential images are ranked (line 8-10) and the images can be retrieved in order of their ranking (line 11).

Algorithm Match
Input: Sample image, IMG
output: Images similar to IMG

1. *cluster* ← extractCluster(IMG, Cl_{query})
2. for each cluster, *cl* ∈ *cluster* {
3.   PTR-list ← search(*cl*, *MOSAIC.root*)
4.   for each *image_id* in PTR-list {
5.   *similarity* ← computeSimilarity()
6.   }
7. }
8. for each *image_id* {
9.   rank(*image_id*)
10.}
11.retrieve the images using the image IDs.

Fig. 2. Algorithm Match.

The search algorithm of the MOSAIC structure is fairly straightforward. Essentially, for each tier, we need to issue a range query to facilitate similarity retrieval of images. For each query cluster, we have the following information: the color ([L, U, V]), size and spatial location ($[X_{min}, Y_{min}], [X_{max}, Y_{max}]$).

In the first layer, color is the search key. To facilitate similarity retrieval, we "enlarge" the L, U and V values by l, u and v respectively. Thus, the first sub-layer is searched with $[L-l, L+l]$, similarly with the second and final sub-layers. This will result in retrieving pointers pointing to the "size" index structure in the next layer. Like the "color" layer, if the size of the query cluster is S, then we generate a range query $[S-s, S+s]$. This allows us to retrieve any node that has value that intersects with the search key. This will result in retrieving pointers pointing to the last layer. Finally in the last layer, the traversal is essentially that of the R-tree searching algorithm. Branches of the R-trees that intersect with the query cluster's spatial location will be traversed. When the leaf nodes are reached, the images whose clusters that intersect with the query cluster are the potential resultant images.

3.3 Insertion of Clusters

Given that an existing MOSAIC structure exists, adding a new image into the database requires inserting its clusters into the MOSAIC structure. The addition of new clusters can be done as follows. First, traverse the indexing structure and insert the cluster into its appropriate R-tree. If the number of clusters in the R-tree exceeds a predetermined number r where r is dependent on the maximum allowable depth of the R-tree, then the R-tree is split into two. Instead of creating a new root node for the R-tree, at the "size" layer, the corresponding range is split into two. Similarly, color layer exceeds s number of clusters (where a possible value for s could be set at twice of its initial value), it will be split and its range updated.

4 Performance Evaluation

In this section, we describe the evaluation of the color-spatial retrieval techniques in VIPER (VIsual Property-based search Engine for image Retrieval), our prototype image retrieval system. We have conducted a large set of experiments, and we report some representative results here.

VIPER is designed and implemented on a SUN Sparc Workstation running Solaris 2.5 using C/C++ programming language. The overall system architecture is shown in Figure 3. It consists of two main modules: the *preprocessing* and *retrieval* modules.

The image database holds the set of 12,000 images used for testing. They are *preprocessed* to extract the appropriate clusters and features information. These are then indexed using the MOSAIC indexing structure. The *retrieval module* of the prototype accepts sample images from the user as queries through a *graphical user interface* module. During querying, the clusters and the associated information of the query image are extracted, and the index and database are searched for matching images. Candidate images are ranked based on the similarity measure and presented to the users. The graphical interface is designed to display the top 60 retrieved images ranked in decreasing order of similarity. Queries are issued by image example. Users are able to specify content-based queries by selecting a sample image or a painted image. The interface also allows the user to "click" on an image to find out more detailed information about the image.

In our experiments, we have examined the efficiency and also the effectiveness of our system on image retrieval. For efficiency, we have timed our runs and also computed the number of IOs needed for each retrieval. And to measure

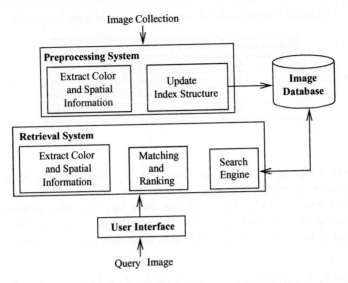

Fig. 3. The architecture of VIPER.

the effectiveness of retrieval, we have used the normalized recall and precision measure [8]. For purpose of comparison, we have also implemented the following retrieval methods:

- **Color Index.** This structure is essentially the first layer of our MOSAIC structure. By comparing with this approach, we can have a feel of how critical are the other features, and study the benefit of multiple feature retrieval.
- **Color-Spatial Index.** This structure comprises two of the layers of the MOSAIC structure — the color and spatial location layers. This structure would serve as a representation of color-spatial techniques proposed in the literature. Comparing with it will also allow us to have a feel of the significance of the size feature.

In our experiments, we have set $Cl_{dominant}$ to 5, i.e., the 5 largest clusters and their information are maintained. For our 12000 image collection, we have altogether $12000 * 5$ clusters in the index structure. For each experiment, a few queries are submitted to our system and an average value for each measurement is recorded. For each query image, their major clusters are also extracted. In this paper, due to space constraint, we shall just present the results when 5 query clusters are used. Table 1 shows the results for the color index structure. For retrieval using the color index structure, we searched the bucket which holds similar color as that of the query cluster. And this search was repeated for each color cluster in the query. The search space using the index structure varies as we include different amount of allowances (to form the range queries) for the attributes of the query clusters.

The experiment is repeated with the color-spatial technique. Table 2 shows the results. The results confirm earlier work that color alone is not sufficient

Table 1. Performance of retrieval using only color indexing

%Allowance	time(sec)	IO	P_{norm}	R_{norm}
0	6	7029	0.2897	0.5861
2	8	9450	0.3058	0.5946
5	10	10667	0.3058	0.5946
10	10	10667	0.3058	0.5946

to represent an image. The results clearly show that by considering the spatial distribution of colors, the effectiveness can be improved. We note that the color-spatial scheme is also more efficient than the color-only scheme. This is because the additional layer can prune the search space even further, resulting in searching only those portion of the trees that may contain relevant images.

Table 2. Performance of retrieval using only color-spatial indexing

%Allowance	time(sec)	IO	P_{norm}	R_{norm}
0	4	2060	0.3782	0.6286
2	4	2842	0.4484	0.6709
5	4	3129	0.4481	0.6709
10	4	3129	0.4481	0.6709

Finally, the results of the MOSAIC structure is shown in Table 3. Comparing Table 2 and Table 3, we see that the effectiveness of both techniques are on par. But by taking a closer look, we see that by using the 3-level index structure, we can achieve a better efficiency (less IO count) than just using index on color and spatial arrangement. The *time* comparison for both may become more obvious if we were to use a larger database. More studies are currently being conducted. All in all, we believe that our proposed index structure, when used for retrieving similar images with large color clusters, would eventually outperform many methods suggested in the literature in terms of efficiency.

Table 3. Performance of retrieval using the 3-level indexing

%Allowance	time(sec)	IO	P_{norm}	R_{norm}
0	4	814	0.3429	0.6116
2	4	1426	0.4369	0.6625
5	4	2279	0.4356	0.6625
10	4	2458	0.4355	0.6625

5 Conclusion

Many multimedia applications require accurate and fast retrieval of data from the multimedia databases. These databases are large and are expected to be larger as time passes. Hence, designing good indexing structure is a promising step to speed up the retrieving process. The indexing structure in our proposed system allows the flexibility to increase and decrease the amount of space to search, depending on how we want to balance between having speed or accuracy. But on average, our system has been proven through experiments to have achieved good retrieval rate and at the same time with an acceptable retrieval precision. Thus, we conclude that with the assistance of a well chosen indexing structure, the rate of retrieval from a large collection of images, generally outperforms other retrieval system with simple or no indexing technique.

Acknowledgement

This project is partially supported by the research grant RP3982694 funded by National University of Singapore.

References

1. J. Beck. Perceptual grouping produced by line figures. *Percept. Pyschophys.*, 2:491–495, 1967.
2. S. Belongie, C. Carson, H. Greenspan, and J. Malik. Recognition of images in large databases using color and texture. In *http://elib.cs.berkeley.edu/papers.html*, 1997.
3. Chin-Chen Chang and Chin-Feng Lee. A spatial match retrieval mechanism for symbolic pictures. *The Journal of Systems and Software*, 44(1):73–83, December 1998.
4. S.T. Goh and K.L. Tan. Retrieving similar images from large image collections efficiently and effectively (available upon request).
5. A. Guttman. R-trees: A dynamic index structure for spatial searching. In B. Yormack, editor, *sigmod*, pages 47–57, Boston, MA, June 1984. acm.
6. W. Hsu, T. S. Chua, and H. K. Pung. An integrated color-spatial approach to content-based image retrieval. In *The Third ACM International Multimedia Conference and Exhibition (MULTIMEDIA '95)*, pages 305–314, New York, November 1996. ACM Press.
7. B.C. Ooi, K.L. Tan, T.S. Chua, and W. Hsu. Fast image retrieval using color-spatial information. *The VLDB Journal*, 7(2):115–128, May 1998.
8. G. Salton and M.J. McGill. *Introduction to Modern Information Retrieval*. McGraw-Hill, New York, 1983.
9. J. Smith and S.-F. Chang. VisualSEEk :A fully automated content-based image query system. In *Proceedings of the Fourth ACM Multimedia Conference (MULTIMEDIA '96)*, pages 87–98, New York, NY, USA, November 1996. ACM Press.
10. B.C. Ooi T.S. Chua, K.C. Teo and K.L. Tan. Using domain knowledge in querying image databases. In *Proceedings of The Third International Conference on Multimedia Modeling*, pages 339–354, Toulouse, France, November 1997.

Enhancing Data Warehousing with Fuzzy Technology *

Ling Feng and Tharam Dillon

Hong Kong Polytechnic University, {cslfeng, csdillon}@comp.polyu.edu.hk

Abstract. A data warehouse integrates large amounts of extracted and summarized data from multiple sources for direct querying and analysis. While it provides decision makers with easy access to such historical and aggregate data, the real meaning of the data has been ignored. For example, "*Whether a total sales amount* **1000** *items indicates a* **good** *or* **bad** *sales performance is still unclear.*" From the decision makers' point of view, the semantics rather than raw numbers which convey the meaning of the data is very important. In this paper, we explore fuzzy technology to provide this semantics for the summarizations and aggregates developed in data warehousing systems. A three-layered data summarization architecture, namely, *quantitative (numerical) summarization, qualitative (categorical) summarization,* and *quantifier summarization,* is proposed. To facilitate the construction of these three summarization levels, two operators are introduced. We provide query capabilities against such enhanced data warehouses by extensions of SQL.

1 Introduction

Data warehouses have gained in importance in recent years [4]. A data warehouse integrates large amounts of enterprise data from multiple and independent data sources consisting of operational databases into a common repository for querying and analysis. Often, data warehouses are designed for online analytical processing, where the queries aggregate large volumes of data in order to detect trends and anomalies. To reduce the cost of executing aggregate queries in such an environment, warehousing systems usually precompute frequently used aggregates and store each materialized aggregate view in a summary table. These summary tables group the base data along various dimensions, corresponding to different sets of group-by attributes, and compute different aggregate functions on measures. *Sum, avg, min, max, count* are the most commonly used aggregate functions. For example, consider a data warehouse with historical sales data for a large chain of departmental stores. Assume that all the member stores sell the same products no matter where (i.e., *east, west, north,* or *south*) they are located. Sales data is collected daily. At the end of each year, each member store will report the total sales amount of each product to the headquarters. Table 1 shows part of an aggregate view mapped into a summary table. Executives at the headquarters can then use it to analyze the activities of the chain stores.

---

* Supported by the Hong Kong Government UGC CERG PolyU 5074/98E.

Example 1. One indicator of the activities of the chain stores may be the sales performance, which can be obtained via the following query:

Q_1: "For each member store, find the total sales amount in 1998".

Also, users can query those products with total sales above a certain value:

Q_2: "For each member store, find products whose sales in 1998 are above 230."

The growth trend of products in sales can be obtained by queries such as:

Q_3: "Find products whose sales difference in the past two years are within 100."

Table 1. Summary data of a chain store

Product	Year	Store	Sales
PC	1997	east	490
PC	1997	west	200
PC	1998	east	480
PC	1998	west	450
PC	1998	south	300
PC	1998	north	50
Workstation	1997	east	500
Notebook	1997	east	460
..	..	..	..

As data warehousing systems provide easy access to both historical and aggregate data which are derived across several data sources beforehand, the analysis-oriented queries such as those given in Example 1 can often be evaluated much more cheaply using warehouse data than using the base relations.

Nowadays, data warehousing has become a key technology to assist management in making quick and competitive business decisions. From the viewpoint of both industry and the research community, data warehousing related problems have sparked vigorous discussions [15], including the use of multidimensional models and OLAP [1], materialized view selection [9], warehouse maintenance [8], query language and processing [3, 6], and physical warehouse design [16, 11]. With more and more data warehousing tools and products developed and applied to decision support systems, we ask one question: Is it enough? or what technologies do we still need for data warehousing?

Currently, most analysis that data warehousing systems perform is *numerically* oriented such as counting the total (average) sales of products. Although the numbers give some indications of the sales behavior, their real *meanings* are missing. For example, whether a total sales **1000** items indicates a **good** or **bad** sales performance is still unclear. From a manager's viewpoint, the semantics conveyed by *linguistic labels* are actually more natural and understandable. The meaning of these linguistic labels will necessarily involve an agreed interpretation between users and knowledge workers which is captured by agreement over the membership functions.

Example 2. Instead of querying detailed sales amounts via Q_1, Q_2, Q_3 in Example 1, users would prefer to know sales performance conveyed by natural language terms like:

Q'_1: "What's the sales performance (**good/medium/bad**) of each store in 1998?"

Q'_2: "For each member store, find products whose sales performance in 1998 are **good**."

Q'_3: "Find the products whose sales in the past two years are **nearly unchanged** (accepting minor differences)."

To answer these queries, warehousing systems need more techniques to build up the meaning of numbers. This has been constantly missing before.

Fuzzy technology provides a framework for modeling the interface between human conceptual categories and data. As [21] says " *It reduces cognitive dissonance in problem modeling, so that the way that humans think about the decision process is much closer to the way it is represented in the machine.*" Since its introduction by L.A. Zadeh [20], fuzzy technology has been widely used in a number of areas [5]. In the fuzzy database community, research on fuzzy databases has been conducted for about twenty years, with the emphasis on handling of imprecise, uncertain, or fuzzy data; flexible querying; and defining and using fuzzy dependencies [7]. However, compared with the areas of expert and control systems, fuzzy database systems have not found wide application. Indeed they have remained outside the main stream database world. This might be due to the less expressed demand for uncertain and imprecise representation and management in the database field. Usually, a simply NULL value is adopted in databases to describe these unknown or uncertain data. In contrast, although a data warehouse is an integration of a number of databases, it aims at providing online analysis and direct querying to business managers, who would prefer linguistic labels to crisp numbers. Under such circumstance, it will be more natural and necessary to apply fuzzy technology to capture the linguistic expressions and semantics of the data. We believe that with the aid of fuzzy techniques, warehousing systems can offer more powerful decision support than currently exists.

In this paper, we provide an investigation of the potential applications of fuzzy technology in data warehousing systems. The remainder of the paper is organized as follows. In section 2, we provide a brief review of the basic concepts of fuzzy sets and membership functions relevant to our work. With the aid of fuzzy techniques, a three-layered data summarization architecture for data warehouses is proposed in section 3. In section 4. we provide query capabilities against such enhanced data warehouses by extensions of the SQL language. Finally, section 5 concludes the paper.

2 Brief Review of Membership Functions and Fuzzy Sets

The concept of a fuzzy set extends the notion of a regular crisp set in order to express classes with ill-defined boundaries (corresponding in particular to linguistic values such as tall, young, well-paid, important, etc.). Within this framework, there is a gradual rather than sharp transition between nonmembership and full membership. A degree of membership is associated with every element x of the universal set X. It takes its value in the interval $[0, 1]$, instead of the pair $\{0, 1\}$.

Such a membership assigning function ($\mu_A : X \to [0,1]$) is called a *membership function* and the set defined by it is a *fuzzy set* [12, 5]. Figure 1 shows an example concept *middle aged* modeled as a bell curve.

Fig.1. *"middle aged"*
Membership function

Fig.2. predicate *"price = medium"*
Membership function

The operation known as the alpha-level set or "α-cut" of a fuzzy set F delivers a subset, made of those elements whose membership degree is over or equal to α: ($F_\alpha = \{x \in X \mid \mu_A(x) \geq \alpha\}$). A fuzzy predicate expresses the content to which the arguments fit the predicate. An elementary predicate (single or multivariable) allows for comparison between variables and constants or between variables [2]. Figure 2 describes the predicate *"price=medium"* with α-cut 0.2. In this case, any price between 24 and 26 is considered medium and fully satisfies the predicate. A price of 20 or 30 satisfies this same predicate at a degree of 0.2, whereas any value under 19 or over 31 is not *medium* at all.

3 Integrating Fuzzy Technology Into Data Warehousing Systems

We divide the summary data in data warehouses into three different levels: *quantitative (numerical) summarization level, qualitative (categorical) summarization level*, and *quantifier summarization level*. Figure 3 is a graphical representation of the three summarization levels on a data cube.

3.1 Level-1: Quantitative (Numerical) Summarization

This level is made up of various aggregate views in traditional data warehouses. Since the view data is often calculated and derived by numerical aggregate functions like *sum, avg, count, min, max* over base resources, we name the level as quantitative (numerical) summarization level. The summary data in Table 1 belongs to this bottom level. As the approach to aggregating data is widely known and published in the literature, we will not discuss this any further here.

3.2 Level-2: Qualitative (Categorical) Summarization

Considering the fact that a human's perception and thinking are generally based on linguistic labels instead of crisp numbers, we further summarize the numerical data of Level-1 into descriptive and categorical concepts so that the way

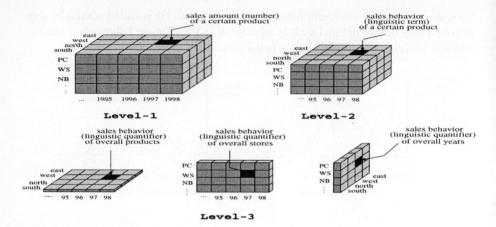

Fig. 3. A graphical representation of three summarization levels for data warehouses

decision makers think about a problem's solution is much closer to the way it is represented in data warehouses.

Here, we apply the fuzzy set techniques developed by [20, 21] to facilitate the process. For example, according to the total sales of products in Level-1, we can categorize different products by *good* (*medium* or *bad*) sales performance in Level-2 using certain membership functions, and later, users can directly invoke these linguistic terms to query the warehouse.

Table 2. Summary data at level 2

Product	Year	Store	F-Sales	F-SalesDegree
PC	1997	east	good	0.96
PC	1997	west	medium	0.75
PC	1998	east	good	0.92
PC	1998	west	good	0.8
PC	1998	south	medium/good	0.75/0.2
PC	1998	north	bad	0.5
Workstation	1997	east	good	1.0
Notebook	1997	east	good	0.84
..	..	..	..	..

As a measure (attribute) can usually be associated with many concepts (e.g., *sales* can be described by the performance of {*very good, good, medium, bad, very bad*}, or it can be expressed through the comparison with its previous behavior like {*greatly changed, slightly changed, nearly unchanged*}, etc.), we introduce an operator **FUZZ-TERM** to enable users to specify a basic set of linguistic terms that are of interest and importance to the decision making process, and they span the universe of discourse for that attribute.

FUZZ-TERM \<linguistic term set\> \<membership function set\>
ON \<aggregate attribute\>   FROM \<table\>

Example 3. Consider a table *R (Product, Year, Store, Sales)* which could be a base table or an aggregate view of the base tables from Level-1. The following statement will summarize the sales performance of products by different stores in different years using the linguistic terms.

FUZZ-TERM {*bad, good, medium*} {

$$bad(x) = \begin{cases} 0 & x > 100 \\ -0.01x + 1 & 0 \le x \le 100 \end{cases} \qquad good(x) = \begin{cases} 0 & 0 < x < 250 \\ 1 & x \ge 500 \\ 0.004x - 1 & 250 \le x \le 500 \end{cases}$$

$$medium(x) = \begin{cases} 0 & x < 50 \text{ or } x > 450 \\ 0.005x - 0.25 & 50 \le x < 250 \\ -0.005x + 2.25 & 250 \le x \le 450 \end{cases}$$

}   *ON Sales FROM R*

Table 2 shows part of the summarization results. An '*F-*' is prefixed with the fuzzified attribute *Sales* – *F-Sale*, whose membership degree is denoted by *F-SalesDegree* attribute. Note that the fifth record PC sales in 1998 in the south can be captured by two terms, i.e., "*medium*" with the membership degree 0.75 and "*good*" with the membership degree 0.2.

Note that the linguistic term set must be complete, i.e., it should provide a fuzzy partitioning of the domain of the attribute variable. For example, if the attribute is *age*, a linguistic term set could be {*young, middle-aged, old*}. The membership functions of linguistic terms can be set by either experts or software tools which derive the functions based on historical data [13, 14, 10].

3.3   Level-3: Quantifier Summarization

Besides the numerical and categorical summarization on *individual* records, often, business managers want to have some insight into the *overall* performance of the whole database.

Example 4. Some simple summarizations in natural language are like:
Q''_1: "How did **most** of products behave last year?"
Q''_2: "What was the **average** performance of products in the southern area?"
Q''_3: "At least what percent of products' behavior was **good**?"

Each of the above queries involves two kinds of linguistic terms such as {most, about half, at least, few} and {good, medium, bad}. In the fuzzy area, the former are called *linguistic quantifiers*[22]. Essentially, linguistic quantifiers can be regarded as fuzzy proportions or fuzzy probabilities. Zadeh represented these linguistic quantifiers as fuzzy sets on the unit interval. The membership grade of any proportion $x \in [0,1]$, $\mu_Q(x)$ is a measure of the compatibility of the proportion x with the linguistic quantifier represented by fuzzy set Q. For example, if Q is the quantifier *most*, then *most*(0.9) represents the degree to which 0.9 satisfies the concept *most* [22].

Here, the third summarization level of data warehouses aims at presenting information contained in the whole database using such linguistic quantifiers. Similar to the definition of linguistic terms, users can declare interesting linguistic quantifiers by the operator **FUZZ-QUANTIFIER**:

FUZZ-QUANTIFIER <linguistic quantifier set> <membership function set>
FOR <quantified attribute> ON <aggregate fuzzified attribute> FROM <table>

Example 5. Consider the table R' *(Product, Year, Store, F-Sales, F-SalesDegree)* from Level-2. The following statement will quantify the attribute *Product* by {*most, around-half, few*} according to the linguistic terms defined on the aggregate fuzzified attribute *F-Sales* before. Table 3 illustrates its summarization result, with an 'Q-' prefix denoting the summarization attributes at Level-3.

$FUZZ\text{-}QUANTIFIER \quad \{most,\ around\text{-}half,\ few\} \quad \{$

$$most(x) = \begin{cases} 0 & x < 0.5 \\ (2x - 1)^{1/2} & x \geq 0.5 \end{cases} \qquad around\text{-}half(x) = exp^{-(\frac{x-0.5}{0.25})^2}$$

$$few(x) = \begin{cases} 0 & x > 0.5 \\ (1 - 2x)^{1/2} & x \leq 0.5 \end{cases}$$

$\}\quad FOR\ Product\quad ON\ F\text{-}Sales\quad FROM\ R'$

Table 3. Summary data at level 3

Year	Store	Q-Product	Q-F-Sales
1997	east	most (*of products*)	good
1997	west	few (*of products*)	bad
1998	east	around half (*of products*)	good
..	..	..	..

Before the summarization, the data in the lower Level-2 table should be grouped by all the attributes except any *aggregate attributes* and *quantified attributes*. Quantifier summarization is then performed against each group. Thus, each summary at Level-3 describes a data group at Level-2. In the above Example 5, each quantifier summary describes the overall product performance in a certain year and a certain area. Similarly, we can get the overall performance regarding years for a certain product in a certain region by:

FUZZ-QUANTIFIER {most, around-half, few} {(*can be the same as before*)}
FOR Year   ON Sales   FROM R'

One example summary obtained from the above statement is like "*In most of the years, PC sold well in the east.*"

Upon the generation of the quantifier summary information about the database, there are many possible pairs <linguistic quantifier, linguistic term> to consider. Based on the considerable work of Yager [19, 17, 18], here, we adopt an entropy like measure to select the most representative linguistic term and quantifier pair to describe the database.

Definition 6. Let $T = \{T_1, T_2, \ldots, T_m\}$ be a set of fuzzy terms and $Q = \{Q_1, Q_2, \ldots, Q_n\}$ be a set of fuzzy quantifiers defined by users. $G = \{r_1, r_2, \ldots, r_{|G|}\}$ is a group of records of the table to be summarized. For simplicity, let $T_i(r_k)$ $(r_k \in G)$ denote the membership degree of record r_k satisfying T_i. We define a **validity function** $\mathcal{F}(T_i)$ on linguistic term $T_i \in T$ against the whole group G as: $\mathcal{F}(T_i) = \sum_{k=1}^{|G|} T_i(r_k) \, / \, |G|$ $\quad (0 \leq T_i(r_k) \leq 1, \; 0 \leq \mathcal{F}(T_i) \leq 1)$ Let us write $v = \mathcal{F}(T_i)$, then let $Q_j(v)$ $(v \in [0,1])$ be the membership grade of the quantifier Q_j. We use $Q_i' = \mathrm{Max}_j(Q_j(\mathcal{F}(T_i)))$ to denote the the maximum membership grade of the quantifiers in Q.

For each linguistic term $T_i \in T$, we have a corresponding Q_i': (T_i, Q_i'). We select the pair which has the smallest value, $\mathrm{Min}_i(-e_i \log e_i)$ where $e_i = Q_i'(\mathcal{F}(T_i))$, to describe the group G of the table.

4 Queries Against the Enhanced Data Warehouses

In order to provide users with easy and flexible access to the enhanced multi-layered data warehouses, in this section, we propose an extension of the well-known SQL query language by incorporating linguistic terms and quantifiers in users' queries. We have chosen to extend SQL so as not to stay too far from the form of queries currently used by the relational database community. The basic block of the extended query language has the following constructs:

SELECT [n] [distinct] <attribute list> FROM <table list>
[WHERE <predicate list>] [GROUP BY <grouping attribute list>]
[HAVING <group predicate list>]
[ORDER BY <attribute list>] [DESC | ASC]

<attribute>	::=	<normal attribute> | <fuzzified attribute> | <fuzzified membership attribute>
<predicate>	::=	<normal predicate> | <fuzzy predicate>
<fuzzy predicate>	::=	<fuzzified attribute> = <linguistic value> | <fuzzified membership attribute> < op > <numerical values>
<linguistic value>	::=	<linguistic term> | <linguistic quantifier>
< op >	::=	= | < | > | <> | ≤ | ≥

The SELECT clause lists the attributes to be retrieved. The FROM clause specifies all tables needed in the query. The WHERE clause specifies the conditions for selection of records from these tables. <predicate list> expresses a list of predicates connected by logical operators AND, OR, or NOT. GROUP BY specifies grouping attributes, whereas HAVING specifies a condition on the groups being selected. Note that all the fuzzified attributes as well as the associated membership attributes like the previously defined *F-Sales, F-SalesDegree, Q-Product,* and *Q-F-Sales* are treated in the same way as the normal attributes. Thus, they can appear in any <attribute list> of the query block as well. Similarly, we can incorporate linguistic terms (e.g., *good, bad, medium*) and linguistic quantifiers (e.g., *most, few, around half*) as linguistic values inside any condition expressions to evaluate the fuzzified attributes. These conditions are called fuzzy predicates in section 2.

The parameter 'n' in the SELECT clause specifies the size of the answer, i.e., the number of desired response records. Its appearance must always be accompanied by the ORDER BY clause, indicating only the top most sorted 'n' number of records should be returned. Here, the default order is in ascending order of values. We can specify the keyword DESC if we want a descending order of values. For example, we can rank-order the result records of *good sales products* according to their *membership grades* from the highest to the lowest through "ORDER BY F-SalesDegree DESC" statement. The keyword ASC can be used to specify ascending order explicitly. We illustrate the usage of the above constructors through a set of queries. Consider two summary tables R1 and R2 from Level-2 and Level-3, respectively: *R1(Product, Year, Store, F-Sales, F-SalesDegree) R2(Year, Store, Q-Product, Q-F-Sales)*

Query-1: *Find the best 2 products whose sales in the east are good in 1997.*

SELECT	2 *Product* FROM *R1*
WHERE	*Store=*"*east*" and *Year=1997* and *F-Sales=*"*good*"
GROUP BY	*F-SalesDegree* DESC

The execution of this query will return 2 products whose membership degrees of "good" are ranked among the top two in the east in 1997. Assume the records of table R1 are within Table 2, from which three products, i.e., *PC, Work-station,* and *Notebook,* sold well (with membership grades *0.96, 1.0* and *0.84* respectively) in the east in 1997. The above query will return two products, *PC* and *Workstation,* as the query result, since the membership grades of *PC* and *Workstation* are among the top two.

Query-2: *Find yearly sales performance of PC in the east (with α-cut=0.8).*

SELECT	*Year, F-Sales* FROM *R1*
WHERE	*Product=*"*PC*" and *Store=*"*east*" and *F-SalesDegree*$\geq$ 0.8

Query-3: *Find the best 3 years and regions in which workstations sold well.*

SELECT	3 *Year, Store* FROM *R1* GROUP BY *Year, Store*
HAVING	*Product=*"*Workstation*" and *F-Sales=*"*good*"
ORDER BY	*F-SalesDegree* DESC

Query-4: *Find the years in which most products' sales performance is bad .*

SELECT	*Year* FROM *R2*
WHERE	*Q-product=*"*most*" and *Q-F-Sales=*"*bad*"

Query-5: *Find the overall sales situation of products in the west.*

SELECT   *Q-Product, Q-F-Sales* FROM *R2* WHERE *Store=*"*west*"

5 Conclusion

In this paper, we explore the use of fuzzy technology to provide semantics to the data in data warehouses. Future work includes efficient storage plan of summary data from different abstract levels, and investigation of aggregate operators defined on fuzzy sets in a data warehousing environment.

References

1. S. Agarwal, R. Agrawal, P. Deshpande, A. Gupta, J.F. Naughton, R. Ramakrishnan, and S. Sarawagi. On the computation of multidimensional aggregates. In *Proc. 22th Intl. Conf. Very Large Data Bases*, Mumbai, India, September 1996.
2. P. Bosc. Some approaches for processing SQLf nested queries. *Intelligent Systems*, 11(9):65–74, September 1996.
3. L. Cabibbo and R. Torlone. From a procedural to a visual query language for OLAP. In *Proc. IEEE Intl. Conf. Very Large Data Bases*, Bombay, India, 1996.
4. S. Chaudhuri and U. Dayal. An overview of data warehousing and OLAP technology. *SIGMOD Record*, 26(1):65–74, 1997.
5. Earl Cox. *The Fuzzy Systems Handbook*. Academic Press, Inc., 1994.
6. P. Deshpande, K. Ramasamy, A. Shukla, and J.F. Naughton. Caching multidimensional queries using chunks. In *Proc. ACM SIGMOD Intl. Conf. Management of Data*, pages 271–282, 1998.
7. D. Dubois, F. Esteva, P. Garcia, L. Godo, D.M.R. Lopez, and H. Prade. Fuzzy set modelling in case-based reasoning. *Intelligent Systems*, 13:301–374, 1996.
8. H. Garcia-Molina, W. Labio, and J. Yang. Expiring data in a warehouse. In *Proc. 23th Intl. Conf. Very Large Data Bases*, New York, USA, August 1998.
9. H. Gupta. Selection of views to materialize in a data warehouse. In *Proc. 23th Intl. Conf. Very Large Data Bases*, Athens, Greece, 1997.
10. R. Jang. ANFIS: adaptive-network-based fuzzy inference system. *IEEE Transactions on Systems, Man, and Cybernetics*, 23(3):665–685, 1993.
11. T. Johnson and D. Shasha. Some approaches to index design for cube forests. *IEEE Data Engineering Bulletin*, 20(1):27–35, March 1997.
12. G.J. Klir and T.A. Folger. *Fuzzy Sets, Uncertainty and Information*. Prentice Hall, Inc., 1988.
13. S. Smith and D. Comer. Automated calibration of a fuzzy logic controller using a cell state space algorithm. *IEEE Control Sytems Magazine*, pages 18–28, 1991.
14. T. Takagi and M. Sugeuo. Fuzzy identification of systems and its applications to modelling and control. *IEEE Transactions on Systems, Man, and Cybernetics*, 15(1):116–131, 1985.
15. J. Widom. Research problems in data warehousing. In *Proc. Intl. Conf. Information and Knowledge Management*, 1995.
16. M.C. Wu and A.P. Buchmann. Encoded bitmap indexing for data warehouses. In *Proc. Intl. Conf. Data Engineering*, pages 220–230, 1998.
17. R.R. Yager. Quantifiers in the formulation of multiple objective decision functions. *Information Science*, 31:107–139, 1983.
18. R.R. Yager. Connectives and quantifiers in fuzzy sets. *Fuzzy Sets Systems*, 40:39–76, 1991.
19. R.R. Yager. Database discovery using fuzzy sets. *Intelligent Systems*, 11(9):691–712, September 1996.
20. L.A. Zadeh. Fuzzy sets. *Information and Control*, 8:338–353, 1965.
21. L.A. Zadeh. Outline of a new approach to the analysis of complex systems and decision processes. *IEEE Transactions on Systems, Man, and Cybernetics*, 3(1), 1973.
22. L.A. Zadeh. A computational approach to fuzzy quantifiers in natural languages. *Comput. Math. Appl.*, 9:149–184, 1983.

Mining Several Data Bases with an Ensemble of Classifiers

Seppo Puuronen[1], Vagan Terziyan[2], and Alexander Logvinovsky[2]

[1]University of Jyväskylä, P. O. Box 35, FIN-40351 Jyväskylä, Finland
sepi@jytko.jyu.fi
[2]Kharkov State Technical University of Radioelectronics, 14 Lenin Avenue,
310166 Kharkov, Ukraine
vagan@kture.cit-ua.net

Abstract. The results of knowledge discovery in data bases could vary depending on the data mining method. There are several ways to select the most appropriate data mining method dynamically. One proposed method clusters the whole domain area into "competence areas" of the methods. A metamethod is then used to decide which data mining method should be used with each data base instance. However, when knowledge is extracted from several data bases knowledge discovery may produce conflicting results even if the separate data bases are consistent. At least two types of conflicts may arise. The first type is created by data inconsistency within the area of the intersection of the data bases. The second type of conflicts is created when the metamethod selects different data mining methods with inconsistent competence maps for the objects of the intersected part. We analyze these two types of conflicts and their combinations and suggest ways to handle them.

1 Introduction

The modern data base technology enables the storage of huge amounts of data, but does not yet offer high level intelligent support to analyze, understand, or visualize the stored data. Data mining is a knowledge extracting process which tries to discover valid, previously unknown, and useful patterns that are not directly obvious to the user [4]. Recently the research in the field of knowledge discovery in data bases has rapidly emerged producing several new data mining methods and techniques for their evaluation, learning and integration [3,5,6,9]. Some of these methods are static and do not analyze a new instance in its context. Dynamic data mining methods, as [8,11,12], take into account the context of a new instance and are even able to take benefit from an ensemble of classifiers. Most of the data mining algorithms assume a single data set, but real world application practitioners have usually to discover knowledge from several data bases [7] and thus there is a need to apply several data mining methods with several data bases.

The brute–force application of statistical methods is unable to take into account the context of the methods and the context of the knowledge. Our goal is to develop methods that can take into account inconsistencies of numerical data when the most appropriate method(s) is chosen. We proposed one technique to handle a single data base using dynamic integration of multiple classifiers in [10] and developed it further in [11]. The technique consists of two phases: the training phase and the classification phase. During the training phase the characteristics and classifications of the training instances are collected into the performance matrix $Q_{n \times m}$, where n is the number of the training instances, m is the number of the classification methods, and q_{ji} is equal to 1 if the classification produced by the method i for the instance j is incorrect and 0 otherwise. In the classification phase a new instance is classified using the weighted k -nearest neighbor algorithm. The weights of the k -nearest neighbors are calculated as a function of the distances between the neighbors and the new instance and the most appropriate method is selected based on the weights and the values of the matrix $Q_{n \times m}$. In a way the performance matrix is used as a competence map of the classifiers included in the ensemble.

The above technique is planned to be used with a single data base and it cannot be applied as such with several data bases because it cannot handle conflicts arising within the intersecting areas of the data bases. There are at least two types of problematic conflicts. The first type arises when there exist different classification results caused by data inconsistency within the intersecting part of the data bases. The second type arises when the technique selects different data mining methods (classifiers) for the instances of the intersected part and there is inconsistency between the competence maps of the classification methods.

Chan [1,2] has proposed the arbiter meta-learning approach which uses the conflicting intersection area of the two subsets of the learning set to generate more accurate classification result. It is obvious that when the arbiter (classifier) is derived only a subset of the whole data is taken into account. Thus a classifier of the lowest level in the classifier structure handles the context of a single subset only. The classifiers of the higher levels of the structure are built using the union of the subsets of the lower levels. Thus the higher a classifier is in the structure, the bigger amount of the contexts of the subsets it handles. This is very similar with the above technique. The main difference between those two ones is that a group of samples not a single sample is considered. In this paper we generalize both the above approach to take into account the contexts of the data bases during classification.

In Chapter 2 we analyze the inconsistencies of the competence maps and the data and present ways to handle them. In Chapter 3 we describe one approach to handle the inconsistency of the data by decontextualizing it. We end up with conclusions in Chapter 4.

2 Data mining with an ensemble of classifiers and several data bases

In this chapter we analyze the inconsistencies of the competence maps and the data and present ways to handle them for three cases: one data base and an ensemble of classifiers, several data bases and one classifier, and an ensemble of classifiers and several data bases.

Let there be n data bases and a training set for each data base including k instances with the vector of the attributes x_j, $j=1,...,k$ and the known classification result $c_j = class\ (x_j)$. Let there also be m classifiers that can be applied to the training sets. The classification results of the classifiers may differ over the same training set and the results of each classifier may differ over the training sets of the different data bases. In the general case all m classifiers can be applied over all the n data bases. Let there be a new unclassified instance. The primary problem is to develop a method which classifies the new instance taking into account all the training sets and all the classifiers (Figure 1).

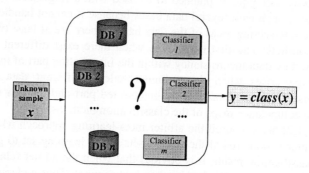

Fig. 1. The data mining problem when several classifiers are used with several data bases

We discuss first the case when there are m classifiers and one data base. Then we discuss the case when there is one classifier and n data bases. Last we discuss the general case with several classifiers and several data bases. The trivial case of one classifier and one training set is not discussed.

2.1 An ensemble of classifiers and one data base

We apply the approach suggested in [10] to integrate the classifiers based on the performance matrix of them. The integration technique selects the most appropriate component classifier from the ensemble. The advanced dynamic integration of multiple classifiers in [11] is one variation of the stacked generalization method using the assumption that each component classifier is the best inside certain areas of the application domain. In the learning phase a performance matrix of each component classifier is derived and these matrixes are used in the application phase to predict the performances of each component classifiers with a new instance. We present here another variation that takes into account the degree of the error made by the classification method in the classification of numerical data.

We change only the step 4 of the above mentioned Jackknife method and the resulting learning phase consists of the following five steps:

1. Unmark all the instances of the training set.

2. Take an unmarked instance j from the training set. If there is no unmarked instance then stop.

3. Derive the classification result for the instance j using the remaining training set (without the instance j) and the classifier i ($i=1,\dots,m$).

4. Give q_{ji} value ε_{ji} where the value ε_{ji} is the absolute difference between the classification result of the step 3 for classifier i and the value of the classification result c_j of the training instance j in the training set.

5. Go to the step 2.

Let us denote the weight of the classification method i over the instance j as ω_{ji}. There are many different possibilities to define the weights. The only requirement is that the weight ω_{ji} should satisfy the following conditions: $\omega_{ji} \to 1$ when $\varepsilon_{ji} \to 0$ and $\omega_{ji} \to 0$ when $\varepsilon_{ji} \to \pm\infty$. We propose the following function to calculate the weights:

$$\omega = \frac{1}{1+\varepsilon^2} \qquad (2.1)$$

The weight of a classification method for a new instance is calculated by inter- or extrapolating the errors of the training set instances and then the weight is evaluated using this error value.

Let us denote the error function of the classification method i for the instance x as $\varepsilon^i(x)$ and the weight function of the classification method i for the instance x as $\omega^i(x)$. The function $\omega^i(x)$ can be interpreted as a competence map of the method i. The competence maps of all the classification methods together form a competence map of the data base.

An example of the competence map for one-dimensional instance x is shown in Figure 2. The curves are obtained calculating first the error values for all the instances in the training set and interpolating these error values to the whole space of the x parameter.

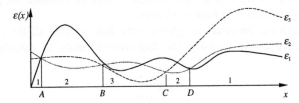

Fig. 2. An example of the competence map for three classifiers with one-dimensional instance data base

The most appropriate classification method for a new instance y is selected in the following way. First the values of the functions $\omega^i(x)$, $i=1,\dots,m$ are calculated and then the classification method giving the highest value is selected. When there is a tie one of the classification methods with the highest value is selected randomly. In the above example the intervals AB and CD are the competence areas of the method 2 and for example in the point C both the method 2 and the method 3 are as competent.

This selection mechanism can be easily adapted to take into account all the classification methods so that each method effects according its weight using the following formula to calculate the final result y:

$$y = \frac{\sum_i y^i \omega^i}{\sum_i \omega^i}, \qquad (2.2)$$

where y^i is the value obtained by the method i and ω^i is the weight of the classification method i.

Thus the weights of the classification methods over the instances can be either used to select the most appropriate classifier or to calculate the final result taking into account the predictions of all the available classifiers.

2.2 One classifier and several data bases

Let us denote the classification result of the method for the instance x over the data base j as $y_j(x)$. The weight of the classifier for the instance x over the data base j is denoted $\omega_j(x)$. The integral weight of the classifier over the data base j can be taken as the mean weight:

$$v_j = \frac{1}{b-a} \int_a^b \omega_j(x) \qquad , \qquad (2.3)$$

where a and b are the boundaries of the instances, $\omega_j(x)$ is the weight of the classifier over the instance x of the data base j, v_j is the integral weight of the classifier over the data base j, and the integral sign means the sum of the weights of all training instances of the data base. This integral weight is used to estimate the performance of the classifier over each data base separately.

This mechanism can be easily adapted to take into account all the data bases in the evaluation of a classifier using the following formula to calculate the final weight y:

$$y = \frac{\sum_j y_j v_j}{\sum_j v_j}, \qquad (2.4)$$

where y_j is the value obtained by the classifier over the instance x of the data base j and v_j is the integral weight of the classifier over the data base j.

This is one possible approach to resolve data inconsistency between separate data bases either using the mean result or the condition $V = \max V_j$ to select the most representative one.

2.3 Several classifiers and several data bases

Let us denote the classification result of the classifier i for the instance x over the data base j as $y_j^i(x)$. The weight of the value and the integral weight of the classifier are denoted $\omega_j^i(x)$ and V_j^i respectively.

The variants of the application of the classifiers to the data bases and the appropriate weights are shown in the Table 1.

Table 1. Weighting classifiers in the general case

	Classifier$_1$	...	Classifier$_m$	
DB$_1$	$y_1^1, \omega_1^1\,(V_1^1)$	...	$y_1^m, \omega_1^m\,(V_1^m)$	y_1, ω_1
DB$_2$	$y_2^1, \omega_2^1\,(V_2^1)$	...	$y_2^m, \omega_2^m\,(V_2^m)$	y_2, ω_2
...	...	...	...	...
DB$_n$	$y_n^1, \omega_n^1\,(V_n^1)$	...	$y_n^m, \omega_n^m\,(V_n^m)$	y_n, ω_n
	y^1, ω^1	...	y^m, ω^m	y, ω

Each row of the table describes the results and weights of all classifiers over a single data base. The total classification result y_j and the weight ω_j of the data base j can be calculated by the following formulas:

$$y_j = \frac{\sum_{i=1}^{m} y_j^i \omega_j^i}{\sum_{i=1}^{m} \omega_j^i}, \text{ and } \omega_j = \frac{\sum_{i=1}^{m} \omega_j^i v_j^i}{\sum_{i=1}^{m} v_j^i}, \tag{2.5}$$

where y_j, ω_j are the total classification result and the weight of the data base j and y_j^i, ω_j^i, v_j^i are the classification result, the weight and the integral weight of the classifier i over the data base j respectively.

Each column of the table describes the results and the weights obtained by one classifier over all the data bases. The classification result y^i and the weight ω^i obtained by the classifier i over all the data bases can be calculated as follows:

$$y^i = \frac{\sum\limits_{j=1}^{n} y_j^i v_j^i}{\sum\limits_{j=1}^{n} v_j^i} \text{, and } \omega^i = \frac{\sum\limits_{j=1}^{n} \omega_j^i v_j^i}{\sum\limits_{j=1}^{n} v_j^i}, \tag{2.6}$$

where y^i, ω^i are the total classification result and the weight evaluated by the classifier i over all the data bases respectively and y_j^i, ω_j^i, v_j^i are the classification result, the weight and the integral weight of the classifier i over the data base j respectively.

The result value y and the weight ω in the bottom-left cell of the table are obtained as a combination of the classification results of all the classifiers over all the data bases.

Thus there exists at least two possibilities to handle the general case. The first one uses formulas (2.5) to convert the general case to the case "one data base and an ensemble of classifiers". The second one uses formulas (2.6) to convert the general case to the case "one classifier and several data bases". Both cases lead to the trivial problem "one data base and one classifier" (more precisely "one virtual data base and one virtual classifier") as it is shown in Chapters 2.1 and 2.2.

There exist at least the next four variants of how to determine the total classification result and the weight over all the data bases using several classifiers:

Evaluate classification results y^i and weights ω^i, $i=(1,\ldots,m)$, using formulas (2.6) (i.e. through the columns of the matrix) and then determine the total result with the formula:

$$y = \frac{\sum\limits_{i=1}^{m} y^i \omega^i}{\sum\limits_{i=1}^{m} \omega^i}. \tag{2.7}$$

Evaluate classification results y_j and weights ω_j, $j=(1,\ldots, n)$, using formulas (2.5) (i.e. through the rows of the matrix) and then determine the total result with the formula:

$$y = \frac{\sum\limits_{j=1}^{n} y_j \omega_j}{\sum\limits_{j=1}^{n} \omega_j}. \tag{2.8}$$

Evaluate the total result based on the values obtained by the two previous methods (2.7, 2.8), for example as a mean value.

Evaluate the result through the whole matrix at once:

$$y = \frac{\sum_{i,j} y^i_j \omega^i_j}{\sum_{i,j} \omega^i_j} \quad . \tag{2.9}$$

3 The Sliding Exam Technique with Decontextualization

In this chapter we present one algorithm to improve the Jackknife (sliding exam or leave one out cross-validation) method used in the learning phase with an ensemble of classifiers. Let us denote the classification result by y^+, when all the instances of the training set are used and y^- when the classification is made excluding the instance i. It is obvious that y^+ depends on the contexts of all the training set instances and that the classification result y^- does not depend on the context of the instance i. Comparison of y^- and y^+ can be used to determine the decontextualization trend of the data base instances.

For the decontextualization process of the values describing the trend of a context decrease when we use the following formula:

$$y_{res} = \frac{y_i \cdot y_j}{y_i + y_j} \quad . \tag{3.1}$$

The main property of (3.1) is that the resulting value of the decontextualization y_{res} is smaller than the values y_i and y_j.

Thus when the value y^+ which depends on the contexts of all the instances and the value y^- which depends on the contexts of all the other instances than i are known for an instance y then we can find the decontextualized value y' using the formula:

$$y' = \frac{y^+ \cdot y^-}{y^+ + y^-} \quad . \tag{3.2}$$

It is possible to take into account all the subcontexts that can be formed from the training set using the following formulas:

$$y^- = \frac{\prod_i y^{i-}}{\prod_i y^{i-} \cdot \sum_j \left(\frac{1}{y^{j-}}\right)} = \frac{1}{\sum_j \left(\frac{1}{y^{j-}}\right)} ; \tag{3.3}$$

$$y' = \frac{y^+ \cdot y^-}{y^+ + y^-} = \frac{1}{\frac{1}{y^+} + \sum_j \left(\frac{1}{y^{j-}}\right)} . \tag{3.4}$$

The difference between the decontextualized value and the precise classification value y is $\varepsilon = y - y'$ which can be calculated for all the instances y_i of the training set.

This evaluation of differences between the decontextualized and precise values enables the improvement of the precision of the statistical methods at any instance x applying the following procedure.

Evaluate the decontextualized values $y_i{}'$ and the differences ε_i for every training set instance i, $i=1,..., k$, where k is the number of the instances in the training set.

Evaluate the decontextualized value $y'(x)$ for instance x as follows

$$y'(x) = \frac{1}{\dfrac{1}{y^+(x)} + \sum_j \left(\dfrac{1}{y^{j-}(x)} \right)} .$$

(3.5)

Evaluate the difference $\varepsilon(x)$ for the instance x as the result of interpolation on the set of the values $\varepsilon_1,...,\varepsilon_k$, where k is the number of the instances in the training set.

Evaluate y(x) using the formula $y(x) = y'(x) + \varepsilon(x)$.

In the case of single data base, the $\varepsilon(x)$ function determines the context of the data base. Let us call it as a self-difference. By analogy with the process of finding the self-difference we can find the inter-difference between two data bases as follows $\varepsilon_{ij} = y_j - y_i{}'$, where y_j is the precise value in the data base j, $y_i{}'$ is the decontextualized value in the data base i, and ε_{ij} is the mutual difference between the data bases.

This inter–difference ε_{ij} determine the context of a data base j in the terms of the data base i. Hence based on the values of the data base i it is possible to derive corresponding values in the context of the data base j by $y_i(x) = y_j{}'(x) + \varepsilon_{ij}(x)$.

4 Conclusion

This paper describes an approach to handle inconsistencies with multiple data bases. We distinguish two types of inconsistencies: data inconsistency and competence map inconsistency. We have considered different cases of applying methods over the data bases and suggested ways to determine the total classification result based on the results of all the methods over each data base. We have also shortly considered the decontextualization process which improves the classification and the handling of the mutual inconsistencies between the data bases. The results are mostly theoretical ones and good real world examples are needed to verify the usefulness of the suggested methods.

5 Acknowledgment

This research is partly supported by the grant from the Academy of Finland.

References

1. Chan, P.: An Extensible Meta-Learning Approach for Scalable and Accurate Inductive Learning. Ph.D. Thesis, Columbia University (1996)
2. Chan, P., Stolfo, S.: On the Accuracy of Meta-Learning for Scalable Data Mining. Intelligent Information Systems 8 (1997) 5-28
3. Dietterich, T.: Machine Learning Research: Four Current Directions. AI Magazine 18 (1997) 97-136
4. Fayyad, U., *et al.*: Advances in Knowledge Discovery and Data Mining. AAAI/MIT Press (1997)
5. Kohavi, R.: A Study of Cross-Validation and Bootstrap for Accuracy Estimation and Model Selection. In: The Proceedings of IJCAI'95 (1995)
6. Koppel, M., Engelson, S.: Integrating Multiple Classifiers by Finding their Areas of Expertise. In: AAAI-96 Workshop On Integrating Multiple Learning Models (1996) 53-58
7. Liu, H., Lu, H., Yao, J.: Identifying Relevant Databases for Multidatabase Mining. In: The Proceedings of the PAKDD'98, Melbourne, Australia, Springer Verlag (1998)
8. Merz, C.: Dynamical Selection of Learning Algorithms. In: Fisher, D., Lenz, H.-J. (eds.), Learning from Data, Artificial Intelligence and Statistics, Springer Verlag, NY (1996)
9. Skalak, D.: Combining Nearest Neighbor Classifiers. Ph.D. Thesis, Dept. of Computer Science, University of Massachusetts, Amherst, MA (1997)
10. Terziyan, V., Tsymbal, A., Puuronen, S.: The Decision Support System for Telemedicine Based on Multiple Expertise. International Journal of Medical Informatics 49 (1998) 217-229
11. Tsymbal, A., Puuronen, S., Terziyan, V.: Advanced Dynamic Selection of Diagnostic Methods. In: Proceedings of the CBMS'98, IEEE CS Press, Lubbock, Texas (1998) 50-54
12. Wolpert, D.: Stacked Generalization. Neural Networks 5 (1992) 241-259

WebTool: An Integrated Framework for Data Mining

F. Masseglia[1,2], P. Poncelet[3,4], and R. Cicchetti[3,4]

[1] LIRMM, 161 Rue Ada, 34392 Montpellier Cedex 5, France
E-mail: massegli@lirmm.fr
[2] PRiSM - Univ. de Versailles, 45 Av. des Etats-Unis 78035 Versailles Cedex, France
[3] LIM - Faculté des Sciences de Luminy, , Case 901, 163 Av. de Luminy, 13288
Marseille Cedex 9, France, E-mail: {poncelet,ciccheti}@lim.univ-mrs.fr
[4] IUT Aix en Provence

Abstract. Large volumes of data such as user address or URL requested are gathered automatically by Web servers and collected in access log files. Analysis of server access data can provide significant and useful information for performance enhancement, and restructuring a Web site for increased effectiveness. In this paper, we propose an integrated system (WebTool) for mining user patterns and association rules from one or more Web servers and pay a particular attention to handling of time constraints. Once interesting patterns are discovered, we illustrate how they can be used to customize the server hypertext organization dynamically.

keywords: data mining, Web usage mining, sequential patterns, time constraints, association rules.

1 Introduction

With the growing popularity of the World Wide Web (Web), large volumes of data such as address of users or URLs requested are gathered automatically by Web servers and collected in access log files. Analysis of server access data can provide significant and useful information for performance enhancement, restructuring a Web site for increased effectiveness, and customer targeting in electronic commerce. Discovering relationships and global patterns that exist in access log files, but are hidden among the vast amounts of data is usually called Web Usage Mining [5, 15].

The groundwork of the approach presented in this paper addresses the problem of exhibiting behavioural patterns from one or more servers collecting data about their users. Our proposal pays particular attention to time constraint handling. We propose an integrated system for mining either association rules or sequential patterns. In our context, by analyzing informations from Web servers, an association rule could be, for

893

instance, *"50 % of visitors who accessed URLs* plaquette/info-f.html and labo/infos.html *also visited* situation.html" or *"85% of visitors who accessed URLs* iut/general.html departement/info.html *and* info/program.html *also visited URL* info/debouches.html". Handling time constraints for mining sequential patterns could provide relationships such as: *"60 % of clients who visited* /jdk1.1.6/docs/api/Package-java.io.html *and* /jdk1.1.6/docs/api/java.io.BufferedWriter.html *in the same transaction, also accessed* /jdk1.1.6/docs/relnotes/deprecatedlist.html *during the following month"* or *"34 % of clients visited* /relnotes/deprecatedlist.html *between September the 20th and October the 30th"*. Once interesting patterns are discovered, they can be used to dynamically customize the hypertext organization. More precisely, the user current behaviour can be compared to one or more sequential patterns and navigational hints can be added to the pages proved to be relevant for this category of users.

The rest of the paper is organized as follows. Our proposal is detailed in section 2. In section 3, we present a very brief overview of the implementation. Section 4 addresses the problem of using discovered patterns in order to customize the hypertext organization. Related work, presented in section 5, is mainly concerned with mining useful information from Web servers. Finally section 6 concludes with future directions.

2 Principles

For presenting our approach, we adopt the chronological viewpoint of data processing: from collected raw data to exhibited knowledge. Like in [5], we consider that the mechanism for discovering relationships and global patterns in Web servers is a 2-phase process. The starting point of the former phase is data automatically gathered by Web servers and collected in access log.

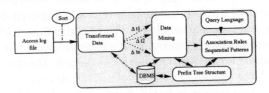

Fig. 1. An overview of the WebTool system

From such a file, the preprocessing phase removes irrelevant data and performs a clustering of entries driven by time considerations. It results in a populated database containing the meaningful remaining data. In the second phase, data mining techniques are applied in order to extract useful patterns or relationships and a visual query langage is provided in order to improve the mining process. Our approach is supported by an integrated system enforcing the described capabilities. Its architecture, close to that of the WebMiner system [5], is depicted in figure 1.

2.1 Data preprocessing

An input in the file log generally respects the *Common Log Format* specified by the CERN and the NCSA [4] and contains address IP of the customer, the user identifier, the access time, the method o f request (e.g. PUT/GET), the URL of the reached page, the protocol used, a possible error code and the number of transmitted bytes. Nevertheless, without loss of generality, we assume in the following that a log entry is merely reduced to the IP address which originates the request, the URL requested and a time stamp. Figure 2 illustrates a snapshot of the access log file from the Web server of the "IUT d'Aix en Provence".

```
132.208.12.150 - - [29/Nov/1998:18:02:30 +0200] "GET /info/RECRUT.gif HTTP/1.0" 200 1141
132.208.12.150 - - [29/Oct/1998:18:03:07 +0200] "GET /info/recrut.html HTTP/1.0" 200 1051
132.208.127.200 - - [16/Oct/1998:20:34:32 +0100] "GET /geaaix/home.html HTTP/1.0 " 200 14617
148.241.148.34 - - [31/Oct/1998:01:17:40 +0200] "GET /info/index.html HTTP/1.0" 304 -
148.241.148.34 - - [31/Oct/1998:01:17:42 +0200] "GET /info/recrut.html HTTP/1.0" 304 -
192.70.76.73 - - [22/Nov/1998:11:06:11 +0200] "GET /info/program.html HTTP/1.0" 200 4280
192.70.76.73 - - [22/Nov/1998:11:06:12 +0200] "GET /info/MATIERES.gif HTTP/1.0" 200 2002
192.93.19.14 - - [07/Dec/1998:11:44:15 +0200] "GET /queldept.html HTTP/1.0" 200 5003
```

Fig. 2. An example of entries in an access log file

During the data processing, three types of manipulations are carried out on the entries of the server log. First of all, a data filtering step is performed in order to filter out irrelevant requests. Then the remaining access log file is sorted by address and time. Finally, entries sufficiently close over time can be clustered. Most of Web log analysis tools operates a cleaning step during which they filter out requests for pages encompassing graphics as well as sound and video (for example, removing log entries with filename suffixes such as *.GIF, .JPEG*).

The WebTool system provides such cleaning facilities. Nevertheless, like in [15], we prefer to avoid their use because we believe that eliminated data may capture interesting and useful information about Web site structure, traffic performance, as well as user motivations. Of course, such a choice requires the implementation of efficient algorithms for extracting knowledge because the size of the access log file remains very large (during our experiments, we observe that removing pages encompassing graphics results in handled data size reduced from 40% to 85%).

The next step aims exhibiting users transactions and organizing data for an increased efficiency. It operates a sort of the file all along encoding data: URLs and visitors are mapped into integer, and date as well as time fields are expressed in relative time from the smallest date of the file.

In the market basket problem, each transaction is defined as a set of purchases bought by a customer at a time. In our context, user transaction has not counterpart because handled data does not capture user working session. Instead, each requested URL, in the access log file, is provided with a time stamp and could be seen as a single transaction. To avoid that situation, we propose like in [10] to cluster together entries, sufficiently close over time by using a maximum time gap (Δt) specified by user. Thus, the preprocessing phase results in a new database containing coded transactions. Each transaction provided with a relative data concerns a visitor, and groups together URLs visited during a common time range. Data can then be dealt for exhibiting knowledge.

2.2 Knowledge Discovery

This section widely resumes the formal description of the Web usage mining proposed in [10] and enhances the problem with useful information for handling time constraints proposed by [13]. From the transformed data yielded by the preprocessing stage, two techniques of knowledge discovery can be applied for fully meeting the analyst needs.

Mining association rules

The techniques used in mining association rules are generally applied in databases where each transaction is made up of a set of items. As we have already noticed in the preprocessing phase, it is necessary within the Web mining framework to gather the items between-them [10]. Let TA be a set of all association transactions obtained from Log. An association transaction t, $t \in TA$, is a tuple $t = <ip_t, UR_t>$ where UR_t, the URL set for t, is defined by $UR_t = ([l_1^t.url]...[l_m^t.url])$, such that for $1 \leq k \leq m$, $l_k^t \in Log$, $l_k^t.ip = ip_t$, $l_k^t.url$ must be unique in UR_t, and $l_{k-1}^t.url < l_k^t.url$.
In other words, an association transaction does not take into account transaction cutting and for each transaction, URLs are sorted in lexicographic order.

Definition 1 Let the database $D = \{t_1, t_2, ..., t_n\}$ be a set of n association transactions, each one consisting of a set of URLs, UR, and associated with a unique identifier corresponding to the visitor id ip_t. A transaction $t \in D$ is said to contain a set UR if $UR \subseteq t$. The *support* of UR is the percentage of transaction in D containing UR: $support(UR) = ||\{t \in D | UR \subseteq t\}||/||\{t \in D\}$. An association rule is a conditional implication among a set of URLs. The *confidence* of an association rule $r: UR_1 \Rightarrow UR_2$, where UR_1 is called the antecedent of the rule and UR_2 is called the consequent, is the conditional probability that a transaction contains UR_2, given that it contains UR_1. In other words, $confidence(r) = support(UR_1 \cup UR_2) / support(UR_1)$.

The problem of mining association rules in D is defined as follows. Given user defined minimum support and confidence, find all associations rules that hold with more than the given $minSupp$ and $minConf$. This problem can be broken into two sub-problems [1]: (i) Find all frequent URs in D, i.e. URs with support greater or equal to minSupp. (ii) For each frequent set of URs found, generate all association rules with confidence greater or equal to minConf. The second sub-problem can be solved very quickly and in main memory in a straightforward manner once all frequent URs and their support are known. Hence, the problem of mining association rules is reduced to the problem of finding frequent URs and we focus, in the WebTool system, on how efficiently extract frequent URs.

Mining sequential patterns Taking into account time for mining sequential patterns requires defining the concept of sequence within the framework of the Web mining.

Definition 2 Let T be a set of all temporal transactions. A temporal transaction t, $t \in T$, is a triple $t = < ip_t, time_t, \{UT_1, UT_2, ..., UT_n\} >$ where for $1 \le i \le n$, UT_i is defined by $UT_i = ([l_1^t.url, l_1^t.time]...[l_m^t.url, l_m^t.time])$, such that for $1 \le k \le m$, $l_k^t \in Log$, $l_k^t.ip = ip_t$, $l_k^t.url$ must be unique in UT_t, $l_{k+1}^t.time - l_k^t.time \le \Delta t$, $time_t = max_{1 \le i \le m} l_i^t.time$.

From temporal transactions, data sequences are defined as in [10]. Discovering sequential patterns resembles closely to mining association rules. However, elements of handled sequences are sets of URLs and not URL, and a main difference is introduced with time concerns. However, the above definition has the following limitations: the user often wants to specify maximum and/or minimum time gaps between adjacent URLs of the sequential patterns, or the user can decide that it does not matter if URLs were accessed separately as long as their occurrences enfold within a given time window. Widely inspired from [13], a frequent sequence is defined as follows:

Definition 3 Given a user-specified minimum time gap ($minGap$), maximum time gap ($maxGap$) and a time window size ($windowSize$), a data-sequence $d = < UT_{t_1}^d UT_{t_2}^d ... UT_{t_m}^d >$ is said to *support* a sequence $S = < UT_{t_1}^S UT_{t_2}^S ... UT_{t_n}^S >$ if there exist integers $l_1 \le u_1 < l_2 \le u_2 < ... < l_n \le u_n$ such that: (i) UT_i^s is contained in $\cup_{k=l_i}^{u_i} UT_k^d$, $1 \le i \le n$; (ii) $UT_{u_i}^d.time - UT_{l_i}^d.time \le windowSize$, $1 \le i \le n$; (iii) $UT_{l_i}^d.time - UT_{u_{i-1}}^d.time > min\text{-}gap$, $2 \le i \le n$; (iv) $UT_{u_i}^d.time - UT_{l_{i-1}}^d.time \le max\text{-}gap$, $2 \le i \le n$. The *support* of s, $supp(s)$, is the fraction of all sub-sequences in D supporting s. When $supp(s) \ge minSupp$ holds, being given a *minimum support* value $minSupp$, the sequence s is called *frequent*.

Mining sequences with time constraints allows a more flexible handling of the visitor transactions, insofar the end user is provided with the following advantages: (i)To gather URL accesses when their dates are rather close via the windowSize constraint. For example, it does not matter if URLs in a sequential pattern were present in two different transactions, as long as the transaction-times of those transactions are within some small time window. The windowSize constraint is rather similar to that of Δt but it generally relates to a longer range of time (a few hours or a few days). (ii)To regard sets of URLs as too close or distant to appear in the same frequent sequence with the minGap or maxGap constraints. For example, the end user probably does not care if a visitor accesses URL "/java-tutorial/ui/animLoop.html", followed by "/relnotes/deprecatedlist.html" three months later.

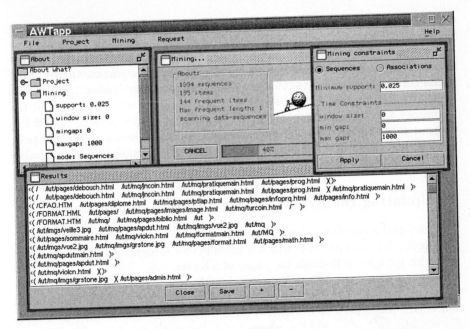

Fig. 3. A snapshot of the graphical interface of the WebTool system

An efficient algorithm for Web mining In the WebTool system we propose a very efficient algorithm which is described in [9]. The PSP algorithm (*Prefix-tree for Sequential Patterns*), used in the WebTool system was firstly defined for mining sequential patterns in market basket applications.

The principle fully resumes the fundamental principles of the GSP algorithm proposed in [13]. Its originality is to use a different hierarchical structure than in GSP in order to improve efficiency of retrievals of sequential patterns.

Arguing that the problem of the mining association rules is included in the mining sequential patterns problem, the principle adopted by WebTool is to use a common structure and the same algorithms to obtain association rules. The adaptation of PSP is done considering that all the transactions took place at the same time. Thus, during the application of PSP, transaction cutting is no longer considered and the yielded result is a frequent set of URLs. The rule generation from these sets of URLs is carried out by the visualization tool. In the figure 3, a snapshot of the WebTool system is depicted.

3   Experiments

We implemented the WebTool system on Ultra Sparc Station. Algorithms for mining association rules or sequential patterns are implemented using C++. The user interface module is implemented using Java (JDK 1.1.6). This module also concerns the preprocessing phase, i.e. the mapping from an access log file to a database of data-sequences according to the user defined time window (Δt), and the visualization tool.

For instance, Let us consider the following association rule extracted by the mining process on the LIRMM access log file:`<(lirmm/plaquette/info-f.html lirmm-infos.html)>`$\Rightarrow$ `<(situ.html /autour.html mtp/index.html)>` *conf* = *13*. It indicates that 13% of the visitor who obtained information about the laboratory LIRMM and more particularly about computer science, would like to know more about the geographical location of the laboratory (`situ.html`), how coming to LIRMM (`autour.html`) as well as informations on Montpellier (`mtp/index.html`).

4   Updating the hypertext organization dynamically

We developed a generator of dynamic links in Web pages using the rules generated from sequential patterns which is intended for recognizing a visitor according to his navigation through the pages of a server.

Since we are only interested in navigation through pages, we assume, in the following, that the hypertext document is defined as graphs with typed nodes and edges. An hypertext navigation for a visitor C is thus defined as a tuple $E_C = < id_C, \{n_1^{t_0}, n_2^{t_1}, ... n_{t_n}^{t_m}\} >$ where $1 \leq k \leq n$ and $1 \leq t \leq m$, n_k^t is the node accessed by the visitor and its associated time stamp, i.e. n_k is the URL of the reached page for the visitor C and the associated time.

Definition 4 Let us assume user defined parameters standing for the confidence (*conf*) and time constraints (Δt, *windowSize*, *minGap* and *maxGap*). A rule R is a triple $R = << a_1 \ a_2 \ ... \ a_i >, < c_1 \ c_2 \ .... \ c_j >, conf_R >$ where $1 \leq k \leq i$, a_k stands for a set of URLs in the antecedent part, $1 \leq k \leq j$, c_k stands for a set of URLs in the consequent part and $conf_R$ is the confidence of R such as $conf_R \geq conf$ and the antecedent as well as the consequent part respect time constraints.

For performing the insertion of a dynamic link from the antecedent part of a rule, let us introduce the interesting subset notion.

Definition 5 Let us consider a rule R, and a user defined parameter *minPages*, standing for the minimal number of pages from which a link can be added. The *interesting subset* of R, noted Is_R, is defined as follows: $\forall a_k \in \{a_1 \ a_2 \ ... \ a_k\}$, $a_k \in Is_R$ if and only if $k \leq minPages$.

An hypertext navigation satisfying a rule is defined as follows:

Definition 6 Let us consider E_C the hypertext navigation of the client C. Let us consider a rule R. Let us consider the transformed paths of E_C according to time constraints, $E_{C_T} = < id_c, \{p_1, \ p_2, \ ..., \ p_l\} >$ where, for $1 \leq k \leq l$, p_k is a sequence encompassing sets of URLs grouped together according to Δt. Furthermore, $\forall p \in \{p_1, \ p_2, \ ..., \ p_l\}$, p respects time constraints. The client navigation E_C *satisfies* R if and only if $\exists p \in E_{C_T} \mid Is_R \subseteq_{seq} p$ where $\subseteq_{seq}$ stands for the inclusion of a sequence into another one [13].

Example 1 Let us consider the following visitor path: p $=<$ (X^{t0}) $(A^{t1}$ Y^{t2} $B^{t3})$ $(Z^{t4}$ $C^{t5})$ $>$. Now, let us consider a rule R where the set of URLs of the antecedent part is: $a =< (A\ B)\ (C)\ (D\ E) >$. Let us assume that $minPages = 3$, thus to be considered as interesting three pages must be accessed by the same visitor. The *interesting subset*, IS_R, is the following $< (A\ B)\ (C) >$. The visitor satisfies the rule since $(A\ B) \subseteq (A^{t1}\ Y^{t2}\ B^{t3})$ and $(C) \subseteq (Z^{t4}\ C^{t5})$.

Implementation issues The technique presented so far was implemented using the functional architecture depicted in figure 4. The Web server (*http* daemon)

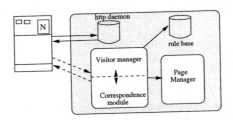

Fig. 4. General architecture

reacts to a customer request returning an applet encharged of the connection to the *visitor manager module* in order to transmit visitor IP address, required URL and a cookie encompassing the visitor navigation. The visitor manager module is a Java application running on the Web server site and using a client/server mechanism. When receiving IP address and required URL, the *visitor manager* examines the customer behaviour by using the *correspondence module*. The latter checks if the customer behaviour, i.e. the client navigation, satisfies a rule previously extracted by the data mining process. When an input satisfies a rule in the *correspondence module*, the required page is modified by the *page manager* which dynamically adds links towards the consequent of the recognized rule. The applet then recovers the URL and displays page on the navigator. If no rule corresponds to the current behaviour of the customer, the URL towards the required page is turned over to the applet which can display it.

Example 2 In the different rules obtained from the IUT access log file, we have noticed that 85% of visitors who visited the "Présentation générale de l'IUT" and the "Présentation générale du Département" pages in the same transaction, followed by the "Programme du Département Informatique" within 2 days, request the server on the "Débouchés avec un DUT" after an additional visit to the "Présentation générale du Département" (C.f. Figure 5). Let us consider a client accessing the pages $< (index.html\ info/genera.html)\ (info/program.html)>$ during his navigation. Let us consider that the navigation satisfies the previous rule. A link corresponding to each consequent of this rule is added to the page. In our case, a link to the page "Débouchés" is dynamically inserted in the URL concerning the Program (C.f. Figure 5).

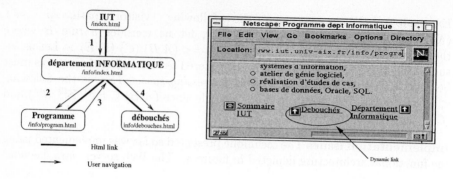

Fig. 5. Part of the hypertext organization and dynamically inserted link

5 Related Work

This section focuses on Web mining. The reader interested by an overview of data mining could refer to [1–3, 6, 11]. Using user access logs for exhibiting useful access patterns has been studied in some interesting approaches. Among them, we quote the approach presented in [10, 5]. A flexible architecture for Web mining, called WEBMINER, and several data mining functions (clustering, association, etc) are proposed. For instance, even if time constraints are not handled in the system (the minimum support is only provided), an approach for mining sequential patterns is addressed: an association rule-like algorithm [2], where the joining operation for candidate generation has been refined, is used. Various constraints can be specified using an SQL-like language with regular expression in order to provide much more control all along the discovery process. For example, the user can specify that he is only interested in clients from the domain **.edu** and in visits occurred after jan, 1, 1996. The WUM system proposed in [12] is based on an "aggregated materialized view of the Web log". Such a view contains aggregated data on sequences of pages requested by visitor. The query processor is incorporated to the miner in order to indentify navigation patterns satisfying properties (existence of cycles, repeated access, etc) specified by the expert. Incorporating the query language early in the mining process allows to construct only patterns having the desired characteristics while irrelevant patterns are removed. On-line analytical processing (OLAP) and multi-dimensional Web log data cube are proposed by [15]. In the WebLogMiner project, the data is split up into the following phases. In the first phase, the data is filtered to remove irrelevant information and it is transformed into a relational database in order to facilitate the following operation. In the second phase, a multi-dimensional array structure, called a data cube is built, each dimension representing a field with all possible values described by attributes. OLAP is used in the third phase in order to provide further insight of any target data set from different perspectives. In the last phase, data mining techniques can be used on the Web log data cube. The use of access patterns for automatically classifying users on a Web site is discussed in [14]. In this work, the authors identify clusters of users that access similar pages using user access logs entry. This lead to an improved organization of the hypertext documents. In this case, the organization can be customised on the fly and dynamically link hypertext pages for individual users.

6 Conclusion

In this paper, we presented an architectural framework for Web usage mining. We applied the approach for two differents servers and showed that association rules and sequential patterns extracted from Web server acces logs allows to predict user visit patterns and a dynamic hypertext organization. We are currently studying how to improve the process extraction using an incremental mining. This problem is very important in the Web mining context since the log files (access log, error log, etc) are always growing. We think that an incremental approach focusing on relationships previously extracted by a miner coud be very efficient.

References

1. R. Agrawal, T. Imielinski, and A. Swami. Mining Association Rules between Sets of Items in Large Databases. In *Proc. of the SIGMOD'93*, Washington, May 1993.
2. R. Agrawal and R. Srikant. Fast Algorithms for Mining Generalized Association Rules. In *Proc. of the VLDB'94*, Santiago, Chile, September 1994.
3. S. Brin, R. Motwani, and al. Dynamic Itemset Counting and Implication Rules for Market Basket Data. In *Proc. of the SIGMOD'97*, Tucson, Arizona, May 1997.
4. World Wide Web Consortium. In *http://lists.w3.org/Archives*, 1998.
5. R. Cooley, B. Mobasher, and J. Srivastava. Web Mining: Information and Pattern Discovery on the World Wide Web. In *Proc. of the ICTAI'97*, November 1997.
6. U.M. Fayad, G. Piatetsky-Shapiro, P. Smyth, and R. Uthurusamy, editors. *Advances in Knowledge Discovery and Data Mining*. AAAI Press, Menlo Park, 1996.
7. H. Mannila, H. Toivonen, and A.I. Verkamo. Discovery of Frequent Episodes in Event Sequences. *Data Mining and Knowledge Discovery*, 1(3), February 1997.
8. F. Masseglia. Le pré-calcul appliqué à l'extraction de sequential patterns en data mining. Technical report, LIRMM, France, June 1998.
9. F. Masseglia, F. Cathala, and P. Poncelet. The PSP Approach for Mining Sequential Patterns. In *Proc of the PKDD'98*, Nantes, France, September 1998.
10. B. Mobasher, N. Jain, E. Han, and J. Srivastava. Web Mining: Pattern Discovery from World Wide Web Transactions. Technical Report, Univ. of Minnesota, 1996.
11. A. Savasere, E. Omiecinski, and S. Navathe. An Efficient Algorithm for Mining Association Rules in Large Databases. In *Proc. of the VLDB'95*, Zurich, 1995.
12. M. Spiliopoulou and L.C. Faulstich. WUM: A Tool for Web Utilization Analysis. In *Proceedings of EDBT Workshop WebDB'98*, Valencia, Spain, March 1998.
13. R. Srikant and R. Agrawal. Mining Sequential Patterns: Generalizations and Performance Improvements. In *Proc. of the EDBT'96*, Avignon, September 1996.
14. T. Yan, M. Jacobsen, and al. From User Access Patterns to Dynamic Hypertext Linking. In *Proc. of the WWW Conference*, Paris, May 1996.
15. O. Zaïane, M .Xin, and J. Han. Discovering Web Access Patterns and Trends by Applying OLAP and Data Mining Technology on Web Logs. In *Proc. on Advances in Digital Libraries Conference (ADL'98)*, Santa Barbara, CA, April 1998.

Local and Federated Database Schemas Evolution
An Impact Propagation Model

L. Deruelle[1], M. Bouneffa[1], G. Goncalves[2], and J.C. Nicolas[2]

[1] Laboratoire d'Informatique du Littoral, B.P. 719. 3, rue Louis David,
62228, Calais, Cedex, France
{deruelle, bouneffa}@lil.univ-littoral.fr
[2] Laboratoire de Gestion de Production, Faculté des sciences appliquées,
Technoparc Futura,
62400 Bethune, France
{goncalves,nicolas}@univ-artois.fr

Abstract. The software evolution is a challenge for engineers. In fact, the high complexity of the software makes it difficult to perform the change. This may cause serious damage in the information system. Within the information system cooperating by the way of federation, the effects are more critical. It appears necessary to provide tools that support the *a priori* change impact analysis. In this paper, we propose the Source Code Software Components Structural Model (SC^{2}SM). This models applications manipulating persistent objects, stored in an ODMG-compliant database system. The SC^{2}SM defines software components multigraphs, that represent local and federated database schemas, programs source codes and their relationships. The multigraph representation is the way to process the *a priori* change impact analysis, using a knowledge base system.

1 Introduction

The software evolution is often a critical task. Without tools and methodologies to control it, the software change may cause serious damage to the information system. In fact, the high complexity of the software makes it difficult to perform the change with avoiding its side effects. Within the information system cooperating by the way of federation, the effects are more critical. The financial cost resulting from the change is colossal. The paper addresses the change that concerns applications manipulating persistent objects, stored in ODMG-compliant local and federated object databases. We shall focus especially on the local database evolution and its impacts on the federation.

Sheth and Larson describes the federated database as a collection of cooperating and autonomous component database systems [19]. The federated database is the way to various database cooperating. The federated information provides the decision support system design [13], based on existing information stored in distributed databases. This is built from the existing autonomous database schemas.

The information stored in databases is represented by several schemas : the local schema, the component schema, the import schemas, the export schemas, the federated schema and an external schema [14], [19]. The local database schema consists of a class hierarchy, that models the persistent objects stored in the local object database [6].

The federated database schema is the integration of multiple export schemas to access the local information. The external schema presents a coherent view of the information. To translate the query commands and data results through each schema level, Sheth and Larson define the processors [19]. The evolution

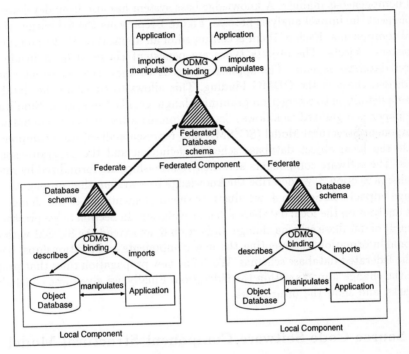

Fig. 1. Federation of two database schemas

of the real world and enterprise organization requires object database schemas changes. The changes cause incoherence and inconsistent states in the programs and the object databases. It is very important to identify this damage before the software exploitation. In the related work, one can find many strategies to control the schema evolution. One of them, the *instances adaptation* concerns the instances that are inconsistent with the new class definition [5], [9]. The *emulation* strategy is based on the class versionning. When a change is performed on a class, a new version is generated. The old programs should refer to the previous version to work correctly [15]. The view mechanism is a way to make the schema change impact transparent for the instances [4]. These approaches do not deal with the application programs manipulating the affected instances. The major drawback is the observation *a posteriori* of the efficient or damage caused by the changes. In this paper, we shall discuss the *a priori* change impact analysis, by simulating the change on software components [7] [3] [2][18]. These components represent the local database schema, the federated database schema and the programs manipulating persistent objects. The simulation provides information to estimate the change effects and their cost. It prevents the incoherence and the damage caused by the changes on both the database schemas and the programs. In [7] [3], we deal with the *a priori* change impact analysis on the local programs manipulating persistent objects. This is performed by a model that represents the database schemas and the program source codes in a unified and homogeneous manner. A knowledge base system has also been developed to implement the impact analysis process. Figure 1 represents the federation of two local components. Each of them is composed of an application that manipulates persistent objects. The objects types are persistent classes defined inside the object database schema. The application needs to know the persistent classes definition, through the ODMG binding. This allows to translate the database schema definition to a target programming language, like C++, Java, Smalltalk. The paper is organized as follows: Section 2 presents the Source Code Software Component Structural Model (SC²SM), that represents all software components inside the local object database schemas definition and the programs source codes. The software components and their relationships are formalized by multigraphs. In Section 3, we describe the knowledge base system that propagates the change impacts. In Section 4, we illustrate the implementation of the change impact analysis on the local database schema evolution. In Section 5, we present an example of database schema change. In Section 6, we extend the SC²SM with additional information, representing the new components and relationships, based on the federated database schemas. We define new propagation rules that propagate the change impacts within the federation. Finally, we give some concluding remarks, and show the future work.

2 Source Code Software Component Structural Model

The Source Code Software Component Structural Model (SC²SM), described in [7] and [3], represents the various software components and their relationships. These are extracted from the object databases schemas files, and programs source codes, by means of a parsing tool [17]. In the SC²SM, we classify the software components following a granularity criterion. So, we consider:

- the coarse grained components that may be source code files, libraries, packages or database schemas.
- the middle grained components that may be effective or generic classes[20][1], persistent classes[6], methods, attributes, free functions, global variables and objects.
- the fine grained components, like statements, database queries and individual symbols.

These components are linked by various relationships that drive the change impacts. Such relationships may be:

- the *Import/Export* relationship, that allows the access of software compo-
nents like local database schema files. In fact, the local database schema change causes impacts on the applications that import it.
- the *Inheritance* relationship that exists between the classes of the application programs or database schemas.
- the *Call* relationship between methods. The change simulated on the called method, like parameter type update, causes impacts on the caller method.
- the *Manipulate* relationship, represents the programs that querying persistent objects. The query syntax needs information about the persistent classes, representing the manipulated objects. The queries are wrote in the Object Query Language defined by the Object Database Management Group standard [6].

A more detailed description of the SC^{2}SM can be found in [7], [3].

The multigraph is a way to formalize the set of links between software components. Let us give a definition of such multigraphs.

Definition:

Let $C = \{c1, c2, ..., cn\}$ be a finite set representing software components, called vertices, and $E = \{e1, e2, ..., en\}$ be a finite set of relationships between components. A multigraph noticed G is defined as follows:

- $G =< C, E >$ with:
- $E \subseteq \mathcal{P}(C)$ and $\forall E_i \in \mathcal{P}(C), |E_i| \leq 2$.
- The vertices and the edges belonging to G are labeled respectively with the software components name and the relationship type.

Nonetheless we shall not consider the isolated points of a graph to be vertices.

In the next section, we define the knowledge base system to perform the impact analysis process, resulting from a change applied on a multigraph node.

3 Knowledge Base System to Process Changes Impacts Analysis

The knowledge base system is a declarative and incremental way to represent the knowledge of the evolution experts. The evolution experts are in charge of the schema database and source code evolution, by performing changes. When the change is simulated on a node or edge of the multigraph, the system processes the change impact using an knowledge base system [10]. The knowledge base system is based on representing the multigraph as a set of facts, that fires propagation rules. The propagation rules are defined in accordance with a change typology. These rules retrieve the set of affected software components and propagate the impacts to the others, by the way of the relationships. The affected components nodes are marked in the graph with the label *Affected*.

We describe here some rules, used in the knowledge base system :

- *DeleteClass(X)*, this rule propagates the impacts of deleting the class X to :
  - the attributes and methods defined in the class X,
  - the objects belonging to the class X repository, manipulated by queries,
  - the inheritance class hierarchy, linked to the class X by the way of the inheritance relationship,
  - the methods and functions calling the method of the class X, by the way of the call relationship.
- *DeleteAttribute(X)*, this propagates the impacts of deleting the attribute X to :
  - the methods using the attribute X inside their body, by the way of a use relationship,
  - the objects using the attribute X,
  - the class inheriting the attribute X,
  - the queries that manipulate the attribute X.
- *DeleteMethod(X)*, this propagates the impacts of deleting the method X to :
  - the methods calling the method X inside their body, by the way of the call relationship,
  - the objects calling the method X,
  - the class inheriting the method X,
  - the queries that call the method X.

A more exhaustive formalization of the propagation rules can be found in [7], [3].

In the next section, we present the implementation of the tools managing the local database schema evolution.

4 Implementation of the Local Database Schema Evolution

The prototype, implementing the SC^{2}SM and the knowledge base system is composed of the following tools :

- the *ObjectStore DBMS* [8] that is used to store the multigraphs, as sets of persistent objects ;
- the *Parsing tool* that extracts the multigraph by parsing the source code of the application. The considered applications are composed of O2 Database schemas and Java or C++ programs manipulating O2 persistent objects ;
- the *Impact Analyzer tool* that provides the simulation of the changes and processes the impact analysis by means of a knowledge base system. The impacts analyzer is implemented by the mean of Jess [10], that is a java clone of CLIPS [12] ;

The implementation details can be found in [7].

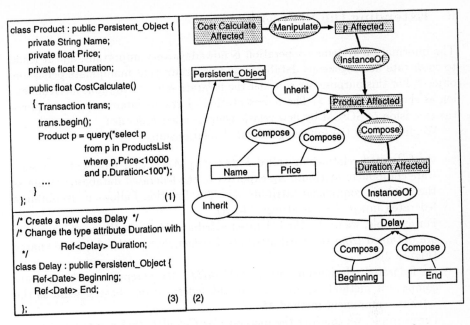

Fig. 2. Source Code schema multigraph representation, based on the SC²SM

5 Example of Local Object Database Schema Change

We propose an example of object database schema definition (box 1 of Figure 2), composed of the persistent class *Product* which is characterized by the product name, its purchase price, the delivery delay, and a method that computes the cost production of a product from the price of its components. The classes that inherit the predefined class *Persistent_Object* are persistent, in accordance with the Object Database Management Group standard [6].

The box 2 of Figure 2 shows the representation of the object database schema by the way of a software components multigraph.

The SC²SM takes into account a component change taxonomy like delete, insert or update [7]. For instance, let us consider the update of the attribute *Duration* type from *float* to *Delay* (box 3 of Figure 2). To perform the change on the attribute *Product.Duration*, we define the class *Delay*, that represents the new attribute type. The class *Delay* defines the beginning and the end of the production time. The change simulation, performed on the attribute *Duration*, causes impacts on the class *Product*, and on the query that manipulates this attribute. The impacts are propagated through the multigraph to the nodes linked to the node *Duration*. Figure 2 shows the results of the impact analysis process, that are nodes marked with the *affected* label.

6 Extending the SC²SM

The information systems cooperation is nowadays very important, and it leads to cooperate heterogeneous databases and programs that manipulate persistent objects. For this purpose, we consider the federation as multigraphs interconnexion as shown in Figure 3. The representation of graphs interconnexion requires the extension of SC²SM by new relationships, called *Federated*.

We distinguish the following federated relationships :

- the federated relationship called *FedAttr(A_L,A_F,f)* that represents the software component attribute A_L exported to the federated database schema as the software component attribute A_F. The function f allows us to obtain a federated image A_F not identical to A_L.

  For example, we define the federated attribute *MajoratedPrice* which values are obtained from the local attribute *Product.Price* with additional charge (Figure 2).
- the federated relationship called *FedMeth(M_L,M_F,f)* represents the software component method M_L exported to the federated database schema as the software component method M_F.

  For example, we consider the method *CostCalculate* that computes the production cost, and the corresponding federated method *RealProductionCost-Calculate*. The method *RealProductionCostCalculate* computes the article production cost with the financial market variation.
- the federated relationship called *FedMethAttr(M_L,A_F,f)* that represents the software component method M_L exported to the federated database schema as the software component attribute A_F.

  For example, we define the federated attribute *ArticleCost* as the result of the local method *Product.CostCalculate*.

The federated relationship named *FedClass(C_L, C_F)* may be derived from the previous ones, as follows :

$$\forall C_i \in C_L, \exists C_j \in C_F, FedAttr(C_i, C_j, f) \vee FedMeth(C_i, C_j, f) \vee FedMethAttr(C_i, C_j, f) \quad (1)$$

That means, for all software components C_i (attributes or methods) of the class C_L, defined in a local database schema, the federation relationship named FedClass(C_L, C_F) exits when :

- an attribute C_i is Federated in C_j (FedAttr(C_i, C_j, f)), or
- a method C_i is federated in C_j (FedMeth(C_i, C_j, f) or FedMethAttr(C_i, C_j, f)).

These federated relationships will allow the knowledge base system to propagate the change impact to the linked software components.

In the next section, we propose an extension of the knowledge base system (described in Section 3), to consider the impacts propagation rules inside the federated system.

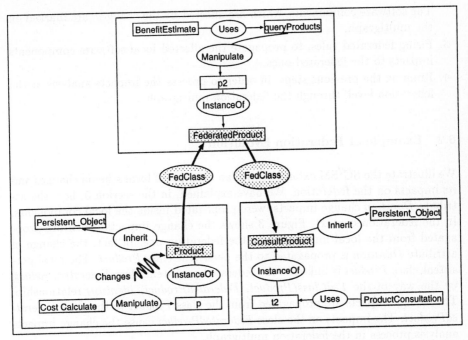

Fig. 3. Graphs cooperation, based on the extending of SC^2SM

6.1 Extending the Knowledge base system for the federation

We consider the changes performed on the software components defined inside the local schema database, and its impacts on the federated software components. To propagate the change impacts to the federation, we define federated propagation rules based on the local propagation rules. We extend the knowledge base system to take into account the change impacts on the federation :

- *DeleteClass(CL)*:
  $Delete(C_L) \wedge Class(C_L) \wedge FedClass(C_L, C_F) - > Delete(C_F)$
- *DeleteAttribute(AL)*:
  $Delete(A_L) \wedge Attribute(A_L) \wedge FedAttr(A_L, A_F) - > Delete(A_F)$
- *DeleteMethod(ML)*:
  $Delete(M_L) \wedge Method(M_L) \wedge (FedMethod(M_L, M_F, f) \vee FedMethAttr(M_L, M_F)) - > Delete(M_F)$

We present, here after, the four steps for the changes impacts analysis at federation level:

1. The simulation of a local component change by the experts to perform the software evolution. The changes are performed on software components, representing database schema.
2. Firing local propagation rules to estimate the affected software components, inside the local multigraph without considering the federated components.

The software components, which are affected by the changes, are marked on the multigraph.

3. Firing federated rules, to propagate the affected local software components impacts to the federated ones.

4. Running the previous steps, in order to process the impacts analysis at the federation level, through the federation multigraph.

6.2 Example of Federation Evolution

We illustrate the SC^{2}SM extension with an example of local schema changes and its impacts on the federation. We have explained, in the section 5, how the attribute *Duration* change impacts, were propagated inside the local components. In the federation context, Figure 3 shows the change impacts which are propagated from the local multigraph to the federation one. In fact, the change of attribute *Duration* is propagated to the persistent class *Product*. The local persistent class *Product* is linked to the federated persistent class *FederatedProduct*, by the way of the *FedClass(Product, FederatedProduct, identity)* relationship. The change impacts are propagated from the class *Product* to the class *FederatedProduct*. The impacts on the class *FederatedProduct* cause the change impacts analysis process in the federation multigraph.

7 Conclusion

We have proposed and implemented an approach for the *a priori* software change impact analysis. This has been applied to propagate the database schema change impact to the application programs that may be a part of a federated information system. The approach is also used in order to analyze any change affecting an object-oriented application, that deals with the ODMG-compliant database management systems.

We consider both database schemas and programs source codes as multigraphs implementing a Source Code Software Components Structural Model (SC^{2}SM). This leads to propagate the change impact by navigating through the paths of such multigraphs. The SC^{2}SM takes into account all kind of software components even if they represent large ones like files and database schemas or more fine ones like statements and individual symbols. This makes the analysis more exhaustive. The prototype that implements our approach is based on the use of a knowledge base system (KBS), that makes it more flexible.

Subsequently, the rules set of the KBS is continuously enriched in order to achieve more exhaustiveness and to consider several aspects of software evolution like analyzing the change impact on the software performances [16]. Otherwise, we are refining the relationships between the federation components within the framework of databases interoperability, provided by the standard services of the Object Management Group (CORBA) [11].

References

1. Edith Au and Dave Makower. *Java Programming Basics*. 1996.
2. S. Barros. *Analyse a priori des conséquences de la modification de systèmes logiciels: de la théorie à la pratique*. PhD thesis, Université Paul Sabatier Toulouse, 1997.
3. H. Basson. Contrôle de l'évolution des logiciels : modélisation pour l'analyse d'impact des modifications. *Document HDR, Université de Nancy I*, Déc 1998.
4. Z. Bellahsene. Extending a view mechanism to support schema evolution in federated database systems. In *Procedings of the eigth International Conference on Database and Expert Systems Aspplication*, pages 573–582, September 1997.
5. M. Bouneffa and N. Boudjlida. Managing schemas changes in oject-relationship databases. In *Proc. of the 14th. International Conference On Entity-Relationship and Object-Oriented Modeling, LNCS*, Brisbane, Qweensland Australia, dec 1995. Springer-Verlag.
6. Rick G. G. Cattel. *ODMG-93 Obejct-Oriented Databases Standard*. International Thomson Publishing, 1995.
7. L. Deruelle. Analyse de l'impact de l'évolution des applications orienté-objet, mémoire de d.e.a. Technical report, Université de Lille, 1998.
8. Object Design. *Bookshelf for ObjectStore PSE Pro Release 3.0 for Java*. http://www.objectdesign.com/, January 1998.
9. Fabrizio Ferrandina, Thorsten Meyer, and Roberto Zicari. Schema and database evolution in the o2 object database system. In *Proceedings of the 21th International Conference on Very Large Databases, Zurich, Switzerland (VLDB '95)*, September 1995.
10. Ernest J. Friedman-Hill. *Jess 4.3 User's Manual*. Sandia National Laboratories, December 1998.
11. J.M. Geib, C. Gransart, and P. Merle. *Corba des Concepts à la Pratique*. InterEditions, 1997.
12. Joseph C. Giarratano. *CLIPS User's Guide*, August 1998.
13. JM. Hannoff, JC. Nicolas, and F. Hemery. Approach to services uses in federated information systems. In *8th. International Conference on Database and Expert System Application (DEXA'97)*, Toulouse, France, Septembre 1997. IEEE.
14. D. Heimbigner and D. MacLeod. A federated architecture for information management. *ACM Transactions on Office Information Systems*, pages 253–278, July 1985.
15. Won Kim. Object-oriented databases definition and research directions. Microelectronics and Computer Technonology Corporation 3500 West Balcones Center Drive Austin, Texas 78759, 1989.
16. N. Melab, H. Basson, M. Bouneffa, and L. Deruelle. Object-oriented Code: Profiling and Instrumentation. In *The proc. of the IEEE Intl. Conf. on Software Maintenance (IEEE-ICSM'99), Oxford,*, 1999.
17. Sun Microsystems. *The Java Compiler Compiler Documentation*. http://www.sun.com/suntest/products/JavaCC/, January 1999.
18. G. Murphy. *Lightweight Structural Summarization as an Aid to Software Evolution*. PhD thesis, University of Washington, July, 1996.
19. A.P. Sheth and J.A. Larson. Federated databases systems for managing distributed, heterogenous, and autonomous databases. *ACM Computer Surveys*, pages 183–236, September 1990.
20. B. Stroustrup. *C++ Programming Language*. Adison Wesley, 1991.

Adaptive Caching Management for Multimedia Support

Frederic Andres, and Kinji Ono

R&D Department, National Center for Science Information Systems
Otsuka 3-29-1, Bunkyo-ku, Tokyo, Japan
E-mail: {andres,ono}@rd.nacsis.ac.jp

Abstract. The Active HYpermedia Delivery System (AHYDS) within the NACSIS R&D department is an experimental advanced platform developed for delivering hypermedia documents over distributed and heterogeneous systems. The evolution of the network technology and the requirements of multimedia applications suggest that hypermedia and multimedia delivery systems need to be improved in terms of media caching to guarantee data delivery to a large scale of users and also to reduce information traffic within large scale multimedia information systems. Remote main-memory accesses require combining main memory access in a same LAN.

In this article, we address the main memory caching capabilities of the AHYDS platform used in a multi-server/multi-client architecture, to optimize the use of the uniform storage management of the underlying data structure. It provides a high performance support in terms of distributed and heterogeneous hypermedia management. We propose two cache algorithms: the "Temperature Adaptation Cache", and the "States Adaptation Cache" for distributed information systems. Performance evaluations show that our proposal reduces the data access latency and increase the hit ratio of accessing data in main memory in a rate between 10 and 20%. The caching algorithms also eliminate the CPU overhead in a range of 50-95% maintaining a high hit ratio.

Keywords: **Application Oriented Database Systems, Caching Management, Access Optimization, and Distributed Multimedia Systems.**

1 Introduction

Applications through the World Wide Web, such as cultural hypermedia or media applications generate new challenges of ensuring a high quality of services in a scalable distributed and heterogeneous environment such as caching improvement [10] based on hierarchical servers. Several new standards and technologies such as XML and SMIL (Synchronous Multimedia Interface Language) have impacted both the way to access to the data, and the way to process data and exchange results over large scale distributed systems or over internet. The evolution of the requirements of the users and of the information engine technology has pushed the integration at different levels including information format integration or system integration of database services and communication services. Managing documents in large scale distributed and heterogeneous system also requires the use of proxies, intermediate components between user web browsers and data servers inside the cyberspace environment. Main memory caching algorithms provide many benefits in terms of improvement network traffic, and user response time as it has been shown in several research works on distributed caching management [15] and on caching over web servers and proxies [6, 7, 9].

However, the effectiveness of these solutions is limited due to the low integration between data structure, data processing and cache services to maximize distributed in-memory data management.

The performance metrics of interest are in this context: latency, and hit ratio. The only way to reduce data access latency for distributed information servers is to include a cache management for the local main memory management combining both local and remote main memory information management, and also single and multiple information copies. Latency can be reduced if the requested information is found either in the local memory or in a remote memory in the same LAN as it is has been shown in [16]. Thus, cache algorithms are needed at the main memory level in order to reduce the data access latency and to maximize the main memory hit ratio. Otherwise, memory access latency becomes a performance bottleneck for the entire system.

In this paper, we investigate the issue of distributed scalable caching management in large-scale multimedia information systems. We propose two adaptive caching algorithms to adjust the in-memory data set according to application requests and to provide efficient cache management for a large scale distributed environment. Experiments have been done to validate our approach using the Active HYpermedia Delivery System (AHYDS) workload. The adaptation is ease by the architecture of the Phasme engine, the underlying component of the AHYDS platform.

The remainder of the paper is organized as follows: Section 2 overviews the Active Hypermedia Delivery System, its features and its uniform storage management. Section 3 describes the two adaptive caching algorithms used inside AHYDS. In Section 4, we provide performance experiments and evaluate our approach using the underlying data structure of AHYDS as test-bed. The experiments enable us to show that our proposal achieves better performance compared to traditional approaches. Section 5 describes related works. Finally, Section 6 presents concluding remarks and future works.

2 AHYDS Overview

In this section, we overview the AHYDS platform used as the test-bed of our investigation in new caching algorithms.

2.1 The AHYDS platform

The Active HYpermedia Delivery System (AHYDS) platform [3] is a delivery system to provide hypermedia documents according to the requirements of the application. It has been developed inside the COE (Center of Excellence) Program under the Japanese Ministry of Education and a French-Japanese cooperation since 1996. We remind its distinguish capabilities. First, AHYDS is based on the Phasme engine [2] vertically customizable from the data type to the execution layout. So it can integrate specific data retrieval and processing for a wide variety of applications and caching web server purpose [1].

Second, The AHYDS Platform leverages a uniform data management (named Extended Binary Algebra) for media data using a uniform interface based on the many-sorted algebra concept: the Phasme Interface Language. The users specify the resolution, and the destination of the output result using a Phasme query and according to the desired format.

Third, the AHYDS platform is targeted towards distributed and heterogeneous environments – The dynamic query supervision based on neural network and equidepth histogram cost evaluator enables dynamic adaptation to evolving wide area network environments.

We used the workload of the Active HYpermedia Delivery System for the evaluation of the caching management. The AHYDS interface combines different application data models accessing a uniform set of data and invoking active and adaptive strategies. The multimedia support includes text, sound, image, and video. AHDYS platform provides multi-resolution and multi-language information retrieval support. The AHYDS interface is based on standard interfaces (SQL, HTML/XML, OO navigation) extended to support multimedia retrieval. The semantic of each interface customizes the data access on-line. AHYDS consists of 5 parts: the Treeview module, the SQLview module, the HTML browser, the Video and Audio presentation and the multi-criteria viewer. The AHYDS application panels and their active capabilities allow the user interactions inside the uniform data set according to his needs, and according to his profile. AHYDS is also a sample of adaptive and interactive distributed caching system using the customizability of the Phasme system.

2.2 Data Management

The AHYDS platform uses the Extended Binary Graph structure [2] as storage structure (see Figure 1).

The EBG structure includes one EBG cache (an in-memory table) and EBGs themselves (including oid-value relationship or oid-oid relationship). An EBG data structure is an extended binary graph based on 2 sets: one source set (OID), and one destination set (values).

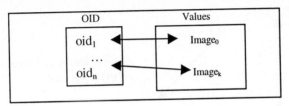

Figure 1: EBG Management

The major feature of the EBG is the storage of unique complex values such as string or media data. Duplication is managed directly at the link level. The EBG cache is based on the EBG Adaptive Cache Management (EAC).

EBGs can have different in-memory types (transient, permanent and persistent) according to their origins and according to the application requirements. EBGs are stored in a LRU ordered-based list. Two other LRU ordered-based lists are used to store duplicate EBGs and single EBGs. The replacement policy follows a first replacement for duplicated EBGs in the distributed information system, then single EBGs are replaced. Furthermore, the default main memory cache evaluates the expected access cost of an EBG or an access part of it as a ratio between the actual cost to access to the required EBG or its part and the elapsed timed consumed for the last access to the EBG.

3 AHYDS Main Memory Caching Algorithms

In the following, we propose two adaptive caching algorithms to extend the main memory cache mechanism used on the EBG data structure of the AHYDS Platform: the "Temperature Adaptation Cache" management (named TAC), and the "States Adaptation Cache" management (named SAC). The implementation is an extension of [1]. We overview cache management and point out how various workloads (pull, and push based workload) get high data service rates.

The major issue of these algorithms is to optimal user response time according to the workload behavior.

3.1 The Temperature Adaptation Cache Algorithm

For each EBG, we define a temperature. Figure 2 shows the variation of temperature for an EBG. When an EBG is accessed, the EBG temperature becomes hot. Each EBG varies according to the EBG in-memory type and according to a linear temperature function within the EBG type. The applied rules is based on a linear function with different weights according to the type of the transactions (short, long, update, read, etc) and according to the type of EBG placement type such as local only, distributed and number of copies, replicated. Further details on the cache architecture are given in [4].

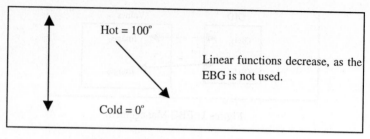

Figure 2: EBG Temperature Variation

Once the heat of an EBG becomes zero, the EBG is returned to its permanent storage space or retained as a temporary in the swap area. The EBG does not include any hard pointer into the structure, so the memory manager is free to re-allocate space of cold EBGs when it processes EBG replacement policies.

3.2 The States Adaptation Cache Algorithm

Each data item (smallest entity inside an EBG) has still a temperature which can in this case varied according to three states: the vapor state, the liquid state, and the frigid state. The use of 3 states enables to include a finer knowledge about the use of each item: (1) item heavily requested and broadcast for proxy cache updates, (2) item not so used, and (3) the item which has not been requested for a while and the temperature is converging to 0.

The adaptation behavior of this algorithm follows the approach used by [13]. We will describe only in the following the specific contribution upon EBGs. The interested reader is referred to [4]. As it is shown in Figure 3, the global system is split into logical groups in order to provide a hierarchical cache management. It provides a hierarchical cache topology inside the global information system. The AHYDS server pushes document items to update AHYDS proxies. Pull data transfers are done by the AHYDS platform for traditional client-server data transfers. AHYDS also processes both cache resolution and data placement. The in-memory cache table provides the information about how the cache location should be resolved. Each AHYDS platform is autonomous and can also have a private cache. So it enables each AHYDS platform to decide which data can be shared to other servers and when those data are available. The load-balancing supervisor is not addressed in this paper.

One of the key components of the AHYDS platform is the item data exchange and updates. This component includes a dynamic protocol and the policy management for adding and suppresses item entries, mechanisms for initializing in-memory cache table, collision resolution, and locale private caching. This enables to test and demonstrate cooperation web browsers sharing URL addresses as a cooperative resource or managing local URL addresses.

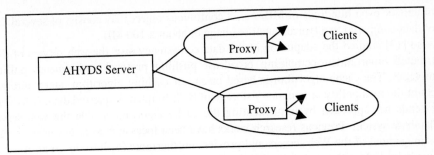

Figure 3: State Adaptation Cache Update

4 Related Works

Several studies have addressed caching management for continuous or conventional data over cyberspace, although none have considered the general framework for distributed and heterogeneous Web server-based engine for multimedia systems.

Data Replacement Policy

The major work [15] in this field has considered multiple client-server architecture, proposing an algorithm, remote load sensitive caching (RLS-caching), for page replacement between servers and the client caches. In this framework, as assumption, the number of read only of the workload is larger than the write only rate. To address the issues introduced by a distributed and heterogeneous environment with multi-servers, we modified and extended this replacement policy for the AHYDS platform. The RSL algorithm is compared with our approaches in Section 5. Some extensions of this approach have been done in [7] in terms of memory management and optimization for media management. Cache management and data replacement policies are studied for continuous data support. But multiple media servers are not considered in this research.

Data Replication and Consistency Management

Main researches [11] and [9] have investigated how the performance of Web server systems is affected by the share of summary cache over large scale wide-area distributed Web. Works [11] performed an analysis on the effect of "maintaining strong cache consistency in a distributed Web environment" on performance. The database integration as a key component of the Web environment including replication management is not addressed in this work. In the work by [9], a new cache sharing protocol Summary-Cache Enhanced ICP using "Bloom filter" based summaries. Their results show that number of inter-proxy protocol messages has been reduced by a factor of 25 to 60%, and that the bandwidth consumption by over 50%. Their approach, however, has not been apply to media data in which size is often in the order of tens or even hundreds of MB, *i.e.*, a continuous object may consist of several GB of data compared to a typical satellite image of about a 100 MB.

Also [13] studied the adaptation of the data consistency over the web servers of distributed environment-combining broadcast pushing protocol and unicast pulling protocol. The cache algorithm is based on an air-caching algorithm, taken into account the availability of temporary storage of high frequent requested data. Our work extends his approach by implementing the cache algorithm inside the web server database system. Previous research works have been focussing on issues of the cache management of the Web servers and proxies. Furthermore [6] introduced an innovative hybrid algorithm for managing the client cache in a distributed persistent information system. This algorithm is a hybrid between page and object caching. Our work is similar to this work as we also provide a caching management for the AHYDS client side but the granularity is different.

5 Performance Evaluation

To compare the different caching algorithms inside the AHYDS platform, we use a Sun ultra 30 and Sun ultra 2 as test-bed server machines. The Sun ultra 2 includes 2x200 MHz processors and a 256-MB memory with about 1.6 GB/sec as throughput. The Sun ultra 30 includes one UltraSPARC II 296 MHz and 256 MB of Memory with about 1.6GB/s as throughput. In these environments, we configured the two machines with the AHDYS servers. In our environment, remote cache-miss latency is equal to 2.4 microseconds. We used the Quantify tool [12] to get performance statistics and profiles from the experiments.

In picking the AHYDS workload (see description in 2.2), we had two goals. First, we want to use multimedia processing that representative of large retrieval users' jobs (query in our case) that would run in large-scale multimedia systems. Second, the AHYDS platform is used in distributed and heterogeneous environment. We compared three generic cache algorithms (*Client/Server Cache Algorithm* (CS), *Client/Server Reserve-based Cache Algorithm* (CSR), and *Remote Load Sensitive Cache Algorithm* (RLS)) with three user-semantic-based adaptive algorithm (*the EBG Adapted Cache Algorithm* (EAC), *the Temperature Adaptation Cache Algorithm* (TAC), and *the State Adaptation Cache Algorithm* (SAC)). The implementation of the CSR algorithm follows the results shown in [14].

5.1 Experimental results

By varying the size of the multimedia data and the rate of the idle memory, we can explore the ability of the adaptive-based cache algorithms to manage multimedia data. Figure 4 shows the workload response time plotted against the percentage of idle memory. Client/Server cache cannot compete compared to other caching algorithms. The results show clearly that generic algorithms result in poor performance for all the type of workloads as the percentage of idle memory decreases. There is no special self-adaptation to application's data structure. The performance of traditional approach is competitive with our proposal only when the size of the multimedia data is large (Figure 4 (a) 3 MB). In this case of large size data access with 46% of idle memory, the caching effect of multiple copies improves the response time. For smaller size (Figure 4 (b) 1.2 MB), our approach based on the EBG structure provides a gain of performance compared to other. The Client/Server cache algorithm with reservation (CLS) degrades the performance due to the increase of the number of exchanged messages between the servers. Comparing the three user-semantic-based adaptive algorithms (Figure 4 (c)), the States Adaptation Cache Algorithm provides a better performance, as the average time for a multimedia data to be kept in the cache is longer for this algorithm. The introduction of three states favors this effect.

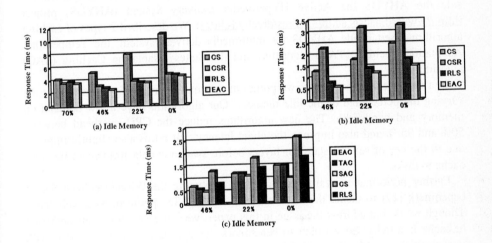

Figure 4: Response Time as function of the percentage of idle memory. In (a) data size is set to 3 MB, in (b) and (c) data size is set to 1.2 MB

Our second experiment based on navigation processing focuses on getting statistics on the number of messages exchanged between the servers to update the caches and statistics on CPU overhead between the different cache algorithms. Client machine is a pentium 333 Mhz.

The results (see Table 1) show that the " States Adaptation Cache (SAC)" Algorithm reduces the CPU overhead significantly, while increasing also the hit ratio due to a larger number of states of the cache management. The decrease of the client latency is due to the remote access data as remote cache hits. Experiments using the Quantify tool show that the CPU time increase is due to servicing remote requests in the EAC, CS and RLS algorithms. Our results indicate that the "States Adaptation Cache" algorithm solves overhead problems of traditional cache algorithms in case of navigation processing.

Table 1: Performance of the Cache Algorithms – Navigation workload

Algorithm type	Hit ratio	Client Latency	User CPU	System CPU
EAC	30%	3.42	50.20	235.33
TAC	45%	3.32	60.24	225.41
SAC	50%	3.01	59.04	220.45
CS	19%	3.75	65.15	260.12
RLS	25%	3.63	64.03	259.26

6 Conclusions and Future works

In this paper, we described user-semantic based adaptive caching management inside the AHYDS the Active HYpermedia Delivery System (AHYDS) project (http://www.rd.nacsis.ac.jp/~andres/db/ahyds.html). We described 2 types of caching algorithms used inside AHYDS for multimedia delivery system: the Temperature Adaptation Caching (TAC) algorithm and the States Adaptation Caching (SAC) algorithm.

In a first set of experiences, we point out the improvement of the response time varying the percentage of the idle memory. Our algorithms have a low demand on memory and bandwidth. The new algorithms reduce the CPU overhead between 50% and 95 % and also improve the client latency. Hit ratios also slightly improve due to the use of several states or layers before swapping data from main memory cache to disks.

Further performance evaluation is being done using the Wisconsin Web Server benchmark [17] to tackle the issue of using the AHYDS platform as a webserver. Though we do not address the issue in this paper, we can easily apply our approach to cache hierarchy. So we plan to benchmark our approach and compared it with new partitioning algorithms [5]. We also would like to apply the study of these algorithms to various cache consistency protocols.

Acknowledgement

We would like to thank NACSIS R&D Department and Washington University/CDOC team for the support to this research. We thank Tredej Toranawigrai for his invaluable help during this work.

References

1. [ABO96] Andres F., Boulos J., and Ono K. "Accessing Active Application-oriented DBMS from the World Wide Web" in the Proceedings of the Intern. Symp. on COoperative DAtabase Systems for Advanced Applications (CODAS), Dec 1996, pp 232-234.

2. [AO97] Andres F., and Ono K. "Phasme Un Systeme parallele de Gestion de Bases de Donnees Oriente Application" F. Andres, K. Ono, in the French Journal Calculateurs Paralleles Edition speciale BD paralleles et distribuees, 1997.

3. [AO98] Andres F., and Ono K. "The Active HYpermedia Delivery System", in the Proceedings of ICDE98, Orlando, USA, 1998, pp 600.

4. [AO99] Andres F., and Ono K. "Caching Management in the AHYDS platform: optimisation and tuning", NACSIS, Technical report 99/1, March 1999.

5. [BMK99] Boncz P., Manegold S., and Kersten M. "Database Architecture Optimized for the new Bottleneck: Memory Access", to appear in Proceeding of the 25th VLDB Conference, Edinburg, Scotland, 1999.

6. [CALM97] Castro M., Adya A., Liskov B., and Myers A.C. "HAC: Hybrid Adaptive Caching for distributed Storage Systems" in The Proceedings of the ACM Symposium on Operating System Principles (SOSP'97), Saint Malo, France, October 1997.

7. [CG97] Chang E., and Garcia-Molina H. "Effective Memory Use in a Media Server" in Proceedings of the 23rd VLDB Conference, Athens, Greece, 1997, pp 496-505.

8. [CI97] Cao P., and Irani S. "Cost-aware WWW Proxy Caching Algorithms" in The Proceedings of the 1997 USENIX Symposium on the Internet Technology and Systems, Dec 1997, pp 193-206.

9. [FCAB98] Fan L., Cao P., Almeida J., and Broder A. Z. "Summary Cache: A Scalable Wide-Area Web Cache Sharing Protocol" in SIGCOMM'98, 1998.

10. [JAC95] Van Jacobson "How to kill the internet", in SIGCOMM'95 Middleware workshop, August 1995, ftp://ftp.ee.lhl.gov/talks/vj-webflame.ps.Z.

11. [LC97] Liu C., and Cao P. "Maintaining Strong Cache Consistency in the World Wide Web", in The Proceedings of ICDCS'97, May 1997, pp 12-21.

12. [QUA99]   Quantify   4.2,   Rational   Software, http://www.rational.com/products/quantify.

13. [SRB97] Stathatos K., Roussopoulos N., Baras J. S. "Adaptive Data Broadcast in Hybrid Networks", in Proceedings of the 23rd VLDB Conference, Athens, Greece, 1997, pp 326-335.

14. [VNL95] Venkataraman S., Livny M., Naughton J., "The Impact of Data Placement on Memory Management for Multi-Server OODBMS", International ICDE, 1995, pp 355-364.

15. [VNL98] Venkataraman S., Naughton J.F., Livny M. "Remote Load Sensitive Caching for Multi-Server Database Systems", in Proceedings of the ICDE, Florida, USA, 1998, pp 514-521.

16. [VR97] Verghese B., and Rosenblum M. "Remote Memory Access in Workstation Clusters", Technical Report CSL-TR-97-729, Computer Systems Laboratory, Stanford University, Stanford, CA, July 1997.

17. [WPB98] Wisconsin Proxy Benchmark 1.0, http://www.cs.wisc.edu/~cao/wpb1.0.html

18. [ZFJ97] Zhang L., Floyd S., and Jacobson V. "Adaptive Web Caching" in The Proceedings of the 2nd Boulder Cache Workshop'97, Colorado, June 1997.

2 Some Basic Concepts

Some basic concepts of the data model used by VHDBS are summarized in this section. We proposed an object-oriented data model (ODM) [9], and such a data model offers a high level of abstraction by the data modeling. This model provides the most necessary and needed concepts for modeling different data, so that it is easy to map data models of existing database systems and database applications to ODM and vice versa. By the design of the data model we take the ODMG 2.0 [1] object model as a basis and are closely related to the InORM project [7] [8], which uses an object-relational data model to model relational and multimedia databases. Some adaptations and extensions are made to the ODMG 2.0, which are necessary for cooperative use of distributed databases in a heterogeneous environment, as the focus of ODMG 2.0 is on the standardization of logical centralized object-oriented database systems, and is therefore different from ours. Such extensions are for example the repository concept and the metadata.

Repository is a basic concept of ODM. By means of repositories the integrated and interoperable schemas of the global information system are defined. Repositories are the first class constructs of the system VHDBS, and the objects are organized as well as stored into repositories. The queries are always formulated on the basis of the repositories, and the results of the queries are put into repositories. Thus, repositories are the storage of the objects (virtual or logical storage on the federated level) and the entry points to reach the objects. The repositories are also the anchor to browse objects at the graphical interface FGRAPH [6]. By means of the repositories, VHDBS provides users the views on the objects. These objects are actually stored in local databases.

There are two kinds of repositories: mirror repositories and combi-repositories (combi-repository stands for combined repository). By means of mirror repositories the definitions (not the contents) of physical repositories of local databases will be mirrored to the global information level. Physical repositories are storage units of local databases, which are for instance relations in relational databases and database entries by some object-oriented databases. There is a one-to-one relationship between a mirror repository and a physical repository, i.e. a physical repository will be reflected to exactly one mirror repository.

Combi-repositories are defined through combining some existing repositories, which could be mirror repositories or themselves combi-repositories. Thus, a combi-repository can be used to define a rather complex relationship between the objects, which are stored as well as managed in some local databases. To specify such a relationship, restrictions and conditions should be given. Therefore, combi-repositories are defined and formulated with queries (combi-repositories are therefore also called query repositories).

VHDBS is based on the object-oriented data model ODM. All things are modeled as objects that belong to some types. Thus, types have also to be determined and assigned to dynamically defined repositories, regardless whether they are defined explicitly or implicitly. In general, a repository is of type CollectionType<ElementType>. ElementType may be arbitrary types and CollectionType is Set, Bag, List, or Collection. Repositories are usually defined with a query. The type for the repository is derived from its select-project part:

$Rep_T = $ SELECT $r1.X_{TX}$, $r2.Y_{TY}$, ...

FROM r1 in Rep1, r2 in Rep2, ...

The types for Rep1 and Rep2 can be traced easily by means of metadata, because they are either mirror repositories or combi-repositories. As explained, a combi-repository is defined recursively, and the base for the recursive definition consists of some mirror repositories managed by the metadata. Therefore the types of the project parts (the dot notations) in the select clause are determinable. They are denoted as TX and TY. The repository Rep has now the implicit type T=CollectionType(ElementType). The ElementType is determined as a tuple type (TX, TY, ...). The CollectionType is derived from the Collection Types of the participating repositories.

3 The Architecture of VHDBS

The multi-layered architecture of VHDBS consisting of a number of components, which can be distributed over several heterogeneous hosts and which cooperate via CORBA2 [5] as well as Orbix [4].

All components of the architecture and all object types defined in the architecture are defined and constructed as modules with interfaces, which are specified in the interface definition language (IDL) of CORBA. The components, which constitute the architecture, are found on four layers. They include the interfaces layer, the federated server layer that conrresponds to the global information layer, the database servers layer and the local database systems layer. VHDBS is accessible through interactive and programmatic interfaces. Currently, three interactive interfaces are supported. One interactive interface is a command-line interpreter for OQL. The global queries are formulated in standard ODMG/OQL [1], which is extended bei us for high-level descriptive manipulation, while distribution remains transparent. The second one is the graphical interface FGRAPH [6]. It allows the user to retrieve the database with graphical displays. The third one is the interface FWEB for web users. VHDBS also supports a C++ programming interface (VHDBS API), by which OQL can be used as a embedded language within C++.

The kernel components in this architecture are found on the federated server layer. It aggregates all services for providing global information (resulting in the VHDBS-API) and coordinates all servers of the federated server layer, consisting of the schema subsystem (ODL parser and meta server), and the query subsystem (OQL parser, query optimizer and query interpreter).

The metadata server manages the metadata, which is used to provide the information about the definitions of types, schemas and repositories of the system, databases and users as well as the locations of the data. Thus, the metadata server component is important for both develoment and management of the global information system by means of supporting cooperative use of distributed and heterogeneous component databases. Metadata is mainly entered via the ODL parser. Additional meta data can be entered via FGRAPH.

Global queries are formulated in standard ODMG/OQL, which is extended for high-level descriptive manipulation, while distribution remains transparent. Queries are analysed by the OQL parser, and correct queries are sent to the query optimizer and then to the query interpreter by the global information server. The optimizer mainly minimizes data transfers. Without optimization, the performance of global queries is only acceptable for small amounts of data. With the aid of the metadata server, the query processing subsystem establishes an execution plan for a query. The query interpreter splits the optimized query into sub-queries for all related component databases, which are executed by them in parallel through the database adapters. All partial results are imported into the Fed-DB, and there they are combined to the final answer under control of the query interpreter (see [10] for our early work on query processing).

With the help of the data model ODM a uniform interface is defined for all database servers, which correspond to all kinds of component database systems. This interface includes typical server operations that can be used commonly by different applications to access the data within any component database. Under this interface there are a number of DBMS adapters, each of which is responsible for a concrete local DBMS and enables the mapping of the global schema to the local schema. These adapters function as sockets and local DBMSs can be plugged into the global information system.

Each component may be instantiated multiple times to scale the VHDBS system. There may be clients connecting to their own federated server and others sharing a federated server. Each federated server instantiates all lower-level servers including the DBMS adapters. The open, modular, multi-tier architecture of VHDBS enables a transparent, flexible distribution of objects and data across a heterogeneous network platform. The system is flexible, scalable and extensible, both at database level and at schema level.

4 Plug&Play

The different databases are integrated or plugged into VHDBS by means of database adapters. The capability of the database plug-in provides the flexibility and scalability of VHDBS. The key issue for plug-in is how to implement an adapter and how far the implementation can be automatically generated. There are two kinds of plug-in: plug-in of databases and plug-in of database systems. We discuss in the following how the two kinds of adapters are developed as well as generated.

4.1 Plug-in of Databases

Instead of having to implement a new adapter by the binding of a new database system, it would be better to possess a generic DBMS adapter which is usable for all database systems, or at least a small number of DBMS adapters, each of which covers as large a class of database systems as possible.

We developed adapters for two kinds of database systems. One for relational database systems (RDBMS adapter) and another for object-oriented database systems (ODBMS adapter). The RDBMS adapter is based on the SQL as well as embedded SQL standard, and the ODBMS adapter is based on the ODMG language mapping. To plug in a database of these two kinds of database systems , e.g. a relational database, what we need to do is to generate an adapter instance of the RDBMS adapter.

To each kind of DBMS an adapter must be developed, and to each database therein an adapter must be instantiated. Each database can contain several repositories, which are available all over an adapter instance.

The different component data base systems differ, depending upon their architectures, considerably in their characteristics. In order to plug in dynamically the data bases in the system, and for that purpose to instantiate the appropriate adapter, their substantial characteristics have to be known to as well as registered in the VHDBS system.

Furthermore, for the query handling the dynamic characteristics, such as current cardinalities of repositories, are relevant. Also these are stored for performance purpose and updated according to the actual status.

To generate an adapter instance, the database characteristics are entered into meta database over FGRAPH (the GUI of the VHDBS), and the Metaserver manages the database characteristics. The analysis and evaluation of the database characteristics occurs in the optimizer, first during the query tree classification, then in individual optimization rules. The result of the evaluation is used to generate the database adapter instance and to register the adapter instance.

4.2 Plug-in of DBMSs

In relatively rare cases it needs to include a new kind of database system into the VHDBS system, for example, if we have to plug in a database system that is not compliant with SQL or ODMG standard. For that purpose a new DBMS adapter is to be implemented. In this case we do expect some support, which supplies a generation assistance for DBMS adapter.

By means of our adapter generation assistance one can proceed as follows: The integration templates and detailed procedure statements are supplied, from which further automizable steps are derivable.

For DBMS adapter all IDL methods and ODM methods that have effects on the database system, have to be implemented with the help of the database system APIs. An abstraction layer should be created, in order to be able to reuse the upper sections of the database system adapter, if later on the adapter of another database system will possesses a similar architecture.

The IDL files, the Makefile and the main program main.cc are to be implemented in detail. For the implementation files, i.e. for repserver_imp.cc and odm_imp.cc, example templates can be supplied. These files constitute roughly 80% of the DBMS adapter source codes. The most costly work is to implement IDL methods, the implementations of which have to be supplied to one or more files manually. This requires an extensive know-how of the database system concerned and at least one person month of a specialist. For many database systems it is however simpler to adapt an existing DBMS adapter to the new DBMS than to implement the functions from scratch, i.e. if a similar adapter exists already, then it can serve as a draft or a pattern.

The implementation files and the database system API files must be entered in the marked places in the supplied Makefile. Now the DBMS adapter is up to configuration work ready for use.

5 Application Domains and Benefits of VHDBS

The following two scenarios of using VHDBS illustrate its wide application domain from Intranet to Extranet. Both scenarios can be realized either by using a possibly emerging VHDBS Telekom service (thus outsourcing IT management and maintenance to a service provider) or by installing VHDBS servers within the enterprise itself. Moreover, the scenarios are variable according to the locations at which VHDBS components (export and/or query components) are accessible.

5.1 Application Domain "Enterprise-wide Information System"

The following scenario illustrates the use of VHDBS as a means for integrating distributed information into an enterprise-wide information system: A public relations agency has branch offices in different locations nationwide or worldwide. Each office runs PR campaigns for a variety of customer companies and products. Corresponding records are kept in local files or databases. To gain a new contract for a particular PR campaign, an office needs a list of references to successful campaigns with similar requirements already performed by the agency. Thus, the office has to check the records of all other offices. Contacting colleagues often results in a time-consuming data collection process with callbacks and follow-up calls. Using VHDBS would provide the desired information automatically within minutes. This sample scenario also holds for many other application domains. It depends on whether only a central department may access all data, or whether each department is allowed to collect enterprise-wide information.

5.2 Application Domain "Integration of Business Partners"

Given an enterprise with a number of suppliers having a partially overlapping range of products or parts, in order to procure a particular part, the enterprise has to query all relevant suppliers and evaluate their offers. Even in business fields with very short reaction times such as the automobile industry, this process takes several hours. Using VHDBS, procurement may be optimized as follows: all suppliers provide VHDBS access to their products and supply databases. Then the enterprise can quickly access and sort all relevant supplier information. The suppliers do not have to change their IT infrastructure, they only need to install a VHDBS database adapter and may still control which information is provided via VHDBS.

Virtual enterprises may benefit even more using VHDBS as a Telekom service: A broker combines offers of his business partners to construct his own product catalogue, which in a second step can be easily imported into an Internet storefront built up by means of existing solutions like Intershop [3] or IBM's Net.Commerce [4]. Providers only have to install a VHDBS adapter for their product catalogue and the broker uses a VHDBS interface to compose and store his offers.

5.3 A Sample Application

We describe a VHDBS sample application in the plant in the following: A wholesaler or trader/broker composes his product catalogue via VHDBS access to all his "providers", condensing, combining and updating all information found. This is achieved by defining a federated repository using VHDBS and the query language OQL, which combines information exported by the providers. The broker copies the result into his local catalogue and provides it to potential customers using standard Internet techniques or again VHDBS.

This scenario can be implemented using VHDBS as follows: (1) the federated schema including all interfaces and mirror repositories is defined, (2) the federated schema is homogenized with the help of combi-repositories, and (3) some queries (i.e. combi-repositories) can be provided to Web users via the external schema. Each plant grower exports his product catalogue to VHDBS. For this purpose the federated schema including all mirror repositories is described in (slightly extended) ODL, a superset of OMG/IDL, reflecting the structure of, e.g., database tables for offered articles, used at that location or enterprise. Here, object-oriented features like inheritance can be used:

```
INTERFACE Article {
            ATTRIBUTE STRING artNo;
            // typical attributes in product catalogues
            ATTRIBUTE STRING name;
            ATTRIBUTE LONG price;
            ATTRIBUTE LONG amount;
            ATTRIBUTE SET<STRING> properties;
            // in case of an OO database
            VOID put_to_shopping_box();
            // federated methods for broker
            VOID order (IN STRING name, address, ...);
};
INTERFACE ArticleMM : Article {
// article with multimedia
data ATTRIBUTE Multimedia picture;
};
INTERFACE ArtMM {
... // not shown here, similar to ArticleMM,
// but with other attribute names
};
REPOSITORY SET<Article> Trees_Smith;
REPOSITORY SET<ArticleMM> Flowers_Powell;
// mirror repositories of all suppliers
REPOSITORY SET<ArtMM>   Cactus_Miller;
```

For each plant grower, such a type and mirror repository description as sketched above is provided. If some providers use homogeneous data schemas, the interfaces need only be provided once to VHDBS. In our example, Powell and Miller use similar schemas in their local databases, but some attribute names and the order of attributes differ, while Smith does not provide any pictures for his trees. Then, combi-repositories are defined, completing the federated schema, and at this step heterogeneous data can be homogenized and horizontal and/or vertical fragmentation of overall logical data is expressed and made transparent. In our example, the broker, Tropical Garden, selects interesting offers from all his providers. Slightly simplified, this is:

```
INTERFACE MyArticle : ArticleMM {
    ATTRIBUTE LONG orig_price;
    ATTRIBUTE STRING orig_number;
    MyArticle compose_offer (IN Article offer2, offer3);
    // see below
```

```
    BOOLEAN isCompatible (IN Article plant2, plant3);
    // see below
};
REPOSITORY MyTrees IS
    "SELECT MyArticle(T+artNo, name, 1.1*price, amount,
              properties,no_picture, price, artNo)
           FROM Trees_Smith WHERE <condition1>";
REPOSITORY MyFlowers IS
           // includes name mapping
    "SELECT MyArticle(T+no, flow_name, 1.05*Price, 1, description, pict, Price, no)
    FROM Flowers_Powell
    WHERE <condition2>";
REPOSITORY MyCactus IS
    "SELECT MyArticle(T+artNo, name, 1.1*price, amount, properties, picture, price, artNo)
              FROM Cactus_Miller
              WHERE <condition3>";
REPOSITORY MyPlants IS "MyFlowers UNION MyTrees UNION MyCactus";
```

The first three definitions homogenize all data to type MyArticle. Here, only relevant articles are selected via any optional conditions, and new prices and article numbers are calculated by the broker. These repository definitions will typically be defined as "macros", i.e. their definitions are inserted at the place where they are referenced. The last definition expresses the horizontal fragmentation (via unions) of overall logical data. The broker may either migrate this data into an Internet storefront, or provide VHDBS Web access. For the latter purpose, parameterized queries over global data can be predefined or defined on-the-fly in the external schema, e.g.:

```
DEFINE Special_Offers (Property, PriceLimit) AS
    SELECT Article(artNo, name, price, amount, properties, picture)
    // orig_price and orig_number are hidden
    FROM MyPlants
    WHERE Property IN properties AND price < PriceLimit;
```

Schema-specific search functions can be provided to Web users in this way by predefined queries, and the result is saved in the Fed-DB to be browsed using FWEB. For example, if a Web user clicks on Special_Offers, he is asked to enter properties and price limits of searched plants, and after specifying these attributes, blocks of plant records including pictures (if provided) are transferred to him and can be browsed. The display type Article used here may provide methods which the Web user can activate on selected objects, e.g. to submit orders or fill a shopping box. The broker Tropical Garden may also provide a second repository to his Web customers, which automatically combines some plants of different kinds, based on some common properties, e.g.:

```
DEFINE Special_Combinations (season) AS
    SELECT f.compose_offer(t,c)
    FROM f IN MyFlowers, t IN MyTrees, c IN MyCactus
    WHERE f.isCompatible(t,c) AND season IN f.properties;
```

Here, operations defined on data type MyArticle above are used to combine the plants.

6 Conclusion

In this paper we presented some main design aspects of the architecture of the system VHDBS, a global information system. VHDBS has been developed by an industrial research project of the Deutsche Telekom. The goal of the research is to provide for industry an acceptable solution as well as a suitable architecture for managing virtual global data that is distributed and heterogeneous in nature, and for supporting cooperative use of existing as well as legacy database systems. Based on OMG and ODMG standards, an object-oriented data model is used as common data model (being adequate to integrate heterogeneous data) and a CORBA Object Request Broker is included in the system architecture. We introduced the repository concept into VHDBS, which can be used to describe and provide the association as well as integration of schemas from distributed and heterogeneous databases or to transparently and cooperatively retrieve data from the local databases. We presented our plug&play mechanism and described how to build adapters systematically. Moreover, we discussed how VHDBS could be used to build an enterprise information system for an enterprise or a virtual enterprise for some business partners.

References

[1] R. G. G. Cattell el al (ed.). The Object Database Standard ODMG 2.0. Morgan Kaufmann Publishing Inc., 1997.

[2] IBM. Internet Business Opportunities with IBM Net.Commerce. See http://www.internet.ibm.com/commercepoint/net.commerce/lit.html

[3] INTERSHOP Communications Inc. White paper on Intershop Online. See http://www.intershop.de/products/online/whitepaper.html, May 1997

[4] IONA Technologies. Orbix 2.2 Programming Guide. 3/1997.

[5] OMG. The Common Object Request Broker: Architecture and specification. Object Management Group, Inc., Revision 2.0, Updated July 1996.

[6] X. Wu and N. Weißenberg. A graphical Interface for cooperative access to distributed and heterogeneous database systems. In Proceedings of the 1997 International Database Engineering & Applications Symposium (IDEAS), Montreal, Canada, Aug. 1997, pp. 13-22, IEEE Computer Society Press.

[7] X. Wu. A type system for an object-oriented database system. In Proceedings of the Fifteenth Annual International Computer Software & Applications Conference, pages 333-338, Tokio, Japan, September 11-13 1991. IEEE Computer Society Press.

[8] X. Wu. A query interface for an object management system. In Proceedings of the 2nd International Conference on Data Base and Expert Systems Applications, Berlin, Springer Verlag, 1991

[9] X. Wu. An architecture for interoperation of distributed heterogeneous database systems. In Proceedings of the 7th International Conference on Data Base and Expert Systems Applications, Zürich, Springer Verlag, LNCS 1134, 1996.

[10] X. Wu. An Approach to Query Translation in a Federation of Distributed Heterogeneous Database Systems. In Proc. 4th Int. Conf. on Object-Oriented Information Systems (OOIS), Brisbane, Australien, Springer-Verlag, Nov. 1997

[11] X. Wu. A component-Based Architecture for Building and Managing Global Information Systems. In Proc. of ICSE Workshop on Component-Based Software Engineering, Kyoto, Japan, April 1998

Transaction Shipping Approach for Mobile Distributed Real-Time Databases

Kam-yiu Lam[1], Tei-Wei Kuo[2], Wai-Hung Tsang[1] and Gary C.K Law[1]

Department of Computer Science[1]
City University of Hong Kong
83 Tat Chee Avenue, Kowloon
HONG KONG
Email: cskylam@cityu.edu.hk

Department of Computer Science and
Information Engineering[2]
National Chung Cheng University
Chiayi, 621 Taiwan, ROC
Email: ktw@cs.ccu.edu.tw

Abstract. Due to the unpredictability of mobile network, it is difficult to meet transaction deadlines in a mobile distributed real-time database system (MDRDTBS). We propose the idea of transaction shipping to reduce the overheads in processing a transaction over mobile network and in resolving priority inversion. We consider a distributed lock-based real-time protocol, the Distributed High Priority Two Phase Locking (DHP-2PL). to study the impacts of mobile network on real-time data access. A detailed model of a MDRTDBS has been developed, and a series of simulation experiments have been performed to evaluate the performance of our approach.

1 Introduction

The realization of "instant" information access over mobile network relies on efficient real-time transaction processing techniques which are suitable to mobile environments. As a result, research in *mobile distributed real-time database systems* (MDRTDBS) is receiving growing attention in recent years [9,12,13]. However, owing to the intrinsic limitations of mobile computing systems, such as limited bandwidth and power supply for client systems, frequent disconnection, and mobility of users, the design of an efficient and cost-effective MDRTDBS requires techniques that are quite different from those adopted in distributed real-time database systems (DRTDBS) over a wired network. It is much more difficult to meet transaction deadlines in a mobile environment. There exist many factors which can seriously affect the system performance: low communication bandwidth often makes the network be the bottleneck resource. Mobility of clients also affects the distribution of workload in the entire system. Disconnection, while a transaction is processing, may even introduce the inconsistency problem. Such poor quality of mobile network can seriously affect the effectiveness of a concurrency control protocol in resolving data-access conflicts.

Although different real-time concurrency control protocols have been proposed for single-site and distributed RTDBS, they are not suitable to MDRTDBS, due to the unique characteristics of mobile environments. The poor qualify of services provided by mobile network also seriously increases the overheads of a concurrency control protocol in resolving data-access conflicts. In this paper, we propose the idea of transaction shipping to process transactions issued by mobile clients. We aim at reducing the overheads for processing transactions over a mobile network and for resolving priority inversion. We consider a distributed lock-based real-time protocol, Distributed High Priority Two Phase Locking (DHP-2PL), to study the impacts of mobile network on real-time data access, where DHP-2PL is derived from the well-known High Priority Two Phase Locking (HP-2PL) [1] for MDRTDBS.

2 Model of a Mobile Distributed Real-time Database System

2.1 System Architecture

A MDRTDBS consists of four major components: the mobile clients (MC's), the base stations, the mobile network, and the main terminal switching office (MTSO) [6,7,9], as shown in Figure 1. The mobile network is assumed to be a radio cellular network, and the entire service area is divided into a number of connected cell sites. Within each cell site, there is a base station which is augmented with a wireless interface to communicate with the MC's within its cell site. The cellular radio network is assumed to be the Global Systems for Mobile Communication (GSM) 900 in which the bandwidth is divided into a number of channels.

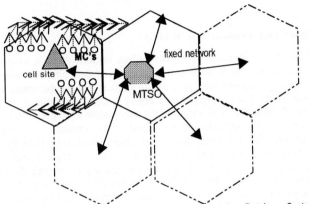

Figure 1: System Architecture of the Mobile Distributed Real-time Database System

The base stations at different cell sites are connected to the MTSO by a point-to-point wired network. Thus, the communications between the base stations and the MTSO are much more efficient than the communications between the base stations and their mobile clients. The MTSO is responsible for active call information maintenance, performance of handoff procedure, channel allocation, and message routing. Attached to each base station is a real-time database system containing a local database which may be accessed by transactions issued from MCs within its cell site or from other cells via the MTSO.

An MC may move around within the same cell site or across the cell border into another cell site. Periodically, it sends a location signal to its base station through the uplink channel. The strength of the location signal received by a base station is dependent on several factors, such as the distance between the MC and the base station, and the surrounding buildings. When an MC is crossing the cell border, the signal will become very weak. If the signal received by a base station is lower than a certain threshold level, the MTSO will be notified, and the MTSO will perform a handoff procedure. It sends out requests to all the base stations, and the base stations must respond by returning the strength of the location signals received from the MC. The MTSO will then assign the MC to the base station which has received the strongest signal. Usually, this is the base station which is responsible for the cell site which the MC is entering.

The processing of an MC transaction may need to access databases at several base stations. The MC first attempts to issue a call request to the base station of its cell site. A channel is granted to the MC after the completion of a setup procedure. The execution of the setup procedure incurs a fixed overhead as it involves communications amongst the MC, the base stations, and the MTSO. Since the number of channels between a base station and its MC's is limited, it is possible that the channel request may be refused due to no free channel available. The queuing for the channels is based on the priorities of the transactions. If the number of attempts exceeds a specified maximum number, the call and the transaction will be aborted. Due to channel contention and slow (and unreliable) communication, the time required to establish a channel is highly unpredictable. Once a channel has been established, the transaction will be sent out through the RF transmitter, which is connected to the antenna from the MC, to the base station of the cell site where the MC currently resides. When an MC is crossing the cell site border while it is communicating with its base station, a new channel will be created with its newly assigned base station after a setup procedure. However, it is still possible that there is no channel available at the new cell. In this case, it will retry for a specified number of times. If it is still not able to get a channel, the transaction will be aborted. Due to noise and interference, the signal, which carries data, may be corrupted while it is being transmitted. In this case, the data will be re-transmitted. Because of high error rate and non-stability of signal transmission, the effective data transmission rate over a mobile network is also highly unpredictable.

2.2   Database and Transaction Models

The entire database is partitioned over different base stations. At each base station, there is a local real-time database, which consists of two types of data objects: *temporal* and *non-temporal* data objects. Temporal data objects are used to record the status of the external objects in the real world. Each temporal data object is associated with a timestamp which denotes the age of the data object. If a transaction may update a temporal data object, then the transaction is given a timestamp when it is initiated. If the transaction commits successfully before its deadline, then the timestamp of any data object which is updated by the transaction will be set as the timestamp of the transaction. The validity of a temporal data object is defined by an *absolute validity interval (avi)* [11]. A temporal data object satisfies the *avi* constraint if the age of the data object is up to date, i.e., the difference of the current time and the age is no more than *avi*. A *relative validity interval (rvi)* may be given to a transaction which requires that the maximum age difference of data objects read by the transaction is no larger than *rvi*. Non-temporal data objects are either derived by operations of transactions or are statically set during system initialization.

Each transaction is given a deadline and a criticality. The priority of a transaction is derived based on its deadline and criticality. It is assumed that the EDF scheduling is used for scheduling the transactions in using the CPU at the base station. It is assumed that the transactions are firm real-time [10]. If the system cannot complete a transaction before its deadline, the transaction will be aborted. Each transaction consists of a sequence of operations. Each operation requires the access of one to several data objects. Operations may access data objects residing at several base stations. When an operation of a transaction accesses a data object residing at a base station outside the cell site of the MC, the operation will be routed to the base station via the MTSO. When all of the operations of a transaction have been processed, a commit protocol will be performed to ensure the failure atomicity of the transaction. It is assumed that the well-known two phase commit (2PC) is adopted because of its simplicity.

3   A Distributed Real-time Locking Protocol for MDRTDBS

In this paper, we propose a distributed locking approach based on both restart and priority inheritance to resolve the problem of priority inversion in MDRTDBS. By extending the well-known HP-2PL, a distributed extension of HP-2PL, called Distributed HP-2PL (DHP-2PL), is proposed. In the design of DHP-2PL, we shall reduce the number of transaction restarts and resolve lock conflict between higher priority and lower priority transactions globally or locally because transaction restarts and conflict resolution can be very expensive in a mobile environment. Unlike other blocking-based protocols such as those based on priority inheritance, DHP-2PL is free of deadlock because priority inheritance is used restrictively for resolving lock conflict with committing transactions in the DHP-2PL.

It is assumed that the local database system at each base station has a lock scheduler which handles the lock requests for data objects residing at that base station. The definition of DHP-2PL is as follows, where T_r and T_h are the lock requesting and lock holding transactions, respectively:

```
Lock Conflcit (T_r, T_h)
Begin
        If       Priority(T_r) > Priority(T_h)
                 If      T_h is not committing or restarting
                         If      T_h is a local transaction
                                 Restart T_h locally
                         Else
                                 Restart T_h globally
                         Endif
                 Else
                         Block T_r until T_h releases the lock
                         Priority(T_h) :=    Priority(T_r)    +    fixed
                         priority level
                 Endif
        Else
                 Block T_r until T_h releases the lock
        Endif
    End
```

A transaction is local if it only has accessed data objects residing at one base station. Otherwise, it is a global transaction. Similar to the HP-2PL, the DHP-2PL uses a restart approach to resolve lock conflicts between non-committing transactions. Restarting a local transaction is simply done by restarting the transaction at the conflicting base station. To restart a global transaction, restart messages must be sent to the base stations where some operations of the global transactions are executing. Global restart takes a much longer time and requires much higher overhead. Usually, a global transaction takes more resources for execution. Restarting a global transaction implies that a lot of resources will be wasted. Thus, it should be minimized. So, if a global transaction is committing, it is allowed to hold a lock until it has finished the commit procedure, even though a higher priority transaction is requesting the lock. Although this will create the priority inversion problem, the blocking time of the higher priority transaction is minimized by priority inheritance. In the DHP-2PL, the priority of the committing transaction will be raised up by two factors: Firstly, its priority is no less than the highest priority of all its blocked transactions. Secondly, a fixed priority level is added to its priority to let its priority higher than all the other executing transactions. No deadlock is possible for the priority raising of any committing transaction because the committing transaction will not be blocked by any other executing transactions. It is because a committing transaction will not make any lock request during its commit procedure.

4 Transaction Shipping for MDRTDBS

To improve the system performance and to reduce the impact of a mobile network on the performance of the DHP-2PL in a MDRTDBS, we propose a *transaction shipping* approach to process the transactions from the mobile clients. The purpose of the approach is to reduce the amount of communications between the mobile client and the database server to alleviate the dependency of the system performance on the underlying network in a MDRTDBS.

In the transaction shipping approach, the entire transaction will be "shipped" to the server for processing instead of shipping every operation or data request to the database server. Although the idea is simple, there exist several difficult practical issues needed to be solved, such as how to identify the path of a transaction before its execution, how to define the execution model of a transaction in a mobile environment, and how to deal with the dynamic properties in transaction execution. For some mobile applications, they may even require users to input parameters while the transactions are executing in order to determine the path of execution. The problem is further complicated by the limited processing power and memory sizes of the mobile clients. Due to these limitations, the client structure is usually very simple with limited information about the whole system e.g., the location of the data objects. In order to solve the problem in transaction shipping, we suggest a pre-analysis approach. The practicality of the pre-analysis comes from the fact that the behavior of many real-time transactions is more predictable, compared with other conventional database systems.

4.1   Pre-analysis Phase

In the transaction shipping approach, the execution of a transaction is divided into two phases: the *pre-analysis phase* and the *execution phase*. Figure 2 shows the system architecture of the processing of a transaction under the transaction shipping approach. Once a transaction is initiated at a mobile client, a coordinator process, called *master coordinator*, will be created at the client side. Before shipping a transaction to the database server, the system will perform a pre-analysis on the transaction to derive its characteristics, e.g., what the operations of the transaction are and what the execution path of the transaction is. The concept of pre-analysis is similar to the two phase methods discussed in [5]. However, it should be noted that [5] is concerned about how to reduce the unpredictability in data access by using the concept of access invariant. In here, we use the pre-analysis to predefine the execution path of a transaction in order to reduce the number of communications between mobile clients and the base stations.

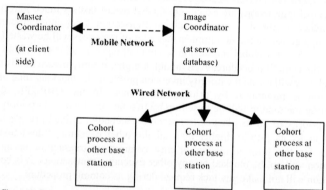

Figure 2: Process Architecture under Transaction Shipping Approach

Although transaction pre-analysis is considered to be difficult and impractical in many conventional database systems due to their dynamic nature, it is quite feasible for many real-time database applications [4,5] *as the properties and behavior of transactions in many real-time database applications are much more well-defined.* Furthermore, in a real-time database system, transactions can often be classified into different types in which each transaction type has certain pre-defined characteristics, e.g., the set of operations and their required data objects, for performing specific user operations [4]. For such real-time database applications, partial pre-analysis can even be done in an *off-line fashion.*

The pre-analysis is started at the mobile client upon the generation of the transaction. It consists of two phases. In the first phase, the *set of operations* in the transaction will be identified. It is usually not difficult to identify the operations in a transaction. For example, if SQL statements are used to access the database, SELECT and INSERT statements are read and write operations, respectively. Note that transactions are assumed to have a simple flat structure. At this stage, it may not be necessary to identify the set of data objects required by the operations. Actually, it may not be easy to be done at the client side as it only contains limited information about the database system and the location of the data objects in the system. The required data objects of an operation can be determined when the operation is being processed at the base station.

In the second phase, the *execution path* of the transaction, e.g., the precedence relationships of its operations, will be determined. For some transactions, the whole execution path can not be determined until the data objects required by the transactions have been identified. For such transactions, the pre-analysis may identify the transaction type first and then, based on the pre-defined characteristics of that transaction type, to make the prediction. After the completion of the pre-analysis, a signature of the transaction will be created in which the operations of the transaction and their precedence relationships are defined.

4.2   Execution Phase

The signature transaction is forwarded to the base station of the MC through the mobile network. Once the server receives the transaction signature, it will create a process, called *image coordinator*, for the transaction. The image coordinator will take over the job from the master coordinator at the MC to process the transaction. Other cohorts for the executions of the operations (issued by the transaction) will be created at other base stations if the operations need to access the data objects located at that base stations.

The benefit of defining an image coordinator at the base station instead at the MC is that the connections amongst the base stations are much better than the connection between the MCs and its base stations. This approach can facilitate the management of transactions and improve the performance of the atomic commitment protocol. Whenever a transaction has to be restarted, all its cohort processes (excluding the master coordinator and the image coordinator) will be destroyed after the completion of undo operations. The image coordinator will be responsible for restarting the transaction from its beginning if its deadline has not been expired.

4.3   Dynamic Properties of Transactions

Due to the dynamic nature of transactions (although transactions in real-time database applications are more well-defined, compared with transactions in traditional database systems, they may still have some dynamic properties) and the interactivities between transactions and mobile clients, data input from MC users may still be needed. As a result, the pre-analysis of a transaction may need to be re-done while it is executing. In this case, the transaction may have to go back to its MC after the completion of an operation. It is obvious that the performance gained from the pre-analysis is dependent on the accuracy of the pre-analysis. In the best case, one single communication between the MC and the base station is required for each transaction execution. In the worst case, the number of communications between the mobile client and the base station for each transaction execution is equal to the number of operations in the transaction, which is equal to that required in the query shipping approach. If the system can make a good estimation in the pre-analysis, a lot of communication cost can be saved.

Note that the transaction shipping approach does not require the transmission of a large number of data objects to the clients, as required in the data shipping approach. This is a very attractive feature for MDRTDBS. Although the processing of the entire transaction at the database server may increase the workload at the base stations, it can ease the management of transactions because all of the cohorts for the execution of a transaction are located at the base stations connected by wired network through the MTSO. Also, the processing power of a mobile client is usually much lower than the servers at the base stations. A mobile client is more suitable for performing simple jobs, e.g., the pre-analysis. The actual processing of the transactions is performed at the base stations which are much more powerful and stable, and the base stations contain much more information about the system.

5   Performance Experiments

In order to evaluate impact of mobile communication on the performance of the proposed protocol DHP-2PL and the transaction shipping approach, a detailed simulation program of a MDRTDBS is implemented according to the MDRTDBS model defined in Section 2.

5.1   Model Parameters and Performance Measures

The deadline of a transaction, T, is defined according to the expected execution time of a transaction [1,2,3,8,9] such as:

$$Deadline = ar(T) + pex(T) \times (1 + SF)$$

where SF : the slack factor is a random variable uniformly chosen from a slack range;

$ar(T)$: the arrival time of transaction T;

$pex(T)$: the predicted execution time of T. It is defined as:

$$pex(T) = (T_{lock} + T_{process} + T_{update}) \times N_{oper}$$

where N_{oper}: the number of operations in a transaction;

T_{lock}: the CPU time required to set a lock;

$T_{process}$: the CPU time required to process an operation; and

T_{update}: the CPU time to update a data object (for write operations) .

The baseline setting of the model is shown as follows:-

Parameters	Baseline Values
Number of MTSO	1
Number of Cell Sites	7
Location Update Interval	0.2 second
Transmission Speed for Channel	10 kbps
Number of Channels for Each Cell Site	10
Think Time	8 seconds
Transaction Size	7 to 14 operations (uniform distribution)
Proportion of write operations	1.0
Slack range	10 – 20 (slack factor is uniformly distributed in the slack range)
Number of Mobile Clients	84
Channel Connection time (CL)	1 second
Call Update Interval	0.2 second
Number of Local Databases	7 (1 in each base station)
Database Size	200 data objects per local database
Concurrency Control	Distributed High Priority Two Phase Locking (DHP-2PL)
Fraction of Temporal Data Objects	10%
Temporal Data Object Update Interval	0.5 update per second per data object
Absolute Threshold (avi)	12 seconds
Relative Threshold (rvi)	8 seconds
CPU Scheduling	Earliest Deadline First
Deadline Missing Treatment	Firm deadline, abort the transaction once the transaction deadline is found missing

Table 1: Model parameters and their baseline values

The primary performance measure used in the simulation experiments is the *miss rate* which is defined as the number of transactions which missed deadlines over the total number of transactions generated. In addition to miss rate, we also measure the *restart probability* which is defined as the total number of transaction restarts over the number of committed transactions. The restart probability can be used as an indicator of data conflict probability. Other measures are *call blocking probability, mean call waiting time, mean turn around time* of a transaction and the *CPU utilization*. The call blocking probability is defined as the number of failed channel requests over the total number of channel requests.

5.2 Performance Results and Discussion

In this section, we study the performance of the transaction shipping approach (TS) as compared with the query shipping approach (QS). We have tested the performance of the transaction shipping approach under different workload overhead and return probability. Under the transaction shipping approach, a transaction has to go back to the mobile client when: (1) it has to receive input data from the mobile client; or (2) when the prediction done at the pre-analysis is incorrect. For the later case, the prediction has to be performed again at the client side. The return probability defines the probability of a transaction to go back to the mobile client after the completion of an operation in the transaction shipping approach. Its value depends on the accuracy of the prediction done at the pre-analysis.

Figure 3 shows the miss rate under the transaction shipping approach (TS) at different return probability and at a zero overhead for the pre-analysis as compared with the query shipping approach (QS). (The impact of the overhead for pre-analysis will be studied in the next set of experiments.) It can be seen that the performance of the system is greatly improved with the use of the transaction shipping approach especially when the return probability is low (a high accuracy of prediction in the pre-analysis). When the return probability is smaller than 0.6, the improvement is more than 75% when the channel connection time is 1 second (CL = 1) and the improvement is about 50% when the channel connection time is 2 second (CL = 2). Again, this is due to smaller channel blocking probability and call waiting time as can be seen in Figure 4 and Figure 5, respectively. The use of transaction shipping approach greatly reduces the amount of communication between the mobile clients and the base stations required for processing the transactions. This also makes the mean turn around time of transactions much shorter as shown in Figure 6. Due to the lower channel contention, part of the workload is shifted from the mobile network to the CPU when the return probability is low (as shown in Figure 7). However, when the return probability and the channel connection time are high, the network will still be the bottleneck resource.

The use of the transaction shipping approach also reduces the lock conflict probability as the lock holding time by a transaction is shorter. The smaller conflict probability can be observed in Figure 8. The restart probability drops greatly with a decrease in return probability when the channel connection time is 1 second. However, when the channel connection time is long (CL = 2), the restart probability drops slightly only when the return probability is very high. It can be explained as follows. For a high channel contention due to a larger return probability and longer channel connection time, some transactions may miss their deadlines even before they have started the processing. Thus, the number of lock holding transactions will be smaller and the probability of lock conflict will be lower. Since the number of restart with the transaction shipping approach is much smaller, the degree of channel contention is lower.

Figure 9 shows the impact of different overheads (defined in terms of the amount of time) for the pre-analysis in the transaction shipping approach on the miss rate. It can be observed that the overhead does not have any observable effect on the performance of the transaction shipping approach. Although the overhead will make the deadlines more tight as the time required to complete a transaction becomes longer, it also releases the degree of resource contention in the system (the mobile network and the base stations) especially on the channels as the transactions now spent more time at the mobile client side instead at the mobile network and base stations.

6   Conclusions

Due to the poor quality of services provided by a mobile network, it is not easy to meet the deadlines of transactions in a mobile distributed real-time database system (MDRTDBS). The performance of any adopted concurrency control protocol in MDRTDBS will be very different from its performance in a DRTDBS over wired network. In this paper, we propose the idea of transaction shipping to process transactions issued by mobile clients. We aim at reducing the overheads for processing a transaction over mobile network and for resolving priority inversion. We consider a distributed lock-based real-time protocol, the Distributed High Priority Two Phase Locking (DHP-2PL), to study the impacts of mobile network on real-time data access, where DHP-2PL is derived from the well-known High Priority Two Phase Locking (HP-2PL) [1] for MDRTDBS. Extensive simulation experiments have been conducted to investigate the impact of mobile network on the performance of the DHP-2PL protocol. Since bandwidth is one of the most scarce resources in a mobile environment, the study shows that the call duration has a significant impact on the performance of DHP-2PL. With the transaction shipping approach, the number of deadline violations is greatly reduced as the contention for channel, the time spent on communication, the probability of lock conflict, and the amount of resources wasted on restarted transactions are much reduced.

References

[1] R. Abbott and Hector Garcia-Molina, "Scheduling Real-Time Transactions: A Performance Evaluation," *ACM Trans. on Database Systems*, vol. 17. no. 3, pp. 513-560, Sep. 1992.

[2] J.R. Haritsa, M. Livny, M.J. Carey, "On Being Optimistic about Real-Time Constraints", in the *Proceedings of the 9th ACM Symposium on Principles of Database Systems*, 1990.

[3] J. Huang, J. Stankovic & K. Ramamritham, "Priority Inheritance in Soft Real-Time Databases", Journal of Real-Time Systems, vol. 4. no. 3, pp. 243-268, 1992.

[4] Y.K. Kim, S.H. Son, "Supporting Predictability in Real-Time Database Systems", *Proceedings of Real-Time Technology and Applications Symposium*, Brookine, Massacgusetts, June 1996, pp. 38-48.

[5] P. O'Neil, K. Ramamritham & C. Pu, "A Two-Phase Approach to Predictably Scheduling Real-time Transactions", in *Performance of Concurrency Control Mechanisms in Centralized Database Systems*, edited by V. Kumar, Prentice Hall, New Jersey, 1996.

[6] OPNET Modeler/Radio 3.0.B©, MIL 3, Inc., 1996.

[7] E. Pitoura and B. Bhargava, "Dealing with Mobility: Issues and Research Challenges," Technical Report, Purdue Univ., Nov. 1993.

[8] O. Ulusoy, " A Study of Two Transaction Processing Architectures for Distributed Real-time Database Systems", *Journal of Systems and Software*, vol. 31, no. 2, pp. 97-108, 1995.

[9] O. Ulusoy, "Real-Time Data Management for Mobile Computing", *Proceedings of International Workshop on Issues and Applications of Database Technology (IADT'98)*, Berlin, Germany, July 1998.

[10] P.S. Yu, K.L. Wu, K.J. Lin & S.H.Son, "On Real-Time Databases: Concurrency Control and Scheduling," *Proceedings of IEEE*, vol. 82, no. 1, pp. 140-57, 1994.

[11] M. Xiong, K. Ramamritham, R. Sivasankaran, J.A. Stankovic, and D. Towsley, ``Scheduling Transactions with Temporal Constraints: Exploiting Data Semantics," *Proceedings of IEEE Real-Time Systems Symposium*, December 1996, pp. 240-251.

[12] P. Xuan, O. Gonzalez, J. Fernandez & K. Ramamritham, "Broadcast on Demand: Efficient and Timely Dissemination of Data in Mobile Environments", *Proceedings of 3rd IEEE Real-Time Technology Application Symposium*, 1997.

[13] Ersan Kayan and Ozgur Ulusoy, "Real-Time Transaction Management in Mobile Computing Systems" in Proceedings of 6th International Conference on Database Systems for Advanced Applications, Taiwan, April 1999.

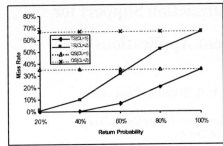

Figure 3 Miss rate at different return probabilities

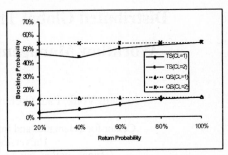

Figure 4 Blocking probabilities at different return probabilities

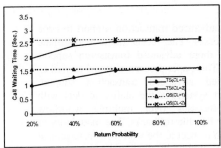

Figure 5 Call waiting time at different return probabilities

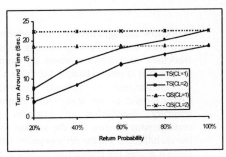

Figure 6 Turn around time at different return probabilities

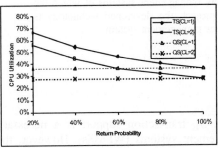

Figure 7 CPU utilization at different return probabilities

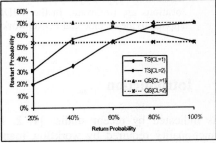

Figure 8 Restart probabilities at different return probabilities

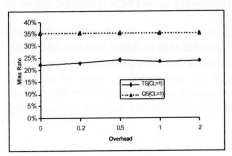

Figure 9 Miss rate at different overhead for pre-processing

Distributed Global Transaction Support for Workflow Management Applications ♣

Jochem Vonk, Paul Grefen, Erik Boertjes, Peter Apers

Center for Telematics and Information Technology (CTIT)
University of Twente
{vonk, grefen, boertjes, apers}@cs.utwente.nl

Workflow management systems require advanced transaction support to cope with their inherently long-running processes. The recent trend to distribute workflow executions requires an even more advanced transaction support system that is able to handle distribution. This paper presents a model as well as an architecture to provide distributed advanced transaction support. Characteristic of the transaction support system is the ability to deal with arbitrary distribution of business processes over multiple workflow management systems and the support for flexible rollbacks. The modularity of the architecture and the orthogonality with respect to the workflow management system allows the transaction system to be applied in other application areas as well. The high scalability of the architecture allows an arbitrary combination of transaction support systems and workflow management systems of which the locations are irrelevant. In the WIDE project, the developed technology is applied to the commercial FORO workflow management system.

1 Introduction

As indicated by recent studies [1, 2, 17, 5], transaction support is a necessary functionality required by workflow management systems (WFMSs). However, the traditional ACID transaction paradigm is too strict for the inherently long-running processes of WFMSs. Because of the characteristics of WFMSs a relaxed notion of atomicity and isolation is required [15, 12, 5].

Another functionality required for WFMSs is the support for distributed workflow executions. Large organizations are usually divided into multiple business units, each operating their own WFMS. However, the overall business processes concerning the business goals of the complete organization are performed by some or all of the separate business units, i.e., the business processes are distributed over the multiple business units of the organization. WFMSs should therefore support the distributed

---

♣ The work presented in this paper is supported by the European Commission in the WIDE Project (ESPRIT No. 20280). Partners in WIDE are Sema Group sae and Hospital General de Manresa in Spain, Politectnico di Milano in Italy, ING Bank and University of Twente in the Netherlands.

execution of the workflow processes. This requires the transaction support system to cope with the distributed execution as well.

In the WIDE project, a two-layer transaction management system has been designed [12, 14]. The upper layer caters for the requirements of long-running processes by offering global transactions with relaxed ACID properties and is based on the saga model [11]. A global transaction is divided in steps whose actions are committed to the database after the step finishes. Rolling back already finished steps relies on compensating actions that semantically undo the effects of completed actions. In the WIDE project, the saga model has been extended to support flexible rollbacks. The lower layer of the transaction model is based on the nested transaction model [18], which provides the more strict traditional ACID properties required by the individual global transaction steps. It is completely orthogonal to the upper layer and is thus not influenced by the extensions made to the upper layer. The lower layer is not relevant in this paper and the reader is referred to [4].

This paper discusses the extension to the WIDE upper layer providing support for the distributed execution of workflow processes, i.e. distributed global transactions. The developed distributed transaction model offers different abort modes to allow for flexible rollbacks. It also offers a mechanism to handle concurrent aborts. The architecture of the non-distributed global transaction support system [14] is extended with a communication protocol to coordinate the different systems. The architecture allows for an arbitrary distribution of transaction support systems and WFMSs.

The paper is structured as follows. Section 2 describes related work. Section 3 discusses distribution of workflow executions. The distributed global transaction support is described in Section 4, of which the architecture is presented in Section 5 together with implementation issues. Section 6 presents concluding remarks.

2   Related Work

Numerous advanced transaction models have been proposed in the past [9, 17, Chic98]. The aim of the WIDE project is not to propose yet another advanced transaction model, but to reuse what is already available. A combination of two models, each supporting different requirements of workflow management systems, is chosen as a basis and both are extended to provide for more advanced features. This paper discusses the extensions made to upper layer of the WIDE transaction with respect to distributed workflow executions and flexible rollbacks.

The transaction model used in the Exotica project [1] is also based on the saga model, but relies on statically computed compensation patterns. The process structure supported by Exotica is more limited than the one supported in WIDE, e.g. cycles are not allowed. Consequently, its functionality is limited compared to the work presented in this paper.

A transaction model similar to ours is discussed in [8]. Different failure sources and failure classes are analyzed. However, the distributed execution of workflows and the required transactional support for it is not covered.

Distributed workflow execution support is described in [3] by introducing Information Carriers (INCAs) All information necessary (data, control flow, etc.) to execute a workflow is contained in INCAs, so there is no real notion of a WFMS. INCAs are passed to the autonomous processing stations involved in the distributed execution. The transactional functionality offered depends on the transactional functionality offered by the processing stations. If a processing station provides the ACID properties, compensating steps are used to undo the completed steps. Which compensating steps need to be executed is specified by rules in the INCAs.

In the Mentor project [23], distributed workflow execution is addressed. A transaction processing monitor (Tuxedo) is used to provide for failure tolerance and reliable message passing. Transactions in Mentor are more restrictive and comply to the strict ACID paradigm, while the model presented in this paper allows for relaxed ACID properties.

The Workflow Management Coalition has specified a standard interface to facilitate the interoperability between different WFMSs [22] allowing for distributed workflow execution, even in a heterogeneous WFMS environment. Transactional issues are not addressed, except for writing an audit log. The work presented in this paper can thus be seen as complementary to the standard interoperability interface.

Commercial workflow products, like Cosa and Staffware, do not offer much transaction support [6, 21]. For example, Cosa treats every workflow activity as a separate ACID transaction.

3 Distributed Workflows

Large organizations are usually divided in multiple business units which have to work together to perform the business processes that involve the entire organization. The WFMSs in use by the separate business units need to interoperate to support the overall business processes, i.e. those business processes that are distributed throughout the organization.

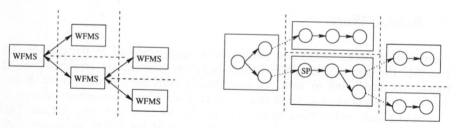

Figure 1a: Distributed WFMSs topology.   1b: Distributed workflow process

The distribution of a process over multiple business units can be seen as the delegation of parts of the process, called subprocesses, from one business unit to another business unit. For example, a billing department performs some actions (the subprocess) for the purchase department. A delegation model is therefore adopted for the distribution of processes over the different business units, and thus over the different WFMSs. In the delegation model, WFMSs can delegate the execution of subprocesses to other WFMSs. This implies that the distributed workflow execution topology is tree-shaped, i.e., one WFMS can delegate to multiple other WFMSs, but a delegated subprocess cannot originate from more than one other WFMS, see Figure 1a in which the dotted lines represent site boundaries. Note that the workflow execution topology might be different than the WFMS topology. Although the execution topology is tree-shaped, the WFMS topology might not be, e.g. in the case where one WFMS executes multiple delegated subprocesses.

An example of a distributed workflow process specification is shown in Figure 1b which represents the workflow process "selling a holiday trip to a customer" of a large travel agency. The travel agency consists of several business units that are involved in the process, the customer buys the holiday trip at the sales office, the financial department handles the invoices, and the booking department arranges the travel documents and vouchers. All involved business units have to perform their own subprocess using their own WFMS. The subprocesses together form the complete "selling trip" process.

In the figure, each distributed subprocess is represented by a global transaction which is a graph consisting of circles and solid arrows. The circles represent actions, called global transaction steps, and the solid arrows indicate the order in which the global transaction steps can be performed. The circle marked with 'SP' is a global savepoint, which is explained in the next section. The dotted arrows indicate the delegation of a subprocess to another WFMS.

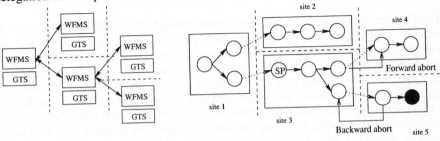

Figure 2a: Distributed WFMSs and global transaction systems

2b: Backward and forward abort

As each separate subprocess is a global transaction, executed by a certain WFMS, it can per site be supported by the non-distributed global transaction support (GTS) system as described in Section 1, see Figure 2a. The connection of the subprocesses, represented by the dotted arrows, implies the order in which the subprocesses are executed. The connected global transactions can therefore be seen as one large distributed global transaction. Only the distribution aspect requires an extension to the global transaction support system to handle the delegation of subprocesses. This extension is described in the next section.

4   Distributed Global Transaction Support

As described before, the upper layer of the transaction model developed in the WIDE project relies on compensating actions to semantically undo the effects of completed global transaction steps in case of failures. Compensating an entire workflow, thereby undoing all the work that has been done so far is called a complete abort. A complete abort is usually too strict and undoing only part of the process would suffice. For this purpose the global savepoint concept is introduced to allow for flexible, partial aborts. When a partial abort is initiated because of some failure in the workflow execution, the executed workflow is only rolled back (compensated) to one or more savepoint(s), thereby avoiding rolling back the entire workflow execution [13]. The part of a workflow that needs to be rolled back is dynamically calculated by the global transaction support.

In the distributed workflow execution scenario, as presented in Figure 2a, every WFMS is supported by a global transaction system, which can handle aborts of global transactions for that specific site. This means that the extension to the global transaction system to cope with distribution does not change the algorithms to calculate a compensating global transaction for one site, i.e. in a non-distributed scenario. In the distributed scenario however, an additional communication protocol is required that decides which other sites need to abort as well and in which abort mode (partial or complete abort). It then signals those other sites to actually start an abort in the correct abort mode.

4.1 Backward and Forward Aborts

To illustrate the way aborts are propagated through the workflow execution, an example is presented in Figure 2b. In the figure, the black circle at site 5 is the workflow activity that fails, thereby causing an abort. Suppose the abort request should be performed in partial abort mode. The transaction system at site 5 finds no savepoint at that site to roll back to. It signals the parent site to abort, called backward abort, in partial abort mode. The subprocess aborted at the parent site can roll back to a savepoint so no more backward aborts are necessary. However, since the part of the subprocess that is rolled back has delegated a subprocess to site 4, that subprocess must be aborted as well. The transaction system will therefore signal the child site to abort, called forward abort. A forward abort implies that the site receiving the forward abort request must abort in complete abort mode as all the actions done at that site are dependent on an action that has been rolled back and are therefore invalid.

In summary, an abort involves multiple sites if the following situations occur:

- A complete abort request is issued by a WFMS that is executing a delegated subprocess; at least one backward abort is issued.
- A complete abort request is issued by a WFMS that has delegated a subprocess; at least one forward abort is issued.
- A partial abort request is issued by a WFMS that has delegated a subprocess and for which the global transaction step that delegated a subprocess has to be compensated; at least one forward abort is issued.
- A partial abort request is issued by a WFMS for which there is no savepoint in the subprocess to roll back to on that site, see example above; at least one backward abort is issued.

If the global transaction support system has computed that other sites need to abort as well, the communication protocol will signal those sites to abort in the abort mode that depends on the following two rules:

1. The parent site: backward abort in the abort mode that was issued by the failing site
2. The child site: forward abort in complete abort mode.

As each WFMS might independently decide that it needs to abort, concurrent aborts can occur. If those aborts trigger forward and/or backward aborts, the concurrent aborts might come together at one site, causing an abort conflict. The way this is handled is described in the next section.

4.2 Concurrent Aborts

Inherent to distributed workflow execution is the possibility that different subprocesses concurrently issue an abort request. Because of the backward and forward aborts, which might follow an abort request, the occurrence of concurrent aborts might lead to abort conflicts. Abort conflicts occur when one site must handle different abort requests, e.g. a subprocess at one site receives a partial abort request from one child site, while another child site request a complete abort. The way in which the abort conflicts are resolved depends on the state in which a subprocess resides at the time an abort request is received. Figure 3 shows the state diagram of a subprocess. A subprocess can reside in the following states:

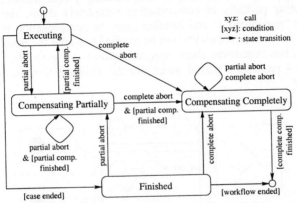

Figure 3: State diagram for concurrent abort requests

- Executing, i.e. the subprocess is being executed normally by the WFMS,
- On Hold, i.e. the subprocess is stopped while a compensating process is being created by the transaction system. This state is not shown in the diagram to keep it readable as the subprocess is always put on hold whenever an abort request is issued and a compensating global transaction is being calculated.
- Compensating partially, i.e. the WFMS is executing a compensation process that has been created by the transaction system based on a partial abort request from the failing subprocess,
- Compensating completely, i.e. the WFMS is executing a compensation process that has been created by the transaction system based on a complete abort request from the failing subprocess, and
- Finished, i.e. the subprocess has been completely executed.

A backward or forward abort request can be received while the subprocess resides in any of the five states. The reaction to the backward or forward abort request can be seen in the state diagram: If a subprocess is in execution or finished state, no abort conflict can occur and an abort request is handled as described in the previous subsection. However, abort conflicts can occur when the subprocess is in one of the other three states and are handled in the following way, see also Figure 3:

- If the subprocess is in the on hold state and thus a compensating global transaction is being created, the following table shows the occurring conflicts and the reaction of the distributed global transaction support:

	Receiving abort request in partial mode	Receiving abort request in complete mode
Creation of compensation in partial abort mode	Finish creation and execution of compensation, then handle the received abort request	Cancel creation, then create and execute the compensation in complete mode
Creation of compensation in complete abort mode	Ignore receiving abort request	Ignore receiving abort request

- If the subprocess is executing a compensating global transaction, i.e. in the compensating partially or compensating completely states, the received abort request is "remembered" and handled after the compensation process has been executed, i.e. concurrent aborts will be handled one after the other.

An example of two concurrent abort requests is shown in Figure 4 in which the failing action on site 4 requests a partial abort and the failing action on site 5 requests a complete abort.

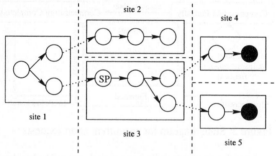

Figure 4: Concurrent abort requests

Both failing sites will issue a backward abort request to site 3. Suppose the partial backward abort request is handled first. During the creation of the partial compensation request, a forward abort is issued to site 4. Site 4 has already handled a complete abort request so no additional abort is necessary at site 4. When the backward complete abort request from site 4 is received by site 3, which is executing the partial compensation request, it first finishes the partial compensation (leaving only the savepoint as the rest of the actions are compensated) after which it handles the complete abort request. In this case no forward abort request is issued as site 5 has already been compensated.

The architecture that has been designed to support the discussed distributed transaction model is described in the next section.

5 Architecture of the Distributed Global Transaction Support

The architecture of the distributed global transaction (DGTS) support does not differ much from the non-distributed global transaction support (GTS). As described before, the necessary communication protocol needs to be added. A non-distributed GTS consists of two parts: a global transaction manager (GTM) and global transaction (GT) objects [12]. Each global transaction, i.e. workflow execution, is represented by one GT object. GT objects are dynamic objects that are created when a global transaction is started and destroyed when a global transaction finishes. They keep track of workflow executions by administrating events like starting and ending of global transaction steps.

5.1 Distributed Global Transaction Manager

The distributed global transaction manager (DGTM) is composed of multiple modules. The most important module with respect to the transactional support for distributed workflow executions is the communication module. It is responsible for the coordination of the different sites in case of an abort that involves multiple sites The WFMSs involved in a distributed workflow execution have a communication mechanism that allows them to interoperate, e.g. using interface 4 specification of the Workflow Management Coalition [22]. This communication mechanism could be used by the DGTS to signal forward and backward aborts to other sites, but that requires the WFMS to handle some of the transactional functionality, reducing the orthogonality between the DGTS and the WFMS. The architectural choice has therefore been made to have a separate and direct communication mechanism between GTS systems. This makes the DGTS and the WFMS as orthogonal as possible, thereby shielding the WFMS from transactional issues and increasing the portability of the transactional support system. The complete architecture with the communication infrastructure is shown in Figure 5a. In the figure, the solid arrows represent the communication between the WFMSs and the dotted arrows represent the communication between the different GTS systems.
The logic module of the DGTM contains the algorithms that are used to calculate compensating global transactions for one site. A formal specification of those algorithms, i.e. for non-distributed workflow executions, can be found in [13].

5.2 Extended Architectural Considerations

The workload of the DGTS depends on the amount of failures that occur in workflow executions. If few failures occur, it is not necessary to have a transaction system on every site where a WFMS is running which only wastes resources. In case of many failures, it is more efficient if the WFMS can use more than one transaction support system. Both requirements can be satisfied by making it possible for any WFMS to use any GTS system that is available, i.e., one WFMS may use multiple GTS systems and one GTS system can be used by multiple WFMSs.
This can be realized using a middleware system such as a CORBA [19] compliant object request broker. In this case it is possible to arbitrarily distribute the GTS

systems over multiple sites. The GTS systems can then be called by any of the WFMSs, which may or may not be on the same site. This way a very flexible and adaptable architecture is offered, of which an example is shown in Figure 5b. Whenever more or less GTS systems are required, a new GTS system can be instantiated or an existing one can be shut down. For the non-distributed global transaction support system the arbitrary distribution of GTS systems is already realized in the WIDE project.

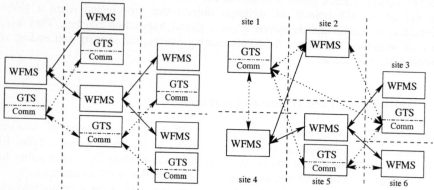

| Figure 5a: Distributed WFMS and GTS Architecture | 5b: Arbitrary distribution of multiple multiple GTS systems |

6   Conclusions and Future Work

This paper describes a model and architecture to provide transactional support for distributed workflow executions. The transaction model relies on compensating actions to semantically undo the effects of completed actions. Specifying savepoints in the workflow process allows to partially compensate a workflow. The WIDE global transaction support system is extended with a communication protocol to provide support for distributing workflow executions over multiple sites. The communication protocol coordinates the calculation of the sites that are involved in an abort, in which abort mode the compensation for those sites must be performed, and the enactment of the distributed global transaction support system at those sites.

In the WIDE project, the non-distributed version of the global transaction support system has been implemented in a prototype environment to support the commercial workflow management system FORO, marketed by SEMA Group [10]. The environment is based on ILU [16], which is a CORBA compliant object request broker and the Oracle database management system [20]. The realization of the extensions to support the distributed execution of workflows as described in this paper is currently considered and can be achieved with little effort. Because of the modularity of the global transaction support system and the orthogonality to the workflow management system, only the communication module needs to be specified and implemented, which can be easily integrated into the global transaction support system.

The transaction model and architecture are othogonal to the workflow management system and can therefore be easily applied to other application areas dealing with long-running processes. The work presented in this paper is currently under consideration to be used in the CrossFlow project [7].

References

[1] G. Alonso, D. Agrawal et al.; Advanced Transaction Models in Workflow Contexts; Procs. Int. Conf. on Data Engineering, New Orleans, USA, 1996.

[2] G. Alonso, D. Agrawal, A. El Abbadi, C. Mohan; Functionality and Limitations of Current Workflow Management Systems; IEEE Expert; Vol. 12, No. 5; 1997.

[3] D. Barbará, S. Mehrotra, M. Rusinkiewicz; INCAs: Managing Dynamic Workflows in Distributed Environments; Journal of Database Management – Special Issue on Multidatabases 7(1): 5-15, 1996.

[4] E. Boertjes, P. Grefen, J. Vonk, P. Apers; An Architecture for Nested Transaction Support on Standard Database Systems; Procs. 9th Int. Conf. on Database and Expert System Application (DEXA); Vienna, Austria, 1998.

[5] A. Cichocki, A. Helal, M. Rusinkiewicz, D. Woelk; Workflow and Process Automation: Concepts and Technology; Kluwer Academic Publishers, 1998.

[6] COSA Solutions Gmbh; Cosa Solutions: Turning Workflow into Cashflow; http://www.cosa.de.

[7] The CrossFlow Project Web Site: http://www.crossflow.org/

[8] J. Eder, W. Liebhart; Workflow Recovery; Procs CoopIS '96, Brussels, Belgium, 1996

[9] A. Elmagarmid, ed.; Database Transaction Models for Advanced Applications; Morgan Kaufmann; USA, 1992.

[10] SEMA Group sae; FORO Web Site: http://dis.sema.es/projects/FORO.

[11] H. Garcia-Molina, K. Salem; Sagas; Procs. ACM-SIGMOD, California, USA, 1987.

[12] P. Grefen, J. Vonk, E. Boertjes, P. Apers; Two-Layer Transaction Management for Workflow Management Applications; Procs. 8th Int. Conf. on Database and Expert System Application (DEXA); Toulouse, France, 1997.

[13] P. Grefen, J. Vonk, E. Boertjes, P. Apers; Semantics and Architecture of Global Transaction Support in Workflow Environments; Procs. CoopIS '99, Edinburgh, Scotland, 1999.

[14] P. Grefen, B. Pernici, G. Sánchez (Eds.); DatabaseSupport for Workflow Management: The WIDE Project; Kluwer Academic Publisher, 1999. ISBN 0-7923-8414-8.

[15] M. Hsu (Ed.); Special Issue on Workflow and Extended Transaction Systems; IEEE Data Engineering Bulletin Vol. 16, No. 2., June 1993.

[16] ILU Web Site: ftp://ftp.parc.xerox.com/pub/ilu/ilu.html.

[17] S. Jajodia, L. Kerschberg (Eds.); Advanced Transaction Models and Architectures; Kluwer Academic Publishers, 1997.

[18] J. E. B. Moss; Nested Transactions: An Approach to Reliable Distributed Computing; The MIT Press, Cambridge, Massachusetts, 1985.

[19] Object Management Group; The Common Object Request Broker: Architecture and Specification, Version 2.0; 1995.

[20] Oracle Corporation. Oracle Web Site: http://www.oracle.com.

[21] Staffware Web Site: http://www.staffware.com.

[22] The Workflow Management Coalition; Interoperability Abstract Specification; Document Number WFMC-TC-1012; 1996.

[23] D. Wodtke, J. Weissenfels, G. Weikum, A. Dittrich; The MENTOR Project: Steps Towards Enterprise-wide Workflow Management; Procs. Int. Conf. on Data Engineering, New Orleans, USA, 1996.

Update Propagation of Replicated Data in Distributed Spatial Databases

Jin Oh Choi[1], Young Sang Shin[2], Bong Hee Hong[2]

[1] Department of Computer Engineering, Kyungdong University, Pongpo Li, Tosung Myun,
Gosung Goon, Kangwon Do, South Korea
jochoi@kyungdong.ac.kr
[2] Department of Computer Engineering, Pusan National University, Jangjun Dong,
Kumjung Goo, Pusan, South Korea
{yosshin, bhhong}@hyowon.cc.pusan.ac.kr

Abstract. When spatial objects are replicated at several sites in the network, the updates of a long transaction in a specific site should be propagated to the other sites for maintaining the consistency of replicated spatial objects. If any two or more transactions at different sites concurrently update some spatial objects within a given region, two spatial objects having spatial relationships should be cooperatively updated even if there are no direct conflicts of locking for them. We present the concepts of *region locking* and *Spatial Relationship-Bound Write locking* for enhancing parallelism of updating the replicated spatial objects. If there are no spatial relationships between the two objects that are concurrently being updated at different sites, parallel updates will be completely allowed. We argue that concurrent updates of two spatial objects having spatial relationships should be propagated and cooperated by using an extended two-phase commit protocol, called *Spatial Relationship-based 2PC protocol*.

1 Introduction

The interactive updates of two replicated spatial objects at different sites should be synchronized for concurrency control. In the interactive transactions, it is very difficult to define the correctness criteria of concurrent transactions since the displayed spatial objects cannot be isolated due to their spatial relationships. We define a *distributed spatial relationship* as the binary spatial relation, for example, disjoin, meets, equals, inside, covers, or overlaps, between two spatial objects which are stored at different sites. Locks on two spatial objects do not conflict with each other, since they are not shared objects. However, concurrent updates of two spatial objects sometimes may make them inconsistent when they have a *distributed spatial relationship*.

In the replicated spatial database, the characteristics of interactive transactions make it difficult to exploit the traditional replication control approaches. As a pessimistic approach, the existing locking-based replication control approach has the following problems. First, locking objects in a long transaction makes other transactions wait for a long time. Second, an interactive transaction that updates spatial objects, has to lock the entire data set or at least a layer, because the replicated spatial objects should be displayed for interactively updating any two or more objects in a long transaction. Third, if two objects have a *distributed spatial relationship*, their concurrent update should be restricted. For example, if the boundary of a spatial object X is shared with the other spatial object Y, a transaction to update Y should be forced to wait until the update of X is completed.

An optimistic approach, like the multi-version control approach [13], allows concurrent updates on the replicated data at several sites, and then, merges the results together. Independent updates of the their own data sets at each site will cause conflicts between them; therefore, resulting in the inconsistent states, when they are merged, calling for the need of rollback in the long transaction.

To deal with the issues of concurrent updates of replicated spatial data, we propose *region locking* and s*patial relationship-bound write locking*, as new locking concepts. We argue that new locking primitives should be introduced to achieve high concurrency and to control the consistency of replicated spatial data. *Region lock* is an extension of the shared lock, which provides a weak READ lock for a group of replicated spatial objects. The *region lock* allows a new long transaction to start at any time without waiting. The possible conflict of concurrent updates of replicated data is filtered by *spatial relationship-bound write locking* during the execution of interactive transactions. The *spatial relationship-bound write lock* is an extension of the exclusive lock to model the update dependency between two interactive transactions due to *distributed spatial relationships*. The *spatial relationship-bound write locking* allows the objects not having any *distributed spatial relationships* to be concurrently updated.

We have introduced a new cooperative update protocol, which is designed on the basis of the existing two-phase commit protocol. The basic protocol of the extended 2PC is the same with that of the existing 2PC except that the decision on collaborative updates or independent updates is based on *distributed spatial relationships*. This protocol is named, *spatial relationship-based 2PC*.

This paper is organized as follows. In section 2, we will briefly describe related works. In section 3, we address the locking problems of spatial objects, which have *distributed spatial relationships*. To deal with the issues of concurrent updates of replicated spatial data, new locking methods are introduced in section 4. Section 5 presents the update propagation protocol based on the distributed spatial relationship-based locking. Section 6 describes an overview of our system implemented on top of a GIS S/W, Gothic. Our conclusions are presented in section 7.

2 Related Work

In distributed databases, replication consistency can be maintained by the synchronous [11] or asynchronous [5] replica control scheme. Synchronous replica control keeps all replicas synchronized at all the sites by the 2PC protocol. Asynchronous replica control propagates replication updates asynchronously to the other sites after committing on a replica-server. In addition, there has been much research to release restriction of synchronous replica control, such as a quorum-based scheme, causality [2][9][12].

The optimistic approach, such as the lazy replication scheme [8], which belongs to the asynchronous replica control method, allows an object to be independently updated at each site. In this approach, locking is not used. Instead, the multi-version concept [13] is employed to control concurrency and ensure the serializability. Concurrent updates of two spatial objects having *distributed spatial relationships* may make them inconsistent even if their READ locks or WRITE locks do not conflict with the other. Thus, the traditional optimistic scheme is difficult to be applied on replica control of spatial objects.

For the increase of the concurrency of long transactions, we have developed a new protocol, named, the *mid-commit protocol* [1] based on the existing 2PC. The main premise of our earlier work was to use the delta-merge protocol to resolve the update conflict problem of long transactions. The work on this paper is an extension of the *mid-commit protocol* for supporting replica control and concurrency of long transactions, which can ensure the serializability of concurrent updates of replicated spatial objects.

3 The Locking Problems of Spatial Objects

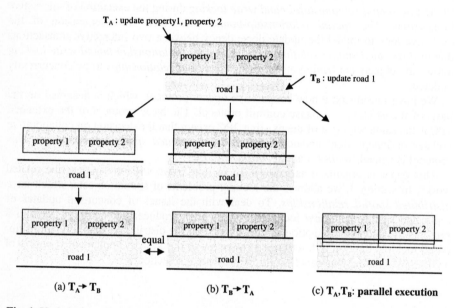

Fig. 1. Updating the objects that have spatial relationships

We will describe the problems of concurrently updating replicated spatial objects, and identify update dependencies of two remote spatial objects. Fig. 1 shows a scenario of updating two spatial objects. Two interactive transactions, T_A and T_B, update replicated data, 'property' and 'road' respectively. If T_A and T_B are executed sequentially, as Fig. 1 (a) or (b), these serially scheduled transactions preserve a correct state.

Not all concurrent execution of long transactions result in a correct state. Consider the schedule of Fig. 1 (c). Since the WRITE locks (property 1, property 2) of T_A do not conflict with the WRITE lock (road 1) of T_B, the locking protocol does not delay any of two transactions. However, the schedule (c) leads to an incorrect state. The schedule leads to an undesirable result because two objects, property 1 and road 1, are independently updated in spite of having a spatial relationship, 'meets'.

Because of the possibility of giving an incorrect state, two spatial objects having a spatial relationship should not be updated concurrently. This is an update constraint of two different spatial objects, which have a spatial relationship. The traditional locking protocol can not ensure the serializability of concurrent updates of two spatial objects with the dependency due to this spatial relationship.

A spatial relationship is defined as a relationship between two spatial objects having Egenhofer's spatial relations. In [6], Egenhofer classified spatial relationships into 8 types, Disjoint, Meets, Equals, Inside1, Inside2, Covers1, Covers2, and Overlaps.

A spatial relationship dependency can also be defined for remote spatial objects. Now, we define *distributed-SR dependency* as follows:

Definition 1. Two objects, O_i and O_j are *distributed-SR dependent* if and only if two objects have a spatial relationship except 'Disjoint' relation, and where O_i and O_j are the objects to be updated by T_i and T_j at remote sites S_i and S_j respectively.

If two objects are *distributed-SR dependent*, concurrent update of them does not guarantee a correct state. Therefore, when two objects, O_i and O_j, are *distributed-SR dependent*, two transactions, T_i and T_j, that update two objects, must update them cooperatively.

4 *Region Locking* and *SR-bound write Locking*

We propose *region locking* and *SR-bound write locking*, which are extensions of two-phase locking. The key idea upon which the extensions are based, is to restrict the unit of concurrency control of interactive transactions to a window of spatial objects displayed on the screen.

4.1 The Definition of *Region Locking* and *SR-bound write Locking*

Region locking sets shared locks on all the objects within the region that is interactively defined by user. *Region lock* is a weak shared lock because the lock allows us to set WRITE locks on some objects in the region later on. This lock mode is similar to *share intention exclusive* lock (*SIX* lock) in multiple granularity locking. When a replicated spatial object is being updated at a remote site, it is desirable to allow interactive transactions to be able to display it at the same time in order to access or update some spatial objects by interacting with displayed objects. Thus, we call the mode of a *region lock* as a *weak SIX lock*, and define it as follows:

Definition 2. A *weak SIX lock* is a lock mode that holds locks on a set of objects in the shared mode and allows the other transactions to acquire exclusive locks on some of the objects. It tolerates shared locks and *weak SIX locks* of other transactions.

The definition of the *region lock* using definition 2 is as follows:

Definition 3. Let D be the whole data set of a map, R be the entire region of the map, R_i be sub-region of R viewed by users who are running a long transaction T_i, and D_{Ri} be all the objects which is totally contained in R_i. We define the *region lock* of T_i as a set of *weak SIX locks* on D_{Ri}.

If there exists a *distributed-SR dependency* between two objects at different sites, concurrent update of the two objects should not be allowed. We introduce a new WRITE lock mode based on *distributed-SR dependency*, and define it as follows:

Definition 4. A *DSRX lock* (Distributed Spatial Relationship-bound eXclusive lock) is a lock mode that sets the exclusive lock to the remote objects being *distributed-SR dependent* on the locally updated object, and also holds an exclusive lock on it. It also tolerates shared locks and *weak SIX locks* of other transactions.

The definition of *SR-bound write lock* using *DSRX lock* is as follows:

Definition 5. Let X be a group of objects in a *region lock* of a transaction T_i. We define *Spatial Relationship-bound Write locks* of T_i as *DSRX locks* on X.

Table 1. Compatibility Matrix for two-phase locks, *weak SIX* and *DSRX*

	READ	WRITE	weak SIX	DSRX
READ	yes	no	yes	yes
WRITE	no	no	no	no
weak SIX	yes	no	yes	yes
DSRX	yes	no	yes	no

Lock compatibility matrix is extended to include *weak SIX lock* and *DSRX lock* as shown in Table 1. In the lock compatibility of Table 1, *weak SIX lock* and *DSRX lock* modes are compatible with the READ lock mode.

4.2 Concurrency Control by *Region Locking*

We name the *region lock* of a transaction T_A, as RGL_A. In Fig. 2, when RGL_A, the *region lock* of transaction T_A, and a RGL_B, the *region lock* of transaction T_B, are sent to remote sites, two *region locks* might have eight kinds of relations, like *distributed spatial relationships*. Except 'Disjoint' relationship, two *region locks* have non-disjoint area, denoted as NDJ_{AB} (Non-DisJoint area of T_A and T_B). In the case of 'Overlaps', NDJ_{AB} is the overlapped area ($RGL_A \cap RGL_B$). For 'Meets' and 'Equals', NDJ_{AB} is the union of two regions ($RGL_A \cup RGL_B$). If two *region locks*, RGL_A and

RGL_B, have NDJ_{AB}, we say, two transactions, T_A and T_B, are in the relation, *region-NDJ*. If two *region locks* don't have an NDJ area, we say, two transactions, T_A and T_B, are in the relation, *region-DJ*.

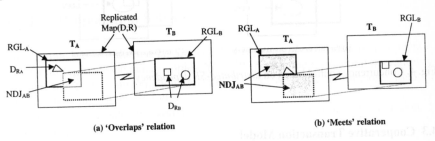

(a) 'Overlaps' relation	(b) 'Meets' relation

Fig. 2. Topology of *region locking*

In this paper, we assume that T_A can only update the objects among D_{RA} after acquiring *SR(Spatial Relationship)-bound write lock* and there is only one transaction at each site at a time. An object, which is updated by T_A and is set to *SR-bound write lock*, is called UDO_A (*UpDating Objects* of T_A, $UDO_A \subset D_{RA}$).

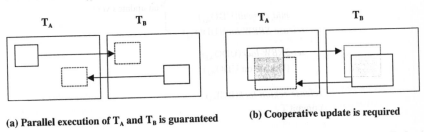

(a) Parallel execution of T_A and T_B is guaranteed   (b) Cooperative update is required

Fig. 3. Concurrency control by *region locking*

We use *region locks* as a means of synchronizing the read access of a group of replicated spatial objects. In Fig. 3 (a), the two transactions, T_A and T_B, can be executed concurrently, because there is no *distributed-SR dependency* between two *region locks*. However, in Fig. 3 (b), concurrent execution of the two transactions must be forbidden, because of the *distributed-SR dependency* between the two *region locks*.

Region locking does not always limit the concurrent execution of two transactions having *distributed-SR dependency*. Some transactions, which have an NDJ between their two *region locks*, can be executed at the same time without affecting each other. Fig. 4 (a) shows that if UDO_A and UDO_B are not *distributed-SR dependent*, update conflict may not occur even if these are updated concurrently. Only when there are the *region lock* conflict and *distributed-SR dependency* between two transactions, concurrent execution of them should be delayed until they obtain exclusive locks on the object to update.

5.2 Notification and Release of *SR-bound write Lock*

```
set-SRBW-lock {

    define the object set for DSRX lock and get UDO_A

    propagate UDO_A to Participants

    FOR(timeout)

        wait for response

    IF(receive any reply-SRBW-conflict)

        THEN write conflict transactions to log

            FOR(all conflict transactions)

                wait for release-SRBW-lock

    write its own UDO_A to log

}
```

```
rcv-set-SRBW-lock(UDO_A) {

    IF(there is its own UDO_B)

        THEN check distributed-SR dependency

            IF(dependent)

                THEN send reply-SRBW-conflict

                    write blocked transaction to log

                ELSE send reply-SRBW-ok

    write UDO_A to log

}
```

Fig. 7. The algorithm of *SR-bound write locking*

The *set-SRBW-lock* operation defines *UpDating Objects*(UDO), and propagates them to all the *Participants* of which *region locks* may conflict with their sources, as shown in Fig. 7. Lock conflicts between a *Coordinator* and its *Participants* mean that *Participants* already hold the *SR-bound write lock* on some of UDO. In such cases, the *Coordinator* writes *Participants* to log, and should wait until the *SR-bound write lock* is released. The *rcv-set-SRBW-lock* operation returns the message, *reply-SRBW-conflict* or *reply-SRBW-ok*, according to lock compatibility.

The release of the *SR-bound write lock* is done by the *release-SRBW-lock* operation. This operation is invoked after executing the *mid-commit*, and the lock release signal is notified to *Participants*.

5.3 SR-based 2PC

We have introduced the *mid-commit* operation to accomplish two purposes: replication control and collaborative work. First, we have to deal with the update propagation problem of replicated data in two or more long transactions. The idea is to decompose an interactive transaction into sub-transactions which contain only one update cycle each, and then perform update propagation incrementally. Second, the collaborative work is required to guarantee the correctness of long transactions. The collaborative work is performed by propagating the DELTA of an updated object to others.

For these purposes, we extend the traditional 2PC for implementing the collaborative work. The basic protocol of the extended 2PC is same with that of existing 2PC. However, the scope of participant sites communicating with the sender is determined by identifying *distributed-SR dependencies*. The extended 2PC, named as *SR-based 2PC*, is operated between a *Coordinator* and its SR-based *Participants*. In this paper, we assume that there is no communication failure and all the sites are always available to limit the scope of this paper.

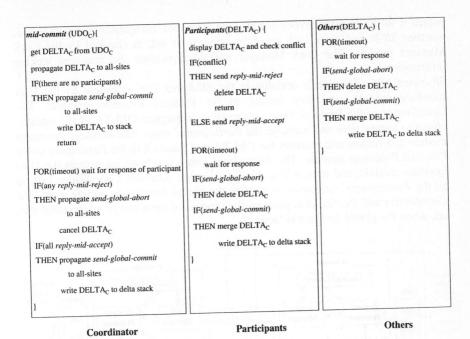

mid-commit (UDO$_C$){	*Participants*(DELTA$_C$) {	*Others*(DELTA$_C$) {
get DELTA$_C$ from UDO$_C$	display DELTA$_C$ and check conflict	FOR(timeout)
propagate DELTA$_C$ to all-sites	IF(conflict)	wait for response
IF(there are no participants)	THEN send *reply-mid-reject*	IF(*send-global-abort*)
THEN propagate *send-global-commit*	delete DELTA$_C$	THEN delete DELTA$_C$
to all-sites	return	IF(*send-global-commit*)
write DELTA$_C$ to stack	ELSE send *reply-mid-accept*	THEN merge DELTA$_C$
return		write DELTA$_C$ to delta stack
	FOR(timeout)	}
FOR(timeout) wait for response of participant	wait for response	
IF(any *reply-mid-reject*)	IF(*send-global-abort*)	
THEN propagate *send-global-abort*	THEN delete DELTA$_C$	
to all-sites	IF(*send-global-commit*)	
cancel DELTA$_C$	THEN merge DELTA$_C$	
IF(all *reply-mid-accept*)	write DELTA$_C$ to delta stack	
THEN propagate *send-global-commit*	}	
to all-sites		
write DELTA$_C$ to delta stack		
}		
Coordinator	**Participants**	**Others**

Fig. 8. The algorithm of *SR-based 2PC*

The *SR-based 2PC* operates among the *Coordinator*, *Participants*, and *Others*. The *Coordinator* is a site that issues the *mid-commit*. *Participants* are those updating the remote objects which are *distributed-SR dependent* or could be potentially *distributed-SR dependent* on the object being updated by the *Coordinator*. *Others* are the sites who are neither the *Coordinator* nor *Participants*. The algorithm of *SR-based 2PC* is shown in Fig. 8.

6 Implementation

For building the replicated spatial database, we have decided to use an object-oriented spatial database system, called 'Gothic 3.0' [14], being operated on two workstations (HP C200 and DEC 500/400). The Gothic system still provides no concurrency control scheme for updating spatial objects. The system sets a WRITE lock on the entire data set before starting any update transactions. We assume that two sites can store and update replicated spatial objects.

We have developed the Replica Manager (R-manager in Fig. 9) on top of the Gothic. The Replica Manager is composed of 5 modules. User Interface, Lock Manager, Protocol Processor, Message Processor, and Catalog Manager.

The implementation issues are how to realize *region locking*, *SR-bound write locking*, and *SR-based 2PC*. The detail implementation techniques and processing mechanisms are as follows:

- *region locking* and *SR-bound write locking*: The User Interface module allows users to define the region to set READ locks to a set of displayed objects, and passes it to the Protocol Processor module. The lock compatibility, for example, whether *SR-bound write lock* could be allowed or not, is checked by the Lock Manager module. The Lock Manager module represents and manages locking information.

- *SR-based 2PC*: The user's decision in the *SR-based 2PC* is caught by the User Interface module, and then passed to the Protocol Processor module. The *Coordinator* in the Protocol Processor module propagates DELTA of the updated object to remote sites and waits for the *Participants'* votes. The Message Processor module at a remote site receives the DELTA and passes it to the *Participant* in the Protocol Processor module. The *Participant* gets a user's decision from the User Interface module, and returns it to the *Coordinator*. After the *Coordinator* gathers all the *Participants'* responses, it notifies the global decision to remote sites. The *Coordinator* and *Participants* perform the process of delta-merge on the local data set, when the global decision is 'accept'.

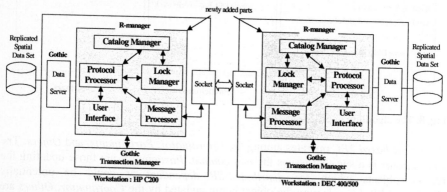

Fig. 9. Architecture for Replicated Spatial Databases

7 Conclusions

In this paper, our goal was the development of new techniques for guaranteeing the concurrency and replication control in replicated spatial databases. To achieve these goals, we proposed new lock modes and an extended update propagation protocol. Because *region locking* does not block the entire data set, it can maximize the concurrency of long transactions. *SR-bound write locking* ensures the correct update of spatial objects. We discovered that the *distributed spatial relationships* between spatial objects are a new dependency factor in the environment of concurrently updating replicated spatial data. *SR-bound write locking* could control the consistency of replicated spatial data having the *distributed spatial relationships*.

The contributions of this paper are as follows: First, we discovered that replicated spatial objects have *distributed spatial relationships*, and the objects are dependent on each other when they are updated at the same time, although they are not the same objects. Second, we proposed new distributed spatial relationship-based locking (*region locking* and *SR-bound write locking*), which support concurrency and replication consistency of long transactions. Third, we developed the extended update propagation protocol for supporting cooperative work and replication control of spatial data. The cooperative work is achieved by *SR-based 2PC protocol*.

Our implementation results showed that high concurrency could be achieved with little overhead. The update conflict caused by *distributed spatial relationships*, could be solved using *SR-bound write locking* and *SR-based 2PC protocol*.

References

1. Am-suk Oh, Jin-oh Choi, Bong-hee Hong:An Incremental Update Propagation Scheme for a Cooperative Transaction Model. Int. Workshop on DEXA (1996) 353-362
2. P. Chundi, D.J. Rosenkrantz, S.S. Ravi: Deferred Updates and Data Placement in Distributed Databases. Proc. Int. Conf. on Data Engineering (1996) 469-476
3. K. Stathatos, S. Kelly, N. Roussopoulos, J.S. Baras: Consistency and Performance of Concurrent Interactive Database Applications. Proc. Int. Conf. on Data Engineering (1996) 602-608
4. A. Kemper, G. Moerkotte: Object-Oriented Database Management : Applications in Engineering and Computer Science. Prentice Hall Press (1994)
5. G. Coulouris, J. Dollimore, T. Kindberg: Distributed Systems : Concepts and Design, 2ED. Addison-Wesley Publishing (1994)
6. M.J. Egenhofer: Reasoning about binary topological relations. 2th Int. Symposium, SSD'91 (1991)
7. H.F. Korth, G.D. Speegle: Long-Duration Transaction in Software. Proc. Int. Conf. on Data Engineering (1990) 568-574
8. J.Gray, P.Helland, D.Shasha: The Dangers of Replication and a Solution. Proc. of the 1996 ACM SIGMOD (1996) 173-182
9. E.Pitoura: A Replication Schema to Support Weak Connectivity in Mobile Information Systems. Int. Workshop on DEXA (1996) 708-717
10. M.H. Nodine, S.B. Zdonic: Cooperative Transaction Hierarchies: A Transaction Model to Support Design Applications. Proc. Int. Conf. on VLDB (1990) 83-94
11. P.A. Bernstein, N. Goodman: An Algorithm for Concurrency Control and Recovery in Replicated Distributed Databases. ACM Tran. Database Systems, vol.9, no.4 (1984) 596-615
12. D. Agrawal, A.E. Abbadi: The Tree Quorum Protocol: An Efficient Approach for Managing Replicated Data. Proc. Int. Conf. on VLDB (1990) 243-254
13. H. berenson, P.Nernstein, J.Gray, J.Melton, E.O'Neil, P.O'Neil: A Critique of ANSI SQL Isolation Levels. Proc. of the 1995 ACM SIGMOD (1995) 1-10
14. The Gothic Object Server Module Reference Manual. Laser Scan Ltd. (1998)

Split Algorithms for
Sets of High-Dimensional Objects

Jukka Teuhola

Turku Centre for Computer Science (TUCS), Univ. of Turku
Lemminkäisenkatu 14 A, FIN-20520 Turku, FINLAND
Email: teuhola@cs.utu.fi

Abstract. This study compares general, heuristic algorithms for splitting a set of high-dimensional objects. The algorithms aim at minimizing the overlap of the created subsets, while simultaneously satisfying a
given balancing condition for their cardinalities. The intuitive goal is to
enhance clustering and disjointness, and thereby to improve retrieval performance. Three categories of complexity are studied: $O(N)$, $O(N \log N)$,
and $O(N^2)$, when splitting a set of N objects. A representative algorithm
is suggested for each category, the main contribution being a new class
of quadratic algorithms which take advantage of existing heuristics for
the traveling salesman problem. All algorithms are quite general, making
minimal assumptions about the underlying object domain. However, for
low-dimensional (e.g. spatial) objects, specialized split techniques produce better results. The experiments are therefore restricted to splitting
a set of signatures (bit-vectors in general). The trade-off between computation effort and result quality is clearly established.

1 Introduction

Data structures for storing database objects on paged secondary storage often
require an algorithm for page splitting, due to *overflows*. If the access key is one-
dimensional, such as with normal *B-trees*, splitting is no problem; it can always
be done trivially at the middle of the sorted array of objects, so that the ranges
of key values for the two subsets will be disjoint, enabling unique branching in
the tree.

In multi-attribute (multi-dimensional) retrieval the situation is quite different. Normally we cannot define a unique ordering of the objects because all dimensions should be supported more or less equally in the queries. Especially for
point data, having atomic values for each attribute, this is often accomplished so
that the split dimension is changed in a cyclic manner in repeated splittings (cf.
k-d-tree, [3, 11]). This results in disjoint subareas, and guarantees a logarithmic
depth for the search tree, for a fixed number of dimensions.

For *spatial objects* (rectangles, for example, see [13]), splitting into disjoint
sets is no more trivial, if possible at all, because the objects may overlap arbitrarily. In a way, the same holds for objects of bit-vector type (*signatures*, see [5,
6, 12]); each bit position represents a 'dimension' of its own, although the related

domain consists of only two values. The number of bit positions is normally so large, that splitting according to one position at a time cannot be considered sufficiently symmetric, since most of the positions never get their turn. Some advantage may yet be gained in queries, as shown in [16].

Examples of possible 'client' data structures for split algorithms are the different versions of *R-trees* [2, 7], as well as other *spatial data structures* [13], developed for storing rectangles with sides parallel with coordinate axes. For storing signatures, a data structure analogous to R-trees is the so called *S-tree* [4]. All these data structures are, of course, already equipped with recommended split algorithms, but we shall suggest some new alternatives.

Splitting is closely related to *clustering* algorithms, see for example [8, 14, 15]. We restrict ourselves to splitting a given set into two clusters, the sizes of which must satisfy an additional balancing constraint.

The common motivation for all page splitting algorithms is to improve subsequent retrieval by aiming at as small overlap between disk pages as possible, because that means better discrimination of subareas on search paths. Many of the data structures supporting retrieval are tree-like, the depth of which partly dictates the worst-case performance. Their depth is kept low by performing *balanced* splits of pages, keeping the loading factor high.

Our goal is to study a set of heuristic, balanced split algorithms, independent of the related object domain and data structure. Only a few general functions, such as *distance, weight* and *overlap*, must be defined for the domain. Three categories of complexity are studied, $O(N)$, $O(N \log N)$ and $O(N^2)$, and a representative algorithm given for each. The trade-off between computation effort and result quality is observed, using superimposed signatures as the test domain. The main contribution, producing the best results, is a quadratic split algorithm, which takes advantage of heuristics developed for the *traveling salesman problem*. Although the suggested heuristics are quite general and applicable under minimal assumptions about the object space, they are mainly meant for high-dimensional cases, where the optimal solution takes too much time.

2 Problem specification

We consider objects from an arbitrary domain A, for which the following functions have been defined:

1. *weight* (also called *extent* or *area*) of an object: $w(x) : A \to I\!R$,
2. *cover* of two objects, as an algebraic infix operator: $x \oplus y : A \times A \to A$,
3. *overlap* of two objects, as an algebraic infix operator: $x \odot y : A \times A \to A$.

For example, for two-dimensional axis-oriented rectangles, $w(x)$ would be the area of x, while $x \oplus y$ would be the *minimum bounding rectangle (MBR)*, and $x \odot y$ would be the intersection rectangle, possibly empty. An example is given in Fig. 1(a). For bit-vector domain, the interpretations might be as follows: $w(x)$ is the number of 1-bits in the vector, $x \oplus y$ is the logical (inclusive) OR of the

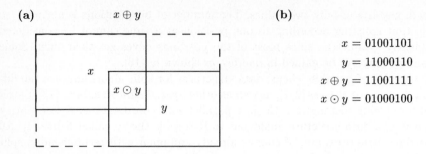

Fig. 1. Examples of cover and overlap functions for (a) rectangles, (b) bit-vectors.

bit vectors, whereas $x \odot y$ is the logical AND of them, see Fig. 1(b). Note that cover and overlap are both *symmetric* and *associative* functions.

Now we can formulate our problem precisely as follows. Given a set $S \subseteq A$ of N elements, and a *balancing parameter* $r \in (0, 0.5]$, choose two subsets of S, denoted $X = \{x_1, \ldots, x_k\}$ and $Y = \{y_1, \ldots, y_m\}$, such that

- $X \cup Y = S$, $X \cap Y = \phi$,
- $k, m \geq \lfloor rN \rfloor$,
- $(x_1 \oplus x_2 \oplus \ldots \oplus x_k) \odot (y_1 \oplus y_2 \oplus \ldots \oplus y_m)$ is minimized.

A typical value for the balancing parameter is $r = 0.4$, restricting the subset size to 0.4...0.6 of the original set.

We still define a *distance* function $d : A \times A \to I\!\!R$ between objects, which is not needed in specifying the problem, but which is useful in developing various heuristics. The function is typically defined so that it supports achieving the primary goal. Thus, after splitting S into X and Y, objects within X should be close to each other, but far from those in Y, and vice versa. A typical distance function is the *symmetric difference* (also called *anti-difference*), defined as

$$d(x, y) = w(x \oplus y) - w(x \odot y) \tag{1}$$

For bit-vectors, the normal *Hamming distance* is obtained like this, i.e. as the weight of the *exclusive OR* of the arguments. For rectangles, the distance formula means the area of MBR outside the overlap of the two arguments. Notice that the former is a *metric distance* (satisfying the triangle inequality), whereas the latter is not. This is not even necessary, but for our main heuristic metric distances are preferred.

For rectangles, still some other (non-metric) alternatives for defining d have been suggested in the literature. For example, the so called *dead space*, which is in MBR, but outside both argument rectangles, is a reasonable choice. Formally:

$$d'(x, y) = w(x \oplus y) - w(x) - w(y) + w(x \odot y) \tag{2}$$

Some algorithms use an *asymmetric* function, which cannot be called distance, at all, but rather *weight increase*, see [7]:

$$inc(x, y) = w(x \oplus y) - w(x) \tag{3}$$

Argument x represents the cover of a cumulatively growing subset, and the *inc* function is used in finding the minimal weight increase.

Some popular heuristics for splitting sets of rectangles [2] are based on projected distances along a single dimension, only. A separate heuristic is needed for choosing the most profitable dimension.

3 Assorted split algorithms

Becker et al have shown [1] that for spatial splits in d dimensions, the optimal solution can be computed in $O(dn \log n + d^2 n^{2d-1})$ time, which is polynomial in n. For two dimensions this is $O(n^3)$, which might still be practical. Generally, the splitting problem is exponential; for some domains and distance functions even NP-complete, being similar to the Graph Partitioning Problem, cf. [9]. Thus, heuristics are the only alternative in all but very small problems.

In describing the R-tree for storing rectangles [7], Guttman suggested both linear and quadratic heuristics, whereas Beckmann et al. decided to use a sorting-based $O(N \log N)$ algorithm in their R*-tree [2]. Deppisch, on the other hand, proposed only a linear alternative for his S-tree [4], a storage structure for signatures.

We shall present one representative algorithm from each of the three classes, using the general framework of the previous section. By varying the distance function, different versions of heuristics are obtained. Moreover, we suggest a new class of heuristics, having quadratic complexity. In measuring the complexity we assume that each evaluation of the above functions (weight, cover, overlap, distance, weight increase) costs one unit, independent of the dimensionality.

3.1 Greedy split

The basic idea is to first choose two *seeds*, as distant as possible, for the two subsets to be created. The rest of the objects are then inserted into the closer subset, using the *inc* function as the measure. If at some point the larger subset reaches its maximum size, the rest of the objects are added to the smaller subset.

In the next algorithm, we follow Deppisch's presentation [4], because it suits better for generalization than Guttman's technique [7].

O(N) algorithm:

Step 1. Find object x with the maximum weight, i.e.
$w(x) = \text{Max}\{w(a)|a \in S\}$. Initialize $S_1 = \{x\}$.

Step 2. Find object y with the maximum weight increase, i.e.
$inc(x, y) = \text{Max}\{inc(x, a)|a \in S\}$. Initialize $S_2 = \{y\}$.

Step 3. Assign each $z \in S \setminus \{x, y\}$ to either S_1 or S_2:
If $|S_1| > (1 - r)N - 1$ then assign z to S_2.
If $|S_2| > (1 - r)N - 1$ then assign z to S_1.
Otherwise, if $inc(S_1, z) < inc(S_2, z)$, the assign z to S_1, else to S_2.

The possible problem of this algorithm is its greedy manner of operation: The best subset is chosen for each object, without looking ahead. When one subset reaches its maximum size, the rest of the objects, being forced to the other subset, may deteriorate the disjointness considerably. In fact, this is rather likely to happen, because a larger subset tends to offer a smaller weight increase, making the subset still larger.

A tie-break rule may be added to the last alternative of Step 3. We should favour the smaller subset if the *inc*-values are equal.

3.2 Sorting-based split

Now we try to avoid the problem of the linear algorithm, which made too hasty decisions. The idea, being analogous to the split in the R*-tree [2], is to arrange the objects into linear order, with the two seeds as endpoints, and then choose the best of the legal cut points within the sequence. As one may guess, sorting is used here as an auxiliary step. More precisely, we use the difference of distances from the seeds as the sorting key. After sorting, the best split point is determined in linear time, by computing the covers of subsets incrementally for each possible split point, and then choosing the one with the minimum overlap.

O(N log N) algorithm:

Step 1. Find object x with the maximum weight, i.e.
$$w(x) = \text{Max}\{w(a)|a \in S\}.$$
Step 2. Find object y with the maximum weight increase, i.e.
$$inc(x,y) = \text{Max}\{inc(x,a)|a \in S\}.$$
Step 3. Create a sorted list $[a_1, \ldots, a_N]$ of the elements of S by using $d(x, a_i) - d(y, a_i)$ as the sorting key.
Step 4. Initialize covers C_0 and C'_{N+1} as empty.
Step 5. Compute cumulative covers:
For $i = 1$ to $\lfloor (1-r)N \rfloor$, compute $C_i = a_i \oplus C_{i-1}$.
For $i = N$ downto $\lceil rN \rceil$ compute $C'_i = a_i \oplus C'_{i+1}$.
Step 6. Find $j \in [\lceil rN \rceil, \lfloor (1-r)N \rfloor]$ minimizing the overlap $w(C_j \odot C'_{j+1})$.
Step 7. Set $S_1 = \{a_1, \ldots, a_j\}$ and $S_2 = \{a_{j+1}, \ldots, a_N\}$.

This non-greedy algorithm is anticipated to produce better results than the linear algorithm. However, it has the feature that consecutive objects in the sequence can be quite far from each other, even though they are almost equally distant from the seeds. This means that their cover may be large, increasing the possibility of a large overlap between subsets. Moreover, in repeated splits of a growing set, it would seem advantageous that neighbouring objects most often get to the same subset. This leads to our next split version.

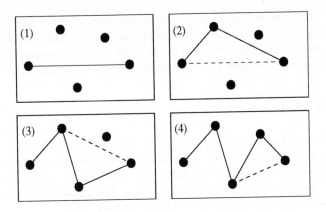

Fig. 2. Illustration of the path building process.

3.3 Path split

We adopt the same goal as above, namely to create a sequence of objects, with the seeds as endpoints, and then find a profitable cut point. Now, however, we try to support proximity of consecutive objects in the sequence. This principle is very similar to the one applied in the *Traveling Salesman Problem* (TSP): Find the shortest path via each of the objects. The difference is that we do not create a cycle, but a so called *Hamiltonian path*. All the numerous heuristics for TSP (see e.g. [10]) can easily be applied to our case, as well.

We suggest the simple *insertion heuristic* of TSP: Start with a two-object path of seeds, and then add all the rest one by one (in random order) into the sequence between two existing objects, so that the increase of path length is minimized at each insert. An example is given in Fig. 2 for a set of points in two dimensions. The applied heuristic has quadratic complexity, and therefore we change also our seed-searching algorithm to quadratic: Find the most distant pair of objects. This is expected to enhance the disjointness of created subsets.

O(N^2) algorithm:

Step 1. Find two most distant objects, $x, y \in S$, as seeds:
$d(x, y) = \text{Max}\{d(x_i, y_j) | x_i, y_j \in S\}$.
Construct a two-object path $P = [p_1, p_2]$, where $p_1 = x$ and $p_2 = y$.

Step 2. For each $z \in S \backslash P$, choose two subsequent elements, $p_k, p_{k+1} \in P$, which minimize the expression $d(p_k, z) + d(p_{k+1}, z) - d(p_k, p_{k+1})$. Insert z between p_k and p_{k+1} in sequence P, and adjust the indexing of elements accordingly.

Step 3. Choose the optimal split point from P in a similar way as in Section 3.2 (Steps 4–7), to minimize the overlap of the subsets.

Notice that this heuristic does not necessarily presume that the distance function is metric, but certainly has advantage if it is. The algorithm can be applied to any kinds of domains with a defined distance between elements, but the selection of the distance function must be done carefully.

4 Experiments

Our purpose was to find out whether using more computing time really pays off in splitting, as one would expect. This has been studied with rectangles in [7] and [2]. The former did not find a big difference, whereas the latter did. The result is probably dependent on the test cases chosen. The related data structures may also have other features which affect the overall success.

We have chosen signatures (fixed-size bit arrays in general) as our test domain of objects, because they represent the higher-dimensional case, with each bit position representing one dimension. There are many applications of signatures, but we picked up a generic case where a set of *keywords*, characterizing an object (e.g. a *document*), is used as the basis of computing the signature. We assume that splitting means physical page splitting, with a certain page capacity.

There are many alternatives of converting the keywords into signatures [5, 6, 16]. We applied *superimposed coding*, where each keyword sets on a certain number of 1-bits in the signature, and the result is obtained as a logical OR of these. The indexes of bits to be set are obtained by suitable hashing functions, applied to the keyword.

In order to be able to use a large profile of cases, we decided to use artificial test data, so that by varying a couple of parameters, we could investigate the behaviour of the algorithms. Notice that there is no sense to split totally arbitrary sets of signatures, because even the optimal split would give only marginal advantage. Therefore, we intentionally chose non-random keywords, so that documents represented two domains, and then let the algorithms do their best to separate the subsets according to their (hidden) domains. This was accomplished by defining a *home class* of keywords for each of the two domains, and then favouring the home class when picking the keywords for documents. The idea of test set generation is illustrated in Fig. 3. The parameters and their default values were:

1. Page size = 4096 bytes.
2. Signature length $s = 64$ bytes = 512 bits.
3. Keywords per class = $10 \ldots 100$ (for each of the two classes).
4. Keywords per document = 10.
5. Number of 1-bits set per keyword = 30.
6. Home proportion $h = 0.5 \ldots 1.0$ (default 1.0); the proportion of keywords taken from the home class.
7. Balance of document counts from the two domains $b = 0.1 \ldots 0.5$ (default 0.5, i.e. equal counts).
8. Split balance factor $r = 0.4 \ldots 0.5$ (default 0.4), specified in Section 2.

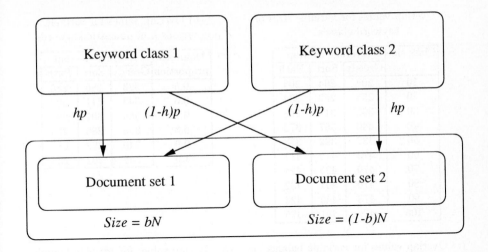

Fig. 3. Schematic view of the signature generation process ($p =$ keys per document.)

We varied parameters 3, 6, 7 and 8 one at a time, assigned default values for others, and observed the overlap (common 1-bits) of the resulting subsets. The average results of 10 repetitions for the three algorithms are given in the tables of Fig. 4. Methods 3.1–3.3 are called 'greedy', 'sort', and 'path', for short.

Test 1. Fig. 4(a) shows that increasing the size of keyword classes makes it more difficult to distinguish between the two domains of documents, or in other words, documents in a certain domain do not resemble each other so much, anymore.

Test 2. Parameter h, the proportion of 'domestic' keywords in documents was here varied. Values close to 0.5 mean that there is no distinction between the document domains, and therefore disjointness cannot be accomplished in split. Fig. 4(b) partially confirms this, but variation also appears; only the case $h = 1.0$ differs clearly from the others.

Test 3. Since our allowed 'slack' in the split is $0.4 \ldots 0.6$, a higher unbalance (parameter b) between the document sets leads to poorer split result, as evidenced by Fig. 4(c), although an anomaly appears for balance ratio 30–70.

Test 4. Having less slack in the split balance (parameter r) also deteriorates the disjointness somewhat, see Fig. 4(d). Values smaller than 0.4 are usually excluded, to keep the overall data structure (e.g. S-tree) sufficiently balanced.

All experiments show also that using more execution time generally improves the quality of the result, although the difference between $O(N \log N)$ and $O(N^2)$ algorithms is not very big.

(a) Overlap values for variable sizes of keyword classes.

Class size	Average overlap		
	Greedy	Sort	Path
10	204	204	204
20	258	252	234
30	392	313	308
40	440	357	373
50	437	392	378
60	473	419	417
70	470	435	424
80	470	441	432
90	473	445	423
100	479	481	475

(b) Overlap values for variable proportions h of domestic keywords.

Domestic proportion	Average overlap		
	Greedy	Sort	Path
0.5	323	280	280
0.6	343	311	307
0.7	366	307	295
0.8	365	286	285
0.9	340	292	288
1.0	258	252	234

(c) Overlap values for variable balances b between document domains.

Balance	Average overlap		
	Greedy	Sort	Path
10–90	315	293	289
20–80	283	261	257
30–70	259	249	229
40–60	316	271	255
50–50	258	252	234

(d) Overlap values for variable bounds r of the split ratio.

Split ratio	Average overlap		
	Greedy	Sort	Path
0.40	258	252	234
0.42	266	252	245
0.44	276	260	255
0.46	276	260	256
0.48	286	266	263
0.50	307	290	286

Fig. 4. Test results for overlap values for different parameter settings.

5 Discussion

We studied three general algorithms of different complexities for splitting sets of high-dimensional objects. The results from experiments show the expected behaviour: More time-consuming algorithms produce better results. On the other hand, in signature files, a small decrease of average page weight (= weight of inclusive OR of signatures within page) may result in large savings in retrieval effort. For example (using the above parameter values), for signature size 512 and query weight 30 (= single-term query), a decrease of page weight from 500 to 490 reduces the probability of page access from 0.49 to 0.27, in a random case. Correspondingly, for a two-term query with average weight 58, the decrease is from 0.25 to 0.08. Anyway, more experimentation is needed with various domains, in order to confirm the generality of the approaches, and to tune the distance function for each special case.

Care must be taken when applying algorithms 3.2 and 3.3 to spatial problems. If the distance is based on the minimum bounding rectangle, the generated sequence of rectangles may 'wind' in the space in a very complicated way, so that the area covered by the subsets is not nearly *convex*. This leads probably to large 'dead space' in the bounding rectangles of the subsets, and thereby to high overlap between them. Therefore, in spatial problems of rectangle domain, we recommend choosing a metric distance function.

The splitting problem was considered detached from the related data structure. The investigation of possible dependencies on e.g. the insert algorithm is left for future work. The same holds for studying the effects of repeated splittings of the same (dynamically growing) set. We conjecture that small advantages of a locality preserving split accumulate into a large overall improvement.

References

1. Becker, B., Franciosa, P. G., Gschwind, S., Ohler, T., Thiemt, G., and Widmayer, P.: "Enclosing Many Boxes by an Optimal Pair of Boxes", Proc. of STACS (1992) 475–486.
2. Beckmann, R., Kriegel, H.-P., Schneider, R., and Seeger, B.: "The R*-tree: An Efficient and Robust Access Method for Points and Rectangles", Proc. ACM SIGMOD Conf. (1990) 322–331.
3. Bentley, J.L.: "Multidimensional Binary Search Trees in Database Applications", *IEEE Trans. on Software Eng.*, Vol. SE-5, No. 4 (1979) 333–340.
4. Deppisch, U.: "S-Tree: A Dynamic Balanced Signature Index for Office Retrieval", Proc. of ACM Conf. on Res. and Dev. in Inf. Retrieval, Pisa, Italy (1986) 77–87.
5. Faloutsos, C., and Christodoulakis, S.: "Signature Files: An Access Method for Documents and Its Analytical Performance Evaluation", *ACM Trans. on Office Inf. Systems*, Vol. 2, No. 4 (1984) 267–288.
6. Faloutsos, C., and Christodoulakis, S.: "Description and Performance Analysis of Signature File Methods", *ACM Trans. on Office Inf. Systems*, Vol. 5, No. 3 (1987) 237–257.
7. Guttman, A.: "R-trees: A Dynamic Index Structure for Spatial Searching", Proc. ACM SIGMOD Conf. (1984) 47–57.
8. Jagadish, H.V.: "Linear Clustering of Objects with Multiple Attributes", Proc. of ACM SIGMOD Conf. (1990) 332–342.
9. Kernighan, B.W., and Lin, S.: "An Efficient Heuristic Procedure for Partitioning Graphs", *Bell System Techn. J.*, Vol. 49, No. 2 (1970) 291–307.
10. Reinelt, G.: "The Traveling Salesman: Computational Solutions for TSP Applications", Lecture Notes in Computer Science 840, Springer-Verlag (1994).
11. Robinson, J.T.: "The K-D-B-Tree: A Search Structure for Large Multidimensional Dynamic Indexes", Proc. ACM SIGMOD Conf. (1981) 10–18.
12. Sacks-Davis, R., Kent, A., and Ramamohanarao, K.: "Multikey Access Methods Based on Superimposed Coding Techniques", *ACM Trans. on Database Systems*, Vol. 12, No. 4 (1987) 655–696.
13. Seeger, B., and Kriegel, H.-P.: "Techniques for Design and Implementation of Efficient Spatial Access Methods", Proc. 14th VLDB Conf. (1988) 360–371.
14. Späth, H.: "Cluster Analysis Algorithms", Ellis Horwood (1980).
15. Teuhola, J.: "Heuristic Clustering of Database Objects According to Multi-Valued Attributes", Proc. 8th DEXA Conf. (1997) 162–171.
16. Zezula, P., Rabitti, F., and Tiberio, P.: "Dynamic Partitioning of Signature Files", *ACM Trans. on Inf. Systems*, Vol. 9, No. 4 (1991) 336–369.

Spatio-Temporal Multimedia Presentations as Database Objects

Michel Adiba and José-Luis Zechinelli-Martini*

LSR-IMAG, University of Grenoble, BP 72 38402 Saint-Martin d'Hères, France
{Michel.Adiba, Jose-Luis.Zechinelli}@imag.fr

Abstract. In this paper, we present a database model and a prototype system which provide a general format for multimedia presentations with spatio-temporal aspects. This representation is independent of any description language and media type and can be used to interpret and to integrate heterogeneous multimedia data coming from different distributed sources. We put a special emphasis on spatial aspects and we provide both qualitative and quantitative relations to compose and query multimedia presentations. The originality of our approach is that presentations can be specified, stored as database objects, queried and executed.

1 Multimedia Presentations

There are now numerous examples of multimedia systems and approaches in the commercial market. These systems have been developed primarily on a case-by-case basis [17]. General multimedia systems need to be supported by frameworks to access, store and present multimedia data in a variety of ways. This involves aspects that span across different areas such as networks, databases, distributed computing, data compression, document processing, user interfaces, etc.

In this paper, we concentrate on a database model and system for multimedia spatio-temporal presentations. Our model is independent of any description language and media type (document, text, audio, etc.). Because spatial and temporal aspects are application dependent, we propose a representation where these aspects can be combined according to different needs.

Our approach is to consider spatio-temporal dimensions as a continuum where any object is defined by its projections over temporal and spatial dimensions. In the spatial dimension, each object is mapped to a rectangle whose sides are projections on the x and y axis. Projections are modeled as intervals. Our spatio-temporal model uses concepts for defining positions, sizes and spatio-temporal presentations. For us, a spatio-temporal presentation is an expression of an algebra of intervals that characterizes the arrangement of one or several objects (texts, images, video and audio data) in space and time.

The remainder of the paper is organized as follows. In Section 2 characterizes a multimedia database system. Section 3 defines spatio-temporal presentations.

---

* Supported by SFERE-CONACyT and ECOS-ANUEIS Project M96E04.

Section 4 discusses the way our model offers a general representation of spatio-temporal aspects. It shows how to support querying and gives several examples that are running in our prototype. Section 5 compares our proposal with other existing works. Finally, Section 6 concludes this paper and introduces some future research directions.

2 Multimedia Database System

Multimedia presentations need to be specified and executed but also stored and reused for defining new ones. Our goal is to answer to these needs from a data base point of view. Figure 1 shows a functional architecture of a Multimedia Database Management System (MDBMS). The architecture separates functionalities and models them as independent specialized modules. Applications can combine them according to their needs.

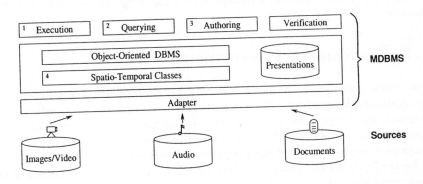

Fig. 1. Architecture.

Multimedia data should be presented taking into account their spatio-temporal characteristics and synchronization restrictions associated to them. For this, different models have been proposed [6] and used for temporal synchronization. An execution module should implement a general model to synchronize multimedia presentations considering also spatial aspects, target systems, process speed, platform characteristics, etc.

A querying module provides powerful facilities to retrieve multimedia objects and/or presentations using object attributes and spatio-temporal characteristics. A data manipulation language should be provided to allow execution, dynamic definition, edition and storing of querying results. Interactive querying and content based retrieval should be also supported.

Defining multimedia presentations implies dealing with the heterogeneous nature of multimedia data, their combination and their integration within a multimedia document. An authoring module should provide a uniform environment for creating and verifying multimedia presentations. Verification is used to detect and eliminate possible conflicts in the user specification in order to ensure consistent presentations.

In recent years, several standards have come up to define and execute multimedia presentations (see Section 5). This has led to an increasing heterogeneity in data that users retrieve and combine to build new presentations. Transparency is needed between multimedia data sources. The MDBMS should be able to store all types of media and documents. Therefore, adapters are needed to transform multimedia data and documents in a general representation.

Our spatio-temporal model enables an MDBMS to define, modify, store and play presentations. Temporal aspects have been treated in our previous work [1, 2, 18, 15]. Currently, we have defined meta-classes that represent our spatio-temporal model (see module 4 in Figure 1) and functions for executing, querying and defining dynamically spatio-temporal presentations (see modules 1, 2, 3 in Figure 1). Queries can be made on descriptive attributes but also on spatio-temporal considerations. Presentations are built by querying existing ones and by defining spatio-temporal characteristics for the result of the query (see Section 4.3).

3 Spatio-temporal Presentations

This section introduces the main concepts for characterizing spatio-temporal presentations. We consider a 3D space (x, y, t), where (x, y) is a coordinate in a 2D space, and t represents a logical time. In our model objects are represented using intervals and we introduce the concept of Spatio-Temporal Shadow (STS) to represent spatio-temporal characteristics of presentations.

Figure 2a shows the general notion of shadow. A shadow is composed of two consecutive intervals δ and d called respectively an offset and a size with specific beginning and ending points. This notion can be applied to any dimension of our 3D space. In each dimension, δ and d have different interpretations.

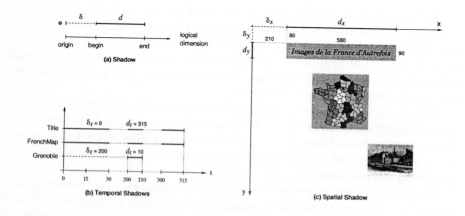

Fig. 2. Spatial and Temporal Shadows.

Shadows are associated to objects (i.e., text, image, audio, video, etc.) for defining presentations. In the temporal dimension, the Temporal Shadow (TS) of an object is defined by δ that represents the delay during which the object is ready to be displayed but not yet "perceptible" and by d, the effective duration of the presentation (see Figure 2b) .

The Spatial Shadow (SS) combines two shadows, one for each dimension x and y (see the title in Figure 2c). The SS describes the position of each object (δ_x, δ_y) and its size (length and width) (d_x, d_y). Thus, the SS describes the spatial attributes of an object in a given presentation. As already said, for spatial aspects we consider that each object can be associated with a rectangle on the screen. To that extent, SS is similar to the notion of Minimum Bounding Rectangle (MBR).

STS combines SS and TS. It is a sextuple (δ_x, δ_y, d_x, d_y, δ_t, d_t), where (δ_x, δ_y, d_x, d_y) defines SS, and (δ_t, d_t), TS. As a first approximation, SS is given in pixels and TS, in seconds. The origin of SS is supposed to be the upper left corner of the screen.

The main idea behind the notion of shadow is that a given object may be associated to different shadows in different presentations. This allows to consider spatial and temporal aspects either separately or not, depending on applications needs.

In our model, a presentation ($\mathcal{P}$) contains explicit knowledge about the objects it is composed of (i.e., their position and their size in space and time). Presentations may consist recursively of other presentations. We make the distinction between single and compound presentations where several objects are associated using spatial and temporal relations.

Single Presentation A single presentation associates an atomic object o (i.e., integer, real, boolean, bits, char, string, Text, Image, Audio, Video) with a spatio-temporal shadow STS. It is a tuple of the form (STS, o). Referring to Figure 2, the title can be defined through a single presentation as follows ((210, 80, 580, 90, 0, 315), **title**). Remember that a given object o may be associated to different STS in different presentations.

Compound Presentation A compound presentation associates two (single or compound) presentations A and B with a spatio-temporal relation $\sigma\tau$. It is a tuple of the form (STS, $\sigma\tau$(A, B)). Offsets δ_x, δ_y, δ_t of the STS are defined with respect to the origin of the 3D space; d_x, d_y, d_t are respectively determined by the spatio-temporal shadows of A and B.

Because we are associating intervals to spatio-temporal presentations, we use interval relations [4] for expressing object composition in space and time. This is possible because spatial relations can be expressed using Allen relations [3]. Let $i \in \{x, y, t\}$ be a dimension and A_i, B_i be the respective intervals in i of A and B. The spatio-temporal relationship $\sigma\tau$(A, B) is composed of predicates r_x(A, B), r_y(A, B), r_t(A, B), where $r \in \{$none, seq, par, before, meet, overlap, start, during, finish, equal, bi, mi, oi, si, di, fi$\}$. Each predicate $r_i : \mathcal{P} \times \mathcal{P} \to$ boolean is verified if the shadows of A_i and B_i are arranged according to the constraints of r_i as defined in [3].

In the following, we introduce predicates that describe interval relations in terms of shadows:

- $none_i(A, B)$ denotes that two object intervals are independently arranged in one dimension i. For instance, the fact that a title A and an explanation B should be executed at the same time is expressed as follows (STS, $\sigma_T(A = (STS_A, \textbf{title}), B = (STS_B, \textbf{explanation})))$, where σ_T is defined by $none_x(A, B)$, $none_y(A, B)$ and $equal_t(A, B)$.
- $seq_i(A, B)$ describes a sequential arrangement. This relation generalizes relations before (with a gap), meet (with no gap), and their inverses bi, mi.
- $par_i(A, B)$ describes a parallel arrangement, where intervals A_i and B_i overlap. It generalizes relations overlap, start, during, finish, equal, and their inverses oi, si, di, fi.

4 Building and Querying Multimedia Presentations

We conducted an implementation of our spatio-temporal model on an experimental MDBMS built upon the O_2 system [5]. In this section, we show how to build presentations combining and reusing pre-existing data and presentations stored in the MDBMS.

4.1 An Object Schema for Generic Presentations

We defined an object schema for presentations that implements our spatio-temporal model. Our approach extends O_2 to offer multimedia presentation management considering spatio-temporal aspects. We take advantage of OQL (Object Query Language) functional aspects and we define methods (suitable for multimedia extensions) that implement spatio-temporal relations. The extensions address (i) characterization of spatio-temporal presentations with spatio-temporal relations and attributes, (ii) functions to build new presentations and to present multimedia query results.

Figure 3 shows our UML object schema. Six classes implement our spatio-temporal extension. Presentations are instances of the Graph_show class. A Graph_show consists of a set of elements that are instances of the abstract class SO. The SO models any Object to be presented describing its spatial and temporal attributes, i.e., the position and the size in space and time.

An SO may be SO_Single or SO_Compound. An SO_Single is specialized to represent text, image, audio and video. Spatio-temporal relations are instances of the class ST_relation that describes the relation between two components A and B. Components are SO instances. The ST_relation class offers boolean methods to verify spatio-temporal relations.

For temporal aspects, we have implemented Allen interval relations as methods. Spatial aspects are not naturally expressed using interval relations. For

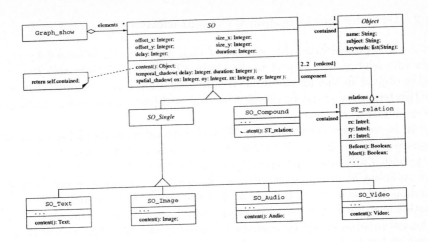

Fig. 3. Schema.

building or querying presentations users specify the way a set of objects are synchronized in time and space (i.e., on the screen). As shown before, interval relations are a way to express object synchronization. However, we do not expect users to use them at definition time. First, because it is not a natural way for defining spatial aspects. Second, we assume that specific languages and user friendly interfaces are provided for that purpose.

We adopt the approaches of geographical and spatial database systems [8, 9, 20] to express them. Spatial relations are classified in topological, directional and metric. Topological relations characterize the fact that spatial areas may overlap, touch or be disjoint. Directional relations concern the order of spatial objects. They are used as a selection criterion dividing the space in partitions, e.g., Grenoble is contained in the southeast region of France. Metric relations evaluate spatial distances between objects, e.g., Lyon is near Grenoble, Paris is far from Grenoble, etc.

We chose topological and directional relations because they can be expressed using interval relations. We exclude metric ones because their semantics is application dependent and subject to fuzzy interpretations. Further, an interesting particularity of directional and topological relations is that combining them in spatial descriptions allows to express distances in qualitative terms. For instance, a title on top of a map may be described using *north* and *touch*.

The SO class defines methods that associate new spatial and temporal attributes to an Object: spatial_shadow, temporal_shadow. This means that we create new presentations for an object. We also implemented three functions to construct and execute presentations. The function present(p: set(SO)) builds and plays a presentation. Similarly, the function present_seq(p: set(SO)) builds presentations where objects are sequentially arranged in time. Finally, create_presentation($name$: $string, p$: set(SO)) stores presentation p with $name$ as a persistent root.

4.2 Defining Spatio-temporal Presentations

In a given presentation, the position of each object is characterized by (1) an absolute relation with respect to the origin; (2) relative relations with respect to other objects in this presentation. Relative relations can be expressed in qualitative terms (by spatio-temporal relations) with(out) quantitative information (e.g., duration, distances).

In [3] we describe the mapping between interval relations and spatial definitions represented by the SS. Each SS component provides quantitative knowledge, either absolute or relative. However, for some relations, their semantics is not sufficient to interpret quantitative knowledge. For instance, the compound relation A *disjoint* B and B *south* of A characterizes absolute and relative information in y, but it does not characterize absolute and relative information in x. This information should be computed using d_{A_x} and d_{B_x}: if A *disjoint* B and B *south* of A with $d_{A_x} > d_{B_x}$ (as in the previous example), then δ_{A_x} is an absolute distance and δ_{B_x} is a relative one.

As in [10], we make the distinction between topological relations which may (not) be naturally combined with directional relations. The first group is composed by disjoint, touch, overlap, cover and cover_by [3]. The second group is composed by inside, contain, and equal. When used with topological relations of the second group, directional relations do not add information about space configuration (equal) or they do not specify a direction using only qualitative information (inside and contain). The use of the quantitative information of SS_A and SS_B allows to deduce a directional relation. This may lead to fuzzy interpretations and this is part of our future work (see Section 6).

4.3 Building presentations as Query Results

The objects that belong to a presentation can be retrieved and presented according to new spatio-temporal specifications. Consider the multimedia presentation of Figure 2 stored as a collection of SO instances accessible through the database entry point Show. The following query retrieves objects in Show that appear to the south of the French map.

```
present_seq(
        select   r.A.spatial_shadow( 100, 100, r.A.size_x, r.A.size_y )
                    .temporal_shadow( 0, 5 )
        from     e in Show.elements, r in e.relations
        where    r.South and r.B.content.name = "FrenchMap"   )
```

The resulting presentation shows objects sequentially without delay between them (present_seq), each one at position (100, 100) during five seconds. Furthermore, each object has descriptive attributes and membership relations with different presentations. Thus, presentations can also be specified referring to object attributes (e.g., name, subject, keywords, etc.), independently of spatio-temporal characteristics.

A Taxonomy for Spatio-temporal Queries Because there exists a rich variety of spatial, temporal and spatio-temporal configurations, we classify queries to build presentations. We identify a total of 15 spatio/temporal types. Depending on the type of information used to specify spatio-temporal presentations, queries are absolute, relative and absolute-relative Moreover, if spatial and temporal queries are combined, 6 additional types can be defined. In the following we give examples assuming that *left and lower parts of the screen* are defined respectively by $x < 300$ and $y > 700$.

Absolute queries refer to locations (in space and/or in time) according to the origin. For example, *which objects are presented in the lower part of the screen during the first 200 seconds of the presentation* Show?

```
select   e
from     e in Show.elements
where    e.offset_x >= 700 and e.delay + e.duration <= 200
```

Relative queries are specified using qualitative (i.e., spatial and/or temporal relations) and/or quantitative information with respect to a given object. For example, in the query: *which objects of* Show *overlap Grenoble and are presented before it?* Grenoble is the reference object from which relative information is specified: *objects that overlap Grenoble and are presented 30 seconds before it.*

```
select   r.A
from     e in Show.elements, r in e.relations
where    r.Spatial_Overlap and
         r.Before and r.B.delay >= 30 and r.B.content.name = "Grenoble"
```

Absolute-Relative queries build presentations from objects that match absolute and relative relations. Consider a configuration where images of French cities appear at the *left part of the screen*. Also, assume that an image of Grenoble is presented in another part of the screen. We may be interested in retrieving objects presented at the *left part of the screen* and to the *northwest* of the image of Grenoble.

The above description addresses both absolute spatial information (i.e., at the *left part of the screen*) and relative one (i.e., to the *northwest* of Grenoble). Temporal absolute-relative restrictions can be added. For example, we do not want objects that appear before second 70 and retrieve objects which presentation starts *70 seconds after the beginning* of Show and *before* Grenoble. Note here the mixing of absolute and relative restrictions.

Finally, we can combine absolute and relative (temporal)spatial restrictions. This is shown in the following query: *objects that start 70 seconds after the beginning of* Show *and before Grenoble. The objects must be presented at the left part of the screen and to the northwest of Grenoble.*

```
select   r.A
from     e in Show.elements, r in e.relations
where    r.Northwest and r.A.offset_x < 300 and
         r.Before and r.A.delay > 70 and r.B.content.name = "Grenoble"
```

So far, we have studied fully specified presentations but it is important to notice that δ and d may have also free (undetermined) values [1]. Free values represent open intervals. For instance, a free delay models the fact that the user is required to do a specific action in order to trigger the presentation which will last for a duration d. If d is itself undefined, this means that the user is requested to stop the presentation. This is useful for modeling interactive multimedia presentations and hypermedia links.

Our work can be extended to address presentation interaction, considering aspects such as synchronized operations (e.g., a particular object is displayed when the narrator in the audio starts talking about it), control buttons (e.g., buttons known from video-recorders, such as stop, fast-forward and rewind) and hyper-links (presentation interaction). We believe that free values are a general representation for defining and executing presentations that include these types of attributes.

Free values impact also on definition and querying aspects: How to answer queries that concern undetermined values? How to extend query languages to support such values? Even if some works have been done for extending multimedia query languages (MOQL) [14], free values are still an open problem that we want to explore.

Other research interests concern definition, querying and execution of presentations in a 4D-space. We aim to extend our approach by incorporating virtual space modeling (VRML) and consider aspects such as orientation, views, etc. Finally, few works have addressed indexation for multimedia applications. We are interested in studying indexation algorithms in order to define a semantic-based indexation environment.

Acknowledgments Thanks to C. COLLET for her careful reading and useful discussions and in general to all the members of the group STORM who have contributed to this work.

References

1. M. Adiba. STORM: an object-oriented multimedia DBMS. In K.Nowsu, B. Thuraisingham, and B. Berra, editors, *Multimedia Database Management Systems. Design and Implementation Strategies*, chapter 3, pages 47–88. Kluwer Academic Publishers, 1996.
2. M. Adiba, R. Lozano, H. Martin, and F. Mocellin. Management of multimedia data using an object-oriented database system. In *Proc. of DEXA'97 Workshop on Database and Expert Systems Applications*, September 1997.
3. M. Adiba and J. L. Zechinelli-Martini. Managing spatio-temporal multimedia presentations as database objects. Technical Report to be published, LSR - IMAG, Grenoble - France, 1999.
4. J. F. Allen. Maintaining knowledge about temporal intervals. *Communications of the ACM*, 26(11):832–843, November 1983.
5. F. Bancilhon, C. Delobel, and P. Kanellakis. *Building an Object-Oriented Database System: The story of O_2*. Morgan Kaufmann, 1992.

6. E. Bertino and E. Ferrari. Temporal synchronization models for multimedia data. *IEEE Transactions on Knowledge and Data Engineering*, 10(4), July/August 1998.
7. M. Echiffre, C. Marchisio, P. Marchisio, P. Panicciari, and S. Del Rossi. MHEG-5—Aims, concepts, and implementation issues. *IEEE MultiMedia*, 5(1), 1998.
8. M. Egenhofer and R. Franzosa. Point-set topological spatial relations. *International Journal of Geographical Information Systems*, 5(2):161–174, 1991.
9. V. Gaede and O. Günther. Multidimensional access methods. *ACM Computing Surveys*, 30(2):170–231, June 1998.
10. D. Hernández. *Qualitative Representation of Spatial Knowledge*, volume 804 of *Lecture Notes in Artificial Intelligence*. Springer-Verlag, 1994.
11. Information processing - Text and office systems - Standard Generalized Markup Language: SGML (ISO 8879). International Standards Organization, 1986.
12. Information processing systems - Computer graphics and image processing - Presentation Environment for Multimedia Objects (PREMO). Working Draft ISO/IEC JTC 1/SC 24 WG 6 N 032, International Standards Organization, 1994.
13. Information technology - Hypermedia/Time-based structuring language: HyTime (ISO/IEC 10744). International Standards Organization, 1997.
14. J. Z. Li. Modeling and querying multimedia data. Technical Report TR 98-05, Department of Computing Science, University of Alberta, March 1998.
15. R. Lozano and H. Martin. Querying virtual videos using path and temporal expressions. In *Proc. of the ACM Symposium on Applied Computing Multimedia Systems Track*, February 1998.
16. R. Lozano, F. Mocellin, M. Adiba, and H. Martin. An object DBMS for multimedia presentations including video data. In *Demonstration Proc. of the 12th European Conference on Object-Oriented Programming*, July 1998.
17. S. Marcus and V.S. Subrahmanian. Towards a theory of multimedia database systems. In V.S. Subrahmanian and Sushil Jajodia, editors, *Multimedia Database Systems. Issues and Research Directions*, pages 1–35. Springer-Verlag, 1996.
18. H. Martin. Specification of intentional multimedia presentations using an object-oriented database. In *Proc. of the International Symposium on Digital Media Information Base*, November 1997.
19. M. T. Özsu, D. Szafron, G. El-Medani, and C. Vittal. An object-oriented multimedia database system for a news-on-demand application. *ACM Multimedia Systems*, 3:182–203, 1995.
20. D. Papadias, N. Karacapilidis, and D. Arkoumanis. Processing fuzzy spatial queries: A configuration similarity approach. *To appear in International Journal of Geographic Information Science*, 13(2), 1999. http://www.cs.ust.hk/faculty/dimitris/publications.htm.
21. M. Vazirgiannis, Y. Theodoridis, and T. Sellis. Spatio-temporal composition and indexing for large multimedia applications. *ACM/Springer-Verlag Multimedia Journal*, 6(4), 1998.
22. Extensible Markup Language (XML). Recommendation REC-xml-19980210, World Wide Web Consortium (W3D), 1998. http://www.w3.org/TR/REC-xml.
23. Synchronized Multimedia Integration Language (SMIL). Recommendation REC-smil-19980615, World Wide Web Consortium (W3D), 1998. http://www.w3.org/TR/REC-smil.

WWW Bookmark Modeling and Visualization: A Fuzzy Based Approach

Costas Petrou, Dimitrios Charitos, Drakoulis Martakos

Department of Informatics, National and Kapodistrian University of Athens
TYPA Buildings, Ilisia, 15771, Athens, Greece
{cpetrou, virtual, martakos}@di.uoa.gr

Abstract. Bookmarks are the facilities found in current web browsers, which allow a user to revisit a WWW page. Due to the large number of bookmarks stored by the majority of WWW users, a series of problems, which may hinder the search for information within bookmarks, are identified. This paper proposes a novel system, which supports the organization of bookmarks and also suggests a 3D spatial metaphor as a visualization technique for navigating within bookmark collections.

1. Introduction

Due to the vast amount of information currently available on the WWW and its continuously encountered prolific growth, web browsers have been geared with facilities that would allow a user to revisit a node. Jakob Nielsen [1] defines the purpose of bookmarks as: the "marking" of a hypertext node which characterizes it as "interesting", for the purpose of gaining direct access to it at some later point in time. Extending this argument, he remarks that bookmarks can also be seen as objects in their own right. The obvious advantage of this approach is the added flexibility to move bookmarks around and to build different kinds of collections of bookmarks for different purposes. A set of requirements has been proposed in [2], regarding the design of a bookmarking system. We have refined these requirements and concluded the following points:

- The size of a typical bookmark list is significantly smaller than any kind of digital document repository. Therefore, we expect that the system can afford to store and manipulate a rich set of descriptive meta-information regarding bookmarks.
- The collection is highly evolutionary, as the user continuously updates it during his browsing sessions. This implies that the re-organization of the collection should follow any shift to user's conceptual space.
- The collection retains a subjective, user-oriented profile. Therefore, the subjectivity, which is inherent in bookmark categorization, must be captured and represented by the system. Originating from the theory of semantic nets, the idea of modeling bookmarks using graph-based representations has been previously tested (e.g., object-oriented modeling in General Magic's Magic Cap user interface [1]).

− The frequency of adding bookmarks is expected to be a small proportion of the frequency of visiting nodes. This allows for analyzing and processing the contents of the node without adding a considerable overhead to the system.

Irrespective of the approach that has been followed in terms of bookmarks organization, the user still has to cope with searching amongst a large number of bookmarks for choosing the most relevant to his interests. It is a current practice in web browsers to organize bookmarks in hierarchies, for facilitating bookmark search. However, a problem that users are usually faced with is that they end up with large hierarchies, which they cannot fully expand and effectively manipulate at the same time. Furthermore it is not possible to easily re-arrange bookmarks in a way that reflects users' ad hoc informational requirements.

As an answer to the aforementioned issues, this paper proposes a semantic modeling framework for shaping the bookmark "space" and suggests a corresponding 3D visualization for this "space". The proposed framework is able to capture both human and system derived meta-information which describes bookmarks. It also incorporates inference capabilities by exploiting fuzzy set theory and fuzzy logic.

2. Semantic framework of WWW bookmarks

2.1 Types of meta-information

We suggest an orthogonal categorization space for bookmark meta-information. The two axis of this space are:

− Reliability: denotes the degree of confidence that the meta-information remains valid, e.g. if the meta-information was captured in time T, it remains valid until the next time T+t when it is updated.
− Source: denotes the supplier of meta-information, ranging from system provided to human described. The intermediate values denote semi-automatically defined meta-information.

A visualization of this space is presented in Fig. 1.

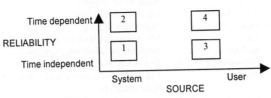

Fig. 1. The proposed meta-information space

Accordingly, the four limits of the space denoted by the boxes one to four, may be described as follows:

1. Meta-information is automatically extracted and always remains valid.
2. Meta-information is automatically extracted, its validity degrading through time.
3. Meta-information is user provided and time-invariant.
4. Meta-information is user provided and its validity degrades during time.

Thereafter, we use these four limits to characterize meta-information as *Type-1* through to *Type-4*. The prototype that has been built is capable of handling the following types of meta-information:

Type-1: Last time that the user has visited a node (in date/time). Mean-time spent during previous visits (in min). Mean-time for transferring the contents (in sec). Availability of the host (requests satisfied/total requests).

Type-3: A semantic model comprising Concepts, Relationships and Weights.

Between Type-1 and Type-3: A set of inference Rules, which augments the semantic model with deductive capabilities.

Between Type-1 and Type-2: A keyword index for the terms found in nodes. Size of the node in terms of bytes. "Profile" of the node: what type of content the bookmark has (dominating text, images, tables).

It has to be noted that the more the meta-information is concentrated nearby the start of the axis, the more system-provided and time-insensitive it is; thus it is "easier" and "safer" to obtain and use. The meta-information, supported by our prototype, conforms to this remark, without underestimating user-provided meta-information, which would be impossible for the system to automatically elaborate.

2.2 A Semantic model of bookmarks

The proposed model adopts a user-centered, domain-depended approach to adaptive bookmark modeling, based on semantic nets. The proposed Semantic model is effectively a kind of user defined semantic net ([3], [4]), enhanced with deductive elements. Fuzzy set theory and fuzzy logic have been employed for implementing this last feature. On the basis of the proposed semantic model, a bookmark is defined as Table 1 explains:

Table 1. Bookmark definition

Attribute	Domain	Comments
ID	number	Unique value for every bookmark
Title	text	Node's title
Reference	text	Node's URL
Size	number	Node's size in bytes
LastVisit	date/time	Last visit timestamp
SMeanTime	time	Mean time in node
TMeanTime	time	Mean time to transfer node
Availability	number	Requests satisfied/ total requests
Keywords	[keywordID]	List of keyword references
Profile	number	Encoded profile for the node, such as text, text with images etc.
Semantics	[(ConceptID/value)]	List of pairs (ConceptID/value)

The next paragraphs discuss the four building elements of the model:

Concepts provide user defined semantics for the bookmark. These semantics can be assigned with various gradients, which express the notion that the bookmark is partially described by the Concept. To accomplish this feature, each Concept corresponds to a fuzzy set. As suggested in [5], [6], systems which require human/expert involvement and rely heavily on human experience benefit more from the use of fuzzy modeling. User provided, lexical characterizations of bookmarks are mostly subjective and subject to user's perception of the node's content. Having to deal with such characterizations, we found that a semantic modeling of Concepts based on and exploiting fuzzy set theory and fuzzy logic may constantly model human knowledge and provide for approximate reasoning ([7], [8]).

Relationships represent user defined notional relationships between Concepts. They are uni-directional, one-to-one and named. The direction defines the way the relationship should be interpreted.

Rules are Multiple Input Single Output (MISO) Fuzzy Logic Controllers (FLCs). The input is Concept fuzzy values, while the output is a dynamically computed Concept value. The dependency graph of the input/output Concepts of the Rules is restricted to be a Directed Acyclic Graph.

Weights: Fuzzy variables. Every Concept is connected with a Weight that provides its domain of definition.

By defining instances of the aforementioned elements, the user constructs a semantic net in the form of a Schema. A user may create more than one Schemata, each of them representing a specific knowledge domain. To illustrate the notion of the Schema, let us consider the following scenario: a user searches the WWW for information about conferences. In such a scenario, the user could have defined a Schema (Fig. 2) for storing his conclusions about the nodes he has visited.

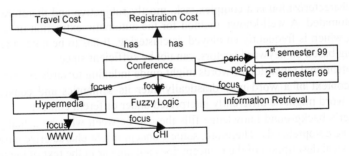

Fig. 2. A schema example

Suppose that given the previously described schema, the user adds a new Concept named "Worth Visit". He would like the system to automatically assign Concept values to newly added bookmarks under the assumption that if the bookmark is described as "Conference", it has a low registration cost, it focuses on fuzzy logic, and it is scheduled for the end of the 1st semester then the more worthy it is to participate in. Our prototype allows for the definition of Rules like this, using a format that imitates natural language. More than one sub-rules compose a Rule instance. For example, the following definition could be considered:

```
RULE1
SubRule1:IF Conference.has.RegistrationCost = "LOW" AND Con-
ference.focus.FuzzyLogic = "VERY" AND Confer-
ence.period.1stSemester = "BEGINNING" THEN WorthVisit =
"VERY"
```

3.1 3D visualization of complex data sets

It is generally accepted that graphical representations are a good way of communicating relationships among objects ([10]). The use of a graphical, three-dimensional spatial context for visualizing information may exploit the intrinsic skills that humans have for navigating in three-dimensional space and for detecting visual patterns there. Moreover, it is understood ([11], [12]) that three-dimensional space allows for a more effective arrangement of a large set of informational objects and for visualizing more attributes for each of these objects, than two-dimensional space does. Accordingly, recent advances in VR technology [13] have suggested that interactive visualizations of large information sets in a three-dimensional context may increase the amount of information that people can meaningfully manage.

Navigating within a complex and extensive informational space, such as WWW, may lead a user into suffering disorientation or the "lost in hyperspace" syndrome. For the purpose of decreasing the effect of such phenomena, several attempts have been made for visualizing the hypergraph structure of WWW. As relevant research ([2],[9],[11],[12],[14],[15]) suggests, at least three different types of requirements have to be considered:

Orientation/ Navigation Requirements: The user must know his current "position" within navigational space, perform more or less drastic "movements" within this space, be presented with an indication of how he reached his current location and, finally, have a visual clue of which are the permitted moves that he can proceed with.

Decision Support Requirements: The user must be supported in deciding his next move. This implies that the user must be provided with meta-information, which describes each possible destination and may aid him in differentiating amongst these destinations.

Usability Requirements: the user must be able to adjust the space in terms of details shown as well as to "reposition" himself so that the visualized part of the space that seems to be of more of interest is highlighted.

Relationships amongst WWW nodes are explicitly defined by links. A set of bookmarks, on the other hand, is a user-specific subset of the overall WWW content, where each node can be accessed directly and where existing links between nodes become irrelevant. Therefore, WWW links are not taken into account in the proposed visualization.

Following the relevant literature review ([13],[16],[17],[18]) it is hypothesized that it would be preferable to develop a three-dimensional visualization of the rich bookmarks meta-information, for the purpose of supporting user navigation within these bookmarks. To achieve that, an effective way of visualizing each type of meta-information as well as groups of relevant types had to be identified. A dynamic arrangement approach, in terms of arranging the elements of the visualization in 3D space, has been followed. This approach provides a user-centric visualization, well adapted to ad-hoc informational needs. In effect, a three-step procedure is proposed:

Firstly, the user poses certain selection criteria based on the semantics of bookmarks, in the form of a selection query. Secondly, the system parses the query and retrieves all bookmarks that partially satisfy the query, constructing an ordered list. Finally, the list order and the meta-information, which describes bookmarks, determine the visual form of each bookmark and the way it is positioned within the 3D space. The development of the system, based on the VRML 2.0 standard and Java, is in progress. Meanwhile, a prototype of such a system has been developed by utilizing Sense8's WorldUp® for simulating the proposed solution.

3.2 Posing selection criteria

A user can pose his preferences defining a SELECT query that better describes his current interests. 3D space is then shaped in order to "highlight" those bookmarks that better match (e.g. have a greater weight value) for the specified concepts. A simple Query has the form of:

```
SELECT Conference.focus.Hypermedia = "very" AND Hyperme-
dia.focus.WWW = "very" AND Conference.has.TravelCost = "Me-
dium"
```

This SELECT statement provides an example of a filtering of bookmarks according to user's preferences. For every bookmark that has been selected, an overall similarity with the selection criteria is computed. A weighted ordered list of bookmarks, which feeds the visualization component for further rendering, is then produced. Alternatively, the user may select a certain bookmark as representative of his current interests. The minimum distance of all bookmarks that share common Concepts is then computed in order to discover most similar bookmarks. In this case also, a weighted ordered list of bookmarks is produced.

3.3 Description of the 3D visualization

As suggested in 3.1, physical links amongst nodes are not taken into account in this paper. In any case, these links are likely to be of low density and represent conceptual relationships which have been determined by the author of the link and not by the reader. As a result, the proposed visualization exploits the meta-information, which has been either explicitly or implicitly derived by user actions and chooses not to render links. In contrast with the information relating to links, meta-information is rich, extensive and user defined. Each web page is represented by an orthogonal parallelepiped box. It is significant to take advantage of perspective as a spatial quality, which may aid users in differentiating between boxes positioned at different depths in relation to the user's viewpoint. Due to difficulties regarding the appreciation of the scale of objects in virtual environments [19], it is proposed that all boxes should be of the same size; as size degrades so distance from the user's viewpoint increases (Fig.3). By utilizing the ordered list, each bookmark is positioned in 3D space according to its relevance to the specific query. The environment extends over a "floor", which is represented by a horizontal plane at a 0 y-coordinate. Visualized bookmarks are arranged around the user's viewpoint, their distance from the pole being inversely proportional to the weight of the corresponding list item.

The content of each page is represented by a sphere, which is concentrically placed inside each box. The size of the sphere indicates the size of the page file (Size attribute) and the types of content that the page includes (Profile attribute) are represented by certain images, texture-mapped onto the sphere. Meanwhile, the transparency of the box's material corresponds to how recently this page was visited by the user (LastVisit attribute). The use of different rates of transparency on the box's material aims at utilizing Type-1 meta-information for visualizing Type-2 meta-information. The height at which each visualized bookmark is positioned, in relation to the "floor" (value of the y-coordinate) represents past experience gained regarding the destination of the link, in terms of difficulty with which the contents of a certain web page may be retrieved.

Fig. 3. View of a small selection of bookmarks from the base of the pole

In order to enhance user's orientation within the 3D space, a ray was designed for indicating the position of the user at all times. This ray emanates from the user's viewpoint and leaves a trace on the central pole as well as on the surface.

4. Conclusions and future work

The semantic framework described in this paper has several distinct features for modeling and visualizing WWW bookmark spaces. A number of conclusions are drawn based on these features:

- The Semantic model provides for capturing both the explicitly and implicitly obtained semantics of the bookmarked nodes. It also provides a great flexibility for constructing simple or more complex models, according to user's preferences and experience.
- The partial assignment of Concept values to bookmarks enriches the expressive capabilities of the model and also ensures the capturing of human ambiguity.
- The framework supports three different types for conceptually characterizing bookmarks: user-provided, based on user's preferences expressed in Rules, and system-provided. To the best of our knowledge, no other attempt has succeeded in supporting both of these types in a single, flexible and coherent framework.
- A 3D visualization metaphor has been constructed on top of the Semantic model, for rendering the elicited knowledge. The dynamic arrangement of the bookmarks in the 3D space results from user-defined selection criteria, thus providing a navigational "space", well adapted to current informational needs

Initial experimental results have demonstrated that the proposed visualization conforms with the prescribed visualization requirements for WWW bookmark visualization, as these have been stated in this paper. Implementation of a fully functioning visualization is under way and experimental evaluation of this system's effectiveness is scheduled for the immediate future.

References

[1] Nielsen, J.: Multimedia and Hypertext: The Internet and Beyond. AP Professional (1995)

[2] Maarek, Y., Shaul, I.: Automatically Organizing Bookmarks per Contents. WWW5 Conference, Paris, France (1996) 1321-1333

[3] Stillings, Neil, et al.: Cognitive Science: An Introduction. MIT Press (1995)

[4] Luger, G., et al.: Cognitive Science: The Science of Intelligent Systems. Academic Press (1994)

[5] Ross, T.: Fuzzy Logic with Engineering Applications. McGraw Hill (1995)

[6] Yan, J., Ryan, M., Power, J.: Using Fuzzy Logic Towards intelligent systems. Prentice Hall International (1994)

[7] Petrou, C., Martakos, D., Hadjiefthymiades, S.: Hypermedia Linking and Querying: A Fuzzy Based Approach. IEEE International Conference of Systems, Man, and Cybernetics (SMC'98), San Diego CA, USA (1998) 1235-1240

[8] Petrou, C., Martakos, D., Hadjiefthymiades, S.: Adding semantics to Hypermedia towards Link's enhancement and Dynamic Linking. Hypertext-Information Retrieval-Multimedia '97 Conference (HIM'97), Dortmund, Germany (1997) 175-190

[9] Chen, C.: Structuring and Visualizing the WWW by Generalized Similarity Analysis. Hypertext 97 Conference, Southampton, UK (1997) 177-186

[10] Fairchild, K. M.: Information Management Using Virtual Reality-Based Visualizations. In: Wexelblat, A. (ed.): Virtual Reality Applications and Explorations. Academic Press Professional, London (1993)

[11] Fowler, R., et al.: 3D Visualization of WWW Semantic Content for Browsing and Query Formulation. WebNet 96 Conference, San Francisco, CA, USA (1996)

[12] Mukherjea, S., Hara, Y.: Focus+Context Views of World-Wide Web Nodes. ACM Hypertext '97 Conference, Chaper Hill, NV, USA (1997) 187-196.

[13] Robertson, G.G., Mackinlay, J.D. and Card, S.K.: Cone Trees: Animated 3D Visualizations of Hierarchical Information. CHI '91 Proceedings: Human Factors in Computing Systems, New York, USA (1991) 189-194

[14] Carriere, J., Kazman, R.: WebQuery: Searching and Visualizing the Web through Connectivity. WWW6 Conference, Santa Clara, CA, USA (1997)

[15] Huang, M., et al.: Dynamic Web navigation with information filtering and animated visual display. APWeb98 Conference, Beijing, China, (1998) 63-71

[16] Fairchild, K.M., Poltrock, S.E. and Furnas, G.W.: SemNet: Three-Dimensional Graphic Representations of Large Knowledge Spaces. In: Cognitive Science and Its Applications for Human-Computer Interaction. Fairlawn, NJ. Lawrence Erlbaum Associates (1988)

[17] Benford, S., et al.: Networked Virtual Reality and Cooperative Work. Presence: Teleoperators and Virtual Environments, Vol.4, No.4. MIT Press (1995)

[18] Andrews, K.: Visualising Cyberspace: Information Visualisation in the Harmony Internet Browser. Proceedings of the 1st IEEE Symposium on Information Visualisation, Atlanta GA (1995) 97-104

[19] Charitos, D.: The Architectural Aspect of Designing Space in Virtual Environments. PhD Thesis submitted at the University of Strathclyde, Faculty of Engineering, (1998)

PTA – A Personal Translation Assistant for Accessing the World Wide Web

Werner Winiwarter

Institute of Applied Computer Science and Information Systems,
University of Vienna, Liebiggasse 4/3, A-1010 Wien, Austria
`winiwarter@acm.org`

Abstract. In this paper we present PTA, a Personal Translation Assistant for the simple access to foreign Web pages through the World Wide Web. For that purpose we have designed and implemented a language learning environment, which uses normal Web browser technology to display foreign Web pages. Before displaying a foreign Web page, we analyze it at the word and sentence level to add links to translations of words and sentences, which are displayed in a separate frame after clicking at the corresponding entry in the source text. The translation rules are completely transparent to the user and can be freely adapted to match the user's personal linguistic preferences.

1 Introduction

The last few years have witnessed a rapid expansion of the World Wide Web, in particular regarding non-English Web pages. This wealth of available multilingual information also led to a renewed interest in learning foreign languages. After a language student reaches a certain level of competence in a foreign language, the reading of written material in this language provides an excellent means for increasing the fluency in this language. The student can learn new terminology or grammatical structures in their natural context without much effort. For that purpose the Web supplies a large number of online material in many languages, e.g. newspapers or journals.

Our aim was therefore to build a *Personal Translation Assistant (PTA)*, which assists the language student in reading foreign texts but only to that extent as it is really necessary for the student. We have designed and implemented a language learning environment, which applies normal Web browser technology to the display of Web pages in foreign languages. Before we display a foreign Web page in the browser, we analyze the page at the word and sentence level and add links to translations. These translations are displayed in a separate frame only after clicking on the corresponding position in the source text.

This design concept differs from traditional online dictionaries and machine translation systems in that it keeps the attention of the student at the source text. In particular it avoids the continuous switching between two parallel texts as in full machine translation systems, which hinders rather than promotes the student from thinking in the new language.

In PTA we follow the *transfer-based translation* approach (for good reviews on machine translation see [1, 2]). For the transfer step we apply *translation rules*, which are fully transparent to the language student. The simple syntax makes it easy for the student to modify existing rules or to add new rules to the rule base. This feature is essential to enable the adaptation of the translation component so that it can be tuned to the user's linguistic preferences.

We have implemented PTA by using the deductive database system *XSB* [3]. XSB supplies a powerful framework for the development of PTA. In particular, XSB enables pure declarative logic programs in contrast to the restrictions of the SLD evaluation strategy of Prolog. Since XSB was especially developed for data-oriented applications, one of its main aims is the ability to load large amounts of data quickly. Therefore, it provides fast asserting and retracting as well as the efficient execution of asserted code, which is essential for the scalability in large language learning applications.

The rest of the paper is organized as follows. First we give a brief overview of the system architecture and the user interface. Next we explain the components for the natural language analysis and generation. Finally, we provide a detailed description of the translation rules used in PTA. Throughout this paper we use examples from a first case study for the access to Portuguese Web pages, which has been carried out with German-speaking language students at the University of Vienna.

2 System Architecture

The system architecture of PTA is displayed in Fig. 1. Web pages in the source language are first *segmented* into words and sentences. Then we perform a morpho-lexical *analysis* of the source text by accessing a *source lexicon*. For full translation we apply the *translation rules* during the *transfer* step. Finally, the *generation* step produces the output in the target language by means of a *target lexicon*. The output of PTA is one of the following four choices:

- *Links to dictionary forms:* For each word of the source text which can be found in the source lexicon a link to the dictionary form of the word in the source lexicon as well as a list of its translations into the target language is created. Figure 2 shows an example of the output for a CNN story about John Glenn's recent space adventure.
- *Links to inflected forms:* In contrast to the links to the dictionary forms, the inflected form of the word in the source text and the corresponding correct inflections of the translations into the target language are displayed.
- *Links to word translation:* For each sentence of the source text a literal translation of each word in the sentence is generated.
- *Links to full translation:* Finally, this output consists of a full translation for each sentence.

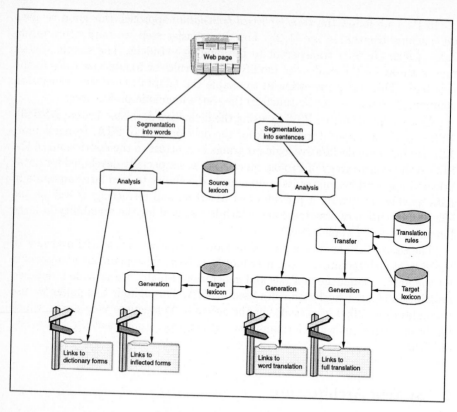

Fig. 1. System architecture

3 Analysis and Generation

We explain the details of the analysis and generation component by making use of the example in Fig. 3. The details of the transfer step are omitted; they are treated separately in Sect. 4. The user input is first analyzed by accessing the source lexicon. To guarantee a compact and efficient representation of the lexical knowledge, we only store the *canonical forms* of the words (i.e. word stems). Word endings of inflected words are represented as separate entries in the lexicon. An exception to this principle is only made for irregular word forms, for which we store the inflections explicitly. Syntactic features such as case, number, etc., are assigned to the appropriate entries for words and word endings. The prototypes of the example entries in Fig. 3 are defined as follows:

- sverb(Verb_stem, Translation_list, Conjugation_class).
- sconj(Conjugation_class, Ending, Mood, Tense, Number, Person).
- sart(Article, Translation, Definitness, Gender, Number).
- sadj(Adjective_stem, Translation_list, Declension_class).
- sadjdecl(Declension_class, Ending, Gender, Number).

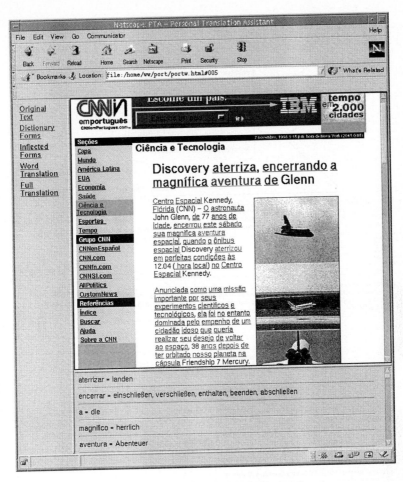

Fig. 2. Example of links to dictionary forms

- snoun(Noun_stem, Translation_list, Declension_class, Gender).
- snoundecl(Declension_class, Ending, Number).
- sword(Word, Word_class, Translation_list).

Each word token in the sentence is *lemmatized*, i.e. it is reduced to its word stem. The result of the analysis process is a *token list*, which indicates for each entry: the word stem, the translation into the target language, and the syntactic features. If there exist several entries in the list of translations of a word, the first entry is selected as default translation. This decision can be overruled by an appropriate translation rule during the transfer step, e.g. for the translation of the verb "encerrar" in Fig. 3.

The value of a syntactic feature is left uninstantiated if it cannot be derived from the user input or if it is controlled by the target language. An example of the former condition is the declension according to the case, which does not

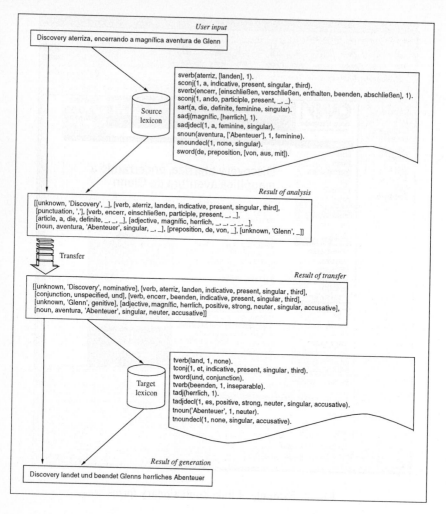

Fig. 3. Example of analysis and generation

exist in Portuguese, an example of the latter is the gender of nouns, which might differ between Portuguese and German. Besides certain changes to the sentence structure and the translation of words and phrases, the transfer step instantiates all the syntactic features with the correct values according to the translation rules. If the transfer step inserts new words into the token list, the word stem in the source language is left unspecified.

The generation step looks up the canonical forms of the word translations in the target lexicon. It considers the restrictions of the indicated syntactic features in the token list and creates the correct morphological surface forms of the individual word tokens.

The arguments of the predicates for the target lexicon in Fig. 3 have the following meaning:

- tverb(Verb_stem, Conjugation_class, Prefix).
- tconj(Conjugation_class, Ending, Mood, Tense, Number, Person).
- tword(Word, Word_class).
- tadj(Adjective_stem, Declension_class).
- tadjdecl(Declension_class, Ending, Comparison, Inflexion, Gender, Number, Case).
- tnoun(Noun_stem, Declension_class, Gender).
- tnoundecl(Declension_class, Ending, Number, Case).

The indication of the prefix for verbs is of special importance to the formation of the past participle. It has to be distinguished between verbs with no prefix, inseparable or separable prefix. In addition to irregular word forms we also consider word derivations, compound nouns, and the important morphological phenomena ablaut, elision, and binding sounds. For a more detailed discussion of the morpho-lexical treatment of the German language see [4].

An important feature of PTA is its user-friendly module for the addition of new terms to the source or target lexicon. The system makes guesses about the word class and the syntactic features of the word to make the task of inserting new lexical entries as easy as possible for the user. The user only has to correct the suggestions of the system to consider exceptional cases. Besides the addition of new words, it is also of high relevance that the user can freely edit existing lexicon entries, in particular to append additional word senses to the list of translations. Furthermore, we also provide the possibility to directly import a large number of new words from a vocabulary list.

4 Translation Rules

For a full translation of sentences from a foreign language, the *transfer step* is the crucial component because it bridges the gap between the analysis of the sentence in the source language and the generation of the corresponding sentence in the target language. In contrast to many commercial machine translation products, PTA performs this transfer step based on a flexible set of translation rules, which is fully transparent to the user. For each translated sentence the user can activate an *explanation component*. It provides the user with the information about which rules have been applied in which sequence and for what reason. With the help of this data the user can freely edit the rule base to improve the performance of the translation component. He can add new rules to cover new linguistic phenomena or he can generalize or refine existing rules to adapt the translation component to his personal linguistic preferences. Each *translation rule* consists of the following four parts:

- the *category*,
- the *rule number* within the category,
- a list of *conditions*, which have to be satisfied to make the rule applicable,
- a list of *actions*, which have to be performed on the token list.

The *category* indicates different types of linguistic tasks during the translation process. So far, we consider the following 7 categories:

1. the translation of compounds,
2. the selection of the correct entry from the list of translations of a word,
3. syntactic changes,
4. the translation of prepositions,
5. the selection of the correct case for prepositions with ambiguous case,
6. long-distance syntactic changes,
7. the determination of uninstantiated syntactic features.

Within each category the rules are numbered to indicate the sequence of the rule application. This means that the order of rule application is controlled by the category and within each category by the *rule number*. This control mechanism allows an efficient performance of the rule application component and makes it possible for the user to tune the system behavior to his specific needs.

We have implemented a large number of different types of *conditions*. For that purpose we distinguish between *absolute conditions* and *relative conditions*. Whereas absolute conditions can take any position in the list of conditions, relative conditions rely on a preceding absolute condition for their interpretation. Therefore, relative conditions must always follow absolute conditions in the list of conditions. The following list shows those conditions which turned out to be most useful for the translation process:

1. *absolute conditions:*
   - `find(C)`: the sentence must contain a word belonging to the class `C`,
   - `findfeat(C, F, V)`: the sentence must contain a word belonging to the class `C` and the value of the feature `F` must equal `V`,
   - `findword(W)`: the sentence must contain the word `W`.

2. *relative conditions:*
   - `prevword(W)`, `nextword(W)`: the previous/next word must be `W`,
   - `prevfeat(C, F, V)`, `nextfeat(C, F, V)`: the previous/next word must belong to the class `C` and the value of the feature `F` must equal `V`,
   - `prev(C)`, `next(C)`: the previous/next word must belong to the class `C`,
   - `nphead(W)`: the head noun of the noun phrase for the qualifier in the absolute condition must be `W`,
   - `pphead(W)`: the head noun of the prepositional phrase for the preposition in the absolute condition must be `W`,
   - `vphead(W)`: the head verb of the verb phrase for the qualifier in the absolute condition must be `W`,
   - `objhead(W)`: the head noun of the object for the verb in the absolute condition must be `W`.

Besides the default interpretation of a condition as required, it is also possible to define a condition as optional, recursive, or negated.

Regarding the *action part* of the translation rules, we also support a large collection of different transformations of the token list. To specify the position in the token list where the action should be applied, we use the position information from the condition part as a reference. This means that we indicate *relative positions* in the action part, which correspond to the sequence number of the corresponding entry in the list of conditions. The action is then performed at the position of this list entry in the token list.

The following predicates are the most common ones, they form a redundant set of commands because we added many shortcuts for the convenience of the user:

1. *general transformations:*
   - neworder(P, L): removes all entries of the condition part from the token list and inserts them in a new order after the word at position P according to the sequence information in L, which is written as a list of positions [P1,P2,...],
   - delete(P): deletes the word at position P,
   - insert(P, W): inserts the word W after the word at position P,
   - insbef(P, W): inserts the word W before the word at position P,
   - replword(P, W): replaces the word at position P with the word W,
   - replsense(P, S): replaces the translation of the word at position P with the new sense S.

2. *specific transformations:*
   - sepprep(P): breaks the fusion of an article and a preposition, which is written as one word at position P, into two separate entries,
   - fuseprep(P): fuses the preposition at position P and the preceding article,
   - dernv(P): derives a noun from the verb at position P,
   - insdefart(P): inserts a definite article before the word at position P,
   - movend(P): moves the verb at position P to the end of the clause (German word order in dependent clauses).

3. *manipulation of syntactic features:*
   - chfeat(P, F, V): changes the value of the feature F to V for the word at position P,
   - chimp(P): changes the tense of the verb at position P to "imperfect",
   - chinfzu(P): changes the mood of the verb at position P to "zu-infinitive" (infinitive with "zu", specific German construction),
   - genitive(P): changes the case of the word at position P to "genitive",
   - dative(P): changes the case of the word at position P to "dative",
   - accusative(P): changes the case of the word at position P to "accusative",
   - copyfeat(P1, P2): copies the syntactic features from the word at position P1 to the word at position P2,
   - copyprep(P): copies the case of the preposition at position P to the other members of the prepositional phrase,
   - copynoun(P): copies the gender and the number of the head noun at position P to the other members of the noun phrase,

- `detverb(P)`: determines the case of the subject and the object for the verb at position P,
- `detnoun(P)`: determines the gender of the noun at position P and changes, if necessary, the number of the noun, e.g. for plural nouns in the source language that are expressed as singular nouns in the target language,
- `detadj(P)`: determines the correct comparison and inflexion of the adjective at position P,
- `detposs(P)`: determines the correct gender of the possessive pronoun at position P if the possessive pronoun in the source language possesses no gender; the information is derived from the gender of the preceding antecedent.

To obtain the necessary information about the syntactic features of the words in the target language, the transfer step accesses the target lexicon (see Sect. 3). The language for the specification of translation rules is very comprehensive and generic to equip the user with a powerful tool for his personal translation needs. According to his individual preferences, the user can select the most useful subset of commands. Furthermore, the user can also define his own specific predicates for conditions or actions based on more general predicates, e.g. the above-mentioned predicate `dative(P)` can be defined as: `dative(P) :- chfeat(P, case, dative)`. Figure 4 shows the application of the translation rules for the example sentence from Fig. 3.

5 Conclusion

In this paper we have presented the PTA system, which aims at providing a new kind of language learning environment that goes beyond the limitations of existing online dictionaries and machine translation systems. By making full use of the powerful logic programming facilities of the deductive database system XSB, we have implemented a flexible and user-friendly translation assistant for the access to foreign Web pages.

After finishing the implementation of PTA, we have started a first case study with German-speaking language students for an advanced course in Portuguese. First reactions by the students were very positive. The definition language used for the specification of the translation rules is easy to learn and after a short training session the students can start immediately to formulate their own translation rules. A detailed evaluation study to measure the impact of PTA on language instruction along the dimensions engagement, effectiveness, and viability is still the topic of ongoing research.

Future work will concentrate on the extension of the PTA system to other language pairs. In particular, we have already started to develop a new version for the translation of Japanese Web pages (for first results see [5]). Finally, we also plan to tackle the challenging task of learning the translation rules automatically. This means that the user only has to supply the improved version of a translation and the system performs the automatic adaptation of the rule base.

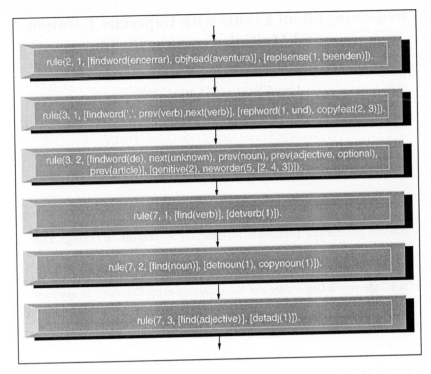

Fig. 4. Example of translation rules

We believe that our personal translation assistant PTA represents a first step towards the important goal of providing new intelligent tools for managing the available wealth of information in the coming multilingual information society. Human language technology products such as PTA will represent the key to both accessibility and usability in future global markets.

References

1. Hutchins, W. J., Somers, H. L.: An Introduction to Machine Translation. Academic Press, London (1992)
2. Lewis, D.: Machine Translation in a Modern Languages Curriculum. Computer Assisted Language Learning, **10**:3 (1997) 255–271
3. Sagonas, K., Swift, T., Warren, D. S.: XSB as an Efficient Deductive Database Engine. In: Proc. of the ACM SIGMOD International Conference on Management of Data (1994) 442–453
4. Winiwarter, W.: MIDAS – the Morphological Component of the IDA System for Efficient Natural Language Interface Design. In: Proc. of the International Conference on Database and Expert Systems Applications (1995) 584–593
5. Winiwarter, W.: A Language Learning Environment for Assisting Foreigners in Reading Japanese Web Pages. In: Proc. of the International Congress on Terminology and Knowledge Engineering (1999)

Reasoning about Events with Imprecise Location and Multiple Granularities

Luca Chittaro and Carlo Combi

Dipartimento di Matematica e Informatica, Università di Udine,
Via delle Scienze, 206, 33100 Udine - ITALY
{chittaro|combi}@dimi.uniud.it

Abstract. In many real-world applications, temporal information is often imprecise about the temporal location of events (*indeterminacy*) and comes at different granularities. Formalisms for reasoning about events and change, such as the Event Calculus (EC) and the Situation Calculus, do not usually provide mechanisms for handling such data, and very little research has been devoted to the goal of extending them with these capabilities. In this paper, we propose TGIC (Temporal Granularity and Indeterminacy event Calculus), an approach to represent events with imprecise location and to deal with them on different timelines, based on the EC ontology.

1 Introduction

In many real-world applications, temporal information is often imprecise about the temporal location of events (*indeterminacy*) and comes at different granularities [8]. Temporal granularity and indeterminacy are thus emerging as crucial requirements for the advancement of intelligent information systems which have to store, manage, and reason about temporal data. Consider, for example, these events taken from the application - a temporal database for cardiological patients - we are considering in our research [4], [6]: "between 2 PM and 4 PM on May 5, 1996, the patient suffered a myocardial infarction", "he started the therapy with thrombolytics in July 1995", "on October 12, 1996, he had a follow-up visit". The three events happened at the hours, months, and days timelines, respectively. Moreover, the first event cannot be precisely located on its timeline.

The two well-known formalisms for reasoning about actions, events and change, i.e. the Situation Calculus [10] and the Event Calculus (EC) [9], do not provide mechanisms for handling temporal indeterminacy and granularity, and very little research has been devoted to the goal of extending them with different granularities. In this work, we propose, using the EC ontology, a novel approach (TGIC, Temporal Granularity and Indeterminacy event Calculus) to represent events with imprecise location and to deal with different timelines.

The notions of event, property, timepoint and time interval are the primitives of the EC ontology: *events* happen at *timepoints* and initiate and/or terminate *time intervals* over which some *property* holds. Properties are assumed to persist until the occurrence of an event interrupts them (default persistence). An event occurrence can be represented by associating the event to the timepoint at which it occurred, e.g. by means of the happens(event,timePoint) clause. EC derives the maximal validity intervals (MVIs) over which properties hold. A MVI is maximal in the sense that it cannot be properly contained in any other validity interval. MVIs for a property p are obtained in response to a mholds_for(p, MVI) query. A property has not to be valid at both endpoints of a MVI: in the following, we thus adopt the convention that time intervals are closed to the left and open to the right.

2 Motivating Examples

In this section, we present two simple clinical examples concerning patients with cardiological pathologies. In particular, the examples are related to the problem of diagnosing and following up heart failure [1]. We concentrate here on a small fragment of expert knowledge concerning the evaluation of the property hfRisk, i.e. the presence of an heart failure risk which requires special surveillance by clinicians in a considered cardiological patient. Among various factors, this property can be initiated by four different events: (i) smDeltaBP: a measurement of systolic and diastolic blood pressure (BP) on the patient reveals an abnormal difference (too small) between the two values; (ii) saD: sudden appearance of dyspnea is detected; (iii) anginaOnset: the patient starts to experience chest pain; and (iv) amnesiaOnset: the patient starts to experience loss of memory. The smDeltaBP event is acquired from a physiological measurement, saD from a monitoring device, while the other two events are acquired from symptoms reported by the patient. Examples of events terminating the property are a measurement of relevant physiological parameters (blood pressure, heart rate, ECG parameters) with normal values (normPar), or the administration of a specific cardiological drug (cardioDrug). Occurrences of all these events can be given at different calendric granularities (days, hours, minutes, or even seconds with some intensive care devices) and with indeterminacy, depending on what the patient remembers of the symptoms, and what is the accuracy in recording data related to therapies or to physiological measurements.

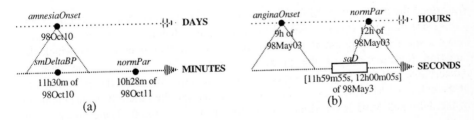

Fig. 1. Case A (a), Case B (b)

Case A. An amnesiaOnset happened on October 10, 1998, a smDeltaBP happened at 11:30 on October 10, 1998, and a normPar happened at 10:28 on October 11, 1998.

This case is illustrated in Figure 1a. Considering for example the minutes timeline, a temporal reasoning system should provide a single MVI that initiates between 0:00 and 11:30 on October 10 (indeed, after 11.30 we are sure that at least one of the two initiating events - amnesiaOnset and smDeltaBP – actually happened), and terminates at 10:28 on October 11, 1998.

Case B. On the same day (May 3, 1998), an anginaOnset happened at 9, and a normPar happened at 12. Moreover, a saD is reported with an indeterminacy of ten seconds: it happened between 11:59:55 and 12:00:05. This case is illustrated in Figure 1b. Considering for example the hours timeline, a temporal reasoning system should be able to conclude that the property holds necessarily between 9 and 12 hours. Being unknown the relative order of occurrence for saD and normPar, the property could also possibly hold after the saD event if the actual occurrence of saD is after normPar. While the first conclusion is certain, the second one is hypothetical. In this paper, we deal with determining necessary conclusions: this is the perspective adopted in the following sections.

3   Representing events and MVIs in TGIC

In TGIC, we allow the assignment of an arbitrary interval of time (at the chosen level of granularity) to an event occurrence. This interval specifies the time span over which it is certain that the (imprecise) timepoint is located. More formally, indeterminacy is represented by generalizing the second argument of happens.[1] We use the happens(event, IOI) clause, where IOI (*Interval Of Indeterminacy*) is a convex interval over which event happened, and is assumed to be closed to the left and open to the right (according to the adopted time interval convention). For example, happens(e,[t1,t2]) states that the occurrence time of event e is greater or equal than t1 and lower than t2.

TGIC adopts the standard calendric granularities (years, months, days, hours, ...), with the associated mappings among timelines. More generally, it allows one to use any set of granularities where mapping contiguous timepoints from a given granularity to the finest one results in contiguous intervals. Special granularities such as business days or business months [2], which do not meet the general requirement above, are thus not considered.

We extend the definition of MVI to accommodate the more general concept of event: a MVI has the form ⟨Start,End⟩ where Start (End) denotes at a given granularity either a specific timepoint, if it is known, or the minimal interval over which the initiation (termination) of the property is necessarily located, in the case of indeterminacy. If Start (End) is a precise instant, it is trivially the left (right) endpoint of the delimited MVI; if Start (End) is itself an interval, then the left (right) endpoint of the delimited MVI is the right (left) endpoint of Start (End). Therefore, a Start

---

[1] In this paper, we concentrate on algorithmic and practical aspects, limiting the discussion of formal aspects to a minimum. A formalization of the presented concepts is instead provided in [3].

(End) determines (i) the minimal interval over which the initiation (termination) of a property is necessarily located, and (ii) the timepoint at which the property initiates (terminates) to be necessarily valid. For example, suppose to have only two events in the database: happens(e1,94Oct10), and happens(e2, [12h of 94Dec10, 14h of 94Dec10]), and e1 initiates property p, while e2 terminates p. In this case, we know that the initiation of the property is necessarily located at 94Oct10 and the termination is located over the interval [12h of 94Dec10, 14h of 94Dec10]. We represent this knowledge, by saying that ⟨94Oct10, [12h of 94Dec10, 14h of 94Dec10]⟩ is a MVI for property p. Therefore, property p is necessarily valid after 94Oct10 and until 12h of 94Dec10.

For conciseness, when an event e initiates (terminates) property p, we refer to the associated IOI as an initiating (terminating) IOI for p.

4   Deriving Maximal Validity Intervals in TGIC

The relative ordering of a set of events with imprecise occurrence times and/or different granularities can be often only partially known (e.g., in Case B, it is not known if saD happens before, simultaneously, or after normPar). Since we are concerned with deriving necessary MVIs, every MVI we derive must be valid in all possible orders consistent with the partial order [7], resulting from imprecise locations of event occurrences. The approach we propose to derive MVIs is organized in three general steps: (i) the (possibly imprecise) occurrence times of events are mapped to the finest granularity level; (ii) an algorithm which handles partially ordered events is applied only at the finest level to derive necessary MVIs; (iii) the obtained results are mapped at the upper granularity levels required by the user.

4.1   Mapping to the finest granularity

TGIC provides a granularity mapping function to map times between any pair of calendric granularities. This is simply achieved by applying standard mappings among calendric units: for example, hour k is mapped into the interval of minutes $[k*60, (k+1)*60]$.

In the first step, the function is used to map the occurrence time of each event to the finest granularity (in our case, the granularity of seconds). For example, the predicate happens(smDeltaBP, 11h30m of 98Oct10) of Case A is mapped into the predicate happens(smDeltaBP, [11h30m00s of 98Oct10, 11h31m00s of 98Oct10]).

4.2   Handling partially ordered events

We distinguish the three possible kinds of intersection among IOIs the algorithm has to deal with: intersection among initiating IOIs, among terminating IOIs, and among both types of IOIs. Hereinafter, we refer to these three different situations, as I_ALONE, T_ALONE, and I_T_INTERSECT, respectively.

Intersection among initiating IOIs.

Let us consider some initiating IOIs for a property p, such that their intersection is non empty, and there are no intersections with terminating IOIs for p (I_ALONE situation). Let us assume that there are no preceding events, which have already initiated p, so that it is important to derive one single IOI to use as a Start in a MVI. The solution to the problem is given by the interval whose left and right endpoints are the minimum left and right endpoints, respectively, of the given IOIs. Indeed, property p cannot initiate before the minimum left endpoint because there are no other preceding events which initiate it, but it necessarily initiates after or at the minimum left endpoint, and before the minimum right endpoint. The latter delimits the interval of necessary validity for property p, because at least one initiating event happens before it, and there is no lower time that guarantees the same. For example, take the three initiating IOIs (anginaOnset, saD, smDeltaBP) for property hfRisk in Figure 2. In this case, in each of the three intervals [t1,t5], [t2,t3], and [t4,t6], an initiating event happened. The derived Start is thus [t1,t3]: the initiation of hfRisk is necessarily located over [t1,t3].

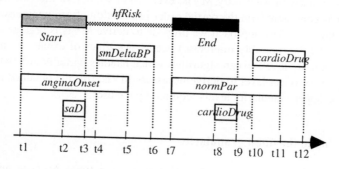

Fig. 2. Examples of I_ALONE and T_ALONE

Intersection among terminating IOIs.

Let us consider some terminating IOIs for a property p, such that their intersection is non empty, and there are no intersections with initiating IOIs for p (T_ALONE situation). Let us assume that p has been initiated by preceding events and no preceding events can terminate it, so that it is important to derive one single IOI to use as an End in a MVI. The solution to the problem is again given by the interval whose left and right endpoints are the minimum left and right endpoints, respectively, of the given IOIs. Indeed, property p cannot terminate before the minimum left endpoint because there are no other preceding events which can terminate it, but it necessarily terminates after or at the minimum left endpoint, and before the minimum right endpoint (when the minimum right end point is reached, it is certain that at least one terminating event has occurred). The necessity of the validity for property p thus terminates at the minimum left endpoint, because a terminating event can happen after or at that point. For example, considering the three terminating IOIs (normPar and the two cardioDrug) for property hfRisk in Figure 2, the derived End is [t7,t9], and ⟨[t1,t3], [t7,t9]⟩ is a MVI for hfRisk.

Intersection among initiating and terminating IOIs.

When an initiating and a terminating IOI for the same property have a non empty intersection (I_T_INTERSECT situation), it is impossible to establish in what order the corresponding initiating and terminating events happened. As a consequence, it is not possible to conclude anything about the necessary effects of the initiating IOI (a Start could be derived only if we knew that the initiating event happened after the terminating one), while terminating IOIs maintain their capability of being used in an End with respect to previous Starts. For example, if in Figure 3 we considered only the three pairs of intersecting IOIs, nothing could be concluded about the necessary validity of hfRisk: there would be no derivable MVI which is valid in all possible orders of the six indeterminate events. Considering all the (seven) IOIs in the database, the first IOI is a Start for hfRisk, and the first terminating IOI is an End. These two IOIs delimit the only necessary MVI in the database.

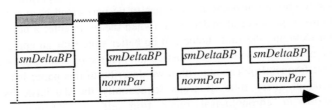

Fig. 3. Three examples of I_T_INTERSECT

If an I_T_INTERSECT occurs when the property does not hold, it is possible (but not necessary) that the property initiates to hold. In these cases, the intersecting IOIs do not allow one to generate a Start, but they have to be considered in relation to a possible subsequent I_ALONE situation. For example, consider the events smDeltaBP and cardioDrug in Figure 4a: since the relative ordering between their occurrences is unknown, they just allow one to conclude that the property hfRisk might have been initiated. Considering also the subsequent event saD, we can conclude that property hfRisk is necessarily valid after t5, because saD has no intersection with terminating IOIs (I_ALONE situation), but to determine the minimal interval for Start, we have to consider also smDeltaBP and cardioDrug. The initiating event for hfRisk can be both smDeltaBP and saD. The IOI of saD will belong completely to Start, while only a part of IOI of smDeltaBP will be included in Start, because when smDeltaBP is the initiating event for the necessary instance of hfRisk, it is impossible for the occurrence of smDeltaBP to be located before the IOI of cardioDrug (the instance of hfRisk initiated by smDeltaBP would be terminated by cardioDrug). Therefore, the Start for hfRisk is given by IOI [t1,t5]: the initiation for the property is necessarily located in that interval.

In general, we call Ext the part of Start, which is produced by considering the I_T_INTERSECT situation preceding the I_ALONE one. The Ext interval in Figure 4a is [t1,t4]. In the general case, a Start needs not to be necessarily convex. This is exemplified in Figure 4b, where, as in the situation of Figure 4a, we can conclude that property hfRisk is necessarily valid after t5, and then we have to similarly consider smDeltaBP and cardioDrug to determine Start. Unlike the case of Figure 4a, smDeltaBP and saD currently do not overlap. Therefore, the Start for hfRisk is given by a non convex IOI which comprises [t1,t3] and [t4,t5]: property hfRisk is necessarily valid after t5, and it has been necessarily initiated over the non convex interval [[t1,t3], [t4,t5]], which is the union of [t1,t3] (the Ext interval, obtained from I_T_INTERSECT) and [t4,t5] (the interval obtained from I_ALONE).

The algorithm.

In the following, we show how TGIC derives necessary MVIs at the finest level of granularity for a given property p, thus providing the set of solutions to the mholds_for(p, MVI) query. We give an high level formalization of the algorithm, representing it as a finite state machine. In general, one preliminary decision has to be taken in order to optimize the performance of such kind of algorithm. It has to be decided if the temporal reasoning activity has to be performed at query time (when the user submits a query) or at update time (when the users enter a new event in the database): for example, the first choice can be better suited for an application where the system is more often updated than queried (so that the reasoning activity has to be performed less frequently). The algorithm we describe in this paper is optimized for being executed at query time. It scans sequentially the database, by moving a temporal window in chronological order from left to right, and processing (as shown in the previous sections) the situation contained in the window.

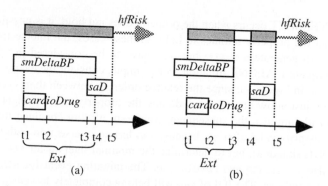

Fig. 4. Example of convex (a) and non-convex (b) Start

The algorithm can be concisely formalized in terms of a finite state machine (FSM), depicted in Figure 5. The input to the FSM is given by the *Situation* procedure (described in the following), which determines the temporal window, providing the

classification of its content (I_ALONE, T_ALONE, or I_T_INTERSECT). The FSM has three different states:
- NOT_HOLDING - the property for which MVIs are being derived does not currently hold (this is also the initial state);
- HOLDING – the property currently holds;
- POSS_HOLDING – the property may possibly hold, but there is no evidence that it necessarily holds.

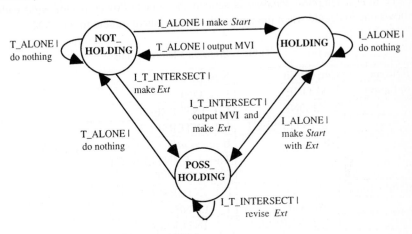

Fig. 5. MVIs derivation as a finite state machine

The current state of the property affects how IOIs are processed in the current temporal window as follows:
- NOT_HOLDING: if the situation in the temporal window is I_ALONE, the property starts to hold (transition to HOLDING), and the Start of a MVI is derived; if it is classified as I_T_INTERSECT, the property may start to hold (transition to POSS_HOLDING), and an Ext is derived for possible use in subsequent processing.
- HOLDING: if the situation in the temporal window is T_ALONE, the property stops to hold (transition to NOT_HOLDING), and a MVI is derived, by associating an End to the previously derived Start; if it is classified as I_T_INTERSECT, a MVI is analogously derived, but the property may start to hold again (transition to POSS_HOLDING) and an Ext is derived.
- POSS_HOLDING: if the situation in the temporal window is T_ALONE, nothing is done (the algorithm must derive only MVIs which certainly hold) and there is a transition to NOT_HOLDING; if it is I_ALONE, the property starts to hold (transition to HOLDING), and a Start for a MVI is derived, taking into consideration also the previously derived Ext; if it is classified as I_T_INTERSECT, there is still no evidence that the property certainly starts to hold (we remain in the POSS_HOLDING state), and the previously derived Ext is updated.

Determining the temporal window. The *Situation* procedure processes each endpoint of every IOI, starting from the leftmost and following the chronological order. When more than one endpoint is located at the same instant, right endpoints are processed before left endpoints.

Processing of *left* endpoints determines the situation in the current temporal window (I_ALONE, T_ALONE, or I_T_INTERSECT); *Sit* is the variable which identifies the current classification (it is initialized to NIL at the beginning of processing and after every time a temporal window is sent to the FSM). Processing of *right* endpoints allows one to decide when the temporal window has to be sent to the FSM.

Table 1. Processing left endpoints

IOI type	Current Sit	New Sit
initiating	I_ALONE	I_ALONE
	T_ALONE	I_T_INTERSECT
	I_T_INTERSECT	I_T_INTERSECT
	NIL	If (*current left endpoint is in a terminating IOI*) Then I_T_INTERSECT Else I_ALONE
terminating	I_ALONE	I_T_INTERSECT
	T_ALONE	T_ALONE
	I_T_INTERSECT	I_T_INTERSECT
	NIL	If (*current left endpoint is in a initiating IOI*) Then I_T_INTERSECT Else T_ALONE

Table 1 illustrates in detail the processing of left endpoints: the considered left endpoint can belong either to an initiating or to a terminating IOI (this is shown in the first column of the table); the second column shows the current classification of the temporal window, determined with the already considered endpoints; the third column gives the possibly new classification after considering the current left endpoint. For example, the first case of the table states that if we encounter a left endpoint for an initiating IOI and the current classification is I_ALONE, the classification does not change. The fourth and the eighth cases deal with NIL, and have thus to determine also if at the considered timepoint there is an intersection among terminating and initiating IOIs.

Table 2 illustrates in detail the processing of right endpoints: the meaning of the first two columns is analogous to that of Table 1; the third column prescribes the action that has to be performed. There are three possible actions: the "Send temporal window" action concludes the construction of a temporal window, by sending it to the FSM; the "Proceed to next endpoint" action extends the width of the temporal window in construction by forcing the consideration of further endpoints (as a result, the width is extended until a right endpoint of a terminating IOI is found); the "Discard window" action throws away the current temporal window and is thus performed only for NIL temporal windows (the IOIs contained in them have been already processed in previous windows).

Table 2. Processing right endpoints

IOI type	Current Sit	Action
initiating	I_ALONE	Send temporal window
	I_T_INTERSECT	Proceed to next endpoint
	NIL	Discard window
terminating	T_ALONE	Send temporal window
	I_T_INTERSECT	Send temporal window
	NIL	Discard window

Figure 6 shows an example of the algorithm running: the temporal windows classified by *Situation* are highlighted in boxed form under the timeline; arrows point out state changes of the FSM; the derived MVIs are shown at the top of the figure.

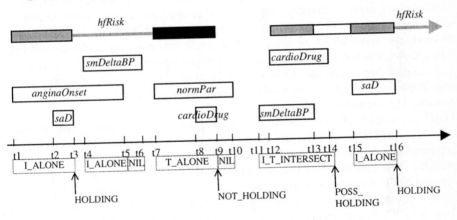

Fig. 6. Temporal windows and state transitions by the FSM

4.3 Answering queries at multiple granularities

TGIC extends the query predicate `mholds_for`, to allow one to perform queries at different levels of granularity. The predicate `mholds_for(p,⟨Start,End⟩, granlev)` returns the MVIs for property `p` at the granularity `granlev`. For example, in Case A (Figure 1a), TGIC derives the MVI ⟨[00h00m00s of 98Oct10, 11h31m00s of 98Oct10], [10h28m00s of 98Oct11, 10h29m00s of 98Oct11]⟩ for the property `hfRisk` at the finest level of granularity. The solution for the query `mholds_for(hfRisk, MVI, minutes)` is ⟨[00h00m of 98Oct10, 11h31m of 98Oct10], 10h28m of 98Oct11⟩. The query `mholds_for(hfRisk, MVI, days)` returns the MVI ⟨98Oct10, 98Oct11⟩ as solution.

Finally, TGIC provides the predicate `msg_mholds_for(p, ⟨Start,End⟩)`, which tries to automatically choose the most suitable granularity level for `Start` and `End`. The most suitable granularity for a `Start` (`End`) of an MVI is chosen as follows: starting from the `Start` (`End`) derived at the finest level, we move to the coarser levels by using granularity mapping predicates, stopping at the first level where the `Start` (`End`) reduces to a time point. For example, for Case A, the query `msg_mholds_for(hfRisk, MVI)` returns the MVI ⟨98Oct10, 10h28m of 98Oct11⟩ as solution. Considering Case B, the latter query returns ⟨09h of 98May03, 12h of 98May03⟩.

5   Discussion and Conclusions

To the best of our knowledge, the only other proposal to deal with temporal granularity in EC is described in [11]. The usefulness of that approach is limited by three serious factors: (i) the possibility of having I_T_INTERSECT situations is prohibited by explicit integrity constraints (that approach is thus often unable to derive the expected MVIs, e.g. in the cases represented by Figures 1b, 3, 4, and 6); (ii) the user can associate to an event only a single timepoint on a chosen timeline (indeterminacy is not allowed); and (iii) the implementation is given only in terms of a declarative logic program. Chittaro and Montanari have shown how declarative implementations of EC are inevitably plagued by a scarce performance, due to a generate-and-test strategy [5].

TGIC overcomes all the above described limitations: it allows and handles I_T_INTERSECT situations; it allows the user to associate any interval of indeterminacy to any event; and an efficient procedural implementation has been provided. It is easy to show that an upper bound for the worst-case complexity of deriving MVIs for a property is quadratic with respect to the number of IOIs in the database for the property (informally, given n IOIs, the temporal window can stop at most at each IOI, and consider the presence of at most $n-1$ other IOIs in the temporal window). We are studying the precise worst-case complexity, considering that database indexing techniques are used for the set of IOIs.

TGIC has been implemented in C, and tested on a large data set, including both clinical examples and automatically generated combinations of initiating and terminating IOIs (produced in such a way to test TGIC behavior on all its execution branches).

References

1. ACC/AHA Task Force: Heart Failure Guidelines. Journal of American College of Cardiology, 26 (1995) 1376-1398

2. Bettini, C., Wang, X., Jajodia, S.: A general framework for time granularity and its application to temporal reasoning. Annals of Mathematics and Artificial Intelligence, 22 (1998) 29-58
3. Chittaro, L., Combi, C.: Temporal Indeterminacy in Deductive Databases: an Approach Based on the Event Calculus. In Andler, S.F., Hanssson, J. (eds.): Active, Real-time and Temporal Database Systems (ARTDB-97), Lecture Notes in Computer Science, Vol. 1553. Springer-Verlag, Berlin Heidelberg New York (1998) 212-227
4. Chittaro, L., Combi, C., Cervesato, E., Cervesato, R., Antonini-Canterin, F., Nicolosi, G.L., Zanuttini, D.: Specifying and Representing Temporal Abstractions of Clinical Data, by a Query Language Based on the Event Calculus. In: Proceedings of the 1997 Annual Conference of Computers in Cardiology. IEEE Press, (1997) 633-636
5. Chittaro, L., Montanari, A.: Efficient temporal reasoning in the Cached Event Calculus. Computational Intelligence 12(1996) 359-382
6. Combi, C., Chittaro, L.: Abstraction on Clinical Data Sequences: an Object-Oriented Data Model and a Query Language Based on the Event Calculus. Artificial Intelligence in Medicine (1999) in press
7. Dean, T., Boddy, M.: Reasoning about Partially Ordered Events. Artificial Intelligence, 36 (1988) 375-399
8. Dyreson, C.E., Snodgrass, R.T.: Temporal indeterminacy. In Snodgrass, R.T. (ed.): The TSQL2 temporal query language. Kluwer Academic Publishers, Boston (1995) 327-346
9. Kowalski, R., Sergot, M.: A logic-based calculus of events. New Generation Computing, 4 (1986) 67-95
10. McCarthy, J., Hayes, P.: Some philosophical problems from the standpoint of artificial intelligence. In Meltzer B. and Michie D. (eds), Machine Intelligence 4 (1969): 463-502
11. Montanari, A., Maim, E., Ciapessoni, E., Ratto, E.: Dealing with Time Granularity in the Event Calculus. Proc. 1992 Internat. Conf. Fifth Generation Computer Systems (FGCS-92), IOS Press, (1992) 702-712

Effective Temporal Aggregation Using Point-Based Trees

Jong Soo Kim[1], Sung Tak Kang[1], and Myoung Ho Kim[1]

Department of Computer Science,
Korea Advanced Institute of Science and Technology,
373-1, KuSung-Dong, YuSung-Gu, Taejeon, Korea, 305-701
{jskim, stkang, mhkim}@dbserver.kaist.ac.kr

Abstract. Temporal databases introduce the concept of time into underlying data, and provide built-in facilities that allow users to store and retrieve time-varying data. The aggregation in temporal databases, that is, temporal aggregation is an extension of conventional aggregation on the domain and range of aggregates to include time concept. Temporal aggregation is important for various applications, but is very expensive. In this paper, we propose a new tree structure for temporal aggregation, called PA-tree, and aggregate processing method based on the PA-tree. We show that the time complexity of the proposed method is better than those of the existing methods. The time complexity of the proposed method is shown to be indeed the lower bound of the problem. We perform comparative experiments and show the performance advantage of our proposed method in practice.

1 Introduction

While conventional database systems store the most recent snapshots of the real world, temporal database(TDB) systems maintain past, present, and future-planned data. They can be applied to many areas where temporal properties of underlying data are important, such as trend analysis and forecasting in decision support systems, version control in computer-aided design, and so on.

Early researches in TDBs were mainly focused on the conceptual issues, such as temporal data modeling [1]. Recent works on TDBs have also considered many implementational issues. For example, indexing techniques, query processing strategies, and storage structures have been studied [2–4]. Many researches on TSQL[5, 6] that is a temporal extension of the standard query language SQL, and SQL/Temporal[6] that is an effort to introduce temporal aspects into the SQL3 standard, are also performed. In the recent works on TDBs, design and implementation of various temporal operators are playing an important part.

Among the database operators, aggregate functions are expensive but very important components. They are essential to statistical tasks and decision support applications. Although there have been several proposals for temporal aggregate processing, the tree-based approach is known to be a promising solution [7]. In the tree-based approach, a special tree structure is built for the tuples that are filtered by a given query, and the temporal aggregate results for the qualified tuples are computed by using the constructed tree structure. Here the construction of a new tree and the aggregate computation on the tree are occurred frequently because each different query generates a different set of qualified tuples. Therefore, efficient tree construction and aggregate computation techniques are essential to the improvement of the query response time in the tree-based approach.

As a tree-based temporal aggregate method, *the aggregation tree*[7] was proposed. However, the aggregation tree has several drawbacks. The aggregation tree can be severely skewed if the time intervals of tuples are in a near sorted order. This situation may occur frequently because tuples are likely to be stored in the order of their time values. The space requirement of the aggregation tree is also too much.

In this paper, we propose *the Point-based Aggregation tree(PA-tree)*, a new balanced tree structure for efficient temporal aggregation, and the aggregate processing techniques on the PA-tree. The time complexity of our method is $O(N \cdot \log N)$, which is indeed the lower bound of the problem while those of other existing methods are $O(N^2)$. Performance experiments also show the advantages of the proposed method in practice.

The remainder of the paper is organized as follows. We describe some preliminary knowledge in Section 2. In Section 3, we propose the structure of the PA-tree. The tree construction and aggregate computation techniques are explained in detail. The performance of the proposed method is evaluated in Section 4. Finally, we conclude with a summary of our work in Section 5.

2 Preliminaries

2.1 Temporal aggregates

There are two major concepts of time in TDBs: *valid time* and *transaction time*.[1] Valid time denotes the time interval during which a fact is valid in reality. Transaction time, on the other hand, represents the time interval during which a fact exists in the database [8]. In this paper, we assume that temporal aggregation is performed only on a single time dimension, either valid time or transaction time. We also assume that temporal data are represented in the tuple time-stamped manner as in [9].

SQL, the standard query language in relational data model, supports basic aggregate functions such as COUNT, SUM, AVG, MIN, and MAX. These aggregate functions can be classified into two different categories: *the computational aggregates* and *the selective aggregates*. The value of the computational aggregate is obtained by accumulating certain computations on tuples. On the other hand, the value of the selective aggregate is obtained by selecting a representative value among the values of tuples. COUNT, SUM, and AVG are the computational aggregate functions, while MIN and MAX are the selective aggregate functions.

---

[1] There is another concept of time, *user-defined time* whose value is not interpreted by DBMS.

Since the TDB allows each tuple to have its valid or transaction time interval, the domain and range of aggregates on these tuples must be extended to include time [7]. The time-line is partitioned into a number of intervals by using the time intervals of tuples, and each partitioned interval may have different aggregate value. Hence, the temporal aggregate values must be computed over these intervals. The maximal continuous intervals on which we have the same aggregate values are called *constant intervals*. The process of grouping tuples over the constant intervals and computing their aggregate values is called *temporal grouping*. *Temporal aggregations* denote the operations that partition time-line into constant intervals and perform temporal grouping on the constant intervals. Figure 1 shows an example of the temporal aggregates MAX and COUNT. Here, the constant intervals for MAX are [0, 9], [10, 15], [16, 16], [17, 19], [20, 28], and so on. Those for COUNT are [0, 2], [3, 5], [6, 9], [10, 11], [12, 12], and etc.

Temporal aggregation can be performed by various approaches. As a simple solution, the following two steps can be iterated for each tuple: (1) comparison of the time interval of a given tuple with the currently obtained constant intervals, (2) construction of new constant intervals and adjustment of the aggregate values for the constant intervals. However, there exists some difficulties in such a simple solution. For instance, in step (1) of the solution, suppose that the constant intervals for the six tuples in Figure 1 (a) have already been constructed. Now consider a new tuple with a time interval [0, 30] that is about to be processed. Then, we must compare this tuple with all the previously constructed constant intervals in order to obtain the constant intervals for the seven tuples. Hence, in the worst case, a tuple must be compared with all the previous constant intervals, which means that the time complexity is $O(N^2)$ where N denotes the number of tuples.

2.2 Previous works

There have been several proposals for temporal aggregate processing, such as the simple one that extends Epstein's algorithm[10] for conventional aggregates. Tuma proposed a technique by extending the existing aggregation methods [4]. In this approach, constant intervals are determined by reading all tuples first, and the aggregate values of the constant intervals are computed by reading the tuples again. However, reading the same relation twice in its entirety causes serious I/O overhead. This approach also has the problem that it compares a tuple with the aggregate values of all the overlapping constant intervals [7].

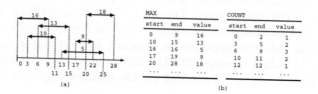

Fig. 1. Temporal aggregations, MAX and COUNT

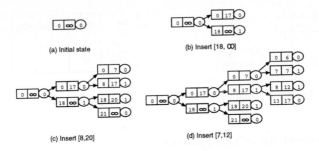

Fig. 2. The construction of the aggregation tree for COUNT

A binary tree, called *the aggregation tree* was proposed for efficient partitioning of constant intervals and computation of aggregate values. Computing temporal aggregates based on the aggregation tree consist of two steps, i.e., tree construction and aggregate value computation with depth-first-search on the tree. A node in the aggregation tree contains a time interval and a value. Time intervals of child nodes *partition* its parent interval. That is, the intervals of sibling nodes are disjoint, and the union of them becomes their parent interval.

In a leaf node of the aggregation tree, the time interval represents a constant interval, and the value is a part of the aggregate value for the constant interval. The real aggregate value of the constant interval is computed at the second step, by depth-first-search on the aggregation tree. That is, the aggregate value of a leaf node is computed by using the values of the nodes on the path from the root to the leaf node. Figure 2 illustrates the construction of the aggregation tree for COUNT. In the figure, each node has the start time and the end time with a value in the circle. The value denotes the number of data items in the node's time interval. In Figure 2 (d), the value of COUNT for the constant interval [8, 12] is the summation of all the values from the root to the leaf node, i.e., 2.

When a new tuple is inserted into the aggregation tree, new child nodes are generated by partitioning the time intervals of leaf nodes that partially overlap the inserted interval. Since the number of child nodes that can be generated on a single insertion is four, the space overhead is not negligible. Moreover, the aggregation tree can be skewed if the time intervals are not uniformly distributed. In the worst case, the aggregation tree almost degenerates into a linked list, and hence the time complexity is $O(N^2)$ where N denotes the total number of tuples [7]. The aggregation tree must be re-constructed for each different query because different conditions of queries may produce different sets of qualified tuples. Each different set of tuples generates different constant intervals and aggregate values. Therefore, efficiency on the tree construction is very important.

3 New temporal aggregation technique

In this section, we propose the PA-tree which is a new tree structure for temporal aggregations, and present an aggregate processing mechanism on the PA-tree.

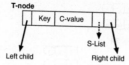

T-node

Left child   Right child

S-List

Fig. 3. The tree node of the PA-tree

name	salary	start time	end time
Richard	40	18	30
Karen	45	8	20
Nathan	35	7	12
Nathan	37	14	21

Fig. 4. The relation *Employee*

3.1 The structure of the PA-tree

Contrary to the aggregation tree, the PA-tree stores information only for the start and the end time of tuples instead of every partitioned time intervals for the tuples. There are two types of nodes in the PA-tree: *a tree node* and *a node for additional linked list*. A tree node(denoted by *T-node*) contains a time-stamp(either "start time" or "end time +1") that plays a role of the key, a value for the computational aggregates(denoted by *C-value*), and a pointer to its linked list(denoted by *S-list*) for the selective aggregates. Figure 3 shows the structure of the tree node. Note that "key" in the figure denotes a time-stamp.

Figure 5 illustrates the construction of the PA-tree for the computational aggregates on the *Employee* relation[3] given in Figure 4. Since the S-list is only for selective aggregates, the trees in the figure do not have S-lists. Two T-nodes that have "the start time" and "the end time + 1" as their key values respectively are inserted for each time interval of a tuple. The C-values of the nodes are set to the amount of the change in the aggregate values at the time of the key values of the nodes as in the figure. During the insertion of the T-nodes, the tree is balanced by using the same technique as in the AVL-tree [11].

For the selective aggregates, we need additional linked lists(S-lists) as well as the T-nodes. A list node(denoted by *L-node*) contains the length of the time interval of a tuple whose start time is the key value of the corresponding T-node, and a value for the selective aggregates(denoted by *S-value*). Figure 6 shows the structure of the node for the selective aggregates in the PA-tree.

---

[3] This example is taken from [KS95]

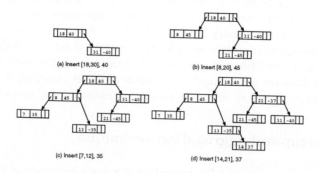

(a) Insert [18,30], 40

(b) Insert [8,20], 45

(c) Insert [7,12], 35

(d) Insert [14,21], 37

Fig. 5. The construction of the PA-tree for the computational aggregates

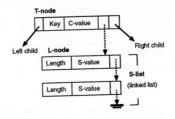

Fig. 6. The nodes of the PA-tree for the selective aggregates

On the selective aggregations, two T-nodes that are explained in the above are inserted for each time interval. Also an L-node for the time interval is inserted into the S-list of the T-node that has the start time as its key value. The length of the interval and the corresponding aggregate value are stored on the L-node. Note that L-nodes in the S-list are only for the selective aggregates.

Figure 7 illustrates the construction of the PA-tree for the selective aggregates on the *Employee* relation.

If an L-node has no effect on the computation of the selective aggregate value for the interval, it can be eliminated from the S-list in order to reduce the processing time. For example, in Figure 7 (a), if a new tuple ([18,30], 45) is inserted after the insertion of the tuple ([18, 30], 40), then the existing L-node can be removed for the MAX aggregate. The formal description of the construction algorithm of the PA-tree is given in Figure 8.

3.2 Aggregate computation on the PA-tree

In the PA-tree, in-order traversal of the tree is used for computational aggregates while post-order traversal is used for selective aggregates. Two traversal mechanisms can be implemented together in a single recursive algorithm.

The computational aggregates on the PA-tree are quite simple. The in-order traversal allows us to visit the T-nodes in the ascending order of time values, and each C-value of the visited node represents the amount of change in the

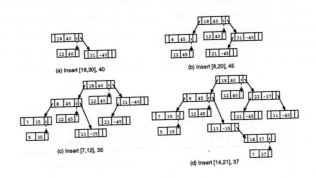

Fig. 7. The construction of the PA-tree for the selective aggregates

> Assume that a tuple t is represented as follows:
> t.Ts: the start time of the time interval of t
> t.Te: the end time of the time interval of t
> t.val: the value of the time-varying attribute of t

For each qualified tuple t do the followings:

1. Insert a T-node whose key value is t.Ts and C-value is t.val;

2. Insert a T-node whose key value is (t.Te + 1) and C-value is (-1)*(t.val);
   The insertions in step 1 and 2 are processed as in the AVL-tree;

3. If the target aggregate type(s) contains only the computational one,
   then skip step 4;

4. Let N denotes the T-node inserted in step 1. Insert an L-node into
   the S-list of N. In the L-node, the Length field is set to (t.Te - t.Ts) and
   the S-value field is set to t.val;

Fig. 8. The construction algorithm of the PA-tree

aggregate value at that time. Therefore, the computational aggregate value of each constant interval can be obtained by accumulating the C-values of visited nodes on the in-order traversal. For instance, suppose that the SUM operator is processed on the tree in Figure 5 (d). The in-order traversal visits the T-nodes as in the following order: <7, 35>, <8, 45>, <13, -35>, <14, 37>, and so on. Thus, the result of the aggregate SUM is as follows: 35 at the time 7, 35 + 45 = 80 from the time 8 to the time 12, 80 - 35 = 45 at the time 13, and etc.

The selective aggregates are processed by using the S-lists of the tree. The selective aggregates based on the S-lists can be considered as *the skyline problem* [12]. The skyline problem finds the maximum values where intervals and the values on the intervals are given. The solution of the skyline problem is a list of pairs (*int, max*), where *int* denotes an interval with a constant maximum value *max*. The problem is identical to the selective aggregate with the MAX operator. The case of the MIN operator is the same except for changing the sign of the values. Therefore, the technique to solve the skyline problem can be applied directly to the selective aggregates MAX and MIN on the PA-tree.

Figure 9 shows an instance of the skyline problem and the corresponding solution. In the PA-tree, the outlines of the buildings of the problem are constructed by using the information in the S-list of a T-node – the length and the aggregate value. Though positive and negative numbers are mixed in C-values or S-values, it is easy to see that the correct outlines can be constructed with a certain encoding scheme. The skyline problem can be solved with a simple algorithm in a divide-and-conquer fashion as in [12]. Since the PA-tree is a balanced binary tree, the divide-and-conquer approach can be applied without any

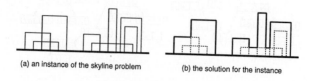

(a) an instance of the skyline problem   (b) the solution for the instance

Fig. 9. The skyline problem

difficulty. For example, suppose that the MAX operator is processed on the tree in Figure 7 (d). The post-order traversal visits the T-nodes as in the following order(we list here only the T-nodes having S-lists): <7, 35>, <14, 7>, <8, 45>, <18, 40>. First, two skylines { ([7, 12], 35) } and { ([14, 21], 37) } are merged with the skyline { ([8, 20], 45) }, and the skyline { ([7, 7], 35), ([8, 20], 45), ([21, 21], 37) } is produced. Then, the result skyline is merged with the skyline { ([18, 30], 40) }. And the final skyline, which is the result of temporal MAX operator, { ([7, 7], 35), ([8, 20], 45), ([21, 30], 40) } is produced.

4   Performance analyses

In this section, we compare the performance of the temporal aggregate method based on the PA-tree with the one based on the aggregation tree. Since the performance of the aggregation tree-based method is shown to be better than other existing methods in [7], we compare our method only with the aggregation tree-based method. We provide the result of experimental evaluation as well as the analysis of the worst case time and space complexity.

4.1   Complexity analyses

Before we describe time complexities of our methods and the aggregation tree-based method, let us investigate the lower bound of the time complexity for the given problem. In fact, the ordering rule of the items that are generated as the results of a temporal aggregation is not defined exactly. However, it is desirable for the time-related analytic applications that the temporal aggregate results are provided according to their time order. Hence we take the temporal aggregation which returns its results in time order as the target of our complexity analysis.

Intuitively, the temporal aggregation of N tuples has a lower bound of $O(N \log N)$ because it converts an arbitrary sequence of time intervals into a time-based sorted form. The following theorem gives a formal basis of the proposition.

Theorem 1. *The lower bound of the time complexity for temporal aggregation on the N number of tuples is $O(N \cdot \log N)$.*

Proof:
We will show that the sorting problem can be transformed into the temporal aggregation problem in $O(N)$ time. Let the problems **SORT-N** and **T-AGG** be defined as follows:

SORT-N: Sorting N distinct natural numbers without any previous information about input numbers.

T-AGG: Temporal aggregation(i.e., computing one of temporal aggregates MIN, MAX, COUNT, SUM and AVG) of N temporal data items.

We will get a lower bound of the time complexity of **T-AGG** by transforming **SORT-N** into **T-AGG**.

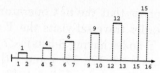

Fig. 10. The instance of **T-AGG** that corresponds to the given instance of **SORT-N**

1. The lower bound of **SORT-N** is $O(N \cdot \log N)$.
2. For any instance $\{ a_1, a_2, \ldots, a_N \}$ of **SORT-N** where a_i's are distinct natural numbers, let us generate the corresponding instance $\{ t_1, t_2, \ldots, t_N \}$ of **T-AGG** as follows.

$$t_i.start = a_i, \; t_i.end = a_i + 1, \; t_i.val = a_i$$

Here, $t_i.start$ and $t_i.end$ denote the time attributes of the tuple t_i, i.e., the start time and the end time of its time interval respectively. Also $t_i.val$ denotes the value of the time-varying attribute of t_i. It is easy to see that this transformation can be done in $O(N)$. For example, if an instance of **SORT-N**, $\{ 12, 4, 9, 6, 1, 15 \}$ is given, the corresponding instance of **T-AGG** is as in Figure 10.

3. Now, for the instance of **T-AGG** in step 2, let us compute temporal aggregate MAX. We can see that the result of temporal aggregation as in Figure 11, i.e., $\{ t_{i_1}, t_{i_2}, \ldots, t_{i_N} \}$ is in fact the result of sorting $\{ a_1, a_2, \ldots, a_N \}$.

4. As we mentioned before, transformation of a **SORT-N** instance into a **T-AGG** instance can be done in $O(N)$. Therefore, if we assume that temporal aggregate MAX can be computed in less than $O(N \cdot \log N)$, this means that we can also solve **SORT-N** in less than $O(N \cdot \log N)$. This is a contradiction. Also it is easy to see that temporal aggregates MIN, COUNT, SUM and AVG cannot be computed in less than $O(N \cdot \log N)$ by using the same argument as in the MAX operator. Hence, **T-AGG** has a lower bound of $O(N \cdot \log N)$.
□

The tree-based temporal aggregate processing is performed in two phases: *the tree construction phase* and *the aggregate computation phase*. Both phases need to be done for each different aggregate query because each query produces

The result for the example

start	end	val		start	end	val
ti_1	ei_1	ti_1		1	2	1
ti_2	ei_2	ti_2		4	5	4
ti_3	ei_3	ti_3		6	7	6
...	...	...		9	10	9
				12	13	12
ti_N	ei_N	ti_N		15	16	15

Fig. 11. The result of temporal aggregate MAX

a different set of qualified tuples and the different tuple set generates a different tree. Hence, the two phases must be considered together for the worst case time complexity. In the followings N denotes the number of tuples that qualify for aggregation.

The aggregation tree is a binary tree that has no balancing mechanism. It can be skewed in the worst case, and hence the time complexity for tree construction is $O(N^2)$. On the other hand, the PA-tree is balanced as in the AVL-tree. Thus, its time complexity for tree construction is $O(N \cdot \log N)$ [11].

The computational and the selective aggregates are processed by using the depth-first-search in the aggregation tree. Thus, both the computational and selective aggregate computation can be done in $O(N)$ after the aggregation tree is constructed. In the PA-tree, the computational aggregates are processed by using the in-order traversal, and the time complexity is $O(N)$. The selective aggregates are processed by traversing the tree nodes in the post-order. On the tree traversal, the skyline problem is solved for each S-list, and two solutions for the S-lists of sibling nodes are merged in order to build the skyline of their parent node. That is, the skylines of T-nodes are constructed in the bottom-up fashion, and the top-most skyline becomes the result of the selective aggregation. This can be considered as the process of solving the problem in a divide-and-conquer manner. The PA-tree partitions a set of time intervals effectively, and hence confines the target of comparison for each time interval to a partition. In this case, the worst case time complexity is $O(N \cdot \log N)$ that is larger than the selective aggregate computation on the aggregation tree. However, the total time complexity is dominated by the tree construction phase. The summary of the result is shown in Table 1.

Now, consider the space requirement of the aggregation tree and the PA-tree. In the aggregation tree, a single tuple insertion may cause splittings of two nodes. These two splittings produce four new nodes. Therefore, if there are N tuples, the corresponding aggregation tree has approximately $4N$ nodes in the worst case. In the PA-tree, since only the start and the end time of a tuple are

Table 1. The time complexities on temporal aggregates

	Tree construction	Computational aggregate on the tree	Total complexity for computational aggregate
The aggregation tree	$O(N^2)$	$O(N)$	$O(N^2)$
The PA-tree	$O(N \cdot \log N)$	$O(N)$	$O(N \cdot \log N)$

(a)

	Tree construction	Selective aggregate on the tree	Total complexity for selective aggregate
The aggregation tree	$O(N^2)$	$O(N)$	$O(N^2)$
The PA-tree	$O(N \cdot \log N)$	$O(N \cdot \log N)$	$O(N \cdot \log N)$

(b)

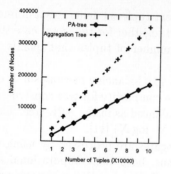

Fig. 12. The number of nodes in both trees

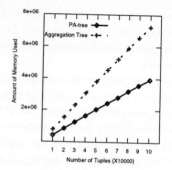

Fig. 13. The amount of memory used on tree construction

inserted, at most two new T-nodes are produced for each tuple. Also an L-node is inserted into the S-list that is attached to the T-node having the start time as its key value. Hence, for N tuples, the PA-tree has maximum $2N$ T-nodes and N L-nodes, which result in $3N$ nodes in the worst case. Thus, the space requirement of the PA-tree is less than that of the aggregation tree in the worst case.

4.2 Experimental results

We have conducted experiments to measure the amount of memory used and the number of memory accesses for the performance of tree-based temporal aggregate methods. The details of the experiments are as follows.

Initially, a synthetic set of tuples in a temporal relation is generated, and the corresponding tree structures, the PA-tree and the aggregation tree for the data set are constructed. The total time range is set to [0, 1000000], which denotes the time range of about 100 years if we consider one hour as the minimum time unit. The start and the end time of each tuple are randomly generated. We assume that the start and the end time values are uniformly distributed.

On the tree construction, the number of nodes and the amount of memory used are measured. We assume that the size of the time attribute and the tree pointer are four bytes each, and the balancing element(as in the balancing element in the AVL-tree [11]) of the PA-tree is one byte. After tree construction, we perform two temporal aggregations – one computational aggregate and one selective aggregate – on the trees.

In the experiments, we repeated the same experiments twelve times for more reliable results. Each result presented here is the average of ten values with the exception of the maximum and the minimum values. Figure 12 and Figure 13 show the number of nodes and the amount of memory used in the aggregation tree and the PA-tree respectively. As in Figure 12, the number of nodes in the PA-tree is about the half of the nodes in the aggregation tree. For actually used amount of memory, the PA-tree also requires about the half of that required in the aggregation tree as shown in Figure 13.

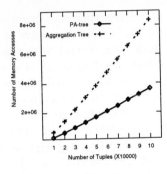

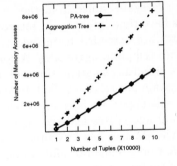

Fig. 14. The number of memory accesses on the computational aggregate processing

Fig. 15. The number of memory accesses on the selective aggregate processing

On the computational aggregate processing, our proposed PA-tree and the aggregation tree have the same worst case time complexity, $O(N)$ for the aggregate computation phase. That is, all the nodes are visited once in the specific orders in both trees. Figure 14 shows the number of memory accesses on the computational aggregate processing including both the tree construction phase and the aggregate computation phase. As shown in Figure 14, we can notice that our proposed method based on the PA-tree requires less number of memory accesses than the method based on the aggregation tree on the computational aggregates. This result can be explained by the fact that (i) constructing a PA-tree takes less time than constructing an aggregation tree, and (ii) the PA-tree has less number of nodes than the aggregation tree. Figure 15 shows the number of memory accesses on the selective aggregate processing. For the selective aggregation, the time complexity of the aggregate computation phase in the PA-tree is $O(N \cdot \log N)$, which is larger than that in the aggregation tree. However, the overall performance of our proposed method is better than the aggregation tree-based method as shown in the figure. This result follows from the fact that the overall time complexity is dominated by the tree construction phase.

In general, if there are many tuples having the same start time, the number of memory accesses on the selective aggregates in the PA-tree may increase since the length of the S-lists becomes larger. However, this performance deterioration can be minimized if we eliminate meaningless elements in the S-lists according to the types of the aggregates on the tree construction phase. For example, let's assume that we are processing a temporal aggregate MAX. Then, on the tree construction phase, we may generate an S-node only when its S-value is greater than or equal to the S-values of the existing S-nodes on the S-list.

5 Conclusion

Aggregations are very expensive but important operations in temporal databases. They are essential to statistical tasks and decision support applications. Temporal aggregates differ from the conventional aggregates since the underlying tuples have time intervals. In temporal databases, the domain and range of aggregates are extended to include time. There have been several proposals to compute temporal aggregates. Among them the tree-based approach is known to be a promising solution. However, the existing tree-based method for temporal aggregation has relatively high time complexity and much space requirement.

In this paper, we have proposed a new tree structure called *the PA-tree* for temporal aggregates and the aggregate computation method on the proposed tree. The PA-tree has less number of nodes than the existing aggregation tree since it stores temporal information on the basis of only the start and the end time of tuples not the partitioned intervals as in the aggregation tree. The PA-tree is balanced, which is not the case in the aggregation tree. The experimental results as well as the analysis of the worst case time complexity have been presented, and have shown that the temporal aggregate method based on the PA-tree outperforms the existing method.

References

1. Gregersen, H., Jensen, C.S.: Temporal Entity-Relationship Models - A Survey. Technical Report R-96-2039. Aalborg University. (1996)
2. Kim, J.S., Kim, M.H.: On Effective Data Clustering in Bitemporal Databases. In Proc. of the 4th International Workshop on Temporal Representation and Reasoning. (1997) 54–61
3. Soo, M.D., Snodgrass, R.T., Jensen, C.S.: Efficient Evaluation of the Valid-Time Natural Join. In Proc. of the 10th ICDE. (1994) 282-293
4. Tuma, P.A.: Implementing Historical Aggregates in TempIS. Master Thesis. Wayne State University. (1992) Nov.
5. Snodgrass, R.T., Ahn, I., Ariav, G., et al: The TSQL2 Temporal Query Language. Kluwer Academic Publishers. (1995)
6. Snodgrass, R.T., Bohlen. M.H., Jensen, C.S., Steiner, A.: Adding Valid Time to SQL/Temporal. ANSIX3H2-96501r2. ISO/IEC JTC 1/SC 21/WG 3 DBL-MAD-146r2. (1996)
7. Kline, N., Snodgrass, R.T.: Computing Temporal Aggregates. In Proc. of the 11th ICDE. (1995) 222–231
8. Jensen, C.S., Clifford, J., Gardia, S., et al: A Consensus Glossary of Temporal Database Concepts. ACM SIGMOD Record. Vol. 23. No. 1. (1994)
9. Jensen, C., Soo, M., Snodgrass, R.: Unifying Temporal Data Model via a Conceptual Model. Information Systems, Vol. 19. No. 7. (1994)
10. Epstein, R.: Techniques for Processing of Aggregates in Relational Database Systems. Technical Report UCB/ERL M7918. Computer Science Department. University of California at Berkeley. (1979)
11. Lewis, H.R., Denenberg, L.: Data Structures and Their Algorithms. HarperCollins Publishers Inc. (1991)
12. Manber, U.: Introduction to Algorithm: A Creative Approach. Addison-Wesley Publishing Company. (1989)

Temporal Indexing with Multidimensional File Structures

Ludger Becker, Andreas Voigtmann[1], Klaus H. Hinrichs

FB15, Institut für Informatik, Westfälische Wilhelms-Universität
Einsteinstr. 62, D-48149 Münster, Germany
{beckelu, avoigt, khh}@math.uni-muenster.de

Abstract. Multidimensional file structures designed for storing point data can be used to store spatial objects if the objects can be transformed into n-dimensional points. We adapt this *transformation technique* to design a flexible indexing technique for temporal databases. This approach can be used to support valid-time, transaction-time, and bitemporal indices. The evaluation of various kinds of temporal selections on such indices is discussed, and we present an experimental comparison with an indexing technique for valid-time databases.

1 Introduction

In the past decade temporal databases have been an active field of research [32]. Several techniques have been developed to handle *valid-time* and *transaction-time*. In contrast to valid-time which is the time an attribute or object is valid in the real world transaction-time describes the time between two modifications of an attribute or an object in the database.

Several temporal index structures have been proposed to support the evaluation of temporal queries, comprehensive surveys can be found in [27] and [22]. For indexing valid-time ranges the *time index* [9], the *time index$^+$* [15], the *TP-index* [29], the *interval B-tree* [1], and the *MAP21 approach* [21] have been presented. These structures do not require any insertion order of the time ranges. In contrast, the *monotonic B$^+$-tree* [10], the *append-only tree* [12], and the *snapshot index* [31] can only be used when the insertion order of the intervals is determined by their start times. Although this insertion order is a transaction-time characteristic, these structures have also been proposed for valid-time indexing. The *time split B-tree* [19] can only be used to index transaction-time databases since it is assumed that the end time of one version is the start time of another version. In [20] the *multiple incremental valid-time tree* (M-IVTT) has been presented as an index structure for bitemporal databases.

In addition to the methods mentioned, valid-time and bitemporal indices may also be constructed based on spatial access methods which support indexing of sets of intervals, e.g., the R*-tree [2]. Basically *now-relative data*, i.e., data which is valid until the current time or which is part of the current database state, can be represented (1) by the *maximum-timestamp approach*, (2) by storing the intervals in a separate R*-tree which does not use the upper bound of the interval for the organization of the tree [7], [25], or (3) by modifying the underlying spatial access method [8], [17]. The maximum-timestamp approach uses a timestamp which is larger than all other timestamps to represent the current time. For the R*-tree this results in directory nodes covering large areas of the data space which cause a poor query performance. The approaches (2) and (3) try to overcome this disadvantage.

In this paper, we propose a flexible indexing technique which can be used for valid-time databases, for transaction-time databases, and for bitemporal databases. Moreover, this method supports attribute- and object-timestamping. In contrast to many of the methods men-

---

1. Current address: Alcatel SEL AG, Research Center Stuttgart, Dept. ZFZ/SN, Lorenzstr. 10, D-70435 Stuttgart

tioned above, our approach can provide index access for additional non-temporal keys. This paper includes an experimental comparison with the MAP21-approach [21], showing that our flexible approach performs well. We have chosen MAP21 since it is easy to implement and it has been shown that the performance of MAP21 is comparable to other temporal index structures [21]. MAP21 maps a bounded interval $r = (a, b)$, $(a < b)$ to a number $M(r) = a * 10^d + b$ where d denotes the maximum number of digits needed to represent any non-negative number in the system, and a B^+-tree is used to index this set of numbers.

The well known *transformation technique* [14], [23] has originally been proposed to store spatial objects in index structures supporting access to multidimensional point-objects. We use this technique in connection with the maximum-timestamp approach to transform intervals of time into two-dimensional points and construct a spatio-temporal index by storing the transformed intervals in a data structure supporting the storage of multidimensional points. In our experiments we used the grid file [24] as the underlying file structure since we have a stable and efficient implementation of the grid file, which supports various kinds of queries including user defined range and join queries incorporating arbitrary predicates.

The research reported in this paper was initiated by a project which tries to provide the benefits of current object-oriented database technology for the implementation of geo-information systems (GIS). In this project we design and implement the GIS database kernel GOODAC (Geo Object Oriented DAtabase Core). The data model underlying GOODAC is the Object-Oriented Geo-Data Model OOGDM [33], [36] which supports timevariant 2-D and 3-D raster- and vector-based data [35]. Concrete GIS-applications define their application-dependent classes based on the OOGDM class hierarchy. The spatial and temporal properties of OOGDM are supported by the Object-Oriented Geo Query Language OOGQL [34]. Since our performance studies have shown that our indexing approach presented in this paper works well, we plan to incorporate a multidimensional file structure into GOODAC to provide a flexible spatio-temporal index structure satisfying the requirements of OOGDM.

The remainder of the paper is organized as follows: In Section 2 we briefly review the temporal aspects of OOGDM and its demands to a spatio-temporal index structure. Section 3 presents an overview of the transformation technique and the grid file. In Section 4 we discuss our method for indexing in temporal databases. Section 5 presents a performance comparison with the MAP21-approach [21]. Section 6 concludes this paper.

2 Temporal Aspects of OOGDM

OOGDM is an object-oriented data model supporting the modeling of GIS-applications. Its core is formed by a hierarchy of classes covering most kinds of GIS-data and a set of operations commonly needed by GIS-applications ([3], [34], [35], [36]). Since OOGDM is extensible by deriving new classes from the predefined class hierarchy, the individual data modeling needs of arbitrary GIS-applications can be satisfied.

In OOGDM the timestamps for *valid-time* are applied to simple types or to relationships referencing other objects. OOGDM supports both *chronon-timestamps* to represent data which is only valid at a specific point in time and *interval-timestamps* to represent data which is valid during specific time intervals. Interval-timestamps of now-relative data are unbounded and have the form [a, *now*]. Timestamps for *transaction-time* can only be intervals. If an object is inserted into the database at transaction-time a and modified or deleted later at transaction-time b, this object obtains the interval-timestamp [a, b] for the transaction-time. A newly inserted object is now-relative (b equals *now*).

The *temporal predicates* available in OOGQL are shown in Figure 1. Further predicates, like *follows*, *during*, *starts*, *finishes*, etc. [26] can be expressed by the predefined predicates or can be realized via the extension mechanism provided by GOODAC. In section 4 we show

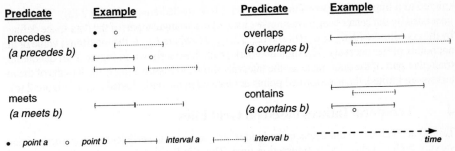

Fig. 1. Temporal predicates for OOGQL.

how queries which are based on the predicates of Figure 1 can be realized by special range queries on multidimensional file structures realizing a valid-time index.

3 Multidimensional File Structures

A d-dimensional file f is a collection of records $R = (K, I)$. $K = (k_1, \ldots, k_d)$ is the *key value* of the record R and I is the *non-key information* of R which is not used for the organization of the multidimensional file. Each *atomic key value* k_i $(1 \leq i \leq n)$ is drawn from a totally ordered, bounded domain X_i. Records are accessed via their key values. We can represent a record R as a point in the underlying d-dimensional *data space* $D(f) = X_1 \times \ldots \times X_d$. In general, the data space is partitioned into cells. At least one *data bucket* on secondary storage is assigned to each cell of this partitioning to hold the data contained in this cell. Access to buckets corresponding to a given cell can be provided either by hash functions or *directories*.

Although primarily designed for point data, multidimensional file structures can be used to store (non-point) geometric objects by applying various techniques (e.g., [14], [28]). File structures using the *transformation* technique [14] represent geometric objects by higher-dimensional points. These points can be stored in any multidimensional file structure. Complex geometric objects must eventually be approximated by simpler objects ([14], [23], [16]).

An interval on a straight line (Figure 2 (a)) can be represented in a two-dimensional space by its left and right endpoints (*endpoint transformation*), or by its center and its half length (*center transformation*). Since the right endpoint of an interval is always larger than the left endpoint, the points representing intervals under the endpoint transformation always lie in the triangular part of the data space located above the diagonal (light and dark shaded areas shown in Figure 2 (b)). If the lengths of the intervals are limited by a fixed value, the points are re-

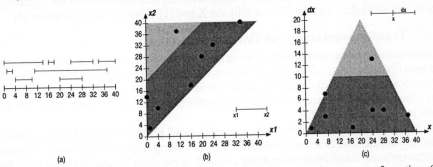

Fig. 2. A set of intervals (a), their endpoint transformations (b), and their center transformations (c). The dark shaded areas in (b) and (c) represent the areas in which the transformed intervals are located if the lengths of the intervals are limited to 20.

stricted to a trapezoidal part of the data space (dark shaded area in Figure 2 (b)). The points generated by the center transformation are located in a triangular part of the data space defined by the coordinates $(0, 0)$, $(i_{max}, 0)$, and $(i_{max}/2, i_{max}/2)$ where i_{max} is the maximum value of the endpoints of the intervals. The light and dark shaded areas shown in Figure 2 (c) denote this triangular part of the data space for the intervals shown in Figure 2 (a). If the lengths of the intervals are limited, the transformed points are located in the dark shaded area of Figure 2 (c).

4   Temporal Indices based on Grid Files

Temporal databases require specialized index structures for the efficient management of data varying both in valid- and in transaction-time. These index structures are similar to multidimensional file structures used for indexing spatial data since they must be capable of storing points and intervals of time.

Except for the R^*-tree, the GR-tree, and the M-IVTT the index structures mentioned in section 1 only support either valid- or transaction-time. Hence, two index structures must be combined for indexing in a bitemporal database. This is basically realized by choosing a suitable index structure for transaction-time which manages for each transaction-time interval an instance of an index structure for valid-time [22]. Although this two-level approach allows an easy subdivision of the database into partitions according to the transaction-time, a bitemporal database is managed more efficiently if valid- and transaction-time information is processed within a single index structure. The temporal index structures mentioned above do not support access to additional non-temporal keys. To provide this functionality we have to combine a temporal index structure with a non-temporal index structure. But this is more difficult than the two-level approach for bitemporal indexing mentioned above since in general the non-temporal index is independent of the valid-time index and must therefore keep track of all records in the database (at least for a particular transaction-time).

In OOGDM valid-time is supported by chronon- and interval-timestamps for attributes and relationships, transaction-time by interval-timestamps for complete objects. In the following, we propose an approach for constructing temporal indices based on grid files which meets the requirements of OOGDM and allows the retrieval of objects based on a set of temporal and non-temporal keys. We decided to use grid files [24] having a 2-level BR^2-directory ([4], [11], [13]) since this implementation can handle non-uniform data distributions efficiently. Obviously, also any other multidimensional file structure satisfying this requirement can be used. Since the number of dimensions may become quite large for an index supporting access via transaction-time, valid-time, and other non-temporal keys, it is still an open question whether our approach can be further improved by using an index structure designed for organizing high-dimensional data, e.g., the TV-tree [18], the X-tree [5], or the Pyramid-technique [6].

4.1   Transformation of Interval-Timestamps

Interval-timestamps can be transformed using either the endpoint or the center representation. The upper bound of interval timestamps for now-relative data is the current time *now*. Hence, the center and the length of an interval-timestamp of now-relative data continuously increase. This causes serious problems with the center transformation which explicitly stores both the center and the interval length.

Consider the transformation of a time interval $[t_i, now]$ at different times $t_j > t_i$ into points in the two-dimensional data space $[min_t, max_t] \times [min_t, max_t]$ (Figure 3). The points obtained with the endpoint transformation are always located on the upper horizontal boundary of the extending occupied triangular area of the data space. The points obtained with the center transformation are located on the right border of the extending occupied triangular area of the data space, i.e., on the line segment $[(t_{current}, 0), (t_{current}/2, t_{current}/2)]$ ($t_{current}$ is the current time).

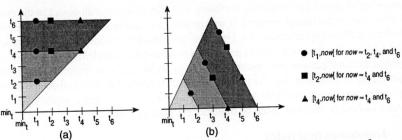

Fig. 3. Endpoint transformation (a) and center transformation (b) of interval-timestamps of now-relative data for different points in time (note that the distance between t_i and t_{i+1} is not specified).

Since many multidimensional file structures partition the data space by an orthogonal grid, the changing spatial location of the transformed interval-timestamps of now-relative data at different points in time can be handled easily for the endpoint transformation if the (upper) endpoint of these intervals is described by the special symbol *now*. For each point $t_{current}$ in time, $now = t_{current}$ denotes the upper bound of the occupied part of the data space in the endpoint dimension. Hence, records representing interval-timestamps of now-relative data are tied to this upper boundary in the endpoint dimension. The transformed interval-timestamps of now-relative data can be kept in the buckets covering the maximum endpoint value $t_{current}$ when a bucket split with respect to the endpoint dimension occurs. Records which are currently valid can be retrieved efficiently by performing an appropriate partial match query.

For the center transformation, there is no obvious way to use the special symbol *now* for representing interval-timestamps of now-relative data. Since both coordinate values of a transformed interval-timestamp of now-relative data change as time goes by (see Figure 3), the record is stored in different buckets at different times even without a modification of the file. The endpoint transformation does not have this disadvantage due to the introduction of *now* and the special location of the transformed interval-timestamps of now-relative data in the data space. Since the endpoint transformation is superior for representing interval-timestamps of now-relative data, we decided to use this transformation for our approach.

In our realization, each of the two dimensions covers the complete interval $[min_t, max_t[$ of possible (chronon) timestamps. We interpret the upper bound max_t as *now*. In summary, we use the transformation technique in connection with the maximum-timestamp approach to store interval timestamps. In contrast to our approach, other proposals [7] and [25] use a second index structure to represent now-relative data by a single temporal key.

4.2 Valid-time Indices

Consider a class having a timestamped attribute a which is represented by a k-dimensional point $(a_1, ..., a_k)$, $k \geq 1$. A (spatio-) temporal index can be constructed as follows. If a is chronon-timestamped the index is realized by a $(k+2)$-dimensional grid file consisting of one dimension for the chronon-timestamp, k dimensions for representing a by the keys $a_1, ..., a_k$, and one dimension for the object identifier denoting the object the attribute belongs to.

If a is interval-timestamped the index is realized by a $(k+3)$-dimensional grid file having two dimensions for representing the interval timestamp via the transformation technique, k dimensions for representing attribute a by the keys $a_1, ..., a_k$, and one dimension for the object identifier denoting the object the attribute belongs to.

A relationship referring to a single object is realized by storing an object identifier in a single key, i.e., $k = 1$. A relationship referring to a set of objects is timestamped by storing the set in the non-key information part of the record which reduces the dimensionality of the file by one.

The approach described above can be applied to construct primary and secondary indices.

A primary index stores the remaining attributes and relationships of an object in the non-key information part of the object's record. If we construct a secondary index, the complete object is stored in a different (primary) index. Hence, if we consider the object identifier as a logical object reference, the object identifier can be used to access the complete object.

Besides the timestamped key mentioned above, additional (non-temporal) keys may be used for organizing the grid file. For indices which are constructed as described above we can realize query processing methods supporting the evaluation of queries involving temporal predicates and predicates which can be transformed to range conditions.

4.3 Transaction-time Index

A transaction-time index supporting object-timestamping as required by OOGDM can be constructed by a three-dimensional grid file consisting of one dimension for the object identifier and two dimensions for representing the interval-timestamp via the transformation technique. The attributes and relationships of the objects are stored in the non-key information part of the records. Obviously, a transaction-time index supporting attribute-timestamps can be constructed similar to the valid-time index presented in the previous section.

4.4 Bitemporal Indices

A bitemporal index can be constructed by combining the methods presented for valid- and transaction-time. A single grid file now contains objects varying with respect to both valid- and transaction-time. For valid- and transaction-time we may use attribute or object-timestamps. To meet the requirements of OOGDM, we have to support object-timestamps for transaction-time and attribute-timestamps for valid-time. A bitemporal index for OOGDM supporting access to a time-varying attribute a represented by $k \geq 1$ keys $a_1, \ldots, a_k$ has $k+4$ or $k+5$ dimensions depending on the kind of timestamps used for the valid-time: two dimensions for the interval timestamp of the transaction-time, one dimension for the chronon-timestamp or two dimensions for the interval-timestamp of the valid-time, k dimensions for representing attribute a by the keys $a_1, \ldots, a_k$, and one dimension for the object identifier denoting the object to which the attribute belongs. Obviously, a bitemporal index can be defined over an additional

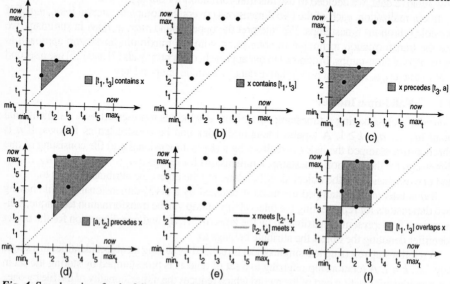

Fig. 4. Search regions for the following temporal predicates of OOGDM.

set of non-temporal keys of that class. The remaining data members of an object are again stored in the non-key information part of the corresponding record.

4.5   Query Processing

We can evaluate a selection with a temporal predicate P, i.e., a condition $P(t, x)$ comparing a given chronon- or interval-timestamp t with chronon- or interval-timestamps x stored in a grid file, by performing a range query covering the corresponding search region of the data space (Figure 4). Note that the query timestamp t must lie inside the interval $[min_t, now]$.

In our grid file implementation the empty part of the data space (e.g., below the diagonal) is mapped to a special (empty) bucket, which is always in main memory. Hence, no overhead is incurred by range queries covering an empty part of the data space. The method for processing joins with grid files [4] can also be used for processing temporal joins.

5   Performance Studies

In this section we present some performance studies using the grid file in connection with the transformation technique and the B^+-tree in connection with the MAP21 approach [21]. In order to perform a fair comparison of the two approaches we implemented the grid file and the B^+-tree on top of the same storage system.

5.1   Primary Temporal Index

We used the grid file and the MAP21 approach to set up primary temporal indices, i.e., buckets and leaves of the grid file and the B^+-tree contain complete objects. In our experiments the indices realized object-timestamps, i.e., the grid file has three dimensions. The capacity of buckets, directory pages, leaves, and internal nodes was 4096 bytes and the object size was 25 bytes. Figure 5 presents the results of performing temporal queries on the grid file and the B^+-tree. For each diagram the x-axis denotes the number n of records stored in the indices, and the y-axis shows the time t which is required to answer a query. Another set of experiments using larger objects (object size 100 bytes) showed similar results. Table 1 presents the parameters for the queries. min_t and max_t denote the lower and upper boundary of the data space, t_{min} and t_{max} denote for each grid file the lower and upper boundary of the occupied part of the data space. The fourth column shows the size of the query range in the starttime dimension.

The query ranges directly affect the performance of the queries. Query regions are only poorly approximated by buckets in the MAP21 approach since every leaf containing intervals of now-relative data covers the whole endtime dimension. In contrast, the orthogonal partitioning of the data space induced by the grid file allows a much better approximation of the query regions by the buckets. Therefore, fewer records have to be tested in a grid file query and as a result our grid file-based approach outperforms the MAP21 approach. Exceptions are the queries "$[t_2, t_4]$ meets x" and "$[a, t_2]$ precedes x". For the query involving meets the B^+-tree-based approach must only retrieve a few leaves starting at t_4. For the query involving precedes the B^+-tree-based approach performs better than the grid file since we only have to retrieve the leave b possibly containing intervals with start time t_2 and all leaves located on the right-hand side of b in the B^+-tree.

An important query in a temporal database environment is the retrieval of all records whose endtime is now, i.e., all records which are currently valid. The whole B^+-tree must be searched for valid records which results in a poor performance. The grid file, on the other hand, must consider only those buckets which cover the current time in the endtime dimension. Hence, the performance of the grid file-based approach is much better.

According to our experiments the size of the query ranges does not affect the relative performance of the grid file and the B^+-tree approach.

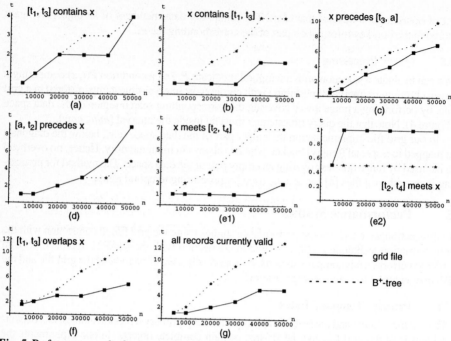

Fig. 5. Performance results for temporal queries on a primary index realized by grid file and B+-tree.

Table 1: Parameters for queries.

Query	Related figures	Query range $[x_1, y_1] \times [x_2, y_2]$	$\dfrac{x_2 - x_1}{t_{max} - t_{min}}$
$[t_1, t_3]$ *contains* x	4(a), 5(a)	$x_1 = t_1 = t_{min} + (t_{max} - t_{min})/3, y_1 = t_1,$ $x_2 = t_3 = t_{min} + 2 * (t_{max} - t_{min})/3, y_2 = t_3$	33%
x *contains* $[t_1, t_3]$	4(b), 5(b)	$x_1 = min_t, y_1 = t_3,$ $x_2 = t_1 = t_{min} + (t_{max} - t_{min})/3, y_2 = max_t$	33%
x *precedes* $[t_3, a]$	4(c), 5(c)	$x_1 = min_t, y_1 = min_t,$ $x_2 = t_3 = t_{min} + (t_{max} - t_{min})/2, y_2 = t_3$	50%
$[a, t_2]$ *precedes* x	4(d), 5(d)	$x_1 = t_2 = t_{min} + (t_{max} - t_{min})/2, y_1 = t_2,$ $x_2 = max_t, y_2 = max_t$	50%
x *meets* $[t_2, t_4]$	4(e), 5(e1)	$x_1 = min_t, y_1 = y_2 = t_2, x_2 = t_2 = (t_{max} - t_{min})/3$	33%
$[t_2, t_4]$ *meets* x	4(e), 5(e2)	$x_1 = x_2 = t_4, y_1 = t_4, y_2 = max_t$	«1%
$[t_1, t_3]$ *overlaps* x	4 (f), 5 (f)	$x_1 = min_t, y_1 = t_1,$ $x_2 = t_1 = t_{min} + (t_{max} - t_{min})/3, y_2 = t_3$ and $x_1 = t_1 = t_{min} + (t_{max} - t_{min})/3, y_1 = t_3,$ $x_2 = t_3 = t_{min} + 2 * (t_{max} - t_{min})/3, y_2 = max_t$	66%
all currently valid	5 (g)	$x_1 = min_t, y_1 = max_t, x_2 = max_t, y_2 = max_t$	100%

5.2 Secondary Temporal Indices

The results for secondary indices do not differ significantly from the primary indices due to the following reasons:

- The size of the records is smaller than the size of the records for similar primary indices. However, our tests with primary indices have shown that the grid file outperforms the B^+-tree/MAP21 approach both for small records (25 bytes) and for large records (100 bytes). Hence, obtaining the (logical) object-identifiers from the secondary temporal indices is more efficient for the grid file-based approach.
- The access to the records is similar for both secondary temporal indices. If the object-identifier for a record has been obtained from the secondary index, another bucket access is required to retrieve the bucket of the primary index storing the record.

6   Conclusions

We have combined the transformation technique which has originally been proposed for storing spatial objects in a multidimensional file structure with the maximum-timestamp approach for representing interval timestamps of now-relative data. We have used this technique to realize valid-time indices for attribute and object timestamps, transaction-time indices for attribute and object timestamps, and bitemporal indices. Furthermore, we have discussed processing of temporal selections. The techniques presented in [4] for processing joins with grid files can also be used for processing temporal joins. This is subject to future work.

The comparison of our approach with the MAP21-technique storing the interval timestamps in a B^+-tree has shown that the grid file having a 2-level BR^2-directory can handle data distributions arising from the maximum-timestamp approach efficiently and provides a better performance than MAP21. Obviously, one may generalize this result to all point access methods which are capable of handling such non-uniform data distributions.

Since the results reported in this paper are quite promising, we plan to integrate multidimensional file structures in our GIS-kernel GOODAC to serve as flexible spatial and temporal access methods.

References

1. C.-H. Ang, K.-P. Tan: *The Interval B-Tree*, Information Processing Letters, 53(2), 1995, 85 - 89.
2. N. Beckmann, H.-P. Kriegel, R. Schneider, B. Seeger: *The R*-tree: An Efficient and Robust Access Method for Points and Rectangles*, Proc. ACM SIGMOD Conf. 1990, 322 - 321.
3. L. Becker, A. Voigtmann, K. Hinrichs: *Developing Applications with the Object-Oriented GIS-Kernel GOODAC*, in: M.J. Kraak, M. Molenaar (Eds.): Proc. SDH '96, Vol. I, 5A1 - 5A18.
4. L. Becker, K. Hinrichs, U. Finke: *A New Algorithm for Computing Joins with Grid Files*, Proc. ICDE 1993, 190 - 198.
5. S. Berchthold, D. Keim, H.-P. Kriegel: *The X-Tree: An Index Structure fir High-Dimensional Data*, Proc. VLDB 1996, 29 - 39.
6. S. Berchthold, C. Böhm, H.-P. Kriegel: *The Pyramid-Technique: Towards Breaking the Curse of Dimensionality*, Proc. ACM SIGMOD Conf. 1998, 142 - 153.
7. E. Bertino et al.: *Indexing Techniques for Advanced Database Systems*, Kluwer 1997.
8. R. Bliujute, C. S. Jensen, S. Saltenis, G. Slivinskas: *R-tree Based Indexing of Now-Relative Bitemporal Data*, TR-25, Time-Center Technical Report, 1998.
9. R. Elmasri, G.T.J. Wuu, Y.-J. Kim: *The Time Index: An Access Structure For Temporal Data*, Proc. VLDB 1990, 1 - 12.
10. R. Elmasri, G.T.J. Wuu, Y.-J. Kim: *The Time Index and the Monotonic B^+-tree*, in [30], 433-456.
11. U. Finke, K. Hinrichs, L. Becker: *The Binary-Radix Bucket-Region Directory: A Simple New Directory for the Grid File*, Proc. Panel'92, 460 - 472, 1992.
12. H. Gunadhi, A. Segev: *Efficient Indexing Methods for Temporal Relations*, IEEE Transactions on Knowledge and Data Engineering, 5(3), 496 - 509, 1993.

13. K. Hinrichs: *Implementation of the Grid File: Design, Concepts and Experience*, BIT 25, 1985, 569 - 592.

14. K. H. Hinrichs, J. Nievergelt: *The grid file: a data structure to support proximity queries on spatial objects*, in: M. Nagl, J. Perl (eds.): Proc. WG'83, 100 - 113.

15. V. Kouramajian, R. Elmasri, A. Chaudhry: *The Time Index$^+$: An Incremental Access Structure For Temporal Databases*, Proc. ICDE 1994, 232 - 242.

16. H.P. Kriegel, H. Horn, M. Schiwietz: *The Performance of Object Decomposition Techniques for Spatial Query Processing*, Proc. 2nd SSD 1991, 257 - 276.

17. A. Kumar, V. J. Tsotras, and C. Faloutsos: *Designing Access Methods for Bitemporal Databases*, IEEE Transactions on Knowledge and Data Engineering, 10(1), 1-20, 1998.

18. K.I. Lin, H. V. Jagadish, C. Faloutsos: *The TV-Tree: An Index for High-Dimensional Data*, VLDB Journal, 3(4), 1994, 517 - 542.

19. D. Lomet, B. Salzberg: *Transaction Time Databases*, in [30], 388 - 417.

20. M.A. Nascimento, M.H. Dunham, R. Elmasri: *M-IVTT: An Index for Bitemporal Databases*, Proc. DEXA '96, 779 - 790.

21. M.A. Nascimento, M.H. Dunham, V. Kouramajian: *A Multiple Tree Mapping Based Approach for Valid-Time Index Ranges*, Journal of the Brazilian Computer Society, 2(3), 1996.

22. M. A. Nascimento, M. H. Eich: *An Introductory Survey to Indexing Techniques for Temporal Databases*, Technical Report 95-CSE-01, Southern Methodist University, Dallas, TX, 1995.

23. J. Nievergelt, K. Hinrichs: *Storage and Access Structures for Geometric Data Bases*, Proc. Intern. Conf. on Foundations of Data Organization, 335 - 345, 1985.

24. J. Nievergelt, H. Hinterberger, K.C. Sevcik: *The Grid File: An Adaptable, Symmetric Multikey File Structure*, ACM TODS 9(1), 38 - 71, 1984.

25. B.-C. Ooi, C. H. Goh, and K.-L. Tan: *Indexing Bitemporal Databases as Points*, Information and Software Technology (40), 327 - 337, 1998.

26. J.F. Roddick, J.D. Patrick: *Temporal Semantics in Information Systems - A Survey*, Information Systems, 17(3), 1992, 249 - 267.

27. B. Salzberg, V. J. Tsotras: *A Comparison of Access Methods for Time Evolving Data*, Technical Report NU-CCS-94-21, College of Computer Science, Northeastern University, 1994.

28. B. Seeger, H.-P. Kriegel: *Techniques for Design and Implementation of Efficient Spatial Access Methods*, Proc. VLDB 1988, 360 - 371.

29. H. Shen, B.C. Ooi, H. Lu: *The TP-Index: A Dynamic and Efficient Indexing Mechanism for Temporal Databases*, Proc. ICDE 1994, 274 - 281.

30. A.U. Tansel, J. Clifford, S. Gadia, S. Jajodia, A. Segev, R. Snodgrass (eds.): *Temporal Databases - Theory, Design, and Implementation*, Benjamin-Cummings, Redwood, CA, 1993.

31. V.J. Tsotras, N. Kanelagris: *The Snapshot Index, an I/O Optimal Access Method for Timeslice Queries*, Information Systems, 3(20), 237 - 260, 1995.

32. V.J. Tsotras, A. Kumar: *Temporal Database Bibliography Update*, ACM SIGMOD Record, 25(1), 1996, 41 - 51.

33. A. Voigtmann, L. Becker, K. Hinrichs: *An Object-Oriented Data Model and a Query Language for Geographic Information Systems*, Bericht Nr. 15/95.-I, Institut für Informatik, Universität Münster, Germany, 1995.

34. A. Voigtmann, L. Becker, K. Hinrichs: *A Query Language for Geo-Applications*, Bericht Nr. 5/96-I, Institut für Informatik, Universität Münster, Germany, 1996.

35. A. Voigtmann, L. Becker, K. H. Hinrichs: *Temporal extensions for an Object-Oriented Geo-Data-Model*, Proc. SDH'96, 11A.25-11A.41.

36. A. Voigtmann: *An Object-Oriented Database Kernel for Spatio-Temporal Geo-Applications*, Ph.D.-Thesis, Institut für Informatik, Universität Münster, Germany, 1998.

Communicating Time-Oriented, Skeletal Plans to Domain Experts Lucidly

Silvia Miksch and Robert Kosara

Vienna University of Technology, Intitute of Software Technology (IFS)
Resselgasse 3/188, A-1040 Vienna, Austria, Europe
{silvia, rkosara}@ifs.tuwien.ac.at, www.ifs.tuwien.ac.at/~{silvia, rkosara}

Abstract. Practical planning systems for real-world environments imply a striking challenge, because the planning and visualization techniques available are not that straightforwardly applicable. Skeletal plans are an effective way to reuse existing domain-specific procedural knowledge, but leave room for execution-time flexibility. However, the basic concepts of skeletal plans are not sufficient in our medical domain. First, the temporal dimensions and variability of plans have to be modelled explicitly. Second, the compositions and the interdependencies of different plans are not lucid to medical domain experts. The aim of our paper is to overcome these limitations and to present an intuitive user interface to the plan-representation language *Asbru*. We explored different representations and developed a powerful plan visualization, called *AsbruView*. AsbruView consists of two views, first, a *topological* view, which utilizes the metaphor graphics of "running tracks" and "traffic" and, second, a *temporal* view, which utilizes the idea of LifeLines.

1 Introduction

Currently, there are some plan-representation languages and various planning techniques available. However, for someone who wants to engineer a *practical* planning system for a particular real-world domain, it is not that straightforward to simply select a representation and a technique and proceed.

We are trying to bridge the gap between theory and practice providing concrete support for *medical treatment planning*. We have encountered two main problems when applying planning techniques in real-world environments: (1) traditional plan-representation languages are not appropriate in dynamically changing environments, like medicine; (2) it is next to impossible to communicate such complex abstract concepts to domain experts, like physicians. Therefore, we focused on a plan-representation language and a suitable visualization of this language. Our final aim is to support the authoring and the execution of clinical protocols seen as time-oriented, skeletal plans. Such skeletal plans turned out to be beneficial to capture domain-specific procedural knowledge.

Section 2 discusses the problem area and the related techniques. Section 3 gives an overview about the time-oriented, skeletal plan-repesentation language, called *Asbru*. Section 4 explains the main features of our plan visualization, called *AsbruView*, using the medical scenario of mechanical ventilation. Finally, we end up with conclusion and future plans.

2 Problem Area and Approaches

Medical Treatment Planning. In recent times, physicians have tried hard to improve the quality of health care through increased awareness of proper disease management techniques while simultaneously the physicians have to reduce costs without adversely affecting the quality of patient care. Treatment planning from scratch typically is not necessary, as general procedures exist which should guide the medical staff. These procedures are called *clinical guidelines* or *protocols*.

Authoring clinical protocols is a non-trivial task. Mostly, these protocols are expressed in natural language or flow diagrams, but these kinds of representation can not easily be transformed into a formal and structured framework [7]. The benefits of existing representations are: (1) writing in free text is easy; (2) medical experts are used to working with free text or flow diagrams; (3) flow diagrams are useful for representing sequential states and actions in a graphical way.

However, these techniques have significant limitations when used in *practical* planning systems: (1) existing clinical protocols are partly vague concerning their intentions and their temporal, context-dependent representations; (2) the variability of clinical protocols is hard to represent in a structured way (e.g., a medical goal can be achieved by different therapeutic actions); (3) it is quite difficult to cope with all possible orders of plan execution and all the exception conditions that might arise; (4) it is hard to represent the concurrent actions, the different temporal dimensions, the high numbers of possible transitions, and the mutual dependencies of parameters in an easy to comprehend way. Therefore, hardly any of the existing protocols are formulated in an appropriate way, which would facilitate computer support.

Representing Time-Oriented Plans. Clinical protocols can be seen as plans, procedures, or algorithms, which need to be executed depending on a patient's health conditions within a certain time interval.

The planning and scheduling problems have been attacked in two major ways: approaches which try to understand and solve the general problem without using of domain-specific knowledge (*domain-independent* approaches) and approaches which use domain heuristics directly (*domain-dependent* approaches). The "classical" domain-independent approach that many planners use describes states and operators in a restricted language known as the STRIPS language [3], or in extensions thereof. The STRIPS language is based on situation calculus [10]. Therefore, all approaches that descended from STRIPS are unable to handle durative events and actions, uncertainty and variability in the utility of available actions, and concurrent and cyclical execution of plans. STRIPS's search space is close to situation space. The usual assumptions are that only the agent affects the state of the world, that all actions occur instantaneously, that effects of actions are instantaneous, and that all actions follow one another with no break inbetween. Finally, classical planning and scheduling assume complete and deterministic information about the world's states and the effects of actions. These assumptions are inappropriate in medical domains.

To overcome some of these limitations, approaches as the planning initiative "Shared Planning and Activity Representation" (SPAR [17]), the procedural reasoning systems (PRSs, [6]), situated and reactive planning ([4], [16], [20]) or O-Plan [18] were proposed. However, we need to have greater temporal reasoning power and to focus on new issues such as temporally extended goals [1].

Another way is representing procedural knowledge as a library of skeletal plans. Skeletal plans are plan schemata at various levels of detail that capture the essence of procedures, but leave room for execution-time flexibility in the achievement of particular goals [5]. However, the basic concepts of skeletal plans are not sufficient in the medical domain, either. The temporal dimensions and variability of clinical protocols have to be modelled explicitly in skeletal plans.

Plan Visualization. Graphical representations support the understanding of complex coherences. In the last years, many visualization techniques were introduced to improve the understanding of the relationship between several variables (e.g., [13], [8], [19]). Cole and Stewart [2] suggested to use metaphor graphics to display a collection of different parameters over time (e.g., minute-ventilation rectangles representing the mechanical ventilator data) and found that human performance on interpreting mechanical ventilator data can be improved significantly [2]. This approach assumes that *"metaphor graphics are custom tailored visual displays designed to look like the real world situation from which the data is collected, but not in a literal sense of 'look like'"* [2]. We extended the idea of metaphor graphics in the literal sense of "metaphor" [9]. A metaphor supports comprehending an unknown complex concept using a well-known concept.

We are more interested in plan visualization than in visualization of multidimensional data. Besides flow charts, graphical animation languages, visual (programming) languages, and process modeling techniques, LifeLines [12] provide an excellent way to represent data and actions over time. LifeLines are diagrams with time lines proceeding from left to right. These lines are drawn in different vertical areas, with a label to the very left-hand side of the area. While events whose dates are known (e.g., past events) are captured very well by this approach, it does not deal with temporal uncertainty, different temporal orders of plans, and compulsory or optional plans.

Which Features Do We Need? We have already developed a plan-representation language, called Asbru, which explicitly defines all the necessary knowledge roles. However, we ended up with a quite complicated and difficult to comprehend language (compare Section 3). We could not communicate the basic concepts to the domain experts – the physicians. Therefore, we need a plan visualization, which is able to capture:

1. *hierarchical decomposition* of plans (which are uniformly represented in a plan-specification library);

2. *compulsory* and *optional* plans;
3. *temporal order:* sequential, concurrent, and cyclical execution of plans;
4. *temporal uncertainty;*
5. *continuous* (durative) states, actions, and effects;
6. *intentions* considered as high-level goals; and
7. *conditions,* that need to hold at particular plan steps.

3   Asbru Language

Considering all shortcomings of traditional plan-representation languages, we defined a temporal, skeletal plan-specification language, called *Asbru* [11]. Asbru is part of the Asgaard project[1] [15], in which we are developing task-specific problem-solving methods (PSMs) based on such time-oriented, skeletal plans written in the Asbru notation. These PSMs will support the design and the execution of skeletal plans by a human executing agent other than the original plan designer (e.g., plan verification, plan selection, plan revision).

Components of Asbru. A plan consists of a name, a set of arguments, including a time annotation (representing the temporal scope of a plan), and five components: *preferences, intentions, conditions, effects,* and *a plan body (layout),* which describes the actions to be executed. The plan name is compulsory and all other components are optional. Table 1 explains the different components of Asbru.

Table 1. Components of Asbru.

Component	May Consists of	Explanation
Preferences		*constrain the selection of a plan*
	strategy	a strategy for dealing with the problem
	utility	a set of utility measures
	select-method	a matching heuristic for the applicability of the whole plan
	resources	a set of prohibited, recommended, discouraged, and obligatory resources
	responsible-actor	a set of actors, who are entitled to adapt the protocols (e.g., physician, nurse)
Intentions		*are high-level goals at various levels of the plan, an annotation specified by the designer; intentions are temporal patterns that should be maintained, achieved, or avoided*
		continued on next page

---

[1] In Norse mythology, *Asgaard* was the home and citadel of the gods. It was located in the heavens and was accessible only over the rainbow bridge, called *Asbru* (or *Bifrost*) (For more information about the *Asgaard* project see http://www.ifs.tuwien.ac.at/asgaard/).

continued from previous page		
Component	**May Consists of**	**Explanation**
	intermediate-state	the state(s) that should be maintained, achieved, or avoided *during* the applicability of the plan
	intermediate-action	the action(s) that should take place *during* the execution of the plan
	overall-state-pattern	the overall pattern of state(s) that should hold *after* finishing the plan
	overall-action-pattern	the overall pattern of action(s) that should hold *after* finishing the plan
Conditions		*are temporal patterns, sampled at a specified frequency, that need to hold at particular plan steps to induce a particular state transition of the plan instance*
	filter-preconditions	the preconditions which need to hold initially if the plan is applicable, but can not be achieved and are necessary for a plan to become **possible**
	setup-preconditions	the preconditions which need to be achieved to enable a plan to start and allow a transition from a **possible** plan to a **ready** plan
	activate-condition	a token which determines if the plan should be started manually or automatically
	suspend-conditions	the conditions which determine when an **activated** plan has to be **suspended**
	abort-conditions	the conditions which determine when an **activated, suspended,** or **reactivated** plan has to be **aborted**
	complete-conditions	the conditions which determine when an **activated** or **reactivated** plan can be completed successfully
	reactivate-conditions	the conditions which determine when a **suspended** plan has to be **reactivated**
Effects		*describe the possible effects of plans*
	functional relationship	relationship between the plan arguments and measurable parameters
	overall effect	overall effect of a plan on parameters independent of plan's arguments
Plan-body (layout)		*is a set of plans to be executed in sequence, in parallel, in any order, or in some frequency*
	sequential (`do-all-sequentially`)	a set of plans that are executed in sequence (executed in total order)
	concurrent : parallel (`do-all-together`)	a set of plans that are executed in parallel – all plans must start together; no **continuation-condition**
		continued on next page

continued from previous page		
Component	May Consists of	Explanation
	concurrent : parallel (do-some-together)	a set of plans that are executed in parallel – some plans must start together; the continuation-conditions specified as subset of plans, which must be completed
	concurrent : any order (do-all-any-order)	a set of plans that are executed in any order – all plans must be completed; no continuation-condition
	concurrent : any order (do-some-any-order)	a set of plans that are executed in any order – some plans must be completed; the continuation-conditions specified as subset of plans, which must be completed
	cyclical (every)	a repeated plan with optional temporal and continuation arguments that can specify its behavior

Hierarchical Decomposition of Plans. The aim is to specify different plans, which are uniformly represented in a plan-specific library. Therefore, all plans and their subplans have the same structure. A *plan* in the plan-specification library is composed hierarchically of a set of plans with arguments and time annotations. The execution interpreter always attempts a decomposition of a plan into its subplans, unless the plan is not found in the plan-specification library, thus representing a nondecomposable plan (informally, an *action*). This is called *"semantic" stop-condition*.

Time Annotations. Intentions, states, and prescribed actions are temporal patterns. A simple temporal pattern is a *parameter proposition*: a parameter (or its abstraction), its value, a context, and a time annotation (e.g., the *state*

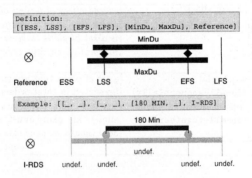

Fig. 1. Asbru's Time Annotations. The upper part of the figure presents the generic annotation and the lower part shows an example.

abstraction of the blood-gas parameter is *normal,* as defined in the context of weaning therapy, during a certain time period).

The time annotations allow us to represent uncertainty in starting time, ending time, and duration [14]. This time annotation supports multiple time lines by providing *reference annotations.* Temporal shifts from the reference annotation are defined to represent the uncertainty in starting time, ending time, and duration, namely earliest starting shift (ESS), latest starting shift (LSS), earliest finishing shift (EFS), latest finishing shift (LFS), minimal duration ($MinDu$), and maximal duration ($MaxDu$). The temporal shifts are associated with time units (e.g., minutes, days) and can be "unknown" or "undefined" to allow incomplete time annotation, denoted by an underscore "_". To allow temporal repetitions, sets of cyclical time points and cyclical time annotations are defined. Figure 1 illustrates these time annotations.

4   AsbruView: Topological and Temporal View

Our plan-visualization approach was influenced by the idea of metaphor graphics ([2], [8]), LifeLines [12], and the graphical-timetable design of Shinkansen Lines (Japanese National Railroad) described in [19]. However, we are utilizing the idea of metaphors more literally. Instead of using an abstract diagram or object (e.g., rectangles, growing and shrinking circles), we are applying signs from the (more-or-less) daily life to communicate the various components of our plan-representation language Asbru.

Our approach, called AsbruView, consists of two views, a topological view and a temporal view. The topological view is eligible to depict the overall flows of the different plans, the hierarchical decomposition of plans, the compulsory and optional plans, and several time-oriented components of the plans. However, this view is incapable for representing the temporal uncertainty in an appropriate way. Therefore, we needed the temporal view to embody this dimension, too.

4.1   Topological View

The topological view is qualified to communicate the basic concepts of Asbru and the overall control and decompositions of plans to be executed. We are utilizing the metaphor of "running tracks" to visualize such a plan. The 3-dimensional objects sketch the "running tracks". The width represents the time axis, the depth represents parallel plans on the same level of decomposition, and the height represents the decomposition of plans into subplans. The cube is rotated to the left to ensure readability in case of multiple tracks. Figure 2 presents a screenshot of the AsbruView program. The upper part of Figure 2 shows parts of a treatment protocol for infants' respiratory distress syndrome (I-RDS). The general rule of *undefined components* is that these icons appear in gray.

Plans can be stacked on top of each other to represent the hierarchical decomposition. For example, the plan *One-of-Controlled-Ventilation* is decomposed into three subplans, called *Controlled-Ventilation, Permissive-Hypercapnia,* or

Crisis-Management (Figure 2). These three subplans will be executed in any order (do-some-together). However, *Controlled-Ventilation* is compulsory (displayed with plain background) and the other two subplans are optional (displayed with question-mark texture). The finishing-line (flag) stands for the complete-conditions.

We are using the metaphor of "traffic" to visualize the other five kinds of conditions (Figure 2). The sign "No Entry with Exceptions" symbolizes the filter-preconditions. The supplementary sign stands for the exeptions, like "Except Buses", which we are using to name the filter-conditions (e.g., "Except Females" allows only females to enter the track). A barrier, which illustrates the fact that this condition can be achieved, embodies the setup-preconditions (and thus the barrier will be opened). The traffic light includes three kinds of conditions: the red light symbolizes the abort-conditions, the yellow light the suspend-conditions, the green light the reactivate-conditions.

4.2 Temporal View

The strengths of the temporal view are to grasp the temporal uncertainty and to explain the plans, their subplans, and their components in more detail. We have adapted the idea of LifeLines (compare Section 2) to represent temporal uncertainty, different temporal orders of plans, and compulsory or optional plans.

The lower part of Figure 2 shows the temporal view. We are using facets [12] for all of Asbru's components: plan body (layout), preferences, intentions, conditions, and effects. Facets can be opened and closed at any time, and share a common time axis. Thus, the relation between different parts of the display is very easy to understand. Vertical scrolling of the different facets is independent. However, vertical scrolling within the topological or temporal view is dependent.

A plan is represented with uncertainty in starting time, ending time, and duration. The time-annotation can be constrained implicitly by the plan's conditions (e.g., complete-conditions) or explicitly by defining starting time, ending time, or duration (compare Section 3). Since time annotations play an important role in all aspects of Asbru, the same kind of representation can be used in all facets (explanations of the time annotations are given in Figure 1). If all the different components are defined, the upper bar has to lie at least on the two diamonds, because the minimal duration must be equal or less than the difference between latest starting shift and earliest finishing shift ($MinDu \leq EFS - LSS$). If the LSS or the EFS are undefined, the black diamonds are converted to gray circles. The two diamonds have to stay on the lower bar accordingly. The visualization of the time annotations is the only metaphor, which breaks our rule of using only signs of the daily life instead of abstract objects.

The symbol next to every plan's name shows its type. In the example, *Initial-Phase* is a sequential plan and *One-of-CPAP-Extubation* is an any-order plan; two parallel lines would indicate a parallel plan and a cyclical arrow would illustrate a cyclical plan. The order of execution is also indicated by the position of the time annotation along the time axis. In case of plans that are to be executed

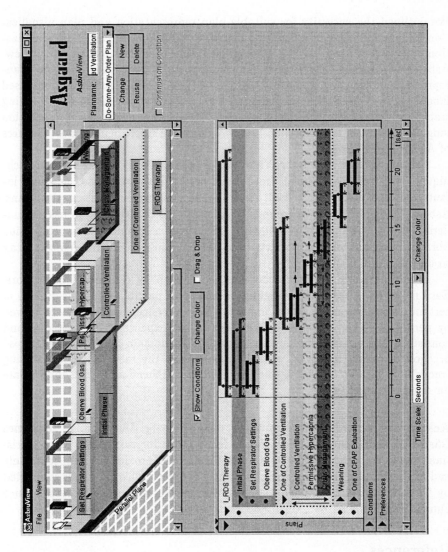

Fig. 2. A screenshot of the *AsbruView* program. The upper part illustrates the topological view showing an example of a real clinical protocol for treating infants' respiratory distress syndrome (I-RDS). The lower part depicts the temporal view.

in any order, the time annotations are displayed with arrows pointing to other possible execution times (e.g., the subplan *Controlled-Ventilation*).

5 Conclusion and Future Plans

We outlined the necessity for suitable plan representation and plan visualization for practical planning systems in real-world domains. Our plan visualization approach is based on metaphor graphics and LifeLines, called AsbruView. AsbruView consists of two views, which support different features of our plan-representation language Asbru. Asbru is a time-oriented and intention-based language to represent skeletal plans. We have utilized the metaphors of "running tracks" and "traffic". These metaphors clarify the complex plan-representation language Asbru in a comprehensible way. We have implemented most features of AsbruView in *Java*^{tm}.

The applicability of AsbruView was evaluated with scenario-based techniques. We applied treatment protocols of mechanically ventilated newborn infants and analyzed AsbruView's expressiveness with collaborating physicians. AsbruView is able to visualize most of the features of Asbru in an easy to understand way and supports the navigation through a complex plan-specification library. Therefore, domain experts need not be familiar with the Asbru syntax to understand a plan.

According to [9], abstract concepts are defined by clusters of metaphors. Each metaphor gives a partial definition and these partial definitions overlap in certain ways. Therefore, better understanding of concepts may best be served by permitting alternative metaphors even at the expense of completeness and consistency. Alternative metaphors of our problem domain could be "road maps" or "golf courses". However, we have first chosen the metaphors of "running tracks" and "traffic", which seemed easier to comprehend and more appropriate for our domain experts.

Acknowledgements. The authors thank Georg Duftschmid, Johannes Gärtner, Klaus Hammermüller, Werner Horn, Peter Johnson, Franz Paky, Christian Popow, Andreas Seyfang, and Yuval Shahar who provided helpful comments and discussions on previous versions of this document. This project is supported by "Fonds zur Förderung der wissenschaftlichen Forschung" (Austrian Science Fund), P12797-INF.

References

1. F. Bacchus and F. Kabanza. Planning for temporally extended goals. In *Proceedings of the Thirteenth National Conference on Artificial Intelligence (AAAI-96)*, pages 1215–1222, Menlo Park, CA, 1996. AAAI Press/The MIT Press.
2. W. G. Cole and J. G. Stewart. Human performance evaluation of a metaphor graphic display for respiratory data. *Methods of Information in Medicine*, 33:390–396, 1994.

3. R. E. Fikes and N. J. Nilsson. STRIPS: A new approach to the application of theorem proving to problem solving. *Artificial Intelligence*, 2(3-4):189–208, 1971.

4. R. Firby. Adaptive execution in complex dynamic worlds. Ph.D. Thesis YALEU/CSD/RR #672 Thesis, Yale University, 1989.

5. P. E. Friedland and Y. Iwasaki. The concept and implementaion of skeletal plans. *Journal of Automated Reasoning*, 1(2):161–208, 1985.

6. M. P. Georgeff, A. L. Lanskey, and M. J. Schoppers. Reasoning and planning in dynamic domains: A experiment with mobile robots. Technical Report Tech Note 380, SRI International, AI Center, 1986.

7. S. I. Herbert. Informatics for care protocols and guidelines: Towards a european knowledge model. In C. J. Gordon and J. Christensen, editors, *Health Telematics for Clinical Guidelines and Protocols*. IOS Press, Amsterdam, 1994.

8. W. Horn, C. Popow, and L. Unterasinger. Metaphor graphics to visualize ICU data over time. In *Proceedings of the Intelligent Data Analysis in Medicine and Pharmacology (IDAMAP-98)*. Workshop Notes of the ECAI-98 Workshop, 1998.

9. G. Lakoff and J. Mark. *Metaphors We Live By*. University of Chicago Press, Chicago, 1980.

10. J. McCarthy and P. J. Hayes. Some philosophical problems from the standpoint of artificial intelligence. In B. Meltzer and M. Michie, D. andSwann, editors, *Machine Intelligence 4*, pages 463–502. University Press, Edinburgh, Scotland, 1969.

11. S. Miksch, Y. Shahar, and P. Johnson. Asbru: A task-specific, intention-based, and time-oriented language for representing skeletal plans. In E. Motta, F. van Harmelen, C. Pierret-Golbreich, I. Filby, and N. Wijngaards, editors, *Proceedings of the 7th Workshop on Knowledge Engineering: Methods & Languages (KEML-97)*. Open University, Milton Keynes, UK, 1997.

12. C. Plaisant, R. Mushlin, A. Snyder, J. Li, D. Heller, and B. Shneiderman. Life-Lines: Using visualization to enhance navigation and analysis of patient records. In *Proceedings of the 1998 American Medical Informatic Association Annual Fall Symposium*, pages 76–80, 1998.

13. S. M. Powsner and E. R. Tufte. Graphical summary of patient status. *The Lancet*, 344(6):386–389, 1994.

14. J.-F. Rit. Propagating temporal constraints for scheduling. In *Proceedings of the Fifth National Conference on Artificial Intelligence (AAAI-86)*, pages 383–388, Los Altos, CA, 1986. Morgan Kaufman Publishers, Inc.

15. Y. Shahar, S. Miksch, and P. Johnson. The Asgaard project: A task-specific framework for the application and critiquing of time-oriented clinical guidelines. *Artificial Intelligence in Medicine*, 14:29–51, 1998.

16. L. A. Suchman. *Plans and Situated Actions: The Problem of Human/Machine Communication*. Cambridge University Press, Cambridge, 1987.

17. A. Tate. Roots of SPAR - shared planning and activity representation. *The Knowledge Engineering Review*, 13(1), 1998.

18. A. Tate, B. Drabble, and J. Dalton. O-plan: A knowledge-based planner and its application to logistic. In *Advanced Planning Technology*, pages 213–239. Morgan Kaufmann, 1996.

19. E. R. Tufte. *Envisioning Information*. Graphics Press, Cheshire, CT, 1990.

20. D. E. Wilkins and K. L. Myers. A common knowledge representation for plan generation and reactive execution. *Journal of Logic and Computation*, 5(6):731–761, 1995.

More BANG for your Buck: A Performance Comparison of BANG and R* Spatial Indexing

Michael Freeston [1,2], Steven Geffner [1], Mike Hörhammer [1]

Alexandria Digital Library Project
[1] Department of Computer Science, University of California, Santa Barbara
[2] Department of Computing Science, University of Aberdeen, Scotland

freeston@alexandria.ucsb.edu   horhamm@cs.ucsb.edu

Abstract. A current trend in database architecture is to provide 'data blades' or 'data cartridges' as 'plug-in' indexing methods to support new data types. The research project which gave rise to this paper aims to test the practicality of a diametrically opposite approach: the development of a new, generic indexing technology i.e. a single indexing technique capable of supporting a wide range of data types. We believe that BANG indexing [Fre87] is now a viable candidate for such a technology, as a result of a series of extensions and refinements, and fundamental improvements in worst-case characteristics made possible by recent theoretical advances [Fre95, Fre97]. The task is therefore to test whether this single generalized technique can match the performance of several other specialized methods. This paper is devoted to the indexing of spatial extents. It describes a simple refinement of an earlier approach to spatial extent indexing based on a dual BANG representation, and compares its performance with that of the R*-tree. The results are surprising. In essence, they show that BANG indexing is able to match - and in many cases significantly surpass - the query performance of the R*-tree without incurring the heavy index optimization costs of the R*-tree. This leads to dramatic improvements in indexing times.

1. Introduction

Since its introduction in 1984 [Gut84], the R-tree and its later refinement the R*-tree [BKS+90] have gained wide acceptance in the academic database community as the preferred spatial indexing method. Despite the many alternatives which have subsequently been proposed, none so far seems to threaten its pre-eminent position. The original appeal of the R-tree design may be confidently attributed to its conceptual and algorithmic simplicity, and its relationship to the familiar B-tree. It has not, however, always been plain sailing for the R-tree. Although the original design displayed the attractive "grow and post tree" [Lom89] insertion characteristics of the B-tree, it had two significant weaknesses: clustering deteriorated over time; and, unlike a B-tree, it could not guarantee the result of an exact-match query in logarithmic time. Both of these are more serious deficiencies today than when the original design was proposed. At that time, the main application area was GIS, in which the data sets tended to be extremely static and processing almost exclusively batch-oriented. Today, new application areas such as virtual reality, scientific visualization and on-line analytical processing (OLAP) demand fast and fully dynamic multi-dimensional indexing methods. And the increasing use of spatial database systems to control on-board navigation systems requires that the worst-case search performance of spatial indexing methods should be as fast and predictable as possible.

Early attempts to solve the clustering problem led to "packing algorithms". These improved the initial clustering and query efficiency, but relied on the assumption that there would be few if any subsequent updates to disturb this optimal arrangement.

The R^+ -tree [SRF87] was an attempt to overcome the unpredictability of R-tree exact-match queries by using non-overlapping subspace partition boundaries. This however could only be achieved by splitting objects, or at least allowing multiple instances of a single object cover. This in turn led to completely uncontrollable and unpredictable update characteristics. The R*-tree returned to the original R-tree approach and succeeded in significantly improving query performance with a new algorithm to optimize clustering. This improvement, however, was achieved at the cost of a considerable additional overhead in insertion and update times.

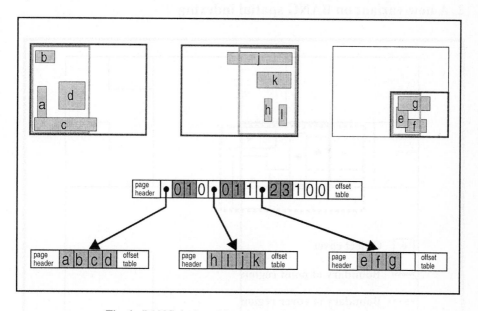

Fig. 1. BANG dual partitioning of a dataspace of extents

In [Fre89b] an alternative structure was proposed for spatial extent indexing based on an extension of BANG (point) indexing [Fre87, 89a]. The principle of the approach is summarized in figure 1. It is based on a dual representation, in which a centre point is associated with each extent. Although it is not required that the extents of the indexed objects are rectilinear (i.e. 'bounding boxes'), we will assume that this is so, since it reflects almost universal practice. There is then no difficulty in defining the centre point of an extent, and the data space can be partitioned into subspaces of centre points according to the BANG technique for multi-dimensional point indexing. As each subspace S is generated, a corresponding dual subspace S' is recorded whose boundary is the smallest which can both be represented by a BANG index key (i.e. a Peano key), and completely encloses the boundaries of all the extents whose associated centre points lie within S. The representation of the dual index entry utilizes the property that the index entry defining subspace S' is a prefix of the Peano code defining the subspace S. It is therefore only necessary to add a second integer to every index entry to indicate the length of the dual prefix. The result is a very compact representation of the dual index structure (figure 1).

The simplicity of this representation must however be weighed against its potential inaccuracy. The worst case occurs when the bounding box of an object intersects the line/plane which divides the entire data space in half i.e. the first partition of the data space. The cover region enclosing the object must then cover the entire data space. For a random distribution, the larger the objects the greater the proportion which will trigger this effect. A similar - though less drastic - effect occurs for bounding box intersections with any lesser partition boundaries.

2. A new variant on BANG spatial indexing

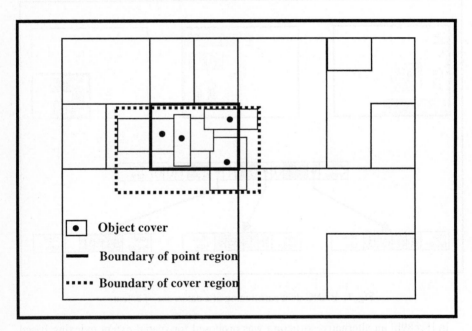

Fig. 2. A minimal cover region

We have recently experimented with an alternative dual representation, in which the cover region is defined in the same way as that of the R*-tree i.e. the smallest rectangular region which completely encloses the minimum bounding boxes of every object in the corresponding point region. We term this a *minimal cover region* (figure 2). The R*-tree of course uses a different object cluster algorithm which is ostensibly independent of the centre points of the covers. However, in the tests described below we have found that, in intersection queries using minimal cover regions, the number of region intersections is little different from that of the R*-tree. The tests also clearly demonstrate the advantage of the BANG approach: the dual representation allows containment queries significantly faster than those for the R*-tree, and index build times are dramatically reduced.

3. Performance tests

Four data sets were used throughout the following tests, each consisting of 100,000 square spatial extents in two dimensions. Three had extents of side 0.1%, 1% and 10% of the range of the domains of the data space respectively, while the fourth contained a mixture of 1/3 each of these three sets. Several spatial distributions were studied, of which we show two here: a pseudo-random distribution of the centers of the extents throughout the data space (which we refer to below as a *uniform* distribution), and a random distribution of 100 clusters of 1000 extents each (referred to below as *clustered*). We deliberately restricted this initial study to square extents, with the intention of introducing the effects of mixtures of increasingly elongated rectangles in a controlled way subsequently.

4. Index creation

We first examined relative performance in building an index. Questions addressed were:
1. In what way is the cost model affected by the hardware/network architecture?
2. How far is the index build time independent of the indexed data?
3. Is the build cpu or i/o bound?
4. In what way does build time depend on index page size?

We assume that, whether dealing with a stand-alone workstation or a central server, the creation of a new index on a data set or on a set of intermediate query results will always occur under the conditions of a shared-nothing architecture. In that case, the overheads of concurrency control do not need to be taken into account, and the only question is whether the file and associated index are small enough to fit entirely into main memory. Given the ever-increasing size of main memories, the latter becomes a possibility for ever-larger files. In that case the efficiency of the indexing algorithm becomes the dominant factor, as measured by the cpu time which it requires. We do not consider the transfer time of the data and index to persistent storage under these circumstances, since this is independent of the indexing method

For seriously large files, however, page access times must be taken into account, and may become the dominant cost. For this case we applied a cost model which assumes that a complete index page or data page read costs a single disk access. (We thus henceforth use the terms *disk access* and *page access* interchangeably). We also assumed that page writes cost nothing in a cpu-bound indexing method. This assumes that the indexing algorithm is constructed in such a way that the next page to be read is always accessed before any previously updated page is written, so that no processing is ever delayed by a write.

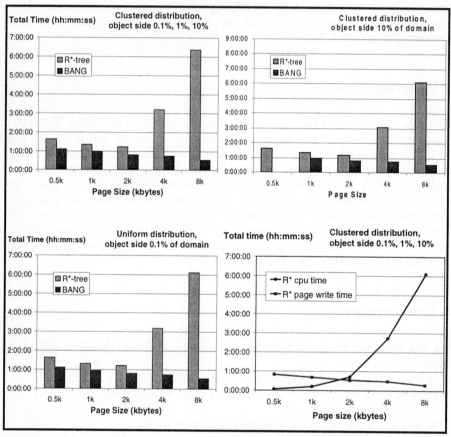

Fig. 3. Index build costs: secondary storage model

The definition we have taken for a *cpu-bound* process in this restricted context is that the total cpu-time is greater than the total disk write time. Thus a cpu-bound indexing method costs only cpu-time + page read time, while an i/o-bound method costs only page read time + page write time. This simple model is almost certainly over-generous to cpu-bound methods in practice, since it assumes optimal coordination of reads and writes in the indexing algorithm.

We therefore measured cpu-time (i.e. user process time) and the number of page reads and writes in a series of tests to compare the cost of BANG and R* index builds for different data sets, data distributions and page sizes. In each case the same page size was used for data and index pages. We then computed a time cost for both the main-memory and secondary-memory models, on the assumption that each disk read or write takes 10 milliseconds. This assumption will tend to favor i/o-bound indexing methods if the actual disk access speed is slower than 10mS, since the slower the disk accesses, the less likely is a method to be cpu-bound. However, the model is not very sensitive to this figure, because both cpu-bound and i/o-bound methods incur page-read costs on the same cost basis, and any error in page write times is restricted to the difference between the total page-write time and the total cpu time. Representative results for the secondary storage model are shown in in figure 3.

The three bar-charts in figure 3 demonstrate that the index build times were remarkably independent of extent (object) size, mixture of sizes, or spatial distribution. The most striking feature is the rapid rise in R* index build times with page size, after an initial slow fall. The graph in figure 3 shows the reason for this behaviour. The cost model assumes that the time for a page access is independent of page size. As the page size increases, the total number of data and index pages falls, and thus the total page access cost also falls. But the graph also shows the rapid rise in R* cpu-time with page size, as a result of its quadratic insertion and page reorganization strategy. The two effects cross over at a page size of 2k, which hence appears to be the optimal page size for R*-tree indexing, at least on this cost model. In contrast, the BANG index build, with its much simpler insertion algorithm and no page reorganization apart from page splitting, is never cpu-bound and thus continues to benefit from increasing page size. Evidently, the cost of building an R*-tree index increases prohibitively as the page size increases beyond 2k. This is therefore an important figure to bear in mind when we come to consider the effect of page size on query performance.

In absolute terms, the BANG index build is never less than 25% faster than the R* index build for any page size, and becomes over an order of magnitude faster for 8k pages.

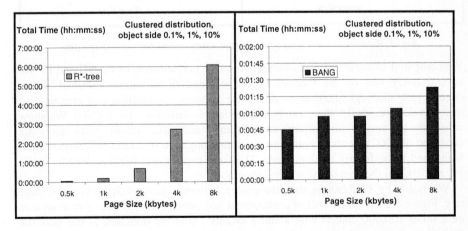

Fig. 4. Index build costs: main memory storage model

Figure 4 shows a representative comparison of index build costs for the main-memory model, based purely on cpu-time. The disparity between the BANG and R* times is so great that they are shown on separate charts with different scales. With 2k pages for example, the R* build takes 40 minutes, while the BANG build takes less than 1 minute. With 8k pages, the BANG build becomes 250 times faster than R*. As with the secondary storage model, we found this performance to be remarkably stable over different data sets and distributions, both in absolute and relative performance terms. Although the BANG build cost increases with page size in the main memory model (in contrast to the secondary storage model), it does so only very slowly, due to its simple logarithmic insertion algorithm. The cpu-bound R* build demonstrates the same quadratic increase in cost with page size in both models.

5. Spatial queries

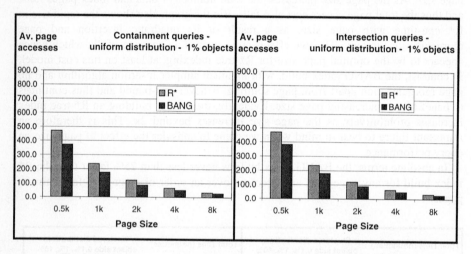

Fig. 5. Relationship between average page accesses and page size in queries

We compared containment and intersection query performance of BANG and R* for several query sets on the indexed object sets and distributions described above. (Recall that, although there is no difference between intersection and containment query evaluation for R*, there can be a considerable difference for BANG). We show here only the results for uniform and clustered data distributions. Each query set consisted of 1000 extents of uniformly random elongation (i.e. ratio of x to y extents) with fixed or uniformly random areas. The fixed areas were: 0.001%, 0.01%, 0.1%, 1% and 10% of the area of the whole data space.

We began by establishing the relationship between query performance and page size. Figure 5 shows the result of containment and intersection queries of random area on a set of 100,000 objects with x and y extents 1% of the domains. In this case the BANG containment query performance was almost identical to its intersection performance but, as we shall show later, this is by no means always so. The point of the figure is that it clearly demonstrates that the number of page accesses is almost exactly inversely proportional to the page size. This seems obvious, but we confirmed it over the variety of data sets used in these tests. It was therefore not necessary to perform further query performance measurements at different page sizes: we chose to use 1k pages. Below we give containment and intersection query performance measurements for uniform and clustered distributions of our test data and query sets.

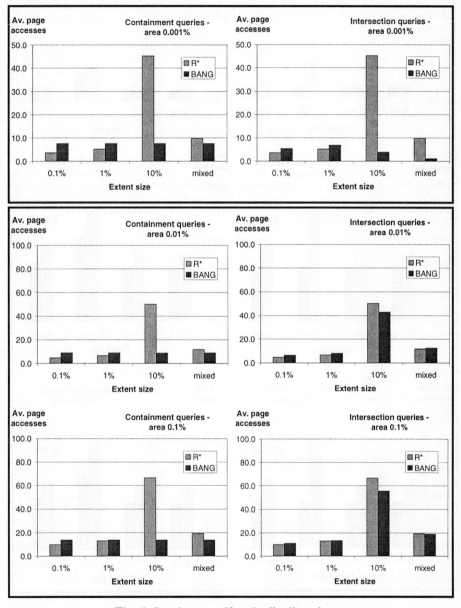

Fig. 6 Queries on uniformly distributed extents

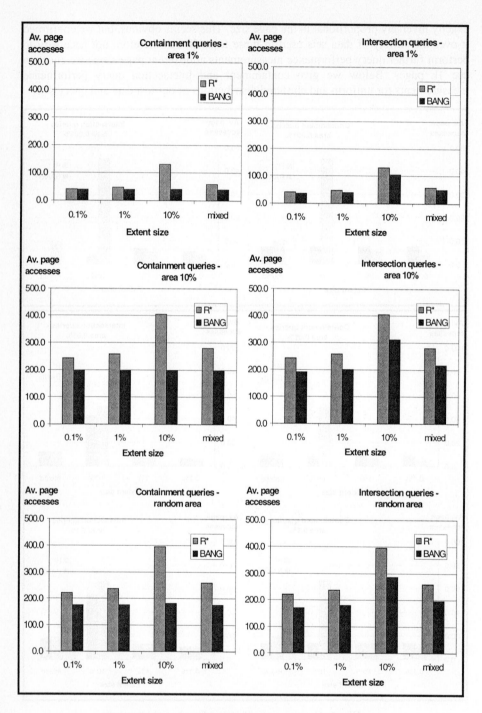

Fig. 7. Queries on uniformly distributed extents (continued)

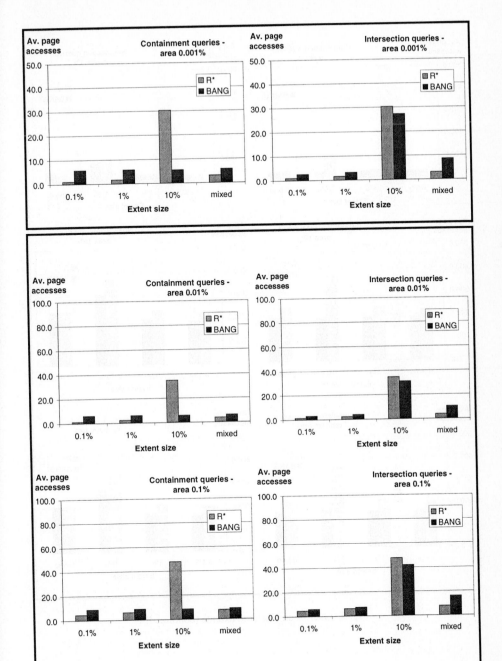

Fig. 8. Queries on clustered extents

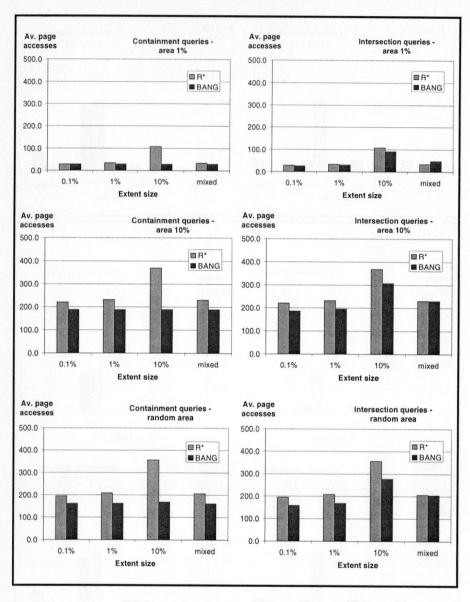

Fig. 9. Queries on clustered extents (continued)

6. Discussion

Two patterns immediately stand out in the test results shown in the bar charts of figures 6 to 9:

1. For the R*-tree, there is no distinction between intersection and containment queries in terms of the number of page accesses required.

2. For BANG, there is a substantial difference. We also see that, for containment queries, the number of page accesses is independent of the area of the extents.

The latter observation is a simple consequence of the fact that BANG uses the centre point partitioning of its dual representation to execute containment queries. This representation does not 'see' the extent boundaries at all so that, provided the size of the data set, the position of the centre points, and their distribution does not change, the partitioning of the data space will be the same. A specific containment query will then always require the same number of page accesses, and return the same number of centre points. Only at that stage are 'false drops' eliminated i.e. extents whose centre points are contained within the query region, but whose boundaries lie partially outside. When the area of the containment query is less than that of the extents, then all the extents with centre points satisfying the query will be false drops.

All four figures show that this approach really pays off for containment queries of all sizes on large extents. The explanation is that, with large extents, there is substantial overlap between them and with the query boundary. This immediately makes a lot of extents false candidates for the R* result set. Note that this is particularly bad when all the candidates are false drops: in the left-hand charts of figures 6 and 8, none of the queries (of areas 0.001%, 0.01% and 0.1%) can contain an extent of size 1%.

BANG does not have it all its own way. The same figures show that, for small containment queries on small extents, R* is on average about twice as efficient as BANG. This may be accounted for by the fact that, for small extents, the minimal cover region may lie partially or completely inside the corresponding point partition region. The smaller the extents, the higher this effect will propagate up the index tree. BANG on the other hand must still rely on the point partition boundaries at every index level.

However, it is clear from all the figures that the R* advantage is always restricted to this special case i.e. the case which requires the fewest page accesses. In fact, we see that BANG is always better over 50 page accesses, and in all but a very few cases it is better over 10 page accesses. For queries which require large numbers of page accesses, BANG is always as good as R*, and frequently 20% to 30% better.

For intersection queries, we see that, as one would expect, the pattern of performance of BANG and R* is closely similar. It was a surprise to us that BANG outperformed R* on intersection queries at all. A notable exception, however, occurs with mixed-sized extents, where R* matches BANG. In this case BANG fails to maintain the advantage it shows with single-sized extents.

7. Conclusion

The primary objective of the project which gave rise to this study is to develop a new, generic indexing technology based on the principles of BANG indexing and the properties of BV-trees. The aim is to reduce the software complexity which is an inevitable consequence of building several different indexing methods into a single database system. But this will only be accepted if the single new technique can be shown to match the performance of each of the old.

This was our motivation in re-examining our previous efforts to extend BANG point indexing to spatial extent indexing, and in developing an improved design. The results reported here are very encouraging, and considerably exceed our original expectations. Taking the R*-tree as the most widely accepted method of spatial extent indexing at the present time, we have shown that the new variant of BANG spatial indexing offers significantly better query performance than the R*-tree. Even better, it does not suffer from the index creation and update overhead of the R*-tree, which increases quadratically with page size. This effectively limits the R*-tree page size to 2k. Since query times are inversely proportional to page size, this means that a BANG spatial index with, for example, 8k pages would perform queries at least 4 times faster than the R*-tree with 2k pages, while still building and updating the index over twice as fast as the (2k page) R*-tree. Conversely, in order to approach BANG query performance in 8k pages, the R*-tree indexing time would have to increase to an order of magnitude more than the corresponding BANG indexing time. The BANG advantage in query and index speeds increases with page size.

In addition to these advantages, the partitioning strategy of BANG spatial indexing has the properties required for a BV-tree implementation [Fre95] i.e. it does not allow subspace boundaries to overlap (a condition not satisfied by the R*-tree), and it supports the enclosure of one subspace by another. With a BV-tree implementation, it will become possible to guarantee exact-match spatial queries in logarithmic time i.e. in a time logarithmic in the number of indexed objects -and, equally importantly, to guarantee a lower limit to the base of the logarithm. No dynamic spatial point or extent indexing method has so far been able to achieve this. We anticipate that this guaranteed performance will become increasingly important in mission-critical and real-time spatial applications, particularly in on-board navigation systems.

We have not attempted a BV-tree implementation in the study described here, in order to keep a clean separation between the BANG spatial and BV-tree implementation and performance issues. We do not anticipate, however, that the combination of the two will cause any significant degradation in performance. This will however be the subject of a subsequent study.

Finally, a number of further refinements have suggested themselves to us during this work, and it seems likely that there is still considerable scope for improvement in performance.

Acknowledgements

The authors are indebted to Ravikanth Kothuri, whose implementation of the R*-tree was used in this study.

This research was supported by the National Science Foundation under grant IRI-96-19915. Additional support was provided by the Alexandria Digital Library project funded jointly by DARPA, NASA and NSF under NSF grant IRI-94-11330.

References

[BKS+90] Beckmann, N., Kriegel, H-P., Schneider, R., Seeger, B.: *The R*-Tree: An Efficient and Robust Access Method for Points and Rectangles.* Proc. ACM SIGMOD Conf., Atlantic City, New Jersey, 1990.

[Fre87] Freeston, M. *The BANG file: a New Kind of Grid File.* Proc. ACM SIGMOD Conf., San Francisco, 1987.

[Fre89a] Freeston, M. *Advances in the Design of the BANG File.* 3rd Int. Conf. on Foundations of Data Organization and Algoritms (FODO), Paris, June 1989. [Lecture Notes in Computer Science No. 367, Springer-Verlag].

[Fre89b] Freeston, M. *A Well-Behaved File Structure for the Storage of Spatial Objects.* 1st Symposium on the Design and Implementation of Large Spatial Databases, Santa Barbara, California, 1989. [Lecture Notes in Computer Science No. 409, Springer-Verlag].

[Fre95] Freeston, M. *A General Solution of the n-dimensional B-tree Problem.* Proc. ACM SIGMOD Conf., San Jose, California, 1995.

[Fre97] Freeston, M. *On the Complexity of BV-tree Updates.* ESPRIT-NSF Workshop on Constraint Databases and their Applications, Delphi, Greece, January 1997. [Lecture Notes in Computer Science No. 1191, Springer-Verlag, 1997].

[Gut84] Guttman, A. *R-trees: a Dynamic Index Structure for Spatial Searching.* Proc. ACM SIGMOD Conf., Boston, 1984.

[KSS+89] Kriegel, H.-P., Schiwietz, M., Schneider, R. and Seeger, B. *A Performance Comparison of Multidimensional Point and Spatial Access Methods .* 1st Symposium on the Design of Large Spatial Databases, Santa Barbara California, 1989. [Lecture Notes in Computer Science No.409, Springer-Verlag].

[Lom89] Lomet, D. *Grow and Post Index Trees: Role Techniques and Future Potential.* 2nd Symposium on the Design of Large Spatial Databases, Zürich, Switzerland, 1989. . [Lecture Notes in Computer Science No.525, Springer-Verlag].

[SRF87] Sellis, T., Roussopoulos, N., and Faloutsos, C. *The R+ Tree: a Dynamic Index for Multi-dimensional Objects.* Proc. 13th VLDB Conf., Brighton, 1987.

A High-Performance Spatial Storage System Based on Main-Memory Database Architecture

Jang Ho Park, Kihong Kim, Sang K. Cha,
Min Seok Song, Sangho Lee, Juchang Lee

Knowledge and Data Engineering Laboratory
School of Electrical Engineering
Seoul National University
Korea
{jhpark, next, chask, mssong, sangho, juch}@kdb.snu.ac.kr

Abstract. Newly emerging spatial applications such as the intelligent transportation system require high-performance access to databases. Although research prototypes and spatial extensions on top of commercial DBMSs have been built, the high-performance requirement is difficult to satisfy because most of them employ the traditional disk-based database architecture. With the steadily increasing memory capacity of computer systems, the main-memory database architecture becomes a feasible approach to meeting the requirement, and a few commercial products are developed recently. However, there has been little work on applying the main-memory database to the spatial domain. This paper presents Xmas-SX, a high-performance spatial storage system based on the main-memory database architecture. It provides the core subset of the OpenGIS geometry types, operators, and spatial indexes. Variable-length spatial data are efficiently managed by storing each of them as a sequence of fixed-size fragments. An experiment shows that, compared with a disk-based ODBMS with data fully cached, Xmas-SX shows only 6% better performance for the spatial range query. Before data fully cached, however, the performance gap is much bigger. For the update, Xmas-SX outperforms the ODBMS by more than ten times.

1 Introduction

Recently, new applications emerging in the spatial domain such as the intelligent transportation system (ITS) require high-performance access to databases as well as the functionality of spatial data management. For example, in the Automatic Vehicle Location (AVL) domain of ITS, the vehicles in the delivery and pick-up service report their location updates to the management center through the wireless network, and the center makes decision on which vehicle to dispatch upon the customer request [Wan98]. Because of frequent location updates and simultaneous service requests, high-performance access to the location management database is a crucial requirement for the success of this service.

There has been much research on implementing spatial database systems. Research prototypes such as Paradise [DKL+94] and Monet [BQK96], and many spatial extensions on top of commercial DBMSs including Oracle SDO [Ora97], ESRI SDE [Esri98], GeoToolKit [BBC97], and Spatial DataBase eXtension (SDBX) [CKS+99] have been built. However, most of them are based on the traditional disk-based database architecture, thus limited in meeting the high-performance requirement. With the steadily increasing main-memory capacity of computer systems, the main-memory database architecture becomes a feasible approach to meeting the requirement by eliminating disk I/Os for data access and taking memory-optimized algorithms [GS92]. Although a few research prototypes and recently their commercialized products such as TimesTen [Nei99] and DataBlitz [Ras99] have shown the utility of the main-memory database concept, there has been little work on applying it to the spatial database domain.

This paper presents Xmas-SX, a spatial extension of an extensible main-memory storage system named Xmas [PPC97, PC+98]. Following the OpenGIS geometry model [BM+96], Xmas-SX incorporates the spatial data management layer on top of Xmas. The layer provides spatial data types, operators, and indexes. Spatial applications use the types and operators through the C++ client programming interface. Because spatial data are generally in variable-length, it is important to store those data efficiently. Xmas-SX treats a variable-length data as a sequence of fixed-size fragments for this purpose. An experiment with a synthetic data set shows that, compared with a disk-based object-oriented DBMS with data fully cached, Xmas-SX shows only 6% better performance for the spatial range query. Before data fully cached, however, the performance gap is much bigger. For the update, Xmas-SX outperforms the ODBMS by more than ten times.

Xmas has been developed with a focus on extensibility since 1995 [PPC97]. The object-oriented approach has been taken in the Xmas implementation to facilitate its extension and maintenance. The incorporation of the spatial data management layer presented in this paper takes advantage of the approach. For example, we define a new container type for variable-length data by inheriting the `Container` class, where a container is a collection of records with the same structure, thus sharing the common interface while refining the implementation details.

The paper is organized as follows. Section 2 presents the architecture of Xmas-SX. Section 3 describes the data model and the C++ client programming interface. Section 4 discusses the management of variable-length data in Xmas-SX. Section 5 describes the implementation and experimental evaluation of the prototype. Finally, Section 6 summarizes the paper with future work.

2 Xmas-SX Architecture

Fig. 1 shows the overall architecture of Xmas-SX, which interacts with spatial applications. Xmas provides the functionality of transaction management, data persistence, concurrency control, and recovery management. Taking advantage of the underlying functionality, the spatial data management (SDM) layer supports spatial data types and operators selected from the OpenGIS geometry model, and two spatial indexes, R-tree [Gut84] and R*-tree [BKSS90]. Finally, SDM incorporates a library

Spatial Applications

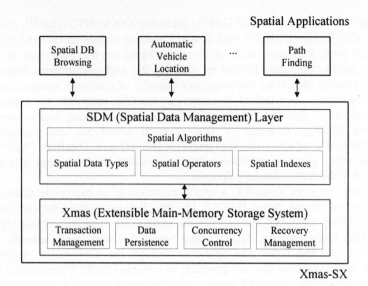

Fig. 1. Xmas-SX Architecture

of spatial algorithms such as the nearest neighbor query [RKV95] using the data types and operators.

The Xmas-SX server process is multi-threaded to run multiple transactions concurrently and to perform disk write for logging and checkpointing in parallel with normal transaction processing. A transaction is processed through interactions among functional modules called managers [PPC97]. The transaction manager supports transaction begin, commit, and abort. The database manager provides operations on the memory-resident primary database. The recovery manager performs restart recovery by ARIES-based logging [MHL+92] and fuzzy checkpointing. The lock manager implements the two-phase locking protocol.

The Xmas-SX database consists of user-defined containers and indexes, and the dictionary. A container is a collection of records with the same structure. A record consists of a fixed number of fields, each of which is either in fixed-length or variable-length. Besides the spatial indexes, Xmas-SX provides the hash index for the exact value search and the T-tree index [LC86] for the range query. An index entry has only the pointer to a record because the key value can be cheaply extracted by chasing the pointer to a memory-resident record. The dictionary maintains the schema describing the structure of all the containers in the database and the information on the physical storage layout of containers and indexes.

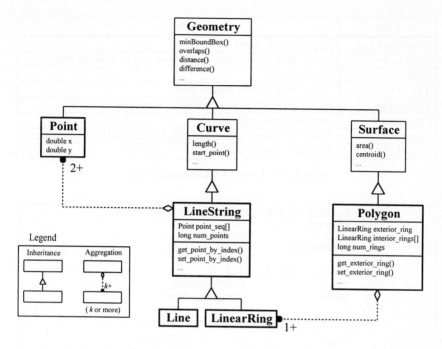

Fig. 2. Inheritance Hierarchy of Spatial Data Types supported by Xmas-SX

3 Data Model and Programming Interface

Xmas-SX takes the OpenGIS geometry model as its spatial data model to benefit from the ongoing OpenGIS standard activity to provide a common representation of spatial information. Fig. 2 shows the spatial data types of Xmas-SX following the core subset of the OpenGIS geometry model. Those surrounded by a bold box such as LineString and Polygon represent concrete types, which can be instantiated. Abstract types such as Geometry and Curve only capture the commonality among the subtypes. LineString models a piecewise linear abstraction of the curve with a sequence of Point objects. Inheriting LineString, Line is a straight segment represented by two end points, and LinearRing is a piecewise linear abstraction of the closed curve. Polygon represents two-dimensional objects with area and has LinearRing objects to represent its outer and inner boundaries.

When creating a container, a data type must be specified for it. Xmas-SX data types are classified into three groups: primitive, domain-specific, and application-specific types. Any of the three can be used as the data type for a container. Primitive and domain-specific types are built-in. Primitive data types include integer, string, and double. Spatial data types above are an example of domain-specific built-in data types. An application-specific type can be defined using these built-in types.

Class	Methods
Transaction	*begin, commit, abort*
Container	*create, drop, open, close, insert, read, update, remove, find*
Index	*create, drop*
Iterator	*insert, read, update, remove, find*
Database	*create, drop, insert, read, update, remove, find*
AggFunc	*min, max, sum, average, count*
Geometry	*overlaps, distance, difference, equals, disjoint, touches, contains*
SpatialApp	*knn_query, range_query*

Table 1. C++ Client Programming Interface

```
create Type RoadSegment (
        integer          ID,
        double           Length,
        LineString       Shape );

create Container BusLine (
        Type             RoadSegment,
        index            Rtree on Shape );
```

(a) Definition of BusLine Container

```
void searchBusLine(Line& aSegment)
{
    Transaction* trans = new Transaction(TIMED_WAIT);
    trans->begin();

    Iterator* itr = new SeqIterator("BusLine", SHARED);
    while (itr->read(&aBusLine, NEXT))
        if (aBusLine.Shape.contains(aSegment))
            cout << aBusLine << endl;

    trans->commit();
}
```

(b) Program searching all the BusLines passing through aSegment

Fig. 3. Example of Xmas-SX Application

Table 1 summarizes the Xmas-SX C++ client programming interface currently supported. The Transaction class provides the methods for transaction begin, commit, and abort. The Iterator class is used to access a set of qualified records one by one. With three subclasses, TtreeIterator, HashIterator, and RtreeIterator, the specified index is used to find records to be accessed. The Geometry class and its subclasses provide methods implementing a subset of the OpenGIS spatial operators. A library of spatial algorithms is implemented as the class SpatialApp.

Fig. 3(a) shows the definition of an application-specific type and a container. By separating the definition of types and containers, multiple containers with the same

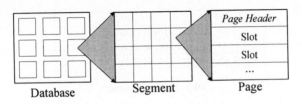

Fig. 4. Database Storage Structure

data type can co-exist in a database. The RoadSegment type has three fields: *ID*, *Length*, and *Shape*. Note that the type of *Shape* is LineString, which is a built-in spatial data type. The container BusLine is created using the RoadSegment type. Fig. 3(b) shows the program that searches all the BusLines passing through a given aSegment. Two classes, Transaction and Iterator, are used. When creating a Transaction object, the strategy to resolve lock conflict, TIMED_WAIT in the example, is specified. When creating an Iterator, the container name and the lock mode, BusLine and EXCLUSIVE, are given. The spatial operator contains, implemented as a method of the LineString class, is used to find whether aBusLine passes through aSegment.

4 Variable-Length Data Management

The efficient handling of variable-length data is important in the spatial domain because spatial data are generally in variable-length. Xmas-SX treats a variable-length data as a sequence of fixed-size fragments. This approach is better than storing the entire data in a contiguous space because it can reduce many in-memory copies and large log records incurred by resizing updates. When stored in a contiguous space, the data may be moved into a newly allocated space as it grows and shrinks. In contrast, Xmas-SX allows to allocate only additional fragments for the increased portion of the data without moving it.

This approach also facilitates the extension of the Xmas container to hold variable-length data by retaining the underlying storage structure of the database. Fig. 4 shows the database storage structure of Xmas, which is the same in Xmas-SX. The database consists of a number of fixed-size segments. A segment is divided into fixed-size pages, and a page is again divided into fixed-size slots. The Xmas container can store only fixed-length records, and each record is stored in one slot. In Xmas-SX, a record consists of fixed-length and/or variable-length fields. The fixed-length fields are all stored in a slot while each variable-length field is split into fixed-size fragments, and one slot is allocated to each fragment. Slots allocated to a variable-length field are managed as either a linked list or a binary tree.

Fig. 5 shows the physical storage layout of the BusLine container defined in Fig. 3(a). It takes the linked-list organization of a variable-length field. A separate page list is maintained to store the variable-length field *Shape*. If there is another variable-length filed, one more page list is created. The page list for the fixed part of records

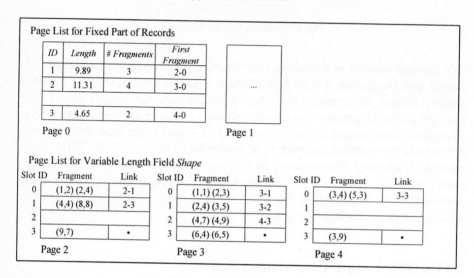

ID	Length	Shape
1	9.89	(1,2) (2,4) (4,4) (8,8) (9,7)
2	11.31	(1,1) (2,3) (2,4) (3,5) (4,7) (4,9) (3,9)
3	4.65	(3,4) (5,3) (6,4) (6,5)

(a) BusLine Container

Page List for Fixed Part of Records

ID	Length	# Fragments	First Fragment
1	9.89	3	2-0
2	11.31	4	3-0
3	4.65	2	4-0

Page 0 ... Page 1

Page List for Variable Length Field *Shape*

Slot ID	Fragment	Link
0	(1,2) (2,4)	2-1
1	(4,4) (8,8)	2-3
2		
3	(9,7)	•

Page 2

Slot ID	Fragment	Link
0	(1,1) (2,3)	3-1
1	(2,4) (3,5)	3-2
2	(4,7) (4,9)	4-3
3	(6,4) (6,5)	•

Page 3

Slot ID	Fragment	Link
0	(3,4) (5,3)	3-3
1		
2		
3	(3,9)	•

Page 4

(b) Storage Layout of BusLine

Fig. 5. Physical Storage Layout of Container

maintains the information necessary to access variable-length fields, the number of fragments and the link to the first fragment. For example, the *Shape* field of the record whose ID is 2 is split into four fragments, and the first fragment is stored in slot 0 of Page 3. Following the link, the next fragment of the *Shape* field can be accessed.

5 Implementation and Experimental Evaluation

The Xmas-SX prototype system is operational on Solaris 2.x. It consists of about 50,000 lines of C++ code with roughly 200 classes. Fig. 6 shows a spatial application on top of the prototype. This Java applet allows a user to browse through a map database of Seoul metropolitan area and to pose two types of queries: the overlapping block search and the nearest neighbor query. The posed query is passed to the Xmas-SX server process, and the query result is displayed on the applet window.

To verify the performance of Xmas-SX, we compared the execution time of the spatial range query and the update on both Xmas-SX and a commercial disk-based object-oriented DBMS (ODBMS). To handle spatial data, we implemented a spatial database extension layer (SDBX) on top of the ODBMS [CKS+99]. The test database

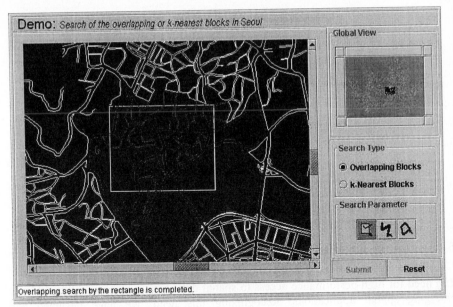

Fig. 6. Spatial Application on top of Xmas-SX

consists of 300,000 synthetic objects. Each object has three attributes, an integral identifier, a square-shaped rectangle, and a 16-byte character array. The identifiers are assigned sequential from 1 to 300,000. The center points of rectangles are uniformly distributed within the two-dimensional unit data space, and each rectangle covers one millionth of the data space. Two indexes, a hash for the identifier attribute and an R-tree for the rectangle attribute, were built.

The spatial range query finds objects whose rectangle attribute intersects the given square-shaped query rectangle and reads all the three attributes of found objects. The size of each query rectangle is 0.1% of the data space area. The update experiment updates the array attribute of an object selected by looking up the hash for randomly generated numbers. The query execution time was measured in the Xmas-SX server process running on a SUN Enterprise3000 server with 167MHz UltraSPARC CPU, 256MB memory, and SCSI disks.

Fig. 7(a) shows the performance of the spatial range query. 10,000 queries are sequentially executed. When data are fully cached after 1,000 query executions for the ODBMS, Xmas-SX shows only 6% better performance over the ODBMS. However, the performance gap is bigger before data fully cached. The average elapsed time of the first 100 executions in the ODBMS is over 860ms. In contrast, the elapsed time of Xmas-SX remains constant, about 18.6ms, because the entire database is loaded into the memory when the server starts up.

Fig. 7(b) shows the update performance. Each transaction updates ten randomly-selected records. Xmas-SX outperforms the ODBMS by more than ten times because, unlike the ODBMS that writes updated data pages on random disk locations at transaction commit, Xmas-SX writes only log records at the end of the append-only log file.

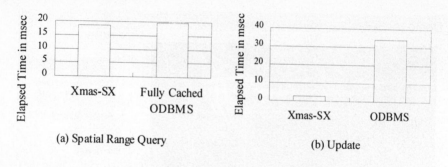

(a) Spatial Range Query

(b) Update

Fig. 7. Comparative Performance of Xmas-SX

6 Summary and Future Work

The need for high-performance access to spatial databases is rising rapidly with new emerging spatial applications. Recognizing this need, we have designed and implemented Xmas-SX, a main-memory storage system focusing on the support of high-performance spatial data management. This paper has presented its OpenGIS-based spatial data model, the C++ client programming interface, and the variable-length spatial data management. Also, with an experiment, the paper has shown that Xmas-SX outperforms a disk-based object-oriented DBMS.

Our future work includes an extension of Xmas-SX to an embedded object storage system supporting ODMG model [CB+97]. It can then support application domains where high-performance access to complex data is required. Also planned is to employ Xmas-SX as an underlying storage system for Spatial DataBase Connectivity (SDBC) [CKS+99], which is under development as a middleware architecture for transparent access to multiple spatial object databases. An extension for the location management database in the telecommunication domain is also pursued.

Acknowledgement. This research has been partially supported by the Engineering Research Center for Advanced Control and Instrumentation in Korea.

References

[BBC97] O. Balovnev, M. Breunig, and A. B. Cremers. From GeoStore to GeoToolKit: The Second Step. In *Proceedings of the 5th International Symposium on Spatial Databases*, pages 223-237, 1997.

[BKSS90] N. Beckmann, H.-P. Kriegel, R. Schneider, and B. Seeger. The R*-Tree: An Efficient and Robust Access Method for Points and Rectangles. In *Proceedings of ACM SIGMOD International Conference on Management of Data*, pages 322-331, 1990.

[BM+96] K. Buehler, L. McKee, et al. *The OpenGIS Guide: Introduction to Interoperable Geoprocessing.* Technical Report, OpenGIS Consortium, Inc. 1996.

[BQK96] P. A. Boncz, W. Quak, and M. L. Kersten. Monet And Its Geographic Extensions: a Novel Approach to High Performance GIS Processing. In *Proceedings of International Conference on Extending Database Technology*, 1996.

[CB+97] R. G. G. Cattell, D.K. Barry, et al. *The Object Database Standard: ODMG 2.0.* Morgan Kaufmann, 1997.

[CKS+99] S. K. Cha, K. H. Kim, C. B. Song, J. K. Kim, and Y. S. Kwon, *Interoperating Geographic Information Systems.* Chapter 22. A Middleware Architecture for Transparent Access to Multiple Spatial Object Databases, pages 267-282. Kluwer Academic Publishers, 1999.

[DKL+94] D. J. DeWitt, N. Kabra, J. Luo, J. M. Patel, and J. Yu. Client-Server Paradise. In *Proceedings of VLDB Conference*, 1994.

[Esri98] ESRI. *Spatial Database Engine.* An ESRI White Paper, 1998. (available at "http://www.esri.com/library/whitepapers/pdfs/sde.pdf").

[GS92] H. Garcia-Molina and K. Salem. Main Memory Database Systems: An Overview. *IEEE Transactions on Knowledge and Data Engineering*, 1992.

[Gut84] A. Guttman. R-Trees: A Dynamic Index Structure for Spatial Searching. In *Proceedings of ACM SIGMOD International Conference on Management of Data*, pages 47-57, 1984.

[LC86] T. J. Lehman and M. J. Carey. A Study of Index Structure for Main Memory Database Management Systems. In *Proceedings of VLDB Conference*, 1986.

[MHL+92] C. Mohan, D. Haderle, B. Lindsay, H. Pirahesh, and P. Schwarz. ARIES: A Transaction Recovery Method Supporting Fine-Granularity Locking and Partial Rollback Using Write-Ahead Logging. *ACM Transactions on Database Systems*, 17(1), March, 1992.

[Nei99] M.-A. Neimat. In-Memory Data Management for Consumer Transactions: The TimesTen Approach. In *Proceedings of ACM SIGMOD International Conference on Management of Data*, 1999.

[Ora97] Oracle. *Oracle 7 Spatial Data Option User's Guide and Reference*, Oracle Corporation, March 1997. (available at "http://web-intranet.ethz.ch/oracle/ora73/doc/server/doc/ A48124 /title.htm")

[PC+98] J. H. Park, S. K. Cha, et al. Xmas: An Extensible Main-Memory Storage System for High-Performance Applications. In *Proceedings of ACM SIGMOD International Conference on Management of Data*, pages 578-580, 1998.

[PPC97] J. H. Park, B. D. Park, and S. K. Cha. Xmas: An Extensible Main-Memory Storage System. In *Proceedings of ACM International Conference on Information and Knowledge Management*, pages 356-362, 1997.

[RKV95] N. Roussopoulos, S. Kelly, and F. Vincent. Nearest Neighbor Queries. In *Proceedings of ACM SIGMOD International Conference on Management of Data*, 1995.

[Ras99] R. Rastogi. DataBlitz Storage Manager: Main Memory Database Performance for Critical Applications. In *Proceedings of ACM SIGMOD International Conference on Management of Data*, 1999.

[Wan98] R.-M. Wang. A Real Time Fleet Management via GIS/GPS Platform. In *Proceedings of the 5th World Congress on Intelligent Transportation Systems*, 1998.

On the Feasibility of Website Refresh Queries

HAIFENG LIU   WEE-KEONG NG   EE-PENG LIM

Centre for Advanced Information Systems, School of Applied Science
Nanyang Technological University, Singapore 639798, SINGAPORE
awkng@ntu.edu.sg

Abstract. Several factors complicate the coordination of information refresh to websites from corporate databases; a complex website contains information from different portions of the databases; websites have different refresh frequencies; different refresh queries have different execution times; and limited resources are available to perform the refresh. Given the information refresh requirements of a set of websites, we must find a suitable set of queries that timely refresh the websites. In this paper, we first formulate the problem formally as the Website Refresh Problem (WRP) and define four problem instances along two parameters: website refresh interval and execution time of refresh query. For each case, we give sufficient and necessary conditions for the feasibility of executing a set of refresh queries.

1   Introduction

Nowadays WWW can not only be used for business corporations to advertise themselves but also be used to support Intranet applications, with information coming from the corporation's databases. Some applications such as financial marketing and order tracking where clients are allowed to track the progress of their orders at a high level through production require resource intensive Intranet web pages *timely* refreshing in response to updates of databases; i.e., refresh work must be completed before the next change of the source data. Usually, two approaches are employed for this refresh work. One is base on a "pull" mechanism where the web pages initiate refresh requests and pull information from appropriate databases which are updated periodically. Another approach is based on a "push" mechanism opposed to "pull" mechanism where whenever databases are changed they in turn initiate updates to the web pages. In this paper, we are concentrating on studying the first case where appropriate set of *refresh queries* must be made periodically to corporation databases so that query results can be distributed to refresh the correct websites, while the "push" mechanism is more concerned about web pages refreshed randomly.

For a large corporation with multiple websites spread across countries and continents, coordinating the refresh of information to websites from corporation databases is a complex task. There are several complications:

- A website contains information that come from different portions of the cor-poration databases. For instance, a single web page alone may contain differ-ent types and amount of information from different parts of the databases.

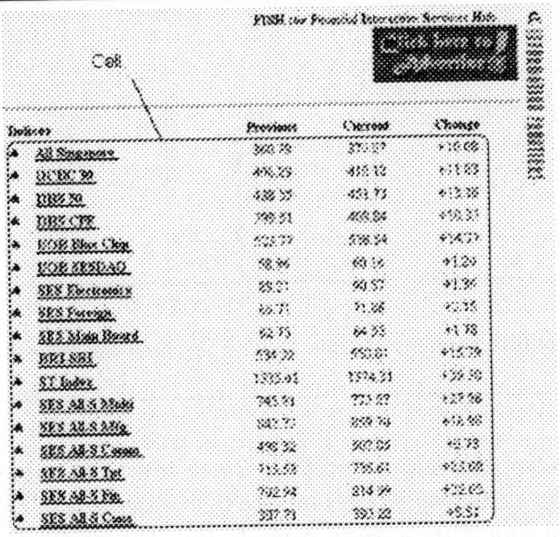

Fig. 1. Cell in the web page http://www.fish.com.sg/stockpage.html

— Websites have different refresh frequencies. Pages in the same host machine may also have different refresh frequencies. Even different parts of the same page have different refresh frequencies.

In order to keep websites up-to-date, an appropriate set of queries must be made to corporation databases so that query results can be distributed to refresh the correct websites. We call a piece of web information refreshed at constant interval by a *refresh query* on source database as a *web cell*. Queries must be made regularly so that fresh information arrive within the refresh frequencies of web cells. Figure 1 show us one page located in the web site "http://www.fish.com.sg" where a set of web pages containing cells refreshed by different queries at different frequencies can be found. For instance, the cell in Fig 1 may be refreshed by executing the query

```
SELECT name, previous, current, current-previous
FROM   Indice
```

every day.

This diversity further complicates the website refresh task because refreshing consumes resources, in particular, processor time for query processing and I/O delay in database access. Thus, to determine whether a set of web cells can be timely refreshed by a set of queries is a non-trivial problem. We start our first step of research from the *uni-processor* environment, which is necessary for establishing the theory for studying the multi-processor case.

With a uni-processor *refresh manager* in charge of initiating refresh requests and performing refresh queries, we implies that one web cell cannot initiate refresh request before the refresh work of another web cell is completed. Let us illustrate by the following example:

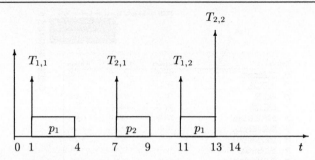

Fig. 2. A conflict happens at time 13 with an infeasible refresh query set.

Example 1. Consider web cells c_1 and c_2, which are to be refreshed at every 10 and 6 time units by executing queries q_1 and q_2 respectively. The execution times of q_1 and q_2 are 3 and 2 time units respectively. The first refresh request of c_1 and c_2 are made at time 1 and 7 and are satisfied by instantaneously executing q_1 and q_2 respectively. Although the second refresh request made by c_1 at 11 is also satisfied, a conflict arises at time 13 when q_2 is to be executed in order to satisfy the second refresh request of c_2; q_1 has not completed the second execution (Figure 2). Thus, the refresh query set $\{q_1, q_2\}$ is infeasible and cannot satisfy the refresh requirement of the cell set. ∎

The above simple example allows one to determine the feasibility of the refresh query set easily. However, with a large amount of refresh information, to determine the feasibility of a refresh query set satisfying the given refresh requirement may be difficult. In this paper, we show how to determine feasibility results for query sets.

We refer to this kind of problem as the Websites Refresh Problem (WRP). The rest of the paper is organized as follows: In Section 2, we review some results in the area of hard-real time systems and view maintenance where our work is related, and distinguish our work with previous works. In Section 3, we give a formal problem definition and introduce some terminology. Section 4 presents some feasibility results. We conclude in Section 5 with a discussion of the remaining open problems and issues for future work.

2 Related Research

2.1 Real-Time Scheduling

If we let queries in the refresh query set be tasks to be scheduled for executions, the problem domain resembles that of a *periodic task system* in a *hard real-time* environment. In a periodic task system [2, 5, 6, 7], each task makes a request for processor time at regular periodic intervals. Every time a request is made by a task, it has to be allocated the necessary amount of processor time (the *execution time* of the task) before a specific deadline. In a hard real time environment, none of the deadlines should be missed. A task system is said to be feasible if any legal set of requests has a corresponding schedule in which no deadlines are missed. The main problem in a periodic task system in a hard real-time environment is to determine the feasibility of the task system. Our WRP is similar to this problem when all deadlines are equal to their task periods (refresh request intervals).

Our work differs from previous works in the following aspects:

- We have restricted ourselves to an environment where no refresh requests are initiated simultaneously. Whenever one request is raised, its corresponding query is executed instantaneously.
- Tasks (queries) are not independent in that a request may be satisfied by different tasks.
- We are investigating more specific problem cases classified by cell refresh interval and query execution time and presenting detailed results for each case.
- Our ultimate goal is to find an appropriate query set to satisfy all requests with the minimal system costs (the least access to database) and our work is the integration of task scheduling and query optimization.

2.2 View Maintenance in Data Warehousing

A *data warehouse* can be thought of as defining and storing integrated materialized views over the data from multiple, autonomous information sources. Once the source has been changed, the view should be recomputed in response to it. Many incremental view maintenance algorithms such as [4, 8, 3] have been developed. A web cell updated periodically by a refresh query can also be viewed as a traditional view since it is also derived from source database tables. With the source database changed, web cell also need to be changed correspondingly. However, our work is not concerned with the maintenance of single view as previous work has done, but focuses on globally maintaining a set of views with the timing constraints satisfied.

3 Problem Formulation

This section describes terminology used in this paper and formally defines WRP considered by us.

A web *cell* is an *atomic* portion of a web page that must be refreshed at some regular interval with information from a corporation's database. Let $C = \{c_1, c_2, \ldots, c_n\}$ be the set of cells in a website where c_i, $1 \leqslant i \leqslant n$, has refresh interval of f_i time units and there exist a *refresh query* q_i that executes in time t_{q_i} to yield c_i. Let $F(C) = \{f_1, f_2, \ldots, f_n\}$ be the set of refresh intervals of cells in C where f_i is constant for cell c_i. Let $\Phi(q)$ denote the result set of query q. Then, $\Phi(q_i) = \{c_i\}$, $1 \leqslant i \leqslant n$, is singleton, and we say that q_i is *atomic*.

Definition 1 Candidate Query Set. Given a cell set C and a query set $Q(C)$, if the result of $Q(C)$ covers all cells in C, i.e., $\Phi(Q(C)) = \bigcup_{q \in Q(C)} \Phi(q) = C$, we say $Q(C)$ is a candidate query set for C. ∎

We refer to the initial candidate query set $Q_0(C) = \{q_1, q_2, \ldots, q_n\}$ of C where q_i's are atomic as a *trivial* candidate query set for C.

Let $T_{i,j}$ be the time when the jth refresh request of c_i occurs. Then, $T_{1,1}$, $T_{2,1}$, $\ldots$, $T_{n,1}$ are the starting times of the first refresh requests for all cells. We can determine all time instants when cells make their refresh requests if all refresh intervals keep constant such that for $j > 1$, we have

$$T_{1,j} = T_{1,1} + f_1(j-1)$$
$$T_{2,j} = T_{2,1} + f_2(j-1)$$
$$\vdots \quad \vdots$$
$$T_{i,j} = T_{i,1} + f_i(j-1)$$
$$\vdots \quad \vdots$$

These time instants form an infinite series per cell. We may refer to each series to be a *request pattern* for a cell and we define the *request pattern set* for C as follows:

Definition 2 Request Pattern Set. The collection of request patterns of all cells in C can be represented as $R(C) \stackrel{F(C)}{=} [T_{1,1}, T_{2,1}, \ldots, T_{n,1}]$ where $F(C) = \{f_1, f_2, \ldots, f_n\}$, and

(i)
$$T_{i,1} < T_{j,1} \text{ for all } i < j,$$

(ii)
$$T_{i,1} \leq T_{1,1} + f_i \text{ for all } i \neq 1. \tag{1}$$

Then, we say $R(C)$ is the *request pattern set* for C. ∎

To satisfy a request occurred at time $T_{i,j}$, query q_i whose result includes c_i needs to be executed after $T_{i,j}$ and that c_i receives refreshed information before $T_{i,j} + f_i$.

Before going further, we first impose restrictions in our environment:

(i) At any time instant, only one request can be initiated, i.e., $T_{i,j} \neq T_{u,v}$ for any i, j, u, v, and to satisfy this request a corresponding query will be executed with negligible delay. We say that the query is executed *instantaneously*.

(ii) Before the current request is satisfied, no other requests can be initiated.

(iii) The execution of one query cannot be interrupted before it finishes (non-preemptive).

(iv) The execution time of any one query is much less than the refresh interval of any one cell.

(v) Time satisfies the *integer boundary constraint*—all the execution requirements and periods are integers.

With these, we define the notion of *timely satisfaction* as follows:

Definition 3 Timely Satisfaction. Given a set of web cells C with a request pattern set $R(C)$ and a candidate query set $Q(C)$, if queries in $Q(C)$ can be independently executed at their respective frequencies and all c_i's can be refreshed within their refresh intervals, we say that $Q(C)$ *timely satisfies* the refresh requirements of C. ∎

Since queries in $Q(C)$ need to be executed periodically, we use ω_p to denote the constant interval between two executions of query $p \in Q(C)$, i.e., the period of p. *If $Q(C)$ timely satisfies C with a request pattern set $R(C)$, we equivalently say that $Q(C)$ is feasible with a request pattern set $R(C)$.*

With the above definitions, we formally restate Website Refresh Problem as follows:

Definition 4 WRP. Given a set of web cells C with request pattern set $R(C)$ and trivial candidate query set $Q_0(C)$, how do we determine the feasibility of $Q_0(C)$? ∎

The complexity of WRP mainly originates from different cell refresh intervals and query execution times besides the irregular starting times of requests of cells. In order to take them into account, we define them as parameters α, β of WRP:

$$
\alpha = \begin{cases}
\alpha_0 & \text{if } f_i = \mu, \mu \text{ is a constant, for } 1 \leqslant i \leqslant n, \\
\alpha_1 & \text{if } f_i = k_i f_{min}, k_i \in Z^+, f_{min} = \min(f_1, \ldots, f_n), \text{ for } 1 \leqslant i \leqslant n, \\
\alpha_2 & \text{otherwise}
\end{cases}
$$

$$
\beta = \begin{cases}
\beta_0 & \text{if } t_q = \varepsilon, \varepsilon \text{ is a constant, for } q \in Q(C), \\
\beta_1 & \text{otherwise}
\end{cases}
$$

Thus, WRP(α, β) defines all problem variations of WRP. Although there are six combinations of α, β values for WRP, two combinations WRP(α_2, β_0) and WRP(α_2, β_1) make no sense since both cases have random cell refresh intervals and have disorderly request pattern sets. Therefore, we exclude them from instances of WRP.

4 Feasibility Results with Trivial Candidate Query Set

This section answers the first portion of WRP (Definition 4). We introduce a series of theorems to obtain sufficient and necessary conditions for feasibility determination of the four WRP cases. Due to space limitations, we omit the proofs of the theorems. The results provide a theoretic basis for succeeding sections.

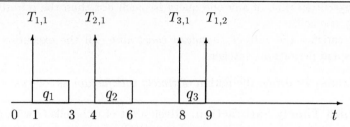

Fig. 3. An infeasible refresh query set in WRP(α_0, β_0)

4.1 WRP(α_0, β_0): Constant Cell Refresh Interval and Constant Query Execution Time

We begin with the simplest case: WRP(α_0, β_0), where all cells in C have the same refresh interval μ and all queries in $Q_0(C)$ have the same execution time ε. For convenience, we use $R(C) \stackrel{\mu}{=} [T_{1,1}, T_{2,1}, \ldots, T_{n,1}]$ to represent the request pattern set of C instead of $R(C) \stackrel{F(C)}{=} [T_{1,1}, T_{2,1}, \ldots, T_{n,1}]$. The feasibility of $Q_0(C)$ depends on the length of time interval between two adjacent starting requests in $R(C)$. That is, $Q_0(C)$ is feasible if and only if the time interval between two adjacent starting request in $R(C)$ is greater than the query execution time ε. We formulate this dependency formally as a necessary and sufficient condition for $Q_0(C)$ feasibility in the following theorem:

Theorem 1. *In* WRP(α_0, β_0), $Q_0(C)$ *is feasible* $\iff R(C) \stackrel{\mu}{=} [T_{1,1}, T_{2,1}, \ldots, T_{n,1}]$, *where* $T_{i,1} + \varepsilon \leqslant T_{j,1}$ *for all* $i < j$, *and* $T_{n,1} + \varepsilon \leqslant T_{1,2}$. ∎

The following example illustrates an infeasible $Q_0(C)$ in WRP(α_0, β_0) (Figure 3).

Example 1. Cells c_1, c_2, c_3 *need to be refreshed by* $Q_0(C) = \{q_1, q_2, q_3\}$. $f_1 = f_2 = f_3 = 8$, $\varepsilon = 2$, $T_{3,1} = 8$, $T_{1,2} = T_{1,1} + f_1 = 9$. *Thus,* $T_{3,1} + \varepsilon > T_{1,2}$ *and* $Q_0(C)$ *is infeasible because the first refresh request of* c_3 *is not satisfied when the second request of* c_1 *is initiated at time 9.* ∎

4.2 WRP(α_1, β_0): Regular Cell Refresh Interval and Constant Query Execution Time

In this case, we relax the restriction so that $f_i = k_i f_{min}$ for all $1 \leqslant i \leqslant n$, where $k_i \in Z^+$ and f_{min} is the shortest refresh interval among all cells in C. For convenience, we assume that c_1 is the cell which has the shortest refresh interval among cells and the starting time of 0 is used when the first refresh request of c_1 is made, i.e., $f_{min} = f_1$ and $T_{1,1} = 0$. Then, for all $1 \leqslant i \leqslant n$,

$$T_{1,i} = (i-1)f_1$$

Next, we introduce the concept of *request phase* of cells to facilitate our exposition:

Definition 2 Request Phase. For all $i \neq 1$, if $T_{1,s_i} < T_{i,1} < T_{1,s_i+1}$, then we define $\phi_i = T_{i,1} - T_{1,s_i}$ as the request phase of c_i. ∎

Thus, we have

$$T_{i,1} = T_{1,s_i} + \phi_i$$

and as we have restricted $T_{i,1} < T_{1,1} + f_i$ (from Eq.1), we have $T_{1,s_i} < f_i$ that leads to

$$s_i < k_i + 1$$

A candidate query set is feasible if the time difference between any two adjacent requests during $[T_{1,i} + \varepsilon, T_{1,i} + f_1]$ is greater than ε, i.e., the request phase difference is larger than ε. Otherwise, there is insufficient time to execute the query to satisfy the first of the two requests and a conflict results if a query is started to satisfy the second request. By noting when two requests from different cells will occur during some interval $[T_{1,i}, T_{1,i} + f_1]$, we now give the conditions to determine the feasibility of $Q_0(C)$ with a given request pattern set in $\mathrm{WRP}(\alpha_1, \beta_0)$ in the following theorem:

Theorem 3. In $\mathrm{WRP}(\alpha_1, \beta_0)$, $Q_0(C)$ with $R(C) \overset{F(C)}{=} [T_{1,1}, T_{2,1}, \ldots, T_{n,1}]$ is feasible (f_1 is the smallest one among $F(C)$) $\Longleftrightarrow$

(i) for all $i \neq 1$, $\phi_i \geqslant \varepsilon$ and $\phi_i + \varepsilon \leqslant f_1$;
(ii) for all $i \neq j \neq 1$, $f_i = k_i f_1$, $f_j = k_j f_1$, $T_{i,1} = T_{1,s_i} + \phi_i$, $T_{j,1} = T_{1,s_j} + \phi_j$,

    (a) if $s_i = s_j$, then $|\phi_i - \phi_j| \geqslant \varepsilon$;
    (b) if $s_i \neq s_j$ and $\gcd(k_i, k_j) = 1$, then $|\phi_i - \phi_j| \geqslant \varepsilon$;
    (c) if $s_i \neq s_j$, $g = \gcd(k_i, k_j) \neq 1$, then either $(s_i - s_j) \bmod g = 0$ and $|\phi_i - \phi_j| \geqslant \varepsilon$ or $(s_i - s_j) \bmod g \neq 0$.

Also, we present an example to illustrate our theory.

Example 2. Cells c_1, c_2, c_3 need to be refreshed by $Q_0(C) = \{q_1, q_2, q_3\}$. $f_1 = 2$, $f_2 = 2 * f_1 = 4$, $f_3 = 3 * f_1 = 6$, thus $k_2 = 2$, $k_3 = 3$ and $\gcd(k_2, k_3) = 1$. $T_{2,1} = T_{1,2} + 1 = 3$, $T_{3,1} = T_{1,3} + 1 = 5$, thus, $\phi_2 = 1$ and $\phi_3 = 1$. $\varepsilon = 2$. Therefore, $|\phi_2 - \phi_3| < \varepsilon$ and and $Q_0(C)$ is infeasible because the third refresh request of c_2 meets the second refresh request of c_3 at time 11 and they cannot be satisfied together. ∎

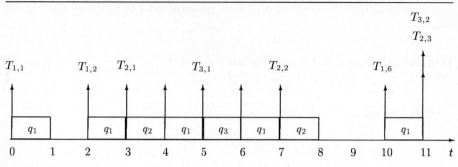

Fig. 4. An infeasible refresh query set in $\text{WRP}(\alpha_1, \beta_0)$

4.3 $\text{WRP}(\alpha_0, \beta_1)$: Constant Cell Refresh Interval and Random Query Execution Time

In this case, our problem is characterized by cells that have the same constant refresh interval μ, and whose queries have different execution times with a basic restriction that for all $1 \leqslant i \leqslant n$, $t_{q_i} \ll \mu$. Actually, $\text{WRP}(\alpha_0, \beta_0)$ is a special instance of this case. As in $\text{WRP}(\alpha_0, \beta_0)$, we determine the feasibility of $Q_0(C)$ below:

Theorem 4. *In* $\text{WRP}(\alpha_0, \beta_1)$, $Q_0(C)$ *is feasible* $\Longleftrightarrow R(C) \overset{\mu}{=} [T_{1,1}, T_{2,1}, \ldots, T_{n,1}]$ *where* $T_{i,1} + t_{q_i} \leqslant T_{j,1}$ *for all* $i < j$ *and* $T_{n,1} + t_{q_n} \leqslant T_{1,2}$. ∎

4.4 $\text{WRP}(\alpha_1, \beta_1)$: Regular Cell Refresh Interval and Random Query Execution Time

In this case, queries in $Q_0(C)$ have different execution times. Since we have assumed that query execution time is far less than cell refresh interval, different query execution times have little effect on our result. Thus, as in $\text{WRP}(\alpha_1, \beta_0)$, we have the following conditions:

Theorem 5. *In* $\text{WRP}(\alpha_1, \beta_1)$, $Q_0(C)$ *with* $R(C) \overset{F(C)}{=} [T_{1,1}, T_{2,1}, \ldots, T_{n,1}]$ *is feasible* (f_1 *is the smallest one among* $F(C)$) $\Longleftrightarrow$

(i) *for all* $i \neq 1$, $\phi_i \geqslant t_{q_1}$ *and* $\phi_i + t_{q_i} \leqslant f_1$;
(ii) *for all* $i \neq j \neq 1$, $f_i = k_i f_1$, $f_j = k_j f_1$, $T_{i,1} = T_{1,s_i} + \phi_i$, $T_{j,1} = T_{1,s_j} + \phi_j$, *if*
    (a) $s_i = s_j$ *or*
    (b) $s_i \neq s_j$ *and* $\gcd(k_i, k_j) = 1$ *or*
    (c) $s_i \neq s_j$, $g = \gcd(k_i, k_j) \neq 1$ *and* $(s_i - s_j) \bmod g = 0$,
    then $\phi_i \neq \phi_j$ *and* $\phi_i - \phi_j \geqslant t_{q_j}$ *if* $\phi_i > \phi_j$; *Otherwise,* $s_i \neq s_j$, $g = \gcd(k_i, k_j) \neq 1$ *and* $(s_i - s_j) \bmod g \neq 0$. ∎

5 Conclusions

In this paper, we have introduced and formulated a new form of queries called *refresh* queries; in particular, queries that are used periodically to refresh a website. We have studied the feasibility of a set of refresh queries for a cell set.

Several assumptions have been made in the preliminary investigation of refresh queries. The most important one is that the refresh manager is composed of the single processor and refresh queries are exclusively executed on this processor. Realizing that it is not too difficult for an enterprise to own multiple processors with multiple databases, part of our future work will focus on the relaxation of this and other assumptions and to study their impact on the theoretical results we have obtained so far. The concept of web cell is similar to the concept of *view* [1] in data warehousing. Our future work will elaborate on web refresh with *view maintenance* together.

References

1. ASHISH GUPTA, INDERPAL SINGH MUMICK. Maintenance of materialized views: Problems, techniques, and applications. *IEEE Data Engineering*, 18(2):3–18, June 1995.
2. C. L. LIU, J. LAYLAND. Scheduling algorithms for multiprogramming in a hard-real-time environment. *Journal of the Association for Computing Machinery*, 20:46–61, 1973.
3. NAM HUYN. Multiple-view self-maintenance in data warehousing environments. In *VLDB'97, Proceedings of 23rd International Conference on Very Large Data Bases*, pages 26–35, 1997.
4. J. V. HARRISON, S. W. DIETRICH. Maintenance of materialized views in a deductive database: An update propagation approach. In *Proceedings of the 1992 JICLSP Workshop on Deductive Databases*, pages 56–65, 1992.
5. A. MOK. Fundamental design problems of distributed systems for the hard real-time environment. *PhD thesis, MIT Laboratory for Computer Science*, 1983.
6. K. RAMAMRITHAM. Allocation and scheduling of precedence-related periodic tasks. *IEEE Transactions on Parallel and Distributed Systems*, 6(4):412–420, April 1995.
7. S. BARUAH, R. HOWELL, L. ROSIER. Algorithms and complexity concerning the preemptive scheduling of periodic, real-time tasks on one processor. *Real-Time Systems*, 2:301–324, 1990.
8. YUE ZHUGE, H. GARCIA-MOLINA, J. HAMMER, J. WIDOM. View maintenance in a warehousing environment. In *Proceedings of the 1995 ACM SIGMOD International Conference on Management of Data*, pages 316–327, San Jose, California, 22–25 May 1995.

Building CyberBroker in Digital Marketplaces Using Java and CORBA

Pin-Kwang Eng   Beng Chin Ooi   Kian-Lee Tan

Dept. of Computer Science, National University of Singapore

Abstract. A Digital Marketplace provides services that facilitate the searching and integrating of diverse data. In this paper, we describe a component in the Digital Marketplace called CyberBroker which carries out resource discovery and automates selection of goods and services. We present its architectural design and the middleware technologies that make it possible. We also present a prototype developed to demonstrate the viability of the proposed architecture.

1   Introduction

The Internet has opened the way for instant global access to information and services. However, to realize its full potential, two particular problems have to be addressed. First, as the number of information sources increases, it is nearly impossible to search the whole information space. In fact, different providers may "sell" the same service or content; some at the same while others at different "cost". Currently, users select their services and determine the sequence to access them manually. Such a process is not only tedious and costly, but has a high chance of creating a sub-optimal sequence. Second, integrating information from multiple sources is difficult to realize because of the heterogeneity and autonomy of sources. Furthermore, the meaning of the information could vary widely across different sources. Consider the data found in the web. It can range from structured (database) to semi-structured (HTML documents) to unstructured (text files and images) data. An attempt to integrate these data would require a lot of time and effort.

In this paper, we address the first issue in the context of a Digital Marketplace (DigiMart). We propose the novel design of a component called CyberBroker in a DigiMart that automates users' tasks of locating and querying the sources in an optimal way. We believe that such a component is invaluable in the face of large information space and limited resources and thus, can result in a more efficient exchange of information goods and services.

While there is no restriction on the type of content and services that can be provided in a DigiMart, in this paper, we have restricted our discussion to structured data that are typically found in file systems and databases. For unstructured data such as those found in html documents, we would require a wrapper that presents the content as structured data. By considering structured data, the concept of cyber-brokering in a marketplace resembles that of query optimization in multidatabases [9]. However, we have identified several marked differences: (1) The processing capability of the multidatabase system is given by that of the query language, i.e., any expression that can be specified by the query language can be processed. On the other hand, the power of the marketplace depends on the services that are provided. (2) In multidatabases, there is typically one copy of a dataset, many copies of a dataset may be provided by different providers in a marketplace. This increases the search space significantly. (3) In multidatabases, the set of operations to be performed is explicit in the query. On the other hand, in a marketplace, a query may involve a collection of services. The broker must determine this collection and facilitate their interoperable use. This again increases the search space significantly. (4) Because of point 1, a feasible solution can always be obtained in multidatabases. In a marketplace, it is possible that a query cannot be evaluated. Moreover, even for a simple query that can be evaluated, the search space has to be fairly large, if not exhaustive, in order to be sure that no feasible solution is missed. In other words, careless pruning of the search space may bypass all feasible solutions!

Our work is closely related to works on two main areas: internet marketplaces and multidatabases. Internet marketplaces allow customers to access a broad range of different computational and data resources while enabling providers to make their data and computational services available to a broad public. In [1], the challenges of designing *spatial internet marketplace* were presented. *Multidatabase systems* [3] provide uniform access in sharing data with a set of autonomous and heterogeneous distributed data sources. Several recent multidatabase projects have employed CORBA to achieve interoperability among heterogeneous data sources and Java to realize portability [11, 2]. However, these works focus on building the system, while we address the design and implementation of the CyberBroker.

Due to space constraint, we are unable to include every technical details in this paper. For more details, please read the extended version [4].

2   The Digital Marketplace

We assume the existence of a Digital Marketplace as shown in Figure 1.

The DigiMart consists of the following key features:

- *Platform independence through message-oriented middleware based on CORBA.* Middleware is a communication software (usually a separate product) that serves as the glue between two applications. In DigiMart, the middleware used is based on the Common Object Request Broker Architecture (CORBA). CORBA allows applications to communicate with one another regardless of where they are located or who created them. Object Request Broker (ORB) is the middleware that enables platform independence to be achieved in DigiMart. In Section 3, we will describe the middleware technologies used in greater detail.
- *Schematic and semantic transparency through Context Interchange middleware services.* DigiMart also provides services that mediate information from

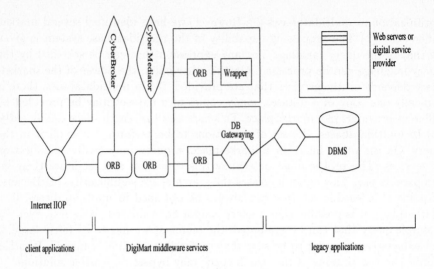

Fig. 1. A Digital Marketplace

disparate contexts. We first note that it is unlikely that data exists in a standard format and data structure. Secondly, the data may have different meaning across various sources. Hence, data should be mediated when their meanings differ and subsequently, converted to a standard format for processing. Wrapped technologies are also required for information retrieval from legacy applications and websites. A component called Cyber Mediator in DigiMart is used to provide such facilities.

– *Data and service brokerage with the CyberBroker.* The CyberBroker is used in the Digital Marketplace to ease the arduous process of resource discovery and provides automatic planning to assist the user in the search for relevant information. This paper describes this component in detail.

From Figure 1, we observe that there are 3 main groups in the Digital Marketplace:

1. The *client applications* are the consumers of information goods and services in the Digital Marketplace. Communication between clients and the server uses the Internet Inter-ORB Protocol (IIOP) which allows different vendor's ORB to communicate over TCP/IP networks, meaning that clients can virtually connect from any part of the world via the Internet.
2. The *DigiMart middleware services* provide the glue between the clients and the legacy applications. The two most important modules are the **Cyber-Broker** and the **Cyber Mediator** which have been discussed above. The middleware also provides other services that allow new service providers to register and join the marketplace.
3. *Legacy applications* are generally referred to as "providers" in the Digital Marketplace. Different providers may provide the same service or content. A provider is required to specify its capability via its properties when it

registers (i.e., joins the marketplace). One expects a provider to specify its capability accurately since it will not be able to remain in the marketplace (as nobody will go to it for services) if consumers find it unable to provide what it claims to. Once registered, it can accept or reject service requests pass to it. Wrapper technology, similar to that in [12], is used to minimize data misinterpretation and facilitate the communication process. As most providers are legacy applications, using wrappers for communication can provide a more uniform access and reduce complexity.

For ease of discussion, the rest of the paper will adopt a context of Digi-Mart where the service providers are used to answer SQL queries. Hence, some providers will provide the necessary datasets while others will provide services in terms of SQL operations such as Join and Project operations for answering SQL queries from the user. We also consider a group of special service providers. This group of providers provide auxiliary services such as sorting and currency conversion services or even graphical display of results. These service providers add value to the current set of services offered and is highly desirable in the Digital Marketplace.

3 Enabling Middleware Technologies

One of our objectives in building DigiMart and CyberBroker is to reuse available technologies. The design of CyberBroker is based on two important technologies - Java and CORBA. This section provides an overview of these two technologies and how they complement each other when used together.

3.1 CORBA

The Common Object Request Broker Architecture (CORBA) is a standard developed by the Object Management Group (OMG) [10]. CORBA defines a standard set of protocols and services for building applications using an object model in a distributed environment. Some advantages of CORBA are [13]:

- *IDL defined interfaces.* The Interface Definition Language (IDL) is a programming language used for defining interfaces. Interface is a popular term used to express the implied contract between two individual entities. IDL allows the separation between the interface and implementation of an entity. This separation aids in managing software component evolution.
- *Programming language independence.* CORBA supports many programming language mappings for OMG IDL. This implies that different parts of the system can be implemented in different languages. For example, a system consisting of C++ and COBOL servers can all communicate fluently. This is especially important when there is a need to communicate with applications implemented in legacy code that support the standard. It removes the need to rewrite every function of the legacy application, saving valuable time and effort.

- *Location transparency.* CORBA provides location transparency meaning that an object can be identified independently of its physical location. It can also easily change its location with minimal impact to the system.
- *Reuse of CORBA services and facilities.* CORBA also provides a set of fundamental services necessary for any non-trivial distributed applications. These services are collectively known as CORBA Services. The CORBA Services are designed to promote a greater amount of software reuse. Each service has been defined and engineered such that it is generic (i.e., domain-independent) and should perform only one specific task thoroughly [7]. In CORBA 2.0 Services Specification, 15 services are defined [5]. Of particular interest is the Trading Service which acts as a yellow page service for distributed objects. It provides the capability to locate objects based on the services they provide. As we shall see later, in the design of our CyberBroker, the registry is actually an implementation of the Trading Service.
- *ORB interoperability across vendors.* CORBA 2.0 and later versions of the CORBA specification define the ways by which different objects implemented using different ORB implementations can interoperate. Hence, it is possible to communicate with applications developed with other vendors' ORB. This implies that the Digital Marketplace can integrate an even wider spectrum of service providers, each using the ORBs of their choice.

3.2 Java

Java is a platform independent object-oriented programming language. Being platform-neutral, it is possible to run Java programs across a range of systems. This greatly helps to simplify many deployment issues.

For distributed applications, several Java technologies such as Java Remote Method Invocation (RMI) and Java Database Connectivity (JDBC) can be used. The latest release of Java, JDK 1.2 even included its own ORB. Java can complement CORBA in the following ways [10]:

- *Simplifies code distribution in large CORBA systems.* Java code can be deployed and managed centrally from the server. If the code in the server is updated, there is no need to update the clients immediately. Instead, clients can receive the updated code whenever they need it. In other words, management of various installations is easier as it is not necessary to update every client manually.
- *Ease of writing CORBA objects.* Java contains several desirable features such as automatic garbage collection, exception handling and integrated multi-threading. These features make it easier to write robust networked objects.
- *Make CORBA ubiquitous on the Web.* With the Java language bindings, CORBA clients can be implemented as applets embedded in web pages. This enables the applet to access CORBA objects which may be legacy applications.
- *Complements CORBA's agenting infrastructure.* CORBA is defining an agenting framework for distributed objects. This framework will let *roaming objects* move from node to node based on defined rules. A roaming object

typically carries its state, itinerary and behavior in its travels. Java byte-codes are ideal for shipping behavior around.

3.3 Binding Java and CORBA

From the above two subsections, we can see that the marriage of Java and CORBA is synergistic in nature. On one end, Java solves the problem of code distribution and on the other end, CORBA solves the problem of intercommunication between distributed components. Put simply, CORBA deals with network transparency while Java deals with implementation transparency. Hence, by using a combination of Java and CORBA, it is possible to create distributed applications that can deploy themselves and run in a cooperative fashion across a network. In Section 5, we will give our experience on using these two technologies in implementing our prototype.

4 CyberBroker Architecture

As mentioned, the CyberBroker is one of the most important component in the Digital Marketplace. It provides the mechanism for identifying the services available (resource discovery) and sequencing their operations more optimally (automatic selection). Figure 2 shows the architecture of the CyberBroker.

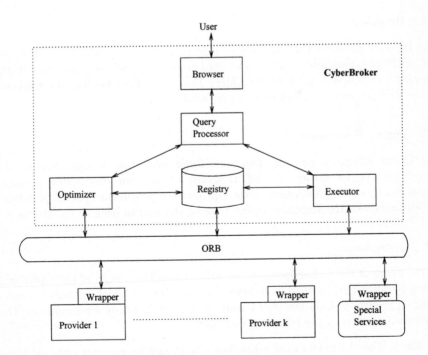

Fig. 2. Architecture of CyberBroker

The CyberBroker works as follows. The browser will display the interface (possibly a Java applet) for the user to submit the query. The query will be passed to the Query Processor which will process the query e.g. check that there is no syntax errors in the case of a SQL query. Once the query is verified, it would be passed to the Optimizer. The Optimizer analyzes the query and converts it to an internal form for more efficient access. The query is then broken up into subqueries, each of which is submitted to the relevant service providers. During this process, the Optimizer will make use of the Registry to search for the relevant providers.

When the providers receive the subqueries, they do not process them immediately. Instead, they develop a set of *access plans* that can be used to process the subquery and return them to the Optimizer. Once the Optimizer receives all the plans for the subqueries, it will generate a final, optimal plan for the initial query, adding new operations to the plan, if necessary, to carry out the whole operation.

Eventually, the winning plan will be passed to the Executor via the Query Processor for execution. The Registry is used again to help the Executor finds the relevant providers. Lastly, the results will be returned to the browser for displaying. One thing to note is that the ORB is used extensively to provide location transparency throughout query processing. This enables the real system to be implemented with less programming effort. The following subsections will discuss the key components in the CyberBroker architecture.

4.1 Browser

The Browser provides the user interface to CyberBroker in the form of a Java applet. Hence, the applet can be executed from any machine connected to the Internet to communicate with the Query Processor. Results that are displayed in the Browser can be text-based or graphical.

4.2 Query Processor

The Query Processor provides two main functions. First, it runs through the query checking for errors. Second, it serves as the coordinator during query processing by sending the query to the Optimizer and then the optimal plan from the Optimizer to the Executor before passing the results back to the Browser.

4.3 Optimizer

At the heart of the CyberBroker is the Optimizer. The design of the Optimizer is largely influenced by the Garlic system's optimizer [6] which extends the rule-based approach of Lohman [8] to work in a heterogeneous environment. The Optimizer consists of the following modules:

- *Rules.* The Optimizer used a rule-based approach to generate optimal plans for the query. This set of rules is stored in the Rules component which is essentially a set of objects each implementing a particular rule. The rule-based approach is selected because it makes the Optimizer highly extensible by simply adding new rules i.e. implementing new rule objects.

- *Glue.* The Glue component is used by the plan generator to evaluate the generated plans and check their integrity. For example, a sort-merge operator would expect the relations to be joined to be sorted. Glue checks for this constraint and if any of the relations is not sorted, it will insert sort operators into the existing plan to enforce the integrity constraint. Besides performing a checking function, Glue can also add service enhancement functions. For example, when sales data are being queried, Glue might add in a currency conversion operator to convert the sales amount from its current currency to the currency preferred by the user. Other additional services might include an encryption function to encrypt sensitive data accessed from the databases etc.

- *Plan Generator.* As the name implies, the Plan Generator is used to enumerate the set of possible plans for a query. Its operation is as follows. First, when the query is received, it will break the query into subqueries. It then queries the Registry to find the relevant providers to send the subqueries to. Upon receiving the subqueries, the service providers will evaluate it and produce access plans on how to execute the subquery. Plans are created based on the capabilities of individual providers and each is characterized by a set of plan properties such as estimated cost and number of tuples output. Once all the plans are received, the Plan Generator will fire rules from the Rules component to generate all possible execution plans for the query. The Plan Generator uses a dynamic programming-based approach similar to [6].

- *Plans Repository.* The Plans Repository acts as a holding place for generated plans. As new plans are generated by the Plan Generator, they are stored in the Plans Repository and subsequently retrieved to further enumerate new plans.

- *Evaluator.* The Evaluator acts as a pruning mechanism to remove equivalent plans to minimize the impact on generating bushy plans. The Evaluator is implicitly invoked whenever a plan is added to the Plans Repository. Plans which are of equivalent properties are eliminated. Thus, by preventing the number of plans from increasing at a rapid rate, the overall system can perform better. Furthermore, as a standalone component, it is relatively easy to customize the pruning behavior of the Evaluator without impacting other components. By just modifying the Evaluator, plans can be pruned according to the criteria set by the user, increasing the flexibility of the Optimizer.

- *Registry.* The Registry would contain information on the various dataset and service providers. The Registry is implemented using the CORBA Trading Service. The CORBA Trading Service defines the IDL interfaces necessary to allow registration and searching of objects based on descriptions and service properties. The service providers will export the data or services they are offering to the Trader. For example, the Optimizer queries the Trader whenever it needs the references to the dataset providers that it wants to send the subquery to. In this case, a property for this reference would be the names of relations that this dataset provider has access to. The Trader can also store a number of links to other Traders to which it can pass on queries. This enables the DigiMart to scale up as the number of providers increase in future.

4.4 Executor

When the final plan is generated by the Optimizer, it will be passed to the Executor via the Query Processor. The Executor will then execute the plan by getting the data from the dataset providers and sending the data to the service providers for processing. Eventually, the final results would be sent back to the Query Processor.

5 Prototype Implementation

In order to illustrate the viability of the CyberBroker in a Digital Marketplace, a prototype of the CyberBroker is implemented. However, the CyberBroker cannot exist without a Digital Marketplace. Hence, we built a Digital Marketplace for a book retailing application. In this marketplace, users can submit the common Select-Project-Join SQL queries as well as queries involving Group By and Having. The full description of the framework can be found in the extended version [4]. We will describe some of the insights gained from building the prototype in this section.

Firstly, our experience with the development of the various components is that Java and CORBA mixes fairly well together. Both technologies complement each other, helping to reduce a lot of development time. For example, all the network communications between objects are greatly simplified by CORBA, thus making the coding simpler. Secondly, the CyberBroker can greatly ease the task of searching for information resources for the users. It not only automates the searching process, but is able to come up with an optimal or close to optimal sequence of accessing the various services. Hence, we believe that it will be an indispensable tool in the real Digital Marketplace. However, a number of problems arise when we deployed and tested the system. The key problem is efficiency. As Java bytecodes are interpreted, a speed penalty is incurred. Trying to use Java to run computationally and I/O intensive operations such as joining of large datasets could take some substantial amount of time. Nevertheless, though slow, implementing in Java allows our code to be ported across different platforms. Besides, there are many advantages in using Java despite the inefficiency issue (see section 3). The other problem is communication overheads. As the data during execution is shipped from location to location, the communication overhead is quite large and thus, will slow down the overall performance. We are currently looking at solutions to these two problems.

6 Conclusion

We have presented the design of the CyberBroker in the context of a Digital Marketplace. We have examined in detail the architectural design of the Cyber-Broker as well as the middleware technologies that make such a design feasible. Our experience from the prototype implementation show that the combination of Java and CORBA is a powerful one when the clients are connected across the globe via the Internet. We believe that the CyberBroker once fully implemented will greatly ease the process of searching for resources and optimal sequencing of services.

Acknowledgements

This project is partially supported by the university research grant RP3982694. Pin-Kwang Eng is also partially supported by the grant RP3982705.

References

1. D.J. Abel. Spatial Internet Marketplaces: A Grand Challenge? In *SSD'97*, 1997.
2. A. Bouguettaya, B. Benatallah, M. Ouzzani, and L. Hendra. Using java and corba for implementing internet databases. In *ICDE'99*, 1999.
3. A. Elmagarmid. *Management of heterogeneous and autonomous database systems*. Morgan Kuaffman, 1999.
4. P.K. Eng, B.C. Ooi, and K.L. Tan. Building cyberbroker in digital marketplaces using java and corba (available upon request).
5. Object Management Group:. CORBA Services Specifications. http://www.omg.org/library/csindx.html.
6. L.M. Haas, D. Kossmann, E.L. Wimmers, and J. Yang. Optimizing Queries across Diverse Data Sources. In *VLDB'97*, 1997.
7. R. Hoque. *CORBA 3*. IDG Books Worldwide, 1998.
8. G. Lohman. Grammar-like Functional Rules for Representing Query Optimization Alternatives. In *SIGMOD'88*, 1988.
9. H. Lu, B.C. Ooi, and C.H. Goh. On Global Multidatabase Query Optimization. *SIGMOD Record*, 20(4), 1992.
10. R. Orfali and D. Harkey. *Client/Server Programming with JAVA and CORBA*. John Wiley & Sons, Inc., 1998.
11. F. Ozcan, S. Nural, P. Koskal, C. Evrendilek, and A. Dogac. Dynamic Query Optimization in Multidatabases. *Data Engineering*, 20(3), 1997.
12. M.T. Roth and P. Schwarz. Don't Scrap it, Wrap it! A Wrapper Architecture for Legacy Data Sources. In *VLDB'97*, 1997.
13. A. Vogel and K. Duddy. *Java Programming with CORBA*. John Wiley & Sons, Inc., 1998.

Experiments in Adaptable and Secure Multimedia Database Systems*
(*Invited Paper*)

Bharat Bhargava[1] and Shunge Li[2]

[1] Purdue University, West Lafayette, IN 47907, USA
[2] GTE Corporation, Irving, TX 75038, USA

Abstract. In the lack of system and network support for guaranteed services, application-level QoS control mechanisms become indispensible. This paper presents several adaptive QoS control techniques for video conferencing under run-time resource constraints. Due to the importance of multimedia security to QoS, this paper also presents a fast MPEG video encryption alrogithm that bounds computation time for any video frame size and is robust to both plaintext and ciphertext attack. Our implementation shows that the algorithm adds only small overhead to video compression process, therefore minimizing its QoS impact on video streams while offering security to digital video applications.

1 Introduction

Real-time distributed multimedia systems such as video conferencing demands a lot of system and network resources in order for their quality of service (QoS) requirements to be satisfied. In the lack of support from underlying networks and operating systems for guaranteed services and resource reservation, an application has to share or compete resources with other applications. Moreover, various anamolies further prevent the application from running in a satisfactory state. This paper intends to show that adaptability is an approach to dealing with run-time resource constraints and various anamolies by showing how a video conferencing system maintains its QoS in a user-satisfactory manner when the network bandwidth decreases. By exploring the adaptability of video conferencing application, this paper reveals that adaptability is a characteristics of digital video systems and can be exploited in environments where resources are limited and shared among multiple applications and where the anamolies occur frequently and unpredictably.

2 Adaptability for Video Conferencing

The key idea of performing adaptive QoS control for video conferencing is to trade some aspects of video quality for others. When the available network bandwidth decreases, to maintain a reasonable frame rate (that is, the smoothness) of

* This research is supported by NSF under grant number NCR-9405931 and CERIAS grant from Purdue University

a video session, some less important aspects of video quality, such as color depth or frame resolution, have to be sacrificed to accommodate decreased network bandwidth.

We have identified several QoS parameters for video conferencing applications [4] and developed techniques to adaptively control these QoS parameters when network conditions change. These QoS control mechanisms have been implemented in Network Video (NV) [2], a popular Internet video conferencing tool developed at XEROX PARC. We modified the NV software and extended its functionality to provide adaptability to network characteristics. Using a probing module, which dynamically monitors the network traffic and computes network bandwidth, the deliverable video quality can be determined and QoS control can be performed through system reconfiguration based on its adaptability features such as color depth, frame resolution, and frame size.

2.1 Color Depth Compression

One approach to accommodate decreasing bandwidth is to encode colors with fewer bits. Figure 1 shows a dual-thresholding scheme for color/gray-scale conversion. This scheme eliminates color fluctuation incurred in a single thresholding when the bandwidth frequently goes across a threshold. The curve in the figure indicates multi-level colors between full-color and gray-scale.

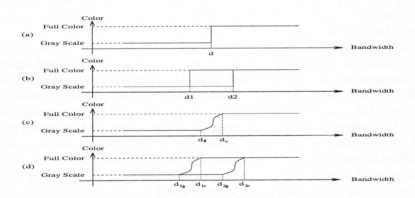

Fig. 1. Thresholding for Color/Gray-Scale Conversion

Two color models are often used in practice: RGB and YUV. Y stands for the luminance component of a pixel; U and V represents the chrominance components of a pixel. YUV model allows separate manipulation of color and brightness of a pixel. In NV, frames represented in RGB space are first captured and then converted into those in YUV space. Since human eyes are less sensitive to chrominance than to luminance, UV is further *subsampled* with an adjacent pixel pair sharing a common UV value while Y component is retained for each pixel. After a 4:2:2 subsampling, each pixel has 8 bits Y component and each adjacent pixel pair has 16 bits UV components. Color depth compression further takes advantage of human perception system by eliminating the redundancy of Y and/or UV components and uses fewer bits to encode them. Apparently, in order to maintain as good frame quality as possible, only less significant bits of Y and/or UV components are discarded.

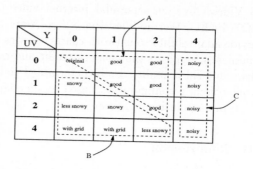

UV \ Y	0	1	2	4
0	original	good	good	noisy
1	snowy	good	good	noisy
2	less snowy	snowy	good	noisy
4	with grid	with grid	less snowy	noisy

Fig. 2. Effect of Color Depth Compression on Image Quality

We have experimented with various compression scenarios by separately compressing Y and UV components each by 1, 2, and 4 bits. The resulting video quality after color depth compression falls into three regions, with *Region A* corresponding to good image quality, *Region B* to tolerable (accetable) image quality, and *Region C* to poor image quality (Figure 2).

Based on these observations some conclusions can be drawn: (1) One should stay in *Region A* and obtain really good image quality if the combined number of compressed bits of Y and UV components of a pixel is not expected to exceed 4 bits. (2) One should enter *Region B* where not-so-bad image quality can be obtained when the combined number of compressed bits of Y and UV components of a pixel is greater than 4 bits, but is no larger than 6 bits. (3) One should go to *Region C* only when a higher compression ratio is needed in the combined number of bits to encode Y and UV components of a pixel. However, image quality is degraded substantially when this is done. Due to the relative importance of the luminance components, the Y components should *not* be compressed for more than 4 bits if one wants to maintain a recognizable image quality.

2.2 Frame Resolution Reduction and Resizing

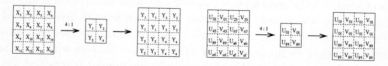

Fig. 3. Resolution Reduction for Y and UV Components

Resolution reduction and frame resizing are two alternative ways for video conferencing systems to adaptively accommodate decreasing bandwidth while trying to maintaining a reasonable frame rate. Figure 3 shows an approach of reducing the frame resolution by a factor of 2 and the frame size by a factor of 4.

By dividing a frame into a matrix of pixel blocks and compressing each block into one pixel, frame resolution is reduced. Termed *compression factor*, a global variable is defined to indicate the size of the block being compressed into one pixel. For example, a compression factor of 2 means a 2 by 2 block in an original frame is replaced with one pixel, resulting in a compression ratio of 4. The new pixel value is a function of all pixel values in the corresponding 2 by 2 matrix, and can be computed using the following function:

$$Y_i = (X_{4i-3} + X_{4i-2} + X_{4i-1} + X_{4i})/4 \qquad i = 1, 2, 3, 4$$

The receiver reconstructs the frame to original size by replacing every pixel with a 2 by 2 matrix. The easiest way of reconstructing a frame is to construct a 2 by 2 matrix by replicating a single pixel, as shown in Figure 3. This lossy process causes the resulting frame blurred. Since averaging does not apply for UV components, a different formula is used to compute the UV components of new pixels (Figure 3). Frame resizing is very similar to frame resolution reduction except that the logical frame size is also affected along with the physical frame size. Both theoretical analysis and experimental study show that resolution reduction provides a finer degree of QoS control than frame resizing [3].

3   A Real-time Video Encryption Algorithm - RVEA

Security is critical to business video conferencing applications. It is important to ensure that only authorized individuals or oragnizations can join the conference and share the data. A common approach to data security is encryption using secret key cryptography algorithms such as DES or IDEA [6]. Two challenges of video encryption are large data size and real-time transmission and processing requirements. Heavy-weigh encryption and decryption algorithms aggrevate the problem and adversely affect QoS such as communication latency. A straightforward way to protect MPEG video is to treat the video as a bitstream and encrypt it with DES. However, a software DES implementation is too slow to meet the real-time requirement of MPEG video playback. One solution to this problem is to selectively encrypt portions of MPEG video. Our previous work [5] uses a secret key randomly changing the sign bits of all DCT coefficients and the sign bits of motion vectors. Although the algorithm can achieve satisfactory encryption results with little computation, it is very weak under plaintext attack.

Real-time Video Encryption Algorithm (RVEA) is a selective encryption algorithm which operates only on the sign bits of both DCT coefficients and motion vectors of an MPEG-encoded video. It can use any secret key cryptography algorithms (such as DES or IDEA) to encrypt selected sign bits. RVEA improves

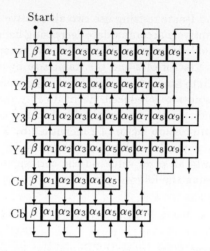

Fig. 4. Bits selection order

our previous work in two ways. First, it adopts secret key cryptography algorithms to encrypt video. Second, it bounds the computation time by limiting the maximum number of bits selected.

RVEA selects at most 64 sign bits (8 bytes) from each macroblock. Let us denote an MPEG compressed 8×8 block as a bitstream of $\beta \alpha_1 \alpha_2 \alpha_3 \ldots \alpha_n$, where β is the code of DC coefficient and α_i is the code for ith nonzero AC coefficient. Each 16×16 macroblock contains six 8×8 blocks. They are Y_1, Y_2, Y_3, Y_4, C_r, and C_b. Figure 4 shows the order in which RVEA selects the sign bits of β and α_i from each macroblock. The reason behind such a selection is that DC coefficients are more significant than AC coefficients and lower frequency ACs are more significant than higher frequency ACs.

To test RVEA encryption results, we implemented RVEA algorithm in Berkeley's *mpeg_encode* software. We used IDEA in our RVEA implementation because it is faster than DES. IDEA is generally considered to be very secure because it uses a key of 128 bits to encrypt a plaintext block of 64 bits. No practical attack on it has been published.

We found that the time spent on encryption with RVEA during video compression is only 2.55% of the total computation time. Hence, a software implementation of RVEA is fast enough to secure MPEG video in real-time MPEG applications.

4   Discussions and Conclusions

Adaptive QoS control techniques can go beyond what we presented so far. We have developed video conferencing session recording feature [4] for NV software and incorporated it with a distributed video-on-demand system [1]. The QoS of the recorded video sessions can be adaptively controlled by a set of parameters such as recording interval or frequency. We have also implemented several codec schemes for NV systems and have successfully demonstrated adaptive switching among codec schemes. Readers are referred to [3] for more details.

RVEA only selectively encrypts a fraction of the whole video. It is faster than encrypting the whole video stream. We found that in a typical MPEG video sign bits occupy less than 10% of the whole video bitstream. Therfore, RVEA can save 90% of encryption time comparing to algorithms that encrypt the whole video stream. For example, to process video frames of 320×240 at a rate of 30 frame per second, RVEA needs to encrypt data 20 72 Kbps, which is far below the encryption rate of 300 kbps on a 66Mhz 486 PC using IDEA.

We do realize that applying RVEA encryption to the units of video slices implies that decryption can start only after the full slice is available; and the sign correction following decryption may incur certain delay. Since the time spent in encryption is much longer than communication latency, RVEA is still much faster than encrypting whole video streams.

One desirable property of RVEA is that it always encrypts at most 64 bits of data for each macroblock regardless of the frame size and type (I, P, or B), suggesting that the burstiness of data does not affect RVEA's encryption speed. The overhead of RVEA encryption is therefore a constant. It is believed that RVEA can be applied to secure video-on-demand applications and pay-per-view programs. Its idea can be extended to non-MPEG compression scheme such as H.263-based video conferencing applications.

References

1. Bharat Bhargava, Shunge Li, Shalab Goel, and Jin Huai. A Distributed Video-on-Demand System for Video Conferencing. In *Proceedings of the International Conference on Multimedia Information Systems (MULTIMEDIA 96), New Delhi, India*, pages 83–93. IETE, February 1996.
2. Ron Frederick. Experiences with Real-Time Software Video Compression. In *Proceedings of the Packet Video Workshop*, Portland, Oregon, September 1994.
3. Shunge Li. *Quality of Service Control for Distributed Multimedia Systems*. PhD thesis, Department of Computer Sciences, Purdue University, 1997.
4. Shunge Li, Shalab Goel, and Bharat Bhargava. VC Collaborator: A Mechanism for Video Conferencing Support. In *SPIE Photonics East '95 Symposium – First International Symposium on Photonics Technologies and Systems for Voice, Video, and Data Communications, SPIE Proceedings Vol. 2617*, pages 89–99, Philadelphia, Pennsylvania, October 1995.
5. Changgui Shi and Bharat Bhargava. An Efficient MPEG Video Encryption Algorithm. In *Proceedings of the 17th IEEE Symposium on Reliable Distributed Systems*, West Lafayette, Indiana, USA, 1998.
6. Douglas R. Stinson. *Cryptography Theory and Practice*. CRC Press, Inc., 1995.

Author Index

Lecture Notes in Computer Science

For information about Vols. 1–1606
please contact your bookseller or Springer-Verlag

Vol. 1645: M. Crochemore, M. Paterson (Eds.), Combinatorial Pattern Matching. Proceedings, 1999. VIII, 295 pages. 1999.

Vol. 1647: F.J. Garijo, M. Boman (Eds.), Multi-Agent System Engineering. Proceedings, 1999. X, 233 pages. 1999. (Subseries LNAI).

Vol. 1648: M. Franklin (Ed.), Financial Cryptography. Proceedings, 1999. VIII, 269 pages. 1999.

Vol. 1649: R.Y. Pinter, S. Tsur (Eds.), Next Generation Information Technologies and Systems. Proceedings, 1999. IX, 327 pages. 1999.

Vol. 1650: K.-D. Althoff, R. Bergmann, L.K. Branting (Eds.), Case-Based Reasoning Research and Development. Proceedings, 1999. XII, 598 pages. 1999. (Subseries LNAI).

Vol. 1651: R.H. Güting, D. Papadias, F. Lochovsky (Eds.), Advances in Spatial Databases. Proceedings, 1999. XI, 371 pages. 1999.

Vol. 1652: M. Klusch, O.M. Shehory, G. Weiss (Eds.), Cooperative Information Agents III. Proceedings, 1999. XI, 404 pages. 1999. (Subseries LNAI).

Vol. 1653: S. Covaci (Ed.), Active Networks. Proceedings, 1999. XIII, 346 pages. 1999.

Vol. 1654: E.R. Hancock, M. Pelillo (Eds.), Energy Minimization Methods in Computer Vision and Pattern Recognition. Proceedings, 1999. IX, 331 pages. 1999.

Vol. 1655: S.-W. Lee, Y. Nakano (Eds.), Document Analysis Systems: Theory and Practice. Proceedings, 1998. XI, 377 pages. 1999.

Vol. 1656: S. Chatterjee, J.F. Prins, L. Carter, J. Ferrante, Z. Li, D. Sehr, P.-C. Yew (Eds.), Languages and Compilers for Parallel Computing. Proceedings, 1998. XI, 384 pages. 1999.

Vol. 1661: C. Freksa, D.M. Mark (Eds.), Spatial Information Theory. Proceedings, 1999. XIII, 477 pages. 1999.

Vol. 1662: V. Malyshkin (Ed.), Parallel Computing Technologies. Proceedings, 1999. XIX, 510 pages. 1999.

Vol. 1663: F. Dehne, A. Gupta. J.-R. Sack, R. Tamassia (Eds.), Algorithms and Data Structures. Proceedings, 1999. IX, 366 pages. 1999.

Vol. 1664: J.C.M. Baeten, S. Mauw (Eds.), CONCUR'99. Concurrency Theory. Proceedings, 1999. XI, 573 pages. 1999.

Vol. 1666: M. Wiener (Ed.), Advances in Cryptology – CRYPTO '99. Proceedings, 1999. XII, 639 pages. 1999.

Vol. 1667: J. Hlavička, E. Maehle, A. Pataricza (Eds.), Dependable Computing – EDCC-3. Proceedings, 1999. XVIII, 455 pages. 1999.

Vol. 1668: J.S. Vitter, C.D. Zaroliagis (Eds.), Algorithm Engineering. Proceedings, 1999. VIII, 361 pages. 1999.

Vol. 1671: D. Hochbaum, K. Jansen, J.D.P. Rolim, A. Sinclair (Eds.), Randomization, Approximation, and Combinatorial Optimization. Proceedings, 1999. IX, 289 pages. 1999.

Vol. 1672: M. Kutylowski, L. Pacholski, T. Wierzbicki (Eds.), Mathematical Foundations of Computer Science 1999. Proceedings, 1999. XII, 455 pages. 1999.

Vol. 1673: P. Lysaght, J. Irvine, R. Hartenstein (Eds.), Field Programmable Logic and Applications. Proceedings, 1999. XI, 541 pages. 1999.

Vol. 1674: D. Floreano, J.-D. Nicoud, F. Mondada (Eds.), Advances in Artificial Life. Proceedings, 1999. XVI, 737 pages. 1999. (Subseries LNAI).

Vol. 1675: J. Estublier (Ed.), System Configuration Management. Proceedings, 1999. VIII, 255 pages. 1999.

Vol. 1976: M. Mohania, A M. Tjoa (Eds.), Data Warehousing and Knowledge Discovery. Proceedings, 1999. XII, 400 pages. 1999.

Vol. 1677: T. Bench-Capon, G. Soda, A M. Tjoa (Eds.), Database and Expert Systems Applications. Proceedings, 1999. XVIII, 1105 pages. 1999.

Vol. 1678: M.H. Böhlen, C.S. Jensen, M.O. Scholl (Eds.), Spatio-Temporal Database Management. Proceedings, 1999. X, 243 pages. 1999.

Vol. 1679: C. Taylor, A. Colchester (Eds.), Medical Image Computing and Computer-Assisted Intervention – MICCAI'99. Proceedings, 1999. XXI, 1240 pages. 1999.

Vol. 1680: D. Dams, R. Gerth, S. Leue, M. Massink (Eds.), Practical Aspects of SPIN Model-Checking. Proceedings, 1999. X, 277 pages. 1999.

Vol. 1682: M. Nielsen, P. Johansen, O.F. Olsen, J. Weickert (Eds.), Scale-Space Theories in Computer Vision. Proceedings, 1999. XII, 532 pages. 1999.

Vol. 1684: G. Ciobanu, G. Păun (Eds.), Fundamentals of Computation Theory. Proceedings, 1999. XI, 570 pages. 1999.

Vol. 1685: P. Amestoy, P. Berger, M. Daydé, I. Duff, V. Frayssé, L. Giraud, D. Ruiz (Eds.), Euro-Par'99. Parallel Processing. Proceedings, 1999. XXXII, 1503 pages. 1999.

Vol. 1688: P. Bouquet, L. Serafini, P. Brézillon, M. Benerecetti, F. Castellani (Eds.), Modeling and Using Context. Proceedings, 1999. XII, 528 pages. 1999. (Subseries LNAI).

Vol. 1689: F. Solina, A. Leonardis (Eds.), Computer Analysis of Images and Patterns. Proceedings, 1999. XIV, 650 pages. 1999.

Vol. 1690: Y. Bertot, G. Dowek, A. Hirschowitz, C. Paulin, L. Théry (Eds.), Theorem Proving in Higher Order Logics. Proceedings, 1999. VIII, 359 pages. 1999.

Vol. 1691: J. Eder, I. Rozman, T. Welzer (Eds.), Advances in Databases and Information Systems. Proceedings, 1999. XIII, 383 pages. 1999.

Vol. 1692: V. Matoušek, P. Mautner, J. Ocelíková, P. Sojka (Eds.), Text, Speech, and Dialogue. Proceedings, 1999. XI, 396 pages. 1999. (Subseries LNAI).

Vol. 1694: A. Cortesi, G. Filé (Eds.), Static Analysis. Proceedings, 1999. VIII, 357 pages. 1999.

Vol. 1701: W. Burgard, T. Christaller, A.B. Cremers (Eds.), KI-99: Advances in Artificial Intelligence. Proceedings, 1999. XI, 311 pages. 1999. (Subseries LNAI).

Vol. 1704: Jan M. Żytkow, J. Rauch (Eds.), Principles of Data Mining and Knowledge Discovery. Proceedings, 1999. XIV, 593 pages. 1999. (Subseries LNAI).

Vol. 1705: H. Ganzinger, D. McAllester, A. Voronkov (Eds.), Logic for Programming and Automated Reasoning. Proceedings, 1999. XII, 397 pages. 1999. (Subseries LNAI).